CARIBBEAN SLAVE SOCIETY AND ECONOMY

A Student Reader

Editors: HILARY BECKLES & VERENE SHEPHERD

THE NEW PRESS, NEW YORK

Published in the United States by The New Press, New York
Distributed by W.W. Norton & Company, Inc.
500 Fifth Avenue, New York, NY 10110

LIBRARY OF CONGRESS CATALOGING-IN-PUBLICATION

Caribbean slave society and economy : a student reader / Hilary
Beckles and Verene Shepherd, editors. — 1st ed.
p. cm.
Includes bibliographical references.
ISBN 1-56584-086-0
1. Slavery—Caribbean Area—History. 2. Slave-trade—Caribbean
Area—History. 3. Plantation life—Caribbean Area—History.
4. Sugar workers—Caribbean Area—History. 5. Slaves—Caribbean
Area—Emancipation. I. Beckles, Hilary, 1955– . II. Shepherd,
Verene.
HT1071.C34 1993
305.5′67′09729—dc20 93-6739 CIP

First Published by Ian Randle Publishers Limited, Jamaica.

Established in 1990 as a major alternative to the large, commercial publishing houses, The New Press is intended to be the first full-scale nonprofit American book publisher outside of the university presses. The Press is operated editorially in the public interest, rather than for private gain; it is committed to publishing in innovative ways works of educational, cultural, and community value, which despite their intellectual merits might not normally be "commercially" viable. The New Press's editorial offices are located at The City University of New York.

Printed in the United States of America.

10 9 8 7 6 5 4 3 2 1

Contents

Introduction

Six European nations succeeded in establishing colonial empires in the Caribbean between 1492 and the end of the eighteenth century. The most important of these, from the point of view of impact upon the region's socio-economic development, were Spain, England, France and Holland. The other nations, Denmark and Sweden, were minor powers whose presence did little to shape the direction and nature of the colonial enterprise. What they all held in common by the middle of the eighteenth century, however, was an overwhelming dependence upon African slave labour to sustain expansion and economic viability.

Since the colonial period, the historiography of these slave systems depicted not only the interests and sensibilities of imperialist groups, but has increasingly reflected the consciousness and activities of the 'insider' creole community. In recent years, the volume of published work has reached such large proportions that scholars now speak in terms of an historiographic revolution. Michael Craton, a leading historian of Caribbean slave systems, has suggested, for example, that slave studies are now more than a vogue, but *nouvelle vague*.

One result of this historiographical development is that scholars who shoulder the additional responsibility of conducting large-scale student seminars, now find the task of comprehensively assimilating the literature rather immense. The process of systematically searching through dozens of journals, not to mention the financial strain of purchasing increasingly expensive monographs, poses a range of special problems for students and tutors alike.

The preparation of this volume of essays con stitutes a modest attempt to redress at least two of these difficulties. It is conceived and designed as a student/tutor companion, and has as its target, the debate environment of the University and College seminar on Comparative Caribbean Slave Systems. The wide range of coverage reflects the main themes of recent research and publication. Essays are selected in order to provide macro-perspectives on the slave mode of production (its internal and external dimensions) as well as its constituent parts along with their socio-economic and ideological expression.

They cover the sociology and economics of slavery, illustrating the dynamic relations between modes of production and social life.

The superstructures of slave systems have fascinated scholars perhaps to a greater degree than their economic substructures; as such the debates on race and colour relations, health and morality, religion, recreational culture, women, family organization and kinship patterns, as well as the endemic problems of social reproduction are represented in a number of essays. Also, the fundamental and unifying characteristics of these slave societies — maturing anti-slavery consciousness and politics — are addressed as one central element to the discourse on social control and resistance. This theme provides part of the general background to investigations of the disintegration of the slave systems, from the Haitian Revolution to Spanish Caribbean emancipation towards the end of the nineteenth century.

Though no general guiding principle was used in the selection of essays, two important objectives were kept firmly in mind: (i) to provide a pan-Caribbean, trans-imperial thematic focus, sensitive to the formation of creole culture and identity that imposed a binding socio-cultural trajectory on the region; (ii) to illustrate the many patterns and forms of socio-economic life and activity that shaped the region's heterogeneous slave societies and to account for their uneven pace and diversity of development.

It took over 100 years for the system of Slavery to sink and spread its roots deeply into the social, institutional and market responses of Caribbean inhabitants. It also took over 100 years of concerted constitutional efforts, by revolution and reform, to remove them in their entirety. The complex, and dialectical relations between these two sets of historical processes are central to the thematic flow of this collection. We hope that it makes a contribution, no matter how small, to students' understanding of Caribbean history and society, and that it acts as an energy source for scholars in their search for new evidence and interpretations.

Hilary McD. Beckles
Verene A. Shepherd

July 1991

Acknowledgements

With the exception of Verene Shepherd's essay *Trade and Exchange in Jamaica in the Period of Slavery* all the essays in this book were previously published in various books and journals. The Editors and Publishers are grateful for permission to reproduce them in this volume and list below the original publication details.

Amerindians and Slavery

David Henige, 'On the Contact Population of Hispaniola: History as Higher Mathematics' Editors: Hispanic American Historial Review, Duke University Press, 6697 College Station, Durham, North Carolina, 27708, U.S.A.

Hispanic American Historial Review, Vol. 58, No. 2, 1978, pp. 217–37.

Alvin O. Thompson, 'Amerindian-European Relations in Dutch Guyana' Dept. History, U.W.I. Cave Hill, Barbados.

Alvin O. Thompson, *Colonialism and Underdevelopment in Guyana, 1580–1803* (Caribbean Research and Publications, Bridgetown, 1987), pp.191-213.

J. Paul Thomas, 'The Caribs of St Vincent: A Study in Imperial Maladministration, 1763–73' Dr. Bridget Brereton, c/o Dept. History, U.W.I. St. Augustine, Trinidad.

Journal of Caribbean History, Vol. 18, No. 2, 1984, pp. 60–73.

Origins of Large-Scale Slavery

Robert Carlyle Batie, 'Why Sugar? Economic Cycles and the Changing of Staples on the English and French Antilles, 1624–54' See Dr. Bridget Brereton.

Journal of Caribbean History, Vols 8-9, 1976, pp. 1-41.

Francisco Scarano, 'The Origins of Plantation Growth in Puerto Rico' University of Wisconsin Press, 114 North, Murray St., Madison, Wisconsin, 53715, U.S.A.

Francisco Scarano, *Sugar and Slavery in Puerto Rico: The Plantation Economy of Ponce*, (Madison, 1984), pp. 16–34.

Franklin Knight, 'The Transformation of Cuban Agriculture, 1763-1838' As above.

Franklin Knight, *Slave Society in Cuba During the 19th Century* (Madison, 1970), pp. 3–24.

Production, Profitability and Markets

J. R. Ward, 'The Profitability of Sugar Planting in the British West Indies, 1650–1834' Economic History Review, Basil Blackwell Ltd., 108 Cowley Rd., Oxford, OX4 1JF, U.K.

Economic History Review, Vol. 31, No. 2 (1978), pp. 197–213.

Robert Stein, 'The French West Indian Sugar Business' Louisiana State University Press, Baton Rouge, 70893, Louisiana, U.S.A.

Robert Stein, *The French Sugar Business in the 18th Century* (Baton Rouge, 1988), pp. 74–89.

K. G. Davies, 'The Origins of the Commission System in the West India Trade.' Royal Historical Society, Univ. College, London, Gower St. London WC1 6BT.

Verene A. Shepherd, 'Trade and Exchange in Jamaica in the Period of Slavery' Unpublished.

Transactions of the Royal Historical Society (London), Fifth Series, 001-2, (1952), pp. 89–107.

Caribbean Slavery and the Capitalist World Economy

Eric Williams, 'Capitalism and Slavery.'

Andre Deutsch, 105 Gr. Russell St., London WC1, U.K.

Eric Williams, *From Columbus to Castro: The History of the Caribbean, 1492–1969* (London, 1970), pp. 136–55.

C. L. R. James, 'French Capitalism and Caribbean Slavery'.

C. L. R. James, *The Black Jacobins: Toussaint L'Ouverture and the San Domingo Revolution* (Vintage Books, 1963), pp. 47–61.

Seymour Drescher, 'The Decline Thesis of British Slavery since *Econocide*' Frank Cass Co. Ltd., Gainsborough House, 11 Gainsborough Rd., London E11 1RS.

Slavery and Abolition, Vol. 7, No. 1 (1986), pp. 3–23.

Race, Colour and Ideology

Arnold A. Sio, 'Marginality and Free Coloured Identity in Caribbean Slave Society' See Frank Cass *previous page*.

Slavery and Abolition, Vol. 8, No. 2 (1987), pp. 166–82.

Gwendolyn Midlo Hall, 'Saint Domingue' The Johns Hopkins Univ. Press, 701 West 40th St., Baltimore, Maryland 21211, U.S.A

Health, Nutrition and the Crisis of Social Reproduction

Kenenth F. Kiple and Virginia H. Kiple, 'Deficiency Diseases in the Caribbean', I.T. Press Journals, 55 Hayward Street, Cambridge, MA 02142-9949, U.S.A.

Journal of Interdisciplinary History, Vol. 11, No. 2 (1980), pp. 197–215.

Michael Craton, 'Death, Disease and Medicine on Jamaican Slave Plantations: The Example of Worthy Park, 1767–1838' The editor, Histoire Sociale/Social History, c/o Dept. of History, Univ. of Ottawa, Ottawa, Ontario, Canada K1N 6N5.

Humphrey E. Lamur, 'Demographic Performance of Two Slave Plantations of the Dutch Speaking Caribbean' CEDLA, Keizersgracht, 395-397, 1016 EK, Amsterdam, The Netherlands.

Boletin de Estudios Latino Americanos y del Caribe, No. 30 (June, 1981), pp. 87–102.

Barry W. Higman, 'The Slave Populations of the British Caribbean: some nineteenth-Century Variations'.

Histoire Sociale — Social History, Vol. 9, No. 18 November (1976), pp. 237–55.

Richard B. Sheridan, 'Mortality and the Medical Treatment of Slaves in the British West Indies', Princeton University Press, 41 William St., Princeton, New Jersey, 08540, U.S.A.

Stanley Engerman and Eugene Genovese (eds), *Race and Slavery in The Western Hemisphere: Quantitative Studies* (Princeton, 1975), pp. 285–307.

University Presses of Florida, 15 NW 15th St., Gainesville, Florida 32603, U.S.A.

Samuel Proctor (ed.), *Eighteenth Century Florida and the Caribbean* (Florida, 1976), pp. 60–70.

Slave Women, Family and Households

Michael Craton, 'Changing Patterns of Slave Families in the British West Indies' See above, by Kiple & Kiple.

Journal of Interdisciplinary History, Vol. X, No. 1 (1979), pp. 1–35.

Barry Higman, 'Household Structure and Fertility on Jamaican Slave Plantations: A Nineteenth-Century Example' Population Investigation Committee, L.S.E., Houghton Street, Aldwych, London WC2A 2AE.

Population Studies, Vol. 27, Pt. 3 (November 1973), 527–50.

Marietta Morrissey, 'Women's Work, Family Formation, and Reproduction Among Caribbean Slaves' University Press of Virginia, Box 3608, University Sta., Charlottesville, V.A. 22903, U.S.A.

Review, IX, 3 (Winter 1986), pp. 339–67.

Social Culture and Autonomy

Humphrey E. Lamur, 'Slave Religion on the Vossenburg Plantation (Suriname) and Missionaries' Reactions' Vinson H. Sutlive *et al.* editors Studies in Third World Societies, Dept. Anthropology, College of William and Mary, Williamsburg, Virginia, 23185, U.S.A.

Monica Schuler, 'Myalism and the African Religious Tradition in Jamaica' The Johns Hopkins Univ. Press, 701 West 40th St., Baltimore, Maryland 21211, U.S.A.

M. Crahan and F. Knight (eds), *Africa and the Caribbean. The Legacies of a Link* (Baltimore, 1979), pp. 65–79.

Dale W. Tomich, 'The Other Face of Slave Labor: Provision Grounds and Internal Marketing in Martinique' The Johns Hopkins University Press. As above.

Dale W. Tomich, *Slavery in the Circuit of Sugar: Martinique and The World Economy, 1830–1848* (Baltimore, 1990), pp. 259–80.

Sidney Mintz and Douglas Hall, 'The Origins of the Jamaican Internal Market System'

Sidney Mintz (ed.), *Papers in Caribbean Anthropology*, No. 57 (New Haven, 1970), pp. 3–26.

N. A. T. Hall, 'Slaves Use of Their "Free" time in the Danish Virgin Islands in the Later Eighteenth and Early Nineteenth Century' Dr. Bridget Brereton, as above.

Journal of Caribbean History, Vol. 13 (1980), pp. 21–43.

Control Resistance and Revolt

Elsa V. Goveia, 'The West Indian Slave Laws of the Eighteenth Century' Originally printed in *Revista de Ciencias Sociales*, IV, No. 1 (1960), pp. 75–105. Editorial de la Universidad de Costa Rica, Apdo. 75, 2050 San Pedro de Montes se Oca, Costa Rica. Also in Laura Foner and Eugene Genovese (eds), Slavery in the New World: A Reader in Comparative History (New Jersey, 1969).

Hilary McD. Beckles, 'Caribbean Anti-Slavery: The Self Liberation Ethos of Enslaved Blacks' Dr. Bridget Brereton, as above.

Journal of Caribbean History, Vol. 22, Nos. 1–2 1988, pp. 1–19.

Monica Schuler, 'Akan Slave Rebellion in the British Caribbean' Editors, Journal of Social History. Carnegie-Mellon University Press, Schenley, Pittsburgh 15213, U.S.A.

Savacou, Vol. 1, No. 1 (June 1970).

N. A. T. Hall, 'Maritime Maroons: *Grand Marronage* from the Danish West Indies' Editors, William and Mary Quarterly, Box 220, Williamsburg, Virginia, 23187, U.S.A.

William and Mary Quarterly, 3rd Series, Vol. XLII, October 1985, pp. 476–97.

Revolution, Reform and Emancipation

David Geggus, 'The Haitian Revolution' The University of North Carolina Press, P.O. Box 2288, Chapel Hill, North Carolina, 22515-1188, U.S.A.

Franklin Knight and Colin Palmer (eds.), *The Modern Caribbean* (University of North Carolina Press), 1989, pp. 21–50.

N. A. T. Hall, 'The Victor Vanquished: Emancipation in St. Croix, its Antecedents and Immediate Aftermath' Prof. Harry Hoetink, Brediusweg 56, 1401 AH Bussum, Netherlands.

Nieuwe West-Indische Gids, Vol. 58, No. 1–2, (1984) pp. 3–36.

Selwyn Carrington, 'The State of the Debate on the Role of Capitalism in the Ending of the Slave System' c/o Dr. Bridget Brereton, Dept. History, St. Augustine, Trinidad.

Journal of Caribbean History, 22, 1–2 (1988), pp. 20–41.

Andre Midas, 'Victor Schoelcher and Emancipation in the French West Indies' *This Journal collapsed in 1954 (Eric Williams was editor) check if we need permission.

Caribbean Historial Review Vol. 1 (1950), pp. 110–30.

Rebecca Scott, 'Explaining Abolition: Contradiction, Adaptation, and Challenge in Cuban Slave Society, 1860–86' The Johns Hopkins University Press, 701 West 40th St., Baltimore, Maryland 21211, U.S.A.

SECTION ONE
Amerindians and Slavery

Caribbean slave societies were established in space occupied and formerly under the control of a heterogeneous, but well-entrenched native people. All European colonists arriving in the region, following the Columbus Mission of 1492, considered it necessary to use their more developed military technology in an effort to subjugate these Amerindians as a prerequisite to successful colonization. The native Caribbean people fought wars of resistance, but were generally defeated and reduced to a range of servile relations. Many were enslaved, and others forced into dishonourable socio-economic conditions of marginalization and servitude. The results of these developments were extremely tragic demographically. These essays examine the quantitative dimensions of the 'genocidal' consequences of colonization, as well as the complex commercial, political and social relations established between Amerindians and Europeans.

On the Contact Population of Hispaniola: History as Higher Mathematics

DAVID HENIGE*

But is it certain that antiquity was so much more populous, as it is pretended?[1]

The most dramatic recent development in Latin American historical demography has been the changing interpretation of the size of the population of the New World at the arrival of the Europeans.[2] Figures as much as ten times greater than those most commonly advanced only a few decades ago are widely accepted today. In this trend the work of Sherburne Cook and Woodrow Borah, particularly for central Mexico, has been exceptionally influential, as shown by the incorporation of their postulated figures into works of a general nature.[3] Willingness to accept extremely high population figures (75 million or more) for the aboriginal New World appears to have reached a point where proponents of middle-range figures (35–75 million) often seem to be functioning as devil's advocates, while those favoring even lower figures are voices crying in the proverbial wilderness. Why such a consensus is developing is not at all clear, but it would seem to be attributable in part to the tenacity of the advocates of a high population and in part to bedazzlement by their extensive use of quantitative tools. In any case, it is not principally the result of any signal increase in data directly and unambiguously supporting arguments for a large precontact population.

Since confidence in these high estimates (or in any estimates) can be no greater than confidence in the means by which they were generated, I propose to discuss in this paper certain aspects of the methods used by proponents of high population estimates. 'Method', in this essay, will include the handling of sources; the assumptions implicit in their statistical procedures (rather, I hasten to add, than the procedures themselves); their explicit and implicit argumentation; and problems of *petitio principii*. Let me emphasize that I will confine myself here to an examination of the attempt by Cook and Borah to estimate the population of Hispaniola in 1492.[4] However, since the authors have brought some of the methods they used in studying central Mexico to their essay on Hispaniola, it is possible that some of the comments offered here may be of use to those attempting to evaluate their more important Mexican work. Angel Rosenblat has covered some of the same ground, but with differing purposes and emphases.[5]

Briefly, Cook and Borah conclude that about 8 million Indians were probably living on Hispaniola when Columbus landed there; that this population was halved during the next four years; that it was reduced to some 30,000 Indians by 1514; and that there were almost no Indians alive by the middle of the sixteenth century.[6] The last two points are well documented and enter into the present discussion only marginally. The earlier figures (for 1492 and 1496) result partly from a logarithmic projection based on a series of later figures, and partly from a series of assumptions whose validity it is one of the purposes of this paper to test.

From all appearances the Cook and Borah

*The author is African Studies Bibliographer at the University of Wisconsin, Madison. He would like to thank John Smail and Mary Braun for their help and comments on an earlier draft of this paper.

Hispanic American Historical Review, Vol. 58, No. 2, 1978, pp. 217–37.

microstudy has thus far been received with approval, even enthusiasm, and its conclusions accepted as reasonable and valid.[7] This ready acceptance is rather puzzling, particularly in view of the fact that previous modern estimates of Hispaniola's contact population ranged between 60,000 and 600,000.[8] It seems that many reviewers, while granting that the essay is provocative, have been persuaded by the authors' handling of their sources and their imaginative statistical procedures. It is to the first of these aspects of their argument that I now turn.

Every truth has two sides; it is well to look at both before we commit ourselves to either.[9]

Borah has recently asserted that his and Cook's work on Hispaniola was characterized by 'careful textual criticism' using the methods developed by the Bollandists and others.[10] Given the importance of a very few sources to any discussion of Hispaniola's aboriginal population, this assertion deserves to be tested rigorously. In their discussion Cook and Borah concentrate on three groups of sources: the reports of Columbus recorded in the journal of his first voyage; the figures adduced by Bartolomé de las Casas in some of his major works; and the evidence for a repartimiento of Indians reportedly undertaken in or about 1496. I would like to examine each of these in turn, discussing both the nature of their evidence and the ways in which the authors used these data.

Columbus' Testimony

Quite properly Cook and Borah begin by citing several passages from Columbus' journal for December 1492 and January 1493, since this is the only available eyewitness account of Hispaniola at that time. However, there are several problems in using this material. Columbus saw and described only a portion of the northern coast, and offered occasional observations of conditions in the near hinterland. Then, too, the only extant manuscript copy of the journal is in the handwriting of Las Casas, who was himself working from a second-hand copy.[11] Inevitably this introduces imponderables regarding the accuracy of the transcription. Finally, there is the crucial matter of Columbus' well-known and long-documented penchant for the metaphor and hyperbole, an appreciation of which is fundamental to any precise interpretation of his 'initial impressions'.[12] Cook and Borah discuss none of these problems.

Turning to their appraisal of Columbus' data, the analysis consists of little more than selecting those passages in which Columbus rhapsodized on the beauty and populousness of the island, transcribing his original language, and juxtaposing their own translations which are sometimes debatable in themselves.[13] In addition to Columbus' assertions about the charms of Hispaniola, which were usually expressed in grandiloquent but opaque language, his journal contains many passages suggesting in more concrete and realistic terms the existence of a sparse population in many parts of the island which fell within his purview. Apparently few people lived along the coast, perhaps from fear of Carib attacks. But even efforts to locate towns and large numbers of people in the interior were usually unfruitful.[14] The authors do not mention these passages.

Viewed in toto, then, Columbus hardly offers a coherent and unambiguous picture of the island's population, although on balance it seems to me to suggest a relatively small population. Nor is it very difficult to account for Columbus' exaggerations. He had hoped to reach the Far East, the land of 'the Great Khan'. He believed he had done so when compiling his journal (and perhaps until his death) and was convinced that Hispaniola was actually Marco Polo's Cipangu.[15] In these circumstances it was all too easy to fall victim to, as one writer has aptly phrased it, 'psychological illusions', which justified and sustained this hope.[16] So it was that, after sailing along the coast for some 75 miles, Columbus was already believing that Hispaniola was larger than England when it was only half its size.[17] He was also able, after seeing by his own estimation fewer than 10,000 Indians, to predict that the remainder of the island contained twice as many people as Portugal.[18]

In sum, Cook and Borah's use of Columbus' testimony to support their contention of a large and 'dense' population can be faulted on two grounds: the selection and analysis of only those passages which might support that view, and the failure to come to grips in any way with the probable validity of that testimony. By culling this source so discriminatingly, the authors cultivate an impression which they seek to reinforce by arguing that there was 'unanimity' as to the existence of a dense population. This claim — and its corollary that 'none of the earliest testimony reported an exiguous population' — is both incorrect and misleading.[19] And this would be true even if every statement of Columbus they cite, however extravagant on its face, could be taken seriously, even literally.[20]

The Estimates of Las Casas

As the only sources to offer comprehensive estimates of early Indian demographic decline under Spanish rule, the works of Bartolomé de las Casas inevitably serve as points of departure for modern investigators seeking to do the same in whole or part. For Cook and Borah, though, Las Casas' figures for Hispaniola serve as constant justification for their own arguments. Where others have seen these figures as inflated, the authors regard them as internally consistent and uncharacteristically conservative.

It need hardly be emphasized that the writings of Las Casas, insofar as they dealt with Spanish treatment of the Indians, were relentlessly and unabashedly polemical. As it relates to the size of the Indian population of Hispaniola, his work can be shown to be curiously dichotomous as well. In order to document and buttress his claims of harsh treatment — scarcely deniable in any case — Las Casas brought to bear a formidable arsenal of numbers, particularly in his *Brevísima relación de la destrucción de las Indias*, representing his view of the enormity of this treatment.[21] Some of his estimates of Indian population appeared in his major works, *Brevísima relación, Apologética historia*, and *Historia de las Indias*, but even more can be found in his many letters, memorials, and lesser tracts. Since Cook and Borah overlooked these materials, I have arranged them in chronological order to illustrate the point I wish to make about Las Casas' values:

1516 'se han disminuidos de un cuento [million] de ánimas que había en la isla Española . . . '[22]

1518 'un cuento y cient mil ánimas que había en la isla Española . . . '[23]

1531 'el cuento e cient mill *de toda esta isla* [Española] . . . '[24]

1535 ' . . . y mataron un cuento y cient mill ánimas *que yo ví en ella por mis ojos*.'[25]

1542 ' . . . que habiendo en la isla Española sobre tres cuentos de ánimas *que vimos*.'[26]

1542 ' . . . y es la cuenta que han dado de tres cuentos de ánimas que había en sola la isla Española.'[27]

1543 ' . . . perdidos que están de los muchos cuentos de ánimas *que vimos por nuestros ojos* en la isla Española, San Juan y Cuba.'[28]

1555 ' . . . la grande isla Española donde . . . sobre tres cuentos de ánimas.'[29]

1552/1560 'Yo creo cierto que [Española] pasaban de tres y de cuatro cuentos los que hallamos vivos.'[30]

The *Historia de las Indias* was begun in 1527 but not completed until the early 1560s and hence cannot be fitted into this schema. In it Las Casas presented three more estimates of this population. In one of these he accepted the figure of 1.1 million while his other estimates were about 3 million.[31]

Viewed in this way, a clear pattern emerges from Las Casas' various attempts to estimate the Indian population on Hispaniola. Obviously, sometime between 1535 and 1542 he tripled his early estimate, without ever accounting plausibly for the change. Thus Las Casas' figures, long regarded as prima facie unlikely, are even less reasonable when viewed *en ensemble*. For not only are his two groups of figures widely different, but he repeatedly contradicted himself in advancing his ocular 'proofs'.[32]

Why this abrupt change? We can only speculate. From all indications the figure of 1.1 million regularly offered by Las Casas in his first twenty years of writing sprang from information obtained from the Archbishop of Seville and from Bernardo de Santo Domingo, who apparently prepared a legal opinion for the Hieronymites on their arrival in 1517.[33] These estimates in turn referred to reports of a repartimiento allegedly carried out by Bartolomé Colón.[34] Before 1535, Las Casas always presented this figure without qualification and we must presume that he accepted it as accurate. Later, though, he would argue, rather unconvincingly, that this count *must* have included only parts of the island, despite his earlier explicit statement to the contrary.[35]

Influenced by his reading of certain classical authors' estimates of population in antiquity, Las Casas came to believe that Hispaniola was capable of supporting 'a much greater number' even than the 3 million he was by then attributing to it.[36] Perhaps, too, the passions aroused during the compilation of *Brevísima relación* made it easier for him to accept this reasoning. Or perhaps it was merely the result of becoming further removed in time and space from Hispaniola.[37] But whatever the stimuli may have been, the disconcerting fact of his abrupt and unaccounted change remains.

It has generally been held that his population estimates speak more to the depth of Las Casas' outrage than to his skills as a demographer; that is, it is impossible to distinguish Las Casas the historian from Las Casas the Defender of the Indians. In contrast, by arguing that Las Casas was consistent in his citations and that he actually erred on the low side in his estimates for

Hispaniola, Cook and Borah create a symbiosis in which certain of Las Casas' data are used to support their own high figures, which in turn are used to exonerate him from charges of pardonable exaggeration. It is important to try to appreciate Las Casas' purposes in offering his figures, to explore as far as possible his sources for them, and to relate the various arguments he adduced to an analytical and temporal framework. Ignoring the vast interpretative literature on Las Casas as well as much of his own work, Cook and Borah fail to do any of these.

The Repartimiento of ca. 1496

Two allotments of Indians loom large in the authors' calculations. One of them, carried out in 1514, is not at issue here.[38] The other, which, following Carl Sauer, they date to 1496, is not well documented, even though they are able to cite several references to it, all dating from 20–50 years later.

In constructing their population decline curve, Cook and Borah first mention three estimates made between 1519 and the mid-1540s. All three suggest that there had been 2 million Indians when Columbus arrived.[39] One of these sources suggested that this figure resulted from an actual census while the others presented the figure without comment. The authors then proceed to the information in Peter Martyr who, in his *De Orbe Novo*, spoke of reports of a population of 1,200,000.[40] Martyr was exceptionally well informed, but there are risks in citing him for details about the condition of Indian society on the arrival of the Spanish. Martyr was a charter member of the school of historical and philosophical thought which idealized the native cultures of the New World, saw the Indians as having existed in a kind of golden age, and contrasted this idyll with the depravity and corruption of Europe.[41] In fact, the chapter in which Martyr cited this figure is, perhaps not inappropriately, principally a catalog of wonders and marvels.[42] All things considered, his attribution of any particular population does not induce easy acceptance.

Cook and Borah next cite several other sources, each hovering around a figure of 1 million Indians. They concentrate on four of these and the relevant information in them is schematized in Table 1.[43] Some of these sources mentioned a count by Columbus or his brother Bartolomé; some merely alleged that the Indians had been counted; and others maintained only that about 1 million Indians had been living on the island when it was discovered.[44] Later I will discuss the uses to which Cook and Borah put these data; for the moment I propose to mention a few interpretative problems in accepting them.

The authors give pride of place to the figure of 1,130,000 Indians mentioned by the licenciado, Alonso de Zuazo.[45] First, on the basis of their own problematic translation, they argue that Zuazo had access to documentary evidence for his figure.[46] Then, too, they are impressed with 'the exactness' of Zuazo's number, in much the same way as biblical scholars of long ago sought to justify belief in antediluvian longevity because of the precise life-spans attributed to many of the biblical patriarchs. We do not really know from where his information came. It could easily have resulted from inferences of his own based on rumor, oral testimony or incomplete data.[47]

In fact the tenor of most of the allusions to a reported count (and Cook and Borah are not unaware of this) is one of hearsay. Obviously there was a popular belief in such a repartimiento. But rumor does not constitute evidence of any event — only of a subsequent belief in it. Cook and Borah recognize the ambiguous and contradictory nature of later accounts and the variety of the numbers cited and attempt to make a virtue of this deficiency by asserting that this very disparity is 'very strong evidence' of such a count and that rounding off is common to oral transmission.[48] While admitting the force of the latter argument, students of oral tradition and oral testimony would, I am sure, be chagrined at this example of the desire to know fabricating its own rationale. In effect, the authors

Table 1: Early Estimates of Aboriginal Population of Hispaniola

Source/Date	Figure cited	Unit described	Area encompassed
Anonymous (1516–17)	1,000,000	Souls	Entire island
Dominicans (1519)**	1,100,000	Persons	Not stated
Bernardo de Santo Domingo (1517)**	1,100,000	Vecinos	Entire island
Alonso de Zuazo (1518)	1,130,000	Indians	Entire island

**Those sources marked (**) referred to a count as well as an allotment. The two should not be thought to be necessarily synonymous.

like exact figures *because* they are exact; and they like inexact figures as well, *because* they are inexact!

What evidence is there against a repartimiento in or around 1496? We cannot reasonably expect to find sources from the time explicitly denying its occurrence, so we must argue by indirection. While any *argumentum e silentio* is at worst foolish and at best inconclusive, I propose a modest exercise of it here.[49] There were two occasions which are reasonably well documented and in which mention of any count would have been appropriate, though by no means necessary. When Nicolás de Ovando was sent to govern Hispaniola in 1501 he was issued a long set of instructions, several of which referred to relations with the Indians. This would seem to have been a good opportunity to allude to any formal arrangements that may already have existed. In the instructions the Indians were regarded as tributary (they were, of course, never thought of in any other way), but there was no mention of an earlier allotment. In fact, one of Ovando's charges was to institutionalize Spanish–Indian relations.[50]

In 1516, the Hieronymites went to Hispaniola to inquire into ways and means of alleviating the maltreatment and depopulation of the Indians there. A commission established soon after their arrival elicited testimony from several long-time settlers. The verbatim record of the testimony has survived in the form of a series of standard questions and the replies to them.[51] Several of the witnesses had resided in Hispaniola continuously since 1494 and some of these mentioned previous allotments in passing, but always referred only to those carried out under Ovando and later.[52] Apparently they knew of no earlier repartimiento, referring most often to Ovando's because it established a precedent in their minds.

All in all, the documentary evidence for a repartimiento under Columbus is far from convincing; it can be argued either way. We can reach only a slightly more satisfying conclusion by asking whether the Spanish had the capability to undertake such an allotment. The accounts of Las Casas and others picture Bartolomé Colón scurrying about the island trying to tamp down incipient Spanish disaffection on the one hand and growing Indian hostility on the other.[58] A chain of small outposts had been established to secure control of the auriferous areas but, despite the defeat of the cacique Caonabo and his allies the previous year, the Spanish were in a position only to try to establish their authority in most of the island through terrorism, since they could no longer rely on friendly caciques for support. Cook and Borah follow Sauer in choosing 1496 as the year of the count and Sauer's choice was based merely on eliminating all other times during the regime of Bartolomé.[54] However, the chroniclers' record of Spanish activities does not lead one to accept effective Spanish control much beyond the immediate area of their main settlement at Isabela. However much they may have wished to do so, they were simply not yet able to enforce a large-scale formal allotment of Indians.[55]

The Evidence of Other Early Sources

In several cases the same sources which mention a million or more Indians when speaking abstractly about Hispaniola leave a very different impression when describing specific events. In addition to imputing an extremely dense population to the small island of Saona (which, perhaps not coincidentally, he thought his own), Michele de Cuneo described the capture of 1,600 Indians. Five hundred of these dispatched to Spain, some were distributed among the settlers, and the remaining 400 were allowed to return to their homes. However, the latter fled to the mountains, causing Cuneo to lament that 'from [then] on scarcely any [slaves] will be had.'[56] In other words, the dispersal of 1,600 Indians apparently resulted in the virtual depopulation of the area around Isabela.

For the years after 1494, we have several references to the size of Indian armies which from time to time attempted to stem the Spanish tide. By far the largest of these figures was Columbus' claim to have defeated an army of 100,000 Indians at La Vega Real in 1495.[57] This Indian force was a coalition of several major caciques, but Columbus' figures were, as usual, certainly much inflated. In this case the exaggeration was part of an attempt to claim that the victory resulted from divine intervention.[58] Cuneo, writing about the time of the battle, reckoned that Caonabo, the major Indian leader in the battle, could field 50,000 men, but when the Spanish moved to occupy the Cibao, where he ruled, they were opposed by an army of no more than 5,000 men.[59] Later Guarionex and several other caciques made a concerted attempt to resist Spanish encroachment, hoping, we are told, to raise an army of 15,000. This mobilization never occurred because the Spanish learned of the preparations, so we cannot know if even this small number of men could have been assembled.[60] Yet, the Spaniards regarded Caonabo and Guarionex as the most powerful caciques on the island.[61] All these figures, even those cited by Columbus for La Vega Real, are remarkably modest under the circumstances hypothesized by Cook and Borah.[62] Certainly they do not suggest an island teeming with 5 or 6 million people.[63]

In sum, it is difficult to share Cook and Borah's enthusiasm for their sources. The documentary evidence they marshal does not provide the consensus on which they so meticulously insist, and they have failed to weigh critically even those data which at first glance might seem to support their argument. Despite chiding Rosenblat for failing to attempt 'the massive critical examination of sources customary in medieval and ancient European studies', Cook and Borah resolutely ignore their own advice.[64] The choices they make are not random, but systematic — designed always to support arguments for a high population. Sound scholarly procedure, it seems to me, requires that research be approached with questions in hand rather than answers in mind and that the more the data seem to fit a hypothesis, the more they demand the closest scrutiny before they can be accepted. But Cook and Borah seem not to agree with this.[65]

I began this discussion by referring to Borah's belief that he and Cook had adopted the methods of the Bollandists in their source analysis. For comparison, let me close by citing the opinion of an early Bollandist leader regarding that exegetical method. He emphasized that it was predicated on 'the duty to explain their view concerning the degree of veracity and the circumspection of the witnesses on whose testimony they support their preference . . . and no one should imagine that the obligation of providing original texts eases the burden. [Rather] it occasions additional studies and work, obliged as they are to collate minutely several manuscripts . . . and there is no place for adroit reticences and oversights.'[66]

When I use a word it means just what I choose it to mean — neither more nor less.[67]

Leaving the subject of source credibility temporarily aside, I intend now to concentrate on method. Having found the information they needed in the sources they used, Cook and Borah proceed to give precision to ambiguity, providing numbers where they had been lacking and offering new numbers in place of earlier estimates. Their method involves developing a population curve for the documented period and then projecting it backwards to 1492. There are three crucial points on this curve: reports of a vestigial population in the 1540s; the repartimiento of 1514 for which figures survive; and the reported repartimiento of 1496. Here we can grant that by the 1540s the Indians were nearly extinct, and that the count of 1514 might have represented as many as 30,000 Indians (even though only about 23,000 were actually recorded).[68] For the years 1508–10, the authors postulate a decline from about 92,000 to 66,000. These figures are modest enough but they are uniquely theirs, and they represent an increase of about 50 per cent above those cited in the sources.

This augmentative aptitude is most clearly manifested in their discussion of the reported 1496 count. Remember that the citations used by Cook and Borah ranged from less than 1 million to 2 million, but clustered around the 1,000,000–1,200,000 level. Table 1 shows that three of the four major sources specified that about 1 million human beings were involved, and three of them stated explicitly that their figures encompassed the entire island. It is at this point that the authors do engage in questioning their sources and conclude that the figures are much too low to indicate the total population. As a result 'persons' and 'Indians' become 'human units', enabling them to argue that this count included only 'able-bodied adults of 14 and above' on the grounds that in later usage the term 'indio' came to have this connotation among others.[69]

Once accepting this assumption, the rest of the argument flows swiftly and easily. Relying on Sauer's conclusion that 'a scant half' of Hispaniola was then under Spanish control, Cook and Borah double Zuazo's figures and attempt to convince the reader that to do so is in reality a conservative procedure. At this point, then, they argue, there were actually about 2,250,000 able-bodied adults on Hispaniola. The remainder of the population is calculated at 40 per cent, yielding a total of 3,770,000, as 'the most probable single figure with which to operate'.[70] It is the figure they employ to infer the size of the population four years previously.

A towering edifice constructed entirely of non-load-bearing 'possible to probable' assumptions may seem risky to the occupants of the top floor. Cook and Borah's 'most probable' figure can be no more likely than the product of the probability of each inference. At this point, in any event, they have reached the limit of the numerical sources; beyond 1496, they are left with the vague observations of Columbus. Undismayed, they look to mathematics in the hope that where historical evidence fails, statistical procedures will not.

They begin by attempting to eliminate any awkward imponderables (ecological constraints, epidemiology, warfare, for example) by boldly arguing that population decline may be 'a logarithmic function of time', and support this startling suggestion by asserting that such a decline in the early sixteenth century 'conforms entirely [sic] to our knowledge' for that period.[71] Having closed the circle of their argumentation in this fashion, they find it easy to project their population curve backwards — a procedure which elicits a population figure of about 8 million for 1492.

Cook and Borah are well aware that this extraordinarily large figure requires a net decline of over 20 per cent per year between mid-1493 and mid-1496 (their chosen parameters). They do not hesitate, however, to try to explain it. Ignoring the rugged terrain of much of the island, they characterize Hispaniola as 'predominantly low-lying tropical coast' capable of supporting dense populations.[72] In modern times, though, it is estimated that only about one-third of Haiti and one-half of the Dominican Republic is arable.[73] The authors rely, of necessity, on the capacity of the agricultural resources of Hispaniola and the agricultural sophistication of the Indians and speak of 'unusually favorable food resources', including maize, cassava, fish, and local fauna.[74] Inevitably this brings us to the matter of the explicatory powers of the 'carrying capacity' argument. Carrying capacity is, of course, an optimal concept — what *could* be if all constituent factors operated optimally. Sauer emphasized the nutritive value of the food crops native to Hispaniola, their quick and easy harvesting, and the advanced agricultural techniques of the Taino.[75] Yet, despite the development of the *conuco* field systems, they had apparently just begun to discover means of fertilizing the soil artificially, and their practices in this regard were still characterized more by magic than method when the Spanish arrived.[76]

Even more important, we know very little about the ethnography of the Hispaniola Indians. Yet, in order to know the efficiency of an agricultural system (that is, actual production measured against hypothesized carrying capacity), we need to know a great deal about those social and cultural factors such as marriage patterns, age of marriage, kinship relationships, and land tenure practices which help to determine the growth and density of a particular population.[77] None of the little we know about these aspects of fifteenth-century Taino society leads us to believe that they put any emphasis on building up population. As a ceiling concept, carrying capacity can directly support an argument against a large population, but it is not useful in supporting an argument for such a population.[78]

Sauer also characterized the Taino as living in 'peace and amity', but from all indications Carib attacks on the Arawak inhabitants of the Greater Antilles were at their height during the fifteenth century.[79] At the same time, Carib occupation of the Lesser Antilles prevented fresh immigration from northern South America, hitherto the major source of Arawak expansion.[80] It is possible, then, that the population of Hispaniola actually may have been declining during the period just before the arrival of the Spanish.

Having argued, though, that Hispaniola could (and did) support a huge contact population, Cook and Borah are left with the task of explaining an equally large decline in so short a time. Unlike Sauer, who emphasized societal disruption with resulting social and psychological malaise, they place primary emphasis, in a process of a priori reasoning, on epidemics which, they argue, must have ravaged the island almost from the day Columbus first anchored.[81] An early epidemiological catastrophe would indeed provide both explication of the decline and some justification for arguing large pre-contact populations, but the complete silence of the sources with regard to epidemics of any kind before the introduction of smallpox in 1518–19 somewhat vitiates the case for it.[82]

Could the death of more than 1 million Indians each year have escaped the notice of the Spanish who were, by Cook and Borah's own argument, in effective control ('occupation') of half the island during the mid-1490s? Could they, in their preoccupation with securing adequate manpower, have failed to mention the effects of disease and taken some sort of precautions against them? Would Columbus' host Guacanacarí have maintained his hospitable attitude in the face of such tragedy? Despite the authors' suggestions to the contrary, the most reasonable answer to these questions is no.

It is unfortunate that the very sources in whose reliability Cook and Borah repose such faith have failed them in accounting for such a decline. While it is bold to argue that something did not happen, it is even more so in the absence of any mention of that occurrence. That so overwhelming a decimation of a huge population could have happened within the purview of sources which resolutely ignored it is difficult to accept.

Although it would be unfair to argue that the arrival of the Spaniards could not have had immediate epidemiological effects, the only disease specifically identified in our sources is 'the French disease' or syphilis.[83] However communicable syphilis was, it was seldom immediately lethal — especially, we are told by Las Casas, among the Indians of Hispaniola where it had long been endemic.[84] In short, the early arrival of epidemics needs to be argued on the basis of some sort of evidence. To produce the specter of epidemiological disaster merely as a deus ex machina to explain the otherwise unaccountable results of a chosen statistical procedure simply fails to persuade.

He had been for Eight Years upon a Project to extract Sun-Beams out of Cucumbers.[85]

Historians like to believe that they approach the record of the past with due regard for the data and free of inhibiting predispositions. Cook and Borah have, I think, given evidence in the essay under review how very difficult it is to subordinate theory to evidence. But if one cannot agree with their methods or their conclusions, one may still be grateful to them for prompting us to ask questions about just what historians are, or ought to be. The authors frame two of the several alternatives clearly: should we approach a problem such as determining the size of the contact population of Hispaniola by a thorough and judicious scrutiny of all the evidence we can muster, or should we use conventional evidence only selectively and for illustration and rely on, say, mathematical techniques for our conclusions? Put another way, should we think of processes such as population decline as responding to a great number of variables — disease patterns, ecological changes, and cross-cultural impact — or should we consider them as completely susceptible to statistical analysis? Can a chapter of human experience really be 'a logarithmic function of time'?

An interest in numbers and a knowledge of statistical method can be useful tools in historical reconstruction and explanation, but they should never become an infatuation which blinds the ardent suitor to the defects of his inamorata. Historians who will become quantifiers must realize what statisticians already know — that, although sophistication of technique might temporarily disguise the weaknesses of the data, it can never really transcend them. All too often numbers have become will o' the wisps, in the frantic search for which the hunter seems to feel obliged to shed one layer of caution after another in hopes of becoming as protean as his elusive quarry.

If there is a correlation between density of population and level of culture, however defined, then it would undeniably be useful to gain some fairly precise understanding of the magnitude of the populations of various parts of the New World at the time of contact. Nor should the meagerness of the data by itself deter investigation. But the investigation must involve carefully structured hypotheses which, if not demonstrably true, at least represent the most reasonable interpretation of the available evidence. Or, as is to be greatly preferred from the historian's point of view, it must produce new evidence.

The intent of this paper has not been to offer yet another estimate of the population of Hispaniola in 1492, nor even to comment extensively on the many different estimates which have already been propounded. On the contrary, I would argue that it is futile to offer any numerical estimates at all on the basis of the evidence now before us. It can readily be granted and, indeed, hardly doubted, that whatever the population of Hispaniola and the rest of the New World was in 1492, there was a tragically precipitate decline during the first several decades of Spanish rule which in some cases led to extinction. But for the moment it is not possible to measure the rate of this decline for the earliest period of colonial rule, as is convincingly demonstrated by the attempt of Cook and Borah to do just that.

Notes

1. David Hume, *On the Populousness of Ancient Nations*.
2. For the extent of the literature see William M. Denevan (ed.), *Native Population of the Americas in 1492* (Madison, 1976), pp. 299–331, and Henry F. Dobyns, *Native American Historical Demography* (Bloomington, 1976).
3. See, for example, John H. Parry, *The Spanish Seaborne Empire* (New York, 1966), pp. 215–16; Thomas H. Hollingsworth, *Historical Demography* (Ithaca, NY, 1969), pp. 135–36; Ralph Davis, *The Rise of the Atlantic Economies* (London, 1973), p. 54; William H. McNeill, *Plagues and People* (Garden City, 1976), p. 203.
4. Sherburne F. Cook and Woodrow Borah, 'The Aboriginal Population of Hispaniola', *Essays in Population History*, 2 vols (Berkeley, 1971–74), I, 376–410.
5. Angel Rosenblat, 'The Population of Hispaniola at the Time of Columbus' in Denevan (ed.), *Native Population*, pp. 43–66. This is a translation of parts of his *La población de América en 1492: Viejos y neuvos cálculos* (México, 1967) and, although there is an addendum, Rosenblat does not comment specifically on Cook and Borah's essay.

6. Cook and Borah suggest a range from 4,070,000 to 14,560,000 but, not surprisingly, the figure most often cited in reviews is their mid-point figure of 8,000,000 and this figure, if any, is that most likely to be subsumed into the literature.
7. See the following reviews of the first volume of *Essays: Historical Methods Newsletter*, no. 5 (June 1972), 120-22 [Sims]; *American Historical Review*, 78 (April 1973), 512-13 [Cooper]; *Ibero-Americana Pragensia*, 6 (1972) 204 [Vebr]; *Ethnohistory*, 20 (Summer 1973), 292-96 [Dobyns]; *HAHR*, 53 (February 1973), 109-12 [Mörner]; *American Studies*, 5 (November 1973), 1809-810 [Crawford]; *Journal of Latin American Studies*, 5 (November 1973), 289-90 [Denevan]; *Rivista Storica Italiana*, 85 (September 1973), 795-98 [Carmagnani]; *Historia Mexicana*, No. 98 (October-December 1975), 316-18 [Gerhard]; *Geographical Review*, 66 (January 1976), 106-08 [Veblen]; *Annals of the Association of American Geographers*, 66 (September 1976), 464-96 [Robinson/Licate]. Only Mörner and Denevan express doubts about Cook and Borah's conclusions.
8. Charles Verlinden, 'La population de l'Amérique précolumbienne: Une question de méthode' in *Méthodologie de l'historie et des sciences humaines: Mélanges en honneur de Fernand Braudel* (Paris, 1973), pp. 453-62 [60,000]; Rosenblat, 'Population', pp. 43-66 [100,000]; Manuel A. Amiama, 'La población de Santo Domingo', *Clío*, no. 115 (1959), 118-19, 132-33 [100,000]; Alejandro Lipschutz, 'La despoblación de los indios después de la conquista', *América Indígena*, 26 (July 1966), 238-40 [100,000-500,000]; Samuel E. Morison, *Admiral of the Ocean Sea* (Boston, 1948), p. 393 [300,000]; Efrén Córdova, 'La encomienda y la desaparición de los indios en las Antillas mayores', *Caribbean Studies*, 8 (October 1968), 23 [500,000]; Frank Moya Pons, *Española en el siglo XVI, 1493-1520* (Santiago, 1971), pp. 66-7 [600,000]. Moya Pons' estimate seems to result from a misreading of Las Casas' account of a population of 60,000 in 1508. Las Casas did not state that this represented 'a tenth part' of the contact population, but that it showed that during the preceding seven or eight years, the Indian population had declined 'more than nine-tenths'. Las Casas, *Historia de las Indias*, II, xiv, in his *Obras escogidas* (hereafter cited as *OE*), 5 vols. (Madrid, 1957-58), II, 43. Others, like Carol O. Sauer, *The Early Spanish Main* (Berkeley, 1966, p. 66, and Pierre Chaunu, 'Las Casas et la première crise structurelle de la colonization espagnole', *Revue Historique*, 299 (January-March 1963), 76-77, accept the repartimiento count of *ca.* 1496 discussed below but do not offer their own estimates.
9. Aesop, *Fables*, 'The Mule'.
10. Borah, 'The Historical Demography of Aboriginal and Colonial America: An Attempt at Perspective', in Denevan (ed.), *Native Population*, p. 33.
11. Morison, 'Texts and Translations of the Journal of Columbus' First Voyage', *HAHR*, 19 (August 1939), 237-38.
12. Cook and Borah, 'Aboriginal Population', p. 376.
13. For example the authors translate 'mayor que' in the phrase 'toda la gente de aquella isla, que estimaba ya por mayor que Inglaterra' as 'more populous', *ibid.*, p. 378. Cf. Cristoforo Colombo, *Diário de Colón* (Madrid, 1968), p. 128. It is just possible that Columbus meant this, but it is more likely that he was comparing the size of 'isla' with 'Inglaterra' rather than its population — the position taken by all previous translators of the journal. Cook and Borah offer no explanation for their innovation.
14. Colombo, *Diário*, pp. 100-17. Rosenblat, 'Population', pp. 59-61, discusses these entries at some length. I mention them only to emphasize the unduly selective nature of Cook and Borah's examples.
15. See, for instance, Colombo, *Diário*, pp. 103, 129-130, 136-37. For a discussion of the importance of the chimera of the Great Khan to Columbus, see Antonio Ballesteros y Baretta, *Cristóbal Colón y el descubrimiento de América*, 2 vols (Buenos Aires, 1945), I, 83-91, and Henry Wagner, 'Marco Polo's Narrative Becomes Propaganda to Inspire Columbus', *Imago Mundi* [London], 6 (1949), 3-13. More generally see Wilcomb E. Washburn, 'The Meaning of "Discovery" in the Fifteenth and Sixteenth Centuries', *American Historical Review*, 68 (October 1962), 1-21.
16. Leonardo Olschki, 'What Columbus Saw on Landing in the West Indies', *Proceedings of the American Philosophical Society*, 84 (July 1941), 633-59, discusses this and related points. Later Hispaniola grew in Columbus' mind until he remembered it as comparable in size to Spain. Columbus to Luís de Santagel, February 1493, in Morison (ed.), *Journals and Other Documents on the Life and Voyages of Christopher Columbus* (New York, 1963), p. 185. Columbus' attitudes toward numbers of Amerindians is illustrated by the transformation in his accounts of an effort to locate large populations on Cuba in 1492. Two men were sent out for this purpose and, according to Columbus' journal, they reported that they had found only a single large village of about 1,000 inhabitants and several small clusters of houses. Colombo, *Diário*, p. 61. A few months later, when writing to Santangel to plead his case for royal support, he stated that these scouts had found 'an infinite number of small villages and people without number'. Morison (ed.), *Journals*, p. 182.
17. Throughout his first voyage Columbus overstated sailing distances, sometimes by two or three times. Among others see Morison, 'The Route of Columbus Along the North Coast of Haiti and the Site of Navidad', *Transactions of the American Philosophical Society*, 31 (December 1940), 239-44 *passim*.
18. Colombo, *Diário*, p. 138.
19. Cook and Borah, 'Aboriginal Population', p. 380. In this assessment they include the testimony of Michele de Cuneo discussed below.
20. As late as 1502, Columbus thought that Hispaniola was 'Tarsis, Scythia, Ophir, Ophaz, and Cipango' rolled into one — an impressive triumph of credulity over disappointment. Columbus to Alexander VI, [Febuary], 1502, in Colombo, trans. by Rinaldo Caddeo, *Relazioni di viaggio e lettere di Cristoforo Colombo, 1493-1506* (Milan, 1941), pp. 244-45.
21. On this see André Saint-Lu, 'Acerca de algunas "contradicciones" lascasianas' in *Estudios sobre Fray Bartolomé de las Casas* (Seville, 1974), pp. 1-3; Charles Bayle, 'Valor histórico de la *Destrucción de las Indias*', *Razón y Fé*, no. 147 (April 1953), 379-91.
22. Memorial of Las Casas to Cardinal Ximénez de Cisneros, in *Colección de documentos inéditos relativos al descubrimiento, conquista y organización de las antiguas posesiones españolas* de América y Oceania (hereafter cited as *CDI*), 42 vols (Madrid, 1864-84, I, 225.
23. Petition to Charles V, *ibid.*, VII, 106.
24. Letter to the Council of the Indies in Las Casas, *Opúsculos, cartas y memoriales, OE*, V, 48, with emphasis added.
25. Letter to Charles V, October 15, 1535, Benno M. Biermann, 'Zwei Briefen von Fray Bartolomé de las Casas, 1534-1535', *Archivum Fratrum Praedicatorum* 4 (1934), 213, with emphasis added.

26. *Brevísima relación de la destrucción de las Indias* (Buenos Aires, 1973), p. 25, with emphasis added. Though published in 1552, the original draft of this work was presented in 1542.
27. *Entre los remedios*, likewise written in 1542, but published only ten years later. Las Casas, *Opúsculos*, p. 75.
28. Las Casas and Fray Rodrigo de Andrada or [Ladrada] to Council of the Indies, 1543. Lewis Hanke, 'Un festón de documentos lascasianos', *Revista Cubana*, 16 (July-December 1941), 169, with emphasis added.
29. Las Casas to Fray Bartolomé Carranza de Miranda, August 1555. *CDI*, VII, 302, Elsewhere in this letter Las Casas claimed that the contact population had been greater than that of 'all Spain' and that each of the five major *cacicazgos* on Hispaniola was larger than Portugal. *Ibid.*, 297, 302.
30. *Apologética historia*, xx, *OE*, III, 65.
31. *Historia de las Indias*, iii, 94, *OE*, II, 397; ii, 18, *OE*, II, 51–52; iii, 19, *OE*, II, 217.
32. Cf. Sancho Panza's observation: 'He that told me the story said that it was so certain and true that when I told it to others I could affirm and swear that I had seen it all myself.'
33. *Historia de las Indias*, iii, 94, *OE*, II, 396–97. Las Casas resided in Hispaniola for many years and may have had other, unidentified, sources for his earlier estimates.
34. We know of this *parecer* only from Las Casas' allusions to it. Another *parecer* prepared at the same time and for the same purpose, and signed by nine other Dominican friars, mentioned neither a repartimiento nor a population estimate. 'Parcecer de los religiosos de Santo Domingo sobre los indios', *CDI*, XI, 211–15. For the repartimiento see below.
35. *Historia de las Indias*, ii, 18, *OE*, II, 51–52.
36. *Apologética historia*, xx, *OE*, III, 65.
37. Note that as Las Casas' numbers increased, so too did his explicit accusation of direct Spanish responsibility for this population decline.
38. For the repartimiento of 1514 see Cook and Borah, 'Aboriginal Population', pp. 380–85, and the sources cited there. In addition see Emilio Rodríguez Demorizi, *Los Domínicos y las encomiendas de indios de la Isla Española* (Santo Domingo, 1971), pp. 73–248.
39. Cook and Borah, 'Aboriginal Population', p. 387.
40. *Ibid.* Pietro Martire de Anghiera, *Décadas del Nuevo Mundo* (ed.) by Edmundo o'Gorman, 2 vols (México, 1964), I, 363. This part of Martyr's work was published in 1516. His principal informants for Hispaniola seem to have been Columbus and Andrés de Morales, cited in Sauer, *Early Spanish Main*, pp. 41–42.
41. This aspect of Martyr is discussed by María Olmedillas de Péreiras, *Pedro Mártir de Angleria y la mentalidad exotística* (Madrid, 1974), and Alberto Salas, 'Pedro Mártir y Oviedo ante el hombre y las culturas americanas', *Imago Mundi* [Buenos Aires], No. 1 (December 1953), 16–25. More generally, John B. Lynch, 'Apocalyptic, Utopian, and Aesthetic Conceptions of Amerindian Culture in the Sixteenth Century', *Comparative Literature Studies*, 4:3 (1967), 363–70.
42. Anghiera, *Décadas*, I, 359–68.
43. To their list add the letter of Pedro de Córdova, the Dominican Vice Provincial, to the Spanish King, May 28, 1517, *CDI*, XI, 217. Córdova spoke of 'more than a million' Indians 'destroyed or dead' but did not relate this figure to any count. It seems more likely that he was referring to a cumulative total.
44. Cook and Borah, 'Aboriginal Population', pp. 388–91.
45. Zuazo, Santo Domingo, to Guillaume de Croy, Comte de Chièvres [Xev(b)res], January 22, 1518, *CDI*, I, 310.
46. Zuazo wrote: 'Digo que a lo que se alcanza de los repartimientos pasados' which Cook and Borah translate as 'I say that according to what may be found in the records of past allotments of Indians for service'. 'Aboriginal Population', p. 388, whereas a more reasonable rendering would be: 'I say that from what may be gleaned from past allotments.' As it happens, they follow this with a series of qualifications that in effect swallow the original statement but the aftertaste remains — that Zuazo's statement is certain evidence that records of a Columbian repartimiento existed in his time.
47. An even more exact figure was cited in the middle of the seventeenth century when Juan Melgarejo Ponce de León stated that there had been 1,006,000 Indians when Columbus 'occupied' Hispaniola. Rodríguez Demorizi, (ed.), 'Relaciones históricas de Santo Domingo,' *Boletín del Archivo General de la Nación* [Santo Domingo], No. 20–21 (January-April. 1942), 117. Ponce de León had been governor of Hispaniola and presumably would have had access to any records. Why, then, the discrepancy, if Zuazo was citing the same records?
48. Cook and Borah, 'Aboriginal Population'. p. 393.
49. Rosenblat, 'Population', pp. 47–55, presents his views on the quality of the evidence for this repartimiento.
50. Instructions to Ovando, September 16, 1501, *CDI*, XXXI, 13–25. Nor did the instructions to Bobadilla in 1499 mention an allotment, but this is less surprising since his mission was to settle disputes among the Spanish. J. Marino Incháustegui Cabral, *Francisco de Bobadilla* (Madrid, 1964), pp. 505–11.
51. Rodríguez Demorizi, *Dominicos*, pp. 273–354 *passim*.
52. *Ibid.*, pp. 276–78, 293–96, 330–32. Manuel Giménez Fernández, *Bartolomé de las Casas*, 2 vols (Seville, 1953–60), I, 309–18, discusses what is known about these informants.
53. Las Casas, *Historia de las Indias*, i, 113–17, *OE*, I, 306–18. For discussions of Bartolomé Colón's administration see Gustavo Mejía Ricart, *Historia de Santo Domingo*, 8 vols (Ciudad Trujillo, 1949–56), III, 179–207, and Troy S. Floyd, *The Columbus Dynasty in the Caribbean, 1492–1526* (Albuquerque, 1973), pp. 33–38.
54. Sauer, *Early Spanish Main*, p. 66.
55. It seems inexplicable that none of the chroniclers mentioned a repartimiento in their accounts of Spanish activities during this period. Given Las Casas' close attention to all Spanish mistreatment of the Indians, including the encomienda system, and that his father was a settler on the island at the time, this omission (if omission it was), is strange.
56. Cuneo's letter, October 15/28, 1495, in Morison, *Journals*, p. 226. See also Cuneo, 'De novitatibus insularum Oceani Hesperii repertorum a Don Christoforo Colombo Genuensi', *Revista de Historia* [Caracas], 4 (January 1965), 54. Cuneo also mentioned the short lifespan of the Indians, declaring that he had seen none he thought older than fifty. *Ibid.*, p. 61.
57. Ferdinand Colón, *Vida del Almirante Don Cristóbal Colón* (Buenos Aires, 1947), pp. 180–81.
58. For the miraculous aspects of the tradition of the battle see Apolinar Tejera, 'La cruz del Santo Cerro y la batalla de la Vega Real', *Boletin del Archivo General de la nación*, no. 40–41 (May-August 1945), 101–119.
59. Cuneo, 'De novitatibus', p. 48; Anghiera, *Décadas*, I, 148.
60. *Ibid.*, p. 155; Gonzalo Fernández de Oviedo y Valdés, *Historia general y natural de las Indias*, 14 vols (Madrid, 1851–55), II, 60; Antonio de Herrera y Tordesillas, *Historia general de los hechos de los castellanos en las*

islas y tierrafirme del mar océano, 17 vols (Madrid, 1934–57), I, 314.

61. Tejera, 'Caonabo y Manicaotex', *Boletín del Archivo General de la Nación*, No. 52–53 (May–August 1947), 103–22 for early views of Caonabo.
62. In conditions of full mobilization it is usually reckoned that one-quarter to one-fifth of the populace bears arms. Stanislas Andreski, *Military Organization and Society* (Berkeley, 1968), pp. 33–74; Hollingsworth, *Historical Demography*, pp. 227–32. For New World applications see Cook and Lesley B. Simpson, *The Population of Central Mexico in the Sixteenth Century* (Berkeley, 1948), pp. 26–30; Robert C. Eidt, 'Aboriginal Chibcha Settlement in Colombia', *Annals of the Association of American Geographers*, 49 (December 1959), 379–91; Juan Friede, *Los Quimbayas bajo la dominiación española* (Bogotá, 1963), pp. 20–21; Horacio A. Difrieri, 'Población indígena y colonial' in *La Argentina: Suma de geografía*, 9 vols (Buenos Aires, 1958–63), VII, 25–28.
63. That is, a figure midway between 8 million in 1492 and 4 million in 1496. Peter Martyr mentioned a famine about this time which he thought had resulted in the death of 50,000 men. Anghiera, *Décadas*, I, 145.
64. Cook and Borah, 'Aboriginal Population', p. 376.
65. From time to time the authors have spoken of the need for such scrutiny but have not put principle into practice, at least for Hispaniola.
66. *Acta Sanctorum, Martii*, 3 vols (Antwerp, 1668), I, xx, quoted in H. Delehaye, *L'oeuvre des Bollandistes, 1615–1915* (Brussels, 1920), pp. 100–01.
67. Humpty-Dumpty in *Through the Looking-Glass*.
68. Cook and Borah, 'Aboriginal Population', pp. 397–99, 401. The authors attribute repartimiento counts to 1508, 1509, and 1510, but one of the witnesses at the Hieronymite inquiry specified that there had been but three allotments during his fifteen years (1502–17) on Hispaniola. Rodríguez Demorizi, *Dominicos*, p. 282. There may have been counts without allotments, but this would have been a wasteful and unlikely procedure.
69. Cook and Borah, 'Aboriginal Population', p. 394.
70. *Ibid.*, p. 397.
71. *Ibid.*, p. 403.
72. Cook and Borah, *Essays*, I, xii; and 'Aboriginal Population', p. 408.
73. Marc A. Holly, *Agriculture in Haiti* (New York, 1955), p. 31; Gérard Pierre-Charles, 'Haití: Esencia y realidad del desarrollo', *Revista Mexicana de Sociología*, 31 (July–September 1969), 595–97; *Area Handbook for the Dominican Republic*, 2d edn (Washington, 1973), pp. 7–8, 12–14, 180. Each of these estimates assumes a wider practice of irrigation than seems to have existed among the Taino.
74. Cook and Borah, 'Aboriginal Population', p. 408.
75. Sauer, *Early Spanish Rule*, pp. 51–59, 68–69.
76. Adolfo de Hostos, 'Plant Fertilization by Magic in the Taino Area of the Greater Antilles', *Caribbean Studies*, 5 (April 1965), pp. 3–5. William G. Sturtevant, 'Taino Agriculture' in Johannes Wilbert (ed.), *The Evolution of Horticultural Systems in Native South America* (Caracas, 1961), pp. 69–82, demonstrates that some early estimates of Taino field size were impossibly large.
77. Direct knowledge of Taino ethnography on Hispaniola derives almost entirely from the account of Taino cosmology and religious practices by Fr. Ramón Pane in Ferdinand Colón's life of his father. See Colón, *Vida*, pp. 183–208, and Edward G. Bourne, 'Columbus, Ramón Pane, and the Beginnings of American Anthropology', *Proceedings of the American Antiquarian Society*, 17 (April 1908), 310–48. For Taino culture generally see Sven Lovén, *Origins of Tainan Culture* (Göteborg, 1935).
78. Recent discussions of the problems in determining and applying carrying capacity are Brain Hayden, 'The Carrying Capacity Dilemma: An Alternative Approach' in Alan C. Swendlund (ed.), *Population Studies in Archaeology and Biological Anthropology: A Symposium* (Washington, 1975), pp. 11–12, and Stephen B. Brush, 'The Concept of Carrying Capacity for Systems of Shifting Agriculture', *American Anthropologist*, 77 (December 1975), pp. 799–811.
79. Sauer, *Early Spanish Main*, p. 69.
80. Marcio Veloz Maggiolo, 'Las Antillas precolombinas: Ecología y poblatión', *Revista Dominicana de Arqueología y Antropología*, 2 (July 1971–June 1972), 165–69.
81. Cook and Borah, 'Aboriginal Population', pp. 409–10. Cf. Sauer, *Early Spanish Main*, p. 203.
82. On the epidemiological consequences of the discovery of the New World see, among others, Alfred W. Crosby, *The Columbian Exchange* (Westport, Conn., 1972), pp. 35–63; Wilbur R. Jacobs, 'The Tip of the Iceberg: Pre-Columbian Indian Demography and Some Implications for Revisionism', *William and Mary Quarterly*, 2nd ser., 31 (January 1974), 123–32; Crosby, 'Virgin Soil Epidemics as a Factor in the Aboriginal Depopulation of America', *William and Mary Quarterly*, 2nd ser., 33 (April 1976), 289–99.
83. Colón, *Vida*, p. 230.
84. Las Casas, *Apologética historia*, xix, *OE*, III, 58–60.
85. Jonathan Swift, *Gulliver's Travels*, Pt. 3, chap. 5.

Amerindian–European Relations in Dutch Guyana

ALVIN O. THOMPSON

In the book from which this article has been taken we have dealt peripherally with the ways in which European, largely Dutch, contacts with the Amerindian communites affected the lives of the latter. At this point it is necessary to focus attention more closely on this subject. All the Amerindian societies were affected to a greater or lesser extent by their contacts with the Europeans. These contacts had to do mainly with trade and military assistance, but the Dutch were able to exploit Amerindian manpower in a variety of other ways, such as in cultivating provision grounds and acting as boat hands, messengers, timber cutters, baggage carriers and guides. The Dutch would have found it impossible to trade, reconnoiter and carry on their other activities in the hinterland without the Indians' assistance. These people influenced the material culture of the Dutch in Guyana in several minor ways, but the Dutch influenced their life more deeply. Still, taken as a whole, the Indian culture-systems remained substantially intact. This was due to some extent to the fact that the Dutch did not generally try to impose their way of life on the Indians, so that their political and social systems embraced very few Indians. In one area, however, the European contact was traumatic.

In Guyana, as in other parts of the Americas, the European advent and colonization had a catastrophic effect upon the demography of the Indian communities. A number of factors account for this situation, such as European diseases, the development of the Indian slave trade, intense warfare often relating to questions of trade, and forced migration resulting from the military and social pressures exerted by the other factors just identified. Warfare and forced migration tended to cause the Indian groups to split into even smaller units than before. Fission led to further vulnerability and further fissioning and so the process of decimation unfolded, as both cause and effect of these fissiparous tendencies. The impression gained from the Dutch contemporary records and from more recent documents is that there was excessive fragmentation of Amerindian political and ethnic groups. In few instances during the period under consideration was the process of aggregation noticeable, and certainly no Amerindian group increased significantly its territorial or political control. The military mastery of the Dutch in the more northerly areas was underscored by the continual expansion of the plantation system there. On the other hand, they had very little jurisdiction over the areas beyond the plantations.

Two kinds of Indian migration are discernible in the context of Guyana during this period: interior migration, that is, from one area to another within Guyana; and inward migration, chiefly from Spanish and Portuguese territories into Guyana. It is difficult at present to trace any pattern or sequence of migration; all that will be attempted here is to give some indication of the general and specific factors relating to such migrations and the groups involved in the same.

The European presence is the obvious factor with which to begin the discussion. As Sheridan points out:

> Not only were the Europeans accompanied to the New World by invisible microparasites, but these conquerors and colonists were themselves macroparasites.[1]

The early Dutch pushed the Indians out of their homelands, and those whom they could not push out they attempted to wipe out with

Colonialism and Underdevelopment in Guyana, 1580–1803 (Caribbean Research and Publications, Bridgetown, 1987), pp. 191–213.

superior military technology and strategy. In some instances the Indians offered physical resistance, but at other times they quietly retreated to areas less accessible to the new invaders. This pattern of migration was noticed in Berbice in the 1670s, and in Demerara in the second half of the eighteenth century. Hartsinck notes that in the early days it was possible to find relatively large villages of sixteen to eighteen households in the lower (most northern) parts of the colonies, but that the situation was quite different by 1770. The villages were now located much further inland, while only two or three households could be found living together in the lower areas.[2]

The Dutch presence in Guyana resulted mainly in the interior rather than the outward migration of the Indians. This was due to two main factors. Firstly, the upper reaches of the rivers and some other areas of the hinterland were never occupied or controlled by the Dutch and in several instances they had nothing more than a trading presence there. Secondly, the Spanish and Portuguese presence had created similar pressures on several Indian groups in those localities, so that there was strong disincentive to migrate to those areas.

Spanish presence and activities in the northwest district and the Cuyuni area during the second half of the eighteenth century led to fissile multiplication and migration of the Indians further east. Thus in 1758 and 1762, as a result of Spanish activities around the Dutch post in Cuyuni, many Caribs fled the area and sought new homes in upper Essequibo. As late as 1769-70 the Dutch were reporting the continual withdrawal of these people from Cuyuni.[3] In the northwest, too, Spanish attacks on Post Moruka in 1769 and 1744 led to extensive dislocation of the Indians living there. According to the Dutch authorities, before the Spanish attacks some 700 Indians could be found around the post, but by 1772 most of them had disappeared from the area. In 1774 they were said to be seeking refuge in Corentyne. The Pomeroon Indians were also greatly dislocated at this time by the Spanish activities.[4] The Spanish had earlier been responsible for the retreat of many Indians from Orinoco into Moruka in fairly large numbers, though actual statistics are unavailable.

As early as 1685 the Caribs are recorded as migrating from the Spanish to the Dutch zone in face of reprisals for an attack (along with some Frenchmen) on Santo Thomé in the previous year. They sought refuge in Amacura, Barima and Waini in northwest Essequibo. In 1752–54 the Dutch records noted the retreat of the Caribs from Orinoco to the Dutch side as a result of continual Spanish harassment. In 1755 these records mentioned that a Spanish priest had recently come to claim some Indians of the Chima (Shiamacotte) nation, who had deserted the Spanish missions for Post Moruka some ten years previously. In 1767 and 1769 some Warraus were also recorded as retreating from Orinoco to Barima; while in the latter year a large number of Caribs were also said to have migrated from the Spanish missions to Mahaicony, some of them clad in priestly garments and ornaments.[5]

Northwest Essequibo witnessed the greatest incidence of inward migration and also the greatest degree of dislocation. But inward migration also took place occasionally from the Spanish zone into the Cuyuni-Mazaruni district. Thus in 1755 Gravesande reported that the chiefs of the Panacay people in upper Cuyuni had paid him a visit recently. They were at loggerheads with the Spanish and were offering their assistance to the Dutch against possible Spanish encroachment on territory which the Dutch held as their own. The Panacays even promised to settle down around the Cuyuni post, but we do not know whether they made good this promise. In 1769, again, it was rumored that a group known as the Cerekous (Cerekon) had moved from Spanish territory into the area just below Post Arinda and were annoying the Akawois. Finally, in 1790 four Indian chiefs along with their followers migrated from the Spanish missions into Dutch territory in Mazaruni.[6]

More to the south and southwest of Guyana, the migrants came from the area of modern Brazil, specifically the Rio Branco–Rio Negro district. The factors leading to migration from this area are less certain, but the most general one was again the European (this time mainly the Portuguese) presence and activities. These activities may be summarized as slave raiding, founding mission stations by the use of force, and establishing a politico-military administration. Dutch activities in the Rio Branco area also played some part in the migration of Indians. The obvious factor was the trade, and especially the slave trade, which the Dutch traders and their cohorts pursued here, as in Orinoco. Groups, perhaps seeking refuge from the Portuguese, Dutch, Carib and other slave raiders, crossed the Ireng and Takutu rivers and made their way into secluded areas within the vast expanse of virtually uninhabited territory in the Rupununi district. This was true of the Macusis, as we shall see shortly.

Another factor which might have accounted for inward migration was the attraction or pull of Dutch trade on one or two groups in the Rio Branco. For instance, the Manaos, a people inhabiting the middle-upper reaches of the Rio Negro, who wanted to establish direct and regular trading contact with the Dutch, found that their efforts were being thwarted by the Caribs and Akawois who occupied strategic areas along the established trade routes. The Akawois feared that their own trading interests might be compromised by their more southern neighbours, but they seem also to have feared that the Manaos would use any opportunity to enslave them and lord it over them.

Actually, the first reference to the Manaos in connection with the Dutch trade occurred in 1719, when they were mentioned in Portuguese records as trafficking with the Dutch in the headwaters of the Rio Branco, though their residence appears to have been on the Rio Negro. They are referred to in a Portuguese source of a later period as being the nation of greatest renown throughout the Rio Negro, on account of their numbers, valor, language and customs. In the 1720s they were the most notorious slave dealers of that district.[7] Their first appearance in Essequibo seems to have been in 1722. In the following year they paid another visit to the area, arriving in three boats carrying about thirty persons, including some slaves whom they hoped to sell to the Dutch. However, their advent produced quite a stir among the Caribs and Akawois there, who warned the Dutch officials that they had come with hostile intentions. The colonial government reacted swiftly to this supposed threat by sending a party to apprehend the Manaos and take them to the fort for questioning. Most of them escaped but about eight or nine of them were caught. This incident shook them quite a bit. Later investigations revealed that they had in fact come with amicable intentions and mainly to improve trade relations with the Dutch. In 1724, no doubt because of the incident mentioned above, they were attacking the Akawois and Caribs in upper Essequibo and threatening to kill all the Dutch. The colonial government resolved to send a force comprising Europeans and Indians to drive them away.

The Manaos were not heard of again in Guyana for some time and virtually disappeared from the Dutch records until 1751, when they were reported by the postholder of Arinda to be harassing the Indian inhabitants of upper Essequibo. This is somewhat surprising, for the Portuguese records in 1727 mentioned their Paramount Chief, Ajuricaba, as being in alliance with the Dutch, and even flying their flag. He had become the scourge of the Rio Negro and Rio Branco, enslaving the inhabitants of those places and selling them to the Dutch. Even after the Portuguese got rid of Ajuricaba in the following year, the Manaos remained a powerful slave-raiding group, obviously in close association with the Dutch traders. But curiously enough, in 1754 Gravesande referred to them as being in alliance with the Portuguese, while in reality they were often at each other's throats.[8] In 1763 Gravesande was thinking of forming an alliance with them, which he believed would further Dutch trading interests in the Rio Branco, while holding the ring politically against the Portuguese, who wanted to promote their interests there. On the other hand, he did not want to antagonize the Caribs, useful allies and, in fact, the most redoubtable military auxiliaries of the Dutch. The Caribs were trying to oppose the alliance; the postholder of Arinda reported that an attempt made in the previous year by the Manaos to send an embassy to the Dutch government in Essequibo had been hindered by them. A sharp encounter had actually taken place between the two groups and the Caribs had been defeated, but the losses sustained by the Manaos had been sufficiently heavy to force them to postpone their visit until the following year. Meanwhile, the Caribs were rallying their forces for the expected confrontation, so that Gravesande feared that the largest Indian war during his administration was imminent. In order to avoid this he send word to the Manaos that they should send only a small force to Arinda, from where they would be escorted to headquarters.[9] As it turned out, the alliance never came about, nor were the Manaos able to establish their own corridor of trade with the Dutch, a circumstance which Gravesande attributed to 'a political dodge of the Carib nation'.[10] Instead, the Manaos had to be content to allow the Dutch and their Indian auxiliaries to come and purchase their slaves from the Rio Branco.

The events outlined above show clearly the pull that Dutch trade had on groups even in the far interior, and also the conflicts which the trade could and did generate among interested parties. This was seen on a much smaller scale in relation to the Wapisianas. In 1753 it was reported that they had killed three white traders who had gone to upper Essequibo to trade with the Portuguese. The incident probably took place somewhere close to the lower-middle Rupununi river, which was the normal route for access into the Portuguese zone. We are not aware of what transpired as a result of the attack, but we know that Gravesande contemplated employing the Caribs who, along with the Macusis, had also been attacked by them, to drive them away from the route they were obstructing or, as he put it, 'away inland far from the River Essequibo'.[11] It is possible that he either made good this threat or that the Indians migrated from fear of reprisals. When the postholder met them some years later, in 1769, he reported that they were occupying both banks of the Ireng river and that they had not seen a white man for sixteen years. He also stated that they lived in the plains during the day but slept in inaccessible rocks and cliffs during the night, and heavily palisaded and defended their nocturnal dwellings for fear of the Manaos, with whom they were always in conflict.[12] They seem to have been divided into a number of families, living apart from each other and shifting their dwellings periodically. In 1739 Horstman had found them south of the Takutu and Uraracuera rivers in what is today modern Brazil. The eighteenth- and nineteenth-century descriptions of them located them roughly between the Rupununi on the east and the Ireng, Takutu and Rio Branco on the west. Schomburgk estimated the number of those living in Guyana around 1840 at 500 souls.[13] From all appearances they were a predatory group (or groups) who found themselves frequently in conflict with their neighbours. It is thought that they forced the Macusis to move further north, and that they absorbed the Atorais.

The Macusis themselves were another group of migrants who entered Guyana at a relatively early period. Iris Myers suggests that a reference on Du Val d'Abbeville's map of 1654 to the Muchikeriens (a people inhabiting the area around Lake Parima), might be applicable to them.[14] The first Dutch document available to us on the subject was written in 1753. It mentions them specifically and strongly implies that they were already well known to the Dutch. This is not surprising for they appear to have been among the chief victims of the Caribs, Manaos and others who sold them as slaves to the Dutch. They were regarded as the least warlike of the groups in the Rio Branco.[15] Their main homeland was probably the Rio Negro area, from where a number of them migrated to Guyana towards the middle of the eighteenth century. The Dutch source just referred to mentions them as the neighbours of the Wapisianas. One view is that they occupied the southern Rupununi savanna first and that they were forced northward by the Wapisianas. Around 1840 Schomburgk declared that their occupation sites included the savannas of the Rupununi and Rio Branco, and the mountain chains of the Pakaraima and Kanuku. He estimated their total number at 3,000, and those living in Guyana at 1,500,[16] a figure which made them one of the largest groups in the country at that time (if his figures are reasonably accurate). By 1786, according to the Portuguese Commandant of the Rio Branco district, they were one of two groups there who were very attached to the Dutch.

The Paravilhanos (Paravianas) were another group originally inhabiting the Brazilian area who migrated in small numbers into Guyana, possibly in the eighteenth century. They are mentioned in Portuguese records as occupying several sites along the Rio Branco and Takutu rivers, and by 1770 they had become the dominant group in that region. Their presence in Guyana is barely mentioned in Dutch records. In 1739 Horstman seems to have found some of them on the Essequibo, about a day's journey above its confluence with the Siparuni. According to Gravesande in 1769, during his early administration they used to live 'up in Essequibo', but because the Caribs repeatedly harassed them they were forced to move to the Ireng river, in close proximity to the Wapisianas.[17] In 1788 they were mentioned in Portuguese records as dwelling close to the headwaters of the Takutu, along the ranges between that river and the Rupununi. They had gained notoriety as dealers in human flesh. According to Farabee, they had become extinct by 1914.

Finally, we must mention the Tarumas in connection with inward migration. We do not know the date of their migration but it is generally thought that they entered the country sometime in the eighteenth century. In 1764 Gravesande mentioned them as a 'numerous and powerful nation' living in upper Essequibo.[18] In the 1720s some of them were living along the Takutu river, from where they probably migrated to the area close to the sources of the Essequibo river.

The migrations into southern Guyana did little to people that region, which throughout the eighteenth century remained largely uninhabited. The main occupation sites were located in the region between the Rupununi in the east and the Takutu and Ireng in the west. Virtually no inhabitants could be found to the east of the upper reaches of the Essequibo river. On the other hand, Indian groups in the north spread out over a much wider area than formerly. Refugee groups found their way as far east as the Corentyne, while others sought asylum along the middle reaches of the Essequibo and Berbice rivers, and in upper Demerara.

A factor which ought not to be overlooked in this discussion as a probable cause of fission and migration is the warfare carried on by groups traditionally residing in Guyana. The problem here, however, is that the records available to us have little to say about these wars, and even less about their effects on Indian migration. Therefore, all that can be attempted here is a summary of the wars to which the records attest. These wars involved mainly the Caribs and to a lesser extent the Akawois, the two groups that the Dutch generally regarded as the most warlike of those dwelling in Guyana.

In 1673 the Dutch records reported that the Caribs and Arawaks of Barima had just concluded a peace agreement. In 1680 the Caribs and Akawois of the Cuyuni–Mazaruni–Essequibo area were engaged in a relatively large-scale war which had not been resolved up to 1683. In 1684 the Barima–Orinoco area was the scene of petty warfare, while in 1686 the Akawois and Caribs of Mazaruni were locked in a power struggle leading to the loss of several families. Conflicts also occurred between the Caribs and Warraus of the Barima–Orinoco area in 1748. But the most sustained war seems to have taken place from 1765 to 1768, between the Akawois and Caribs in upper Demerara and the middle Essequibo–Mazaruni areas. At one stage it even threatened to merge with a conflict between similar groups in the Corentyne.

The conflicts between the various Amerindian groups upset the balance of life among them and caused considerable anxiety. They led on several occasions to the stoppage of trade with the Europeans. Indeed, the hinterland trade depended to a large extent on the goodwill of the Indians and their ability to maintain amicable relations among themselves and also with the Europeans, particularly the Dutch. This was an important reason why the Dutch officials always attempted to keep the peace with them and on several occasions to act as intermediaries between belligerent groups. Thus they intervened in Indian disputes in 1680, 1683, 1686, 1765 and 1766, but they were not always able to bring about peace. In 1680, for example, the Akawois in Cuyuni refused to accept bribes from them or allow them to act as peacemakers in their war with the Caribs.

One of the main problems which the Dutch officials faced in this respect was their limited political authority over the hinterland. Of course, several contemporary and modern writers have asserted that by the late eighteenth century the Dutch had established a kind of protectorate over the Indians. For instance, in the arguments put forward in 1898 by the British authorities in their boundary dispute with Venezuela they asserted that the Amerindian chiefs became 'formally accredited officers of the Dutch Colony, and exercised their authority with the sanction of the West India Company'.[19] A more recent writer declared in 1977 that the Indians had 'unquestionably recognized the protectorate of the Dutch, and the Dutch had assumed the responsibilities of a protecting power'.[20] The British authorities had made virtually the same statement earlier, specifically in relation to the Caribs,[21] while Rodway had said much the same thing in 1896.[22] These views demonstrate a complete misunderstanding of the relations between the two parties during the period under discussion. In general, it was the Dutch and not the Indians who needed to be protected — from threatened Spanish invasion, maroons and even the ravages of hunger. They were the ones who were dependent on the Indians, and not the latter on them. Nevertheless, they were to some extent responsible for fostering the myth of their role as protectors of the Indians. Especially in their boundary disputes with the Spanish, they were bent upon demonstrating their political, military and commercial hegemony over the region under dispute. The rights of the Indians were never considered by them when it came to the question of territorial jurisdiction, any more than they were considered by the Spanish, British, French or Portuguese. The Europeans simply viewed them as having no territorial rights (and very few other rights). According to the so-called 'law of nations' of that period, which was completely Eurocentric, their lands were open to expropriation and colonization, provided they were not already under the jurisdiction of some Christian (European) power. But since effective occupation was regarded by the Europeans as the clearest expression of sovereignty, the Dutch tried hard to create the impression that they were the effective occupants of a much wider area than they actually administered.

One must also distinguish between the language sometimes used in official correspondence between the WIC and the local Dutch administrators, and the reality of the situation on the ground. Sometimes this official correspondence seems to imply that the Indians were under Dutch control but in moments of greater lucidity and honesty Dutch dependence on the goodwill and substantial assistance of the Indians becomes manifest. On balance, the sources indicate a delicate alliance between the so-called 'colonizer' and the 'colonized'.

It is obvious that from the point of view of the vast majority of the Indians in Guyana the Dutch did not exercise the slightest jurisdiction over them. Without doubt, Dutch influence was felt over a wide area, as we have seen already. However, we must not confuse influence with jurisdiction, alliance with allegiance, fraternalism with paternalism. No formal empire of any significant territorial size was established by the Dutch and it is quite doubtful whether we should even regard the degree of Dutch influence as constituting an informal empire. It should perhaps be said here that the same argument holds good in relation to Spanish jurisdiction over the sprawling provinces of Guayana, Barcelona, Cumaná, Santa Fé, etc.

Effective Dutch jurisdiction touched relatively few Indians, chiefly the Arawaks and Warraus, who came to reside either around the Dutch hinterland posts or on the peripheries of the estates, and who underwent the most extensive acculturation. It is true that the Indians were sometimes required by the Dutch to obtain passes to go beyond the posts, but these appear to have been Indians living below the posts. In 1763 the Commander of Demerara issued a permit allowing a Carib chief to go to Berbice. Similar passes were issued to Indians by other Dutch officials in 1778 and 1779.[23] Dutch merchants had to pay a small sum of money to obtain such passes, but this does not appear to have been the case with the Indians.[24] What is clear is that official Dutch policy — in contrast to that of the Spanish and Portuguese — was to eschew the use of force to restrict the movement and way of life of the Indians. The Dutch tried to use persuasion rather than coercion to keep the Indians in alliance with them and in close proximity to their settlements. This was the rationale behind the postholdership system and the periodic distribution of gifts to the Indians. It is necessary to stress here that this distribution was not an act of patronage but rather one of friendship. Dutch records leave us in no doubt that without these gifts the friendship and services of the Indians could not be assured.

The custom of regular distribution of gifts to the Indians seems to have originated in the late seventeenth century. According to Van Berkel, each Indian captain or chief at that time received biennially from the Dutch in Berbice (and perhaps also in Essequibo) a red worsted dress and a hat, with which he appeared at the fort.[25] Another source of the same period makes it clear that such gifts were necessary 'to keep on friendly terms with the Chiefs'.[26] As time went by the practice embraced a large number of chiefs from an increasingly wider area, and was put on a more official footing in 1778 when a number of chiefs were invited to the Dutch headquarters in Essequibo and presented with hats having broad silver rims, and staves with silver knobs. At the same time the Indians were encouraged to show fidelity to the Dutch government at all times, to give their assistance whenever requested to do so, and to refer their disputes to the Dutch authorities. They were told that the instruments they had just received were indicative of the Dutch government's recognition of them as chiefs, and that whenever they wanted to appoint new chiefs they should choose those proposed by the Dutch government. It is also said that the chiefs and their followers were elaborately entertained at Duinenburg, the Company's plantation, and that they expressed loyalty and friendship to the Dutch government.[27]

In the following year similar gifts were distributed to a large number of chiefs of the Carib, Arawak and Warrau peoples. The staves were engraved with the WIC's seal, a practice which soon became customary. In 1784 the WIC approved an elaborate plan put forward by the colonial authorities in Essequibo and Demerara to honor the chiefs, especially those of the Caribs. They were to be invited to come to the fort in Essequibo from the various districts of the country, and were to be offered lands on which to settle permanently, close to the Dutch settlements. In addition, they were to be given the staves, as mentioned above, and also silver ring-collars and rum. In return, they were to pledge themselves to return to the fort once annually to give a list of the men under their command, and to renew their pledge to assist the Dutch in times of military need. In order to induce them to do so, they were to be given gifts on such occasions.[28] Here, then, is the system which several writers have regarded as tantamount to a recognition by the Indians of the paramountcy of Dutch authority, a view strengthened by Hartsinck's statement in 1770, some years before the system was elaborated fully, that the chiefs were being appointed by the Dutch Governors.[29]

On the contrary, a close look at the situation reveals that for three important reasons the Dutch cannot really be said to have exercised paramountcy over the Indians in general. In the first place it must be realized that the reason for putting forward the scheme was because the Indians were withdrawing from the neighbourhood of the Dutch settlements. The scheme was therefore designed to attract them once again to the lower reaches of the rivers, where their services would be more readily available in times of need, particularly against runaways and maroons. This was actually stated in the document of 1784 which set out the scheme, while it is implied in those relating to the convocation of 1778.

Secondly, the minutes of the Court of Policy of 1778, which recorded the actual visit of the chiefs in that year, declare that the presents were given to them as 'a token of friendship', not to make vassals of them.[30] In 1785, also, when three chiefs and 105 of their followers from upper Essequibo visited the fort, the chiefs were given silver ring-collars as 'tokens of friendship'.[31] While it is possible that a few of the chiefs were raised to the office or had their power enhanced by the Dutch, in general their power emanated solely from their kinsmen, to whom they were ultimately responsible. This point was made by Hilhouse, who was well-acquainted with the Indians. He indicated in 1825 that the chief's authority was still subject to that of his people, and that the Akawois elected their own captains (chiefs), acknowledged no white protector, and rejected any interference in their domestic affairs.[32] Several years earlier, in 1769, Gravesande had stated that when the principal chiefs visited him they immediately took a chair, sat down, and refused to eat and drink anything but what he himself had. They referred to him only as 'mate' and 'brother'.[33] It was only during the governorship of Sir Henry Light (1838–48) that the colonial government really began to appoint chiefs, and only then can they be said to have become the accredited agents of the colonial government.[34]

The third major reason relates to the land grants. It appears that few if any Indians accepted the offer of such grants. They preferred to retain their independence and mobility, rather than come under the thumb of the Dutch, as would certainly have been the result if they had accepted the land grants. It was only under the British that the system of creating Indian reservations, first mooted by the Dutch, came into operation.

The tendency of the Indians to withdraw a fair distance from the seat of Dutch power was one of the clearest expressions of their independence. The Dutch continued to coax them to return, or at least not to move farther afield. Thus in 1803, in their instructions to their postholders, they enjoined strict application of the regulations concerning the humane treatment of the Indians. When the British occupied the colony later in the same year they showed a similar concern about the Indian question. They felt that their earlier occupation (1796–1802) had led to the withdrawal of a considerable number of Indians to more remote districts in the country, a circumstance which might have had grave consequences for their colonies. They therefore reintroduced the system of annual presents that thad lapsed temporarily. Gradually, however, they extricated themselves from this system as they felt more confident of their control over the colonies and the hinterland. In 1831 they made the presents triennial, and on the eve of the final abolition of slavery in 1838 they discontinued the practice altogether. The result was a significant withdrawal of the Indians from the main colonial areas to more remote positions.[35] This circumstance reinforces the view that the presents were the nuts and bolts of the alliance between the Europeans and the Indians. The British, like the Dutch, saw the alliance mainly as a security in times of slave uprisings; while the Indians were only prepared to stay close to the Europeans as long as they were willing to give them gifts, allowances and rewards for military service against the slaves. The friendship between the two parties was no love relationship but rather a business arrangement. During the Dutch regime giving presents to the Indians was an ineluctable necessity for the colonial administrations. In fact, by the nineteenth century the Indians had even begun to view the presents and allowances as a form of tribute. In 1813 Colonel Edward Codd, Acting Governor of Demerara, had this to say:

> It is obvious that our Colonies are tributaries to the Indians; whilst the proper system of policy would be to make them allies, looking to us for protection.[36]

He had good reason to be apprehensive about this arrangement. In 1810 Mahanarva, a Carib chief, had moved into the capital with his men, threatening to use physical force unless the customary presents and allowances withheld from him by the British were paid. The government decided to appease the chief rather than risk his taking umbrage on this occasion. The presents were given but the government reserved the right — at least so the Governor wrote — to decide whether it would make presents in future. As noted above, the presents continued for another two decades.

It is sometimes asserted that even if the Indians were not politically, they were at least militarily, subordinate to the Dutch, that they could be summoned in times of military need, and that they were committed to placing their forces under Dutch officers. There is some ambiguity in the Dutch records on this matter. Sometimes these records convey the impression that the Indians were under some compulsion to respond to the Dutch call for assistance, and indeed the Dutch records at times contain such words as *summoned* and *ordered* when referring to the call for assistance. However, the term *requested* or an analogous term is used as commonly. On each occasion when military assistance was rendered, material rewards had to be given to the Indians, apart from the annual presents. In 1763, for instance, when the assistance of the Caribs was being sought by the Director-General of Essequibo to quarantine the colony from the slave uprising in Berbice, this is what he had to say to the WIC:

> I shall write to Post Arinda as soon as possible to instruct the Postholder to induce the Carib nation, by the promise of a recompense, to take up arms in this matter.[37]

Such requests and rewards were quite common. In one sense, therefore, the Indian military auxiliaries may be viewed as mercenaries rather than allies.

It is also somewhat inaccurate to say that the Indians generally fought under Dutch officers. Again, there are instances when the Dutch records state that Dutch officers were being sent to head the Indian contingents. In 1769 the Commander of Demerara stated that he had appointed a persom whom the Arawaks respected as commander over them in order to prevent them from migrating to Berbice. The person was almost certainly a white burgher officer.[38] A few years later, in 1744, an Essequibo burgher officer, Stephanus Gerardus van der Heyden (Heijden), was appointed by the Dutch authorities there as colonel over the Indians of that territory, while his sons were appointed captains.[39] Though the evidence on the subject is at present rather scanty, it appears that during the second half of the eighteenth century the Dutch began to appoint officers to act on their behalf in their military dealings with the Indians. These officers, however, were only liaisons between the Dutch and Indian forces, and were not commanders superimposed by the Dutch over the Indians. They attempted with varying degrees of success to coordinate the efforts of the whites and Indians in bush expeditions. But they were never recognized by the Indians as their superiors, and on some occasions it proved virtually impossible to achieve coordination between the two forces. Thus in 1769 when Backer, the Dutch Commandant, attempted to get a Carib chief to put his forces under Dutch command, he replied: 'No, I am master of the Caribs. You can be master of the whites and of the other nations, and then we can together become masters of everything.'[40] Hilhouse indicated in 1825 that when expeditions were composed of whites and Indians there was 'always considerable confusion and insubordination', and that this could only be avoided by dividing the forces along racial lines.[41]

The Indians were never formally recruited and constituted by the Dutch into a military corps. The nearest they came to this was to attract several of them to the most important posts established in the hinterland. In the late eighteenth century about twenty-five of them were receiving small monthly stipends as military auxiliaries attached to Post Moruka. Even so, no attempt was made to train them in European combat tactics. It is certainly untrue, then, to state that the Indians were generally militarily subordinate to the Europeans.

Some writers regard the fact that on several occasions the Indians sought redress from the Dutch government for wrongs they had suffered at the hands of the colonists as evidence that they were amenable to Dutch law. However, we must also challenge this view on the basis that the referral of such disputes was the result of a clear understanding between the Dutch colonial authorities and the Indians that the two parties would eschew the use of force, as far as possible, in their relations with each other. Thus the Indians complained, not from a position of subordination, but from one of alliance. It hardly needs to be said that the fact that a complaint has been lodged by someone against another person to a third party does not necessarily mean that the complainant is under the jurisdiction of the third party, but rather that the accused is under such jurisdiction. This was the situation between the Dutch and the Indians. The latter always reserved the right to resort to the arbitrament of force if they should fail to obtain redress through the Dutch judicial process. In fact, when grave offenses were committed against them they sought immediate retribution by appeal to arms, rather than referring the matter to the colonial authorities. Thus Amerindian–Dutch relations were often punctuated by physical conflicts, as happened in 1747, 1750 and 1755–56.

The colonial authorities were quite sensitive to the need to court the favor of the Indians and therefore published laws periodically prohibiting the colonists from ill-treating them. As early as 1627 Abraham van Pere, the proprietor and founder of the colony of Berbice, had agreed as one of the conditions of his proprietary grant to treat the Indians justly and honestly.[42] Similar instructions were given to Abraham Beekman, Commander of Essequibo, in 1768, and to the postholders. Laws were actually published on this matter for the information of the colonists in 1729 and around 1760. According to the edict of 1729 delinquents were to be fined f.50 for the first offense and f.100 for the second, while a third offense was to meet with a much heavier penalty.[43] In spite of these laws the Indians were often abused by the colonists.

An important reason for this was that even when the Indians lodged complaints against the miscreants the Dutch courts rarely dispensed justice impartially. For one thing, Indians, like Africans, were considered as an inferior and untrustworthy species of humanity whose testimony could not be admitted against whites in Dutch law courts. The result was that even when the colonists were obviously guilty they usually got off very lightly, as we can see from two cases brought before the colonial judiciary in 1750. The first was against Pieter Marchal, a planter in Mazaruni, whom the Caribs accused of refusal to pay them for services rendered him over a period of four months. Although the Court of Justice found the evidence heavily weighted against him, it simply admonished rather than compelled him to keep the peace with the Indians and pay them their dues. The other case concerned the ill-treatment of another group of Caribs by the colonist Pieter de Bakker. This time the Indians' testimony was corroborated by that of another white person. Nonetheless, the court simply reprimanded him.[44] Again, in 1752 the actions of one Christian Tonsel in seizing the children and friends of some Caribs of Barima met with only reprimand and an order to restore the persons seized to their relatives.[45]

Generally, the colonial judiciaries were not interested in dealing out even-handed justice in cases involving Europeans and Indians. But there were a few occasions on which *raisons d'état* made it imperative to rule in favour of the Indians, as can be illustrated by reference to two incidents which took place in 1760 and 1772. The first concerned Nicolas Stedevelt, a trader who had put a Carib from Cuyuni in fetters and taken away his wife for allegedly stealing his goods. Though he had a white witness who confirmed that the Indian had confessed to committing the crime, the Court passed judgement against him. He was fined f.250 and cautioned that he would be banished from the colony for a similar offense in future.[46] Two probable reasons account for this unusual judgement. A law had recently been passed prohibiting the whites from mistreating the Indians and Stedevelt's actions seemed a flagrant disavowal of the authority of the government. More importantly, Spanish activities in Cuyuni were a constant source of bother to the Dutch. They were therefore sparing no efforts to maintain friendly relations with the Indians in that area, whom they hoped to use as a counterfoil to the Spanish. Stedevelt's actions threatened to embroil the Dutch in a conflict with the Indians at a time when the former could least afford it.

The second instance concerned one F. W. Gerds, who was imprisoned for twenty-four hours, heavily fined, and ordered to pay f.50 as compensation to an Indian whom he had whipped. Again, in this case Dutch 'humanitarianism' and 'sense of fair play' must have been mixed with the leaven of enlightened self-interest. It is interesting to note that the same dispatch that carried the story about Gerds also mentioned that a slave revolt was taking place on the sea coast and that the assistance of the Indians was being sought; hence the need to ensure that the Indians did not have fresh cause for umbrage against the Dutch.[47]

Apart from cases where the Indians brought complaints against the colonists, there were a few instances when the Dutch courts tried Indians for wrongs committed by them. In 1765 an Indian was charged with committing murder in the Moruka district; in 1783 a similar event took place.

A third incident involving the Carib chief Aritanna in 1755 became a *cause celèbre* some years after the event, for the British (in their main argument concerning their boundary dispute with Venezuela in 1898) used it as evidence-in-chief of Dutch jurisdiction over the Indians. They alleged that the chief had been *summoned* by the Dutch authorities to appear before the Court of Justice, because he had killed certain Akawois in the Mazaruni district. But this allegation was not completely correct.[48] In the first place, the person on trail was not Aritanna but rather the colonist Pieter Marchal who had incited him to commit the act. He confessed to having killed the Indians at Marchal's instigation, but no action was taken against him. Moreover, although Gravesande wrote to the WIC on January 5, 1765, that the Court of Justice had sent someone to *summon* the chief

(*Indiaen op te ontbieden*), in an earlier dispatch of November 24, 1755, he had stated that the Court had decided to invite (*te versoeken hier te weesen*) the chief to testify at the trial.[49] This incident cannot therefore be used as conclusive evidence of Dutch jurisdiction over the Indians in Mazaruni.

The entire rationale behind Dutch claims that they were offering the Indians protection against the whites can be gathered from Gravesande's candid statement in 1769:

> There is no one, Your Honours, who is more convinced how advantageous and necessary the friendship of the Indians is to this Colony . . . I therefore neglect no possible opportunity of cultivating the friendship of the same and of protecting them from all the ill-treatment and tyranny of the whites as far as it is expedient to do.[50]

This was it. For a brief moment the Director-General exposed the naked truth: the cause of the Indians was only espoused as long as it was expedient for the Dutch to do so. Expediency, however, sometimes made the colonial officials consider playing off one group of Indians against the other. Thus in the Dutch–Akawois conflict of 1755–56 Gravesande contemplated requesting the assistance of the Caribs to fight the Dutch cause, but we have no evidence that he actually had recourse to this measure. In 1763 he expressed the hope that his Carib allies would 'get a good hiding' from the Manaos because he felt that they were obstructing the latter from making direct contact and permanent alliance with the Dutch. Later in the same year an expedition comprising Dutchmen and Caribs, *en route* to assisting the whites to put down the Berbice slave uprising, killed several Indians on the contention that they had come to kill an Akawois chief. It was often the colonists, rather than the colonial authorities, who played off the Indians against each other for their unscrupulous ends and who were also responsible for instances of impassioned invective and armed hostilities between the Dutch and the Indians. Up to the end of the Dutch period there were still several instances of festering grievances between the two parties.

On a few occasions the Dutch offered military assistance or gave moral support to their Indian allies against outsiders, but on each occasion that we have come across a particular Dutch interest was at stake. In 1724 they decided to assist the Caribs of upper Essequibo to repel the Manaos, but this was done because they had received a report that the latter had threatened to kill all Dutchmen, and also because their attacks on the Caribs and Akawois might have led to the migration of these people to other areas, to the detriment of the Dutch fisheries there.[51] In 1746 the Dutch offered military assistance to the Indians in Waini who had been attacked by other Indians from Orinoco. This was the time when the boundary problem with the Spanish in Orinoco was becoming a major issue and the Dutch suspected that the attacks had been instigated by the Spanish in Cumaná. The Dutch were therefore hoping, in effect, to use the Indians of Waini and the other rivers in the northwest to hold the ring against the Spanish, instead of shielding the Indians from attacks. Again, in 1769 they gave their blessings to a Carib expedition which was about to attack some Cerekous Indians in upper Essequibo, who were alleged to have arrived from Orinoco under Spanish instructions to harass those Indians in alliance with the Dutch. Needless to say, important Dutch territorial and trading interests were at stake. Curiously enough, however, when in 1757 the Caribs were preparing to attack a new Spanish religious mission in Cuyuni in an area which the Dutch claimed as belonging to them, the government in Essequibo not only refused to provide them with arms but sent an emissary to Orinoco to apprize the colonial government there of the intended attack. The Dutch reasoned on this occasion that their action would secure the goodwill of the Spaniards.[52] This proves once again that it was narrow self-interest which was the crucial variable in Dutch relations with the Indians. The latter were often used as pawns in the game of diplomatic and military chess between the various European colonial powers. As far as the Dutch were concerned, once their own interests were not at stake the Indians could kill themselves or each other without their batting an eye at what was taking place.

While issues relating to war and trade dominated Amerindian–Dutch relations, the exigencies of life forced the Dutch to forge links with the Indians at other levels. As already indicated, one of the vital ways in which the Indians assisted the Dutch in the daily running of the plantations was by providing bread and fish for them, or more precisely for their slaves. Indian methods of preparing cassava and fish were also commonly employed on the plantations. The Indians affected the culture of Dutch plantation society in these and several other ways, such as through the use of hammocks in place of European-style beds; Indian boats, which were admirably suited to riverine navigation; and the local palms for thatching roofs. The *troolie* palm was particularly widely used. When laid properly, it forms thatching which is very durable and quite resistant to rain. It was used by the Dutch to thatch their boiler rooms, slave huts and other buildings.

Although contact between the two parties was regularly maintained, most Indians, even those who gave some service to the plantations and the posts, preferred to live some distance away from the Dutch establishments. Nonetheless, some of them found it convenient to live on or close to the Dutch settlements — especially the Arawaks and Warraus. The Dutch considered the former to be the most docile, sedentary and civilized of all the Indians. They were certainly the ones who underwent the greatest degree of acculturation to European values, a circumstance which must have had a lot to do with the European view of them. On the other hand, the Caribs and Akawois, who rarely gave any but military service,[53] were vilified as the most barbarous and incorrigible groups, to whom raid and rapine were the normal way of life. The Dutch, of course, never bothered to address the question of the impact of their own presence and activities on the escalation of Indian warfare.

As a rule, the Indians were sensitive about their rights, as we gather from both Van Berkel and Hartsinck. They refused to be coerced into doing a job or to be ordered about, and allowed no impairment of their rights as freemen.[54]

In return for their services they received a wide assortment of European manufactured goods — cloth, hats, mirrors, beads, fish hooks, pins, needles, scissors, pots, basins, cutlasses, axes, adzes, firearms, powder, shot, etc.[55] Iron tools were the most important of these commodities, from the point of view of the economic improvements they were capable of bringing about in Indian societies. The iron axes made it easier to clear the dense forest, while the cutlasses were quite handy for light cutting purposes. These tools therefore were in great demand; nevertheless, it would be a gross exageration to suggest, as Seggar does, that these tools revolutionized the economic life of the Indians.[56] The fact is that they had a surprisingly limited impact on Indian agriculture. They were not introduced in sufficiently large quantities to make them commonly available throughout the country during the Dutch period. Stone tools therefore survived for a long time after the introduction of the new tools, as was also the case in West Africa for over a thousand years after iron technology had been introduced there. The iron tools which the Dutch sold the Indians were also quite shoddy and anything but durable,[57] nor did the Dutch make their knowledge of iron smelting available to the Indians. While iron ore has not been discovered in large quantities in Guyana, the knowledge of iron smelting might have enhanced Indian societies appreciably.

The Dutch also failed to influence Indian agricultural technology, apart from the use of iron tools. We must record a series of negatives on this score: no animal manure or artificial fertilizers, no wheel and plow, no rotation of crops, no soil conservation methods. Instead, they continued to use their old methods well into the nineteenth century: slashing and burning, planting a variety of crops in a single field, and leaving the land fallow after three or four years.[58]

Even in relation to new crops the Dutch had little to offer. The sugar cane was the only exotic crop of note which they introduced, and, even so, the Indians made very limited use of it. They cultivated it as a secondary crop alongside their other crops. In fact, nineteenth-century sources dealing with Indian domestic crops generally do not mention sugar cane, but only crops of local origin. Cassava remained by far the most important Indian crop.

Apart from European agricultural tools, there were other tools (especially the adze) which were used to manufacture boats and other wooden items. The European contribution in this area was quite significant, mainly in lightening the various tasks and providing a better finish. However, once again we notice the absence of any substantial modifications in either shapes, sizes or methods of construction of Indian boats.

Iron was used for a wide variety of other purposes. It often replaced the bone or wooden points at the tip of javelins and arrows, thus giving these implements sharper and more durable points. Sometimes, also, iron hunting and fishing tools were used side by side with the traditional tools. For fishing, of course, the Indians utilized the metal fish hooks which were imported in seemingly large quantities. (Among the items which the British distributed to the Indians in 1827 were 11,972 fish hooks.)[59] But for a long time fishing with hooks did not displace the traditional method of fishing, which entailed damming and poisoning the rivers and using nets and arrows to obtain large catches.[60]

Firearms were perhaps the most significant innovation and certainly the most coveted implement introduced by the Dutch, even though their impact was largely negative. Of course, up to at least the last years of the eighteenth century gun technology was still not highly advanced.

Moreover, the 'trade guns' exported from Europe were usually the worst of their kind, as was certainly the case with the majority of Dutch trade guns introduced into Guyana.[61] Even in the late nineteenth century, under the British regime, the Indians were receiving guns which are said by Im Thurn to have been of 'a most trumpety kind'.[62] Occasionally, more efficient weapons found their way through illicit trade into Indian hands, but even these often became rusty and defective in the tropics because of the climate and, more importantly, neglect to service them regularly. There must also have been problems in repairing them and obtaining adequate supplies of gunpowder and ammunition. In spite of these limitations, guns gave their users a certain military advantage over opponents using such traditional weapons as spears, bows and arrows. Consequently, the Indians made every effort to acquire them. In practice, however, the supply of guns was always limited, even for European personnel in the colonies. Relatively few Indians therefore acquired them, so that they never completely displaced the traditional weapons. The Caribs seem to have obtained more than their neighbours, which increased their striking power considerably and allowed them to prosecute the slave trade virtually with impunity. Both Spanish and Portuguese documents attest to this fact.

After a while the Dutch authorities began to show some uneasiness over the trade in guns to the Indians or even putting such weapons in their hands to assist the whites in their military undertakings. In 1755 Gravesande expressed fears that the possession of such weapons would considerably increase the difficulty of keeping the Indians in check and that one day they might turn the guns against the whites. They were not trustworthy, since their friendship with the whites was based upon 'fear or by reason of the profit they make out of trading with us than from inclination'.[63] A few years earlier, in 1750, he complained to the Zeeland Chamber that occasionally they obtained good guns, and that their acquisition of firearms made them lose their awe of these weapons, which he obviously saw as the ultimate security of the whites. He suggested that the surest way to eliminate this overarching threat was to abolish the gun trade completely, under stiff penalties against delinquents.[64]

Actually, the Chamber prohibited the trade on at least two occasions, in 1735 and again in 1752, no doubt acting on the Director-General's suggestion. However, these embargoes did little to stop the flow of arms to the Indians, especially since the suppression of the trade was likely to lead to a rupture of the alliance between the Indians and the Dutch. In fact, in 1762 the Caribs laid the cards on the table: they were not prepared to fight the white man's wars without firepower. Thus the authorities were forced to equip the Indians with firearms to fight for them in 1762, 1763, 1778 and 1785, and no doubt on other occasions.[65]

Firearms added a new and significant factor to Indian warfare during the eighteenth century, though this did not mean that they invariably ensured success by their possessors against groups using mainly traditional weapons. They remained a prized possession for a long time, as Seggar noted in 1965: 'The shot-gun eventually became, and still is the greatest prestige or status possession [among the Indians].'[66]

European manufacturers also modified Amerindian societies in areas of dress and ornamentation, mainly in relation to the use of new materials. Glass beads commonly replaced seeds, shells, bark, etc, as the basic material for making women's aprons, especially among the groups in regular contact with the Dutch; the notable exceptions were the Warraus.[67] Imported beads were also used to make necklaces, but traditional materials held their own for a much longer time in the manufacture of these ornaments. Blue cloth was now used to make men's laps, but we do not know how common this practice had become by the end of the Dutch period. What we know is that cloth formed an increasingly important item of the trade. Bolingbroke, writing around the end of the period, indicated that the Indians used their cloth laps when visiting the European headquarters. On such occasions the chiefs were more 'elaborately' clad, in full European garb.[68] We also learn from Im Thurn, who wrote about three-quarters of a century later, that only the Warraus retained the use of bark cloths at that time instead of imported cloths.[69]

The Europeans were much less successful in introducing domesticated animals into the Indian societies in Guyana. This is quite surprising when we note that the introduction of such animals constituted a major input into many Indian societies in the Americas. The introduction of the horse, for example, revolutionized Indian warfare in several parts of the Americas. However, in the case of Guyana, it was not the horse but the dog which was the major innovation, and its impact was in respect of hunting rather than warfare. Even so, the Indians owed the introduction of this animal more to the

Spanish and the Portuguese than to the Dutch. The small breeds of hunting dogs formerly possessed by the Indians were increasingly displaced by dogs imported from Spanish and Portuguese territories. Schomburgk stated that the Akawois went to Colombia and Brazil to obtain these animals.[70] The Tarumas in upper Essequibo had become breeders of these dogs by the late nineteenth century,[71] by which time they were equal in value to a good gun or a large canoe.

Apart from dogs, no other animal had a major impact on Indian societies in Guyana. Horses were expensive and suffered a high mortality rate, at least in the plantation area. Their limited utility was also due to their unsuitability to the terrain in which the majority of the Indians lived. They simply could not compete with the canoe and the Indian's bare feet in mobility and versatility along the rivers and over the paths. The animals which the Europeans used for food were considered by the Indians well into the nineteenth century as unclean.[72] It is only in more recent times that they — mainly those in the Rupununi savanna — have taken to raising cattle, pigs, sheep and goats.

Speaking more generally, the Indian-European contact led to a much more highly developed barter economy among the former. By the end of the Dutch period this had led, if not to the emergence of a specialized trading class, at least to certain groups taking the leading role in trade. These came mainly from the Akawois and to some extent the Carib communities.

Outside of the purely material aspects of Indian life, contact with the Dutch affected the Indians in a few other ways. From the early days the Dutch cohabited with Indian women and produced a small mixed group. In the early nineteenth century they were living mainly at Bartica, at the junction of the Mazaruni and Essequibo rivers, by which time they had become considerably mixed with African blood. They were chiefly engaged in cutting timber and salting fish for the Europeans. They often spoke a hybrid language known as Creole Dutch, which had become the lingua franca of the slaves and several Indians by the late eighteenth century.[73] Dutch lexical items had also found their way into the Amerindian languages, for instance, *negotiae* for 'trade' and *kleine flinte* for 'small arms'.[74]

In the field of religion, almost nothing was done to Christianize the Indians. The Moravians and Roman Catholics were the only groups which showed some interest in them. The Moravians turned to them after encountering planter opposition to their efforts at converting the slaves. They turned to the Arawaks in Berbice, where they founded a mission in 1738. They established their headquarters at a place called Pilgerruh (Pilgerhuth), at the junction of the Wiruni (Wironje) and Berbice rivers, and lived a simple life, fishing, hunting and engaging in tailoring and shoemaking to obtain a livelihood. In time they learnt the Arawak language and began to translate the Bible into it, and also to compile a dictionary. By 1759 they had about 300 Indians under their spiritual charge, but shortly afterwards a number of their followers died of an epidemic which swept the colony at that time. The mission survived until 1763, when it was destroyed by the slaves during the uprising in that year. The missionaries moved to Corentyne (Ephraim), where their coreligionists had established another mission in 1757; this survived until 1806 when it was destroyed by fire and eventually abandoned. After the Moravians departed the Indians quickly forgot most of the missionaries' teachings, though some memories survived for a long time.[75]

The Indians in Essequibo and Demerara did not undergo any Christian instruction. In 1729 A Roman Catholic priest from Orinoco visited Essequibo and requested permission to start work among them, but the Commander turned down the request.[76] This seems to have been the only attempt to start a mission among the Indians there.

On the whole, it can be said that the Amerindians were as much in the mainstream of developments in Guyana, both positive and negative, as the Africans and the Europeans. The advent of the Europeans had quite a negative impact on their political structures. Many Indian communities became fragmented and some were destroyed, a situation which reflected in vivid miniature what had taken place and what was still going on throughout the continent of North and South America where whole civilizations were destroyed. This was all part of the process of underdevelopment characteristic of the European impact on autochthonous societies. New communities sprang up from the devastation and destruction, but these were small and perhaps less cohesive than their predecessors, and were sometimes pitted against each other in an interlocking struggle for survival. This is certainly the picture which emerges of the Caribs and Arawaks around the mid-eighteenth century. Without doubt, the European advent multiplied the incidence of warfare within

Indian communities, while Indian-European wars, and animosities bred between Indians and Africans due to the use of Indians as slave catchers, added further dimensions to the military factor. Our preliminary investigations strongly suggest that in several instances relatively peaceful zones in the pre-European period, such as the middle Essequibo-Mazaruni area, became battlegrounds in which the use of firearms escalated the conflicts. More peaceful pursuits also took place. A more sophisticated network of trade developed, with the Indians exchanging a variety of local goods for exotic products. But even here the military factor was intrusive, especially in relation to the slave trade, the repercussions of which were felt over a wide area.

The Dutch needed the Indians, as they needed the Africans, in order to develop viable colonies. They needed them for trade, military purposes, manpower availability, and a variety of other purposes. Indian initiative and response to the new groups did much to determine the pattern of plantation and hinterland development. In time the Dutch found it possible to arrange a *modus vivendi* with several Indian groups, but only relatively few of them came under effective Dutch jurisdiction. What the Dutch hoped to do, and what they actually did in a number of instances, was to establish a sphere of influence over various groups in the hinterland. This allowed them to further their commercial objectives, and also gave them some claims vis-à-vis their European neighbours to possession of territories, particularly in those areas where their postholders and Indian allies resided.

Notes

1. R. Sheridan, *Doctors and Slaves: a Medical and Demographic History of Slavery in the British West Indies 1680–1834*, (Cambridge, 1985), p. 40.
2. Jan J. Hartsinck, *Beschrijving van Guiana of de Wildekust in Zuid-America* (Amsterdam, 1770), pp. 290–91, 293.
3. British Guiana Boundary Arbitration with the United States of Venezuela. The case on behalf of the Government of Her Britannic Majesty (London, 1898), hereafter BGBV, Appendix ii, pp. 143, 214, 217; British Guiana Boundary Arbitration with the United States of Brazil. The case on behalf of the Government of Her Britannic Majesty (London, 1903), hereafter VGB, Appendix, i, p. 83; United States Commission on Boundary between Venezuela and British Guiana; Report and Accompanying Papers of the Mission Appointed by the President of the Unites States . . . (Washington, 1897), hereafter USC, i, p. 340.
4. *BGBV*, App. ii, pp. 8–9, 12; App. iv, pp. 101, 127.
5. *BGBV, App. i, pp. 11, 188; App. ii, pp. 76, 100, 119; App. iv, p. 2; USC, i, pp. 249, 259; C. A. Harris and J. A. J. de Villiers, Storm van Gravesande: The Rise of British Guiana* 2 vols (London, 1911), ii, p. 624.
6. *BGBV*, App. ii, p. 119; App. iv, pp. 7, 78.
7. *FGB*, App. i, pp. 24–25, 113.
8. *Ibid.*, p. 67.
9. *Ibid.*, p. 70.
10. *Ibid.*, p. 73.
11. *Ibid.*, p. 61.
12. *Ibid.*, pp. 61, 86.
13. *Ibid.* W. Farabee, *The Central Arawaks* (Anthropological Publications, Univ. of Philadelphia), 9 (1918), p. 13; G. W. Bennett, *An Illustrated History of British Guiana* (Georgetown, 1866), p. 87.
14. I. Myers, 'The Makushi of British Guiana', *Timehri*, 27, (1946), p. 18.
15. *FGB*, App. i, p. 139. See also R. M. Schomburgk, *Travels in British Guiana 1848–1844*, 2 vols (originally published 1834, rpt. Georgetown, 1922–23), ii, pp. 318, 343.
16. Schomburgk, *Travels*, i, p. 280, ii, p. 246.
17. *FGB*, App. i, p. 86.
18. *Ibid.*, p. 72.
19. *BGBV*, App. i, p. 91.
20. M. N. Menezes, *British Policy Towards the Indians in British Guiana, 1803–1873* (Oxford, 1977), p. 128
21. *BGBV*, App. i, p. 98.
22. J. Rodway, 'The Indian Policy of the Dutch', *Timehri*, new ser., 15, (1896), p. 28.
23. *BGBV*, App. iii, p. 104; App. iv, pp. 189–90; App. v, p. 73.
24. *Ibid.*, App. iii, p. 112.
25. A van Berkel (trans W. E. Roth), *Adriaan van Berkel's Travels in South America Between the Berbice and Essequibo Rivers and Surinam 1670–1689* (Georgetown, 1941), p. 70.
26. *BGBV*, App. i, p. 90.
27. *Ibid.*, App. iv, p. 188; *FGB*, App. i, p. 134.
28. *BGBV*, App. v, pp. 25–26.
29. Hartsinck, p. 291.
30. *BGBV*, App. iv, pp. 187, 188. *FGB*, App. i, p. 134.
31. *FGB*, App. i, p. 159.
32. V. Roth, 'Hillhouse's "Book of Reconnoissances" ', *Timehri*, 25 (1934), pp. 20, 23.
33. Harris & De Villiers, ii, pp. 598–99.
34. *BGBV*, App. i, p. 103.
35. *Ibid.*, p. 105.
36. *Ibid.*, App. v, p. 216.
37. *Ibid.*, App. ii, p. 223.
38. *Ibid.*, App. iv, p. 5.
39. *Ibid*,, p. 124; see also pp. 190, 192.
40. *Ibid.*, p. 11.
41. V. Roth, *op. cit.*, p. 23.
42. J. Rodway, 'Indian Policy', p. 14.
43. *BGBV*, App. ii, p. 9.
44. *Ibid.*, p. 64.
45. *Ibid.*, p. 72–73.
46. *Ibid.*, pp. 182–83.
47. Harris & De Villiers, ii, pp. 661–65.
48. *BGBV*, App. i, p. 86.
49. *Ibid.*, App. ii, pp. 123, 125.
50. Cited by Harris & De Villiers, i, pp. 87–88.
51. *BGBV*, App. ii, pp. 2–3.
52. *Ibid.*, pp. 130–31.
53. Hartsinck, *op cit.*, p. 270. Actually, there were always a few Caribs and Akawois who were willing to give non-military service to the Dutch but their numbers were much smaller than those of the Arawaks and Warraus.
54. *Ibid.*, p. 17; Van Berkel, p. 29.
55. *BGBV*, App. iv, p. 16.

56. W. H. Seggar, 'The Changing Amerindian', *Journal of the British Guiana Museum and Zoo*, 40, (1965), p. 13.
57. *BGBV*, App. iii, p. 76.
58. E. Im Thurn, 'A Journey in the Interior of British Guiana', *Proceedings of the Royal Geographical Society*, 2 (8) (1880), pp. 251, 253.
59. *Royal Gazette*, December 21, 1826, Guyana National Archives.
60. H. A. Bolingbroke, *A Voyage to Demerary 1799–1806* (originally published 1808; rpt. Georgetown, 1941), p.106; C. B. Brown, *Canoe and Camp Life in British Guiana* (London, 1876), p. 57.
61. *BGBV*, App. ii, p. 67.
62. Im Thurn, *op. cit.*, p. 36.
63. Harris & De Villiers, i, p. 342.
64. *Ibid.*, App. ii, pp. 217, 220–21, App. iv, p. 193; App. v, p. 40.
66. W. H. Seggar, *op. cit.*, p. 14.
67. Im Thurn, *op. cit.*, pp. 194–95, 201; Brown, pp. 22–23.
68. Bolingbroke, p. 126.
69. Im Thurn, *op. cit.*, p. 194.
70. Schomburgk, *Travels*, i, p. 154.
71. Im Thurn, *Among the Indians*, p. 232.
72. *Ibid.*, p. 259; Bennett, p. 95.
73. See, for instance, Schomburgk, *op. cit.*, i, pp. 246–47.
74. *Ibid.*, ii, p. 138; Brown, pp. 26, 131.
75. Hartsinck, *op. cit.*, p. 290; P. M. Netscher, (trans. W. E. Roth), *History of the Colonies Essequibo, Demerary and Berbice* (originally published 1888; Georgetown, 1929), p. 86; W. H. Brett, *Mission Work Among the Indian Tribes in the Forests of Guiana, 1840–1880* (New York, 1880), p. 3; P. A. Beatty, *A History of the Lutheran Church in Guyana* (Georgetown, 1970), pp. 13, 14.
76. *USC*, ii, pp. 250–51.

The Caribs of St Vincent: A Study in Imperial Maladministration, 1763–73

J. PAUL THOMAS

In late 1772, at a time when the corruption and cruelty of British rule in India were subjects of massive concern, publicly voiced in Parliament and press, disquieting reports on a military expedition to an obscure West Indian island were taken up by the parliamentary opposition. Reports concerned the sending of two regiments from America to aid local troops in the suppression, and possible deportation or even extermination of a group of free Negroes in St Vincent, whose main crime appeared to be their refusal to sell or exchange their lands to planters, speculators and investors. These, thus thwarted, had appealed to the government for help. There was much material inviting opposition scorn, not only on the grounds of the injustice of the expedition's aims, but also over the foolishness of sending ill-equipped troops in the unpleasant rainy season, when fever, disease and desertion afflicted the force quite as much as the successful tactics of well-armed and resourceful Caribs.[1]

The outcry over the Carib question was not comparable with the great debate in the contemporary press on the American question, or over Indian maladministration. Whereas these latter regularly spawned popular, profitable pamphlet literature, widely reprinted in the periodical press at each successive crisis, the only lengthy piece inspired by the St Vincent question was *Authentic Papers relative to the Expedition against the Caribs and the sale of Lands in the Island of St Vincent*, published by John Almon in February 1773, and this was merely a reprinting of the material laid upon the table of the Commons for consideration in the debates.

This lengthy collection, however, is of immense use to the historian, partly for its ready availability, occupying sixty-five pages of the *Parliamentary History* and finding its way into a number of contemporary periodicals, and partly because its contents, a chronological compendium of official correspondence, reportage and local petitioning, afford a detailed view of the development of a crisis involving a vulnerable native population, an ignorant administration and a number of land-hungry, profiteering colonial adventurers. Irrespective of the rights or wrongs of the Carib question, it was, like Bengal, or indeed the Pennsylvanian frontier, an example of how interested men on the spot could ignore or override the central government's wishes, or even force government intervention in their favour.[2]

The timing of the debates on St Vincent, during the East Indian crisis, was in itself significant. The promoter of the motion of censure on the question, Thomas Townshend Jr, consciously and adroitly remarked on the connection. He asserted, 'such a spirit of gaming is gone forth, that the rapacity of the planters in St Vincent is nearly connected with that rage for making of fortunes, by the most destructive means, which gave such a shock to public credit in the course of last summer.'[3] This was a direct reference to the problems of the banking system and of the East India Company in 1772. Not only was this parallel noted in newspaper correspondence by 'A. Proprietor' in the *Gazetteer*, linking government reluctance to bring to justice 'robbers and murderers of the Moghul' with the 'St Vincent exterminating scheme', but was mischievously compared with the massacre at St George's Fields, in the *Public Advertiser*.[4]

The criticism faced by the government was undoubtedly inconsistent, for Townshend and his parliamentary supporters in these debates, the 'Bostonian', Barlow Trecothick and the Chathamite, Isaac Barré, were as likely to attack administrative land policy and restrictions on

Journal of Caribbean History, Vol. 18, No. 2, 1984, pp. 60–73.

frontier adventurism in America. Sir Richard Sutton indeed pointed out the government's problem when he asserted that the opposition would as happily have attacked the government's failure to protect the allegedly threatened St Vincent planters.[5] This dilemma showed in the court's reluctance to decisively intervene in India's affairs where such intervention would arouse partisan accusations of encroaching on East Indian patronage.

It is difficult to accuse the government of deliberate inhumanity over the St Vincent affair, yet positive morality was by no means conspicuous in the official handling of the Caribs. Certainly, the *Authentic Papers* show official distaste for the planters and no great eagerness to endorse their representations.[6] Official reluctance to countenance the claims and aspirations of frontier and island land speculators and planters, however, did not necessarily derive from humanitarian regard for the rights of native populations already in possession of colonial lands. It stemmed rather from the spirit of the 1763 proclamation, and the Grenvillite policy of limiting expansion, with particular reference to the western American frontier. If this policy of containment involved garrisoning expense, it retained a degree of government control and in revenue projects implied potential in colonial patronage, rather than proliferation of expensive and damaging frontier warfare and the expansion of colonial populations beyond the geographical limits of official control. The Pontiac rebellion had given Whitehall a taste of the dangerous effects of land speculation upon aggrieved natives.[7]

Reluctance to endorse the planters' complaints also stemmed from official distaste for the kind of adventurers and speculators attracted by the opportunities offered by the new lands of the empire. St Vincent offered a quintessential example of the impact of colonial adventurers upon the tentative policy-making of the administrators of 1763. It was to the gaming spirit of these adventurers that Townshend was alluding in his speeches. Such men were making fortunes exploiting the riches of a more sophisticated native civilization in Bengal, and were financing and mortgaging fraudulent stock-jobbing schemes in the ceded islands. Prominent names among such adventurers were those of Lauchlin Macleane, Richard and William Burke and Sir George Colebrooke, all of whom may be implicated in dubious land purchases in Grenada and St Vincent from 1762 onwards, and be shown to have damaged national and company credit in East India stock-boosting schemes during the period.[8] Equally distasteful to traditional-minded administrators and parliamentarians at this time were the West Indian slavers, absentee landlords and planters, and the returning East Indian nabobs whose riches, real and imagined, seemed to be wreaking havoc on the domestic economy, and threatening the traditional grip of 'property' upon Parliament as the newly rich sought to purchase seats in Parliament.[9]

The 'good faith' of such 'avaricious and interested men' was pledged against the Caribs.[10] The latter race was variously described by contemporary commentators, depending on their degree of attachment to the St Vincent land lobby. There were two distinct 'races' of Caribs. The 'yellow' or 'red' Caribs were generally accepted to be a harmless and inoffensive people. They were the original inhabitants of the island and seemed content to co-operate with the European settlers, remaining in proximity with them in the coastal settlements of the island. The 'black' Caribs were, it appears, the descendants of the union of a cargo of shipwrecked slaves marooned about a century previously. They had been accepted by the 'red' Caribs at first but the mixed race, who were universally agreed to be either more aggressive or enterprising, subsequently feuded with their neighbours. Increasingly, neighbouring French colonists came to be involved, and once French settlement of the island proceeded, the black Caribs retreated from the coastal settlements and set up on the rich soil and woodland of the interior and north of the island.

The motives for this separation were sympathetic ones. The black race feared possible French plans to enslave them, and were at all times anxious to emphasize their distinctive status *vis-à-vis* the black slaves brought by the French. Fear of renewed slavery and possibly of the English reclaiming their property (the original shipwrecked slaves were alleged to have been on an English slaver), was evinced in explanation of black reticence and obstruction in the 1760s, with some suspicion being voiced that the French were playing on these fears. The slavery issue was of considerable significance, not only because of Carib sympathy and occasional asylum for British and French 'runaways', but also in determining British racial attitudes to the negroes during the disputes of the 1760s and 1770s.[11]

Attitudes to native races were equivocal at this time. There appears to have been a certain fascination for continental endorsement of the notion of the 'noble' savage. The ideas of Montesquieu and Rousseau were to be found alongside Locke's in popular British and American tracts of the period, while races such as the North American Indians and the Eskimos received a great deal of attention in the popular prints of the era, and a degree of romanticization of their lifestyle and mores. Although the Red Indians were often depicted as scalping, murdering savages, especially by the frontiersmen who had most violent contact with them, British and British American regulars like Major Rogers and Lieutenant Henry Timberlake wrote idealistic accounts of the bravery and virtue of the Delawares and the Cherokees. Enlightened Americans, notably the Pennsylvanians Benjamin Franklin and Anthony Benezet, who were later associated with anti-slavery campaigns, were outspokenly sympathetic to Indian rights.[12]

The acquiescent 'red' Caribs were warmly approved by all accounts, but the blacks were tainted with Negro, slave blood. Sympathy for the Negro was at this time a very individual affair, the successes of Granville Sharpe's activities in England being originally guided by personal acquaintance over the case of Jonathan Strong in 1765, and by opportunism in forcing an important test case over the Negro Somerset in 1772.[13] Moreover, just as Red Indians were subject to popular infamy, even anti-slavery campaigners such as Arthur Lee described Negroes as 'a race the most detestable and vile that ever the earth produced'.[14]

Contempt and distrust of the Negroes showed among Carib sympathizers. Thus, 'Sagitta', in the *Gazetteer*, while realistically noting the Caribs' fears for their security and suspicions of the motives of the land speculators, insisted that, 'After all savages are not to be treated upon the same maxims with polished nations', for they were 'a people accustomed to employ treachery for all the purposes of policy'.[15] 'W.W.' in the *Public Advertiser* also threw light upon contemporary attitudes. Evincing 'The sacred legend of our Holy Faith' and 'the fixed law of nature' in support, he argued that 'the weaker shall be subject to the stronger', which advantage he maintained 'we evidently enjoy over the aborigines, as well as the black inhabitants of St Vincent'.[16]

The evidence of the planters and their supporters, both in Parliament and press, and most persuasively in their official correspondence with governors Melville, Leybourne and Fitzmaurice, was primarily concerned with emphasizing the Caribs' character defects, their links with the neighbouring French islands, and their affinity with their slave ancestors and with contemporary slave runaways. Much of the official correspondence which Townshend had called for in the debates of December 1772 dwelt on these themes, their prejudicial effect reinforced by the testimony of Alexander Campbell, a prominent council member, planter and land speculator, later to pass into history as the plaintiff in the 1774 *Campbell* v. *Hall* judgement, and that of Messrs Sharpe and Maitland, also planters and council members from the island. Campbell retailed the story of the blacks' approach to M. Denerie, governor of neighbouring Martinique, seeking advice and support, while Sharpe 'represented the Caribs to be a set of men void of faith and every sentiment of morality', who 'loved plurality of women and drinking'.[17] The written evidence of Harry Alexander, president of the Council of St Vincent, and of Richard Maitland, the island's agent, showed that from 1769 onward the local planter community and council, stirred by Carib resistance, were concerned to arrange local self-defence, and to call for extra troops from within the empire.[18]

Why the Caribs had resorted to arms was well documented. They were reluctant to sell or exchange the woodlands they had occupied since the days of French settlement. How these woodlands had come to be a matter of contention lay within the vague arrangements for St Vincent in the 1763 settlement. The island had been occupied by the French, who had, after some friction, tacitly accepted black Carib ownership of and independence within the woodlands. Their terms of surrender did not comprehend the fate of this independent people. Instructions to bear gently on them and not disturb their lands had been handed out in 1764, but the *Authentic Papers* show that with mounting pressure from land-hungry settlers, and with official interest growing in perhaps gaining profit from what could, under asserted sovereignty, be termed Crown lands, moves were made in 1769 to properly survey the black Caribs' territory.

It was the surveying party and its building of a road into the disputed area which led to what can only be termed passive resistance from the blacks who surrounded a body of troops called in to support the alarmed surveyors, and having taken them prisoner returned them unharmed, once assured that the territorial dispute would be referred to the Crown.

Government and private interest in Carib land was not unconnected with the high quality of the property. A memorial from Sir William

Young, first land commissioner for the area, remarked in 1767 that 'the soil was found superlatively excellent — by far more extensive, more level, and a finer country than the part already disposed of; and as the soil is perhaps the best in the world, and it is admirably supplied with rivers, it would probably soon become a more valuable sugar colony than any possessed by the Crown', except Jamaica. Young commented on French acknowledgement of the Caribs' property and suggested the reservation of lands for the blacks, quit rent free and inalienable, in return for making these richer territories available.[19]

Instructions from the lords of the Treasury to the land commissioners followed up Young's suggestions, counselling caution and tolerance in dealing with the blacks, suggesting their separation from the 'red' Caribs and giving guidelines for suitable prices for cleared land sold. The plan was to give the Caribs a price and time to clear or abandon their land.[20] The resulting surveys saw Carib resistance, and, to the credit of the local authorities, a pause for consultation with the government. Sadly, the papers showed that these consultations were coloured by planter emphasis upon Carib unreliability and the physical threat they posed to whites. Official correspondence from the *de facto* Governor of Grenada, Ulysses Fitzmaurice, detailed the negotiations the blacks had had with Martinique, and shrewdly commented on the religious and linguistic links retained with the French, and upon the resentment of dispossessed French and St Lucians who 'consider the present possessors as usurpers of their property and retain an irreconcilable hatred to the English name — these people are exceedingly diligent in working the weak minds of Caribs already prejudiced and suspicious'. Fitzmaurice's testimony was the realistic assessment of a governor actually in trouble for his own acceptance of French Grenadian rights within the council of Grenada. Himself unprejudiced against the local French and enjoying 'a good understanding' with the Governor of Martinique, he recognized that the suspicions of the blacks 'cannot easily be reconciled to the vicinity of white people, whose gradual and successful intrusions upon their Carib neighbours they are sagacious enough to have remarked'.[21]

The government's response to the surveying problems came in a letter from Hillsborough to Fitzmaurice in August 1769 approving the arming of the local settlers and advising a call for reinforcement from the North American establishment if events got out of hand.[22] From then on representations from St Vincent increasingly sought to indicate just such a crisis with depositions in late 1769 alleging further Carib violence. By 1771 an address of the Council and Assembly of St Vincent to the King spoke of 'The dangerous and distressed situation of this colony' and spoke of 'Your Majesty's natural born subjects, who, had purchased lands at very high prices, with an intention of cultivating them, and had met with success — till unexpectedly their properties are rendered very precarious, and their lives endangered by a rebellion of the negroes — without the least provocation from the inhabitants — daily enticing their slaves to join them.' The blacks were accused of violence and genocide against their red counterparts, and the aim of 'totally extirpating the white inhabitants'.[23]

Whether or not these charges were true, it was significant that local representative institutions were totally dominated by the planters and by would-be land speculators whose interests were served by such charges, and by 1772 the government's scepticism seemed to have changed to total acceptance of the planters' viewpoint, as a letter from Hillsborough to Governor Leybourne indicated. He cautioned against 'unnecessary severities that may have the appearance of cruelty and oppression' and looked to secure 'a full submission' from the blacks.[24] The blacks had apparently renounced, or more accurately, denied allegiance to the British Crown during negotiations over land sales in 1770–71, a stance understandable in the light of their history. The dangers inherent in accepting the independence of a free, French-influenced and -speaking Negro race of slave descent in an area of small white and large Negro slave populations were obvious. Fears were bolstered by typical contemporary incredulity that any population within the empire could voluntarily reject the much-vaunted political benefits and freedoms concomitant with submission to the English Crown and constitution. A similar rejection of British values had occurred in Acadia earlier that century; now, prompted by planter suggestions, the government resorted to the policy of forced deportation formerly employed against French, white Acadian habitants, to solve the Carib problem.[25]

The evidence of Messrs Maitland, Otley and Sharpe had suggested that 'any unoccupied tract of 10,000 acres of woodland upon any part of the coast of Africa would afford them [the blacks] all the necessaries of life which they have been accustomed to'. Following this up, Hillsborough advised: 'If necessary demand the removal of the Caribs, do take up such vessels as can be procured, to serve as transports for the conveyance of them to some unfrequented part of the coast of Africa, or to some desert island adjacent thereto'. These instructions, with others to the Governor of the Leeward Islands, were separate and secret 'lest those infatuated savages should become desperate'.[26] 'W.W.' of the *Gazetteer* had expressed similar fears that the Red Indians of America should become desperate if they heard news of this less than enlightened native policy.[27] In the context of often more enlightened policy towards the American Indian at this time, this policy departure is eloquent testimony to the success of the local land lobby and official local representation, and to the awkward position of the mixed, independent Negro race in geographical proximity to French possessions and to a slave economy.

Amid the meagure historiography of this episode, L. J. Ragatz, chronicler of the West Indian planter class, denigrated Townshend and other critics as 'well-meaning but ill-informed individuals' and sternly maintained that the policy was necessary for the proper development of the island as a colony.[28] The well-meaning individuals thus dismissed included a horrified Horace Walpole, and Edmund Burke, as well as a number of distinguished parliamentary critics. If these latter could fairly be accused of having a partisan axe to grind in the debates, this was not necessarily the case with Walpole, already horrified by revelations of the maltreatment of the Bengalese, or of Edmund Burke, whose absence from the debates may well have been due to the possibility of embarrassment over the deep involvement of his younger brother, Richard, in a particularly imprudent land purchase in the Carib territories actually at the centre of the dispute.

Although paradoxically Burke's intense clannishness led him to fervently support the rectitude of Richard's premature and dubiously financed purchases in the area, his private correspondence showed sympathy for the unhappy natives. He attacked 'those who acted in that part' who 'were not possessed of the skill of governing them, or perhaps of the desire of it; and having found or rather made them troublesome neighbours, they could think of no other method to free themselves from that uneasiness, but by removing them by force from their habitations'. He condemned this 'weak and sinister policy' of using troops against 'those unhappy savages'.[29]

Walpole was particularly indignant, like Burke perceiving the malign influence of the governor, council and land commission at work. He sympathized with 'the Caribs' who 'have no representatives in Parliament; they have no agents but God, and he is seldom called to the bar of the House to defend their cause'. Walpole remarked of the note in February on the affair: '206 to 88 gave them up to the mercy of their persecutors'.[30] The Carib cause was defended stoutly within the House and continuing the flavour of military inquiry which had occasioned Townshend's original motion in December, it was the correspondence of serving soldiers on the island and the verbal evidence of senior officers which condemned the military and administrative arrangements for the expedition and called into question the morality behind it all. Lieutenant-Governor Grove cited the peaceable nature of the blacks, and remarked the pressure from white settlers upon their land; Lieutenant-Colonel Fletcher thought them 'well affected to our Government' and 'peaceable until the surveyors had begun to make inroads into their country'. The report of Lieutenant-General Trappaud from the expedition itself confirmed the military attitude. He maintained, 'the poor Caribs have been ill-used — we have only been able to penetrate four miles into the country. God knows how this petty expedition will end; all we hope for is that the promoters and contrivers of it will be brought to a speedy and severe account.'[31] This distaste among the military was voiced in the press, too, with a letter from an officer off the coast of St Vincent who opined at large upon 'the infamy that it will bring upon the national character to butcher a parcel of innocent savages in cold blood'.[32]

The local planters came under some odium. The *Annual Register*, of which Edmund Burke was editor, gave a lengthy and considered account of the expedition and the debates that surrounded it, in which the 'fear and avarice' which 'operated strongly to make them wish removal of the black inhabitants' was remarked. The *Register* made much of the planters' disappointment that they were unable to proceed in 1769 with the reduction of the blacks.[33] In the debates both Isaac Barré and Townshend were severe upon the evidence that planters Sharpe and Alexander had been reluctant to quit the rich inroads made into Carib territory at that time and had regretted 'his Majesty's unfortunate clemency'.

Sharpe in particular was castigated by Townshend as 'a clever, artful, diffuse man — an interested planter' who thought 'sending the Caribs to the coast of Guinea was an eligible plan'.[34] This opinion was backed by at least one newspaper piece, by 'Britannicus' in the *St James's Chronicle*, who likened the planters to the East Indian nabobs, both groups benefiting from a ministry which 'carried on a farce of an enquiry in this as they did in the India Business — the unrighteous Nabobs are to enjoy their millions and *jaghires*, and the St Vincent settlers the estates and plantations seized by force from the natives. Each injured party appeals in vain to English justice.'[35]

Less convincing was the opposition's overzealous depiction of the blacks as defenders of liberty, cast in the mould of English constitutional libertarians. The presumed attractions of allegiance to the British Crown were considered enormous. The offer of the benefits of the British constitution, the settling of provincial assemblies and English laws and customs, had been key clauses in the Proclamation of 1763 relating to the newly acquired territories of the empire. In December Trecothick and Townshend, aided by Whitworth, were right to raise the question of the honour of the British flag, but Barré's heated espousal of the blacks' cause, depicting them as 'in arms for the preservation of their liberty' while calling on 'every English heart' to 'applaud them', strained credulity in its use of conventional Whiggish political jargon.[36] Given such a stance it is unsurprising that opposition oratory received the standard response, voted down in February by a large Northite majority.

The government claimed they were not unduly responsive to settler pressure, and indeed the crux seems to have been reached in 1771 when Carib resistance to further planter negotiations and less attractive offers for their land were met by their references to an independence of ownership and sovereignty, prompting at least one newspaper commentator to remark 'on this occasion, without the least reserve, and in express terms' that the blacks 'denied all allegiance to the King'.[37] This point was reiterated in the local petitions to the Crown. It was notable that, with the military expedition successful but at high cost in sick and wounded, the general approach once the Caribs had submitted, seemed to be lenient, reserving to them rights and privileges as subjects of the British king. When later hostilities with the French saw a further weakening of Carib allegiance, the exasperated authorities finally deported them. Thus, from 1797 the black Caribs were to be located in central America.[38]

If powerful lobbying and a question of sovereignty had stirred the government sufficiently to act against the Caribs, any reluctance was attributable to the low esteem in which the older established West Indian lobbyists were held, and to the suspicion of speculators and *arrivistes* like Macleane and the Burkes. These had made life difficult for the local administrations of Grenada and St Vincent in the early postwar period. Richard Burke was at this time continuing to disrupt local politics through his speculatory activities and his attempts to secure the functions of the local Treasury, and through the procedural wrangling of his 'friends' in the local assembly. His activities centred around purchases of 'red' Carib land in 1770, unsanctioned by local or central government, possibly through the agency of French entrepreneurs known to be operating illegally at that time.[39] Interest in land sales involved not only local officials and planters like Sharpe, Alexander and Campbell, all identifiable as a united and coherent interest group, but outsiders, including the French, and Burke who was identified with the Fitzmaurice interest at Grenada, and whose feud with the officialdom of the ceded islands went back some years. Moreover, the government's insensitivity and ignorance complicated matters such as Richard Burke's land suit in the area by pledging St Vincent property, including Carib land, and indeed land ceded 'inalienably' to the Caribs in the treaty of 1773, to placate the interests of General Monckton, and Dalrymple, the head of the 1772–73 expedition.[40]

The Carib expedition of 1772–73 hinted at problems awaiting imperial administration elsewhere. Although debate on its rights and wrongs never competed with other contemporary outbursts, most notably the East India revelations, the parliamentary proceedings over this episode were covered in detail, including the humanitarian arguments of the opposition, which linked the Carib affair, by inference and coincidence, with the scandal and injustice revealed in Bengal. Moreover, speeches and newspaper correspondence, and detailed and sympathetic coverage by the *Annual Register* provide the imperial historian with useful illustrations of the confused thinking on treatment of indigenous peoples within the empire. There is clear evidence of the fantasy of savage innocence at work, most notably in the ready acceptance by all interested groups of the virtues of the harmless 'red' Caribs, and the doubts over the mixed blood of the blacks. Ambivalence of attitude to the Negro was to be found, for although Trecothick, Barré and various correspondents were eager to equate Carib resistance with more

English, sophisticated concepts of libertarian struggle, just as there had been a certain Whiggish enthusiasm over the case of the slave, Somerset, in the preceding summer, it is clear that the Caribs' association with tainted, slave blood, their own fears of renewed slavery, and geographical proximity to slave populations underlay many of their problems.[41]

Interesting from the racial viewpoint, the Carib episode is most revealing, perhaps, for its evidence of what Edmund Burke termed weak policy. Whitehall knew little of the Caribs or their history. As the *Annual Register* commented, the French surrender terms actually overlooked their existence. There was distaste and distrust, not only from Whitehall of the West India planters, but from the older, established planting class, of the temptations of cheap smallholdings in the new islands which could draw away poorer whites from their employment and control.[42] There was the influence on local and metropolitan politics, both of the older interest and that of maverick investors like the Burkes, and contractors like Sir George Colebrooke who had already made their mark upon East Indian speculations and seemed eager to make a 'quick buck' wherever available. Distrust of irresponsibility and adventurism underlay much of the talk of the good name of the English flag which characterized criticism of the expedition.

The government, based as it was upon response to interest and lobbying, was particularly dependent for advice and information in this affair upon a local hierarchy of planters and politicians who stood to gain by the removal of the Caribs. Whitehall's dependence for information upon local politicians and influence groups, themselves shaped by opportunities for local patronage and aggrandizement, was a feature not only in St Vincent, but in North America. Where in St Vincent the metropolitan authorities were dragged reluctantly into insensitive and ill-judged action, so later in the year, the breakdown of local authority in Boston, and the reports and viewpoint of the Hutchinson-dominated administration led to precipitate clumsy parliamentary reaction. Time and again the history of Whitehall and Parliament's intervention in imperial affairs from 1763 up to the American war was one of reluctance born of ignorance; of foolish and over-enthusiastic implementation of pet theories; or of over-reaction to stimulus from interests and influence on the spot. The Carib affair was an encapsulation in miniature of the problems raised by interaction of central, cautious but ignorant government, and local aims and interests, within a newly expanded empire. As was to happen too often in the future, the interests of indigenous peoples suffered in the resulting confusion.

Notes

1. Commons debate, 9 December 1772: *Parliamentary History of England from the Norman Conquest in 1066 to the year 1803*, ed. W. Cobbett, 36 vols (London, 1886–70), xvii, pp. 568–71.
2. *Ibid.*, pp. 575–639. See also *London Chronicle*, 13–16, 16–18, 23–25 February, 1773; *Critical Review*, xxxv, January 1773, p. 154; *St. James's Chronicle*, 16–18 February 1773.
3. *Parliamentary History*, xvii, pp. 572–73.
4. 'A. Proprietor', *Gazetteer*, 24 February 1773; 'Alfred', *Public Advertiser*, 22 April 1773.
5. *Parliamentary History*, p. 735.
6. See *Authentic Papers relative to the Expedition against the Caribs and the sale of Lands in the Island of St Vincent* (J. Almon, 1773).
7. For newspaper accounts of the effects of frontier expansion and land speculation upon the Indians see *Public Advertiser*, 25 August, 11 November 1763.
8. For the East India speculations of Lord Shelburne, his secretary, Lauchlin Macleane, of the Burkes, Colebrooke *et al.* see L. S. Sutherland, *The East India Company in Eighteenth Century Politics* (Oxford, 1952), pp. 206–12; also L. S. Sutherland and J. Woods, 'The East India Speculations of William Burke', in *Proceedings of the Leeds Philosophical and Literary Society*, xi, 1962.

   For details of Macleane's involvement see particularly J. N. M. Macleane, *Reward is Secondary, the life of a political adventurer and an inquiry into the identity of Junius* (London, 1963), pp. 63, 73–75, 82–85, which discusses his post-war land syndicate in Grenada. See also Dixon Wecter, *Edmund Burke and his Kinsmen* (Boulder, Colorado, 1939), which details the Burkes' speculations in both the East and West Indies.
9. J. M. Holzmann, *The Nabobs in England. A study of the returned Anglo-Indian, 1760–85* (New York, 1926), is also instructive on contemporary hostility in England to the West Indian *nouveaux riches*.
10. *Parliamentary History*, xvii, pp. 730–31, T. Townshend on the evidence of Mr Sharpe, 10 February 1773.
11. See *Annual Register*, 1773, p. 83 on Carib origins. See also C. Shephard, *An Historical Account of St Vincent* (London, 1831), pp. 22–25. For contemporary accounts see 'Sagitta', *Gazetteer*, 7 January 1773; 'Candidus', *London Chronicle*, 1 January 1773; Memorial of Richard Maitland to Lord Hillsborough (not dated), *Parliamentary History*, xvii, pp. 594–95.
12. See, for example, 'G.L.D.', *Gazetteer*, 1 February 1773 on the Esquimaux; Major Rogers' Journal was extensively featured in *London Chronicle*, December 1765, 28–30 January 1766; for Timberlake see *Monthly Review*, January 1776.

    For sympathetic articles see e.g. *London Chronicle*, 21–24 September 1765, 3–6 August 1771, 26–29 October 1771; *Gentleman's Magazine*, August 1765, February 1772. For more savage accounts see *London Chronicle*, 30 July–2 August 1763, 5–8 April 1766. For Franklin and Benezet see G. S. Brookes, *Friend Anthony Benezet* (Philadelphia, 1937), pp. 120–22; L. W. Labaree (ed.), *The Papers of Benjamin Franklin* (New Haven, Conn.,

1957) xi, pp. 69–74, 103–04; *Gentleman's Magazine*, April 1764.
13. See Sir R. Coupland, *The British Anti-Slavery Movement* (London, 1933) pp. 48–56.
14. A. Lee, *Vindication of the Continental Colonies* (London, 1764), p. 25.
15. 'Sagitta', *Gazetteer*, 7 January 1773.
16. 'W.W.', *Public Advertiser*, 15 March 1773.
17. *Parliamentary History*, xvii, pp. 727–28 (Alexander Campbell's testimony); *ibid.*, p. 727 (Mr Sharpe's testimony); *ibid.*, pp. 728–30 T. Townshend on both.
18. *Ibid.*, pp. 580–85, Maitland and Alexander correspondence.
19. *Ibid.*, pp. 575–79.
20. *Ibid.*, pp. 582–87.
21. *Ibid.*, pp. 587–88. For coverage of the scandal of French Grenadian Councillors see Anon, *London Chronicle*, December 1769, pp. 26–29; 'British Indignation', *Ibid.*, January 1770, pp. 25–27.
22. *Parliamentary History*, xvii, p. 597.
23. *Ibid.*, pp. 595–97. Charges of genocide were reiterated by 'Candour', 'Questions from St Vincent', *London Chronicle*, February 1773, pp. 20–23.
24. *Parliamentary History*, xvii, pp. 632–35.
25. For the Acadian affair see Sir R. Coupland, *The Quebec Act: a study in Statesmanship* (Oxford, 1925), pp. 11–14.
26. *Parliamentary History*, xvii, pp. 634–35.
27. See note 15.
28. L. J. Ragatz, *The Fall of the Planter Class in the British Caribbean, 1763–1833* (New York, 1928), p. 116.
29. E. Burke to James de Lancey, 20 August 1772: T. W. Copeland (ed.), *The correspondence of Edmund Burke* (Cambridge, 1860), ii, p. 328 and note.
30. A. F. Steuart (ed.), *The Last Journals of Horace Walpole* (London, 1810), i, pp. 169–71. *Correspondence of H. Walpole* (ed.), Toynbee, viii, pp. 228–41: Walpole to Sir Horace Mann, 21 January, 17 February 1773.
31. Groove, Fletcher and Trappaud's evidence is taken from the account of the Commons proceedings printed in the *Lloyd's Evening Post*, 10–12, 12–15 February 1773.
32. *London Evening Post*, 22 January 1773.
33. *Annual Register*, 1773, pp. 85, 86–87.
34. *Parliamentary History*, xvii, pp. 728–30.
35. *St James's Chronicle*, 16–18 February 1773.
36. *Parliamentary History*, xvii, pp. 569–71; debate of 10 December 1772. A fuller account is available in *Gentleman's Magazine*.
37. 'Candidus', *London Chronicle*, 1 January 1773.
38. The terms of surrender are fully reprinted from the *St Vincent's Gazette* of 27 February in the *London Chronicle*, 10–13 April 1773, and in C. Shephard, *An Historical Account of St Vincent* (London, 1831) pp. 34–36. Sir A. Burns, *History of the British West Indies* (London: 1954) pp. 505–06, details the subsequent treachery and deportation of the black Caribs.
39. See Gov. Melvill to Lord Hillsborough, 16 December 1770, quoted in D. Wecter, *Edmund Burke and his Kinsmen*, p. 57. See also *ibid.*, pp. 60–68.
40. For Burke's and Macleane's political sympathies in the area see, J. N. M. Macleane, *Reward is Secondary*, pp. 171–250. For details of the government land grants see *Burke Correspondence*, ii, pp. 460–64; E. Burke to Rockingham, 21 September 1773.
41. See Franklin's caustic remarks on such 'Whiggish' sympathy over the Somerset affair, *London Chronicle*, 20 June 1772; *Franklin Papers*, xvii, p. 269.
42. L. J. Ragatz, *The Fall of the Planter Class*, pp. 115–17, makes this point.

SECTION TWO
Origins of Large-Scale Slavery

The extensive use of servile labour, both Amerindian and African, has origins within the mining and agricultural sectors of Spanish colonies in the Greater Antilles during the sixteenth century. But the establishment of African slavery as the principal labour institution is related more specifically to the expansion of the sugar industry. As large-scale sugar production spread through the entire region, the demand for African slave labour increased at a phenomenal rate. The emergence of the industry gained revolutionizing proportions in the Lesser Antilles during the seventeenth century, and in the Greater Antilles during the eighteenth and nineteenth centuries. Everywhere, the relations between sugar and black slavery were similar. In this section, the peculiar characteristics of sugar and slavery development are explored, mostly for Barbados, Martinique, Puerto Rico and Cuba. Explanations are given for the uneven pace of development in the use of slave labour throughout the region, and the relations between differential growth and patterns of economic activity accounted for.

Why Sugar?
Economic Cycles and the Changing of Staples on the English and French Antilles, 1624–54

ROBERT CARLYLE BATIE*

One of the enigmas facing scholars investigating the 17th-century West Indies is the phenomenal economic expansion that, from 1624 to 1654, elevated the Caribees into a prominent place among the world's colonies.[1] During most of the 17th and 18th centuries, the English and French Antillean possessions experienced few abrupt changes. Until 1789, no revolutionary waves wracked the islands, intellectual life was negligible, and social and economic patterns remained largely constant. Events of the first thirty turbulent but formative years of settlement, however, stand in sharp contrast to these generalizations. From 1624, when Englishmen founded their first enduring colony on the islands, until 1643, the date when sugar became a significant export, Europeans flocked to the region to raise tobacco, cotton, indigo and ginger. Then in 1643 the Barbadians abruptly turned to sugar, so abruptly in fact that by 1655, when they shipped an estimated 7,787 tons to England,[2] their settlement had achieved very near its full growth. How near will be discussed later, but it is useful to remember that Jamaica, conquered in 1655, required roughly sixty years before its sugar output consistently equalled the level its rival attained in twelve. The differential in their growth rates has hitherto never been adequately explained, but it enabled Barbados to become the most prosperous 17th-century insular colony on the globe. As surprising as the suddenness of that island's transformation is the fact that from 1643 to 1654 other Antillean dominions continued to produce their previous exports. Why this was the case, why the newly founded colonies enjoyed an unusually high growth rate, why their inhabitants waited until the 1640s before plunging heavily into sugar, and why Barbados enjoyed an advantage over its sisters, constitutes the subject of this article.

The cause of these changes is obscured by the standard and disarmingly simple explanation held by scholars for the popularity of sugar cane during the next two centuries, namely that settlers found it more profitable to raise than alternative products.[3] Having made this assumption, historians have found it reasonable to conclude that, until sugar cane cultivation became widespread, the Caribee enclaves enjoyed only a marginal existence. For a current view of this interpretation, one need but turn to recent works by two eminent historians, Richard S. Dunn and Carl Bridenbaugh. The latter most bluntly stated this thesis: Caribee farmers obtained 'their first truly profitable staple' only with sugar and 'to maintain that the white men made a success of their colonies prior to 1645 is to press the evidence too hard'.[4] Dunn, while also believing that 'no one made much money' from Antillean tobacco and that sugar 'fetched a far higher and steadier profit than any other American commodity', was nevertheless perplexed by the implications of this line of thought. He therefore qualified it by stating 'there are a number of small mysteries about the introduction of sugar culture to Barbados', one presumably being 'that the Barbadians struggled with tobacco and cotton so long

*I am indebted to Dauril Alden, Robert Paul Thomas and Richard Bean for their constructive criticisms of earlier drafts of this paper.

Journal of Caribbean History, Vols 8–9, 1976, pp. 1–41.

before they tried making sugar'.[5] He might also have added that if pre-sugar agriculture was unremunerative, it is almost impossible to explain why thousands of Europeans migrated to the islands during that period.

In contrast to the traditional interpretation, it is a contention of this essay that the pre-sugar era was one of great economic opportunity. The case for this view rests primarily on commodity price data, which serves as a measure of colonial incomes, and on the remnants of both English and French correspondence and travel accounts. That the two groups of colonies experienced the same economic trends is to be expected since their settlers lived under similar free market institutions, raised nearly identical commodities, and bought their slaves from and sold their products to the same Dutch merchants. This placed all planters on as much the same competitive footing as if they were members of a single nationality.

The source of the price data utilized in this paper deserves mentioning. Almost no Caribbean information survives concerning the worth of tropical exports, but scholars have compiled at least two lists of published Chesapeake prices for tobacco,[6] the first staple exported from the Antilles. These figures serve as a reasonable proxy for West Indian values since all planters produced for the same Atlantic seaboard market, raised, with the exception of Barbadians, a quality leaf and paid substantial shipping fees when sending their product to the Old World, fees which dwarfed any transportation advantage the Antillean settlements might have had over Virginia. No accurate substitute exists for New World prices of other Caribbean commodities, but since each was sold in Europe, there remains a record of how much they bought on the Amsterdam exchange,[7] tobacco excepted. This record, which is far fuller, and therefore more reliable, than the spotty series of Virginia tobacco values, largely parallels Caribee price trends, since competition among European merchants forced price changes to be passed back to the original producers. Still the Netherlands market fluctuations are not identical to the New World variations because, as economic theory indicates, the huge trans-Atlantic carriage costs constituted an unknown but nearly constant burden.[8] As a result, percentage changes in Virginia figures cannot be compared directly with shifts in Dutch values even though the two series convincingly demonstrate that, despite two brief recessions, from 1624 to 1654 settlers enjoyed remarkable prosperity. The evidence for this view is presented in Figures 1 and 2 which show that at no time later

Figure 1

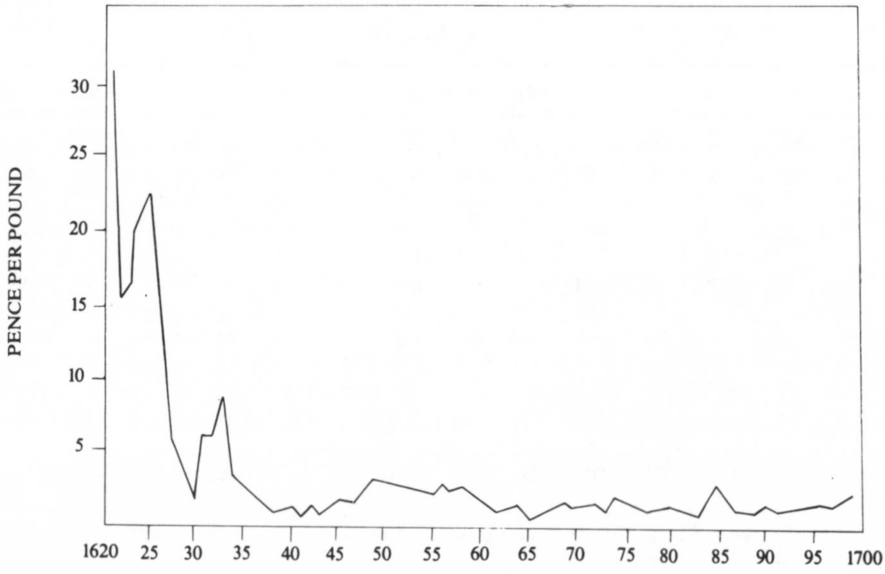

Source: Table 1 and Robert P. Thomas and Terry L. Anderson, 'The Economic Growth of the Chesapeake in the Seventeenth Century', unpublished paper, Department of Economics, University of Washington, n.p.

Figure 2 Netherlands Prices of Sugar and Indigo, 1624–1700

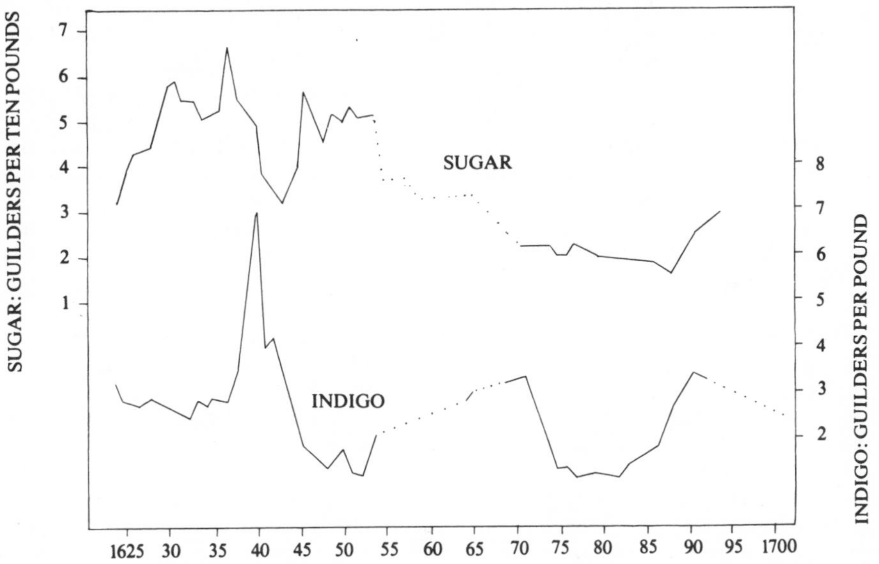

Source: Nicholas W. Posthumaus, 'Inquiry into the History of Prices in Holland' (Leiden, 1946), I, 119–20, 134–5, 415–16.

in the century did the average value of Antillean products attain as high a level as it then achieved. Clearly the first decades of Caribee colonization were boom times. As the next section indicates, the economic basis for that prosperity was laid during an earlier period.

1 The Profitability of Tobacco Cultivation, 1624–34

Historians describing the English colonization of North America have focused much of their attention on either the religious motives contributing to the Puritan migration or on the well-organized and heavily capitalized nature of the Virginia Company and have often lost sight of the economic incentives that led thousands to venture across the Atlantic. Yet for the American habitations to thrive and to be able to import European essentials, they had to export some product of such great value that it could bear the expensive trans-Atlantic shipping costs. Tobacco proved to be the first such staple discovered outside non-Hispanic America, which perhaps explains why over half-a-dozen English colonies,[9] started during the first two decades of the century, but before the leaf became a sure commodity, failed.

Tobacco served as a profitable export because it was in great demand relative to its supply. In the middle of the 16th century, the Spanish introduced it to Europe where it sold as a medicine, until Sir Walter Raleigh popularized pipe smoking.[10] By the early 1600s, the new fashion had become so widespread that Hispanic planters, whose ability to expand commodity output when prices increased was constrained by government regulations and a limited Caribbean labour force, found themselves unable to meet the needs of the new market. As a result, the value of tobacco soared[11] until only the wealthiest gentlemen could afford it. At this time, around 1616, Virginians discovered that they could raise the plant, and in 1619 one New World writer noted that it fetched 3s. 6d. a pound and that a grower could make £200 yearly. Another author stated that a settler could raise 25 bushels of corn and 700 pounds of tobacco a year, which suggests that the latter brought him £122 10s.[12] In either instance the sum was extraordinary, for from 1613 through 1622 unskilled farm labourers in England received an average wage of about 4s. a week or around £10 8s. a year,[13] provided that they were employed throughout each season which was generally not the case. Even after leaf prices had started declining, earnings remained for some time substantial. For instance, from 1624 to 1629, tobacco planters received on an average 19s. 5d. a pound for their product or thirteen times as much as they usually obtained from 1655 to 1700,[14] the half century following the period treated in this article. It is small wonder then that after 1616 the inhabitants of Jamestown rightly believed that they had discovered in tobacco the means by which their faltering village could become a thriving community, and it is also small wonder that thousands of English labourers, unable to afford the passage to America, chose to sell themselves into indentured servitude in the hope of making their fortunes once their terms expired. A great migration wave thus began, and the settlement of the English and French Antilles must be viewed in its context.

The Caribees, which consist of a chain of small islands stretching from Puerto Rico to the Main, provided logical places for Northern Europeans to found tobacco colonies: all but Trinidad were uninhabited by the Spanish; the direction of the prevailing trades placed the islands upwind from Hispanic America, thereby protecting them from attack; and they lay near the famous Spanish tobacco producing areas of Venezuela and Trinidad,[15] a point which led prospective planters to believe that a quality leaf could be raised in the Caribbean. As a consequence, during the 1620s and early 1630s, the English and French founded settlements on seven Caribee islands: St Christopher (1624), Barbados (1627), Nevis (1628), Antigua (1632), Montserrat (1632), Guadeloupe (1635) and Martinique (1635). In addition, Englishmen also settled two isles closer to the mainland, Old Providence (1629) and Tortuga (1630).

The circumstances surrounding the inception of the Lesser Antillean enclaves underscores the early profitability of tobacco farming. Future inhabitants, mainly young males, migrated to the region with the expectation of making a quick killing and then returning to Europe. The promoters who led the procession had similar motives. Thomas Warner, founder of the first successful colony, was typical of such men, nearly all of whom were unwealthy adventurers. A member of Roger North's short-lived settlement on the Amazon, he arrived at St Christopher in 1624 with less than two dozen men. Despite the destruction of one tobacco crop by a hurricane, in 1625 he returned to England with 9,500 pounds of the leaf. This fetched such a high price that in 1626 he was able to sail back to St Christopher with 400 recruits.[16] The French plantations were begun in an equally modest manner. In 1625, a French privateer which had unsuccessfully attacked a Spanish vessel stopped at St Christopher for repairs. After talking with the Englishmen, the officers decided that farming would be more profitable than buccaneering, and they formed habitations on the unclaimed ends of the island. From there, they later branched out to Martinique and Guadeloupe.[17] Even the Puritan colony of Providence developed because of the efforts of ambitious entrepreneurs seeking to make their fortunes in tobacco. The Puritans had founded a settlement on Bermuda in 1612, but the climate proved inimical to the cultivation of a quality leaf. Aware of Warner's success, Philip Bell, Governor of Bermuda in the late 1620s, decided to plant in the Caribbean, for he believed that a small tropical island could 'in short time be made more rich and bountiful either by tobacco or any other commodities than double or treble any man's estate in all England'.[18] After sending forth settlers from Bermuda, he offered his resignation to the London directors while at the same time asking them for assistance, particularly in obtaining a royal charter for his new venture. The Earl of Warwick, the principal investor in Puritan overseas enterprises, faced with this *fait accompli*, accepted Bell's proposal, formed the Providence Company, made his erstwhile employee its governor, and gave him substantial financial aid.[19] Of course, not all the individuals founding West Indian settlements were of inconsequential stature. The possibility of acquiring wealth appealed to men of all classes and occupations, and two separate groups of powerful London merchants contested for jurisdiction over Barbados, the most windward of the Lesser Antilles. One faction ultimately obtained the assistance of the King's companion, the Earl of Carlisle, who became proprietor of the English Caribees. The Earl then gave his merchant supporters 10,000 acres on Barbados in return for which they voided his considerable debts to them.[20]

Throughout the 1620s, settlers made extraordinary profits from tobacco, even though increased New World production forced its price steadily downward. As late as 1628, when Barbadians apparently sold their leaf, which all agreed was of inferior quality, for 9d. a pound, expected profits were so high that twenty Barbados servants were contracted on a one year lease for £1,000.[21] Given the risk from disease and natural catastrophe, the leasees obviously expected an average net return per person of well above £50. An indirect but more systematic method of determining profits relies on productivity estimates. Assuming that the typical worker raised between 1,000 and 1,500 pounds of tobacco annually,[22] a conservative estimate, yearly incomes would have varied from £37 10s.

to £56 5s., nearly all of which sum would have been net profit since production costs were limited to the purchase of a hoe, an axe and land, each of which cost little. Land, the one item of potential value, was so abundant relative to the population that even by 1640 it fetched only around 10s. an acre on Barbados, making it possible at that late year for an unassisted farmer to more than meet his field needs with an initial investment of only £2. On the French islands settlers experienced even fewer costs, for Martinique and Guadeloupe remained sparsely colonized until near the end of the century, with the result that uncleared property was virtually worthless. This led the Crown to give new planters free tracts 200 paces by 1,000 paces.[23]

With Caribee incomes four to six times as high as those in England, the islands took on the appearance of boom towns, a designation which also aptly fitted contemporary Virginia.[24] Planters put all their efforts into raising the weed: they lived in hastily constructed huts, imported their foodstuffs, which sometimes led to shortages, and avoided expending time on non-essential improvements to their land. As Sir Henry Colt, who visited Barbados in 1631, wrote, 'your grownd & plantations . . . lye like ye ruines of some village lately burned, . . . all ye earth couered black wth cenders nothinge is cleer. What digged or weeded for beautye?' The inhabitants, many of whom were 'younge & hott bloods', did however spice their labour with an 'excesse of drinkinge' and engaged in quarrels stemming from their 'fyery spiritts'.[25] The tropical enclaves were indeed boom communities with the violence and rough living conditions associated with early Virginia and the later gold mining towns of the American West.

The adventurers who swarmed over the Caribees usually acquired their substantial incomes with their own hands, a point which gave the islands an egalitarian appearance. Servants could be purchased, but price theory indicates that settlers would bid the price of indentures up to a point nearly equal to their expected earnings, thereby making the shippers who sold the bondsmen the primary beneficiaries of the white slave trade. That this happened is supported by evidence from Edmund Morgan who cites one case where in 1623 a Virginia servant sold for £150 sterling.[26] It is likely that indentures, purchased at inflated values, often failed to repay their original cost. For tobacco prices declined irregularly for nearly two decades, and during that period colonists, uncertain that the trend would continue, probably tended to overestimate future revenues. It is understandable, then, why most planters chose not to invest heavily in servile labour but rather kept their work force small. One notable exception consisted of setttlers like Warner and the later famous Colonel James Drax, men who returned to England where they obtained indentures cheaply, that country then being in the midst of a depression.[27] Another exception concerns colonists who luckily had merchant relatives able to send them a steady stream of inexpensive servants, generally in return for a partnership in the estate. Such business arrangements proved advantageous to both parties, for planters without cheap, exploitable labour could never hope to enter the small circle of truly successful West Indians. In all likelihood the later well-known connection between leading settlers and merchants began at this point. It was a case where to become an insular magnate, one had to engage in trade, the area where major profits lay, and not a situation where wealthy colonists chose to invest previously acquired fortunes in shipping.

The confidence of this world of men-on-the-make received a rude shock in 1630 when tobacco values temporarily plummeted to around a pence a pound, an unanticipated low level. The price decline, which was naturally accompanied by a profusion of colonial complaints that may have influenced those scholars who have believed that the pre-sugar era was economically disappointing, can be attributed in part to an abrupt increase in the Antillian tobacco output. For, although in 1629 a Spanish expeditionary force destroyed the Nevis and St Christopher crops, by 1630 the inhabitants of those places had renewed their production; Barbados, founded in 1627, was just coming into its own; and planters on Providence were marketing their first harvest.

Despite the glut, the depression of 1630 was short-lived, with prices rebounding in the following year so that from 1631 to 1634 the leaf sold for an average of 5–6d. a pound and planters found it more profitable to cultivate than other commodities. Among the foremost reasons for tobacco's resurgence in 1631 were Governor Harvey's laws designed to restrict Virginia's production, laws which he apparently enforced until dissatisfied colonists removed him from office in 1635. In addition, in 1632 the English Crown reduced imposts on Virginia leaf from 6d. to 2d. a pound and on that from the Antilles from 9d. to 4d.[28] But the new prosperity proved ephemeral, for Englishmen and Frenchmen, attracted by the still substantial profits to be made in agriculture, continued to flock to

America, causing the tobacco supply to increase rapidly. As a result, prices steadily declined, falling from up to 6d. a pound in 1634 to around 2.5d. in 1635.[29] They would not reach the 1624–34 levels again in the century, and the era when unassisted planters could make their own fortunes had ended.

2 A Growing Depression and the Search for a New Staple, 1635–40

During the next five years, 1635 to 1640, tobacco values steadily deteriorated. Colonists complained when prices fell to 2.5d. a pound, even though that figure was still well above the future long-run average of 1.5d., and they were truly distressed when in 1638 and 1639 a bumper Virginia harvest forced leaf values down to 0.75d. a pound. As might be expected, it was during these last years that Antillean planters earnestly began to investigate raising other commodities, one of which was sugar cane, a product whose potential they did not immediately grasp. The breadth of the search for a new staple can be gleaned from the Providence Company correspondence. Concerned about the stability of tobacco prices, the directors wrote Governor Bell as early as 1632, 'Wish silk grass (like hemp) to be planted and sent home, and sugar canes for private use; cotton to be made trial of; mulberry trees to be procured, also bees and fruits from the main'. Pomegranates, peppers and fig trees were also planted that year.[30] Most of these products proved of little commercial value, if only because spoilage during shipping was excessive. But a few appeared highly profitable, for enduring circumstances had combined to reduce the supply of tropical and semi-tropical commodities reaching Europe from elsewhere in the world, a point enhancing their worth. Warfare handicapped the Brazilian economy; high shipping fees restricted the importation of Indian staples; piracy and unfavourable climatic conditions reduced the quantity of cotton and sugar raised in the Southern Mediterranean; and a complex of factors joined to impair Spanish American agriculture, central to them being a merchantile system which impeded the flow of labour to the New World, taxed goods from there at a rate of roughly 27% *ad valorem*, and placed all shipping in the hands of a monopolistic trade guild.[31]

Yet, even with international circumstances favourable for English and French planters to shift to other commodities, colonists hesitated before abandoning tobacco. Unknown products required new and sometimes complex cultivation skills which were difficult to acquire in the 17th century. In addition, European agriculture revenues then fluctuated widely from year to year, and consequently settlers came to realize that leaf values would not rebound only after the 1638 price decline created a crisis in the industry which led to many Antillean producers leaving it. By the end of the decade, the exodus was largely complete, for in 1638–39 English officials on the Antilles and in Virginia formed a cartel designed to drastically reduce the leaf supply. By its terms Caribbean settlers ceased growing the plant almost entirely.[32] That they agreed to do this without serious argument indicates that most colonists believed that other commodities were more profitable to raise.

Fearing that without French participation the cartel would fail to significantly reduce tobacco supplies, Thomas Warner requested that his neighbours also join it. They declined, perhaps because they hoped to capitalize on the expected higher prices. But Warner was not so easily dissuaded, and by threatening to attack Gallic St Christopher, in May 1639 he forced Sieur Lonvilliers de Poincy, the French governor-general, to support the Anglo-Saxon scheme.[33] Yet even with all the non-Hispanic colonies involved, the crop restriction programme clearly failed to achieve its purpose, partly because Chesapeake planters could not be easily policed.[34] The French left the cartel in late 1640 after their eighteen-month agreement with Warner expired, but by then the leaf offered neither them nor anyone else much immediate future.

It may appear that colonists should have begun turning to sugar during the tobacco ban, but they were then still in the process of acquiring information concerning how to make that difficult staple, and so instead planters started raising cotton, a commodity which required little special knowledge to grow and which solitary farmers could easily cultivate without purchasing expensive equipment. A few colonists, whom others could copy, had already produced it commercially, especially on Barbados where the tobacco was so rank that Richard Ligon, an earlier traveller, called it 'the worst I think that grows in the world'[35] and where the southeast littoral, one of the first areas settled, received insufficient rainfall to produce other commodities luxuriantly.[36] Barbadians began exporting cotton around 1630 when leaf values took their first dip, and in 1631 Sir Henry Colt wrote that 'now ye trade of cotton fills them all with hope'.[37] The rebounding of tobacco prices from 1631 to 1634 temporarily slowed the movement to cotton, but the change in the terms of trade after that period again inspired settlers to grow it. In this respect, they, and other West Indians, had the encouragement of proprietary officials. The Company of the Isles of America, for instance, recommended in 1636 that its colonists raise the product.[38] In May of the following year, the proprietary agent on Barbados, Peter Hay, was told to 'incourage every planter to plant Cotton for Barbados Cotton of all other is esteemed best... and it is a staple commoditie that will ever be worth money',[39] while in 1637 Providence Island Company officials notified their governor that cotton was more valuable in England than was tobacco.[40]

But despite the shift to a new staple, planters still found themselves plagued by unstable market conditions, for so many settlers turned to cotton in 1638 that in 1639 the extra supply forced the bottom out of the English market. Prices remained depressed for the next four years. Smyrna cotton, for instance, sold at an average of 0.478 guilders a pound in Amsterdam from 1635 through 1638[41] but brought only 65% of that from 1640 to 1644. The reduction in value, however, had desirable side benefits, for it made cotton fabrics less costly to consumers and contributed to the establishment of the English cotton weaving industry. It also meant, however, that Caribee settlers had failed to find a permanent alternative to tobacco.

In searching for a new staple, colonists began experimenting with ginger, long a major export from Santo Domingo and Puerto Rico.[42] Few records remain of this crop, which was soon to be eclipsed by sugar cane, but all indications suggest that it played a large role in West Indian economies. For instance Father Dutertre, author of a respected 17th-century history of the islands, wrote that, when tobacco cultivation was banned, French planters turned primarily to ginger because 'it had a better price'.[43] But ginger faced an inelastic European demand with the result that, as in the case of cotton, the addition to its supply drove its value rapidly downwards.[44]

Thus by 1640, the English and French Antilles were caught in the throes of a depression, one only slightly mitigated by planter attempts to shift from tobacco to cotton and ginger. Islands where only a few years earlier colonists had been tantalized by the dream of affluence now offered their inhabitants a standard of living little, if any, better than that of Europe. As one Barbadian afterwards wrote, 'this island was in a very low condition... and small hopes appeared of raising any fortunes there for the future'.[45] Henry Ashton, Governor of Antigua, described planters on St Christopher as reduced 'to this pointe of undoeing',[46] while on Providence the bleak economic outlook influenced many settlers to emigrate, thereby reducing the island's military strength and paving the way for the 1641 Spanish reconquest. The French inhabitants of course fared no better than their rivals, which perhaps explains why Sieur Loinvilliers de Poincy pessimistic about his future capacity to muster enough men to repel Anglo-American assaults, proposed to the Company directors that part of St Christopher be sold or abandoned.[47]

3 The Appearance of Large Plantation Crops: The Coming of Sugar, 1624–43

By 1640, the West Indian economy had deteriorated to the point where a Barbados proprietary agent wrote 'unlesse some New Inventions be founde oute to Make A Commodytie on the Inhabitants are noe wayes able to subsist'.[48] That new invention was fast making its appearance. Starting sometime near 1635 when tobacco prices crumbled, a limited number of colonists began experimenting with indigo, a prominent blue dye, and shortly afterwards a few commenced testing sugar.[49] It is, of course, not at all surprising that settlers waited until those years before raising these products. In fact, any other economic behaviour would have been inexplicable given the earlier profitability of tobacco.

The introduction of indigo and sugar cane must have occurred only gradually, for to produce either commodity required a heavy capital outlay, sizeable labour force and sophisticated knowledge of manufacturing processes, none of which was needed to grow tobacco, cotton or ginger. The distinction was due to the necessity of processing the dye material and cane juice into finished products before marketing them. In the case of indigo, colonists had to erect large stone vats in which the leaves were steeped and their precipitate oxidized,[50] and although some planters employed as few as half-a-dozen workers, upwards of 17–25 men laboured on particularly efficient estates.[51] The cost of these properties served as an obstacle which dissuaded many West Indians from entering the industry, but the barriers to making sugar were even greater. The milling and refining equipment, which on one Jamaican plantation were inventoried at £199 in 1672,[52] and the minimal number of slaves, cost far more than anything used in manufacturing indigo. The smallest competitive sugar plantations, for instance, contained several dozen workers, while noticeably successful properties had between 60 and 200 hands.[53] The latter estates were worth at least £1,000, and during the 1640s one sold for £14,000.[54] In addition to these expenses operators needed a wealth of information that the first sugar planters were forced to acquire through the costly process of trial and error. To provide some idea of the complexity of this lore, in the boiling house alone the refiner had to know how much lye to add to the syrup, how long to heat each type of juice, how hot to maintain the furnaces and when to strike the final cauldron.[55] Clearly, the mastery of the art of making sugar required time, skill and money. It is no wonder, then, that colonists waited until tobacco values reached very near their long-run levels before seriously committing themselves to learning how to produce muscovado, the common brown sugar later exported from the islands. Nor is it any wonder that settlers experimented with indigo first.

By about 1637, West Indians exported enough of the dye for English officials on St Christopher to levy taxes of 'halfe a pound . . . per poll' for 'powder Shott and other Ammunicion'.[56] But the industry began to blossom only as the decade closed when the value of indigo in Amsterdam rose abruptly from 4.43 guilders a pound in 1638 to 8.10 guilders in 1640.[57] This dramatic change was due to the 1639–41 near collapse of the trans-Atlantic Spanish convoy system, a breakdown which was heightened by the secession of Portugal and by the Catalonian revolt, which served to block the shipment of indigo from Guatemala, then Europe's foremost supplier.[58] As a result, from 1640 through 1642 the dye sold for more than at any other time in the century[59] and temporarily became the most profitable commodity raised in the West Indies, a point which induced settlers with capital to prefer it to sugar.

This was true despite abnormal international market conditions in the sugar industry which made the sweetener also unusually high priced. In the last half of the 16th century, Brazil became the major source of the muscovado consumed in Europe; and since she and her mother country, Portugal, had become components of the Spanish empire in 1580, both were drawn into the struggle that began when a twelve-year truce between Madrid and the Netherlands expired in 1621. That war proved unusually disastrous for Brazil in that the directors of the West India Company, a firm created to conduct the Dutch maritime offensive against the New World Luso-Spanish empire, decided to seize prominent Portuguese slave stations in West Africa and to capture Portuguese America, a land particularly vulnerable because it had been settled only along the coast, making the entire area open to seaborne assault. After several years of abortive attacks, in 1630 the Dutch took Recife, the main port of Pernambuco and the capital of one of the two major Brazilian sugar-producing regions, and, during the decade of fighting that followed, they gradually expanded the territory under their control until, by 1641, it included the entire area from Maranhão in the far North to the São Francisco River in the South.[60] During this warfare, however, the object of the conquest, the sugar estates, were largely destroyed, and with their output reduced, muscovado prices on the Amsterdam exchange rose from a year average of 0.32 guilders a pound in 1624 to never less than 0.50 guilders a pound during the 1630s. With prices like these, Caribee settlers were likely to find the commodity profitable to grow once they mastered its intricate production processes.

As a prerequisite to accomplishing this feat, planters not only had to find sugar cane relatively more remunerative to cultivate than indigo, but their colonies had to mature to a point where wealthy sugar estates would be secure from confiscation or attack. The threat of invasion particularly worried wealthy investors who stood to loose a fortune in slaves and equipment during even the briefest seaborne raid, for although the Caribees contained few accessible landing places, they straddled the main Hispanic convoy route from Iberia to Peru, which made them a tempting target for passing fleets. The danger became a reality when Spaniards laid ruin to the Nevis and St Christopher colonies (1629) and twice attacked Old Providence (1635 and 1641). In addition, Spain fortified the small island of St Martin from whence supply ships picked off straying Englishmen and Frenchmen. Barbados excepted, Indians also threatened the colonies. Caribs toppled English settlements on Trinidad, St Lucia and Tobago, and in 1640 overran Antigua. At the same time they isolated and harassed the French on Guadeloupe to the extent that until 1640 that community remained on the verge of collapse, and even as late as 1654 they almost conquered Martinique.[61] There remained only one defence against these dangers; namely, for the English and French to increase their insular populations to the point where potential invaders would avoid attacking them; but until the mid-1630s, little advance was made in this direction.

Harried by depression and the ever growing threat of civil war, Englishmen left their homeland in such numbers during the 1630s that their exodus was called the 'Great Migration'. The 1635 collapse of the tobacco market reorientated that human flow, causing many individuals who otherwise would have gone to Virginia to sail to the West Indies where they could cultivate the more profitable cotton, ginger, indigo and later sugar cane. Thus, while the citizenry of Virginia increased from 4,914 in 1635[62] to an estimated 7,738 in 1639,[63] the population of Barbados alone, whose dry climate proved especially appropriate for raising cotton, mushroomed from 1,227 in 1635 to 8,707 in 1639.[64] By that time the island was too heavily settled to succumb easily to foreign invasion. The same was less true of the other Caribee settlements. Under 20,000 Englishmen[65] and perhaps a third as many Frenchmen dwelt on the Antilles by 1640,[66] but only Barbados and St Christopher contained substantial populations, and the joint inhabitants of the latter island lived in mutual fear of each other. The resultant instability so retarded St Christopher's development that its economy fully flourished only after England permanently acquired the French sector in 1713. By 1640, then, Barbados was easily the most heavily populated and securely held West Indian colony, which gave it a substantial advantage over its insular neighbours.

Planter properties were also threatened by the arbitrary actions of Antillean governors, who ruled largely independent of home control until the success of the subsequent sugar boom attracted European attention to the Caribees. Since most of these officials went to the islands expecting to make their fortunes and since they lacked the supportive power sources which both gave and checked authority granted to local leaders in their homelands, they sometimes levied heavy fines on wealthier rivals who committed minor transgressions. Governor Henry Hawley of Barbados exemplifies such a leader. In 1630, he arraigned and executed his predecessor, Sir William Tufton, on flimsy charges following Tufton's protest at the governor's arbitrary rule. Hawley then managed with an iron hand the colony for nearly a decade during which time he once even exiled the Earl of Carlisle's kinsman and proprietary agent, Peter Hay. Upon being given recall orders in 1639, Hawley changed his stand, created an island assembly, and temporarily defied his former patron. Yet the revolt was short-lived, for Hawley lacked widespread popular support and was forced to surrender to Crown officials, leaving behind an established legislature which gave Barbadians a means not found on the other Caribees of countering arbitrary government.[67] For this reason also, the settlers on that island experienced a decrease in investment risks towards the end of the 1630s.

It is no wonder then, that with risk costs and tobacco prices having declined simultaneously on only Barbados, colonists there were more aggressive than those elsewhere in turning to sugar. The precise date when cultivation began remains unclear, but one account stated that the original trials were made in 1637 by a Dutchman, Peeter Brower.[68] At least talk of raising sugar cane was in the air by that time, for in 1638 the Earl of Warwick attempted to purchase the colony's proprietary charter for apparently £12,000 in order to make the commodity.[69] Even so, the year when planting began is unimportant, for the initial experiments were largely unsuccessful. As Richard Ligon noted,

> some of the most industrious men, having gotten Plants from Pernambock, a place in *Brazill*, and made tryal of them at the Barbadoes; and finding them to grow, they planted more and more . . . till they had such considerable number, as they were worth the while to set up a very small Ingenio [mill and boiling house] . . . But, the secrets of the work being not well understood, the Sugars they made were very inconsiderable, and little worth, for two or three years. But they finding their errours by their daily practice, began a little to mend; and, by new directions from *Brazil*, sometimes by strangers, and now and then by their own people, who . . . were content sometimes to make a voyage thither, to improve their knowledge in a thing they so much desired . . . And so returning with more Plants, and better knowledge, they went on upon fresh hopes.[70]

Thus, at the earliest, Barbadians became familiar with the intricacies of cultivating sugar only after 1639 when it superseded indigo in profitability.

The French sugar industry was created shortly after that of the English. In 1635, officials of the proprietary firm, the Company of the Isles of America, directed settlers on Guadeloupe 'to work their people principally at cotton and at sugar' and to de-emphasize tobacco.[71] The recommendation concerning muscovado was not followed, but the potential of cane was recognized, and in 1640 one traveller wrote that in time 'it will be far more common to make sugar than tobacco, principally on the islands of Guadeloupe and Martinique, which will be able someday to supply France'.[72] That was on the eve of the founding of the French sugar industry. In 1639, the Company had granted a

Dutchman, Daniel Trezel, a six-year monopoly on all sugar produced on Martinique if he would establish a plantation there. Trezel began clearing land and planting cane, but he also experienced financial difficulties, and in 1642, reportedly when he was ready to produce 25 tons of sugar, Governor Du Parquet, who gained nothing from the arrangement, permitted his milling equipment to be sold for what some said were minor debts.[73]

But despite Trezel's ill fortune, the industry was taking root on the other islands. The first recorded shipment from Barbados reached England in 1643, and according to an enthusiastic proprietary agent, the colony had become 'the most flourishing Island in all those American parts, and I verily believe in all the world, for the producing of sugar Indico Ginger'.[74] According to tradition, the industry began on St Christopher in the same year,[75] and in 1644 the French proprietary company, dissatisfied with what had happened on Martinique, financed the founding of an estate on Guadeloupe, but only after appointing a member of its board of directors, Charles Houel, as governor.

By that time sugar had again replaced indigo as the most remunerative product on the islands. Why this occurred can only be understood in terms of commodity price changes. With the re-establishment of the Spanish convoy system, the value of Amsterdam indigo fell from an average of 8.10 guilders a pound in 1640 to 4.58 guilders in 1643, 3.15 guilders in 1645, 2.78 guilders in 1646, and 2.31 guilders in 1648, with the result that from 1645 to 1649 the dye sold for an average of only 2.70 guilders a pound, well below its long-run value.[76] If the terms of trade during the more competitive and stable second half of the century are any guide, the critical year in this steady decline, when indigo and sugar appeared equally profitable to cultivate, was 1643. For over a decade thereafter, the sweetener easily held the first position.

Much of the credit for the new primacy of muscovado was due to changes in its supply. Following the secession of Portugal and Luso-Brazil from Spain in 1640 and the Dutch consolidation of its conquests during the early 1640s, warfare nearly ceased in Brazil, sugar output expanded, and Dutch prices fell from 0.49 guilders a pound in 1649 to a low of 0.31 guilders in 1643, a point which helps to explain why Trezel failed. But at the same time, the Dutch West India Company, which was experiencing difficulty paying its debts, decreased its Brazilian garrison, ordered its overdue loans collected, and recalled (1644) its popular New World governor-general Johan Maurits, whose expansive economic policies struck the directors as extravagant. The foreclosure on delinquent loans, a policy implemented by Maurits' successors, threw the colony's financial system into disarray, causing interest rates to rise to as much as 4 per cent a month. With the region in economic upheaval, the Portuguese citizenry revolted in 1645, capturing the hinterland. For the next nine years, the Dutch held the ports and the rebels controlled the agricultural areas.[77] Under such circumstances, sugar cultivation was again thoroughly disrupted, and, with the decrease in supply, prices rose, averaging 0.51 guilders a pound from 1646 through 1654. The new and extraordinary profitability of sugar production was reflected in an abrupt shift in the Amsterdam terms of trade, and consequently it took on an average almost three times as much indigo to purchase a pound of sugar from 1645 to 1649 as it had during the previous five years.

4 The Sugar Boom, 1645–54

With Barbadians secure from foreign invasion or confiscatory decrees, they were in an ideal position to take advantage of the resurgence in sugar prices. As a result, almost overnight the colony was thrust into a boom period much like that of the earlier tobacco era. As a measure of the new prosperity, Ligon wrote that planters sold their muscovado for 50s.–54s. 6d. a cwt, prices far above the 23s.–25s. they received in the late 1650s.[78] The difference between the two levels was nearly all profit for planters and it furthered their buoyant psychology and their get-rich-quick talk. Ligon, for instance, believed that sugar 'will make' Barbados 'one of the richest Spots of earth under the Sun', and he described one man, Colonel James Drax, who had arrived on the island with, at the most, £300 and yet who by 1650 expected to return soon to England with sufficient money to buy an estate large enough to provide a yearly income of £10,000. Colonel Thomas Modyford, who immigrated to Barbados with Ligon in 1647, had similar ambitions, and he also by 1650 was saying that he would not return to the Old Country until he had realized £100,000 on his investment of only £1,000.[79] At the same time William Powrey, who like many other settlers sought financial assistance in England, assured an uncle that £1,000 spent to equip a property with slaves and mill would return £2,000 annually after three years.[80] By any standard, these men expected astronomical profits.

The exceptional value of sugar led to a reduction in the sum needed to enter the industry. James Parker, for instance, wrote in 1646 that 'a man with about 200 off pounds . . . might quickly gaine an estate by sugar',[81] for even a plantation too small to function efficiently could return a good profit. This made it very easy for colonists who had already developed a work force large enough to raise indigo to switch to sugar cane. Moreover, while £200 was then a substantial figure, amounting to nearly twenty times the yearly wage of unskilled labourers in England, money flowed freely on Barbados. Numerous English gentry, who had shown the bad judgement to side with the King during the Civil War and had fled to the island, were inspired by the price of sugar to invest their funds in the industry. Indicative of the economic and numerical importance of such men is the fact that by 1650 they dominated the Barbados Assembly and helped cause the island to side with the royal family whose prospects were then bleak.

The Dutch also contributed to the availability of capital and, incidentally, of labour. After the Brazilians revolted in 1645, the West India Company directors, believing that the insurrection would soon be squelched, ordered their governor on the Gold Coast, Van der Wel, to continue sending slaves to Brazil. The High Council in Pernambuco, faced with an influx of blacks it could not use, shipped them to the Lesser Antilles where they were sold on lenient credit terms.[82] Of the islands, Barbados lay nearest to Recife, and with conditions on it propitious for cultivating cane, the Dutch found it expedient to sell nearly all their slaves to that colony, a situation aptly described by Sir Robert Harley, who wrote that 'the Dutch being ingaged on the coast of Giney in Affrick for Negros slaves having lost Brasille not knowing where to vent them they trusted them to Barbados, this was the first rise of the Plantacion'.[83] By perhaps 1650 and certainly by 1654, at least 20,000 blacks dwelt on the island,[84] a number equal to over twice what its white population had been only fifteen years earlier.

The influx of slaves and the size requirements for sugar estates altered the nature of Barbados society and led to the creation of a planter elite. The Dutch, forced to dump their blacks in the Caribees, inundated the market and were unable to obtain a price for their slaves even close to their worth. Ligon wrote that a 'best man *Negroe*' cost £30 sterling and that a woman brought £25–£27.[85] This was 60–100% higher than the Royal African Company had charged planters during the first twenty years it serviced Barbados,[86] which indicates that the Dutch received a return that more than covered their cost of granting credit. But the income colonists obtained from their slaves was proportionately much higher. One source noted that a black could produce enough sugar to pay for his original cost in only eighteen months,[87] while Ligon's figures show a net profit of £57 10s. yearly per labourer on a plantation containing 130 workers.[88] Consequently, slaves appeared cheap and settlers invested heavily in them. This trend was in sharp contrast to the boom years of the late 1620s, and it resulted in wealth patterns becoming strikingly unequal, with a few planters buying out surrounding small farmers in order to have estates large enough to make sugar.[89]

Adding to this economic growth was an enormous influx of English servants attracted to Barbados by its opulence. These people were sold at rates competitive with slave prices, making it profitable for planters to employ them as field hands. Only too late did indentures discover that on sugar estates men laboured under frightful conditions. As Ligon wrote, 'I have seen an Overseer beat a Servant with a cane about the head, till the blood had followed, for a fault that is not worth the speaking of; and yet he must have patience, or worse will follow. Truly, I have seen such cruelty there done to servants as I did not think one Christian could have done to another.'[90] Additional Englishmen, political prisoners and felons, also found themselves sentenced to the West Indies where they served lengthy indentureships. Cromwell shipped no less than 12,000 captured soldiers to Barbados,[91] while judges sent convicts there in such numbers that Henry Whistler wrote in his journal, 'this Illand is the Dunghill wharone England doth cast forth its rubidg: Rodgs and hors and such like peopel are those which are generally brought heare.'[92]

The impact of this influx of labourers on the insular economy was softened only by their high death rate. In 1647 alone an epidemic, probably of yellow fever, killed an estimated 6,000–10,000 Barbadians.[93] Dysentery, otherwise called the 'bloody flux', also accounted for numerous deaths, perhaps because colonists were unaware of basic sanitary practices. As it was, slaves and evidently servants drank from the same still ponds at which animals were watered. These ponds were further used 'upon all occasions, and to all purposes: to boil their meat, to make their drink, to wash their linen, for it will beare soape'.[94] Despite the ensuing toll, the population continued to increase, and by 1654 perhaps 25,000–30,000 Englishmen inhabited Barbados.[95]

Apart from population changes, the magnitude of the sugar boom can be seen in the extension of the frontier line. When colonists first began to grow cane, Barbados was only partially settled. Ligon indicated that in 1647 at least one-third of it was not cultivated, especially the higher parts where 'passage was stopped by gullies'. Yet the frontiersmen, who probably made their living girding and burning trees, planting provisions and tobacco, and then selling the land, were fast extending the inhabited area, for Ligon also wrote, 'at the time we came first there, we found both *Potatoes, Maies* and *Bonavists*, planted between the boughes, the Trees lying along upon the ground: so far short was the ground then of being clear'd'.[96] In 1652, five years later, the frontier was so far extended that Colonal Modyford wrote, 'this island of Barbados cannot last in an height of trade three year longer especially for sugar, the wood being almost already spent'.[97] He could have added that men already imported lumber from as far away as Surinam.[98] Still, contrary to the impression he gave, the colony was not yet fully settled, for its population stood at only about 70% of the 66,170 who dwelt there in 1684 or 83% of the 54,498 who inhabited the place in 1712.[99] Even so, by 1654 it contained more people per square mile than any agricultural area in Europe.

As the Barbados frontier receded and planters grew affluent, primitive living conditions began to disappear. Ligon had found the dwellings alive with insects and shabbily constructed. Made of roughly cut local wood, the houses were built so low that he could hardly stand upright while wearing his hat. They also lacked window glass. This forced colonists to construct their homes without openings on the side towards the trade winds in order to avoid having rain blown inside during storms. The breezeless rooms were consequently hot and stuffy. In addition, flies, cockroaches, ants and mosquitoes from the undrained swamps so pestered the inhabitants that, to stop insects which crawled, settlers set table legs and bed posts in bowls of water and hung hammocks and shelves containing meat by tarred ropes. Planters also placed sugar at one end of the dinner table to attract flies from food at the other.[100]

Yet the island was fast changing. Father Biet, visiting it in 1654, wrote that the 'plantation master's house is ordinarily handsome and has many rooms'. He also noted that 'one furnishes his house sumptuously. Things that are the finest in England or elsewhere are found in the island',[101] and a year later Henry Whistler wrote, 'the genterey heare doth liue far better than ours doue in England'.[102] The wealth and labour which flowed into Barbados during the sugar boom years had transformed that colony from a raw and primitive frontier region into a mature and affluent settlement.

During those same years, the remaining Caribees failed to turn fully to sugar or to become completely inhabited, partly because most prospective colonists sailed to Barbados but also because an unusual degree of political turmoil swept the other islands. For instance, rebellion intermittently racked the English sector of St Christopher from December 1641 to at least March 1642,[103] after which Governor Warner carefully exiled, or executed, his enemies. Affairs probably remained somewhat unstable for some time following that because Warner was by then an old man according to West Indian standards (he was to die in 1649), and people were perhaps unsure what type of government would replace his autocratic rule. In comparison to this short-lived upheaval, a protracted revolution of major proportions convulsed the French territories. Since their founding, their leading officials had managed with little outside assistance, and when, in 1645, the French proprietary company recalled its governor-general, Sieur de Poincy, he refused to relinquish his command of St Christopher, the only area over which he exercised actual authority. In the struggle which followed, the other governors sided first with the Company of the Isles of America and tried to seize de Poincy; but when this failed and the Crown, which was also involved in a civil war at home and the Thirty Years War abroad, chose not to provide the firm with financial of military support, the governor of Guadeloupe, Charles Houel, also rebelled. There ensued a lengthy and violent rebellion during which major planters who were reluctant to turn against their King found themselves pitted against their governors. These latter, arguing that the Company sought to impose extra duties on settlers, enlisted the assistance of small farmers and confiscated the property of their opponents. The trouble even spread to Martinique, the single island which remained loyal to the firm. The civil war drew to a close in the late 1640s when the Company, which was near bankruptcy, sought to recoup its losses by selling its proprietary claim to the by then clearly victorious governors, thereby legalizing their independent positions. This it did between 1649 and 1651, ending half a decade of strife.[104]

During that period, the French sugar industry remained in an undeveloped state[105] with, primarily, the governors investing heavily in it. A visitor to Guadeloupe wrote around 1647 that Houel had a plantation containing 100 Negroes with 80 more ordered and that he expected to make 75 tons of sugar yearly,[106] but as late as 1656 only about ten mills existed on the island.[107] A traveller staying on St Christopher in 1646 and early 1647 wrote that de Poincy owned over 100 slaves, a sugar mill and an indigo works. Advised by a man called 'Dom Paul Espagnol', the governor supposedly earned annually 30,000 *écus* from sugar, and the commodity was described as 'the first merchandise of our islands', no doubt because of its price. Yet despite this favourable description, the sugar industry appeared relatively undeveloped. De Poincy possessed the largest plantation in the French sector, but his boiling house contained only three cauldrons which made his works of minimal efficient size.[108] Even so, he apparently took advantage of the high sugar prices and rapidly increased his production, for Father Pelleprat, who visited St Christopher in 1654, believed that he owned 600 or 700 slaves.[109] If true, this would have made him very nearly the most wealthy planter on the Antilles, a position in striking contrast to that of his subjects who owned slaves and raised mainly tobacco.

With planters living outside Barbados unable to shift fully to sugar cane, it might be expected that their insular economies would remain depressed. Yet that was not the case, for with the primary flow of English labourers directed towards Barbados and with Spanish America no longer able to compete for European tobacco markets, the tobacco and cotton supplies reaching the Old World ceased expanding at previous rates and may even have decreased. Prices for these commodities consequently rose to profitable levels. The average value of Virginia tobacco, for instance, increased from 0.9d. per pound in 1640–43 to 1.5d. in 1645–49 and 3d. in 1649–50. As a result, all the English Caribbean colonies prospered, and their populations steadily expanded. The citizenry of Anglo-St Christopher, for instance, was estimated at more than 6,000 in 1645 and 12,000–13,000 in 1648.[110] While these figures lack reliability, by 1655 so many people inhabited the colony that one observer wrote, 'this island is almost worne out by reason of the multituds that live upon it'.[111] Even the less defended Leewards participated in the prosperity, and the number of Englishmen on Antigua rose from about thirty families in 1640 to 350 armed men or 750 'soules' in 1646 and close to 1,200 men in 1655.[112]

Despite the divisive civil war wracking the French colonies, their populations also grew rapidly. In 1642, the Company of the Isles of America, which had every reason to inflate its accomplishments since it sought support from the Crown, declared that over 7,000 Frenchmen lived on the Antilles.[113] Three years later, a priest put the number at 5,000. Of these, 3,000 dwelt on St Christopher and 1,000 each inhabited Guadeloupe and Martinique.[114] Their populations increased substantially during the next decade, and by 1655 the islands contained around 13,000 whites and 10,000 slaves.[115] To put this expansion of perhaps threefold to fivefold over a thirteen-year period into perspective, during the next forty-five years their citizenry increased only one and one-half times.[116] Equally important, during this period the population of Martinique and Guadeloupe surpassed that of French St Christopher: the 1645 estimate of 3,000 living on the latter island is higher than any that followed, while in 1655 Guadeloupe was said to contain 12,000 whites although in 1664 it actually had, according to a census, only 5,009.[117] That was very near the 5,303 persons said to inhabit Martinique in 1658.[118] During the sugar boom era, the French thus became thoroughly entrenched on what later became their two Caribee strongholds.

The end of that period was sealed in January 1654 when the Portuguese expelled the Dutch from Recife, the main port of Pernambuco, thereby enabling Brazilian producers to again market their commodities in Europe. As a result, tropical staple prices dropped to competitive levels, ending the most lucrative age in West Indian agriculture. For Barbadians, however, the period had lost much of its lustre even earlier. In May of 1650, royalists in the island assembly passed a declaration of loyalty to the son of Charles I. Parliament retaliated in August by forbidding Englishmen to trade with the island. Then, in 1651, Cromwell sent a fleet to the Caribees which blockaded the colony; and in January 1652, after James Modyford, then a leading militia officer, defected with his regiment, the insurgents surrendered. Because the warfare interrupted trade, planters doubtless fared poorly.

Since Holland played a major role in the Barbados economy, trade was further disturbed by the Anglo-Dutch War of 1652–54. That engagement however, did benefit the French islands, for the Amsterdam merchants were temporarily forced to orient the bulk of their Caribee shipping to them. Relations became so close between the two nationalities that when Indians attacked Martinique in 1654, Dutch soldiers were used to bear the brunt of the assault and when Protestant refugees fled Brazil, following the Portuguese reconquest, they bypassed the English possessions for Catholic Guadeloupe.

With the 1654 decline in muscovado prices, the Caribee economies experienced a sharp reverse. Numerous sugar-cane planters, hoping to minimize their losses, turned to cotton or ginger, increasing the supply of those commodities so much that their values also fell. Ginger, for instance, declined by 1655–56 from £5 sterling a cwt, to £1.25, a drop in percentage very near that which had occurred in the price of sugar.[119] The ramifications of the recession touched most aspects of Antillean life. Among the noticeable consequences, the number of whites willing to migrate to the region decreased, and as a result the islands experienced a loss in their European populations. The number of Englishmen on Barbados fell from perhaps 25,000 in 1654, apparently the highest figure in its history, to 19,568 by 1684,[120] while the population of sparsely settled Martinique declined by over 1,000.[121] Antiguans expressed the prevailing feeling of the time in a 1656 petition to Cromwell in which they asked for aid because 'many plantations have been deserted'. Their statement further noted that 'no supplies of servants have of late arrived from England' and that the 'number of fighting men is very inconsiderable', so that 'unless some speedy course is taken to remedy these evils, the island will be quite deserted'.[122] Antiguans were not the only ones seeking a political remedy for their economic ills. Barbadians petitioned the home government in 1654 to enforce the law prohibiting the cultivation of tobacco in England,[123] and in 1655–56 they presented the Protector with a carefully prepared request asking that he levy prohibitive duties on Brazilian sugar and reduce tariffs on English colonial commodities. As a result of these and other New World pressures, he revised the customs schedule.[124] In addition, he declared that all earlier loans made by the Dutch to settlers were to be paid to the English government. Colonial officials, who were themselves often planters, failed to collect these accounts, and consequently Englishmen emerged from the boom period largely unencumbered by debts.

The depression of 1654, and the competition characteristic of the following era, hardly proved disastrous for planters. Antigua did not, as the petitioners feared, become deserted, and while Martinique did temporarily lose settlers, it soon became the foremost French colony of the century. These successes, however, occurred in large part because of the firm foundation established during the prosperous years, 1624–54,

Table 1 Anglo-American Tobacco Prices, 1624–50 (pence per lb)

Year	Price	Year	Price
1624	36,[1] 24,[2] 6	1639	4/5
1625	12, 36[3]	1640	1 1/5
1628	3,9[4]	1641	1/2
1630	2, 1[5]	1642	1 1/2
1631	6	1643	4/5
1632	6	1645	1 1/2
1633	9	1646	1 1/2
1634	1,[6] 6,[7] 4/5, 4–6[8]	1647	1 1/2
1635	2–3, 2–3	1649	3
1636	2	1650	3
1638	4/5		

[1] All uncited prices come from Robert P. Thomas and Terry L. Anderson, 'The Economic Growth of the Chesapeake in the Seventeenth Century'. unpublished paper, Department of Economics, University of Washington, n.p. and Irene W. D. Hecht, 'The Virginia Colony, 1607–40: A study in Frontier Growth' (Ph.D. dissertation, University of Washington, 1969), 356–58.
[2] Edmund S. Morgan, 'The Firth American Boom: Virginia 1618 to 1630', *William and Mary Quarterly*, 3rd ser., 28 (April 1971), 177.
[3] *Ibid.*
[4] *CSP Dom., 1628–1629*, ser. 2, III, 411.
[5] George Louis Beer, *The Origins of the British Colonial System 1578–1660* (1908; rpt. Gloucester, Mass., 1959), 93.
[6] Lewis Cecil Gray, *History of Agriculture in the Southern United States to 1860* (1933; rpt. Gloucester, Mass., 1958), I, 260.
[7] Beer, *British Colonial System*, 94.
[8] *Ibid.*

Table 2 Netherlands Prices of Sugar, Cotton and Indigo, 1624–54 (guilders per Dutch lb)

Year	Sugar[1]	Cotton[2]	Indigo[3]	Year	Sugar	Cotton	Indigo
1624	0.32	0.81	4.13	1640	0.49	0.34	8.10
1625	0.38	0.84	3.85	1641	0.38	0.33	4.95
1626	0.42		3.76	1642	0.34	0.29	5.25
1628	0.44	0.60	3.90	1643	0.31	0.29	4.58
1630	0.57	0.53	3.72	1645	0.39	0.56	3.15
1631	0.59	0.48	3.55	1646	0.57	0.61	2.78
1632	0.54	0.50	3.45	1648	0.43	0.28	2.31
1633	0.54	0.48	3.83	1649	0.52	0.29	2.57
1634	0.50	0.48	3.75	1650	0.49	0.28	2.79
1635	0.51	0.56	3.90	1651	0.53	0.34	2.30
1636	0.52	0.50	3.83	1652	0.50	0.34	2.18
1637	0.67	0.47	3.90	1653	0.51	0.43	2.53
1638	0.54	0.38	4.43	1654	0.51	0.46	3.13

[1] Nicholaas Posthumus, *Inquiry into the History of Prices in Holland* (Leiden, 1946), I, 119.
[2] *Ibid.*, 281.
[3] *Ibid.*, 415–16.

successes which elevate those three decades to a prominent place in West Indian history. Yet events during that time are also much misunderstood. Scholars have overlooked the extraordinary incomes planters originally received from producing tobacco and how this influenced the founding of ten English and French colonies in the Caribbean between 1624 and 1635. Also overlooked have been the accompanying increase in tobacco output and consequent decrease in leaf prices, a trend which culminated in a depression around 1640 and which motivated settlers to feverishly search for a new staple. As a result of their investigations, Barbadians and to a lesser extent other colonists began raising sugar and there occurred another intense boom that lasted until 1654. By then the growth in West Indian populations had placed England and France in a position where they felt obliged to assert themselves as major Antillean powers, while Barbados, the most developed of the Caribees, exhibited all the characteristics that prompted men later in the century to call her 'the garden of the world'[125] and Henry Whistler to write in 1655 'This island is one of the riches spotes of ground in the wordell and fully inhabited'.[126] Neither Jamaica nor the larger French colonies of Martinique, Guadeloupe, and later St Dominique would overtake her in population until the 18th century which, as much as anything, indicates the strength and formative influence of the economic forces at work during this early period.

Notes

1. Historians have often stated that, for unspecified reasons, sugar cane cultivation was exceptionally profitable and economic growth unusually rapid during the 1660s. For instance, Richard Sheridan described this period as a 'golden age'. See *The Development of the Plantations to 1750: An Era of West Indian Prosperity 1750–1775, Chapters in Caribbean History*, I (Barbados, 1970), 83, Aside from explaining in detail the causes of that prosperity, this article seeks to move back the chronology of that era to before 1654.
2. Richard S. Dunn, *Sugar and Slaves: The Rise of the Planter Class in the English West Indies, 1624–1713* (Chapel Hill, 1972), 203. This is easily the finest book published on the 17th-century Antilles. Most of the sugar was shipped to London where the customs on the white import amounted to £1,419 12s. and the custom on brown sugar (muscovado) totalled £10,002 10s. See W. Noel Sainsbury (ed.), *Calendar of State Papers, colonial series, American and the West Indies, 1754–1660* (London, 1860), I 434, (hereafter *CSP Col. AWI, 1574–1660*). It should be noted that sugar cane was cultivated on the Caribees quite early, perhaps because the juice from the stalks served as a raw sweetener and as a base for alcoholic beverages. During the 16th century, Indians apparently carried the plant from Puerto Rico to the larger French islands, for the first settlers found it growing wild, while Captain Powell introduced it to Barbados in 1627. Because of the plant's availability, colonists possibly exported some crude molasses during the 1630s, but until *ca.* 1640 they evidently failed to invest the capital in equipment and knowledge necessary to make a quality product.
3. Accepting this unproven belief makes it difficult to explain why planters turned to sugar cane in the 1640s, for one is then faced with the perplexing question of why Caribee settlers waited nearly twenty years after founding their colonies before raising their most remunerative product. It is the thesis of this paper that sugar was not always their most profitable commodity and that colonists turned to it only when the sweetener increased in value relative to alternative staples. For a different explanation of events, see Matthew Edel, 'The Brazilian Sugar Cycle of the Seventeenth Century and the Rise of West Indian Competition', *Caribbean Studies*, IX (April 1969), 24–44.
4. *No Peace Beyond the Line: The English in the Caribbean 1624–1609* (New York, 1972), 33, 98.
5. *Sugar and Slaves*, 19, 49, 60–1, 188. The appearance of this and the above recent works enables us to delineate the frontiers of Caribbean scholarship. Both authors introduce new archival findings, and both view the early sugar era as a prosperous time, but neither writer systematically utilized price data, the primary basis for the conclusions of his article, to throw light on the course of economic development. For that reason, perhaps, neither noted that the early West Indian economies were subject to violent economic cycles.
6. See Table 1.
7. Nicholaas W. Posthumus, *Inquiry into the History of Prices in Holland* (Leiden, 1946), I, 119, 169–70, 281–86, 413–16.
8. The Amsterdam price of tobacco, or any other New World staple, was the sum of its American price, transportation costs and transaction expenses. Competition rapidly drove the latter down to a point where additional shippers and merchants had little incentive to enter the field, thereby minimizing changes in average profits. Until 1651–52, basic operating costs in these two areas also remained relatively constant for there occurred no major shifts in the balance of sea power, no break in New World Anglo-French hostilities with Spain, and no significant cost reducing shipping innovations. Consequently, European market fluctuations were consistently passed directly to planters, causing colonial incomes to oscillate from one extreme to another. The dynamics of that situation can more fully be understood by examining a hypothetical case. Assume that, as in the 1685 sugar industry, Barbadians sold their produce for 10s. a cwt and that transportation and transaction charges added an additional 10s. burden to the commodity so that it fetched 20s. a cwt wholesale in London. A 4s. or 20% decrease in the London figure, then, would result in a 4s. or 40% decline in its West Indian value.
9. Among these were two on the Amazon, two in Guiana, two on the Caribees and one in New England.
10. F. W. Fairhold, *Tobacco Its History and Associations* (London, 1859), 50. The curative powers of tobacco were widely advertised in natural histories. See John Gerard, *The Herball or General Histoire of Plantes* (London, 1597), 287 and Jacques Gohory, *Instruction sur l'herbe petum ditte en france l'herbe de la Royne ou Medicée* (Paris, 1572), *passim*.
11. Huguette and Pierre Chaunu, *Séville et l'Atlantique* (Paris, 1956), VI, Pt 2, 1033.

12. Lewis Cecil Gray, *History of Agriculture in the Southern United States to 1860* (1933; rpt. Gloucester, Mass., 1958), I, 218–19.
13. In comparison, the lesser gentry lived well. James E. Rogers described one landowner, a man educated at Cambridge, who on £300 or £400 a year kept a stable of horses, lived in some luxury and maintained a considerable number of servants. See *A History of Agriculture and Prices in England* (Oxford, 1887), V, 28-9, 673.
14. See Table 1 and Thomas and Anderson, 'Growth of the Chesapeake'. n.p.
15. Trinidad was actually little more than a contraband centre for Venezuelan tobacco, but many Northern Europeans believed it to be a major producer. John Gerard, for instance, wrote that the best tobacco came from that island but did not mention Venezuela. See *The Herball*, 285, and Eric Eustace Williams, *History of the People of Trinidad and Tobago* (New York, 1964), 14.
16. James A. Williamson, *The Caribee Islands Under the Proprietary Patents* (London, 1926), 22 and John Cordy Jeaffreson, *A Young Squire of the Seventeenth Century* (London, 1878), I, 18.
17. Nellis M. Crouse, *French Pioneers in the West Indies, 1624-44* (New York, 1940), 16–18; and Jean Baptiste Dutertre, *Histoire générale des Antilles habitées par les François* (Paris, 1667), I, 1–113.
18. Arthur Percival Newton, *The Colonising Activities of the English Puritans* (New Haven, 1914), 33.
19. *Ibid.*, 31–34, 44–46.
20. The early history of Barbados is described by Vincent T. Harlow, *A History of Barbados, 1625-85* (1926; rpt. New York, 1969), N. Darnell Davis, *The Cavaliers and Roundheads of Barbados, 1650-1652* (Georgetown, British Guiana, 1887) and Williamson, *The Caribee Islands*. Richard S. Dunn provides the best overview of the colonization of all of the islands in his *Sugar and Slaves*.
21. John Bruce, (ed.), *Calendar of State Papers, domestic series, Charles I, 1628-1629*, ser. 2 (London, 1859), III, 411 and Harlow, *History of Barbados*, 12.
22. Thomas and Anderson have noted seven productivity estimates for Virginia between 1624 and 1645. They are 800 lbs, 800–1,000 lbs, 1,500 lbs, 1,530 lbs, 2,000–2,400 lbs and 2,000–3,000 lbs. To these I added one of 1,000 lbs from the early French Caribbean and took the median which was 1,000–1,500 lbs. This is a conservative figure, for the lower productivity estimates probably applied to planters who spend much of their time raising corn. See 'Growth of the Chesapeake', Appendix Two, and (Anon.), 'La plus ancienne relation de voyage aux colonies françaises des Antilles' (*ca.* 1640), ed. Louis-Philippe May, *Terre-air-mer, la geographie*, XVIII (July-August 1932), 16. Virginia's productivity estimates clearly provide a reasonable proxy for Caribbean figures. For one thing, cultivation techniques were nearly identical in the two regions, partly because the English and French were unable to improve already existing Spanish husbandry practices. For an understanding of the virtually unchanging state of the art from *ca.* 1620 to 1779, one need only glance at the works of Vázquez de Espinosa, Father Labat and Jonathan Carver. Second, several West Indian productivity estimates exist for the years following 1645 and these closely resemble those coming from Virginia. John Scott (*ca.* 1668), for instance, stated that a man who raised his own provisions could grow 2,500 lbs of tobacco yearly while Father Labat (*ca.* 1700) placed the figure at 1,330 lbs. See Antonio Vázquez de Espinosa, *Description of the Indies* (*ca.* 1620), trans. Charles Upson Clark (1942; rpt. Washington DC, 1968), 56–57; Jean Baptiste Labat, *Nouveaux voyage aux isles de l'Amérique* (The Hague, 1725), I, Bk 4, 169–71; Jonathan Carver, *A Treatise on the Cultivation of the Tobacco Plant* (London, 1779), *passim*; and John Scott, 'Description of Barbados', *The Bulletin of the Barbados Museum and Historical Society*, No 11 and 12 (November 1967 and February 1968), n.p.
23. Dunn, *Sugar and Slaves*, 66. Dutertre, *Histoire générale*, II, 452–53. For a more detailed discussion of French land policy, see Mme. G. Desportes, 'Mode d'appropriation des terres', *Annales de Antilles*, No 2 (1955), 71–88. Land began to increase significantly in value only towards the end of the 1630s. Before then it was so cheap that Barbados and St Christopher planters found it advantageous to create patent offices for registration of titles only around 1639. Public surveyors appeared on both the English and French Caribees only in the 1640s, but titles remained vague throughout the century, causing numerous lawsuits when property became valuable. See 'Papers Relating to the Early History of Barbados and St Kitts', ed. N. Barnell Davis, *Timcehri*, new ser., VI (1892), 339–40.
24. Edmund Morgan, 'The First American Boom: Virginia 1618 to 1630', *William and Mary Quarterly*, 3rd ser., 27 (April 1971), 169–98.
25. Henry Colt, 'The Voyage of Sir Henry Colt' (1631), *Colonising Expeditions to the West Indies and Guiana, 1623–1667*, ed. Vincent T. Harlow, Hakluyt Society, 2nd ser., Vol. LVI (1924; rpt. Nendeln/Liechtenstein, 1967), 65–66. Colt considered the planters lazy, in part because they had difficulty controlling their servants. Food shortages were common during the 1620s, but as tobacco prices fell settlers began raising their own eatables, and Barbados apparently even started exporting foodstuffs to the other Caribees.
26. 'The First American Boom', 197.
27. Real wages in England were then very near the lowest levels recorded during the period 1250–1950. One of the foremost causes of this depression was the deterioration of the English woollen industry. See E. H. Phelps Brown and Sheila V. Hopkins, 'Seven Centuries of the Prices of Consumables, Compared with Builders' Wage-rates', *Economica*, new ser., XXIII (November 1956), 302 and B[arry] E. Supple, *Commercial Crisis and Change in England, 1600-1642* (Cambridge, 1959), 5-6, 33–38, 120.
28. George Louis Beer, *The Origins of the British Colonial System 1578-1660* (1908; rpt. Gloucester, Mass., 1959), 204.
29. See Table 1. According to the independent but non-quantitative work by the French historian Louis-Philippe May, tobacco prices broke in 1635. See his *Histoire économique de la Martinique* (*1635-1763*) (Paris, 1930), 87.
30. *CSP Co AWI, 1574–1660*, I, 146, 148.
31. Clarence H. Haring, *Trade and Navigation Between Spain and the Indies* (1918; rpt. Gloucester, Mass., 1964), 77–78, 84–88.
32. Gray, *History of Agriculture*, I, 261–62, and J. Harry Bennett, 'Peter Hay, Proprietary Agent in Barbados, 1636-1641', *The Jamaican Historical Review*, V (1965), 16. This was not the first time a cartel was attempted. In 1629, 1630, 1631, 1632 and 1633 Virginians attempted to restrict tobacco cultivation, apparently with little success, and in 1634 the Crown succumbed to colonial requests and appointed a commissioner who was to sit on the Council and establish rules for reducing production. See *CSP Col. AWI, 1574-1660*, I, 117, 190. The man, however, died on his way to America. In the Caribbean, there also appears to have been an unsuc-

cessful attempt to reduce the tobacco supply in 1633 or 1634. See Davis (ed.), 'Early History of Barbados and St Kitts', p. 339.

33. M. Moreau de Saint-Méry, *Loix et constitutions des colonies françoises de l'Amérique sous le vent* (Paris, 1784), I, 43–4; and Dutertre, *Histoire générale*, I, 143–45.
34. The total quantity of tobacco imported at the Port of London amounted to 1,516,050 lbs in 1637, 3,117,600 lbs in 1638, 1338,360 lbs in 1639 and 1,207,100 lbs in 1640. Of this the share from Barbados fell from 124,590 lbs in 1637 and 204,906 lbs in 1638 to 28,010 lbs in 1639 and to 66,900 lbs in 1640, while the share from St Christopher declined from 263,600 lbs in 1637 and 470,730 lbs in 1638 to 107,310 lbs in 1639 and 138,970 lbs in 1640. See 'Imports of Tobacco, 1637–1640', *Caribbeana*, ed. Vere Langford Oliver (London, 1914), III, 197–98. The quantity of Virginia tobacco imported into London greatly exceeded the quantity from the Caribees because the West Indian leaf was more heavily taxed in England. This led Antillean planters to ship their product directly to the Netherlands.
35. Richard Ligon, *A True & Exact History of the Island of Barbados* (1657) (1673; rpt. London, 1970), 113. In the late 1630s, another observer called Barbados tobacco, 'the worst of all tobaccos'. See Bennett, 'Peter Hay', 15.
36. Scott, 'Description of Barbados', n.p.; and David Watts, *Man's Influence on the Vegetation of Barbados, 1627 to 1800*, University of Hull Occasional Papers in Geography, no. 4 (Hull, England, 1966), opposite 16.
37. Colt, 'Voyage of Sir Henry Colt', 69.
38. May, *Histoire économique*, 87–88.
39. Bennett, 'Peter Hay', 16.
40. *CSP Col. AWI, 1574–1660*, I, 277.
41. Posthumus, *Prices in Holland*, I, 119, 284.
42. The detailed Stanto Domingo census of 1606 demonstrates that ginger was the foremost economic product of that island. See Antonio Ossorio, 'Autos y testimonios tocantes a las cossas del estado de la isla Españo*la', in Relaciónes históricas de Santo Domingo*, ed. E. Rodigrues Demorizi, (Ciudad Trujillo, 1945), II, 443–44. Ginger also served as a prominent Puerto Rican export and was grown on Jamaica and Cuba. See Irene Wright, 'History of Sugar-IX', *The Louisiana Planter and Sugar Manufacture*, LV (July 17, 1915), 46 and Robert Batie, 'A Comparative Economic History of the Spanish, French, and English on the Caribbean Islands during the Seventeenth Century', (Ph.D dissertation, University of Washington, 1972), 22–27.
43. Dutertre, *Historie générale*, II, 7.
44. Don Diego de Torres Vargas, 'Descripción de la isla y ciudad de Puerto Rico, y de su vecindad y polbaciónes, presidio, gobernadores y obicpos; frutos y minerales' (1647), *Boletín histórico de Puerto Rico*, IV (September–October 1917), 261.
45. Nicholas Foster, *A Briefe Relation of the Late Horrid Rebellion Acted in the Island Barbados, in the West Indies* (1650; rpt. London, 1879), 1–2.
46. J. Harry Bennett, 'The English Caribees in the Period of the Civil War, 1642–1646', *William and Mary Quarterly*, 24 (April 1967), 360.
47. Sieur Lonvilliers de Poincy, 'Mémoires envoyés aux seigneurs de la Compagnie des Iles de l'Amérique' (1640), in *Tricentenaire des Antilles Guadeloupe 1635–1935, documents inédits*, ed. J.[oseph] Rennard, (Basse-Terre, Guadeloupe, 1935), 40.
48. Bennett, 'Peter Hay', 16–17.
49. Scott, 'Description of Barbados', n.p.
50. For background on indigo, see W. A. Vetterli, 'The History of Indigo', *Ciba Review*, No. 85 (April 1951), 3066–3087, a succinct and balanced study; J. Bridges-Lee, *On Indigo Manufacture: A Practical and Theoretical Guide to the Production of the Dye* (Calcutta, 1892), provides a detailed explanation of the reason for each step in the manufacturing process; James Crokatt (ed.) *Observations Concerning Indigo and Cochineal* (London, 1746), translated selections from authors like Jean Baptiste Labat; George Watt, *Dictionary of the Economic Products of India* (London, 1890), IV, 383–469, or the abridged edition, *Commercial Products of India*, (1908; rpt. New Delhi, 1966), 660–85; Dauril Alden, 'The Growth and Decline of Indigo Production in Colonial Brazil: A Study in Comparative Economic History', *The Journal of Economic History*, XXV (March 1965), 35–60; William F. Leggett, *Ancient and Medieval Dyes* (Brooklyn, 1944), 17–31; and Batie, 'Caribbean Islands during the Seventeenth Century', 68–72.
51. The 18th-century planter-historian Edward Long noted that a twenty-five acre plantation required twenty men, while Patrick Browne wrote that 'seventeen negroes are sufficient to manage twenty acres of indigo'. Neither author stated that estates were commonly that size, but both seemed to assume it. Since techniques for producing indigo appear nearly identical throughout the 17th and 18th centuries, there is no reason to expect the ideal plantation size to have changed. See Edward Long, *The History of Jamaica* (London, 1774), I, 407, and Patrick Browne, *The Civil and Natural History of Jamaica* (London, 1789), 304–05.
52. J. Harry Bennett, 'Cary Helyar, Merchant and Planter of Seventeenth-Century Jamaica', *William and Mary Quarterly*, 21 (January 1964), 74.
53. How many labourers were needed remains difficult to pinpoint, but the number probably varied. Ward Barrett noted that on thirteen 17th- and 18th-century estates the work force ranged from 50 to 500 labourers. But both 50 and 500 were atypical figures, for the second smallest number was 150 and the third largest number was 300. Since estates sufficiently prominent to attract attention might well have been unusually large, it is useful to compare Barrett's findings with those of Richard S. Dunn who, utilizing the Barbados census records of 1679–80, discovered that the 175 settlers who possessed 60 or more slaves owned 53% of the island's acreage and 54% of its Negroes. See Barrett, 'Caribbean Sugar-Production Standards in the Seventeenth and Eighteenth Centuries', in *Merchants and Scholars*, ed. John Parker (Minneapolis, 1965), 166; and Dunn, 'The Barbados Census of 1680: Profile of the Richest Colony in English America', *William and Mary Quarterly*, 26 (October 1969), 12, 17.
54. Ligon, *Islands of Barbadoes*, 22.
55. Accurate accounts of the sugar-making process and of plantation life are rare. See Barrett, 'Caribbean Sugar-Production Standards', 147–70 and his *The Sugar Hacienda of the Marqueses del Valle* (Minneapolis, 1970); Noel Deerr, *The History of Sugar*, 2 vols (London, 1949–50), Labat, *Nouveaux voyage*, II, Bk 3, 224–360, one of the most detailed and useful works available; F. Depons, *A Voyage to the Eastern Part of Terra Firma of the Spanish Main in South America, During the Years 1801, 1802, 1803, and 1804*, trans. (New York, 1806), II, 196–229; Batie, 'Caribbean Islands during the Seventeenth Century', 112–69; Michael Craton and James Walvin, *A Jamaican Plantation* (Toronto and Buffalo, 1970), 95–154; and J. Harry Bennett, *Bondsman and Bishops, Slavery and Apprenticeship on the Codrington Plantations of Barbados,*

1710-1838, *University of California Publication in History*, LXII (Berkeley and Los Angeles, 1958).
56. N. Darnell Davis (ed.), 'Early History of Barbados and St Kitts', 336.
57. Posthumus, *Prices in Holland*, I, 416.
58. Chaunu, *Séville et l'Atlantique*, VIII, pt. 2, sec. 2, 1797-1848; John Lynch, *Spain Under the Habsburgs* (New York, 1969), II, 94-115.
59. Posthumus, *Prices in Holland*, I, 415-16.
60. C. R. Boxer, *The Dutch in Brazil 1624-1654* (Oxford, 1957), *passim*.
61. Dunn summarizes the well-known English colonizing failures in *Sugar and Slaves*, 17. Thomas G. Mathews, in 'The Spanish Domination of Saint Martin (1633-1648)', *Caribbean Studies*, IX (April 1969), 3-23, insightfully presents the Spanish response to foreign incursions. Details of Indian attempts to obstruct the French colonizing activity are found in C. A. Banbuck, *Histoire politique, économique et sociale de la Martinique sous l'ancien régime (1635-1789)* (Paris, 1935), 30-35; Maurice Satineau, *Histoire de la Guadeloupe sous l'ancien régime (1635-1789)* (Paris 1928), 21-32; and above all Dutertre, *Histoire générale*, 70-2, 81-95, 113-15, 145-53, 496-504. For a discussion of Indian customs by a priest who lived among the natives, see Raymond P. Breton, *Les Caraibes de La Guadeloupe 1635-1656* (1656), ed. Joseph Rennard (Paris, 1929), 45-74.
62. *CSP Col. AWI, 1574-1660*, I, 201.
63. I am in debt to Kevin P. Kelly of the Institute of Early American History and Culture for providing me with this figure.
64. Bennett, 'Peter Hay', 13.
65. *CSP Col. AWI, 1574-1660*, I, 295.
66. Early authors gave widely varying accounts as to how many planters they believed lived on the Caribees, but most scholars tend to accept a report by company officials who place the population at 7,000 in 1642. See May, *Histoire économique*, 55. The French were heavily outnumbered because the English depression and Civil War impelled numerous people from that island to sail to America while the more stable economic conditions within France reduced the incentives for individuals from that country to migrate.
67. Harlow, *History of Barbados*, 7-20.
68. Scott, 'Description of Barbados' [7].
69. Bennett, 'Peter Hay', 20.
70. Ligon, *Island of Barbadoes*, 85.
71. Ch[ristian] Schnakenbourg, 'Note sur les origines de l'industrie sucrière en Guadeloupe au XVII siècle (1640-1670)', *Revue française de'historie d'outremer*, LX No. 200 (1968), 270.
72. [Anon.], 'La plus ancienne relation', 16.
73. Rennard, ed. *Tricentenaire des Antilles*, 49-53.
74. Bennett, 'English Caribbees', 372.
75. Labat, *Nouveaux voyage*, I, Bk 3, 228.
76. Posthumus, *Prices in Holland*, I, 416.
77. This account relies heavily on Boxer, *Dutch in Brazil*, *passim*, and Hermann Watjen, 'The Dutch colonial Empire in Brazil', trans. Peter Guldbrandesn, typescript trans. of a work published at The Hague in 1921 (Bancroft Library, University of California at Berkeley). The sugar supply reaching Europe was also reduced due to a shortage of vessels and to high trans-Atlantic shipping costs, both of which were the result of warfare at sea. From 1623 through 1636, Dutch West-India Company raiders captured 547 Spanish-Portuguese ships valued at 6,710,000 florins, while in 1647 and 1648 they took 259 vesels trading with Bahia alone. See Watjen, 'Empire in Brazil', 125 and Boxer, *Dutch in Brazil*, Appendix III.
78. The 50s.-54s. 6d. estimate was calculated from an anonymous statement that in 1650 slaves cost 1,000-1,100 pounds of sugar apiece and from Ligon's belief that slave prices varied from £25-£30. Ligon wrote in one place that Barbadians received 70s.-124s. per cwt for brown sugar and in another that the lowest price was 25s. The figures are irreconcilable even though it may be surmised that the lower one referred to values after 1654 when he wrote his book. Certainly Posthumus' price data indicate that from 1645 to 1654 sugar was worth a great deal, in fact far more than the 28s. which it fetched in 1658. Other sources support this view. In 1685, a petition to the Crown stated that in earlier times 'our sugar then yielded very high rates in England as from three pounds unto four pounds per cent for our muscovado sugars, and white sugars from 6 lbs to 7 lbs per cent, whereas now our white sugar cleers not the halfe part of what our musco sugar heretofore yielded'. See Ligon, *Island of Barbadoes*, 46-7, 92, 95; [Anon.], ' Breife Discription of the Ilande of Barbados' (1650), in *Colonising Expeditions to the West Indies and Guiana, 1623-1667*, ed. V[incent] T. Harlow, the Hakluyt Society, 2nd. ser., LVI (1925; rpt. Nendeln/Liechtenstein, 1967), 45 and [Anon.], 'Groans of the Plantations' (1685), *The Journal of the Barbados Museum and Historical Society*, XVI (November 1948 and February 1949), 27.
79. Ligon, *Island of Barbadoes*, 86, 96, 22.
80. Dunn, *Sugar and Slaves*, 59.
81. Bridenbaugh, *Beyond the Line*, 79.
82. Watjen, 'Empire in Brazil', 505-06.
83. Elizabeth Donnan (ed.), *Documents Illustrative of the History of the Slave Trade to America* (Washington, DC, 1930), I, 125. Another author wrote, 'the Hollanders . . . did at the first attempt of makeing sugar give great credit to the most sober inhabitants, and upon the unhappie Civill warr that brake out in England, they managed the whole Trade in or Westerne Collonies, and furnished the Island with Negroes, Coppers, Stills, and all other things Appertaining to the Ingenious for making of sugar'. See Harlow, *History of Barbados*, 42.
84. Harlow, *History of Barbados*, 338.
85. Ligon, *Island of Barbadoes*, 46.
86. K. G. Davies, *The Royal African Company* (New York, 1970), 364.
87. Donnan (ed.), *History of the Slave Trade*, I, 124.
88. Ligon, *Island of Barbadoes*, 116.
89. Richard Pares who examined Barbadian land records believed that settlers began enlarging their estates around 1646. See *Merchants and Planters, Economic History Supplement*, No. 4 (Cambridge, England, 1960), 57. The long-run economic forces which ultimately resulted in slaves displacing white servants are analyzed by Richard N. Bean in 'The British Trans-Atlantic Slave Trade, 1650-1755' (Ph.D. dissertation, University of Washington, 1971), 103-18.
90. Ligon also noted that both white males and females laboured in the fields alongside blacks (*Island of Barbadoes*, 44, 115). After 1654, Antillean slave prices fell and real wage rates in England rose. As a result fewer people sold themselves into servitude while those men who did fetched comparatively high prices and were generally placed in managerial or skilled labouring positions where they enjoyed improved working conditions. Similar trends occurred, although more slowly, on the French islands. Concerning brutality, for instance, a visitor to Martinique wrote in 1660 that servants were so cruelly handled that they would be better off as slaves among the Turks. See Cosimo Brunetti, 'Three Relations of the West Indies in 1659-60', ed. Susan Heller Anderson, *Transactions of the American*

Philosophical Society, LIX (September 1968), 15.
91. Harlow, *History of Barbados*, 119.
92. Henry Whistler, 'Extracts from Henry Whistler's Journal of the West Indies Expedition' (1655), in *The Narrative of General Venables with an Appendix of Papers Relating to the Expedition to the West Indies III*, ed. C. H. Firth, Royal Historical Society, new ser. (London, 1900), 146.
93. Harlow, *History of Barbados*, 273, and Beauchamp Plantagent, ' Description of the Providence of New Albion', (1648), in *Tracts and Other Papers*, ed. Peter Force, (Washington DC, 1838), II, 5.
94. Ligon, *Island of Barbadoes*, 28–9.
95. Harlow has compiled a list of population estimates. Only three figures exist for the number of whites dwelling on that island at the end of the sugar boom: 30,000 in 1653, 23,000 in 1655, and 'at least' 25,000 in 1655. Considering how many people must have lived there in order to produce the recorded sugar exports, I feel that 25,000 is a conservative figure. See *History of Barbados*, 338.
96. *Illand of Barbadoes*, 24, 94.
97. *CSP Col. AWI, 1574–1660*, I, 374.
98. Father Antoine Biet, '. . . Visit to Barbados in 1654' (1654), ed. and trans. Jerome S. Handler, *The Journal of Barbados Museum and Historical Society*, XXXII (May, 1967), 56.
99. Dunn, *Sugar and Slaves*, 87.
100. *Illand of Barbadoes*, 40, 59, 63–64, 94.
101. Biet, 'Visit to Barbados', 65, 67–68.
102. Whistler, 'West India Expedition', 146.
103. Bennett, 'English Caribees', 361–65.
104. The fullest account of these struggles was written by Dutertre, *Histoire générale*, I, 146–448, whose interpretation was later closely followed by Crouse, the only modern historian to treat this subject in English. See his *French Pioneers, passim*. The Knights of Malta, of which de Poincy was a member, acquired St Christopher along with St Martin, St Croix and St Bartholomew on 24 May 1651 for 120,000 livres. Du Parquet bought Martinique and the French claims to St Lucia, Grenada and the Grenadines on 27 September 1650 for 60,000 livres, while Houel and his brother-in-law, Boisseret, purchased Guadeloupe, Mariegalante, Desirade and the Saints on 4 September 1649, for 73,000 livres.
105. Planters believed that their principal problem was an inability to acquire sufficient capital for slaves and equipment. As early as 1639, Du Parquet wrote that 'there is not one hero [on Martinique] rich enough' to erect sugar works. At the end of the sugar era, the problem still remained, and Father Breton noted that 'one will make more profit from this merchandize [sugar] than from tobacco, but it takes a great deal of money in order to erect a mill'. In fact, capital may have been scarce because risk costs remained excessive, a point which led investors to place their money elsewhere. See Dutertre, *Histoire générale*, I, 109, and Breton, 'L'îsle de la Guadeloupe', 44.
106. Stewart L. Mims, *Colbert's West India Policy* (New Haven, 1912), 34.
107. Schnakenbourg, 'Origines de l'industrie sucrière', 300.
108. F. Maurile de Saint-Michel, *Voyages des isles Camercanes en l'Amérique* (Le Mans, 1652), 44–45, 120.
109. P. Pierre Pelleprat, 'Relation des missions des pères de la Compagnie de Jesus' (1655), in *Mission de Cayenne et de la Guyane Française* (Paris, 1857), 46.
110. Pacifique de Provins, *Breve relation du voyage des îles de l'Amérique* (1645) (Paris, 1939), 16 and Jeaffreson, *Young Squire*, I, 34.
111. Vere, L. Oliver, *The History of Antigua* (London, 1894), I, xxv.
112. *Ibid.*, xxv and Bennett, 'English Caribbees', 37.
113. May, *Histoire économique*, 55. One even higher estimate exists. In about 1640, an anoymous source wrote that 8,000 French bachelors lived on St Christopher, 2,000 on Martinique, and 1,000 on Guadeloupe. While the estimate is obviously excessive, the distribution is informative. [Anon.] 'Plus ancienne relation', 14.
114. de Provins, *Îles de l'Amérique*, 16–17, 20.
115. Only two estimates exist of the total number of people then living on the French Antilles. Father Pelleprat, who visited the Caribbees in 1654, wrote that altogether they contained 15,000–16,000 Frenchmen and 12,000–13,000 slaves, but an examination of the various estimates of specific island populations suggests that these figures are too high. In 1658, Charles Rochfort wrote that there were 9,000–10,000 whites on the French Antilles and nearly as many Indians and Negroes. The present author feels that 13,000 Frenchmen and 10,000 slaves constitutes a reasonable estimate but that either figure could be in error by as much as 2,000. See Pelleprat, 'Missions des pères', 6, 47. May, *Histoire économique*, 54–55.
116. Batie, 'Caribbean Islands during the Seventeenth Century', 174–75.
117. Schnakenbourg, 'Origines de l'industrie sucrière', 300.
118. J. B. Delwarde, *Les défricheurs et les petits colons de la Martinique au XVII siècle* (Paris, 1935), 18.
119. Harlow, *History of Barbados*, 93. The French also complained about the decline in ginger prices. See Dutertre, *Histoire générale*, II, 95–6.
120. By 1684, the Barbados slave population had risen to 46,602. In 1712, just before Queen Anne's War ended, the island contained 12,528 whites and 41,970 blacks, in 1809, 15,556 whites and 69,119 Negroes, and in 1922, 15,000 whites and 180,000 blacks. See Dunn, *Sugar and Slaves*, 87 and Harlow, *History of Barbados*, 338.
121. Brunetti, 'Relations of the West Indies', 28.
122. Oliver, *History of Antigua*, I, xxvii.
123. *CSP Co. AWI, 1574–1660*, I, 417.
124. Harlow, *History of Barbados*, 91–3.
125. John Houghton, *A Collection of Letters for the Improvement of Husbandry and Trade* (London, 1681), I, 2–3. During the second half of the 17th century, English and French colonists expanded sugar production and enjoyed a high standard of living partly at the expense of Brazilian planters. Luso-American sugar output revived briefly following the expulsion of the Dutch but then entered a period of protracted decline, primarily because the Crown levied heavy taxes on its producers, taxes which in 1624 amounted to perhaps 30% of the value of their output and which tended to increase in later years, thereby placing Brazilians at a competitive disadvantage. See Frederic Mauro, *Le Portugal ét l'Atlantique au XVII siècle (1570–1670), Étude économique* (Paris, 1960), 225.
126. Whistler, 'West India Expedition', 145. The rapid economic expansion of the Caribees up to 1654 was a major factor in causing Cromwell to implement the Western Design which led to England conquering Jamaica in 1655. Not realizing that the English Antillean growth rate, and particularly that of Barbados, was artificially high, a view also not grasped by his West Indian advisers such as the optimistic Modyford, Cromwell vastly overestimated the wealth that would accrue to England were she to enlarge her Caribbean dominions. At the same time, he was acutely aware of the fact that by 1654 Barbados had become nearly completely settled and that continued Antillean economic growth depended on seizing one of the larger Spanish islands.

The Origins of Plantation Growth in Puerto Rico

FRANCISCO SCARANO

In attempting to understand the rise of sugar in Puerto Rico, one is impressed by the rather cursory treatment afforded the important societal process of plantation evolution in scholarly literature. In the absence of thorough studies of the nineteenth-century economy, useful guidelines are found only in textbooks and general histories, and in barely a handful of specialized monographs conceived primarily in a legalistic framework.[1] As a result, the standard interpretation suffers serious shortcomings, particularly in regard to two crucial issues: the origins of economic change, and the nature of the plantation labor system, or more precisely, the economic role of slavery in sugar. Because clarification of these issues is essential to an understanding of Puerto Rico's economy and society during the nineteenth century, it is at this point necessary to address several prevailing misconceptions.

The standard interpretation of the resurgence of commercial agriculture in the early 1800s is inadequate primarily because of its excessive emphasis on the administrative measures dictated by Spain and its colonial representatives to promote economic growth. In their sometimes unconscious attempt to explain the historical process as a function of institutional change or political events, historians have offered what amounts to a monocausal explanation of a complex, multifaceted process. With the exception of a few scholars who have stressed the need to view Puerto Rican developments in a broader context, there has been wide agreement on the 'determining' effects of the so-called *Cédula de Gracias*, a royal decree of 1815 which endeavored to promote cash-crop agriculture through increased trade, freer technological exchange, and the attraction of foreign capital. Enacted to 'give renewed impulse to the prosperity and welfare of the natives of that Island',[2] the Cédula allowed (among other things) the opening of all ports to foreign trade, the abolition of the ecclesiastical tithe and other taxes, the promotion of immigration from friendly Catholic countries, and a reduction of duties on imports of slaves and agricultural implements and machinery. The decree came in the wake of the restoration of Ferdinand VII to the Spanish throne and the conclusion of the first wave of anti-Spanish revolutionary activity in the continental colonies — a rebellion to which segments of the Puerto Rican Creole elite had shown some sympathy, but had not yet resolved to follow. In a way, therefore, the Cédula was designed to appease the island's liberals, whose ideological disposition, though not yet transformed into outright anti-Spanish and pro-independence feelings, alarmed imperial authorities who were conscious of the colony's value as a strategic base for counter-campaigns. In the conception of policymakers in Spain at this difficult junctive insurgency, colonial economic growth was not just an end in itself; it was also a means to obtain the support of influential Creole groups and to thwart the rise of an independence movement.

Regardless of underlying intent, with the Cédula the Spanish crown removed a series of obstacles in the path of plantation development, and partly because of this the production of cash crops took off soon after the decree's promulgation — slowly at first, and more rapidly after about 1825. But the changes in trade regulations, immigration policy, and taxation embodied in the Cédula were hardly sufficient in themselves to spark the plantation boom. Though often overlooked by historians, the facts are that the reform measures actually adopted reduced the scope of the original

---

Sugar and Slavery in Puerto Rico: The Plantation Economy of Ponce, (Madison, 1984), pp. 16–34.

Table 1 Concentration of Sugar Plantations in Puerto Rico, 1828

Sugar production[a] (tons)	Number of municipalities	Number of plantations[b]	Total production (tons)	% of total output
0	15	2	—	—
1-50	18	17	322.9	2.3
51-200	10	44	1,168.4	8.3
201-1,000	11	125	4,962.4	35.2
More than 1,001	3	88	7,622.4	54.2
Total	57	276	14,076.1	100.0

Source: Córdova, *Memorias geográficas*, Vol. 2, *passim*.
[a] Many districts not reporting sugar output produced molasses in home-made wooden mills.
[b] In one district, Sabana Grande, two plantations were reported but no sugar output was recorded.

decree, and more important, that the ordinance was neither a radical departure from ongoing imperial policy nor a potent catalyst of the larger, pan-Caribbean forces that ultimately sustained Puerto Rico's full incorporation into the international economy. All too frequently in the historical literature these points have been sidelined in favor of a simpler, rigid, causal connection between policy change and economic growth.[3] One would be remiss, however, to accept this conceptualization; reform was an important ingredient in the formula of plantation development, but more as a permissive condition than as an independent agent of change.

The reformist intent of Ferdinand VII's new policy toward Puerto Rico immediately faced several practical challenges. Far from pleasing all of the colonial elites, the Cédula de Gracias aroused the suspicion of Spanish merchants and raised the specter of a total collapse of the island exchequer. It theatened, in other words, two of the most solid foundations of Spanish colonial power. To thwart a dangerous depletion of the treasury and to appease the peninsular merchants, Spanish officials in Puerto Rico did not enforce all of the Cédula's provisions, choosing instead to modify some and postpone others. In the months following the king's declaration, intendant Alejandro Ramírez and governor Salvador Meléndez promulgated a series of regulations governing the Cédula, most of which sought to balance the need for a progressive economic policy with the preservation of merchant interests and the protection of the treasury's solvency. Thus, while the Cédula exempted foreign colonists from all regular taxes for a period of ten years, Ramírez and Meléndez reduced the period to five years; while it authorized forcing trade through all of the island's ports for a period of 15 years, they limited the period to one year, and in the case of the import trade, to the port of San Juan exclusively; and although the Cédula abolished the ecclesiastical tithe and the *alcabala* (an old sales tax), the two highest ranking officials devised a new tax on gross income, the *subsidio*, to take their place, which amounted to a larger levy than the tithe and alcabala combined.[4] The scope of other minor measures was enlarged, to be sure, and few of the restrictions were later rescinded. But on the whole the limitations imposed on key provisions of the Cédula reduced its potential impact on trade, procurement of outside capital, internal accumulation, and free access to the slave trade — the crucial prerequisites of economic growth.

In the context of long-term Spanish policy toward its Caribbean possessions, moreover, the Cédula did not mark a new departure. Most of the reforms prescribed in 1815 specifically for Puerto Rico had been dictated for the Caribbean in general at various times during the earlier Bourbon reformist period. As Morales Carrión has noted, the Cédula marked 'the formal abandonment of the old Spanish exclusivism in practice as well as in theory . . . [as it] brought together principles and measures which at different times had been adopted but never systematized in an official policy'.[5] Restrictions on the immigration of wealthy foreigners and skilled workers had been relaxed in 1778; the slave trade had been declared free of duty and open to foreigners in 1789; and by 1797, when Spain allowed its colonies to conduct trade with 'neutral' nations on a temporary basis — a move which hastened the expansion of trade between Spanish America and the United States — *de facto* commerce with foreign powers had existed for some time.[6]

Institutionally, then, Spain has consistently sought to promote cash-crop agriculture in its Caribbean possessions long before Ferdinand VII handed down his reform packages for Cuba and Puerto Rico. Indeed the consensus among historians is that the revival of Spanish mercantilism in the late colonial period, and its tolerance of colonial trade with the bourgeoning Spaniard periphery (Catalonia and the Basque provinces especially), prescribed a concerted effort to create cash-crop economies oriented towards overseas markets, albeit through the mediation of Spanish merchants and shippers whenever possible.[7] This policy, and the general expansion of markets for tropical staples, enlarged the demand for Puerto Rico's coffee and (to a lesser extent) tobacco, and significant advances in the export of these products were recorded. Yet sugar cane cultivation and sugar exports did not increase correlatively. Why?

In addressing this question it is fruitful to compare the Cuban and Puerto Rican cases, for despite the basic similarity of Spanish policy toward both islands before 1800, Cuba developed the foundations of its industry early, and Puerto Rico did not. In the comparative framework, the critical point turns on differences in economic endowment and possibilities rather than on policy. Given a Spanish policy that was fundamentally the same toward both islands, what accounted for the difference in timing between the two? The answer rests heavily on one factor: the rate of prior capital accumulation and the attendant existence (or lack) of a capital reserve to invest in sugar once the demand arose. There is no doubt that a large gulf separated Puerto Rico and Cuba in this respect during the eighteenth century.

The greater extent to which Creoles participated in the onset of sugar production in Cuba is one clear indication of a difference in prior capital accumulation. Knight has indicated that Creole ownership of the industry predominated in Cuba until the early nineteenth century:

> The sugar revolution derived its greatest impetus from the entrepreneurial skills of the oldest families in Cuba. These families, having become rich in land and having access to public offices, found themselves strategically positioned to take every advantage of the early economic development. Until the early nineteenth century — indeed, until the technical and capital transformation of the period beginning around 1838 — this oligarchy maintained control and prominence. Eventually they gave way to new men and newly acquired wealth and the new economies of scale which the industrial age required. Between 1760 and 1810, these old oligarchs had increased per mill production from the vicinity of 165 tons to more than 400 tons [of sugar]. They increased the acreage of sugar cane, and expanded the number of mills. The largest producers remained unchanged: Arango, Montalvo, Duarte, Peñalver, Córdova, Herrera, O'Reilly.[8]

In addition to the sources of accumulation pointed out by Knight, there were in eighteenth-century Cuba other sources from which the Creole elite derived capital that was later invested in sugar. Tobacco was one of them, and the provisioning of Spanish ships at Havana for their return voyage across the Atlantic was another. With the rise of contraband after the peace of Utrecht (1713), the tobacco economy

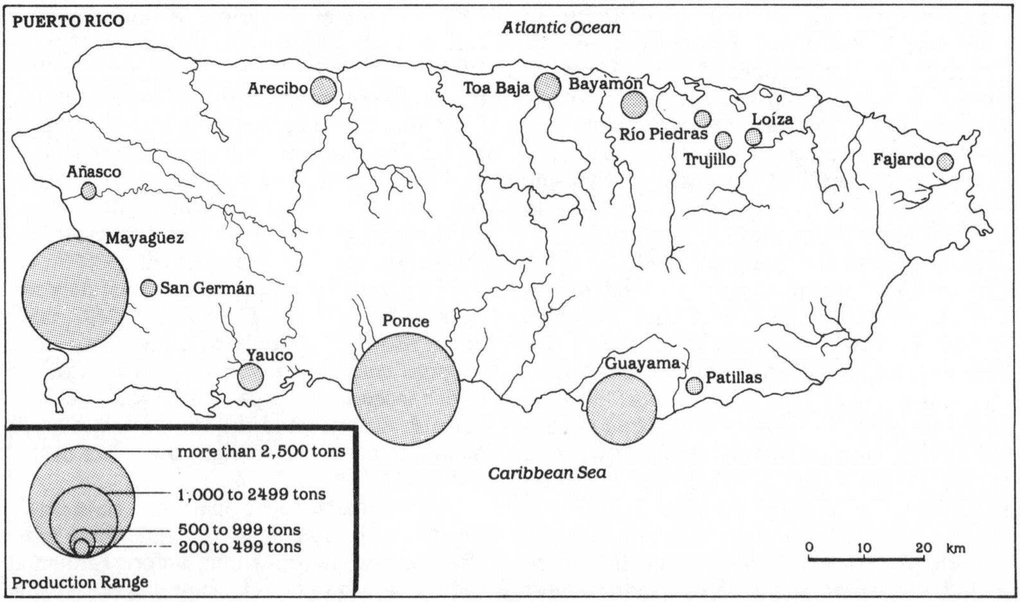

flourished, and although a Crown monopoly established in 1717 curtailed its potential for greater expansion, it became in the first half of the century an important source of commercial wealth.[9] Similarly, the myriad of activities revolving around the use of Havana as a rendezvous for returning Spanish ships received a strong stimulus with the recuperation of intra-imperial trade from its depression of the late seventeenth century. Thus, by the time the English captured Havana during the Seven Years' War — an occupation that lasted several months in 1762–63 — contacts with the European economy, making possible an accumulation of wealth that was soon to be funneled increasingly into the sugar economy.[10]

Puerto Rico, in contrast, remained relatively isolated from European trade during this period, and in its external relations confined mainly to a contraband trade with foreign colonies that was marked by high deficits. Usable to initiate any commercial activity on a scale analogous to Cuba's, Puerto Rican Creoles were generally incapable of harnessing sufficient capital to invest in the machinery and slaves required to begin commercial sugar production. Hubert Aimes, paraphrasing a Crown report of 1781 on ways to develop the colonial economies, summarizes the situation well: 'There are scarcely half a dozen persons in Puerto Rico able to buy twenty negroes each; little advancement can be expected from them.'[11] Nevertheless, the situation had begun to change with the increase in commerce that occurred after 1765, the spread of coffee and tobacco planting, and the Spaniards' investment of enormous sums on military construction in San Juan from the 1760s to the 1780s; by the time of the Crown report the possibility of accumulation had greatly improved. Still, at the turn of the nineteenth century Creoles were not sufficiently wealthy to propel the sugar economy forward, and the export boom owed much of its impetus to foreigners who eagerly seized on the opportunity to settle in Puerto Rico when other plantation colonies began to wane. While Creoles had controlled most of the sugar wealth in Cuba in the early stages of the industry there, foreigners and peninsular Spaniards constituted the bulk of the Puerto Rican planter class at an analogous stage of the Puerto Rican industry's development.

Ultimately, then, the most important objection to the policy-centered conceptualization of structural change is that it does not credit developments taking place outside the island society that both conditioned the demand for sugar and stimulated the migration of foreign planters, merchants, and skilled sugar workers to Puerto Rico. Against a backdrop of sweeping changes throughout the Caribbean, Spanish reforms legitimized and reinforced broad economic trends which sooner or later would have had an impact on Puerto Rican society, regardless of imperial policy. The havoc created in the international sugar market by the destruction of the Saint Domingue industry; the large and growing demand for the product in the United States, as well as that country's enhanced mercantile power in the Caribbean region; the economic decay of neighbouring plantation colonies; the abolition of the British slave trade; and the increasing importance of Saint Thomas as a clearinghouse for all types of plantation commerce — all of these together account for the Puerto Rican ascendence more adequately than enlightened colonial policy. Although the careful implementation of a long-standing Bourbon policy of export promotion undoubtedly facilitated and accelerated it, the shift to cane cultivation in Puerto Rico may be more fruitfully interpreted as part of a complex chain of events that displaced the locus of plantation agriculture in the Caribbean from the exhausted soils of the classic sugar colonies to the virgin lands of the larger Spanish colonies, and to some of the newly opened continental territories (British Guiana, for example).[12] In legitimizing the plantation system in Cuba and Puerto Rico through the liberalizing measures of the 1810s, Spain effectively guaranteed the continuation of its political control of the last of its American colonies. The costs of this transaction were considerable, however, for in so acting the metropolis, which could neither absorb the colonies' exports nor control their productive structures, relinquished many of the economic advantages of the imperial relationship.

Of all the major reorientations that occurred within the Caribbean during the age of revolutions, perhaps none was more instrumental in the development of Puerto Rico's plantation system than the commercial ascent of the Danish free port of Saint Thomas. The Haitian Revolution and the Napoleonic wars precipitated extremely favourable market conditions; the avalanche of the United States–Caribbean commerce created efficient linkages with distant markets; but it was the presence of nearby Saint Thomas that cemented these beneficial conditions for Puerto Rico. 'At the time,' Alejandro Tapia y Rivera reminisced of the 1820s and 1830s, 'St Thomas was... our Liverpool and

Paris in commercial matters'.[13] This assessment refers basically to the Danish colony's relations with San Juan, but the assessment can easily be extended to the enormous influence Saint Thomas exercised in outports' economies as well. As a centre for commerce, shipping, finance, and the slave trade, and as a source of sugar entrepreneurs, the importance of Saint Thomas to developing sugar districts in Puerto Rico was unsurpassed, in the early period at least.

Unlike its sister colony of Saint Croix in the Danish Virgin Islands, Saint Thomas evolved from earliest times not as a plantation colony, but as a trade depot, one of several commercial links with Europe and North America in the eastern Caribbean. Declared a free port in 1764–67, several years after the abolition of the Danish West India Company, its commercial prosperity benefited from the chaos of Caribbean trade in the 1790s, brought about by war and revolution. In the words of one early chronicler, the Reverend John P. Knox,

> an immensely increased impetus was given to the commerce of St Thomas by the breaking out of war in 1792, consequent upon the French revolution. The island then profited by the neutrality maintained by Denmark. It became the only market in the West Indies for the products of all the colonies, and the only channel through which they could be conveyed to the countries in the North of Europe. The resort to it of mercantile speculators from all quarters, brought a large addition to its population; and... [J. P. Nissen] informs us, that many stores and houses were built, and that in the year 1793 one hundred and four persons took out burgher briefs; that is, paid the tax required to qualify them to begin business in the colony.[14]

The occupation of the island by the British for a brief period in 1801–02 and again between 1807 and 1815 eliminated the advantages of neutrality and curtailed the growth of its commercial wealth. But it is significant that the Puerto Rican branch of the Saint Thomas trade did not suffer correspondingly, particularly during the second British occupation. Relations between the two colonies, which had been close ever since the first half of the eighteenth century (Saint Thomas was considered the nerve centre of the contraband trade at the time) intensified in the early 1810s.[15] Shipping statistics for Saint Thomas in 1811 reveal, for instance, that intercourse with the Spanish islands (mostly Puerto Rico and Santo Domingo) predominated over all other contacts with non-British territories, a situation no doubt reinforced when Great Britain imposed an embargo on United States merchantmen in 1812 — the second such action in five years.[16] On both geopolitical and economic grounds the trend toward greater interdependence between Puerto Rico and Saint Thomas was inevitable. On the one hand, diplomatic events brought the islands closer together than perhaps at any other time in history, since the provisional Spanish government, recognized by the authorities in Puerto Rico, was allied with Great Britain in a joint struggle against Napoleon, whose armies had invaded Spain the previous year. Thus Saint Thomas became a full ally for most of the duration of the British regime, a status Puerto Rican authorities must have welcomed as a legitimate excuse for a trade which, although deeply rooted in tradition, violated the spirit of Spanish mercantilist policy. On the other hand, the change in the imperial colors of Saint Thomas could not have been more timely from an economic point of view. With peninsular trade disrupted by the war, and the flow of traditional fiscal subsidies (*situados*) from the viceroyalty of New Spain halted by the rebellion in New Spain, Puerto Rico's external commerce and finances came dangerously close to collapse.[17] This crisis and the outbreak of war between the United States and Great Britain in 1812 created a dilemma for Spanish officials in Puerto Rico: how to balance the conflicting interests of the two powers in order to sustain commerce with both, the sum of which was a significant portion of the Puerto Rican total. The ensuing compromise policy both welcomed the intensified relations with British traders (now including the Saint Thomas merchants) and promoted the arrival of North American vessels, a part of whose merchandise was reportedly sent, oddly enough, to Saint Thomas.[18]

The significance of the British occupation of Saint Thomas for the development of the port's crucial ties with Puerto Rico therefore rests on the unique opportunities it created for reinforcing the islands' commercial and financial interdependence. In Saint Thomas in 1807 the British encountered a rich merchant group made wealthier by war. When they curtailed its activity, they inadvertently strengthened the merchants' disposition to finance commercial and agricultural venture in Puerto Rico. The associations thus established outlived the wartime occupation, and flourished when the island was returned to Danish sovereignty.

When peace was re-established in Europe in 1815, and Saint Thomas regained the advantages of the free port under Danish rule, its merchants recuperated most of the estranged transit trade.

Contacts with the British, French, and Dutch colonies resumed, and the volume of shipping handled by the port steadily increased. 'In the decade 1821–1830,' Waldemar Westergaard notes, 'the tonnage of ships annually visiting St. Thomas harbor was more than double what it had been during the two decades preceding. An average of not less than 2,809 ships of a combined tonnage of 177,444 called there each year.'[19] This frantic pace continued into the 1840s. Through it all, the momentum of the Puerto Rican trade accelerated, partly because of beneficial Spanish legislation and partly because of the collapse of wartime partnerships cultivated by Saint Thomas merchants elsewhere in the Caribbean region. Such was the fate of that island's contacts with the Spanish Main, whose trade had enriched many a Saint Thomas merchant during the independence wars. But as Knox saw it, the penetration of British and other European traders into the new republics of northern South America did not greatly damage the prosperity of the Danish emporium, which only became more dependent on its close ties with Puerto Rico:

> When it became evident to the European powers that the South Americans could succeed in throwing off the yoke of the mother country, their enterprising merchants began to mediate the opening of a direct trade with these rich and fertile regions, and as early as 1824 direct importations were made at various of the Colombian ports. This, of course, was so much withdrawn from the commerce of St. Thomas; but, in the meantime, the island of Puerto Rico so increased its population and productions, as in a great degree to make up the loss of South American trade.[20]

Saint Thomas would enjoy its dominance over Puerto Rican plantation commerce for several decades, though it would not be long before traders in the United States and Europe seized on the opportunity to establish direct contacts with the merchants and planters of the booming Puerto Rican outports. In time, Saint Thomas would be edged out — but not before it mediated in the transformation of the Puerto Rican coastal lowlands into sprawling cane fields that thrived on the toil of a subjected population.

Plantation Labor

In the abundant literature on plantation systems of the Americas, Puerto Rico is often singled out as an anomalous case: an economy and society which developed an advanced sugar industry during times of a farily open Atlantic slave trade, yet did not rely to any significant degree on the labor of African slaves. The notion that nineteenth-century Puerto Rico was an exception to the slave-based sugar systems of the time has gained wide historiographical appeal, both in national and international scholary circles. In his authoritative history of sugar, for instance, Noel Deerr asserts that 'a peculiar feature of the Porto Rican industry is that it owes but little to African labor.' And Luis M. Diaz Soler, whose general history of Puerto Rican slavery stands as the only full-length study of the subject, concludes that 'slavery was an accident in the nineteenth century'.[21] The data suggest, however, that as an economic institution slavery flourished co-extensively and in conjunction with the sprouting of sugar haciendas in the first half of the nineteenth century, not by accident, but as a result of the powerful economic rationale of the emerging dominant institutions of the lowland countryside. The haciendas needed a mass of inexpensive disciplined workers, and for nearly three decades after 1815 the African slave trade satisfied that demand. Except on very small farms using a balanced combination of slaves and jornaleros, slaves constituted the majority of sugar workers in the principal producing districts until well beyond the middle of the century.

In reviewing the scholarship on plantation labour, one is impressed by the extent to which the free-labor argument rests on the writings of one observer, George D. Flinter. An Irishman who for 21 years served as an officer of the British Army in the West Indies, Flinter visited Puerto Rico in 1829–32 and wrote two books on his experiences there: *A View of the Present Condition of the Slave Population in the Island of Puerto Rico, Under the Spanish Government*, a short treatise published in 1832; and *An Account of the Present State of the Island of Puerto Rico*, a lengthier work published in London in 1834.[22] Since Flinter, at greater length than any other contemporary observer, addressed the question of the relative importance of free and slave labor, his views have carried particular weight in the writings of modern scholars, just as they shaped the opinions of his contemporaries. Yet in positing his defense of Puerto Rican slavery on the twofold argument that the masters were benevolent with their slaves and that the institution itself was economically unsound, Flinter at best deliberately misled his readers to believe that his generalizations applied to all sectors of the island society and economy; at worst, and probably no less deliberately, he portrayed a false picture of the reality he so fully observed.

Flinter's first work on Puerto Rico — of the two, the only to deal exclusively with slavery — appeared at the height of international agitation over the expectation of British abolition. Published simultaneously in English and Spanish, it was a propaganda piece unquestionably aimed at portraying a benign image of Spanish slavery at a time when Caribbean slavery was coming under severe abolitionist pressures abroad. True to the propaganda genre, the book was an awkward piece. The title was only marginally related to the content, about two-thirds of which was devoted to a philosophical defense of very gradual, long-term abolition. In the section devoted to Puerto Rico, Flinter articulated a defense of the island's slave system which was meant to divorce that system on qualitative grounds, from other slave regimes that were beginning to collapse around it. He skillfully conveyed the impression, so favorably to the interests of the local planter class, that slavery in Puerto Rico was not only of trifling importance to the export economy, but that it was also extremely easy on the slaves themselves because of the 'wise and philanthropic' provisions of the Spanish slave codes. 'The object of this work,' he said in the introduction, 'is to demonstrate the convenience and happiness that black slaves enjoy in this island and in all the Spanish colonies, compared to their previous condition in the colonies of other nations.' To 'substantiate' this, he in effect argued that: (*a*) Puerto Rican slaves were humanely treated in strict observance of the laws; (*b*) they generally owned property; (*c*) all slaves on the plantations cultivated subsistence plots; (*d*) they lived in family units which promoted stable unions and normal reproduction; (*e*) the growth of the slave population 'does not in any way owe to importations of African slaves, which have been limited in recent times due to the lack of capital; nor can it be attributed to introductions by new colonists . . . '[23]

I will not attempt a detailed discussion of the issues of slave treatment and the structure of the slave family, for although they are important, they transcend the scope of this work. It is interesting to note, however, that for the most part Flinter's generalizations on these issues rested on the need to explain the 'insignificance' of slave imports in the early 1820s and early 1830s. Because he could not publicize the existence of a full-scale clandestine slave trade — the revelation would have seriously undermined his defense of the Puerto Rican regime, especially for British readers — Flinter needed an alternative explanation for the enormous recent increase in the slave population, which had grown from 19,000 persons in 1815 to 32,000 in 1828. The only possibility, short of admitting the continuation of the trade, was to portray the slaves' material and family conditions in the most favorable terms possible, on the assumption that under the normally harsh conditions of New World slavery the population would not reproduce itself — indeed, that it would take abnormally high slave incomes and family stability to achieve positive rates of growth. What Flinter perhaps did not realize was that in the period 1815–28 the slave population increased at an annual rate of 4.2 per cent, a phenomenon he would have found almost impossible to explain solely on the basis of stable unions and normal reproduction.

This difficulty underscores the basic problem of Flinter's credibility. Although he lived in Puerto Rico during some of the most intense slave-trading years, he purported to show the outside world that little such activity had occurred. One must suspect, too, his generalizations about slavery which were phrased in such a manner as to conceal differences between plantation and non-plantation phenomena. Undoubtedly familiar with the peculiarities of the emerging hacienda system, he did not endeavor to distinguish between the practice of slavery in the haciendas and its practice in other sectors of the economy. The distinction was a crucial one to make in discussing the economic importance of slavery, for as he knew too well the sugar industry was the raison d'être for the extension of slavery. He must also have known that at least half of the slaves in sugar plantations were of recent importation.

In his second book, which dealt exclusively with Puerto Rico and was based on more extensive observations, Flinter elaborated on his earlier themes but avoided any application of the arguments of free labor and benevolent treatment to the sugar industry. The Puerto Rican experience, he indicated, demonstrated the superiority of free over slave labour 'in security, in economy and in productiveness', as 'free labor on a large scale and attended by the most beneficial consequences, has been for some years in practical operation in Puerto Rico, and . . . the free black and the slave work together in the same field as the white man.'[24] As a general description of labor in a wide range of activities, from subsistence farming to coffee and tobacco production, this statement was probably not incorrect. But Flinter did not clearly specify this range of applications. Instead, he left readers of this voluminous work to discover for themselves how vague and misleading the generalization was in reference to a society in which labor- and capital-intensive agriculture coexisted with several types of small-scale, peasant production.

Furthermore, Flinter's observations concerning sugar labor indicated an exception. In a section of the book dealing with the relative inputs of slave labor in the sugar, coffee, tobacco, and cattle industries, he estimated that fully 80 per cent of the island's sugar was produced by slaves.[25] Accordingly, his detailed description of the principal sugar districts of Mayagüez, Ponce, and Guayama did not once mention the occurrence of free labor (although it existed on a small scale); on the contrary, it abounded in references to the haciendas' reliance on slaves. The remainder of the book offered no further evidence to support his initial implication that free labor 'on a large scale' existed in the plantation context.

David Turnbull's influential book on Cuba and the slave trade, published in 1840, gave notoriety to Flinter's misrepresentation of Puerto Rican slavery and added a new dimension to the incipient argument about free labor: Turnbull applied Flinter's thesis specifically to the sugar industry. Citing Flinter, the British consul in Havana concluded that

> the most remarkable fact connected with the history and the present state of Puerto Rico is that the fields are cultivated, *and sugar manufactured*, by the hands of white men under a tropical sun. It is very possible that this might never have occurred had not the island been treated as a penal settlement at an early period of its history. The convicts themselves were condemned to hard labour as a part of their punishment; and when the term of their sentence arrived, they were compelled to continue it in order to obtain the means of subsistence . . . [;] their descendants present at this day a permanent solution to the problem, that white labour can be profitably applied to the cultivation of the sugar-cane, and the manufacture of its products, in one of the warmest regions of the West Indies [emphasis added].[26]

Turnbull also referred in his chapter on Puerto Rico to a population census of 1834 that classified nearly half of the slave population of about 40,000 as African-born, an indication, he thought, that the slave trade had intensified in recent years with the proliferation of sugar estates. This contradiction notwithstanding, his distortion of Flinter's ambiguous conclusions has been accepted literally by many a reputable scholar, and represents today one of the standard sources of the free-labor argument.[27]

The Flinter-Turnbull thesis contrasts sharply with the testimony of Victor Schoelcher, the renowned French abolitionist, who visited Puerto Rico in 1841 with the purpose of obtaining first-hand knowledge of slavery there — a trip that shocked him deeply and influenced his conversion to radical abolitionism, according to one biographer.[28] In his little-known notes on the Puerto Rican journey, Schoelcher asserted that the primary function of the island's slave system was to sustain the sugar economy and that, consequently, the beneficial aspects of the slave codes were universally violated. He claimed that the 41,000 overworked, mistreated slaves of Puerto Rico, by themselves and without any significant collaboration from the peasantry, produced at least two-thirds as much sugar as the 78,000 slaves of Martinique. His argument was that in the French colony the proportion of elderly slaves and children was higher, and that the planters, unable to purchase new slaves since 1831, had deemed it in their best interst to ameliorate the working and living conditions of the slaves they had.[29] Flinter's 'senseless opinion' on these issues, he thought, was the product of a man who sought to justify slavery in general, and Spanish slavery in particular, on the basis of spurious comparisons between the living conditions of the slaves and those of the laboring classes in Europe.[30] Contrary to Flinter's assertions, Puerto Rican planters were, with few exceptions (Schoelcher cited Cornelius Kortright, owner of a large hacienda on the north coast) exceedingly brutal to their slaves:

> One is tempted to praise the charity of our planters when one sees how the unhappy creatures bowed under the great evil of slavery are treated in Puerto Rico. Completely given over to the discretion of the master, their work is only limited by his pleasure. At harvest time one sees the blacks going to the mill by three o'clock in the morning and continuing until eight or nine o'clock in the evening, having as their only compensation, the pleasure of eating cane. They never even get twenty-four hours of respite during the year. On Sundays and feast days they still have to go to work for two hours in the morning and often for two hours in the evening.[31]

Such an inhuman regime, Schoelcher thought, could not be sustained without ample recourse to the African slave trade, which recently had provided as many as 3,000 new slaves in one year.

Schoelcher's remarkable testimony to the Puerto Rican plantations' heavy reliance on

Table 2 Changing Population Balances, Puerto Rican Sugar Municipalities, 1812–28

Sugar production, 1828 (tons)	Municipality	Population in 1812 Free	Slave	% Slave	Population in 1828 Free	Slave	% Slave	Pop. growth 1812–28 % Free	% Slave
More than 1,001	Mayagüez	8,640	994	10.3	14,407	3,860	21.1	67	288
	Ponce	8,780	1,060	10.8	11,723	3,204	21.5	61	296
	Guayama	2,191	328	13.0	5,501	2,373	29.8	156	623
	Subtotal	19,611	2,382	10.8	31,631	9,437	23.0	61	296
201–1,000	Bayamón[a]	6,047	1,364	18.4	5,351	899	14.4	– 12	– 34
	Loíza	2,220	696	23.9	3.456	742	17.7	56	7
	Trujillo[b]	2,173	406	15.7	7,576	610	12.9	133	50
	Rió Piedras	1,717	618	26.5	2,063	969	32.0	20	57
	Toa Baja	3,048	337	10.0	3,040	410	11.9	0	22
	Arecibo	6,176	432	6.5	9,048	915	9.2	45	112
	Añasco	7,301	447	5.8	9,257	627	6.3	27	40
	San Germán	15,242	1,281	7.8	30,550	1,673	5.2	105	31
	Yauco	5,447	570	9.5	10,271	834	7.5	89	46
	Patillas	2,531	338	11.8	3,278	407	9.8	47	20
	Fajardo	3,750	444	10.6	3,750	367	8.9	0	– 17
	Subtotal	55,652	6,933	11.1	88,090	8,453	8.8	58	22
	Total	75,263	9,315	8.2	119,721	17,890	13.0	59	92

Sources: AGI, Indiferente General, leg. 1525; Córdova, *Memorias geográficas*, Vol. 2, *passim*.
[a] Loose territory between 1812 and 1828 because of the establisment of new towns.
[b] Segregated into two municipalities between the census dates. The data for 1828 represent the sum of both subdivisions (Trujillo Alto and Trujillo Bajo).

slave labor finds corroboration in quantitative data collected by the colonial government, which is summarized in Table 2. The three major sugar-producing districts (Mayagüez, Ponce, and Guayama), where more than half of the added sugar output of the first few decades of the century was recorded, experienced enormous increases in their slave populations between 1812 and 1828. While the expansion of the free population in those districts averaged 62 per cent, the growth of the slave population averaged 296 per cent. In contrast, in the eleven districts that produced only between 201 and 1,000 tons of sugar in 1828, the free population increased by an average of 58 per cent, and the slave population by only 22 per cent. These differences clearly point to a dichotomy in the effects of economic change on the population structures of the various coastal districts of Puerto Rico. In districts that experienced only mild economic change the slave population increased at a fairly rapid pace, but its growth rate fell below that of the non-slave groups. There the connection between sugar and slavery was not overwhelmingly positive, although one cannot overlook the possibility that changes in the nature of the slave regime occurred in those areas in response to the challenge of sugar production, and that, as a result, the figures on population growth may conceal potentially significant changes in the organization of labor. On the other hand, in the major sugar areas the data on population change point to a very positive correlation between plantation development and slavery. As the districts most affected by foreign colonization and investment, Puerto Rico's three prime sugar municipios replicated, in their early stages, the previous Caribbean pattern in which a rapid expansion of sugar production entailed a sizeable increase in the African slave population.

The extent to which the islandwide pattern conformed to, or was influenced by, the trend in Mayagüez, Ponce, and Guayama can be statistically ascertained. In order to measure the degree to which a hypothetical prevalence of slave labor in the sugar industry held for all of Puerto Rico, a correlation analysis was performed using Córdova's 1828 data — a large collection of economic and demographic statistics, containing for each of 58 municipios a breakdown of the population into five socio-racial categories, as well as figures on land use, production, and (in the case of sugar farms) type of processing machinery. As Table 3 makes plain, the degree of correlation between sugar

Table 3 Correlation of Population Groups, Land Use, and Mill Technology, 1828

Variable	(1)	(2)	(3)	(4)	(5)	(6)	(7)	(8)	(9)	(10)	(11)	(12)
(1) Whites	1.00	.62	.51	.69	.55	.71	.19	.45	.83	.58	.13	.73
(2) Mulattoes		1.00	.64	.46	.51	.62	.37	.51	.58	.31	.14	.70
(3) Free blacks			1.00	.35	.48	.33	.39	.46	.33	.04	.11	.54
(4) Peasant squatters				1.00	.62	.58	.26	.52	.54	.66	.27	.53
(5) Slaves					1.00	.39	.74	.92	.38	.69	.18	.56
(6) Wooden mills						1.00	.10	.35	.66	.48	.07	.64
(7) Iron mills							1.00	.89	.14	.43	.10	.40
(8) Sugar lands								1.00	.31	.60	.14	.52
(9) Subsistence lands									1.00	.64	.15	.72
(10) Coffee lands										1.00	.09	.47
(11) Tobacco lands											1.00	.24
(12) Livestock												1.00

Source: Córdova, *Memorias geográficas*, Vol. 2.
Note: This table makes use of the Pearson Correlation Matrix. Pearson's product-moment coefficient of correlation is a statistical measure of the strength of a bivariate relationship. For two variables suspected of exhibiting a linear relationship (as when, for instance, change in the value of one variable provokes a concomitant change in the value of the other), Pearson's coefficient (*r*) indicates the direction and strength of the association. When *r* approaches +1.0 or −1.0, a strong linear relationship can be assumed.

cane farming and slavery was very high indeed.

The even greater correlation between the slave population and the capitalized segment of the sugar industry that was represented by the haciendas and associated with the use of iron-roller mills is highly significant. It distinguishes the industry as an economic sphere with a labor organization that differed sharply from the labor systems in other sectors of the economy, in which free labor predominated. This distinction brings up the important issue of the motivation of Puerto Rican hacendados in choosing to stock their estates with imported Africans, rather than resorting to the potentially abundant pool of free labor embodied in the peasantry. The population censuses of this period give evidence of a substantial increase in the free group — from 202,276 persons in 1815 to 267,837 in 1828, and to 317,018 in 1834 (the intercensal annual growth rates were 2.3 and 2.8 per cent, respectively). Yet the slave population grew even faster, from 18,616 persons in 1815 to 31,874 in 1828, and to 41,818 in 1834 (at intercensal average rates of 4.2 and 4.7 per cent).[32]

Why did planters prefer to purchase African slaves if such a large free population existed? Part of the answer may be found in Schoelcher's argument that the foreign planters, many of whom had been engaged in the sugar business in other slaveholding areas, were predisposed to favor slavery as the only profitable method of sugar labor. 'The increment in the slave population,' Salvador Brau wrote of the first decades of the nineteenth century, 'was sustained by the erroneous belief that only the African race could withstand with impunity the hard labor of the haciendas; the notion that without slaves sugar could not be produced attained the character of an axiom.'[33] Had the incipient planter class encountered objective economic reasons to employ wage workers in the demanding chores of the plantations, these attitudes would probably not have persisted. There is every reason to believe that the planters would have employed free workers instead of slaves if the cost and work discipline of the former matched that of the enslaved blacks.

The problem is, of course, that the existence of a large peasant population — a potential supply of non-slave labor — need not be tantamount to an effective labor supply. For such a correlation to hold, as Witold Kula and others have argued, the peasantry would have had to be in an advanced stage of deterioration, particularly in regard to the means of economic independence — the land.[34] As we have seen, this was not the situation in Puerto Rico during the first half of the nineteenth century, when land to own or to squat on was still available in the interior sections of the country. There are documented cases of peasant migrations from plantation zones to the uplands, where large-scale agriculture had not yet taken hold.[35] Future research on this question may reveal that these were not isolated cases, but part of a widespread movement of freeholders into marginal lands of the interior that were unsuitable for sugar cane and which had not yet been encroached on by coffee haciendas. As long as these lands remained an alternative to the peasantry, the supply of wage labor to the sugar haciendas was bound to remain scarce, and consequently, expensive.

The preceding observations must not be construed as a categorical denial of the occurrence of wage labor on the plantations before 1849. One of the characteristics of the Cuban and Puerto Rican experience with sugar in the nineteenth century, a heritage of three centuries of society-building, was that there was no succession of slave labor to free labor, but a simultaneous juxtaposition of both, as Moreno Fraginals has observed of the Cuban situation.[36] Especially during the harvest, haciendas employed a few jornaleros to complement their permanent slave work force, which normally took care of all the industrial tasks. In the early years there were reports that prospective planters turned to the peasantry for most of the tasks entailed in the founding of new estates. In Guayama, for example, several hundred peasants from all over the region were employed in clearing the land and in hoeing and planting for several years after 1816, but the introduction of large contingents of African slaves terminated the practice, which suggests that the experiment with free labor failed. Most contemporaries believed, moreover, that the trouble with jornaleros was not so much the difficulty in persuading them to work, but their high cost and notorious absenteeism. The cost factor reflected the scarcity of supply, as only the prospect of very high wages could lure peasants away from their subsistence plots, even temporarily, for the demanding work of cane harvesting. Even if population growth may have progressively lowered the cost of free workers, however, there remained the serious problems of irregularity in work attendance and resistance to the intensity of sugar labor. These were critical difficulties in a production process that required uninterrupted labor to avoid grave losses of raw materials and lowered sugar yields; canes must be milled within 48 hours of harvesting lest they begin to rot. This was the crux of the problem: because of their lack of regular work attendance and resistance to prevailing working conditions, jornaleros were ill-suited to the processing phase, which was widely recognized as the bottleneck of sugar production before the advent of the central-mill system. '[The planters] have great difficulty in getting the freemen to work in the manufacture of sugar,' exclaimed John Lindegren, the British consul in San Juan, 'and there are few estates in which they can get them into the boiling houses. . . . '[37] If they succeeded in doing so, one might add, the planters would have desired to bind the workers to the haciendas in any way possible to preclude costly interruptions. Unable as yet to coerce jornaleros legally, hacendados preferred to employ them in field work, and, as a safeguard against absenteeism, to institute a system of piecework.

The Reglamento of 1849 imposed a series of coercive measures to hold down the price of wage labor and, more important, to force jornaleros into a slavelike productive system on the plantations.[38] Enacted in the wake of a sharp depression in sugar income resulting from low prices, the news of abolition in the French colonies, and the disclosure of at least two serious slave conspiracies (one of them in Ponce), this law attempted to undermine the independence of the peasantry by placing limitations on traditional access to the land and by formulating a legal definition of 'jornaleros' which encompassed peasant smallholders as well as the truly landless.[39] The history of this legislation is the story of a partly successful attempt to maneuvre a Caribbean peasantry into virtual slavery when the possibility of extending black slavery had ended. While I will not attempt to describe this history, it is fitting to observe that for the planters the experiment was not altogether a happy one. Between 1849 and 1873, although armed with legal authority to bind jornaleros to plantation work, hacendados tried desperately to obtain alternative sources of servile labor, whether by contracting with workers in the foreign West Indies, planning to import Chinese coolies, or promising to 'care for' several hundred *emancipados* (freedmen) from the slaver *Majesty* shipwrecked off the coast of Humacao in 1859. Planters enthusiastically backed these plans, but the colonial government opposed them.

Such plans were obvious signs of the failure of the coercive laws to satisfy the haciendas' demand for abundant, constant, and disciplined labor; so, too, were the planters' lamentations about the negative impact of abolition in 1873. Slavery continued to be the basis of labor in many coastal estates until the time of emancipation, and the crisis that concerned the Diputación Provincial in 1880, and which echoed throughout the colony's ruling circles, was in part a result of slavery's demise.

Notes

1. Examples of this scholarship are Lidio Cruz Monclova, *Historia de Puerto Rico (Siglo XIX)*, 6th ed., 6 vols (Rio Piedras, 1970); Tomás Blanco, *Prontuario histórico de*

Puerto Rico, 6th ed. (San Juan, 1970); Isabel Gutiérrez del Arroyo, *El reformismo ilustrado en Puerto Rico* (Mexico, D. F., 1953); and Labour Gomez Acevedo, *Organización y reglamentación del trabajo ent el Puerto Rico del siglo XIX* (San Juan, 1970). Several noteworthy exceptions to the legalistic interpretation of social change may be found in the anthropological literature: Fernández Méndez. *Historia cultural*; Julian Steward *et al.*, *The People of Puerto Rico: A Study in Social Anthropology* (Urbana, 1956); Sidney W. Mintz, 'Labor and Sugar in Puerto Rico and in Jamaica, 1800-1850', *Comparative Studies in Society and History*, Vol. 1, No. 3 (March 1959), pp. 273-83; and Sidney W. Mintz, 'The Role of Forced Labor in Nineteenth Century Puerto Rico', *Caribbean Historical Review* 1, No. 2 (December 1951), pp. 134-51.

2. King Ferdinand VII in the Cédula's preface, cited in Cruz Monclova, *Historia de Puerto Rico*, 1:77. See the text of the decree in Cayetano Coll y Toste, 'La Cédula de Gracias y sus efectos, rectificaciones históricas', Bulltín Histórico de Puerto Rico (*BHPR*) 14:3-24.
3. See, for instance, Coll y Toste, 'La Cédula de Gracias'; and Salvador Brau, 'Las clases jornaleras de Puerto Rico,' *Ensayos* (*idsquisiciones sociológicas*) (Río Piedras: Editorial Edil, 1972), p. 23. In fairness to Brau, he later embraced a more sophisticated interpretation of the rise of the sugar industry in his essay, 'La caña *de azúcar', Ensayos*, pp. 271-94.
4. Cruz Monclova, *Historia de Puerto Rico*, 1:79-83. The agreements have been transcribed by Coll y Toste, 'La Cédula de Gracias'.
5. Arturo Morales Carrión, *Puerto Rico and the Non-Hispanic Caribbean: A Study in the Decline of Spanish Exclusivism* (Río Piedras, 1952), p. 141.
6. *Ibid.*, pp. 118-32.
7. Manuel Moreno Fraginals, *El Ingenio: Complejos Económico-Sociales Cubana del Azúcar* 3 vols. (Havana: Editorial de Ciencias Sociales, 1978) vol. 2; J. H. Parry, *The Spanish Seaborne Empire* (London: Hutchinson, 1966), chap. 16.
8. Franklin W. Knight, 'Origins of Wealth and the Sugar Revolution in Cuba, 1750-1850', *The Hispanic American Historical Review*, 57, No. 2 (May 1977), pp. 231-53. Pablo Tornero has recently identified a large number of Cuban hacendados of this period, corroborating Knight's observations on the predominance of the old Creole families. See Pablo Tornero, 'Hacendados y desarrollo azucarero cubano (1763-1818)', *Revista de Indias* 38, Nos. 153-54 (July-December 1978), pp. 715-37.
9. Hubert H. S. Aimes, *A History of Slavery in Cuba, 1511 to 1868* (New York and London, 1907), pp. 20-23.
10. Julio Le Riverend, *Historia económica de Cuba* (Barcelona, 1972), pp. 147-48. A detailed account of the Cuban sugar industry in the early eighteenth century may be found in Leví Marrero, *Cuba: economía y sociedad*, 7 vols to date (Madrid, 1971-78), 7:1-39.
11. Aimes, *op. cit.*, p. 41.
12. Ramiro Guerra y Sánchez, *Sugar and Society in the Caribbean (New Haven, 1964); Joseph L. Ragatz, The Fall of the Planter Class in the British Caribbean, 1753-1833* (New York: The Century Co., 1928); and Sidney W. Mintz, 'Labor and Sugar'.
13. Alejandro Tapia y Rivera, *Mis memorias, o Puerto Rico como lo encontré y como lo dejo* (Barcelona, 1968), p. 17.
14. John P. Knox, *A Historical Account of St. Thomas, W.I.* (New York, 1852), p. 100.
15. For accounts of contraband trade between Saint Thomas and Puerto Rico, see Morales Carrión, *op. cit.*, pp. 83-86; Manuel Gutiérrez de Arce, *La colonización danesa en las Islas Vírgenes: estudio histórico-jurídico* (Seville, 1945), p. 54; and Birgit Sonesson, 'El papel de Santomás en el hasta 1815', *Anales de Investigación Histórica*, 4, nos. 1-2 (1977), pp. 42-80.
16. The first embargo was imposed in 1807-09. Sonesson, *op. cit.*, pp. 74-75.
17. Luis E. González Vales, *Aljandro Ramírez y su tiempo: ensayos de historia económica e institucional* (Río Piedras, 1978).
18. Sonesson, *op. cit.*, pp. 74-75.
19. Waldemar Westergaard, *The Danish West Indies Under Company Rule (1671-1754)* (New York, 1917), p. 252. In comparison, the port of Havana — then one of the busiest in the Americas — saw 1,057 arrivals of merchant vessels (excluding a large number of slave ships) in 1828 and 2,524 in 1837. Knight, 'Origins of Wealth', p. 246.
20. Knox, *op. cit.*, p. 104.
21. Noel Deerr, *The History of Sugar*, 2 vols (London, 1948), Vol. 1, p. 126; Luis M. Díaz Soler, *Historia de la Esclavitud Negra en Puerto Rico* (Río Piedras, 3rd edn, 1970), p. 349.
22. The first of his works was published in English in Philadelphia (1832), while a Spanish version appeared the same year in New York. All references in this study are to the Spanish translation: George Flinter, *Examen de estado actual de los esclavos de la Isla de Puerto Rico bajo el dominio español* (1832; rpt, San Juan, 1976). The second work was published in London by Longmans in 1834.
23. Flinter, *Examen*, pp. 16, 46-50.
24. George Flinter, *An Account of the Present State of the Island of Puerto Rico* (London, 1834), p. vii.
25. Significantly, this calculation was flawed by a mathematical error. Having estimated the number of field slaves at 30,000 and the total number of sugar and coffee haciendas at 448, Flinter's average for all slaveholdings should have been 67, not 37 as he indicated in his text. If one accepts his (incorrect) implicit estimate of labor productivity in the sugar sector (obtained by dividing sugar output per estate, of which there were 300, by his incorrect estimate of slaves per unit), scarcely one-third of the 30,000 field slaves would have sufficed to produce the entire crop of 21,000 tons of sugar.
26. David Turnbull, *Travels in the West: Cuba, with Notices of Porto Rico and the Slave Trade* (London, 1840). pp. 559-60.
27. Among the scholars who have referred to Turnbull on these issues are Eric Williams, *From Columbus to Castro: The History of the Caribbean* (New York, 1970); Deerr, *History of Sugar*; Díaz Soler, *Historia de la esclavitud*; and Mintz, 'Labor and Sugar'.
28. Cited by Thomas Mathews. 'The Question of Color in Puerto Rico', in *Slavery and Race Relations in Latin America*, ed. Robert Brent Toplin (Westport, Conn., 1974), pp. 299-323.
29. Victor Schoelcher. *Colonies étrangères et Haiti*, 2 vols (Paris, 1843), 1:320-22.
30. *Ibid.*, 1:332-33.
31. *Ibid.*, 1:330.
32. Censuses of the populations of Puerto Rico, AGI, Indiferente General, leg. 1525; Córdova, *Memorias geográficas*, 2:400; Ormaechea, 'Memoria acerca de la agricultura'.
33. Brau, 'Las clases jornaleras', p. 25.
34. Witold Kula, *Teoría económica del sistema feudal*, trans. Estanislao J. Zembrzuski (Buenos Aires, 1974), pp. 16-17.

35. Félix M. Oritz, in 'Análisis de los registros de matrimonios de la parroquia de Yabucoa, 1813–1850', *Anales de Investigación Histórica* Vol. 1, No. 1 (1974), pp. 73–92, has demonstrated the occurrence of a substantial migration of peasants from Guayama, a plantation district, into Yabucoa. In addition, the 1849–50 jornalero register of the town of Utuado in the interior highlands lists a considerable number of young migrants from coastal areas; see Fernando Picó, comp., *Registro general de jornaleros: Utuado, Puerto Rico, 1849–1850* (Río Piedras, 1977). For an analysis of this migration, see Picó's excellent study of the dispossession of the highland peasantry, *Libertad y servidumbre*, pp. 69–73.
36. Manuel Moreno Fraginals (trans. Cedric Bellfrage), *The Sugarmill: the socio-economic complex of sugar in Cuba, 1760–1860* (New York, 1976), p. 131. From a broader perspective, Mintz writes: 'Indeed, the history of Caribbean plantations does not show a clear break between a slave mode of production and a capitalist mode of production, but something quite different. The succession of different mixes of forms of labor exaction in specific instances reveals clearly how the plantation systems of different Caribbean societies developed as parts of a worldwide capitalism, each particular case indicating how variant means were employed to provide adequate labor, some successful and some not, all within an international division of labor transformed by capitalism, and to satisfy an international market created by that same capitalist system'. Sidney W. Mintz, 'Was the Plantation Slave a Proletarian?', *Review* 2, No. 1 (Summer 1978), pp. 81–98.
37. Great Britain, *Parliamentary Papers* (PP), Vol. 23 (1847–48), Pt 3 (*Accounts and Papers*, Vol. 17), 'Appendix to the Seventh Report from the Committee on Sugar and Coffee Planting', p. 370.
38. See the text of the Reglamento of 1849 in *BHPR* 6:217–21.
39. The news of French abolition and its consequences touched off a wave of panic among the Puerto Rican planters. In part their fears stemmed from a bloody revolt of the freemen of Martinique which soon spread to the Danish island of Saint Croix, and prompted the Puerto Rican governor, Juan Prim, to dispatch troops to aid the French colonial government in restoring order. Fearful of a general uprising in Puerto Rico in response to the deteriorating material conditions of the plantations and the spread of an insurrectionary spirit in the eastern Caribbean, Governor Prim enacted a repressive ordinance (*Bando contra la raza africana*) imposing severe punishment for even minor offenses committed by blacks, whether free or slave. Shortly thereafter the discovery of conspiracies among the slaves of Ponce and Vega Baja confirmed the worse fears of the ruling class. On these events, see Díaz Soler, *Historia de la esclavitud*, pp. 217–22; Arturo Morales Carrión, *Auge y decadencia de la trata negrera en Puerto Rico (1820–1860)* (San Juan, 1978), pp. 149–75; Guillermo A. Baralt, *Esclavos rebeldes: conspiraciones y sublevaciones de esclavos en Puerto Rico, 1795–1873* (Río Piedras, 1982).

    French abolition may have affected some hacendados in another way. Article 8 of the French emancipation decree threatened all French citizens in foreign countries who possessed slaves with abrogation of citizenship unless they disposed of the slaves within three years. Although later it was all but nullified, Article 8 may have intimidated those planters in Puerto Rico who had retained French citizenship. See Lawrence C. Jennings, 'La abolition de l'esclavage par la IIe Republique et ses effets en Louisiane, 1848–1858', *Revue française d'histoire d'outre-mer*, 56, No. 205 (1969), pp. 375–97.

The Transformation of Cuban Agriculture, 1763–1838

FRANKLIN KNIGHT

There is no doubt about it. The era of our happiness has arrived.
Arango Y Parreño, 1793

Over the years from 1763 to 1838, Cuba changed from an underpopulated, underdeveloped settlement of small towns, cattle ranches, and tobacco farms to a community of large sugar and coffee plantations. Any full understanding of the history of slavery in the island after this date must perforce take into account the revolutionary changes in the structure of Cuban society and economy that preceded.

Although Cuban political life had not overcome, by 1838, the uncertainty and corruption which were its bane, the economic condition of the island was extremely promising. The island had 'arrived' among the world's sugar producers. While the other producers of the West Indies complained bitterly about 'rack and ruin', the Cuban sugar cane planters merely complained about the acute shortage of workhands of any color for their estates. The island had become the foremost producer of the world's sugar, but there still remained an abundance of fertile, unworked land of inestimable potential for the growing of sugar cane. The frequent changes of local political leadership in Havana and the incessant alternation of Spanish court parties had hardly affected the steady spread of the plantation throughout the island. From a minor colony in the Spanish imperial domain, Cuba had become the most valuable member of Spain's diminished overseas empire. Indeed, while Isabel II (1833–68) reigned unsteadily in Spain, sugar became 'king' in Cuba. But Cuba was important not merely because it was beginning to make substantial contributions to the Spanish treasury, but also because of the very nature of Cuban production at this time, it had joined the wider world community; metropolitan Spain knew only too well the dire consequences of this development.

The history of the sugar plantation goes as far back as the late sixteenth century in Cuba[1] The early settlers had continually produced small quantities of sugar on the island. And indeed, there were scattered examples of larger plantations, with probably as many as one hundred slaves, both in Cuba and Hispaniola from the late sixteenth century.[2] The technique of production may have been as efficient as that employed anywhere else in the world at that time. Nevertheless, it is important to point out that sugar production was geared exclusively toward internal consumption, and very few producers thought of sugar as a lucrative enterprise.[3] Moreover, the demand for sugar at that time in Europe was adequately supplied from the islands on the other side of the Atlantic and Brazil.

Cuban society at that time was not dominated by the plantation of any sort. It was, instead, an underpopulated island, a settlement colony existing on small ranches, *vegas* (tobacco farms), and in small towns, with a few plantations and a few slaves. Until the second half of the eighteenth century, Cuban agriculture consisted of alternating attempts at monoculture and a mixed economy, neither of which was distinguished in the activities of the overseas Spanish empire taken as a whole. This is not to say that the island was not an important

Slave Society in Cuba During the 19th Century (Madison, 1970), pp. 3–24.

part of the Spanish empire in the New World. It was valuable as a meeting place for ships and men from the diverse parts of the mainland, and it represented a springboard for the colonization attempts on the mainland before it lost its place to the ports and cities of New Spain and New Granada. A few colonists, however, remained in Cuba braving the elements and making a living by raising cattle and planting tobacco. Tobacco was the main export crop; but leather, meat, and dyewoods became important commercial supplements, especially in the immensely valuable inter-island trade.[4] The most important aspect of early Cuban society was the fact that, in accordance with the general pattern of Spanish colonial expansion, the majority of the inhabitants of the island colony lived in towns. Life in Cuba at that time for freedman or slave centered upon the town, the hacienda, or the vega.[5]

As long as the society remained predominantly dependent on the growing of tobacco and the raising of cattle, the labor requirements were low. Since tobacco was not grown as a plantation crop, but as a small-scale cash crop — as indeed it was in the English colonies of the eastern Caribbean before the sugar revolution — and ranching does not require regimented labor, Cuba could remain an island settlement of preponderantly white persons.[6] It is folly to expect that such a society would generate high racial tension, whether or not the whites were racists. The white sector maintained its substantial majority and probably as a result exhibited little or no racial fear of the non-white sector of the population. There was, and could be, little tension of any kind. The society just did not have the kind of divisions which yield strife: no foreigners of note, no Indians, no very rich people, few African slaves. As far as the lack of racial tension went, this resulted less from the benevolence of Spanish legislation or the doctrine and intercession of the single, all-encompassing Roman Catholic Church, than it did from the realities of the situation. In Cuba at this time the African simply represented little economic value and even less economic competition. In terms of services and obligations, therefore, white and non-white complemented each other.[7]

In the pre-plantation era of Cuban slavery, the enslaved persons could live with few rigorous rules. A large number of the slaves were obviously in domestic service, while the others worked in the fields. Often white masters and their slaves worked together in the tobacco vegas, or on the cattle haciendas. In any case, the farms were small and their proprietors poor. Tobacco plantations such as the ones found in Virginia and other areas of the southern United States were the exception in Cuba, where the farmers had few slaves and a lower social position than the cattle rancher. The cattle ranchers tended to be richer than the tobacco growers, but this was not really important since they both used small numbers of slaves and supervised them rather laxly. Regardless of where master and slave found themselves, the relationship tended toward intimacy and patriarchy. In comparison with the other islands of the Caribbean before the late eighteenth century, the relations between masters and slaves were relatively personal. This apparently amiable situation derived less from the differing cultural heritages of the various Caribbean islands than from their varying stages of economic development.

But the placidity and lethargy of Cuban society did not last forever. Between 1762 and 1838 the relatively mixed economy based on cattle-ranching, tobacco-growing, and the small-scale production of sugar gave way to the dominance of plantation agriculture based on the large-scale production of sugar and coffee. There was no single factor which engendered the change in the nature of Cuban society and its agriculture. Instead, a bewildering series of interrelated events and forces over which the Cubans themselves had no control, and which they often did not understand, imposed the radical transformation into a plantation society. Among these powerful agents of change in the history of Cuban society at this time must be included the shifts in international market demands, the English occupation of Havana in 1763–64, the far-reaching economic and administrative reforms of Charles III (1759–88), the sudden destruction of the French colony of St. Domingue, and the disruptive wars of the Latin American independence movement. All these events, occurring in the last decades of the eighteenth century and the early years of the nineteenth, resulted in a truly revolutionary change in the nature of Cuban society.

Once the Cuban agricultural revolution took place, other equally fundamental changes were irrepressible. The entire society began to readjust itself to the new demands of the plantation and the economy. More slaves resulted in a new method of organizing slave labor. More intensive agriculture meant wider markets and greater dissatisfaction with the restrictive measures of Spanish colonial commerce. Greater participation in the international market brought new ideas of economic and political relationship. The Cuban elite which had long complacently accepted Spanish colonial rule began to demand greater intercourse with other countries, particularly France, Great Britain, and the United States. The illegal trade with the British which had always been conducted clandestinely assumed prominent proportions. And the United States became a large market for Cuban sugar as well as the best source of the manufactured goods, skilled laborers, and enlightening ideas so seriously lacking in the island.

The most convenient starting point for this intensification in Cuban agriculture may be taken as the year 1763, when the English captured and occupied Havana for a period of ten months. Of course, seen in isolation that event may not have been crucial to the island's agriculture.[8] The English did nothing that the Cubans were not already doing before they arrived on the scene.[9] Nevertheless, the large number of merchant vessels which visited Havana during the months of the occupation and the importation and sale of more than 10,000 slaves in such a short time constituted a tremendous stimulus to a process already under way. Among other things, the English occupation of Havana emphasized the gigantic gap betwen the prevailing Cuban demand for slaves and its effective supply. It also convinced Charles III and his ministers that the entire colonial situation was ready for the rational reforms which they had already been contemplating.[10]

The real importance of the reforms of Charles III lay in the fact that they were the first major official attempt to integrate the island of Cuba into the mainstream of the wider world. Cuban changes, however, were only a small part of the large scheme of physiocratic ideas to bring Spain up to date by the thorough overhaul of her relations with her overseas colonies. Nor by focusing on the official acts of the Spanish Crown should one lose sight of the important fact that the entire eighteenth century was a period of general European economic progress and enlightenment. To a certain extent, therefore, Charles III was as much the servant of his age as he was the master of his deeds.[11] The island of Cuba was of paramount importance in the imperial plans of Charles III, as a testing ground for the measures that he subsequently applied to the rest of the empire.

Before the late eighteenth century, Cuban property owners had bought their slaves from the English, the French, the Dutch, and the Portuguese.[12] Indeed, before 1792 Spain had never been able to provide her colonies with the required human cargoes, since she lacked the necessary African factories. At first she farmed out the awards for the supply in a series of *asientos*, or contracts. These contracts gave the right to any individual of any country to deliver for sale a stated number of slaves in the Spanish empire. Later the asientos were given to the emerging joint-stock companies of the Portuguese, French, and, after 1713, the British.[13] The companies, like the individuals earlier, promised to transport a specific number of slaves to the Spanish colonies, and to pay a specified tax into the Spanish treasury.

However the awards were made, they were totally inadequate to supply the Spanish colonies. The official asientos were supplemented by a lively, mutually beneficial, inter-island trade throughout the Caribbean. English privateers, often acting on their own initiative, made sporadic trips among the Spanish islands, and by force or judicious bribes sold their cargo of slaves for specie.[14] But there were also well-established markets in Jamaica and Dominica, in which the Cubans regularly made their purchases. Condemned strongly by the Spanish crown, but welcomed openly by the islanders, this inter-island trade fulfilled two acute needs: the Cubans got their slaves, and the English and the French obtained cash, dyewoods, and hides. Spanish silver, dyewoods, and leather products not only enabled the Jamaican and other West Indian merchants to become solvent, but found their way into English domestic industry, and English trade with the Far East.

The Spanish government was always aware of the unsatisfactory conduct of the asiento, and the formation of their own chartered companies in the early eighteenth century was an attempt to rectify the situation. In the case of Cuba, the Real Compañía Mercantil de La Habana was the first attempt to boost the trade in slaves and to stir the waning interest in agriculture[15] The company was formed in 1740 to take over the transportation to and sale of Africans in the island. It disposed of its slaves for cash, credit, or pledged crop returns. In this way the company dominated, though it never monopolized, the island's major exports of sugar, tobacco, and hides before 1763. In the first twenty-six years of its operation the company brought into Cuba and sold officially 9,943 slaves. But of this number, more than 50 per cent were sold in the three years immediately following the British occupation.[16]

The Real Compañía had other counterparts in Spanish America. The Caracas Company, chartered in 1728, monopolized the trade of the Venezuelan coast. A company from Galicia received a charter to trade with the Campeche region in 1734, and the Barcelona Company, chartered in 1755, intended to carry on trade with Puerto Rico and Hispaniola. Most of these new companies had the financial backing of the merchants from the northern provinces of Spain. Only the Caracas Company proved successful over the long run. Nevertheless, the organization of the companies represented Bourbon attempts to liberalize trade in the empire and to break the monopoly of Andalusia.

The organization of the Real Compañía was extremely important, but from the planter's point of view it proved more a liability than an asset. On the one hand it failed to supply an adequate amount of goods or slaves at reasonable or satisfactory rates. On the other hand, it bought the planters' products at the lowest possible prices. Under these conditions, contraband trade became probably the largest outlet for Cuban products and the best method of obtaining necessary imported goods. But the prevalence of the contraband trade made it monumentally difficult to arrive at credible estimates for the island's commerce, or its slave population and annual rate of slave importation. This study takes into account the possibility that the official figures represent the minimum for any particuar time. Nevertheless, I think that the earlier figures may not be too inaccurate since the demands were low; and the later figures at least represent an index of volume.

On the basis of official estimates and intelligent guesswork, Hubert Aimes set the total number of slaves imported into Cuba between 1512 and 1761 at about 60,000 — a figure which seems eminently reasonable for the period.[17] For 1762–1838, the same author put the total at somewhere in the region of 400,000.[18] The mean annual import figure for the first period of nearly 250 years comes to about 250 slaves per year. The mean annual figure for the 76 years prior to 1838 comes to nearly 5,000 slaves per year. These figures dramatically reflect the demographic changes which were brought about in the society as a consequence of the transatlantic slave trade. But the trade, for its part, was merely a local response to the agricultural demand. Cuban planters wanted more adult Africans to provide the labor for the cultivation of their land. And even though they knew that it meant a fundamental change in the composition of their island's population, they were quite prepared for that eventuality. The demand, after all, preceded the fateful events in St. Domingue and France at the end of the century, and so there was less need for worry.

The commercial importance of Havana increased tremendously after the British occupation. During the eighteen years after 1860, the number of ships calling at the port rose from six to more than two hundred per year.[19] As part of the system of modified free trade which had been instituted during the reforms of Charles III, the port became a focal point for the entire gulf area, handling larger and larger quantities of European manufactured goods and slaves. Commodities which were usually scarce became more available, and in the case of slaves a greater supply seemed to be consistently below the local requirements. As far as the Cuban planters were concerned, African laborers were the most valuable commodity which could be imported into the island at that time. The liberalization of the trade afforded by the crown unwittingly paved the way for a succession of unforeseen events towards the end of the eighteenth century which would begin the promotion of the island of Cuba as the foremost producer of sugar in the world.

Once the Creoles in Cuba had begun the agricultural transformation of the island, the supply of slaves became the main concern. For at this time the international competition in the production of tropical staples depended on a sufficient labor force. The continuous agitation by the Cubans led to the complete reexamination of the island's slave supply. Not surprisingly, the consensus was that the means and measures by which the Cubans procured their slaves were totally inconsistent with the agricultural requirements of the island. Over a period of years, therefore, the crown granted permission for an unrestricted number of slaves to be brought to the island.[20] Finally, a royal cedula of February 28, 1789, permitted foreigners and Spaniards to sell as many slaves as they could in a specified number of free ports, including Havana.[21] This was exactly what the Cuban planters had been anxious to achieve for more than a decade. The royal order removed all the previous restrictions on the trade of slaves, suspended all taxes for a period of three years, and allowed the merchants to sell at any price determined by the local market conditions. Indeed, the planters were so delighted by the new situation that they persuaded the royal court in Madrid to extend the free trade beginning in 1792 for a further period of six years.[22] And so great was the interest in Cuban agriculture and the commerce in slaves that a total of eleven royal pronouncements was made between 1789 and 1798 expanding the trade in black workers to the Spanish Indies.[23]

This declaration of a virtual free trade in slaves at the end of the eighteenth century, then, provided the necessary impetus for the development of the plantation society. Nevertheless, the greater trade must also be seen against the general background of events in the Caribbean and elsewhere at that time. For exactly during this period of time international events favored the growth of Cuba's economy and importance. And perhaps the most significant single event was the destruction of the sugar-producing capacity of the French colony of St. Domingue, and the later creation of the independent republic of Haiti.

Until 1789, St. Domingue was the most highly developed plantation society in the world. It was the paragon among sugar islands of the West Indies. Situated on the western part of the island of Hispaniola, and comprising a total area of only 10,700 square miles, the colony's population of 40,000 white persons and 480,000 slaves and free persons of color had long become the ideal of, and comparison for, every other colony in the area that hoped to become rich by growing sugar cane and coffee. The Cubans reasoned that with four times the land area of St. Domingue, and undoubtedly greater soil fertility, they could easily outproduce their neighbors. The only handicap they had was the acute shortage of slaves, which, however, was being rectified at last. And like the sugar producers in St. Domingue a little before, they would have faced the unhappy restrictions of their own exclusive imperial commercial system.[24] But before they could worry about that, there was the immediate concern of raising their sugar production to a competitive level.

The extension of the French revolution to the Caribbean brought two unexpected results beneficial to the Cuban producers. In the first place, the principal producer of the world's sugar and coffee was almost instantly and completely destroyed. The price of sugar on the European market rose sharply as the demand outstripped the available supply, and brought a windfall to producers elsewhere. But in the immediate aftermath of the events in St. Domingue, the Spanish crown was hesitant to sanction the creation of a new slave society in Cuba, even though it would give permission to the continued increase in the number of Africans imported into the island. Nevertheless, the Cuban planters won a resounding victory over the crown when they got a concession in 1792 for the first Spanish ship ever to sail directly from Africa to Cuba bringing Africans to the slave market in the Antilles. In the second place, from St. Domingue came a number of refugees who brought their skills, their slaves, and an uncertain amount of capital, and initiated the plantation agriculture of coffee in the eastern sections of the island.[25] It seemed, despite the confustion of that era, very clear to Don Francisco de Arango y Parreño, the intelligent, articulate representative of the Cuban planters in Madrid, that the age of their happiness had indeed arrived.

From its very inception, the Cuban plantation agriculture depended upon imported skills, imported capital, and an imported labor force. An uncertain part of the skills and capital came from the early immigrants from St. Domingue. These were joined later by other French emigrés from Louisiana who preferred to go into exile than to endure life under the Anglo-Saxons after Napoleon sold the territory to the United States of America. And even some defeated royalist supporters of the mainlaind Latin American wars settled in Cuba, bringing at least their initiative, if they had no cash.[26]

Cuba derived enormous benefits from the unsettling external situation at the beginning of the nineteenth century. Wars in the area considerably augmented the available supply of capital devoted to agriculture. This led to other necessary changes as well. For since tropical agriculture depended at this time on the availability of land and slaves, intensified agriculture necessitated a fundamental change in the pattern of landholding and land use, and in the demographic composition of the island. In short, to accommodate the newcomers, black and white, the Cubans had to alter the basic structure of landholding in their island.[27]

The old tobacco and cattle holdings rapidly gave way in certain areas to the sugar and coffee plantations. Specific zones developed for each particular form of activity. Tobacco became the principal crop in the region mainly west of Havana. Sugar dominated the central plains and the lowlands around Santiago de Cuba in the eastern end of the island. Coffee, after failing to hold its own on the plains against the inexorable expansion of the sugar plantation, retreated to the mountainous area of the eastern division. But before this pattern attained its final form, it was imperative to abolish the antiquated nature of landholding and land use in Cuba. Only then could valuable land be free for new settlements and new crops.

To understand the revolution in landholding which took place at this time, it is necessary to go back to the early days of Spanish colonization in the new world and to trace the complicated growth of a system of landholding fettered by lethargic, ancestral latifundism. This system, incidentally, was common throughout Latin America before the nationalist wars of liberation in the early eighteenth century. The general pattern was the enormous hacienda with its ill-defined boundaries. Designed to be self-sufficient as much as possible, these estates also produced a few cash crops to meet the royal tax and support the luxurious life of their occupants. This type of hacienda had its roots far back in the frontier conditions of Spanish society, but it underwent some modification when it was transplanted to the New World.

After America was discovered, all land became the personal domain of the Castilian monarch, who had the prerogative to dispose of it either in usufruct or outright grant to any deserving person. Both methods of distribution were used. Originally, each occupied territory was divided into towns which had contiguous boundaries. Within the towns, the land was parceled among the settlers, and enclosed by a common pasture. Beyond this common pasture, the royal lands (*realengos*) were distributed in haphazard, often overlapping grants called *mercedes*, of usufructal tenure.[28] It must, however, be emphasized that the royal grants were modest in size. Latifundism was certainly not the intention of the crown and had its own peculiar historical genesis in the following years.

Each merced was given for the cultivation of a particular crop. Recipients of these mercedes were forbidden to change the designated crop for which they had originally received their parcel of land. The usufructal landlords paid a special annual fee that was determined by the size of the plot or its agricultural purpose. And although the land could be inherited, it could not be sold, sublet, or subdivided. This, then, was the system, which, fraught with abuses and legal complications, prevailed throughout the centuries and was to provide the basis for Creole wealth by the early nineteenth century in Cuba. Over a period of time marriage, as well as other agreements of local interest and dubious legality, converted the modest holdings into larger farms, sometimes of astonishing dimensions.

The absence of a real estate market was only one handicap to the accumulation of wealth by the landholding group. For although a planter may have had the use of his land, he could not cut a large number of the hardwood trees on his hacienda without express royal permission. Until the late eighteenth century, the crown had first lien on all hardwood trees in the island in order that the fleet construction continually taking place at Havana would not be jeopardized.[29] But as the years passed, the rise of the large sugar plantation and the preservation of the hardwood forests became mutually antagonistic. Part of the entire scheme to change the pattern of landholding, therefore, was an alteration of the system of hardwood forest preservation. The sugar revolution — indeed, the entire structure of Cuban society in the nineteenth century — cannot be understood without recognizing the importance of the fundamental change in landholding and land use between the late eighteenth and the early nineteenth century.

The big opportunity for the landholders came with the gradual insolvency of the Spanish crown. As the resources of the treasury decreased the crown ceded for cash the land which its representatives — or local municipal councils — had offered in usufruct. By these means, a small number of wealthy colonists had persevered in the time-consuming legal disentanglements, and finally bought titles in fee simple, to use the Anglo-Saxon term, to the land they used or hoped to own. Nevertheless, by the end of the eighteenth century there had been few concrete achievements in the way of legal security for land. As more immigrants came the demand for land dramatically grew. In order to capitalize on the new source of wealth from land, it became urgent to straighten out the existing confusion or uncertainty over land. That, therefore, became the first obsession of the Sociedad Económica de Amigos del País, or the Havana Economic Society.

The Havana Economic Society, founded by twenty-seven Creole landholders, received its royal sanction in 1791.[30] It was not the only such organization in the island, but another attempt to form a group of the Creoles of Santiago de Cuba ended in failure, leaving the Havana group as the only dynamic social and economic association dominated by the Creoles. Despite the fact that the Havana group later expanded into a body with a membership of nearly two hundred persons, at no time did its influence and activity extend beyond a small enthusiastic core mainly domiciled in Havana. Of the 126 members registered in 1793, 113 resided in the capital city, Havana. The Economic Society was, in every respect an exclusive club, a tightly organized elite group bent on the pursuit of economic power and political influence.

The formation of economic societies was a common response in Latin America to the ideas of the European enlightenment, although this development was interrupted by the wars of separation from Spain in the early nineteenth century. But in Latin America, unlike in Europe, there was a greater emphasis on the pure and applied sciences than on philosophy.[31] In Cuba, the emphasis was on scientific activity and economic interests. The program of the Havana Economic Society encompassed science and arts, commerce and industry, beautification, and agriculture and education. Nevertheless, throughout the long life of the society, agriculture remained its consuming passion.

The Economic Society became the chief advocate for radical changes in the structure of Cuban landholding. Not surprisingly, its members were among the most articulate and influential men on the island. Yet the ultimate success of the society's pleas rested with the nature of political leadership in Havana, and the prevailing state of the Spanish treasury. Interested captains-general and impoverished monarchs were the ingredients of success.

The two most successful periods of the Economic Society coincided with the terms in office of Luis de Las Casas y Arragori (1790–96) and Alejandro Ramírez (1816–19). The supreme political head of the island was also the titular head of the Economic Society (acting in the name of the Spanish monarch) and was able to exert official influence in Madrid, helping or hindering any measure according to his fancy. Regardless of the political ideas held by both Las Casas and Ramírez, they both were themselves landholders in Cuba and probably had a personal interest in reforming the system of land ownership and land use.[32] It was evident that during the periods of office of these two men the landowners would have friends in high places.

On the other hand, the Spanish crown was hardly in a position to resist colonial requests that offered the opportunity of financial rewards. For over a century the royal treasury had barely been solvent, and the long Napoleonic wars further depleted the already slender resources. The Spanish troops and naval forces which at first fought reluctantly with the French emperor in Europe — and then, after experiencing the occupation of their homeland, turned against him — cost a lot of money to maintain. Neither Charles IV nor Ferdinand VII could be oblivious to the constant need to find new ways of securing money according to the necessities of the state. One such new way, of course, was to accept the advocated changes in the legal nature of land tenure. Unfortunately, the crown derived far fewer returns from that gesture than it had anticipated, and the poverty of the Spanish treasury remained a constant factor throughout the nineteenth century.[33]

Between 1795 and 1820, the landholders won such major concessions from the crown that they altered irrevocably the entire system of land ownership in Cuba. A royal cedula of 1800 broke up the hereditary pattern of the existing *señorios*, or large estates, and permitted the outright ownership of lands previously held in usufruct. Even crown lands became fast-selling real estate. Further royal decrees in 1815 and 1816 gave landowners the right to parcel, sell, sublet, and use their land without legal intervention. But most important of all for the future development of the sugar estate, royal approval was finally given for the destruction of the hardwood forests in the interest of agricultural expansion. After a long dispute, sugar at last took precedence over the royal navy: the Spanish crown had cleared the way for the sugar revolution in Cuba.

The immediate effect of the series of royal decrees was to open the way for real estate speculation. Land values rose rapidly, sometimes as high as five times what they had been in the late 1790s. And as the sugar belt moved out of the area around Havana, it further stimulated the rise in the market price of land. In the Matanzas sugar belt, for example, land that before the turn of the century was priced at 80 pesos per hectare was sold at prices in excess of 500 pesos afterwards. The Economic Society of Havana bought a number of estates and resold them to the new immigrants at moderate profits.[34] Private investors such as Juan Poey, a wealthy Creole planter of Havana, dreamed of making millions of pesos in real estate speculation, though it is unlikely that they made quite that amount. Nevertheless, many new schemes produced new towns, mainly settled by immigrants, such as Guira, Alquizar, Nueva Paz, Palos, Bagäes, and Güines in the outskirts of Havana. The construction of towns was even carried on by private individuals, like Agustín de Cárdenas, marquis of Cárdenas de Monte Hermoso, who founded the town of San Antonio de los Baños on his estate. He also leased small farms to the new immigrants. The exemption from the payment of the alcabala, or sales tax, by the purchasers of new land also served to further encourage a lively real estate market.[35]

The ability to cut and use the timber on private lands did not result in the instant deforestation of the island. Until the middle of the nineteenth century, the landowners zealously protected the forests as their primary source of fuel for their boilers, and timber for general building and the construction of the boxes in which they transported their sugar. Major deforestation only came with the advanced technological era, especially after the use of railroads had become general throughout the sugar-cane-producing area. Rail transport eventually proved so convenient and economical that the cane growers derived more profits by replacing their forests with canefields, and importing their lumber, firewood, and coal. Even the railroads, which had used locally mined coal, found it necessary to import this fuel as local supplies dwindled.[36] By the late 1860s the central section of the island had been almost completely deforested.

The leaders of the Cuban agricultural phenomenon of the nineteenth century were extremely intelligent men, fervently desiring that Cuba should stand second to none in gross agricultural production. Francisco Arango y Parreño and Francisco Frías y Jacott, Count of Pozos Dulces, were amazingly farsighted. They knew that Cuban prosperity had come latest among the West Indian producers of sugar and coffee. Unlike the plantation owners of Jamaica, Barbados, Antigua, and St. Domingue, the Cubans lacked the numbers of slaves to catapult them into competitive production. But this liability, they reasonably assumed, was offset by the vast stretches of deep fertile land in Cuba.[37] Moreover, the Cubans were starting when science and technology offered new scope for profits and production in the sugar industry. With no obsolete machinery on their hands, the Cubans began with the latest equipment and the most proven formula for sugar production.

The Cuban Creoles, in agriculture as in politics, were a restless group. They were always ready to grasp at any innovation which promised to boost the total output, or to cut the costs of production.[38] As the sugar industry got under way, private individuals and public commissions made long trips through the other sugar islands, reporting in detail upon every aspect of the production of sugar and coffee.

In 1795, along with Ignacio Montalvo y Ambulodi, Count of Casa-Montalvo (who died soon afterwards), Arango y Parreño made the first official trip abroad for the Cuban sugar planters. The long voyage took the indefatigable and curious representative of the city of Havana to England, Portugal, Barbados, and Jamaica. Everywhere he went, the extremely inquisitive Arango reported back to his keenly interested audience on a bewildering range of topics, with particular emphasis on agriculture and relevant proposals for adaptation to Cuban conditions.[39]

In his reports from Europe, Arango noted the superior advantage of the English and Portuguese in the slave trade. Both countries, he pointed out, had factories on the African coast. This measure facilitated a steady supply of African slaves to their colonies, and reduced the price of the slaves at the delivery point because the initial cost was lower. English industrial development impressed him most. He sent back models of the newly invented sugar mills, and a detailed description of the refining process. His opinion was that the Cubans stood to gain a far greater advantage from importing 'those marvelous European machines' and thus completing the entire refining process in Cuba, than from selling muscovado (unrefined brown sugar) to the European refiners. This was, perhaps, his most valuable observation. It was partly the result of the British West Indians' failure to mechanize and to refine their sugar which weakened their competitive position in the European market.

In Barbados and Jamaica, Arango visited the foremost sugar producers among the British islands. Nothing in the political, social, and economic position of the islands escaped his careful scrutiny. Long reports relayed information ranging from the total area of land under cane cultivation to the most minute aspect of the production of sugar and rum.

Arango's journey convinced the Cubans that soon Cuba would be the world's leading sugar producer. As a result of his persuasive advocacy new varieties of cane, partiuclarly the Otaheiti, and new types of processing employing steam, water, and wind power were introduced to the island.[40] But along with the imported technique came a new awareness on the part of the Cuban Creole elite. They had joined the stream of ideas of the wider world. A mounting wave of criticism — carefully tendered under the guise of 'suggestions' — of Spanish colonial and economic policies originated in Havana. As the Cubans realized the magnitude of their economic potential, they realized the stifling restrictions of being a part of the Spanish empire. They demanded free international trade to buy the slaves, food, and manufactured goods that Spain could not supply, and to sell in a market larger than that offered by the Iberian peninsula. The Cuban attraction towards Britain and the United States in the early nineteenth century was, therefore, one of practical economic necessity.

Arango's fact-finding tour of Barbados and Jamaica in 1795 became the first of a frequent general practice. To any Cuban sugar producer, the grand tour of the British West Indies became a source of personal prestige, establishing the traveler as an authority on the subject of sugar production. And in some cases, the trip became the prerequisite for the founding of an *ingenio* (sugar estate with factory).[41] The curiosity value aside, the trips did provide much useful knowledge of methods and machines which were brought to Cuba. The 'Jamaican train', the boiling process of sugar manufacture, became standard in the early days of Cuban sugar production. Yet the true value of these trips over the long term came from the restless desire of the Cuban planters to find a process which would combine speed, efficiency, economy, and labor-saving devices. Because they were never able to stock their plantations with slaves the way the Jamaicans or Barbadians did, they had to find some alternative. In the fiercely competitive sugar market, survival depended on the volume of production. To the British West Indies and to Brazil, increased volume resulted from more slaves and more acreage under cane. But in the nineteenth century the British were waging a relentless crusade to abolish the slave trade and, ultimately, slavery. The essential problem for Cuba, therefore, was to devise a method of increasing the total output using the available manpower or, better, less manpower.

By 1828, Cuba had clearly surpassed her British West Indian neighbors in sugar production. A commission of Ramon de Arozarena and Pedro Bauduy made a thorough tour of Jamaica in that year, and reported back to the Cuban government.[42] In a lengthy report filled with interesting and knowledgeable observations, the commissioners described their journeys through the island, and the state of its sugar, coffee, and pimento operations. There were only three aspects in which the Cubans were not as distinguished as their neighbors: in the large-scale manufacture of rum, as a byproduct of sugar; in the extensive use of guinea grass as cattle fodder; and in the possession of pimento, which was native to Jamaica. They clearly supported the immediate adoption of those three measures. But they thought that Cuba, with her vast areas of virgin land, her large forests, water supply, and mountains would always be in a position to outproduce the sugar and coffee planters of Jamaica. They were amazed, too, that English chemical developments were completely unknown in the Jamaican sugar industry, which produced only muscovado sugar. Jamaica's economic glory lay in her past; Cuba was the land with the future.

The economic and political activities resulting from the progressive reforms of Charles III initiated the complete renovation of Cuban society: a steep rise in population, agricultural production, and profits; a new political awareness as new ideas crept back along the routes of economic and educational contact. The old order slowly dissolved. The new prosperity based on land speculation, slave trading, and sugar and coffee plantations brought to the forefront of Cuban society a new economic elite which accepted the old order on its own terms. This was extremely important, especially for the race relations which were to develop from the demands of plantation management and operation. Men like Muguel Aldama, Juan Poey, Julian Zulueta, Gonzalo José de Herrera y Beltran de Santa Cruz, Count of Fernandina, and Franciso Arango y Parreño were men who had become wealthy during their lifetimes, when the island was undergoing the changes of economy and demography which made it a classic, late-flowering example of the plantation society and the South Atlantic System. But the real importance of this new slave-owning class was that they would not, and could not, be bounded by the patriarchal conventions of the prevous era of Cuban slavery. Their attitude to the Church, the state, and their plantations was one which they themselves worked out — an attitude which reflected the new political power position of the Cuban Creole class.

Between 1775 and 1838 the island underwent profound changes in the composition of its population. In 1775, Cuba had a population of 171,500 persons. Of this total, 96,400 were white persons; 36,300 were free persons of color; and 38,900 were African slaves. But even then, a large proportion of the African slaves were recently imported — a trend which was to continue throughout the period of slavery on the island. By 1841, the official census reported a permanent population of 1,007,624 persons, of whom 418,291 were white, 152,838 were free

Table 1 Cuban Population Growth, 1774–1841

Class	1774	%	1827	%	1841	%
White	06,440	56.9	311,051	44.1	418,291	41.6
Free colored	36,301	20.3	106,494	15.1	152,838	15.1
Slave	38,879	22.8	286,942	40.8	436,495	43.3
Total population	171,620	100.0	704,487	100.0	1,007,624	100.0

Sources: For the census of 1774, Guerra y Sánchez, *Historia*, 2:78. For 1827 and 1841, *Resumen del censo de la población de la isla de Cuba . . . 1841 . . .* (Havana, 1842), p. 19.

persons of color, and 436,495 were slaves (see Table 1). In two generations the black element of the population had risen to be a majority in the society. The phenomenal growth of the slave population — from less than 23 per cent of the total population in 1774 to more than 43 per cent in 1841 — may be understood and explained only by looking at the profound concomitant change in the nature of agricultural activity. But the volume of trade to Cuba in the nineteenth century is more surprising, because of Great Britain's hostility to the trade at that time and her attempts to put an end to it.

The volume of trade in Africans to Cuba, had, despite fluctuations from year to year, tended to increase generally as the demand grew for workers on the island, and especially since the attempt to import white workers was not succeeding. With the abolition of the English slave trade in 1807, the most efficient suppliers of slaves in the Caribbean were removed. But from the Cuban planters' point of view, the greatest calamity was the agreement of 1817, forced by the English upon a war-weakened Spain, whereby the Spanish agreed to stop the trade to their colonies after 1820.[43] Of course, as an incentive to do so, the English government had paid the Spanish crown £400,000 as 'compensation'. No amount of money, however, especially when it was paid in Spain, could have induced the Cuban planters at that time to cooperate in the cessation of the slave trade. Instead, the Cubans regarded the British offer as a 'monstrous, hypocritical plot' designed to undermine their expanding sugar cane and coffee plantations and eventually stifle their economic progress.[44] The Anglo-Spanish agreement had the effect of increasing the numbers of Africans brought to the island of Cuba. Indeed, with the fear that the trade might be terminated in 1820, the mean annual importation figures between 1816 and 1820 were more than three times the figures for the period between 1812 and 1815.[45] Despite their awareness of the racial tragedy in St. Domingue, and despite the foreboding of the metropolitan power, the Cubans gambled on the risks: the plantation society had, by then, become the *sine qua non* in the Caribbean for wealth, stability, civilization, and patriotism.[46]

Yet, after the establishment of the independent republic of Haiti in 1804, slaveowners in the area could never be as complacent as they used to be in the unquestioned days of the eighteenth century. And after about 1817, the official relations between the metropolis and the colony, between Cuba and Spain, changed considerably as a result of the increased inflow of Africans. The white population suddenly became more and more aware of the heightening possibilities of a racial confrontation in the island.[47] Some white persons became fearful. The planters began to see the Spanish government — and especially the Spanish military power on the island — as the best guarantee of their personal safety and the security of their property.[48] Even the native Cubans began to see self-interest and self-preservation as the overriding concerns of the moment. Cuba would remain a faithful colony as long as the planters needed Spain.

Notes

1. José Antonio Saco, *Historia de la esclavitud de la raza africana en el nuevo mundo . . .* 4 vols (Havana, 1938), 2:96–97.
2. Hubert H. S. Aimes, *A History of Slavery in Cuba, 1511–1868* (New York, 1907), p. 13.
3. Actually, sugar cane growing had declined markedly by the end of the seventeenth century. See H. E. Friedlaender, *Historia económica de Cuba* (Havana, 1944), pp. 18–31.
4. Francisco de Arango y Parreño, *Obras* 2 vols (Havana, 1952), 1:81; Elizabeth Donnan (ed.), *Documents Illustrative of the Slave Trade to America* 4 vols (New York, 1965) 2:204–5, 211–12, 254; Allan Christelow, 'Contraband Trade between Jamaica and the Spanish Main, and the Free Port Act of 1766', *Hispanic American Historical Review*, 22 (1942), 309–43.
5. See Ramiro Guerra y Sánchez *et al.* (ed.), *Historia de la nación cubana* 10 vols (Havana, 1952), 1.
6. Aimes, *op. cit.*, p. 8.
7. See Herbert S. Klein, *Slavery in the Americas: A Comparative Study of Virginia and Cuba* (Chicago, 1967), pp. 131–33.
8. Aimes quite correctly points out that the English

occupation did not 'cause' the awakening and economic development of Cuba (*op. cit.*, p. 33). He does, nevertheless, agree that it marks a period of significant change (*ibid.*, p. 69).

9. Donnan, *op. cit.*, 2: xlv; Aimes, *op. cit.*, pp. 22–25.
10. J. H. Parry, *The Spanish Seaborne Empire* (New York, 1966), pp. 314–25; John E. Fagg, *Latin America: A General History* (New York, 1963), pp. 292–303. My information on the reforms of Charles III is condensed principally from the following: Cayetano Alcázar Molina, *Los virreinatos en el siglo XVIII*, (Madrid, 2nd edn, 1959); R. A. Humphreys and John Lynch, (ed.), *The Origins of Latin American Revolutions, 1808–1826* (New York, 1965); Salvador de Madariaga, *The Fall of the Spanish American Empire*. (New York, rev. edn, 1963); R. J. Shafer, *The Economic Societies in the Spanish World (1763–1821)* (New York, 1958).
11. Richard Herr, *The Eighteenth-Century Revolution in Spain* (Princeton, 1958).
12. J. H. Parry and P. M. Sherlock, *A Short History of the West Indies* (London, 1956), pp. 95–107.
13. Aimes, *op. cit.*, pp. 35–37; Jerónimo Becker y González, *La política española en las Indias* (Madrid, 1920), pp. 412–15.
14. Allan Christelow, *op. cit.*, pp. 309–43; Parry and Sherlock, *op. cit.*, p. 103.
15. Aimes, *op. cit.*, pp.29–30; Donnan, *op. cit.*, 2:xlv.
16. Aimes, *op. cit.*, pp. 23, 36.
17. These figures are taken from Aimes, *op. cit.*, p. 269, who derived them from Alexander von Humboldt, *The Island of Cuba*, trans. J. S. Thrasher (New York, 1856), pp. 216–24. Cuban import figures for this period compare closely with those for Jamaica during its heyday of slavery. See Orlando Patterson, *The Sociology of Slavery* (London, 1967), pp. 290–91.
18. Aimes, *op. cit.*, p. 269.
19. Parry, *op. cit.*, p. 316; Aimes, *op. cit.*, p. 35.
20. Aimes, *op. cit.*, pp. 45–48; Becker y González, *op. cit.*, pp. 412–15.
21. *Real cédula por la que Su Majestad concede libertad para el comercio de negros con las islas de Cuba, Sto. Domingo, Puerto Rico, y provincia de Caracas a los españoles y extranjeros* (Madrid, 1789).
22. Aimes, *op. cit.*, p. 50.
23. Manuel Moreno Fraginals, *El ingenio* (Habana, 1964), p. 8.
24. Arango y Parreño, *op. cit.*, 2:134.
25. Francisco Pérez de la Riva y Pons, *Origen y régimen de la propiedad territorial en Cuba* (Havana, 1946), p. 136; Humboldt, *op. cit.*, p. 46.
26. Antonio Gallenga, *The Pearl of the Antilles* (London: *op. cit.*, 1873), pp. 10–11; Juan Pérez de la Riva, 'Documentos para la historia de las gentes sin historia. El tráfico de culíes chinos', *Revista de la Biblioteca Nacional José Martí*, 6 (1965), 77–90.
27. Moreno Fraginals, *op. cit.*, pp. 18–19; Pérez de la Riva y Pons, *op. cit.*, p. 91; Duvon C. Corbitt, 'Mercedes and Realengos: A Survey of the Public Land System of Cuba', *Hispanic American Historical Review*, 19 (1930), 262–85.
28. Pérez de la Riva, *op. cit.*, pp. 20–21; Corbitt, *op. cit.*, pp. 262–78.
29. Pérez de la Riva, *op. cit.*, pp. 137–48.
30. Shafer, *op. cit.*, pp. 151–54, 183–98; R. Guerra y Sánchez trans. Marjorie M. Urquidi, *Sugar and Society in the Caribbean*, (New Haven, 1964), pp. 56–57.
31. See Arthur P. Whitaker (ed.), *Latin America and the Enlightenment* (Ithaca, N.Y., 2nd edn, 1961).
32. Pérez de la Riva, *op. cit.*, pp. 127–28.
33. See Raymond Carr, *Spain 1808–1939* (Oxford, 1966), pp. 155–319.
34. Moreno Fraginals, *op. cit.*, pp. 14–15; Guerra y Sánchez, *Historia*, pp. 157–63.
35. Pérez de la Riva, *op. cit.*, pp. 132–34; Guerra y Sánchez, *Sugar and Society*, pp. 33–36.
36. Moreno Fraginals, *op. cit.*, pp. 74–78.
37. Arango y Parreño, *op. cit.*, 1:114–74.
38. For a variety of interesting local inventions, especially designed for the sugar cane industry, see the records in Archivo Histórico Nacional, Madrid, Seción de Ultramar (hereafter AHN, Ultramar), Fomento, leg. 49(19, 27, 28).
39. Arango y Parreño, *op. cit.*, 1:234–47.
40. Francisco J. Ponte Dominguez, *Arango Parreño, el estadista colonial* (Havana, 1937), pp. 84–87.
41. Moreno Fraginals, *op. cit.*, p. 24.
42. AHN, Ultramar, Fomento, leg. 37, fol. 91: *Informe sobre... Jamayca. Por D. Ramon de Arozarena, y D. Pedro Bauduy* (Havana, 1828).
43. *Ibid.*, Esclavitud, leg. 3547, fol. 1333: governor of Cuba to minister of war and colonies, July 2, 1861 (confidential).
44. Justo Zaragoza, *Las insurrecciones en Cuba*, 2 vols (Madrid, 1872–73), 1:512.
45. Aimes, *op. cit.*, p. 269. gives the imports as follows:

1812:	6,081	*1816:*	17,737
1813:	4,770	*1817:*	25,841
1814:	4,321	*1818:*	19,902
1815:	9,111	*1819:*	15,147
		1820:	17,194

Since these figures are based on official calculations, they probably represent the lowest import statistics.

46. Arango y Parreño, *op. cit.*, 1:148–50.
47. Rafael M. de Labra y Cadrana, *La abolición de la esclavitud en el orden económico* (Madrid, 1873), p. 251; AHN, Ultramar, Esclavitud, leg. 3552(2), ind. 6, fol. 3: confidential despatch of Captain-General O'Donnell, September 30, 1844.
48. *Ibid.*

SECTION THREE
Production and Profitability

The historiography of the sugar industry's profitability during the slavery period is quite extensive, and is being enlarged steadily. It has not been denied that capital was generated and accumulated at high levels in the sugar industry. Debate centred on changes and fluctuations in profitability, and the circumstances under which attractive returns on investments were made possible. Ward points to a gradual decline in British West Indian profitability between the 'Golden Age' of the seventeenth century and the end of slavery in the 1830s.

Stein and Davies approach the subject from a different angle, focusing more on production, the acquisition of input by sugar plantations and the disposal of output through legal or illicit means.

Davies concentrates on the Commission System which was an outstanding characteristic of West Indian external trade, being both a system of marketing and a means by which credit was transmitted from the Mother country. Unlike Stein and Davies, Shepherd is concerned with the relations between the sugar economy and other producing units in a diversified economy. Her focus is on the internal system of exchange as opposed to the external trade.

These essays illustrate some of the major concerns which have gained attention in the past two decades.

The Profitability of Sugar Planting in the British West Indies, 1650–1834

J. R. WARD*

How profitable were the plantations of the British West Indies during the years of slavery? The question is interesting for several reasons. First, colonists went there, when they went of their own accord, in order to make money, and it is worth asking how well they succeeded. Then there is the problem of the effect of the plantations upon the mother country. It is generally considered that they were profitable to their owners, at least during the early years. But were they equally profitable to society at large? The British West Indies were developed and held under the navigation laws, and these laws gave them a virtual monopoly of the British market for the products of tropical agriculture. But for much of the eighteenth century the planters of the British colonies were unable to deliver sugar to Europe as cheaply as the planters of the French, Dutch, and Danish islands. So it can be argued that in consequence of British West Indian settlement under a peculiar form of economic organization, the British consumer had to pay more for his sugar than he would have under free trade. Also the West Indian colonies became objects of international rivalry and brought large expenditures on defence. These points were first made in a coherent way by Adam Smith, and his economic indictment of the British West Indies lay at the heart of his attack on the system of regulated trade.[1] More recently they have been the subject of debate in this *Review*.[2] The problem is, did the private profits of the sugar planters exceed by a large enough margin the social costs that their business entailed? Clearly the first step in its resolution must be to estimate what those profits were.

Finally, the subject of profitability is important for the history of the plantations during the seventy years before the abolition of slavery in 1834. There are various points of view on this. On the other hand, L. J. Ragatz has told a gloomy story of almost continuous decline.[3] The prosperity of the sugar planters, he considers, reached its height about the middle of the eighteenth century, but even then it was clouded. They were overcommitted to a crop which exhausted the soil, they could not or would not improve their techniques, and many were absentees employing dishonest or incapable managers. In the following decades they were ruined by a remorseless sequence of misfortunes. The settlement of more fertile lands in the newly acquired Ceded Islands, Trinidad, and British Guiana glutted their markets; the rebellion of the North American colonies cut them off from their traditional source of plantation supplies; and the abolition of the British slave trade in 1808 raised the cost of their labour. Plantation agriculture was on the point of collapse through most of the British West Indies even before the slaves were freed; emancipation only consummated a longer process of decline. The breadth of its scholarship and the force of its argument have given Ragatz's account great influence, but more recently it has been criticized. R. B. Sheridan and W. A. Green have taken a less pessimistic view of the planters' capacity for technical improvement.[4] R. K. Aufhauser has examined

*This article is part of a larger study of the British West Indies between 1624 and 1834. I am grateful to the archivists and their staffs who have made material available to me. I have profited from conversations with Prof. Stanley Engerman and Mr George Tyson and their advice on sources, and from comments made on an earlier draft read to the Conference of Scottish Economic Historians held at Edinburgh in December 1975.

Economic History Review, Vol. 31, No. 2 (1978), pp. 197–213.

the records of some Barbados plantations on the eve of emancipation and found that they were making profits.[5] Hence one of the purposes of this article is to extend the discussions and put the period studied by Ragatz into wider perspective. It is based upon the study of a sample of plantation records.[6] First, it considers the form of plantation accounts and the way in which they may be used to estimate the rate of profit. Second, it presents the results that these accounts yield for the sample of plantations chosen and discusses their limitations. Third, it draws some conclusions on the subjects mentioned here.

I

The rate of profit is the ratio between net income and a stock of capital, and a means of estimating these is required. Income is the balance of receipts and expenses, net of capital appreciation or depreciation; sometimes this is stated in planters' papers but more usually we must make the estimates ourselves. Plantation receipts came from the sale of sugar, rum, and molasses, and sometimes also from livestock, provisions, and the hiring out of slaves. To be deducted from these are the three main categories of expenditure: first, the so-called Island Expenses, that is expenses incurred locally in the colony in taxes, salaries, and the purchase of food, lumber, slaves, and livestock; second, the Invoice, that is the shipments from Europe of plantation stores; and third, the costs of marketing the sugar, that is factorage, insurance, and freight. Ideally, we should have information about all of these as the basis for our estimates, but we are not always so fortunate. The most important components of the balance are the income from the sales of sugar and rum, and the Island Expenses; where no information on these survives no estimate of profit has been attempted. For the sugar it is best to use detailed accounts of sales which give the price obtained and the proceeds net of marketing expenses. But sometimes there is an account only of the weight, or of the volume (number of hogsheads) of production, or in shipments leaving the plantation, or reaching Great Britain. In such cases the proceeds of sales have been estimated by assuming that the weight per hogshead was the average for the time and place, that 96 per cent of production was shipped to market from the plantation, that the loss of weight in shipment through leakage was 14 per cent, and that the sugar when it reached its destination was sold at the average current London price as reported in the main published series.[7]

The rum was usually sold locally to meet the Island Expenses, and for information on these the Island Account is necessary. At it happens, because this was the main instrument by which owners supervised their property, it was the class of record which was kept most carefully and which survives most often. The second component of expenditure, the Invoice, was less considerable, and less subject to unpredictable variation. So where the necessary accounts do not survive I have estimated it as a ratio of the number of slaves on the plantation, calculating this ratio from other contemporary data. Thirdly there are the marketing costs. Where the details are not known they can be estimated. The factor's commission was standardized throughout the period at 2½ per cent; rates for freight and insurance were quite uniform for each island or groups of islands in any particular year. The details are set out in Tables 1 and 2.

Table 2 glosses over a number of complications. The seaworthiness of ships varied, as did the reputations of their owners and captains; also rebates were often given if a ship left the Caribbean before the start of the hurricane season in July or August, and, in wartime, if it took convoy. The rates listed are the average of rates quoted, deducting these rebates, and adding the usual charges for commission (½ per cent) and for making out the policy (¼ per cent).

Table 1 Freight Rates on Sugar from the West Indies to London (per cwt)

		Jamaica		Other West Indies	
		s.	d.	s.	d.
1689–97	War	14	5	8	9
1698–1702	Peace	6	6	3	7
1703–13	War	15	9	7	4
1714–38	Peace	4	0	3	6
1739–48	War	10	0	8	0
1749–55	Peace	4	0	3	6
1756–62	War	8	0	6	0
1763–75	Peace	4	0	3	6
1776–82	War	8	0	8	0
1783–92	Peace	4	0	3	6
1793–98	War	9	0	7	0
1799–1801	War	10	0	8	0
1802–03	Peace	6	0	4	6
1804–07	War	9	6	7	6
1808–15	War	11	0	9	0
1816–34	Peace	6	0	5	0

Sources: R. Davis, *The Rise of the English Shipping Industry* (1962), p. 283; plantation records.

Table 2 Insurance Rates on Sugar from the West Indies to London (per cent)

		Jamaica	Other West Indies
1689–97	War	17	17
1698–1702	Peace	6	4
1703–13	War	11	11
1714–38	Peace	6	4
1739–48	War	15	10
1749–55	Peace	6	4
1756–62	War	15	10
1763–75	Peace	4	3
1776–82	War	10	13
1783–92	Peace	4	3
1793–1800	War	11	8
1801	War	8	6
1802	Peace	5	3
1803–08	War	7	6
1809–15	War	5	4
1816–24	Peace	4	3
1825–34	Peace	3	2

Sources: Plantation records.

But in practice not all ships sailed before the hurricane season or took convoy in wartime, although most did. So in this way the procedure will tend to understate the average net premium paid. On the other hand, many planters did not insure at all, particularly in time of peace, and while over the long term they would pay a price in uncompensated losses, this price would on average be less than the premiums whose costs were saved, because these included an element of broker's and underwriter's profit. Thus we have a complete record of shipments from the Parham plantations in Antigua between 1749 and 1781.[8] The average rate of loss in peacetime was 1.6 per cent and in wartime 3.9 per cent, much below the prevailing rates of insurance. So in this way insurance rates overstate the dangers of war and the sea. This probably cancels out the understatement introduced by the treatment of rebates. I think that on balance Table 2 rather exaggerates the cost of insurance.[9]

The last point to consider in the calculation of net income is capital appreciation and depreciation. Capital expenditure, whether for the maintenance of an existing stock or for additions to it, was usually included in the Island Account and Invoice. So when a plantation's equipment does not change, the estimates of income made in the way already described can be accepted without further adjustment. But where the capital stock changes substantially special account must be taken. Few complete variations of assets were made, but their most important component, the number of slaves, was recorded regularly. So the capital stock of each plantation has been calculated as a multiple of the number of its slaves. Account is taken of capital appreciation and depreciation when the number of slaves changes by more than 5 per cent in the period for which the estimate of profits is made.

The multiplier required for this, the average stock of capital employed per slave, has been estimated from plantation records. Valuations made at current market prices have been accepted as they stand, except for land, and after 1808, for slaves. During much of the period, land in the West Indies was scarce and so commanded a rent which appeared in its price. Therefore, I have valued it at the current cost of clearing and cultivating. Similarly, after the prohibition of the African slave trade in 1808 and of the inter-colonial trade in 1825, slaves also became scarce, at least in the more productive colonies. Thus in the years before emancipation the average market price of slaves ranged from £115 in British Guiana to £33 in Antigua.[10]

If the market price was no longer a true measure of the economic cost of a slave, however, it is not easy to establish a more satisfactory alternative. Certainly, estimates of the cost of rearing slaves were published, but these were worthless exaggerations put out by the planters' pressure groups to show that they could not compete with Cuba or Brazil, where the slave trade continued.[11] I have seen no authentic account among plantation records and it would be very difficult to make. The main expense of rearing a slave was its food, but how much did this cost? The slaves grew much of it for themselves on their own provision grounds. But no one knows, and perhaps no white man ever knew, how a child's needs were met there, whether through its own labour, through increased efforts by its parents (and what did this cost their master in the canefields?), or by their sacrifice of income from sales of the surplus in the markets. The rest of the slaves' needs were met by the master's purchases — these alone are easily accounted for — and by gang labour under his instructions. But what price should be put on this? Much of it was done outside the cane-planting and harvesting seasons, which were the times of greatest demand for labour. Also, on some plantations, particularly in Barbados and the Leeward Islands, food crops were grown on the cane lands as part of a system of rotation. Therefore, the opportunity cost of labour devoted to growing food is uncertain. In short, it is impossible to estimate directly the cost of raising a slave. But for many years before

Table 3 Annual Maintenance Costs per Slave (£ sterling)

	Indian corn	Herrings	Clothing	Medical attendance	Taxes	Total	Index number
1799–1807	2.535	0.930	0.49	0.20	0.30	4.455	100
1808–19	3.250	1.250	0.64	0.25	0.35	5.470	129
1820–34	1.625	0.625	0.42	0.25	0.25	3.170	71

Sources: Plantation accounts.

the abolition of the slave trade planters consistently urged their managers to encourage breeding and avoid purchases 'from the ships'.[12] If this policy was rational then the cost of breeding a slave in the West Indies must have been equal to or less than the market price of a slave of similar quality brought from Africa. For the sake of simplicity I assume that the business of slave supply was in long-run competitive equilibrium and that costs equalled prices, that is, £55 sterling for a plantation slave of average quality in the years 1799–1807.

The economics of slave breeding are not likely to have changed substantially, so I estimate the economic cost of a slave in later years by adjusting the price of 1799–1807 for movements in the price of the food and clothing required for its maintenance and in the costs of medical attendance and taxes. I assume that each slave received annually 6.5 bushels of Indian corn, 56 lbs of pickled herrings, 5 yards of linen, and 4 yards of woollen cloth. The composition of the index of average costs derived on these assumptions is set out in Table 3.[13] The index yields £71 as the average economic cost of a slave for 1808–19, or £64 for 1799–1819, and £39 for 1820–34.

There is one further point. The procedure takes no account of changes in the composition or average quality of the slave labour force. But after the ending of the African slave trade in 1808, and perhaps also before, the proportion of African-born slaves on the plantations fell, and that of Creoles — locally born slaves — rose. Creoles were more valuable than Africans; they had more skills, including a better command of English, and they were more amenable to plantation discipline. So in this way the average quality of plantation slaves was rising. However, in another way it was falling. Most slaves imported from Africa were aged between 10 and 30 years. Therefore, because they were no longer imported after 1808 an unfavourable change occurred in the age distribution of plantation slaves. The most productive slaves aged between about 20 and 40 became relatively less numerous, older and less productive slaves became relatively more numerous. Table 4 sets out the details of these changes, and of the relative values of the different classes of slaves, taken from plantation listings and valuations. In estimating relative values all variables except the ones under consideration have been held constant. Thus, for example, the average value of Creoles in relation to Africans is the average relative value of Creoles of similar age and employment. Relative values may reasonably be used as a measure of quality. On this

Table 4 Relative values and age distributions of slaves, 1799–1834

		1799–1819		1820–34	
Ages	Relative values (Average value age 20–9 = 100)	Age distribution (%)	Percentage of creoles in age group	Age distribution (%)	Percentage of creoles in age group
0–4	15	11	100	11	100
5–9	35	9	100	10	100
10–19	80	18	80	17	100
20–29	100	20	50	18	85
30–39	80	19	50	18	50
40–49	65	12	50	12	50
50–59	40	6	45	9	50
60–	10	5	40	5	45
Percentage of creoles in total population			65		75

Average relative value of Africans 1799–1834 = 100.
Average relative value of creoles 1799–1834 = 120.

Sources: Plantation valuations and listings.

Table 5 Capital employed per slave (£ sterling)

	Slave	Livestock	Buildings utensils	Cultivated land	Total
Lesser Antilles				(2 acres per slave)	
1650–1748	22	5	8	10	45
1749–82	35	5	15	14	69
1783–91	40	6	20	16	82
1792–98	45	7	25	20	97
1799–1819	64	8	30	24	126
1820–34	39	6	25	20	90
Jamaica				(3 acres per slave)	
1670–1748	22	10	10	15	57
1749–82	35	10	25	21	91
1783–91	40	12	30	24	106
1792–98	45	13	35	30	123
1799–1819	64	14	40	36	154
1820–34	39	1	35	30	116
British Guiana				(2 acres per slave)	
1820–34	29	1	45	35	120

Sources: Inventory data in Sheridan, *Sugar and Slavery*; plantation records.

assumption the information set out in Table 4 has been used to compile the following index of the average quality of plantation slaves:

1799–1819	100.0	1820–34	100.2

The change that occurs is trivial: most of the effect of the increasing proportion of creoles is cancelled out by the deterioration of the age distribution. I have therefore ignored it in my calculations.

The estimates of capital employed per slave yielded by these procedures are set out in Table 5. Between the middle of the eighteenth century and the early nineteenth century prices rose; in the 1820s they fell. Equipment became more elaborate; for example wind- and water-mills replaced the cattle-mills of the pioneers. In Jamaica more livestock was kept and more cultivated land was needed to pasture it. British Guiana used more fixed capital per slave than the other colonies, for example, steam engines and unusually large boiling-houses for year-round operation, and its drainage systems made the cost of developing land for cultivation greater. But less livestock was needed because of the natural fertility of the soil and the transport facilities provided by its canals.

II

Table 6 summarizes the results of these calculations. It gives for each colony or group of colonies the average rate of the plantations studied, weighted by the number of their slaves. It distinguishes the main periods of West Indian history, of war and peace, and of high and low prices. How representative is the sample of plantations likely to be? That is the first problem raised by these estimates. It has been chosen to give, so far as is possible, a fair coverage of British West Indian sugar planting as it extended over time and space, but the distribution of evidence is uneven. Before the middle of the eighteenth century plantation records are comparatively scarce; they are scarce also for the colonies of Trinidad and British Guiana, which were added to the British Empire much later, and probably this is not fortuitous. West Indian plantation

Table 6 Average Rate of Profit of Sample Plantations (number of plantations in brackets)

		Barbados (%)	Leeward Islands (%)	Jamaica (%)	Ceded Islands (%)	Trinidad, British Guiana (%)
1689–97	War	—	10.3 (1)	2.1 (1)	—	—
1698–1702	Peace	—	13.6 (1)	7.3 (2)	—	—
1703–13	War	6.2 (1)	8.3 (1)	3.2 (2)	—	—
1714–38	Peace	13.7 (2)	16.1 (1)	4.1 (1)	—	—
1739–48		—	16.4 (1)	13.4 (1)	—	—
1749–55	Peace	3.4 (1)	10.6 (1)	13.0 (2)	—	—
1756–62	War	11.2 (4)	12.9 (1)	14.8 (2)	—	—
1763–75	Peace	5.6 (4)	12.3 (2)	8.9 (2)	5.2 (1)	—
1776–82	War	2.3 (4)	2.4 (3)	3.0 (3)	7.0 (1)	—
1783–91	Peace	5.3 (3)	12.1 (2)	6.4 (4)	15.5 (1)	—
1792–98	War, high prices	6.1 (3)	12.0 (2)	13.9 (2)	22.2 (3)	—
1799–1819	War	5.8 (3)	9.1 (6)	9.6 (3)	10.0 (7)	—
1820–34	Peace, low prices	7.7 (1)	3.9 (6)	5.3 (5)	5.7 (3)	13.3 (2)

Sources: Plantation records.

Table 7 Slave Hiring Rates

	(1)	(2)	(3)	(4)	(5)
	Hiring rates* (pence sterling per day)		Slave values† (£ sterling)		
	Barbados	Jamaica		(1) ÷ (3)	(2) ÷ (3)
1670–1725	6	8	22	0.0011	0.0015
1761–63	6	—	35	0.0007	—
1783–91	7½	16	40	0.0008	0.0017
1792–98	9	22	45	0.0008	0.0020
1799–1819	12	24	64	0.0008	0.0016
1820–34	11	22	39	0.0012	0.0024

Sources: Plantation records; British Library, Sloane 3984, f. 216; Scottish R.O., Airlie Papers, GD 16/27/291.
* Rates for adult field hands.
† Average values for all slaves.

records survive most frequently if their owners became country gentlemen in England or Scotland. In the eighteenth century it was quite easy for them to do so, but changing circumstances made it more difficult for anyone acquiring a plantation for the first time in the last years of slavery. Some obvious problems arise from this. We have no estimates for Jamaica or the Leeward Islands before 1689, or for Barbados before 1703. The rates of profit suggested for Jamaica between 1689 and 1739 are almost certainly too low, for they are taken from the accounts of the Bybrook and Spring plantations, which were being seriously mismanaged during these years.[14] The Ceded Islands between 1763 and 1775 are represented only by two years of the Grand Bras plantation, and the figure of 5.2 per cent seems too low for territories as productive as these. On the other hand, the estimate for them of 22.2 per cent in the years 1792–98 seems too high, for many plantations in Grenada and St Vincent were seriously disturbed by the French and Carib revolts of 1795, but this episode does not appear in the records which have been studied.[15] Lastly, no calculations have been made from plantation records for Trinidad and British Guiana between 1799 and 1819 because none has been found.

As early plantation records are so scarce, it may never be possible to establish conclusively what were the usual rates of profit before the middle of the eighteenth century, but the meagre information can be supplemented with the evidence of hiring rates for slaves. If the market for hirings was competitive — and there is no reason to suppose that it was not — then the ratio between the value of a slave and the rate at which it could be hired should reflect the rates of return usual on this type of capital. Table 7 gives information on this subject. In the late seventeenth and early eighteenth centuries the ratio between a slave's daily hire rate and its market value was much the same as it was to be a hundred years later; presumably the usual rates of profit were much the same also, that is about 10 per cent in Jamaica and 5 or 6 per cent in Barbados where the productivity of the slaves had fallen with the fertility of the soil.[16] We can only guess what the situation was in the Leeward Islands. Before the middle of the eighteenth century their sugar plantations progressed more rapidly than Jamaica's, and therefore they were probably more profitable. Perhaps they yielded as much as 15 per cent on average; this was the experience of the Parham plantations in Antigua.

From 1749 the sample of plantations becomes larger and it is worth trying to make the estimates more precise. On the plantations of the Ceded Islands between 1763 and 1775 the average output of sugar per slave was probably about 12 cwt (see Table 8). During these years the average rate of profit on three plantations of similar productivity on other islands was 10.6 per cent, and I substitute this for the estimate of 5.2 per cent.[17] As for the Ceded Islands in the period 1792–98, it seems that the rebellions of 1795 affected almost all the plantations of Grenada and a fifth of St Vincent's; it cost these estates on average three years' output and a quarter of their slaves. On these assumptions I revise the sample estimate of profit downwards from 22.2 per cent to 13.8 per cent.[18] The average output per slave in Trinidad and British Guiana was about 19 cwt. I suggest as their proxy for the years 1799–1819 Amity Hall, Jamaica, and Calliagua and Pembroke, St Vincent. At this time the average output per slave on these plantations was 17.8 cwt and their rate of profit was 16 per cent. These additions and corrections are combined with the sample

Table 8 Average Sugar Production per Slave (production per slave on sample plantation in brackets) (cwt)

	Barbados	Leeward Islands	Jamaica	Ceded Islands	Trinidad, British Guiana
1650–59	14.5	—	—	—	—
1660–88	9.0	14.0	9.0	—	—
1689–1702	9.0	11.0	9.0 (7.6)	—	—
1703–13	5.2 (4.4)	11.0	9.0 (7.6)	—	—
1714–38	5.2 (6.1)	10.9 (11.6)	8.4 (8.5)	—	—
1739–48	3.5	9.1 (12.2)	7.8 (11.5)	—	—
1749–55	3.7	9.1 (10.1)	8.0 (10.6)	—	—
1756–62	4.0 (3.8)	10.4 (10.2)	8.4 (11.5)	—	—
1763–75	3.9 (3.6)	8.9 (9.7)	9.2 (9.7)	n.d. (14.8)	—
1776–82	2.4	6.9 (6.9)	7.6 (6.3)	n.d. (12.3)	—
1783–91	n.d. (3.9)	n.d. (8.5)	n.d. (10.6)	n.d. (12.5)	—
1792–98	n.d. (5.0)	n.d. (6.9)	10.5 (14.8)	n.d. (12.9)	—
1799–1819	5.5 (7.1)	9.9 (10.1)	12.0 (13.7)	10.9 (15.7)	n.d.
1820–34	6.0 (6.2)	8.3 (9.2)	11.1 (11.7)	13.2 (12.2)	18.9 (19.4)

Sources: Sugar production estimated from statistics of sugar imports into England and Wales or Great Britain (adding 30 per cent to take account of losses in shipment and sales in other markets) from Dunn, *op. cit.*, p. 203; Sheridan, *Sugar and Slavery*, pp. 487–92; N. Deerr, *The History of Sugar*, 2 vols (1949–50), I, 193–202; Ragatz, *Statistics*, p. 20. Number of slaves in each colony from Dunn, *op. cit.*, pp. 87–88, 127, 141, 155, 169, 171; Sheridan, *Sugar and Slavery*, pp. 124–233, 452–59; R. Pares, *Merchants and Planters* (Cambridge, 1960), p. 84; Ragatz, *Statistics*, p. 5; *Number of Slaves Registered Originally and at each Subsequent Registration* (P.P. 1833, xxvi, 474); *Population Returns Received from the Slave Colonies by the Colonial Registry Office since 1833* (P.P. 1835, LI, 289). I assume that the following proportions of each colony's slaves were employed on sugar plantations: Jamaica 1670–1748, 1792–1834, 50 per cent; Jamaica 1749–91, Dominica, St. Lucia, 60 per cent; Barbados, Trinidad, British Guiana, 70 per cent; Leeward Islands, Grenada, St Vincent, Tobago, 80 per cent.

estimates for 1749–1834 in Table 9. The calculation of the British West Indian average rate of profit has been weighted by an estimate of the amount of capital employed on sugar plantations in each colony.

Having made these adjustments, may we now accept the sample of plantations as representative? It comes out well by the two criteria most readily available: the productivity of their slaves was close to the average for their colonies, and the quality of their sugar, as measured by the prices that it fetched, was close to the market average.[19] But in one way the sample is certainly unrepresentative: it is composed almost wholly of the estates of absentees, while among plantation owners in general the rate of absenteeism probably did not exceed 50 per cent for most of the eighteenth century, although it had reached about 70 per cent by the 1820s.[20] But it has been suggested that absenteeism caused much inefficiency and waste, so is it not possible that on this account the sample seriously understates the average rate of profit?

Unfortunately, there is information for only a handful of estates owned wholly or in part by residents, to compare with the performance of those owned by absentees. Ownership of the Jamaican plantations Bybrook and Spring was

Table 9 Adjusted Estimates of Average Rates of Profit (per cent)

	Barbados	Leeward Islands	Jamaica	Ceded Islands	Trinidad, British Guiana	All British West Indies
1749–55	3.4	10.6	13.0	—	—	10.1
1756–62	11.2	12.9	14.8	—	—	13.5
1763–75	5.6	12.3	8.9	10.5	—	9.3
1776–82	2.3	2.4	3.0	7.0	—	3.4
1783–91	5.3	12.1	6.4	15.5	—	8.5
1792–98	6.1	12.0	13.9	13.8	—	12.6
1799–1819	5.8	9.1	9.6	10.0	16.0	9.6
1820–34	7.7	3.9	5.3	5.7	13.3	7.1

Sources: Plantation records.

shared between a resident and an absentee. Both yielded low profits early in the eighteenth century, but from the 1750s Spring improved greatly. There are also John Pinney's accounts for his Mountravers plantation on Nevis, which cover both his years as a resident between 1768 and 1783 and his subsequent experience as an absentee. For the period 1768–75 his profits, at 10 per cent per annum, were no better than those of many absentee estates, but during the difficult years of the American War of Independence they were exceptionally good. As an absentee, Pinney found his rate of profit slightly reduced, to about 9 per cent on average. But probably much of this shortfall was due to the arrival at Nevis in 1787 of the borer worm, a highly destructive cane parasite. This affected all plantations on the island more or less, whether they were owned by residents or absentees.[21] So on this subject the plantation accounts are inconclusive: residence might be accompanied by either high or low profits. It has already been noticed that the quantities and qualities of sugar produced by the plantations of the sample, most of which belonged to absentees, did not differ much from the averages for their colonies. So what evidence there is suggests that absenteeism had little effect upon profits and that the sample is representative.

III

What conclusions may now be drawn on the problems mentioned in the introduction? First, it seems that sugar planting in the British West Indies was profitable throughout the years of slavery. In the 1650s the pioneers of Barbados probably made very large profits indeed, perhaps as much as 40 or 50 per cent,[22] but these were the result of special circumstances, in particular the disruption of the plantations of Brazil by the war between the Dutch and the Portuguese. The reduction of sugar prices through the normal processes of competition seems to have brought West Indian profits to a more modest level by the later seventeenth century. They declined furthest in Barbados, where a fall in yields accompanied the fall in prices, and the clamours of this colony were mainly responsible for the protective laws passed in favour of the sugar planters in the 1730s, and for the spread of the notion of 'soil exhaustion' as the nemesis of West Indian agriculture. The other colonies were more prosperous. On the whole, West Indian profits compare well with those made elsewhere. Dr Grassby has suggested that a return of about 10 per cent was usual for seventeenth-century merchants.[23] Prof. Anstey has estimated an average rate of 9.5 per cent for the British slave trade between 1761 and 1807, and the profits of other businesses are not likely to have been any higher than this in the eighteenth century, except perhaps during the early years of important technical innovations.[24]

With planters' profits averaging about 10 per cent, is it likely that the British West Indies were profitable to society at large when account has been taken of their incidental costs? This is not the place to discuss fully the examinations of this subject by Profs. Sheridan and Thomas, but it should be noticed that the estimates of profits from planting which they use seem too low. Their calculations are made for Jamaica in the early 1770s and scaled up for the British West Indies as a whole. They derive from Edward Long's *History of Jamaica* a figure of £450,000 for profits on production in the economy. Perhaps £300,000 of this can be attributed to the sugar plantations, which suggests a yearly profit of about £3 per slave and a rate of return of 3 per cent on capital.[25] But this is much less than my sample estimate for Jamaica in the years 1763–75 (8.9 per cent), less than the rate suggested by Long himself as usual for particular plantations (about 10 per cent),[26] and indeed less than Long's average earnings from his own estate (9.5 per cent).[27] The sample estimates suggest instead an annual profit on sugar production of £800,000 in Jamaica and £1,700,000 in the British West Indies as a whole, or about £1,200,000 and £2,500,000 respectively if profits from other staples were included. Perhaps discussion of the social profitability of the British West Indies could usefully be reopened.

Lastly, what was happening to the plantations during the last half-century before emancipaiton? Were they sliding towards bankruptcy as Ragatz argued? It seems to me, as to other recent writers, that his story of dilapidation and futility is too pessimistic. Certainly the years of the American War of Independence were miserable. For the first and only time in the eighteenth century Britain lost command of the sea to her commercial rivals, supplies from North America were cut off, and the slaves starved. But profits recovered well in the next decade and were maintained through the vicissitudes of the French wars; production costs may have risen, but sugar prices rose also. Depression came only in the 1820s. Then prices fell with the end of wartime scarcities, and with the growth of production in the newly acquired territories the older colonies lost their monopoly power in the British market. Also the burden of the sugar duties, levied at specific rates, increased with the postwar deflation. The effective rate *ad valorem* on British West Indian muscovado sugar, which had been 20 per cent in the 1770s and 35 per cent during the Napoleonic Wars, reached 50 per cent in 1829. The rates of duty were kept up, with some slight relief in 1830, partly for fiscal reasons, partly from political convenience (the sugar planters were one of the weakest interest groups in contemporary society), and partly to put pressure on the colonies to improve the condition of their slaves. In this way it was the growth of anti-slavery feeling in England that caused the decline of plantation profits and not the decline of profits that encouraged anti-slavery feeling, as some have supposed. But in spite of their difficulties the plantations were still viable, covering their costs and yielding modest profits. Productivity was maintained everywhere and increased in Barbados with improved techniques. However much they complained, the planters still sought to maintain their capital and go on making sugar.

University of Edinburgh

Notes

1. A. Smith, *The Wealth of Nations*, 2 vols (1776). See esp. Bk IV, Chap. 7, 'Of Colonies'.
2. R. B. Sheridan, 'The Wealth of Jamaica in the Eighteenth Century', *Economic History Review*, 2nd ser., XVIII (1965), 292–311; R. P. Thomas, 'The Sugar Colonies of the Old Empire: Profit or Loss for Great Britain?', *ibid.*, XXI (1968), 30–45; R. B. Sheridan, 'The Wealth of Jamaica in the Eighteenth Century: A Rejoinder', *ibid.*, 46–61.
3. L. J. Ragatz, *The Downfall of the Planter Class in the British Caribbean, 1763–1833* (New York, 1928).
4. R. B. Sheridan, *Sugar and Slavery* (Barbados, 1974), Chap. 16; W. A. Green, 'The Planter Class and British West Indian Sugar Production, before and after Emancipation', *Economic History Review*, 2nd ser., XXVI (1973), 448–63.
5. R. K. Aufhauser, 'The Profitability of Slavery in the British Caribbean', *Journal of Interdisciplinary History*, V (1974), 45–67.
6. They are listed in the Appendix.
7. The assumptions about hogshead capacity, proportions shipped, and losses in transit are based upon plantation records. Sugar prices for 1674–1775 from Sheridan, *Sugar and Slavery*, pp.496–97; 1776–89, 'The Average Price of Antigua Sugars at the British Market since 1769. Taken from the Books of a Mercantile House in London', *House of Commons Papers, 1731–1800, Accounts and Papers*, XXVI, 1789, No. 646a, Pt 5. Antigua; 1790–91, 1818–19, 1834, plantation records; 1792–1817, 1820–33, annual average of sugar prices from the *London Gazette* printed in L. J. Ragatz, *Statistics for the Study of British Caribbean Economic History, 1763–1833* (1927), p. 8. Usually prices were slightly higher in the outports than in London, but apparently this was because their markets were narrower and their means of payment less secure. The published prices for 1726–58 have been criticized as likely to understate the true average because they are derived from the sales of sugar paid to the crown on account of the 4½ per cent export duty, which may have been of low quality. But insofar as it has been possible to check this, crown sugar does not seem to have been much worse than the average. Between 1749 and 1758 its mean price was 34s. 5d. while sugar from the Parham plantations, Antigua, sold for 35s. 1d. Somerset Record Office (R.O), Tudway Papers, Box 12.
8. Somerset R.O., Tudway Papers, Box 12.
9. For further details see R. Pares, *War and Trade in the West Indies* (Oxford, 1936), pp.495–500.
10. *Averages of Sales in the Colonies Affected by the Slavery Abolition Act* Parliamentary Papers, 1837–38, XLVIII, 329; D. Eltis, 'The Traffic in Slaves between the British West Indian Colonies, 1807–33', *Economic History Review* 2nd ser., XXV (1972), 55–64.
11. See, for example, *Statements . . . relating to the Commercial, Financial, and Political State of the British West India Colonies*, House of Lords Sessional Papers, 1831, VI, 120–28.
12. See, for example, National Library of Scotland, Nisbet Papers, MS 5477, Letter Book of William Chisholme, 1797–1810; Somerset R.O., Dickenson Papers, DD/DN 468, Letter Book of William Dickenson, 1792–94.
13. These assumptions, and information about prices, the costs of medical attendance, and taxes per slave, are taken from plantation accounts. See also J. H. Bennett, *Bondsmen and Bishops: Slavery and Apprenticeship on the Codrington Plantations of Barbados, 1710–1838* (Berkeley, 1958), especially pp.37–43, 102, 132. Of course, as I have already indicated that only a part of the slaves' food was usually bought in, it is inconsistent to use market prices as a measure of costs. But this seems to be the least satisfactory solution that is possible for the problem. On another occasion I hope to discuss more thoroughly the economics of food-growing on sugar plantations.
14. For Bybrook plantation see R. S. Dunn, *Sugar and Slaves* (1973), pp.212–22; for Spring see D. K. Jones, 'The Elbridge, Woolnough and Smyth Families of Bristol in the Eighteenth Century, with Special Reference to the Spring Plantation, Jamaica' (unpublished M. Litt. thesis, Bristol University, 1972).
15. Of the plantations studied only Grand Bras was affected by rebellion, and its accounts do not survive for the period 1795–1801.
16. Slaves were usually hired by the day. It is difficult to convert a daily rate of hiring into an annual return without knowing how regularly they were employed or what were the incidental costs of ownership. But in the late eighteenth and early nineteenth centuries the usual rate of return to owners of hired slaves was considered to be about 10 per cent. (Rhodes House Library, Oxford, Ramsay Papers, MS Brit. Emp. s. 2, f.91; Young Papers, MS West Ind. t. 1, vol. III, f.11, vol. v, f.48). It may seem puzzling that hiring rates fell so little in Jamaica in the 1820s when plantation profits were almost certainly reduced. I think that the discrepancy is due to the nature of the market for hirings. Slaves were usually hired to dig cane holes, the hardest of plantation work. Much of this kind of labour was provided by specialist jobbing gangs built up for the purpose by middle-class whites as a form of investment. Before the

ending of the slave trade these jobbing gangs had usually been recruited by purchase from Africa. So because of this, and because of the nature of their work, their rate of depletion after 1808 was particularly high. At the same time plantation owners were increasingly reluctant to hire out their slaves, because they were anxious to raise fertility and reduce mortality. For both these reasons the supply of labour for hire was greatly lessened. The decline in the value-to-hire ratio may reflect the increased pessimism of slave owners because of the deterioration of the economic climate and the progress of the British campaign for emancipation.

17. The plantations are Spring, Jamaica, Mountravers, Nevis, and Parham, Antigua. Their average output per slave was 10 cwt.
18. See Ragatz, *Downfall of the Planter Class*, pp.220–23; G. Turnbull, *Narrative of the Revolt and Insurrection of the French Inhabitants of the Island of Grenada* (Edinburgh, 1795), p.163; Greater London Record Office (Middlesex Records), Cooper-Franks Papers, Acc. 775/953/13.
19. For productivity see Table 8. To assess quantity the average prices of sugar reported in the *London Gazette* have been compared with the London prices for sugar from the following estates: Newton, Barbados, 1793–1802; Parham, Antigua, 1791–1832; Windward and Clare Hall, Antigua, 1815–24; Dickenson, Jamaica, 1821–29; Cane Garden, St Vincent, and Hillsborough, Dominica, 1796–1828; Calliagua and Pembroke, St Vincent, 1809; Success and Veedenhoop, Demerara, 1824–32. The price of sugar from the sample estates was on average 1.4 per cent higher than the *Gazette* average.
20. Absentees owned 30 per cent of Jamaica's sugar estates in 1775, and 84 per cent in 1832: R. B. Sheridan, 'Simon Taylor, Sugar Tycoon of Jamaica, 1740–1813', *Agricultural History*, XLV (1971), 287. For the 1820s see also P.R.O. Colonial Registers of Slaves, T71, which usually indicate whether the return for a plantation was made by its owner or by his attorney.
21. For the borer's effects on other plantations on Nevis, see Department of Manuscripts, University College of North Wales, Bangor, Stapleton-Cotton Papers, especially Bundle 18.
22. Output per slave was about 14.5 cwt. The average price of a hundredweight of sugar in Europe in the 1650s was about 54s. or 38s. to the planter net of marketing costs: N. W. Posthumus, *Inquiry into the History of Prices in Holland* (Leiden, 1946), p.119. Revenue per slave: £27 6s. On the evidence of plantation accounts for later years costs per slave are not likely to have exceeded £6–7. Profits per slave: £21 on a capital of £45.
23. R. Grassby, 'The Rate of Profit in Seventeenth-Century England', *English Historical Review*, LXXXIV (1969), 733.
24. R. Anstey, *The Atlantic Slave Trade and British Abolition* (1975), Chap. 2; F. Crouzet (ed.), *Capital Formation in the Industrial Revolution* (1972), pp.195–96.
25. Sheridan, 'Wealth of Jamaica', 305; Thomas, *loc. cit.*, 34–36. Sheridan, 'Rejoinder', 56, revised his estimate of profits upwards from £450,000 to £534,700. About 114,000 of Jamaica's 190,000 slaves worked on sugar plantations at this time.
26. E. Long, *The History of Jamaica*, 3 vols (1774), I, 459–62.
27. F. W. Pitman, 'The Settlement and Financing of British West India Plantations in the Eighteenth Century', in *Essays in Colonial History presented to Charles McLean Andrews by his Students* (New Haven, 1931), p.275.

Appendix

This Appendix sets out the estimates of plantation profits summarized in Table 6 and the sources upon which they are based.

Name of colony and plantation	Average annual profits (£ sterling)	Average number of slaves	Average rate of profit (%)
1. BARBADOS			
Newton			
1706–13	477	171	6.2
1714–16, 1724	1,448	171	18.8
1756–62	1,777	243	10.6
1763–75	1,068	255	6.1
1776–82	391	242	2.3
1783–91	1,570	251	7.6
1792–8	1,495	262	5.9
1799–1815	2,313	255	7.2
Seawells			
1756–62	1,103	103	15.5
1763–75	1,119	162	10.0
1776–82	829	179	6.7
1783–91	575	189	3.7
1792–8	1,509	186	8.4
1799–1804	837	180	3.7
Mount Alleyne			
1756–62	642	158	5.9

1768–75	721	161	6.5
1776–82	709	161	6.4

Source: London University Library, Newton Papers, MS 523.

Codrington			
1722–30	1,003	227	9.8
1750–55	469	198	3.4
1756–62	1,879	194	14.0
1763–75	412	287	2.1
1776–82	– 546 (loss)	284	– 2.8 (loss)
1783–91	958	270	4.3
1792–98	1,215	261	4.8
1799–1819	2,151	293	5.8
1820–29	2,472	359	7.7

Sources: United Society for the Propagation of the Gospel, London, Codrington Plantation Papers; F. J. Klingberg (ed.), *Codrington Chronicle* (Berkeley, 1949), pp.78–82.

2. LEEWARD ISLANDS

Parham, Antigua			
1689–97	694	150	10.3
1698–1702	915	150	13.6
1703–13	561	150	8.3
1714–38	1,235	170	16.1
1739–48	2,106	285	16.4
1749–55	2,401	329	10.6
1756–62	3,375	379	12.9
1763–75	4,190	464	13.1
1776–82	1,996	515	5.6
1783–91	5,457	502	13.3
1792–98	6,385	532	12.4
1799–1819	5,009	561	7.1
1820–6	2,349	574	4.5

Source: Somerset R.O., Tudway Papers.

Windward, Antigua			
1776–82	– 863 (loss)	900	– 1.4 (loss)
Windward and Clare Hall, Antigua			
1815–19	14,758	1,100	10.6
1820–30	4,376	1,100	4.4

Source: Gloucestershire R.O., Codrington Papers, D1610, A12, A49.

Mountravers, Nevis			
1768–75	1,217	174	10.1
1776–82	1,554	186	12.1
1783–91	1,436	191	9.2
1792–8	2,221	209	11.0
1799–1802	1,574	206	6.1
Stoney Grove, Nevis			
1826–34	– 45 (loss)	209	– 0.2 (loss)

Sources: Bristol University Library, Pinney Papers; R. Pares, *A West-India Fortune* (1956), pp.89, 91.

Hill Estate, St Christopher			
1816–19	3,309	206	12.7
1820–24	851	196	4.8
Lower Estate, St. Christopher			
1816–19	435	103	3.4
1820–24	97	97	1.1

Source: Berkshire R.O., Estridge Papers, D/EX 292 El.

3. JAMAICA

Bybrook			
1687–91	520	139	6.6
1697–98	−410 (loss)	103	−7.0 (loss)
1698–1702	297	109	4.8
1703–13	196	121	2.8

Source: Somerset R.O., Helyar of Coker Court Papers.

Spring			
1700–02	439	69	11.2
1703–13	149	69	3.8
1714–38	163	69	4.1
1746–48	543	71	13.4
1749–55	1,123	83	14.9
1756–62	1,415	103	15.1
1763–75	1,048	132	8.7
1776–82	782	124	0.7
1783–91	199	90	2.1
1792–98	1,904	84	18.4
1799–1800	2,014	100	13.1

Source: Bristol Archives Office, Smyth of Ashton Court Papers, AC/WO/16.

Mesopotamia			
1751–55	3,150	280	12.4
1756–62	3,580	268	14.7
1763–75	2,124	260	9.0
1776–82	870	261	3.7
1783–87	3,704	274	12.8
1821–31	1,509	382	3.4
Island			
1822–27	2,388	184	11.2

Source: Bodleian Library, Oxford, Clarendon Deposited Papers.

Dickenson Estates			
1779–82	1,351	468	3.2
1783–87	2,328	480	4.6
1821, 1827, 1829	3,209	631	4.4

Sources: Wiltshire R.O., Dickenson Papers, 282/1, 282/3; Somerset R.O., Dickenson Papers, DD/DN 469, 478–80.

York			
1785–91	2,563	452	5.3

Source: Exeter University Library, Gale-Morant Papers.

Trouthall			
1792–98	2,600	179	11.8

Source: National Library of Scotland, Nisbet Papers, MS 5479.

Dundee			
1803–14	628	219	1.9

Source: Scottish R.O., Thomson, Dickson & Shaw Papers, GD 241/172.

Amity Hall			
1805–19	5,788	253	14.9
1820–33	1,845	248	6.4

Source: Surrey R.O., Goulburn Papers.

4. CEDED ISLANDS			
Grand Bras, Grenada			
1774-75	1,512	421	5.2
1776-82	2,002	416	7.0
1783-91	5,036	395	15.5
1792-95	7,828	430	18.8
1802-08, 1811-13	2,107	360	4.6
Source: Greater London R.O. (Middlesex records), Cooper-Franks Papers, Acc. 775/953.			
Hillsborough, Dominica, and Cane Garden, St. Vincent			
1796-98	6,612	240	28.4
1799-1819	2,747	230	9.5
1820-22	1,551	230	7.5
Sources: Royal Commonwealth Society Library, London, Greg Papers; Rhodes House Library, Oxford, Greg Papers, MS West Ind. t. 2.			
Melville Hall, Dominica			
1802-07	2,678	18	10.7
Source: Scottish R.O., Balfour-Melville Papers, GD 126.			
Pembroke, St. Vincent			
1801-06	5,741	261	17.5
Calliagua, St. Vincent			
1801-06	3,672	185	15.8
Source: Rhodes House Library, Oxford, Young Papers, MS West Ind. t. 1.			
Richland Park, St. Vincent			
1810-17	216	131	1.3
1826-34	236	120	2.2
Source: Bristol University Library, Pinney Papers.			
5. DEMERARA			
Success			
1821, 1825, 1827-31	7,489	485	12.9
Vreedenhoop			
1823, 1827-30	6,567	394	13.9
Source: Clwyd County R.O., Gladstone Papers, CH 39, 79, 144.			

The French West Indian Sugar Business

ROBERT STEIN

Political reason insists the the colonies always be dependent upon the mother country.
— 'Sur les retours des colonies' (anonymous memoir)

Once the cane was grown and processed, it remained for the plantation director to sell the sugar, preferably at a profit. In selling his sugar, the planter entered into a complex relationship with French or colonical merchants that was often characterized by bitterness on both sides. The planters believed that the merchants were abusing their monopoly privileges over trade with islands, while the merchants accused the planters of subverting the entire colonial system by illegally trading with foreigners. The debate became particularly acrimonious late in the eighteenth century, when colonial debts to French merchants reached unprecedented heights. It is against the background of increasing colonial indebtedness and growing French frustration that the West Indian aspects of the sugar business must be considered.

Any examination of the sugar trade in the colonies must begin with the quantities involved, both per plantation and per colony. In spite of limited and occasionally conflicting evidence, it appears that the average sugar plantation in the French West Indies produced anywhere from 100,000 to 250,000 pounds of sugar. The most reliable figures come from Christian Schnakenbourg's study of Guadeloupe: he estimated that in the late eighteenth century the average Guadeloupe sugar plantation of 181 carrés, of which 57.5 were planted in cane, produced some 900 quintaux (about 90,000 pounds) of sugar. This was clayed sugar, however, and must be converted into its equivalent in muscovado. Using Seymour Drescher's conversion factor of 1.42, the average Guadeloupe plantation produced 1,250–1,300 quintaux of muscovado. This was considerably lower than contemporary estimates of good or even modest yields. Tascher de la Pagerie, for example, claimed in1787 that an average 100-carré plantation should yield 3,500 quintaux of sugar, and a good one 4,000 quintaux. Even if Tascher was talking about muscovado and even if he meant 100 planted carrés, his figures would still be almost double Schnakenbourg's. D'Auberteuil was even more extravagant in 1776, believing that a 150-carré plantation should yield 12,000 quintaux of muscovado. Similar discrepancies existed in productivity-per-slave figures. Schnakenbourg has calculated that on Guadeloupe it took 112 slaves (of whom 85 were adult) to produce 900 quintaux of clayed sugar, each adult slave yielding some 1,500 pounds of muscovado. But contemporary estimates were again much higher. Tascher believed that 100 (adult?) slaves could produce 3,500–4,000 pounds of muscovado, a figure unequalled even by d'Auberteuil, who claimed 2,400 pounds each on a good plantation. D'Auberteuil admitted elsewhere that his figures were somewhat optimistic and that planters could hope to get 2,000 pounds per slave only on exceptionally fertile land.[1]

The contemporary estimates for Saint Domingue seem more reliable, although the data are incomplete. In 1791 Saint Domingue planters exported some 163 million pounds of sugar to France, a figure that rises to 192 million pounds when the 70 million pounds of clayed sugar it includes are converted to their equivalent in muscovado.[2] This was produced on 800 sugar plantations for an average yield of nearly 240,000 pounds (2,400 quintaux) each; the 350 muscovado plantations produced 93

The French Sugar Business in the 18th Century (Baton Rouge, 1988), pp. 74–89.

million pounds, or 270,000 pounds (2,700 quintaux) each, while the 450 clayed-sugar plantations produced a bit more than 200,000 pounds (2,000 quintaux) each (muscovado equivalent). These figures are much higher than their Guadeloupe counterparts, reflecting the larger plantation sizes on Saint Domingue and, perhaps, their greater fertility. Some Saint Dominque plantations were immense, like Grande Place, owned by the Marquis de Gallifet.[3] With nearly 400 slaves, it produced up to 650,000 pounds of sugar (muscovado equivalent) in one year. This was nearly ten times the output of a small plantation on Martinique, such as the one at Anse à l'Ane owned by the Comtesse de la Rochefoucault and the Marquise de Cheylarfont. There some 150 slaves produced about 70,000 pounds of sugar per year (muscovado equivalent) in the 1770s.[4]

Colonial production figures would be even higher if they were complete. Unfortunately, reliable statistics exist only for exports to France, and there is no sure way of ascertaining gross production figures. There are a few eighteenth-century estimates of colonial sugar production, but these are of limited value and usually ignore the problem of smuggling.[5] In spite of numerous laws to the contrary, smuggling was a major business in the French West Indies, and it undoubtedly consumed a significant portion of the French colonial sugar crop. The most notorious smugglers were the Guadeloupeans, although they may well have been rivalled by residents of the south of Saint Domingue. Schnakenbourg has estimated that between 1667 and 1789, anywhere from 17 to 60 per cent of the annual Guadeloupe sugar crop went to smugglers, with the overall average approaching 40 per cent.[6] This is probably higher than the rest of the French colonies, but there is no way of knowing for sure. It is dangerous enough to assume a constant rate of smuggling, let alone attempt to identify that rate.[7] All that can be said for certain is that Saint Domingue produced from two-thirds to three-quarters of all French West Indian sugar late in the Old Regime.

In selling his quarter of a million pounds, or 250 barrels, of sugar each year, the typical planter wanted both high prices and the security of a guaranteed market, a combination not always feasible. In practice, therefore, planters had to decide whether to use the services of a middleman based either in the colonies or in France. Although most planters opted for these services, many did not and instead tried to market their own sugar. Basically, there were two ways of disposing of sugar without having recourse to merchant intermediaries.[8] Planters could sell directly to ship captains or to foreigners. Selling directly to captains was the time-honored means that had been so useful in the colonies' early days. It was essentially a barter system: the passing ship captain traded flour, wine, or manufactured goods from Europe to the planter for sugar either on hand or to be produced after harvest. Although such a system was apparently declining by the eighteenth century, it was still used until the Revolution, particularly by small shippers and out-of-the-way planters. Now, however, the shippers exchanged slaves for sugar, with both sides saving the commissions charged by merchants.

The second direct-sale system was illegal because it involved selling sugar to foreigners. Throughout most of the Old Regime, it was illegal for French West Indian planters either to sell sugar to foreigners or to purchase most commodities from them. However, in areas that proved to be unpopular with French merchants, such as the Lesser Antilles and the south of Saint Domingue, many planters came to depend upon the services of British, American, or even Dutch smugglers. Although present from the earliest days of colonial settlement, smuggling first became a major factor in the colonial economy during the War of the Austrian Succession (1744–48). As the Conseil Supérieur of Martinique notes in 1759: 'That war, so glorious for the nation through its victories, became harmful for our colonies through the weakness of our navy . . . . The need to turn abroad forced the creation of a trading system.'[9] This new system relied upon the sale of French colonial commodities to foreigners in return for flour, cod, manufactured goods, and especially slaves.

Illegal deals with foreigners took place in several ways.[10] One was quite traditional, with transfers of merchandise made in secluded inlets at night. Variations of this method were numerous and sophisticated, but all involved some nocturnal sleight of hand, such as this sugar-for-slaves trade described in 1730:

> To go to this island [the Dutch Colony of Saint Eustatius] in total security to buy Negroes with the intent of reselling them, the French on Martinique make simulated declarations to the Bureau des Domaines claiming that they are shipping to Saint Domingue a certain number of local Negroes that [in reality] they have borrowed from their neighbors. The declaration made for form's sake, the Negroes return to their masters, and during the night the false claimants load their boats with sugar or other

commodities and sail to Saint Eustatius, where they trade their cargo for the number of Negroes claimed on their declaration and proceed to sell them on Saint Domingue.[11]

Another means of smuggling was more innovative; it involved filling barrels labelled SYRUP with sugar and selling them openly to foreigners. After the Seven Years' War, the government allowed the colonists to sell the largely unwanted beverages to foreigners under the well-defined — but scarcely obeyed — conditions. The planters viewed this as an open invitation to fraud and were encouraged to do so by the generally benign neglect of the colonial administration. As one observer put it: 'Whole lots are sold in molds to be shipped to Havana and new England. How many other Americans are there who, while declaring "syrups" and "tafias", are actually exporting [clayed sugar] . . . ?' So common were these and similar practices that the French consul in Boston wrote to his superior that 'the illegal commerce is conducted openly between our islands and my department'.[12]

Illicit transactions affected the colonial economy and aroused the ire of French merchants. According to the merchants, massive foreign purchases raised sugar prices in the islands, but low foreign shipping costs plus government subsidies prevented similar price increases in Europe.[13] Unaided by subsidies and faced with high shipping costs, the French merchants were hurt by high purchase prices and low sale prices. The French merchants also lost when foreigners illegally sold goods to the French West Indian planters. Although the French merchants had a theoretical monopoly over most kinds of sales to the islands, foreigners subverted that monopoly, particularly from 1744 to 1783, and introduced vast quantities of slaves, flour, cod, and manufactured goods. In 1765 one person observed, 'The English are selling Negroes all over Saint Domingue.' And the previous year he noted that 'English flour continues to be introduced freely and with all kinds of abuses.' The Dutch also participated in the illicit trade, although they specialized in selling manufactured goods to the planters. As Frances Armytage remarked: 'The Dutch at St. Eustatius were rich and prosperous solely because they were the distributors of European manufacturers to all the French islands in the vicinity. . . . The French had not been able to supply their own colonies with enough provisions and manufactures for some time, and St. Eustatius had become their chief source of supply.' These purchases claimed a significant quantity of French West Indian commodities: 'A paper . . . stated that the French West Indian produce loaded at St. Eustatius was enough to fill forty or fifty large ships in a year.[14]

Even so, most exports of sugar were legal and were facilitated by the services of one or two merchants. Basically, the planter had his sugar shipped to a French merchant, either with or without the intermediary of a local merchant, and then the sugar was usually sold to a Dutchman or a German. The contractual relationships, first, between the planter and the local and/or French merchant and, then, between the colonial and the metropolitan merchants varied according to the size and financial health of all concerned. Depending on the relative strength of the parties involved, the planter was either in control of the entire affair or very much at the mercy of the merchant(s).

Owners of small plantations had to limit their dealing to local merchants or, in the special case of Guadeloupe before the Seven Years' War, to merchants on Martinique.[15] The production of these small plantations was too small to necessitate direct dealings with the French ports, and local intermediaries were capable of handling it all. The colonial merchant, usually located in the larger towns, such as Cap Français, Port-au-Prince, or Saint Marc on Saint Domingue, Fort Royal on Martinique, and Pointe-à-Pitre or Basse Terre on Guadeloupe, could purchase the sugar from the planter for resale to French captains. More often, he could act as a commissioned agent, finding a buyer for the sugar and taking a substantial (usually 5 per cent) commission on the transaction. In either case the merchant profited from the deal, and the small planter made a quick sale.

Larger planters required more sophisticated arrangements involving the active participation of merchants in France. The planter's sugar was shipped to France, where it was sold by a merchant who kept a commission on the sale and remitted the rest to the planter. Financially healthy planters had great freedom in choosing which French merchants to patronize and were under no obligation to be faithful to any one agent. Of course, sugar tended to follow family lines, with planters preferring to use the trustworthy services of relatives, but in the absence of convenient family connections good service was the only criterion to adopt. Not having a long-term contract with a French merchant house, the planter was free to ship his goods on the first available ship going to the preferred destination, and solvent planters could deal with merchants in several French ports.

Once planters were in financial difficulties, their range of options was limited, at least on paper. They had to accept long-term arrangements with French merchant firms even though such arrangements were often draconian.[16] In extreme cases, hard-pressed planters had to abandon real control over their plantations to the French merchants, who in turn took over the often substantial debts of the plantation. Some French merchant houses specialized in this type of transaction, and the Bordeaux firm of Henry Romberg, Bapst and Company had contracts with nearly sixty planters on Saint Domingue in the 1780s.[17] Romberg, Bapst and Company agreed to pay off plantation debts, guarantee the delivery of European merchandise and African slaves to the plantations, and run the estates efficiently; in return the company had exclusive rights to sell the products of one plantation and priority in shipping the commodities in its ships. Such arrangements had certain advantages for the planters. Relieved of his debts and usually guaranteed a reasonable pension by the merchant, the planter was put back on his feet while retaining ownership of, albeit not control over, his plantation. The merchant, on the other hand, was drawn into the quagmire of colonial debt and could be extricated only in the unlikely case of the plantation turning a profit. But to transform virtually bankrupt plantations into profitable enterprises took more time and more money than most companies could afford, and the new plantation owners — the French merchants — quickly became overextended.

As Françoise Thésée noted, indebted planters used the French merchants more as bankers than as commissioned agents. Planters in effect used their merchant associates to finance inefficient operations, and by the end of the Old Regime the colonies were in considerable debt to the port merchants. Most of this money represented slave purchases that the planters had made but could not afford. This was not necessarily a new phenomenon; even in 1765 Stanislas Foache of Le Havre remarked, 'The old cargo debts are almost all for Negroes; there are very few for merchandise.'[18] Since it was difficult to force colonial debtors to pay, especially with foreclosure almost unknown on the islands, the only way the merchants could get their money back was to lend or invest even more money, take over running the plantations, and once again hope to make a profit. The planter was well protected by local custom and had little reason to fear the loss of his estate. Local authorities were reluctant to force planters to pay their debts and all but refused to consider seizing real property. The problem originated in the early days of colonial settlement, when it appeared that a period of planter indebtedness was inevitable before profits could accrue. In order to protect the pioneering planters, laws were passed prohibiting the seizure of parts of the estate; in other words, slaves could not be seized by creditors. With the colonies developed, planters used their legal immunity to force loans from metropolitan merchants; they did this simply by contracting debts that they had no intention of repaying.[19]

Needless to say, merchant creditors did not acquiesce in this matter, but they had little chance of winning the battle. The legal administration on Saint Domingue sided with the planters, and exasperated merchants could only lament 'the sad job of recovering debts on Saint Domingue'. Actually, persistent efforts could reap come rewards, but only at the expense of alienating the debtor and losing future business. Most merchants simply considered it impossible to get anywhere with the authorities. 'Real seizures,' wrote one merchant in 1749, 'although permitted in America as in France, have not yet been concluded [successfully] on Saint Domingue. Some have tried this route more than once, but the infinite number of formalities, the lengths of time, and the dearth of legal procedures have disgusted all who have been involved with it.'[20] Ship's captains seemed to have somewhat better luck in dealing with colonists, but even they had to give up when faced with the expenses involved. After a while it simply became too expensive to wait for all payments to be made.

The impossibility of foreclosing left the merchant with little leverage over the planter once the initial commitment was made. The merchant could refuse to make a commitment; he could simply serve as a commissioned agent with no banking role. This, however, was to run the risk of accepting a secondary position permanently. By not offering any exceptional services to the planter, the merchant could not hope to attract as much business. Of course, not all planters were in desperate straits, but it seems that enough were to affect the health of the entire system by the 1780s. On the eve of the French Revolution, economic difficulties put into sharper relief both the similarities and the differences between merchant and planter. On one hand the colonists had to rely heavily on the frequently willing merchant for money; on the other hand the colonists viewed this money as a long-term capital investment, while the merchant thought it was a short-term loan. The result was considerable misunderstanding and bitterness.

In the middle of the dispute were the major colonial merchants. Whereas the smaller colonial merchants were independent retailers purchasing European goods from arriving ships and speculating in small quantities of colonial commodities, larger merchants were usually associated with French commercial houses and acted primarily as representatives of French interests.[21] The major colonial merchants served almost as frontline soldiers in the battle waged against the planters. As such, they had somehow to balance the unrelenting demands of the home office with the realities of colonial life. This was not always an easy task, a fact to which numerous impatient letters bear witness. As one colonial merchant complained to the head office, 'We are between the hammer and the anvil, between your interests and those of our landowners.'[22] The French merchant wanted all of his money immediately, the planter wanted to postpone repayment indefinitely, and the colonial merchant wanted to receive as much as possible from the former without forever losing the latter as a customer.

Most of the major colonial merchant houses were subsidiaries of French companies, although they did not necessarily begin that way. It was not at all unusual for small merchants in the French ports to go to Saint Domingue and make modest fortunes as commissioned agents; they then returned to France to establish major commercial houses using the services of the colonial companies they had created. But whether formed originally by a French merchant temporarily residing in the colonies or by one who had never left France, most significant colonial companies were accountable to parent companies in France. The French company always retained a controlling interest in the colonial one. For example, Stanislas Foache of Le Havre organized a company in Saint Domingue in 1777; Foache held a 50 per cent interest, and two colonial merchants split the remaining 50 per cent. Five years later, Foache reorganized the company as Stanislas Foache, Morange and Company, but again kept a 50 per cent interest personally, in addition to advancing money to two of his three partners. This was quite typical, and similar arrangements existed for other colonial companies.[23] The French supplied the capital and the colonial agent the labor; profits were split accordingly.

Large colonial merchant houses handled all the French merchant's affairs in the area. Among other things, this included running plantations either owned or managed by the merchant; acting as commissioned agents on purchases and sales of slaves, colonial commodities, and European goods; and collecting debts. One overworked colonial merchant complained of his burden in a letter to the main office: 'I beg you to pay a moment's attention to our affairs and to their nature: five plantations in sugar that require constant surveillance: trials, credits . . . and all the costs of exploitation. Three coffee plantations that have the same needs to fill as the sugar plantations. In the office; books, letters, accounts, purchases, barreling, goods to sell, and finally recovering debts, this terrible thing in town and country.'[24]

The colonial merchant also had to be a shrewd observer of the colonial scene: he frequently speculated in sugar or other commodities and had to know what, when, and at what price to buy and sell. Such a wide range of activities required a large staff, and the major colonial merchant houses employed several skilled workers. Preparing to return to France from Cap Français in 1777, Stanislas Foache described his staff in a lengthy letter to his brother in Le Havre.[25] Foache was particularly pleased with the abilities of his workers, whom he preferred above almost all others in the town. The chef de maison described no fewer than eight office workers, at least two of whom later became partners in the company. These two were Hellot, pictured as an honest, intelligent young man of twenty-two who already handled many of the legal affairs of the company and who was to assume responsibility for the company after Foache's departure, and Morange, the meticulous cashier from Saint Domingue who had never been outside Cap Français or seen a plantation. The other employees included the hard-working Pellier; Gerard, the book-keeper from Martinique; Corneille, a local Creole who kept the books rather unsatisfactorily; La Croix, the director of the store or warehouse; and two travelling clerks.

Colonial agents were probably the only people in the colonies certain to make the profits from colonial commerce. Taking a commission on all transactions, they were able to avoid the problems besetting the planters. Although it was commonly believed that sugar planters made vast sums of money, such as was not the case. In spite of hypothetical calculations showing that a well-run estate should net profits of 25 per cent per year, few planters ever realized such profits in practice, and plantation records show losses almost as frequently as gains.[26] Even large, well-organized, and presumably well-run plantations did not necessarily make money. This was the case with the five plantations owned by the Marquis de Gallifet.[27] Worth some 5,500,000 livres in 1784, Gallifet's three sugar plantations (worth 5 million livres) and two coffee plantations (worth 500,000 livres) produced up to 300,000 livres' worth of goods per year. Unfortunately, expenses could be just as high, and in the thirty-two quarters from July 1, 1783, through June, 1791, the estate showed a profit in only sixteen. After eight years the five plantations actually had a net loss of 2,507 livres, even though revenues were nearly 3 million livres. The more modest Bongars sugar plantation did little better in the 1770s.[28] With about 200 slaves it produced 200,000 pounds of sugar per year, and from 1769 to 1779, total income was 1,114,000 livres. Expenses over the same period were 1,108,000 livres, leaving the plantation with a trivial surplus of 6,000 livres on what probably amounted to a capital investment of nearly 1 million livres. Individual plantations were clearly not always prosperous.

The overall picture was similar, especially later in the Old Regime. Very rough estimates indicate that the French colonists sold a maximum of 300 million livres' worth of goods annually before the Revolution. Jean Tarrade estimated that from 1784 to 1790 'imports from the colonies and from the Newfoundland fisheries' were worth some 200 million livres per year, a figure that should be augmented by a maximum of 50 per cent to account for smuggling and losses in transit. Colonial imports during the same period probably amounted to some 175 million to 200 million livres per year: close to 90 million livres for goods shipped directly from France, some 80 million livres for slaves, and the rest for goods purchased illegally from foreigners.[29]. Thus, the colonies had an annual profit of from 100 million to 125 million livres. This, however, was based on a total capital investment of over 2,000, million livres, for a profit of some 5–6 per cent.[30] This figure must be lowered somewhat to ascertain the planters' net profit; commissions charged by middlemen, taxes, and the like prevented the planters from actually receiving all of their money. Indeed, the comité intermédaire of Martinique estimated in 1787 that net profits for all plantations on the island were in the neighborhood of only 2 per cent.[31]

It is commonly assumed that profit rates were higher earlier in the eighteenth century, but the data are not entirely convincing. Indeed, many historians seem to accept the notion of diminishing profits in order to explain the apparently unprecedented rancor that characterized merchant-planter relations following the American Revolution. Christian Schnakenbourg, for example, wrote of an economic crisis afflicting Guadeloupe, the other French West Indies, and perhaps even the entire Caribbean area from 1785 to 1790, an argument also advanced by Jean Tarrade for the French islands. Similar crises have been discerned in the French ports: Jean Meyer spoke of Nantes's declining profits, and François Crouzet implied much the same for Bordeaux.[32] The evidence for such statements, however, is often slight and usually rests on an unproven belief in an earlier golden age of high profits. Unfortunately, such a golden age, if it ever existed, was probably brief and of little significance. It is possible, as Schnakenbourg believes, that the first planters on Guadeloupe made annual profits of 25 per cent or, as Meyer implies, that early slave traders made profits of over 100 per cent, but such examples testify more to the high-risk nature of the early colonial and slave trades than to a subsequent crisis of declining profits. Once transatlantic commerce ceased being the preserve of a few adventurous souls and became another business run by calculating businessmen, it followed the normal laws of the marketplace, reflecting competition and supply and demand. In such conditions, astronomical profits were most unlikely and were due to some exceptional stroke of fortune, such as a sudden and unexpected dearth of ships in port. These quirks notwithstanding, colonial commerce normally provided a 5 per cent annual profit, about the same as good investments in France. Colonial trade did involve greater risks, but it also held out the possibility of greater profits and perhaps the prospect of greater or at least more rapid growth based on loans. In other words, credit was much looser in the colonies than in France.

What was unique about the last decade of the Old Regime was the very size of the entire operation, the increasing needs for captial to keep it functioning smoothly, and the sources of that capital. After the American war, the volume of trade between France and the colonies doubled, and debts increased accordingly. Instead of a recession, as in France, there was a tremendous boom in the 1780s for colonial commerce, and this boom was ultimately financed by credits provided — often voluntarily — by French port merchants on the verge of overextention. The central problem was with the slave trade, and for French slavers the American war was a critical turning point. Before the war, English slavers provided the French West Indies with a large proportion of its slaves, perhaps up to 50 per cent.[33] These slaves were notoriously cheap and provided the French planters with an economical source of labor. After the war the English were effectively excluded from the French West Indian slave market just when that market was expanding appreciably. Now the French merchants were supplying the colonies with virtually all the required slaves, and the French slave trade nearly doubled relative to prewar levels, going from an average of less than 60 expeditions per year to 110 per year. This meant that more than twice as much of the merchants' capital was being tied up for lengthy periods of time in slaving, and colonists' delays in repaying debts provoked an exceptionally strident response from the merchants.[34] Also, it should be noted that during the last decade of the Old Regime more medium-sized merchants were involved in slaving than ever before; these men had far smaller reserves than the large merchants who had dominated slaving in earlier periods, and they were affected more directly by the delays in payment.

Things looked no better from the planters' point of view. Expansion forced them to purchase more slaves than ever before, and the slave population of Saint Domingue alone went from an estimated 260,000 in 1775 to 465,000 in 1789.[35] The new slaves were supplied almost exclusively by French traders and were much more expensive than prewar English (or even French) slaves. In short, planters' expenses were rising rapidly, but revenues were temporarily lagging behind. It would be two or three years before the large labor force affected harvest sizes and plantation income, and it was the question of who was to finance the waiting period that sharply divided merchants from the planters during the 1780s. Thus, the impressive growth of colonial trade created short-term problems of considerable proportion. Had there been sufficient time available, these problems probably would have been resolved to the satisfaction of both planter and merchant, but the French and Haitian revolutions brought the postwar period to an early end and made any such readjustments impossible.

The problems of the 1780s were 'growing pains', aggravated by the intense dislike of the merchants by the planters and the deep suspicions of the planters by the merchants. Tied together in a colonial economy and dependent upon that economy for their prosperity, the merchant and planter nonetheless pursued conflicting short-term policies and had opposing views of their respective roles in the system. The planter believed that the health of the colonial economy was the first priority; as one planter said in 1791 or 1792: 'There are two classes of men on Saint Domingue: the planter and the merchant. The first is the true colonist; he belongs to the land, either through possession or his work. Behold the citizen. The merchant . . . sacrifices all to his cupidity. He lives in Saint Domingue as a gambler lives by a gaming table. Behold the troublemaker.'[36] The French merchant, on the other hand, believed in the subordination of colonial interests to French commercial ones. The colonies should consume French goods and produce exotic commodities that French merchants could sell throughout Europe. Typical were the sentiments of the deputies of commerce: The colonies, they declared, 'consume the excess of the production of our soil and our manufactures . . . . They deliver in return luxury commodities that we lack and that habit has made necessary . . . . It is through sales of colonial commodities — after our own consumption — that we obtain a tribute of 70 million livres from foreign lands.'[37]

Thus, on the eve of the Revolution, there was a split between merchant and planter, but this must not overshadow the close ties between the two throughout the Old Regime. Although neither was completely satisfied with the colonial system and although both tried to gain advantages during the early days of the French Revolution, they realized that their fates were closely linked and that they both relied on the continuation of the slave trade and the slave system for their livelihood. The eighteenth-century French colonial economy depended on the use of slave labor, and slaves bore the burden of the entire operation. In determining just who profited and who lost from the system, it appeared that all were winners save the slaves, Planters, colonial merchants, French merchants, and African merchants made profits from the sales of either slaves or sugar or both, while the use of slave labor helped keep sugar prices relatively low in eighteenth-century Europe.[38] By keeping prices down, merchants helped to create a demand for sugar and coffee, which alone seemed to justify the entire operation.

Notes

1. C. Schnakenbourg, *Les sucreries de la Guadeloupe* (Paris, 1972), 88–89; Seymour Drescher, *Econocide* (Pittsburgh, 1977), 192; Tascher de la Pageine, 'Mes délassements', III, 110–11; Hilliard d'Auberteuil, *Considérations*, I, 236.
2. *Archives de la Chambre de Commerce, masseiles* (hereafter ACCM), H19 (printed in M. Avalle, *Tableau comparatif des pronitions des colonies françaises aux Antilles avec celles des colonies complanises, espagales et hollandaises de l'anneé 1787 à* 1788 (Paris, 1799), Table 11). The manuscript says 1794, but this is clearly impossible; internal evidence suggests 1791.
3. *Archives Nationeles* (hereafter AN), 107AP127, May 22, 1775; AN, 107AP128, dossier 4, May 12, 1784. For production figures see AN, 197AP130, dossier 1 (1790–91).
4. AN, T256/2.
5. See, for example, AN, F12 1639A, 'Mémoire sur les sucres', by an anonymous author. This claims that the French West Indies produced 160,000,000 lbs of sugar annually, but it does not break this figure down by colony or by type of sugar. It also ignores smuggling.
6. Schnakenbourg, *op. cit.*, 118, See also Jean Tarrade, *Le commerce colonial de la France à la fin de l'annien régime* (Paris, 1972), 111.
7. Drescher, *Econocide*, 46–47, 195–96, assumes a 'steady rate of smuggling from 1770 to 1787' and sets his rate at 11.1 per cent of total production. Unfortunately, evidence for these statements appears to be lacking. For a contemporary estimate of illegal sales to foreigners, see M. Weuves, *Réflexions historiques et politiques sur le commerce de France avec des colonies de l'Amérique* (Geneva, 1780), 54, Weuves believed that one-quarter of the production of the Lesser Antilles and one-eight of that of Saint Domingue went to smugglers. Avalle, *op. cit.*, Table 8, put the value of smuggled goods from the French islands at 5 per cent of total production in 1787.
8. On sales see Schnakenbourg, *op. cit.*, 100–26.
9. *Archives Départementales, Bouches du Rhône* (hereafterADBR), C2561, March 7, 1759.
10. Schnakenbourg, *Les sucreries de la Guadeloupe*, 120–21. See also C. Frostin, *Histoire de l'autonomisme colon de la partie française* de Saint Domingue anx XVIIe et XVIIIe siècles (Paris, 1975), Chaps. 9–11; Tarrade, *op. cit.*, 101–12; Frances Armytage, *The Free Port System in the British West Indies*, 1766–1822 (London, 1953), Chap. 3.
11. *Archive Départementales, Loire Attantigne* (hereafter ADLA), C735, mémoire by the Chamber of Commerce of Guienne (Bordeaux), September 2, 1730.
12. ADSM, BDM, 1.48, January 28, 1784; AN, Col F2B 8, July 21, 1784.
13. This was a common complaint. See for example, *Archives commerce Bordeuax* (hereafter ACB), HH49, April 22, 1786, and ADSM, BDM, 1.48, January 28, 1784. On the problems caused by the smugglers, see P. Butel, *La croissance commerciale bordelaise dans la seconde moitié du XVIIIe siècle* (Paris, 1976), 216–21.
14. *Archive Départementales, Seine Maritime* (herafter ADSM), Funds Begoven Demeaux, 1.47, January 14, 1764 [*sic*; it should read 1765], and September 19, 1764; Armytage, *op. cit.*, 35–36.
15. Schnakenbourg, *op. cit.*, 111.
16. Pierre Léon, *Marchands et speculateurs dauphinois dans le monde antillais au XVIII siècle* (Paris, 1963), 81.
17. This company is the subject of F. Thésée, *Les négociants bordelais et les wlons de Saint Domingue* (Paris 1972), upon which this section is largely based.
18. ADSM, BDM 1.47, June 13, 1765.
19. Thésée, *op. cit.*, 261. See also ADSM, BDM, 1.47, May 22, 1765, ADSM, BDM 1.48, February 7, 1784; and Article 48 of the Code Noir.
20. ADSM, BDM, 1.48, February 7 and August 25, 1784; ACCM, BDM, 1.48, June 4, 1749. According to Schnakenbourg, *op. cit.*, 235, there were but six foreclosures on Guadeloupe from 1778 to 1788, and this was a time of economic crisis.
21. For a description of the purchases made by merchants, see Weuves, *op. cit.*, 29.
22. ADSM, BDM, 1.48, May 18, 1784.
23. ADSM, BDM, 1.53, December 28, 1777, and May 15, 1782. For other companies, see Thésée, *op. cit.*, 29–30.
24. ADSM, BDM, 1.47, May 18, 1784.
25. ADSM, BDM, 1.47, January 3, 1777.
26. For example, see Tascher, 'Mes délassements', III, 110–11.
27. AN, 107AP128, dossier, 4, May 12, 1784, and dossier 1, July 1, 1783, to June 30, 1784 (brouillard).
28. AN, T520/2.
29. Tarrade, *op. cit.*, 740 says that 70,000,000 livres' worth were exported, but the colonists paid far more than that once commissions, taxes, and profits — all paid by the colonists — were added.
30. On total investment, see ACCM, H19, which evaluates Saint Domingue plantations at 1,488,000,000 livres. Schnakenbourg, *op. cit.*, 88–89, estimates Guadeloupe's sugar plantations to have been worth 155,000,000 livres; other Guadeloupe plantations plus all of Martinique's plantations would easily amount to more than 357,000,000 livres. For a comparison of profits, see Richard B. Sheridan, *The Development of the Plantations* (Barbados, 1970), 102, which estimates a similar profit on investments in Jamaica at this time. J. R. Ward, 'The Profitability of Sugar Planting in the British West Indies, 1650–1835', *Economic History Review*, XXXI (1978), 208, says that profits averaged about 10 per cent in the eighteenth century.
31. AN, Col F3 84, 'Examen des observations du commerce de la Martinique sur le procès verbal colonial par le comité intermédaire de cette assemblée', 1787.
32. Schnakenbourg, *op. cit.*, 127–239; Tarrade, *op. cit.*, 776, 783; Jo Meyer, *L'armement nantais dans la deuxième moitié du XVIIe siècle* (Paris, 1969), 248, 250; François Crouzet in François Pariset (ed.) *Histoire de Bordeaux* (Bordeaux, 1968), V, 316–17.
33. P. Curtin, *The Atlantic Slave Trade* (Madison, 1969), 211, 216, as corrected by Stein, 'Measuring the French Slave Trade', *Journal of African History*, XIX (1978), 519–20.
34. Stein, 'Profitability of the Nantes Slave Trade, 1753–92, *Journal of Economic History, xxxv (1975)*, 791.
35. C. Frostin, *Les révoltes blanchesà St Domingue aux XVIIe et XVIIIe siècles* (Paris, 1975), 28.
36. *Discours historique sur la cause des désastres de la partie française de Saint Dominque* (Paris, [1792?]), 56–57.
37. AN, Col F2B 8, 'Avis de deputés du commerce', 1785.
38. Robert Paul Thomas and Richard Nelson Bean, 'The Fishers of Men: The Profit of the Slave Trade', *Journal of Economic History*, XXXIV (1974), 885–914.

The Origins of the Commission System in the West India Trade

The Alexander Prize Essay

K. G. DAVIES, M.A.

Read 16 June 1951

The half-century which followed the capture of Jamaica in 1655 was characterized by the consolidation rather than by the expansion of the English interest in the West Indies.[1] In the political sphere this consolidation took several forms. The acquisition of Jamaica, by far the largest English West Indian colony, and the termination of proprietary rule in the Caribee Islands in 1663 brought the greater part of the English West Indian empire under the direct adminstration of the Crown.[2] As a corollary to this extension of Crown rule, the creation of effective institutions for the government of these and other colonies became a matter of urgent necessity. After a series of experiments in the decade following the Restoration, the constitution in 1672 of the Council of Trade and Plantations inaugurated 'a more thorough system of colonial control than had been established by any of its predecessors'.[3] The sum effect of these developments was that London became, in a way that it had never been before, the place where all the major decisions affecting the destinies of the West Indies were taken. From London there issued not only Crown-appointed governors and a stream of Orders-in-Council, but also declarations of the King's pleasure on such minor questions as appointments to colonial judgeships and seats in colonial councils.[4] To London there flowed, besides acts of colonial legislatures for approval or rejection, a torrent of complaints and petitions for redress.

To such a process of centralization the West Indians could not be expected to remain indifferent. Their immediate reaction was to seek for some representation at the centre of business whereby they could obtain reliable, up-to-date information, and through which they could bring pressure to bear on those in whose power they found themselves. These objects were achieved by the formation of associations of West Indian planters resident in England together with London merchants with West Indian connections, and by the appointment of political agents nominated and paid by the several colonial legislatures. The first of these associations, the Committee for the Concern of Barbados, was established in 1671, and shortly afterwards the Jamaica Coffee-House in St. Michael's Alley became a recognized meeting-place for persons interested in that colony.[5] Such associations, whether formal record-keeping bodies like the Barbados Committee or informal like the Coffee-House, provided not only a medium for the exchange of views and co-ordination of private interests but also a repository of expert knowledge and opinion on which the government could and did draw. The political agents, on the other hand, were more directly representative of the interests of the colonies; their duties included the presentation and management of petitions, lobbying of all kinds and the transmission of information.[6]

The growth of absenteeism, especially amongst the planters of substance, helped to divert the interests of many away from the colonies to the wider stage which England afforded. The first generation of English settlers in the West Indies may have been genuine exiles

Transactions of the Royal Historical Society (London), Fifth Series, 001-2, (1952), pp. 89-107.

seeking a fresh start and a clean break from home. But by the later seventeenth century a different type was in the ascendant, and in Barbados at least had already established itself. To some of the second and third generation of planters the West Indies were no more than a point of departure; to others they offered a tolerable fortune followed by retirement to quiet estates in Kent; to others their West Indian estates were mere appendages to more valuable property in England.[7] Some West Indians, like John Blake of Barbados, were already in the seventies of the seventeenth century sending their children to be educated in England.[8] Many, like the Littletons, the Merricks and the Freres, retained family ties with England. Almost, it seems, as soon as the 'frontier phase' in a West Indian colony's history was ended and the estate put on a working footing, the planter and his family began to aspire to the pleasures of civilized life 'at home'.

This focusing of the political interests and social aspirations of the West Indies upon England has its economic counterpart in the post-Restoration period. It is with the concentration of the economic interests of the sugar colonies upon the London market and the machinery by which this concentration was effected that this paper is concerned.[9] Just as the last 40 years of the seventeenth century witnessed the development of political agencies, so they saw also the foundations laid of the commission or 'factorage' system which in the eighteenth century was to become an outstanding characteristic of the West India trade.[10] In its heyday this commission system grew to be something more than a widely adopted method of marketing the most important commodity produced by the Old Empire: it became the means whereby credit, the very life-blood of the West Indies in the eighteenth century, was transmitted from the mother country. For this reason its origins and early development deserve a brief inquiry.

During the seventeenth century trade between England and the West Indies was carried on in at least four different ways. The first settlers had to rely on the fortuitous arrival of a ship bringing reinforcements, stores and provisions, for which they could barter their tobacco, indigo, cotton and other products. But as soon as a settlement had demonstrated its will to survive and its ability to pay, a more regular form of trade sprang up. In 1628, for example, Thomas Littleton, a London merchant, sent three ships to Nevis with provisions, munitions and clothing to the value of £5,000. These goods were consigned to Littleton's factor or agent, whose duty it was to sell them and make suitable returns.[11] This mode of trading was particularly apt for the early years of a new colony's existence. The merchant in London (or in many instances the Dutch merchant) supplied the capital which enabled the necessities of life and labour to be brought to the colonist.[12] In these early days the planter's main concern was to plant, to produce larger crops, to buy more food, more land and more labour. Individual holdings of land in Barbados and the Leeward Islands before the elevation of sugar to the status of main crop tended to be small; and planters to be men of little fortune. In such a trade, the merchant, English or Dutch, made the running, and could and no doubt did exploit the initiative which he held. But the small planter drew certain benefits from his subordinate position. By selling in the island, he could without any delay translate his crops into the commodities he needed; no calls were made on his small capital for customs, freight or insurance, though all three would be reflected in the value set upon his crop; and if the ship which carried the produce of his land was lost on the homeward voyage, not he but the merchant was the sufferer.

This method of trading begat in the islands a class of merchants or 'shop-keepers' who handled the goods of their principals, collected debts and made up return cargoes. Richard Ligon described how during his residence in Barbados from 1647 to 1650 an English merchant might accumulate the money to buy a plantation by trading in this way.[13] Ten years later Thomas Povey's letter-book shows us Edward Bradbourn acting as factor in Barbados for Povey and Martin Noell in London.[14] Although this method of trading began to be superseded soon after the Restoration it did not die out altogether; during the remainder of the seventeenth century and in the eighteenth, middlemen factors continued to ply their trade in the islands. Azariah Pinney, on his arrival in Nevis in 1686, set up as factor for his family and soon began to gather other commissions from England.[15] The yearly cargoes which William Stout, the Lancaster Quaker, sent to Barbados between 1699 and 1702 were consigned to factors resident in the island.[16] Alternatively, the roles might be reversed, the island merchant setting up in business on his own account and himself employing an agent in England to make consignments to him.[17] Unpopular as they were and the target of spiteful legislation which doubled the difficulties of their business, these island merchants and factors served a useful purpose in reducing the demands put upon the capital of the smaller planter.

But the future belonged neither to the speculative ship, nor to the London merchant with his island factor, nor to the island merchant with his English factor. The future belonged to a trade in which the planter himself assumed responsibility for the marketing of his products, consigning them on his own account to an agent, at first in London and later in other towns, who for a consideration saw to their ultimate disposal. This system reached its full flowering in the eighteenth century, when it can be studied in the records of such firms as Pinney and Tobin, and Lascelles and Maxwell. But it was in full working order, though on a smaller scale, by the end of the third quarter of the seveteenth century. The great commission houses which later dominate the scene have their seventeenth-century counterparts in firms such as Bawden & Gardiner and John Eyles & Company, and in individuals such as Thomas Tryon, Anthony Wallinger and Nathaniel Bridges.

The duties performed by the London agent of a West Indian planter in the later seventeenth century were much the same as those undertaken in the eighteenth century. He received the goods off the ship, having previously made whatever insurance on them might be necessary; he obtained the certificate of discharge and paid the customs; he warehoused the goods; and either personally or through a broker he conducted the sale. From the gross proceeds he first deducted his own commission of $2\frac{1}{2}$ per cent, plus an additional $\frac{1}{2}$ of 1 per cent for brokerage if he had himself negotiated the sale. Further deductions were made in respect of charges which the agent had defrayed on behalf of his correspondent for freight, customs, and so on. The net proceeds were then placed to the credit of the planter and could be used either for the purchase of goods which he might order out from England (on which the agent collected a further $2\frac{1}{2}$ per cent) or as a fund on which bills could be drawn for the payment of debts due in England or in the West Indies.[18] To the planter therefore his English factor stood at once as selling and buying agent and as banker.

The bill of exchange, by means of which the planter was enabled to draw upon the funds he had accumulated in the hands of his agent, represented a credit transaction involving at least three parties, the drawer (in this case the planter), the drawee (his agent in London) and the payee (the planter's creditor). The principal evidence for the operation of commission agents in the West India trade in the later seventeenth century derives from the records neither of a planter nor of an agent, but of a payee, the largest single business engaged in that trade, the Royal African Company.[19] The nature of the trade pursued by this company is well known. Goods of English, European or East Indian manufacture sent out from London were bartered on the coast of West Africa for negro slaves; these were shipped to the West Indies where they were sold sometimes to contractors but more often directly to the planters. Payment for the Company's slaves could be made in one of three ways. First, the Company's accepted coin, for the most part the Spanish pieces-of-eight which circulated in Barbados and Jamaica. Secondly, payment might be in kind, usually sugar but sometimes indigo, cotton or other products. This method was almost universally practised in the Leeward Islands where sugar was current, and it was by no means rare in the other colonies. The third mode of payment was by the planter's bill of exchange drawn on his London agent or on some other person in England and made payable to the Company in London. It is these bills, entered in the Company's books, which with scattered references from other sources provide the material for studying the commission system in the early stages of its development. For the years 1672–94 record is preserved of about 1,500 bills, of a gross value of nearly £350,000. The yearly average for the whole period is £16,000, and for the years of the Company's greatest activity, 1676–87, it is over £21,000.[20]

Not all these 1,500 hundred bills are evidence of the operation of a commission system. Nearly a half of the two hundred persons on whom they were drawn were concerned in only one bill. The acceptance and payment of a single bill does not make the acceptor a commission agent; nor need it imply the existence of any well-founded commercial relationship between the parties concerned. It may denote merely the discharge of an obligation of a non-commercial nature; and in many instances in which a single bill was drawn the parties appear to have had some family connection.[21] If we may take the five bills spread over a period of at least two years as evidence of a regular correspondence between planter and agent, nearly 60 such attachments can be discerned in these years. The degree of permanence which they enjoyed varied widely. Generally the practice seems to have been for the planter to employ only one agent at a time and to continue with him over a number of years. The

Bulkeleys, the Farmers, the Silvesters and the Hothersalls, all planters of Barbados, retained their agents for thirteen years or longer, while John Gibbes was associated with the firm of Eyles & Co. for nineteen years. But that the planter retained some freedom of action is clear. John Davies, for example, who had a 200-acre estate in Barbados, employed Robert Chaplin as his factor from 1672 to 1682. But while continuing to drawn on Chaplin, he began in 1676 to draw also on Eyles & Co. In 1682 he gave up both agents and began to draw on a third, John Eston. Similarly Humphrey Waterman, after two years with Edward Thornburgh, transferred his commission to Christopher Fowler, while John Pierce, whose 1,000-acre estate was one of the largest in Barbados, employed simultaneously Robert Chaplin and the firm of Bawden & Co. as his factors. At the end of the seventeenth century, therefore, it was still possible for a planter to change his correspondent. Thus the agents of the African Company in Barbados reported in 1693 that several of the planters who employed John Gardiner 'have such regrett at his unkind useage that they Change theire factors'.[22] In the eighteenth century a planter might have no alternative but to confine his business to the agent to whom he owed money.[23] But in the seventeenth century these bonds of debt had not been firmly or finally riveted. Chronic indebtedness was already a West Indian characteristic,[24] but the principal creditors do not as yet seem to have been the London agents. The largest single creditor in the West Indian colonies in the last quarter of the seventeenth century was the Royal African Company itself. The standing debt owing to it never fell below £100,000 and frequently rose above £150,000.[25] Credit for the purchase of labour, the commodity of most vital importance to the planter, was thus being supplied from outside the commission mechanism. The replacement in the early eighteenth century of the African Company by private slave-traders, less able and less disposed to sell on trust, deprived the planters of a source of credit which they could ill afford to lose, and probably threw a heavier burden upon the commission agents.[26]

Without the records of a seventeenth-century commission agent, it is difficult to reconstruct the precise relationship which existed between his kind and the West Indian planters. It is possible that even at this date such agents as John Bawden, John Eyles and John Gardiner were making advances to their correspondents on the security of their West Indian estates. But no evidence has so far come to light to confirm such an hypothesis. What is fairly certain is that agents were not disposed to make advances on the bills drawn upon them. Ideally the planter should have kept a sufficient reserve in the hands of his agent to meet all contingencies. But it was general practice to draw on the bill of lading, that is to say, to send off the bills of exchange at the same time as the goods which were intended to meet them.[27] In other words, planters were writing cheques and then hastening to the bank to pay in sufficient to cover them. If the goods and the bill came to hand together, well and good. But if the ship which carried the planter's sugars was lost, his bill could expect no mercy; it was promptly protested and returned to drawer.[28] To some extent this contingency could be provided for by long-dated bills, but in fact these were uncommon. Thirty or forty days after sight were the periods at which the majority of West India bills became payable in the seventies of the seventeenth century, though somewhat longer-dated bills became more common in later years.[29] Attempts by the planters to anticipate the proceeds of their consignments were met by firm protests from the agents. In the early years of the war which began in 1689, the West India trade was severely dislocated by embargoes, shipping losses and a scarcity of freight. Two bills drawn at this time by Thomas Walrond of Barbados were entered in the Company's books with a note: 'Mr. Walrond does not doubt but thro' the blessing of God to have Sugars timely for the full discharge of these bills of Exchange If Fraight may then be had.' [30] Freight was apparently not to be had, and the bills were protested. In normal times very few bills had to be returned to drawer. Between 1672 and 1687 Bawden & Co. protested only six, Eyles & Co. seven, Hinchman two and Tryon three. But with the outbreak of war the number rose steeply. Of eighteen bills drawn on John Gardiner between 1689 and 1694, all but four were protested;[31] Eyles & Co. protested nine of the bills drawn on them in the early years of the war, and Henry Hale ten. Of twenty-eight bills which the African Company received on 7 November 1692, only seven were paid. This manifestation of the factors' unwillingness to make advances on bills came at a time when the planters were in particular need of credit; for sugar prices were booming and maximum output was called for.[32] It is therefore reasonable to suppose that agents were not yet convinced either of the necessity or of the profit to themselves of making advances to planters on their bills. Only further inquiry can show if they were supplying extensive credit in any other form.

The intimate social relationship which was later to subsist between planter and factor[33] does not appear to have fully developed in the seventeenth century. John Blake, for example, employed a distant kinsman to oversee the education of his children in England, whereas a century later he would probably have commended them to Nathaniel Bridges, his factor.[34] On the other hand, there are signs that already the relationship was growing into something more than a business convenience. When John Hothersall of Barbados made his will in 1694, he appointed his good friends Sir John and Francis Eyles guardians of his children and besought them to advise his widow in her investments.[35] Eyles & Co. had been factors for the Hothersalls for at least fourteen years, and by the will were made receivers of the products of the plantation during the minority of the children.

The task of inquiring into the origins of this commission system is somewhat simplified by the knowledge that as yet it did not extend to the trade of every West Indian colony. We have already noticed the persistence into the eighteenth century of the earlier forms of trading controlled either by London or by island merchants. Of the 1,500 bills which the African Company received between 1672 and 1694, only 58 originated in Jamaica and 25 in the Leeward Islands; the remainder were drawn in Barbados. This is not to suggest that the commission system was unknown outside the trade of Barbados; Christopher Jeaffreson has left evidence of its existence in the trade of the island of St. Christopher's.[36] But the extensive use of the bill of exchange in Barbados and its rarity elsewhere imply that it was to the conditions which prevailed in Barbados that the system was thought to be particularly apt.

Barbados at the Restoration was unique amongst the English colonies, and not only on account of her riches. As the first island to cultivate sugar as a commercial crop she had a start of several years over her rivals, and throughout the seventeenth century she continued one or more jumps ahead of them. The concomitants of sugar planting, a large slave population, intensive cultivation of the soil, and the large estate, all manifested themselves first in Barbados. While Jamaica continued a 'frontier colony' until well into the eighteenth century,[37] Barbados was already in the fifties of the seventeenth century so fully settled that she could afford, indeed was constrained, to get rid of her surplus population to the newer colonies.[38] By 1676 it could be said that 'there is not a foot of land in Barbados that is not employed even to the seaside', and, despite the falling price of sugar, land values were high.[39] The rapid growth of the slave population in the fifties and sixties is itself evidence of the heavy capitalization and intensive cultivation of the soil.[40] With the possible exception of the little island of Nevis, Barbados alone in the last quarter of the seventeenth century had reached a point beyond which further economic progress could take place only at a much reduced rate.

Although the average size of a plantation was certainly under 100 acres,[41] Barbados in the second half of the seventeenth century was already a land of comparatively large estates.[42] In 1673 she could boast of no less than 74 'eminent planters' with estates of 200–1,000 acres,[43], many of whom were aristocrats by birth as well as by inclination. 'Whoever will look over the Map of Barbadoes,' wrote John Oldmixon, 'will find the Country is not possessed by such a set of Men as inhabit the other Plantations', but by 'families of the most ancient and honourable in England'.[44] Such were the Draxes, the Stedes, the Codringtons, the Littletons, the Willoughbys and the Fortescues. Though they might be debtors, they were still men of substance, men whose promissory bills might be expected to command acceptance, men whose estates were such that they did not feel the same urgency as their lesser brethren to turn their crops immediately to account, men, in short, who could forbear returns long enough to send their products to the best accessible market, however distant it might be. The commission system was in origin the method of disposal for the sugar produced by the large, intensively cultivated, highly capitalized estate; and since it was in Barbados that such estates were mainly to be found in the seventeenth century, it was in the trade of that colony that the system made its first appearance. In the eighteenth century, as Jamaica began to be more intensively cultivated and families like the Pinneys built up large estates in other islands, the system spread into the entire West Indian trade.

The evidence for this statement lies in the bills of exchange already mentioned. Of the 74 'eminent planters' of Barbados, all but fourteen appear in the records as drawing bills in favour of the Company, and the majority of them did so regularly and may therefore be assumed to have employed London agents. Of the 122 bills drawn between 1672 and 1680 on the three leading agents of the time, John Bawden, John Eyles and Edward Thornburgh, 82 were drawn by 'eminent planters',[45] and ten others by men who, though not appearing in this list of 'eminent planters', are found a few years later holding offices in the island which tended to be the preserves of the greater landowners.[46] From the point of view of the London agent it is understandable that this should have been so. Only the larger fish could have been really worth the catching. The labour of correspondence and accounting could scarcely be recompensed if consignments of sugar were not to be large enough for the commission thereon to amount to a worthwhile sum.

The growth of the large estate and the emergence of a class of substantial planters were the prerequisites of the commission system. But other factors help to explain its rise, in particular the concentration of the economic interests of the West Indies upon England to which reference has already been made. In the main this concentration was arbitrary; the planters did not want it and never ceased in the seventeenth century to campaign against it. The imperial economic programme which took shape between 1650 and 1665 was not intended to benefit them. By the Navigation Act of 1660 and the Staple Act of 1663 their interests were completely subordinated to those of the mother country. They lost above all the right to buy from and sell to the Dutch traders whose ready acceptance of 'moderate gains by Trade' had done so much to set the English colonies on their feet. The planters were left at the mercy of the English and island merchants, and as early as 1655 they were resenting the position in which they found themselves.[47] 'The Merchants,' they complained in 1661, 'having us in their power that wee can send our sugars noe where else, they give us what they please and soe having the markett in themselves to send it for other countryes, they sell it for what they list, and make us simple planters only the propertie of their gaine, and sell the poor for bread and the rich for shoes.'[48] In such straits any planter who could afford to do so must have been encouraged to reach out to a wider and freer market than that provided by his own island. Since Europe was closed to him, he could look only to England. In London he would find at least a measure of competition for his sugars amongst English grocers, refiners, distillers and re-exporters. Thus the invasion of the London market by the West Indian planters may be seen partly as a reply to the prohibition of free trade and the alleged excesses of the local merchants and factors.[49]

Fundamentally there could be only one motive for a planter to switch his products from the island market to London. Richard Ligon told the Barbados planter of the early fifties that he could expect 3d. a lb for muscovado sugar sold in the island. 'But if,' he continued, 'you run the Hazards of the Sea, as all Marchants doe and bring it for England, it will sell in London for 12d. a lb.' [50] Already, therefore, an incentive existed for the planter to forbear his returns in the expectation of a greater profit. Later in the century it is less easy to assess the relative margins of profit to be gained from the two alternative methods of trade. They certainly may not be regarded as constant; a heavy sugar crop could mean high freight charges as shippers competed for cargo space, but low wholesale prices in London. On such occasions the planter's profit might disappear altogether.[51] But the fact that in the later seventeenth century planters were making consignments to England on their own accounts of itself suggests that generally this method of disposal through London agents was thought to be the more profitable.

At the time when Ligon wrote, sugar was a crop of such golden possibilities that the risks and trouble of making consignments to London may not have been compensated by the extra gain accruing. But the sellers' market which Barbados enjoyed in the forties and early fifties disappeared under the impact of an increase in world production of sugar with which consumption did not keep pace. From the mid-fifties almost until the outbreak of war in 1689 prices were falling; in June 1686 good Barbados sugar was selling for no more than 15s. 9d. a 100 lbs in the London wholesale market, a price such as would obtain only two or three times in the next 200 years.[52] These falling prices magnified the difference in the margin of profit accruing to the planter by the alternative methods of marketing his sugar. When profits were being cut to the bone and possibly in some years annihilated, the chance of an extra shilling or even of a few pence on 100 lbs of sugar could not be ignored by those planters who could afford the delay involved in dispatching their goods to London. Like the navigation laws, falling prices bore equally on all the sugar islands; yet only in the trade of Barbados did the commission system play an important part in the seventeenth century. As yet it was only in Barbados that there was to be found a sufficiency of planters of substance wedded to a one-crop method of agriculture.[53] For the most part the products of Jamaica continued to be sold in the old way and the planters of that island remained in subjection to local merchants and factors long after those of Barbados had emancipated themselves.[54] The navigation laws and the falling price of sugar, which promoted the commission system in Barbados, produced different effects in the other English islands because those colonies were at different levels of economic development and specialization. As Jamaica and Antigua came more into line with Barbados in the eighteenth century, the commission system became practically universal.

It remains to consider briefly the London agents themselves, the first generation of new-style West Indian merchants, who operated the system. It has already been pointed out that the 1,500 bills of exchange which are the principal evidence for this paper were drawn on more than 200 people and that only a small number of these men were acting as commission agents. In fact, a group of about twenty engrossed nearly two-thirds of the business.[55] The connection between these leading commission agents and the West Indian political agencies is notable; Edward Thornburgh, the first agent appointed by Barbados, Thomas Hinchman, chosen for the same office in 1671, John Gardiner, nominated for the position in 1694, Bartholomew Gracedieu, agent for Jamaica from 1693 to 1704, Robert Chaplin, personal agent to the governors of Barbados, all these in their private capacities were commission agents to West Indian planters.[56]

These new West Indian merchants were of diverse origins. Some like John Bawden were absentee planters whose commission business may have grown out of the practice of receiving the products of their own and their friends' estates for sale in London.[57] Some like Thomas Tryon knew the colonies from experience but had no territorial interest in the island whose planters they served.[58] Others like John and Francis Eyles had no apparent hereditary or personal connections with the plantations or their trade.[59] Few as yet were specialists. Bawden for instance had trading interests in Holland and the Canaries, dabbled in the slave trade and was part-owner of a number of ships plying for hire.[60] His West Indian affairs, however, were his main concern, and his usual designation was that of West Indian merchant. His commission business certainly prospered. In 1682 he was able to take John Gardiner into partnership, and these two, according to Oldmixon, 'had then the largest Commissions from Barbadoes of any Merchants in England, and perhaps the largest that ever were lodg'd in one House in the West-India Trade', a verdict which coincides exactly with the evidence of the bills of exchange.[61]

Bawden's greatest competitors were Eyles & Co. With the two partners in this firm is associated one of the great mercantile dynasties of eighteenth-century London. The eldest daughter of John Eyles, the senior partner, married a nephew of Robert Stiles, the 'millionaire' merchant of Amsterdam, while two other daughters married into the gentry. The two sons of Francis Eyles, the junior partner, John and Joseph, are too well known in eighteenth-century political and business history to need any comment. The founder of the firm, John Eyles, son of a Devizes mercer, applied himself to the West Indian commission business at least as early as 1674. From the African Company's records we can see that at different times more than 30 people drew bills on him from Barbados. Like Bawden's, his agency was large enough to warrant a partner, and the volume of business which the firm handled was only a little less than that of Bawden & Gardiner. That his career was successful and that he died a wealthy man there can be no doubt. Member for Devizes in the Exclusion Parliament, under James II he became successively knight, alderman of the City of London and Lord Mayor. How much of the property which he left at his death, and how much of the £29,000 which he lent to the government in 1689, represented the profits of his commission business it is impossible to say.[62] One fact, however, does emerge clearly: the leading commission agents of the seventeenth century were men of substance and influence who can stand comparison with the great houses of 50 or 100 years later.

One final piece of evidence of the growth of the commission system remains, the curious project sponsored by Dalby Thomas in 1687 for a West India Company. The objects of this scheme were two-fold, first to make loans to the colonies, and second, in the words which the projector addressed to the planters:

> to have had all your Goods that came to England brought to one Body of Men, which we call'd a Common Factory, and they constantly to be chosen by you in your Assemblies, and they to have been Accountable to every Consignor for the Nett proceed of every parcell of Goods Sold.[63]

The project failed, killed (so it was said and so it might be expected) by those who stood to lose most by it, the commission agents led by Bawden and Gardiner.[64] The significance of this storm-in-a-teacup could easily be exaggerated; it was never anything more than a project. But it does show that the commission business had made such progress that a projector could contemplate erecting it into an organized system; and the failure of the scheme itself testifies to the strength of the established agents. The foundations of the system which, it is hardly too much to say, was to keep the English West Indies in being during the eighteenth century had been well and truly laid.

Notes

1. Barbados 'expanded' in the sense that she helped to people other colonies; many left in the sixties and seventies of the seventeenth century to settle Surinam, Jamaica and St. Lucia. But taking the West Indies as a whole, the movement was an increase and redistribution of population rather than a territorial expansion. See A. D. Chandler, 'The Expansion of Barbados', *Journal of the Barbados Museum and Historical Society*, xiii 1945–46, 106–36.
2. J. A. Williamson, *The Caribee Islands under the Proprietary Patents*, Chapter X.
3. C. M. Andrews, *British Committees, Commissions and Councils of Trade and Plantations, 1622–1675*, p. 111.
4. For example, *Calendar of State Papers, Colonial* (*Cal. S. P. Col.*), *1677–80*, Nos. 387 and 889; Public Record Office (P.R.O), Treasury (Expired Commissions), 70, 169, fo. 45r.
5. L. M. Penson, *The Colonial Agents of the British West Indies*, pp. 181–83.
6. *Ibid.*, Chapters II, III, IX.
7. Sir Peter Colleton, Sir Edwin Stede and Christopher Jeaffreson are examples of these three types of West Indian.
8. Blake family records, described in *Caribbeans*, ed. V. L. Oliver, i. 51–57.
9. The principal authorities are the works of G. L. Beer; C. M. Andrews, *The Colonial Period in American History*, especially Vols II and IV; V. T. Harlow, *A History of Barbados, 1625–1685*; C. S. S. Higham, *The Development of the Leeward Islands under the Restoration*; F. W. Pitman, *The Development of the British West Indies*; Richard Pares, *A West-India Fortune*; O. P. Starkey, *The Economic Geography of Barbados*; Noel Deerr, *A History of Sugar*; *Caribbeana*, ed. V. L. Oliver; *A Young Squire of the Seventeenth Century*, ed. J. C. Jeaffreson; *Autobiography of William Stout*, ed. J. Harland; Richard Ligon, *A True and Exact History of the Island of Barbadoes*, (1673); Dalby Thomas, *An Historical Account of the Rise and Growth of the West-India Collonies*, (1690); John Oldmixon, *The British Empire in America*, (1708); Edward Littleton, *The Groans of the Plantations*; Thomas Tryon, *Letters Domestick and Foreign to Several Persons of Quality*, (1700). The manuscript sources used in this paper are the Entry Books of Bills of Exchange of the Royal African Company, P.R.O., Treasury 70, 269–77 and 282, and the Letter Books of the same Company, principally T.70/1, 10, 12, 15–17, 20.
10. A brilliant picture of the working of a commission house in the later eighteenth century has been given by Professor Pares in *A West-India Fortune*. Unfortunately the Pinneys did not go into the business until 1783. The subject of the rise of the commission system was touched upon by Professor Penson, *The Colonial Agents of the British West Indies*, pp. 10 ff. Material for comparison is to be found in J. S. Bassett, 'The Relations between the Virginia Planter and the London Merchant', *Annual Report of the American Historical Association for 1901*, i, 553–75, and in Elizabeth Donnan, 'Eighteenth-Century English Merchants: Micajah Perry', *Journal of Economic and Business History*, iv, 1931–32, 70.
11. *Caribbeana*, ii, 2–7, for a description of a Chancery suit, Littleton *v.* Bullock.
12. For the extent of Dutch trade, see G. L. Beer, *The Origins of the British Colonial System*, pp. 357–59; British Museum add. ms. 11411, fos. 3v–5v; Dalby Thomas, *An Historical Account of the Rise and Growth of the West-India Collonies*, pp. 36–37.
13. *A True and Exact History of the Island of Barbadoes*, pp. 109–12.
14. British Museum add. ms. 11411, fos. 78v–79v, Thomas Povey to Edward Bradbourn.
15. *A West-India Fortune*, pp. 32–35.
16. *Autobiography*, pp. 54 ff.
17. *A West-India Fortune*, p. 35.
18. J. Oldmixon, *The British Empire in America*, ii, 155. An account rendered by Edward Thornburgh to the Assembly of Barbados of the sale of 30 butts of sugar illustrates the type and scale of charges which an agent defrayed, P.R.O., Colonial Office, 31, 2, pp. 112–13. Three per cent was the regular charge for commission and brokerage combined; see a report by John Eyles, Benjamin Skutt and John Bawden (all commission agents) on the accounts of the Barbados Four-and-a-half Per Cent Duty in *Calendar of Treasury Books, 1679–80*, p. 513.
19. P.R.O., T.70/269–77 and 282. The entry books for the years 1700–27 are of little value.
20. These are gross figures, including bills drawn not by planters but by syndicates of contractors who bought negroes from the Company. They include also the very small (until 1690) number of bills which were protested.
21. Thus Justus Birkin drew on James Birkin, Katherine Bentley on Sir Martin Bentley, Emanuel Hulson on Thomas Hulson, etc.
22. P.R.O., T.70/14, fo. 61r.
23. *A West-India Fortune*, pp. 172, 254–58.
24. For example, *A Young Squire of the Seventeenth Century*, ed. J. C. Jeaffreson, ii, 50.
25. In 1681 the debt stood at £120,000; in 1685 at £136,000; in 1690 at £170,000; in 1694 at £128,000; in 1696 at £140,000; details from annual statements of the assets of the Company in P.R.O., T.70/101. The floating debt must at times had made the total outstanding very much larger.
26. In 1700 the Governor of Jamaica (a former agent of the Company and possibly a prejudiced witness) wrote to the Council of Trade and Plantations: 'Another fatal thing to the settling and increasing these Plantations is the merchants of London have never left soliciting against the Royal Company under pretence they would supply negroes more plentiful and cheap, till they have gotten them out and themselves in, and whereas the Royal Company usually supplied negroes at £22 and £24 per head and gave 6, 8 and 12 months' credit, now the

Merchants sell for £34 per head and give no credit at all' (*Cal. S. P. Col.*, 1700, p. 19).

27. J. Oldmixon, *op. cit.*, ii, 167.
28. J. Oldmixon, *op. cit.*, ii, 167. Three copies of a bill were normally sent by different ships, so that if one miscarried the others would arrive.
29. Of the first 112 bills received by the Company between 1672 and 1675, 61 were payable at 30 or 40 days' sight, and 40 at 50 or 60 days' sight. Of 55 bills drawn in 1688, 26 were payable not at so many days' sight but on a certain date written into the bill, generally from six to twelve months after the bill was drawn. An interesting and (amongst these bills) rare form is a bill in which the date of payment was made contingent upon some event, for example, 'Three months after the safe arrival of the *George*, Samuel Jones, Commander, in the Port of London.'
30. P.R.O., T.70/276, under date 7 November 1692.
31. This action made Gardiner unpopular in Barbados and may have prejudiced his candidature for the political agency of the island. His conduct, the African Company's agents reported, 'extreamly disobligeth his freinds by exposeing Theire reputation and for Bringing it into contempt here to there Greate Damage (P.R.O., T.70/17, fo.61r.).
32. The average London wholesale price of Barbados sugar in December 1688 was 23s. 6d. a 100 lbs; in December 1689 it was 33s. 6d.; in November 1690, 34s.; in December 1693, 38s.; in December 1695, 55s.; details from an index of sugar prices compiled from the records of the African Company's sales.
33. *A West-India Fortune*, pp. 186–87.
34. *Caribbeana*, ed. V. L. Oliver, i, 51–57.
35. P.R.O., Chancery Proceedings, C. 5, 238/47.
36. *A Young Squire of the Seventeenth Century*, ii, 213–14.
37. F. W. Pitman, 'The Settlement and Financing of British West India Plantations in the Eighteenth Century', *Essays in Colonial History presented to C. M. Andrews*.
38. V. T. Harlow, *A History of Barbados*, p. 203; A. D. Chandler, 'The Expansion of Barbados', *Journal of the Barbados Museum and Historical Society*, xiii, 1946, 106.
39. *Cal. S. P. Col., 1675–76*, p. 421.
40. In 1680 Barbados had 37,000 slaves; *Cal. S. P. Col., 1677–80*, No. 1336, xxiv. In 1748 she had 47,000, an increase of only 27 per cent; F. W. Pitman, *The Development of the British West Indies*, Appendix I. Jamaica, on the other hand, had 9,000 in 1673 and 112,000 in 1746, an increase of 1,150 per cent (*ibid.*).
41. 80 acres in 1712 (Pitman in *Essays in Colonial History presented to C. M. Andrews*, p. 260).
42. Harlow, *op. cit.*, pp. 306–07.
43. *Cal. S. P. Col., 1669–74*, No. 1101, ii.
44. J. Oldmixon, *op. cit.*, ii, 111.
45. If owners employed managers or attorneys with power to draw bills, the number emanating from the large estates might well be greater than appears.
46. British Museum, Sloane MS., 2441, fos. 21r–22r.
47. Butler to Cromwell, 'The islanders heer much desire commerce with strangers, our English merchants traffiquing to those parts being generally great extortioners', quoted in Harlow, *op. cit.*, p. 88.
48. P.R.O., C.O. 1/15, No. 70. Further evidence of the notorious animosity between planters and merchants is to be found in C.O. 1/23, No. 20, and in Oldmixon, *op. cit.*, ii, 155.
49. Compare L. M. Penson, *The Colonial Agents of the British West Indies*, pp. 10–11.
50. *A True and Exact History of the Island of Barbadoes*, pp. 95–96.
51. Limitation of production was preached by Thomas Tryon, *Letters, Domestick and Foreign to Several Persons of Quality*, Nos. xxxii and xxxiii.
52. This quotation and the evidence for falling prices derive from an index of wholesale sugar prices for the years 1674 to 1695 compiled from the records of sales of sugar by the African Company. Cf. N. Deerr, *A History of Sugar*, ii, 530–31.
53. Jamaica, presumably because sugar slumped before she was too deeply committed to it, remained an island of 'mixed planting' in the eighteenth century (F. W. Pitman, *Essays in Colonial History presented to C. M. Andrews*, pp. 263–64).
54. An instance of what this subjection could mean is to be found in the records of the African Company. In 1682 the Company's agents entered into an agreement with other factors in Jamaica to depress the price of sugar by holding up their purchases. So strong was the combination that the agents believed nothing could mar its success but the insistence of principals in England upon early returns (P.R.O., T.70/10, fo. 28r, T.70/15, fos. 30r, 31r).
55. The names of the most active agents with the number of bills drawn on them in favour of the African Company are: Paul Allestree (53 bills), Sir John Bawden, trading in his own name and as Bawden & Co. (136), Robert Chaplin (26), Thomas Clarke (47), Sir John Eyles, in his own name and as Eyles & Co. (126), Christopher Fowler (39), Henry Hale (24), Thomas Hart (24), John Harwood (46), Thomas Hinchman (39), John Hill (20), Thomas Robson (23), John Sadler (30), Benjamin Skutt (22), Edward Thornburgh (37), Richard Tilden (37), Thomas Tryon (40), Anthony Wallinger (39) and Richard Worsam (21).
56. L. M. Penson, *The Colonial Agents of the British West Indies*, pp. 250–51; *Cal. S. P. Col., 1677–80*, Nos. 197 and 413; *Cal. S. P. Col., 1681–85*, No. 274.
57. Compare Christopher Jeaffreson, who marketed his own sugars but refused the commissions of his friends (*op. cit.*, ii, 213–14).
58. *Some Memoirs of the Life of Mr. Thomas Tryon* (1705), pp. 40–41. Tryon spent five years in Barbados making hats.
59. The Eyles were a Wiltshire family; see below.
60. P.R.O., Chancery Proceedings, C.5/455/40 and C.5/97/4; T.70/79–82 for hiring of ships belonging to Bawden; *Cal. S. P. Col., 1681–85*, No. 1106.
61. J. Oldmixon, *op. cit.*, ii, 47–48. Bawden was knighted in 1687 and in the same year became an alderman of the City of London.
62. For the Eyles family, see *Wiltshire Notes and Queries*, i, 213, 265, 301, 366–67. 390–1; v 431; vi 371; vii 444; viii 145–51; P.R.O., Chancery Proceedings, C.8/242/138, C.7/405/40, C.7/530/76; Will of John Eyles, P.C.C. 109 Degg; *Calendar of Treasury Books, 1689–92*, Part V, 1972, 1974, 1983, 1984.
63. Dalby Thomas, *op. cit.*, Dedication and pp. 48–49.
64. Oldmixon, *op. cit.*, ii, 47–48.

Trade and Exchange in Jamaica in the Period of Slavery

VERENE A. SHEPHERD

I

Traditional accounts of commercial transactions in British Caribbean sugar plantation societies have been located within the context of external trading relations. Where domestic trade and exchange have been addressed, the focus has been on the marketing system of the slaves. Scholars have been less concerned with the other dimension of local trade — that which developed among the different rural agrarian units. Such inter-property relations were most evident in Jamaica among Britain's mercantilist empire in the Caribbean; for unlike in the classical plantation economies of the Eastern Caribbean, sugar monoculture was never a persistent feature of the island's colonial economy. Jamaica produced and exported, in addition to sugar, significant quantities of coffee, cotton, ginger, pimento, dyewoods and hardwood. The island also produced food and livestock. Most of these commodities were produced on properties geared towards the export market although some output was exchanged locally from the estates and 'minor' staple plantations. Indeed, Barry Higman indicated that towards the time of emancipation, the flow of goods and labour from one unit to another resulted in about 17% of the total production on sugar estates and coffee plantations remaining in Jamaica.[1] Unlike sugar estates, coffee plantations and other monocultural 'minor staple' units, however, the island's livestock farmers catered primarily to the domestic market. Livestock farmers were able to sustain a vibrant trade with other properties, but especially with the sugar estates which needed large numbers of working animals (as well as grass and pasturage facilities) for the production of sugar. Animals were especially vital where planters did not utilize wind, steam or water power. Even where alternative forms of power existed, 'standby' 'cattle' mills were often maintained.

This essay, using examples from the Accounts Produce,[2] illustrates another dimension of the domestic system of trade and exchange which developed during the period of slavery — the economic relations which developed between the locally based 'pens' (livestock farms) and the dominant sugar estates, arguably the best example of inter-property trade in the island. It examines the pens' transition from primarily export-based production in the 17th century to the dominant form of domestic trade and exchange by the 19th century. The essay, while intended as a contribution to the empirical base of knowledge on commercial relations in Caribbean plantation societies, has the potential to contribute to theoretical discussions on the nature and socio-economic implications of diversification of commodity production in colonial economies within a region characterized by sugar monoculture.

II The Transition from Export to a Dominant Local Trade

The Accounts Produce show quite clearly that by the mid-19th century Jamaica's livestock farms participated only minimally in the direct export trade. This was in contrast to their participation in the export trade in the preceding century. Indeed, the early history of the livestock industry in the 16th and 17th centuries indicates that the export dimension of trade was highly developed. In that period, these farms had an independent economic dynamic, exporting hides, lard and dried meat to the Spanish Indies and Spain. By 1740, the majority of the livestock farms disposed of their output on the domestic market, principally the sugar estates. Quantitative data on the disposal of pen output are not abundant, especially for those units owned by resident proprietors. The available trade statistics provided by the Accounts Produce from 1740 relate primarily to the properties of absentees; nevertheless, they can be used effectively to demonstrate some broad trends in the extent of pen participation in the export trade.

From the data available, it would seem that from the mid-18th century, where pens produced goods for export, the value of such goods did not, in general, exceed the proceeds from local transaction. Before 1800, the commodities exported were ginger, pimento, cotton, dyewoods and hardwood (logwood, fustic, mahogany). These products could be related clearly to specific parishes. Ginger was sold from the pens in St. Andrew; pimento from St. Ann and Trelawny, but mostly from the former; dyewoods, fustic and cotton from St. Elizabeth with some cotton also from the pens in St. Catherine.

Two distinct patterns of trade seemed to have existed. One method was to ship the commodity to Britain, presumably to an agent who handled the sale there. The most frequently observed practice, however, and one which was in direct contract to the usual method of disposing of sugar, was to sell the product to merchants in Kingston, who then arranged the sale.

Evidence of the participation of pens in the export trade was most available from the 1770s. Accounts for the earlier period were scanty, perhaps because of the greater residency of the penkeepers then. In 1740, for example, whereas it was evident that estates were exporting minor staples in addition to sugar (such crops also being exported from plantations of minor staples), only two of the eighteen pens for which returns were seen exported any commodity, in this case, cotton. In this period, most of the pens were located on the southside, particularly St. Catherine, and supplied primarily grass and provisions to the urban markets.[3] Forty years later, of the 21 returns relating to livestock farms, only five participated in the export trade. From Dornoch, Riverhead and Gordon Valley pens in St. Ann were shipped 118 bags of pimento valued at £256 17s. Several other bags valued at £161 0s.4d. were sold in Kingston, presumably for later export. In all then, pimento sales totalled £417 17s. 4d., but this represented only 11 per cent of the total earnings of the pen which amounted to £38,587 7s. 7d.[4]

Taking the period 1776–85 together, it is evident that the pens continued to export ginger, pimento, fustic, mahogany, logwood and cotton. A similar commodity-parish relationship existed as in 1740.[5] The just over 40 returns seen (representing 25 pens), showed a mere seven pens active in the export market. In all cases, the value of exports fell far below the receipts from internal transactions. The best example in this period is from Luana Pen in St. Elizabeth which had eight separate returns in the period under review. Between 1776 and 1785, Luana exported 58 tons of fustic (£340 16s. 9d.), 65 tons of logwood (£325) and 995 lbs of cotton (£87 1s. 3d.), totalling £1,083 10s. 6d; but over the same period, receipts from livestock sales and pen services totalled £3,156 12s. 0d. Exports thus represented 34% of total earnings of just over £4,240.[6] In the other accounts, the percentage represented by exports was lower. The receipts of Dornoch, Riverhead and Gordon Valley pens from exports together represented 11 per cent of all goods and services sold.

Accounts for 1800 and 1820, the other years sampled, also replicated these earlier trends with respect to commodities produced, parishes in which produced, patterns of trade and comparative receipts from sales — with one important exception, the addition of coffee to the list of exports. In 1800, coffee was shipped from pens in St. Ann, Clarendon and St. James. Cotton, logwood and fustic continued to be produced in St. Elizabeth and Westmoreland, by this time an important exporter of logwood. One pen in St. Dorothy shipped a quantity of lignum vitae wood, and pimento continued to be associated with the St. Ann pens.[7]

Unlike in the preceding period, the value of exports from the pens in 1800 and 1820 at times exceeded earnings from internal transactions. Two notable examples were firstly Bellemont Pen which in 1800 exported coffee valued at £1,117 6s. 8d., 67% of total receipts for that year. The second case was Patherton Pen whose coffee exports formed 82 per cent of total earnings. As not all the accounts contained the volume and value of the commodities and as it is not at all times safe to assign current prices to the crops (if sold in Jamaica, for example, commodities fetched a different price from those exported directly to Great Britain), it is impossible to ascertain the extent to which Patherton and Bellemont typified the situation with the pens in 1800 with respect to value of exports *vs* internal trade. A further complication limiting generalization about the trend is that it would seem that it is those pen/coffee combined units, mostly in Manchester, which showed an increase of exports over internal sales. Pens like Luana, which were primarily devoted to livestock rearing, continued to show an excess of internal transactions over exports. In 1800, Luana earned 32% from export sales, for example. Indeed, of the eight complete accounts seen for this year, six recorded that sales from internal transactions exceeded those from exports. It should also be added that of 73 returns of pens in 1800, 21 (29%) participated in the external trade — a significant enough improvement over previous years in numbers, though not necessarily in percentage. This improvement seemed attributable to the increase of pens producing and exporting coffee.

In 1820, 153 returns of pens were seen. Of this number 43 or 28% participated in the direct export trade. The products exported were coffee, pimento, fustic, lignum vitae, logwood and hides. One pen, Castille Fort, provided ballast for outgoing ships. Most pens exported only one commodity. Only a minority[8] exported two. The usual combination was pimento and coffee (four pens) or logwood and fustic (two pens). One pen exported both pimento and fustic. St. Ann's pens continued to be overrepresented in the export of pimento. The combined pen/coffee units in Manchester most likely dominated the export of coffee, but because of the high residency among the coffee farmers, were underrepresented in the Accounts Produce. In the 1820 returns, it is the St. Ann pens which seemed to be exporting most of the coffee.

Most of the products were recorded as having been 'sent to Kingston'. Again, as not all commodity prices were included, only tentative statements can be made about the value of the products sold abroad. What seems clear is that of the 18 pens which had detailed information on prices and volume of goods, only three seemed to have earned more from exports than from internal transactions, the percentage from exports ranging from 59% to 71%. The others earned between 0.2% and 39% from external trade. The limited quantitative data, therefore, serve to reinforce the impression from qualitative sources that unlike the sugar estates, by the 19th century, pens catered essentially to the domestic market in the island.

III The Domestic Trade

In contrast to their relatively minimal involvement in the direct export trade, Jamaican pens participated actively in the domestic system of exchange. The pens conducted two levels of exchange locally. One was the domestic trade in provisions and livestock in which money was used as a medium of exchange. The other was a form of barter, an informal, non-monetary exchange of commodities among properties. A variety of goods were involved in the internal system of exchange among Jamaican properties. The primary product was livestock, comprising working steers, spayed heifers, breeding cows, mules, horses, bulls, calves, asses, fat cattle, old, wornout estate cattle and small stock. Other goods included food provisions (mainly corn and plantains), grass, milk, bricks, white lime, shingles, fresh beef, fish, timber, staves, sugar, rum, coffee and miscellaneous items. Most of these goods were sold by the pens. Those sold or exchanged by estates were sugar, rum and old working cattle. Where pen/coffee units or monocultural coffee units were involved in the trade, they sold coffee and livestock in the case of the former.

Various services (including labour) were also provided. The principal services provided by pens were jobbing, pasturage and wainage (cartage). Sugar estates rented excess land, at times in exchange for more pastureland from nearby properties. They also jobbed their tradesmen. Jobbing was, however, probably dominated by pens and specialized, independent jobbing gangs.

Of the goods listed above, the trade in livestock was the most lucrative for pens. According to Bryan Edwards, an eighteenth-century estate spent a minimum of £300 per annum to replace 'stock'.[9] The majority, indeed, spent far more. In 1783, Simon Taylor, the attorney for Golden Grove estate in St. Thomas-in-the-East, reported that that estate needed 100 working steers annually.[10] At around £30 each in 1820, this would cost this estate £3,000 per annum. As estates also bought mules and spayed heifers annually, pens stood to gain considerably from the trade in working stock, especially around 1820 when the price of a mule was £40 and for a young, spayed heifer, £22 10s.–26 each. J. B. Moreton recorded that an estate with even 100 acres of cane needed to buy 40 mules annually and maintain 100 always on the estate in the late eighteenth century.[11] Horses, proof asses and fat stock sold to the butchers also fetched considerable sums.

Of the services provided by pens, jobbing was the most financially rewarding. Jobbing consisted chiefly of digging cane holes and planting the spring canes on estates. In 1834, the have . . . '.[17] Third, pen-keepers or pen overseers themselves visited estates to enquire about the availability of livestock for sale. Over time, estates developed a relationship with particular pens, getting to know their routine and approximate selling time for young steers, heifers and mules.

In the majority of cases, pen slaves supplied the orders sent in by estates for livestock. The driving of cattle and horsekind to and from estates provided the slaves involved with a great deal of mobility. On 27 July 1750, for example, Charles Guy and Julius left Vineyard Pen with 15 steers, two young horses, ten heifers and two mules for a property in Westmoreland. They did not all return until August 2. Their explanation was that they had been delayed unduly because several people asked them to collect and deliver letters.[18] Pen slaves often covered longer distances than were involved in the case of Vineyard Pen's labourers. Slaves from Agualta Vale Pen in St Mary, for example, drove animals to Spring Estate in St Andrew, approximately 34 miles away.[19] Slaves from other properties, or those belonging to individual butchers, also went to the pens to collect goods for their masters. Mr. Markham, for example, 'sent his negroes for one dozen crabs caught by Titus and a he-lamb'.[20] Markham similarly sent his slaves to purchase fat cattle from Vineyard Pen. According to Thistlewood, however, his 'hands' were inadequate to manage the nine cows and calves; so that Charles and Cuffie had to help with them as far as Black River.[21] In some cases, the butchers, or estate overseers, visited the pen personally to make arrangements for purchase.[22]

In addition to driving livestock to 'markets', pen slaves fetched animals bought for the pen or to be pastured on its lands. In 1807, for example, the overseer of Thetford Hall Pen in St John sent slaves from that property to Mile Gully in Clarendon for a bull purchased from that pen.[23] Similarly, Thistlewood sent the slaves Dick, Guy, Charles, Julius and Simon to Mr. Allen's pen to fetch the mares for pasturage.[24] When pen slaves themselves delivered livestock to markets, or fetched and returned animals for fattening or pasturage, an extra cost was added.

The method by which other pen products were disposed of seemed less systematic. On Vineyard and Breadnut Island pens, for example, no letters were exchanged respecting the sale of vegetables and food crops. Also, no advertisements appeared in the newspapers relating to the sale of products other than large stock and its by-products. Products such as

cost of digging cane holes was £8 per acre. In this and previous years, some pens profited considerably from this service provided by their hired slaves. Stoneyfield Pen in St. Ann, for example, earned £660 1s. 6d. in 1820 for jobbing done on Fellowship Hall estate. This represented 52.54% of its total earnings from internal transactions.[12]

Pasturage, particularly for St. Catherine's pens, was also quite lucrative. In the eighteenth century, the typical rates charged for this service were 15s. per month for each horse or mule, and 10s. per month for each head of cattle. If pastured in batches of 20, rates were slightly lower. For example, 7s. 6d. for each animal was charged where cattle were pastured in batches of 20 or more. Rates increased in the nineteenth century to a maximum of 20s. for each horse.[13]

For sugar estates, the sale of their old, meagre or fat cattle after the crop to pens or butchers gave them handsome returns on their initial investment in young working stock. James Stevenson, the attorney for the Scarlett's estates in Jamaica, noted in 1800 that fat cattle from the estates sold at around £40 each. He stressed that formerly, old, fat cattle sold at between £18 and £25 each, but now fetched almost as much as for young cattle. Even though estates then had to buy fresh beef from such stock, at 1s.–1s. 8d. a pound, he felt they still made a profit in the sale of fat stock.[14] The army used a substantial proportion of the fresh beef sold by pens, at times up to 425 head per annum.[15]

The internal sale of rum also provided estates with money to help with local contingencies. As most of this product would have eventually been re-exported by Kingston merchants, however, this was, perhaps, not a true part of the domestic trade. However, sugar estates still participated in local transactions by providing the sugar and rum needs of non-sugar producing units.

The availability of goods and services provided by Jamaican pens was made known to potential customers in one of three ways. First, the sale of livestock was advertised in various newspapers. One hundred and twenty pens advertised the sale of animals in various newspapers sampled between 1780 and the end of slavery.[16] Second, pen-keepers or overseers, utilizing the services of slave couriers, sent letters to sugar planters or their representatives and butchers indicating the availability of planters' stock and fat cattle respectively. Thomas Thistlewood, owner of Vineyard Pen, noted in 1751, for example, that he 'sent Julius to Mr. Markham [a butcher in Black River] with a letter to let him know what fat cattle we capons, crabs, poultry,[25] eggs, fruits, sheep, goats and vegetables were sent to market in Westmoreland or Black River each week.[26] These were clearly not marketed by slaves on their own account as such sales were not usually made on Saturdays or Sundays. On some Saturdays, however, products were prepared for sale the following week.[27] In addition to these producta, Phibbah, Thistlewood's 'house-keeper', frequently sold cloth (usually check) in Westmoreland.

Few pens returned in the Accounts Produce established butcheries in the period under review. Those that did also developed significant links with properties and individuals within and outside of the area of their location. The best example of the scale of transactions in fresh beef from a pen is provided by Batchelor's Hall Pen's accounts. In 1833, this pen earned £2,120 2s. 11d. from its sale of fresh beef to estates, individuals, the troops and ships. This represented 57.63% of its total earnings for that year.[28]

The participation of the various units in the internal commodity trade varied in extent, volume and value from year to year. In 1740, when the Accounts Produce returns begin, 175 accounts were sent in by overseers. These represented 85 sugar estates, 20 pens, five plantations of minor staples, 19 jobbing gangs, 19 multiple crop combinations and 27 returns relating to merchants' earnings or house rents collected. Eighteen of the 20 pens, 20 of the 85 estates and the plantations of minor staples participated in the internal trade. Unfortunately, there is no detailed accounts of the buyers involved, so that the extent of economic links for 1740 cannot be measured.

The returns for 1760 indicate that interproperty transactions remained essentially the same as for 1740 in terms of the total number of properties involved. Sugar estates had, however, improved their participation, moving from 23.52% in 1740 to 35.68% in 1760. Pens basically remained at the same level, but the participation by plantations had declined. By 1780, 120 properties of the 266 returned were involved in local transactions. The number of properties involved continued to increase along with the increase in the number of returns. These indications are for units owned by absentees, but resident proprietors also participated in the trade, though the extent of their involvement cannot be ascertained. In the post-slavery period, however, the nature of transactions underwent slight changes. While the sale of livestock continued between pens and estates, there was a drastic reduction in the jobbing of pen labourers on the estates. Indeed, only five such cases were noted in the 152 returns of pens in 1840, compared with 64 of the 145 such units in the 1820 return.

The extent of trade is clearer in the nineteenth-century returns. The majority of estates relied either on pens or local butchers to buy their old stock. Pens dominated this trade, however, as they were better placed than the butchers to fatten such animals prior to their being killed for fresh beef. Only five of the pens returned in 1820 had their own butcheries, and the supply of beef — a form of final demand linkage — was probably in the hands of urban butchers and independent pens not returned.

The volume of livestock being sold in the island can be partially ascertained from the Accounts Produce. In the first return when pens were not as numerous as later on, these units supplied only 34 head of working stock to estates. In that year, few pens were monocultural livestock units, and St. Catherine's units, in particular, sold more sheep and small stock than cattle and mules. By 1780, 21 of the 266 returns were pens. The latter were involved in the sale of livestock to the number of 942. This represented 50.7 per cent of the 1,881 sold by the 120 units involved in local trading. Table 1, showing the specific breakdown of the numbers traded, indicates the relative importance of each type of livestock in the eighteenth century. It is clear that in the late eighteenth century, heifers and mules were overrepresented in terms of working animals. The mule, indeed, was recognizedly unsurpassed in its hardiness as a work animal. The horses, on the other hand, and the 'steers' were underrepresented as work animals, the

Table 1 Breakdown of Livestock Sales by Type and Volume, 1780

All properties		Pens only	%
Working steers	278	137	49.28
Heifers	19	15	78.94
Cows	30	24	80.00
Calves	56	38	67.85
Horses	123*	91	73.98
Old/fat/cattle	1,039	407	39.17
Bulls	3	—	—
Sheep	140	95	67.85
Mules	181	131	72.37
Asses	12	4	33.33
	1,881	942	50.70

*Including six mill horses.
Source: J.A., A.P., 1780, 18/11/4/9.

former being more important for transportation and the horse-racing industry. This was in contrast to the trend in England where by 1850, English farmers, with some regional variations, had virtually dispersed with the working of cattle in favour of the use of horses. This was because after the Napoleonic Wars, more favourable price conditions and the increasing efficiency of horses in farming caused the emphasis in cattle husbandry to shift to beef production.[29] In Jamaica, however, competition from horse-racing and the expensiveness of procuring and maintaining horses determined their unattractiveness as draught animals.

By the mid-nineteenth century, however, mules had largely been displaced by steers and spayed heifers. A partial indication of this shift is that by 1820, and in contrast to 1780, an estimated 3,162 steers, 1,162 spayed heifers and only 511 mules were sold or exchanged internally. By the post-slavery period, the number of mules sold by the pens represented in the Accounts Produce had fallen significantly. In 1840, for example, the 283 mules compared with 2,461 steers and 1,006 heifers were sold from the pens.[30]

Contemporary sources provide no explanations for this shift, but one can speculate that the dual income yielded by oxen was attractive to both planters and pen-keepers. Unlike the oxen, mules realized little of a return on initial investment at the end of their working life. Indeed, the table also reinforces qualitative statements about the lucrative nature of the sale of old stock from the estates and the dominance of pens in the trade in working stock.

By 1820, when the total number of livestock traded internally was 14,134 head, pens were responsible for 8,267 or 54.49%, an improvement over their 1780 level. In the former year, the returns included 145 pens and 470 sugar estates. As in previous years, sugar estates dominated the sale of old, meagre stock, while pens controlled the sale of working animals. Pens acted as 'middlemen' in the trade in old stock which could not be sold straight to the butcher. These were fattened on the pens' pastures prior to sale to urban butchers. This enabled them to make a profit on their purchases from the estates.

As a result of the trade in livestock, therefore, a significant degree of economic links developed among the island's main economic units. These links typified the relations between estates and pens throughout the island.

The Accounts Produce give some indication of the relative value of each type of good and service to properties involved in the internal trade, as is demonstrated by Table 2, based on examples drawn from the 1820 Accounts (which are far more detailed than previous samples

Table 2 Sample of Interproperty Trade, 1820

	Property	Type	Parish	Total earnings from the internal trade £	s.	d.	Proportion earned from dealings with estates/pens £	s.	d	%
1	Golden Grove	Sugar estate	Hanover	2,405	2	0	84	2	0	3.5
2	Silver Grove	Sugar estate	Hanover	1,923	14	0	157	2	0	8.2
3	Steelfield	Sugar estate	Trelawny	1,318	10	6	135	0	0	10.2
4	Unity Hall	Sugar estate	St. James	2,300	16	6	179	0	0	7.8
5	Seven Rivers	Sugar estate	St. James	267	3	0	267	3	0	100
6	Old Montpelier	Sugar estate	St. James	3,896	18	0	219	0	0	5.6
7	Grange	Sugar estate	Hanover	1,540	15	8	115	0	0	7.5
8	Fontabelle	Sugar estate	Westmoreland	695	9	4	622	0	0	89.4
9	Frome	Sugar estate	Westmoreland	178	15	7	82	4	7	46.0
10	Spring Garden	Sugar estate	Westmoreland	186	0	0	128	0	0	56.06
11	Silver Grove	Sugar estate	Trelawny	169	10	0	136	0	0	80.2
12	Golden Grove	Sugar estate	Trelawny	134	10	0	119	10	0	88.8
13	Harding Hall	Sugar estate	Hanover	1,348	5	8	108	0	0	8.0
14	Old Shafston	Pen	Westmoreland	1,321	0	6	204	0	0	15.4
15	Carysfort	Pen	Westmoreland	3,998	19	3½	3,396	19	3½	84.9
16	Midgham	Pen	Westmoreland	1,451	12	11	1,251	15	0	86.2
17	Paradise	Pen	Westmoreland	790	6	8	218	18	0	27.6
18	Mount Edgecombe	Pen	Westmoreland	2,120	13	0½	1,350	8	10½	63.6
19	Hamstead	Pen	St. Mary	428	8	0	428	8	0	100

Source: J.A., A.P., 1B/11/4/54–6.

Table 5 The Internal Trade: Relative Value of Goods and Services from Selected Properties, 1820

	Property	Livestock			Jobbing			Pasturage			Wainage			Provisions			Wood, staves shingles			Misc. rents, etc		
		£	s.	d.	£	s.	d	£	s.	d.	£	s.	d.	£	s.	d.	£	s.	d.	£	s.	d.
1	Forest Pen	4,027	16	8	75	0	0		—			—			—			—			—	
2	Maverly Estate	137	0	0		—			—			—			—		363	7	6	134	4	11
3	Lyndhurst Plan.	620	0	0		—			—			—			—		554	7	7		—	
4	Pindar's River Estate	124	0	0		—			—		20	0	0		—			—		150	0	0
5	Phantilland's Pen	356	13	4	746	16	8	45	6	8					—			—		122	4	5
6	Chudleigh Plan	1,326	10	0		—			—			—			—			—			—	
7	Brazellitta Est.	174	0	0	294	0	9½		—		40	0	0		—			—		37	3	4
8	Crescent Park Pen	787	0	0	20	0	0		—			—			—			—			—	
9	Batchelor's Hall Pen	1,304	0	0		—			—		84	0	0	2,272	3	9		—			—	
10	Petersville Est.	1,655	10	0		—			—			—			—			—			—	
11	Monymusk Estate		—		60	0	0		—			—			—			—		45	0	0
12	Spring Gdn. Pen	1,740	13	0		—		18	10	0		—			—			—		16	5	0
13	Worthy Part Est.	225	0	0		—			—			—			—			—				
14	Aboukir Plan.	72	10	0		—			—		97	0	0	38	1	3	70	16	0		—	
15	Paynestown Pen	640	0	0	1	5	0		—		3	0	0		—			—			—	
16	New Forest Pen	219	16	0	47	10	0	207	2	6	263	13	4	39	0	0		—			—	
17	Chesterfield Est.	220	0	0		—			—		10	0	0	32	8	4		—		25	0	0
18	Crawle Pen	2,379	0	8	211	7	9	446	5	10	393	3	8½		—			—			—	
19	Lower Works Pen	1049	0	0½		—		375	0	0½		—			—			—			—	
20	Palmyra Pen	167	6	8	662	0	0		—		50	18	9		—			—			—	
21	Rosehall Estate	148	0	0	50	10	0		—		5	6	8		—			—			—	
22	Cherry Gdns. Est	52	0	0		—			—			—			—			—			—	
23	Holland Estate	400	0	0		—			—			—			—			—			—	
24	Sevens Plan	300	0	0		—			—			—		88	5	0		—			—	
25	Santa Cruz Park Pen	924	0	0	72	0	0		—			—			—		10	0	0		—	
26	Ramble Pen	1,450	0	0		—			—		105	5	0	78	0	0	427	15	0	155	0	0
27	St. Faith's Pen	1,386	7	0	99	14	10½	6	18	4		—			—		403	1	6		—	
28	Ardoch Pen	574	10	0	190	9	7½	20	8	0		—			—		16	0	0		—	
29	Bryan's Pen	980	7	8	476	0	0		—		368	0	0	115	0	0		—		78	17	6
30	New Ground Est.	108	0	0		—			—		38	0	0		—			—			—	
31	Dunbarton Est.		—		80	0	0		—					522	0	2		—			—	
32	Phoenix Park Pen	2,028	6	8		—			—			—			—		202	0	0		—	
33	Prospect Est.	368	8	0		—			—			—		88	8	0		—		47	0	0
35	Roaring River Est.	32	0	0		—			—			—		58	4	6		—			—	
35	Williamsfield Est.	12	10	0	85	0	0		—			—			—			—			—	

Source: J.A., A.P., 1B/11/4/54–6.

returned). In 1740, for example, though 35 units indicated earnings from the domestic trade, the purchases of these goods and services were rarely given. Values were equally generally absent, making calculations based on known price rates virtually impossible. Table 2 indicates that 11 of the 16 pens involved earned most from the sale of livestock and its by-product, beef. It should be stressed that not all transactions involved money, but all could be reduced to monetary value. Where goods were exchanged for other goods or services, however, a money value was not given. Flamstead Estate in St. James, for example, bartered 110 gallons of rum for stock in 1780.[31] Unlike in other West Indian islands, however, the products of the island were not made legal tender after 1751, despite an attempt to get the Assembly to sanction this. Where it occurred, it was more custom than law. Indeed, Edward Long confirmed that 'money is the chief agent for carrying on any trade'.[32] Increased draining of money from the island by American and Spanish merchants, however, not only made bartering common, but according to Long, 'credit became a part of Commerce'.[33] Although pens diversified their activities to a greater extent after the abolition of slavery, up to 1840, earnings from the livestock trade still accounted for the largest share of their income. A sample of 24% of the pens returned in 1820 (representing 9–10% of the estimated island total) reveals earnings of £25,990 5s. 8½d. from livestock sales to estates. These pens earned more from such sales (69%) than from other important income-generating activities such as jobbing, wainage, pasturage, the sale of food (ground provisions and fresh beef) and wood. These other sales and services combined yielded £11,974 19s. 0d. or 31 per cent of the total earnings of £37,965. Taken singly, jobbing represented 8%, pasturage 3%, wainage 4%, provisions 9% and miscellaneous items (rents, shingles, wood, staves) 7%. These percentages varied, of course, from pen to pen. Forest pen, for example, earned only 2% from non-livestock sources.

It should be pointed out that on the whole, estates and pens were unequal partners in the internal trade. In the majority of cases, as Table 3 illustrates, estates accumulated less from their internal transactions with pens than they did from other sources such as the sale of rum to Kingston merchants and fat cattle to butchers. On the other hand, pens relied on the estates for the greater portion of their earnings. Additionally, the estates' gains from the internal trade represented an insignificant part of their total earnings from the domestic export trade. For example, Prospect Estate in Hanover earned £12,650 18s. 0d. from the sale of sugar and rum and only £183 10s. 0d. from internal transactions. Of the money accumulated locally, £128 10s. 0d. resulted from trade with pens. Similarly, Mint Estate in Westmoreland earned £7,818 17s. 0d. from the export of sugar and rum and £420 14s. 0d. from the domestic trade.[34]

Conclusion

It should be clear from the foregoing analysis that commercial relations in 18th- and 19th-century Jamaica did not conform to the trade patterns in monocultural or classic plantation economies. The island's colonial economy was diversified and led not only to the availability of a wider range of export crops, but to the emergence of non-staple producers who traded their goods on the domestic market.

Despite the importance of this domestic trade in livestock, however, local producers were never able to supply the total livestock requirements of the island. The competition between estates and pens for land made the pens unable to maintain the required livestock density which would cater to the island's needs. Furthermore, the high cost of production of local livestock made pen-keepers unable to compete with external producers, notably Hispanic America. This lack of self-sufficiency in working animals encouraged the development and maintenance of a vibrant import trade with Spanish America. Between 1815 and 1825, for example, the Spanish Main and Islands supplied 57,704 of the total 59,182 mules, horses, asses and cattle imported into the island.[35] Nevertheless, the domestic trade in livestock reduced the island's dependence on foreign sources and supplied locally a larger share of Jamaica's total demand for plantation animals than did any other island in the British Caribbean.

Notes

1. B. W. Higman, 'Slave Population and Economy in Jamaica at the time of Emancipation' (Ph.D. diss., UWI, Mona, 1970), p. 313.
2. Accounts Produce contain returns of commodities produced, method of disposal and value of goods and services in some cases. These accounts related to the properties of absentees, but information pertaining to pens owned by residents is available where the latter traded with the former.

3. Jamaica Archives (J.A.), Accounts Produce (A.P.), 1B/11/4/1.
4. *Ibid.*, 1B/11/4/9.
5. *Ibid.*
6. *Ibid.*
7. *Ibid.*, 1B/11/4/27-28.
8. *Ibid.*, 1B/11/4/54-56.
9. B. Edwards, *The History of the West Indies*, 2 vols (London, 1793), I, p. 259.
10. Simon Taylor to Chaloner Arcedeckne, 29 October 1782, Jamaica Estate Paper, Vanneck Manuscripts, Box 2, Bundle 10.
11. J. B. Moreton, *Manners and Customs in the West Indian Islands* (London, 1790), p. 57.
12. A.P. 1B/11/4/56.
13. *St. Jago de la Vega Gazette*, 4-11 April 1801, p. 93.
14. James Stevenson to Mrs Scarlett, 8 April 1800. Scarlett Family Collection, DDCA/41/17, Hull University Library (Brynmor Jones).
15. *Jamaica House of Assembly Votes* (*J.H.A.V.*) 1795-6, p. 282.
16. *Royal Gazette*, 1780-1834; *St. Jago de la Vega Gazette*, 1791-1831; *Falmouth Post*, 1791-1836.
17. Thomas Thistlewood's Journal, Vineyard Pen, 15 January 1751, Monson 31/2 fol. 8, Lincolnshire Archives Office.
18. *Ibid.*, Monson 31/1, fols. 342, 348.
19. V. Shepherd, 'Problems in the Supply of Livestock to Sugar Estates in the Period of Slavery', UWI, Mona, 1987.
20. Thistlewood's Journal, 26 January 1751, Monson 31/2, fol. 14.
21. *Ibid.*, 10 April 1751, fol. 58.
22. *Ibid.*, 23 April 1751, fol. 59.
23. Thetford Hall Pen Accounts, 1807. D.M. 444, Special Collections, Bristol University Library.
24. Thistlewood's Journal, 11 April 1751, Monson 31/2, fol. 25.
25. *Ibid.*, 5 September 1750, Monson 31/1, fol. 374.
26. *Ibid.*, 1750-51, Monson 31/1-2.
27. *Ibid.*, 11 July 1750, Monson 31/1, fol. 355.
28. Accounts Produce, Batchelor's Hall Pen, January-December 1833, Vanneck MSS; Jamaica Estate Papers, Box 2, Bundle 60.
29. J. A. Perkins, 'The Ox, the Horse, and English Farming, 1750-1850', Working Papers in Economic History, 3/1975, University of New South Wales, Dept, of Economic History, School of Economics, pp. 2-15. (I am grateful to Prof. Barry Higman for this source).
30. A.P. 1B/11/4/84-5, 1840.
31. *Ibid.*, 1B/11/4/9, 1780.
32. Add. MS 12,404, fols. 450-2, E. Long, *History of Jamaica*, 3 vols. (London, 1774), I, fols. 450-52.
33. *Ibid.*, fol. 450.
34. A.P. 1B/11/4/54-56.
35. V. Shepherd, 'Pens and Penkeepers in a Plantation Society', Ph.D., Cambridge, 1988, p. 163.

SECTION FOUR
Caribbean Slavery and the Capitalist World Economy

The conclusions of Eric Williams and C. L. R. James were clearly stated before 1945. Firstly, they stated that both the slave and sugar trades were lucrative, and that the plantation system provided a significant amount of that critical surplus capital which propelled England and France into self-sustained economic growth in the eighteenth and nineteenth centuries. Secondly, that with the ability of European capitalism to reproduce, internally, its own surplus capital, largely associated with the ascendancy of industrial capital over merchant capital in the late eighteenth century and early nineteenth century, came the economic context for the reduced economic significance of the West Indian plantation system. Declining importance and adverse market forces led to long-term crisis in the West Indian plantation economy and hence the movement towards the abolition. Over these theses, rigorous polemics, with transatlantic dimensions, have developed. The intention of these essays is simply to provide a brief summary of the intellectual loci of the various arguments involved in these polemics.

Capitalism and Slavery

ERIC WILLIAMS

'There is nothing which contributes more to the development of the colonies and the cultivation of their soil than the laborious toil of the Negroes.' So reads a decree of King Louis XIV of France, on August 26, 1670. It was the consensus of seventeenth-century European opinion. Negroes became the 'life' of the Caribbean, as George Downing said of Barbados in 1645. Without Negroes, said the Spanish Council of the Indies in 1685, the food needed for the support of the whole kingdom would cease to be produced, and America would face absolute ruin. Europe has seldom been as unanimous on any issue as it has been on the value of Negro slave labour.

In 1645, before the introduction of the sugar economy, Barbados had 5,680 Negro slaves, or more than three able-bodied white men to every slave. In 1667, after the introduction of the sugar industry, the island, by one account, contained 82,023 slaves, or nearly ten slaves to every white man fit to bear arms. By 1698, a more accurate estimate of the population gave the figures as 2,330 white males and 42,000 slaves, or a ratio of more than eighteen slaves to every white male.

In Jamaica the ratio of slaves to whites was one to three in 1658, nearly six to one in 1698. There were 1,400 slaves in the former year, 40,000 in the latter. The ratio of slaves and mulattoes to whites increased from more than two to one in Martinique in 1664 to more than three to one in 1701. The coloured population amounted to 2,434 in 1664 and 23,362 in 1701. In Guadeloupe, by 1697, the coloured population outnumbered the whites by more than three to two. In Grenada in 1700 the Negro slaves and mulattoes were more than double the number of whites. In the Leeward Islands and in St. Thomas the whites steadily lost ground.

By 1688 it was estimated that Jamaica required annually 10,000 slaves, the Leeward Islands 6,000, and Barbados 4,000. A contract of October, 1675, with one Jean Oudiette, called

---

From Columbus to Castro: The History of the Caribbean, 1492–1969 (London, 1970), pp. 136–55.

for the supply of 800 slaves a year for four years to the French West Indies. Four years later, in 1679, the Senegal Company undertook to supply 2,000 slaves a year for eight years to the French Islands. Between 1680 and 1688 the Royal African Company supplied 46,396 slaves to the British West Indies, an annual average of 5,155.

The Negro slave trade became one of the most important business enterprises of the seventeenth century. In accordance with sixteenth-century precedents its organisation was entrusted to a company which was given the sole right by a particular nation to trade in slaves on the coast of West Africa, erect and maintain the forts necessary for the protection of the trade, and transport and sell the slaves in the West Indies. Individuals, free traders or 'interlopers', as they were called, were excluded. Thus the British incorporated the Company of Royal Adventurers trading to Africa, in 1663, and later replaced this company by the Royal African Company, in 1672, the royal patronage and participation reflecting the importance of the trade and continuing the fashion set by the Spanish monarchy of increasing its revenues thereby. The monopoly of the French slave trade was at first assigned to the French West India Company in 1664, and then transferred, in 1673, to the Senegal Company. The monopoly of the Dutch slave trade was given to the Dutch West India Company, incorporated in 1621. Sweden organised a Guinea Company in 1647. The Danish West India Company, chartered in 1671, with the royal family among its shareholders, was allowed in 1674 to extend its activities to Guinea. Brandenburg established a Brandenburg African Company, and established its first trading post on the coast of West Africa in 1682. The Negro slave trade, begun about 1450 as a Portuguese monopoly, had, by the end of the seventeenth century, become an international free-for-all.

The organisation of the slave trade gave rise to one of the most heated and far-reaching economic polemics of the period. Typical of the argument in favour of the monopoly was a paper in 1680 regarding the Royal African Company of England. The argument, summarised, was as follows: firstly, experience demonstrated that the slave trade could not be carried on without forts on the West African coast costing £20,000 a year, too heavy a charge for private traders, and it was not practicable to apportion it among them; secondly, the trade was exposed to attack by other nations, and it was the losses from such attacks prior to 1663 which had resulted in the formation of the chartered company; thirdly, the maintenance of forts and warships could not be undertaken by the Company unless it had an exclusive control; fourthly, private traders enslaved all and sundry, even Negroes of high rank, and this led to reprisals on the coast; finally, England's great rival, Holland, was only waiting for the dissolution of the English company to engross the entire trade.

The monopolistic company had to face two opponents: the planter in the colonies and the merchant at home, both of whom combined to advocate free trade. The planters complained of the insufficient quantity, the poor quality, and the high prices of the slaves supplied by the Company; the latter countered by pointing out that the planters were heavily in debt to it, estimated in 1671 at £70,000, and, four years later, at £60,000 for Jamaica alone. The British merchants claimed that free trade would mean the purchase of a larger number of Negroes, which would mean the production of a larger quantity of British goods for the purchase and upkeep of the slaves.

The controversy ended in a victory for free trade. On July 5, 1698, Parliament passed an act abrogating the monopoly of the Royal African Company, and throwing open the trade to all British subjects on payment of a duty of 10 per cent *ad valorem* on all goods exported to Africa for the purchase of slaves.

The acrimonious controversy retained no trade of the pseudo-humanitarianism of the Spaniards in the sixteenth century, that Negro slavery was essential to the preservation of the Indians. In its place was a solid economic fact, that Negro slavery was essential to the preservation of the sugar plantations. The considerations were purely economic. The slaves were denominated 'black ivory'. The best slave was, in Spanish parlance, a 'piece of the Indies', a slave 30–35 years old, about five feet eleven inches in height, without any physical defect. Adults who were not so tall and children were measured, and the total reduced to 'pieces of the Indies'. A contract in 1676 between the Spaniards and the Portuguese called for the supply of 10,000 'tons' of slaves; to avoid fraud and argument, it was stipulated that three Negroes should be considered the equivalent of one ton. In 1651 the English Guinea Company instructed its agent to load one of its ships with as many Negroes as it could carry, and, in default, to fill the ship with cattle.

The mortality in the Middle Passage was regarded merely as an unfortunate trading loss, except for the fact that Negroes were more costly than cattle. Losses in fact ran quite high, but such concern as was evinced had to deal merely with profits. In 1659, a Dutch slaver, the *St. Jan*, lost 110 slaves out of a cargo of 219 — for every two slaves purchased, one died in transit to the West Indies. In 1678, the *Arthur*, one of the ships of the Royal African Company, suffered a mortality of 88 out of 417 slaves — that is, more than 20 per cent. The *Martha*, another ship, landed 385 in Barbados out of 447 taken on the coast — the mortality amounted to 62, or a little less than 15 per cent. The *Coaster* lost 37 out of 150, a mortality of approximately 25 per cent. The *Hannibal*, in 1694, with a cargo of 700 slaves, buried 320 on the voyage, a mortality of 43 per cent; the Royal African Company lost £10 and the owner of the vessel 10 guineas on each slave, the total loss amounting to £6,650. The losses sustained by these five vessels amounted to 617 out of a total cargo of 1,933, that is, 32 per cent. Three out of every ten slaves perished in the Middle Passage. Hence the note of exasperation in the account of his voyage by the captain of the *Hannibal*:

> No gold-finders can endure so much noisome slavery as they do who carry Negroes; for those have some respite and satisfaction, but we endure twice the misery; and yet by their mortality our voyages are ruin'd, and we pine and fret our selves to death to think we should undergo so much misery, and take so much pains to so little purpose.

The lamentations of an individual slave trader or sugar planter were drowned out by the seventeenth-century chorus of approbation. Negro slavery and the Negro slave trade fitted beautifully into the economic theory of the age. This theory, known as mercantilism, stated that the wealth of a nation depended upon its possession of bullion, the precious metals. If, however, bullion was not available through possession of the mines, the new doctrine went further than its Spanish predecessor in emphasising that a country could increase its stock by a favourable balance of trade, exporting more than it imported. One of the best and clearest statements of the theory was made by Edward Misselden, in his *Circle of Commerce*, in 1623:

> For as a pair of scales is an invention to show us the weight of things, whereby we may discern the heavy from the light . . . so is also the balance of trade an excellent and politique invention to show us the difference of weight in the commerce of one kingdom with another: that is, whether the native commodities exported, and all the foreign commodities imported do balance or over-balance one another in the scale of commerce . . . If the native commodities exported do weight down and exceed in value the foreign commodities imported, it is a rule that never fails that then the kingdom grows rich and prospers in estate and stock: because the overplus thereof must needs come in in treasure . . . But if the foreign commodities imported do exceed in value the native commodities exported, it is a manifest sign that the trade decayeth, and the stock of the kingdom wasteth apace; because the overplus must needs go out in treasure.

National policy of the leading European nations concentrated on achieving a favourable balance of trade. Colonial possessions were highly prized as a means to this end; they increased the exports of the metropolitan country, prevented the drain of treasure by the purchase of necessary tropical produce, and provided freights for the ships of the metropolis and employment for its sailors.

The combination of the Negro slave trade, Negro slavery and Caribbean sugar production is known as the triangular trade. A ship left the metropolitan country with a cargo of metropolitan goods, which it exchanged on the coast of West Africa for slaves. This constituted the first side of the triangle. The second constisted of the Middle Passage, the voyage from West Africa to the West Indies with the slaves. The triangle was completed by the voyage from the West Indies to the metropolitan country with sugar and other Caribbean products received in exchange for the slaves. As the slave ships were not always adequate for the transportation of the West Indian produce, the triangular trade was supplemented by a direct trade between the metropolitan country and the West Indian islands.

The triangular trade provided a market in West Africa and the West Indies for metropolitan products, thereby increasing metropolitan exports and contributing to full employment at home. The purchase of the slaves on the coast of West Africa and their maintenance in the West Indies gave an enormous stimulus to metropolitan industry and agriculture. For example, the British woollen industry was heavily dependent on the triangular trade. A parliamentary committee of 1695 emphasised that the slave trade was an encouragement to Britain's woollen industry. In addition, wool was required in the West Indies for blankets and clothing for the slaves on the plantations.

Iron, guns and brass also figured prominently in the triangular trade and the ancillary West Indian trade. Iron bars were the trading medium on a large part of the West African coast, and by 1682 Britain was exporting about 10,000 bars of iron a year to Africa. Sugar stoves, iron rollers, nails found a ready market on the West Indian plantations. Brass pans and kettles were customarily included in the slave trader's cargo.

The triangular trade presented an impressive statistical picture. Britain's trade in 1697 may be taken as an illustration.

	Imports £	*Exports £*
British West Indies	326,536	142,795
North America	279,582	140,129
Africa	6,615	13,435
Antigua	28,209	8,029
Barbados	196,532	77,465
Jamaica	70,000	40,726
Montserrat	14,699	3,532
Nevis	17,096	13,043
Carolina	12,374	5,289
New England	26,282	64,468
New York	10,093	4,579
Pennsylvania	3,347	2,997
Virginia and Maryland	227,756	58,796
Total	*1,220,121*	*575,283*

Barbados was the most important single colony in the British Empire, worth almost as much, in its total trade, as the two tobacco colonies of Virginia and Maryland combined, and nearly three times as valuable as Jamaica. The tiny sugar island was more valuable to Britain than Carolina, New England, New York and Pennsylvania together. 'Go ahead, England, Barbados is behind you,' is today a stock joke in the British West Indies of the Barbadian's view of his own importance. Two and a half centuries ago, it was no joke. It was sound politics, based on sound economics. Jamaica's external trade was larger than New England's as far as Britain was concerned; Nevis was more important in the commercial firmament than New York; Antigua surpassed Carolina; Montserrat rated higher than Pennsylvania. Total British trade with Africa was larger than total trade with Pennsylvania, New York and Carolina. In 1697 the triangular trade accounted for nearly 10 per cent of total British imports and over 4 per cent of total British exports. Barbados alone accounted for nearly 4 per cent of Britain's external trade.

Mercantilists were jubilant. The West Indian colonies were ideal colonies, providing a market, directly as well as indirectly, through the slave trade, for British manufactures and foodstuffs, whilst they supplied sugar and other tropical commodities that would otherwise have had to be imported from foreigners or dispensed with entirely. The West Indies thus contributed to Britain's balance of trade in two ways, by buying Britain's exports and by rendering the expenditure of bullion on foreign tropical imports unnecessary. On the other hand, the mainland colonies, Virginia and Maryland, and, to a lesser extent, Carolina excepted, where the conditions of labour and production duplicated those of the West Indies, were nuisances; they produced the same agricultural commodities as England, gave early evidence of competing with the metropolitan countries in manufactured goods as well, and were rivals in fishing and shipbuilding.

The British economists enthused. Sir Josiah Child in his *New Discourse of Trade* in 1668, wrote:

> The people that evacuate from us to Barbados, and the other West India Plantations . . . do commonly work one Englishman to ten or eight Blacks; and if we keep the trade of our said plantations entirely to England, England would have no less inhabitants, but rather an increase of people by such evacuation, because that one Englishman, with the Blacks that work with him, accounting what they eat, use and wear, would make employment for four men in England . . . whereas peradventure of ten men that issue from us to New England and Ireland, what we send to or receive from them, doth not employ one man in England.

In 1690, Sir Dalby Thomas stated that every white man in the West Indies was one hundred and thirty times more valuable to Britain than those who stayed at home:

> Each white man, woman, and child, residing in the sugar plantations, occasions the consumption of more of our native commodities, and manufactures, than ten at home do — beef, pork, salt, fish, butter, cheese, corn, flour, beer, cyder, bridles, coaches, beds, chairs, stools, pictures, clocks, watches; pewter, brass, copper, iron vessels and instruments; sail-cloth and cordage; of which, in their building, shipping, mills, boiling, and distilling-houses, field-labour and domestic uses, they consume infinite quantities.

Charles Davenant, perhaps the ablest of the seventeenth-century economists, estimated at the end of the century that Britain's total profit from trade amounted to £2,000,000. Of this figure the plantation trade accounted for £600,000, and the re-export of plantation produce for £120,000. Trade with Africa, Europe and the Levant brought in another £600,000. The triangular trade thus represented a minimum of 36 per cent of Britain's commercial profits. Davenant added that every individual in the West Indies, white or Negro, was as profitable as seven in England.

What the West Indies had done for Seville in Spain in the sixteenth century, they did for Bristol in England and Bordeaux in France in the seventeenth. Each town became the metropolis of its country's trade with the Caribbean, though neither Bristol nor Bordeaux enjoyed the monopoly that had been granted to Seville. In 1661 only one ship, and that ship a Dutch one, came to Bordeaux from the West Indies. Ten years later twelve ships sailed from that port to the West Indies, and six returned from there. In 1683 the number of sailings to the sugar islands had risen to twenty-six. La Rochelle for a time eclipsed Bordeaux. In 1685 forty-nine ships sailed from that port to the West Indies. Nantes also was intimately connected with West Indian trade; in 1684 twenty-four ships belonging to the port were engaged in West Indian trade.

As a result of the triangular trade Bristol became a city of shopkeepers. It was said in 1685 that there was scarcely a shopkeeper in the city who had not a venture on board some ship bound for Virginia or the West Indies. The port took the lead in the struggle for the abrogation of the Royal African Company's monopoly, and in the first nine years of free trade shipped slaves to the West Indies at the rate of 17,883 a year. In 1700 Bristol had forty-six ships in the West Indian trade.

The basis of this astounding commercial efflorescence was the Negro slaves, 'the strength and sinews of this western world'. In 1662 the Company of Royal Adventurers trading to Africa pointed to the 'profit and honour' that had accrued to British subjects from the slave trade, which King Charles II himself described as that 'beneficial trade . . . so much importing our service, and the enriching of this Our Kingdom'. According to Colbert in France, no commerce in the world produced as many advantages as the slave trade. Benjamin Raule exhorted the Elector of Prussia, on October 26, 1685, not to be left behind in the race: 'Everyone knows that the slave trade is the source of the wealth which the Spaniards wring out of the West Indies, and that whoever knows how to furnish them slaves, will share their wealth. Who can say by how many millions of hard cash the Dutch West India Company has enriched itself in this slave trade!' At the end of the seventeenth century all Europe, and not England only, was impressed with the words of Sir Dalby Thomas: 'The pleasure, glory and grandeur of England has been advanced more by sugar than by any other commodity, wool not excepted.'

The Negro slave trade in the eighteenth century constituted one of the greatest migrations in recorded history. Its volume is indicated in the following table, prepared from various statistics that are available.

Years	*Colony*	*Importation*	*Average importation per year*
1700–86	Jamaica	610,000	7,000
1708–35 & 1747–66	Barbados	148,821	3,100
1680–1776	Saint-Domingue	800,000	8,247
1720–29	Antigua	12,278	1,362
1721–30	St. Kitts	10,358	1,035
1721–29	Montserrat	3,210	357
1721–26	Nevis	1,267	253
1767–73	Dominica	19,194	2,742
1763–89	Cuba	30,875	1,143
1700–54	Danish Islands	11,750	214

Average annual importations do not provide a complete picture. In 1774 the importation into Jamaica was 18,448. In fourteen of the years 1702–75, the annual importation exceeded 10,000. Imports into Saint-Domingue averaged 12,559 in the years 1764–68; in 1768 they were 15,279. In 1718 Barbados imported 7,126 slaves. During the nine months in which Cuba was under British occupation in 1762, 10,700 slaves were introduced. The British introduced 41,000 slaves in three years into Guadeloupe whilst they were in occupation of the island during the Seven Years' War.

These large importations represented one of the greatest advantages which the slave trade had over other trades. The frightful mortality of the slaves on the plantations made annual increments essential. Consider the case of Saint-Domingue. In 1763 the slave population amounted to 206,539. Imports from 1764 to 1774 numbered 102,474. The slave population in 1776 was 290,000. Thus, despite an importation of over 1,000,000, without taking into account the annual births, the increase of the slave population in thirteen years was less than 85,000. Taking only importations into consideration, the slave population in 1776 was 19,000 less than the figure of 1763 with the importations added, and the imports for one year are not available.

A much clearer illustration of the mortality is available for Barbados. In 1764 there were 70,706 slaves in the island. Importations to 1783, with no figures available for the years 1779 and 1780, totalled 41,840. The total population, allowing for neither deaths nor births, should, therefore, have been 112,546 in 1783. Actually, it was 62,258. Thus despite an annual importation for the eighteen years for which statistics are available of 2,324, the population in 1783 was 8,448 less than it was in 1764, or an annual decline of 469. The appalling mortality is brought out in the following table.

Year	*Slaves*	*Imports*	*Potential pop. of next year*	*Actual pop. of next year*	*Decrease*	*Decrease as % of imports*
1764	70,706	3,936	74,642	72,255	2,387	60
1765	72,255	3,228	75,483	73,651	1,832	57
1766	73,651	4,061	77,712	74,656	3,056	75
1767	74,656	4,154	78,810	76,275	2,535	61
1768	76,275	4,628	80,903	75,658	4,345	90
1769	75,658	6,837	82,495	76,334	6,161	90
1770	76,334	5,825	82,159	75,998	6,171	106
1771	75,998	2,728	78,716	74,485	4,231	155
1764–71		35,397	106,103	74,206	31,897	90

Thus, after eight years of importations, averaging 4,424 a year, the population of Barbados was only 3,411 larger. 35,397 slaves had been imported; 31,897 had disappeared. In 1770 and 1771 the mortality was so high that the importation in those years, heavy though it was, was not adequate to supply the deficit. Half the population had had to be renewed in eight years.

In 1703 Jamaica had 45,000 Negroes; in 1778, 205,261, an average annual increase from all causes of 2,109. Between 1703 and 1775, 469,893 slaves had been imported, an average annual importation of 6,807. For every additional slave in its population, Jamaica had had to import three. The total population in 1778, excluding births and based only on imports, should have been 541,893, and that figure excludes imports for 1776, 1777 and 1778. Allowing 11,000 a year for those three years, the total population in 1778 should have been 547,893. The actual population in that year was less than 40 per cent of the potential total.

Economic development has never been purchased so high a price. According to one of the leading planters of Saint-Domingue, one in every three imported Negroes died in the first three years. To the mortality on the plantations must be added the mortality on the slave ships. On the slave ships belonging to the port of Nantes in France, that mortality varied from 5 per cent in 1746 and 1774 to as high as 34 per cent in 1732. For all the slave cargoes transported by them between 1715 and 1775, the mortality amounted to 16 per cent. Of 100 Negroes who left the coast of Africa, therefore, only 84 reached the West Indies; one-third of these died in three years. For every 56 Negroes, therefore, on the plantations at the end of three years, 44 had perished.

The slave trade thus represented a wear and tear, a depreciation which no other trade equalled. The loss of an individual planter or trader was insignificant compared with the basic fact that every cargo of slaves, including the quick and the dead, represented so much industrial development and employment, so much employment of ships and sailors, in the metropolitan country. No other commercial undertaking required so large a capital as the slave trade. In addition to the ship, there was its equipment, armament, cargo, its unusually large supply of water and foodstuffs, its abnormally large crew. In 1765 it was estimated that in France the cost of fitting out and arming a vessel for 300 slaves was 242,500 livres. The cargo of a vessel from Nantes in 1757 was valued at 141,500 livres; it purchased 500 slaves. The cargo of the *Prince de Conty*, of 300 tons, was valued at 221,224 livres, with which 800 slaves were purchased.

Large profits were realised from the slave trade. The *King Solomon*, belonging to the Royal African Company, carried a cargo worth £4,252 in 1720. It took on 296 Negroes who were sold in St. Kitts for £9,228. The profit was thus 117 per cent. From 1698 to 1707 the Royal African Company exported from England to Africa goods to the value of £293,740. The Company sold 5,982 Negroes in Barbados for £156,425, an average of £26 per head. It sold 2,178 slaves in Antigua for £80,522, an average of £37 per head. The total number of Negroes imported into the British islands by the Company in these years was 17,760. The sale of 8,160 Negroes in Barbados and Antigua, less than half the total imports into all the islands, thus realised 80 per cent of the total exports from England. Allowing an average price of £26 per head for the remaining 9,600 Negroes, the total amount realised from the sale of the Company's Negroes was £488,107. The profit on the Company's exports was thus 66 per cent. For every £3 worth of merchandise exported from England, the Company obtained an additional £2 by way of profit.

The Negroes taken on by the *Prince de Conty* on the coast of Africa averaged 275 livres each; the survivors of the Middle Passage fetched 1,300 livres each in Saint-Domingue. In 1700 a cargo of 238 slaves was purchased by the Danish West Indies at prices ranging from 90 to 100 rixdollars. In 1753 the wholesale price on the coast of Africa was 100 rixdollars; the retail price in the Danish West Indies was 150–300 rixdollars. In 1724 the Danish West India Company made a profit of 28 per cent on its slave imports; in 1725, 30 per cent; 70 per cent on the survivors of a cargo of 1733 despite a mortality in transit of 45 per cent; 50 per cent on a cargo of 1754. It need occasion no surprise, therefore, that one of the eighteenth-century slave dealers admitted that, of all the places he had lived in, England, Ireland, America, Portugal, the West Indies, the Cape Verde Islands, the Azores and Africa, it was in Africa that he could most quickly make his fortune.

The slave trade was central to the triangular trade. It was, in the words of one British mercantilist, 'the spring and parent whence the others flow'; 'the first principle and foundation of all the rest', echoed another, 'the mainspring of the machine which sets every wheel in motion'. The slave trade kept the wheels of metropolitan industry turning; it stimulated navigation and shipbuilding and employed seamen; it raised fishing villages into flourishing cities; it gave sustenance to new industries based on the processing of colonial raw materials; it yielded large profits which were ploughed back into metropolitan industry; and, finally, it gave rise to an unprecedented commerce in the West Indies and made the Caribbean territories among the most valuable colonies the world has ever known.

Examples must suffice. In 1729 the British West Indies absorbed one-quarter of Britain's iron exports, and Africa, where the price of a Negro was commonly reckoned at one Birmingham gun, was one of the most important markets for the British armaments industry. In 1753 there were 120 sugar refineries in England — eighty in London, twenty in Bristol. In 1780 the British West Indies supplied two-thirds of the 6,500,000 pounds of raw cotton imported by Britain. Up to 1770 one-third of Manchester's textile exports went to Africa, one-half to the West Indian and American colonies. In 1709 the British West Indies employed one-tenth of all British shipping engaged in foreign trade. Between 1710 and 1714, 122,000 tons of British shipping sailed to the West Indies, 112,000 tons to the mainland colonies. Between 1709 and 1787, British shipping engaged in foreign trade quadrupled; ships clearing for Africa multiplied twelve times and the tonnage eleven times.

The triangular trade marked the ascendancy of two additional European ports in the eighteenth century, Liverpool in England and Nantes in France, and further contributed to the development of Bristol and Bordeaux, begun in the seventeenth century. Liverpool's first slave ship, of 30 tons, sailed for Africa in 1709. In 1783 the port had 85 ships, of 12,294 tons, in the trade. Between 1709 and 1783, a total of 2,249 ships, of 240,657 tons, sailed from Liverpool to Africa — an annual average of 30 ships and 3,200 tons. The proportion of slave ships to the total shipping of the port was one in a hundred in 1709, one in nine in 1730, one in four in 1763, one in three in 1771. In 1752, 88 Liverpool vessels carried upwards of 24,730 slaves from Africa. Seven firms, owning 26 vessels, carried 7,030 slaves.

Liverpool's exports to Africa in 1770 read like a census of British manufactures: beans, brass, beer, textiles, copper, candles, chairs, cider, cordage, earthenware, gunpowder, glass, haberdashery, iron, lead, looking glasses, pewter, pipes, paper, stockings, silver, sugar, salt, kettles.

In 1774 there were eight sugar refineries in Liverpool. Two distilleries were established in the town for the express purpose of supplying slave ships. There were many chain and anchor foundries, and manufacturers of and dealers in iron, copper, brass and lead in the town. In 1774 there were fifteen roperies. Half of Liverpool's sailors were engaged in the slave trade, which, by 1783, was estimated to bring the town a clear annual profit of £300,000. The slave trade transformed Liverpool from a fishing village into a great centre of international commerce. The population rose from 5,000 in 1700 to 34,000 in 1773. It was a common saying in the town that its principal streets had been marked out by the chains, and the walls of its houses cemented by the blood, of the African slaves. The red brick Customs House, blazoned with Negro heads, bore mute but eloquent testimony to the origins of Liverpool's rise by 1783 to the position of one of the most famous — or infamous, depending on the point of view — towns in the world of commerce.

What Liverpool was to England, Nantes was to France. Between 1715 and 1775, vessels belonging to the port exported 229,525 slaves from Africa, an annual average of 3,763. In 1751 Nantes ships transported 10,003 Negroes. Slave ships constituted about one-fifth of the total shipping of the port. But the slave trade conditioned all others. The slavers brought back sugar and other tropical produce. The number of sugar refineries declined from fifteen in 1700 to four in 1750. But five textile factories were established by 1769, together with manufactures of jams and sweetmeats dependent on sugar. As in Liverpool, a slave trading aristocracy developed, of big capitalists each owning four or six ships.

The West Indian trade was worth twice as much to eighteenth-century Bristol as the remainder of her other overseas commerce. In the 1780s the town had 30 vessels engaged in the slave trade, and 72 in the West Indian trade. Some of its most prominent citizens were engaged in sugar refining. The Baptist Mills of Bristol produced brass manufactures for the slave trade.

As Nantes was the slave trading port *par excellence* of France, Bordeaux was the sugar port. In 1720, Bordeaux had 74 ships, of 6,882 tons, in the West Indian trade; in 1782, 310 ships, of 108,000 tons. In 1749 the town's trade with the West Indies exceeded 27 million livres; in 1771, at its peak, it approximated 171 million. An enormous stimulus was given to shipbuilding: 14 ships, of 3,640 tons, in 1754; 245 totalling 74,485 tons, between 1763 and 1778. Sugar imports into Bordeaux, less than 10 million livres in 1749, attained the huge figure of 101 million in 1780. A mere 22 livres of coffee were imported in 1724; in 1771, the figure was 112 million. Indigo, less than 5 million livres up to 1770, amounted to 22 million in 1772. Bordeaux, in return, exported codfish from Newfoundland, salted fish from Holland, salted beef from Ireland, flour and wine to the West Indies. There were 26 sugar refineries in the town in 1789. Population rose from 43,000 in 1698 to 110,000 in 1790.

The West Indian basis of Bordeaux' prosperity was symbolised by the aggrandisement of a naturalised Portuguese Jew, Gradis. The founder of the dynasty was David, who became a citizen in 1731. Devoting himself exclusively to West Indian trade, he established a branch in Saint-Domingue, which he entrusted to a brother-in-law, Jacob, and another in Martinique, which was supervised by a nephew. His son, Abraham, became the greatest merchant in eighteenth-century Bordeaux. At the government's order, he supplied Canada in the Seven Years' War, six ships in 1756, fourteen in 1758. He loaned large sums to the state and to the greatest in the land. He died in 1780, leaving a fortune of 8 million livres, having lived to hear himself denominated by contemporaries, 'the famous Jew Gradis, King of Bordeaux'.

The remarkable value of the triangular trade can best be presented statistically. As for the seventeenth century, we shall take as an illustration the British West Indies. The table that follows gives British imports from, and British exports to, the several colonies for the year 1773 and the period 1714 to 1773.

Thus Jamaica in the eighteenth century was what Barbados had been in the seventeenth century, the most important colony in the British Empire. Its exports to Britain from 1714 to 1773 were three times those of Barbados; its imports from Britain more than double. In these years one-twelfth of total British imports came from Jamaica, nearly one-fortieth of total British exports went to Jamaica. In 1773 one-ninth of total British imports came from the island, one-twenty-second of British exports went to it. Jamaica's exports to Britain were ten times those of New England; the exports to the two colonies were about the same. Jamaica's exports to Britain from 1714 to 1773 were one-fifth larger than those of Virginia and Maryland combined; its imports from Britain about one-tenth less.

From 1714 to 1773 Barbados' exports to Britain were more than one quarter larger than those of Carolina, imports from Britain about one-tenth less. Antigua's exports to Britain were 15 per cent larger than those of Pennsylvania; imports from Britain about two-fifths the figure for that mainland colony. St. Kitts' exports to

Colony	*Imports (1773)*	*Exports (1773)*	*Imports (1714–73)*	*Exports (1714–73)*
Total British	11,406,841	14,763,252	492,146,670	730,962,105
Antigua	112,779	93,323	12,785,262	3,821,726
Barbados	168,682	148,817	14,506,497	7,442,652
Jamaica	1,286,888	683,451	42,259,749	16,844,990
Montserrat	47,911	14,947	3,387,237	537,831
Nevis	39,299	9,181	3,636,504	549,564
St. Kitts	150,512	62,607	13,305,659*	3,181,901*
Tobago	20,453	30,049	49,587†	122,093†
Grenada	445,041	102,761	3,620,504‡	1,179,279‡
St. Vincent	145,619	38,444	672,991	235,665
Dominica	248,868	43,679	1,469,704§	322,294§
Tortola	48,000	26,927	863,931‖	220,038‖
Carolina	456,513	344,859	11,410,480	8,423,588
New England	124,624	527,055	4,134,392	16,934,316
New York	76,246	289,214	1,910,796	11,377,696
Pennsylvania	36,652	426,448	1,115,112	9,627,409
Virginia & Maryland	589,803	328,904	35,158,481	18,391,097
British West Indies	2,830,583	1,270,846	101,264,818	45,389,988
Mainland Colonies	1,420,471	2,375,797	55,552,675	69,903,613
Africa	68,424	662,112	2,407,447	15,235,829

*1732–73 †1764–73 ‡1762–73 §1763–73 ‖1748–73

Britain were seven times the figure for New York; its imports more than one-quarter those of New York. Grenada's exports to Britain in twelve years, 1762–73, were more than five times as large as Georgia's in forty-two, 1732–73; Grenada's imports were half as large as those of Georgia.

In 1773 total British imports from the British West Indies amounted to one quarter of total British imports, British exports to the West Indies to about one-eleventh of the total export trade. Imports from the mainland colonies were one half the West Indian figure; exports less than double. For the years 1714–73, British imports from the West Indies were one-fifth of the total import trade; from the mainland colonies they were slightly more than half the West Indian figure; from Africa they were 0.5 per cent. British exports to the West Indies during the period were one-sixteenth of the total export trade; to the mainland, they were one-tenth; to Africa, one-fiftieth. For these sixty years the triangular trade accounted for 21 per cent of British imports; 8 per cent of British exports; and nearly 14 per cent of Britain's total external trade.

The population of the British West Indies in 1787 was 58,353 whites; 7,706 free Negroes; 461,864 slaves — a total of 527,923. The annual British export of slaves from Africa by 1783 was approximately 34,000. This was the human and social basis of one in every five pounds of British imports, one in every twelve of British exports, and one in every seven of Britain's total trade.

The situation in the French West Indies was essentially similar. In 1715 France's external trade amounted to 175 million livres — imports, 75; exports, 100. West Indian trade accounted for one-sixth of the whole, 30 million; their imports, of 20 million, amounted to one-fifth of France's export trade; their exports, 10 million, constituted one-eighth of France's import trade. In 1776, though France had lost some of the smaller West Indian islands, exports from the French West Indies amounted to 200 million livres, imports to 70 million, the total external trade of the islands representing more than one-third of total French commerce, which oscillated between 600 and 700 million livres; West Indian trade employed 1,000 ships, outward and inward cargoes in the proportion of 5 to 4. The population of the French West Indies about 1780 amounted to 63,682 whites, 13,429 free Negroes, and 437,738 slaves — a total of 514,849. France's annual export of slaves from Africa was estimated at 20,000.

Magnum est saccharum et prevalebit! Great is sugar, and it will prevail! Mercantilists were jubilant. The colonies, wrote Horace Walpole, were 'the source of all our riches, and preserve the balance of trade in our favour, for I don't know where we have it but by the means of our colonies'. The statistics given above identify the colonies which Walpole had in mind. An annual profit of 7s per head was sufficient to enrich a country, said William Wood; each white man in the colonies brought a profit of over £7 pounds, twenty times as much. The Negro slaves, said Postlethwayt, were 'the fundamental prop and support' of the colonies, 'valuable people', and the British Empire was 'a magnificent superstructure of American commerce and naval power on an African foundation'. Rule Britannia! Britannia rules the waves. For Britons never shall be slaves.

But the sons of France arose to glory. France joined in the homage to the triangular trade. 'What commerce,' asked the Chamber of Commerce of Nantes, 'can be compared to that which obtains men in exchange for commodities?' Profound question! The abandonment of the slave trade, continued the Chamber, would be inevitably followed by the ruin of colonial commerce; 'whence follows the fact that we have no branch of trade so precious to the State and so worthy of protection as the Guinea trade'. The triangular trade was incomparable, the slave trade precious, and the West Indies perfect colonies. 'The more colonies differ from the metropolis,' said Nantes, 'the more perfect they are... Such are the Caribbean colonies; they have none of our objects of trade; they have others which we lack and cannot produce.'

But there were discordant notes in the mercantilist harmony. The first was opposition to the slave trade. In 1774, in Jamaica, the very centre of Negro slavery, a debating society voted that the slave trade was not consistent with sound policy, or with the laws of nature and of morality. In 1776 Thomas Jefferson wrote into the Declaration of Independence three paragraphs attacking the King of England for his 'piratical warfare' on the coast of Africa against people who never offended him, and for his veto of colonial legislation attempting to prohibit or restrain the slave trade. The paragraphs were only deleted on the representations of the states of South Carolina, Georgia and New England. Two petitions were presented to Parliament, in 1774 and 1776, for abolition of the slave trade. A third, more important, was presented in 1783 by the Quakers. The Prime Minister, Lord North, complimented them on their humanity, but regretted that abolition was an impossibility, as the slave trade had become necessary to every nation in Europe. European public opinion accepted the position stated by Postlethwayt: 'We shall take things as they are, and reason from them in their present state, and not from that wherein we could hope them to be.... We cannot think of giving up the slave-trade, notwithstanding my good wishes that it could be done.'

The second discordant note was more disturbing. Between 1772 and 1778, Liverpool slave traders were estimated to have lost £700,000 in the slave trade. By 1788 twelve of the thirty leading houses which had dominated the trade from 1773 had gone bankrupt. Slave trading, like sugar production, had its casualties. A slave trader in 1754, as his supreme defence of the slave trade, had adumbrated that 'from this trade proceed benefits, far outweighing all, either real or pretended mischiefs and inconveniencies'. If and when the slave trade ceased to be profitable, it would not be so easy to defend it.

The third discordant note came also from the British colonies. The British government's ambition was to become the slave carriers and sugar suppliers of the whole world. Britain had fought for and obtained the *asiento*. The supply of slaves to foreign nations became an integral part of the British slave trade. Of 497,736 slaves imported in Jamaica between 1702 and 1775, 137,114 had been re-exported, one out of every four. In 1731, imports were 10,079; re-exports, 5,708. From 1775 to 1783, Antigua imported 5,673 slaves and re-exported 1,972, one out of every three. Jamaica resorted to its seventeenth-century policy, an export tax on all Negroes re-exported. In 1774, the Board of Trade, on the representation of the slave traders of London, Liverpool and Bristol, disallowed the law as unjustifiable, improper and prejudicial to British commerce, pointed out that legislative autonomy in the colonies did not extend to the imposition of duties upon British ships and goods or to the prejudice and obstruction of British commerce, and reprimanded the Governor of the island for dereliction of duty in not stopping efforts to 'check and discourage a traffic... beneficial to the nation'.

French Capitalism and Caribbean Slavery

C. L. R. JAMES

The slave trade and slavery were the economic basis of the French Revolution. 'Sad irony of human history,' comments Jaurès. 'The fortunes created at Bordeaux, at Nantes, by the slave trade, gave to the bourgeoisie that pride which needed liberty and contributed to human emancipation.' Nantes was the centre of the slave trade. As early as 1666, 108 ships went to the coast of Guinea and took on board 37,430[1] slaves, to a total value of more than 37 million, giving the Nantes bourgeoisie 15–20 per cent on their money. In 1700 Nantes was sending 50 ships a year to the West Indies with Irish salt beef, linen for the household and for clothing the slaves, and machinery for sugar-mills. *Nearly all the industries which developed in France during the eighteenth century had their origin in goods or commodities destined for the coast of Guinea or for America.* The capital from the slave-trade fertilized them; though the bourgeoisie traded in other things than slaves, upon the success or failure of the traffic everything else depended.[2]

Some ships took on the way wine from Maderia for the colonists and dried turtle from Cape Verde for the slaves. In return they brought back colonial produce to Nantes whence Dutch vessels took it to Northern Europe. Some made the return journey by the way of Spain and Portugal, exchanging their colonial cargo for the products of those countries. Sixty ships from Rochelle and Oberon brought their salted cod to Nantes, to go to the inland market or out to the colonies to feed the slaves. The year 1758 saw the first manufactory of Indian cloth, to weave the raw cotton of India and the West Indian islands.

The planters and small manufacturers of San Domingo were able to establish themselves only by means of the capital advanced by the maritime bourgeoisie. By 1789 the Nantes merchants alone had 50 million invested in the West Indies.

Bordeaux had begun with the wine industry which gave its ship-builders and navigators an opportunity to trade all over the world; then came brandy, also to all ports, but above all to the colonies. By the middle of the eighteenth century, 16 factories refined 10,000 tons of raw sugar from San Domingo every year, using nearly 4,000 tons of charcoal. Local factories supplied the town with jars, dishes and bottles. The trade was cosmopolitan — Flemings, Germans, Dutchmen, Irishmen and Englishmen came to live in Bordeaux, contributing to the general expansion and amassing riches for themselves. Bordeaux traded with Holland, Germany, Portugal, Venice and Ireland, but slavery and the colonial trade were the fount and origin and sustenance of this thriving industry and farflung commerce.

Marseilles was the great centre for the Mediterranean and Eastern trade, and a royal decree at the beginning of the century had attempted to exclude it from the trade with the colonies. The attempt failed. San Domingo was the special centre of the Marseilles trade. Marseilles sent there not only the wines of Provence: in 1789 there were in Marseilles 12 sugar refineries, nearly as many as in Bordeaux.

In the early years most of this trade had been carried in foreign-built or foreign-owned ships. But by 1730 the maritime bourgeois began to build themselves. In 1778 Bordeaux ship-owners constructed seven vessels, in 1784 they constructed 32, with a total of 115 for the six years. A Marseilles ship-owner, Georges Roux, could fit out a fleet on his own account in order

The Black Jacobins: Toussaint L'Ouverture and the San Domingo Revolution (Vintage Books, 1963), pp. 47–61.

to take vengeance on the English fleet for the prizes it had taken.

Nantes, Bordeaux and Marseilles were the chief centres of the maritime bourgeoisie, bur Orlenas, Dieppe, Bercy-Paris, a dozen great towns, refined raw sugar and shared in the subsidiary industries.[3] A large part of the hides worked in France came from San Domingo. The flourishing cotton industry of Normandy drew its raw cotton in part from the West Indies, and in all its ramifications the cotton trade occupied the population of more than a hundred French towns. In 1789 exchanges with the American colonies were 296 million. France exported to the islands 78 million of flour, salted meats, wines and stuffs. The colonies sent to France 218 million of sugar, coffee, cocoa, wood, indigo and hides. Of the 218 million imported only 71 million were consumed in France. The rest was exported after preparation. The total value of the colonies represented 3,000 million, and on them depended the livelihood of a number of Frenchmen variously estimated at between two and six million. By 1759 San Domingo was the market of the new world. It received in its ports 1,587 ships, a greater number than Marseilles, and France used for the San Domingo trade alone 750 great vessels employing 24,000 sailors. In 1789 Britain's export trade would be £27 million, that of France £17 million, of which the trade of San Domingo would account for nearly £11 million. The whole of Britain's colonial trade in that year amounted to only £5 million.[4]

The maritime bourgeoisie would not hear of any change in the Exclusive. They had the ear of the Minister and the Government, and not only were the colonists refused permission to trade with foreign countries, but the circulation of all French currency, except the very lowest, was forbidden in the islands, lest the colonists use it to purchase foreign goods. In such a method of trade they were at the mercy of the bourgeoisie. In 1774 their indebtedness was 200 million, and by 1789 it was estimated at between 300 and 500 million.[5] If the colonists complained of the Exclusive, the bourgeoisie complained that the colonists would not pay their debts, and agitated for stricter measures against the contraband.

Rich as was the French bourgeoisie, the colonial trade was too big for it. The British bourgeois, most successful of slave-traders, sold thousands of smuggled slaves every year to the French colonists and particularly to San Domingo. But even while they sold the slaves to San Domingo, the British were watching the progress of this colony with alarm and with envy. After the independence of America in 1783, this amazing French colony suddenly made such a leap as almost to double its production between 1783 and 1789. In those years Bordeaux alone invested 100 million in San Domingo. The British bourgeois were the great rivals of the French. All through the eighteenth century they fought in every part of the world. The French had jumped gleefully in to help drive them out of America. San Domingo was now incomparably the finest colony in the world and its possibilities seemed limitless. The British bourgeoisie investigated the new situation in the West Indies, and on the basis of what it saw, prepared a bombshell for its rivals. Without slaves San Domingo was doomed. The British colonies had enough slaves for all the trade they were ever likely to do. With the tears rolling down their cheeks for the poor suffering blacks, those British bourgeois who had no West Indian interests set up a great howl for the abolition of the slave trade.

A venal race of scholars, profiteering panders to national vanity, have conspired to obscure the truth about abolition. Up to 1783 the British bourgeoisie had taken the slave trade for granted. In 1773 and again in 1774, the Jamaica Assembly, afraid of insurrection and seeking to raise revenue, taxed the importation of slaves. In great wrath the British Board of Trade disallowed the measures and told the Governor that he would be sacked if he gave his sanction to any similar bill.[6] Well-meaning persons talked of the iniquity of slavery and the slave trade, as well-meaning persons in 1938 talked about the native question in Africa or the misery of the Indian peasant. Dr. Johnson toasted the next slave insurrection in the West Indies. Stray members of parliament introduced Bills for the abolition of the slave trade which the House rejected without much bother. In 1783 Lord North turned down a petition against the trade:[7] the petition did credit to the Christian feelings, and to the humane breast, etc, etc, but the trade was necessary. With the loss of America, however, a new situation arose.

The British found that by the abolition of the mercantile system with America, they gained instead of losing. It was the first great lesson in the advantages of free trade. But if Britain gained the British West Indies suffered. The rising industrial bourgeoisie, feeling its way to free trade and a greater exploitation of India, began to abuse the West Indies, called them 'sterile rocks',[8] and asked if the interest and independence of the nation should be sacrificed to 72,000 masters and 400,000 slaves.[9]

The industrial bourgeois were beginning their victorious attack upon the agricultural monopoly which was to culminate in the Repeal of the Corn Laws in 1846. The West Indian sugar-producers were monopolists whose methods of production afforded an easy target, and Adam Smith[10] and Arthur Young,[11] the forerunners of the new era, condemned the whole principle of slave labour as the most expensive in the world. Besides, why not get sugar from India? India, after the loss of America, assumed a new importance. The British experimented with sugar in Bengal, received glowing reports and in 1791 the first shipments arrived.[12] In 1793 Mr. Randle Jackson would preach to the company's shareholders a little sermon on the new orientation. 'It seemed as if Providence, when it took from us America, would not leave its favourite people without an ample substitute; or who should say that Providence had not taken from us one member, more seriously to impress us with the value of another.'[13] It might not be good theology, but it was very good economics. Pitt and Dundas saw a chance of capturing the continental market from France by East India sugar. There was cotton and indigo. The production of cotton in India doubled in a few years. Indian free labour cost a penny a day.

But the West Indian vested interests were strong, statesmen do not act merely on speculation, and these possibilities by themselves would not have accounted for any sudden change in British policy. It was the miraculous growth of San Domingo that was decisive. Pitt found that some 50 per cent of the slaves imported into the British islands were sold to the French colonies.[14] It was the British slave trade, therefore, which was increasing French colonial produce and putting the European market into French hands. Britain was cutting its own throat. And even the profits from this export were not likely to last. Already a few years before the slave merchants had failed for £700,000 in a year.[15] The French, seeking to provide their own slaves, were encroaching in Africa and increasing their share of the trade every year. Why should they continue to buy from Britain? Holland and Spain were doing the same. By 1786 Pitt, a disciple of Adam Smith, had seen the light clearly. He asked Wilberforce to undertake the campaign.[16] Wilberforce represented the important division of Yorkshire, he had a great reputation, all the humanity, justice, stain on national character, etc, etc, would sound well coming from him. Pitt was in a hurry — it was important to bring the trade to a complete stop quickly and suddenly. The French had neither the capital nor the organisation to make good the deficiency at once and he would ruin San Domingo at a stroke. In 1787 he warned Wilberforce that if he did not bring the motion in, somebody else would,[17] and in 1788 he informed the Cabinet that he would not stay in it with those who opposed.[18] Pitt was fairly certain of success in England. With truly British nerve he tried to persuade the European governments to abolish the trade on the score of inhumanity. The French government discussed the proposal amicably, but by May, 1789, the British Ambassador wrote sadly that it seemed as if all the French government's negotiations had been to 'compliment us and to keep us quiet and in good humour'.[19] The Dutch, less polite, gave a more abrupt negative. But here a great stroke of luck befell Pitt. France was then stirring with pre-revolutionary attacks on all obvious abuses, and one year after the Abolitionist Society had been formed in Britain, a group of Liberals in France, Brissot, Mirabeau, Pétion, Condorcet, Abbé Grégoire, all the great names of the first years of the revolution, followed the British example and formed a society, the Friends of the Negro. The leading spirit was Brissot, a journalist who had seen slavery in the United States. The society aimed at the abolition of slavery, published a journal, agitated. This suited the British down to the ground. Clarkson went to Paris, to stimulate 'the slumbering energies'[20] of the society, gave it money, supplied France with British anti-slavery propaganda.[21] Despite the names that were to become so famous and a large membership, we must beware of thinking that the Friends of the Negro represented a force. The colonists took them seriously, the maritime bourgeoisie did not. It was the French Revolution which, with unexpected swiftness, would drag these eloquent Frenchmen out of the stimulating excitement of philanthropic propaganda and put them face to face with economic reality.

These then were the forces which in the decade preceding the French Revolution linked San Domingo to the economic destiny of three continents and the social and political conflicts of that pregnant age. A trade and method of production so cruel and so immoral that it would wilt before the publicity which a great revolution throws upon the sources of wealth; the powerful British Government determined to wreck French commerce in the Antilles, agitating at home and intriguing in France among men who, unbeknown to themselves, would soon have power in their hands; the colonial world (itself divided) and the French bourgeoisie, each intent on its own purposes and, unaware of the approaching danger, drawing apart instead of closer together. Not one courageous leader, many courageous leaders were needed, but the science of history was not what it is today and no man living then could foresee, as we can foresee today, the coming upheavals.[22] Mirabeau indeed said that the colonists slept on the edge of Vesuvius, but for centuries the same thing had been said and the slaves had never done anything.

How could anyone seriously fear for such a wonderful colony? Slavery seemed eternal and the profits mounted. Never before, and perhaps never since, has the world seen anything proportionately so dazzling as the last years of pre-revolutionary San Domingo. Between 1783 and 1789 production nearly doubled. Between 1764 and 1771 the average importation of slaves varied between 10,000 and 15,000. In 1786 it was 27,000, and from 1787 onwards the colony was taking more than 40,000 slaves a year. But economic prosperity is no guarantee of social stability. That rests on the constantly shifting equilibrium between the classes. It was the prosperity of the bourgeoisie that started the English revolution of the seventeenth century. With every stride in production the colony was marching to its doom.

The enormous increase of slaves was filling the colony with native Africans, more resentful, more intractable, more ready for rebellion than the Creole Negro. Of the 500,000 slaves in the colony in 1789, more than two-thirds had been born in Africa.

These slaves were being used for the opening up of new lands. There was no time to allow for the period of acclimatisation, known as the seasoning, and they died like flies. From the earliest days of the colony towards the middle of the eighteenth century, there had been some improvement in the treatment of the slaves, but this enormous number of newcomers who had to be broken and terrorised into labour and submission caused an increase in fear and severity. In 1784 the administrators, who visited one of the slave shops which sometimes served as a market-place instead of the deck of the slaver, reported a revolting picture of dead and dying thrown pell-mell into the filth. The Le Jeune case took place in 1788. In 1790 de Wimpffen states that not one article of the Negro Code was obeyed. He himself had sat at table with a woman, beautiful, rich and very much admired, who had had a careless cook thrown into the oven.

The problem of feeding this enormous increase in the slave population was making the struggle between the planters and the maritime bourgeoisie over the Exclusive more bitter than ever, and the planters after 1783 had forced a slight breach in the straitjacket which clasped them. Having tasted blood, they wanted more.

Mulattoes educated in Paris during the Seven Years' War had come home, and their education and accomplishments filled the colonists with hatred and envy and fear. It was these last years that saw the fiercest legislation against them. Forbidden to go to France, where they learnt things that were not good for them, they stayed at home to increase the strength of the dissatisfied.

With the growth of trade and of profits, the number of planters who could afford to leave their estates in charge of managers grew, and by 1789, in addition to the maritime bourgeoisie, there was a large group of absentee proprietors in France linked to the aristocracy by marriage, for whom San Domingo was nothing else but a source of revenue to be spent in the luxurious living of aristocratic Paris. So far had these parasites penetrated into the French aristocracy that a memoir from San Domingo to the King could say: 'Sire, your court is Creole', without too much stretching of the truth.

The prosperity affected even the slaves. More of them could save money, buy their freedom, and enter the promised land.

This was the San Domingo of 1789, the most profitable colony the world had ever known; to the casual eye the most flourishing and prosperous possession on the face of the globe; to the analyst a society torn by inner and outer contradictions which in four years would split that structure into so many pieces that they could never be put together again.

It was the French bourgeoisie which pressed the button. This strange San Domingo society was but a garish exaggeration, a crazy caricature, of the *ancien régime* in France. The royalist bureaucracy, incompetent and wasteful, could not manage the finances of France; the aristocracy and the clergy had bled the peasantry dry, impeded the economic development of the country, gobbled up all the best places, and considered themselves almost as superior to the able and vigorous bourgeois as the white planters considered themselves superior to the mulattoes.

But the French bourgeoisie too was proud

and no members of it were prouder than the maritime bourgeois. We have seen their wealth. They knew that they were the foundation of the country's prosperity. They were buying up the land of the aristocracy. They built great schools and universities, they read Voltaire and Rousseau, they sent their linen to the colonies to be washed and to get the right colour and scent, they sent their wine for two or three voyages to the colonies and back to give it the right flavour. They, along with the other bourgeois, chafed at their social disadvantages; the chaotic state of French administration and finance handicapped them in their business. A hard winter in 1788 brought matters to a head. The monarchy was already bankrupt, the aristocracy made a bid to recover its former power, the peasants began to revolt, and the bourgeoisie saw that the time had come for it to govern the country on the English model in collaboration with its allies, the radical aristocracy. In the agitation which began the French Revolution, the maritime bourgeoisie took the lead. The bourgeoisie of Dauphiné and Brittany, with their ports of Marseilles and Nantes, attacked the monarchy even before the official opening of the States-General, and Mirabeau, the first leader of the revolution, was the deputy for Marseilles.

From all over the country the *cahiers*, or lists of grievances, poured in. But the French people, like the vast majority of Europeans today, had too many grievances of their own to be concerned about the sufferings of Africans, and only a few *cahiers*, chiefly from clergymen, demanded the abolition of slavery. The States-General met. Mirabeau, Pétion, Mayor of Paris, Abbé Grégoire, Condorcet, all members of the Friends of the Negro, were deputies, all pledged to abolition. But abolition for the maritime bourgeois was ruin. For the moment, however, the States-General grappled with the King.

While the French bourgeoisie led the assault on the absolute monarchy at home, the planters followed suit in the colonies. And, as in France, the geographical divisions of San Domingo and their historical development shaped the revolutionary movement and the coming insurrection of the slaves.

The pride of the colony was the great North Plain of which Le Cap was the chief port. Bounded on the north by the ocean, and on the south by a ridge of mountains running almost the length of the island, it was about 50 miles in length and between 10 and 20 miles in breadth. Cultivated since 1670, it was covered with plantations within easy reach of each other. Le Cap was the centre of the island's economic, social and political life. In any revolutionary upheaval, the planters of the North Plain and the merchants and lawyers of Le Cap would take the lead. (But the slave-gangs of the North Plain, in close proximity to each other and the sooner aware of the various changes in the political situation, would be correspondingly ready for political action.)

Very different was the West Province, with its isolated plantations scattered over wide areas. In districts like the Artibonite, Verrettes, Mirabelais, and St Marc, there were many mulatto proprietors, some of great wealth.

The South Province was a sort of pariah, somewhat sparsely populated, with a majority of mulattoes. The eastern end, Cape Tiburon, was only some 50 miles from Jamaica and here the contraband trade was particularly strong.

Early in 1788 the North Province took the lead. It formed a secret committee to secure representation in the States-General. In Paris the group of wealthy absentee noblemen formed a committee for the same purpose, the two groups collaborated and the Paris noblemen refused to accept the veto of the King. At the end of 1788 the colonists summoned electoral assemblies and elected a delegation, some of whom consisted of their allies in Paris. In their *cahier* they claimed abolition of military justice and the institution of a civil judiciary; all legislation and taxes to be voted by provincial assemblies subject only to the approval of the King and a Colonial Committee sitting at Paris but elected by themselves. By restricting political rights to owners of land the planters effectively excluded the small whites who took little interest in all this agitation. Of the slaves and mulattoes, they said not a word. Slaves did not count, and the mulattoes secured permission from the frightened bureaucracy to send a deputation to Paris on their own account. But a number of the planters at home, and quite a few in Paris, the Club Massiac, viewed this desire to be represented in the States-General with distrust. The agitation for abolition of the slave trade in England, the propaganda of the Friends of the Negro, the revolutionary temper of France, filled them with foreboding. Representation in the States-General by a few deputies could effect nothing, and it would bring the full glare of publicity and awakening political interest on the state of society in San Domingo, which was exactly what they did not want. But while the pro-representation group were in a minority, having a positive aim they were bold and confident. Their opponents, with bad consciences and aiming only at avoiding trouble, could oppose no effective resistance. Colonial representation in a metropolitan assembly was an innovation unheard of at that time, but the San Domingo representatives, profiting by the revolutionary ferment in Paris, circumvented the objections of the King and Minister. They petitioned the nobility who cold-shouldered them. But when Louis tried to intimidate the Third Estate, and the deputies went to the tennis-court and swore that being the representatives of the people they would never adjourn, Gouy d'Arsy, leader of the colonists, boldly led his group of colonial noblemen into this historic meeting. Out of gratitude for this unexpected support, the bourgeoisie welcomed them, and thus France admitted the principle of colonial representation. Full of confidence these slave owners claimed 18 seats, but Mirabeau turned fiercely on them: 'You claim representation proportionate to the number of the inhabitants. The free blacks are proprietors and tax-payers, and yet they have not been allowed to vote. And as for the slaves, either they are men or they are not; if the colonists consider them to be men, let them free them and make them electors and eligible for seats; if the contrary is the case, have we, in apportioning deputies according to the population of France, taken into consideration the number of our horses and our mules?'

San Domingo was allowed only six deputies. In less than five minutes the great Liberal orator had placed the case of the Friends of the Negro squarely before the whole of France in unforgettable words. The San Domingo representatives realised at last what they had done; they had tied the fortunes of San Domingo to the assembly of a people in revolution and thenceforth the history of liberty in France and of slave emancipation in San Domingo was one and indivisible.

Unaware of these portentous developments, the colonists in San Domingo were going from victory to victory. As in France, the last months of 1788 in San Domingo had been hard. France had had to prohibit the export of grain, and under these circumstances the Exclusive was a tyrannical imposition threatening the island with famine. The Governor opened certain ports to foreign ships; the Intendant, Barbé de Marbois, agreed to the first small breaches but refused to sanction their extension. The matter went to the King's Council which repudiated the Governor, recalled him, and appointed a new Governor, with the colonists calling for the blood of the Intendant. This was the situation when on a day in September a boat sailed into the harbour, and the captain, hurrying ashore, ran down the streets of Le Cap, shouting the news of July 14th. The King had been preparing to disperse the Constituent Assembly by force, and the Paris masses, arming themselves, had stormed the Bastille as the symbol of feudal reaction. The great French Revolution had begun.

Notes

1. This section is based on the work of Jaurès, *Histoire Socialiste de la Révolution Francaise*, (Paris, 1922), pp. 62–84.
2. Gaston-Martin, *L'Ere des Négriers, 1714–1774*. Paris, 1931, p. 424.
3. L. Deschamps, *Les Colonies pendant la Revolution* (Paris, 1898), pp. 3–8.
4. H. Brougham, *The Colonial Policy of the European Powers*, 2 vols (Edinburgh, 1803), Vol. II, pp. 538–40.
5. Deschamps, *op. cit.*, p. 25.
6. Great Britain, *House of Commons: Accounts and Papers, 1795–1796*, Vol. 100.
7. *Parliamentary History*, XXIII, pp. 1026–27.
8. *The Right in the West Indian Merchants to a Double Monopoly of the Sugar Market of Great Britain, and the Expedience of all monopolies examined*. (n.d.).
9. J. Chalmers, *Opinions on Interesting Subjects of Law and Commercial Policy arising from American Independence* (London, 1784), p. 60.
10. A. Smith, *The wealth of Nations*, Vol. I, p. 123.
11. A. Young, *Annals of Agriculture* (1788), Vol. IX, pp. 88–96.
12. *East India Sugar*, 1822, Appendix I, p. 3.
13. *Debate on the Expediency of Cultivating Sugar in the Territories of the East India Company*, East India House (1793).
14. *Report of the Committee of Privy Council for Trade and Plantations* (1798), Pt IV, Tables for Dominica and Jamaica.
15. T. Clarkson, *Essay on the Impolicy of the African Slave Trade* (London, 1784), p. 29.
16. R. Coupland, *The British Antislavery Movement* (London, 1933), p. 73.
17. R. Coupland, *Wilberforce* (Oxford, 1923), p.93.
18. *Fortescue MSS*. (Historical Manuscripts Commission, British Museum). Pitt to Grenville, June 29, 1788. Vol. I, p. 342.
19. *Liverpool Papers*. (Add. MSS. British Museum), Lord Dorset to Lord Hawkesbury, Vol. 38224, p. 118.
20. R. I. and S. Wilberforce, *Life of Wilberforce* (London, 1838), Vol. I, p. 228.
21. *Cahiers de la Révolution Francaise* (Paris, 1935), No. III, p. 25.
22. Written in 1938.

The Decline Thesis of British Slavery since Econocide

SEYMOUR DRESCHER*

Part One: The Decline Thesis and its Opponents

Appearing in 1944, *Capitalism and Slavery* was a comprehensive attempt to explain the rise and fall of British colonial slavery in relation to the evolution of European world capitalism.[1] In dealing with the final stages of slavery, Eric Williams developed a two-pronged argument linking its demise to changes in the British imperial economy. The first prong related to changes in the structure of economic relationships between the metropolis and the colonies. Down to the American Revolutionary War, concluded Williams, British slavery, including the Atlantic slave trade, was a growing and complementary element of the imperial economy. The slave system provided an ever-increasing amount of tropical staples, protected market for British manufactures, and a source of British metropolitan capital. In a number of ways, the slave economy thus helped to fuel the industrial revolution. Williams' second prong related to political economy, to an economic ideology designated as mercantilism. It sustained the multiple linkages of the system by assuming the need for a protected imperial zone in which British manufactures, trade and maritime skills could develop.

For Williams, the American War dramatically changed the economies and ideological relationship which had sustained the slave system. British colonial production, under increasing competition from its French counterpart, ceased to provide what was needed by the empire amply or cheaply enough. *In Capitalism and Slavery*, 1776 began the 'uninterrupted decline' of the British West Indies both as a producer of British staples, as a consumer of British industrial output and as a contributor to British capital. The very capitalism that had been nurtured by slavery now destroyed the fetter on its own further development. At precisely the same moment a new political economy was adumbrated, in Adam Smith's *Wealth of Nations*. It viewed protected colonial trade as a brake on the creation of national wealth. The demise of slavery was thus perfectly congruent with the rise of laissez-faire.[2]

At a less global level *Capitalism and Slavery* also provided a detailed set of rigorous economic motivations for the short-run successes and failures of British abolition. The failure of the British West Indies to recover its rate of profitability after the American war combined with the growth of alternative staple sources to set the stage for the rise of abolitionism in the 1780s. The St. Domingue revolution momentarily stemmed the tide, but colonial overproduction induced abolition of the slave trade in 1806–07 and emancipation in 1833. All of this was set against the background of a continuous decline in West Indian profits, the imperial significance of British slavery and its metropolitan economic supports. One by one those interests which had once supported slavery turned against it.[3] Each and every tightening of the noose could be explained by reference to the interplay of economic patterns and motives. *Capitalism and Slavery* also contained two interesting but basically post-scriptural chapters on the roles of the abolitionist 'Saints' and the colonial slaves but

*This essay was prepared during a fellowship at the Woodrow Wilson Center for Scholars. I wish to express my appreciation to the participants at the Bellaggio conference on British Capitalism and British Slavery in 1984 for their extensive comments, and to Stanley Engerman in particular for his advice.

Slavery and Abolition, Vol. 7, No. 1 (1986), pp. 3–23.

the main story was carried along the path of its putative economic determinants.

In the three decades following the appearance of *Capitalism and Slavery* a number of objections were raised to some of Williams' short-run interpretations. Its major structural elements, however, remained deeply entrenched in the historiography of British anti-slavery: the rise of abolitionism was closely correlated with the rise of laissez-faire and the decline of the British West Indies. One of these elements rested on a tradition of British imperial history which divided an 'old' mercantilist from a 'new' laissez-faire empire by the American Revolution. The other element rested on the work of a number of historians of the Caribbean, above all Lowell Ragatz's *Fall of the Planter Class in the British West Indies, 1763–1833*. The striking novelty of *Capitalism and Slavery* lay in Williams' vigorous fusion of these two historiographical streams.

In approaching the discussion of Williams' most famous work during the past decade one should begin by observing that the systematic discussion of *Capitalism and Slavery* is itself little more than a decade old. Apart from Roger Anstey's initial foray in the *Economic History Review* (1968),[4] *Capitalism and Slavery* was either praised in passing or summarily dismissed, both without extended analysis. It therefore percolated, rather than flowed, into historiographical discourse for reasons which would make an interesting study in its own right.[5] By the mid-seventies, the Williams decline theory was being described by some historians as the new orthodoxy.

A major challenge appeared with the publication of two works. In 1975 *The Atlantic Slave Trade and British Abolition*, by Roger Anstey, attacked some of Williams' short-run interpretations, especially the motives for British abolition in 1806–07. In *Econocide* (1977) I challenged both the long- and short-term premises of *Capitalism and Slavery*. With the same data used both by contemporary actors and by Williams to show the 'amazing value' of the British West Indies before 1775, I found no decline in the value of the British slave system until well after the abolition of the slave trade.[6] There was in other words a disjuncture between the dramatic rise of political abolitionism and the economic value of its target. *Econocide* also took sharp issue with the premise that there was a major shift in the political economy of the British Empire following the American Revolution. Here too, I found that the change required by the Williams thesis was not tangibly operative until *at least* three-quarters of the age of British abolitionism (1788–1838) had expired, if then. The thrust of *Econocide's* attack was quite clear. If British slavery was economically expanding at the moment that its growth was decisively inhibited by political action, its economic decline was contingent upon, not determinative of, abolitionism. Economic decline may well have eased the later stages of destruction. Likewise, a structural change in imperial political economy could not have been determinant at the beginning or the middle of the abolition process. One might even question whether it was clearly so at the end, in 1833. Some of *Econocide's* subordinate arguments will be considered at the appropriate place. The basic point is that *Econocide* challenged the validity of these two givens in the explanation of British abolition. It neither precluded hypotheses based on indirect economic arguments nor urged a reversion to the old humanitarian narrative of the victory of the Saints.

Part Two: After *Econocide* Defenders of the Decline Theory

In dealing with the Williams decline thesis since *Econocide* one initial difficulty presents itself. There have been few further extended discussions of the Williams thesis. In this sense the discussion of the critique of the Williams thesis has been almost as slow in getting off the ground as Williams' original critique of the 'Coupland' tradition. One extended essay on the status of the question was published by Stanley Engerman and David Eltis in 1980.[7] Another was produced by Cecil Gutzmore for the Hull Sesquicentennial in 1983.[8] A much lengthier critique of *Econocide*, by Selwyn Carrington, appeared, with an appended reply, in June 1984.[9] Otherwise the decline theory has been discussed more casually in books, essays, and introductions to other collective enterprises. For our purposes, one valuable vein of discussion can also be assayed — reviews and review essays on *Econocide*. To their authors my procedure might be viewed as sacrilege or, at the very least, as hitting well below the intellect. Scholars never expect to have what they say in reviews held against them. Yet the large number of reviews offer a very broad sampling of the general reaction to the issues raised by *Econocide*. There is already some precedent for using the reviews. Walter E. Minchinton's essay, 'Williams and Drescher: Abolition and Emancipation', in the September 1983 issue of

Slavery and Abolition, extensively quotes from the most critical ones. I will therefore use them to highlight typical reactions, including areas of agreement, disagreement, and designated directions for future orientation.

One may logically begin with the decline theory. *Capitalism and Slavery* posited that the British Caribbean had attained an 'amazing value' for Britain on the eve of American independence. Its value depreciated from 1776 on. Williams' empirical demonstration was founded on the data of British overseas trade, drawn from official records from 1697 to 1773, as compiled by Sir Charles Whitworth.[10] It should be noted that Williams broadly and explicitly included both the African and foreign slave trades sectors in his accounting system.[11] He also compared the British Afro-Caribbean system with others. *Econocide's* first major step was to carry Williams' systemic analysis of 1697–1773 forward half a century, using the same database and 'filling in' the void in the Williams account for the period between the Declaration of Independence and Waterloo.[12]

The central indicator used by both *Capitalism and Slavery* and *Econocide* as a measure of value is conceptually important in another respect. It was the one measure most available to, and overwhelmingly used by, contemporaries in the political debate over abolition. Its use therefore avoids severe epistemiological problems which arise from employing measures of value which were either unclear to contemporaries or not central to their arguments. I must return to this problem below. *Econocide* portrayed the impact of the trade data graphically by superimposing the Williams 'rising' years (until the early seventies) with the putative 'decline' period thereafter (see figure 1).[13] One might easily perform similar operations in tabular form.

Table 1 shows the British West Indian percentage of British overseas trade using key pivotal years ranging from 1763 to 1783. In each case the period *after* exceeds the share of the period *before* the pivotal date, both for the medium and the long term. To judge from the general reception of *Econocide*, most scholars have accepted the idea that the systematic extension of the Williams database requires some revision of *Capitalism and Slavery's* argument in its classical format of '1776 and all that'.[14]

One statistical demolition did not of course end the discussion. One way of responding to any given data series is to extend it. Perhaps the Williams database doesn't work for the 50 years

Figure 1

British West Indian Trade, 1722–1822

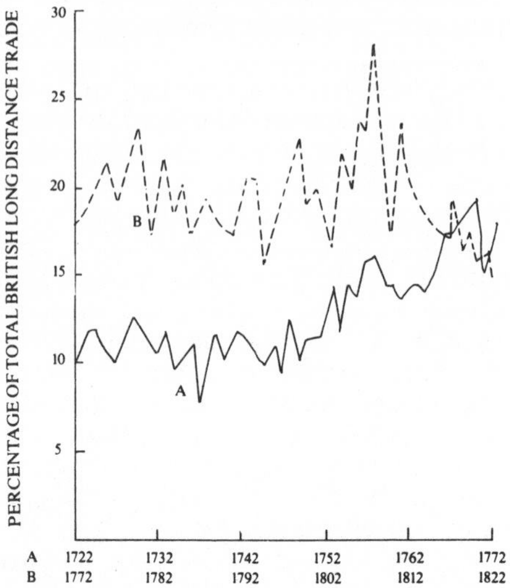

Source: Mitchell and Deane, Abstract, pp. 309–11, 'Overseas Trade'.

Table 1 British West Indian Shares of British Trade (Imports, Exports, and Re-exports) for Various 'Pivotal' years 1763–83

		Prior – equivalent period	
Years	%	Years	%
Pivot of 1763 (Ragatz)			
1763–92	18.30	1782–62	11.99
1763–97	18.24	1723–62	11.88
1763–1802	18.69	1718–92	11.90
1763–1807	19.08	1713–62	11.62
Pivot of 1776 (Williams)			
1777–1806	19.36	1737–76	14.50
1777–1811	19.82	1732–76	14.16
1777–1816	19.46	1727–76	13.96
1777–1821	18.97	1722–76	13.76
Pivot of Peace of Versailles			
1783–1807	19.42	1758–82	17.54
1783–1812	19.76	1753–82	17.04
1783–1817	19.36	1748–82	16.36
1783–1822	18.71	1743–82	15.82

Source: Mitchell and Deane, *Abstract of British Historical Statistics*, (Cambridge, 1962), pp. 309–11.

after 1763 or 1776, but what if we use Ragatz's 'falling planters' of 1763–1833 or Williams' 'rising free-traders' of 1776–1846?[15] Isn't decline visible toward the end? The answer is yes, but the point also strikes me as wide of the original mark. *Econocide's* own first table shows that by 1828–32 the British West Indies was relatively back where it had been in the mid-eighteenth century. (One might still be tempted to say that Britain's slave system had, at long last, declined only to the point where it was as valuable as in its Ragatzian 'golden age'.) Such a line of argument already grants the basic point of the original argument against the Williams thesis no matter how deeply or steeply the slave system declined after the abolition of the slave trade. It is clear that thereafter the limits to the value of anti-slavery were political rather than economic. It is also difficult to see how any scholar inclined toward economic determinism can take much comfort in the observation that the 'real' decline in West Indian fortunes was political.[16] The unique strength of *Capitalism and Slavery* resides in the affirmation of a conjuncture between economic and political change. No correlation, no thesis.

Econocide did not suppose that all political limitations on the slave system were ineffectual until the moment of emancipation. That seemed irrelevant. Lengthening the frame of reference to 1833 or even to 1983 does not alter the basic Williams hypothesis — that economic decline induced the abolitionist-capitalist attack in 1788–92, or the victory in 1806–07. The relationship between imperial economic policy in the final stages of abolition and apprenticeship may therefore be treated quite independently of the crucial policy decision to limit its further growth. Even beyond this the Williams scenario faces other difficulties which have not yet been faced by those who see the period 1823–46 as a saving remnant for *Capitalism and Slavery*. The final 'stage' of the Williams decline theory is based on the following argument. By 1833 a Parliament had been elected in Britain which, said Williams, 'was perfectly responsive to the needs and aspirations of British capitalists'.[17] Hence, British capitalism destroyed slavery as a first step in the destruction of the West Indian monopoly (p. 169). Yet the fact is that emancipation was not coordinated with a step against West Indian monopoly but with one which gave it a new lease of life.

If the protection of British slave sugar produced resentment after the Napoleonic wars, whether from East Indian or consumer interests, relief was clearly no priority in Parliament during the debates over emancipation and apprenticeship between 1823 and 1838. As late as 1841 the government was defeated in the Commons when it attempted to reduce the protection accorded to British colonial sugar. Therefore it seems that by 1833 either a Parliament had been elected which was not 'perfectly responsive' to the aspirations of the capitalists, or the capitalists in 1833 did *not* aspire to anti-monopoly, or emancipation was not taken as a step toward the end of West Indian monopoly, or Parliament aspired more to destroy slavery than West Indian monopoly. From Williams' account I do not believe it is possible to sustain the sequence of his argument.

Alongside the role of the slave system as an imperial trading partner, *Capitalism and Slavery* stressed a second aspect of economic development — the putative profit decline of the West Indian planters. Here Williams challenged the economic viability of the British plantation system after the American Revolutionary War. He stressed not only the 'monopoly' character of the West Indies, 'but that it was so unprofitable that for this reason alone its destruction was inevitable'.[18] *Capitalism and Slavery* therefore argued for a sharp fall in Jamaica profits after 1774. Since the link between unprofitability and destruction is made so forcefully at the general level, recent scholars have rightly introduced more detailed and systematic analysis to this aspect of the Ragatz and Williams decline thesis.

It should be pointed out that there is a difference between the rate of plantation profits to the planters or African merchants, and the value of their system to the Empire. The happiness of the planters over their profit conditions was no more central to their utility to the metropolis than the happiness of the slaves over their working conditions.

In any event, the viability of slavery to the planters may have been less impaired by the abolition of the slave trade than was slavery's relative significance in the trade system. On this question J. R. Ward has done much to systematically demonstrate that the West Indian colonies as a whole were operating at a profit down to the eve of emancipation. His data seem to indicate that profit rates were as high or higher after the American War as before, and that, at least until 1820, an average return of 10 per cent was as characteristic of the period following as for the period before the American War, at least down to 1820. Ward also seems to agree that the Ragatzean picture of progressive decrepitude has to be modified.[19]

Econocide was also criticized for insufficient attention to the issue of shifting patterns of capital investment in the slave property of the British West Indies.[20] Using Caribbean slave population growth as an index of capital growth, it would appear that capital investment was increasing at a more rapid rate between

1790–1805 than between 1750–70. The capital value of the British slave empire more than doubled between 1785 and 1815 (including conquered areas). The £15 million sunk by British investors into Demerara alone between the British conquest in 1796 and its temporary return to the Dutch in 1802 served as a standing reminder to abolitionists concerning the prospects of slavery as a field for investment before the abolition of the slave trade.

Scholarly attention has also been recently focused on the significance of British slavery in accounting for the growth of British exports before and during the industrial revolution.[21] In this context François Crouzet estimates that the West Indies accounted for 18 per cent of the increase of British exports from 1700/01 to 1772/73. Until the end of the century the West Indies actually increased its share. Considering the three decades 1783/1812 as a whole the West Indies and Latin America (also served by the African slave trade) contributed more to Britain's cumulated additional exports (official values) than any area except the United States. Table 2 shows that the West Indies steadily maintained its relative role in British export growth until the abolition of the slave trade as other areas rose or fell dramatically. Africa's independent role fell as did that of North America and, most dramatically, the export trade east of the Cape of Good Hope.

These are measures which can be placed alongside the trade figures. For some supporters of a 1776+ decline theory, however, the use of trade figures to measure the long-range value of British slavery to the British imperial economy was spurious and beside the point. The same would apparently hold for both planter profits and capital accumulation rates. They were all amassed under protective barriers. For some reviewers, the central shift in the abolitionist victory lies not at all in the trade series but in a decisive shift of the *measurement* of value which presumably occurred under the aegis of a shifting political economy from mercantilism to laissez-faire. For Barbara Solow, as for Mary Turner and Elsa Goveia, *the* major long-run fact of British slave production is that the British consumer paid more for eighteenth-century British sugar than his or her continental counterpart paid for non-British, and especially French, sugar. Fundamentally, this is a cost-accounting argument, using the world market as the basic measure of value. If British importers were paying a higher price for their muscovado than was warranted by the world market the value of the sugar colonies was deceptive. Noel Deerr accounts for this in terms of a qualitative difference between British and French muscovado,[22] but the fact remains that for most of the eighteenth century British plantation sugar did not compete effectively on the continental market except in war years, when French sugars were bottled up by the British navy and privateers.

Whether or not it was Williams' principal line of attack, this point, acknowledged by *Econocide*, was part of an effort to resuscitate the decline thesis. This, says Barbara Solow, 'is the decline that matters'. Fair enough — let us give the price-competitive argument the attention it deserves. The single major problem

Table 2 British Percentage of Area Shares Contributions to Increased Exports, 1700–01 to 1804–06

Area	(Official values) 1700/01 to 1772/73 (1)	(Current values) 1784/86 to 1804/06 (2)	Manufacturing exports only 1784/86 to 1804/06 (3)
West Indies	18.2	21.1	22.3
Latin America		4.0	4.3
Africa	7.8	2.5	2.6
Ireland, etc	14.6	10.1	8.0
East Indies	13.5		
Asia (incl. China)		3.2	2.8
Europe	4.2	30.3	28.7
Continenal North America	41.8	28.3	30.7
Other		0.4	

Sources: Column 1, François Crouzet, 'Toward an Export Economy: British Exports during the Industrial Revolution', *Explorations in Economic History*, 17 (1980), 48–93, p. 72; columns 2 and 3, Ralph Davis, *The Industrial Revolution and British Overseas Trade* (Leicester, 1978), p. 89.

with the 'mercantilist sugar' argument is the same one that attaches generically to a whole set of parallel long-range indictments concerning the efficiency of the British slave system — absenteeism, indebtedness, white flight, demographic deficiency, soil exhaustion, etc. All of these 'disabilities' were identified on both sides of the ocean more than half a century before 1790 without inciting either to abolitionism or abolition.[23] So it is with French sugar. The condition did not, as Solow speculates, begin as early as the 1760s. It was definitively recognized at least as early as the 1730s, using, of course, the same import, export and re-export data used for the volume of trade measures in *Capitalism and Slavery* and *Econocide*. The planters and their friends complained of it, their North American enemies gloated over it, their own allies pled it every time there was an internal squabble over redistribution of mercantilist burdens — whether in the 1730s or the 1780s.

Without too much difficulty one could push the perception back still further. The comparative cheapness of foreign sugar was in fact emphasized by the West Indian planters as early as the Peace of Utrecht.[24] How then could such a hoary fact induce abolition? The neo-decliners claim that a new stimulus to recognition of this fact burst through in the 1780s and held fast thereafter. Why? Various 'candidate' catalysts are offered. Williams himself had offered booming St. Domingue after 1783. The American Revolution left the British sugar planters 'face to face with their French rivals'.[25] *Econocide* showed that the relationship remained 'back to back', as it had for half a century before. Each system served separate markets, and Jamaican sugar was actually expanding faster than that of St. Domingue on the eve of abolitionist take-off in the late eighties. *Econocide* therefore claimed that before 1790 'British planters did not seriously challenge their French rivals and that the metropolis did not seriously challenge the planter monopoly'. Therefore the British planters I concluded 'nestled comfortably in the arms' of their own protected market.[26] The neo-decliners disagree. Mary Turner's catalysts are the fall of the Bastille and the French Revolution. Solow's are Adam Smith in 1776 and Pitt's condemnation of the slave trade in 1791. All of these catalysts were followed (Solow's within a few hours) by Parliament's thumping *rejection* of abolition by a vote of almost two to one.

There is another more fundamental fact of sugar prices, however, which argues against the cheap sugar argument for abolition. Abolition scored its first symbolic victory in 1792, and its second substantive victory in 1806–07, after a decade in which world market sugar prices actually moved in favour of the British consumer.[27] It was precisely in 1791 that British sugar once again massively re-entered the continental market. (As for emancipation, Howard Temperley has also argued that, in the period prior to 1833, a large proportion of the West Indian crop was sold on the world market, which determined its price.[28]) The biggest price gap between the British and the world market reopened as a consequence, not a cause of the advent of a free labour market after apprenticeship. Moreover, the market price economic interpretation of abolition must also account for the reason why planters' spokesmen were more open to laissez-faire on both the carrying and marketing of their sugar at the time of the abolition of the slave trade than was the British Parliament which controlled their destinies. In 1807 the British government served up the Orders-in-Council and protectionism all around. Economists might wish to do another estimate of the value of the Sugar colonies to Great Britain for the period 1790–1807 to see whether the abolitionists attacked and won during the precise period when, by cost-accounting criteria, the metropolis was a loss to the colonies, not vice versa. In the first decade of the nineteenth century, British per capita consumption of sugar was probably at its all-time peak for the entire era of British colonial slavery.

If a neo-classical cheap sugar model has difficulty enough in addressing the timing of abolitionism it gets into even more difficulty in accounting for the targets. If Smithian anti-monopoly sentiment was a source of antagonism to British slavery after 1788, why was the first target that segment of the slave economy (the African slave trade) which did so much of its business in successful competition in the world market? And why was abolitionism's second target (1805) the premier British *cotton* colony (Demerara) whose produce received absolutely no protection whatever in the metropolitan market? Neo-classical economism may wind up with as many facts to explain away as its Marxian predecessor.[29]

Finally, the classical approach must respond to the same epistemological problem as historians who regard trade figures as more central indicators (than planter profit) of value. Empirically, the trade figures were primarily used by contemporary policy makers in abolition debates. The abolitionists pointed to potential alternative sources of British trade, but until well after slave trade ended the abolitionists always had to point toward the bush rather than the hand. Over the course of the 50 years from 1783 to emancipation the abolitionists were always more speculative customer-counters than their opponents.

This approach to decline strikes me as deriving from a broader historical misconception. It assumes, with Williams, that there was a political swing away from mercantilism in the generation after the publication of *Wealth of Nations* and the Peace of Versailles. As P. J. Cain and A. G. Hopkins have argued, there was no widespread conversion to laissez-faire after 1776. There were merely sectoral adjustments for specific targets of opportunity within the old framework.[30] The French Wars gave added impetus to the arguments for strengthening the empire rather than lowering barriers to free competition. The burdens of war, not of the consumer, were the main concern of British governments in the decades before abolition. The ever-ascending proportion of the retail price of sugar determined by fixed rate duties amply demonstrates this. The great shift in the balance of economic power and priorities came during the 30 years after the fall of Napoleon. The Cain-Hopkins reassessment coincides with that of *Econocide* rather than with those theories requiring more of a laissez-faire 'spirit of '76'.

In addition to its neo-classical defenders, the decline thesis has also found new supporters within the mercantilist frame of reference which was less explicitly but in fact more frequently employed by *Capitalism and Slavery*. Given the stubborn persistence of the mercantilist perspective in Britain, indeed its reaffirmation less than two years before political abolition was placed on the parliamentary agenda, it has been re-argued that the very interests united by mercantilism before 1775 were instrumental in undermining the West India interest. Ragatz and Williams, now reinforced by Carrington, emphasize that in 1785 the British shipping interest decisively fought to limit the claims of the West Indians to trade with American carriers.[31] With major exceptions for 'emergencies', this prohibition remained in effect until the mid-twenties. The policy was particularly damaging to the planter interest in the mid-eighties and in 1805–08. The second structural pressure on the planters was the metropolitan policy of heavy fixed duties upon sugar. Duties on imports rose during each conflict and were never substantially reduced before abolition.

Carrington argues that these facts demonstrate the decline of the planter class and, therefore, of British West Indian slavery. This by no means follows. The maintenance of the navigation laws clearly underlined the dependence of the British shipping interest on the West Indies. Within its mercantilist perspective the West Indian shipping interest thereafter supported the West Indies against abolitionists. After slave trade abolition the West Indies in fact supplied one of the few outlets for the re-deployment of former slave ships until the end of the continental blockade. Even more of former slave ships until the end of the continental blockade. Even more clearly, sugar duties were one of the fiscal mainstays of public revenue. No government considered risking a change during the course of, or immediately after, the French wars. Both the sugar revenues and the navigation system force us to recognize the important differences for the empire between the short-run prosperity of the planter and the value of the sugar colonies. This, again, is why trade figures strike me as a better indicator of the significance at the imperial level than profitability or prices. The mercantilist perspective, as *Econocide* emphasizes, did allow abolitionists, regardless of growth or decline, to move separately against the slave trade when they could convince Parliament that no unmanageable short-run damage would accrue to the slave colonies in the circumstances of 1806–07.

Both the neo-mercantilist and laissez-faire arguments assume an imperial or world-market context. Another strategic defence of the decline theory focuses on intracolonial comparisons. As one would expect, this frame of reference is most frequently invoked by historians of the West Indies. In defending *Capitalism and Slavery* these historians maintain that *Econocide* does not sufficiently emphasize differential development within the islands.[32] They point out that some old colonies, at least, had passed their peak. On similar grounds Carrington in his lengthy critique of *Econocide* has systematically attempted to revive the Ragatzian perspective in toto. His own analysis gives to the decline of the old islands primacy of position. Carrington goes even further. He imputes to *Econocide* the argument that 'the older islands (namely Barbados and the Leeward Islands) were not saturated as was generally believed but were developing with renewed strength'. Carrington considers that point critical to Drescher's study. In fact, *Econocide* explicitly argues exactly the opposite. Summarizing British Caribbean conditions in 1790, *Econocide* says: 'Taken as a whole, the slave colonies had exhausted neither their soil nor their potential. *Some, such as Barbados and the Leeward Islands, were considered to be at or past their optimum development. But this was only one segment of the islands*'[33] (italics added).

Econocide reiterates in its closing chapter for the period 1780–1833 as a whole, 'Metropolitan politicians would naturally think in imperial not regional terms. *Barbados had no special economic status as against Jamaica in 1788, and Jamaica had none vis-à-vis Trinidad in 1805 or Demarara in 1815.*' And, 'the dynamic of the colonial system was no more measured by the statistics of the seventeenth-century pioneers than were metropolitan trends by the statistics of Old Sarum.'[34] *Econocide* maintains that at *all* times from the end of the American war to Waterloo, and beyond, there were developing slave sectors. This was as visible to contemporaries as it should be to historians. Eric Williams' own favourite source for pre-1776, Sir Charles Whitworth, showed that as of 1790, Jamaica, Dominica and St. Vincent had clearly expanded beyond their pre-war peaks. Other official sources showed that Jamaica, St. Vincent and Trinidad were frontier *de jure* colonies as of 1802, to which one could add Demerara (*de facto*) in 1807 and Demerara, Mauritius and the Cape Colony (*de jure*) by 1815. Carrington's approach does indicate why many of the smaller islands were less apprehensive (but never to the point of advocacy) of abolition in 1807.

The method of reducing the decline theory of British slavery to the decline of some parts of British slavery does not, in fact, support Williams' turning point. Rather it undermines it and throws into question the very possibility of using such a theory in historical analysis. If, using Carrington's criteria, decline must be dated from the decline of the first slave area in an economic system, American slavery was declining almost before slavery crossed the Appalachians, when Pennsylvania legislated its gradual abolition. Using Carrington's criteria, the decline of slavery in Delaware after 1800 would mean that Southern slavery too was already in decline. In the West Indies Carrington's criteria dispose not only of *Econocide's* nineteenth-century turning point, but of Williams' (1776) and Ragatz's (1763) as well. As Williams himself noted, 'as early as 1663, a mere twenty years after the rise of the sugar industry, Barbados was "decaying fast" and the complaints of soil exhaustion grew more numerous and more plaintive'.[35] This would, it is true, give economic decline a comfortable 150-year lead on abolition. It would, however, also mean that over 98 per cent of the slaves brought to America in British ships between 1620 and 1808 were boarded after the beginning of the decline of British slavery.[36] If, following Carrington, we use Deerr's 'old colony' sugar export figures rather than colonial complaints it still appears that Barbados reached its pre-abolition sugar peak in 1698, more than one hundred years before 1808. Nevis' pre-abolition peak was in 1710, Montserrat's in 1735.[37] Therefore, of the five little-old-islands possessed by Britain on the eve of the Seven Years' War, a majority were already long in decline. We would have to conclude that Ragatz was too late by a full generation and Williams by 40 years in identifying the turning point. A reduction of British slavery to its insular parts reduces the very idea of rise and fall, whether of Drescher, Williams, Ragatz, or most other historians of Atlantic slavery, to chaos.

Carrington also uses the crop by crop performance of the British West Indies between 1775 and 1806 to test and to reaffirm the decline theory against *Econocide*. I again take fundamental issue with his method of disaggregation. *Econocide* showed that the sugar islands were both dynamic and flexible in the face of new opportunities. As new opportunities opened up for sugar, the British colonies became the largest colonial producing area in the world. Far from being exclusively wedded to monoculture, British slavery became *increasingly* polycultural in the decades between the Treaty of Versailles and abolition of the slave trade.

British dependency on slave-grown imports clearly increased during the two decades prior to the abolition of the British slave trade. Table 3 shows that the primary slave products increased their relative contribution to total British imports. The fact that cotton and coffee gained on sugar does not alter the picture of the combined figures. Britain became more dependent not only upon the slave zone but upon the slave importing areas as well. If slave-based cotton production was entirely responsible for the increase in British exports between 1792 and 1806, half of that raw material was still dependent upon slave importing

Table 3 Slave-Grown share of British Imports, 1784–86 to 1814–16

Product	(1) Current value (£000)	(2) % Predominatly grown by slaves	(3) % of total British imports	(4) % grown in slave importing areas	(5) % of total British imports in same
		1784/86			
Sugar	2614	100	11.5	100	11.5
Coffee	158	88	0.6	88	0.6
Cotton	1817[a]	70	5.6	70	5.6
Total			17.7		17.7
All British imports	22761				
		1804/06			
Sugar	6879	97	12.0	97	12.0
Coffee	2458	99	4.4	99	4.4
Cotton	5628	89[a]	9.0	53[b]	5.4
Total			25.4		21.8
All British imports	55558				
		1814/16			
Sugar	11138	98	15.1	—	—
Coffee	2784	79	3.1	—	—
Cotton	8593	96	11.5	35	4.2
Total			29.7		4.2
All British imports	71796				
		1824/26			
Sugar	6722	93	9.4	—	—
Coffee	1022	87	1.3	—	—
Cotton	7452	86	9.7	18	2.0
Total			20.4		2.0
All British imports	66389				

[a] Estimates of contributing areas from *Econocide*, pp. 84–85.
[b] U.S. cotton production is excluded here from the slave-importing zone, although abolition was not effected until 1808. Column 2 represents the actual percentage in 1804/06.
Source: Ralph Davis, *The Industrial Revolution and British Overseas Trade* (Leicester, 1978), appendix on British imports.

economies. Even (prematurely) excluding the United States from the slave importing roster (column 3, 1804–06) does not alter the general picture (column 4). If one also added rice and tobacco to the slave-produced share of British imports the dependency on slavery would rise still higher, to 23 per cent in 1784/86, 27 per cent in 1804/06, and 32 per cent in 1814/16, according to Ralph Davis' figures.

Ralph Davis' post-*Econocide* figures on real trade values from 1794–96 to 1844–46 also show that while cotton and coffee accounted for only 28 per cent of the value of the 'big three' British slave staples in 1784–86, they accounted for more than 39 per cent in 1804–06.[38] On the eve of abolition slave production was tangibly diversifying as well as expanding. All of this remains hidden if each crop is treated in isolation. Not only did coffee emerge as the new 'second' crop to sugar after the American war, but sugar culture itself underwent a 'green revolution'. The introduction of Otaheite cane in the last decade of the eighteenth century increased yields per acre. The British colonies were pioneers in this transformation.[39]

Carrington offers a final structural argument on behalf of the Williams decline dating. This concerns the slave trade itself as an indicator. While most recent scholarship has tended to accept the Anstey-Drescher claim that the British slave trade peaked only after the American War, in the 1790s, David

Richardson's findings seem to modify that claim.[40] His figures apparently indicate twin peaks, one just before the American War of Independence and a second only slightly higher, in the 1790s. By all counts the total American post-war volume exceeded any pre-war equivalent period. Most scholars also agree that the British trade was somewhat reduced by the Slave Carrying Act of 1799, further reduced by the abolition Act of 1806, and virtually annihilated by the Act of 1807. J.E. Inikori argues for a much higher 'hidden' trade than other scholars from 1800 to 1807.[41] *Econocide* was sceptical of the argument but emphasized that the impact of abolition would be magnified by Inikori's estimate.

Carrington disputes not the fact of expansion but its interpretation. He argues that the crucial point is not how *many* slaves were transported by British carriers but what percentage were re-exported from the old islands. 'One of the best indicators of West Indian prosperity during the eighteenth century', he claims, was the ability and readiness of the planters to purchase slaves. 'For most of the period up to 1775–76, the planters retained a majority of the slaves imported into the islands. After the American War, even if more slaves were imported into the islands than in the pre-1775 period, a larger number was also re-exported.'[42]

Jamaican data (the only island for which we have a full run of eighteenth-century re-exports) show that most of the years in which a majority of slaves was re-exported come from the period *prior* to 1775/76.[43] This misreading of the data brings us to the larger issue of Carrington's use of re-exports as an indicator of decline.

Carrington argues that the percentage of re-exports should be used as an indicator of decline. Elsewhere I have argued that, based on Jamaica's data series, there was no direct correlation between the rate of planter profits and the rate of re-exports. I also showed that post-1800 re-export figures could be quite deceptive since a substantial number were recycled to *de jure* British colonies. An even larger number went to *de facto* British planters. Further evidence against any positive correlation between the percentage of retained slave imports and planter prosperity may be observed from Carrington's own Bellaggio paper, 'The Economy of the British West Indies, 1775–1791: The Makings of the Williams/Drescher Controversy', Appendix V.[44] Ignoring for the moment the methodological difficulty in excluding slave import figures into the new frontier regions of

Table 4 Percentage of Received Slaves Re-exported from Jamaica by Five-Year Intervals, 1713–87

Period	% Re-exported	Period	% Re-exported
1713–17	50.2	1758–62	15.0
1718–22	40.1	1763–67	17.0
1723–27	43.9	1768–72	13.0
1728–32	44.5	1773–78	15.3
1733–37	43.6	1778–82	14.6
1738–42	15.5	1783–87	32.0
1742–47	24.0	Years over 50% re-exports:	
1748–52	22.1	1709, 1713, 1714, 1719, 1720,	
1753–57	12.1˙	1723, 1724, 1730, 1731, 1733	
		(peak 69.9%), *1786*	

Source: McKusker, 'The Rum Trade', pp. 615–16.

Trinidad and Demerara, one can easily observe that the planters retained the highest percentage of slaves just when their profits were *lowest*. From 1788 to 1798 planters enjoyed an almost uninterrupted period of high profits. Yet the lowest retention rates are clustered precisely in that period (with the exception of 1798). Correspondingly the years 1800–01 and 1805 were years of low or falling prices, yet they seem to be characterized by high retention rates. There are enough anomalies, even from this pattern, to cast doubt on the relevance of profits to re-exports altogether, but it is at least quite clear that the hypothesis of low profits–high re-exports and vice versa is not borne out.

Finally, I wish to draw attention to the untenability of the whole Carrington premise on even longer-term grounds. In Table 4, I carry the percentage of Jamaican re-exports back to the Treaty of Utrecht. The reader can easily observe that using percentages of re-exports as an indicator of decline places the nadir of the most dynamic old British colony in the 'Asiento' years at the beginning of the *eighteenth* century. As given, Carrington's re-exports theory, like his 'little-old-colony' theory, leads us to a Herodian slaughter of the innocents. It would simply destroy the development paradigms of most historians including Williams. If we accept Carrington's premises, we have truly entered an age of paradigms lost.

Ebb and Flow

In terms of the larger issues one can spend less time with the post-*Econocide* views which draw on *Capitalism and Slavery* to explain the ups and downs of abolitionist fortunes. Like the spatial and product segmentations just discussed, these tend to look to very short-run developments to explain political decisions. Scholars reflecting on these questions do not necessarily take issue with the broader findings of *Econocide* or defend those of *Capitalism and Slavery*. For the post-American War decade Carrington upholds Williams' short-run arguments to the letter. He asserts, with Williams, that the slave system failed to recover its 1774–75 level of profitability during the years between the Treaty of Versailles (1783) and the St. Domingue Revolution. I have again argued elsewhere that profits by and even before 1791 were well above their level of 1775.

Another post-war issue concerns the impact of the restrictions on American carriers to the British islands after 1783. Carrington maintains that shortages lasted until the St. Domingue uprising. I again take the opposite position. In this encounter Carrington sticks with the Ragatzian position *tout court* — that St. Domingue alone, and only momentarily, saved the tottering planters. Some historians slice the post-American War frame of reference even more finely. In an essay on Britain's policy towards St. Domingue, David Geggus focuses on the state of the West Indies just prior to the abolitionist breakthrough in 1788-91.[45] He nods in *Econocide's* direction by noting that production recovered pre-war levels by the mid-1780s. However, he faults the study for relying too heavily on the turbulent years after 1789 to make a case for the West Indies' recovery of its imperial position. If, however, Geggus had compared the '*non*-turbulent' pre-American War years (1771–1774) with only the equally non-turbulent post-war and pre-French revolutionary years (1784–1788), he would have found that the West Indies accounted for a higher percentage of British imports, exports and total trade in the second period than the first. *Econocide* characterized the 1780s as a period of West Indian recovery. As with the whole metropolitan export trade, it was only in the 1790s that recovery gave way to new growth.

Many historians, including Geggus and Carrington, point to annual downturns in production, profits, trade shares and the slave trade during the period 1783–1807. There is no objection to using these for carefully delimited comparisons. But decline theorists could hardly insist that annual or even quinquennial downturns in an economic sector are sufficient to categorize it as a declining trend. Otherwise, almost every major British trade in the Empire, metropolitan and colonial alike, was declining at some point between 1783 and 1806. Even the superstar of the post-1783 period, British cottons, staggered badly in the 1790s. Exceptional critics like Minchinton, who apply such a rigorous criterion of cumulative trends to the British West Indian case, simply fail to note that by such a test no British trading zone in the world rose or fell continuously during every quinquennium of the century before Waterloo (see *Econocide*, table 2). Cyclical and politically induced fluctuations were bound to be part of any economic activity.

Some objections to *Econocide* consisted in quoting 'high authorities' on short-term issues to explain general motives. In *every* case to date this comes down to the pleasant pastime of 'pick your pundit'.[46] Arguing for Williams' overproduction thesis, one historian triumphantly cited a speech by the 'Leading Minister' in the Lords who in 1807 assured his House that abolition would save the planters from ruin. Hence concern about overproduction presumably predisposed the House to vote for abolition. The same historian neglects to observe that two weeks later the 'Leading Minister' of the other House assured *his* audience that abolition would lead to no decrease of production. The House then voted even more overwhelmingly for abolition. May we then conclude that the Commons was even more anxious about underproduction in 1807.

Aside from these possibilities, it is clear that the factors most important to Williams, a coalescence of antagonistic economic interests and a shift in political economy, simply have not been unearthed by further research as playing their allotted role in the decline and fall of slavery outlined by *Capitalism and Slavery*. This does not preclude incorporating negative short-term psychological effects of the American War on the West Indies on the slave interest. It does fundamentally challenge any account of abolition which incorporates either the decline of the West Indies or perceptions of the decline of the value of slavery to Britain during the generation after 1783. Just as Williams may have exaggerated the increasing importance of the West Indies to the imperial economy before 1775 so he appears, at the very least, to have exaggerated the diminution of its importance to Britain before emancipation. It is more likely that as in the case of American slavery two growing, if unequal, social systems faced each other, rather than a rising and a falling one.

Part Three: Alternatives to West Indian Decline

Thus far we have dealt with arguments tending to defend elements of the Williams thesis as given within the parameters of *Capitalism and Slavery*. Some approaches actually narrow the framework of discussion. It is now important to consider some of the alternatives to the Williams economic decline thesis.

We can begin at the extremes. On the one hand, one might conclude, with Roger Anstey, that the sapping of the Ragatz-Williams decline theory means that the case for explaining abolition in 'terms of fundamental economic change is seriously if not totally undermined'.[47] On the other hand, from the Marxist side, Cecil Gutzmore, in his survey of the 'bourgeois' critiques of *Capitalism and Slavery*, similarly assumes that the effect of these critiques is to return the state of the question 'to the rather narrow Christian (even Methodist) humanitarianism of those who originally erected the tradition'.[48] The pendulum presumably swings back from the pristine economic determinism of *Capitalism and Slavery* to the pure moralism of the Coupland school.

Neither the expectations of Anstey nor the fears of Gutzmore have prevailed. The outcome to date is illustrated by many of those who accepted the main critique of the Williams thesis as valid, yet immediately seek alternative explantation somehow grounded in fundamental economic development. Pieter Emmer's was a typical response to *Econocide*: Drescher's new interpretation, he concluded, 'has overturned most of the factual implication of the Williams thesis. But still . . . there remains something unassailable in this thesis concerning the connection between economics and abolition.'[49]

Econocide, some reviewers realized, did not at all dispute this. Philip Curtin noted that a staunch defender of a Marxian point of view could take a more roundabout approach, drawing a class struggle out of the religious ideology that pervaded British middle-class life in the eighteenth century. Alan Adamson, moving the argument toward the post-emancipation period, suggests that economic forces would be much more apparent in the struggle over the sugar duties. Richard Lopper also argues that a Marxist analysis can easily accommodate an abandonment of both the decline thesis and Williams' economic determinist reading of abolition.[50]

Embodied in many reactions, made as reservations or suggestions, are two fundamental propositions. The first of these might be called a historiographical gut feeling. The response goes something like this: 'It is surely no accident that abolition coincided with the industrial revolution.' The second fundamental proposition, however, seems to derive from a recognition, sometimes wholehearted, sometimes grudging, that the abolition of slavery cannot be explained by direct extrapolation from pure economic motives or mechanisms any more than from pure moral consciousness. Most of the alternative approaches thus far lean toward an attempt to find a new ideological base for abolitionism. The attack on the Coupland school of pure ideas by the Williams school of impure interests begins with a search for convincingly impure ideas. The principal target of scholarly concern has become the anti-slavery 'ideology' — some combination of economic and non-economic ideas which called forth the abolitionist crusade and permitted it to triumph. There has also been a renewed search for an ideological combination which will include both the abolitionist spokesmen and the political economists of industrializing Britain.

Perhaps the most apt conclusion to this survey of the decline thesis since *Econocide* would be to emphasize the enduring heritage of *Capitalism and Slavery*, the book which constituted the object of its critique. As long as British slavery and abolition were regarded as *sui generis*, primarily as moral categories, they were more likely to be treated commemoratively than analytically. *Capitalism and Slavery* was therefore a classical demonstration of the value of even deliberately simplistic history. It would be no gain whatever to the historiography of slavery if apparent gaps in the causal chain forged by Williams fragmented slavery scholarship into clusters of specialists with no common framework. Williams cast his story in a global economic setting and that setting must, if anything, be remapped and resynthesized.

Williams' last and most enduring message was that abolition could not have triumphed independently of economic developments linked to industrialization. This simple hypothesis has already proved to be more fruitful than those offered by historians in the whole century before him. *Capitalism and Slavery* changed the way in which we view abolition precisely because it riveted attention on the context rather than on heroes. Historians are unlikely again to suspend disbelief in the existence of 'three or four perfectly virtuous pages in the history of nations'.

Notes

1. Eric Williams, *Capitalism and Slavery* (1944, rpt. 1966), hereafter *C&S*.
2. *Ibid.*, p. 120.
3. *Ibid.*, p. 154.
4. 2nd Ser. xxi, 307–20, No. 2 (1968), See also his 'A Re-interpretation of the Abolition of the British Slave Trade, 1806–07', *Economic History Review*, LXXXVII (1972), No. 343, 304–32.
5. Cf. Cecil Gutzmore, 'The Continuing Dispute over the Connections between the Capitalist Mode of Production and Chattel Slavery, presented at the Sesquecentennial of the Death of William Wilberforce and the Emancipation Act of 1833' (MSS), pp. 2–6.
6. *C&S*, pp. 52–54, 225–26, tables; *Econocide*, pp. 16–25.
7. 'Economic Aspects of the Abolition Debate' in Christine Bolt and Seymour Drescher (eds.), *Anti-Slavery, Religion, and Reform: Essays in Memory of Roger Anstey* (Folkestone, England; Hamden, Conn., 1980), pp. 272–73.
8. See note 4.
9. ' "Econocide" — Myth or Reality — The Question of West Indian Decline, 1783–1806' and the reply, 'Econocide, Capitalism and Slavery: A Commentary' in *Boletin de Estudios Latinoamericanos y del Caribe*, 36 (June 1984), 13–67.
10. See note 6.
11. *C&S*, p. 225, n. 16.
12. See note 5.
13. *Econocide*, p. 20, fig. 5.
14. Those reviews of *Econocide* which evidently accept the undermining of the Williams decline thesis are: W. J. Hausman, J. A. Casada, G. Heuman, L. J. Belliot, R. Anstey, D. Eltis, R. Lopper, J. Hogendorn, B. Hilton, J. Walvin, P. E. H. Hair, P. D. Curtin, R. Koch, I. R. Hancock, J. P. Greene, S. Daget, P. Emmer, J. A. Lesourd, Sv. E. Green-Pedersen. In the most novel portion of his essay on 'Williams and Drescher' in *Slavery and Abolition*, September, 1983, Vol. 4, No. 3, 81–105, Walter Minchinton dismisses the utility of official British trade statistics for measuring trends in the relative significance of global trade zones, including the British West Indies. On grounds that these figures used static official prices, Minchinton insists that they do 'not enable us to assess properly the importance of the British West Indies for Great Britain' (*ibid.*, p. 87). He does not, however, address the fact that the other economic historians of the same period consider it quite feasible to measure relative trade shares on the basis of the official data (see, for example, François Crouzet's 'Toward an export economy', cited in Table 2). More important, he overlooks the fact that Ralph Davis' *real* price data confirm the British West Indian trends at the end of the eighteenth century (see note 37, below). Minchinton also overlooks the fact that the official figures were those used exclusively by contemporary MPs and publicists in arguments about the value of the British West Indies (see *Econocide*, p. 231, note). (Incidentally, Minchinton's summary dismissal of the official data works directly against his own conclusion that *Capitalism and Slavery* remains a 'yardstick' for the study of abolition. If the official series cannot validate *Econocide*'s conclusions about the West Indies after 1775, how can the same data validate *Capitalism and Slavery's* similar conclusions about the period before 1775?)
15. See, *inter alia*, Gutzmore, 'Continuing Dispute', pp. 16–17; Review of A. Adamson.
16. Review of M. Craton. The most systematic and elegant elaboration to date of the implicit tension between abolition and the pattern of economic development yet written is David Eltis' 'Capitalism and Abolition: The Missed Opportunities of 1807–1865', typescript kindly circulated at the Bellaggio conference. It is a foretaste of Eltis' eagerly awaited two-volume synthesis on the nineteenth-century slave trade.
17. *C&S*, p. 134.
18. *Ibid.*, p. 135.
19. J. R. Ward, 'The Profitability of Sugar Planting in the British West Indies, 1650–1834', *Economic History Review*, 2nd ser., XXXI (1978); and his excellent unpublished sequel, 'The Profitability and Viability of British West Indian Plantation Slavery, 1807–1834'.
20. Review by M. Craton.
21. At the Bellaggio conference on British Slavery and British Capitalism, Barbara Solow placed special emphasis on the significance of the eighteenth-century export trade in British economic development. See the general discussion in John J. McKusker and Russel R. Menard, *The Economy of British America, 1607–1789* (Chapel Hill and London, 1985), 39–45.
22. See review essays by B. Solow and M. Turner; review by E. Goveia; Noel Deerr, *A History of Sugar*, 2 vols. (London, 1949–50), pp. 529–31.
23. *Econocide*, pp. 39–41.
24. See *Some Observations Showing the Dangers of Losing the Trade of the Slave Colonies, by a Planter* (1714), from the Huntington Library Collection, no. 146982.
25. *C&S*, p. 122.
26. *Econocide*, pp. 46–51.

Table: Re-exports of sugar compared to 'British'/foreign sugar ratios (1765–1818) (selected periods)

Period	% of British imports re-exported (cwt) (1)	London prices/foreign prices × 100 (per British cwt) (2)
1761–65	23.8	124 (a)
1771–75	4.5	144 (b)
1781–85	10.0	136 (c)
1791–95	24.5	—
1801–05	33.3	83 (d)
1814–18	31.8 (27.9)	88 (e)

Column 1: Parenthetical figure = British West Indian sugar only

Column 2: (a) = London compared with Amsterdam Muscovado; (b) = London compared with Nantes Muscovado; (c) = ditto, but Nantes prices for 1782–84 only; (d) = London/Amsterdam ratio, but Amsterdam prices 1801, 1804, 1806 only; (e) London/Havana, ord. yellow.

Sources: Column 1: 1765–1805, *Econocide*, p. 80, 1814–1818 PP, 1847–48, LVIII; column 2: (a) and (b) London prices from R. Sheridan, *Sugar and Slavery: An Economic History of the British West Indies* (Baltimore, 1974), p. 497; Amsterdam prices, Deerr, *History*, p. 530; *ibid.*; (c) Nantes prices from Deerr, *ibid.*, British prices from *ibid.* Mean of range given by Deerr; (d) same as (c); (e) *PP* 1847–48 (44), p. 3 of *Report*.

27. See Deerr, *History*, p. 530, prices of sugar in London and Amsterdam, 1806. Just prior to the Commons debate of 1792, 5 January–5 March, British re-exports of sugar to Europe were running at about 300% of the rate of average re-exports for 1787–90. (calculated from

A Report from the Committee of Warehouses of the United East-India Company Relative to the Price of Sugar (London, 1792), p. 23). Below, I offer a table, but only suggestively, comparing the ratios of Britsh re-exports to 'British'/foreign sugar prices at points between 1765 and 1818. From the sources used, it is unclear whether different grades of sugar are being compared in the price series in different ports. In the re-export series it is also unclear how much 'foreign' sugar was beng re-exported, especially in the war years: 1761–63; 1781–83; 1793–95; 1801; 1804–05. Five-year intervals are chosen both because Parliament preferred these multi-year averages, and because quantities of foreign sugar, listed as 'retained' for consumption in one year might have been imported in prior years. (See, for example, *PP* 1847–48 LVIII Seasonal Paper No. 400: '*Return of Quantities of Sugar*', etc, p. 3, n. lc.)

28. Temperley, 'Capitalism, Slavery and Ideology', *Past and Present*, No. 75 (May, 1977), 101.
29. *Econocide*, p. 53.
30. P. J. Cain and A. G. Hopkins, 'The Political Economy of British Expansion Overseas, 1750–1914', *Economic History Review*, 2nd ser., XXXIII, No. 4, (November 1980), 463–90. Referring to *Econocide*, Cain and Hopkins write: 'Contrary to a long-standing belief, the slave trade was not overthrown by powerful industrial interests cramped by colonial restrictions. Manufacturers were neither influential enough to overthrow the trade nor driven by economic logic to make the attempt' (p. 473, n.).
31. Carrington, 'Econocide/Myth'.
32. See reviews by Emmer, G. Heuman, and the essay by D. Geggus, 'The British Government and the Saint Domingue slave revolt, 1791–1793', *English Historical Review*, XCVI, No. 379 (April, 1981), 287.
33. *Econocide*, p. 64.
34. *Ibid.*, pp. 165–66.
35. C&S, p. 113.
36. P. Curtin, *The Slave Trade: A Census* (Madison, 1969), pp. 119, 216.
37. Deerr, *History of Sugar*, pp. 193–96.
38. R. Davis, *The Industrial Revolution and British Overseas Trade* (Leicester, 1979), pp. 89–125.
39. Deerr, *History of Sugar*, p. 21.
40. See for example P. E. Lovejoy, 'The Volume of the Atlantic Slave Trade: A Synthesis', *Journal of African History*, Vol. 23, No. 4, (1982), 473–501; James A. Rawley, *The Transatlantic Slave Trade: A History* (New York, 1981), p. 428; and D. Richardson, unpublished figures summarized in his Bellaggio conference paper 'The Slave Trade, Sugar, and British Economic Growth 1784–76.
41. J. E. Inikori, 'Measuring the Atlantic Slave Trade: An Assessment of Curtin and Anstey', *Journal of African History*, 17 (1976), 197–223; *Econocide*, pp. 211–13.
42. Carrington, 'Econocide/Myth', p. 42.
43. *Ibid.*, p. 43, figure XXIII: Slave imports into and exports from the B. W. I., 1783–1805.
44. J. J. McCusker, 'The Rum Trade and the Balance of Payments of the Thirteen Continental Colonies, 1660–1776', University of Pittsburgh, Ph.D. dissertation, 2 vols., 1970.
45. See note 32, above.
46. Another historian cited yet another leading Minister who assured the Governor of Jamaica in 1808 that abolition had been a practical response to overproduction. Yet only nine months earlier the same MP had opposed abolition as impractical on grounds of planter demand for slaves. is there any reason why one should prefer after-the-fact rationalizations to before-the-fact statements in determining motivations?
47. Anstey, *Atlantic Slave Trade*, pp. 51–52.
48. Gutzmore, 'Continuing Dispute', p. 26.
49. Emmer's review.
50. Reviews of Curtin, Adamson, and Lopper.

SECTION FIVE
Race, Colour and Ideology

The dynamics of colour, race and class within Caribbean societies, from the earliest years of colonization in the seventeenth century until present times, have long been popular foci of historical research. Wherever black laboured as slaves and whites mastered in the Caribbean, and indeed the Americas, a prominent feature of society was the existence of people of mixed racial ancestry, their numbers and rate of growth varying according to situational demographic, ideological and economic factors. Since legal codes for governing the enslaved blacks provided that all juveniles should at birth take the socio-legal status of their mothers, most peoples of mixed racial origins, particularly the mulattoes born of slave mothers, were at birth designated slaves. However, partly because some empowered whites could not comfortably enslave their own progeniture, and partly because white supremist ideology required some socio-economic expression, a general tendency was for the manumission of these coloured people. Consequently, a group of free-coloured people emerged, and was to be found in most Caribbean societies. In general, they cherished their legal freedom, the most highly valued commodity in slave society, but were rejected by white society on the basis of their colour — the common mark of servitude and inferiority. Living within these two psychological worlds, the free-coloureds developed a unique perspective on society which has been identified as being worthy of special study.

Marginality and Free Coloured Identity in Caribbean Slave Society

ARNOLD A. SIO*

The structure of Caribbean slave society consisted of a small minority of Europeans who dominated the majority of the population of enslaved Africans. Despite the profound differences in power, culture, and race between the masters and the slaves, the ideal of the masters that the two were to remain totally separate was never realized. The bipolar structure of the society was gradually altered through the genetic intermixture of the masters and the slaves and the emergence of an intermediate racial group. Over time a significant portion of this racial mixed population became legally free. This created an overlap between the free Europeans and the enslaved Africans and promoted questions regarding the boundaries of the respective groups, criteria of identification, and status allocation. In a society in which slavery was associated with race, a free coloured person was 'a third party in a system built for two'. The interpenetration of the masters and the slaves and the appearance of an intermediate group of freedmen or free coloured has been defined 'as one of the most critical problem areas in the historical study of Afro-Caribbean societies'.[1]

*Senior Research Fellow, Department of Sociology and Anthropology, Colgate University, Hamilton, NY 13346, USA. This essay pertains to the British Caribbean and is a revised version of a paper presented at the Centre for Caribbean Studies in Warwick University. I am grateful to Gad Heuman for arranging the presentation and to those present for their helpful comments.

Slavery and Abolition, Vol. 8, No. 2 (1987), pp. 166–82.

Unlike the United States where the literature on the free Negro dates back to the turn of the century, research on this group in the Caribbean is relatively recent and less substantial. The Caribbean freedmen figure in two kinds of studies. The most extensive are those pertaining to race and colour in the Caribbean that often involve comparisons with the rest of the Americas, particularly the United States. Second, are those more recent studies that, although they may take up the matter of race and colour, are for the most part descriptive accounts of the freedmen that include their demographic characteristics, political-legal status, economic activity, religious life, education, and to some extent stratification, relations with whites and with slaves, and culture and social organization.

There are two general features of the research on the free coloured that have given rise to the issues discussed in this paper. The first is that the studies conform for the most part to the observation that much of what has been written is about the 'established free coloured, if not the elite',[2] and to the related observation that the 'plight of the free coloured majority . . . is seldom recorded'.[3] Many of the existing generalizations are based on a 'fraction of the whole'[4] that probably varied from 5 to 7 per cent of the group and in some places might have consisted of a small number of families. The tendency to take the most visible, active, and articulate 'as typical of the whole group'[5] has not gone unrecognized in the literature.[6] While it may be the case that in a particular study reference is made to the narrowness of its base, the implications are not always taken into account when generalizations are actually stated.

The second general feature pertains to the way in which the freedmen have been depicted in the literature. The people of colour were marginal to Caribbean slave society: neither black nor white, neither African nor European, and neither slave nor free. The consequences of this marginality for their identity constitute the content of the depictions of the group in the literature. Although it is recognized that their marginality did not produce a uniform response among the freedmen, including the leadership and the established segment of the group, the free coloured are generally portrayed, sometimes explicitly, more often implicitly, as having identified themselves with the dominant whites.[7] The defining features of this assimilationist depiction are to be found in the following: 'they were loyal to the establishment',[8] 'strongly identified with the master class',[9] 'tended to identify culturally with the whites',[10] and 'were very conscious of their European heritage and extremely proud of it'.[11] Although opposed to the white policy of exclusion based on racial ancestry, they favoured the existing society, including slavery, and 'tended to aspire to white plantocratic or managerial status'.[12]

The concern of this essay is with three problematic or neglected issues that relate to the question of the identity of the free people of colour: culture and social organization, unity and group consciousness, and the style and goals of their political activity. The existing research provides the basis for observations that are often of an exploratory and provisional nature. The tentative parts of this discussion reflect not only the need for more historical information that is comparative and generalizable, but also for more research that is guided by a view of the free coloured as of critical importance to an understanding of Caribbean slave society and Afro-American history.[13]

I

What we know about the culture of people of colour pertains to members of the upper stratum of the population who are said to have emulated the whites. Although this view of the free coloured culture is often extended by assumption and implication to the entire group, little is known about the culture of the majority of freedmen during slavery. It is apparent that this issue is considerably more complex than is conveyed by statements based on a segment of the group. Not only is it the least studied of the three issues, it is also the most difficult to approach. For that reason many of the observations in this section of the paper are likely to be the most exploratory and provisional.

In approaching the origin and nature of the culture of the free coloured we begin with the relationship between the free coloured and the slaves. Since the freedmen emerged in conjunction with slavery, their culture and social organization originally involved a transfer or carry-over from the slave community. The components of this Afro-creole complex were modified as the free coloured became differentiated into separate strata. However, since it appears that during slavery and after a substantial number of the people of colour remained generally removed from sustained interaction with the whites and the Euro-creole complex of that group, this cleavage served to maintain and reinforce the Afro-creole cultural complex among themselves and the slaves.

It is likely that in the early years of the group a number of the free coloured, many of them the miscegenated offspring of wealthy whites who had arranged for their freedom, conformed to the Euro-creole pattern of the dominant group. Even at a later date, however, the number who could adopt and sustain this way of life, as we shall note, must have been quite limited. Our conception of the culture of the freedmen is based largely on the minority who were in a position to take on the cultural complex of the ruling whites.

Within the boundaries created and maintained by the white structure of dominance, the life of the free people of colour was to a large extent removed from that of the whites. Indeed, members of the dominant group were peripheral to most of the relationships in which the freedmen were involved. The ratio of free coloured to whites, the concentration of the free coloured and of the coloured slaves in the towns, the location of most of the freedmen in the lower stratum of the free coloured social order, the racism of the dominant group and its control of the major sources of power — these were among the factors that singly and in combination determined the interaction of the free coloured people and the whites. With the exception of the interaction between free coloured women and white males and a small number of those of the upper stratum and whites, interaction with those of the dominant group was not an important element in the free coloured social structure.

It was the local community of the freedmen that constituted their primary environment, while the work experience, which was most likely to bring them into contact with the whites, was their secondary environment and less important for their life-ways. Considerable social interaction occurred between the freedmen and the slaves of the towns. Just as the distinction between the master and the slave tended to break down in the towns, so the line between the freedmen and the slaves became blurred. Not only did the town slaves have more mobility than those on the plantations, many also worked, lived, and carried on a social life away from their masters. Interaction with the slaves on many levels and in a variety of ways rather than with the whites must then have been a feature of everyday life for most of the free people of colour. Given the concentration of the free coloured and the coloured slaves in the towns, it is likely that relations were mainly between the coloured members of each group.[14]

Many freedmen existed on the margins of an economy that was dominated by the plantation system.[15] They often found themselves and the slaves similarly situated in the towns, especially with regard to work and living conditions. They lived close to each other, they interacted more frequently with each other than either did with the whites and they shared the same familiar life-space. They often participated in the same religious, economic, educational, and social activities. Family and kinship relations based on common origin were another measure of the extensive network in which the freedmen and the slaves were involved. Then, too, there were the numerous informal contacts that must have marked the daily round of freedmen and slaves as they moved about the towns.[16] In spite of the growing difference in legal status and group membership, a substantial number of the free coloured and the slaves, who were concentrated in a similar economic, social, and ecological position, shared the Afro-creole pattern which was in turn reinforced by their participation in a wide range of institutions and activities.[17]

Thus, the conditions that functioned to largely confine the interaction of the majority of the freedmen to themselves and with the slaves, also served to perpetuate the Afro-creole complex of the free coloured group. Moreover, the structure of dominance maintained by the whites, especially their control of the economy and polity, was such that the life chances of the free people of colour were exceedingly limited. Their position was characterized by its static nature. This, too, furthered the stability and continuity of the group's life-ways.

Additions to the group from the slave population through manumission and self-purchase tended to have the same result. The change in status from slave to freedman was a shift from one subordinate group to another, both based on racial ancestry. It is likely that many of those who were freed became incorporated into the lower stratum of the free coloured community. Although an important change occurred in legal status and group affiliation, the freed slave could expect to find significant continuities of colour, cultural patterns and, if an ex-town slave, little change in environment. Given the network that existed between the slaves and the freedmen, the freed slave was likely to have been very familiar with the free coloured social and cultural life even as it changed, especially when, as must often have been the case, there were parents, children, other relatives, and friends among the freedmen. It is unlikely, then, that the change in status from slave to freedman involved a set of unfamiliar institutions and cultural understandings. The freed slave was a source of stability and continuity, for the movement of freed slaves into the free coloured group meant an infusion of Afro-creole life-ways. The transition for the freed slave was relatively simple, causing little personal or group disruption with integration into the group of freedmen being largely a matter of course.

Accretion to the freedmen population also occurred through the birth of children. Throughout the slavery period, the free coloured group appears to have been the only one capable of increasing through natural means. This was an important source of growth. When restrictions were placed on manumission, it became the primary source of population growth. The life-ways that were passed on through the socialization of the children contributed to the cultural continuity of the freedmen and promoted group identification.

The changes that gradually occurred among the free coloured during the slavery period included some degree of social, economic, and cultural differentiation. As mentioned earlier, a small upper stratum emerged who participated in the Euro-creole culture of the dominant group. However, those who could adopt this cultural complex remained a small number throughout the period. Most of those who desired to do so were unable to acquire the education or wealth to maintain the life-ways of the ruling whites. The middle stratum that emerged in the process of differentiation developed a 'Synthetic-creole' culture that was a combination of elements derived from the Afro-creole and Euro-creole patterns.[18]

The process of differentiation did not involve a large number of the freedmen. No significant increase in interaction with the white population appears to have occurred. The social and kinship networks among the free coloured and between them and the town slaves remained relatively unchanged. A substantial proportion of the freedmen, varying in size from colony to colony, remained — and was to remain for a long time — Afro-creole in its life-ways.

II

The issue regarding the unity and consciousness of the freedmen is, like that relating to their culture, part of the larger question of their identity as a group. It has been said that they lacked a 'social organization' and that they were slow in developing a 'group consciousness'.[19] It is clear, however, that a sense of identity was a continuous process and developed with the freedmen's consciousness as a group. The growth of a group consciousness began quite early. Just as they were set apart from the beginning by the dominant group, so they set themselves apart. Their consciousness largely coincided with their position in the society. They were a people of colour, neither black nor white, but coloured and consciously so. Like their counterparts in the United States, they were 'new people'.[20] Since the boundaries between themselves and the slaves were vague and fluid, the continuation of relations with slaves was not a barrier to a free coloured identity. By the late eighteenth century, the larger society was aware that the free coloured had begun to develop a separate identity and were becoming a solitary people.

The development of a group consciousness among the freedmen occurred in conjunction with an increase in population size and density and with the growth of social organization. Over time the increasing size and concentration of the free coloured in the towns meant more than an aggregation of large numbers of people of one's own kind. For there gradually emerged a sense of a sizeable group and a perception of being part of a discernible whole with a distinct history, common origin, and shared concerns.[21] This perception was also fostered by the creation of organizations and associations that contributed to the development of a group identification. The racism of the whites that was institutionalized in the structure of dominance and exclusion reinforced patterns of association and identification among the free people of colour. The limited occupational differentiation among them made for common social and economic interests and for a similarity of life-ways. Thus, the limitations on the economic development of the freedmen that kept them marginal to the main economy of the society contributed to their consciousness as a group and to their solidarity.

As they became conscious of themselves as a group an identity developed that embodied a distinct sense of difference. The sense of identity manifested itself in the definitions of acceptable behaviour among themselves, the terms they used to define themselves, and in their view of themselves in relation to whites, to a particular island, and to the Caribbean region as a whole.

In the course of time, norms and values

developed that were seen as contributing to group identity and pride and that were intended to govern the actions of the freedmen. Those who deviated from these norms and values aroused the displeasure of others. The freedmen of Jamaica who applied for and were granted special privileges by the Assembly, removing various disabilities normally attached to the status of the free coloured, incurred the displeasure of the rest of the group. The practice was scorned by the free coloured newspaper where those 'who chose to avail themselves of *such means* to be blanched' were referred to as having participated in an 'infamous delusion'. While those who were granted the special privileges viewed themselves as having been rewarded for achieving a mode of living that conformed to that of the dominant group and won its approval, the press viewed them as dupes and as a threat to the solidarity of the group. They had been subjected to the '*acme* of political juggling' by the ruling whites.[22]

The terms with which they distinguished themselves as a group reveal that their sense of identity very much involved attachment to a homeland or territory and a region. Most of all they perceived themselves as genuinely indigenous to the area, indeed, as native sons. They were 'natives of the soil', a particular island was 'our native country' or 'native land'. 'This is our native country — we have nowhere else to go.' They were creoles of colour expressing a new ethnicity.

On the other hand, the whites were perceived as 'alien,' as 'transient', and as 'foreigners'. The freedmen of Grenada expressed it as having more of a vested interest than the 'transient white foreigners'. Moreover, 'they', the whites, were aliens and interlopers not only to particular islands but to the Caribbean region as a whole. Throughout, the free coloured make it clear that central to their identity was that 'we', the free coloured, are native sons and our homeland is an island and region, while 'they', the whites, are alien to both.

The regional dimension of the free coloured sense of identity was grounded in an extensive network of similar groups in the Spanish, French, Dutch, and Danish colonies as well as the British. Information was communicated through this network regarding the general situation, political activities, and goals of the several groups in the region. The value of this network was enhanced by the immigration and travel of freedmen to the different colonies where much exchange of information took place and their presence tended to heighten the group consciousness and identity of the free coloured.[23]

The evolution of a separate identity included the way the free coloured conceived of their place in the structure of the society. The whites, of course, intended that they be located between themselves and the slaves, with the free people of colour having their primary identification with the whites. However, although the free coloured accepted their intermediateness in terms of 'colour' and, indeed, made it a central feature of their distinctive identity, they had no intention of occupying an intermediate position in the society. Such a position would have been inherently unstable, with severe limitations on their civil rights and aspirations. Their aggressive pursuit of the rights of citizenship made it apparent to the dominant group that the freedmen rejected being relegated to an intermediate place in the society.

Thus, while they identified themselves as native sons, they also considered themselves as British citizens. Was this a matter of confused identity? That the freedmen may have subscribed to the political values of the dominant group and claimed equal rights as British citizens is hardly to be taken as evidence that they did not perceive of themselves as having a separate and distinctive identity. It did not mean that the free coloured identified with the whites and that the acquisition of citizenship was to be the initial step toward acceptance in the existing society. Rather it was that the rights and privileges of citizens were seen as instrumental not only to inclusion in the polity and as crucial to their efforts in the economy, but potentially as providing access to the power resources with which to have an independent impact on the society and on their future as a group with its own identity. Recent research indicates that the freedmen did not entirely share the white view of Caribbean society and its future, despite the subscription of some of them to the Euro-creole pattern.[24]

We have referred to those of the freedmen who in the course of time were able to assimilate the cultural patterns of the ruling whites. Even by the 1830s, however, when the free coloured had gained their civil rights, the ability to adopt those life-ways was limited to a minority of the group. With the Afro-creole and Synthetic-creole patterns predominating, the differences in culture among the freedmen may not have been very great. It is conceivable that the freedmen shared a view of themselves as native sons and as British citizens who valued and sought equal rights as a means to the realization of their aspirations as individuals and as a group. There is no evidence of a confused identity resulting from their identification of themselves as a distinct people and as British citizens.

III

Their political activity was aimed at gaining the rights and privileges of British citizens, which would resolve the political and legal contradictions confounding their position in the society. Only a small number of the group were involved in articulating the goals of the freedmen and in providing the political leadership. Much of the research has been centred on the activities of these freedmen.

The politicization of the freedmen occurred in connection with certain changes in their situation. These included the growth in the size of the group, the appearance of a significant number of free-born people of colour, the increasing concentration of freedmen in the towns, the social and economic differentiation that meant some economic success and growth in the wealth of the group, and their involvement in the activities of the mission churches.[25] These changes raised their expectations regarding their life chances which, however, came up against the continued exclusionary policies and practices of the dominant white group. The effects of these changes were reinforced and intensified by the restiveness of the freedmen in the other colonies, the revolutionary disturbances in the French colonies, and the changes in the British colonial policy in response to the movement for amelioration and emancipation.

The goals of the freedmen and the means they employed have been depicted as conservative.[26] However, in seeking to gain civil and political rights for themselves — and acting on the premise that they had a legitimate claim to such rights — the freedmen were in fundamental opposition to the existing structure of the society as it was being maintained by the power and racial ideology of the ruling whites. Moreover, the goals and political activity of the free coloured could very well be taken as an indirect attack on slavery, for the same power and ideology informed and maintained the system of slavery. To pursue these goals, then, was to challenge the power and ideology that were integral to the identity, cohesion, and dominance of the whites. To attempt to bring the free coloured into the power structure of Caribbean slave society under these circumstances was hardly a conservative or moderate goal and the whites were quick to perceive it as the radical goal that it, indeed, was at the time. The presence of a politically aggressive group of freedmen pursuing issues that challenged the stability and continuation of the existing political, economic, and social organization of the society convinced the whites that they had been correct from the beginning in their view of the free coloured as potentially as great a threat to the established order as the slaves.[27]

The freedmen engaged in individual, uncoordinated acts of protest and organized political action to gain their civil rights. There was persistent opposition by individuals and small groups of the free coloured to segregation in churches and places of public recreation and to the generally discriminatory behaviour of the whites. The organized political action carried on by the freedmen was legal and aimed primarily at constitutional change: petitions, appeals, expressions of grievances, lobbying in England, and testifying before imperial commissions. Action directed at constitutional change was the primary means used by the freedmen.

The freedmen were fundamentally opposed to living in a society in which 'the structure was rooted in the biogenetic conception of group superiority-inferiority — in short, racism'.[28] From the vantage point of the whites, of course, this represented a rejection of the principle that was fundamental to the hierarchical organization of the society. The status of the free coloured was ascribed on the basis of their non-white ancestry. The whites intended that their status and racial ancestry would correspond in that not only would freedmen be relegated to a subordinate group, but the group would also remain undifferentiated. However, the free coloured did become internally differentiated to the point where, in terms of certain social and economic criteria, there were freedmen who were at the same level or a level above the whites. Yet, since racial ancestry was intended to determine the structure of the society, they were excluded from certain rights that would have been theirs had they been white. It was not that the freedmen were opposed to living in a stratified society. Rather, through their political activity they hoped to create a situation in which their individual efforts and achievements — given full rein as a result of having the rights of citizens — would largely determine their position in the society and not their racial ancestry.

Slavery and the relations with slaves were very

much involved in the strategy pursued by the freedmen in their campaign for civil rights. This is especially evident in the way in which they portrayed themselves to the whites and in the methods used to bring about change. It is clear from the previous discussion of the relations between the slaves and the free coloured that the complex issue of the place and meaning of slavery in the life of the freedmen is far from settled. Some of what follows, then, is of necessity tentative and provisional.

With regard to the direct involvement in slavery through the ownership of slaves, the most recent research indicates that the free coloured owned relatively few slaves, were no more than 20 per cent of the owners in 1832, and owned a much smaller proportion of the slave population than did the whites. A relatively large proportion of the coloured slaves belonged to the freedmen which, as we noted earlier, reflected the concentration in the towns of the two groups. More free coloured females than males owned slaves. They were most likely to have owned slaves in units of rarely more than 10, many of whom would have been domestics. Their owner may well have been someone to whom they were related and who was not wealthy. While there were those among the free people of colour who saw the ownership of slaves as the way to wealth and prestige in a slave society, there were few planters among them.[29]

Challenging the slavery system was not one of the goals in the otherwise aggressive, persistent, and lengthy campaign carried on by the freedmen for their civil rights. Freedmen were not to become involved in political alliances with the slaves. Unless they were willing to challenge the slavery system head on, the freedmen were aware that improvement in their life chances depended on setting themselves apart from the slaves. It seems doubtful, however, that they could have expected to attain equality in the sense that their racial ancestry would no longer be a factor in their life chances. For that would be a long time in coming and called for the unity of all those with African ancestry and the abolition of slavery. Nevertheless, it was perceived that substantial gains were to be made within the existing society by separating themselves from the slaves.

Separating themselves from the slaves meant more than not entering into alliances with the slaves or not attacking slavery. Distinguishing themselves from the slaves socially, culturally, and ideologically was crucial for the image they projected of themselves in their approach to the ruling whites. Thus we find that while, on the one hand, the free coloured expressions of group identity emphasized their separateness — a third group in the society — and tended to be cast in ethnic terms and in language often critical of the whites and of colonialism, in their numerous and various appeals for equal rights, on the other hand, they stressed their identity with the whites.

In validating their claim to the rights of British citizens they portrayed themselves as having achieved ownership of land, property, and slaves, and as sharing many of the values, sentiments, and attitudes of the whites. Throughout they stressed that they had remained an orderly and loyal people. It was an approach to the dominant group that involved refraining from an attack on slavery, distinguishing themselves from the slaves, expressing their identity with the whites, and exploiting the desire of the whites to have the free coloured serve as a buffer group between themselves and the slaves.

The free coloured portrayals of themselves in their approach to the colonial authorities tell us much about their conduct of the campaign for civil rights. There are much less reliable as sources of information about their life-ways, attitudes toward whites, and particularly their views on slavery. After all, the campaign was designed and conducted to bring the ruling group around to the point of granting the freedmen their rights as citizens.[30] Therefore, with the possible exception of those directly involved in the various petitions and addresses, we do not know the extent to which there was acceptance within the free coloured community, particularly among the lower stratum, of a set of goals that prohibited political alliances with slaves and expressions of opposition to slavery.

Although political alliances with the slaves are likely to have been infrequent, we do have some evidence of freedmen becoming allied with slaves, and expressing their opposition to slavery in other ways. Unfortunately, very little research has been done on free coloured involvement in slave rebellions, conspiracies, runaways, and marronage. We have information on alliances of slaves and freedmen in revolts in Grenada,[31] Barbados,[32] and Jamaica,[33] and in aborted plots in Antigua[34] and Tobago,[35] and on the harbouring of runaways.[36] These alliances extended from 1736 in Antigua to 1832 in Jamaica and into the period when the free people of colour were granted their civil rights. What appears to have happened is that, as the freedmen gained their civil rights in the late 1820s and early 1830s, especially the franchise and access to the Assembly, and as their sense of a separate identity continued to develop, there was an increase in their opposition to slavery.

Contrary to what the whites had come to expect after they had granted the freedmen their civil rights, in the end the freedmen did not join with them in a united front against the abolition of slavery. Nor were the expectations of the free coloured fully realized. Caribbean society continued to be one in which the life chances of its people would be determined to a large extent by their racial ancestry. There were gains for the freedmen. While these gains varied from colony to colony, there was a general reduction in the scope of white regulation of the polity and the economy, though they continued to control both areas. Sharing political and legal rights with members of the dominant group did not, of course, mean full acceptance. The exclusion of people of colour from the primary and institutional life of the whites remained almost complete. For 'they continued to suffer the stigma of slave and partial black ancestry'.[37]

IV

At the centre of the research on the free coloured is the marginality of their position in Caribbean slave society. They have been depicted as responding to their marginality by identifying with the whites. Although it is recognized that their response was not entirely uniform, it is the free coloured as assimilationist that is the most prominent, explicitly and implicitly, in the scholarly research and in the popular view of the group. A discussion of this interpretation of their identity has been the objective of this essay. It has involved observations grounded in the documentary materials as well as assertions that are tentative and speculative.

The question of the identity of the free coloured must be examined in relation to the evolving and changing character of the group. The history of the freedmen during slavery is the evolution and assimilation to a new identity.[38] From the beginning they were defined as a marginal people. Accepting this definition of themselves was also the beginning of their consciousness as a new people. As their marginality dissolved during the slavery period, they gradually developed an identity as a people who were creole in colour and culture and in their views of Caribbean society, its people, and its future. Some final observations on these dimensions of their identity are in order.

In making their phenotype a vital part of their identity the free coloured, it has been said, failed to develop a consciousness of their own worth. For they had made as their own the racist ideology and practices of the dominant white group. The 'white bias' of the freedmen, then, is evidence of their identification with the whites.[39]

While there may have been a similarity in form, the so-called white bias of the freedmen did not have the same meaning and purpose as among the whites. To begin with, given the focus of the present research, we know only that during slavery this bias existed among some of the established freedmen. Second, the slaves as well as the free blacks, and free coloured — whether free by manumission, self-purchase or birth — were all subjected to the racism of the whites. The legal disabilities and discriminatory practices of the whites applied to all free non-whites. Likewise, no distinctions were made by the whites between free coloured and free blacks in the extension of civil rights over the years. Third, slaves, free blacks and free coloured were often joined by an extensive network of ties, including kinship, and similar life situations. Fourth, the freedmen carried on a vigorous campaign for their civil rights and against their exclusion from full participation in the society on the basis of their racial ancestry. Most important, the phenotypic bias of the free persons of colour was not justified and supported by a racist ideology as were the racial values and practices of the whites. It was apparent, even before they gained their civil rights and before emancipation, that the freedmen did not intend to institutionalize their bias in a structure of dominance devoted to the maintenance of an hierarchical order based on gradations of colour and the permanent exclusion of those who did not have the proper phenotype. The phenotype, it may be suggested, had the same meaning and purpose, though perhaps not the same weight during slavery, as the socio-economic criteria usually associated with 'class': occupation, income, wealth, education, life-style. That is, among the freedmen the value of the phenotype did not derive from an ideology of biogenetic superiority, but rather from its importance as a determinant of a person's life chances in a society where race was used to justify slavery.

The freedmen were creoles of culture as well as colour. The focus of the existing research gives the impression that they identified culturally exclusively with the dominant white sector in adopting the Euro-creole culture.

Largely missing from the discussion of the

culture of the free coloured group are the lower and middle strata. Given the limited differentiation of the free coloured sector and the restricted interaction with the whites for most of the slavery period, interaction occurred mainly among the freedmen themselves and between those of the lower stratum and the slaves who shared the Afro-creole culture. A substantial number of the freedmen, varying from colony to colony, were involved in this relationship, which continued in the towns after emancipation and into the twentieth century.

The segmented nature of free coloured culture became pronounced as the group became differentiated and gradually gained its civil rights. The result was the Afro-creole, Synthetic-creole and the Euro-creole cultural segments. Most important in this process was the emergence of a middle stratum and the development of the Synthetic-creole pattern. Much later — a century or more after the free coloured had gained their civil rights and the slaves their freedom — when the middle stratum finally gained political control, as in Jamaica, the Synthetic-creole culture was articulated as a national culture and as the basis for solidarity and the integration of all parts of the society.[40]

The development of an identity of their own among the freedmen required that they be free and in order to be free they had to belong — to have their rights as British citizens. It is important, however, that the conflict between themselves and the whites not be seen as limited to the acquisition of civil rights for the freedmen, as part of a drive toward the 'maximization of their status' and eventual incorporation into the existing society, but as a conflict having to do with the way the society was ordered and its future. Their support of the abolition of slavery, the pivotal institution in the society, and their opposition to racism, the ideology that justified both slavery and the severe restrictions on their freedom, involved a conception of society very different in important respects than the existing one, and was a manifestation of their strong identification with the colony as their homeland.

The insular dimension of their identity became most evident in the post-emancipation years when they opposed the ruling whites, whose identity remained predominantly metropolitan, concerning the issues facing the society, especially those pertaining to the newly freed slaves, and the future direction of the society. Rather than identify their interests with those of the whites, they 'engaged in a politics of opposition, of alternative proposals and policies, and enacting rather than reacting'.[41] Moreover, they had a different view of themselves than the whites who were bent on keeping them and the former slaves in a position of subordinancy, while they looked forward to 'ascendancy' in the society for themselves and the freemen. At the same time, however, their commitment to pluralism is evident in their stress on the importance of the whites and certain of their values to the well-being and development of the post-emancipation society.

Notes

1. Sidney W. Mintz and Richard Price, *An Anthropological Approach to the Afro-American Past: A Caribbean Perspective* (Philadelphia, 1976), p. 3. The terms free coloured, free people of colour, and freedmen refer to persons of mixed racial ancestry who gradually came to be defined as a separate socio-racial group.
2. David W. Cohen and Jack P. Green (eds), *Neither Slave Nor Free: The Freedom of African Descent in the Slave Societies of the New World*, (Baltimore, 1972), p. 15.
3. David Lowenthal, 'Free Coloured West Indians: A Racial Dilemma', *Studies in Eighteenth-Century Culture* (Cleveland, 1973), p. 347.
4. Edward Brathwaite, *The Development of Creole Society in Jamaica, 1770–1820* (Oxford, 1971), p. 174.
5. Cohen and Green, *Neither Slave Nor Free*, p. 15.
6. Jerome S. Handler, *The Unappropriated People: Freedmen in the Slave Society of Barbados* (Baltimore, 1974), pp. 212–13; G. J. Heuman, *Between Black and White: Race, Politics and the Free Coloreds in Jamaica, 1792–1865* (Westport, Conn., 1981), p. xvi.
7. The most systematic assimilationist interpretation is Mavis Christine. C. Campbell, *The Dynamics of Change in a Slave Society: Sociopolitical History of the Free Coloreds in Jamaica, 1792–1865* (Rutherford, NJ, 1976), pp. 10, 144–45, 176, and esp. 368. A contrasting interpretation of the free coloured response to their marginality is Heuman, *op. cit.*, esp. Appendix A, and 'Slavery and Emancipation in the British Caribbean', *Journal of Imperial and Commonwealth History*, 6, 1978, 170–1. See Arnold A. Sio, 'West Indian Politicians of Color', *Plantation Society*, 2, 1983, pp. 91–97.
8. Brathwaite, *op. cit.*, p. 193.
9. Orlando Patterson, *Slavery and Social Death* (Cambridge, 1982), p. 257.
10. B. W. Higman, *Slave Populations of the British Caribbean* (Baltimore, 1984), p. 112.
11. Phillip D. Curtin, *Two Jamaicas* (Cambridge, 1955), p. 45.
12. Cohen and Greene, *Neither Slave Nor Free*, p. 12.
13. The interpretation presented in the section that follows owes much to Handler, *op. cit.*, an especially creative and insightful study of the freedmen during the slavery period, and to the dialogue created by the studies of Campbell, *op. cit.*, and Heuman, *op. cit.*
14. Very little has been written on either the cultural or the social relations between slaves and freedmen. However, see Handler, *op. cit.*, 79–80, 98–99, 153, 201–08, and the observations in the more recent study by Edward Cox,

Free Coloreds in the Slave Societies of St. Kitts and Grenada, 1763-1833 (Knoxville, 1984), pp. 25, 45, 71, 75. The emerging research on urban slavery in the Caribbean undoubtedly will involve relations between slaves and freedmen. Heuman has observed that 'an examination of manumission data as well as of free coloured wills might also reveal the close bonds between many free people and slaves. Such research would help to offset the portrayal of the free coloured and slave communities as totally divided and at odds with each other.' See his 'Robert Osborn of Jamaica', paper presented at the Fifteenth Conference of Caribbean Historians UWI (Jamaica), 184, p. 3. The terms Euro-creole and Afro-creole are from Brathwaite, *op. cit.*, pp. 297-305, 309. Also Handler, *op. cit.*, p. 216. Similar terms and distinctions are to be found in Curtin, *op. cit.*, pp. 25, 42, and Orlando Patterson, 'Context and Choice in Ethnic Allegiance', *op. cit.*, Nathan Glazier and Daniel P. Moynihan, (eds), *Ethnicity* (Cambridge, 1975), pp. 316-19.

15. Arnold A. Sio, 'Race and Colour in the Status of the Free Coloured in the West Indies: Jamaica and Barbados', *Journal of Belizean Affairs*, 4, 1976, pp. 35-37; Celia Karch, 'London Bourne of Barbados', Paper presented at the Fifteenth Conference of Caribbean Historians, UWI (Jamaica) April, 1984, p. 12. It is not clear from the study of Grenada and St. Kitts to what extent the freedman were economically marginalized as in Jamaica and Barbados. Indeed, according to Cox, it was not the exclusion of the freedom from the economy that brought them into contact with the slaves, but rather their central position in the economy. Thus, 'meaningful ties with the slaves' were not only to be found among the lower stratum of the free coloured community, (*op. cit.*, p. 75).
16. Minutes of evidence, Select Committee of the House of Lords, the Laws and Usages of the Several West Indies Colonies in Relation to the Slave Population, Part II, 14 July-9 August, 1832, p. 710.
17. Initially, the free coloured were simply no longer the property of another. Beyond that they had no rights and often were treated legally as slaves. Only gradually did the legal status of the free coloured begin to diverge from that of the slaves.
18. The term 'Synthetic-creole' is from Patterson, 'Context and Choice', pp. 317-19. I have retained his definition. However, I view this pattern as emerging before the free coloured gained their civil rights and emancipation. At the same time, I agree with Patterson that the process of creolization was not as advanced during slavery as some have assumed. Moreover, as he and others have pointed out, it was a segmented process that produced Afro-creole, Synthetic-creole, and Euro-creole patterns. It was with the gradual differentiation of the free coloured group that a middle stratum emerged whose limited resources would not allow for the adoption of the Euro-creole life-ways. The result was the synthetic pattern. What I am suggesting is that a significant percentage of people of colour were to be found in the lower stratum adhering to the Afro-creole pattern during slavery and well into the twentieth century.
19. Cohen and Greene, *Neither Slave Nor Free*, p. 12.
20. 'You must take us for ourselves — we are new people.' Charles Waddell Chesnutt, *The House Behind Cedars* (Ridgewood, NJ, 1900, 1968), p. 83.
21. Leonard P. Curry, *The Free Black in Urban America 1800-1850* (Chicago, 1981), pp. 239-43 describes a similar development among free Negroes in the United States.
22. *Watchman and Jamaica Free Press*, 17 December 1831. Italicized in the original. Also Heuman, 'White Over Brown Over Black: The Free Coloreds in Jamaican Society During Slavery and After Emancipation', *Journal of Caribbean History* (1981), pp. 14, 57.
23. Cox, *op. cit.*, pp. 100, 142.
24. This is the main argument presented by Heuman, *Between Black and White* and Karch, 'London Bourne'. It was made much earlier by Curtin, *op. cit.*, p. 44.
25. The importance of the Protestant missions in the politicization of the freedmen — their consciousness and organizational skills — warrants a separate study. In this connection see the excellent study by Mary Turner, *Slaves and Missionaries* (Urbana, Ill., 1982), pp. 15, 27, 57, 85, 91, 163, 179, 198; Handler, *op. cit.*, pp. 154-61; Cox, *op. cit.*, pp. 111-22 for the role of the Catholic Church as well as the missions; Brathwaite, *op. cit.*, pp. 208-11.
26. This a widely-held view. Handler, *op. cit.*, pp. 216-17, is representative.
27. Cohen and Greene, *Neither Slave Nor Free*, pp. 16-17.
28. Donald L. Noel (ed.), *The Origins of American Slavery and Racism* (Columbus, Ohio, 1972), pp. 9, 27.
29. Higman, *Slave Populations*, pp. 101, 107, 112, 153.
30. The major shortcoming of the source materials on the free coloured is that much of it consists of whites who were writing for whites, whether in public documents or travel accounts, and of petitions and addresses prepared by the free coloured leadership for white consumption. These petitions and addresses are important in that they were produced by the freedmen themselves and, therefore, are of value, especially with regard to their political goals and activities and for the manner in which they portrayed themselves to the ruling whites.
31. Cox, *op. cit.*, Chap. 5.
32. Hilary Beckles, 'On the Backs of Blacks: The Barbados Free Coloured Pursuit of Civil Rights and the 1816 Slave Rebellion', *Immigrants and Minorities*, 3, 1984, 167-85; Handler, *op. cit.*, pp. 85-86; M. Craton, *Testing the Chains* (Ithaca, 1982), p. 260.
33. Craton, *op. cit.*, p. 316.
34. David Barry Gaspar, *Bondmen and Rebels* (Baltimore, 1985), pp. 12, 28, 43-61.
35. Craton, *op. cit.*, p. 157.
36. Gad Heuman, 'Runaway slaves in Nineteenth-Century Barbados', in *Out of the House of Bondage*, Gad Heuman (ed.) and *Slavery and Abolition*, 6, 3, December 1985, p. 17.
37. Patterson, *Slavery and Social Death*, p. 257. Indeed, white racism may have intensified after the freedmen gained their civil rights and after emancipation. See David Lowenthal, *West Indian Societies* (New York, 1972), p. 67. Also David Barry Gaspar, ' "The Best Years of My Life": James Johnston of St. Lucia and Antigua, 1819-1832', pp. 2, 4, 5-6, paper presented at the Fifteenth Conference of Caribbean Historians, UWI (Jamaica), 1983.
38. Campbell, on the other hand, concluded that a combination of factors led to an increase in the identification with whites from the 1820s onward. (*op. cit.*, p. 368).
39. Fernando Henriques, *Family and Colour in Jamaica* (London, 1953), p. 49.
40. Patterson, 'Context and Choice', p. 319.
41. Sio, 'West Indian Politicians', p. 97. Also Swithin Wilmot, 'Race, Electoral Violence and Constitutional Reform in Jamaica, 1830-1854', *Journal of Caribbean History*, (1982), 17, 1-13.

Saint Domingue

GWENDOLYN MIDLO HALL

Emancipation and the status of the free population systems in the Americas have been discussed by a number of contemporary historians. They have generally treated the attitudes toward racial differences held by the various colonizing powers as the crucial question in determining the ease of emancipation and the quality of life available to the free people. Neglecting the problem of social control and viewing the slave systems as static, or as developmental in the direction of growing humanitarianism with the passage of time, they have assembled fragmentary and sometimes distorted evidence to prove or disprove a preconceived theory. Saint Domingue is a particularly interesting colony in which to examine the problems of emancipation and the status of a free population in a slave society. Of great economic importance to France, it was administered by a centralized bureaucracy, and documentation is abundant.

From the evidence relating to formulation of policy, it is clear that pre-existing attitudes toward race were relatively insignificant. Pressures upon and within the society were intense, and policies stemming from attitudes toward race were luxuries the policy makers could not afford. Fundamental military, economic, social, and political concerns were crucial. These concerns were conflicting in themselves, and changes in policy toward emancipation and the status of the free reflected which concern, or concerns, was of paramount importance at any given period of time. The metropolis jealously asserted its right to determine policy in its own interests, and little sentimentality crept into policy discussion. 'The property rights of the masters have never been the reason for tolerating slavery in the colonies,' wrote a high colonial official. 'The establishment of the lands was, and is, the sole aim, in the interest of commerce.'[1] Emilien Petit maintained that the French government should encourage or restrict emancipation in the interests of the stability of the colony, regardless of the desires of the masters. His strategy was a middle course: restrict emancipation to keep enough hands, but do not restrict it so much that it produces a dangerous state of despair among the slaves, because 'only the hope for liberty can sustain or animate the fidelity of the slaves in a state of degradation and poverty and attach them to their masters, or to white blood, which amounts to the same thing.'[2]

The Predominance of Military Considerations During the Pre-Plantation Period

During the early years of colonization of the French Caribbean, it was difficult to obtain white colonists. Before the rise of the slave plantation systems, there were few attractions for them. At the same time, rivalry over control of the islands was intense, not because of the economic value of the islands themselves, but because the British and French islands were viewed as bridgeheads to the gold- and silver-producing Spanish mainland colonies. Once the Spanish territorial monopoly of the Caribbean had been breached, the principle of effective occupation determined which power would control which islands. Emancipation was encouraged, and freedmen enjoyed a relatively high status because the colonizers needed to count as many heads as possible, and because the free colored, and at times even the slaves,

Neither Slave Nor Free: The Freedmen of African Descent in the Slave Societies of the New World (Johns Hopkins University Press, 1972), pp. 172–92.

were effectively used for military purposes. While the military role of the slaves and the free colored population was apparently less prominent in the British colonies, which quickly became colonies of economic exploitation and for which white settlers were easier to obtain, the free colored population was the major source of military strength in the Spanish and French Caribbean. In Saint Domingue, Africans were the principal military and police force from the earliest years of colonization, even after the rise of the slave plantation system, and this situation was an important factor in the success of the Haitian Revolution. As Jean-Baptiste Dutertre reported in the middle of the seventeenth century:

> They are valiant and hardy in the face of danger, and during all the desperate encounters which our colonists of Saint Christopher Island have had from time to time with the English, they have been no less redoubtable to this nation than their masters. M. d'Enambuc used them advantageously to repulse the British, and M. le Commandeur de Salles, seeing himself in this year 1666 with the choice between victory and death, used them to chase these irreconcilable enemies of our nation from the island. And they have so well done their duty, setting fires everywhere while our Frenchmen were in battle, that they have made no small contribution to the famous victory which France won over England.[3]

Throughout the history of Saint Domingue, officials in the islands mobilized free blacks, mulattoes, and slaves, not only to participate in the frequent colonial wars of the Caribbean, but also to pursue fugitive slaves and to defend the border with Spain. In 1695, they offered slaves 10 écus for each enemy head and each deserter returned to an officer, and freedom for taking an enemy officer or flag or for saving the live of a subject of the king.[4]

Even after the rise of the slave plantation system, Africans continued to be used for military and police purposes — an important factor in the success of the Haitian Revolution. Thus, in 1709, the government routinely mobilized trusted plantation slaves, 'experience having proved that one can make very good use of the *Nègres des Habitans*',[5] and in 1721 it organized a company composed of whites and mulattoes to guard the Spanish border and provided that, in default of whites, free blacks also could be received into the company.[6] In 1724, the government conscripted free blacks into military service and organized them into the *Compagnie de Nègres-Libres*, which was divided into from three to four squadrons, each under an officer. The main duty of this company was to pursue fugitive slaves.[7] When the *Maréchausée*, a militarized police force, was reorganized in 1733, its archers were chosen from among free blacks and mulattoes.[8] In 1740, the king, complaining that the white colonists were too 'soft', even in defense of 'their own property', recommended an increase in emancipations to augment the military strength of the colony; the free Africans, he noted, had always been regarded as 'the principal force of the colony'.[9]

As the slave plantation system developed, however, internal security problems became more severe and exerted pressure against using Africans for military purposes. Following the Mackandal conspiracy, exposed in 1758, masters expressed their fear that the arming and military training of slaves would undermine discipline, and they insisted upon training and leading their own slaves. It was decided that slaves would in no case be allowed to form a separate body of troops.[10] The government continued to rely heavily upon the free colored population for defense, however, and in 1762 it organized a *Compagnie de Chasseurs de Gens de Couleur* consisting of volunteer free blacks and mulattoes.[11] Though this body of troops was supposed to be disbanded at the end of the war in 1763, it was still in existence in 1768, when the commanders were ordered to use it in the pursuit of fugitive slaves and deserters, and for policing the neighborhoods.[12]

In 1779, the king, expressing full confidence in the attachment and fidelity of his free colored subjects, formed a *Corps de Chasseurs Volontaires de Gens de Couleurs de St. Domingue* consisting of 600 volunteers,[13] and, in 1780, the commander in chief ordered a general conscription of free men of color. Thereafter, all blacks, mulattoes, and free colored men between fifteen and sixteen years of age were ordered to serve one year in the *Compagnies de Chasseurs-Royaux* of their department, and no emancipation could be ratified until the subject had served one year in the said companies.[14] Upon the departure of most of the garrison on a major expedition, the commander in chief ordered the commander of the *limonade* battalion to call up the colored militia to help garrison the island.[15] Two old captains of the *Nègres-Libres*, both aged 96, were given life-time [*sic*] pensions from the government. According to the order, 'The said Etienne Auba has always given to his numerous family as well as to the people of his color the best example of respect, of obedience and of submission to the government as well as to the whites.[16]

Moreau de St.-Méry boasted of the excellent soldier the French had made of the mulatto. His worth had been proven in his conscription into the *Maréchausée*, into the *Chasseurs* formed by M. de Belzince in 1762, and into the *Compagnies de Chasseurs-Royaux*, which marched on Savannah, Georgia, in 1779. It was the mulattoes, he wrote, who usually pursued fugitive slaves. He pointed out that military life had its attractions for the idle and pleasure-loving, and that the mulatto was content with little, living off roots and tropical fruits. He needed almost no clothes, could stand the sun, and could climb mountains with agility. But he should not be confined to the barracks at night, because 'night belongs to pleasure'.[17] It is, unfortunately, only too rarely that poetic justice is dished out as it was in Saint Domingue, where this cynical policy of degrading and exploiting a population to fulfill the military needs of the rulers backfired so thoroughly.

Policy Toward Emancipation and the Needs of Plantation Agriculture

The colonizing powers initiated the slave systems with few pre-conceptions about encouraging or discouraging emancipation. It eventually became evident that, if no restrictions were placed upon emancipation, the free coloured population would grow rapidly. During the pre-plantation period in Saint Domingue, the existence of a large free colored population was a military advantage. The development of a plantation system, however, brought with it hostility toward the emancipation of slaves and vigorous attempts from the metropolis to limit severely the right of the master to emancipate his slave at will, the obvious reason being that a slave plantation system required large numbers of slaves to work in agriculture. Freed slaves tended overwhelmingly either to abandon agriculture and flock to the cities and towns, thus creating a serious problem of social control, or, where land was available, to engage in subsistence agriculture. In either case, they rarely offered themselves on the labor market. This tendency was a major factor leading to the decline of the sugar industry in Jamaica following the emancipation of slaves there.[18] Abolition also resulted in a labor shortage in the coffee regions of Brazil, where freedmen found that they could meet their necessities by working two or three days a week and preferred to 'buy leisure' rather than earn more than enough to acquire the most rudimentary necessities.[19] In contrast, on small islands like Antigua, where neither land for subsistence agriculture nor employment in towns was available, labor costs did not increase after the abolition of slavery, and the plantation system continued to thrive.[20]

In colonies where economic alternatives to plantation labor existed, slavery or another form of forced labor, either direct or indirect, was necessary to ensure the existence of plantation agriculture.[21] Maintaining an adequate labor force on the estates was an essential concern of those policy makers who encouraged plantation agriculture, and, consequently, restrictions upon the right of masters to emancipate slaves at will were characteristic of societies evolving in this direction.

The Evolution of French Policy Regarding Emancipation

French policy evolved from placing no restrictions whatsoever upon emancipation to deliberately increasing limitations that would make it very difficult indeed for the master to emancipate his slave. During the strategic period of colonization, the *Code Noir* allowed masters 20 years of age or older to emancipate their slaves without the consent of their parents. This right was revoked in 1721, for the stated reason that young masters were abusing it and thereby ruining their estates, a fact which resulted in a 'considerable prejudice to our colonies, the principal utility of which depends upon the labor of the Negroes, who give value to the lands'.[22] By the early eighteenth century, a government permit was required for emancipations.[23] The master had to petition for the right to emancipate his slave, stating the reasons why he wished to do so. The petition then had to be approved and ratified by a government official.[24] Hostility was expresssed toward testamentary emancipations on the grounds that sick masters at the mercy of their slaves were often forced to emancipate them against their will and that the impatience of the slaves often hastened the death of the master.[25]

In 1775, a royal ordinance imposed a heavy tax upon emancipations: at least 1,000 livres for each male, and 2,000 livres for each female under the age of 40 for a permit to emancipate, unless the master could prove extraordinary service to himself or to the colony.[26]

Subsequently, tax-free emancipations were allowed only for military service, such as that of a drummer in the army for eight years, chasing fugitive slaves, or performing other military duties or outstanding services.[27] This was a continuation of an earlier policy. Earlier in the eighteenth century, several slaves had been emancipated for service to the colony, usually for the denunciation or capture of fugitive slaves,[28] and some slaves had been promised freedom for outstanding acts of bravery on the battlefield.[29]

The growing hostility of the metropolis toward emancipation was also manifested during the eighteenth century in a steady under cutting of the principle that a slave became free upon touching the soil of France.[30] By 1762, the institution of slavery had taken firm root on French soil, and one official felt called upon to complain that 'Paris has become a public market where men are sold to the highest bidder; and there is not a bourgeois or a worker who does not have his black slave.'[31]

Illegal Forms of Emancipation

Flight and the establishment of colonies of *marons* was a wide spread and effective means by which slaves freed themselves. These techniques dated from the earliest years of colonization in the French Caribbean. Before 1665, the Dutch brought 1,200–1,300 black slaves to Martinique and Guadeloupe and sold them cheaply and on credit.[32] M. Houel, the administrator of the colony, having more confidence in his slaves than in the French colonists, made the mistake of arming his slaves and teaching them to use firearms. The slaves outnumbered the French, and at the end of 1656 there was an uprising led by two slaves named Pedre and Jean le Blanc. Their plan was to massacre the masters, keep their wives, and set up two Angolan kingdoms on the island of Guadeloupe, one at Basse-Terre and the other at Capesterre. Intertribal rivalries carried over from Africa led to disunity, and some of the conspirators failed to show up at the appointed time and place. About 40 slaves armed themselves and seized several plantations. Pursued by the militia, they headed for the woods. The militia hesitated to follow them. For ten or twelve days, they pillaged the plantations and massacred the French settlers. The French militia obtained 20 Brazilian slaves to carry food and serve as guides in pursuit of the rebels. Following the capture of the conspirators, the two Angolan kings were quartered, and several of their followers were subjected to various forms of torture.[33]

Simultaneously, mass desertions of slaves occurred in Guadeloupe. Those who left returned for relatives they had left behind and to convince others to follow them. They fled to the Indians, who received them well at first, but later discovered that the slaves could be profitably sold to the Spanish. Desertions became so massive that every house lost some slaves. In response to a rumor that all the slaves were going to leave on a certain day, masters put their slaves in irons. But in spite of draconian measures, mass desertion spread to even the most devoted slaves. Punishments only made them leave more quickly. 'One was reduced to such an extremity at Martinique,' wrote Dutertre, 'that one dared not say a cross word to a black, nor make the slightest correction without his fleeing to the woods. Even the *Negresses* fled, running off with little infants seven or eight days old.'[34]

Search parties sent after the slaves could not locate them. The slaves led groups of Indians in raiding the plantations in broad daylight, stealing, killing, running off slaves, and burning homes. This situation lasted for two years, until the French authorities decided that the only solution was to clear out the Indians, who were giving the slaves boats in which to escape and offering them asylum. The French authorities finally reached an agreement with the Indians not to receive fugitive slaves.[35]

The fugitive slaves were called *marons*. They developed techniques of guerrilla warfare which closely resemble contemporary methods. The tactics of Francisque Fabulé are a good example. A tall, powerful slave with a martial air, Fabulé declared himself the leader of 300–400 *marons*, organizing his followers into groups of 25 or 30 and dispersing them around the island. They descended on isolated estates at night and stole arms and provisions, though at first they did not kill anyone. The settlers feared the possibilities of the situation and offered Francisque his freedom if he would return and bring in some of his followers. Francisque agreed at first to these terms and then reneged. Instead, he joined the Indians and blocked the roads, burning down estates and massacring their owners. The French settlers decided to fight, but they did not get far. Thick forests, rocks, cliffs, and mountains blocked their path. After hunting the *marons* for a month, the French militia captured only five or six fugitives, who happened to have foot trouble and could not run. 'The rest, not at all wishing to fight, sought their health in flight.' Four or five Frenchmen died of snakebite. Because the pursuit was proving more costly to the French than to the fugitive slaves, the militia asked to be demobilized to attend to neglected crops, and the authorities adopted a new tactic: offering rewards for the return of fugitives, paying the reward, and pardoning the fugitives. These tactics made inroads upon Fabulé's followers, and within a few months he agreed to surrender in return for his freedom. A treaty was signed which stated that the island had been devastated by fugitive slaves, and, since Francisque Fabulé was the leader of a large band, he would be given his freedom and a thousand pounds of tobacco, and no punishment would be inflicted upon the members of his band. He brought in six or seven of his followers, collected a reward, and was given an official hug, his freedom, and a sword to wear. Thereafter, he brought in large numbers of fugitives in return for additional rewards.[36]

The pattern established in the lesser French islands was carried over to Saint Domingue, where maroon colonies also thrived. Escaped slaves set up communities, elected their leaders, cultivated the soil, built houses, and constructed barricades against invaders. Operating from these bases, fugitives hid in the cane fields during the day, robbed passers-by on the highways at night, and went from plantation to plantation seizing cattle. They often hid in the slave quarters, gathering information about what went on in the master's house so that they could steal without being noticed.[37] Mass desertions of slaves, especially in wartime, were common. The authorities complained that

> they leave in bands, and desert to the foreigners with whom we are at war. Several of the colonists have had the misfortune of seeing themselves deprived of the cultivation of their lands, and reduced to seeking the help of their friends to provide for their families. And it is certain that . . . the enemy has not taken as many as those who have given themselves up voluntarily, and a great number who remain do so only for the return of some and the desertion of others from the island.[38]

Colonists lived in fear of being suddenly ruined by the loss of all their slaves. Planters who went to bed at night owning 100 or 200 slaves could not be sure of waking up the next morning with even one.[39]

Flight was greatly facilitated because two-thirds of the island was in Spanish hands. The Spanish part of the island was undeveloped, thinly populated, and its slave system was relatively mild. Colonial rivalries between France and Spain made the authorities of the Spanish part of the island very uncooperative in returning fugitive slaves. Attempts to eliminate the Spanish part of the island as a refuge for fugitive slaves met with little success. In 1728, a secret treaty was signed with the Spanish to allow a French agent to go to the city of Santo Domingo to claim all the fugitive slaves there. The agent spent 23,700 livres in this undertaking, which failed because a revolt took place at Santo Domingo when he arrived. The colonists would not allow themselves to be taxed to pay his expenses, and the cost was eventually assumed by the king of France.[40] It was not until 1776 that a treaty was negotiated between France and Spain for the purpose of mutual restoration of escaped slaves.[41]

Colonial officals were well aware of the danger implicit in the existence of permanent pockets of slave military power: 'A colony which has the misfortune to have to fear establishments of slave deserters enters, from that moment, into a state of war, the danger of which can only increase with time.'[42] Large maroon bands and guerrilla bases were never successfully eliminated during the colonial period in Saint Domingue and were still in existence at the outbreak of the Haitian Revolution.[43]

Theft and the Market

The market was very important to the economic, social, and religious life of West Africa, and the blacks, especially the women, were skilled in buying and selling. Within Saint Domingue, the French colonists depended upon the slave-operated markets to trade goods and especially to provide the cities and towns with food. Colonial authorities had to recognize that the colony depended upon these slave-operated markets. When the *Code Noir* of 1685 outlawed these markets, the authorities in Saint Domingue protested that they were absolutely necessary to the commerce of the colony, and the French government changed the law the next year to allow them to continue.[44]

The West African brought with him complex ideas about property. In Dahomey, which had the greatest cultural influence in Saint Domingue, everything belonged, in theory, to the king: land, horses, implements, slaves, money, even the person of the subject. But no king would dare claim his rights, because of fear of the tribal ancestors. There were two other types of property. One was the propety of the sib, or extended family. It was owned collectively and was administered by the oldest male member. The other was private property, which could be held by men or women. It included the houses a person built and the trees he planted, regardless of who owned the land. Private property was the money earned, the produce of one's labor, utensils, guns, mats, pipes, and magic charms, which often consisted of herbs and medicines discovered in the forest. The discoverer could sell the formula to others for their use. There were complex rules for the inheritance of personal property.[45]

French law denied all property rights to slaves. Anything the slave might acquire through industry, gift, or any other way belonged legally to the master. A slave could not give or will anything he possessed to members of his family or to friends. He could not make a valid contract to dispose of goods.[46] This simplistic view of property rights entirely excluded the slave, but was impossible to enforce in Saint Domingue because the slaves controlled the internal market and because, in addition to the legal market, an illegal one was created by the slaves to dispose of stolen goods. Indeed, the illegal market tended to supplant the legal one. Colonial officials complained that slaves were stealing indigo and other merchandise that was easy to carry and were selling it to black-market operators travelling from plantation to plantation; and this illegal trade was thriving to the exent that the public markets were poorly attended.[47] The *procureur du roi* described the systematic operations of the black market:

> several persons buy indifferently from slaves indigo, horses, clothing, and other merchandise without troubling to find out where the slaves could have obtained these goods. The slaves conspire with the house slaves to steal the indigo from the drying houses and the horses from the field, break into the storehouses, and pass the stolen goods from one neighborhood to another, from hand to hand among the slaves, until it is finally sold to several bad-intentioned individuals, who receive it, give some recompense to the slaves for their thefts, and then resell it to merchants or exchange it for other merchandise.[48]

Slaves used monopoly price-fixing to profiteer on food sold in the cities and towns. They waited along the highways, stopping all the supplies headed for the market, and then resold them at high prices. These practices were so effective that the Council of Cap complained that officers from the merchant fleet, the clergy, the House of Charity, and private families were suffering from lack of eggs, poultry, and vegetables, and some people were being forced to eat meat on the days forbidden by the church, for lack of fresh foods.[49]

The slaves of Saint Domingue used their control of the internal markets, both the legal and illegal ones, to amass sums of money with which to purchase their freedom. Cabarets owned by free blacks became centers of vice, the proceeds of which went toward the purchase of freedom for more individual slaves. Colonial officials concluded that most of the disorder among slaves came from the 'facility which the colonists have of giving them freedom in return for sums of money', because, once a sum was agreed upon, they

> abandon the service of their masters, engaging in private affairs under the pretext of working by the day in return for a small recompense which they promise to their said masters. Others abandon themselves to all kinds of vices to amass the sums agreed upon, getting together in the houses of those who have already been freed, most of them having cabarets, and fraternize with whites who are low enough to receive them and suffer their infamous and immodest commerce.[50]

Through control of the internal market, the blacks in Saint Domingue exercised a considerable amount of economic power, amassing wealth through legal and illegal channels, much of which went toward the increase of the free black population.

Racism as an Instrument of Social and Political Domination

As the slave population began heavily to outnumber the white population in the countryside, the obvious symbol of visible racial differences was seized upon as a means of convincing the slaves of their own innate inferiority. Overt racist policies were instituted during the last half of the eighteenth century in Saint Domingue, and perhaps because this period preceded the flowering of racist theories during the nineteenth century, as the institution of slavery itself was seriously challenged, French ideologists did not find it necessary to attempt to convince themselves of the innate inferiority of the Africans. They contented themselves with trying to convince the Africans. Containing the slaves and maintaining the social order were frankly acknowledged as the reasons for racist policies. *A memoire du roi* dating from 1777 was blunt.

Whatever distance they may be from their origin, they always keep the stain of slavery, and are declared incapable of all public functions. Even gentlemen who descend to any degree from a woman of color cannot enjoy the prerogatives of nobility. This law is harsh, but wise and necessary. In a country where there are fifteen slaves to one white, one cannot put too much distance between the two species, one cannot impress upon the blacks too much respect for those they serve. This distinction, rigorously observed even after freedom, is the principal prop of the subordination of the slave, by the opinion that results that his color is inextricably linked with servitude, and nothing can render him equal to his master.[51]

A book officially endorsed by the French government stated that 'interest and security demand that we overwhelm the black race with so much disdain that whoever descends from it until the sixth generation shall be covered by an indelible stain.'[52] The very spectacle of free blacks was dangerous for slaves, it declared, because color should be absolutely identified with slave status.[53]

Along with the tendency to restrict emancipation, identify blackness with slavery, and degrade the free coloured population, as plantation agriculture flourished, there was also a tendency to create a caste system, which fomented mutual antagonisms among people of varying degrees of African descent by establishing distinct legal and social categories in accordance with the percentage of admixture of European blood, the number of generations of legitimate birth, and the number of generations removed from slavery.

Origin of the Colonial Elite of Saint Domingue

Early egalitarian policies toward race contrasted sharply with discriminatory policies characteristic of the late colonial period. The *Code Noir* guaranteed in unequivocable language full citizenship rights to slaves emancipated in the French islands, considering them the same as native-born French citizens, regardless of where the slaves had been born (Articles 57, 58, and 59).[54] These measures were no doubt motivated by the desire to count as many heads as possible at a time when the principle of effective occupation determined control of the islands. The population factor, especially the shortage of white women, was certainly very important in promoting racial equality in early Saint Domingue.[55] As Dutertre wrote: 'There are many of these mulattoes in the islands who are free and work for themselves. I have seen some fairly handsome ones who have married Frenchmen. This disorder was more common before than it is today because the number of women and girls in the Antilles prevent it; but at the beginning of colonisation it was terrible and almost without remedy.'[56]

Interracial unions, both informal and legalized, continued on a large scale throughout the history of the colony. The *Code Noir* exerted pressure on the master to marry his slave concubine, thereby freeing her and legitimizing their children, under penalty of fine and confiscation of the concubine family (Article 9). Before the promulgation of the *Code Noir*, it was accepted practice that the offspring of unions between white men and black women be automatically emancipated when they reached the age of 21. The *Code Noir* followed the Roman principle that the status of the new-born child followed the condition of the mother, and, thereafter, formal emancipation in writing was required. French colonists in Saint Domingue expressed dissatisfaction with this provision, and an administrator in Saint Domingue proposed in 1697 that a law be passed declaring all mulattoes free as soon as they reached the age of 21. The minister of the colonies agreed to propose such a change in the *Code Noir*, 'which was formulated without having examined this question in depth'.[57] It is evident that Article 9 was frequently violated. Many children were emancipated because they were 'children of free men'. This would have been legal if the father was not the master, or if the master had married his slave concubine. But most of these children were probably sired by their mother's master.[58]

There was strong sentiment in favor of emancipating the natural children of the master throughout the history of the colony, and these children were an important source of the free colored population. As late as 1735, mulattoes were specifically excluded from the policy of sharply restricting the emancipation of slaves. Instructions to the colonial authorites read: 'You should not follow the same policy with the mulattoes. I know that they are the declared enemies of the blacks.'[59] As late as 1777, Emilien Petit favored freeing the mulatto children of white planters and making the fathers responsible for their care until they came of age. He explained:

It is to the affection of their concubines that whites have owed the discovery of several conspiracies . . . the children born of these concubinages form a class of freedmen who are always distinguished from the other classes of free colored people, with whom they have few ties, and whom they despise. The freedmen who depends upon his master or patron for his subsistence will not easily risk seeing himself deprived of it. One would find fewer guilty parties among the mulattoes if they had something to lose.[60]

Racial mixture was not discouraged in pre-plantation Saint Domingue. The *Code Noir* was not concerned about preventing the fusion of the races, either physically or legally.[61] A judgment rendered by the Council of Martinique in 1698 declared that the *Code Noir* aimed only at the vice of concubinage. Far from preventing racial mixture (*le mélange des sangs*), it was concerned only with augmenting the colony, because it discharged the master who married his slave concubine from paying the fine.[62] As late as 1713, the administrators were remarkably free from preoccupation with *le mélange des sangs* typical of the late colony. Pointing to widespread concubinage of slave women, they complained that masters kept their concubines and their children openly in their homes, 'exposing them to the eyes of all with as much assurance as if they had been procreated from a legitimate marriage'.[63]

Throughout the history of the colony, whether by virtue of the provisions of the *Code Noir* or otherwise, legal intermarriage was far from unusual. In 1703, the king refused to receive the titles of nobility of several French noblemen because they had married *mulatresses*.[61] A report dating from 1731 indicated that intermarriage was almost universal in some parts of Saint Domingue:

In the inspection which M. de la Roche-Allard has made in Cayes in the neighborhood of Jacumel, he reported to me that there are few whites of pure blood . . . the whites ally themselves willingly in marriage with the blacks because the latter, through their frugality, acquire property more easily than the whites.[65]

A nephew and cousin tried unsuccessfully in 1746 to prevent their white relative's marriage to a *mulatresse*. The court ordered the publication of the banns and required the curé to proceed with the marriage, under penalty of seizure of his stipend.[66] Even during the last few decades of the colony, marriage between white masters and their slave concubines and between impecunious white Frenchmen and comfortably placed women of color were common enough to inspire bitter comment. Hilliard d'Auberteuil wrote that the *Code Noir* was 'subject to great abuse'.

How many *Negresses* have profited from it and appropriated the entire fortune of their masters, brutalized by libertinage and incapable of resisting their power over feeble and seduced souls . . . . The wealth of families has been sacrificed to passion, has become the price of debauchery, and respectable names have fallen, along with the best lands, to legitimized mulattoes.[67]

On the other hand, white men who married *filles de couleur* were accused of doing so for money. In the 1770s, there were about 300 white men, several born gentlemen, who were married to *sang-melées*. 'They make these women whom cupidity has induced them to marry miserable; [and] their children, incapable of filling any civil function, . . . [are] condemned to share the humiliation of slaves.'[68] Emilien Petit favored outlawing intermarriage, under penalty of nullification, a prohibition which was 'necessary to prevent unions so contrary to the growth of the white population, and to maintain the superiority of white blood, which such misalliances degrade'.[69]

The wealth of the free colored population was a unique feature of Saint Domingue. The *Code Noir* placed no restrictions upon inheritance of property, and the offspring of alliances between master and slave, whether legitimate or not, freely inherited their father's property, land, and slaves. A royal decree dating from 1726 declared free blacks and their children and descendents incapable of receiving from whites any donation among the living or after death, under penalty of confiscation of the property, thus abrogating the *Code Noir* in this respect.[70] But this change came too late to alter the existing customs in Saint Domingue, and the decree was never enforced in the colony.[71]

The courts of Saint Domingue consistently awarded contested legacies to the colored offspring of white masters. There was a case in which the party who was to inherit an estate in the event that the deceased left no legitimate posterity denied that a former slave wife and their legitimized children constituted legitimate posterity. The lower court had held for the mulatto children, and, although the Council of Cap reversed the lower court, the *Conseil d'État* reversed the Council of Cap in 1772, giving the inheritance to the mulatto children.[72] A judgment dating from 1775 awarded two estates and 240 slaves to the mulatto bastards of their white father, who had willed this property to them.[73] A judgment dating from 1782 awarded half of a succession to the brothers and sisters of the deceased and half to the children of Nanette Soreau, *mulatresse libre*, in accordance with the terms of the deceased's will.[74]

The free colored population increased rapidly, in spite of restrictions on emancipation and the social degradation enacted during the last half of the eighteenth century. The census taken around 1700 listed 500 *gens de couleur libres*. By 1715, their number had increased to 1,500. By 1780, the figure reached 28,000. Between 1770 and 1780, there were 7,000–8,000 individual emancipations in the colony, and marriages among *affranchis*, slaves, and French colonists were never more common.[75] It appears that the free colored elite was moving rapidly toward outnumbering, if not absorbing, the white elite during the last few years of the colony. The figures below are for free persons owning property or slaves:[76]

	1784	1788	1789
Whites	20,229	27,727	30,831
Slaves	13,257	21,848	24,848
Free coloured	297,079	405,528	434,429

The total population of Saint Domingue in 1789 was 518,000, including 40,000 white, 28,000 free colored, and 450,000 slaves.

Writing in 1798, after the colony had exploded. P.J. Laborie, a fugitive planter, expressed the opinion that the *Code Noir* was framed too early, when experience with slavery was lacking. Emancipation was unrestricted, no limits had been placed upon acquisition of property by the free colored population, and there was no discrimination against them before the law. Restrictions were imposed later, but they were not very effective.[77] It is easier to prevent the growth of a wealthy and powerful group within a society than to degrade or destroy it once it has come into existence. The wealthy, the educated *gens de couleur*, defended their interests very well, and in the process became the fuse which ignited the colony.

Social Conflict Between the Coloured and White Elites of Saint Domingue

The Haitian Revolution was precipitated by the response of the free colored population to attempts by whites to strip them of legal protection, degrade them socially, and destroy their network of influence with persons and institutions which could offer protection in order to dispossess the free colored population of coveted land, slaves, and other property. The system of racial discrimination was gradually built up over the years and culminated with sharp discriminatory measures during the last two decades of the colony.

The basic conflict was over wealth and over power to protect wealth. Because widespread intermarriage and more informal unions resulted in the passing of some of the best lands to the mulatto offspring of white planters, the economic struggle was also manifested in sexual rivalry. Julien Raimond, eloquent representative of the colored elite of Saint Domingue in the French General Assembly, dated discrimination from shortly before the war of 1744, when the colony began to become prosperous and a large number of Europeans came over, including marriageable white women seeking to marry rich white planters. But the virtues of the white women sent over in those days by the French government seemed 'more than suspect, and their marriages with the whites did not have all the fruit that was anticipated'. They were often passed over for more fertile *filles de couleur*, who also often possessed the added advantage of owning land and slaves. In spite of the presence of white women, white men continued to marry *filles de couleur*, or to choose a woman from among their slaves, 'making them their wives, under the title of housekeepers'. The daughters of the *gens de couleur* often married newly arrived white settlers. As the colony became more cultivated, the colored population grew rapidly and at the expense of the white population, owing to the lack of white women and to the preference for colored women.

Many white families came over after the peace of 1749. They were jealous of the growing fortunes of the *gens de couleur*. After the peace of 1763, there was a new wave of immigration. Educated *gens de couleur* returned from France, where they had served in the house of the king and as officers in various regiments, provoking jealousy of their accomplishments from white settlers, who pushed for the passage of humiliating and oppressive laws. Several governors, including M. Dennery and M. de Bellecombe, tried to control the hostile whites, but the result was a massacre 'at Martinique, on the day of Fête-Dieu, and in the other colonies, we saw the poor whites hunting down and murdering the *gens de couleur*, accusing them of imaginary plots.' Marriages between white men and *filles de couleur* were outlawed in 1768, and these women became concubines instead of wives. Many free colored landowners were deprived of their lands by 'a host of tyrannical acts', but many held on to their property and slaves and maintained a strong position.[78]

The first right which came under attack was access to political positions, because political power is the ultimate arbiter of economic power, and because the denial of political rights was a precondition for denying the free colored population access to public protection. In 1706, a mulatto was appointed *procureur du roi*, despite the protest of the *doyen du conseil* that 'a mulatto bastard cannot be received in any judiciary post'.[79] In 1760, however, the king ordered that no *sang-melé* or white person married to a *sang-melé* could hold office in the judiciary or in the militia, or hold any other public employment in the colony.[80]

The impetus toward racial discrimination was not rooted in the French national character. 'There is so little color prejudice in France,' wrote Emilien Petit, 'that mulattoes, quadroons, and other descendants of the black race are received in the military corps reserved for the young nobility and as magistrates.'[81] Racial discrimination in Saint Domingue stemmed from the cold, calculated ambitions of the white colonists. One free colored man was sold some property by a white man who took the money for the purchase, denounced him as a slave who could not prove he was free, had him legally re-enslaved, and then refused to deliver the property purchased because a slave was incapable of making a contract.[82] Another case was that of M. Boyer, a butcher in the neighborhood of Trou who was selling meat at $1\frac{1}{2}$ *escalin* per pound. Boyer had obtained from the government an exclusive monopoly for selling meat, thus closing down two free colored competitors who were selling the same quality of meat at 1 *escalin* per pound. Because this privilege ate into the pocketbooks of all purchasers of meat, the monopoly was finally set aside, and the right of the free colored butchers to do business was protected.[83] The list of discriminatory laws that flowered during the last three decades of the colony is long and ludicrous.[84]

Manipulation of Racial Conflict in the Face of the Independence Threat

The metropolis had no particular stake in the color of the planters of Saint Domingue. As long as the French government and French commercial interests continued to rake in countless wealth from the slave trade and from the refining and marketing of sugar, the conflict between the white and colored elites of Saint Domingue was a relatively small matter. Because the white elite had more influence at court, it succeeded in getting discriminatory measures passed. But the metropolis was not adverse to backing the colored elite in its struggle against the white elite, if the interests of France demanded it.

The American Revolution raised the specter of a successful independence movement among the white planters of Saint Domingue, and, as part of its effort to control the white planters, the metropolis attempted to abandon discrimination against the colored elite of Saint Domingue, hoping to rely upon the loyalty of the colored elite as a weapon against the independence-minded whites. A memorandum dating from the 1780s communicated the views of His Majesty that 'the most thoughtful people consider the *gens de couleur* as the greatest barrier against troubles from the slaves. This class of men merits concern and care, and it leans toward tempering the established degradation and even bringing it to an end. This delicate subject demands profound thought, and should be carefully considered.'[85]

Racial discrimination became intense during the last few decades of the colony, not only as a means of controlling an ever-growing slave population, but, even more important, as an instrument used by ambitious white colonists to degrade and dispossess a segment of the population which was vulnerable to attack on the grounds of ancestry. Whatever one might say in favor of the current emphasis upon a psychological explanation for the origin of racial prejudice, the history of Saint Domingue confirms Antoine Gisler's conclusion that 'color prejudice with its great repercussions, had largely a political origin . . . the fruit of the methodical effort of an entire century.'[86]

If it is possible to generalize from the history of Saint Domingue, we can conclude that racial antagonism is not a significant, inherent trait in mankind, but an attitude, an emotional response, which in this case was created and manipulated by the state in the interests of promoting a stable slave plantation system and of maintaining political control over a colony which was supplying the metropolis with countless wealth. The obvious implication is that the human mind is malleable, and that it is possible for the state to adopt and implement policies which bring about profound changes in racial attitudes and in social relations.

Notes

1. Emilien Petit, *Traité sur le gouvernement des esclaves*, 2 vols (Paris, 1777), 2: 68. Translations from this and all other sources cited herein are the author's.
2. *Ibid.*, p. 69.
3. Jean-Baptiste Dutertre, *Histoire générale des Antilles habitées par les françois*, 4 vols (Paris, 1667–71), 2: 499.
4. M. L. E. Moreau de St.-Méry, *Loix et constitutions des colonies françaises de l'Amérique sous le vent*, 6 vols (Paris, 1784–89), Arrêt du Conseil de Guerre pour la defense de la Colonie en cas d'attaque, February 17, 1695.
5. *Ibid.*, Ordonnance des administrateurs touchant les Nègres à armer en temps de guerre, September 9, 1709.
6. *Ibid.*, Ordonnance des administrateurs, March 27, 1721.
7. *Ibid.*, Règlement fait par le gouverneur de Cap, pour la Compagnie des Nègres-Libres de la dépendance de la même ville, April 29, 1724.
8. *Ibid.*, Ordonnance des administrateurs, January 20, 1733.
9. *Ibid.*, Lettre du ministre à M. de Larnage sur les milices, June 3, 1740.
10. *Ibid.*, Ordonnance des administrateurs, March 12, 1759.
11. *Ibid.*, Ordonnance du gouverneur général, March 12, 1779.
12. *Ibid.*, Ordonnance du roi, April, 1768.
13. *Ibid.*, Ordonnance du gouverneur général, March 12, 1779.
14. *Ibid.*, Ordonnance du commandant en chef par interim, May 26, 1780.
15. *Ibid.*, Lettre du gouverneur général au commandant du bataillon de limonade, April 15, 1782.
16. *Ibid.*, Ordonnances des administrateurs, July 8, 1776, and August 11, 1779.
17. M. L. E. Moreau de St.-Méry, *Description topographique, physique, civile, politique, et historique de la partie française de l'Isle Saint-Domingue*, 4 vols (Philadelphia, 1797), 1: 103–04.
18. Noel Deerr, *The History of Sugar*, 2 vols. (London, 1950), 2: 362–70.
19. Celso Furtado, *The Economic Growth of Brazil: A Survey from Colonial to Modern Times* (Berkeley and Los Angeles, 1965), pp. 153–54.
20. Deerr, *op. cit.*, 2: 368.
21. For a discussion of forced labor among white settlers of Puerto Rico during the nineteenth century, see S. W. Mintz, 'Labor and Sugar in Puerto Rico and Jamaica', *Comparative Studies in Society and History*, 1, no. 3, March 1959 273–83.
22. Moreau de St.-Méry, *Loix*, Déclaration du roi, December 15, 1721.
23. *Ibid.*, Ordonnance des administrateurs généraux des isles, August 15, 1711, and Ordonnance du roi, October 24, 1713.
24. *Ibid.*, Ordonnance de l'intendant en fonction, portant concession de la liberté à un de ses esclaves, avec la ratification du général, October 10 and 11, 1721.
25. Petit, *op. cit.*, 2: 70.
26. Moreau de St.-Méry, *Loix*, Ordonnance du roi, May 22, 1775.
27. *Ibid.*, Ordonnance des administrateurs, October 23, 1775.
28. *Ibid.* See also Arrêt du Conseil du Cap, August 6, 1708; Ordonnance des administrateurs, February 10, 1710; Ordonnance des administrateurs, June 28, 1734; and Arrêt du Conseil du Cap, July 9, 1750.
29. See, for example, *ibid.*, Arrêt du Conseil de Guerre, February 17, 1695, and Ordonnance des administrateurs, September 9, 1709.
30. *Ibid.*, Extrait de la lettre du ministre à M. Ducasse, February 5, 1698; Extrait de la lettre du ministre à M. Ducasse, March 11, 1699; Lettre du Ministre sur les Nègres amenés en France, June 10, 1707; Ordonnance du roi, April 28, 1694; Déclaration du roi, October 28, 1694; Edit du roi, October, 1716; Déclaration du roi, December 15, 1738; Lettre du ministre aux administrateurs, June 30, 1763; Règlement de l'intendant, August 29, 1769; Déclaration du roi, August 9, 1777; Arrêt du Conseil d'État, September 7, 1777; and Ordonnance du roi, February 23, 1778.
31. Paul Trayer, *Étude historique de la condition légale des esclaves dans les colonies françaises* (Paris, 1887), pp. 95–96.
32. Dutertre, *op. cit.*, 3: 201.
33. *Ibid.*, 1: 500–502.
34. *Ibid.*, 2: 537.
35. *Ibid.*, 1: 502–04.
36. *Ibid.*, 3: 201–04. For the treaty signed with Francisque Fabulé, *see* Moreau de St.-Méry, *Loix*, Arrêt du Conseil de la Martinique, March 2, 1665.
37. *Ibid.*, Arrêt du Conseil de la Martinique, October 13, 1671, and Arrêt de règlement du Conseil de Léogane, March 16, 1705.
38. *Ibid.*, Arrêt du Conseil de Léogane, July 1, 1709.
39. *Ibid.*, Mémoire des administrateurs au Conseil Supérieur du Cap, July 7, 1721.
40. *Ibid.*, Arrêt du Conseil du Petit-Goave, March 6, 1728; Arrêt du Conseil du Cap, December 6, 1728; and Extrait de la lettre du ministre à M. Duclos, January 18, 1735.
41. *Ibid.*, Commission d'un commissaire de la nation françoise auprès du gouvernement Espagnole de Santo Domingo, January 15, 1776; Ordonnance des administrateurs concernant les Nègres Espagnoles pris en marronage, March 30, 1776; Ordonnance des administrateurs concernant les frais de restitution des esclaves fugitifs ramenés de l'Espagnole, April 16, 1776; Traité définitif de police entre les cours de France et de l'Espagne sur divers points concernant leurs sujets respectifs à St. Domingue, June 3 and December 4, 1777; and Lettre de l'intendant à l'ordonnateur du Cap touchant le prix des Nègres françois mariés dans la partie Espagnole, January 28, 1778.
42. Petit, *op. cit.*, 2: 165. Petit was referring to a peace treaty signed between the Assembly of Jamaica and Cudjoe, a leader of fugitive slaves, in 1739. A French translation of the treaty was published in *Ibid.*, 2: 165–77.
43. C. L. R. James, *The Black Jacobins*, (New York, 2nd rev. edn, 1963).
44. Edit du roi, March, 1685, or *Code Noir*, Art. 7. The original complete text is published in Lucien Peytraud, *L'esclavage aux Antilles françaises avant 1789* (Paris, 1897), pp. 158–66.
45. Melville J. Herskovits, *Dahomey: An Ancient West African Kingdom*, 2 vols (New York, 1928), 1: 78–95, 51–63.
46. *Code Noir*, Art. 28.
47. Moreau de St.-Méry, *Loix*, Arrêt du Conseil du Petit-Goave, January 8, 1697.
48. *Ibid.*
49. *Ibid.*, Arrêt du Conseil du Cap, February 7, 1707.
50. *Ibid.*, Ordonnance des administrateurs généraux des isles, August 15, 1711.
51. Antoine Gisler, *L'esclavage aux Antilles françaises (XVIIe–XIXe siècles): Contribution au problème de l'esclavage* (Fribourg, 1964), pp. 99–100.
52. Hilliard d'Auberteuil, *Considerations sur l'état présent*

de la colonie française de St. Domingue, 2 vols (Paris, 1776–77), 2: 73.
53. *Ibid.*, 2: 84.
54. Article 59 reads: 'We give to the freedmen the same rights, privileges, and immunities enjoyed by free-born persons; we will that the merit of an acquired liberty produce in them the same effects upon their persons as well as their property as the good fortune of natural freedom causes to our other subjects.' Some later versions of the *Code Noir* read, 'Voulons qu'ils méritent une liberté acquise', but this is an inaccuracy stemming from the growth of racism. The original *Code Noir* reads, 'Voulons que la mérite d'une liberté acquise'.
55. For some interesting concepts about the impact of population patterns on the racial attitudes and organization of colonial society, see Marvin Harris, *Patterns of Race in the Americas* (New York, 1964), and Winthrop D. Jordan, 'American Chiaroscuro: The Status and Definition of Mulattoes in the British Colonies,' *William and Mary Quarterly*, 19, no. 2, April, 1962, 183–200.
56. Dutertre, *op. cit.*, 2: 513.
57. Moreau de St.-Méry, *Loix*, Extrait de la lettre du ministre à M. Dacasse, February 5, 1698.
58. Peytraud, *op. cit.*, p. 199.
59. Moreau de St.-Méry, *Loix*, Extrait de la lettre à le marquis de Fayet, March 29, 1735.
60. Petit, *op. cit.*, 2: 72–75.
61. Peytraud, *op. cit.*, p. 156.
62. *Ibid.*, p. 202.
63. Moreau de St.-Méry, *Loix*, Ordonnance des administrateurs, December 18, 1713.
64. *Ibid.*, Lettre du ministre au gouverneur général des isles, May 4, 1703.
65. Peytraud, *op. cit.*, p. 207.
66. Moreau de St.-Méry, *Loix*, Arrêts du Conseil du Cap, May 2 and June 13, 1746.
67. Hillaird d'Auberteuil, *op. cit.*, 2: 80, 81.
68. *Ibid.*, 79 and n.
69. Petit, *op. cit.*, 2: 81.
70. Moreau de St.-Méry, *Loix*, Déclaration du roi, February 8, 1726; C. Vanufel and Champion de Villeneuve, *Code des Colons de St. Domingue* (Paris, 1862), pp. 42, 43.
71. Auguste Lebeau, *De la condition des gens de couleur libres sous l'Ancient Régime d'après des documents des archives coloniales* (Paris, 1903), p. 15.
72. Moreau de st.-Méry, *Loix*, Arrêt du Conseil du Cap, December 21, 1769.
73. *Ibid.*, October 5, 1775.
74. *Ibid.*, April 29, 1782.
75. Moreau de St.-Méry, *Description de la partie française*, 1: 68.
76. *Ibid.*, p. 1. The earlier figure for slaves was undercounted. Because slaves were subject to a head tax, slave-owners attempted to conceal the number of slaves they actually had. M. de Marbois, the last intendant, was more vigilant, and arrived at more accurate figures, but even these were considerably undercounted. See P. J. Laborie, *The Coffee Planter of St. Domingue* (London, 1798), App., pp. 56–57. In one case, 68 slaves were confiscated from a master who had concealed their existence from the census. See Moreau de St.-Méry, *Loix*, Ordonnance de l'intendant, June 19, 1756.
77. Laborie, *op. cit.*, App., pp. 44–53.
78. Julien Raimond, *Observations sur l'origine et les progrès du préjugé des colons blancs contre les hommes de couleur* (Paris, 1791).
79. Moreau de St.-Méry, *Loix*, Arrêt du Conseil du Cap, October 24, 1706.
80. *Ibid.*, May 22, 1760.
81. Quoted in Lebeau, *op. cit.*, p. 23.
82. Moreau de St.-Méry, *Loix*, Ordonnance des administrateurs, February 26, 1770.
83. *Ibid.*, Ordonnance des administrateurs touchant la boucherie au quartier du Trou, March 16, 1784.
84. For a brief summary of some discriminatory laws, see J. G. Leyburn, *The Haitian People* (New Haven, Conn., 1941), pp. 18–19. For texts of the laws, see Moreau de St.-Méry, *Loix*, Arrêt du Conseil du Cap, May 22, 1760; Ordonnance du roi, April 30, 1764; Lettre du ministre aux administrateurs, September 25, 1774; Ordonnance du roi, July 23, 1720; Ordonnance du gouverneur général, May 29, 1762; Lettre du ministre à l'intendant des Isles du Vent, December 30, 1741; Arrêt de règlement du Conseil du Cap, April 17, 1762; Arrêt du Conseil du Cap, January 23, 1769; Arrêt du Conseil du Port-au-Prince, January 13, 1770; Lettre du ministre aux administrateurs, May 27, 1771; Règlements des administrateurs, June 24 and July 16, 1773; Arrêt du Conseil du Port-au-Prince, January 9, 1778; Lettre du ministre aux administrateurs, March 13, 1778; and Règlement provisoire des administrateurs, February 9, 1779.
85. Quoted in Gisler, *op. cit.*, 98.
86. *Ibid.*, pp. 98, 99.

SECTION SIX
Health, Nutrition and the Crisis of Social Reproduction

Recent research on slavery has confirmed that slaves were generally malnourished and therefore preyed upon by a range of diseases related to under- and malnutrition. Not only did food availability fluctuate seasonally, but slaves experienced long periods of hunger during and after hurricanes, droughts and war. Crop cycles in Europe and North America also affected food availability. Kiple and Kiple, Craton and Sheridan have suggested that slaves suffered from severe deficiencies in important vitamins and minerals, and that the root cause of their vulnerability to fatal and damaging diseases was malnutrition. These authors, however, recognize the problems inherent in any research that attempts to diagnose symptoms known to be the result of nutritional deficiency that were widespread among slaves. By discussing labour in relation to food supplies within a hostile disease environment, Kiple and Kiple, Craton and Sheridan have provided pioneer accounts of the biological history of slaves.

Poor health and nutrition of slaves and internal demographic and other socio-economic factors contributed to the general inability of Caribbean slave populations to reproduce themselves naturally until the closing years of the slave system. Demographic historians have emphasized the need to analyse the composition of all societies and to identify the variables that determine performance over time.

The essays by Lamur and Higman address the major structural and methodological issues involved in the discourse on slave demography.

Deficiency Diseases in the Caribbean

KENNETH F. KIPLE AND VIRGINIA H. KIPLE*

The history of slavery in the Americas has recently taken on a new biological dimension as historians have begun to appreciate the importance of pathogenic agents in any holistic understanding of their subject. Of special interest is the impact of these agents on slave mortality and, more specifically, the extent of the role that they played in preventing most Caribbean slave populations from sustaining a natural rate of growth.

Historians are also looking beyond pathogens to the nutritional factor, which may have figured prominently in the etiologies of slave diseases. Seldom does a new work appear which does not allege that malnutrition was a serious problem of Caribbean slave health. However, no attempt has been made to single out specific nutritional deficiencies in the Caribbean slave diet and in the process prove that Caribbean bondsmen were malnourished. Nor for that matter has any effort been made to link suspected nutritional deficiencies with some of the more important West Indian slave diseases.

This study makes such an attempt by investigating the West African nutritional heritage of Caribbean slaves, by analyzing the Caribbean slave diet, and by matching nutritional deficiencies revealed by this analysis with the symptoms of the diseases which plagued slaves exclusively.

The African Nutritional Heritage

Although there were some exceptions, West African diets were poor. Prior to the sixteenth century, they consisted of bananas, taro, the small African yam, millet, and rice crops, which researchers believe did little more than sustain life. In the sixteenth century, American cassava and maize were imported, and are credited with stimulating the growth of West Africa's population — a growth that kept pace, or even exceeded, the drain of the slave trade.[1]

Although the introduction of these two starchy plants may have resolved problems of quantity, the quality of West African diets remained deficient. Animal protein has never played a major role in West African nutrition, with much of the blame belonging to the tsetse fly — a bloodsucking insect which imparts African sleeping sickness to animals as well as to man. In much of West Africa the tsetse fly was so prevalent that it made the raising of cattle and other large animals, if not in all cases impossible, at least unprofitable. Thus many West Africans were limited to keeping a few goats, chickens, and dogs and sometimes a pig — animals so scarce and highly prized that they were slaughtered only on special occasions.[2]

Bovine milk was thus excluded fron West African diets, which may be a reason for the

Kenneth F. Kiple is Associate Professor of History at Bowling Green State University. He is the co-author with Virginia H. Kiple of a book-length study on the biological history of blacks in the United States.

This study is an elaboration of the Caribbean portion of the paper 'Slave Nutrition and Disease during the Nineteenth Century: The United States and the Caribbean', which was delivered at the annual meeting of the organization of American Historians (1979). The authors wish to thank the Joint Committee on Latin American Studies of the Social Science Research Council and the American Council of Learned Societies for an award to support the project out of which this research was generated. They are grateful also to the Bowling Green Faculty Research Committee for assistance with supplementary travel funds.

Journal of Interdisciplinary History, Vol. 11, No. 2 (1980), pp. 197–215.

high frequency of lactose intolerance today among blacks of West African origin. Such intolerance occurs among people with a history of low milk consumption. Also excluded in many places were eggs, for some because of taboos against their consumption, and for others because it seemed wasteful to eat the egg rather than wait for the chicken. Finally, because of cultural beliefs, fruit consumption was frequently frowned upon as was the use of most vegetables, except the yam, taro, cassava, and maize.[3]

One consequence of this background was that many West Africans must have reached the New World with a history of malnutrition. Empirical data suggest that this was the case. Research conducted by Fogel, Engerman, and Higman concerning the height of some 25,000 Trinidadian slaves indicates that newly imported Africans were significantly shorter on average than Creole-born slaves. Fraginals has found the same to be true for Cuba. First-generation Creole slaves were significantly taller than freshly imported Africans.[4]

Research has demonstrated that a radical change in dietary habits produces a dramatic increase in height. The rapid growth of New World slaves over the course of a generation or so implies that West Indian diets were at least more protein laden than those of West Africa and were probably also of better overall quality. We discuss West Africa in order to emphasize the poor nutritional status of a sizeable portion of slaves in the Caribbean.[5]

West Indian slave populations were seldom self-sustaining so long as the slave trade endured. Rather, they received massive injections of fresh imports from that traffic until the beginning of the nineteenth century and, in the case of Cuba, through the middle of that century. Hence Caribbean slave populations always had many badly nourished newcomers crowding their ranks — a condition which the circumstances of the Middle Passage could only have aggravated. The standard menu for slaves making the passage was a boiled cereal (usually rice) with a 'sauce' made by boiling salted fish — a diet lacking in many important nutrients. Moreover, the dysentery and diarrhea, always rife aboard a slaver, would have leached away many of those nutrients which such a diet could have provided.[6]

Thus many West Africans, badly nourished to begin with and then subjected to the disastrous nutritional circumstances of the Middle Passage, reached the New World in a malnourished condition. Doubtless some never recovered, which must count as an important reason for the high incidence of 'seasoning' mortality.

Malnutrition, in addition to its own inherent destructiveness, also renders the body susceptible to pathogenic invasion and, in the case of slaves moving into a new disease environment, to pathogens and strains of pathogens against which they had inefficient defenses. Assuming, however, that the newly imported slaves did survive, they did so on a diet which, although in many ways superior to their accustomed diets in West Africa, may nonetheless have been seriously deficient in some nutrients.

Diet

Our technique for constructing the Caribbean slave diet reflected in Table 1 has been to assign to slaves the amount of meat and cereal that planters claimed that they issued — the kind of standardized *ideal* allotment which is mentioned over and over again in everything from instructions to overseers, to travel accounts, to tracts on slave care — and then to 'build up' that basic allotment with the most commonly mentioned and readily available or easy to store supplements to reach a caloric intake of about 3,000 calories daily. Three thousand calories would be too low for a young male laboring during a sugar harvest; 3,200–4,000 calories would be closer to his requirement for this fraction of the year. However, not all islands employed a majority of their slaves in sugar cultivation, and female requirements run in the average about 1,200 calories fewer than males. Thus 3,000 calories seems a reasonable intake for the average adult slave for at least most of the year.[7]

By employing this technique, we may assume that, ideally, Caribbean slaves received an allotment of a little less than a half pound of animal protein daily, either as dried beef or salted fish, and about a pint of cereal in the form of either cornmeal or rice. This core allotment would have provided in the neighborhood of a third of the daily calorie requirements but about twice as much protein as today's recommendations suggest.[8]

Because of a lack of calories provided by the core, Caribbean slaves were dependent upon

Table 1 Analysis of Caribbean Slave Diets Computed on a Daily Basis[a]

	Calories	Protein	Fat[b]	Calcium	Phosphorus	Iron	Vitamin A	Thiamine	Riboflavin	Niacin	Vitamin C
.42 lb beef	387	65	12	38	791	9.7	0	.13	.60	7.2	0
1 pint cornmeal	884	22	8	42	544	4.4	1180	.74	.20	4.6[c]	0
Core plus vegetable supplements (see below)	2630	104	20	374	1941	26.1	4540	1.80	1.40	20.5	142
% RDA	88[d]	189[e]		47	243		91	123	81	108	316
.42 lb fish[f]	440	67	1	311	790	2.5	0	.15	.80	5.2	0
1 pint rice	1416	26	2	94	366	3.2	0	.28	.12	6.2	0
Core plus supplements	3215	110	3	473	1763	17.7	3360	1.35	1.49	20.1	142
% of RDA	107	200		87	220		67	93	88	106	316
Vegetable supplements											
½ lb. yams	197	4		39	135	1.1	0	.20	.08	1.0	17
½ lb. taro[g]	236	3		187	218	4.5	0	.22	.04	1.8	16
1 lb. bananas	386	5		36	118	3.2	860	.23	.27	3.2	45
1 lb. plantains[g]	540	5		32	136	3.2	2500	.27	.18	2.7	64

[a] Unless otherwise specified, all food values have been calculated from C. F. Adams, *Nutritive Value of American Foods* (Washington D.C., 1975).

[b] The fat content of vegetable supplements has not been included because that contribution is negligible.

[c] The niacin figure for corn is particularly misleading, because the niacin contained in corn is chemically bound. Thus without special treatment, most of the vitamin B_3 in cornmeal is unavailable to the consumer.

[d] All RDAS established by the Food and Nutrition Board, National Academy of Sciences, National Research Council (*Recommended Dietary Allowances* [Washington D.C., 1974; 8th revised ed]) are for a male aged 18–35 years, although — except for protein and iron — female allowances are virtually the same. Pregnant and lactating women have increased requirements for all nutrients.

[e] The RDA in the past few years has been lowered from 70 to 55 grams in keeping with an increasingly sedentary life style. However, this seems too low for the nineteenth-century slave, and indeed some experts believe that even 70 grams is too low an RDA to maintain long-term health. See N. S. Scrimshaw, 'Shattuck Lecture — Strengths and Weaknesses of the Committee Approach: An Analysis of Past and Present Recommended Allowances for Protein in Health and Disease'. *New England Journal of Medicine*, CCXCIV (1976), 136–42, 198–203. In agreement are C. Frank Consolazio *et al.*, 'Protein Metabolism during Intensive Physical Training in the Young Adult', *American Journal of Clinical Nutrition*, XXVIII (1975), 29–33, who believe that those engaged in sufficient physical activity to cause perspiration need at least 100 grams of protein every day.

[f] The 3 lbs of fish allotted to Caribbean slaves every week was either dried or pickled cod or herring. Thus we have averaged the nutrients for which information is available yielded by fish submitted to both processes. The difficulty is that no recent reliable data exist to specify the quantity of most minerals and all vitamins provided by dried, salted, or pickled fish. Therefore, we have relied on older data for dried but unsalted cod and herring. (Found in the 1950 edition of the *Agriculture Handbook*.) This means that nutritive values are probably high at least for the B vitamins.

[g] Computed from A. von Muralt (ed.), *Protein-Calorie Malnutrition* (Heidelberg, 1969), Tables, 147–77.

supplements to that core, which explains the importance of their provision grounds and vegetable gardens often mentioned in the literature on Caribbean plantations. Although West Indian plants and dietary preferences varied from place to place, yams, taro, plantains, and bananas are the most frequently cited supplements. The usual practice was to boil all of these foods (save the bananas) with the ration of animal protein and cereal; and, assuming that out of the cooking pot the average slave plucked a half pound of yam, another of taro root, and perhaps a pound of plantains, he would have satisfied his caloric needs for the day.[9]

Surprisingly, despite the usual description of these basic diets as 'starchy' and 'protein poor', they seem to have supplied most of the basic nutrients. The diets were poor in calcium, and with milk — the one food which might have remedied the problem — in short supply and most slaves lactose intolerant, a widespread calcium deficiency must have been a nutritional fact of life. Caribbean slaves seem also to have been slightly deficient in vitamin A, but, superficially at least, the slave diets of the Caribbean might be characterized as not that poor by eighteenth- and nineteenth-century standards.[10]

A closer look, however, reveals some serious problems, in part because of the chemical composition of some of the foods in question and in part because of the peculiar relationships among some of the nutrients. For example, an enormously complicating factor is the absence of sufficient fats. In both the beef and fish slave diets the animal protein and cereal were the only items to supply any amount of fat. However, because of the low fat content of dried fish and jerked beef, this meant only 20 grams of fat daily for West Indian slaves on a beef-corn core, and a measly 3 grams for those on a fish-rice core. Yet the established world standard for fat intake suggests 80–125 grams as a safe minimum.[11]

Although the low fat intake of slaves may have been good for cholesterol levels, such a diet means that the amount of vitamin A that Table 1 shows West Indian bondsmen as receiving is considerably overstated. Vitamin A is fat-soluble; hence a low fat diet impairs the ability of the body to absorb that vitamin. Moreover, the fish or meat allotment to slaves was usually reported as rancid; indeed, slaves allegedly preferred it that way. Unfortunately rancidity has a destructive effect on fat-soluble vitamins. Thus, instead of being only mildly vitamin A deficient, many West Indian slaves, because of an absence of dietary fat and the rancidity of much of the fat that they did ingest, must have been severely vitamin A deficient.[12]

Less well known is the relationship between fat and thiamine or vitamin B_1. Because thiamine is part of the water soluble vitamin B complex, fat has little to do with its absorption. But in the case of low-fat diets, such as those of Caribbean slaves, carbohydrates replace fat as the major energy source, and carbohydrates require thiamine for metabolism. Thus the low fat/high carbohydrate content of the Caribbean slave diets would have greatly accelerated thiamine requirements. For West Indian slaves thiamine requirements would have been higher than for the whites on the islands whose diets were heavily fat-laden. But even more to the point, it is highly doubtful that Caribbean bondsmen actually received as much thiamine as is suggested by Table 1.[13]

The process of pickling, salting, and drying beef or fish treats thiamine poorly. Both alkaline solutions and prolonged dehydration have a destructive effect on thiamine, the least stable of the B complex vitamins. This lack of stability also means that heat is more destructive to thiamine than to riboflavin or niacin. Thus data on the thiamine content of foods are usually given, as they are in Table 1, before cooking because of the losses which occur in the process. The loss from cornmeal, for example, runs between 15 and 25 per cent. In the case of meat, however, that loss can be as high as 85 per cent.[14]

Moreover, because thiamine is so highly soluble in water, it is readily leached out of the food during boiling, the standard method of cooking on most West Indian plantations. Fish or beef was tossed into the family or communal pot where it simmered all day along with yams, plantains, taro root, and, quite possibly, the cereal ration as well. Because of such factors as dehydration and cooking losses, the thiamine delivered by the West Indian slave diet is probably overstated by at least 50 per cent. Those slaves especially whose cereal allotment was rice were bound to be seriously B_1 deficient because, when rice is subjected to a polishing process to retard spoilage, the process also strips away the thiamine-rich husk of the grain.[15]

Finally, it bears repeating that the low-fat diet of Caribbean slaves would have severely exacerbated a condition of thiamine deficiency by elevating thiamine requirements. To this factor should be added two more exacerbating difficulties: a diet high in carbohydrates also accelerates thiamine requirements; and thiamine is the most poorly stored of all of the B vitamins.[16]

Not all Caribbean bondsmen suffered from the deficiencies of calcium, vitamin A, and thiamine. Red peppers provided much in the way of vitamin A, as did mangoes and ackee, both of which came into widespread West Indian use at about the turn of the nineteenth century. Milk was not totally unavailable to Caribbean slaves and, although most blacks were lactose intolerant, a few ounces in cornbread or coffee would have made a nutritional contribution — especially in the areas of sorely needed tryptophan and calcium — without necessarily producing symptoms of lactose intolerance.[17]

Disease

Not all slaves had access to a variety of supplementary comestibles, and many had access to very few. Even assuming that slave diets were marginally, rather than severely, deficient in one or another vitamin, economic, political, and climatic circumstances could quickly have changed those diets for the worse. The English-French global struggle frequently deprived West Indian slaves of their meat and cereal core diet, as did the end of North American imports to the British West Indies after the American Revolution. Hurricanes were always destructive to slave provision grounds, particularly to the fragile plantain and banana trees, and high prices for meat and cereal or low prices for sugar reduced supplies for slave rations.[18]

Even during good times Caribbean slave diets were badly out of balance, and times were often far from good. Yet all that a nutritional analysis of the basic foodstuffs in the slave regimen has done is to create the suspicion of widespread deficiencies of vitamins A and B_1. That suspicion can only be transformed into something more concrete if the diseases triggered by these deficiencies can be found to have afflicted slaves in large numbers. A correlation could then be established beeen a nutritional deficiency and a deficiency disease.

In any search for a deficiency disease one is quickly confronted with the phenomenon of so-called 'Negro diseases', given much prominence by West Indian physicians of the period. These were diseases from which blacks were far more likely to suffer than whites. Yaws, for example, was reportedly an affliction with an enormous color prejudice. The prejudice, however, is easily explicable in terms of a slave trade which constantly introduced persons infected in West Africa. Because of skin-to-skin transmission, the disease flourished among a people who lived in close contact and wore few clothes. Another such disease — a major killer of infants — was the 'jawful', or neonatal tetanus. The affliction singled out black infants for special grim attention because of the frequency of umbilical stump infections. The unsanitary condition of many slave quarters, on the one hand, and West African practices such as packing the stump with mud, on the other, guaranteed a high black as opposed to white death rate from the disease. There are, however, other Negro diseases the etiologies of which are not so easily understood in terms of pathogenic discrimination, but the symptoms of which do suggest problems of nutrition.[19]

Nutritional analysis has suggested that many Caribbean slaves would have been vitamin A and thiamine deficient, both because the diet itself was low in these vitamins and because a low-fat diet meant that much vitamin A was not absorbed and that thiamine requirements were elevated. Considering vitamin A first, one discovers among those peculiarly 'Negro afflictions' which occupied the attention of Caribbean slave physicians the malady 'sore eyes'. Eye afflictions were so widespread among the slaves that whole chapters in books on slave medicine were devoted to the problem, which is characteristic of several nutrient deficiencies. Night blindness, described as a 'disease which is so frequently seen among Negroes', is prominently mentioned in those chapters, and is a classic sign of vitamin A deficiency. Its prevalence among the slaves, along with the high incidence of sore eyes, does much to strengthen the suspicion born of nutritional analysis that many Caribbean bondsmen were vitamin A deficient.[20]

Another sizeable body of literature amassed by Caribbean physicians concerns one of the worst curses to befall a West Indian slave — the *mal d'estomach*. Also called *mal de estomágo*, *hati-weri*, *cachexia africana*, and just plain dirt-eating, the disease afflicted the black population of the West Indies exclusively. In Puerto Rico it was reportedly one of the two worst diseases of the slaves. In Jamaica it was portrayed as 'common upon almost every plantation' and on some estates the cause of about half the deaths. At first, doctors were powerless against it, and iron masks were used to break the pica habit. However, by the last decades of the eighteenth century, physicians were nearly unanimous in their prescibed cure — a better, more balanced diet.[21]

This mysterious malady, as described by eighteenth-century physicians, made its victims 'languid and listless', 'short breathed', and 'giddy', and afflicted them with 'palpitations of the heart' and 'loss of appetite.' With the progression of the sickness, legs swelled, the countenance became bloated and 'dropsy ensue(d)'. These symptoms are a classic portrayal of beriberi advancing from the dry to wet stage — and beriberi is caused by thiamine deficiency.[22]

In addition to these outstanding symptoms of thiamine deficiency, many other reasons exist for suspecting that *mal d'estomach* was in fact beriberi. Pregnant and lactating females were reported as the most susceptible to the disease, and pregnant and lactating females have historically proven the most vulnerable to beriberi because of accelerated requirements for most nutrients, including the B complex. Also vulnerable were young girls who suffered a disproportionately heavy incidence of the disease 'at a certain time in their life . . . (just) before their periodical evacuations appear'. The females in question, who probably consumed less food than their brothers of the same age, would have been experiencing the period of growth when requirements for all the B vitamins accelerate. The children susceptible to *mal d'estomach* were depicted as nutritionally deprived and often rickety in appearance. Whether the disease struck at the young or old, male or female, the remedy that physicians prescribed was 'wholesome food'; that the cure worked does nothing to weaken the hypothesis that the disease was indeed beriberi.[23]

There are other explanations for the symptoms. Slaves who manifested dirt-eating symptoms were sometimes thought to be attempting suicide, and slaves who developed *mal d'estomach* often personally diagnosed their problem as the result of having been poisoned or cursed by an 'obeah man'. More recently *mal d'estomach* has been pronounced to be the result of ankylostomiasis or hookworm infection, and indeed dirt-eating among slaves in the United States has also been attributed to hookworm. Yet this explanation ignores the relative immunity that blacks have to hookworm 'expressed as a resistance both to invasion by the parasite and to the injurious effects after invasion'. Another problem with hookworm infection as the culprit is that the disease was not unknown to colonial physicians; rather it was commonly diagnosed in British troops and thus presumably would have been recognized in blacks had they manifested similar symptoms.[24]

Others have confused the *mal d'estomach* with the dry belly ache, which was also frequently fatal. This affliction, however, was accompanied by enormous intestinal pains that often had individuals begging to be shot or otherwise put out of their misery and which terminated in convulsions or epileptic seizures. Benjamin Franklin became interested in the problem and speculated in a letter to a West Indian physician that the dry belly ache was the result of drinking rum distilled in apparatuses using lead fastenings and pipes. Franklin's speculation may have been correct, for other physicians observed that the dry belly ache often caused lead poisoning. *Mal d'estomach* and dry belly ache were clearly two separate afflictions, with only the former, according to contemporary doctors, having a nutritional etiology.[25]

Evidence of a general B vitamin deficiency in the West Indies is contained in a seasonal phenomenon which occurred at crop time on sugar plantations; despite the long hours of extraordinary hard labor, blacks paradoxically enjoyed better health throughout the harvest. Physicians commented on the 'peculiar glossiness of the skin, so indicative of health (which) is never seen to the same extent at any other season'. Moreover, it was accepted wisdom that slaves purchased during crop time would do better in terms of health than slaves purchased at any other time of the year. Physicians and planters attributed this condition to the drinking of sugar cane juice. Custom allowed slaves to drink as much as they wished of the 'hot liquor' from the 'last copper', which contained a mixture of brown sugar and molasses. Thus slaves who drank from the 'last copper' were imbibing a liquid rich in iron and the B vitamins. If island physicians were not certain why, they nonetheless knew that this annual infusion of minerals and vitamins was beneficial for slaves.[26]

Physicians also (significantly in terms of thiamine deficiency) periodically suspected rice of producing bad health. A Jamaican physician reported early in the nineteenth century that rice had lately 'fallen into disuse' because it caused 'dropsical swellings'. Edema can be symptomatic of many disorders but, because they were linked to rice consumption, the 'dropsical swellings' do suggest beriberi, and dropsy had the reputation of being a major killer of adult Caribbean slaves.[27]

Mortality records bear out dropsy's deadliness; in those consulted for Barbados, dropsy dominated as a cause of plantation deaths. In Jamaica, on the Worthy Park estate between 1811 and 1834, dropsy accounted for fully 10 per cent of the 222 deaths, ranking only behind deaths from old age (53) and fever (23); of 357 slave deaths in St. James Parish, Jamaica, between 1817 and 1820, dropsy accounted for 11 per cent of the deaths, second only to old age. If dirt-eating and *mal d'estomach* deaths are added to those from dropsy, the three accounted for 16 per cent of the deaths. Dropsy alone claimed 11 per cent of the 288 deaths on three other Jamaican estates from 1817 to 1829. If other diseases with symptoms suggestive of beriberi, such as 'fits', 'convulsions', and 'bloated', are included with dropsy, the diseases in question accounted for 22 per cent of the deaths registered.[28]

On the Newton plantation in Barbados from 1796 to 1801 and from 1811 to 1825, dropsy accounted for 9 per cent of the 153 deaths (14), tying with consumption for third place behind old age (22) and 'no cause given' (19). By race the death records for the dioceses of Havana for 1843 recorded a black death rate from *anasarea* (general dropsy) of about three times that for whites. Finally, slave death statistics compiled by a West Indian physician during the 1820s for a Jamaican parish credits dropsy, plus other beriberi-like afflictions, with fully 20 per cent of the victims aged over one year of age in the district in question.[29]

As with *mal d'estomach* and 'cachexias', there was a cure for dropsy. In the words of Long, 'Sometimes they [the slaves] fall into dropsies, which generally prove mortal; for this disorder requires a very nutritious diet'. In the minds of white planters good nutrition was equated with fresh meat, and fresh meat contains that thiamine which could have cured the 'dropsies'.[30]

Fertility and Infant Mortality

Beriberi is one of those nutritional diseases, like pellagra, which escaped identification as a disease *sui generis* for many years, largely because its protean symptoms misled physicians into thinking that they were confronting a number of diseases. Because it was in the Far East that beriberi was finally identified, it subsequently was associated with rice-eating cultures; hence, beriberi is not usually thought of in a Caribbean context. Yet in 1865, early in the effort to conquer beriberi, Hava reported that the disease was epidemic among blacks on Cuban plantations and described all of the symptoms of wet beriberi. In 1871 a French physician observed the disease on Cuban *ingenios* (plantations) and attempted, not very successfully, to treat it with arsenic. Finally in 1873 the disease was reported as raging with virulence on some Cuban plantations, causing a mortality rate of between 60 and 75 per cent. Because the slave diet in Cuba could and did produce beriberi, there are grounds for the suspicion that the disease was fairly widespread among West Indian slaves and that many of those who died from *mal d'estomach*, dropsy, or convulsions were actually dying of beriberi.[31]

If these deaths were caused by beriberi, then the dietary deficiency which produced this disease may have significantly altered the demographic history of West Indian slave populations — not so much because of the adult deaths, but because of infant mortality. For all the major nutritional diseases, only beriberi is a killer of otherwise normal infants receiving an adequate supply of breast milk. Adult slaves in the United States, for example, suffered from pellagra caused by niacin deficiency. Yet it is almost impossible for infants to be niacin deficient, because human milk supplies an adequate amount of both niacin and tryptophan (naicin's precursor), even if the mother is niacin deficient. However, a mother deficient in thiamine will invariably have milk deficient in that vitamin. To complicate matters for medical personnel, she may show few or even no signs of thiamine deficiency herself; in other words, a mother whose child develops infantile beriberi may not display overt signs of the malady.[32]

Infantile beriberi symptoms are very different from adult symptoms, and edema is only occasionally seen. The disease begins with vomiting, pallor, restlessness, loss of appetite, and insomnia and terminates life with convulsions and/or cardiac failure. Clearly the variety of symptoms makes it difficult to pin down the disease on West Indian plantations of yesterday. But if beriberi were fairly widespread, then infantile beriberi had unquestionably to be a major destroyer of West Indian slave infants. How major a destroyer may be gauged by looking at the Philippines, where beriberi has been and still is a chronic problem; in the late 1950s between 75 and 85 per cent of the 25,000 beriberi deaths reported there annually were infants. By the turn of the century, nearly half of all infants born alive in Manila failed to reach one year of age; infantile beriberi bears much of the blame for this mortality.[33]

How major a killer beriberi was in the West Indies can only be speculated upon. The disease usually strikes infants between the first and sixth months of life, before supplements have been added to their diets. If the attack is acute, the infant has difficulty in breathing, becomes cyanosed, and dies of cardiac failure with 'unnerving rapidity'. If it is chronic, the infant grows thin and wasted, edema occasionally occurs, and convulsions are frequently seen in the terminal stages.[34]

To be sure, the infant slave had to live long enough to contract infantile beriberi by first escaping that primary destroyer of the newborn in the Caribbean — neonatal tetanus. The fearsome reputation of this affliction was well deserved; indeed, the ailment has been credited with carrying off about one quarter of all slave infants within their first two weeks of life. However, as pointed out by students of Caribbean slave mortality, 'it is evident that the majority of fatalities among slave children born at Worthy Park occurred not at birth but in the children's early years.'[35]

A consultation of the literature produced by West Indian physicians and of the mortality data suggests that the latter statement applies not only to Worthy Park but to the Caribbean slave population as a whole. Rivaling neonatal tetanus as major causes of infant deaths were marasmus, convulsions, and tetanic convulsions. Researchers today looking for evidence of beriberi's presence in a region scrutinize any death that is classified under the rubric of convulsions or marasmus. Convulsions were also associated with teething difficulties, yet infants do not convulse simply because of teething. However, the months of teething are also those months during which infants would be most likely to succumb to beriberi.[36]

Another signal to researchers is the phenomenon of mothers with a history of losing one baby after another within the first few months of life. The West Indian literature offers many examples of mothers who had produced fifteen children and lost all but two, or who 'had borne ten children, and yet has now but one alive', or 'the instances of those who have had four, five, six children, without succeeding in bringing up one in spite of the utmost attention and indulgence . . . '[37]

Further analysis of mortality data and plantation records is needed. But this study does show that there is a correlation between a thiamine deficiency in the West Indian slave diet and diseases with beriberi-like symptoms, which ranked among the most important causes of slave mortality. If beriberi were as widespread as the evidence gathered thus far suggests, then thiamine deficiency must join with other factors produced by the slave trade and sugar monoculture to explain why Caribbean slave populations did not sustain themselves by natural means as did the slave population of the United States. It has often been urged that low fertility was at fault. Yet none of the islands have adequate birth records either to confirm or refute this suggestion. A possible measure of fertility relates the number of children under one year to the number of women able to bear those children. But if something is killing those infants at a brisk rate, then this kind of fertility ratio is a very misleading statistic.

Finally, it has been suggested that low fertility may have been partially the result of the practice of West African mothers to nurse their children for periods as long as three years. West Indian planters tried to discourage prolonged nursing but were not so successful in combating West African cultural practices as were United States planters, who were dealing with a people much further removed in time from their homeland. United States' slaves tended to nurse their babies for a year or less. Although the ability of lactation to prevent pregnancy after a few months of nursing is in doubt, there seems no question that prolonged lactation substantially increased the risk of death by thiamine deficiency for many West Indian slave infants.[38]

Although the slave diets of both the United States and the West Indies contained the potential for precipitating a B vitamin deficiency disease, pellagra, the deficiency disease of United States slaves, would not have killed the very young. But beriberi, the disease of Caribbean slaves, most certainly would have. The result may well help to account for the 'astounding fact, that while the blacks in the United States have increased *tenfold*, those of the British West Indies [and the West Indies] generally have decreased in the proportion of five to two'.[39]

Notes

1. Oliver Davis, *West Africa Before the Europeans: Archeology and Prehistory* (New York, 1967), 8, 149; Alfred W. Crosby, *The Columbian Exchange: Biological and Cultural Consequences of 1492* (Westport, Conn., 1972), 186–88; Bruce F. Johnston, *The Staple Food Economics of Western Tropical Africa* (Stanford, 1958), 174–81.

2. J. P. Glasgow, *The Distribution and Abundance of Tsetse* (London, 1963), 1–3; John Ford, *The Role of the Trypanosomiases in African Ecology: A Study of the Tsetse Fly Problem* (Oxford, 1971), 88–89; Frederick J. Simoons, *Eat Not This Flesh: Food Avoidances in the Old World* (Madison, 1961), 56.
3. Although West Indian figures are not available, about three-quarters of the Afro-Americans living in the United States are lactose intolerant, meaning that, because they have low levels of the lactase enzyme which breaks down milk sugars, they cannot drink milk. For a discussion, see K. and V. Kiple, 'Slave Child Mortality: Some Nutritional Answers to a Perennial Puzzle', *Journal of Social History*, X, (1977), 284–309. For WestAfrican dietary habits, consult Simoons, *op. cit.*, 73–78; Tadeuz Lewicki. *West African Food in the Middle Ages* (London, 1974), 79, 116–27; Michael Gelfand, *Diet and Tradition in African Culture* (Edinburgh, 1971), 206.
4. Robert W. Fogel and Stanley L. Engerman, 'Recent Findings in the Study of Slave Demography and Family Structure', *Sociology and Social Research*, LXIII, (1979), 566–89; Barry W. Higman, 'Growth in Afro-Caribbean Slave Populations.' *American Journal of Physical Anthropology*, L (1979), 373–85; Manuel Moreno Fraginals, 'Africa in Cuba: A Quantitative Analysis of the African Populations in the island of Cuba', in Vera Rubin and Arthur Tuden (eds), 'Comparative Perspectives on Slavery in New World Plantation Societies,' *Journal of the New York Academy of Science*, CCXCII (1979), 197–98.
5. J. M. Tanner, 'Earlier Maturation in Man,' *Scientific American*, CCXVIII (1968), 26–27; Albert Damon, 'Secular Trend in Height and Weight within Old American Families at Harvard, 1870–1965: Within Twelve Four-generation Families', *American Journal of Physical Anthropology*, XXIX (1968), 45–50; Phyllis Eveleth and Tanner, *Worldwide Variation in Human Growth* (Oxford, 1976), 274.
6. Philip D. Curtin, *The Atlantic Slave Trade: A Census* (Madison, 1969), remains the authority for measuring the magnitude of the various slave trades to the Americas. See also Herbert S. Klein, *The Middle Passage: Comparative Studies in the Atlantic Slave Trade* (Princeton, 1978). For the diets of blacks in the middle passage consult *ibid*, 200–01; John Riland, *Memoirs of a West-India Planter* (London, 1827), 56.
7. Food and Agriculture Organization, *Calorie Requirements* (Washington, D.C., 1950), 23–24.
8. The fish or meat ration in particular varied erratically from the ideal. For example, slave laws in the Leeward Islands required planters to issue a slave 1¼ lbs. of salt fish weekly. Elsa V. Goveia, *Slave Society in the British Leeward Islands at the End of the Eighteenth Century* (New Haven, 1965), 193. Barbadian planters, however, claimed that they issued a pound of fish daily: *A Report on a Committee of the Council of Barbados, Appointed to Inquire into the Actual Condition of the Slaves* (London, 1824), 106, 113. Yet Jerome S. Handler and Frederick W. Lange in *Plantation Slavery in Barbados* (Cambridge, 1977), 87, an investigation on the Newton plantation, found that its slaves received only ½ lb of salt fish every two weeks, although for the island as a whole the norm was about 1 lb weekly. Richard N. Bean, 'Food Imports into the British West Indies: 1680–1845', *Journal of the New Academy of Sciences*, CCXCII (1977), 581–90, also found the average to be 'just a bit over one pound of preserved fish per slave per week' (587). For Cuba, Fraginals, 'Africa in Cuba', 198, states that 'the daily norm was some 200 grams (about one-half pound) of jerked beef'. The point is that by accepting planters' claims of about ½ lb of fish or meat daily, we are doubtless erring on the high side.
9. For two contemporaries who stressed importance of slave provision grounds see Robert Collins, *Practical Rules for the Management and Medical Treatment of Negro Slaves in the Sugar Colonies* (London, 1811; rpt. edn, 1971), 87, 99; Bryan Edwards, *The History, Civil and Commercial, of the British Colonies in the West Indies* (London, 1807; 4th edn), II, 160–63.
10. Ignio Abbad y Lasierra, *Historia Geografica de Puerto Rico* (San Juan, 1886; rpt. edn 1970), 183; Humphrey E. Lamur, 'Demography of Surinam Plantation Slaves in the Last Decade before Emancipation: The Case of Catherine Sophia', *Journal of the New York Academy of Sciences*, CCXCII (1977), 161–73; Michael Craton, 'Hobbesian or Panglossian? The Two Extremes of State Conditions in the British Caribbean, 1783–1834', *William and Mary Quarterly*, XXXV (1978), 345.
11. League of Nations Technical Commission on Nutrition, *The Problems of Nutrition* (New York, 1936).
12. Edward Long, *The History of Jamaica* (London, 1774), II, 413; Michael Craton and James Walvin, *A Jamaican Plantation, The History of Worthy Park* (Toronto, 1970), 135. Leonard W. Autrand and A. E. Woods, *Food Chemistry* (Westport, Conn., 1973), 122.
13. L. E. Lloyd, B. E. McDonald, and E. Crampton, *Fundamentals of Nutrition* (San Francisco, 1978; 2nd edn), 166. Roger J. Williams *et. al. The Biochemistry of B Vitamins* (Austin Texas, 1950), 276, 282; Aurand and Woods, *op. cit.*, 210. The relationship between fat and thiamine requirements may help to explain a puzzle that nutritionists recently encountered in Puerto Rico. The diet of their subjects clearly supplied a sufficiency of thiamine, yet measurements revealed them to be slightly deficient. Throughout the article, frequent mention is made of the extremely *low fat* yield of the diet. Nelson A. Fernandez *et. al.*, 'Nutrition Survey of Two Rural Puerto Rican Areas Before and After a Community Improvement Program', *American Journal of Clinical Nutrition*, XXII (1969), 1639–51.
14. Aurand and Woods, *op. cit.*, 211; E. E. Rice, 'The Nutritional Content and Value of Meat and Meat Products', in J. F. Price and B. S. Schweigert (eds), *The Science of Meat and Meat Products* (San Francisco, 1971; 2nd ed), 307; Lloyd, McDonald, and Crampton, *op. cit.*, 163.
15. A. Barclay, *A Practical View of the Present State of Slavery in the West Indies* (London, 1827; 2nd edn), 307. Analysis of Caribbean diets today consisting principally of rice, beans, bananas, and codfish indicates that they would be seriously thiamine deficient were it not for 'enriched' rice. See for example Diva Sanjur, *Puerto Rican Food Habits: A Socio-Cultural Approach* (Ithaca, 1970), 23.
16. Lloyd, McDonald, and Crampton, *op. cit.*, 163.
17. John H. Parry, 'Plantation and Provision Ground: An Historical Sketch of the Introduction of Food Crops into Jamaica', *Revista de Historia de America*, XXXIX (155), 16–17.
18. David Lowenthal, 'The Population of Barbados', *Social Economic Studies*, VI (157), 445–501; Richard B. Sheridan, 'The Crisis of Slave Subsistence in the British West Indies during and after the American Revolution', *William and Mary Quarterly*, XXXIII (1976), 615–41; Berta Cabanillas, *Origenes de los Habitos Alimenticios del Pueblo de Puerto Rico* (Madrid, 1955), 274–75, 290.
19. For works that deal exclusively with West Indian black-related diseases see Jean Barthelemy, *Observations sur les Maladies des Negres, leurs causes, leurs traitemens,*

et les moyens de les prevenir (Paris, 1892; 2nd edn), 2; James Thompson, *A Treatise on the Diseases of Negroes as They Occur in the Island of Jamaica* (Kingston, Jamaica, 1820).

20. See William Hilary, *Observations on the Changes of the Air and the Concomitant Epidemical Diseases, in the Island of Barbados* (London, 1811; 2nd edn), 297–304, for a discussion of nyctalopia. See also Collins, *Practical Rules*, 287; James Grainger, *Essay on the More Common West Indian Diseases* (London, 1807; 2nd edn), 60.
21. Bengt Ansell and State Lagercrantz, *Geophagical Customs* (Uppsala, 1958), 60; John Stewart, *An Account of Jamaica* (London, 1808), 273; Abbad y Lasierra, *op. cit.*, 207; John Imray, 'Observations on the Mal d'estomach or Cachexia Africana, as it Takes place among the Negroes of Dominica', *Edinburgh Medical and Surgical Journal*, CIX (1843), 314; John Williamso, *Medical and Miscellaneous Observations Relative to the West India Islands* (Edinburgh, 1817), I, 177–82; II, 267; Edwards, *History of British in West Indies*, II, 167; Collins, *Practical Rules*, 274.
22. *Ibid.*, 293, 295; Williamson, *Medical and Miscellaneous Observations*, I, 110, Abbad y Lasierra, *op. cit.*, 207, John Hunter, *Observations on the Diseases of the Army in Jamaica* (London, 1808; 3rd ed.), 249.
23. David Mason, 'On Atrophia a Ventriculo (Mal D'Estomach) or Dirt-Eating', *Edinburgh Medical and Surgical Journal*, XXXIX (1833), 292; Orlando Patterson, *The Sociology of Slavery* (London, 167), 102; Williamson, *Medical and Miscellaneous Observations*, I, 182; II, 267; Collins, *Practical Rules*, 294; Imray, *op. cit.*, 314; Edwards, *History of British in West Indies*, II, 167.
24. This 'very pronounced' black resistance to hookworm infection was discovered by investigators in the American South during the early decades of this century. See for example, A. E. Keller, W. S. Leathers, and H. C. Ricks, 'An Investigation of the Incidence and Intensity of Infestation of Hookworm in Mississippi', *American Journal of Hygiene*, XIX (1934), 629–56.
25. Hillary, *op. cit.*, 182; Hunter, *Diseases of the Army in Jamaica*, 195, 211-216; Grainger, *West Indian Diseases*, 32.
26. Claude Levy, 'Slavery and the Emancipation Movement in Barbados, 1650–1833', *Journal of Negro History*, LV (1970), 6; Williamson, *Medical and Miscellaneous Observations*, I, 73; Long, *History of Jamaica*, II, 548, 551; Frank Wesley Pitman, 'Slavery on the British West Indian Plantations in the Eighteenth Century', *Journal of Negro History*, II (1926), 632; Richard Henry Dana, *To Cuba and Back: a Vacation Voyage* (Carbondale, Ill., 1966; rpt. edn).
27. Collins, *Practical Rules*, 85; Patterson, *op. cit.*, 99: J. Harry Bennett, *Bondsmen and Bishops: Slavery and Apprenticeship on the Codrington Plantations of Barbados, 1710–1838* (Berkeley, 1958), 56–58; George W. Roberts. *The Population of Jamaica* (Cambridge, England, 1957), 175; Richard S. Dunn, *Sugar* and *Slaves: The Rise of the Planter Class in the English West Indies, 1624–1713* (Chapel Hill, 1972), 302, 305–06; Higman, *Slave Population and Economy in Jamaica* (Oxford, 1976), 112–13.
28. Craton and Walvin, *A Jamaica Plantation*, 113, 197–98; Higman, *Slave Population*, 112. Deaths were substantially understated because of a failure to report infant deaths.
29. Handler and Lange, *Plantation Slavery in Barbados*, 99; D. Angel Jose Crowley (ed.), *Un Ensayo Estadistico-Medico de la Mortalitad de la Diocesis de la Habana durante el Ano de 1843* (Havana, 1845); William Sells, *Remarks on the Condition of the Slaves in the Island of Jamaica* (London, 1823; rpt. edn 1972), 19–20.
30. Long, *History of Jamaica*, II, 433; Pittman, *The Development of the British West Indies, 1760–1763* (New Haven, 1917), 13, 386.
31. Juan G. Hava, 'Communicacion Dirigida a la Academia sobre una Epidemia de Beriberi', *Academia de Ciencias Medical de la Habana: Anales*, II (165), 160–61: J. Minteguiaga, 'Lettre sur le Beriberi', *Gazette Medicale de Paris*, XLV (1874), 35; August Hirsch, *Handbook of Geographical and Historical Pathology* (London, 1883), II, 576.
32. C. C. de Silva and N. G. Baptist, *Tropical Nutritional Disorders of Infants and Children* (London, 1969), 114–15; Robert R. Williams, *Toward the Conquest of Beriberi* (Cambridge, 1961), 153, 156–57.
33. Michael Latham *et. al.*, *Scopes Manual on Nutrition* (New York, 1972), 39; Stanley Davidson *et. al.*, *Human Nutrition and Dietetics* (Edinburgh, 1975; 6th ed.), 415; Williams, *Toward the Conquest of Beriberi*, 81.
34. Davidson *et al.*, *Human Nutrition*, 415; Latham *et al.*, *Scope on Nutrition*, 39.
35. Craton and Walvin, *op. cit.*, 134. See also the parochial records for Barbados: the Parish of St. Thomas, for example, buried 168 slave children aged ten and under for the period 1816–34. Only 36 of the deaths were one year of age or less. In St. Phillips Parish, 33 of their 106 burials were infants. The records for other parishes are incomplete, yet what data are available continue to suggest that only about one third of those aged ten and under of those slave children who died were infants aged one or less.
36. Collins, *Practical Rules*, 393–94; Roberts, *Population of Jamaica*, 175; Williams, *Toward the Conquest of Beriberi*, 85.
37. M. G. Lewis, *Journal of a West Indian Proprietor, 1815–1817* (London, 1929), 97, 111.
38. Engerman, 'Some Economic and Demographic Comparisons of Slavery in the United States and the British Indies', *Economic History Review*, XXIX (1976), 264–66; Anrudh K. Jain, 'Demographic Aspects of Lactation and Postpartum Amenorrhea,' *Demography*, VII (1970), 250–71; Lamur, 'Demography of Surinam Plantation Slaves in the Last Decade before Emancipation', 168; Klein and Engerman, 'Fertility Differentials between Slaves in the United States and the British West Indies: A Note on Lactation Practices and their Possible Implications', *William and Mary Quarterly*, XXXV (1978), 357–74; Collins, *Practical Rules*, 146.
39. Josiah Clark Nott and George R. Gliddon (eds), *Indigenous Places of the Earth: or New Chapters of Ethnological Inquiry* (Philadelphia, 1857), 387.

Death, Disease and Medicine on the Jamaican Slave Plantations; the Example of Worthy Park, 1767–1838

MICHAEL CRATON*

Even while condemning the institution of slavery, many modern writers on the subject have echoed the early apologists of slavery in assuming that the health of plantation slaves can be positively correlated with the number of doctors and the amount of medicine used.[1] The motives of the slaveowners are usually acknowledged to have been economic calculation rather than disinterested philanthropy, but the facts that there were more 'doctors' in Jamaica in 1800 than in 1900, that nearly all plantations had their own practitioners, and that medicines featured largely in any list of imported plantation supplies, are taken as evidence that slaves were relatively well cared for. Without such care, it is assumed, slave health conditions would have been far worse; perhaps even as bad as those in the notorious 'graveyard' of the West African coast.[2]

More careful research, however, revises — even reverses — these views. Ignorance of the etiology of tropical diseases placed them largely beyond human control, and this situation was compounded by treatments based upon a purblind ignorance of human physiology, and an irrelevant pharmacopeia. Even at Worthy Park plantation in central Jamaica, which was serviced for 55 years by a doctor famous for his efficiency, slave medicine was a mixed blessing indeed.[3]

Under the Jamaican Consolidated Slave Law of 1792, not only were overseers to hand in to the vestries annual lists of births and deaths on their plantations on a penalty of £50 for non-compliance, but every plantation doctor was also 'on oath, to give-in an account of slaves dying, with, to the best of his judgement, the causes thereof, under penalty of £100 for each neglect'.[4]

Thus, for at least those estates for which records have survived, there exist cause-of-death diagnoses up to the standard attained by eighteenth-century plantation doctors. In addition, at Worthy Park, and some other estates the slave ledgers included, rather less systematically, comments on the health of slaves whose efficiency was impaired, and lists of medicines used. Besides this, Worthy Park's chief slave doctor, John Quier (1739-1822), published an account of seven years of his practice in the district.[5]

What follows is a table (Table 1) showing all the causes of death ascribed in the Worthy Park records between 1792 and 1838, applying to 401 slaves. Wherever possible, the slave doctor's diagnoses have been translated into modern terms, and grouped together into classes along the lines of the World Health Organisation[6] categories. Further on, the significance of the diagnoses given in the 'Condition' columns of the Worthy Park slave ledgers is also discussed, but the Condition listings are so much less systematic and conclusive — so much less final — than Causes of Death, that they cannot easily be tabulated.

The 401 specific causes of death from Worthy Park represent perhaps the largest sample it is now possible to recover from a single Jamaican estate. However, any such single source needs careful preliminary evaluation before its general value is established. The two chief deficiencies of the data are that they are not complete, and that they are derived from a population which

*Department of History, University of Waterloo.

Histoire Sociale — Social History, Vol. 9, No. 18 November (1976), pp. 237–55.

Table 1 Worthy Park: Incidence of Causes of Death Noted, 1783–1838 (Assigned by World Health Organisation Categories)

Worthy Park diagnoses	*Incidences*	*Modern diagnoses* (where different)	*W.H.O.*	*Categories*
Dysentery	10	Bacillary Dysentery	I	004
Flux	25	Diarrhoeal Disease		009
Phthisis Consumption	15	Tuberculosis		011
Coco Bays	2	Leprosy (Arabian)		030
Whooping Cough. Croup	4			033
Locked Jaw	2	Tetanus		037
Measles	5			055
Smallpox	2			056
Diseased Brain. Water on the Brain	2	Encephalitis		062
Yaws	24			102
Dirt Eating	9	Helminthiasis		127
Worms, Worm Fever	14	Internal parasites		129
Fever	26			
Palsy	3	Cerebral palsy	VI	343
Fits, Convulsions, Epilepsy	7	Epilepsy		345
Complaint in Spine	1	Spinal chord disease		349
Apoplexy, Stroke	2		VII	436
Elephantiasis	1			457
Violent Cold, Cough, Catarrh	11	Acute Common Cold	VIII	460
Influenza	2			470
Pneumonia	1			480
Asthma	4			493
Pleurisy	10			511
Abcess in Lungs	2			513
Rupture	3	Hernia	IX	551
Suppression of Menses	2	Menstrual disorder	X	626
Childbed	7			644
Puny from Birth, At Birth, Still Born	18		XI	677
Ulcers, Ulceration	14	Chronic skin ulcers	XIII	707
Spasms	1	Nervous system	XVI	780
Dropsy, 'Cold, Bloated & Dropsical'	38	Cardiovascular. lympathic		782
Lung Trouble, Sore Throat	3	Respiratory system		783
Stomach Complaint	1	Upper gastro-intestinal		784
Bloated, Swelled & Bloated, Inflammation of Bowels	4	Lower gastro-intestinal		785
Swelled Leg, Sore Foot	4	Limbs & joints		787
Old Age, Decline, Weakness, Informity, Invalid (where old)	89	Senility		794
Suddenly, In the Night, Sudden, Act of God, Vindication of God	7	Sudden Death (Unknown Cause)		795
Diseased Many Years, Infirmity, Invalid (not aged), Sick Some Time, Worthless, At Hospital in Kingston	7	Other sicknesses, unspecified		796
Accident	14		XVII	880
Ate Poison, Suicide by Poison	3	Suicide		950
Shot while Stealing	1	Legal Intervention		970
Suffocation	1			994
	401			

changed considerably during the 46 years covered, particularly in the gradual increase in the proportion of Creole (island-born), and thus fully 'seasoned' (acclimatised) slaves. It is likely that between 1792 and 1838 some 1,000 slaves actually died at Worthy Park, so that causes of death are specifically unknown for almost two-thirds. However, the nature of the records determines that these causes of death can be regarded as virtually a random sample, scattered evenly over the entire period and over the whole range of the population.

Causes of death data are deficient for two periods of exceptional mortality, following a large influx of new Africans in the 1790s, and the arrival of more than 100 new Creoles in 1830. This may have led to a slight understatement of the deaths by 'fever' and 'flux'. Yet these periods of exceptional mortality occurred in only about four of the 46 years covered. Were all causes of death in those years specifically known and recorded, this would surely have led to a severe distortion of the overall situation. Moreover, only a minority of Jamaican estates had comparable influxes of population in slavery's last years.

Another area of slight doubt was the degree to which causes of infant death were underrepresented. It is well known that infant mortality itself was commonly understated by plantation records, though not quite to the degree that some writers believe.[7] At Worthy Park, the number of those who were born and died during the intercensal periods and thus went unrecorded was probably no more than one in five overall. Over the period 1792–1838 just over 30 per cent of those born on the estate died in their first five years. Only about 20 per cent of the known causes of death related to deaths in this age range. But since about a third of Worthy Park's slaves were African-born and never were infants at Worthy Park it seems likely that causes of death were not under-represented at all.

It is a commonplace of plantation studies that new African slaves suffered far higher mortality rates and died from different diseases than seasoned Creoles. Yet it should be rememberd that by the beginning of the period covered an established plantation of 500 slaves would, on the average, receive only two or three new Africans a year, and that from the ending of the British slave trade in 1808 the flow dried up altogether. Accordingly, for Jamaica as a whole, and for most long-established estates, the proportion of Africans in the slave plantation declined from only about 50 per cent in 1792, to no more than 10 per cent in 1838. The Worthy Park figures were 42.1 per cent in 1784, soaring to 63.4 per cent in 1794, and then declining gradually to 37.9 per cent in 1813 and 9.6 per cent in 1838.[8]

If it is accepted then that the causes of death from Worthy Park for the last half century of slavery were more or less random and representative, it is worth stating here what were the average demographic characteristics of that plantation during that period, in respect of the sex ratio, age cohorts, mortality and fertility levels, and life expectancies.

Worthy Park was a typical Jamaican sugar plantation in most respects, though somewhat larger, further inland, and consequently even more self-contained than the average. How then did its pattern of death and disease compare with other types of settlement and other areas? Although comparable vital statistics were not obtainable, it has at least proved possible to compare the Worthy Park causes of death figures for 1792–1838 with the only previously published cause-of-death analysis for a West Indian slave population, derived from British Guiana, 1829–32, and with figures for the total population of heavily urbanised St. Catherine's Parish, Jamaica, between 1774 and 1778, including free whites, coloureds and black as well as slaves.[10]

In fact, when looking for comparisons with the Worthy Park causes of death, it was the data from St. Catherine's — a lowland area with some sugar plantations but heavily dominated by Spanish Town, the Jamaican capital — which were first employed. The contrasts between a tightly-knit but closed and rural population of slaves, and largely urbanised and geographically mobile population, including all races and classes, were immediately apparent. This was particularly so in the far greater incidence of death by 'fever' and the far smaller number of deaths by old age in Spanish Town and its environs. A tragically high proportion of those who died from fever in Spanish Town were members of the white army garrison who, during their period of acclimatisation, suffered from one of the highest mortality rates in the world.[11] The evidence for mortality among urban slaves is ambivalent,[12] but it is almost certain that the beneficial effects stemming from the fact that they were largely Creoles, and from rather better food and working conditions than on plantations, were offset by a vulnerability induced by slum crowding, poor sanitation, nearby swamps, and the chances of reinfection by transients, particularly in respect of

Table 2 Worthy Park: Average Population Pyramid, 1784–1813

Cohort	Ages	Numbers in each cohort	% of total in each cohort	Recorded deaths in each cohort	% dead in each cohort	Dead each year per 1,000 (av. mortality 39.37)	Annual death rate (per 1,000)	Probability of dying in cohort period	Dead in each cohort period of 10,000 at year 0	Survivors at end of each cohort period	Expectation of life at beginning of each cohort period
1	0– 4	488*	10.76	63**	14.26	5.61	52.14	.2607	2607	7393	27.4
2	5– 9	447	9.86	24	5.43	2.14	21.70	.1085	802	6591	31.2
3	10–14	393	8.64	17	3.85	1.52	17.59	.0879	579	6012	29.7
4	15–19	350	7.72	13	2.94	1.16	15.03	.0752	452	5560	27.3
5	20–24	459	10.12	55	12.44	4.90	48.42	.2421	1346	4214	24.3
6	25–29	451	9.95	28	6.33	2.49	25.03	.1252	528	3686	26.3
7	30–34	417	9.20	28	6.33	2.49	27.07	.1354	499	3187	24.7
8	35–39	335	7.39	26	5.88	2.31	31.26	.1563	498	2689	22.8
9	40–44	325	7.17	33	7.47	2.94	41.00	.2050	551	2138	20.6
10	45–49	205	4.52	27	6.11	2.41	53.32	.2666	570	1568	19.0
11	50–54	220	4.85	21	4.75	1.87	38.56	.1928	302	1266	18.2
12	55–59	181	3.99	17	3.85	1.52	38.10	.1905	241	1025	15.3
13	60–64	126	2.77	19	4.30	1.69	61.01	.3050	386	639	12.0
14	65–69	69	1.52	26	5.88	2.31	151.97	.7594	485	154	4.9
15	70+	70	1.54	45	10.18	4.01	—	1.0000	154	0	2.5
Totals		4535	100.00	442	100.00	39.37					

* 21 added for under-recording
** Increased by 50 per cent from 42 for under-recording

epidemics. All in all, the mortality rates in tropical towns were probably twice the average for whole colonies, and higher than for any plantations.[13]

Though largely explicable, the very great differences between the causes of death from Worthy Park and from St. Catherine's left the question of the typicality of Worthy Park as a sugar plantation up in the air. The discovery of the remarkable correlation between Worthy Park's figures and those for a far larger sample drawn from sugar plantations in a colony a thousand miles distant in a rather later period, was therefore very exciting. Many contemporary writers spoke of sugar plantations as if they were standard in every respect, and of the contrasts between different types of settlement and locations within the Caribbean. Some analysis has recently been made of differences in overall mortality figures.[14] But here for the first time was statistical evidence by specific causes of death. Moreover, from this it was clear that there were health characteristics common and peculiar to sugar plantations wherever they were found within the Caribbean region. These contrasted to a marked degree with West Indian towns, and probably differed to a lesser but significant degree from smaller, less intensively cultivated plantations growing staples other than sugar, in hillier areas, for which similar work remains to be undertaken.

In drawing up both cause-of-death tables there were many difficulties of classification. Too many of the alleged explanations of death from Worthy Park were non-specific or downright evasive. What, for example, is learned from 'Accident'? And what can be made of 'At Hospital in Kingston', 'Suddenly', 'In the Night', or 'A Vindication of God'? In a dismaying number of cases the doctor was describing — and presumably had been treating — symptoms rather than actual diseases. 'Convulsions' and gastro-intestinal complications were particularly difficult to identify, but even the common diagnoses of 'flux', 'fever', 'ulcers', and ''dropsy' proved troublesome. At first sight there also seemed to be a remarkably high number of different causes of death. However, discriminating reclassification — first along World Health Organisation lines and then, less scientifically, into the categories used for the British Guiana slaves — elicited a much clearer picture.

Despite the depredations of epidemics (not all of which were killers) and the decimation of the 'seasoning' process among new slaves, the chief single cause of death on sugar plantations was still old age — or at least debility among elderly adults. That over a fifth of the slaves lived long enough to die of what were regarded as natural causes surely runs counter to the impression given by *average* survival rates, which suggest a life expectancy at birth of less than 30 years for Creoles, and for newly-arrived Africans an average expectation of no more than a dozen more years.

Epidemics of measles, smallpox and yellow fever carried off numbers of plantation slaves in some years, but the dreaded 'fluxes' struck more regularly and killed even more overall. Known

Table 3 Comparative Causes of Death: Worthy Park, 1792–1838: British Guiana, 1829–32; St. Catherine's (Spanish town), 1774–78[15]

	Worthy Park slaves 1795–1838	British Guiana slaves 1829–32	St. Catherine's (Spanish Town) 1774–78
Old Age, Debility	22.2	19.1	3.6
Dysentery, Flux	8.7	12.0	9.3
Dropsy	9.5	9.2	3.4
Pulmonary Diseases	11.4	9.2	5.7
Fevers (inc. Measles, Smallpox)	9.2	8.1	39.9
Yaws, Ulcers	9.5	6.1	6.1
Inflammations, etc.	2.0	4.4	3.8
Gastro-Intestinal	6.0	4.3	3.8
Accidents	4.3	4.2	1.6
Leprosy	0.5	3.8	—
Convulsions	3.8	3.7	6.3
Lockjaw	0.5	2.6	0.8
Syphilis	—	1.0	1.1
Others & Unknown	12.4	12.3	14.6
Totals	100.0	100.0	100.0

by their symptoms either as the 'white' or 'bloody' flux, these were nearly all varieties of bacillary dysentry, particularly infection by the protozoa *shigella shigae*. Bacillary dysentery could kill quickly by dehydration and poisoning by bacterial toxins. Amoebic dysentery was probably less common, and where fatal was not always identified as a flux, killing more slowly by chronic infection and secondary ulcerations in intestines, liver or lungs.

Plantation deaths from 'inflammation' and 'mortification' were rather less common than might be expected. On the other hand, intestinal and subcutaneous parasites were extremely common, and it was not the most evident types — such as the nauseating tape and guinea worms — which were necessarily the most dangerous. The tiny hookworm in particular was a far more serious and widespread cause of ill health, debility and death than was recognised by contemporary doctors. The larvae of these creatures were picked up by bare feet, causing what was known as 'ground itch' between the toes. Shedding their skin and burrowing, the larvae travelled through the bloodstream to the lymph glands or lungs, where they caused a cough. Migrating to the mouth, they were ingested, finding a home in the intestines, where they came to maturity. Still only about a centimetre long, hookworms, if undisturbed, could live in their host for seven or even ten years. Females in season laid thousands of eggs a day which, deposited in faeces, restarted the cycle.

Where colonies of over 500 hookworms developed, ancyclostomiasis, or hookworm disease, resulted. This was characterised by symptoms often regarded as separate diseases: flux-like emissions, fluid retention ('dropsy'), convulsions, and the mysterious craving to eat strange substances, particularly clay ('dirt eating').[16] Besides this, non-fatal ancyclostomiasis could stunt growth and delay puberty, and caused chronic anaemia, which brought on the fatigue, dullness and apathy which were often regarded as natural African traits.

Dysentery and intestinal parasites were promoted by unhygienic overcrowding, especially where drinking water, earth closets and cooking facilities were in close proximity, and lack of washing water made personal cleanliness difficult. In these respects, Worthy Park, with good running water from an aqueduct, was rather more fortunate than some estates and most of the crowded 'yards' of the Jamaican towns. This may have been the reason why the recorded cases of tetanus, or lockjaw, in infants — normally contracted through umbilical infection in unhygienic conditions, and invariably fatal — were fewer at Worthy Park than elsewhere. Another reason, though, might have been that the doctor was less ready than other plantation doctors to diagnose lockjaw as a cause of death.[17]

At least two fevers which were later recognised as tropical scourges, the food and water-borne typhoid, and the louse, flea and mite-borne typhus, were also encouraged by unhygienic conditions such as were found in West Indian plantations and towns. Unfortunately, certain identification of these fevers in the West Indies during slavery days is now impossible. However, if they did occur, typhoid was probably more common in the towns than on rural plantations, and of the three main types of typhus, scrub typhus, carried by ticks and chiggers and characterised by dropsy-causing myocarditis, was that most likely to have occurred on plantations. Cholera was apparently not known in the West Indies until after British slavery ended, though there were disastrous outbreaks later. Diphtheria, if it existed, was not recognised during slavery days.

Of the endemic fevers, detectable in the records, malaria ('ague') and dengue were widespread, but the chief killer was probably yellow fever. This disease, so-called for the jaundicing that followed from liver infection, was technically endemic, but went through epidemic phases as different strains of virus went the rounds. Doctors correctly associated fevers with marshes, but erroneously attributed infection to 'miasmas' rising from them at night, rather than to the *anopheles and aedes aegypti* mosquitoes that bred in them and carried the viruses. Slaves did what they could to repel mosquitoes by sleeping with permanently smoking fires nearby, but this was to reduce the nuisance rather than through a perception of danger. It was the immunisation process of the passage of time rather than such preventative measures which brought about the gradual decline in deaths from fevers. Many slaves indeed were already less likely to suffer from certain types of disease notoriously fatal to Europeans in the tropics. Most types of malaria and yellow fever were African in origin, and African slaves at least had inbuilt immunities. Sleeping sickness (trypanosomiasis), however, was only known among the African-born, since the infection was carried by the tsetse fly, which never migrated from Central Africa to the West Indies.

Rather more common killers than fever on plantations, even among acclimatised slaves, were the many varieties of pulmonary infection

Worthy Park: Average Population Pyramid, 1784–1813

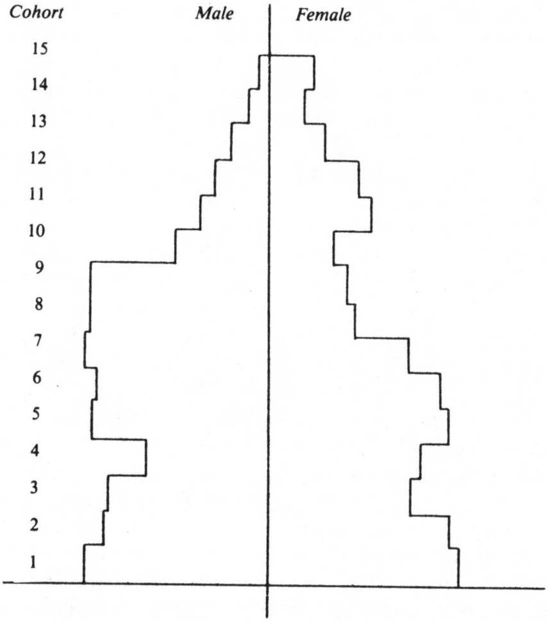

Cohort	Ages	Totals in cohorts	Males	Females	% in cohort of total	% males in cohort of total	% females in cohort of total
1	0– 4	488	242	247	10.76	5.32	5.45
2	5– 9	447	215	232	9.86	4.74	5.12
3	10–14	392	208	184	8.64	4.59	4.05
4	15–19	350	158	192	7.71	3.48	4.24
5	20–24	459	230	229	10.12	5.07	5.05
6	25–29	451	225	226	9.95	4.96	4.99
7	30–34	417	236	181	9.20	5.20	4.00
8	35–39	335	230	105	7.39	5.07	2.32
9	40–44	325	227	98	7.17	5.01	2.16
10	45–49	205	123	82	4.52	2.71	1.81
11	50–54	220	89	131	4.85	1.96	2.89
12	55–59	181	68	113	3.99	1.50	2.49
13	60–64	126	50	76	2.77	1.10	1.67
14	65–69	69	27	42	1.52	0.60	0.92
15	70 +	70	11	59	1.54	0.24	1.30
Totals		4535	2338	2197	100.00	51.55	48.45

imported from Europe. In these cases, resistance was low through lack of immunisation, but also was sapped by overcrowding, overwork and deficient diet. Influenza could kill directly, but even the common cold could accelerate into fatal pneumonia, or a cough or 'catarrh' degenerate into 'galloping consumption'. Whooping cough, though not common, could be fatal to slave children. Diet and vitamin deficiencies also contributed to the high incidence of dropsy, a diagnosis applied to any swelling thought to be caused by an excess of one of the bodily fluids.

Yet dropsies were at least as common among the whites as among blacks in Jamaica, with liver, heart and urinary conditions often exacerbated by excessive drinking. Though some writers deplored the intemperance of town slaves, few slaves in fact had opportunities for such over-indulgence. This probably also explains why they so rarely suffered from the gout, or the myterious 'dry belly-ache' so common among Jamaican whites, now known to have been lead poisoning due to drinking rum distilled in vessels made of lead, and drink from pewter pots.

Some 'dropsies' and 'ulcers' among slaves were symptoms of horrifying diseases originally imported from Africa which remained endemic among blacks, though whites were seemingly immune; elephantiasis, 'coco bays' (alias 'Arabian leprosy'), scrofula, true leprosy, and yaws. Of these, yaws, a highly contagious but non-venereal variant of syphilis, was especially virulent. Often contracted in childhood, it was characterised first by raspberry-like eruptions, then by scarring and ulceration, and, with the prolonged tertiary stages, often by excruciating 'bone-ache' and damage to cartilages, spleen and brain. Many sufferers died of old age or general debility rather than of yaws itself, but the disease progressively sapped energy and will, as well as making the victims pathetically unsightly. On some Jamaican estates about a sixth of the slaves, at any one time, suffered seriously from yaws, and there was a separate 'yaws hothouse', or isolation hospital, where the worst cases withered away.[18] At Worthy Park, however, the disease was rather less serious and a second hothouse was not considered necessary.

From the death diagnoses, true venereal disease seems to have been relatively uncommon at Worthy Park and elsewhere, though the effects of yaws were often indistinguishable from those of syphilis, and gonorrhea may have been so common as to be considered unworthy of notice.[19] Certain other diseases which afflict modern society, such as heart disease, stomach ulcers and cancers, were noticeably rare on slave plantations, either because the slaves did not have the opportunities to contract them, or did not live long enough to develop the symptoms. With the possible exception of the single slave 'shot while stealing', no deaths recorded at Worthy Park were directly attributable to the slave condition. Deaths by accident were no more common than one would expect in any industrial situation with minimal safeguards; and suicides (of whom only three were certainly recorded) were probably no more common than in the British army during National Service, or among undergraduates at a modern university.

The data derived from the Condition listings at Worthy Park are not only more fragmentary and capricious than those for Causes of Death; for several reasons they also seriously understate the low level of general health on the plantation. Even for the years for which full records survive, the health of individual slaves was only noted if their condition incapacitated them. For example, there is no reference at all in the Worthy Park records to eye diseases, though it is unlikely that the plantation was entirely free from all forms of opthalmia common among slaves elsewhere. Short-term or non-fatal illnesses such as colds and malaria were rarely recorded either. Cases of measles and smallpox which did not kill, however, sometimes were; for though immunisation theory was not yet developed, it was already recognised that these diseases rarely recurred.

Many other diseases were too common for diagnosis, not diagnosed in their early stages, or not recognised at all. From the incidence of death from yaws, 'coco bays', scrofula and 'dropsy', it seems likely that at least a third of the slaves suffered from diseases of the skin and tissues at some time during their lives, and perhaps half from serious internal disorders. In most cases these diseases were incurable and progressive, though not invariably fatal in themselves. If the debilitating effects of deficient diet and parasites less crippling than hookworm are included, nearly all slaves were subject to tropical ailments which lowered their efficiency, their fertility and enjoyment of life.

In sum, though seasoned slaves on established sugar plantations were not more subject to fatality than most persons in the tropics — and much less so than those living in towns in the lowlands — the general level of their health was dismally low.

Masters and doctors alike were disposed by

their 'interest' and ignorance to minimise slave ailments. Owners and overseers were determined to keep all but the dying at work, and to trim the costs of medical treatment. To their eyes, a successsful doctor was one who satisfied these requirements. Paid a *per capita* fee, plantation doctors were rewarded positively for cursory treatment, and encouraged to ignore failure and simulate success. Faced with a level of general health that condemned the plantation system by which they lived, or was beyond their care or ken, doctors tended to disguise the inadequacy of the treatments and the ignorance of their diagnoses with accusations of malingering, self-inflicted injury and 'natural' unhealthiness stemming from the slaves' racial origins. In this they perpetuated the malign ignorance of Dr John Trapham, who in 1679 attributed the high incidence of yaws among blacks to the alleged fact that they were an 'animal people', subject to an 'unhappy jumble of the rational with the brutal Nature',[20] or even the distasteful fatalism of a slave trader in 1694:

> [...] What the small-pox spar'd, the flux swept off to our great regret, after all our pains and care to give their messes in due order and season, keeping their lodgings as clean and sweet as possible, and enduring so much misery and stench so long among a parcel of creatures nastier than swine: and after all our expectations to be defeated by their mortality.[21]

The medical profession, like all self-legislating and self-perpetuating 'misteries', has always been a conservatising force. What particularly bedevilled eighteenth- and even nineteenth-century medicine were the persistence of the fallacy of the four 'humours' in the teeth of the clinical evidence, and the tradition that devalued surgery in favour of 'physic'. When Dr Trapham wrote his *Discourse on the State of Health in Jamaica* in 1679, belief in humoral theory was still absolute. Every human ailment, from hookworm to cancer, was said to be due to an excess of one of the four vital fluids which flowed from liver to heart: melancholy, phlegm, blood, choler — the counterparts of earth, water, air and fire. The sole purpose of medicine, it was held, was to keep the elements in balance, the chief methods being blood-letting, 'salivation', blistering and purging. Physicians were neither willing nor able to use the surgeon's knife, save in emergencies such as amputations.

Besides this, doctors made undiscriminate use of at least two dangerous specifics: mercury and opium. The first, beloved of alchemists as 'quicksilver', had some success with 'the pox', but produced crippling side-effects which until recent times were thought to be symptoms of the disease it purported to cure.[22] The second quelled pain but was demoralisingly addictive, including withdrawal symptoms after very little use. That both mercurials and opiates were relatively expensive may have been positively beneficial to such dependent patients as slaves. The herbal remedies preferred for cheapness's sake were, where ineffectual, generally harmless. It might be argued that in the absence of antiseptics and anaesthetics the reluctance of doctors to operate was also to the slaves' advantage.[23]

What medical progress was made during the slavery period was not due to any revolution in theory or dramatic new methods (save inoculation for smallpox), but a slightly more empirical attitude, a greater attention to the individual patient, and the first glimmerings of a belief in cleanliness, rest and restorative diet. In these respects, the pioneers were the English Thomas Sydenham (1624–89) and the Dutch clinicians such as Hermann Boerhaave of Leyden (1688–1738).[24] Hans Sloane, a disciple of Sydenham, displayed a comparatively open mind and a willingness to experiment (honestly recording failures as well as successes) in the descriptions he published of the many cases he treated during his brief stay in Jamaica (1688–89).[25] But neither Sloane nor his eighteenth-century successors made any systematic discoveries concerning causes or cures. At best they simply learned, through bitter experience, that a West Indian doctor was more likely to succeed the less he applied the 'scientific' humoral theory and the pharmacy he had learned in the European schools.

This gradual awareness can be well illustrated by the career of Dr John Quier, graduate of Leyden and London, who was Worthy Park's doctor from 1767 to 1822, from six published letters written to a former colleague during Quier's first years in Jamaica,[26] and from his later practice. From the letters it seems that Quier was not obsessed by humoral theory, but still placed too great an emphasis upon bodily fluids and the efficacy of 'cleansing the blood'. From the descriptions of some of his early treatments it seems that his patients might well have stood a better chance with no treatment at all. For the eye disease he called 'the dry opthalmies', for example, he specified a copious bleeding, 'antiphlogistic' purges, a 'cooling regimen' with nitre, and blisters behind the ears and on the side of the neck, as well as the 'emollient poultices' which alone might have brought any relief.

What caused Dr Quier most concern were smallpox and measles, serious outbreaks of which occurred in Lluidas Vale during his first few years there. Indeed, he has been given credit, almost certainly exaggerated, for advances in the prevention and diagnosis of these diseases.[27] Although distinguishing clearly between smallpox and measles, he attributed quite distinct afflictions such as dysentery, dry bellyache and even tetanus as 'secondary manifestations' of them. In these respects, only in being able to diagnose whooping cough was Dr Quier farther advanced than the Persian medical authority Rhazes (AD 860–932) who, while being the earliest correctly to identify smallpox and measles, was apparently not aware of any other endemic diseases.[28]

At least John Quier differed from the majority of his fellow slave doctors in learning somewhat from his failures. At first he believed that excessive heat made the blood 'putrescent', and he tended to let blood by venesection at the onset of any fever. He also administered savage purgatives such as the mercuric calomel, nitre, or jalap, in almost all cases of serious illness. When in some measles cases these led not to a 'salutary salivation' and gentle evacuation, but to bloody vomiting and diarrhoea, he bled the patients more, applying blisters to the thighs. If the internal spasm and pains became too severe, he administered — literally almost as a last resort — heroic doses, up to four grains a day, of opium.

Although he never admitted that it was the medicine rather than the disease which was killing his patients, John Quier soon realised that excessive purging and bleeding weakened them, and gradually relented. Ironically, strong 'medicine' became reserved for those unfortunates whom the well-intentioned doctor regarded as strong enough to stand them. In the cases of the very old or young, the seriously undernourished and 'naturally' debilitated, nature was 'allowed to take its course', and some patients' clearly gained a fortuitous reprieve. In the eighteenth century it was medicine as often as death itself which acted as a great leveller.

As to inoculation for smallpox, John Quier was certainly no innovator. The technique of inoculation had been introduced into England from Turkey by Lady Mary Wortley Montagu as early as 1717, and there is some evidence that some form of 'variolation', or intentional inoculative infection with the disease, was known in West Africa.[29] Quier himself acknowledged that he used the method developed by Thomas, Baron Dimsdale, consultant to Catherine the Great — infecting those who had not yet had the disease through a scratch on the arm, with matter drawn from smallpox pustules. Although effective in most individual cases — inducing only a mild form of the disease — it did not avert or check the general spread of smallpox, and could lead to serious cases and death. There is no evidence that John Quier or any slave doctor in Jamaica adopted the much more satisfactory system of vaccination by cowpox matter introduced by Edward Jenner, even when it gained widespread acceptance in England after 1800.

John Quier's method was to wait until a smallpox outbreak threatened, and then to inoculate large numbers of slaves together. In 1768 he treated over 700 slaves, receiving a flat fee of 6s. 8d. a head. As with his treatments, at first Quier's methods were almost indiscriminate. Yet experience and empirical observation taught him that it was pointless to 'inoculate' those who already had the disease, and dangerous to infect the young, the old, weakly, those far gone in pregnancy, and anyone he classified as having 'putrid blood'. By exercising such discrimination Quier diminished his income at first; but as his reputation for success grew, the call upon his services increased.

Success for all West Indian doctors indeed came with moderation and common sense. A wise and humane doctor, such as John Quier clearly became, was one who realised that since his medication could rarely cure, and no doctor could — or ought to — persuade planters to improve slave conditions in general, he should concentrate on ameliorating symptoms and, by providing care, cleanliness, fresh air and decent food, encourage any natural tendency towards a cure, as well as the will to survive. Harsh medicine was simply for the peace of mind of those who paid, and those patients strong enough to take it who believed in it.

Thus, while he continued to pay lip service to the crude, irrelevant, and harmful mysteries of his craft such as bleeding, blistering and purging, John Quier more often came to prescribe strengthening diets, emolients, cooling lotions and analgesics such as the opiate laudanum. It was also during his regime that the slave 'hothouse' still standing at Worthy Park was built, as on many Jamaican properties one of the most substantial buildings erected. For women in childbirth, John Quier recommended that they be allowed to 'lie in' at least two weeks. Observing that the blacks who worked in the stillhouse (distillery) were the fattest on the estate, he recommended that infants be drafted there to fatten up. Although Dr Quier disapproved of the African customs of swaddling newborn infants and suckling children into their second year, there is at least one scrap of evidence that he came to place as much credence in 'African' medicine as in his own received pharmacy. Noticing that his black slave 'doctoress' assistant was in the habit of bathing the swollen feet of yaws sufferers in urine he did not tell her to desist, and honesty compelled him to admit that the patients came to no further harm.

To modern eyes, the wisest section of Dr John Quier's letters from Jamaica concerns a regimen for maintaining general health in a tropical climate. It could serve as a model in most respects even today: choose a dry, healthy location; practise temperance, drinking a little wine but selecting a diet more vegetable than animal, including fresh fruit; rise early, take a moderate amount of exercise, and avoid the night-time damp; bathe frequently, and change clothing according to the time of day and season; maintain a cheerful disposition. Unfortunately, however, these excellent suggestions (which John Quier perhaps followed himself, for he lived to 83) were absolutely irrelevant to the lives of slaves. As Hans Sloane had found long before, they were also almost reversed by the habits of most of the Jamaican whites.

From the Worthy Park evidence for 1792–1838 it is clear that the level of health on slave plantations was low. Yet the situation should not be exaggerated. Disease alone did not account for the continuing natural decrease in the population, which was also influenced by purely demographic characteristics.[30] If sugar plantations, with their large cramped populations and intensive agriculture, were less healthy than mountain pens and coffee plantations, estates like Worthy Park in spacious highland areas were healthier than those in the swampy lowlands of St. Catherine, St. Thomas-in-the-East, St. Mary, or St. James; and all were far less disease-ridden than the kennels and yards of Spanish Town, Kingston and the other ports, the ships on the Middle Passage, and the barracoons of the African coast.[31] Besides this, the health situation which the Worthy Park records for 1792–1838 disclosed was almost certainly better than that which obtained in the plantation's earlier days — though the improvement, like that in the population's demographic balance, was largely beyond the understanding or control of planters, doctors and 'amelioration' laws.

The 'triangle trade' of trade goods, slaves and sugar made the West Indies a crossroads for the diseases of Europe, Africa and tropical America. Until immunities built up over the years, newcomers were infected by unfamiliar strains of virus, germ and parasite. This well-documented but unexplained phenomenon accounted for perhaps half of all African slaves between the time of their original seizure and the conclusion of the seasoning process on a West Indian plantation four years later. It likewise killed almost as high a ratio of all whites newly arriving in the sugar islands, and an even higher proportion of white crewmen on the slave ships, or white soldiers cramped and ill-fed in barracks in the West Indies and West Africa.[32]

Owing to the fallacies of humoral theory, medical treatment for diseases was totally inadequate: never curative, at best palliative or innocuous, at worst positively baneful. The greatest improvement came fortuitously, with the process of creolisation. The increasingly closed nature of the plantation population made it a closed disease environment, rather less subject to attack from passing epidemics than towns or villages.

What remained, however, was serious enough; the general debility from ailments associated with unhygienic conditions, poor diet and overwork. Here, it might be argued, 'amelioration' legislation, such as was passed in all British West Indian colonies from about 1787, and particularly after 1823, should have improved health conditions, by regulating the workload, and establishing standards of food, clothing and medical care.[33] Yet these regulations were minimal, reflecting standards rather than improving them, often a form of 'window-dressing'. Medical treatment was effectively beyond the control of legislation. Besides this, towards the very end of slavery the effects of any improvements were offset by the decline in plantation profits, which made masters inclined to work their slaves harder and spend less on their upkeep and care. If slaves towards the end of formal slavery were able to grow more food, to expand their homes, and to improve their clothing, this was mainly through their own efforts. It might also be argued that there was an ironic virtue in necessity, since the decline in expenditure on slave medicine may have been actually beneficial to health.

Notes

1. Not excluding Michael Craton, *Sinews of Empire: A Short History of British Slavery* (New York and London, 1974), 192–94. The ideas in this paper largely stemmed from remarks concerning the dubious benefits of European medicine practised in West Africa, made by Philip D. Curtin while commenting on a paper on West Indian slave-doctors by Richard B. Sheridan at the M.S.S.B. comparative slavery conference at Rochester, New York, in March 1972. Curtin's own article, 'Epidemiology and the Slave Trade'. *Political Science Quarterly*, LXXXIII (June 1968), 2: 190–216, was the pioneer work on this subject. See also Richard H. Shyrock, 'Medical Practice in the Old South', *South Atlantic Quarterly*, XXIX (April 1930) 2, reprinted in *Medicine in America: Historical Essays* (Baltimore, 1966), 49–70. Much of the material here is to be included in a chapter in a forthcoming study of slaves, slave society and ex-slaves, *Searching for the Invisible Man* (Harvard, 1976).
2. For an analysis of the mortality in West Africa, mainly white, which shaped European views, see K. G. Davies, 'The Living and the Dead: White Mortality in West Africa, 1684–1732', in S. Engerman and E. Genovese (eds), *Race and Slavery in the Western Hemisphere; Quantitative Studies* (Princeton, 1975).
3. Hans Sloane's strictures against black doctors (1707) could indeed be turned by modern commentators against such white practitioners as Sloane himself: '[. . .] There are many such *Indian* and Black Doctors, who pretend, and are supposed to understand, and cure several Distempers, but what I could see of their practice [. . .] they do not perform what they pretend, unless in the vertues of some few Simples. Their ignorance of Anatomy, Diseases, Method, &c. renders even that knowledge of the vertues of Herbs, not only useless, but even sometimes hurtful to those who employ them [. . .].' *A Voyage to Madera . . . and Jamaica*, 2 vols (London, 1707, 1725), I, cxli.
4. Jamaican Act of 32 George III, c. xxiii, 33–5.
5. J. Quier, J. Hume *et. atl.*, *Letters and Essays on the Smallpox* (London, 1778).
6. *Manual of the International Statistical Classification of Diseases, Injuries, and Causes of Death, Based on the Recommendations of the Eighth Revision of Conference, 1965, and Adopted by the Nineteenth World Health Assembly*, 2 vols (Geneva: World Health Organisation, 1967).
7. For example, by George W. Roberts, *The Population of Jamaica* (Cambridge, England, 1957), 165–75. Roberts, however, does not prove his contention; he asserts it, substituting figures for a later period of the worst known infant mortality (the 1890s), on the assumption that slavery must have been as bad, or worse.
8. Michael Craton, 'Jamaican Slave Mortality: Fresh Light from Worthy Park. Longville and the Tharp Estates', *Journal of Caribbean History* (November 1971): 1–27. The percentage of Africans at Worthy Park actually rose steeply in 1792 itself because of the influx of over 200 new Africans. It was 45.7 per cent in 1791 and 60.3 per cent in 1793.
9. These tables are all taken from *Searching for the Invisible Man* (*op. cit.*), Chapter III.
10. The British Guiana data are cited in Roberts, *op. cit.*, 175. The St. Catherine's data are derived from Jamaica, Island Record Office, *St. Catherine's Copy Register, Causes of Death*. Vol. I. There is a list of death causes in Edward Braithwaite, *The Development of Creole Society in Jamaica* (Oxford, 1971), but since these refer to the deaths of soldiers in the military hospital, it is not comparable. Barry Higman, 'Slave Population and Economy in Jamaica at the Time of Emancipation' (unpublished Ph.D. thesis, UWI, 1971) also has a cause of death table for parts of Jamaica in the Registration period (1817–29). This suggests close parallels, but cannot be correlated with those given here because of the smallness of the sample (125) and the differing categories. Between 1817 and 1836 the average annual mortality for white troops stationed in Jamaica was 121.3 per 1,000, of whom 101.9 died from fevers. This compared with total figures for black troops of 30 per 1,000 (fevers 8.7). The comparable figures for the Windwards and Leewards station were 78.5 per 1,000 for white troops (fevers, 36.9), and 40 (fevers, 7.1) for black troops. Roberts, 165–72, quoting Tulloch and Marshall.
12. Barry Higman believes that 'race/geographic' origin was more important than rural/urban dichotomy, and that 'urban' slaves were healthier than plantation slaves. However, his definition of 'urban' includes concentrations no larger than a hamlet, as well as the few true Jamaican towns; Kingston, Port Royal, Spanish Town, Montego Bay.
13. As late as 1851, the annual mortality rate in New Orleans was 81 per 1,000, three times as high as contemporary rates in London, New York and Philadelphia. The rate for Jamaica as a whole in the last decades of slavery was about 35 per 1,000, compared with the 1792–1838 average for Worthy Park of 40 per cent.
14. For example, Higman, *op. cit.*
15. Basic categories from British Guiana slave data; Roberts, *Population of Jamaica*, 175. Data for St. Catherine's from Jamaica, Island Record Office, *St. Catherine's Copy Register, Causes of Death*, Vol. 1. Total sample of 472 made up and allocated as follows: Old Age, Debility — 'Old Age', 17; Dysentery, Flux — 'Putrid Fever', 40; 'Flux', 4; Dropsy — 'Dropsy', 16; Pulmonary Diseases — 'Consumption', 25; 'Pleurisy', 2: Fevers (inc. Measles, Smallpox) — 'Fever', 159, 'Fever and Worms', 4, 'Nervous Fever', 2, 'Smallpox', 21, 'Spotted Fever', 1, 'Putrid Sore Throat', 1; Yaws, Ulcers — 'Decayed', 28, 'Sore Leg', 1; Inflammations, etc. — 'Swelling', 1; 'Gout', 9, 'Schirrous Liver', 1, 'Gout in Stomach', 2, 'Bilious Fever', 5, 'Bellyache', 2, 'Swollen Liver', 1, 'Gravel', 1, 'Obstruction', 1; Accidents — 'Accident', 2, 'Murdered', 2, 'A Fall', 3; Convulsions — 'Fits', 26, 'Convulsions', 3, 'Palsy', 1; Lockjaw — 'Lockjaw', 4; Syphilis — 'Sores & Ill Habits', 5; Others and Unknown — 'Unknown', 28, 'Not stated' 7, 'Infancy', 1, 'Childbirth', 6, 'Rheumatism', 1, 'Surfeit, 1, 'Mortification', 1, 'Apoplexy', 3, 'Teething', 1, 'Suspicious', 2, 'Suddenly', 7, 'Hystericks & Broken Hearted', 2, 'Hanged' (for forgery), 1, 'Insobriety', 4, 'Cancer', 1, 'Want', 1. In these St. Catherine's diagnoses 'Decay' might well be a synonym for the 'Debility' used in British Guiana. 'Putrid Fever' may well be a synonym for the 'Flux'. The incidence of fever was disastrously high among the garrison. The two victims of Bellyache were both planters. Some of those listed with convulsions may well have suffered from worms. Leprosy (like Venereal Disease) was probably not specifically diagnosed for social reasons. A high proportion of the population of St. Catherine's was white, coloured and free, though persons were not invariably identified by race or status in the Register.
16. For contemporary views on 'dirt-eating' see Thomas Dancer, *The Medical Assistant: or Jamaican Practice of Physic* [. . .] (Kingston, Jamaica, 1801); James

Thompson, *A Treatise on the Diseases of Negroes as they occur in the Island of Jamaica* (Kingston, Jamaica, 1820), 24, 32: James Stewart, *A View of the Past and Present State of the Island of Jamaica* (Edinburgh, 1823), 307. Some modern commentators have suggested a connection between dirt-eating and the deficiency disease beriberi; Shyrock, 'Old South', 50.

17. In his report to a committee of the Jamaican House of Assembly in 1788, Dr. Quier was reported as saying: 'That he has not in general observed any very great Mortality amongst the Negro Infants, soon after their Birth, in that part of the Country where he practises, nor any peculiar Disease to which they are more subject, than any other Children would be under the same Circumstances [. . .]. That in his Opinion, difficult Labours happen as frequently amongst Negro Women here as amongst the Females of the Labouring Poor in England; but that he has not observed a greater proportion of the Infants of the former perish in the Delivery than of the latter; that he does not conceive the Tetanus or Locked Jaw to be a disease common to Infants in the part where he practices; that he apprehends there may be a reason to suppose that a Symptom which generally attends approaching Death, from whatever Cause it may proceed, in Children vizt. a Paralysis of the Muscle of the Lower Jaw, has been frequently mistaken by People unacquainted with Medicine, for the Tetanus, as he has often observed the same name to be given in common discourse to both those Afflictions though of so very different a Nature [. . .].' *Report of the Assembly on the Slave Issues*, enclosed in Lt. Gov. Clark's No. 92, 20 November 1788, London Public Record Office, *C.O. 137/88*.

    Relative to the common belief that many slave infants died of tetanus before they reached the age of nine days it is worth pointing out both that tetanus is rarely fatal in less than two weeks, and also that slave mothers probably regarded the killing of an ailing infant less than nine days old as abortion, not infanticide, since the humanising spirit was believed to be acquired after the ninth day. For tetanus, see also, Edward Long, *The History of Jamaica*, 3 vols (London, 1774), III, 713: Dancer, *op. cit.*, 269.

18 At Braco Estate, Trelawny, for example, there were an average of 68 slaves 'In the Hothouse, in Yaws house with sores. Pregnant, lying in & attendants' in June 1796, out of a population of 402; *Braco Slave Book, April 1795–December 1797* (Braco: Trelawny).

19. Modern Worthy Park offers an illuminating parallel. When the Sugar Industry Labour Welfare Board clinic was set up on the estate in 1951, the doctor was called upon to treat no less than 331 cases of yaws and 250 of syphilis, but only 28 gonorrhea. In a comparatively short time yaws and syphilis were contained, but the cases of gonorrhea treated multiplied to hundreds. Such is progress. Michael Craton and James Walvin, *A Jamaican Plantation: The History of Jamaica, 1670–1970* (London: W. H. Allen, and Toronto, 1970), 308. That gonorrhea was in fact common among the Worthy Park slaves, at least around 1824, is suggested by the purchase by the estate of six penis syringes included in the list of medicines and equipment appended.

20. Thomas Trapham, *A Discourse on the State of Health in the Island of Jamaica* (London: Boulter, 1679), *passim*. The equating of black slaves with animals by a plantation doctor immediately brings to mind a parallel between slave and veterinary medicine. If planters and their doctors regarded slaves as little more than valuable animals, it is not surprising that slave medicine was little better than 'horse doctor cures'. Veterinary science — probably because the treatment of animals has been required to remain cheap, and animal doctors are even less regarded as colleagues by MBs and MDs than once they were — has made comparatively far less progress than medicine for humans. For example, horses are still poulticed, blistered and cauterised, much like eighteenth-century slaves.

21. Elizabeth Donnan, *Documents Illustrative of the History of the Slave Trade to America*, 4 vols (Washington, 1930–31), I, 410.

22. The miners of quicksilver at Almadén in Spain, the Japanese of Minimata who ate mercury-poisoned fish, and the thousands of Iraquis who ate mercury-dusted seed grain, were alike found to be suffering from *locomotor ataxia* and other manifestations thought to be classic symptoms of tertiary syphilis. It would be instructive to discover how often *locomotor ataxia* and the other symptoms occurred in persons with syphilis before they were treated with mercurials.

23. It was not long since surgery had been entirely in the hands of barbers. Readers of Samuel Pepys' diaries will recall with what trepidation Pepys submitted to surgery for the stone, and his gratitude to the Almighty for allowing him to survive what was technically a very simple operation. In Pepys' case the 'miracle' was almost certainly that the surgeon used a brand new knife. Until the days of Lister, deaths from appendicitis were far more common among those operated on than those with whom nature was allowed to take its course.

24. Douglas Guthrie, *A History of Medicine* (London, revised edn, 1958), 216–31.

25. Hans Sloane, *A Voyage to . . . Jamaica*, I, *passim*. This work was not published until 1707, 18 years after Sloane's sojourn in Jamaica as physician to his kinsman. Governor Albermarle.

26. Quier *et. al.*, *Letters and Essays on the Smallpox*. The letters, dating from 1769 to 1776, were addressed to Dr. Donald Munro of London, a member of the famous Edinburgh medical clan of that name.

27. Heinz Goerke, 'The Life and Scientific Works of Dr. John Quier, Practitioner of Physic and Surgery, Jamaica, 1738–1822', *West Indian Medical Journal*, V, xviii, 22–27.

28. Guthrie, *op. cit.*, 89.

29. Cotton Mather, who promoted inoculation in Boston in 1721, wrote to a fellow member of the Royal Society in London in 1716 that he had heard of variolation from one of his own slaves, a 'Guaramantee' fittingly named Onesimus; Frederick C. Kalgan, 'The Rise of Scientific Activity in Colonial New England', *Yale Journal of Biology and Medicine*, XXII (December 1949), 130.

30. This argument is developed in Craton, 'Jamaican Slave Mortality' (1971); *Sinews of Empire*, 194–99; 'Jamaican Slavery' (1974).

31. The mortality of the slaves on the Middle Passage was probably about 20 per cent per voyage on the average at the beginning of the eighteenth century, and just about 15 per cent by the end of the century. This represented an annual rate of nearly double these figures, since voyages averaged only about six months. These rates of 300–400 per 1,000 per year were probably equalled among the slaves from the time of their capture until the time of shipment: Craton, *Sinews of Empire*, 96–98.

32. The annual rate among white troops stationed in Jamaica of 121.3 deaths per 1,000, though the second highest in the world, was made to seem quite moderate by the West African figures. As late as 1823–6, the death rate for British troops stationed in Sierra Leone was 483 per 1,000, and for the Gold Coast, 668 per 1,000. In the

slave trade, 20–25 per cent of all white crewmen died on each round trip, which averaged about a year, in the 1780s, compared with less than 3 per cent on ships sailing simply between England and the West Indies. Roberts, *Population of Jamaica*, 167; Davies, 'The Living and the Dead': Craton, *Sinews of Empire*, 97.

33. See, for example, Elsa Goveia, *Slave Society in the British Leeward Islands at the End of the Eighteenth Century* (New Haven, 1965), 183–88.

Mortality and the Medical Treatment of Slaves in the British West Indies

RICHARD B. SHERIDAN

Successive waves of peoples have occupied the Caribbean islands, beginning in pre-Columbian times with the Siboneys, Tainos, Arawaks, and Caribs. Only a handful of these indigenous peoples survived the coming of the Spaniard. The Spaniard's exclusive claim to the Antilles was successfully challenged by Dutchmen, Frenchmen, Englishmen, and Danes. For upwards of four centuries the inexorable demand for plantation labor was met by selling Africans into bondage. Following slave emancipation came contract and free laborers from India, China, and elsewhere. Dominating the population of the Caribbean today are the descendants of the African slaves who survived the health hazards of a complex tropical environment in an age of rudimentary medical science.

I

At the outset it may be asked why Europeans transported Africans several thousand miles to the New World instead of establishing plantations in tropical Africa. This question can perhaps be answered briefly by reference to three environments — physical, technological, and social. Technologically superior Europeans found the coastal lowlands of West Africa both inaccessible and inhospitable. Treacherous surf, mangrove swamps, enervating climate, generally poor soils, and the difficulty of supporting animal husbandry in the face of the tsetse fly were some of the reasons for the failure to establish plantations in Africa. Caribbean islands, on the other hand, were capable of supporting livestock and plantation agriculture. They were in the path of the trade winds which determined sailing and trade routes, energized windmills, and made the climate less enervating. Slaves were less prone to run away or rebel when they were confined to small, densely populated islands and denied access to guns and sailing craft. Then it was possible for Europeans to replicate their old-world culture, albeit a culture corrupted by slavery, when they occupied sparsely populated or even depopulated West Indian islands.[1] Finally, as Philip Curtin has so ably demonstrated, Europeans suffered a lower mortality rate in the West Indies than they did in West Africa, while imported Africans worked better and lived longer than Indians and white indentured workers.[2]

Prior to 1816 only crude estimates of the slave population of the British West Indies are extant. In 1680, the colonies of Barbados, Jamaica, and the four Leeward Islands of Antigua, St. Kitts, Nevis, and Montserrat contained some 68,000 Negro slaves, of whom Barbados claimed about two-thirds. In 1700, there were some 116,000 slaves, of whom Barbados and Jamaica claimed 50,000 and 45,000, respectively. Jamaica moved ahead of Barbados in subsequent decades. Its slave population in 1750 was 125,000, while that of Barbados was 68,000, and the Leeward Islands, 64,000. The estimated total population in 1750 was 257,000. By the Treaty of Paris in 1763, Britain acquired the 'Ceded Islands' of Dominica, St. Vincent, Grenada, and Tobago. Meanwhile, the several British Virgin Islands acquired enough slaves to be included in the estimates. By the eve of the American Revolution the eleven Caribbean islands contained some 416,000 slaves, as compared with 460,000 in the thirteen mainland colonies. Colonies acquired by conquest after 1775 included St. Lucia, Trinidad, Berbice, and Demerara. In 1800, fifteen British colonies contained about 674,000 slaves, nearly half of

Race and Slavery in The Western Hemisphere: Quantitative Studies (Princeton, 1975), pp. 285–307.

whom were in Jamaica. In 1834, at the time of slave emancipation, 651,912 slaves were enumerated in the British Caribbean.[3]

'The most striking demographic peculiarity of the South Atlantic System was its failure to produce a self-sustaining slave population in tropical America,' writes Philip Curtin.[4] Whereas the slave population of the American South increased by natural means during and following the era of the slave trade, that of the West Indies depended on annual recruits from Africa merely to maintain the existing population. Only the island of Barbados had a slave population that increased by natural means, and this came after the African slave trade was prohibited by the British Parliament in 1807. Among the numerous causes of slave mortality in the West Indies were the high proportion of male to female slave imports, the difficulty of acclimating or 'seasoning' newly imported slaves, unstable sexual unions which contributed to the low birth rate, high mortality among infants and young children, malnutrition, hard labor, cruel punishment, epidemic and other diseases, and accidents.[5]

Broadly speaking, slavery in the British Caribbean falls into three periods with respect to the mix of demographic and economic factors. Early slavery dates from about 1640 with the launching of the sugar industry in Barbados. It gradually gave way to near-monoculture slavery in that island during the 1680s, and to slave amelioration in the 1760s and 1770s. These stages came later in other Caribbean islands which lagged behind Barbados in developing slave-plantation economies.

The Caribbean colonies were initially colonies of settlement perhaps as much as colonies of exploitation. They attracted numerous smallholders who grew tobacco and other minor staples and foodstuffs with the assistance of indentured servants and a few black slaves. Compared with minor staples, sugar production required more land, labor, and fixed and working capital for efficient production. But for several decades sugar plantations were under-capitalized, depending on both white servants and black slaves to produce not only the sweetening substance but also the greater part of their food requirements. Planters conserved their human capital by assigning slaves to light tasks, feeding and clothing them well, and encouraging family life and reproduction. Contemporary accounts indicate that slave cargoes contained about as many females as males.[6]

Near-monoculture slavery followed in the course of decades the early slave economy. It was characterized by the consolidation of smallholdings into sugar plantations, rising land values, emigration of former smallholders and their servants, annual cropping of cane land, soil depletion and its correction by heavy application of fertilizer, dependence on imported foodstuffs and other supplies and equipment, and a slave population that failed to reproduce itself. Probably the chief cause of the excess of deaths over births was the low cost of imported slaves. Since it was generally cheaper to buy new workers than to bear the cost of breeding and raising a slave to working age in the colony, planters preferred to import more men than women. Not only did the birth rate decline, but the death rate increased because of hard labor, cruel punishment, malnutrition, epidemics, and accidents. Most of the deaths occurred during the seasoning, for the mortality among new slaves was greater than that among Creoles or island-born Negroes.[7]

Amelioration of the slave's condition seems to have been limited to estates of enlightened planters prior to the American Revolution. Trade interruption in conjunction with unusually severe hurricanes during the revolutionary struggle resulted in slave deaths, reputedly as many as 15,000 in Jamaica.[8] Planters not only grew more foodstuffs at a time of uncertain supplies from abroad but they were also concerned to increase the birth rate and longevity of their slaves. After 1790 the long and bitter slave rebellion in St. Domingue threatened to spread to the British colonies. Planters became fearful of large aggregations of African-born slaves and sought to substitute a more tractable and self-generating labor force of Creole blacks. The collapse of the sugar boom of the 1790s brought planter and politician demands to end the slave trade in an effort to deny laborers to foreign competitors and thus limit sugar production and raise prices to the comparative advantage of British planters. Meanwhile, amelioration had been encouraged by higher slave prices. Finally, the anti-slavery movement in England became a force which could not be ignored.[9]

II

Though historians and demographers assign different weights to economic and non-economic factors, they agree that mortality rates declined during the 80–100 years prior to

British slave emancipation. Crude annual rates of population decrease can be computed by relating net slave import figures to unofficial census returns. For Barbados the annual rate of decrease was 4.1 per cent in the quarter century 1676–1700. It then rose to 4.9 per cent in 1701–25, after which it declined to 3.6 per cent in 1726–50 and 3.8 per cent in 1751–75. Import data are spotty for the years from 1776 to the end of the slave trade in 1897, but other evidence indicates that imports played a declining role in recruiting the slave population. Indeed, the Barbadian experience was unique, for the island's blacks increased from about 69,400 in 1809 to 83,150 in 1834.[10].

The mortality experience of Jamaica and Barbados affords interesting points of comparison. My crude calculations for Jamaica gives an annual rate of decrease of 3.1 per cent in 1676–1700, 3.7 per cent in 1701–25, 3.5 per cent in 1726–50, and 2.5 per cent in 1751–75. Though the downward trend was reversed for a time in the 1790s, the annual rate declined to 2.0 in 1776–1800 and to 0.43 per cent from 1817 to 1829.[11] While the computed rates of population of the two islands rose and fell, Jamaica's rate not only lagged behind but was consistently lower than that of Barbados. The lag can be explained by the later economic development of Jamaica, while the consistently lower rates were probably due to the more diversified economy of Jamaica. Barry Higman has demonstrated statistically that in Jamaica the slaves increased generally on coffee plantations and cattle ranches or pens, and decreased on sugar estates. He cites a contemporary observer who attributed the heavy mortality on sugar plantations to cane-hole digging, night work, and the use of the whip.[12]

Recent studies have recounted the mortality experience of individual sugar plantations. J. Harry Bennett, Jr has told the tragic story of the slaves on the Codrington plantations in Barbados from 1712 to 1748. In an average year there was only one birth to every 100 of the population, one out of every two infants died before reaching five years of age, four or five of every 100 seasoned slaves died annually, and deaths during the seasoning claimed four or five in every ten of the Africans imported as replacements. Despite the purchase of an average of nine slaves a year, the Codrington community declined from 292 to 209.[13]

African recruitment and the hiring of seasoned slaves were abandoned by the managers of Codrington in 1761. There followed after some delay a new policy of amelioration to prolong the life of the slaves and encourage them to breed. That the new policy was successful is evident from the increase of the labor force by one-third from 1793 to 1823.[14]

Slavery on Worthy Park estate in Jamaica has been analyzed by Michael Craton and James Walvin. The work force increased from 318 to 357 in 1791. Massive purchases of new slaves during the sugar boom of the 1790s increased the death rate from 3.0 per cent to 5.7 per cent, while the birth rate remained fairly stable at 2.3 per cent. By the turn of the century the mortality rate had probably resumed its downward trend. Over the entire period 1811–37, when a policy of amelioration was vigorously pursued, the annual average death rate was 2.60 per cent and the birth rate 2.33 per cent. This gave a natural decrease of 0.27 per cent, or approximately six slaves every five years out of a population of about 500.[15]

The slave mortality experience can now be summarized briefly. After an initial period of relatively mild slavery, sugar monoculture ushered in a more demanding labor regimen. Most of the slaves who survived the Middle Passage arrived in a debilitated condition. Substantial numbers died during the seasoning. Illnesses multiplied on the plantations after periods of drought, night work, and toil in wet weather. Overwork and malnutrition contributed to the decline of the blacks. From time to time epidemics of smallpox and measles took a heavy toll. When the cost of imported slaves was low in relation to the cost of breeding and rearing children to the age of labor, planters purchased many more males than females. From this followed unstable sexual unions which, in turn, contributed to the low birth rate and that high infant mortality. But far more women tended to survive than men, leading in time to an equalization of the sex ratio. Finally, natural increase depended upon the combination of sexual balance, a reasonably healthy birth rate, and a moderate death rate.

III

It may be argued from the foregoing discussion that demographic conditions improved because of natural forces operating on slave fertility and mortality rates, and that amelioration as a conscious policy of slaveholders was ineffectual. On the other hand, declining mortality might be explained as a consequence of such expedients as lightened discipline and labor tasks and improved food, clothing, housing, and medical attention. A third hypothesis would attribute demographic improvement to a combination of natural and contrived elements. The remainder of this paper will marshal evidence in an effort to support the third hypothesis in its medical dimensions.

'As an economic measure,' writes Harry Bennett, 'amelioration can be defined with substantial accuracy as a system by which money that would otherwise have been spent on hiring and buying Negroes was used to improve the lot of the existing stock of slaves in order to induce them to breed their replacements.'[16] From the standpoint of medical treatment of slaves, amelioration would depend on the number of medical practitioners in the islands, their professional qualifications, the number and quality of medical assistants and nurses, the provision of hospitals and other physical facilities to isolate and treat patients, sanitary measures, the state of medical science and especially tropical medicine, and, of course, the extent to which these resources were concentrated on the black people.

Modern medical progress dates from the sixteenth century when old wisdom was challenged by devastating epidemics stemming from interpenetration of disease environments which accompanied wars, urbanization, and intercontinental migration and trade. Exploration of new lands brought new diseases as well as new drugs with which to treat them. Knowledge of infectious diseases advanced. Physical and chemical discoveries reacted on physiology, medicine, and surgery. In an age when qualified physicians were far outnumbered by quacks and mountebanks, notable developments occurred in immunology, surgery, obstetrics, medicine, and especially medical education.

As the commercial revolution shifted north from Italy, so did the centers of medical education. Padua was the educational center of medicine in Renaissance Italy. In the seventeenth century the center shifted to Leyden, Holland. Here Hermann Boerhaave (1668–1738), the great teacher of clinical medicine, attracted students from many lands: from England, Scotland, and even from the West Indies and North America. Through his students Boerhaave was the founder of the Edinburgh Medical School, which suceeded Leyden as the center of European and American teaching and research.[17]

'The specialty of tropical medicine deals with all diseases prevalent in the tropics and with the complex of interrelationships betwen man and disease in the tropical environment,' writes Dr. Thomas Huckle Weller.[18] Since the navy was Britain's first line of defense and imperial defense extended into tropical latitudes, it is not surprising that a naval surgeon pioneered tropical medicine. Scurvy was the scourge of seamen, and it was James Lind, the Scottish naval physician, who, in 1754, published *A Treatise on Scurvy*, which recommended the use of lemon juice with highly successful results. He also wrote an *Essay on Diseases of Europeans in Hot Climates*, which is said to have opened the campaign for the conquest of the tropics for the white man.[19] Included among the Europeans who ventured into hot climates were numerous doctors. Several of these medical men because famous for their scientific achievements.

Foremost among the physicians who practiced in the West Indies was Sir Hans Sloane (1660–1753). He was born at Killileagh, Ireland, the son of a tax collector. In 1683 he graduated M.D. at the University of Leyden, having earlier studied medicine at Paris and Montpellier. Four years later he went to the West Indies as physician to the Duke of Albemarle, Governor of Jamaica. During his stay of fifteen months on the island, Sloane made many natural history observations and collections, returning to London with some 800 species of plants. His great work was published in 1702 under the title, *A Voyage to the Islands Madera, Barabados, Nieves, S. Christophers, and Jamaica, with the Natural History of the last of those Islands.* During his long life he received many honors, including his appointment as first physician to George II. Sloane is best known for his great collection of natural histroy specimens, manuscripts, and books which he bequeathed to the nation on condition that £20,000 should be paid to his family. Indeed, Sloane's bequest became the first collection of the British Museum.[20]

Although it is uncertain if Sloane ever treated slaves, no such doubt concerns two other medical men who combined practice with scientific pursuits in Jamaica. Testifying before a committee of the Privy Council in 1789 was John Quier (1738–1822), practitioner in physic and surgery. He said that he had studied surgery in London and physic at Leyden and served as assistant surgeon in military hospitals in the former war. For upwards of twenty-one years he had practiced in Jamaica, where he had from 4,000 to 5,000 slaves constantly under his care. Quier reduced infant deaths from tetanus or lockjaw, was a pioneer in inoculation for smallpox, and anticipated European doctors by more than a century in the diagnosis of measles. He closed his testimony by saying that 'within these last Twenty Years the Treatment of new negroes in this Island has been greatly altered for the Better; that these People are now in general treated with great Humanity and Tenderness, both before and after they are become seasoned to the Country; and that he does not conceive the great Mortality amongst them commonly to arise from want of Food or severe Labour.'[21]

The career of Dr. William Wright, F.R.S. (1735–1819), was similar in many respects to that of Dr. Quier. He was born in the village of Crieff, Perthshire, Scotland, where he attended the grammar school. At the age of seventeen he was apprenticed to a surgeon at Falkirk, and in 1756 entered the Edinburgh Medical School. Two years later he was licensed at Surgeons' Hall, London, after which he served as surgeon's mate on several men-of-war as well as in military hospitals in the West Indies. At the end of the Seven Years' War he returned to London and obtained the degree of doctor of medicine.[22]

Because of the scarcity of medical opportunities in England, Dr. Wright was induced to seek his fortune in Jamaica. There he met Dr. Thomas Steel, a young surgeon who had been his fellow student at Edinburgh. Forming a partnership, the young doctors took up residence on Hampden Estate in St. James Parish, the property of James Sterling, who was an absentee in Scotland. According to Dr. Wright's *Memoir*, 'The Negroes under the medical charge of the two partners amounted to 1200, which, at 5 shillings each per annum, produced a considerable item of ascertained revenue.' From the income of his medical practice and his plantation, Dr. Wright was able to retire to Edinburgh after 1776 and, with the exception of two military assignments in the West Indies, devoted his remaining years to scientific and literary pursuits. That many Scots doctors had followed him to Jamaica is suggested by the remittance of some £11,000 which he solicited from his friends in Jamaica to rebuild the University of Edinburgh.[23]

Dr. Wright's medical practice was undertaken with the aim of advancing medical science. He was a close observer of nature and was said to have pried with a curious eye into her most secret recesses. His remedies, while few, were efficacious. Patients, including pregnant women, were kept in well-ventilated airy, and sanitary quarters and black nurses and midwives were properly instructed. For the cure of fevers, and especially lockjaw, he administered cold baths. By these and other means few women died of puerperal fever and the proportion of children who died of lockjaw was small in comparison with the members of former times.[24]

Much of Dr. Wright's fame rested on his natural history collections and the scientific papers he wrote. For many years he collected plants in Jamaica, supplying specimens to the Royal Gardens at Kew and the botanical gardens in Liverpool and Glasgow. He was a voluminous correspondent, a bibliophile, and a member of numerous learned societies. The work which issued from his original mind 'brought him to be favourably known in that select circle of science, where Banks, Solander and Fothergill, Smith, Lind and Pulteney, Black, Hope and Rutherford, Hutton, Home and the two Hunters, were the burning and the shining lights.'[25]

James Grainger, M.D. (1721?–66), had an extensive medical practice among the slaves and also wrote an essay on West Indian diseases and remedies. Born in Scotland, he attended medical classes at Edinburgh Unviersity for three years and was apprenticed to a surgeon of that city. After service as an army surgeon, he toured Europe and then returned to Edinburgh and graduated M.D. in 1753. During the next six years he lived in London. Failing to obtain patients, he depended chiefly on his pen for a livelihood. His poems, essays, and translations from the classics brought him to the attention of such luminaries as Samuel Johnson and Oliver Goldsmith.

Grainger came to the West Indies in 1759 as the companion and tutor of the heir to a sugar fortune. Soon after his arrival in St. Kitts he married the daughter of a leading planter. Grainger not only practiced medicine and managed a plantation which belonged to an in-law, but he also found time to indulge his favorite study of botany and to write poetry. During his rides to different parts of the island to treat patients he composed a poem which was published in 1764 under the title, *The Sugar Cane, A Poem in Four Parts*. The same year saw the publication of his *An Essay on the More Common West-India Diseases*.[26]

The principal design of Grainger's *Essay* was 'to enable those who are intrusted with the management of Negroes to treat them in a more scientific manner than has hitherto been generally practised . . . .' He wrote of the choice of new slaves, their seasoning, the diseases to which they were most exposed, and their management with respect to diet, clothing, punishment, and medical treatment. Grainger was probably an innovator in prescribing medicines concocted from indigenous plants. 'The islands contain innumerable medicines of high efficacy,' he wrote 'not known in Europe; and doubtless a much greater number still remain to be investigated by future inquiry.' Dr. William Wright saw the second edition of Grainger's *Essay* through the press in 1802, to which he added an introduction, practical notes, and a 'Linnean Index'. Wright said that he knew of physicians and surgeons who had profited much by it, 'both in the knowledge of the diseases of the Negroes, and of the indigeneous remedies; in which respects it is, in my opinion, an excellent model for a more scientific and general treatise on tropical diseases, especially among the Blacks.'[27]

Dr. John Coakley Lettsom, F.R.S. (1744–1815), was an eminent Quaker physician and philanthropist. He was born on the island of Little Jost Van Dykes in the British Virgin Islands, the son of Edward and Mary Lettsom, who were Quakers. His father owned about 50 slaves who worked his cotton plantation on Little Jost Van Dykes and his sugar plantation on the neighbouring island of Tortola. Because of his frail health, Lettsom was sent to England to live with Quaker friends of the family. At the age of sixteen he was apprenticed to a surgeon and apothecary at Settle in Yorkshire. He continued his medical education in London under the patronage of Dr. John Fothergill, leading Quaker practitioner and philanthropist. At Fothergill's home Lettsom met Benjamin Franklin and David Barclay, the great city merchant.[28]

Lettsom's experience as a doctor to the slaves was short and dramatic. In 1767 he sailed to Tortola with a view to getting money to finish his medical education. He refused one source of money, for his Quaker anti-slavery scruples impelled him to free the ten slaves that he inherited from his father's estate. Lettsom then turned with great zeal to the practice of medicine on Tortola and neighboring islands. He wrote that he often saw 50–100 people before breakfast. Indeed in the short space of six months his practice yielded the surprising sum of nearly £2,000.[29]

Lettsom studied at the Edinburgh Medical School and the University of Leyden, where he took his M.D. degree in 1769. He succeeded to Fothergill's practice in London and at the height of his career earned £12,000 in a single year. He founded the Medical Society of London, the Royal Sea Bathing Hospital, and was active in the Royal Humane Society and prison reform. From Fothergill he acquired a keen interest in natural science. The botanical garden at his country villa at Camberwell included specimens from remote lands and climates. One of his numerous books was the *Naturalist's and Traveller's Companion* (1772). He also published *Reflections on the General Treatment and Cure of Fevers* (1772), which drew on his medical experience in the West Indies.[30] As a vigorous supporter of causes and no mean controversialist, Lettsom made enemies and did not escape the satrists, who wrote of him:

I, John Lettsom,
Blisters, bleeds and sweats 'em.
If after that they please to die,
I, John Lettsom.

Not all of the white doctors regarded with scorn and ridicule the medical treatment of slaves by slaves. One of these was James Thomson, M.D., a graduate of the Edinburgh Medical School and friend and protégé of Drs. William Wright and John Quier. As a doctor who treated slaves in Jamaica and as a scientist who diligently carried on the work begun by Wright and Quier, Thomson observed closely the relationship between medical plant and the slave doctors who collected, prepared, and prescribed them. He wrote that it was the serious duty of every planter to provide a proper black person to superintend the management of the sick. Thomson candidly acknowledged that the effects of his most labored prescriptions had been often superseded by the perserving administration of the black doctors' most simple remedies. He wrote at length of his and other doctors' experiments with the medicinal plants of Jamaica, of which he recommended that as many as twenty-eight varieties be kept on every estate.[31]

IV

Biographical sketches of leading doctors obviously need to be supplemented with descriptive and quantitative data. Though many gaps in our medical knowledge remain to be filled, the remainder of this essay will summarize the data I have collected from primary and secondary sources pertaining to Barbados, Jamaica, and Antigua.

Doctors may have been attached to Barbadian plantations as early as 1690. In that year Sir Dalby Thomas wrote that a sugar plantation of 100 acres would require fifty black slaves, seven white servants, an overseer, farrier, carter, and a doctor whose salary amounted to £20 per annum.[32] A century later Joshua Steele, a leading planter, submitted evidence on slavery to Governor Parry of Barbados. He testified that it was the general practice in plantations to give a standing salary as far as 5s. per slave 'to some medical person, apothecary, or practitioner, to supply medicines and attendance annually'. Some planters went further and not only gave a salary for daily attendance, but also imported at their own charge the necessary medicines.[33] Dr. George Pinckard, an army surgeon who was stationed in Barbados, wrote in 1796 that the island contained many members of the medical profession who were an honor to their profession and an ornament to society. There were others, however, who were 'pre-eminent in ignorance... and the very *negro doctors* of the estates too justly vie with them in medical knowledge.'[34]

Harry Bennett has calculated the cost of maintaining the Codrington slaves during the eighteenth century. During the first half of the century the average cost per slave was £2 2s. 11¼d. a year. Of this amount £1 11s. was for food, 8s. 5¾d. for clothing, and 3s. 6d. for medical care. In the latter half of the century, the whole of the annual charge had risen to £3 16.5¼d., with £3 for food 8s. 5¼d. for clothing, and 8s.0d. for medical care. Medical care increased from 8.1 per cent to 10.5 per cent of total maintenance charges. Bennett writes that amelioration proved to be the most effective method of insuring a continuing supply of labor. In fact, the slave population which earlier had suffered such a high mortality rose from 266 to 355 from 1793 to 1823.[35]

Jamaica seems to have been well supplied with doctors who differed widely in their professional qualifications. Charles Leslie, who lived on the island before 1740, said that the physicians there of any note generally made fine estates. He went on to say that the island was:

> quite crowded with raw unexperienced Youths, who imagine this the properest Place for a Settlement; and when they come over, are generally set to prescribe to a parcel of Negroes in some Country-plantations. Their numbers make but dull Business for most of them; and in the Towns there are generally one or two eminent Men who have the Employment, and soon get to be rich.[36]

The quality of practice had improved by the later part of the eighteenth century according to Bryan Edwards, the planter-historian. Every plantation that he was acquainted with in Jamaica was under the daily or weekly inspection of a practitioner in physic and surgery who frequently resided on the estate. The planters had become intolerant of 'illiterate pretenders in medicine' and sought for and encouraged 'young men of skill and science'. The usual payment to doctors for attendance and medicines was 6s. a head per annum for all the Negroes on the estate whether sick or well. Extra payments were made for amputations, inoculation, and difficult cases of midwifery. On an estate having 500 slaves the doctor's compensation was about £150 sterling per year, plus such prerequisites as board, washing, and lodging. Edwards was of the opinion that few plantation doctors had less than 500 slaves under their care; while several, with their assistants, had upwards of 5,000.[37]

Early nineteenth-century practices in Jamaica were described by Robert Renny. He maintained that the health of the slaves was very punctually attended to. Newly imported slaves were 'generally inoculated with the small, or the cow pock, matter'. Every large estate had a doctor in residence or in the immediate neighborhood. The slaves were attended in the sick-room, or hospital, over which an aged Negress presided as nurse. The proprietor commonly furnished blankets, rice, sugar, oatmeal, and flour; while those of a more liberal disposition supplied beef and mutton, and even sometimes spices, sago, and wines. Renny said that 'the Negroes are subject to the same diseases as the Europeans; though they are seldom affected, and more seldom carried off, by those fevers, which usually prove so destructive to the white settlers.'[38]

The new policy of amelioration, according to the Jamaican demographer George Roberts, appears to have had some success. The wastage of human life which had been compatible with slavery when Africans could be easily and cheaply imported, would have led to depopulation after the prohibition of the slave trade in 1807 if measures had not been taken to increase fertility and decrease mortality.'[39]

Since a College of Physicians and Surgeons was not established in Jamaica until 1832, and before this no proof of qualification or registration was required, it is difficult to ascertain the number of doctors or pass on their professional standing. Some idea of the number of doctors and their wealthholding can be gained, however, by searching the *Inventorys* series at the Island Record Office at Spanish Town. In the five-year period 1741–45, the personal property inventories of twenty-four physicians and surgeons are recorded. Omitting shillings and pence, they range from £39 to £6,522, the average being £874 in Jamaica currency, or £624 sterling. Thirty years later, in 1771–75, a total of twenty-six doctors' estates were inventoried. They range from £51 to £9,931, and average £2,237 currency, or £1,597 sterling. Whereas the doctors in the first period held most of their personal property in the form of accounts receivable, those in the latter period not only claimed debts outstanding but a sizeable number also owned slaves which they either leased or worked on their own plantations and pens.[40]

Fifty-one doctors' inventories are recorded in the years from 1791 to 1795 in Jamaica. They range from £10 to £56,815, and average £4,481 currency, or £3,199 sterling. At least half of these doctors were Scotsmen or Irishmen, whose personal property inventories were generally on the high side compared with all doctors. Dr. Alexander McLenan of St. James Parish was a man of substance; his personal property amounted to nearly £12,171 currency. Of this amount, nearly £5,520 consisted of claims on individuals in the form of book debts and amounts owing from ten estates and pens presumably for the treatment of slaves.[41]

One of the paradoxes in the demographic history of Jamaica is that within a decade after full emancipation the black population began to grow, while the number of doctors practicing on the island declined sharply. Compared with the 200 doctors in 1830, the number had declined to 87 in 1861 and 84 in 1871. The island's population, on the other hand, increased from 377,400 in 1844 to 506,100 in 1871. Some of the reasons for the growth in population lie outside the practice of medicine and surgery. It seems reasonable to assume, for example, that the high rate of abortion and child neglect that was reported in slave times declined after emancipation when stable sexual unions became more common. Also, the growth of peasant agriculture probably lightened the labor tasks of the blacks by comparison with the slave-plantations, thus helping to reduce mortality.[42]

V

The medical history of Antigua is better documented than that of other British Caribbean colonies. In part, this is owing to the monumental genealogical history of the island by Dr. Vere Langford Oliver, himself a descendant of a prominent Antiguan family and also a medical practitioner. Moreover, the letter books and account books of Dr. Walter Tullideph afford insights not only into his own career as a doctor, merchant, and planter, but also of his doctor friends and business associates who like himself were Scotsmen.[43]

Medical practitioners increased in number and professional attainment as Antigua moved into front rank as a slave-plantation colony. From an estimated between five and ten doctors in the first decade of the eighteenth century, the number increased to twenty-two in 1731, when a roster was drawn up in connection with the assignments of doctors to militia regiments. At least half of the doctors enumerated in 1731 would appear to have been Scotsmen. Beginning in 1732, new doctors had to be certified and licensed. From these records we learn that nineteen new doctors were licensed from 1732 to 1750, of whom twelve arrived on the island after 1742. Most of the entries include only the date and name of the licensee, but a few give more particulars. We learn, for example, that a Dr. Forgus presented his diploma from the faculty of physicians of Angiers in France, Dr. Adam Byrne presented his certificate from Dublin University, Dr. John Tod presented his certificate from a chirurgeon and apothecary at Edinburgh, and Drs. Patrick Malcolm and Ashton Warner presented diplomas from Surgeon's Hall.[41]

Antigua may have had more qualified doctors in the middle years of the eighteenth century than at any other time during slavery. Compared with the nineteen doctors who were certified and licensed from 1732 to 1750, only nine were added to the rolls in the third quarter of the century, and only six in the fourth quarter.[45] That these figures understate the number of practitioners is suggested by the changing structure of medical practice. Whereas the doctors practiced individually for some years, they later employed assistants who treated slaves under their supervision. John Luffman wrote in 1787 that sick slaves were attended by young doctors whose principals contracted with the owners of estates or their attorneys at the common price of 3s.9d. sterling per slave. It was the business of these assistants to make twice weekly visits to the estates that had been put under the care of their employers. Their pay was so meagre that Luffman doubted if it covered their expenses.[46]

At mid-century Antigua had approximately

thirty-two qualified doctors in a population that was predominantly black. At that time the island contained approximately 30,000 blacks and 3,500 whites. The ratio of one doctor to 1,047 inhabitants compares favourably with the Jamaican ratio of one to 1,855 in 1830, and even the Mississippi ratio of one to 1,448 in 1970.[47]

Of the thirty-two Antiguan doctors, nineteen have been identified as Scotsmen or educated in Scotland, seven were Antiguans, one an Irishman, and five not identified. Foremost among the Antiguans was Dr. Ashton Warner (1721–89), descendant of the founder of the colony and member of a prominent planter family. For a time he practiced in London as did his brother Joseph Warner, F.R.S. (1717–1801).[48] But whereas Joseph remained to become one of the city's leading surgeons, Ashton returned to Antigua in 1749. Besides his medical practice, he was President of the Council and owner of two sugar plantations.[49] Dr. George Crump was the son and heir of an Antiguan barrister and planter, and a nephew of a lieutenant-colonel of militia who was made governor of Guadeloupe at the British conquest in 1759. That the Crumps were among the best educated families of Antigua is evident from the fact that the doctor as well as his father and uncle were graduates of Leyden University.[50] The first Jarvis in Antigua was a book-keeper. His son, Dr. Francis Jarvis, married the widow of a leading planter. Dr. William Jarvis, who was licensed to practice in 1746, was first cousin to Dr. Francis Jarvis. Dr. Thomas Jarvis, another cousin, produced a diploma from the College of Physicians at Edinburgh and was licensed to practice medicine in Antigua in 1790. He inherited property on the island which he claimed to be worth £50,000.[51]

Numbered among the nineteen Scots doctors was Walter Tullideph (1703?–72), who had a successful career in the West Indies. He was born at Dumbarney, the son of a Presbyterian minister. After attending the high school at Edinburgh, he was apprenticed to a chirurgeon of that city in 1718. About 1726 he went to Antigua where several friends and relatives were already established as doctors, merchants, and government officials.[52]

We first learn of Tullideph from his letters to Sir Hans Sloane. He wrote from Antigua on 5 July 1727:

> When I had the honor to wait upon you in London you were pleased to recommend to me the Study of our West India Vegetables, in obedience to which desire, I have made it my endeavour to examine several of them in their perfection and to put up a dryed specimen of each of them as often as I could conveniently.[53]

From time to time Tullideph shipped growing plants and dried specimens to Sloane, but his scientific interest soon became subordinated to his professional and business activities. Sloane was informed in a letter of 25 June 1734 that the laborious practice of physic and surgery engrossed most of Tullideph's time. The young doctor had left the country and settled in the town of St. John where he was endeavoring to get a modest fortune.[54]

That the move to town did not interfere with the treatment of plantation slaves seems evident from the entries in Tullideph's medical ledger. Though part of the ledger has decayed, enough remains to show that his practice was considerable. While his white patients were treated individually, his far more numerous black patients were treated mainly on a contract basis. For example, one entry in his account with Samuel Byam's plantation is as follows: 'To yet care of 125 negroes fm. Janry. 25, 1734/5 to Do. 1735/6 is one year @ 6/ . . . [£] 37.10.0.' In other words, Tullideph contracted to treat Byam's slaves on an annual basis at 6s. per head. Twenty-two such accounts are entered in the ledger from 1731 to 1735, some for periods of less than five years. In 1733 Tullideph had 14 accounts for the care of 1,198 slaves at a total charge of nearly £360. The next year he had seventeen accounts for 1,408 slaves at £422.[55]

Other Negro slaves, especially those owned by smallholders and artisans, were treated by Tullideph on an individual basis. For example, he charged £1 8s. for dressing a wound, the same for visiting a Negro wench in labor, £2 for the 'Cure of a Clap', £2 16s. for maintaining two slaves at his hot house with nursing and lodging, and £5 for laying open a mortification in a slave's leg with dressing and care involving several visits.[56]

To augment his modest fortune the young doctor sold medicines and other goods at retail and wholesale. He sent to London for upwards of £160 worth of medicine in the early 1730s, most of it coming from Alexander Johnston, 'Chymist and Druggist at the Golden Stead in Fan Church Street over against Magpie Alley'. Small quantities were retailed to local inhabitants, the greater part being dispensed at wholesale to doctors in Antigua and neighboring islands. Tullideph also acted as Johnston's attorney in collecting debts owed by doctors in the West Indies.[57]

Tullideph came to Antigua at the invitation of

his cousin Dr. Walter Sydserfe, who became a planter, assemblyman, councillor, and lieutenant-general in the militia. Having come out to join his cousin in the practice of medicine. Tullideph, in turn, found that he needed assistance. On 24 March 1735 he wrote to another cousin who was a sugar factor in London: 'If you can agree with any Sober Young Surgeon who has been educated at Edinburgh (if possible) for three years, he to pay his own passage . . . I will give him ye first year £30, ye second 40, and the third £50 . . . .'[58] The following year a Dr. William Mercer was licensed to practice in Antigua, and two years after this Tullideph ordered his London chemist to charge a small invoice of medicines to 'Messrs. Walter Tullideph & Wm. Mercer in Compy'.[59]

The transition from doctor to planter was accelerated in 1736 when Tullideph married a young widow and came into possession of a small plantation. To his brother David, a Scottish merchant trading to Antigua, he wrote in the fall of 1738: 'I have resigned all business in favour of Dr. Mercer, it was too great fatigue & he allowed me in consideration £300 (which keep a secret), & I still hold all business that side of the creek next my self which may be £200 per Ann. gott with much ease. You may acquaint Brother Thomas of this.'[60]

Meanwhile, Tullideph had written to Brother Thomas in Scotland about the prospects for combining medicine with planting in Antigua:

> If any of our nephews will Study Physick and Settle as a Planter I can allow such a one £100 Sterlg. pr. Ann. to manadge my Estate and take care of my negroes when I resolve to come home, besides ye Care of adjoining plantations Tomie [Thomas] don't stand for a small matter in ye purchase of an estate . . . [61]

Although none of his nephews followed his advice. Tullideph found several doctors who eagerly enlisted his support in climbing the ladder of plantership.

As doctor-planters with influential connections in Scotland, England, and Antigua Tullideph and Sydserfe came in time to direct a Scots colonial community consisting of doctors, merchants, book-keepers, overseers, plantation attorneys, and planters. Both of these cousins married into planter families, served in the legislature and militia, managed the estates of absentees, and acted as guardians, executors, and trustees. In these and other capacities they found opportunities to recommend their fellow countrymen. Fourteen of the nineteen doctors who are mentioned in the Tullideph correspondence from 1734 to 1758 were Scotsmen, of whom at least eight became members of the colonial gentry.

Population growth, enclosures, and a low level of material well-being coexisted in eighteenth-century Scotland with a high level of primary and secondary education, the flowering of university life, and intellectual and cultural achievement. As Richard Pares has observed, theological Calvinism was losing its hold on the people, and the great mental and moral energies which it generated were transferred to secular studies and secular interests. Many Scotsmen sought a new life in the colonies. The Scottish family system helped to make the migration a continuous one, for one Scotsman was hardly established abroad before he sent for his brothers, cousins, nephews, and fellow townsmen. Politics aided the outward movement, for the Scottish M.P.s at Westminster generally voted in a bloc and they traded their votes for posts in the colonies which they conferred on their relatives and friends. Another source of strength were the Scotsmen who fought in colonial wars.[62]

VI

It might be concluded that Scots doctors and medical progress did much to improve the health and longevity of slaves in the West Indies. But it should be emphasized that the Scots' contribution was reinforced by other developments. These included the relative rise in the price of slaves, the threat of slave rebellion, competition from rival slave-plantation colonies, the growing proportion of Creole to African slaves, and the rise of the anti-slavery movement in England. Since mortality and medical care began on the Middle Passage, it is interesting to speculate about the relationship between the Parliamentary Act of 1788 which required qualified doctors on all slave vessels and the loss of fewer Africans in transit to the plantations during the later decades of the slave trade.[63] Economic and humanitarian forces combined to induce colonial legislatures to adopt ameliorative measures which included provisions regarding the medical care of slaves. The Leeward Islands Act of 1798, for example, required every plantation to provide a 'commodious' hospital, employ a doctor who was obliged to call at the estate twice a week unless he was notified in writing that his presence was not required, give special attention to pregnant women and infants, and record vital statistics.[64]

Yet it may be argued that what was achieved by investment in medical care of slaves was partly negated by factors that were beyond the control of planter, their medical assistants, and reformers.[65] Orlando Patterson writes that 'the most important factor in any consideration of reproduction during slavery is an analysis of the attitudes toward pregnancy and child-rearing on the part of both masters and slaves.'[66] We have seen that most planters adopted a new policy toward reproduction in the later part of the eighteenth century. There is dramatic evidence that male slaves valued medical services, for only the white doctors were spared in the bloody slave revolts which occurred on the Danish island of St. John in 1733, and in French St. Domingue in 1791.[67]

Most important in negating the policy of reproduction was the attitude of female slaves themselves. Irregular sexual unions were fostered by the excess of black males over females, the large number of unmarried white males attached to plantations, planter opposition to slave family life and their own cavalier attitude toward concubinage. In the absence of venereal disease, irregular relations need not have inhibited reproduction. But there is evidence that such diseases did inhibit the birth rate. Moreover, slave women disliked the idea of bringing more slaves into the world and often found ways to induce abortion. Finally, there is reason to believe that many infants died because of maternal neglect.[68]

Having ventured to analyze some of the mortality and medical variables of Caribbean slavery, I end this essay with a challenge to press forward with improved data and analytical tools, and especially to undertake comparative studies of mortality and the medical treatment of slaves in the Atlantic world.

Notes

1. Richard B. Sheridan, 'The Development of the Plantations to 1750', in *Chapters in Caribbean History* (London, 1970), pp. 12–25.
2. 'Epidemiology and the Slave Trade', *Political Science Quarterly* 83 (June 1968), 190–216.
3. Noel Deerr, *The History of Sugar*, (London, 1949–1950), II, 278–79, 306.
4. Curtin, p. 213.
5. Richard B. Sheridan, 'Africa and the Caribbean in the Atlantic Slave Trade', *American Historical Review* 77, February 1972, 15–21.
6. *Ibid.*, p. 20; Orlando Paterson, *The Sociology of Slavery: An Analysis of the Origins, Development and Structure of Negro Slave Society in Jamaica* (London, 1967), p. 105.
7. Sheridan, 'Africa and the Atlantic Slave Trade', pp. 20–27.
8. William Beckford, *A Descriptive Account of the Island of Jamaica* (London, 1790), II, 311–12.
9. George W. Roberts, *The Population of Jamaica* (Cambridge, England, 1957), pp. 234-35; Eric Williams, *Capitalism and Slavery* (Chapel Hill, 1944), pp. 145–53.
10. Sheridan, 'Africa and the Atlantic Slave Trade', pp. 27–30; Roberts, *op. cit.*, p. 36; Philip D. Curtin, *The Atlantic Slave Trade: A Census* (Madison, Wis., 1969), pp. 52–72; George R. Mellor, *British Imperial Trusteeship 1783–1850*, (London, 1951), pp. 433–42.
11. Gisela Eisner, *Jamaica, 1830–1930: A Study in Economic Growth* (Manchester, 1961), pp. 131–32.
12. Douglas G. Hall, *Free Jamaica, 1838–1865: An Economic History* (New Haven, 1959), pp. 17–18; Barry W. Higman, 'Slave Population and Economy in Jamaica at the Time of Emancipation', unpublished Ph.D. dissertation, UWI, 1970, p. 92.
13. *Bondsmen and Bishops, Slavery and Apprenticeship on the Codrington Plantations of Barbados, 1710–1838*, (Berkeley and Los Angeles, 1958), p. 61.
14. *Ibid.*, pp. 138–41.
15. *A Jamaican Plantation: The History of Worthy Park 1670–1970* (Toronto, 1970), p. 130; Michael Craton, 'Jamaican Slave Mortality: Fresh Light from Worthy Park, Longville and the Tharp Estates', *Journal of Caribbean History*, 3 November (1971), 1–27.
16. Bennett, *op. cit.*, p. 140.
17. Douglas Guthrie, *A History of Medicine* (London, 1945), pp. 193–95, 220–31; Lester S. King, *The Medical World of the Eighteenth Century* (Chicago, 1958), pp. 1–29, 297–325.
18. 'Tropical Medicine', in *Encyclopedia Britannica*, (Chicago, 1955), XXII, 495; H. Harold Scott, *A History of Tropical Medicine* (Baltimore, 1939), I, 1–96, II, 982–1010.
19. Charles Singer, 'History of Medicine', in *Encyclopedia Britannica*, XV, 203.
20. S. Lee (ed.), *The Dictionary of National Biography* (London, 1897), LII, 379–80.
21. Great Britain, *Parliamentary Papers*, 1789, Vol. XXVI, No. 646a, Pt III, Jamaica Appendix, No. 8, 'Report of the Lords of the Committee of Council for Trade and Plantations on the Slave Trade', Heinz Goerke, 'The Life and Scientific Works of Dr. John Quier, Practitioner of Physic and Surgery, Jamaica: 1738–1822', *West Indian Medical Journal* 5 (1956), 23–26. Dr. Quier treated the slaves on Worthy Park estate. See Craton and Walvin *op. cit.*
22. *Memoirs of the Late William Wright, M.D., Fellow of the Royal Societies of London and Edinburgh, etc., With Extracts from His Correspondence and a Selection of His Papers on Medical and Botanical Subjects* (Edinburgh, 1828), pp. 1–19.
23. *Ibid*, pp. 23, 86.
24. *Ibid.*, pp. 90–92.
25. *Ibid.*, p. 175.
26. L. Stephen and S. Lee (eds), *The Dictionary of National Biography* (New York, 1890), XXII, 368–69.
27. James Grainger, M.D., *An Essay on the More Common West-India Diseases; and the Remedies which that Country Itself Produces: To which are added, Some Hints on the Management, etc., of Negroes. The Second Edition, With Practical Notes, and a Linnean Index, by William Wright, M.D.F.R.S.*, (Edinburgh, 1802), pp. i–viii.
28. James Johnston Abraham, *Lettsom: His Life, Times, Friends and Descendants* (London, 1933), pp.1–47.
29. *Ibid.*, pp. 48–60.
30. *Ibid.*, pp. 61–127, 150, 208, 276, 295–98.

31. *A Treatise on the Diseases of Negroes, As they Occur in the Island of Jamaica with Observations on the Country Remedies* (Jamaica, 1820), pp. 1-2, 8-11, 112, 143-168.
32. *An Historical Account of the Rise and Growth of the West-India Colonies* (London, 1690), p. 14.
33. William Dickson, *Mitigation of Slavery, Part I, Letters and Papers of the late Hon. J. Steele* (London, 1814), pp. 150-53.
34. *Notes on the West Indies* (London, 1806), I, 388-92.
35. Bennett, *op. cit.*, pp. 43, 139-41.
36. *A New History of Jamaica from the Earliest Accounts to the Taking of Porto Bello by Vice-Admiral Vernon* (London, 1740), p. 50.
37. *The History, Civil and Commercial, of the British Colonies in the West Indies* (Dublin, 1793), II, 127-28; for another favorable impression of the medical treatment of slaves, see Beckford, *op. cit.*, II, 304-06.
38. *A History of Jamaica* (London, 1807), pp. 176-79.
39. Roberts, *op. cit.*, pp. 238-45.
40. Jamaica Public Record Office, Spanish Town, *Inventorys*, Vols. XXI-XXV, LI-LVI.
41. *Ibid.*, Vols. LXXXIII-XC.
42. Eisner, *op. cit.*, pp. 133-40, 165-66, 337-40.
43. Vere Langford Oliver, *The History of the Island of Antigua* (London, 1894-99); *Letters Books of Dr. Walter Tullideph of Antigua and Scotland*, 1734-67, 3 vols, 'Dr. Tullideph's General Ledger'; 'Dr. Tullidephs Medical Ledger'. I am indebted to the late Sir Herbert Ogilvy, Bart, for permission to quote extracts from these records.
44. Oliver, *op. cit.*, I, xcviii-cix.
45. *Ibid.*, cxxiii-cxlvii.
46. *Brief Account of the Island of Antigua, together with the customs and manners of its inhabitants, white as well as black; as also an accurate statement of the food, clothing, and labor* (London, 1789), reprinted in Oliver, *op. cit.*, I, cxxxiii.
47. Eisner, *op. cit.*, p. 337; Jack Star, 'Where Have Our Doctors Gone', *Look* 35 29 June 1971, 15-17.
48. S. Lee (ed.), *The Dictionary of National Biography* (London, 1899), LIX, 396-97.
49. Oliver, *op. cit.*, III, 186-87.
50. *Ibid.*, I, 184-86.
51. *Ibid.*, II, 96-103.
52. Charles B. Boog Watson (ed.), *Register of Edinburgh Apprentices, 1701-1755* (Edinburgh, 1929), p. 88; Tullideph to Andrew Aiton in Scotland, dated Antigua, 16 May 1757, *Tullideph Letter Book*, Vol. II; Oliver, *op. cit.*, I, 223-25; III, 128-33, 155-62; R. B. Sheridan, 'The Rise of a Colonial Gentry: A Case Study of Antigua, 1730-1775', *Economic History Review*, 2d ser., 13 (1961), 342-57.
53. Great Britain, British Museum, Sloane MSS, 4049, Vol. XIV, fol. 3, 'Original Letters to Mr. H. Sloane'.
54. Tullideph to Sir Hans Sloane, dated Antigua, 25 June 1734, *Tullideph Letter Book*, Vol. I.
55. 'Tullideph's Medical Ledger', fols. 1-247.
56. *Ibid.*, fols. 52, 54, 62, 108, 135.
57. Tullideph wrote to Alexander Johnston on 21 October 1734, 2 February 1735, 22 October 1736, 23 May 1736, 27 June 1737, and 10 August 1738 — all in Vol. I of the *Tullideph Letter Books.*
58. Tullideph to William Dunbar, Merchant in London, dated Antigua, 24 March 1734, *ibid.*
59. Tullideph to Alexander Johnston in London, dated Antigua, 17 April 1738, *ibid.*
60. Tullideph to David Tullideph in England, dated Antigua, 3 November 1738, *ibid.*
61. Tullideph to Thomas Tullideph in Scotland, dated Antigua 28 April 1736, *ibid.*
62. 'A Quarter of a Millennium of Anglo-Scottish Union', in F. A and E. Humphreys (eds), *The Historian's Business and Other Essays*, (Oxford, 1961), pp. 84-94.
63. C. M. MacInnes, 'The Slave Trade', in Northcote Parkinson (ed.), *The Trade Winds: A Study of British Overseas Trade during the French Wars 1793-1815*, (London 1948), pp. 254-55; Curtin, *Atlantic Slave Trade*, pp. 275-86.
64. Elsa V. Goveia, *Slave Society in the British Leeward Islands at the End of the Eighteenth Century*, (New Haven, 1965), pp. 191-98.
65. Cultural barriers which impeded European doctors in treating patients in colonial countries are dicussed perceptively by Frantz Fanon in Chap. 4, 'Medicine and Colonialism', of his book, *A Dying Colonialism* (New York, 1967), pp. 121-45.
66. *Sociology of Slavery*, p. 105.
67. *Ibid.*, p. 105; Waldemar Westergaard, *The Danish West Indies Under Company Rule* (New York, 1917), p. 169, C. L. R. James, *The Black Jacobins: Toussaint L'Ouverture and the San Domingo Revolution* (New York, 2nd edn 1963), p. 88.
68. Patterson, *op. cit.*, pp. 106-12.

Demographic Performance of Two Slave Populations of the Dutch Speaking Caribbean

HUMPHREY E. LAMUR*

1. Introduction

One of the most challenging issues of slave demography in the Western hemisphere is the great difference in the natural increase of the U.S. slave population compared with the slave societies in the Caribbean and Latin America. This differential persisted during the entire period of slavery. The U.S. slave population increased at a rate of 2.4 per cent annually during the 1810–60 period, while in Cuba the slave population declined by 7 per cent between 1816 and 1860. For Jamaica and Brazil the corresponding figures are around 0.5 per cent (1817–32) and 3.5 per cent (between 1798 and 1825) (Fogel and Engerman 1979: 567; Klein and Engerman 1978: 360). One of the few exceptions to this Caribbean pattern of declining slave population growth is the demographic performance of the slaves of the Dutch Antilles. Since their population growth has been so different from that of Suriname, the other Dutch speaking Caribbean country, it will be interesting to draw comparisions between them in order to explain the differentials (Section 3). Before doing so, a brief overview of the demographic evolution of the two slave populations during the second half of the nineteenth century is presented in Section 2. Section 4 summarises the findings of this paper.

2. Natural increase of slaves in Curacao and Suriname

Two sources regarding the Dutch Antilles slave population are of importance. First, the official vital statistics that are provided by the planters and published annually by the *Distrikt-en Wijkmeesters (Curaçaose verslagen van 1840–1862)*. The second source is an 1854 report of *Gouverneurs en Gezaghebbers* of the Dutch Antilles compiled on request of the Dutch government, in connection with the abolition of slavery (*Rapport der Staatscommissie II 1856*). As far as Curaçao, the largest of the six islands constituting the Dutch Antilles, is concerned, the population figures derived from the two sources differ significantly. The higher rates provided by the Governor are justified by the fact that the planners failed to register the slaves aged 60 years or older since these had not been taken into account in computing the tax (*hoofdenbelasting*). The smaller deviation from the census total of January 5, 1857 is another test of the reliability of the material provided by the Governor. Nevertheless, I have decided to use the official vital statistics since they cover a number of consecutive years and provide us with a breakdown of the data according to demographic components. Regarding the nature and reliability of the Suriname data, I refer to an earlier publication (Lamur 1977).

Because of the great availability of information, most of the comparisons will be between Suriname and Curaçao, excluding the other five islands of the Dutch Antilles. For the same reason the article will focus on the second half of the nineteenth century. Moreover, this confinement to the period when the slave imports ceased precludes the effect of factors which can distort the comparison. These variables include the uneven sex ratios, the age

*I am grateful to Bob Scholte for his contribution in preparing the English version of this paper. For their comments and suggestions, I wish to record my debt to S. Engerman, H. Hoetink and Richard Steckel. Richard Steckel was also extremely helpful in providing me with material from his Ph.D. dissertation. I am also grateful to Hanneke Kossen for typing several drafts of the paper.

Boletin de Estudios Latino Americanos y del Caribe, No. 30 (June, 1981), pp. 87–102.

structure of slave women entering Curaçao and Suriname after their child-bearing period had begun.

During the last decades before emancipation both slave societies showed a decline in population size with a 4.3 per cent rate of decrease from 1840 to 1863 and an 11.6 per cent in the case of Suriname for the years 1849–63 (Table 1). The decline in the total slave population of Curaçao resulted from manumissions. As far as the natural increase is concerned, however, Curaçao showed a positive rate during the entire 1840–61 period, while the Suriname rate was negative for nearly all the years between 1849 and 1861. The 0.3 per cent rate of decrease of the Suriname slave population has resulted from a birth rate of 3.1 per cent and a mortality rate of 3.4 per cent. For Curaçao the average annual rate of increase is composed of a birth rate of 4.2 per cent and a death rate of 2.4 per cent (Table 2).

The other islands of the Dutch Antilles have also displayed rates of natural increase between 1850 and 1861, as Table 3 indicates. The trend of the natural increase is another aspect of slave demography which differentiates the two societies. While the Suriname rate has changed from negative to positive after emancipation, in the case of Curaçao Hartog (1961: 446) dates this change as early as 1778. However, he presents no evidence to support his statement and currently available data do not as yet permit an analysis of this issue.

The differences in fertility level between Curaçao and Suriname are also discernible when a more exact guide to the reproductive performance, namely the cohort fertility, is used. For Curaçao, the calculation of this rate is based on the accounts of emancipation (*Archief van de Algemene Rekenkamer* 1863). These plantation records list the ages of female slaves and their children, if there were children living with them (for problems relating to the estimation of demographic variables used in this article, see appendix). Of a total of 148 plantations in 1863, 123 have been omitted from the analysis, since the number of slaves per estate, 25–30, is too small to warrant reliable statistical calculation. Eight of the remaining 25 plantations included mothers aged 45 and have been selected for further analysis. For each of these mothers the average number of children living with her and registered in the archives has been calculated; subsequently the same has been done for the group of women as a whole, yielding a value of 5.5. Table 4 demonstrates that the rate has been highest (7.5) and the average birth interval quite small (3.6) on the smaller units, whilst child-bearing has begun at earlier ages. This seems to be consistent with the findings for the U.S. slave population around 1830 (Fogel and Engerman 1979: 574). Taking into account both the children who were born alive but died before the 1863 census and those unlisted for other reasons (sales, manumissions, runaways), it is safe to conclude that the true value of the cohort fertility rate exceeds the number of 5.5 children computed on the basis of the records. To make an assessment of the correct figure, adjusting only for infant deaths, the following steps have been taken:

1. For the 1840–61 period the birth rate of 4.2 per cent and the death rate of 2.4 per cent which have been computed earlier, are considered as minimum values, taking into account the under-registration of births and deaths.
2. It has been assumed that the Curaçao slave population satisfies the four criteria characterising a stable population, namely, a constant rate of natural increase and age-

Table 1 Population growth

January of the year	Curaçao *	Curaçao **	Suriname
1840	5750	n.a.	n.a.
1841	6023	n.a.	n.a.
1842	5979	n.a.	n.a.
1843	5772	n.a.	n.a.
1844	5793	6869	n.a.
1845	5569	6555	n.a.
1846	5619	6931	n.a.
1847	5436	6923	n.a.
1848	5479	6809	n.a.
1849	5585	6703	41310
1850	5638	6854	40311
1851	5573	6893	39697
1852	5542	6891	39157
1853	5503	6981	38690
1854	5418	n.a.	38545
1855	5615	n.a.	38051
1856	5585	n.a.	38592
1857	6986	n.a.	38404
1858	6309	n.a.	37961
1859	5855	n.a.	38142
1860	5962	n.a.	37796
1861	5398	n.a.	37001
1862	5524	n.a.	36732
1863	5498	n.a.	36484

Source: * Annual reports of the *Distrikt-en Wijkmeesters* and *Koloniale Verslagen*
** *Gouverneu en Gezaghebbers* *Rapport der Staatscommissie II* 1856 pp.136–37
n.a.: not available

Table 2 Rates of natural increase of slave population, Curaçao and Suriname

Year	Curaçao			Suriname		
	Natural increase per 100 slaves					
	Birth	Death	Nat. increase	Birth	Death	Nat. increase
1840	3.7	1.6	2.1			
1841	4.5	2.8	1.7			
1842	3.3	2.3	1.0			
1843	4.1	2.5	1.6			
1844	4.2	2.7	1.5			
1845	2.5	1.7	0.8			
1846	4.1	2.5	1.6			
1847	3.9	2.1	1.8			
1848	4.5	1.6	2.9			
1849	4.4	1.9	2.5	2.7	3.4	−0.7
1850	5.0	2.4	2.6	3.3	3.0	+0.3
1851	4.7	2.4	2.3	3.1	3.9	−0.8
1852	3.7	3.2	0.5	3.1	3.2	−0.1
1853	4.6	2.7	1.9	3.1	2.7	+0.4
1854	5.2	2.7	2.5	3.0	3.2	−0.2
1855	5.1	2.7	2.4	2.8	3.8	−1.0
1856	4.0	2.7	1.3	3.2	3.1	+0.1
1857	3.9	2.0	1.9	3.1	4.1	−0.1
1858	5.0	2.0	3.0	3.3	3.1	+0.2
1859	3.9	2.8	1.1	3.2	4.6	−1.4
1860	4.7	4.1	0.6	3.1	3.4	−0.3
1861	5.2	2.6	2.6	3.1	3.8	−0.7
1840–49	3.9	2.1	1.8	—	—	—
1850–61	4.5	2.6	1.9	3.1	3.4	−0.3
1840–61	4.2	2.4	1.8	—	—	—

Source: (Curaçao): Annual reports of the *Distriki-en Wijkmeesters* and *Koloniale Verslagen*

specific fertility, unchanged age structure and negligible migration rate.

3. Given a 1.8 per cent rate of natural increase computed on the basis of vital statistics and a gross reduction rate of 2.70 (m = 27) which has been calculated as 5.5/2.05, the Coale/Demeny stable population table (United Nations 1967: 85, 89) points to the West model (female) level 9. This choice implies that the birth rate has been somewhere between 3.8 and 4.3 per cent, while the death rate has amounted to 2.3 per cent.
4. But since the cohort fertility rate has exceeded the value of 5.5, as pointed out earlier, the true figure for the gross reproduction rate has also been higher than 2.7, corresponding to 5.5 (= 2.7 × 2.05). This means that the birth rate has also exceeded 4.3, while the death rate has been over 2.3 per cent, which implies a 2.0 per cent rate of natural increase.

This preliminary conclusion is supported by an analysis of the age structure of Savonet, the largest estate of Curaçao during slavery (274 slaves). The 'proportions at age x', one of the criteria for comparing the age structure of Savonet with the stable population model, has not yielded satisfactory results since it does not conform to any of the age structures of the model. The other criteria, 'proportions up to age x', however, points more or less to an age structure of the model corresponding to a value of R equal to 0.025 (Table 5). This rate of natural increase has resulted from a birth rate of 4.86 per cent and a death rate of 2.36 per cent. If this is correct, the estimated cohort fertility rate of the Savonet female slaves in 1863 was 6.4 while their expectation of life at birth amounted to 40.0 years. This finding is more or less consistent with the results for the Curaçao slave population as a whole, which point to vital rates exceeding 4.3 per cent and 2.3 per cent. So it is likely that the values computed for Savonet have

Table 3 Population and vital rates, 1850–61, Dutch Antilles

	Aruba			Bonaire			Curaçao			Saba			St. Eustatius			St. Maarten		
Year	B	D	N	B	D	N	B	D	N	B	D	N	B	D	N	B	D	N
1850	3.6	0.8	2.8	4.7	2.5	2.2	5.0	2.4	2.6	1.5	0.9	0.6	1.9	1.8	0.1	4.2	1.5	2.7
1851	3.9	1.0	2.9	4.2	2.3	1.9	4.7	2.4	2.3	1.9	0.7	1.2	2.1	1.3	0.8	3.3	0.8	2.5
1852	2.4	1.0	1.4	3.5	1.4	2.1	3.7	3.2	0.5	1.2	0.4	0.8	3.5	2.7	0.8	3.6	1.5	2.1
1853	3.8	1.5	2.3	3.9	1.8	2.1	4.6	2.7	1.9	1.0	0.6	0.4	3.1	1.6	1.5	3.3	1.0	2.3
1854	6.2	1.5	4.7	5.6	2.0	3.6	5.2	2.7	2.5	2.4	0.3	2.1	2.7	2.1	0.6	3.5	1.2	2.3
1855	3.0	1.5	1.5	5.7	2.0	3.7	5.1	2.7	2.4	3.5	0.3	3.2	3.3	2.1	1.2	3.1	1.1	2.0
1856	4.3	1.4	2.9	5.1	5.2	0.1	4.0	2.7	1.3	3.7	1.3	2.4	4.1	2.8	1.3	2.7	1.4	1.3
1857	4.2	1.5	2.7	4.1	1.2	2.9	3.9	2.0	1.9	4.3	0.5	3.8	3.2	1.7	1.5	2.0	1.4	0.6
1858	4.5	2.4	2.1	5.7	2.2	3.5	5.0	2.0	3.0	4.0	1.9	2.1	4.1	2.2	1.9	2.9	1.3	1.6
1859	3.6	2.1	1.5	4.0	2.0	2.0	3.9	2.8	1.1	4.3	1.0	3.3	3.7	3.1	0.6	2.4	0.8	1.6
1860	4.8	2.4	2.4	5.7	1.6	4.1	4.7	4.1	0.6	3.5	1.4	2.1	5.2	4.6	0.6	1.4	1.0	0.4
1861	7.0	1.5	5.5	4.6	1.1	3.5	5.2	2.6	2.6	3.9	1.9	2.0	3.5	2.6	0.9	3.0	9.8	2.2
1850–61	4.2	1.5	2.7	2.1	2.6	4.5	2.6	1.9	2.9	0.9	2.0	3.3.	2.3	1.0	2.9	1.1	1.8	

Source: *Koloniale Verslagen*
B = Birth per 100
D = Death per 100
N = Natural increase per 100

Table 4 Cohort fertility rate and its determinants for Curaçao slave population in 1863, before adjusting for unregistered infant mortality

Plant. size	Cohort fert. rate R	Age at first birth F	Age at last birth L	Average child-bearing period (L – F)	Average birth interval S	Proportion ever bearing children
1–50	7.5 (2)	19.5	43.0	23.5	3.6	n.a.
51–100	4.3 (3)	22.0	32.0	10.0	3.5	n.a.
101–150	5.3 (3)	24.0	40.3	16.3	4.2	n.a.
Total	5.5 (8)	22.1	38.0	15.9	3.8	0.80

Source: *Archief van de Algemene Rekenkamer* 1863
( ) Absolute number of women aged 45 years
n.a.: not available

prevailed for the slaves of Curaçao as a whole.

The fertility level of the slaves of the Richardson plantation on St. Maarten is another case which underscores the unusually high rate of reproduction of the Dutch Antilles. Of a total of 69 slaves belonging to Ann Louisa Richardson, 26 have been recorded as living in units consisting of five mothers who were living with their surviving children (*Archief van de Algemene Rekenkamer* 1863). Based on data for the two mothers aged 42 and 51, while excluding the others for reasons indicated in Table 6, a family size of 8.5 has been computed. This figure is even higher than the 6.4 rate calculated for Curaçao, in spite of the fact that no adjustments have been made both for children who have died before registration and those unlisted for other reasons. However, the very small number of women upon which the calcuation has been based does not permit reliable statistical analysis.

An adjustment for the other demographic variables, namely the birth interval and the child-bearing period, can now be made using the

Table 5 Age distribution of the West model, level 9 (females) for R equals 0.025 and 0.030, and the female slave population of Savonet, 1863

Age	R (0.025)	Proportions up to age (x) Sav.	R (0.030)	Age group	R (0.025)	Proportions at age (x) Sav.	R (0.030)
1	4.2	4.2	4.7	0–1	4.2	4.2	4.7
5	17.9	22.8	19.6	1–4	13.6	18.5	14.9
10	32.2	37.8	35.0	5–9	14.3	15.0	15.3
15	44.5	46.4	47.9	10–14	12.2	8.5	12.8
20	55.0	53.5	58.6	15–19	10.5	7.1	10.7
25	63.9	62.8	67.4	20–24	8.9	9.2	8.8
30	71.4	74.2	74.7	25–29	7.5	11.4	7.2
35	77.7	80.0	80.6	30–34	6.2	5.7	5.9
40	82.9	85.0	85.4	35–39	5.2	5.0	4.8
45	87.2	88.5	89.3	40–44	4.3	3.5	3.8
50	90.7	92.1	92.4	45–49	3.5	3.5	3.0
55	93.6	94.2	94.8	50–54	2.8	2.1	2.4
60	95.8	94.2	96.7	55–59	2.2	0.0	1.8
65	97.5	95.0	98.0	60–64	1.6	0.7	1.3
				65–69	1.1	0.7	0.9
				70–74	0.7	2.1	0.5
				75–79	0.3	0.7	0.2
				80 +	0.1	1.4	0.1

Source: *Archief van de Algemene Rekenkamer* 1863

Table 6 Richardson plantations, St. Maarten, November 17, 1862

	Age of the mother			Birth interval										
Name of the mother	on Nov. 17 1862	at birth of first child	at birth of last child	1–2	2–3	3–4	4–5	5–6	6–7	7–8	8–9	9–10	Average	No. of live births
Phillis Richardson*	73	28	37	3	6								4.5	3**
Minverva Richardson***	36	17		2	8	5								
Maria Richardson	42	17	40	3	1	2	2	5	1	2	6	3	2.7	10
Polyninal Richardson****	19	16		3										
Hetty Daniels	51	25	46	3	4	2	3	4	4				3.3	7

Source: *Archief van de Rekenkamer* 1863
* Mother of Minverva, Maria and Polyninal
** Some of the children may have died already since the time when the mother reached age 45
*** Incomplete (age under 45)
**** Incomplete (age under 45)

following equation developed by Steckel (1977: 96–103).

$$R = \frac{(\bar{L} - \bar{F})}{\bar{S}} + 1$$

where:	R	=	cohort fertility rate
	(L – F)	=	child-bearing period
	L	=	age of mother at the birth of her first child
	F	=	age of mother at the birth of her last child
	S	=	birth interval

Based on the data of the plantation records, the average number of live births per mother has proven to be 5.5, while the ages at first and last surviving children have been 22.1 and 38.0 years respectively. Adjustment for the unregistered live births has raised the cohort fertility rate to 6.4. In order to estimate the average birth interval, information on the birth order of the additional child who died before the 1863 registration is required. The following alternatives are of importance:

1. Assuming that the unlisted child was born between the birth dates of the first and the last registered children, the correction for the additional birth lowers the average birth interval to 2.8 years.
2. If the child was born before the birth date of the oldest of the registered children or after that of the youngest, it is not possible to compute the average birth interval since the exact date of birth of the missing child is unknown. However, there is no reason to doubt that the interval is different from the one computed for the surviving children, namely 3.8 (Table 4). This implies a child-bearing period of 19.7 years. Comparison with the Richardson estate of St. Maarten, however, points to birth intervals of 2.7 and 3.3 years for the mothers aged 42 and 51. This tends to suggest that the first assumption is more likely to be correct, which implies an average birth interval of 2.8 years and a child-bearing period of 15.9. This extremely short birth interval, relative to that of the American slave population (Table 7), is surprising and raises a number of questions, which will be dealt with in Section 3.

The unusual high fertility level of the Curaçao slave population is demonstrated if compared with the two other slave populations indicated in Table 7. Curaçao holds a middle position between the U.S. and Suriname. It should be emphasized that in the case of Suriname the fertility has been measured in terms of the total fertility rate instead of the cohort fertility figure based on material of three plantations, namely Andressa (timber), Catharina Sophia (sugar) and Mijn Vermaak (coffee). None of these estates has shown a higher rate than Curaçao.

In trying to explain the differences in fertility level between Curaçao and Suriname, both demographic and socio-economic factors are of importance. The demographic variables include: the age of the mother at the birth of her first and last children, the average birth interval and the proportion of women ever bearing children (Fogel and Engerman 1979: 574). Since the differences in child-bearing period between the two slave societies have been small, as Table 7 demonstrates, it is unlikely that this demographic component can account for the Curaçao-Suriname differential in fertility. Data on the rate of childlessness point to an estimated 29 per cent for Suriname and 20 per cent for Curaçao. While the rate for Curaçao exceeds that of Suriname, the difference is too small to explain a large proportion of the fertility differential between Curaçao and Suriname. As Klein and Engerman (1979: 366) have pointed

Table 7 Fertility rate for three slave populations

Country	Cohort fertility rate R	Average child-bearing period in years (L – F)	Average birth interval in years S	Proportion ever bearing children
US 1830–60	7.2	18.0	2.9	0.76
Curaçao 1840–60	6.4	[15.9 19.7	[2.8 3.8	[0.80 0.80
Suriname 1850–60	3.0	12.1	3.1	0.71

Source: (U.S.)—Fogel 1976; Klein and Engerman 1978: 360–368.

out in the case of Jamaica, these relatively low rates of childlessness for Suriname tend to contradict the notion that infertility (possibly caused by venereal disease) has been widespread in Suriname, and has accounted for the low fertility of slave women of this Dutch speaking Caribbean country. It is more likely that the differential average birth interval has caused the observed differences in fertility between Curaçao and Suriname. But what accounts for the smaller birth interval of the Curaçao slave women? Since no other demographic factor is of importance in this connection, I shall now turn to social variables to investigate their possible contribution to the substantial differences in average birth interval between the two slave populations.

3. Fertility and labour conditions

In dealing with slavery in the Dutch speaking Caribbean it has often been pointed out that the treatment of slaves in Curaçao has been less cruel than in Suriname (among others, Hoetink 1958; 1969; Van Lier 1971: 117–176; Paula 1969; *Rapport der Staatscommissie* 1856; Römer 1977). Hence, it may be useful to discuss whether this factor has contributed to the differences in fertility level. However, the conclusions have to be tentative since the relevant archive material both on this factor and the other social variables has not yet been fully explored.

Because of its favourable geographical location on the coast, Willemstad, the capital of Curaçao, functioned as a commercial centre during the eighteenth and early nineteenth centuries. Slaves brought from Africa to Curaçao were sold to Spanish planters in Colombia, Venezuela and other Latin American countries (Goslinga 1977). Since the slaves were used as merchandise, a less harsh treatment served the interest of their owners (*Brief der Kamer van Amsterdam van 24 december 1694*; Hamelberg 1901. I: *documenten blz.* 107). The decision taken in 1642 to build two hospitals in Curaçao for the treatment of the slaves, long before such facilities existed for civilians and soldiers, was aimed at enhancing the exchange value of the slaves. The appointment of a medical doctor around 1682 charged with the slaves' treatment points in the same direction (Hamelberg 1901. I: 77–78; Hartog 1961: 446–51; Römer 1977: 31–35).

Another factor indicating the less cruel treatment of the slaves in Curaçao in comparison with Suriname is the nature of the work. To the extent that plantation labour existed in Curaçao, it primarily concerned cattle raising, planting of corn and growing of sorghum. Only six months a year were spent on these activities, while during the second half of the year the slaves were kept busy on the pens with turning the cattle out to grass repairing or building fences on the pasture land, cleaning the pastures of weeds, cleaning the wells, timber cutting and so on (*Rapport der Staatscommissie* 1856. II: 134–54, 226). Sugar estates producing for the world market, where heavy physically demanding labour and long working hours usually prevent slave fertility from rising as in Suriname, were non-existent in Curaçao. The importance of this factor in explaining the Curaçao-Suriname fertility differential is supported by a comparison of the slave fertility by crop in Suriname. Preliminary data show that around 1860 the child/woman ratio of the slaves of sugar plantations was 25–30 per cent lower than the rate on plantations growing other crops such as cotton or coffee (Lamur, *Slave Fertility and Plantation Labour in Suriname*).

The findings for Suriname are consistent with Higman's analysis of the Jamaican slave fertility: 'it appears that the only units to approach the extremely high rate of natural decrease on the sugar estates were the jobbing gangs' (1967: 122–123). The fertility-reducing effect of the nature of the work was reinforced by the influence of the size of the plantations. In the case of Suriname, the fertility rate of the slaves of smaller units was higher than the rate for those on the large plantations (Lamur, *Slave Fertility*.). In this respect the Suriname data are also comparable with those for Jamaica (Higman, *op. cit.* 127–28). In addtion, at the end of the eighteenth century the ratio of whites to slaves was about 60 per cent for Curaçao, while in the case of Suriname the rate amounted to 5 per cent in 1834. Since the Curaçao plantations were on the average smaller than those in Suriname (Table 8), it is likely that this factor contributed to the higher fertility rate of the Curaçao slave population.

The smaller size of the Curaçao plantations, the nature of the work as well as the greater share of whites, relative to Suriname, all these factors combined, imply that the Curaçao slaves had more contact with the white society in their daily lives. 'In general the relation of the master to his slaves in Curaçao was one of individual contact, there was no fear on the part of the owners, and therefore no insecurity or sadism' (Hoetink 1969: 182–83; compare also Paula

Table 8 Plantations and plantation slaves by size of slave population, Curaçao and Suriname, 1862

	Plantations		Slaves			
Size of	Number		Number		Percentage	
slave pop.	Curaçao	Suriname	Curaçao	Suriname	Curaçao	Suriname
1–50	128	64	1523	1075	41.9	3.9
51–100	13	57	961	4320	26.4	15.7
101–150	8	51	876	6139	24.1	22.4
151–200	0	15	0	2579	0	9.4
201–250	0	19	0	4291	0	15.7
251–300	1	7	274	1903	7.5	6.9
301–350	0	7	0	2282	0	8.3
351–400	0	5	0	1932	0	7.1
401–450	0	1	0	410	0	1.5
451–500	0	1	0	450	0	1.6
500+	0	3	0	2012	0	7.3
TOTAL	150	230	3634	27393	100.0	100.0

Source: *Archief van de Algemene Rekenkamer*

1967; Römer 1977: 24–64; for Suriname, see Van Lier 1971: 51–84, 117–76). Hence it is conceivable that the Curaçao slaves partly adopted some of the white masters' customs, among them the European childnursing practices which imply shorter birth intervals associated with shorter lactation periods. The Suriname data on the other hand point to the retention of African patterns of a lactation period of two to three years, as well as to the practice of abstention from sexual intercourse during lactation (Lamur, *Slave Fertility*). However, no information is as yet available on the lactational practices of the Curaçao slave women. The only source which provides data which is probably related to this subject is a publication by Brenneker (1973: 1314–15; 1975: 2518) on the folklore of the Dutch Antilles. One of his informants who was interviewed in the 1970s claimed that in older times the lactation period was two years, while only a three months' period of abstention from sexual intercourse during lactation was observed. This information is consistent with the small birth interval for the Curaçao slave population (2.9 years) calculated earlier on the basis of cohort analysis. However, Brenneker provides no indication that the expression 'in older time' refers to the Curaçao slave period (for a discussion of variations in cultural adaptation in analysing the Jamaican-U.S. fertility differential, see Engerman 1976: 265–66; 1977: 607–08).

While important, the medical treatment, the plantation size and the nature of the work are not the only factors which are related to the high fertility level of the Curaçao slave population. It has frequently been argued that a poor diet has a negative effect on human fertility. A deficiency of protein (in meat and fish for example) tends to lower the age of menopause and to raise the age of menarche, while the frequency of irregular and anovulatory cycli is increased. In addition, the probability of a miscarriage and a still-birth is higher than for an inadequately nourished female. And in the adult male, loss of sperm mobility and cessation of sperm production may be the result of undernutrition (Frisch 1978: 22). Fragmentary information shows that regarding nutrition the slaves of Curaçao were also better off than their partners in distress in Suriname. In 1662 provision grounds were established to make the provision of the slaves less dependent on imported food supplies (Hartog 1961: 448). Though some authors claim that the diet of the Curaçao slaves was poor (Goslinga 1961: 381), most contemporaries characterise their diet as adequate and certainly superior to that of the slaves in Suriname. J. J. Putman, a Roman Catholic priest who lived in Curaçao between 1835 and 1853, claims that the food provided by some owners was below legal standards. He adds, however, the even in those cases the slaves did not suffer because of the possibility for stealing food (*Rapport der Staatscommissie* 1856. II: 284, 285; Teenstra 1836 I: 171, 172). In addition, the Curaçao diet consisting of corn, fruit, meat and fish was rich in protein, while the nutritional content of the diet in Suriname was very low, consisting of mainly plantains, yams and some dried fish (Emmer and Van den

Boogaart 1977: 210–13; Van der Kuyp 1958). Putman's observation that low birth rates had been observed in Curaçao in the years of bad harvest, points to a coherence between fertility and the quality of nutrition. In spite of the plausibility of this relationship the evidence for it provided in this paper is quite weak. More information on this factor is required before firm conclusions can be drawn.

The same applies to other factors which may also have contributed to the Curaçao-Suriname fertility differentials. One is the unhealthy, swampy climate of Suriname in comparision with Curaçao (Teenstra 1836. I: 177). Another variable is the presumed breeding of slaves on the Dutch Antillian island Bonaire. The offsprings of this stud farm, situated in a valley called Rincón, are said to have been reared for sale to planters in Curaçao and slave importing countries (Teenstra 1836. I: 188, 189). It may be mentioned in this connection that the Bonaire birth rate was higher than that of the other islands between 1850 and 1861, as Table 3 indicates. An even higher rate, namely 3 per cent, has been observed for Bonaire during the 1817–36 period (*Rapport der Staatscommissie* 1856. II: 10–11). However, since Teenstra presents no evidence to support his statement on the *aanfokkerij van slaven* or its demographic effects, his claim is misleading. Lowenthal and Clark (1977: 512, 527–30) may be correct in stating that the rapid natural increase of the slave population in Barbuda has probably misled modern commentators to conclude that slave breeding occurred. Nevertheless, Lowenthal and Clark's rejection of stud farms in Barbuda, or my remarks in the case of Bonaire, are not sufficient arguments against the plausibility of slave breeding in the Western hemisphere.

The family and household structure of the slaves is a third factor worth mentioning in a study on the fertility differential between slave societies. But here too no information is available for Suriname, while in the case of the Dutch Antilles only the Richardson plantation provides some data on this factor. As indicated earlier, of a total of 69 slaves 26 are listed in the plantation records as living in units, namely five mothers each registered with their surviving children. For the remaining slaves, consisting of seven women of child-bearing age and eleven children below the age of 15, no kinship relation is indicated. So it is not possible to trace whether or not they were residing outside the woman-and-children household type.

Hence, it is too soon to state that only 37 per cent of the slaves of the Richardson plantation were living in units, consisting of a woman and her children. Nor is it correct to assume that these five households were mother-headed. An important aspect of this issue concerns the relative occurrence of two-parent households. As pointed out by Fogel and Engerman (1979: 578), 'recent work has led to a substantial revision of earlier views on the slave family. Earlier writings presumed a relative absence of stable mating patterns among slaves . . . , thus linking the slave experience to issues relating to the twentieth century black family'. This view has recently been questioned for the United States. Data published by Higman (1973; 1975: 266–70) suggest a higher frequency of living in two-parent households among West Indian slaves than was previously believed (see also Fogel and Engerman 1979: 575). For the Dutch speaking Caribbean, data are now being processed to test the plausibility of the view that stable mating patterns were virtually non-existent among the slaves in those areas.

4. Summary

The American slave population grew much faster than the slave societies of the Caribbean and Latin America, even after the closing of the slave trade. Brazil, Cuba, Guyana, Jamaica, as well as Martinique and Suriname, showed a substantial natural decrease. One of the few exceptions to this Caribbean pattern of declining slave population is the demographic performance of the slaves of the Dutch Antilles. A comparison beween Curaçao and Suriname suggests that the fertility rate of the former is twice as high as that of the latter. It is likely that this differential is caused by differences in the average birth interval between the two populations. This demographic variable, in turn, is probably related to differences in both the nature of slavery and the labour conditions on the plantations. Nutrition is another factor which may have contributed to the differences in fertility. No information is as yet available on the role that other variables may have played in causing the differential.

Appendix: Calculation of the age of the mother at the birth of her first child, the number of children ever born, the rate of childlessness

It must be emphasized that some of the demographic variables used in this article have been estimated. Here I only list both the steps involved and the limitations imposed by the nature of the material or the method employed.

Children ever born

In calculating the cohort fertility rate, data on the number of children ever born to a woman are required. However, the exact number is not known since only data on the number of children who survived to be recorded in the plantation archive of 1863 are available. In addition, the records also omit the children no longer living at home; for example, older children who were sold or left the maternal household for any other reason. Besides, it is likely that older women aged 60 or over have been misclassified as non-mothers because their children no longer lived at home (Trussel and Steckel 1978: 488–89). All these biases combined may have produced a cohort fertility rate which is lower than the number of surviving children ever born to a woman. In Section 2 of this paper an attempt has been made to adjust for these biases. The names of the eight Curaçao plantations used in this context are Valentijn, Rondeklip, Zevenhuizen, Suikertuintje, St. Jacob, St. Barber en Fuik, Koraal and Rustenburg. As mentioned earlier, in the case of Suriname, fertility has been measured in terms of the general fertility rate, based on material from the following estates: Andressa, Catharina Sophia and Mijn Vermasak.

Ages at first birth

The plantation records used for this article list the ages of female slaves and their children for the year 1863, if there were children living with them. I have simply subtracted the age of the mother at the birth of her first child. However, there is no guarantee that the children listed with the woman were her own, and in case the eldest is an adopted child the computed age at first birth is biased downwards. No information is available on the occurrence of adoption during slavery in the Dutch Antilles and Suriname. For the U.S., Sutch (cited in Trussel and Steckel 1978: 478) claims that adoption was rare among slaves and 'estimated that only 1 per cent of slave children under age thirteen were orphans'. The nature of the data in the Dutch Antilles and Suriname archives may have caused another bias, though working in the opposite direction, since no information is available on children who were born and died before the registration of the data in 1863. Since it is likely that some first-born children had died before being recorded and since the probability of this occurrence rises with the time elapsed since the first birth, the computed age of the mother at first birth tends to be overstated. This issue has been raised earlier by, among others, Trussel and Steckel regarding the U.S. slave population (1978: 482–83).

Rate of childlessness

Of a total of ten women of the Curaçao plantation Savonet belonging to the 40–49 age category, eight are recorded in the 1863 plantation archive as having borne one or more children. As indicated earlier, the average number of children per mother aged 45 amounts to 6.5, after adjusting for the unlisted child who died before registration. This means that the chance for a child to die before recording is 0.15 (1/6.5). When applied to the two women classified as childless, this chance yields a 0.3 child which is quite small and may be neglected. The rate of childlessness estimated in this way is 20 per cent, two to a total of ten women, but has to be used with caution, taking into account that the calculation is based on only one plantation. This limitation holds also for Suriname since only three plantations are involved in computing the 29 per cent rate of childlessness.

References

Archief van de Algemene Rekenkamer, *Afrekeningen van de Emancipatie in het Archief van de Algemene Rekenkamer* (Schaarsbergen: Algemeen Rijksarchief, 1863).

Brenneker, P., *Sambumbu, Volkskinde van Curaçao, Aruba en Bonaire* (Curaçao, 1973–75).

Engerman, S. L., 'Some economic and demographic comparisions of slavery in the United States and the British West Indies'. *Economic History Review*, 29 (April, 1976), 258–75.

Engerman, S. L., 'Quantitative and economic analysis of West Indian slave societies: research problems', in V. Rubin and A. Tuden (Eds), *Comparative perspectives on slavery in New World-plantation societies* (New York, 1977).

Fogel, R. W., (Lecture given in Amsterdam, 1976).

Fogel, R. W. and Engerman, S. L., 'Recent findings in the

study of the slave demography and family structure', *Sociology and Social Research*, 63, No. 3 (1979) 566-89.

Frisch, R. E., 'Population, food intake and fertility', *Science*, 199, (1978), 22—30.

Goslinga, C. Ch., 'Curaçao as a slave-trading center during the War of the Spanish Succession (1702-1714)', *Nieuwe West Indische Gids*, 1-2 (1977), 1-50.

Hamelberg, J. H. J. 1901 *De Nederlanders op de West Indische Eilanden*, I, (Amsterdam, 1901).

Hartog, J., *Curaçao van kolonie tot autonomie* (2 delen), (Aruba, 1961).

Higman, B. W., 'Household structure and fertility on Jamaican slave plantations', *Population Studies*, 27 (1973), 527-50.

Higman, B. W., 'The slave family and household in the British West Indies', *Journal of Interdisciplinary History*, 6 (1975), 261-287.

Higman, B. W. 1976 *Slave population and economy in Jamaica, 1807-1834*', (New York, 1976).

Hoetink, H., *Het patroon van de oudse Curaçaose samenleving*, (Assen, 1958).

Hoetink, H., 'Race relations in Curaçao and Surinam', in F. Foner and E. D. Genovese (Eds), *Slavery in the New World* (New York, 1969).

Klein, H. S. and Engerman, S. L., 'Fertility differentials between slaves in the United States and the British West Indies, *William and Mary Quarterly*, 35 (1978), 357-74.

Koloniale Verslagen, 1849-63.

Lamur, H. E., 'Demography of Surinam plantation slaves in the last decade before Emancipation: the case of Catharina Sophia', in V. Rubin and A. Tuden *op. cit.*, *Slave fertility and plantation labour in Surinam*.

Lowenthal, D., and Clarke, C. G., 'Slave-breeding in Barbuda: the past of a negro myth', in V. Rubin and A. Tuden.

Paula, A. F., *From objective to subjective social barriers* (Curaçao, 1967).

Rapport der Staatscommissie, *Erste rapport der Staatscommissie benoemd bij K. B. van 29 november 1853 no. 66, tot het voorstellen van maatregelen t.a.v. de slaven in de Nederlandse Koloniën* (The Hague, 1855).

Rapport der Staatscommissie, *Tweede rapport der Staatscommissie benoemd bij K. B. van 29 november 1853 no. 66, tot het voorstellen van maatregelen t.a.v. de slaven in de Nederlandse Koloniën* (The Hague, 1856).

Römer, R. A., *Un pueblo na kaminda*, (1977).

Steckel, R. H., *The economics of U.S. slave and southern white fertility*, Ph.D. dissertation, University of Chicago, (1977).

Teenstra, M. D., *De Nederlandsch West Indische Eilanden* (2 delen) (Amsterdam, 1836).

Trussel, J. and Steckel, R., 'The age of slaves at menarche and their first birth', *Journal of Interdisciplinary History*, 8, No. 3, (1978) 477-505.

United Nations, *Methods of estimating basic demographic measures from incomplete data* (New York, 1967).

Van den Boogaart, E., and Emmer, P. C., 'Plantation slavery in the last decade before emancipation: the case of Catharina Sophia', in V. Rubin and A. Tuden *op. cit.*

Van der Kuyp, E. E., 'De voeding van de slaaf en de betekenis daarvan voor zijn nakomelingen', in *Emancipatieblad* (1958).

Van Lier, R. A. J., *Frontier Society* (The Hague, 1971).

Wijkregisters van de Nederlandse Antillen.

The Slave Populations of the British Caribbean: Some Nineteenth-Century Variations

BARRY W. HIGMAN

In the study of slavery, the comparative method is now firmly established. But in all of the grand systems, such as those of Tannenbaum, Elkins and Genovese,[1] the comparisons are made essentially at the level of the nation or empire. The underlying assumption is that at this level the slave societies were sufficiently uniform to permit useful generalization. But since it can be shown that slave societies changed their character in response to economic change, this assumption has to be questioned.

An important recent example of this questioning is found in Franklin Knight's study of nineteenth-century Cuba. Knight argues that the sugar revolution in Cuba, which began immediately before the American Revolution, produced a slave society which was organized in much the same way as all those societies based on the sugar plantation, from Brazil to Barbados, St. Domingue, Jamaica, and Louisiana. Metropolitan influences and the timing were relatively insignificant factors. Thus Knight concludes that comparative studies of slave society 'should be concerned less with concurrent time spans and metropolitan institutional differences than with equivalent stages of economic and social growth'.[2]

With these considerations in mind, an attempt will be made to look at some limited aspects of the slave populations of the British Caribbean in the early nineteenth century. This enables us to hold the metropolitan framework constant, except that most British colonies had representative assemblies, while the most recently settled (Trinidad, Guyana, and St. Lucia) were Crown colonies. Detailed studies of the slave societies of the British colonies after 1776 have so far been confined to the works of Patterson and Brathwaite on Jamaica, Goveia on the Leeward Islands, and a thesis on the Windward Islands by Marshall.[3] It is not difficult to argue that these studies are more strongly contrasted in terms of their interpretations of the nature and the place of slavery in these societies than in terms of the variations they present among the particular places considered. The historians' viewpoints seem to be more diverse than the islands. This interpretative debate will not be entered directly here but approached through a discussion of the demographic diversity within the British Caribbean.

The importance of the demographic structure of slavery for an understanding of the slave society hardly needs to be stressed. In the first place, the density of the population had an immediate impact on the possibilities of communication. It also determined the chances of slaves achieving quasi-independence (which could be looked for in the provision grounds system), running away, and rebelling. Second, the sex ratio affected not only the level of fertility but also the kinds of family and household patterns which the slaves could establish.[4] Again, the sex ratio was an important indication of the relative balance of Africans and creoles, with cultural consequences. There was also an intimate connection between this balance of Africans and creoles and the age distribution of the population, which in turn determined very largely the pattern of fertility and mortality. These ramifications of demographic structure could be expanded greatly, but enough has been said to indicate their significance. In addition, it may be argued that the demographic pattern provides a potential *index* of the nature of slave society.

Before the British abolition of the slave tade in 1807, the population records of the West Indian slaves were confined to poll tax rolls, of

Eighteenth Century Florida and the Caribbean (Florida, 1976), pp. 60–70.

doubtful accuracy, and to estate journals, few of which have survived. but the slave registration acts passed after 1816 produced a mass of relatively reliable material. The registration of slaves was imposed on the Crown Colony of Trinidad by Order in Council in 1812, but the other colonies passed their own laws independently. As a result, the records are not always strictly comparable, some of the registrations being triennial and others annual, and the data collected vary from place to place.[5] This disparity adds a complicating dimension to the search for genuine demographic diversity. But here only the gross demographic variables will be considered.

The published registration data enable only a crude estimate of the rate of natural increase in the years between 1816 and 1834.[6] Thus all mortality, whether African or creole, has to be compared with the crude birth rate. But even with this rough index, the pattern of natural increase provides a useful means of classifying the colonies into groups. Three major groups can be defined: the first was characterized by natural increases, the second by heavy though lessening natural decreases, and the third by light though deteriorating decreases.

Of the first group, only the Bahamas and Barbados managed to maintain a positive natural increase throughout the period 1816–34. By 1823 both of these colonies had achieved a high rate of natural increase, in excess of 10 per 1,000 per year. Montserrat almost maintained a continuous increase, while St Christopher and Antigua had moved from a decrease to a modest increase by 1825. Unlike these relatively gradual movements into a position of natural increase, two colonies, St. Lucia and the Virgin Islands, moved from heavy natural decreases before 1820 to fairly high increases thereafter. Thus, with the exception of St. Lucia, it is clear that the only places to achieve natural increases in the period before the abolition of slavery were the colonies established by the English in the seventeenth century; of this group of old, established settlements, the only colony not to conform to the trend of natural increase was Nevis, which until 1825 followed the pattern set by Antigua and St. Christopher, but then decreased.

The second group of colonies failed to achieve natural increases before emancipation, though showing some improvement in the rate. The members of this group were the most recently established colonies of Trinidad and Guyana, and the islands of St. Vincent, Grenada, and Tobago, which had been ceded to Britain after the Peace of Paris. The colony with the heaviest consistent natural decrease throughout the period was the ceded island of Tobago, with an improvement to about 1827 followed by a decline. Another of the ceded islands, Grenada, followed a similar course. Until 1820 Grenada's natural decrease was as great as that of Trinidad's, but during the 1820s it managed some actual increases before falling again after 1829.

The third group of colonies was similar to the second in that it sustained consistent natural decreases. But whereas in both the second and first groups there was a general improvement in the rate throughout the period, in the third there was steady deterioration in the rate of natural decrease. Jamaica and Dominica comprised this group. Around 1820 the rate of natural decrease in Jamaica remained less than that in St. Christopher, Nevis, and Antigua, which have been placed in the first group. But the decline in Jamaica's position was so continuous that, by 1830, its rate of natural decrease was similar to that of the second group of colonies.

This grouping of the slave populations into three major types is rather rough, of course. Some of the diversity within each group has already been noticed. On the other hand, the general trends are distinct enough.

In terms of the broad questions posed at the outset, it is necessary to try to explain these three patterns and to investigate the significance of the contrasts. First, it might be argued that the diversity of the populations arose from purely adventitious demographic factors independent of the nature of the slave societies. Second, the contrasts may be attributed to different forms of economy, each with its individual impact on society. Third, the contrasts might not be the result of distinct economic structures but instead simply reflect different stages in the development of a single type of settlement, namely the plantation. In an attempt to weigh these alternatives, it should be possible to throw some light on the significance of natural increase as an index of social and demographic trends. The abolitionists, in the early nineteenth century, regarded the failure of the slave populations to maintain themselves as the final proof of the inhumanity of the slave system.[7]

To begin with the economic structures, it is clear that the three groups of colonies contained a good deal of diversity. The first group contained the most strictly monocultural economies, but it also included the Bahamas, the economy of which depended on cotton, salt-pans, and wrecking. In the Bahamas the seasonal pattern of these activities and the scattered character of the islands meant that the tight, formal organization of the sugar plantation was absent. All of the other colonies depended on sugar to a certain degree. Unfortunately, the registration returns for Belize and the Cayman Islands do not contain any data on fertility or mortality, so it is not possible to compare the pattern there with that of the Bahamas. The Cayman Islands depended on turtle fishing. In Belize the seasonal patterns of the mahogany and logwood industries formed the basis for what seems to have been an even looser type of slave society.[8] But the age-sex structure of the slave population of Belize was similar to that favored by the planters as an ideal for the sugar colonies, which tended to produce natural decreases. Apart from the Bahamas, Belize, and the Cayman Islands, the colonies differed only in the extent to which the plantation sector was founded on sugar, cotton, coffee, or cocoa.

Jamaica, with about 350,000 slaves in 1817, had as large a slave population as all the rest of the British Caribbean. Thus, contrasts within Jamaica, both in terms of economy and settlement stage, were as significant as those among the individual islands of the eastern Caribbean. Within Jamaica the heaviest natural decreases occurred in those areas dominated by sugar plantations. The slaves working on coffee plantations or livestock pens had begun to increase, at least by the end of the 1820s. The slaves located in the towns of Jamaica had also achieved a natural increase by about 1820 and maintained this position up until the time of emancipation.[9]

The evidence from Jamaica suggests that a strong case could be made for arguing that the rate of natural increase was essentially a function of the degree to which sugar dominated the economy and hence the activities of the slaves. But even within Jamaica many sugar estates could be found with natural increases, and one monocultural sugar parish, Vere, showed the same pattern. Vere was one of the old, established planting regions of Jamaica, lacking the provision grounds system which had emerged in the rest of Jamaica both before and especially after the American Revolution. This raises the third alternative explanation of the general pattern of natural increase: namely, the stage of settlement. In the first group of colonies the highest rates of natural increase occurred in the first settled English sugar colonies. Like the parish of Vere in Jamaica, these islands were strictly monocultural, lacking the provision grounds system, and hence importing the greater part of their food supply. These islands were also the most densely settled by the time of the abolition of the slave trade. In 1817 their slave population densities ranged from 188 slaves per square mile in Antigua to 466 in Barbados. The only other colonies with densities greater than 100 per square mile were the small islands of Grenada, St. Vincent, and the Virgin Islands.

Curtin, in *The Atlantic Slave Trade*, has argued that the demographic history of the sugar colonies tended to fall into a regular pattern over time.[10] At first the ratio of slave imports to population would be high. This would produce an abnormal age-sex structure which was necessarily associated with a high level of natural decrease. As the colony reached full production, he argues, the total slave population began to level off. Slave imports continued, but only enough to make up the deficit between deaths and births. Over time, the creoles steadily increased in proportion to the African-born. Finally, the deficit between births and deaths diminished and then disappeared. This, according to Curtin, was the position in Barbados by 1810 and in Jamaica by the 1840s.

Curtin's model is attractive in its simplicity, but it is not completely satisfactory when applied to the sugar colonies of the British Caribbean. In the case of Barbados, it is true that the slave population had achieved a natural increase by 1810 and that it was very dense. But as early as the 1660s, Barbados was as densely settled as any of the other colonies were to become in the early nineteenth century. it is difficult to define what Curtin means by 'full production', but in gross terms it seems that Barbados reached a peak by the 1660s and after about 1730 went into a period of secular decline, from which it began to recover only after 1810. Thus the period of natural increase in the slave population of Barbados coincided with a period of increasing productivity, rather than with a situation of labor saturation. The decline in productivity during the eighteenth century can be attributed to other factors, of course, but it is important to ask whether this situation may not have created the foundation for the emergence of natural growth. The falling off in the level of slave imports was also less noticeable in Barbados because of its location and role as entrepôt. Perhaps this could account for the relatively late emergence of a natural increase in Barbados, in terms of Curtin's model. But it cannot be used to explain the long period between the leveling off in production in the

Leeward Islands and the appearance of a natural increase in the slave population.

There seems to be at least one important untested assumption in Curtin's model. It is founded on the belief that the creole section of a slave population would grow naturally. Thus the observed natural decrease was merely the result of continued imports of Africans who, because of their age-sex structure, contributed much to mortality but little to fertility, thus overwhelming the slow growth among the creoles. But the evidence that creole slave populations tended to support natural increases is somewhat contradictory. Thus, in the case of Jamaica it can be shown that the parish of Vere had a relatively high proportion of creoles, but this pattern was shared by other sugar parishes which had heavy natural decreases. Studies of particular estates are also conflicting. Thus Craton's study of Worthy Park in Jamaica is essentially an argument for Curtin's model.[11] But on other estates it is clear that the creole section tended to be eroded in the same way as the African. So long as the planter believed that there was a cost advantage in purchasing African slaves rather than relying on creole increase, as he generally did until 1807, this is not surprising. Even in the period after 1807, the same erosion of the creole section can be identified on many estates. The reasons are less clear in this period, but it seems that the creoles may have been less fertile than the Africans, so that the initial impetus to fertility from the age-sex structure of the slave trade was removed after 1807.[12]

For the British Caribbean as a whole, the evidence favors the broad outlines of Curtin's model of demographic development. Thus, in the most recently settled colonies of Trinidad and Guyana, the heavy, but improving, rates of natural decrease were associated with a rapid decrease in the sex ratio and hence an increase in the creole section. This pattern was somewhat tempered until the 1820s by the continued movement of slaves to the new colonies, especially from the Bahamas and Dominica.[13] In several colonies, notably Tobago, Dominica, St. Vincent, and Jamaica, the sex ratio continued to decline even after the sexes had been equalized. In the old colonies the sex ratio had already reached low levels by 1815 at least, and natural increases were associated with an increase in masculinity. Thus in the sugar colonies it appears that natural increases did not occur until the populations were disproportionately female.

It is worth emphasizing that these demographic foundations of natural increase in the sugar colonies were not required in the non-sugar islands. In the Bahamas there was a natural increase long before the sexes were balanced and while the males remained dominant. The Bahamas had been affected by the heavy immigration of American loyalists and their slaves after 1783, but, unlike the new sugar islands, these slaves were probably creole rather than African. Yet in the Jamaican coffee parish of Manchester, which was settled only after 1800, there was a preponderance of both males and Africans, together with a natural increase.

In conclusion, it may be worth attempting a typology of the slave populations of the British Caribbean. It is not meant to suggest that demographic structure will necessarily provide an adequate index of the nature of slave societies, but it is at least a useful starting point. First, the sugar colonies must be separated from the non-sugar colonies. Then, the sugar colonies need to be subdivided according to their stage of settlement. In doing this a more complex model than that proposed by Curtin will be required, to account for a range of internal demographic variety. Finally, it must be said, contra Knight, that the sugar plantation cannot be looked at without regard to chronology. The changing attitudes of the planters and slaves have to be taken into account. In terms of this typology, it is clear that the diversity of the slave populations of the British Caribbean is not explicable by reference to any single demographic cycle, but was a genuine diversity.

Notes

1. See Eugene D. Genovese, *The World the Slaveholders Made* (New York, 1969), p. 8.
2. Franklin W. Knight, *Slave Society in Cuba during the Nineteenth Century* (Madison, 1970), pp. 193–94.
3. Orlando Patterson, *The Sociology of Slavery* (London, 1967); Edward Brathwaite, *The Development of Creole Society in Jamaica, 1770–1820* (Oxford, 1971); Elsa V. Goveia, *Slave Society in the British Leeward Islands at the End of the Eighteenth Century* (New Haven, 1965); Bernard Marshall, 'Slave Society and Economy in the Windward Islands, 1763–1820' (Ph.D. diss., University of the West Indies, 1972).
4. See Orlando Patterson's essay 'From Endo-deme to Matri-deme' Samuel Proctor (Ed.), *Eighteenth-century Florida and the Caribbean* (Florida 1976).
5. From a contemporary critique, see *A Review of the Colonial Slave Registration Acts, in a Report of a Committee of the Board of Directors of the African Institution* (London, 1820).
6. *Parliamentary Papers*, 1833, 26 (539):473–77; 1835, 51(235):289. The original documents are in the series T.71 at the Public Record Office, London. See Appendix.

7. See, for example, the evidence of Buxton, *Parliamentary Papers*, 1832 (127), Lords, 2:828.
8. Narda Dobson, *A History of Belize* (London, 1973), p. 149.
9. B. W. Higman, 'Slave Population and Economy in Jamaica at the time of Emancipation' (Ph.D. diss., University of the West Indies, 1970), pp. 73–127.
10. Philip D. Curtin, *The Atlantic Slave Trade* (Madison, 1969), p. 29.
11. Michael Craton, 'Jamaican Slave Mortality: Fresh Light from Worthy Park, Longville, and the Tharp Estates', *Journal of Caribbean History*, 3 (1971):1–27; Michael Craton and James Walvin, *A Jamaican Plantation: A History of Worthy Park, 1670–1970* (London, 1970), pp. 125–54.
12. B. W. Higman, 'Household Structure and Fertility on Jamaican Slave Plantations: A Nineteenth-Century Example', *Population Studies*, Vol. 27, 3 (1973), and this volume.
13. D. Eltis, 'The Traffic in Slaves between the British West Indian Colonies, 1807–1833', *Economic History Review*, 25 (1972):55–64.
14. Calculated from *Parliamentary Papers*, 1833, 26 (539):473–77; *ibid.*, 1835, 51 (235):289.

Appendix Basic Demographic Indexes

	Total slave population	Males per 100 females	Births per 1,000	Deaths per 1,000	Natural increase per 1,000
FIRST GROUP					
Bahamas					
1819–22	10,098	104.6			
1822–25	10,036	103.3	26.9	14.2	12.7
1825–28	9,266	100.2	31.0	14.9	16.1
Barbados					
1817–20	77,919	86.1	31.7	28.3	3.4
1820–23	78,581	86.5	34.9	28.5	6.4
1823–26	79,684	84.9	40.2	28.1	12.1
1826–29	81,227	85.1	38.0	28.0	10.0
1829–32	81,701	85.8	40.7	30.6	10.1
Montserrat					
1817–21	6,558	86.4	31.0	30.4	0.6
1821–24	6,392	86.0	31.4	32.0	−0.6
1824–27	6,270	84.6	34.1	28.1	6.0
St Christopher					
1817–22	19,993	92.3	25.2	28.4	−3.2
1822–25	19,667	91.9	28.2	29.0	−0.8
1825–28	19,413	91.2	29.3	27.5	1.8
1828–31	19,198	91.5	28.3	26.3	2.0
Antigua					
1817–21	31,627	87.4	18.5	22.8	−4.3
1821–24	30,650	87.9	27.1	27.6	−0.5
1824–27	30,077	88.8	25.5	25.2	0.3
Nevis					
1817–22	9,432	96.6	22.5	25.9	−3.4
1822–25	9,274	97.9	23.9	24.9	−1.0
1825–28	9,273	97.9	22.9	22.6	0.3
1828–31	9,201	97.8	23.3	24.6	−1.3
Virgin Islands					
1818–22	6,680	86.7	18.9	26.9	−8.0
1822–25	5,948	85.4	26.6	17.1	9.5
1825–28	5,418	86.2	28.2	17.4	10.8
St Lucia					
1816–19	15,662	83.0	15.5	42.2	−26.9
1819–22	14,417	83.4	21.4	30.8	−9.4
1822–25	13,756	84.8	29.2	25.2	4.0
1825–28	13,689	85.3	29.1	24.4	4.7
1828–31	13,505	84.9	27.9	25.9	2.0
SECOND GROUP					
Trinidad					
1816–19	24,541	125.1	19.3	37.6	−18.3
1819–22	23,463	126.5	21.2	34.5	−13.3
1822–25	23,920	124.0	22.8	24.5	−1.7
1825–28	24,114	117.1	18.0	25.5	−7.5
Demerara					
1817–20	77,622	128.7	20.9	30.3	−9.4
1820–23	76,177	124.4	19.7	31.5	−11.8
1823–26	73,180	120.5	20.5	34.8	−14.3
1826–29	70,425	116.9	22.2	27.1	−4.9
1829–32	67.512	112.6	20.2	34.7	−13.5

Appendix *continued*

	Total slave population	Males per 100 females	Births per 1,000	Deaths per 1,000	Natural increase per 1,000
Berbice					
1817–19	24,159	128.1			
1819–22	23,062	121.9	23.8	2.3	−8.5
1822–25	21,910	114.9	23.0	36.5	−13.5
1825–28	21,182	116.3	28.14	27.3	0.8
1828–31	20,772	116.8	25.5	30.3	−4.8
St Vincent					
1817–22	24,735	100.2	21.5	34.0	−12.5
1822–25	24,016	97.4	25.7	30.6	−4.9
1825–28	23,740	96.1	24.3	29.7	−5.4
1828–31	23,398	95.0	25.4	32.3	−6.9
Grenada					
1817	27,565	95.2	16.3	32.7	−16.4
1818	27,415	94.7	24.0	39.0	−15.0
1819	27,060	94.6	26.4	43.2	−16.8
1820	26,899	93.6	23.8	33.3	−9.5
1821	25,667	93.4	26.6	36.2	−9.6
1822	25,586	93.4	28.2	26.6	1.6
1823	25,310	94.0	28.4	32.6	−4.2
1824	24,972	94.0	27.1	29.0	−1.9
1825	24,897	93.9	27.2	30.5	−3.3
1826	24,581	93.8	26.9	32.3	−5.4
1827	24,473	93.8	28.8	27.3	1.5
1828	24,342	93.7	28.2	29.3	−1.1
1829	24,145	94.2	30.5	30.4	0.1
1830	23,878	94.0	30.7	41.0	−10.3
1831	23,604	93.9	29.0	39.3	−10.3
1820	15,063	96.2	20.2	53.1	−32.9
1821	14,581	95.1	22.8	46.4	−23.6
1822	14,315	94.4	22.1	26.8	−24.7
1823	14,074	93.8	22.6	31.5	−8.9
1824	13,656	92.4	23.6	48.4	−24.8
1825	13,683	91.3	22.7	29.5	−6.8
1826	13,428	90.9	24.4	51.4	−27.0
1827	12,999	89.5	25.7	30.6	−4.9
1828	12,895	89.5	28.6	41.8	−13.2
1829	12,723	90.3	29.4	41.8	−12.4
1830	12,556	87.8	25.5	40.4	−14.9
1831	12,370	87.4	27.6	41.6	−14.0
1832	12,091	86.4	25.3	45.6	−20.3
THIRD GROUP					
Jamaica					
1817–20	344,266	99.7	23.6	24.3	−0.7
1820–23	339,318	98.7	22.8	25.9	−3.1
1823–26	333,686	97.4	23.0	25.1	−2.1
1826–29	326,770	96.5	22.2	25.6	−3.4
1929–32	317,649	95.5	23.2	28.0	−4.8
Dominica					
1817–20	17,257	92.1	27.7	30.4	−2.7
1820–23	16,134	91.3	28.2	31.6	−3.4
1823–26	15,553	91.2	28.1	32.0	−3.9

SECTION SEVEN
Slave Women, Family and Households

Scholars of slavery in the Caribbean have attributed a superordinate role to women in analyses of family and kinship patterns. In most instances their arguments have been related directly to women's predominant role in child-rearing and infant socialization in these undoubtedly patriarchal societies. For these and related reasons, perceptions of the slave family have been more intimately linked with women than with men.

Recent scholarship on the slave family by Higman and Craton, however, tends to present a more realistic analysis of women in the domestic context. For example, Craton has suggested the need to minimize traditional concepts in the light of new evidence which illustrates that the 'myth of matrifocality stems from the planters' emphasis on motherhood because of their need to perpetuate slavery through the female line, and their vain wish to breed rather than to buy new slaves by granting slave mothers relatively easier conditions.' The evidence presented by Higman, however, supports the generalization that African-based family structures and concepts largely gave way to European systems and ideas as the slave society matured and became Creolised.

Changing Patterns of Slave Families in the British West Indies

MICHAEL CRATON

> ...any Attempt to restrain this Licentious Intercourse between the Sexes amongst the Slaves in this Island in the present State of their Notions of Right and Wrong, by introducing the Marriage Ceremony amongst them, would be utterly impracticable, and perhaps of dangerous Consequence, as these People are universally known to claim a Right of Disposing themselves in this Respect, according to their own Will and Pleasure without any Controul from their Masters.[1]

Writers on the West Indies have echoed the negative statements of Alexis de Tocqueville and E. Franklin Frazier on slave and modern black families in the United States.[2] In this vein, Simey, Henriques, and Goode exaggerated the matrifocality and instability of modern Caribbean families as 'deviant' results of an alleged absence of family life in slavery, while Smith and Patterson confidently backed up

*Michael Craton is Professor of History at the University of Waterloo. He is the author of *Searching for the Invisible Man: Slaves and Plantation Life in Jamaica* (Cambridge, Mass., 1978).

This article is the revision of a paper presented at the Organization of American Historians meeting, 1978. Grateful thanks are expressed for help in the compilation of data to Gail Saunders, Archivist of the Bahamas, and her staff in the Public Records Department, Nassau; to Louis Arruda and Geoffrey Dunlop for preliminary work on the 26 Bahamian holdings and Burton Williams' slaves; to Stanley Engerman for some of the Trinidad data and useful comments on an earlier draft; to Colin Clarke and David Lowenthal for material on Barbuda; to Barry Higman and Arnold Sio for sharing ideas and information; and to Gary Brannon for the execution of the map and figures.

Journal of Interdisciplinary History, Vol. X, No. 1 No. 1 (1979), pp. 1–35.

their analyses of modern family with assertions that 'the woman normally acted as the sole permanent element in the slave family, whether or not the male partner was polygynous', and that 'the nuclear family could hardly exist within the context of slavery'.[3]

In work published since 1973, Higman has proved these assertions to be wrong and thus has reopened the whole study of the West Indian family and its roots. Although concentrating on sugar plantation colonies and the period of slave amelioration and registration (1807–34), he has shown that family life — even in patterns recognizable to Europeans — was then the norm for British West Indian slaves. Although polygyny and other African practices persisted, the nuclear, two-headed household was extremely common among the African-born as well as Creole slaves. More remarkably, single-headed maternal households were in a minority in every area studied by Higman, save for the towns. The frequency of matrifocal families and the general disruption of slave families had become exaggerated, he suggested, because of the practices of those slaves with whom whites were most familiar: domestics and urban slaves.[4]

The purpose of this present paper is fourfold. It adds to Higman's evidence by using material chiefly from the Bahamas, a non-sugar, largely non-plantation colony. It also summarizes the evidence hitherto gathered, sketches the varieties of slave family from place to place and time to time, and finally, discusses developmental models. Despite great variations according to location, employment, and ownership (not to mention the difficulties presented by fragmentary and uneven evidence), a consistent pattern does emerge. This suggests both the place that the rediscovered West Indian slave family of the late slave period occupies in the continuum between West African roots and modern West Indian black family, and some of the ways in which the dynamics of West Indian black family have differed from those of the United States and Latin America.

As Stephen noted as early as 1824, slave conditions in the Bahama Islands were at the benign end of a scale on which the sugar colonies further south — particularly the newly acquired colonies of Trinidad and Guyana — represented the opposite extreme. An influx of Loyalist planters after 1783 had changed the tone and pace of the archipelagic colony, doubling the white population and trebling the number of slaves; but the population density remained a twentieth of that of Jamaica and a fiftieth of that of Barbados, while the ratio of black slaves to white freemen and the average size of slave holdings remained among the lowest in the British West Indies.[5]

Most of the Loyalist emigrés settled their slaves on Bahamian 'Out Islands' until then unpopulated, attempting to replicate the plantation conditions they had left behind in the Carolinas, Georgia, and Florida. They found the climate ideal for growing sea island cotton, but the exhaustion of the thin soil and the depredations of the chenille bug left them unable to compete with American cotton once Whitney's gin became effective after 1800. Although a local planter, Joseph Eve, invented a wind-powered variant of the gin, Bahamian cotton production had almost faded away by 1820. Plantations were turned over to stock or the growing of grains and other provisions, and many of the slaves had to fend for themselves.

Figure 1 Population Pyramids, Rolle Slaves and 26 Bahamian Holdings, 1822

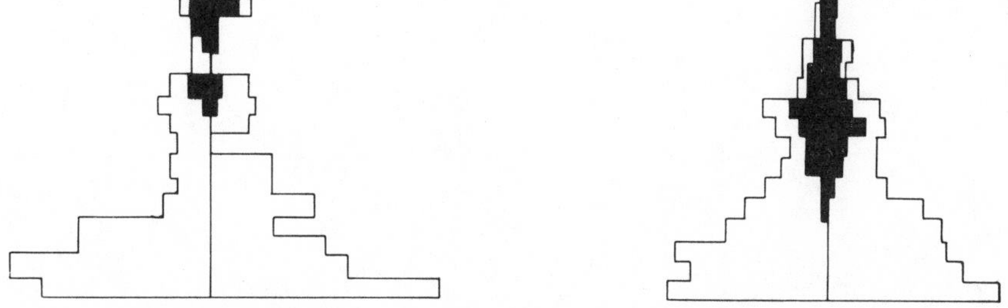

A. Rolle Slaves, Exuma

B. 26 Bahamian Holdings

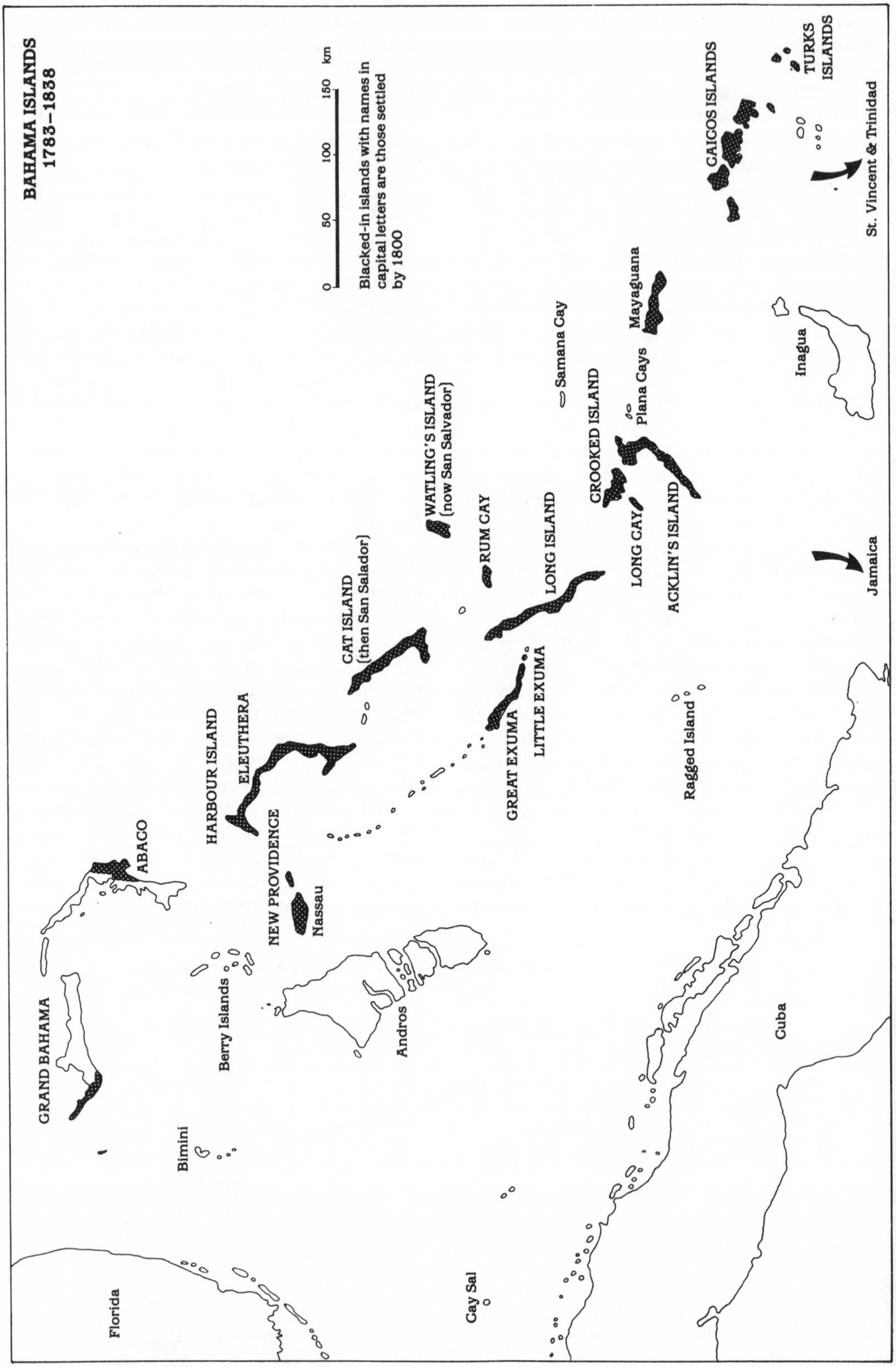
BAHAMA ISLANDS
1783–1838
0 50 100 150 km
Blacked-in islands with names in capital letters are those settled by 1800
GRAND BAHAMA
ABACO
HARBOUR ISLAND
ELEUTHERA
NEW PROVIDENCE
Nassau
CAT ISLAND
(then San Salador)
WATLING'S ISLAND
(now San Salvador)
RUM CAY
LONG ISLAND
GREAT EXUMA
LITTLE EXUMA
Samana Cay
CROOKED ISLAND
Plana Cays
LONG CAY
ACKLIN'S ISLAND
Mayaguana
CAICOS ISLANDS
TURKS
ISLANDS
St. Vincent & Trinidad
Jamaica
Inagua
Ragged Island
Berry Islands
Andros
Bimini
Florida
Gay Sal
Cuba

Those planters who could sold up and migrated once more. Many of them attempted to transfer their slaves to the old colony of Jamaica or the new sugar plantations in Trinidad and St. Vincent, where fresh slaves were at a premium after the African supply had been cut off by the abolition of the Atlantic slave trade in 1808. Although slaves were registered in the Crown Colony of Trinidad as early as 1813, this opportunistic trade was not revealed until the first returns under the Bahamian Slave Registration Act of 1812 reached London, after which it was effectively scotched by the abolitionists under Stephen Lushington in 1823. By then, perhaps 2,000 Bahamian slaves (a fifth) had already been transferred.[6]

The meticulous triennial returns of British West Indian slaves produced by the registration laws were of great value to the emancipationists, who were able to prove the persistence of 'natural decrease' as well as to end the intercolonial trade. Modern demographers, however, can put them to much wider use, reconstituting and comparing whole colony populations by age, sex, African or Creole birth, mortality, fertility, and life expectancy. In at least two colonies, Trinidad and the Bahamas, it is also possible to discover and compare patterns of slave family. Unlike the Trinidadian instructions, the Bahamian law did not require the listing of slaves' families or households-by-name. But approximately a quarter of Bahamian slaves were voluntarily listed by their owners in such a way as to indicate family relationships, though with limits on the range of family types identifiable. Comparison between the original lists of 1821 and 1822 and those of 1825, 1828, 1831, and 1834, moreover, allows both for corroboration of relationships and the testing of their permanence.[7]

In all, it has proved possible to analyze 26 slave holdings in the first Bahamian census of 1821–22 in which owners listed slaves in family groups, rather than by alphabetical order, age, sex or any other method. This sample comprised 3,011 out of a Bahamas grand total of about 12,000, an average of 116 slaves per holding, but with a range between 20 and 840, drawn from eleven different islands. The findings not only illustrate the contrasts between the Bahamian slave population and those in sugar plantation colonies further south, but also point up the typicality of the only Bahamian slave group previously studied, that of the slaves owned by John, Lord Rolle on the island of Exuma.[8]

Ten times the size of the Rolle holding, this widespread fourth of the Bahamian slave population exhibited almost as balanced, 'modern', and 'unslavelike' a demographic pattern, with a broad base of youngsters and a fair number of elderly slaves. The sexes in the fertile age ranges were almost as equally balanced as Rolle's slaves, and the only features reminiscent of slave populations further south were a slight 'bulge' in the age range from 40 to 54, representing in this case survivors from the migration of Loyalists' slaves in the 1780s, and a substantial remnant of Africans, 18.8 per cent

Figure 2 Bahamas, 26 Holdings, 1822; Age differences between Males and their Mates

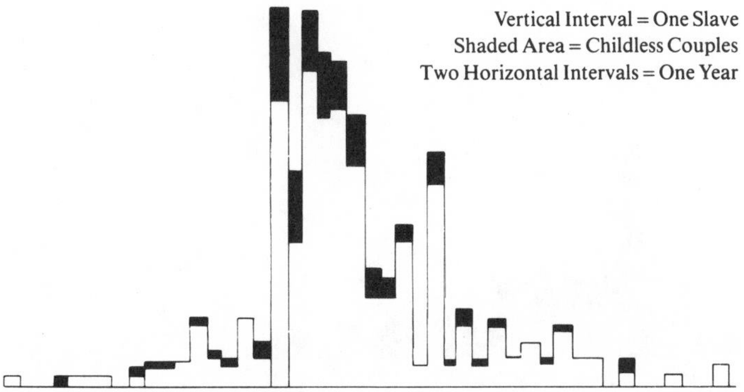

of the total. Unlike the Rolle holding, there also was evidence of considerable miscegenation, 6.9 per cent of the 3,011 slaves being listed as 'mulatto' or 'yellow'.[9]

These slight differences and the less optimal work and living conditions accounted for a rather lower average net population increase than with Lord Rolle's slaves, but the incidence of family in the sample of 26 holdings was very similar. As Table 1 shows, 85.0 per cent were found in some type of family, with no less than 54.1 per cent of the 3,011 slaves indicated as living in simple nuclear families. Of the 1,356 slaves over 20 years old, 854, or 63.1 percent, were listed in couples. The normal pattern was for males to be a few years older than their mates. On the average, males were some 4½ years older, but this figure was skewed by some much older males and by the few older females. Of 397 couples who were the parents in nuclear families or were childless, in 303 cases the males were from 0–10 years older, with an average of three years and 10½ months. Although the presence of elderly mothers whose first children had left the household or had died makes it difficult to count exactly, the average age of mothers at the birth of their first children appears to have been under 20 years. As Table 2 shows, the spacing between children was regular and healthy, with the overall average almost exactly three years. Of all women in the age range from 15–49, a high proportion, 65.8 percent, were indicated as mothers, having had on the average almost exactly three children.[10]

Besides these basic statistical findings, a study of the Bahamian returns allows for some general observations and analysis along lines followed by Gutman and other scholars of slavery in the United States. First, important implications concerning the incidence of endogamy and exogamy — or at least of in-group and out-group mating — arose from the tendency of slave families to appear most clearly in the records of the larger and more isolated holdings, which were mainly in islands distant from Nassau, the colonial capital.[11] In contrast, on New Providence (Nassau's island) and the nearer, long-established settlements of Harbour Island and Eleuthera, conjugal patterns seem to have been more disrupted. Many of the holdings were too small to include whole families and this clearly contributed to the custom of choosing mates from other holdings. But there were other factors. Among a heavily creolized population (with some slaves six generations removed from Africa), in small units, marital mobility was not only possible but probably seen as desirable to avoid too close a consanguinity. Miscegenation was also rather more common in New Providence and Eleuthera than further afield, those slaves listed as mulatto or yellow constituting 8 percent of the few holdings analyzed, and probably more than 10 percent overall.[12]

In general, it seems that these conditions led not to familial cohesion but the reverse, with many male mates absent or even temporary. Female-headed families were most common in

Figure 3 Bahamas, 26 Holdings, 1822; Ages of Mothers at Births of their Children

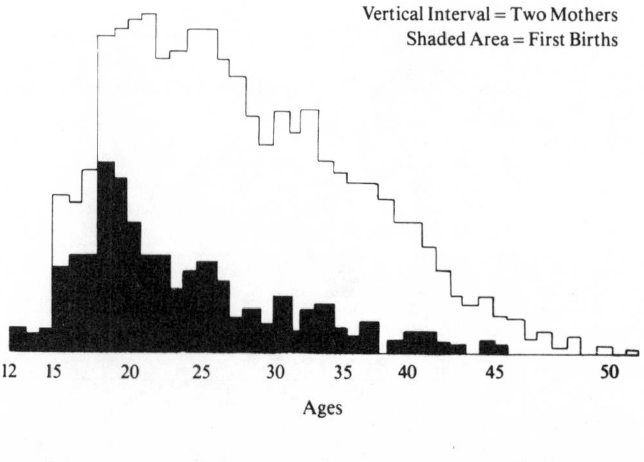

Table 1 Household Patterns, Rolle Slaves, and 26 Bahamian Holdings, 1822

	Rolle Slaves, Exuma				26 Bahamian Holdings			
Family type	Total slaves	Number of units	Mean size of units	Per cent of total in type	Total slaves	Number of units	Mean size of units	Per cent of total type
1. Man, woman, children	110	26	4.23	46.6	1,629	308	5.29	54.1
2. Man, woman	14	7	2.00	5.9	178	89	2.00	5.9
3. Woman, children	40	12	3.33	16.9	377	95	3.97	12.5
4. Man, children	11	2	5.50	4.7	16	3	5.33	0.5
5. Three-generation groups	29	5	5.80	12.3	358	46	7.78	11.9
6. Men Alone, or together	11	—	—	4.7	264	—	—	8.8
7. Women alone, or together	9	—	—	3.8	173	—	—	5.8
8. Children separately	12	—	—	5.1	16	—	—	0.5
Totals	236	—	—	100.0	3,011	—	—	100.0
A. Nuclear family (1,2,5)	153	38	4.03	64.8	2,165	443	4.89	71.9
B. Denuded family (3.4)	51	14	3.64	21.6	393	98	4.01	13.0
C. No family (6,7,8)	32	—	—	13.6	453	—	—	15.1

Table 2 Bahamas, 26 Slave Holdings, 1822 – Average Ages of Mothers at Births and Child Spacing

Which child	Number of mothers	Per cent total mothers in each group	Average ages at births	Average spacing (years)
1st	479	100.0	22.37	
2nd	356	74.3	26.53	3.36
3rd	244	50.9	30.00	2.93
4th	170	35.5	32.60	2.93
5th	105	21.9	33.38	2.42
6th	59	12.3	35.22	2.81
7th	31	6.5	40.10	2.95
8th	8	1.7	43.46	2.67
9th	2	0.4	38.75	1.87
10th	1	0.2	38.00	1.00
Averages			34.84	3.02

the listings for New Providence (where almost a quarter of all Bahamian slaves lived), not only in the several holdings that consisted solely of slave mothers and their children, but also in such groups as the 37 slaves of Elizabeth Mary Anderson, where nine men aged from 22–60 were listed together but separately from five female-headed families averaging five children each. Only in the exceptional holding of William Wylly at the isolated western end of New Providence were families distinct and clearly permanent.

In the distant, more recently established settlements, populations were on the average larger, more isolated and, perhaps of necessity, more cohesive. The choice of mates was limited, and thus relationships were likely to be not only well-known but also more permanent. In relatively large populations, consisting in most cases primarily of first and second generation Creoles, such enforced in-group mating would not yet come into conflict with any customary ban on cousin-mating that may have existed (whether derived from Africa or Europe). In all, it is possible that conditions in the Out Islands, which Nassauvians, both white and black, might consider primitive, were more conducive to stable family formation than those closer to the colonial centre. Certainly, in modern times, Otterbein has documented a greater awareness of the value of stable families in 'primitive' Andros Island than that to be inferred in the less affluent sections of modernized Nassau, which include large groups of displaced Out Islanders. Yet these conditions seem to have also obtained in slavery days, a conclusion that runs counter to Gutman's contention that the dislocating effects of urbanization postdated emancipation, at least in the United States.[13]

The listings of families headed by single females may disguise the existence of serially shifting, or even polygynous, relationships. But in the series of five censuses spread over 12 years (1822–34) there is very little positive evidence of serial monogamy, and only rare and equivocal evidence of polygyny.[14] Naming practices were very little help in tracing family patterns. Bahamian slaves did not universally adopt surnames before emancipation, and then it is by no means certain that surnames were patronymics in the modern style.[15] The practice of taking the surname of the former owner tends to exaggerate consanguinity as well as to confuse relationships — the most extreme case being Lord Rolle's 372 slaves, all of whom took the surname Rolle in order to share common rights in their former master's land. The discernment of immediate relationships was aided, however, by the frequent practice of naming a male child after his father or grandfather, and the occasional custom of naming a female after her grandmother.[16]

Such three-generation links sometimes allowed for the identification of extended family units, but the positive evidence of wider kinship links was disappointingly meager, and the direct evidence from the records of related families living close together in clusters of huts or 'yards' was non-existent, although such groupings are known to have been a feature of Out Island life in later times. However, the frequent listing of a young girl with her first child in the household of her parents, or mother, does permit some inferences about sexual customs. Few girls under 20 cohabited with their mates; few mothers over 20 lived with their parents, and most, as we have seen, lived with mates. Nearly all girls who bore their first children in their mothers' households began separate cohabitation at, or shortly before, the birth of their second children. It therefore seems likely that premarital sex was not uncommon, and even that virginity at marriage was not excessively prized; but that separate cohabitation in a nuclear household was the accepted norm for couples over the age of 20.[17]

The evidence proves the vigorous existence of families among Bahamian slaves during the registration period and, indeed, points to the existence of types of family classified as 'modern' by Europeans among the least modernized groups of slaves. It remains to be decided, though, whether this was a social pattern chosen by the slaves themselves — and thus likely to have existed before the recorded period — or one determined, or at least encouraged, by the Eurocentric, pro-natalist, or publicity-conscious masters.

Strong evidence for the latter conclusion is found in the case of the slaves of William Wylly, Attorney-General of the Bahamas. An ardent Methodist who arranged for a minister to preach regularly to his slaves, he came to be regarded as a crypto-emancipationist by his fellow planters because of a legal decision made in 1816, and was at the center of a bitter wrangle between the plantocratic Assembly and three successive governors, lasting until 1820. Close examination of the evidence, however, shows that Wylly was a strict paternalist, and suggests that if he wished to turn his slaves loose it was because they were no longer profitable.[18]

By 1818, Wylly's three adjacent estates in western New Providence had ceased to grow cotton, Tusculum and Waterloo being turned over to stock raising and Clifton, the largest, being devoted to growing provisions for the slaves and the Nassau market. The Attorney-General's many enemies accused him both of allowing his slaves more time to work for themselves than laid down by Bahamian law, and of supplying them with less than the provisions specified. In response, Wylly produced convincing proof of the degree to which his slaves were self-supporting, and stated, 'My principal object has been, to accustom them to *habits of Industry and Oeconomy* — which I am convinced, never will be found to exist among any Slaves, in this part of the World, who are victualled by their Masters.'[19]

At the same time, Wylly forwarded a revealing set of regulations for his slaves which he had caused to be printed and published in Nassau in 1815. Apart from his concern for religious instruction and regular prayers, and details of clothing, feeding, work, and punishment regulations, these clearly illustrated his views on slave marriage, sexual continence, and motherhood. 'Every man, upon taking his first wife,' read the seventh article of the regulations, 'is entitled to a well built stone house, consisting of two apartments, and is to receive a sow pig, and a pair of dunghill fowls, as a donation from the proprietor.'[20]

'In cases of Adultery,' read Article XI, 'the man forfeits his hogs, poultry, and other moveable effects; which are to be sold, and the proceeds paid over to the injured husband. Both offenders are moreover to be whipt; their heads to be shaved, and they are to wear *Sack cloth* (viz. gowns and caps made of Cotton bagging) for the next half year; during which time they are not to go beyond the limits of the plantation, under the penalty of being whipt.'

With far less Mosaic severity, Article XIX enjoined that, 'On working days, the children are to be carried, early every morning, by their mothers, to the Nursery, where proper care will be taken of them during the day; and their mothers are to call for them when they return from their work in the afternoon. Women who have children at the breast, are never to be sent to any distance from the homestead.'

Predictably, Wylly's slave lists in the registration returns disclose a neat pattern of families and a healthy natural increase. Since his regulations were published and his views on slave management became well known, it is possible that they became normative. The very decision to list slaves according to families and households may indicate owners who shared Wylly's concerns. Certainly, the other two Bahamian owners known to have engaged in correspondence on the management of their slaves, Lord Rolle of Exuma and Burton Williams of Watling's Island, demonstrated an awareness of the value of stable families in producing healthy, fertile, and contented slaves.[21]

It is likely, though, that such planters as Wylly, Rolle, and Williams were self-deluding if not self-serving. The widespread incidence and consistent form of slave families suggest customary choice on the part of the slaves rather than the dictates of the masters. Few plantations were owner-managed, especially in the Out Islands, and it seems strange that orderly patterns of slave family should be more common the further from Nassau (where slaves were commonly under the daily scrutiny of their owners), unless this was the slaves' own choice. Nor can the growing influence of Christianity be given unequivocal credit. The established Anglican Church, which held a monopoly on formal weddings until 1827, did not proselytize the slaves, and the few sectarian missionaries concentrated on Nassau and the nearer islands. The underground 'Native Baptists', who were active among the Loyalists' slaves in Nassau as early as in Jamaica, may have had more widespread influence. But they were known to be tolerant about informal marital ties, being regarded by whites as hardly Christians at all. Indeed, the common impression held by the whites of the mass of the slaves was that those who were not heathen practisers of *obeah* were infidel 'followers of Mahomet'.[22]

This at least suggests strong African cultural retentions, particularly in the Out Islands.

Table 3 Bahamas, 26 Slave Holdings, 1822 Comparison between African-Headed and Creole Families

		A. African-headed families[a]				B. Creole families			
Family type		Total slaves	Number of units	Mean size of units	Per cent of total in type	Total slaves	Number of units	Mean size of units	Per cent of total in type
1.	Man, woman, children	830[a]	154	5.39	61.0	799	154	5.19	48.4
2.	Man, woman	138[a]	69	2.00	10.2	40	20	2.00	2.4
3.	Woman, children	91	21	4.33	6.7	278	72	3.86	16.8
4.	Man, children	11	2	5.50	0.8	5	1	5.00	0.3
5.	Three-generation groups	128[a]	19	6.73	9.4	238	29	8.21	14.4
6.	Men alone, or together	114	—	—	8.4	150	—	—	9.1
7.	Women alone, or together	48	—	—	3.5	125	—	—	7.6
8.	Children separately	—	—	—	—	16	2	8.00	1.0
	Totals	1,360	—	—	100.0	1,651	—	—	100.0
A.	Nuclear family (1,2,5)	1,096	242	4.53	80.6	1,077	203	5.31	65.2
B.	Denuded family (3.4)	102	23	4.43	7.5	283	73	3.88	17.1
C.	No family (6,7,8)	162	—	—	11.9	291	—	—	17.7

[a]African-headed families were taken to be those in which both parents, either parent, or the single parent were of African birth. Thus in categories 1, 2 and 5 in Section A mixed couples were included.

Numerically the Africans were few by the registration period but, as elderly survivors, seem to have been highly respected members of the slave community. Indeed, it became clear on further analysis of the 26 holdings that the African slaves had influence out of all proportion to their numbers, and even that they were dominant in shaping family life in the Bahamas. Although most of the African-born slaves were grouped together toward the end of the rolls, in more than a third of the slave holdings analyzed an African couple was at the head of the list. This usually indicated that the owner had chosen the most prestigious married African as head driver.[23]

As in all slave communities the role of such leaders was ambivalent. They were chosen for what was termed 'confidentiality' — fidelity, reliability, and respectability. But they were known to be effective because they commanded respect and 'reputation', among Creoles as well as African blacks. For example, Wylly's African head driver and under-driver, Boatswain and Jack, practically ran his estates. Strong family men, they were expected to lead prayers at Sunday services and conduct funerals. Boatswain at least was literate, and was paid for each slave taught to read; both were rewarded with 12 guineas a a year, the right to own and ride a horse, and the power to inflict punishment on their own initiative up to 12 stripes. But did their authority, ultimately, stem from their paternalistic master, or from their position as family heads and from African roots? And what did the family pattern at Clifton, Tusculum, and Waterloo owe, respectively, to memories of Africa, the examples of Boatswain and Jack, and the encouragement of Wylly?

Strong clues emerged from the discovery that, when African-headed families — those in which both parents, either parent, or the only parent were African-born — were separated from purely Creole families, it became obvious that Africans were considerably more inclined toward family formation than Creole slaves. Of the Africans, 65.3 per cent lived in couples, compared with less than 60 per cent of the Creoles over the age of twenty. Of all African-headed families, 61.0 per cent were of the simple nuclear type, with an additional 9.4 per cent indicted as extended family households. This compared with 48.4 per cent in nuclear units and 14.4 per cent in extended households among Creole families. Only 11.9 per cent of Africans lived alone, compared with 16.7 per cent of adult Creoles.

By a Bahamian law of 1824, owners were forbidden to separate slave husbands from wives by sale, gift, or bequest, or to take their children away from them before they were fourteen years old. Although the act did not expressly forbid the splitting of families by shifting slaves from island to island, or the separation of children from single parents, it would seem to have provided owners with a motive for discouraging rather than encouraging slave families. Yet the evidence strongly suggests that masters were not only forced to acknowledge slave marital arrangements and to sell or transfer slaves only in families, even before 1824, but also to consider carefully the social consequences before they shifted slaves from their customary houses, plots, and kin at all.[24]

Wylly, although an alleged emancipationist, only manumitted three of his slaves after 1822 and did not scruple to scatter them by sale and transfer between 1821 and his death in 1828. Families, however, were carefully kept together. In another case, Rolle proposed an ingenious scheme in 1826 to shift all of his slaves to Trinidad, where they were to work to earn their freedom in the Spanish style. Fortunately for the slaves, the project was vetoed by the Colonial Office. But the word must have filtered down to Exuma, for in 1828 when Rolle's agent set about transferring some slaves to Grand Bahama, all of the slaves, fearing a move to Trinidad, became so mutinous that troops had to be sent down to keep order. Two years later, when they heard that the agent planned to ship them from Exuma to Cat Island, 44 slaves (five men, eight women, and their families) actually rebelled. Under the leadership of a slave called Pompey they first fled to the bush, then seized Rolle's salt boat, and sailed to Nassau to put their case to Governor Smyth, who was widely thought to be a friend of the slaves. The fugitives were thrown into the workhouse and the leaders flogged (including the eight women). But Smyth was angry when he heard about it and none of the slaves in the end were sent to Cat Island; it can be said that Pompey and his fellows won the principle that Bahamian slaves could not with impunity be shifted against their will.[25]

The largest single transfer of slaves had been the shipment in 1823 of most of the 840 slaves of James Moss from Acklin's Island and Crooked Island to Jamaica, where their fate remains obscure. Yet the most interesting of all Bahamian transfers was that to Trinidad between 1821 and 1823 of the majority of the slaves of Burton Williams of Watling's Island

and his family, since it allows for comparisons between the fortunes of those transferred and other slaves in Trinidad, and between all those and the slaves left behind in the Bahamas.

Early in 1825, after he had been in Trinidad 3½ years, Williams gave evidence to the Trinidad Council about his slaves. He claimed that in '30 odd' years of Bahamian residence he had seen the group of seven slaves inherited and 'about 100' bought augmented by 224 through natural increase. This remarkable growth (as rapid as that indicated for Rolle's slaves, and sustained over a longer period) was attributed by Williams to his own residence among the slaves, to firm management, and to the encouragement of marriage 'by giving a feast to the Gang when they come together and a sharp punishment when they part'.[26]

Certainly, the 450 Williams slaves found in the Bahamas in 1821 exhibited an even healthier demographic balance and a higher incidence of family formation than the Bahamian average, as is shown in Figure 4 and Table 4. The proportion of young children was higher, there were only two thirds as many Africans, and yet a fair number of very elderly slaves. The proportion of slaves in nuclear families, 55.8 per cent, was some 2 per cent higher than the average for the 26 holdings analyzed earlier, and the total in some kind of family more than 5 per cent higher, at 90.2 per cent. Yet, by Williams' account, the situation in the Bahamas had become economically and demographically critical by 1821, so that he could neither clothe nor feed his slaves adequately, although he owned 13,000 acres of land. Taking advantage of the inducements offered by Trinidad, he therefore transferred 324 of his slaves in five cargoes between 1821 and 1823.[27]

Although one or two couples were split and an unknown number of extended family members separated, Williams clearly attempted to transfer his slaves predominantly in family units. Comparison of the slaves settled at

Figure 4 The Burton Williams slaves, 1822, and 1825, compared with Bahamas and Trinidad slaves, 1825; population pyramids

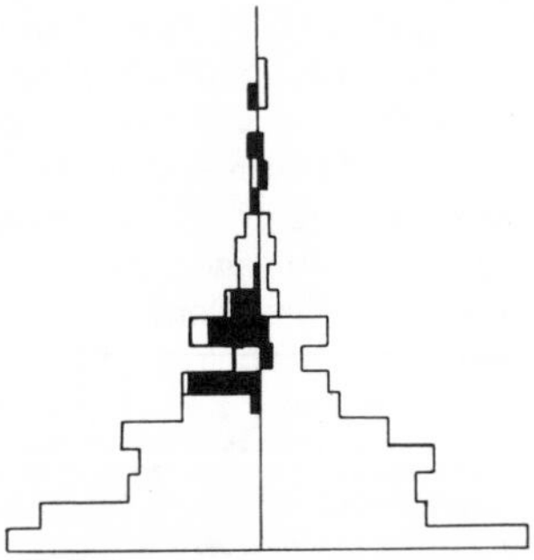

A. Williams Slaves, Bahamas 1821–2

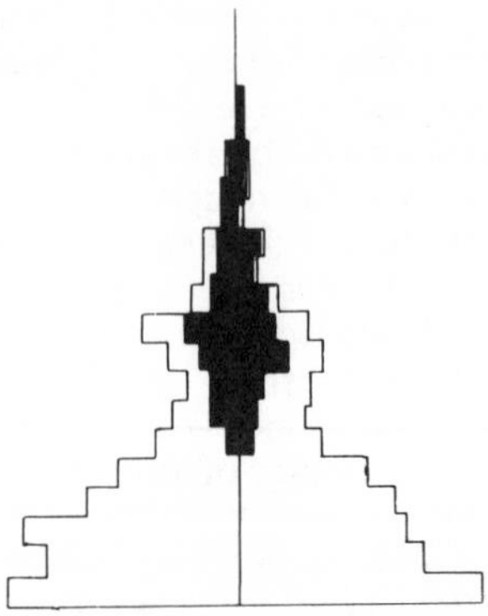

B. Bahamas Slaves, 26 Holdings, 1822

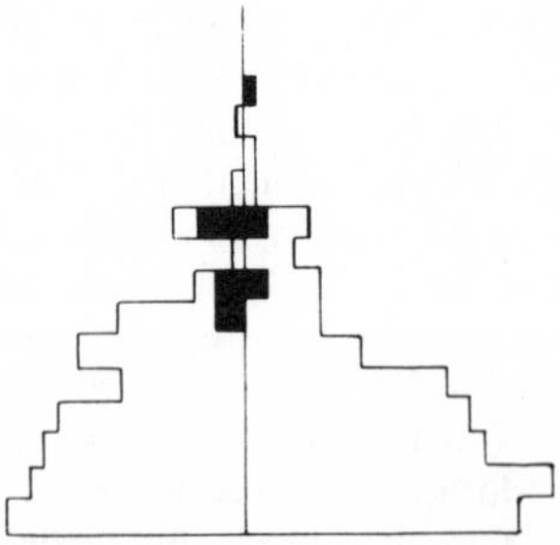

C. Burton Williams Slaves, Williamsville, Trinidad, 1825

D. Trinidad Slaves Overall, 1825 (Hypothetical Reconstruction)
Shaded Area = African Slaves

Table 4 Bahamas, Family Formation, Williams Slaves 1822 and 1825 compared with 26 Holdings, 1822

Family type	A. Williams slaves, 1822				B. Williams slaves, Bahamas, 1825				C. 26 Bahamian holdings, 1822			
	Total slaves	Number of units	Mean size of units	Per cent of total in type	Total slaves	Number of units	Mean size of units	Per cent of total in type	Total slaves	Number of units	Mean size of units	Per cent of total in type
1. Man, woman, Children	251	47	5.34	55.8	103	20	5.15	46.0	1,629	308	5.29	54.1
2. Man, woman	28	14	2.00	6.2	10	5	2.00	4.5	178	89	2.00	5.9
3. Woman, children	45	10	4.50	10.0	38	14	2.71	17.0	377	95	3.97	12.5
4. Man, children	2	1	2.00	0.5	0	0	—	—	16	3	5.33	0.5
5. Three-generation	80	9	8.88	17.8	25	4	6.25	11.2	358	46	7.78	11.9
6. Single men	15	—	—	3.3	22	—	—	9.8	264	—	—	8.8
7. Single women	14	—	—	3.1	8	—	—	3.5	173	—	—	5.8
8. Separate children	15	—	—	3.3	18	5	3.60	8.0	16	—	—	0.5
Totals	450	—	—	100.0	224	—	—	100.0	3,011	—	—	100.0
A. Nuclear family (1, 2, 5)	359	70	5.13	79.8	138	29	4.75	61.6	2,165	443	4.89	71.9
B. Denuded family (3, 4)	47	11	4.27	10.4	38	14	2.71	17.0	393	98	4.01	13.0
C. No family (6, 7, 8)	44	—	—	9.8	48	—	—	21.4	453	—	—	15.1

Williamsville, his new estate in Naparima, in the Trinidadian returns of 1825 with those left behind listed in the Bahamas returns of the same year, indicates also that the majority of the elderly and Africans were left behind, and that rather more young females were carried than young males. The transferred population therefore exhibited many characteristics sharply different from those of the generality of Trinidadian slaves. Only 5.3 per cent of the Williamsville slaves were African-born, compared with the Trinidadian average of over 40 per cent, and females outnumbered males by 7.8 per cent, more than reversing the general Trinidadian pattern. Whether using the categories used elsewhere in this paper or those employed by Higman, the contrast in family formation is even more noticeable. Because of the greater detail given in the Trinidadian registration returns, more types could be differentiated, but the total of Williamsville slaves in some type of family was as high as in the Bahamas sample, and almost twice as high as the Trinidadian average indicated by Higman. The percentage in simple nuclear households, 57.3 per cent, was slightly higher than in the Bahamas, and three times as high as the Trinidadian average. Mothers living alone with their children accounted for only 6 per cent of the Williamsville slaves, half of the Bahamas figure, and little more than a quarter of that for Trinidad as a whole.

As a consequence of the division of the Williams slaves, those left behind in the Bahamas were less well-balanced in composition than the Bahamian average and therefore increased in number rather less rapidly after 1823. Yet those transferred were less healthy than those left behind and increased even more slowly. However, they did increase, in contrast to Trinidadian slaves in general, who suffered an alarming depeletion throughout the registration period. By the end of 1826, 33 of Williams's Trinidadian slaves had died, while 57 were born (49 having been sold and two manumitted), an annual rate of natural increase of roughly 16 per 1,000. This was half the Bahamian rate, and compared with an annual net decrease at least as high for Trinidadian slaves on the average.[28]

Although his 1825 evidence was twisted to justify the transfer, Williams had to admit that the health and morale of his slaves had suffered in the first three years — the seasoning period. 'Fevers and Agues and bowel Complaints,' as well as unfamilar 'Sores', although not great killers, were common among the transferred slaves. These ills Williams attributed to his having arrived in the middle of the wet season, settling in a wooded and marshy area, and being forced to feed his slaves on plantains and saltfish rather than their customary guinea corn (millet or sorghum). He deplored the laxity of Trinidadian morals and the effects on family life of the disparity in the sex ratio. He also pleaded that the demoralizing effects of Colonial Office regulations would encourage the idleness of slaves and limit the powers of correction of their masters. Against the evidence, he denied that the work required of slaves was harder than in the Bahamas, and claimed that slaves had more opportunity in Trinidad to dispose of the surplus food that they grew on their own allotments. However, he remarked that most of the slaves would have returned to the Bahamas if they had been given the choice.[29]

The research undertaken so far not only indicates a far wider existence of family in slave society than hitherto expected, but has also clarified the varieties of family within the range of West Indian slave communities in the late slave period. At one end of the scale were the virtual peasants of the Bahamas, Barbuda and, perhaps, the Grenadines, with locational stability, a small proportion of African slaves, natural increase, and a relatively high incidence of nuclear and stable families. At the opposite pole were the overworked slaves of new plantations such as those of Trinidad, Guyana, and St. Vincent, with a high rate of natural decrease, a majority of slaves living alone or in 'barrack' conditions, and a high proportion of 'denuded', female-headed families. In between came the mass of West Indian slaves, all but 10 per cent living on plantations of one sort or another, with a wide range of demographic patterns but a generally declining rate of natural increase and a rapidly dwindling African population, and varying degrees of practical exogamy, miscegenation with whites, and family formation.[30]

Unfortunately, statistical information on West Indian slave families is practically limited to the registration period, 1813–34, after the slave trade with Africa had ended, when all plantations were starting to decline, amelioration measures were being applied, and missionaries were beginning to make their influence felt. It remains to be seen whether a morphology of slave family during the entire period of slavery can be inferred, or projected, from this material alone; what additional light is shed by the white-produced literary sources from an earlier period; and, finally, what other

Table 5 Family Structure, Williams Trinidadian Slaves, 1825 compared with Trinidadian Total, 1813 (Higman, 1978)[a]

	A. Williams slaves, 1825				B. Trinidadian slaves total, 1813			
Family type	Total	Units	Mean size	Per cent in type	Total	Units	Mean size	Per cent in type
Man, woman, children	142	24	5.9	57.4	4,675	1,162	4.0	18.3
Man, woman	6	3	2.0	2.4	1,036	518	2.0	4.0
Woman, children	15	3	5.0	6.0	5,690	2,066	2.8	22.2
Man, children	0	0	—	—	357	138	2.6	1.4
Polygynists	0	0	—	—	31	7	4.4	0.1
Three-generation and extended[b]	47	8	5.9	18.9	445	97	4.6	1.7
Siblings	14	4	3.5	5.7	} 547	197	2.8	2.1
Siblings, children	9	2	4.5	3.6				
Man, woman, cousins	5	2	2.5	2.0	0	0	—	—
No family[c]	10	—	—	4.0	12,892	—	—	50.2
Totals	248	—	—	100.0	25,673	—	—	100.0

[a] Data from Public Record Office, London, T. 71/513 (1825); T. 71/501–503; Higman, 'Family Patterns in Trinidad,' 32.

[b] In the Williams Population: Man, Woman, Children, their Children (8); Man, Woman, Children, Man's Sister, her Children (7); Man, Woman, Children, Woman's Brother, his Spouse (6); Man, Woman, Child, Man's Brother, his Spouse (5); Man, Woman, Man's Sister, her Child (4); Woman, Children, Spouses (5). In the Higman Total: Woman, her Children, her Grandchildren (227); 'Extended' (218).

[c] In the Williams Population, Men and Women living alone, unrelated separated Children.

arguments can be adduced, including the incorporation of West African material.

Earlier speculation led the present writer and Higman to postulate, and then to refine to the point of dismissal, two successive models. First, if one took the nuclear two-headed family as the quintessentially modern family form, it was beguilingly easy to propose its different incidence during the registration period as relating to the degree of maturation, creolization, or modernization of each slave unit, and thus to suggest a historical progression from some aboriginal African form of family. Such a progression initially seemed borne out by the closer parallels among the modern Jamaican rural communities analyzed by Edith Clarke and the Exumian slaves of Rolle, as compared with Jamaican slave plantation examples, and by the highly developed family patterns traced by Colin Clarke and Lowenthal among the completely creolized peasants of Barbuda in 1851.[31]

However, the discovery by Higman, amply corroborated by the Bahamian material examined here, that Africans were at least as likely as Creoles to form nuclear families, modified the original model. This revision, coupled with the likelihood that the registration records largely concealed the existence of extended families, and the apparent paradox that Creole men were more likely to be polygynous than Africans, led Higman to a second developmental mode, based on the seemingly progressive differences between Trinidad, Jamaica, and Barbados.[32] By this formulation, the establishment of 'elementary nuclear families' was the primary response of the displaced Africans in the first slave generation. This was the stage of fictive kin such as the 'shipmate' relationship described by Edwards. Owing to high mortality, the further shifting of slaves, and a high male ratio, families were able to practice polygyny. A second slave generation began to establish extended families based on the formation of virilocal 'yards' within single plantations; but, because mortality remained high and fresh Africans were continually arriving, the elementary family continued the dominant norm. At this stage polygyny may actually have increased, as an index of status and property. In subsequent generations, kinship networks expanded as slaves increasingly practiced exogamy. This occurred earliest and most rapidly where holdings were small and contiguous, and the proportion of Creoles high. The process tended toward matrifocality rather than the nuclear family, especially where lack of slave-controlled provision grounds, money, and property deprived slaves of the chance of 'marriage strategies'.[33]

It was clearly right to de-emphasize the normative role of the slaveowners and to stress that slaves largely determined their own family arrangements. Higman's schematic formulation also properly recognized that a wide variety of family types coexisted in all periods, since different islands and sectors developed at different rates and in different ways. A closer study of the Bahamian materials, however, suggested that it was the Bahamas rather than Barbados which represented the forward extreme of slave family development. Higman's most recent analysis of the 1813 registration returns also suggested that Trinidad was a more special case than previously thought: an area directly supervized and rapidly expanding on the eve of emancipation and changing technology, rather than a frontier area exactly analogous to Barbados in 1650 or Jamaica in 1720. In particular, his scrutiny pointed up three conclusions apparent or latent in the Bahamian material considered here: the critical importance to slave family development of plantation size; the effects of urbanization; and the difficulty of tracing simple cultural transfers from Africa. Even more critically, Higman's earlier model underestimated the formative changes that occurred over the century and a half before the slave trade ended. These included great changes in the intensity of the plantation system and the gradual evolution of systems of slave management aimed at greater efficiency in general, and thus at increasing slave fertility as well. Perhaps most important of all was small and impermanent, and only for a few privileged slaves: this was the filtering down into the West Indies of evolving concepts of the 'modern' family, which gradually gained hold in the practice of creolized slaves, as well as in the minds of white masters.

It is notable that the two most important early writers on British West Indian slavery gave sympathetic accounts of the slaves' society and customs. Ligon (1657) and Sloane (1707) described the early slaves as having a great sense of decorum. Unlike Europeans, they were not ashamed of nakedness and, though with a healthy sex drive, fastidiously avoided public displays of 'wantonness'. They married when they could, and had a rigorous distaste for adultery. 'They have every one his Wife,' wrote Sloane, 'and are very much concern'd if they prove adulterous, but in some measure satisfied if their Masters punish the Man who does them the supposed injury, in any of his Hogs, or other small wealth. The care of the Masters and Overseers about their Wives, is what keeps their Plantations chiefly in good order, whence they even buy Wives in proportion to their Men, lest the Men should wander to neighbouring Plantations and neglect to serve them.' The males appeared to be dominant and the practice of polygyny by no means uncommon, being enjoyed, 'by certain brave fellows... of extraordinary qualities', from the earliest days. In contrast to later reports there was a strong bond of affection between parents and children, particularly between mothers and infants, who, in African fashion, were carried to work in the fields and not weaned for two years or even longer. Great respect and care were shown for the aged, whether or not they were actual kin.[34]

Ligon and Sloane wrote with exceptional objectivity before the plantation system was intensified, and also in a period when extended families were more important than nuclear families in Europe itself, and modern ideas of childhood and parent affection were still relatively strange. Besides, during Ligon's period in Barbados and Sloane's in Jamaica miscegenation had not yet become institutionalized because there was still a sizeable proportion of whites of both sexes in the laboring population, and the majority of the blacks were unacculturated Africans.

Echoes of Ligon and Sloane could still be heard in later writings, but most gave a far less sympathetic account of the slaves. As Barbados, followed by the Leeward Islands and Jamaica, became dominated by sugar plantations, the planters became more callous and indifferent to slaves' social arrangements. Wedded to the plantations, the slave trade also intensified, and now men imported outnumbered women by three to two. Meanwhile, bourgeois social values increasingly added insult to injury. As far as they were concerned at all, planters disparaged as natural faults characteristics in their slaves for which the white themselves were chiefly to blame, and often similarly guilty. Thus, although marriage and family life were practically discouraged and forcible miscegenation was rife, planters condemned the slaves' 'promiscuity', 'polygamy', and apparent indifference to their children, or even to having children at all.

Behind the planters' ignorance and exaggeration, however, lay the undoubted truth that the quality of slave life had nearly everywhere deteriorated seriously. In this phase, West Indian families were probably at a low point of integration — before extended new kinships had been built up and laws passed forbidding the separation of husbands and wives, and mothers and children. Except for the polygymous favors enjoyed by privileged slaves like drivers — the slaves' 'worst domestic tyrants' — conjugal unions were rare and impermanent, and the majority of infants lived with single mothers or grandmothers — up to 10 per cent of whom were, or had been, the casual mates of plantation whites.

In the last phase of slavery, as the profits of plantations dwindled, the price of slaves rose, and in 1808, the supply of fresh Africans was cut off and the West Indian slaveowners came under economic constraints at the same time as they were coming under pressure from metropolitan philanthropists. Writers on slave society attacked or defended plantation customs, or proposed methods of raising the dismal level of slave fertility. The encouragement of Christianity and family life was seen by some as methods of making slaves contented, peaceable, and fertile. Some measure of local reform would, moreover, vitiate the arguments of the emancipationists and undermine the sectarian missionaries, who shared none of the establishment's reluctance to proselytize the slaves and promote respectable marriage. Accordingly, in the 1820s, plantocratic Assemblies passed acts ostensibly encouraging slave marriage and actually authorizing fees to Anglican ministers for slave baptisms.

Few writers, though, acknowledged the slaves' own motives. Since all slaves yearned chiefly to be free, if adherence to the Church and its formulas were conditions of freedom, a growing number of slaves would aspire to baptism and formal marriage, with their official registrations, as potent indicators of improving social status. Most writers also ignored the degree to which slaves actually possessed property and virtual tenure of houses and plots, which they were able, in custom if not law, to bequeath to whomever they wished. Long before emancipation, a fair proportion of West Indian slaves had ample reasons, on the grounds of respectability and conformability to the laws of inheritance, to adopt the familial norms of the master class.

But nearly every commentator, from Ligon and Sloane to 'Monk' Lewis and Mrs. A. C. Carmichael, did share two absolute certainties: that as to marriage, whatever the masters did, the slaves always had and always would (in the

Table 6 West Indian Family from Slavery to the Present; A Comparison of Trinidad, Jamaica, and the Bahamas in Slavery Days with Barbuda immediately after Slavery, and with Modern Rural Jamaica, 1813–1955

	A. Trinidad, 1813				B. Montpelier, Jamaica, 1825			
Family[a] type	Total slaves	Number of units	Mean size of units	Per cent of total in type	Total slaves	Number of units	Mean size of units	Per cent of total in type
1.	4,675	1,162	4.0	18.3	204	50	4.1	25.1
2.	1,036	518	2.0	4.0	76	38	2.0	9.3
3.	5,690	2,066	2.8	22.2	328	70	4.7	40.3
4.	357	138	2.6	1.4	0	0	—	—
5.	445	97	4.6	1.7	24	6	4.0	2.9
6, 7, 8	12,892	—	—	50.2	182	—	—	22.4
Others	578	204	2.8	2.2				
	25,673	—	—	100.0	814	—	—	100.0
A	6,156	1,777	3.5	24.0	304	94	3.2	37.3
B	6,625	2,408	2.8	25.8	328	70	4.7	40.3
C	12,892	—	—	50.2	182	—	—	22.6

	C. Bahamas, holdings 26, 1822			D. Barbuda, 1851				E. Rural Jamaica, 1955[b] 1. 'Sugartown' 2. 'Mocca'	
Total slaves	Number of units	Mean size of units	Percent of total in type	Total population	Number of units	Mean size of units	Percent of total in type	Per cent of total population in type	Per cent of total population in type
629	308	5.3	54.1	425	76	5.6	67.7	}	
178	89	2.0	5.9	28	14	2.0	4.5	} 46	42
377	95	4.0	12.5	50	12	4.2	8.0	16	117
16	3	5.3	0.5	6	1	6.0	0.7	3	3
358	46	7.8	11.9	90	18	5.0	14.3	18	30
264	—	—	8.8	7	7	1.0	1.1	}	
173	—	—	5.8	10	10	1.0	1.6	} 17	9
16	—	—	0.5	13	6	2.2	2.1	}	
011	—	—	100.0	629	144	4.7	100.0	100	100
165	443	4.9	71.9	543	108	5.0	86.3	65	71
393	98	4.0	13.0	56	13	4.3	8.6	19	20
453	—	—	15.1	30	23	1.3	3.1	17	9

[a]1 = Man, Woman, Children; 2 = Man, Women; 3 = Woman, Children; 4 = Man, Chidlren; 5 = Three Nuclear Family (1, 2, 5); B = Denuded Family (3, 4); C = No Family (6, 7, 8). Generation Groups; 6 = Men Alone, or Together, or Together, 7 = Women Alone, or Together; 8 = Children Separately Edith Clarke, *My Mother Who Fathered Me* (London 1957), 191–94.

words of the Jamaican, John Quier) 'claim a Right of disposing of themselves in this Respect, according to their Own Will and Pleasure without any Controul from their Masters'; and that within certain obvious constraints these voluntary arrangements were African rather than European. We restrain their Actions sufficiently, to our conveniences,' wrote Lindsay, Rector of St. Catherine's, Jamaica, 'tho' we inslave not the Inclinations of the Heart, against their Natural Habits and Native Customs, which may well be injoy'd separately from their Obedience to us.'[35]

Few Africans carried their children with them into slavery, and fewer still accompanied marital partners from West Africa into West Indian plantations, let alone the members of the extended family and kinship groups which were of prime importance in West African society. The ethnic mixing which was standard plantation policy meant additionally that the legacies of Africa were transmitted in a haphazard or generalized way. Yet the impress of Africa was indelible, and African patterns were replicated where possible, and reconstituted as soon as possible where not, surviving slavery itself in modified forms.

On large plantations there were sometimes sub-cultural groups — such as 'Ibo' or 'Congo' — and some forceful cultural traditions, particularly the Akan (or 'Coromantee'), seem to have been normative. Yet the very variety of West African roots allowed for creative syncretism, or the choice of alternative customs — for example, concerning the role of women , and the acceptability of cousin-mating and premarital intercourse — as the slaves made the necessary adjustments to the new environment, the dictates of the plantation system, and the shifting demographic conditions.[36]

Some features of the plantation system, such as the expectation that women would work in the fields, that men would monopolize the skilled and privileged roles, and that slave driver and other elite slaves such as head craftsmen would be likely to practice polygyny, actually facilitated the continuation of West African customs. Other continuities were of necessity more covert, having to exist in the narrow scope of private life left to the slaves by the master class: rites of passage, courtship and pre-marital negotiations, marriage ceremonies and celebrations, and the role of elderly slaves as 'councils of elders' to determine custom and settle domestic disputes. While the slave trade lasted, direct links with Africa were never cut, native Africans being brought in groups to expand plantations or, more commonly arriving in ones and twos to make up the shortfall in slave fertility. As Edwards testified, these Africans were welcomed into family units, especially those of their own tribe and language.[37]

From the simple pairings which were all that the planters provided for, the slaves built up extended family relationship beyond the masters' ken or concern and, in the course of generations, whole new kinship networks based on the cohesive 'village' of a single plantation holding but gradually extending beyond the plantation's bounds into nearby groups. In Barbados, a small island covered with small contiguous plantations, the process of social diffusion had gone on longest; but even there, as in Africa, the primary allegiance remained the village, the birthplace, the home and burial-place of closest family, kin, and ancestors.

In 1808 the direct connection with Mother Africa was cut, but by that time the area of social autonomy had significantly expanded for most slaves. Slaves owned their own property (in some colonies even in law), bequeathed and inherited houses and land, and in some islands virtually controlled the internal market system. On declining plantations they were encouraged to be as nearly self-sufficient as possible, and on decayed plantations were left almost entirely to their own devices. Yet, contrary to the masters' pessimism, the young and the aged were better cared for than under more rigorous slave regimes, and the unfavourable ratio between deaths and births began to reverse. In the phrase of Sidney Mintz, the most fortunate British West Indian slaves were proto-peasants long before slavery ended, and made an easy transition into 'full freedom' in 1838.[38]

Four influences militated against the continued development of peasant lifestyles and family systems: the breakup of the old slave quarters and the consequent 'marginalization' of many ex-slaves; the persistence of plantations in a more impersonal form; an accelerated urbanization; and the spread of the canons of respectability. The closing down of the slave cantonments after emancipation, as plantations decayed or turned to less intensive forms of agriculture (particularly, grazing 'pens'), or ex-slaves who refused to work on the planters' terms were evicted from houses and plots, was as traumatic a change as the cutting of the African link or the ending of formal slavery itself. The more fortunate ex-slaves were able to form their own villages and develop a healthy peasant society; but many others without land of their own were forced into a marginal existence, depending on the increasingly mechanized plantations for wages, but competing with each other, and with newly imported indentured laborers, in a cruelly seasonal economy. Far fewer women worked as plantation laborers, and most of the men became transients, living in barracks or strange villages during crop-time and being unable to form permanent or stable attachments while women provided the only permanence and stability for children. A similar continuation of the worst features of the slave period occurred among the poor of the towns, which burgeoned after emancipation. The new towns had a high proportion of migrants from the countryside, a disproportionately high ratio of women, and thus a majority of impermanent, fractured, and matrifocal families.

As we have noticed, many slaves in the last phase of slavery were attracted by the apparent advantages of respectable, European-type families. After emancipation these became the norm among the small emergent middle class, many of the members of which were the colored descendants of domestic slaves who had engaged in miscegenous relationships. Under the growing influence of the churches, a far wider spectrum of the ex-slaves continued to subscribe outwardly to the canons of respectability, especially in islands like Barbados where the Anglican Church was deeply entrenched and conditions were unfavourable for true peasant development. Yet, as Wilson has plausibly argued, the subscription to respectability is superficial among the majority of British West Indian blacks. Far more deeply engrained are the tenets of 'reputation': those elements of custom which place greater stress on community, kinship, and extended family, and place greater value on social worth, than on introspective family forms, bourgeois manners, and material wealth. In this analysis, reputation provides a continuous thread of tradition passing back through slavery to Africa itself.[39]

Therefore, in assessing the nature of slave family and its place in the continuum we emphasize not the ways that slavery destroyed or distorted family, but the ways in which the slaves' own forms of family triumphed over adversity. In this light, we evaluate slavery not by the manner in which it controlled and shaped slaves' destinies, but by the degree to which it allowed slaves to make family lives of their own.

Notes

1. John Quier, 'Report of the Jamaican House of Assembly on the Slave Issues', in Lt. Gov. Clarke's No. 92, November 20, 1788; Public Record Office, London, C.O. 137/88, Appendix C.
2. Herbert G. Gutman, *The Black Family in Slavery and Freedom, 1750–1925* (New York, 1976), xxi.
3. Thomas S. Simey, *Welfare and Planning in the West Indies* (Oxford, 1946), 50–51, 79; Fernando Henriques, *Family and Colour in Jamaica* (London, 1953), 103; William J. Goode, 'Illegitimacy in the Caribbean Social Structure', *American Sociological Review*, XXV (1960), 21–30; M. G. Smith, *The Plural Society in the British West Indies* (Berkeley, 1965), 109; Orlando Patterson, *The Sociology of Slavery* (London, 1967), 167.
4. Barry W. Higman, 'Household Structure and Fertility on Jamaican Slave Plantations: A Nineteenth-Century Example', *Population Studies*, XXVII (1973), 527–50; *idem*, 'The Slave Family and Household in the British West Indies, 1800–1834', *Journal of Interdisciplinary History,* VI (1975), 261–87; *idem, Slave Population and Economy in Jamaica, 1807–1834* (Cambridge, 1976) Higman's 'Family Property: The Slave Family in the British Caribbean in the Early Nineteenth Century', unpub. paper (1976), is now largely superseded by his 'African and Creole Slave Family Patterns in Trinidad,' paper delivered at the Tenth Conference of Caribbean Historians (1978). See *ibid.*, 12.
5. James Stephen, *The Slavery of the British West India Colonies Delineated* (London, 1824), I, Appendix III, 454–74. The Bahamas, with almost exactly the same total land area as Jamaica (4,400 square miles), had approximately 10,000 slaves against 300,000 in Jamaica. Barbados, with only 166 square miles, had 65,000 slaves. In 1800, the ratio between blacks and whites in the Bahamas was about 4:1; in Barbados it was 8:1; In Jamaica 12:1.
6. David Eltis, 'The Traffic in Slaves between the British West Indian Colonies, 1807–1833', *Economic History Review*, XXV (1972), 55–64. Perhaps through a misunderstanding, there was a partial census of Bahamian slaves in 1821. Most of these were relisted in 1822, but not all. The 1822 census book gives a grand total of 10,808 slaves, but this seems to omit the slaves lised in 1821 and not relisted in 1822. The intercolonial migration was at its peak between 1821 and 1822; its volume may never be known with complete accuracy.
7. Archives of the Bahamas, Nassau; Register of Returns of Slaves, Bahama Islands, 1821–1834. It was fortunate that the Bahamas Registration Act of 1821 required the listing of all slaves every three years, not just an initial census and subsequent triennial increases and decreases as in most other colonies. The Act specified what information should be given but not the order of the lists. Despite this, there seems to have been a remarkable uniformity in the method used by those owners who chose to list their slaves in family and household groups. An absolutely certain distinction between family and household was scarcely possible, but a comparison of the data on slaves transferred from the Bahamas to Trinidad (where the registration returns gave fuller details), and corroboration between the triennial Bahamian censuses, suggested that although extended families were understated, the listings concentrated on families rather than mere cohabitation, and the groups listed were almost invariably cohabiting families, rarely mere 'housefuls'.

8. Craton, 'Hobbesian or Panglossian? The Two Extremes of Slave Conditions in the British Caribbean, 1738-1834', *William and Mary Quarterly*, XXV (1978), 324-56; *idem, Searching for the Invisible Man: Slaves and Plantation Life in Jamaica* (Cambridge, Mass., 1978), 60-118.
9. The proportions of African and colored slaves in the 26 holdings in 1822 were remarkably close to those in the overall slave population, 20.0 and 6.9%.
10. The average age of mothers at the birth of their first children given in Table 2, 22.37 years, is clearly overstated since the 479 mothers included many whose earlier children were old enough to have left the parental household, and were thus not recorded. When the 251 mothers aged 35 or more at the time of the census were excluded, the average age of the remaining 228 mothers at the birth of their first surviving child was 19.27 years. Of the females in the age range 15-49, 65.6% were indicated as mothers. In all, the 479 mothers listed had 1,456 listed children, an average of 3.02 children each.
11. Of the 26 holdings analyzed, 20 were established in the further islands, with a total of 2,634 slaves, an average of 132 per holding. Six were established in New Providence and Eleuthera, with a total of 367 slaves, an average of 61. In 1834 (the only year for which figures have been tabulated), 481 of the 730 Bahamian holdings of 5 or less slaves, and 692 of the 1,088 of 20 or less, were in New Providence and Eleuthera (including Harbour Island), but only 26 of the 107 Bahamian holdings of more than 20 slaves: Archives of the Bahamas, Nassau; Register of Returns of Slaves, Bahama Islands, 1834. The 1834 tabulation has been made by Gail Saunders.
12. The figure for 1834 was 9.6%, but by that date a considerable number had been manumitted.
13. Keith F. Otterbein, *The Andros Islanders; A Study of Family Organization in the Bahamas* (Lawrence, Kansas, 1966). There is as yet no scholarly study of family in New Providence, or of the huge migration that has concentrated more than half the Bahamian population in the capital. Gutman, *op. cit.*, 444-45, 489-91.
14. In the 1822 sample of 26 holdings, 5 possible cases of polygyny occurred. One such was Jack Stewart, a mulatto slave aged 66 belonging to James Moss at Acklin's Island, who appeared to live with Phoebe, an African aged 55, Kate, a Creole aged 37, and 10 children aged between 1 and 15, all listed as mulattoes.
15. Permanent mates and their children generally shared a surname, but in female-headed families and transient unions a practice common later in the Bahamas may have been followed; children went by their mother's surname until they were 21 and then adopted their father's surname.
16. Craton, 'Hobbesian or Panglossian?', 19. Today there are thousands of Rolles in the Bahamas, including, it is said, two thirds of the population of Exuma. Male children often had a prefix or suffix added, as with Young Bacchus, Jack Junior, Little Jim, or the African-sounding Jim Jim, son of Jim. Males were often named after their fathers, females more rarely after their mothers. Out of the 67 family units of the Williams group of slaves transferred to Trinidad there were 22 males named after their fathers and at least 1 after a grandfather; 4 females were named after their mothers, at least 3 after a grandmother, and 1 after a mother's sister.
17. In the populations studied, 28 young mothers lived with their parents, their average ages being 18 years and 9 months. Only 5 were over 20 years old, and the average age at the birth of their first children was 17 years and 8 months. Only 1 of the 28 had a second child.
18. Michael Craton, *A History of the Bahamas* (London, 1962), 173-74, 194-96.
19. William Wylly to President W. V. Munnings, August 31, 1818, C.O. 23/67, 147.
20. *Regulations for the Government of the Slaves at Clifton and Tusculum in New Providence, Printed at the Office of the New Gazette*, 1815, enclosed in *ibid.*
21. Of Wylly's 67 slaves in 1821, as many as 53 lived in 8 two-headed households (in 2 of which the family included a teenage single mother), with 1 female-headed family and a maximum of 9 slaves living alone, averaging 49 years old and including 6 elderly Africans. Almost certainly, 3 of the hosuehold units at Clifton were the extended family of Jack, the African under-driver, and his wife Sue. Twenty of the 67 slaves were under the age of 10 in 1821. See below, 19-23; C.O. 295/66, 53-59; 295/67, 219; 295/71, 26-35; 295/78, 233-265.
22. D. W. Rose, reporting on the slaves of Exuma, 1802; Craton, *History of the Bahamas*, 183.
23. Besides 10 African couples, there were 3 holdings in which an African male headed the list with his Creole mate. In these 13 holdings (half of the total) there were 187 Africans out of a total of 805 slaves or 23.2%, not significantly more than the overall average, 18.8%.
24. Act of 4 Geo. IV, c. 6; *Acts of the Assembly of the Bahama Islands* (Nassau, 1827), V, 227-28.
25. Archives of the Bahamas, Manumissions Index; Register of Returns of Slaves, 1825, 1828, 1831, 1834; Public Record Office, London; Register of Returns of Slaves, St. Vincent, 1822, 1825. Craton, 'Hobbesian or Panglossian?', 19-20; C.O. 295/67, 219; 295/71, 26-35; 295/78, 233-265; Governor James Carmichael Smyth to Lord Stanley, October 27, 1830, C.O. 23/82, 368-420.
26. Evidence given on January 18, 1825, C.O. 295/66, 53-59. A population of 107 increasing at the Rolle rate for 1822-34, 34.5 per 1,000 per year, would have reached 331 in the thirty-fourth year.
27.

		Men	Women	Boys	Girls	Infants	
July	1821	27	43	7	5	23	
February	1822	9	11	6	4	24	
July	1822	6	11	3	3	14	
March	1823	10	10	7	5	33	
June	1823	6	11	6	7	33	
		58	86	29	24	127	324

This compilation was made on September 27, 1823. By that time, 19 children had been added to Williams' slaves by birth, and only 7 of the total had been lost by death. This indicated a crude annual birth rate of 29 per 1,000 and a death rate around 11 per 1,000. However, of 3,239 slaves imported into Trinidad from all sources between 1813 and 1822 (1,678 being males and 1,561 females), 232 males and 156 females had died, 388 in all, against only 236 births; C.O. 295/59, 252, 255.
28. 'Return showing the number of Negroes imported into this Island by Burton Williams Esq.', enclosed in Governor Sir Ralph Woodford to William Huskisson, March 7, 1828, C.O. 295/77, 33-49.
29. C.O. 295/66, 57.
30. Craton, 'Hobbesian or Panglossian?', 19-21; Colin Clarke and David Lowenthal, 'Barbuda; the Past of a Negro Myth', in Vera Rubin and Arthur Tuden (eds), *Comparative Perspectives on Slavery in New World Plantation Societies* (New York, 1977), 510-34.

31. The argument is proposed in Craton, 'Hobbesian or Panglossian?' which was first delivered at the conference on Comparative Perspectives in New World Plantation Societies, New York, 1976. Edith Clarke, *My Mothers Who Fathered Me* (London, 1957).

Barbuda Household Types, 1851

Household type	Number of units	Number of persons	Persons per unit	Per cent total persons per unit type	
1. Man, woman, children	76	425	5.59	67.57	
2. Man and woman	14	28	2.00	4.45	
3. Woman and children	12	50	4.17	7.95	
4. Man and children	1	6	6.00	0.95	
5. Three generations (i.e. two women and children)	18	90	5.00	14.31	(95.23)
6. Men alone	7	7	1.00	1.11	
7. Women alone	10	10	1.00	1.59	
8. Women together	6	13	2.17	2.07	(4.77)
	144	629	4.73	100.00	

Source: Colin Clarke and D. Lowenthal, private correspondence (Codrington records, Gloucester County Record Office, England).

32. What follows is the argument proposed by Higman, 'Family Property', now superseded by his 'Slave Family patterns in Trinidad', 1977. The change was based on the analysis of the full 1813 slave population of 25,673 (a quarter of whom lived in Port of Spain), rather than the rural sample of 1,296 previously used.
33. Bryan Edwards, *The History, Civil and Commercial, of the British Colonies in the British West Indies* (London 1801), II, 155.
34. Richard Ligon, *A True and Exact History of the Island of Barbadoes* (London, 1657), 47; Hans Sloane, *A Voyage to the Islands Madera, Barbados, Nieves, S. Christophers and Jamaica* (London, 1725), II, xlviii; Stanley L. Engerman, 'Some Economic and Demographic Comparisons of Slavery in the United States and the British West Indies', *Economic History Review*, XXIX (1976), 258-75.
35. Quier, 'Report', 492; Lindsay, 'A Few Conjectural Considerations upon the Creation of the Human Race, Occasioned by the Present Quixottical Rage of setting the Slaves from Africa at Liberty', unpub. ms. dated Spanish Town, July 23, 1788, British Museum, Add. Mss. 12439.
36. Higman, 'Slave Family Patterns in Trinidad,' 14-18, 33-35. This strongly stresses the melding effect of the African slave trade to Trinidad. Only among the Ibo was there a recognizable transfer of specific African family patterns, and this was attributed to the high numbers and comparatively even sex ratio. When the African slaves were broken down by 7 general regions of origin there were no really significant variations in the proportions of family types recreated in Trinidad.
37. Edwards, *British West Indies*, II, 155.
38. Sidney W. Mintz, *Caribbean Transformations* (Chigato, 1974), 151-52.
39. Peter J. Wilson, *Crab Antics: The Social Anthropology of English-Speaking Negro Societies of the Caribbean* (New Haven, 1973).

Household Structure and Fertility on Jamaican Slave Plantations: A Nineteenth-Century Example

B. W. HIGMAN

It is generally agreed that the marital instability and casual mating characteristic of West Indian family structure depress fertility.[1] These conditions are traced to the mating organization of the slaves.[2] The stresses placed on the African family systems of the slaves are obvious: the continued importation of slaves, most of them young adult males; the ruthless separation of kin through sale or removal; the overwhelming authority of the master, reducing the dependence of children on their parents and the economic role of the male household head. Yet, in spite of these stresses, there is evidence of strong bonds of kinship and sense of family among the slaves.[3]

Studies of slave family structure and its connection with fertility have so far depended on literary sources. The analysis of actual slave families might be expected to contribute to the search for order in these patterns, but the data necessary for such detailed studies are rarely available. The present study of two Jamaican sugar estates (Old and New Montpelier) and a livestock pen (Shettlewood) is based on a unique set of documents which enables the identification of households, for the year 1825, within the context of data for the period 1817-32. In spite of certain limitations in the data, it does present empirical evidence of slave household structure and its relation to fertility for the first time.

The Data

For the years 1824 to 1828, the Account Book of Old Montpelier estate contains five lists of the slaves on the estate, giving the name, age, sex, colour, country of birth and occupation of each slave.[4] That for January 1827 also notes the state of health of the slaves and their mothers' names (when the mother was living on the estate). That for 1828 gives both the 'old' and 'Christian' names of the slaves, and notes their 'disposition' (towards their masters). The Account Book also contains a 'Report of the State and Condition of Old Montpelier Negro Houses and Provision Grounds and the Number of Stock possessed by each family', dated 1 August 1825. The first column of this report is titled 'Names with their families and dependants, if any' and consists of groups of names, the number of individuals in each group being totalled in the margin. The second column is headed 'Conditions of houses' and links to each of the groups in the first column a description of one or more houses. These groups and their associated houses can be confidently identified as 'households'. Then follow detailed statements of the livestock, gardens and provision grounds belonging to each group, a description of the provisions planted, and remarks on the 'state of culture' of the grounds. A total of 47 households are listed in the report, but it is clear that pages have been lost from the Account Book.

In 1832 Lord Seaford, owner of the properties, presented to the House of Lords 'a report made to me, on my application, by the gentleman managing my estates', dated 1 August 1825.[5] This was a continuation of the Old Montpelier report found in the Account Book, listing 124 households, and similar data for New Montpelier and Shettlewood. Seaford's purpose in producing this report was to impress the opponents of slavery with the comforts and wealth of his slaves, not to make any statement regarding household structure. Thus, the data are relatively neutral.

Population Studies, Vol. 27, Pt. 3, (November 1973), 527-50.

The reports contain no information about kinship. This gap can be filled, in part, by using the returns of registrations of slaves made in 1817, 1820, 1823, 1826, 1829 and 1832.[6] The returns for (28th June) 1817 list the names of the slaves, their age, colour, country and mother's name (when she lived on the same property). The subsequent returns give the same data for all slaves entering or leaving the population, whether by birth, purchase or removal, or death, manumission or sale.

These three sets of data have been collated and analysed using methods analogous to family reconstitution.[7] The problem of the identification of individuals is partly circumvented in this study, since slaves could not enter or leave the population without record. But names did change. In July 1816 almost all of the slaves at Old Montpelier, five-sixths of those at New Montpelier and half of those at Shettlewood were baptized, thus receiving 'Christian' names and surnames before the first registration of 1817.[8] Yet the old names recurred. Three household members could not be identified at Old Montpelier, 15 at New Montpelier, and two at Shettlewood. Consequently, several single-member households and one household of six have had to be excluded from some sections of the household analysis.

The limitations of the data are fairly clearly defined. They say nothing about paternity. Even links through the maternal line are discoverable only if the mother was living (on the same property as her child) in 1817. This, together with the underrecording of births 1817–23, makes it impossible to compute completed family size or the spacing of births. The 1825 household report provides only a static picture of the residential pattern. Fertility for the period 1817–32 can only be related to household structure as it was in 1825.

The Setting

The limitations of the study extend beyond the data to the period and places considered. The period 1817–32 was not typical of slavery in Jamaica since it came after the abolition of the slave trade in 1807. The two estates and the pen were larger than average, and were relatively recently settled. The owner, Charles Rose Ellis (created Lord Seaford in 1826), was described as a 'humane, well-intentioned' absentee proprietor. He was the 'acknowledged head' of the West India interest.[9] In 1797 he brought in a motion which placed in the hands of the colonial legislatures the encouragement of 'a reform in the manners and morality of the negroes' which would end polygamy, a family system he thought unfavourable to population growth.[10] But this was more a delaying tactic than evidence of genuine interest in amelioration. (The Jamaica Assembly had already, in 1791, decreed that slave families should be preserved as far as possible when sold.[11]) In 1831, Seaford invited the Moravians to instruct his slaves, but they declined since they expected the Anglicans to erect a church nearby.[12] Seaford's benevolence seems to have extended little beyond permitting the slaves to run livestock on the estate pastures.[13]

Old and New Montpelier estates were located in the valley of the Great River, in the western parish of St. James, about twelve miles from Montego Bay; Shettlewood pen adjoined, being on the western side of the river, in Hanover. They occupied 10,000 acres in St. James and 2,000 acres in Hanover. Old Montpelier was settled about 1745 and the New Works in 1775. In the 1820s 600 acres were in cane on the former estate and 400 acres on the latter.[14] A total of 7,632 acres were in woodland and ruinate on the two estates.[15] At Old Montpelier the works and slaves' houses covered 45 acres and the Negro grounds 350 acres. The estates produced nothing for sale, other than sugar and rum. Shettlewood pen fattened and butchered their old livestock, and bred planters' steers and mules for sale.[16]

In 1817 there were 958 slaves living on the three properties, by 1832 only 825 (Table 1). Males were in a minority throughout the period. At Shettlewood, where the male proportion declined steadily, there was a corresponding decline in the African group; but the latter process was very similar at Old Montpelier and there the sexes remained fairly evenly balanced. Whereas the rate of natural increase improved at Old Montpelier and, considerably, at Shettlewood, there was a deterioration at New Montpelier. If African mortality and fertility are excluded, it appears that there was a consistent natural increase in the creole population at Old Montpelier, that such a pattern emerged at Shettlewood after 1820, and that at New Montpelier an increase became a decrease from about 1821 (Figure 1).

The causes of all these contrasts are not apparent, but some can be explained by population movements, the maturity of the properties and the related patterns of age distribution. At least 70 slaves were moved to Shettlewood from the eastern end of the island

Table 1 Vital rates

	1817		1820		1823		1826		1829		1832
Old Montpelier Estate											
Slave population	426		412		400		395		395		383
Males per 100 females	98		96		96		96		101		100
Percentage African	39		35		32		30		27		25
Births per 1,000		23		17		18		21		24	
Deaths per 1,000		33		29		22		20		30	
Natural increase		−10		−12		−4		+1		−6	
New Montpelier Estate											
Slave population	303		353		334		319		303		288
Males per 100 females	89		93		98		96		93		91
Percentage African	46		45		42		40		38		38
Births per 1,000		25		12		13		8		13	
Deaths per 1,000		27		30		28		25		29	
Natural increase		−2		−18		−15		−17		−16	
Shettlewood Pen											
Slave population	229		155		146		146		157		154
Males per 100 females	78		70		74		64		63		62
Percentage African	45		37		32		28		24		21
Births per 1,000		5		18		27		37		28	
Deaths per 1,000		41		33		25		13		21	
Natural increase		−38		−15		+2		+24		+7	

Note: Triennia ending 30 June. For 1829–32 the deaths of slaves killed in the rebellion of December 1831 are excluded from the death rates: two at Old Montpelier and four at Shettlewood.

Figure 1 Births, deaths (total) and creole deaths (three-year moving averages)

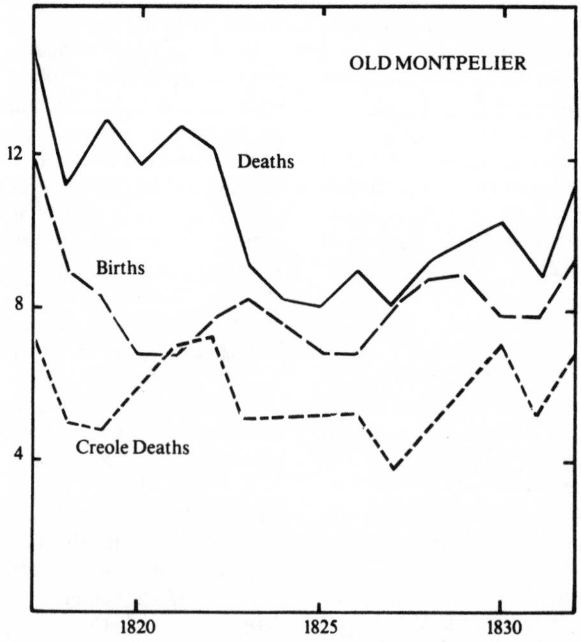

(*a*)

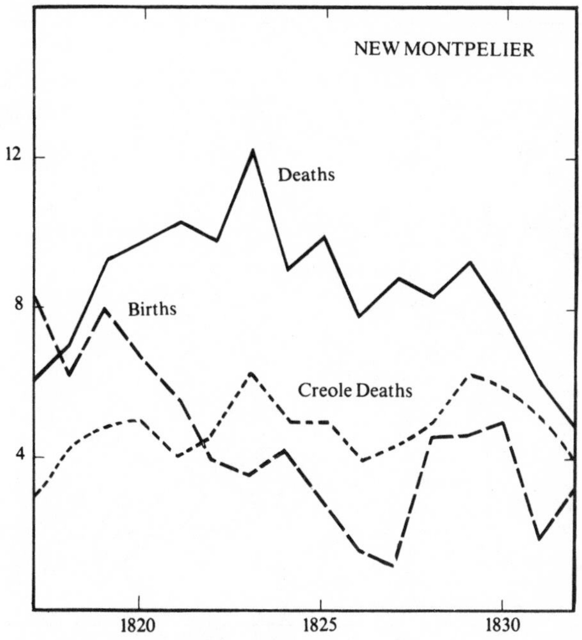
NEW MONTPELIER
Deaths
Births
Creole Deaths
12
8
4
1820
1825
1830

(b)

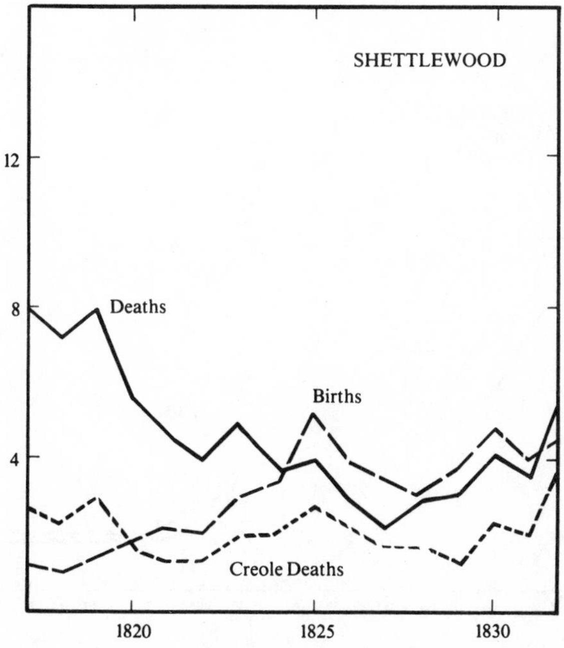
SHETTLEWOOD
Deaths
Births
Creole Deaths
12
8
4
1820
1825
1830

(c)

Figure 2 Age distribution, at 1 January (the chart for Africans shows all three properties together)

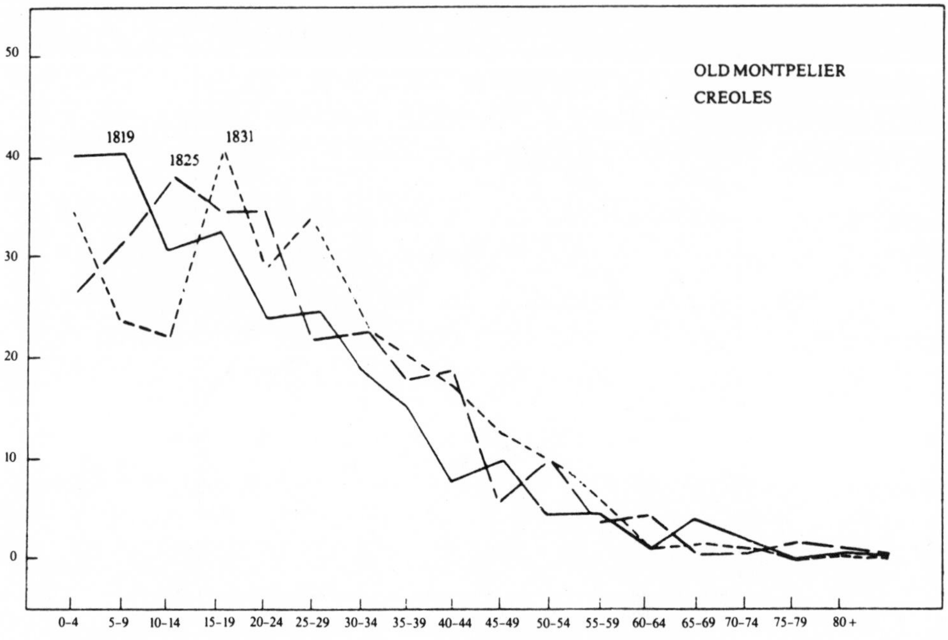

(*a*)

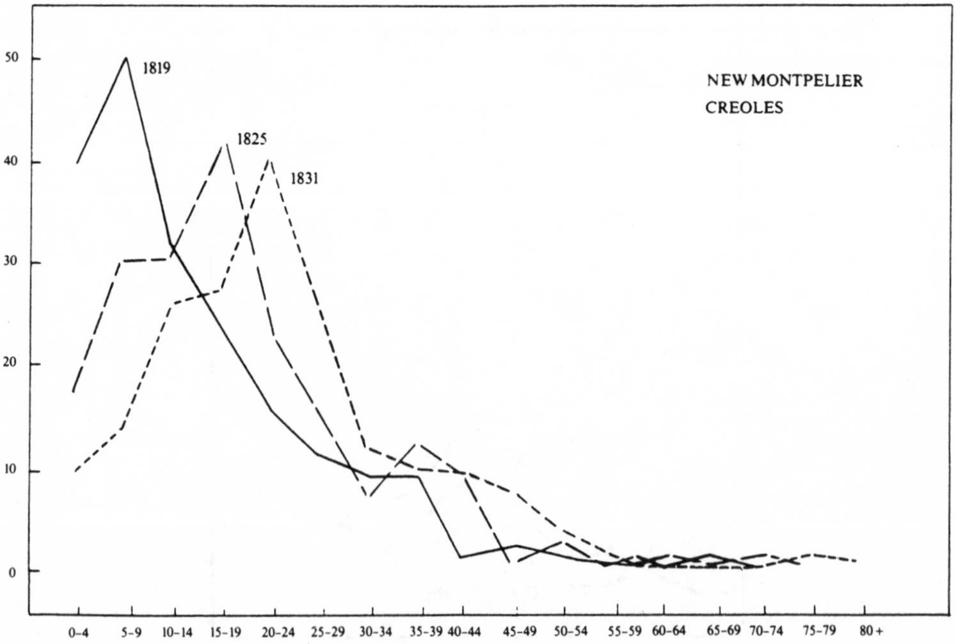

(*b*)

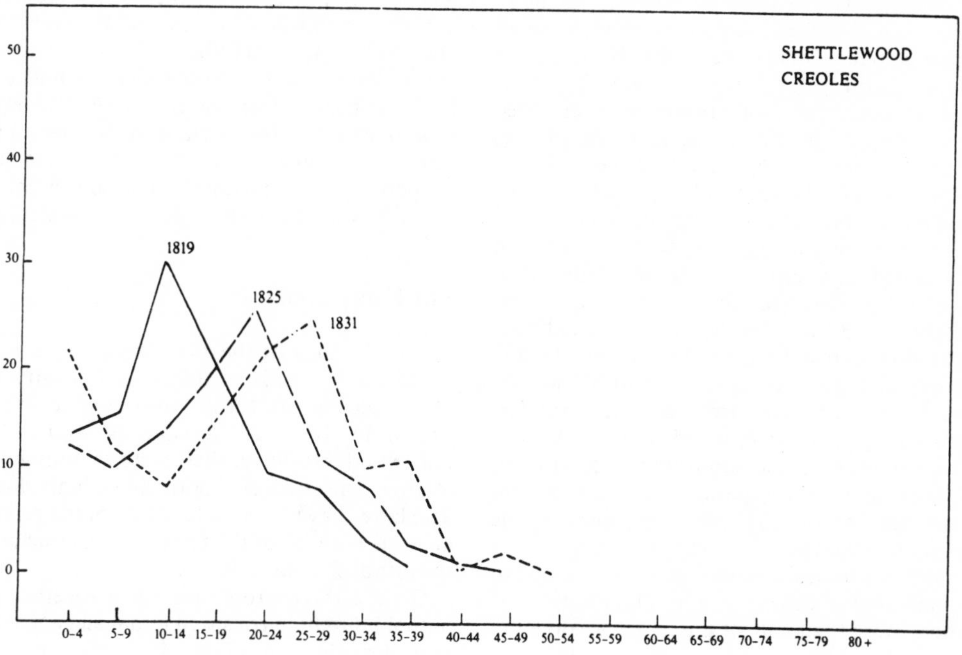
SHETTLEWOOD
CREOLES
50
40
30
20
10
0
1819
1825
1831
0–4
5–9
10–14
15–19
20–24
25–29
30–34
35–39
40–44
45–49
50–54
55–59
60–64
65–69
70–74
75–79
80+

(c)

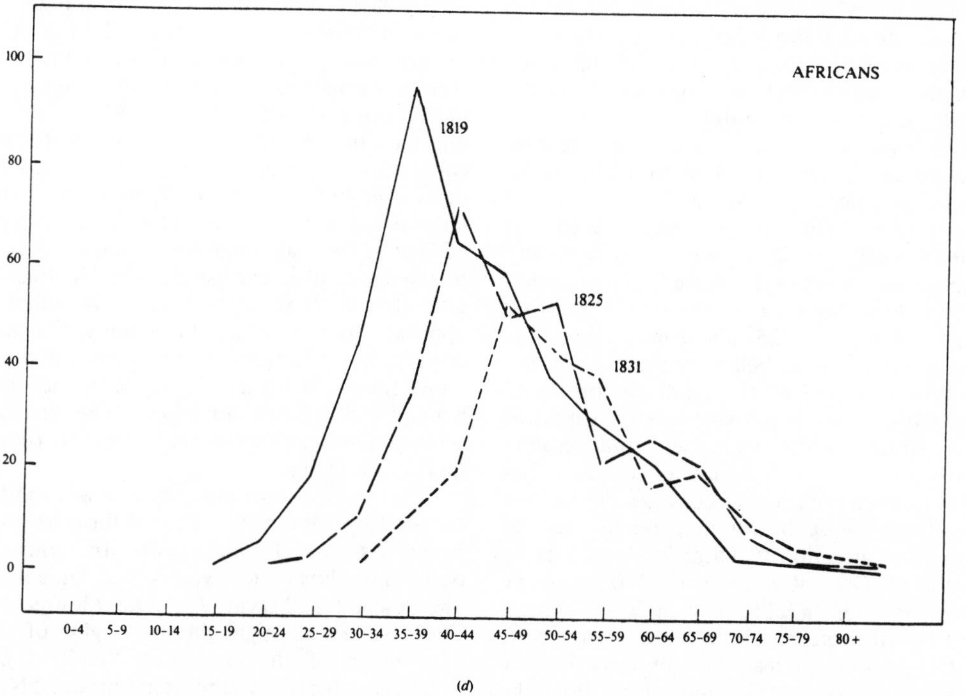
AFRICANS
100
80
60
40
20
0
1819
1825
1831
0–4
5–9
10–14
15–19
20–24
25–29
30–34
35–39
40–44
45–49
50–54
55–59
60–64
65–69
70–74
75–79
80+

(d)

between March 1816 and 1817,[17] and in 1819 the survivors of the 'seasoning' period went to New Montpelier. Of the 53 slaves moved, 13 of the 25 males and 18 of the 28 females were Africans, all aged between 28 and 42 years. None of the creoles in the group was more than 15 years of age. It seems that mothers were not separated from children in this move, and that siblings whose mothers died between 1817 and 1819 were kept together. The youthful age structure of the creoles at New Montpelier in 1819, which resulted from this age-specific migration and associated high fertility could not be sustained, as fertility declined throughout the period (Figure 2). By 1831 the age structure had been heavily eroded in the age-groups under 20 years. A similar erosion occurred at Old Montpelier and Shettlewood, but there growth in the under-ten-years group was renewed by 1831. At New Montpelier, both the youthful age structure at the beginning of the period and the failure to grow again before 1832 can be explained by the large and augmented African section.

The way in which the slaves were allocated to occupations is known only for Old Montpelier. There more than half of the females worked in the fields. Men had a wider range of occupations, especially in the trades. Almost all of the male slaves of colour were put to trades, though they did not dominate the group. The female slaves of colour, however, made up almost all of those who were domestics or washerwomen. Thus, only aged or invalid black females could expect to escape labour in the fields, and it was more difficult for women to attain positions of status or relative independence. The pattern at New Montpelier must have been very similar to that at Old Montpelier. On large pens, such as Shettlewood, the slaves were organized into gangs, but there were more isolated, semi-independent tasks to be performed than on sugar estates. In 1825, about 42 of the estate slaves were listed as being occupied at 'Farm'. Farm was a part of the estate, according to Hakewill, 'which is cultivated for the supply of the estates with vegetables and ground provisions; where a range of cottages has likewise been built for the convalescent negroes or others whose health may require rest or particular attention.'[18] Farm is about 3 miles east of the Great River, elevated 500 feet above the valley floor. In 1825, many of the slaves there suffered from elephantiasis, leprosy and ulcers, but there were at least two or three healthy families whose function must have been the production of provisions.

The slave populations of the three properties were not strictly closed. At the end of 1825 seven whites lived at Old Montpelier, and there was a constant turnover of overseers. Between 1817 and 1832, white men fathered 32 slave children, ten mulattoes, 21 quadroons and one mustee.[19] Mulatto men, either slave or free, had eight sambo children by black slave women. Free coloured people lived on and around the properties, and from time to time large numbers of slaves were hired to work on the estates.

The Households

The limitations of the 1825 household report, noted above, make it difficult to classify the households satisfactorily. An attempt to do so is shown in Table 2. In addition to the 252 households classified, there were 25 households at Farm, most consisting of single individuals. The latter have been excluded from the general analysis because of the temporary character of the establishment at Farm.

On the three properties taken together the modal household consisted of a male, a woman and her children (Type 4). This type was followed by Types 12 (a male and a female), 7 (a woman, her children, and others) and 1 (a woman and her children). More than half the households contained consanguines (identifiable through the maternal line). The picture changes somewhat if the household types are analysed in terms of the number of individuals they accounted for. Almost three-quarters of the slaves lived in households containing consanguines (Types 1–7). Half of them lived in households of Types 4 and 7, the latter being in many cases essentially a sub-type of Type 4. Thus, although fewer than 25 per cent of the slaves lived exclusively with identifiable kin, almost 50 per cent lived in households approximating the elementary family. This has important implications for the understanding of slave family structure. It suggests that the woman-and-children household type was far from dominant, whatever the importance of the mother–child–link.

In terms of households, Type 4 was modal only at New Montpelier, while at the other two properties Type 12 was modal. In terms of occupants, however, Type 4 was modal at Shettlewood and Type 7 at Old Montpelier. These variations highlight the origins of the importance of the elementary family type. Relatively, this type was most important at New Montpelier, the estate that was the most recently

Table 2 Household structure

Household type	Number of households				Percentage of households				Number of occupants			
	Old Montpelier	New Montpelier	Shettlewood	Total	Old Montpelier	New Montpelier	Shettlewood	Total	Old Montpelier	New Montpelier	Shettlewood	Total
1. Woman and her children	10	13	6	29	8.1	15.5	13.6	11.5	38	36	21	95
2. Woman, her children and grandchildren	—	1	3	4	—	1.2	6.8	1.6	—	5	14	19
3. Woman, her children, her nephews and nieces (and their children)	1	—	1	2	0.8	—	2.4	0.8	7	—	8	15
4. Male, woman and her children	19	25	6	50	15.3	29.8	13.6	19.8	72	104	28	204
5. Male, woman, her children and grandchildren	3	1	—	4	2.4	1.2	—	1.6	18	6	—	24
6. Siblings, and others	2	2	4	6	1.6	2.4	4.5	2.4	7	10	5	22
7. Woman, her children, and others	19	13	3	35	15.3	15.5	6.8	13.9	111	68	20	199
8. Male	14	5	6	25	11.3	5.9	13.6	9.9	14	5	6	25
9. Female	13	3	3	19	10.5	3.6	6.8	7.5	13	3	3	19
10. Males	5	1	1	7	4.0	1.2	2.4	2.8	10	2	2	14
11. Females	2	1	1	4	1.6	1.2	2.4	1.6	5	2	2	9
12. Male and female	26	6	7	39	21.0	7.0	15.9	15.5	50	12	14	76
13. Males and females	10	13	5	28	8.1	15.5	11.2	11.1	30	43	20	93
Total	124	94	44	252	100.0	100.0	100.0	100.0	375	296	143	814

settled, suffered the greatest stresses in terms of the movement of slaves, had the highest proportion of Africans and the heaviest mortality. The implications of this pattern must be sought in the composition of the households.

The distribution of Africans among the household types was similar to that for the total populations (Table 3). In absolute numbers, the concentrations of Africans into Type 4 at New Montpelier was greater than that for any of the household types on the other two properties. Thus, when Africans formed households, other than single-member units, they most often established those of Type 4, whereas creoles participated in the more complex Type 7. This might suggest that the Africans attempted to maintain nuclear families, while the creoles, dislocated by the experience of slavery, were unable to do so; or it may simply signify that the ramifications of creole kinship were that much greater.

The distribution of slaves of colour contrasted strongly with that of Africans (Table 3). Those with white fathers (mulattoes and quadroons) lived almost exclusively in households dominated by mothers, grandmothers and aunts. There was no place for slave mates in such households. But it is also true that some slave women had fairly long-term relationships with whites. By contrast, sambo children (whose mothers were almost always black) generally lived in households containing potential male mates (black men), but always lacking potential fathers (mulattoes).

A general consideration of the age structure of the household types is not very useful since it conceals too many other variables. Almost all of them contained the whole spectrum of ages, especially those consisting of consanguines. Slaves living alone tended to be relatively old, most being Africans over 40 years of age. As the slaves aged, the major shift was from households based on consanguines (especially the mother-and-children type) to those containing males and females who were not identifiable kin. But this pattern was confused by the connection between the African/creole ratio and age.

At Old Montpelier, at least, there was a relationship between occupation and household type. Field slaves were to be found in all of the types, except Type 3 (in which all of the slaves were coloured domestics or tradesmen). In general, field slaves comprised about half of the occupants of each type. The drivers most often lived in households containing women and children rather than non-kin. Tradesmen followed a similar pattern, but more often lived alone or in groups of males and females who were not identifiable kin. Domestics tended to live in households dominated by women. Since they were often older, slaves employed in minor field tasks frequently lived with non-kin.

Colour, country, age and occupation were

Table 3 The distribution between the household types of Africans and slaves of colour

	Africans			Slaves of colour		
				Number		
		Percentage*				
Household type	Number	A	B	Mulatto	Quadroon	Sambo
1	21	67.7	22.1	3	7	1
2	3	75.0	15.0	1	1	—
3	—	—	—	6	6	—
4	66	67.3	33.2	2	—	2
5	4	50.0	16.0	—	—	—
6	3	—	13.6	—	—	—
7	56	47.5	28.1	3	2	7
8	17		73.9	—	—	2
9	14		82.3	—	—	—
10	6		42.8	—	—	—
11	4		44.4	1	—	—
12	45		46.8	—	—	1
13	41		45.1	—	—	—
Totals	280			16	16	14

* The A percentages exclude all 'children', while the B percentages are based on the total populations, including 'children'.

not independent but related characteristics, so that some broad patterns emerge. The Africans, the ageing section of the population, formed either elementary families or lived alone. Most of those living alone were over 40 years of age and the men, who were generally employed as watchmen, could not easily find a place in the wider household system. Slaves of colour, however, with their privileged occupations allying them to the great house and the whites, formed households in which slave men had no part but were tightly organized around the maternal connection. Creole blacks, the majority of the population and of the field labour force, were widely distributed among the household types but were a dominant element in Types 7 (mothers, their children, and others) and 10–13 (groups of males and females who cannot be identified as kin). The ramifications of kinship among the creoles were important organizing factors which could not be matched by the common experience of regional origin or of being shipmates for the Africans.

Mates

Household type 4 has so far been defined as comprising a male, a woman and her children. More needs to be known about the 'male' before it can be considered an elementary family. In only three cases can the 'male' and 'woman' be identified certainly as mates. Three weeks after the household report was made, in August 1825, Charles Rose (Ellis) and Ann Ellis 1st of Old Montpelier were married by an Anglican priest.[20] They were creole blacks, Charles Rose (aged 34 years) being a mason and Ann Ellis (31 years) working in the first gang. Ann Ellis's two children lived with them, immediately before the marriage, in a 'good stone house, shingled' with a new kitchen. They possessed two cows, a steer and a bull calf, ten hogs and four chickens, and had the use of six acres of provision grounds in which were planted yams, cocos, corn and plantains. On the same day in 1825, Charles Beckford married Becky Richards of New Montpelier; they, too, were creole blacks, aged 26 and 37 years respectively. Becky Richards' daughter, aged 15 years, lived with them. Their house was of wattle and thatch and the only livestock they had were hogs and chickens; they had but one acre of provision grounds. In 1827, Richard Trail and Elizabeth Miller of Shettlewood were married.[21] Like the other couples, they were black creoles, but were younger (24 and 23 years respectively). In 1825 they had lived together, with Elizabeth Miller's two children, who were both surnamed Trail, suggesting that they were also Richard Trail's children. Their house was wattled and thatched, but in bad condition; they had a cow and three acres planted in yams, cocos and plantains. At Old and New Montpelier the mothers of the married couples had all died by 1825, but the mothers of Richard Trail and Elizabeth Miller, both Africans, lived with their other children. Thus, while marriage was confined to creole blacks who already lived together, with the woman's children, it included a wide range of ages and, probably, of statuses within the slave hierarchy.

The identification of mates in the remaining households must rest on less solid evidence. The two most obvious indicators are the age difference of the potential mates and the ordering of individuals within the household lists. All of those in household type 4 were older than 20 years and most were over 40 years of age (Table 4). At Old Montpelier, 12 of the 'males' and 'women' were separated by less then ten years of age, seven by more than ten years, but only three by more than 20 years. At New Montpelier 13 were separated by less than ten years, 11 by more than ten, but only two by more than 20. At Shettlewood none of the six potential mates were separated by more than 11 years. Thus, the evidence from age suggests that

Table 4 Ages of male and female co-residents in household type 4

	Age of 'women' co-resident						
Age of 'male'	20–29	30–39	40–49	50–59	60–69	70 +	Total 'males'
20–29	2	3	2	—	—	—	7
30–39	—	1	4	—	—	—	5
40–49	1	3	9	2	—	—	15
50–59	1	5	8	1	—	—	15
60–69	—	1	3	1	—	1	6
70 +	—	—	1	—	—	—	1
Total 'women'	4	13	27	4	—	1	

most of the men and women living in household type 4 were mates.

The evidence provided by the ordering of names within the household lists is tantalizing but inconsistent. For Old Montpelier the lists are ordered in a manner suggestive of status within the household. With one exception, all the Type 4 households in which the male and female differed in age by less than ten years are ordered thus: male, woman, her children (listed by age). At Shettlewood the form was, with two exceptions, slightly different: woman, male, the female's children. At New Montpelier the household members were divided by sex: male, the woman's male children, woman, her daughters. Thus, these data cannot be used to determine male or female headship. But only five of the Type 4 households were arranged so that the male was placed at the end of the list, and most of these involved men and women more than 20 years apart in age. Probably 90 per cent of the males and females in this type, then, were mates.

Male mates can also be sought in household types 5,6, 7, 12 and 13. Of the four households of Type 5 (male, woman, her children and grandchildren) only two seem to be extensions of Type 4. The males in the other two households were in their twenties, whereas the women were in their fifties and seventies; they were most probably collaterals. Using the same principles, it seems that roughly half the households of Types 6 and 7 contained mates. For household type 12 (male and female) the only available evidence is that of age, and on this basis it appears that about 75 per cent of the pairs may have been mates (Table 5). In Type 13 (males and females) additional evidence can be found in the ordering of the lists, and this suggests a similar proportion to that found for Type 12; but the possible complexities, of course, are much greater.

In general, probably 100 of the 252 households contained mates. Almost half of these households contained only their — or rather the woman's — children. It is impossible to estimate the number of women who did not live together with their mates, but there must have been at least 30. Some of their mates had died, others lived in separate houses or even on other properties. There is concrete evidence of the latter. In 1825, James Lewis of Shettlewood cut the throat of his 'wife', Ann Thomas of Old Montpelier, and then killed himself.[22] They were aged 30 and 24 years respectively. Both were the children of African mothers who were living in 1825, and both seem to have lived all their lives on their particular properties.

Polygynists

In the 1825 report five men, but no women, were listed for two houses, all of them at Old Montpelier. In the second house for which they were listed their names appear at the end of the list, in parentheses. George Ellis, a creole carpenter aged 54 years, lived with the mother of Ann Thomas (mentioned above), her three children and the son of Ann Thomas. His second house comprised Bessy Ellis, an African nurse, her five children, and an aged invalid woman. Like George Ellis, most of the other men attributed to two houses held positions of authority on the estate. The head driver, David Richards 2nd, a black creole aged 49 years, lived in one house with an invalid creole woman aged 47, and a mulatto washerwoman and her (but not his) quadroon daughter. In his second house, the only occupant was a black creole woman aged 37, who worked in the first gang. William Squires, an African aged 50 years, who was in the first gang and acted as stillerman, lived with an African woman aged 45 years; in

Table 5 Ages of male and female co-residents in household type 12

	Age of female co-resident								
Age of male	0–9	10–19	20–29	30–39	40–49	50–59	60–69	70+	Total males
0–9	—	—	—	—	—	—	—	—	—
10–19	—	—	1	—	—	—	—	—	1
20–29	—	1	1	3	—	1	1	—	7
30–39	—	—	2	5	1	—	—	—	8
40–49	1	1	—	4	3	2	—	—	11
50–59	—	—	—	—	6	2	—	—	8
60–69	—	—	—	—	—	1	—	—	1
70+	—	—	—	—	—	—	1	1	2
Total females	1	2	4	12	10	6	2	1	

his second house lived an invalid African aged 41 years and her two children. Similarly, William Richards 1st was an African aged 49 years who worked in the first gang and as boiler; an African woman lived in each of his houses, one aged 45 and the other 43 years, and both working in the first gang. Finally, James Hedley, a 34-year-old creole of the first gang, lived with a creole woman aged 39 years who worked alongside him; in his second house lived another creole woman, aged 45 years, and her daughter.

Although the available evidence does not make it possible to identify these men as polygynists with certainty, it is probable that they were. Their positions within the slave hierarchy fit closely the contemporary testimony on polygamy. In every case the houses were occupied only by women and their children, excluding the possibility of co-resident mates other than the potential polygynists. It must also be noticed that, with the exception of David Richards, the two houses were always adjacent in the list which, it will be argued below, signified spatial contiguity. The creoles were as significant as the Africans but, unlike the 'monogamous' mates, the 'polygamous' households at Old Montpelier were generally either exclusively African or exclusively creole.

Polygynists living with several women in a single house are more difficult to identify. They can be looked for in household types 7 and 13. About one-third of these 63 households consisted of a man and more than one woman (and their children), but in terms of their age structure only a minority of these could have been mates.

Grandmothers

The 'grandmother family' was virtually unknown on the three properties; that is, no households were discovered consisting of a woman and her grandchildren, the mother of the children living elsewhere. In the households containing identifiable grandchildren (Types 2 and 5) the mothers lived in the same household, with the exception of three cases in which the mothers had died. But the data are limited because the link between a woman and her grandchildren is known only if the mother was alive in 1817. Thus, it is necessary to consider the possibility of grandchildren living with their grandmothers, their mothers having died before 1817. These may be sought in household types 6, 11, 12 and 13, using some basic principles: the woman and potential grandchild must be at least 30 years separated in age, the woman could not be a creole and the child African, and the mother of the child must have been dead by 1817. Applying these rules, only four of the 28 Type 13, two of the 39 Type 12, and one of the four Type 11 households could have contained grandmothers and grandchildren, all but one of them at Old Montpelier, the longest-established of the estates. Thus, even in the widest sense the 'grandmother family' must have been extremely rare.

Since nothing is known about paternity, it is difficult to dissect those households which might have been headed by men in the absence of female mates. A man's potential children are not easily distinguished from potential grandchildren or collaterals. But, even with the most generous assumptions it is certain that fewer than ten households (of Types 10, 12 and 13) could have consisted of fathers and their children or grandchildren. In the absence of their mothers, children rarely lived with their paternal kin.

Movement and Separation

The 1825 household report was made six years after 53 slaves had been moved from Shettlewood to New Montpelier. What was the impact of this disruption on household structure? In 1825, some 33 of them survived at New Montpelier, being distributed among 14 households; another five lived at Farm. Five Africans and one creole (whose mother had died) moved singly into households made up of New Montpelier slaves. All of these households were of Type 13, indefinable groups of males and females, except that an African, Moses Richards, established a house with a New Montpelier African and her three children (aged 14, five and two years). But the remaining 27 Shettlewood slaves lived in eight households which contained no New Montpelier slaves. All but one of the children continued to live with their mothers. Two of the households were of Type 1, one of Type 4, and one of Type 7; the latter contained an African man and woman, her two children, and the daughter of an African who died before the move from Shettlewood. Two African men lived together, while two pairs of Africans (possible mates) established households. An African man lived with a girl, perhaps his daughter, whose mother had died in 1820. In sum, there is little evidence that the movement of the slaves disrupted the relationships of mates or mothers and children. But the Shettlewood slaves probably found it difficult to integrate themselves into the New Montpelier household system. Only Africans, who moved in with other Africans (perhaps shipmates or fellow countrymen) had any success in this respect. The women mothered very few children after going to New Montpelier, so that no child born between 1819 and 1825 was alive in the latter year. This pattern began to change only at the end of the 1820s when the girls who had come from Shettlewood reached maturity.

The impact on family structure of movement to Farm was much more disruptive, because of its selective nature. Two households there consisted of an African man and woman, and each woman's three children. Two other women lived with a single child each, but most of the slaves lived alone or in pairs. Only two of the slaves at Farm had mothers living on the estates. In part, this isolation was a result of the diseases from which the slaves suffered. The slaves living in family groups were all healthy and probably constituted the basic work-force of Farm. Once again, it is noticeable that the slaves who moved from Shettlewood to New Montpelier, and then to Farm, lived in a more tightly knit group than the other slaves.

Spatial Aspects

On each of the properties the slaves' houses were within 200 yards of the works or great house. At New Montpelier the houses were sited on a slope by the Great River; at Old Montpelier, one mile to the east, they were on a hill behind the works. A print produced in 1820 represents the latter, showing 14 of the slaves' houses concealed by trees.[23] These houses appear to be arranged irregularly, unlike some other estates where they were set out in lines, suggesting that the Montpelier slaves were permitted some latitude in the location of their houses. The manner in which the household reports were compiled is unknown, but since the overseer had to make a visual inspection of the houses and grounds, the listing probably follows some sort of route from house to house. Thus, it is likely that houses listed next to one another were spatially adjacent as well.

Some 'households' occupied more than one house. In many cases this was simply part of the process of decay and reconstruction; for example: 'old house, rather bad; wattled and shingled; a small new house' or 'wattled and thatched; small and bad; a new one, Spanish walled and shingled, but not quite finished'. Such cases have been ignored. At Old Montpelier two households occupied three houses, both of them consisting of women, their children and others. One of these comprised nine slaves: a male hospital attendant, a woman and her two black children (and her free brown children), an aged African invalid woman, an adolescent quadroon carpenter, a young woman whose African mother had died in 1819, a sambo woman and her black daughter. The other three-house household contained a black woman and her four sambo children (two masons and a washerwoman), a mother and her daughter, and an invalid woman. These households had the use of 12 and 13 acres of provision grounds, respectively, and held large numbers of livestock. The only other three-house unit was that listed first for New Montpelier; it consisted simply of a man, a woman and her two children, but they had far more livestock than any other household. Households occupying two houses also generally appeared early in the lists. It is evident that these households had more than one house not because of their numbers, but because of their privileged occupations and relative prosperity; many groups of similar size had to hold in a single house.

It is probable that these multiple-house households formed tight units or 'yards', with the houses set out around a central open area. The evidence found in the adjacence of separate households is also suggestive of yard formation. At Old Montpelier, 30 slaves did not live with their mothers, but 13 of them lived in the house listed next to their mothers' and another three were only one house further removed. At Shettlewood three slaves lived next to their mothers, six one house removed, and seven further away. But at New Montpelier only one slave was listed next to his mother, while six lived further away. In general, 50 per cent of the slaves who did not live with their mothers were no further away than one or two houses. It is also clear that at New Montpelier fewer children moved away from their mothers; but when they did they moved much farther. Among the children not living with their mothers the differences between the sexes are of interest:

	Old Montpelier		*New Montpelier*		*Shettlewood Pen*	
	Males	Females	Males	Females	Males	Females
Living in the next house	9	4	—	1	2	1
Living in next house but one	1	2	—	—	4	2
Living further away	5	9	4	2	2	5

Figure 3 Bessy Gardner's connection, Shettlewood

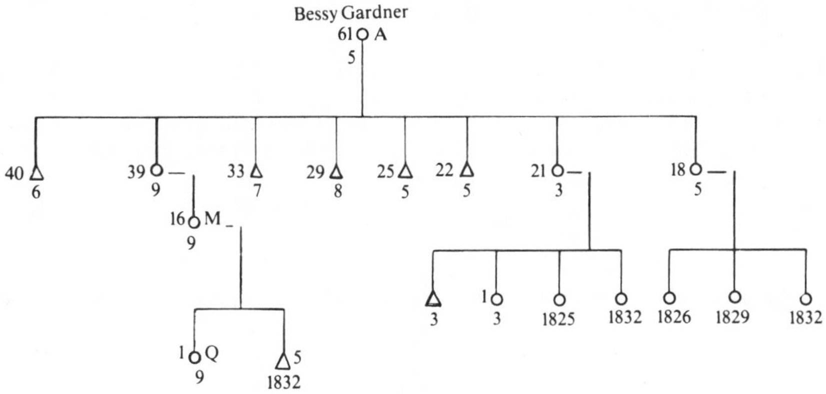

Note: Numbers to the left of the male/female symbol indicate age in 1825. Numbers below the symbol indicate the household in which the slave lived in 1825. Where a date is given, 1825–32, this indicates the year of birth of children born after 1 August 1825, or, if 1817–25, the year of death of a slave dying between 28 June 1818 and 31 July 1825. All of the slaves were black and creole, unless indicated otherwise (to the right of the male/female symbol): A = African; M = Mulatto; Q = Quadroon; Mu = Mustee; S = Sambo.

Sons most often stayed close to their mothers, with the exception of those at New Montpelier, while daughters tended to move away. In part these contrasts were complementary, since it appears that the sons who stayed near their mothers were establishing households with other women's daughters. Daughters either moved away from their mothers to live near the mothers of their mates or, less often, lived with their children in the same house as their mother. Only one woman whose mother was living in 1825 had moved to a household lacking a possible male mate.

This pattern of movement applied not only to individual sons and daughters, but also to sets of siblings, and this resulted in groups of households, probably organized as yards, related by blood to a single woman. A clear example occurred in the households numbered 5 to 9 at Shettlewood (Figure 3). In house 5 lived Bessy Gardner, an African aged 61 years, and her two youngest sons and daughter. Her eldest son lived in house 6. House 7 was occupied by her second son and a woman who was pregnant at the time of the household report (and whose mother, an African, lived with an African man in house 23). In house 8 was her third son and an apparently unrelated man and woman (aged 20 and 22 years). Bessy Gardner's eldest daughter lived in house 9 with her mulatto daughter and quadroon granddaughter. Her other daughter, Elizabeth Miller, had moved away (though not very far, perhaps) to house 3, where she lived with her two children and the man she married in 1827.

Colour also played a role in the formation of linked household groups. At Old Montpelier all of the mulatto slaves and twelve of the 14 quadroons lived in three adjacent houses (25, 26 and 27). Further, the sambo nephew of the mulatto head of house 27 lived in house 28. Most of the slaves were domestics, hence it is probable that they were located close to the great house.

The movement of slaves also seems to have resulted in spatially linked household groups. Of the 33 Shettlewood slaves living at New Montpelier in 1825, 19 were living in houses 29 to 33. These households comprehended almost all who had retained the mother–child residential link. The one Shettlewood man to establish a household with a New Montpelier woman lived in house 31; thus, it seems that he brought her into the centre of the Shettlewood knot of houses. A simple explanation of the unity of the Shettlewood slaves at New Montpelier is that they moved into houses built for them in 1819 at a single site. In 1825 all of these houses were described as 'good; stone, shingled'. Houses 34, 36 and 37 were similarly described but by 1825 they were occupied by slaves who had lived on the estate since 1817 at least. Perhaps the spatial separation was a cause, as well as a measure, of their isolation within the New Montpelier population.

In the above analysis several aspects of the spatial pattern suggest that residence may have been based on patrilocal rules, or that such rules were emerging. The pattern established by the polygynists, identified above, points in the same direction. But unfortunately the trend is not clear enough for this to be more than a suggestion

Household Formation

The mother–child tie was the strongest element in the creation and maintenance of households. So long as their mothers lived, very few slaves moved to separate households and about half of those who did move away went no further than one or two houses distant. All of the slaves who moved away from their mothers were creoles, of course, and almost all were black. Most of them were over 20 years of age, though at Old

Figure 4 The connections of Beneba 1st, Old Montpelier, and Frances Harvey, Shettlewood (for code, see note to Figure 3)

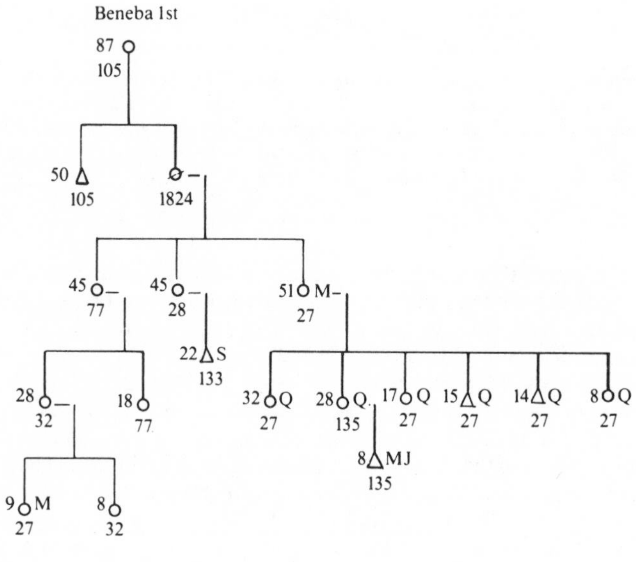

(*a*)

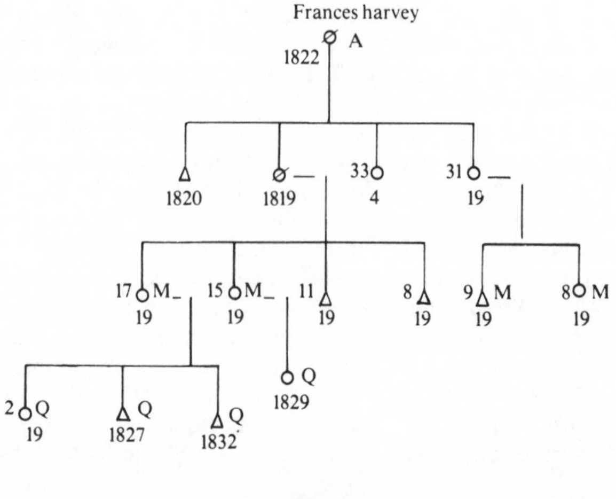

(*b*)

Montpelier a few moved away in their late teens. In 1825 the majority lived in households with their mates and children (Types 4 and 7), or simply with their mates (Type 12). Very few of them lived alone, and it has been noted already that only one woman lived with her children, apart from her mother and without a mate. Sons moved short distances to establish households near their mothers, whereas daughters moved into the ambit of their mates' mothers. Although this pattern was not universal, the point is important since it suggests that men may have played a greater role than women in the establishment of co-resident unions. And, since men living alone continued to live near their mothers, in many cases, they (or their mothers) may also have decided the stability of the relationship.

In so far as daughters whose mothers were alive formed relationships with men, they continued to live in their mothers' houses until they conceived or bore children. But very few lived with their mothers after bearing children, and most of these were coloured slaves who did not form unions within the slave population (Figure 4). The rarity of women living without a mate is suggestive of a more stable pattern of unions than Patterson recognizes,[24] unless it is argued that women parting with co-resident mates either quickly engaged new ones or returned promptly to their mothers' household. It is not improbable that slaves soon contracted new unions, but it is unlikely that these would have been based on co-residence in the first instance. The second possibility would fit neatly, if, as seems often to have been the case, the women had moved into households established by sons close to their living mothers. This point depends on the nature of rights to house and grounds, as does the whole question of stability.

If this case study is unable to solve the problem of stability, it does challenge the accepted view of household structure. Statements such as 'conditions under slavery were such that the woman and children were of necessity that family unit' (Kerr); 'normally the children resided with their mother, and the parents lived apart, singly or with different mates' (Smith); or 'the nuclear family could hardly exist within the context of slavery' (Patterson) require serious reconsideration.[25] Although the evidence is slight, this study also contradicts Patterson's argument that marriage was confined to old couples, under the influence of missionaries, being treated with contempt by the young.

Those creole slaves whose mothers were dead or had been moved to other properties were not subject to the same principles of residence. Yet it is clear that links through the maternal line remained important, so that slaves lived with their siblings, grandmothers, aunts and cousins (Figure 4). Many, however, moved into households lacking identifiable kin and containing Africans.

For the African slaves the mother–child tie and the ramifications of kinship were missing. Thus, they were more likely to live with their mates when they formed unions and also more likely to live alone when they grew old because they lacked opportunities for alternative forms of alignment. When African men contracted creole mates they were more likely to be drawn into the ambit of their mate's mother than were creole men.

If the roots of a chaotic family system are to be traced to slavery they should be evident in the 1820s as well as in the eighteenth century. The abolition of the slave trade did not necessarily stabilize the household system and amelioration seems to have had little impact. M. G. Smith's sample of domestic units in modern rural Jamaica is not strictly comparable with the classification of households used in this study, because of the limitations of the slave data, but the results are very similar.[26] The perception of 'chaos' in either the slave or modern periods may be a subjective matter, depending on categories of 'kinship' genealogically described which simply may not be useful indicators of the system.[27]

Family and Fertility

Before considering the impact of family and household structure on fertility, it is necessary to assess the quality of the data found in the returns of registrations of slaves for the measurement of fertility. Roberts, in particular, has argued that the returns take no account of children born within a triennium and dying before its end.[28] But, in fact, the Jamaica Registry Law required a record of 'the total number of births and deaths since the last return', and the practice was inconsistent.[29] On the three properties under study 14 per cent of the births registered related to children who were born and died within a triennium, the children dying at ages ranging from ten days to two years ten months. For Old Montpelier, the Account Book throws further light on this problem since it contains 'increase' lists for 1825

Table 6 Age-specific fertility by household type and age group, 1817–25 and 1825–32

	Births per 1,000 woman-years (woman-years given in parentheses)							
	15–24 age group		25–34 age group		35–44 age group		15–44 age group	
Household type	1817–25	1825–32	1817–25	1825–32	1817–25	1825–32	1817–25	1825–32
Old Montpelier								
1	— (3)	— (15)	297 (37)	— (4)	135 (37)	250 (20)	208 (77)	128 (39)
2	— (0)	— (0)	— (0)	— (0)	— (0)	— (0)	— (0)	— (0)
3	— (1)	— (6)	— (7)	— (3)	500 (2)	— (4)	100 (10)	— (13)
4	40 (25)	98 (41)	333 (42)	— (22)	96 (73)	87 (46)	157 (140)	73 (109)
5	222 (9)	167 (24)	— (3)	333 (3)	154 (13)	250 (4)	160 (25)	194 (31)
6	— (12)	83 (12)	— (1)	77 (13)	— (0)	— (0)	— (13)	80 (25)
7	91 (66)	151 (93)	164 (55)	156 (51)	58 (52)	— (39)	104 (173)	120 (183)
9	— (8)	— (2)	— (13)	143 (7)	— (5)	— (14)	— (26)	44 (23)
11	— (13)	250 (4)	— (14)	— (9)	— (0)	— (5)	— (27)	56 (18)
12	— (20)	167 (18)	20 (50)	59 (17)	— (68)	— (50)	7 (138)	47 (85)
13	— (28)	59 (17)	— (35)	111 (18)	— (24)	38 (26)	— (87)	66 (61)
New Montpelier								
1	— (24)	61 (33)	56 (18)	— (19)	82 (49)	72 (14)	55 (91)	45 (66)
2	— (2)	— (14)	— (0)	— (0)	125 (8)	— (0)	100 (10)	— (14)
3	— (0)	— (0)	— (0)	— (0)	— (0)	— (0)	— (0)	— (0)
4	130 (23)	28 (72)	310 (29)	— (17)	94 (117)	18 (55)	136 (169)	21 (144)
5	— (0)	— (0)	— (5)	— (0)	— (10)	— (9)	— (15)	— (9)
6	— (2)	— (7)	— (12)	— (4)	— (2)	— (10)	— (16)	— (21)
7	— (24)	79 (66)	38 (52)	43 (23)	97 (62)	23 (44)	58 (138)	53 (133)
9	— (8)	— (1)	71 (14)	400 (5)	— (2)	71 (14)	42 (24)	150 (20)
11	— (7)	— (2)	250 (4)	— (0)	— (0)	— (0)	91 (11)	— (2)
12	— (9)	— (0)	— (11)	— (10)	— (20)	— (10)	— (40)	— (20)
13	— (25)	— (4)	— (46)	100 (20)	— (42)	26 (39)	— (113)	48 (63)

Shettlewood								
1	53 (19)	50 (20)	100 (10)	583 (12)	67 (15)	— (10)	68 (44)	190 (42)
2	133 (15)	67 (15)	— (0)	111 (9)	— (4)	— (4)	105 (19)	71 (28)
3	250 (4)	250 (12)	— (6)	— (0)	— (4)	— (0)	71 (14)	250 (12)
4	105 (19)	91 (44)	— (4)	— (7)	83 (24)	— (10)	85 (47)	65 (61)
5	— (0)	— (0)	— (0)	— (0)	— (0)	— (0)	— (0)	— (0)
6	— (3)	— (14)	— (8)	500 (2)	— (0)	— (4)	— (11)	50 (20)
7	105 (19)	53 (38)	157 (6)	200 (15)	188 (16)	— (2)	146 (41)	(91) (55)
9	— (0)	— (0)	— (0)	— (0)	— (10)	— (7)	— (10)	— (7)
11	— (0)	— (0)	— (0)	— (0)	— (3)	— (0)	— (3)	— (0)
12	— (13)	— (5)	— (4)	300 (10)	— (12)	— (8)	— (29)	130 (23)
13	— (37)	— (42)	— (13)	100 (20)	— (10)	— (9)	— (61)	28 (71)
Total								
1	22 (46)	44 (68)	200 (65)	200 (35)	99 (101)	136 (44)	113 (212)	109 (147)
2	118 (17)	31 (29)	— (0)	111 (9)	83 (12)	— (4)	103 (29)	48 (42)
3	200 (5)	167 (18)	— (13)	— (3)	167 (6)	— (4)	83 (24)	120 (250)
4	89 (67)	66 (157)	307 (75)	— (46)	93 (214)	45 (111)	138 (356)	48 (314)
5	222 (9)	167 (24)	— (8)	333 (3)	87 (23)	77 (13)	100 (40)	150 (40)
6	— (17)	30 (33)	— (21)	105 (19)	— (2)	— (14)	— (40)	45 (66)
7	77 (109)	107 (197)	106 (113)	135 (89)	92 (130)	12 (85)	91 (352)	92 (371)
9	— (16)	— (3)	37 (27)	250 (12)	— (17)	29 (35)	17 (60)	80 (50)
11	— (20)	167 (6)	56 (18)	— (9)	— (3)	— (5)	24 (41)	50 (20)
12	— (42)	130 (23)	15 (65)	108 (37)	— (100)	— (68)	5 (207)	55 (128)
13	— (90)	16 (63)	— (94)	103 (58)	— (76)	27 (74)	— (260)	46 (195)

Note: The periods 1817–25 and 1825–32 are divided at 30 June 1825.

Table 7 African and Creole age-specific fertility, for three-year periods

Age-groups	Births per 1,000 woman-years (woman-years given in parentheses)											
	Africans						Creoles					
	1817–20	1820–23	1823–26	1826–29	1829–32	Total 1817–20	1817–20	1820–23	1823–26	1826–29	1829–32	Total 1817–32
Old Montpelier												
15–19							98 (51)	— (54)	20 (51)	46 (66)	— (60)	32 (282)
20–24							74 (27)	30 (33)	93 (54)	250 (36)	222 (45)	138 (195)
25–29	67 (15)	83 (12)	— (0)	— (0)	— (0)	74 (27)	148 (54)	143 (42)	48 (21)	103 (397)	188 (48)	137 (204)
30–34	83 (24)	— (6)	67 (15)	— (6)	— (0)	59 (51)	102 (39)	71 (42)	125 (48)	91 (33)	167 (18)	106 (180)
35–39	22 (45)	67 (30)	134 (15)	— (12)	— (15)	51 (117)	91 (33)	139 (36)	111 (36)	67 (45)	77 (39)	95 (189)
40–44	— (307	— (45)	22 (45)	— (24)	— (6)	7 (150)	83 (12)	56 (18)	61 (33)	77 (39)	54 (147)	
General fertility rate	44 (114)	32 (93)	53 (75)	— (42)	— (21)	35 (345)	106 (216)	71 (225)	71 (255)	95 (252)	112 (249)	91 (1197)
New Montpelier												
15–19							— (33)	— (30)	18 (57)	15 (66)	19 (54)	13 (240)
20–24							— (21)	37 (27)	111 (36)	48 (21)	137 (51)	83 (156)
25–29	42 (247)	111 (9)	— (3)	— (0)	— (0)	56 (36)	146 (21)	— (24)	— (12)	37 (27)	33 (30)	44 (114)
30–34	111 (45)	111 (36)	— (9)	333 (6)	— (0)	104 (96)	111 (18)	74 (27)	— (15)	— (21)	— (15)	40 (96)
35–39	127 (102)	56 (36)	78 (51)	47 (21)	222 (9)	100 (219)	200 (15)	— (15)	36 (27)	— (12)	— (15)	48 (84)
40–44	111 (18)	11 (81)	13 (78)	— (39)	— (27)	17 (243)	— (0)	— (6)	67 (15)	— (21)	37 (27)	29 (69)
General fertility rate	111 (189)	56 (162	36 (141)	45 (66)	56 (36)	67 (594)	74 (108)	23 (129)	37 (162)	12 (168)	52 (192)	49 (759)

Shettlewood												
15–19							— (33)	48 (42)	22 (45)	111 (45)	74 (27)	52 (192)
20–24							— (12)	167 (12)	119 (42)	83 (48)	41 (51)	97 (165)
25–29	— (0)	— (0)	— (0)	— (0)	— (0)	— (0)	— (18)	— (24)	417 (12)	222 (18)	154 (39)	131 (111)
30–34	167 (12)	— (3)	— (0)	— (0)	— (0)	133 (15)	— (6)	— (0)	— (12)	— (15)	83 (12)	22 (45)
35–39	33 (30)	167 (18)	— (6)	— (0)	— (0)	74 (54)	— (0)	— (6)	— (6)	167 (6)	— (15)	31 (33)
40–44	— (30)	— (27)	83 (24)	— (12)	— (3)	10 (96)	— (0)	— (0)	— (0)	— (3)	— (0)	— (3)
General fertility rate	42 (72)	63 (48)	83 (30)	— (12)	— (3)	42 (165)	— (69)	48 (84)	94 (117)	104 (135)	83 (144)	74 (549)
15–19							43 (117)	16 (126)	19 (153)	51 (177)	21 (141)	32 (714)
20–24							33 (60)	56 (72)	106 (132)	133 (105)	136 (147)	105 (516)
25–29	51 (39)	95 (21)	— (3)	— (0)	— (0)	64 (63)	118 (93)	67 (90)	133 (45)	107 (84)	136 (117)	112 (429)
30–34	111 (81)	89 (45)	42 (24)	167 (12)	— (0)	99 (162)	95 (63)	72 (69)	80 (75)	43 (69)	89 (45)	75 (321)
35–39	89 (179)	84 (84)	83 (72)	31 (33)	83 (24)	82 (329)	125 (48)	88 (57)	72 (69)	63 (63)	43 (69)	75 (306)
40–44	26 (78)	6 (153)	21 (147)	— (75)	— (36)	12 (489)	83 (12)	42 (24)	33 (60)	35 (57)	61 (66)	55 (219)
General fertility rate	77 (377)	49 (303)	41 (246)	25 (120)	33 (60)	53 (1106)	79 (393)	52 (438)	67 (534)	74 (555)	85 (585)	72 (2505)

and 1827. In 1827, all the children born were described as being 'nine days old at date' and all appear in the registration returns for 1829. In 1825, two children who died from tetanus on the sixth and seventh days after birth were listed in the Account Book but not registered. (The mothers of children surviving nine days received 13s. 4d. from the attorney.) It would seem that, for these three properties, the underrecording of fertility was confined to mortality in the first nine days of life. Contemporary estimates placed the mortality within this period at 25–50 per cent of all live births.[30] The data can, however, be used to make comparisons between the three properties, household types and age groups, on the assumption that the extent of underregistration was evenly distributed.

Table 6 shows broad age-specific fertility rates for each of the 11 household types containing women. A basis difficulty in this analysis is that the household type of each woman is known only for 1825. To meet this problem the rates have been divided into two periods, 1817–25 and 1825–32, but it is clear that some births will have been wrongly attributed. For example, a woman living with her children in 1825 may have borne all of them while living with a mate, the man having died before 1825. More importantly, the female children living in such a household frequently moved into the childbearing age groups after 1825, and it is probable that, if they had children, they then lived in households containing a mate. In general, it seems that the 1817–25 rates are more reliable indicators than those for the later period. In household Type 4, for instance, the 'women' bore 48 children between 1817 and 1825 and the 'children' only one, whereas in 1825–32 the 'women' bore only seven children and the 'children' nine. Thus the inclusion of 'children' in the calculation of woman-years does not greatly depress the fertility of the 'women' in 1817–25, but does so considerably for 1825–32.

Concentrating on the 1817–25 period, then, the most fertile women were those who lived with a mate and their children (household Type 4), followed by those who lived in households lacking mates (Types 1 and 2). Thus, the presence of a mate was conducive, though not essential, to relatively high fertility. Households of Type 7 (a woman, her children and others) were not as fertile since they frequently included invalids and unconnected individuals. The very low fertility of women living alone, with other women, with a man, with groups of men and women, or with siblings, may be seen as a corollary of the strong tendency for children to live with their mothers. But the women living in such households demonstrated a significant increase in fertility after 1825, suggesting that they moved into, or created by bearing children, different types. The relatively low fertility of women living apart from their mates may be explained in terms of reduced coital frequency, and this factor probably also affected some of the women living in household Type 7. In summary, the most fertile women were those who lived with a mate, followed by those living exclusively with their offspring, while the least fertile were those living with adults and who were not identifiable kin.

Excepting those household types which accounted for only a few births (Types 2, 3 and 5), the most fertile age group was always the 25–34 years group (Table 6). Within this age group the highest fertility (0.307 births per woman year) occurred among women in household Type 4, followed by those in Types 1 (0.200) and 7 (0.106). At the property level, however, households of Type 4 were the most fertile only at New Montpelier, where they were dominated by Africans (Table 3). At Old Montpelier Type 1 households were more fertile than Type 4, since the latter had a more mature age structure, reducing the fertility of the 'women' and incorporating a larger proportion of female children over 15 years. The pattern of Shettlewood was somewhat aberrant, probably because of the small numbers involved; but if Types 4 and 7 are seen to overlap, the divergence is minor.

The results of this analysis suggest, first, that the planters' belief that fertility would be encouraged by the formation and maintenance of stable monogamous unions was not unrealistic. The missionaries' emphasis on marriage, however, seems to have had little relation to fertility. And, although the evidence is slight, polygyny seems not to have reduced the fertility of women living in such households, contrary to the view of both planter and missionary.[31] At Old Montpelier, where the evidence of polygyny is strongest, the sexes were evenly balanced so that it could hardly have exacerbated the shortage of women complained of in earlier periods. It is possible that, as some planters contended, fertility was reduced by the prolonged residence of children with their parents; certainly daughters rarely moved away before bearing children, and they were particularly infertile during adolescence, though few men remained with their parents after their twentieth birthday. These findings fit the modern consensus that marital instability and casual mating depress fertility in the West Indies.[32]

The limitations of the household data make it impossible to trace effectively changes in fertility through the period, but the general age-specific fertility rates are of interest (Table 7). Patterson has argued that the young creole slaves were indifferent to child-rearing, whereas 'the habit of childbearing was too strongly rooted in the African woman for even the slave system to destroy it'.[33] But the evidence of Table 7 shows the creoles to have been more fertile than the Africans on the three properties. These data include no African women under 25 years, perhaps the most fertile years, but the creoles surpassed the Africans even in the 25–29 years age group. At Old Montpelier, the most thoroughly creolized of the properties, the creoles were most fertile throughout the period, whereas at Shettlewood a decline in African fertility was matched by a rapid increase in that of the creoles. New Montpelier, with the greatest proportion of Africans, presents a different pattern. There the fertility of the Africans exceeded that of the creoles throughout the period, possibly a result of the dominance of household Type 4 and of Africans within the type. Perhaps the high mortality of creoles at New Montpelier (Figure 1) engendered an instability which made it difficult for them to maintain households of this type.

If the evidence regarding African fertility is confused, it is certain that creoles under 20 years were most fertile (Table 7). This might be seen either as a result of quasi-prostitution (associated with abortion) or of the retentiveness of maternal household heads. Only slaves bearing children of colour demonstrated high fertility in this age group. This pattern conforms with that argued by Patterson. But following this initial infertility an early peak was reached, generally around 25 years of age, after which the decline in fertility was continuous. However generous the assumptions made regarding underregistration, the slaves were not a fertile population. If comparison is made with modern times it is seen that the distribution of fertility among the age groups also differed, being relatively very low in the early years but approaching modern levels after 35 years.[34] Thus, to invert the argument, this pattern may be seen as suggestive of early casual mating followed by relatively stable monogamy, which corroborates the accepted view of developmental instability and gives depth to the otherwise static analysis of households.

Notes

1. See G. W. Roberts, 'Some aspects of mating and fertility in the West Indies', *Population Studies*, VIII (1955), pp. 199-227; Judith Blake, *Family Structure in Jamaica: The Social Context of Reproduction* (New York, 1961). Cf. Anthony Marino, 'Family, fertility, and sex ratios in the British Caribbean', *Population Studies*, XXIV, 2 (July 1970), pp. 159-72.
2. M. G. Smith, *West Indian Family Structure* (Seattle, 1926), p. 260.
3. Edward Brathwaite, *The Development of Creole Society in Jamaica, 1770–1820* (Oxford, 1971), p. 204. Cf. Elsa V. Goveia, *Slave Society in the British Leeward Islands at the End of the Eighteenth Century* (New Haven, 1965), pp. 235-237, and Orlando Patterson, *The Sociology of Slavery* (London, 1967), p. 160.
4. Old Montpelier Estate, Account Book (Institute of Jamaica, Kingston).
5. *Parliamentary Papers*, 1832 (127), House of Lords, 'Report from the Select Committee on the state of the West India colonies', p. 88. The report is printed at pp. 1376-93.
6. Returns of Registration of Slaves, Liber 27, f. 37; Liber 30, ff. 42 and 49; Liber 40, ff. 83-84; Liber 48, f. 163; Liber 66, ff. 159-60; Liber 75, f. 100; Liber 85, ff. 60-61; Liber 93, f. 33; Liber 96, f. 213; Liber 100; ff. 214-15; Liber 129, f. 28 and f. 32; Liber 32; Liber 130, f. 170 (Jamaica Archives, Spanish Town). The returns at Spanish Town are copies, the originals being located in the series T. 71 at the Public Record Office, London.
7. See E. A. Wrigley (Ed.) *An Introduction to English Historical Demography* (London, 1966).
8. St. James, Copy Register, Vol. 2: Baptisms, 17 July, 1816 (Island Record Office, Spanish Town).
9. Joseph Sturge and Thomas Harvey, *The West Indies in 1837* (London, 1838), p. 229; *Dictionary of National Biography Gentleman's Magazine*, XXIV (1845), Pt ii, p. 419.
10. *Parliamentary Debates*, 33, p. 257 (6 April, 1797). See also Goveia, *op. cit.*, in footnote 3, p. 33; Alfred Owen Aldridge, 'Population and polygamy in eigtheenth-century thought', *Journal of the History of Medicine*, 4, 2 (Spring 1949), pp. 129-48.
11. Brathwaite, *op. cit* in footnote 3, p.292.
12. Minutes of the Missions Conference, 30 November 1831 (Moravian Church Archives, Malvern, Jamaica).
13. *Parliamentary Papers*, 1832 (127), *op. cit.*, p. 90; Account Book, *op. cit.*
14. James Hakewill, *A Picturesque Tour of the Island of Jamaica, from drawings made in the years 1820 and 1821* (London, 1825), Plate 19.
15. Account Book, *op. cit.*
16. Accounts Produce (Jamaica Archives, Spanish Town). See, for example, Liber 51, ff. 87, 91 and 92; Liber 62, f. 63.
17. *Jamaica Almanack* (1817 and 1818), Poll tax givings-in.
18. Hakewill, *op. cit.*, in footnote 14, Plate 19.
19. A mulatto being the offspring of a black and a white, a quadroon of a mulatto and a white, a mustee of a quadroon and a white, and a sambo of a mulatto and a black.
20. St. James, Copy Register, Vol. 2: Marriages, 25 August, 1825 (Island Record Office, Spanish Town).
21. Baptisms and Marriages of Slaves, St. James, 1827-28: Marriages, 23 December, 1827 (Jamaica Archives, Spanish Town).
22. Returns of Registrations of Slaves, Liber 93, f. 33; Liber 85, f. 60.
23. Hakewill, *op. cit*, in footnote 14, Plate 19. Another

drawing was produced by Duperly following the rebellion of 1831, but it was obviously based on Hakewill. Duperly added a further nine houses on the bare hill behing the overseer's house and stores, but these may have been mere fancy. Duperly's print is reproduced in *Jamaica Journal*, 3, 2 (June 1969), p. 25. An undated, detailed map of Montpelier Estate is to be found at the Institute of Jamaica, Kingston.

24. Patterson, *op. cit.*, in footnote 3, pp. 159–70.
25. *Ibid.*, p. 167; Madeline Kerr, *Personality and Conflict in Jamaica* (London, 1952), p. 93; M. G. Smith, 'Social structure in the British Caribbean about 1820', *Social and Economic Studies*, 1, 4 (August 1953), p. 72.
26. M. G. Smith, *West Indian Family Structure*, p. 161. See also William Davenport, 'The family system of Jamaica', in Paul Bohannan and John Middleton (eds), *Marriage, Family and Residence* (New York, 1968), pp. 247–84.
27. See Rodney Needham (Ed.) *Rethinking Kinship and Marriage* (London, 1971).
28. George W. Roberts, *The Population of Jamaica* (Cambridge, 1957), pp. 3–4. Roberts seems to assume that the Jamaica and Demerara and Essequibo laws were the same, and appears to be quoting Robertson's report on the latter rather than the Jamaica law. See James Robertson's report in *Parliamentary Papers*, 1833, Vol. 26 (700), 'Slave population. (Slave Registries)', p. 447.
29. Jamaica Law, 57 Geo. III, Cap, XV, Section 4.
30. Robert Renny, *A History of Jamaica* (London, 1807), p. 188; John Phillippo, *Jamaica: Its Past and Present State* London 1843), p. 144.
31. See Aldridge *loc. cit.*, in footnote 10, and Geoffrey Hawthorn, *The Sociology of Fertility* (London, 1970), p. 32.
32. Roberts, *loc. cit.*, in footnote 1 (1955). Cf. Marino, *op. cit.*, in footnote 1 (1970).
33. Patterson, *op. cit.*, in footnote 3, p. 109.
34. Joycelin Byrne, *Levels of Fertility in Commonwealth Caribbean, 1921–1965* (University of the West Indies, 1972), pp. 58–59.

Appendix Household size

	Number of households																												
	Old Montpelier										New Montpelier										Shettlewood								
Household type	1	2	3	4	5	6	7	8	9	Household type	1	2	3	4	5	6	7	8	9	Household type	1	2	3	4	5	6	7	8	9
1	—	2	3	2	1	2	—	—	—	1	—	8	2	2	—	1	—	—	—	1	—	1	2	2	1	—	—	—	—
2	—	—	—	—	—	—	—	—	—	2	—	—	—	—	1	—	—	—	—	2	—	—	1	1	—	—	1	—	—
3	—	—	—	—	—	—	1	—	—	3	—	—	—	—	—	—	—	—	—	3	—	—	—	—	—	—	—	1	—
4	—	—	10	3	6	—	—	—	—	4	—	—	11	6	4	2	1	1	—	4	—	—	—	2	4	—	—	—	—
5	—	—	—	—	1	1	1	—	—	5	—	—	—	—	—	1	—	—	—	5	—	—	—	—	—	—	—	—	—
6	—	—	1	1	—	—	—	—	—	6	—	—	—	—	2	—	—	—	—	6	—	1	1	—	—	—	—	—	—
7	—	—	1	6	3	4	4	1	1	7	—	—	1	3	3	4	2	—	—	7	—	—	—	1	—	—	1	—	1
8	14	—	—	—	—	—	—	—	—	8	5	—	—	—	—	—	—	—	—	8	6	—	—	—	—	—	—	—	—
9	13	—	—	—	—	—	—	—	—	9	3	—	—	—	—	—	—	—	—	9	3	—	—	—	—	—	—	—	—
10	—	5	—	—	—	—	—	—	—	10	—	1	—	—	—	—	—	—	—	10	—	1	—	—	—	—	—	—	—
11	—	1	1	—	—	—	—	—	—	11	—	1	—	—	—	—	—	—	—	11	—	1	—	—	—	—	—	—	—
12	—	25	—	—	—	—	—	—	—	12	—	6	—	—	—	—	—	—	—	12	—	7	—	—	—	—	—	—	—
13	—	—	10	—	—	—	—	—	—	13	—	—	10	2	1	—	—	—	—	13	—	—	4	—	—	—	—	1	—
Total households	27	33	26	12	12	7	6	1	1		8	16	24	13	11	8	3	1	—		9	11	8	6	5	—	2	2	1
Total occupants	27	66	78	48	60	42	42	8	9		8	32	72	52	55	48	21	8	—		9	22	24	24	25	—	14	16	9

Women's Work, Family Formation, and Reproduction Among Caribbean Slaves

MARIETTA MORRISSEY

Introduction

The organization of slave families in the American South has received new, sustained attention from Genovese (1976), Fogel and Engerman (1974), Gutman (1977), and others. It is argued, first, that slave families were more likely to be nuclear — a male, a female, and their children — than matrifocal as previously proposed, and, secondly, that families maintained intergenerational ties. Hence, family stability is now said to be prevailed among American slaves. This proposition contradicts the findings of Stampp (1956) and others who argued that slavery broke up families, that with 'these conditions — the absence of legal marriage, the family's minor social and economic significance, and the father's limited role — it is hardly surprising to find that slave families were highly unstable' (Stampp, 1956: 344). And it challenges Patterson's (1979) more recent hypothesis that slaves were 'natally alienated', or symbolically estranged from natal ties by the slave condition.

For the West Indies, it is more difficult to establish the existence of 'stable' family patterns. Slaves were rarely able to reproduce their numbers, certainly not at the level found among slaves in the United States (Fogel and Engerman, 1974). Still, statistical evidence of high levels of nuclear family formation has been found for Jamaica (Higman, 1976a), Trinidad (Higman, 1978; 1979), and the Bahamas (Craton, 1979; 1978). Indeed, Craton concludes that patterned family life, 'even in patterns recognizable to Europeans', was sometimes the norm for West Indian slaves, in particular, 'nuclear, two-headed households' (1979: 2).

The evidence of conjugal domestic units among British West Indian slaves is an important empirical breakthrough in the study of the family, although there is still little quantifiable evidence of intergenerational kinship. But a body of critique has developed, focusing on the failure of contemporary quantitative research to identify fully the meaning and origins of nuclear families among Caribbean slaves and thus to account for the considerable variation in Caribbean slave family organization (Patterson, 1976; 1982). That is, why did nuclear families form, instead of other arrangements? And why are nuclear families found in some settings, while the mother–child unit predominates elsewhere?

Major findings on Caribbean slave families and critical reaction will be reviewed. It is suggested that both propositions of stable nuclear family formation among Caribbean slaves and critical commentary have failed to consider women as a complementary unit of analysis to the family and thus have missed a crucial source of explanation of changing patterns of Caribbean slave families.

Research on Nuclear Families Among British West Indian Slaves

The recent examination of slave registration figures presented to British colonial authorities shortly before emancipation extends aggregate and plantation-specific research on nuclear family formation. The methodological approach and findings differ dramatically from those of earlier research on slave families based on occasional and incomplete plantation records, diaries of slave owners and travelers, and other documents of the period.

Higman studied three plantations in Jamaica and aggregate figures for Trinidad. He

Review, IX, 3 (Winter 1986), pp. 339–67.

concludes that the nuclear family was the modal type on three estates in Jamaica on the eve of emancipation (1976a). His findings for Trinidad in 1813 are similar (1978; 1979). Craton's (1979) study of the Bahamas echoes Higman's work in methods and substance. According to the 1821–22 census, most Bahamian slaves lived in nuclear families.

Three competing but tentative hypotheses have been offered by historians and demographers about the origins of West Indian nuclear families.

First, it has been argued that nuclear families were sometimes a demographic possibility: for example, where sex ratios were even or populations stable and isolated (Craton, 1979). Thus, it is suggested that in the absence of material and ideological constraints, and given the demographic opportunity, nuclear families developed. This explanation is so broad as to be nearly tautological: nuclear families can exist, therefore they do exist. It does not offer in sufficiently specific terms the conditions that unite a variety of New World national and plantation settings that produced nuclear families.

Secondly, it has been hypothesized that African traditions predisposed slaves to stable, co-residential conjugal patterns. Indeed, Africans appear to have been more likely than Creoles to establish stable, two-headed households in urban Trinidad (Higman, 1978: 170), although contradictory evidence has been found in other settings, for example, Martinique (Debien, 1960). Still, no evidence is offered of what particular African family forms were represented in nuclear units, so no hypotheses can be developed about the meaning of slave families based on links to the slaves' African past. Higman suggests, however, that African-born slaves may have perceived the nuclear family as a 'building-block of extended or polygynous family types rooted in lineage or locality' (1978: 171).

Finally, for high-status males or males with productive garden plots and well-developed marketing skills and opportunities, nuclear families served an economic function not unlike that of early Western nuclear families (Patterson, 1969; Higman, 1976a). This is an important explanation of Caribbean nuclear family formation, supported by the statistical evidence of nuclear and polygamous families among slaves with prestigious occupations and/or lighter skin color in Trinidad and Jamaica. However, this explanation applies only to some Caribbean slaves. Field hands were found in equal proportions among all family types in Higman's Jamaican sample, suggesting that the family economic function may have reinforced other tendencies toward nuclear family formation.

Women as a Unit of Analysis

The new scholarship on women has made clear that their roles as producers and reproducers of the future labor force have profound effects on family organization (Goody, 1976; Quick, 1977). A materialist analysis suggests that women's roles are established through the system of production (in particular, the labor market) and reinforced by ideological agents such as the state and church (Boserup, 1970; Blumberg, 1977). An important factor emerges from these assumptions for analysis of West Indian slave families. That is, the time at which New World slave societies reached their peak need for labor relative to the availability of slaves on the world market may have influenced women's work, family membership and fertility. Craton, Higman, and others have distinguished between the demographic profiles (in particular, the sex ratios of older and newer slave societies) in accounting for differential patterns of family formation and reproduction in the study of Caribbean slaves; I suggest refining that distinction to the more fundamental one of societies with labor shortage and those with labor surpluses.

At times of labor shortage, particularly towards the end of the slave trade, when young male slaves were not easily purchased, women were used in increasing proportions as field laborers rather than as household workers. At the same time, slave holders tried to breed new slaves by encouraging nuclear family formation and the reproduction of children. Given the nearly constant historical tendency towards the natural decrease of slaves in the West Indies, stimulation of reproduction was generally ineffective, particularly, it seems, when women's production roles in agriculture were also emphasized. It is hypothesized, then, that women's increased contributions to agricultural production mitigated the effects of planter incentives and reduced women's tendencies to live in nuclear families and to produce children. In formal terms:

1. At time of severe labor shortage, West Indian slave women
   (a) were employed more often than males in field labor;

   (b) lived, in the main, by themselves or with their children;
   (c) produced relatively few children (fewer than 30 per 1,000 population annually)[1]
2. At times of adequate labor supply, West Indian slave women
   (a) were employed in equal numbers to males, or less often, in field labor;
   (b) lived, in the main, in nuclear families;
   (c) produced a relatively large number of children (more than 30 per 1,000).

These propositions will be examined in light of six cases; the Bahamas, the Leeward Islands, Martinique, Jamaica, Barbados, and Cuba. These societies represent three stages in the evolution of New World plantation agriculture. The Bahamas and the Leewards, although different in agricultural and social structure, both had sizable labor surpluses by the late eighteenth and early nineteenth centuries, the time of our inquiry. We can expect women to work in the fields as often or less so than males in the Leewards and the Bahamas, nuclear families to predominate, and slave reproduction rates to be high. Barbados and Martinique, our second set of cases, present a second stage in the evolution of Caribbean plantation agriculture. Both areas suffered a labor shortage at the turn of the nineteenth century. Therefore, we can expect a predominance of single female or mother-child units, low levels of reproduction (below 30 per 1,000 population), and the disproportionate presence of women in field work. However, the competitive position of these islands had diminished in the world sugar market by the era under investigation. Labor shortage was a serious problem, but the high levels of productivity demanded of an earlier slave population in Barbados and Martinique were not required of workers during this era. By introducing a third paired comparison, that of Jamaica and Cuba, we can explore in greater depth the independent variable — labor shortage — and its impact on women's lives. These societies reached peak levels of labor productivity and agricultural capacity as the slave trade ended. We can expect women to predominate heavily in agricultural work, natural production to be extremely low (approaching natural decrease), and mother-child units or women alone to be most common familial patterns.

The Bahamas and the Leeward Islands

British settlers occupied the Bahamas in the 1650s and contributed to the mercantile character that distinguished the area from the agricultural West Indies to the south. Cotton cultivation by slaves was established, but 'in such colonies the conditions did not exist which led, in the West Indies proper, to the development of a fully fashioned slave society of the plantation type' (Lewis, 1968: 309). The area never experienced severe labor shortages, as its agricultural development preceded the intensification and competition of later sugar planting.

As predicted, most of the 10,000 Bahamian slaves (54 per cent) registered from 1821 to 1822 lived in 'simple nuclear families' (Craton, 1979: 7, 11). Craton argues that three factors contributed to the slaves' likely preference for conjugal domestic units: (1) 'Eurocentric, pro-natalist, or publicity-conscious masters'; (2) the widespread existence of provision gardens, apparently in male slaves' control, that required the labor of women and children; and (3) the tendency for nuclear families to be on larger, more isolated estates in a fairly stable cohort.[2]

These factors lead Craton to suggest a continuum of family types among Caribbean slaves. At one pole were the 'virtual peasants of the Bahamas, Barbuda, and, perhaps, the Grenadines with locational stability, a small proportion of African slaves, natural increase and a relatively high incidence of nuclear and stable families. At the opposite pole were the over-worked slaves of new plantations such as those of Trinidad, Guyana, and St. Vincent, with a high rate of natural decrease, a majority of slaves living alone or in 'barrack' conditions, and a high proportion of 'denuded', female-headed families' (1979: 25). Indeed, Craton reports the reluctance of one group of Bahamian slaves to be moved to Trinidad's more productive plantations, where slaves reputedly worked much harder.

The missing factor in Craton's discussion is an account of how relative productivity affected women's work roles. We have little information about what kinds of work women did on Bahamian plantations. The overall sex ratio was nearly even in contrast to more intensely cultivated areas of the Caribbean, where males predominated. This is a probable indication that high productivity was not demanded, as the apparently more productive male slave labor force was still available through trade. Craton (1978: 350–52) offers ample evidence of declining productivity, production, and profitability on the large cotton estate of Lord John

Rolle, said to be typical of Bahamian plantations after the 1790s. Craton suggests that slave masters took advantage of the nearly even sex ratio to pursue pronatalism, but with only moderate success. Higman (1976: 67) finds a natural increase among Bahamian slaves of about 16 per 1,000 population from 1825 to 1828, up from an earlier period and the highest in the British West Indies at the time (see Appendix). But the birth rate climbed to barely more than 30 per 1,000 from 1825 to 1828, well after labor productivity reached its peak in the Bahamas.

The Leeward Islands (St. Christopher, Nevis Montserrat, and Antigua) were settled from 1623 to 1632. These small islands were the sight of wars among the French, English, and Amerindians until the early 1700s, when plantation sugar production became a consistent, lucrative enterprise. Among them there has been considerable variation in productivity, sugar exports levels, and slave populations. Antigua, with 37,808 (mostly slaves) and more than 25,000 acres in cane, surpassed Barbados in sugar exports in the mid-eighteenth century, as indicated in Table 1. The other islands had less agricultural land than Antigua, and fewer slaves (in 1775, St. Kitts recorded 23,462 Blacks; Nevis, 11,000; Monserrat, 9,834 [Sheridan, 1973: 150]).

By the end of the eighteenth century, sugar planting had peaked in the British Leewards, and planters enjoyed a relative surplus of labor. 'Originally the slave system had been intended to relieve the shortage of field labour for the plantations. But by the end of the eighteenth century its influence had created a pattern of profuse consumption of relatively unproductive forced labour, as well as of wealth, which was proving ruinously expensive to maintain' (Goveia, 1965: 150). Goveia offers several indicators of labour surplus. a smaller proportion of slaves was used in the field work, leading to a decline in productivity from a mid-century peak. More slaves were employed in domestic service: 27 per cent of the slave population on Montserrat engaged in domestic service or worked as tradesmen or fisherman (Goveia, 1965: 146). The custom of hiring out slaves was well developed, manumissions were relatively numerous, and a cash economy among slaves were extensive. Slaves customerily supplemented food and clothing allotments through earnings from provision sales and hiring out (Goveia, 1965: 135–39).

The population of the Leewards was highly Creolized by the late eighteenth century. Women outnumbered men on Nevis and probably on Montserrat, and children and old people made up more than a third of the population on both islands (Goveia, 1956: 124). Women's work is not treated directly by Goveia, but we can infer that women were not especially valued as field workers. Most of the numerous domestics were women; some slaves were hired out for domestic service. Other groups commonly able to evade field work along with women workers were able to do so in the Leewards. People of mixed ethnicity, in particular, were not attractive to Leewards' planters for field work.

We expect the Leewards to exhibit a relatively high proportion of nuclear families and a high birth rate. Higman's population estimates are for the 1800s, well after the peak in sugar production. All of the Leewards had an increase in births from 1817 to 1831, with all except Nevis showing a small natural increase, but never more than Montserrat's 6 births per 1,000 population in the period from 1824 to 1827. More relevant to our hypotheses, only Montserrat exhibited a crude birth rate over 30 per 1,000.[3]

Slave families are said by Goveia to have consisted of a mother and her children, all belonging to the mother's owner, regardless of the parentage of the children. Goveia does report on the success of Methodist and Moravian churches in the Leewards, both of which advocated 'Christian monogamy' for their slave converts (1965: 271–99). Goveia is of an earlier school of thought that rejects on logical grounds the possibility of stable conjugal unions among slaves. One set of nineteenth-century observers may partially confirm Goveia's findings. Sturge and Harvey, travelling through Antigua after emancipation, claimed this about the earlier slave condition: 'Husbands and wives are not helpmeets to one another; they rarely reside in the same hut, or even on the same estate' (1838: 76).

What, so far, does our exploration of women's roles reveal about their contribution to nuclear family formation in early Caribbean plantation societies? The Bahamas and the Leewards enjoyed an adequate labor supply in the eighteenth century. A majority of Bahamian slaves lived in nuclear families, although we know little about women's work. In contrast, slave women of the Leewards appear to have worked in domestic service and less demanding areas of field work. Yet nuclear families appear not to have formed in the Leewards, and the crude birth rate was high by early nineteenth-century Caribbean standards only in Montserrat.

Barbados and Martinique

Barbados reached its peak productive capacity in the late 1600s, 'the first [English colony] to transform its society from a smallholder, semi-subsistence base to a slave-plantation, near-monoculture regime which was dominated by a class of wealthy sugar planters' (Sheridan, 1973: 124). An expanding African slave population made possible this dramatic transition. From a reported 6,000 slaves in 1643, the slave population grew to more than 68,000 in 1783 (Sheridan, 1973: 133; Watson, 1975: 48), primarily through the massive purchase of young male Africans. But by the late 1700s, the abolition of the slave trade was certain, and Barbados had entered a stage of productive decline.

Our best source of information on the daily lives of slaves during the transition from highly successful to less lucrative planting in Barbados comes from two Codrington estates, left to the Society for the Propagation of the Gospel in Foreign Parts in 1710 (Bennett, 1958). In the early 1700s, Codrington shared the remarkable good fortune of the Barbados plantocracy, depending on the heavy purchase of highly productive slaves, and thus maximizing their gain from the sugar boom. And, by the end of the century, the Codrington estates suffered labor shortage and financial loss.

> The slave trade lost its relevance for the Codrington plantations in 1761. After fifty years of trial, the policy of restocking with new African Negroes was discarded forever. From 1712 to 1761 the Society had purchased about 450 Negroes at a cost of about £15,000. It had spent two and one-half times the value of the Negroes left by Christopher Codrington, and had added one-half times the number of slaves that had come from him. The outcome of this investment after five decades was a population smaller by more than one-third (Bennett, 1958: 52).

New categories of workers were now brought to the fields. 'Young Negroes who would formerly have been apprenticed to artisans were now kept at work in the secondary great gangs' (Bennett, 1958: 19). Other schemes were tried, including 'recruiting Africans, hiring slaves on an occasional basis, reducing crops and production, concentrating available strength in the field gangs, purchasing parcels of seasoned slaves' (1958: 19). None of these efforts succeeded.

Women became an increased portion of the slave population through purchase and creolization. In 1732, there had been 123 males to 58 females on the Society's estates. Females slightly outnumbered male slaves byu the end of the century. At that time 'one-half of the men worked in the fields, but only one-third of the women were spared the heavy duty on the land' (Bennett, 1958: 13). Table 2 presents the occupational distribution of males and females at Codrington in 1781. Women did some domestic work (personnel workers), but men had more opportunities to evade field work by serving as skilled workers. Moreover, a 1775 price listing indicates that women were engaged in heavy field work, with most in the first gang, and were valued at the same price as first-gang male field hands.

At the same time, estate officials arrived at what they saw as the last resort in solving labor supply problems: 'amelioration' of the slaves' conditions. One goal of amelioration was to 'encourage the Negroes to breed' (Bennett, 1958: 100). Women were now sometimes given a small reward for delivering a child. The resulting birth rate of 2 per cent was an improvement, but was lower than before, and still less than the death rate (2.5 per cent) (1958: 98). Better houses and garden plots were offered, and field work decreased at Codrington with the use of plows in 1812.

Amelioration eventually brought a small natural increase in Codrington's slaves, with a net gain of three slaves in 1795, eleven in 1800, five in 1804, and seven in 1805. By this time, Codrington had moved beyond other estates in Barbados in amelioration and would shortly adopt ways to ease the emancipation of its slaves. The Codrington records are puzzling on marital patterns, as passing sexual unions were often mistaken for polygamous ones (Bennett, 1958: 35). Polygamy was believed to dominate conjugal forms throughout the island. For example, in 1787, Barbados's governor claimed that male slaves generally had several wives (Watson, 1975: 176). It is likely that women and children were often housed separately from men; there are examples in the Codrington records of slaves helping a 'new mother' to build a house (Bennett, 1958: 33). But a mix of single women, mother–child, and polygamous residential patterns probably prevailed, with only some 'enduring monogamous unions' (Bennett, 1958: 35).

The evidence for a natural increase of slaves on the Codrington estates would seem to contradict our hypothesis that labor shortages inhibited reproduction. By 1834, women substantially outnumbered men (173 females to 135 males, counting boys and girls), and worked almost exclusively in field labor, along with girls and boys. Yet 'the breeding program had brought spectacular results in Barbados generally after the abolition of the slave trade in 1807, [with] the Codrington gain thought to be unequaled by any other sugar estate' (Bennett, 1958: 131). Still, the number of new slaves born yearly was small, particularly in comparison with the number purchased earlier. The net gain in slaves was also influenced by the absences of new adult Africans; about 43 per cent of African slaves died soon after reaching Codrington.

Our information on Barbados as a whole, pertaining to a later period, points to the relative success of amelioration. Higman (1976b) calculates Barbados's rate of natural increase at about 10 per 1,000 population by 1823, more than the Leewards' at the same time, but less than the Bahamas'. But as many as 40.7 births per 1,000 population were registered in 1823 (1976b: 68), and 30.6 deaths per 1,000 population. Indeed, the number of slaves increased from 69,400 in 1809 to 82,000 in 1834 (Curtin, 1969: 59). On Codrington, manumissions increased along with task labor as the estate prepared for emancipation. Slaves were also permitted to buy free days (Bennett, 1958: 125). Eventually, slaves were granted plots on which to grow provisions. They paid rent to estate owners in exchange for labor (Bennett, 1958: 129). Women continued to predominate in field work, but it is likely that overall productivity fell as slaves became 'apprentices', and those with lots devoted time to cash crops (1958: 132–33).

It appears, then, that our hypothesis is only partially supported for Barbados. Women experienced an increased role in agricultural production, although reproduction also increased. It is likely, however, that by the 1800s increases in crude birth rate accompanied reductions in labor productivity for both men and women. Although nuclear families seem to have been largely absent, it is unclear whether mother–child units and single females or polygamous family forms prevailed.

Martinique was settled by the French in 1635. Plantation agriculture was quickly established, with more than 21,000 slaves by 1700. Martinique reached its zenith in sugar production from 1763 to 1789 by trading with the United States. On the eve of the French Revolution, Martinique exported more than 8,000 tons of sugar annually, surpassing Barbados (see Table 1).[4] With the start of the nineteenth century, the French West Indies suffered the abolition of the slave trade, changes in colonial administration, and the effects of European wars. By 1815, the sugar industry had recovered, but not to its earlier level of prosperity. French planters purchased some slaves illegally until emancipation in 1848, but maintained a small work force and relatively little agricultural land in cane.

Table 1 Sugar Exports of the Ten Leading Caribbean Islands, 1766–70 (annual averages in tons)

	Exports		Areas in square miles
Saint-Domingue	61,247	(1767–68)	10,200
Jamaica	36,021		4,411
Antigua	10,690		108
Cuba	10,000	(1770–78)	44,206
St. Christopher	9,701		68
Martinique	8,778		380
St. Croix	8,230	(1770)	84
Guadeloupe	7,898	(1767)	619
Barbados	7,819		166
Grenada	6,552		120
	166,936		60,362

Source: Sheridan (1973:101).

Debien's research on Martinique may offer the most complete assessment of women's work roles and family formation for Caribbean slave societies of the mid- to late eighteenth century. Debien studied records from a single plantation, L'Anse-à-l'Ane, from 1743 to 1778. As early as 1746, adult males and females were about equal in number, with 56 men and 52 women (Debien, 1960: 5). No purchases of slaves were made after 1753, resulting in a small natural population increment after 1763 and continuing near parity in sex ratio. This gender distribution was typical of Martinique's estates in the 1800s (Tomich, 1976: 106).

There was never a labor surplus on L'Anse-à-l'Ane, so both men and women were used as field laborers, mostly in the first gang, with teenagers and children in second and third gangs. This distribution of personnel became

Table 2 Occupations of Slaves at Codrington, 1781

Occupation	Men	Women	Boys	Girls	Total
Field workers	37	52	34	39	162
Artisans and watchmen	17	0	1	0	18
Stockkeepers	10	5	7	1	23
Personnel workers	3	15	0	1	19
Non-workers	4	4	19	27	54

Source: Bennett (1958:12).

common on Martinique's estates (Tomich, 1976: 185–88). Indeed, in 1772, the first gang of 60 field slaves was composed of 20 males and 40 females (Debien, 1960: 18). As in Barbados, male slaves worked in skilled tasks and sugar refining. Debien argues further that women's reproduction was not highly valued, as price data indicate that female slaves were considerably less costly than males aged 18–40. 'Their relatively low price underscores that their reproductive function was secondary; and the constant decline shows that masters were not concerned with an increase in women in order to increase the number of children. Children were always numerous at L'Anse-à-l'Ane, but not as a result of a demographic policy. Simply it is a general custom of the island' (Debien, 1960: 44–45).[5] Women had few paths out of field work, as in other areas of labor shortage. This can be attributed, however, to the rate of planter absenteeism and resulting low need for domestic service. Other evidence of labor shortage is manifest in eighteenth-century Martinique: for example, children increasingly performed field labor in the first gang after 1763 (1960: 23).

Still other indicators suggest that labor shortage was not acute, or at least was mitigated by declining production. For example, although women and children were increasingly drawn into field work, the overall number of field workers fell. Proportionately more slaves were old, sick, freed, or in skilled jobs after 1763. The first gang had 98 workers in 1746, and only 66 by 1773 (Debien, 1960: 5). Moreover, women did hire themselves out for domestic work, a phenomenon not generally associated with an intense need for female labor on New World plantations.

There is evidence of low fertility accompanying high levels of nuclear family formation at L'Anse. There were 58 children born of about 50 slave women at L'Anse from 1762 to 1777, a period for which records were fairly well kept (Debien, 1960: 77). The number of children per 100 women from 1753 to 1773 is recorded in Table 3, and ranges from 69.38 in 1753 to 98.14 in 1763, and then falls to 81.48 in 1767 and 60.41 in 1773. This suggests a decline in fertility, perhaps associated with women's expanding agricultural role. Extending data from L'Anse to the society level, the annual crude birth rate would not be high from 1762 to 1777, only about 21 births per 1,000 population. Debien speculates that infant mortality rates were artifically low in plantation computations. Listings by slaves' names suggest high infant mortality with the death of 29 of 58 babies born from 1762 to the end of 1777 (1960: 77).

Successes in reproduction at L'Anse were largely limited to conjugal families, about 52 of which are recorded for the period from 1761 to 1776. These families produced 215 children, slightly more than four per couple (1960: 58). Conjugal families predominated among Creoles, who made up nine-tenths of the L'Anse population from 1746. 'Maternal families' were less numerous than conjugal units, but more frequent than 'passing units'. The relationships 'approached' conjugal units, with a male maintaining a provision garden for the women and her children. Still, women in such families were less fertile than those in conjugal families.

There was a labor shortage in Martinique from 1763 to 1789, and, like Barbados, it confirms some dimensions of our hypotheses. Women participated in field work disproportionately to their numbers at L'Anse, predominating in the first gang. As expected, the birth rate was well below 30 per 1,000 population. Nevertheless, many couples lived in nuclear families, particularly creoles.[6] Their birth rate was probably higher than 30 per 1,000.

Jamaica and Cuba

Jamaica reached its peak in number of slaves, gross output of sugar, and labor productivity from 1805 to 1809. In 1808, 324,000 slaves were owned by Jamaican planters. Owners found it

Table 3 Demographic Indices, L'Anse-à-L'Ane, 1753–73

	Total slaves	Women older than 17	Number of children younger than 11	Number of children per 100 women
1753	152	49	34	69.38
1763	—	54	53	98.14
1767	163	54	44	81.48
1773	154	48	29	60.41

Source: Debien (1960:73).

cheaper to purchase slaves than to breed them, and tried to purchase males from about 15 to 30 years of age. With the rise of sugar production in the French islands and erosion of Jamaican soil, sugar production became more intense. At the same time, labor was in short supply with the abolition of the slave trade in 1807. This labor shortage greatly influenced the demographic profile of the slave population, as it had in Barbados and Martinique.

Like slave populations in our earlier cases, Jamaica's became proportionately more female, older, and lighter through the early 1800s. The sex ratio favored women on Jamaican estates by 1820. For example, at Worthy Park, records from which have been studied extensively by Craton, 65 per cent of the field labor force was female by 1832 (Craton, 1977: 142). At Rosehall, half of the women were in the field, but only one-eighth of the men. Women also remained in the fields longer than did men (Higman, 1976a: 194). At the Irwin estate in St. James, females constituted the majority in the first and second gangs (1976a: 199). At Maryland, a coffee plantation in St. Andrew, women worked in the fields longer than did men; of those in the 20–59 year age group, only nine women were not in the fields, whereas 20 men were not (1976a: 196). There was also an increase in whiteness among Jamaican slaves, and light skin ceased to be an easy path to manumission or to more highly skilled occupations. Slave owners complained also that too many slaves were over 40 or under 20. Higman comments:

> After 1807 the structure of the slave population of Jamaica changed in a manner contrary to the planters' ideal. It became less 'effective' and less 'flexible'. Not only was the number of slaves in the most productive age groups decreasing absolutely and relatively, but the slaves in these groups were also increasingly female and coloured (1976a: 211).

What was the effect on fertility and family form of intensification of women's role in production? Higman (1976a: 156–73) found these relationships on three properties: Old Montpelier, New Montpelier, and Shettlewood Pen. (1) More than half of the 864 slaves on the three properties lived in units with a man, a woman, and her children, or, in a related family type, a women, her children, and others, while 'probably 100 of the [slave] households . . . contained mates' (1976a: 164). (2) Other significant household types includes the slave living alone or with friends (about 30 per cent), polygamous units (in which about 11 per cent of slaves resided), mother-child households (about 11 per cent), and male-female households (including about 11 per cent of the slave population). (3) Africans were more likely to live alone or in simple nuclear families (man, woman, his and/or her children) than were Creoles. (4) Slaves of color 'with their privileged occupations and blood allying them to the great house and the whites, formed households in which slave men had no part and which were tightly organized around the maternal connection' (1976a: 162).

At the plantation level there is little relationship between a tendency for a female to work in the fields and to live in a nuclear family. There was a strong tendency for domestics, mostly colored, to live in female-dominated units, for mulatto and quadroon slaves (with white fathers) to live in female-dominated units. Male slaves with authority in the field constituted the male groups most likely to be in the household with women and children. Athough 'co-residence of a mate was conducive, though not essential, to relatively high fertility', colored females were significantly more fertile than black women. The Colored population of Jamaica was only about 10 per cent in 1832, yet colored births constituted 18 per cent of registered slave births from 1829–32. Among 15–19 year olds, the fertility of colored women was five times that of blacks (Higman, 1976a: 154). Higman concludes that the Colored woman, with a higher status occupation and economic security through her likely links to a white man, was more willing to bear children than was the black woman.

> Thus, because of the essential economic impotence of the slave, the normal relationship between social status and fertility was reversed. The slave woman of colour and status was therefore more prepared to expose herself to the risk of pregnancy than was the black woman (1976a: 155).

There is no direct evidence that colored women were more fertile because they did not work in the fields. On the other hand, that domestic workers produced more children than field workers on the three plantations studied by Higman is consistent with our hypothesis of a tension between female agricultural work and reproduction. Moreover, Jamaican planters did make some efforts to encourage breeding. By the 1820s, planters exempted women from field work as soon as pregnancy was suspected. After birth, women were permitted to remain in the second gang for as long as they nursed their children, which could be two years (Higman, 1976a: 206–07).[7]

Higman presents some evidence that production did intensify on Jamaican plantations during the 1830s. Although supposedly less productive slaves (i.e., women and teenagers) were now used in the fields, productivity remained fairly consistent from 1800 to 1834. 'Productivity declined less rapidly than the slave population and even more slowly than gross output' (1976a: 213). On the other hand, where slave women were fertile, productivity fell — a relationship supporting our hypothesis. 'The more the slaves were able to maintain and augment their numbers the lower their productivity' (1976a: 221). Higman hypothesizes further that manumissions fell and slave rights were eroded as masters faced labor shortages. Jamaican slaves were tied increasingly to plantation sugar production. Probably 90 per cent were on agricultural units in the 1830s; even in 1834, more than 70 per cent of the active slave labor force was field labor (1976a: 36–42).

Craton's (1977) findings for Worthy Park echo Higman's. Worthy Park was one of the largest and best managed of Jamaica's sugar estates, one of twelve with more than 500 slaves in 1820. With the abolition of the slave trade in 1808, the number of slaves at Worthy Park fell, and with it the profits from sugar production declined. The demographic profile of the field gangs also changed. Women were relied upon increasingly for field labor, with males making up 92.4 per cent of the work force for skilled occupations. In the 1790s women made up 58 per cent of the field labor force; and 65 per cent in the 1830s. Craton comments, 'It was indeed a curious society, as well as an inefficient agricultural economy, in which women for the most part were the laborers and men the specialist workers' (1977: 146).

Efforts to ameliorate slaves' lives eased the natural decrease of slaves at Worthy Park, but the birth rate remained less than the death rate. Planters tried to intensify production in response to falling sugar prices. Productivity actually fell with the 'increasing frailty of the slave labor force', but so did the number of slaves at Worthy Park (Craton, 1977: 172).

The effect of amelioration on overall fertility in Jamaica cannot be assessed accurately. Roberts (1957) speculates that Jamaica's rate of natural decrease fell from a higher, although unspecified, rate in the 1700s to about 5 per 1,000 slaves annually in 1829. Given a close ratio of sexes and a fairly young population, it is likely that a rise in fertility accounts for much of the fall in natural decrease (1957: 245). Roberts notes, however, that planters reported disappointment in the results of their amelioration programs. M. G. Lewis, for example, complained that after his various efforts in the early 1800s to improve the birth rate on his estates, there was little change. No more than 12 or 13 new babies were born of 330 slaves annually (Lewis, 1834: 320). Registration figures (Appendix) indicate little change in the birth rate, despite the improved sex ratio, but an increase in slave deaths.

The last great sugar island, Cuba, reached its peak well after the abolition of the slave trade and, thus, with Jamaica, suffered dramatic consequences of labor shortage. Seventeenth- and early eighteenth-century Cuba had been only a modest sugar producer; tobacco was the main Cuban export crop. From 1762 to 1838, a transition to large-scale sugar production was completed (Knight, 1970: 6). During that period, 400,000 slaves were imported to Cuba; the slave population increased from nearly 39,000 in 1774 to well over 400,000 in 1841 (1970: 21).

As Cuban sugar production intensified, male slaves were favored; many estates had exclusively male labor force. Half the population was aged from 16 to 25, the rest from 26 to 40 (Moreno Fraginals, 1978: 39). This highly productive demographic profile changed when the slave trade was abolished and as the Spanish metropolitan government urged the importation of African women to curtail the perceived violence and homosexuality of the heavy male slave population. With the new techniques of sugar production adopted in Cuba, women and children could be employed more productively than ever before in sugar agriculture. From 1850, about 45 per cent of African slaves imported to Cuba were women, and nearly all worked in some phase of sugar production, with virtually no mobility to more skilled positions. Moreno Fraginals contends that productivity per capita dropped as the sex ratio equalized, but indicates also that productivity levels demanded of Cuban women slaves surpassed those of other Caribbean slave societies.

As slaves became more difficult to procure, planters attempted to encourage the reproduction of slaves. Nuclear families were rare, Moreno Fraginals tells us, because couples were so often broken up for slaves; mothers and children constituted the basic kinship unit. Some planters encouraged monogamy to increase the birth rate. Several slave breeding farms were established. But the housing of slaves in barracks on many plantations, the related eradication of garden plots to supplement plantation rations, and the supervision of children in plantation nurseries all inhibited nuclear family formation. Nor were many births effected through planters' coercion. Pregnant women received few rewards for giving birth until the 1860s and 1870s, when they were permitted to work only ten house a day and received prizes for children who survived to two years (Moreno Fraginals, 1978: 43–57).

Amelioration efforts of the mid-nineteenth century did reduce slave mortality, especially among infants, and reproduction rates increased. The overall mortality of Cuban slaves from 1835 to 1841 was 63 per 1,000 population, falling to 61 per 1,000 from 1856 to 1860; infant mortality fell from 575 per 1,000 annually to 283 per 1,000 for the same periods. The natural decrease of population improved only slightly from a loss of 44 per 1,000 population annually from 1835 to 1841 to a loss of 33 per 1,000 from 1856 to 1860 (Moreno Fraginals, 1978: 88). From 1860 to 1880, and the emancipation of Cuban slaves, amelioraton measures increased. Still numbers continued to decline through natural decrease and manumissions. In 1883, there were somewhat fewer than 100,000 slaves registered in Cuba.

The Cuban and Jamaican cases offer the same mixed results as those of Barbados and Martinique. Cuban and Jamaican planters used more women than men in agricultural production, with few alternatives or avenues for mobility; these tendencies are not significantly greater for Jamaica and Cuba than for Barbados and Martinique. It appears, however, that women were under more pressure to maintain high labor productivity in Cuba and Jamaica than in Barbados and Martinique. In neither Jamaica nor Cuba were even low levels of natural increase achieved. As for Martinique and Barbados, family patterns are not related to reproduction in the expected way for either Jamaica or Cuba. Nuclear families were common, if not prevalent, in Jamaica, but nearly non-existent in Cuba. The Cuban case, perhaps along with Barbados, confirms the hypothesized relationships between labor supply and family formation, whereas neither Jamaica nor Martinique does so.[8]

Summary and Conclusions

The two major hypotheses examined are these:

Hypothesis 1: At times of labour shortage, West Indian slave women

- (a) were employed in larger numbers than male slaves in field labor;
- (b) lived mainly by themselves or with children;
- (c) produced relatively few children, resulting in a crude birth rate of less than 30 per 1,000.

Hypothesis 2: At times of adequate labor supply, West Indian slave women

- (a) were employed in field labor in the same numbers as males, or less frequently;
- (b) lived mainly in nuclear families;
- (c) produced relatively large number of children, resulting in a crude birth rate of 30 or more children per 1,000 population.

The cases of labor shortage were late eighteenth-century/early nineteenth-century Barbados, Martinique, Jamaica, and Cuba. The results of my analysis of these cases are presented schematically in Table 4.

All four societies utilized women increasingly in field work as male slaves became scarce. It appears that only slightly larger proportions of the female work force worked in agriculture in Jamaica and Cuba than in Martinique and Barbados. But high levels of labor productivity were probably achieved by women in Jamaica and Cuba. Only Cuba and perhaps Barbados conform to our hypothesis about family patterns. Jamaica and Martinique exhibited higher levels of nuclear family formation than mother–child and single female units. Extensive provision grounds in Jamaica and Martinique

Table 4 Results for Hypothesis 1

	(a) Women outnumber men in fields	(b) Mother–child unit predominates	(c) Crude birth rate is low
Barbados	yes	?	no
Martinique	yes	no	yes
Jamaica	yes	no	yes
Cuba	yes	yes	yes

Table 5 Results for Hypothesis 2

	(a) Women employed equally or less frequently than men in fields	(b) Nuclear families predominate	(c) Crude birth rate is high
Bahamas	yes	yes	yes
Leewards			
Antigua	yes	no	no
Montserrat	yes	no	yes
St. Kitts	yes	no	no
Nevis	yes	no	no

may thus have mitigated the effects of labor shortage on family organization.[9] Reproduction patterns conform more closely to our hypothesis for all societies, although emphasis on amelioration caused dramatic increases in slaves' crude birth rate in Barbados. Nuclear family formation did little to increase reproduction at the aggregate level; amelioration contributed to increased birth rates more powerfully than did nuclear family formation.

The findings related to Hypothesis 2 are presented in Table 5. For the Bahamas and the Leewards, women performed agricultural work as much as or less often than men. In the Bahamas, an adequate labor supply is related to nuclear family formation and increasing birth rate, as predicted. The relationship is not especially strong, however, given that the crude birth rate reached little more than 30 per 1,000 only after 1825. For the Leewards, adequate supplies of labor did not lead to the creation of nuclear families. Only in Montserrat is a crude birth rate over 30 per 1,000 recorded for the early nineteenth century. These cases suggest that labor supply per se does not explain the birth rate of West Indian slaves, and neither does family organization.

This investigation of several West Indian cases suggests that labor shortages did draw women into the most rigorous forms of field labor as the abolition of the slave trade approached. Women's presence in agricultural work seems not to have precluded nuclear family formation in Jamaica and Martinique. Women's agricultural work does seem to have discouraged reproduction in the absence of strenuous amelioration efforts such as those of Barbados in the early 1800s. However, labor supply did not strongly encourage reproduction, as the cases of the Bahamas and Leewards demonstrate.

Theories that unite production and reproduction assume individual or familial incentives for both (Goody, 1976; Boserup, 1970; Blumberg, 1970). In slavery, owners obtained maximum benefits by slaves' reproduction, but had little direct interest in family formation. It may be that in Caribbean slavery family formation related directly to slaves' self-interest, particularly where provision gardening was possible. On the other hand, children may have brought little joy or comfort to Caribbean slaves,[10] given the conditions of life — more difficult than those of more fertile U.S. slaves — and thus reproduction depended on strenuous planter efforts at amelioration.

References

Bennett, J. Harry, Jr. *Bondsmen and Bishops: Slavery and Apprenticeship on the Codrington Plantations of Barbados, 1710–1838* (Berkeley, 1958).

Blumberg, Rae Lesser. *Stratification: Socioeconomic and Sexual Inequality* (Dubuque, IA, 1977).

Boserup, Ester. *The Role of Women in Economic Development* (New York, 1970).

Craton, Michael. *Searching for the Invisible Man: Slaves and Plantation Life in Jamaica*. Cambridge (MA, 1977).

Craton, Michael. 'Hobbesian or Panglossian? The Two Extremes of Slave Conditions in the British Caribbean, 1783–1834', *William and Mary Quarterly*, XXXV, 2 (April 1978), 324–56.

Craton, Michael. 'Changing Patterns of Slave Families in the British West Indies', *Journal of Interdisciplinary History*, X, 1, (Summer 1979), 1–35.

Curtin, Philip. *The Atlantic Slave Trade* (Madison, 1969).

Debien, Gabriel. *Destinées d'esclaves à la Martinique, 1746–1778* (Dakar, 1960).

Dirks, Robert. 'Resource Fluctuations and Competitive Transformation in West Indian Slave Societies,' in C. D. Laughlin, Jr. & Ivan A. Brady (Eds), *Extinction and Survival in Human Populations* (New York, 1978), 122–180.

Fogel, R. W. & Engerman, S. L. *Time on the Cross* (Boston, 1974).

Fraginals, Manuel Moreno. *El Ingenio: Complejo Econmico Social Cubano del Azúcar* (Havana, 1978).

Genovese, Eugene, D. *Roll, Jordan, Roll* (New York, 1976).

Goody, Jack. *Production and Reproduction* (Cambridge, 1976).

Goveia, Elsa V. *Slave Society in the British Leeward Islands at the End of the Eighteenth Century* (New Haven, CT, 1965).

Gutman, Herbert. *The Black Family in Slavery and Freedom, 1750–1925* (New York, 1977).

Higman, Barry W. *Slave Population and Economy in Jamaica, 1807–1834* (Cambridge, 1976a).

Higman, Barry W. 'The Slave Population of the British Caribbean: Some Nineteenth Century Variations', in Samuel Proctor (ed.), *Eighteenth Century Florida and the Caribbean* (Gainesville, 1976b), 60–70.

Higman, Barry W. 'African and Creole Slave Family Patterns in Trinidad', *Journal of Family History*, III, 2 (Summmer, 1978), 163–80.

Higman, Barry W. 'African and Creole Family Patterns in Trinidad', in Margaret E. Crahan & Franklin W. Knight (Eds), *Africa and the Caribbean: The Legacy of a Link* (Baltimore, 1979), 41–64.

Klein, Herbert S. & Engerman, Stanley, L. 'Fertility Differentials Between Slaves in the United States and the British West Indies: A Note on Lactation Practices', *William and Mary Quarterly*, XXXV, 2 (April, 1978), 257–74.

Knight, Franklin W. *Slave Society in Cuba During the Nineteenth Century* (Madison, 1970).

Lewis, Gordon K. *The Growth of the Modern West Indies* (New York, 1968).

Lewis, Matthew Gregory. *Journal of a West Indian Proprietor* (London, 1834).

Mathieson, William Law. *British Slavery and Its Abolition* (London, 1926).

Patterson, Orlando. *The Sociology of Slavery* (Rutherford, NJ, 1969).

Patterson, Orlando. 'From Endo-Deme to Matri-Deme: An Interpretation of the Development of Kinship and Social Organization Among the Slaves of Jamaica, 1655–1830,' in Samuel Proctor (Ed.), *Eighteenth Century Florida and the Caribbean* (Gainesville, 1976), 50–59.

Patterson, Orlando. 'On Slavery and Slave Formations', *New Left Review*, No. 117 (September, 1979), 31–67.

Patterson, Orlando. 'Persistance, Continuity and Change in the Jamaican Working-Class Family', *Journal of Family History*, VII, 2 (Summer, 1982), 135–61.

Quick, Paddy. 'The Class Nature of Women's Oppression', *Review of Radical Political Economics*, IX, 3 (Fall, 1977), 42–53.

Roberts, G. W. *The Population of Jamaica* (Cambridge, 1957).

Sheridan, Richard B. *Sugar and Slavery* (Baltimore, 1973).

Stampp, Kenneth M. *The Peculiar Institution* (New York, 1956).

Sturge, Joseph & Harvey, Thomas. *The West Indies in 1837* (London, 1938).

Tomich, Dale. 'Prelude to Emancipation: Sugar and Slavery in Martinique, 1830–1848', unpubl. Ph.D. diss., Univ. of Wisconsin (1976).

Watson, Karl Steward. 'The Civilised Island, Barbados', unpubl. Ph.D. diss., Gainesville, Univ. of Florida (1975).

Notes

1. The criterion based on crude birth rates during the early nineteenth century. Klein and Eagerman (1978) report that the birth rate among U.S. slaves was 55 per cent 1,000, considered high for mid-nineteenth-century populations in general. Jamaica's low crude birth rate of 23 per 1,000 from 1817 to 1829 is comparable to European birth rates during the same period.
2. Craton (1978) compares the Rolle estate in Grand Exuma in the Bahamas with Jamaica's Worthy Park, and considers many factors important in the higher rates of fertility and nuclear family formation found in the Bahamas. Included among them are the closer sex ratio, the small number of Africans, and a favorable age distribution. He concludes, however, 'The essential differences between the two populations clearly lay in the nature of the economic system in which each was employed. Worthy Park's system was the "factory-in-a-field" of sugar production, while Exuma's was an almost decayed open plantation system with a negligible "industrial" component' (1978: 349).
3. Higman (1976: 65–66) contends that Caribbean slave populations increased their birth rates as the Creole population increased and the sex ratio became more even. 'Thus in the sugar colonies it appears that natural increases did not occur until the populations were disproportionately female' (1976: 66–67). Eventually, feminization, 'aging and wasting' of the population occurred (Craton, 1978), causing a decline in fertility. Sex ratios were similar in St. Kitts, Nevis, Montserrat, and Antigua, and related to an increasing birth rate, but in a strong way only in Montserrat.
4. Martinique was long attractive to France's rival metropoles. English and Dutch attacks had been repulsed in the seventeenth century. The English again tried but failed to capture Martinique in 1759; a British seige succeeded in 1762, but the island was returned to the French by the Treaty of Paris in 1763. The French Revolution threatened Martinique's sugar planters, with talk of rights for black slaves and the free colored population. The French Revolutionary government abolished slavery in 1790, and Martinique's and Guadeloupe's elites surrendered themselves to Britian in 1794. With access to British markets, Martinique once again prospered, until 1802, when Martinique was returned again to France by the terms of the Treaty of Amiens. The British seized Martinique again in 1809, permanently restoring the island to France in 1814. In the meantime, Napoleon had made slavery legal once again.
5. All translations are mine.
6. Debien comments that on the more intensely cultivated Saint-Domingue, there were fewer than two or three families per plantation at any time. The birth rate was also very low.
7. To permit women to nurse their children for two years ran counter to the planters' desire to increase labor productivity. Nursing took women from the fields altogether or removed them to lighter tasks they could complete while breastfeeding a child. Still, planters perceived nursing as a necessary incentive to increase women's fertility, and some associated it with infant health and development — major issues in societies with high infant and child death rates.
8. There is considerable evidence that nuclear families did have more children than other family forms, at the plantation level. At Montpelier, analyzed by Higman (1976a), and L'Anse-à-L'Ane, studied by Debien, nuclear families had more children than did other families. Craton (1978) made the same discovery about slaves at the Rolle estate in the Bahamas.
9. Food allocations and distribution may hold the key to the small population increments and possible propensity for mother–child units in the Leewards. These islands had little non-estate land, although slaves received a small provision garden near their huts to supplement estate-grown and imported provisions. Frequent drought affected ground provisions more than

it did sugar (Mathieson, 1926; 72; Sturge & Harvey, 1838). Rations allotted to slaves were small, 'much less, indeed, than was given in the prisons in Jamaica' (Mathieson, 1926: 72). Slaves in the Leewards may have lacked both the material basis in extensive and productive provision-gardening for the formation of residential conjugal units and the health and welfare conducive to rapid population growth (see also Dirks, 1978).

10. We have no way of knowing how many children were conceived by Caribbean slaves, but were miscarried or stillborn. Craton (1978: 343) reports that 21.8% of 'births' among females at Worthy Park in 1795 were said to be miscarriages in plantation records.

Appendix Basic Demographic Indices, Early Nineteenth-Century Bahamas, Montserrat, Antigua, Nevis, St. Christopher, Barbados, and Jamaica

	Date	Total slave populations	Males per 100 females	Births per 1,000	Deaths per 1,000	Natural increases per 1,000
Bahamas	1819–22	10,908	104.6	—	—	—
	1822–25	10,036	103.3	26.9	14.2	12.7
	1825–28	9,266	100.2	31.0	14.9	16.1
Leewards						
Montserrat						
	1817–21	6,558	86.4	31.0	30.4	0.6
	1821–24	6,392	86.0	31.4	32.0	−0.6
	1824–27	6,270	84.6	34.1	28.1	6.0
St. Christopher (St. Kitts)						
	1817–21	19,993	92.3	25.2	28.4	−3.2
	1821–25	19,667	91.9	28.2	29.3	−0.8
	1825–28	19,413	91.2	29.3	27.5	1.8
	1828–31	19,198	91.5	28.3	26.3	2.0
Antigua						
	1817–21	31,627	87.4	18.5	22.8	−4.3
	1821–24	30,650	87.9	27.1	27.6	−0.5
	1824–27	30,077	88.8	25.5	25.2	0.3
Nevis						
	1817–22	9,432	96.6	22.5	25.9	−3.4
	1822–25	9,274	97.9	23.9	24.9	−1.0
	1825–28	9,273	97.7	22.9	22.6	0.3
	1828–31	9,201	97.8	23.3	24.6	−1.3
Barbados						
	1817–20	77,919	86.1	31.7	28.3	3.4
	1820–23	78,581	86.5	34.9	28.5	6.4
	1823–26	79,684	84.9	40.2	28.1	12.1
	1826–29	81,227	85.1	38.0	28.0	10.0
	1829–32	81,701	85.8	40.7	30.6	10.1
Jamaica						
	1817–20	334,266	99.7	23.6	24.3	−0.7
	1820–23	339,318	98.7	22.8	25.9	−3.1
	1823–26	333,686	97.4	23.0	25.1	−2.1
	1826–29	326,770	96.5	22.2	25.6	−3.4
	1829–32	317,649	95.5	23.2	28.0	−4.8

Source: Higman (1976b:67–69).

SECTION EIGHT
Social Culture and Autonomy

The relations between African cultural and ideological world views and those of their European overlords within the Caribbean environment, have produced a vibrant and facinating literature. Issues surrounding the degree of cultural retention, adaptation of slavery, especially from the perspective of the historian concenred with the nature of nativist consciousness, development and institutional formation. Lamur and Schuler address the important issue of the dynamics of cultural interaction within the social theatre of religious formation and evolution.

The ways in which slaves pursued the right to be autonomous, economic agents, as part of the legitimate use of their 'leisure' times are also major concerns. The culture of marketing emerged as a common expression, and material and social conditions on the plantations as well as in the towns made it particularly attractive for several reasons; it allowed slaves to improve the quality and quantity of their diets in a context of general malnutrition, to own and possess property in a system that also defined them as property, and it allowed them time to travel, and to attempt to 'normalize' their social lives as much as possible under the generally restrictive circumstances. These benefits, however, had to be pursued, and it is here that women, in particular, displayed great tenacity. Marketing symbolized a spirit of independence, and was central to the process of non-violent protest and resistance which characterized day-to-day anti-slavery behaviour.

Slave Religion on the Vossenburg Plantation (Suriname) and Missionaries' Reaction

HUMPHREY E. LAMUR.

In the course of years much has been published on both the religion of slave populations and the proselytizing of the descendants of slaves in the Caribbean and in the United States. Among the recent publications are Simpson (1982) on Haiti, Jamaica, Trinidad; Bilby (1981) on Jamaica; Thoden van Velzen and Van Wetering (1982, 1983) and Wooding (1972) on Suriname. There also exist numerous publications dealing with Afro-Caribbean religions in the Danish and Spanish Caribbean and Brazil.

However, very little is known about the religion of slaves in the Western hemisphere and their proselytizing. In particular, in the seventeenth and eighteenth centuries, the planters were opposed to the conversion of slaves to Christianity for fear that religious instruction would automatically lead to manumission. Only after the mid-eighteenth century had the proselytizing of slaves started, but not even in all slave societies. In most Caribbean slave societies missionary activities began around 1850 (Genovese 1976, 185; Jackson 1931, 168–239; Lamur 1984; Oldendorp 1770; Olwig 1985; Rooke 1979). Most of the available information on this subject concerns primarily the slave population in the American state Virginia. Thus, most of the comparison

Resistance and Rebellion in Suriname: Old and New, Studies in Third World Societies, No. 43, College of William and Mary, pp. 103–17.

which follows will be with this slave society. In the remainder of this paper I shall present a brief overview of the achievements of missionary activities among the slave population in Virginia. In doing so I shall rely on Genovese (1976, 183–209) and Jackson (1931, 168–239). Subsequently, some remarks will be made on the religious beliefs of the slave population on the sugar estate Vossenburg. This is followed by a discussion of the Protestant missionaries' efforts to convert the slaves of this plantation to Christianity.

Black Conversion in Virginia

The history of Christianity of the slave population in Virginia can be divided into three periods, namely 1750–90, 1790–1830, and 1830–60 (Genovese 1976; Jackson 1931). One of the criteria used by the authors to distinguish these periods is the missionaries' attitude toward slavery. In the period 1750–90, the Baptists and Methodists 'expressed hostility towards slavery and a hope that it would vanish'. They argued that the slaves were brothers in Christ. During the period 1790–1830, antislavery attitudes in the churches began to decline under pressure by the slaveowners. The Nat Turner uprising in 1822 meant a turning point in the history of black Christianity in Virginia and ushered in the third phase. 'Whereas previously many slaveholders had feared slaves with religion — and the example of Turner confirmed their fears — now they feared slaves without religion even more.' Hence they began to accept Christianity as a means of social control. In response (Genovese 1976, 186–87), 'several churches embraced the pro-slavery argument. They won the trust of the masters and freed themselves to preach the gospel to the slaves.' However, the slaveowners remained reluctant to the missionaries' wish to teach the slaves to read and write. How did the slave population in Virginia respond to the new efforts of the preachers after 1822 to convert them? It seems that the missionaries failed in eliminating the remnants of African religion of the slaves. Genovese (1976, 184) claims that 'the conditions of their new social life forced them to combine their African inheritance with the dominant power they confronted and to shape a religion of their own'. He examines a number of sources which support this statement. One is Jones, a Presbyterian missionary who preached the gospel to the slaves in Georgia around 1840. Genovese quotes him as saying that the slaves still believed in 'second-sight, apparitions, charms, witchcraft, and in a kind of irresistible Satanic influence' (see also Jones 1847, 127–28). A second source, Hundley (1860, 328–29, cited in Genovese) was a slaveowner. Around 1860 he claimed that the slaves still believed in 'witchcraft, sorcery, conjuring and other forms of paganism'. About the same time, another slaveowner, Eliza Andrews, described the attitudes of the slaves to Christianity as indifferent but not hostile. Several times she attended religious services for the slaves and noticed that they fell asleep through the sermons. Similar remarks on the retention of African religious elements by the slaves were also made by medical doctors who worked in the Southern States around the mid-nineteenth century. Among them were Carpenter (1844, 165), Cartwright (1857, 11), and Wilson (1860, 319). Thus, it may be concluded that the missionaries failed to fully eliminate the African beliefs of the slave population in Virginia. This finding of Genovese is consistent with the conclusion reached by Jernegan in the early twentieth century that the efforts to convert the slaves to Christianity were not successful.

Slave Religion on Vossenburg

Does the conclusion concerning black Christianity in Virginia in the period prior to 1860 hold also for the slave population at Vossenburg, a sugar estate in Suriname? I have chosen this plantation for the following reason. To date, it is the only plantation in Suriname for which the material on missionaries' activities has been analyzed in relation to other aspects of plantation life.

In the late seventeenth and early eighteenth centuries Vossenburg was owned by Adriaan de Graff. It covered 3,000 acres and was situated on the Commewijne river in the coastal area of Suriname. In 1705, the number of slaves amounted to 92, and increased to 196 in 1747. A few years before the abolition of slavery in 1863 the slave force had increased to 240.

As said before, I shall first present some information on the religious beliefs of the slave population at Vossenburg, and then discuss both the missionaries' efforts to convert the slaves to Christianity and the slaves' response to these endeavors. Both the missionaries' account and the oral histories of informants that I collected in the period 1980–82 and thereafter were used to gain an insight into the religion of the slave population at Vossenburg. The information, though fragmentary, shows that the system of belief of the slaves at Vossenburg consisted of the following elements:

- A Supreme being and lower Gods
- Priests and mediums of lower Gods
- Religious objects
- Rituals

Adangra was the name by which the slaves denoted their God. The available information does not reveal in what respect the Gods affected the life of the slaves. The main religious objects were a wooden image of a God used for group worship and some small icons kept in each house for private use. Among the functionaries who played an important role in religious ceremonies were the priest and the obeahman (*lukuman*). In addition there was also the witchdoctor (*wissiman*) who affected the life of the slaves, although he cannot be considered as a religious functionary. The priests were in charge of leading the services intended to worship the God. The primary task of the obeahmen was to divine the cause of sickness or death of fellow slaves. In particular they tried to deduce whether sickness/death was of a supernatural origin for which a human being was to blame, or whether a natural cause was involved. Obeahmen also prescribed medicines for illness. These tasks were performed at the request of the interested party. The obeahman rarely acted on his own initiative. While the obeahman was seen by the slaves as a benefactor, the witchdoctor was perceived as antisocial. The latter was thought to cause illness and death, and acted both at the request of others and on his own initiative. This is a summary of the system of belief of the slave population at Vossenburg which the Moravian Mission confronted when it started its activities on 27 December 1847.

The aim of the Moravian Brotherhood Mission was to convert the slaves to Christianity, and at the same time to eliminate the religion of the slave population since it was considered inconsistent with Christianity. Did the Moravian preachers succeed in this? To answer this question I shall discuss a number of cases of conflicts between the slaves and the missionaries which took place in the period of 1847–77, i.e. the last year for which archival material is available on missionary accounts at Vossenburg.

Conversion of Slaves on Vossenburg

The missionaries visited Vossenburg every six weeks. They arrived on Saturdays and stayed with the director of Vossenburg. The next day, on Sunday, they held two religious services, one in the morning, the other in the evening. The sermons took place in the engineer's or the carpenter's shed. In addition, the missionaries gave religious instruction (catechism) and they baptized both children and adults. In addition, they visited the sick, the needy, and the older people.

One of the problems in analyzing the missionary accounts on the conversion of the slaves at Vossenburg was the question what different missionaries meant by conversion and what religious tactics they applied. Further, it was of importance to know whether the notions held by the missionaries on conversion had changed in the course of years between 1847 and 1877. Unfortunately, it was not possible to find a satisfactory answer to these questions. Yet, to give an impression of the notions of conversion held by the missionaries, I will report two events. In 1861 an epidemic broke out which claimed many victims among the slave population. The missionary saw it as a punishment by God and assumed that the slaves shared his view: 'For the first time ... the Negroes were quiet and attentive, ... The Lord had addressed them seriously, ... ' The next event: a slave who had been excommunicated by the missionary, was later, on his death, 'buried as a pagan'. The missionary claimed that this made a strong impression on another slave, a sick one who had also been excommunicated. The slave showed repentance and asked the missionary to be readmitted to the church. This led the missionary to report that 'God's Spirit has touched his heart'. This case is also interesting because it reveals what religious tactics the missionary used to convert this penitent. He told him that the slave who had beeen buried earlier as a 'pagan' was 'now standing before God's judgement seat' to be punished for his 'idolatry'. Having told the penitent all this, he was proposed to be readmitted as a member of the church, but only on the condition that he would 'publicly in the church in front of the whole idolatrous slave force express his repentance for his wrongdoing'. The slave did so, as the missionary informed us in his monthly report. Let me repeat that this case only shows how that particular missionary went about converting the slaves. Thus, I am not suggesting that this event was representative of the religious tactics applied by other missionaries who worked at Vossenburg between 1847 and 1877, because of the lack of more information on this subject.

J. G. F. Jansa, the first Moravian missionary to preach the gospel to the slaves at Vossenburg, started his work on 28 December 1847. Before doing so he asked the slaves who were gathered if they were in favor of his work. A driver backed by a small group of slaves answered, 'No, we do not want it.' However, the majority reacted favourably. Thus Jansa soon realized that he would face a difficult task among a group which he described as the most superstitious of all slave populations in Suriname. Their God which is the biggest of its kind in this country was called *Andranga* or the 'most secret'. This remark is correct. The cult of the slaves at Vossenburg was apparently so important that the place of worship in the bush where the icon of the Supreme God was located was also attended by slaves from the nearby plantations, namely Breukelerwaard, Fairfield, Fortuin, and Schoonoord. These were plantations where the Moravian Mission had started their activities some years earlier. In 1847 a new wooden image of the God, five feet in height, was built to replace an older one which had rotted. The new one was placed standing in a hut with a roof of leaves, while the old one was placed to the side near the new image. This altar where the God was worshipped was located at a distance of one hour walking from the center of the plantation.

It was at the place of worship, on 16 July 1849, that the first serious confrontation between the missionary Jansa and the slaves took place on. That morning, following the religious service in the converted prayer house, Jansa was invited by a mulatto slave to destroy their God in the bush. The missionary accepted the invitation and in the afternoon went to the slaves' place of worship accompanied by a few slaves, among whom was one of the drivers. Jansa proceeded to destroy the hut and seized the religious images. Subsequently, they returned to the center of the plantation, where the missionary asked the slaves if they had any more religious objects in their huts. The head driver, a slave priest, responded in slave creole that the icons would be delivered to the missionary the next day: 'they will be available tomorrow' ('*Tamara sa de*'). But the missionary insisted and the slaves handed over the objects to the missionary on the spot. Then the missionary went into the huts to see for himself if the slaves had hidden more of the icons.

The news that the missionary had dared to destroy the altar astonished director Uhlenkamp of Vossenburg. He noticed that of old the slaves of this sugar estate were known as 'idolatrous'. Why had the slaves invited the missionary to the center of their religious activities? Is this event a sign that the slaves had deserted their own African beliefs? I do not think so, because the slaves still defended their own religion against criticism by the missionary, as the following event shows. During a service in the prayer house on 26 October 1849 the missionary depicted the slaves as stupid because they worshipped their own God. This remark annoyed the slaves. A driver, who probably acted as spokesman of the group, responded that the missionary should control himself. He did so by using the following rhetorical question, in creole: 'If you are living among the negroes, you have to speak their language.' A more reasonable explanation for the slaves' willingness to destroy their own religious objects is to perceive this behavior as an act of iconoclasm. The replacement of old relics by a new one had probably occurred in the past. Thus, the incident in 1849 was not intended by the slaves as a rejection of their religion as such, but rather as a destruction of the religious objects they had in use at that time. In my view the missionary's demand was only a cause for the slaves to do what they had done periodically in the past.

Similar events have recently occurred in West Africa. This is clear from an analysis of the anti-witchcraft movement among the Bashilele (le Mupele); here too relics were destroyed (Ngokwey 1978).

There is another possible explanation for the slaves' willingness to hand over their religious objects to the missionary. Their behavior can also be judged as a gesture of goodwill in return for the missionaries' readiness to accept them as equals. Whatever explanation is correct, the destruction of the religious objects did not mean that the slaves had lapsed from their own African beliefs. This is clear from the following case. On Sunday morning 22 May 1850 a conflict broke out between the director of the plantation, Uhlenkamp, and the slaves. They declined an order by the director to work on that day because Sundays were usually a day off. Some time later, during the sermon in the prayer house, the missionary tried to persuade the slaves to obey the director and to carry out his orders after the service. The slaves rejected the missionary's plea and made clear that they had already made numerous sacrifices for the church. They reminded him that his predecessor, the missionary Jansa, had taken away their beloved religious objects a year ago. They also threatened to reclaim all this if they did not get the whole Sunday off to attend the church meeting. From this incident it is also clear that the slaves began to see the missionary as an appendage of the director and they resented it.

The following event also shows that the introduction of Christianity in 1847 had not resulted in a full surrender to Christian ideas. On 20 November 1853, the slave woman Dina went to the missionary to inform him that she no longer wanted to live together with the slave October. The latter did not let it pass and a few hours later, after the sermon, he also made his way to the missionary to give his version of their matrimonial problems. Dina was ill which led her sister Paulina to consult an obeahman. The latter consulted the gods and then concluded that Dina's sickness was of a supernatural origin, for which October was to be blamed. This, October claimed, was the real motive for Dina to leave him, despite his humble appeal not to do so.

Another indication that the slaves still defended their own belief, concerns the so called '*kwa kwa banji*', small benches, which the missionary considered one of the slaves' religious objects. When the issue was first raised on 11 August 1857, the slaves responded with reserve. They were reluctant to discuss the subject and they only admitted that a certain man named Staars was 'the father of the seats'. Staars, at that time living as a free black at the nearby plantation of Fairfield, was a slave at Vossenburg before his manumission. One month later, on 25 September 1857, the 'religious' seats were a cause of a dispute again, when the missionary discovered three of them in the prayer house during the service. Moreover he learned that many converted slaves owned these seats and used them as drums at their religious dances. At that sermon, another driver was one of the slaves who had brought his seat to the prayer house. In a discussion with the missionary that followed he denied that the seats were used as objects of worship and thus he refused to put away his bench. Following the dispute the missionary explained that it was sinful to possess the seats. However, the slaves did not share that view and were determined not to give in. The missionary went to the director and the white overseer to discuss the conflict. On his return to the prayer house he told the slaves that he had decided to postpone the ceremony of baptism to his next visit on 9 November 1857. Probably, he expected that the slaves would change their minds after some time. At this next visit he made a third effort to persuade them to dispose of the seats. However, he failed again.

Two years later another incident occurred which reveals that even baptized slaves had not fully accepted Christian ideas. In 1859 the slave Hiob Hermanses complained that his sickness was of a supernatural origin, for which he blamed Abraham Hermanus. The missionary was astonished to learn that Hermanses, who had only recently been baptized a Christian, still believed in what he described as witchcraft. As he saw it Hermanses had slid back into 'paganism'.

A major blow to the work of the Moravian Mission was the discovery by the missionary on 25 July 1860 that 22 converted male slaves had continued to hold religious meetings at their altar in the place of worship in the bush. He also learned that these slaves had built a new wooden image of their god. In addition he was informed that the slaves were performing *Pakasaka*, a religious ritual, in their huts. Apparently, on the same day that the missionary received the information on the new wooden image, it was agreed that the slaves would take the idol from the bush to the slave quarters to show it to the missionary at his next visit to Vossenburg. However, six weeks later, on 14 September 1860 on his arrival at the plantation, the missionary found that the icon was removed but not destroyed and probably installed in another place. He demanded that the image be delivered to him immediately, as missionary Jansa had done some 13 years ago. But this time the slaves refused to grant his request, despite his threat that a curse would rest on them as long as their god was among them. The missionary also decided not to baptize new candidates at that time. It seems that this incident had depressed the missionary. He considered it as a sign of the influence of Satan but continued to believe that Jesus Christ would finally gain the victory.

Not long after this incident the missionary had to admit that he had not yet succeeded in converting the slaves to Christianity. On 22 October 1860 it came to his attention that a few slaves had taken part in a dance ritual near the sluice gate. When questioned, the slaves — all the 15 participants and 6 spectators — gave their names. Three of the fifteen participants, all of them converted males, promised to refrain from further participation. The remaining 12, none of them converted, refused to make such a promise. All of these, except one, were female slaves.

The small number of slaves who attended the services in the prayer house was also a disappointing experience for the Moravian

Mission. In 1861 this led the missionary to conclude that the devil had got the upper hand:

When I arrived at the prayer house for the afternoon service only 50 people were present. The others did not consider it worth attending the sermon, but preferred to pursue their pleasures instead . . . (Lamur 1984, 94)

Whether the small number of slaves that attended the services points to indifference rather than hostility toward Christianity is not clear.

On 1 July 1863, slavery was abolished in Suriname. The ex-slaves remained on Vossenburg as (semi-) free laborers and the Moravian Mission continued to preach the gospel to them. Did this change in the legal status of the slaves affect their relationship to the missionaries? To answer this question let us consider a few more cases. On Christmas Eve of the year 1863 a child died. According to former slave Leptonis, it was caused by a witchdoctor who had used supernatural means. Hence, Leptonis decided to find out which of his fellows was to blame for it. To do so, he took the corpse and, while carrying it on his head, walked along the huts in the old slave quarters in order to divine the cause of death. This case is interesting since it shows that witchdoctors were considered as antisocial individuals who should be punished. But more important is to note that the slaves' African-based religion still affected their behavior.

The slaves often spoke out openly in defending their religion against criticism from the missionaries. On 8 February 1869 a conflict arose between a few freedmen and the missionary. He had learned from Heering, who had succeeded Uhlenkamp as director, on 21 June 1864, that the ex-slaves were still holding the bench dance-rituals. When they were gathered the missionary demanded them to stop these activities. Samson Winston, a 29-year-old field hand who had been baptized on 1 September 1866, stepped forward in the direction of the missionary. Furiously he looked at the missionary and gave him to understand that he did not intend to grant this request and that the 'bench' had cost him a lot of money. 'I shall not stop playing, preacher. You can take against me whatever measure you like, the bench has cost me money,' he said in the Creole language. Consider also the following incident. On 22 April 1869, the missionary told the blacks during a service that he believed most of them were still worshipping their 'idols'. One of those present confirmed this on behalf of the audience by saying: 'Yes Sir, that is correct.'

A few months later on 19 August 1879, the missionary suffered another setback in his work. On that day he learned that the blacks were again 'worshipping the *Mamasneki*' (a serpent deity). A member of the church council, an ex-slave who was questioned by the missionary, said that he was unaware of it. 'If the snake finds himself in one of the houses, he certainly has got there on his own efforts', the member of the council added soberly. Then all began search for the snake and it was found in the garret of the prayer house. At the request of the missionary the reptile was killed and the Christian services could be started.

Even the blacks who were converted to Christianity did not accept all regulations imposed on them by the missionaries. On 14 July 1872 Markus Vreede Cornelius told the missionary that he was not prepared to pay more than 32 cents ('*drisren*') as financial contribution for the church. When the missionary told him that it was not enough, he became angry and threatened to pay nothing. The missionary in turn took a strong position and threatened to expel Cornelius as a member of the church if he did not reverse his decision.

The cases presented above reveal that the Moravian Mission made little progress in converting the slaves to Christianity at the sugar estate Vossenburg. Nor did the missionaries succeed in eliminating the African-based religion of the slave-population. Quite the opposite. The slaves retained their own system of beliefs and practiced their religion along with attending the religious services of the Mission.

While it is difficult to give a sufficient explanation of the retention of slave religion at Vossenburg, it may be concluded that the role played by the slave priests was an important factor. When the missionary Jansa introduced Christianity at Vossenburg in 1847, it was a black slave driver who opposed this effort. Two years later the missionary visited the place where the slaves worshipped their god. That time the head driver, who also was a slave priest, played a crucial role in the discussion with the missionary. Three months later the missionary criticized the slaves for what he described as their idolatrous way of life, and again it was a driver who admonished the missionary to control himself. On 2 July 1850, the missionary expelled a slave from the prayer house during a service, just because he did not like the remarks he made. It concerned the slaves' admiration for a driver. In one of the clashes in the prayer house over the benches ('*kwa kwa banji*') on 25

December 1857 the slave who declined the demand of the preacher to put away his bench was the second-driver. In 1864 Leptonis tried to uncover the witchdoctor who he thought to be responsible for the death of a child. While it was not possible to know the social position of Leptonis in the slave community, apparently he was one of the obeahmen, since it was they who were responsible for finding out the causes of sickness or death of fellow members in the community. Finally, the case of Samson Winst can be mentioned. He said that he did not care a bit about the missionary's demand to stop holding ritual dancings, Samson was a 29-year-old driver. In sum, in most of the recorded clashes or cases of deliberation with the missionary concerning the religion of the slaves, it was the drivers (acting at the same time as religious functionaries, priests or obeahmen) who were involved. They did so as spokesmen of the slave community or of a group of slaves.

The missionaries were aware of the fact that the drivers/priests had a great influence on the success or failure of the Moravian Mission. Consider the following case. On 24 February 1851 a driver expressed his wish to become a member of the Moravian church. When the missionary responded in astonishment to the slave's intentions, the latter assured him that he was serious. This incident led the missionary to write the following in his monthly report to the headquarters: 'If he becomes so faithful to the Saviour as he now is to the Devil, then he can be of great help to the Saviour's affair.'

Why was it in particular the drivers/priests who opposed the Moravian Mission and tried to retain their own religion? To answer this question it should be kept in mind that the religion of the slaves at Vossenburg emerged as a response to oppressive slavery conditions and, psychologically, it offered some protection against exploitation by the planters. However, the Moravian Mission considered the religion of the slaves as pagan and attempted to destroy it. In doing so the mission threatened the emotional support, the feelings of security, and group solidarity rendered to the slaves by their beliefs. No wonder the missionaries clashed with the drivers/priests who were looked upon by the fellow slaves as functionaries responsible for maintaining the slaves' religious system. There is another factor which helps to explain why the missionaries clashed with the slaves. Some missionaries interfered in the conflict between the slaves and the director of Vossenburg. Often they called on the slaves to obey the members of the dominant white group, the director, the overseers, the book-keeper, the artisans, and to carry out their orders. In some cases the missionaries made their appeal because they were fearful that the conflicts between the blacks and the whites would get out of control. But whatever the motives of the missionaries to interfere, by trying to inculcate in the slaves such virtues as patience, submission, and obedience, they hoped to contribute to maintaining the social order. The mere fact that they acted this way provoked resentment among the slaves and thus led them to depict the Moravian preachers as an appendage of the dominant white planter class. Thus, the slaves also saw the missionaries as preservers of the interests of the planter class.

How to explain the missionaries' attitudes in this respect? To answer this question we have to go back to the year 1734 when the Moravian Mission negotiated an agreement with the Society of Suriname. This governing board of Suriname represented the interests of the planter class. In this agreement the conditions were spelled out under which the society allowed the Moravian Mission to preach the gospel to the slaves in Suriname. To indicate what conditions were involved, let me quote a paragraph from the letter of agreement dated 7 December 1734:

> On 4 December I met again with the directors in the West Indian House, to have talks. They only asked me how I felt about the slaves. I replied that one should try to convert them, but at the same time to admonish them to be loyal and industrious and therefore not to long for freedom. However, to accept it with thanks when it is granted to them. They were satisfied with my answer (Lamur 1984, 112).

To fully understand this paragraph it should be kept in mind that cooperation between Christian churches and private Western organizations in the colonies was quite normal, in particular in the eighteenth and nineteenth centuries. In Suriname, for example, the Dutch Reformed Church held a similar view. One of its preachers, J. W. Kals, who lived in Suriname between 1731 and 1756, linked the need to preach the gospel and the importance of the mission to the planter class (Van der Linde 1987, 141–56).

The missionaries admitted that slavery conditions were harsh, but they considered slavery as a system that was imposed by God and that it should only be abolished by Him (on the slant of the Moravian Mission, see Van Raalte 1973, 113–25; Zeefuik 1973, 31–42; 138–52). This point of view held by the Moravian Mission led to inconsistency, contradiction, and a lack of clarity in the behavior of the missionaries who preached the gospel at Vossenburg and elsewhere in Suriname. One of the few missionaries who openly criticized his colleagues for interfering in conflicts in favor of the dominant white group is N. O. Tank, who lived in Suriname between 1846 and 1848. His view was that the missionaries were used 'to keep the negroes in subordination and under control, as if one had a presentiment that the whip would once prove insufficient' (Tank 1848, 24, 25).

Whether the missionaries who preached the gospel at Vossenburg thought that way is not clear to me. Ironically, they depised the morals of the dominant white group and saw them as godless and lapsed Christians.

Conclusion

In both slave societies, namely Virginia and Vossenburg, the missionaries failed to fully eliminate the African-based religion of the slave populations. In the case of Vossenburg the slave population apparently retained more elements of their religion than did the slaves in Virginia. At Vossenburg the missionaries started their activities much later compared with Virginia, as at Vossenburg the history of Christianity began in 1847, when major changes in the occupational structure of the slave population had already taken place. These changes include the emergence of a group of relatively privileged slaves. It was they who contributed most to the retention of the African-based religion of the slave group. As spokesmen of the slave community, these drivers/priests spoke out openly and defended the slaves' religion. Thus, I found no indication that Christianity rendered the slaves docile. However, neither did it lead them to rebel.

References

Bilby, K. M., 'The Kromanti dance of the Windward Maroons of Jamaica', *Nieuw West Indische Gids* (1981) 55.1.-2: 52–101.

Carpenter, W. M., 'Observations on the Cachexia Africana. New Orleans'. *Medical and Surgical Journal* (1844), 1: 146–65.

Cartwright, S. A., *Ethnology of the Negro or Prognathous Race* (New Orleans, 1857).

Earnest, J. B, *The Religious Development of the Negro in Virginia* (Charlottesville, Va, 1914).

Genovese, E. D., *Roll, Jordan Roll* (New York, 1976).

Hundley, D. R., *Social Relations in our Southern States* (New York, 1860).

Jackson, L. P., 'Religious development in the Negro in Virginia from 1760 to 1860', *Journal of Negro History* (1931), 16: 168–239.

Jernegan, M. W., 'Slavery and Conversion in the American Colonies', *American Historical Review* (1916), 21: 504–27.

Jones, C. C., *Suggestions on the Religious Instruction of the Negroes in the Southern States* (Philadelphia, 1847).

Lamur, H. E., *De kerstening van de Slaven van de Surinaamse plantage Vossenburg, 1847–1877* (Amsterdam, 1984).

Linde, J. M. van der, *Jan Willem Kals, 1700–1781* (Kampen, 1987).

Ngokwey, Ndolamb, 'Le désenchantement enchanteur ou d'un mouvement religieuse à l'outre', *Les Cahiers du Cedaf* (1978), No. 8.

Oldendorp, C. G. A., *Geschichte der Mission der evangelischen Brueder auf den caraibischen Inslen St. Thomas, S. Croix und S. Jan. Johann Jakob Bossard* (Barby, 1770).

Olwig, K. F., 'Slaves and Masters on Eighteenth-Century St. John', *Ethnos* (1985), 50.3/4: 2124–30.

Van Raalte, J., *Secularisatie en zending in Suriname* (Wageningen, 1973).

Rooke, P. T., 'The World they Made: the Politics of Missionary Education to British West Indian Slaves, 1800–1833', *Caribbean Studies* (1979), 18.3/4: 47–68.

Simpson, G. E., *Religious cults of the Caribbean: Trinidad, Jamaica and Haiti* (Puerto Rico, 1982).

Tank. N. O., 'Circulaire aan de Heeren Eigenaars en administrateurs van plantaadjes in de kolonie Suriname', in E. van Emden *et al.*, *Onderzoek ten gevolge der circulaire van de heer Otto Tank* (Paramirbo, 1848).

Thoden van Velzen, H. U. and van Wetering, W., 'Voorspoed, angsten en demonen', *Antropologische Verkenningen* (1982), 1.2: 85–118.

Thoden van Velzen, H. U. and van Wetering, W., 'Affluence and the Flowering of Bush Negro Religious Movements', *Bijdragen tot de Taal-, Land en Volkenkunde* (1983), 139: 99–139.

Wilson, J. S., 'The Pecularities and Diseases of Negroes', *American Cotton Planter and Soil of the South* New Series: 4 (1860).

Wooding, J. C., *Winti: een afroamerikaanse godsdienst in Suriname* (Meppel, 1972).

Zeefuik, K. A., *Herrnhutter Zending en Haagsche Maatschappij, 1828–1867* (Utrecht, 1973).

Myalism and the African Religious Tradition in Jamaica

MONICA SCHULER*

Religious movements have played a central role in Jamaican history for three centuries. Impossible to ignore, they have proved difficult to understand because scholars have tended to interpret them primarily as the frustrated expressions of marginal or oppressed people, emphasizing their psychological rather than their sociopolitical functions.[1]

If there is a certain similarity and continuity detectable in Jamaican religious movements from Myalism in the eighteenth century through Revivalism in the nineteenth and Rastafarianism in the twentieth, it is not solely because they are lower-class responses to colonial oppression. That explanation accounts only for the circumstances of the movements' development. Their shape and content are derived from an older, precolonial African tradition that posits a world in which, 'under ideal circumstances, good prevails absolutely and exclusively'. Such a perfect world is rarely achieved, however, because malevolent forces permeate the universe and produce evil through the malicious thoughts and feelings of selfish, antisocial people. Such people, placing personal goals above those of the community, employ ritual to satisfy their self-centered desires, that is, they practice magic or sorcery. To prevent the misfortune they occasion, and to maximize good fortune for the entire community are major functions of religious ritual which, unlike magic, is always community centered.

This is the religious tradition to which Afro-Jamaican religious movements belong. It is a dynamic, present-world-oriented tradition which refuses to accept as natural dissension, poverty, corruption, illness, failure, oppression — 'all the negative, disappointing, tragic experiences of life.' Believing these evils to be caused by sorcery, this religious tradition claims to have the weapons with which to eradicate them.[2] This tradition has been a powerful catalyst for African and Afro-Jamaican resistance to European values and control. It also explains why sociopolitical protest has usually been expressed in religious terms in Jamaica.[3]

Myalism, a religious movement which originated in eighteenth-century Jamaica, is the first documented Jamaican religion cast in the 'classical' African mold, and an examination of Myalism can provide us with a model for studying later Jamaican religious movements. Myal can be examined for a hundred-year period from the 1760s to the 1860s at least. It emerged in the 1760s as a pan-African religious society to protect slaves against European sorcery. By the early nineteenth century it had adopted Christian elements. In 1831-32 Myalists assumed a leading role in the last Jamaican slave rebellion. The postslavery period saw it reemerge stronger than ever from a period of persecution, acquiring new converts and openly challenging Christian missionaries in the early 1840s, only to be driven underground by the Jamaican government. In the early 1860s it gained new life under the aegis of a religious revival whose missionary sponsorship Myalists soon rejected.

Although undoubtedly syncretic, Myalism demonstrates many of the characteristics of classical Central African religious movements as outlined recently by Willy de Craemer, Jan Vansina, and Renée C. Fox. First is a collective group's acceptance of a new religious form consisting of rearranged existing rituals, symbols, and beliefs combined occasionally with new

*Written with the support of a grant from the Wenner-Gren Foundation for Anthropological Research.

Africa and the Caribbean. The Legacies of a Link (Baltimore, 1979), pp. 65-79.

beliefs. Second, the originator is a charismatic leader, inspired by dreams or visions. Third, the aim, in a culture which believes that good can and should prevail, is to prevent misfortune and maximize good fortune for the community. As a result Central African movements are always millennial and always involve witch or sorcery hunting. Fourth, a movement must move beyond its original community. As it does, a specific group in each community assumes responsibility for it, its members sometimes incorporating their own visions in the movement, extending and modifying it in such a way that it may last a quarter of a century or more despite unfulfilled millennial promises. A movement may even seem to have disappeared when, in fact, political hostility may have driven it underground to reemerge under more favorable conditions. Fifth, the focus of all classical movements is a charm for the protection of the community from disease and death. Charms, however, may be absent from or peripheral to movements which have adopted non-classical elements such as Christianity. Finally, de Craemer, Vansina, and Fox stress that modern Central African movements have not been purely or even primarily reactions to the stresses of the colonial experience or modernization, but rather form 'an integral part of the precolonial Central African tradition and they were primarily religious in nature'.[4]

The planter-historian Edward Long was the first European to record the existence of the Myal religion, referring to it as a new society in the 1760s, open to *all*. Its initiation ritual, which he called the 'myal dance', provided invulnerability to death caused by Europeans, that is, European sorcery. According to Long, candidates enacted a ritual of death and rebirth in the Myal dance by drinking a mixture of cold water and the herb-branched calalu[5] and then dancing until they reached a state of dissociation resembling death. The application of another mixture to the body revived the candidate.[6] While Long's is the only description of Myalism available for the eighteenth century, accounts of the 1830s and 1840s make it clear that Myalists believed that all misfortune — not just slavery — stemmed from malicious forces, embodied in the spirits of the dead. The Myal organization provided specialists — doctors — trained to identify the spirit causing the problem, exorcise it, and prevent a recurrence. All problems, including bodily illness, were thought to stem from spiritual sources and required the performance of appropriate ritual.[7]

The appearance of the new Myal religion in the 1760s symbolized a spirit of cooperation among enslaved Africans of various ethnic backgrounds that had not hitherto been the case in Jamaica. Indeed, Myalism may actually have fostered pan-African cooperation where once only ethnic division had existed. The Africans who poured into Jamaica as slaves in the seventeenth and eighteenth centuries had entered a new, permanent situation in which *all* slaves, regardless of previous rank or national origin, were considered equally inferior. All probably shared the common African conviction that malicious sorcery played a part in their misfortune.[8] Yet so strong was national identity, so linked was it to the rituals and customs that ensured survival, that despite their common predicament the different nations tended to isolate themselves from each other, none more so than the Akan. They organized exclusively Akan uprisings throughout most of the eighteenth century, led by ritual specialists who, like their counterparts in the Akan homeland, offered protection from European bullets. The Akan failed to recognize the inherent weakness of such national resistance in a heterogeneous slave population, but toward the end of the eighteenth century a trend towards pan-African solidarity may be detected. Several factors may have encouraged this: the increase of Jamaica-born (Creole) slaves, who comprised 75 per cent of the slave population by 1789; a decrease in Akan imports; a corresponding increase in Central African and Yoruba slaves; and Myalism which, by defining the cause of misfortune and its remedy, influenced the values and norms of plantation society for increasing numbers of slaves, and constituted an important form of social control by and for the enslaved.[9]

Part of the trend toward pan-African cooperation saw slave revolts organized along cooperative lines. Akan, Kongo, and Mandinka people participated in the slave revolt of 1798, and the rebellion of 1831–32 had a Creole stamp.[10] It was no coincidence that this uprising was popularly known as 'The Baptist War', referring to the so-called 'Native' or 'Black' Baptists who led it and whose blend of African and European religious beliefs and practices was really Myalist, not Baptist.

Myalism had passed into a new stage after 1791 when it absorbed certain congenial aspects of the Baptist version of Christianity. During and after the American War of Independence, a number of United Empire Loyalists fled to the Bahamas, and some eventually made their way to Jamaica. Some of the Afro-American servants and slaves who accompanied them introduced the Baptist religion to Jamaica. Moses Baker, for example, aided by a Quaker planter, settled in St. James parish in 1791 to preach the Baptist faith to slaves. The geographical limits of Baker's following coincide almost exactly with the core area of an aggressive Myal movement of the 1840s. Because of strict laws against non-Church-of-England preachers, Baker had great difficulty maintaining regular contact with his followers; he could visit them only at night and could not hold Sunday services outside his employer's property. Nevertheless, he served congregations many miles apart.

The Black or Native Baptist preachers, as men like Baker came to be called, developed an organization that the English Baptists, Wesleyan Methodists, and Presbyterians later found useful. They issued tickets indicating each individual's status — member, candidate, or inquirer — and for instruction they divided their flock into classes, each with its own leader. The leaders became almost totally independent of the preachers and ruled their classes with an iron hand. In time, Baker and his fellow preachers found it impossible to control the content of the leaders' teaching and their ritual, which grew less and less 'orthodox' from the Baptist viewpoint.

Myalists extracted and emphasized two central elements of the Baptist faith because they seemed to correspond with beliefs or symbols already familiar to them — the inspiration of the Holy Spirit; and Baptism, in the manner of John the Baptist, by immersion. Some members actually referred to their church as 'John the Baptist's Church'. The leaders developed a technique for attaining possession by the Holy Spirit and 'dreams' experienced in this state were crucial to a candidate's acceptance for baptism. Without them they could not be born again, 'either by water or the Spirit'. Today, descendants of nineteenth-century Central African immigrants in St. Thomas parish like to have their children baptized, even though they belong to the Kumina cult, because they believe that the sacrament confers on the child the Holy Spirit's special protection against evil spirits. They also profess a special attachment to Revivalists and Baptists who practice baptism by immersion in the river, the dwelling place of African spirits who are believed to protect them. The Afro-Jamaican religious tradition, then, has consistently reinterpreted Christianity in African, not European, cultural terms.

At the urging of Baker and his colleagues who were frustrated by this reinterpretation, the English Baptists sent a missionary to the north coast in 1814. His work among Baker's flock had scarcely begun when he died, and not until 1824 did his successor, Reverend Thomas Burchell, arrive. At Baker's urging most of his followers accepted Burchell's leadership, but many who joined the Baptist church eventually left. Baptist orthodoxy obviously had little to offer them, and they preferred a religion which combined Baptist and Myal elements in a way that deserves to be called Myalist rather than Black Baptist.[11]

The Myal notion of sin as sorcery, an offense not against God but against society, made it far more this-world oriented than the Baptist faith. Myal ritual offered a cure for society's ills which, since they were caused by sorcery, could be eradicated by antisorcery ritual. For this reason Myalism was far more relevant to many Afro-Jamaicans than any missionary version of the Christian faith. It attracted new followers on the north coast in the 1830s and 1840s and mounted anti-European offensives in both decades, demonstrating a continued Afro-Jamaican awareness of the major source of their misfortune in the nineteenth century.

Repression of a work strike by slaves in St. James parish in late 1831 transformed the strike into a slave rebellion which spread to other parishes. The opportunity to eradicate European sorcery appeared to be at hand, and through the agency of a European prophet, the Reverend Thomas Burchell. In England at the time, Burchell was believed to be returning with the emancipation edict which the planters were thought to be withholding from the slaves. The year had been hard, with drought followed by floods, rumors concerning emancipation, and a fervent religious revival. No wonder the missionaries, articulate advocates of emancipation, appeared like prophets of the millennium.

The missionaries turned out not to be prophets after all, and instructed the slaves that, since Burchell could not bring freedom, they should return to work. The slaves, however, preferred to heed their leaders' message — that resistance was the work of God. Baptist and Presbyterian congregations accused their pastors of deserting them and of being 'paid by the magistrates to deceive them' and threatened revenge. Severe repression of the rebellion followed, with deliberate military destruction of slave houses and kitchen gardens. Slave attendance at church declined, for the missionaries had been discredited by their failure to support the rebellion, by Burchell's failure to bring freedom, and, ironically, by the wave of persecution they faced from planters and Jamaican authorities who suspected them of having fomented the uprising.

Even though the rebellion did hasten the passage of the Emancipation Act in 1833, the coming of emancipation in 1834 did not confer the 'full free' for which Afro-Jamaicans longed.[12] Four years of apprenticeship followed during which freed people had to continue working for their former owners, although wages were paid. For many, little had changed. The end of apprenticeship in 1838 brought the unwelcome news that the houses the slaves had built on the land they had cleared and cultivated on their masters' property were not theirs, and they were ordered to pay rent or move. Rent and wage disputes became the rule after 1838, hinging on the Afro-Jamaicans' determination that, if they had to work on the plantations, they would do so only for just wages and just rents. On their side planters were equally determined to get back in rent what they had paid in wages — to make free labor cheaper than slave, even as they mourned the loss of their slaves. Planters harassed adamant workers in a number of ways — workers' kitchen gardens and sometimes their homes were destroyed; garden produce was seized on its way to market and charges of theft brought against workers; eviction notices were issued. In many parts of the land there was an exodus from the plantations, both voluntary and involuntary, as former slaves sought work in the towns, or purchased marginal plantation land from financially ruined planters.[13]

By 1841 the wage situation had improved and rents had been lowered, but African immigrants were not introduced to provide competition in the labor market and drive wages down. A family of four or more could not subsist on plantation wages alone, or even on the food and income from a small plot of land; it needed both sources of income. Plantation laborers enjoyed the most comfort and security and had the best chance of saving money to purchase land if they worked on sugar estates with unused land in adjacent mountainous areas. These areas, such as the Plantain Garden River and Blue Mountain Valley of St. Thomas-in-the-East and the enclosed basin of Upper Clarendon, contained adjacent uplands usually well watered by rivers and rainfall. Other districts were not so blessed, notably the lowland coastal areas of St. James, Trelawny, and the plains of Westmoreland. Here all tillable lowland was planted with sugar cane, and workers' provision grounds had to be located in hills and mountains a considerable distance from the plantations. These plantation workers, therefore, had to divide their time unproductively between their lowland jobs and their mountain plots, wasting many hours travelling between the two. Capricious rainfall and poor soil made food crop cultivation unremunerative but affected sugar cultivation less, so sugar estates in this area continued to prosper while those elsewhere failed, and proprietors here did not feel the need to break up their adjacent hill and mountain lands for sale to workers who, more than most, remained trapped on the estates. The results were still evident in the twentieth century with poor, unsubstantial houses reflecting the fact that people had neither time nor motivation to improve their estate dwellings, nor to erect more than lean-tos in the mountains.[14]

The hardships experienced in the northern Jamaican parishes of St. James and Trelawny, center of Myalism in the 1820s, 1830s, and early 1840s, produced a revival among Myalists which gained the movement new members as it set out to eradicate the sorcery that was causing misfortune. This new stage of the Myal movement began in December 1841 and lasted until repression drove it underground in November of the following year. A plantation movement for the reasons described above, it began on Spring estate on the St. James coast about 6 miles from Montego Bay, and eventually affected some 22 plantation villages.

Since 1838 a number of unexpected deaths had occurred in the Spring estate village; these were ascribed to obeah, which was then blamed for every misfortune. During Christmas of 1841, tenants of Spring invited Myalists from nearby Ironshore estate to cleanse Spring of obeah, and everyone but the Presbyterians in the village participated in the ceremonies. A second Myal band from Flower Hill estate performed the anti-obeah ritual on Blue Hole estate in July or August 1842. Villagers from Millennium Hall and Palmyra estates requested Myal help in September. The ritual performances increased and spread southwest and southeast of Spring, encompassing 16 or 17 sugar estate villages in St. James, bounded on the south by the Montego River. By October 1842 the movement had crossed parish boundaries, entering Trelawny and, some said, Westmoreland. Although primarily a north coast phenomenon, it turned up as far away as St. Thomas-in-the-Vale the same year.[15]

The Myal religion in the 1840s recognized

three grades of membership — Archangels, Angels, and Ministering Angelics. The Archangels, both men and women, were the leaders whose chief function was that of divination, which the other two ranks represented lower levels of expertise and had special ritual functions. The Angels spoke readily of their visions and their ability to detect obeah and its devotees. The Ministering Angelics usually operated in groups of 9–20 people and concentrated on making converts, digging up buried obeah charms and catching shadows. Myal believers were of both sexes, single as well as married, and of all ages, although some observers commented on the large number of young men among them. They led well-regulated lives and did not drink alcohol. When engaged in anti-obeah activities they wore cords or handkerchiefs tied tightly around their heads and waists and carried bottles of liquid and other ritual objects.[16]

Myalists in 1841–42 preached in prophetic and millennial terms that they were God's angels, appointed by Him to do His work. God, they said, had observed that the world had become 'contrary' and so 'he appointed we for to put it right again'. Myalists were called 'to do the work of the Lord, and do it, they must. . . . Their bodies may be punished here, but above all they will be rewarded according to their zeal'. When urged to return to the plantation labor they had deserted, Myalists retorted, 'We cannot keep peace till Jesus tell us to keep it. The spirit is all over the world.' Aware that their message would fall on more or less orthodox Christian ears — indeed, intending it to do so — Myalists explained that although their teachings were not in the Bible, 'God ordain it for all that.' And they justified their mission by claiming a new dispensation — 'Minister to baptize them right, theirs is the true Baptism, and foretime God speak to his prophets and disciples, and why not now also?' The Myal task, they preached, was to clear the land for Jesus Christ, who was coming among them, and they predicted that their movement would soon spread throughout Jamaica.[17]

Clearing the land for Jesus Christ meant eradicating obeah through special public rituals which only Myalists could perform. The first, a ceremony to discover the sources of obeah, required the drinking of a mixture containing the root of a lily plant. This, followed by singing and dancing, produced a state of dissociation in which participants claimed guidance by the Myal spirit to buried obeah charms and, in some cases, to the person responsible for buying them. The offending objects would then be dug up, and if a guilty person was uncovered, he or she would be subjected to a trial and ordeal, thereby forcing a confession and a vow of repentance. The Myal dance, usually held in the evening, started as early as six o'clock and often did not end until one in the morning. Since it could take more than a single performance to achieve results, the dance could continue for many nights.[18]

Most accounts of Myal anti-obeah activity fail to provide detailed information about either the persons involved or the diagnoses of Myal doctors. On occasion, old Africans were accused of practicing obeah, and if many Myalists were young men, self-promotion might well have been a cause of their accusing the elderly of sorcery. Such accusations might also reflect a Creole-African cleavage owing to fear of African ritual powers or simply a fear of job competition from new African arrivals. On at least one occasion African recaptives rescued from a Cuban slave ship and settled in St. James were accused of obeah. On Running Gut estate in St. James such accusations led to a riot. Millennium Hall Myalists accused a colored shopkeeper of obeah because he testified against them in court. They probably already had grievances against him — both his color and his occupation symbolized privilege, and plantation workers all over Jamaica resented their dependence on estate shops. Competition for choice estate jobs also caused conflict, and on one occasion a Myal doctor diagnosed that an estate head stillerman who lost his job had been bewitched by his successor who had stolen his shadow.[19]

Myal wrath targeted two groups of Europeans — planters and missionaries. 'I cannot do other work but my Lord work,' Myalists tried for disturbing the peace said constantly (Myalism was not at this time illegal). Since 'other work' meant plantation labor, the work stoppages connected with Myalism in 1841–42 may well have been a form of 'industrial action' against employers. The planters, at any rate, reacted as if this were indeed the case, summoned the police to stop performances of Myal ritual on their estates. Police action produced considerable unrest — people attacked constables on their way to make arrests, threatened to burn down a police station, and denounced the authorities, beginning with the Queen and proceeding downward to the governor and local magistrates.[20]

The missionaries were as alarmed as the

planters, and denounced the new Myal prophecies. Myalists reacted to missionary castigation and interference abusively and aggressively. When Reverend Hope M. Waddell, a Presbyterian with many parishioners on the affected estates, tried to break up the Myal ritual on Blue Hole by accusing female Myalists of madness, members turned on him in anger:

'They are not mad.' 'They have the spirit.'
'You must be mad yourself, and had best go away.'
'Let the women go on, we don't want you.' 'Who brought you here?' 'What do you want with us?'

Most estates had meeting houses erected by missionary organizations, and Myalists attempted to gain possession of these as well as missionary churches. In one case a Baptist class voluntarily turned over their meeting house to Myalists. Thus, competition for members became an issue between European missionaries and Myalists.[21]

Myalism made an attempt at that time to create the more perfect world the missionaries themselves had promised but had failed to deliver — a state where spiritual salvation matched economic and social self-sufficiency. The missionaries might buy land and create new settlements, they might champion Afro-Jamaicans in petition after petition, but they were not part of the island's power structure, although when the chips were down they tended to support it. They had neither economic nor political power. They could lighten but not eradicate the burdens of the people. In 1841 — 50 years after the Baptist word was first preached on the north coast — Myalists offered something more hopeful: quite simply, the millennium.[22]

Severe measures taken by the authorities against Myalists temporarily checked its public manifestations. Within three years, however, the dance was performed again on Trelawny estates, and sporadic accounts of Myal practice continued to trickle in from various parishes throughout the troubled 1850s.[23]

Through their continued control of an economy based on monoculture as well as their control of the government, Jamaican planters perpetuated the very afflictions Myalism had been designed to counteract. They understood correctly that Myalism threatened that control. Had they let Myalism as a public regeneration movement go unchecked in 1842 it may well have challenged European control more aggressively as it had done in 1831–32.

The late 1840s and the 1850s were years of extreme hardship for Jamaicans. Severe cholera, smallpox, and measles epidemics struck in the 1850s. Drought and food shortages marked both decades, and manmade hardships like lower wages, higher prices, and taxes combined with disease to create an atmosphere of despair and apocalypse. These festering troubles produced periodic eruptions. Violent protests occurred in 1859 over extortionist road tolls in Westmoreland and a land tenure dispute in Trelawny.[24] An occasional educated urban Jamaican warned of bloody revolution, but after the riots of 1859, working-class Jamaicans resorted, not to greater violence, but to restorative ritual as they had done in 1840.

Beginning in the Moravian church and spreading rapidly to Baptist and Wesleyan congregations, a movement known as the Great Revival swept over Jamaica; it subsided in 1861 but resurfaced in 1866 in the wake of the Morant Bay tragedy of late 1865. The revival soon left missionaries behind, frowning in disapproval at the Myal elements such as dancing, drumming, and spirit possession which revivalists practiced — evidence that Myalism, far from defunct, had been kept alive by the struggle against misfortune and evil through the 1840s and 1850s. It could be argued that the Great Revival was more Myalist than Christian. Certainly when Myalism once more tested its strength against Christianity, Myalism proved the more vital of the two. In subsequent years black revivalist sects multiplied and flourished. The Myal movement was once more undergoing transformation.[25] 'Eventually,' according to de Craemer, Vansina, and Fox, 'all movements end up being replaced by others that seem very similar to outsiders, but look brand new to the congregations.' The acid test comes when people feel that misfortune is not being eradicated, and they turn to what they hope will prove to be a more effective movement, receiving at least 'a sense of renewal' from it. The new movement must show many of the features of the old, however, and 'this the underlying process which accounts for the fact that all Central African religious movements are variants of a single tradition. However different they may be, they retain the attributes of the paradigm.'[26]

The visions revealed in the wake of the Great Revival may not all have been as revolutionary as the following warning from 'A Son of Africa' posted on a wharf gate in Lucea, Hanover in 1865, but it is nevertheless suggestive of the Great Revival's conception of the nature of misfortune at that time:

I heard a Voice speaking to me in the year 1864, saying 'Tell the Sons and Daughters of Africa, that a great deliverance will take place for them from the hand of Oppression; for, said the Voice, they are oppressed by Government, by Magistrates, by Proprietors, and by Merchants.' And this voice also said 'tell them to call a solemn Assembly, and to sanctify themselves for the day of deliverance which will surely take place; but, if the People will not hearken, I will bring the Sword into the land to chastise them for their disobedience, and for the iniquities which they have committed. And the Sword will come from America. If the people depend upon their Arms, and upon our Queen, and forget Him who is our God, they will be greatly mistaken, and the mistakes will lead to great distress'.... But great will be the deliverance of the sons and daughters of Africa, the children of Nlaweh... for the Voice said, if we wait until the thing takes place before we cry unto Him, the cry will be in vain, but if we pray truly from our hearts, and humble ourselves we have no need to fear. If not... there will be Gog and Magog to battle.[27]

Even after the bloody suppression of the Morant Bay disturbances of 1865 in which the original demonstration had been led by a separatist preacher, Revivalists were not cowed, nor did they go underground as they might have. Sharing a common core of belief and a spirit of solidarity similar to that of the Myalists, they defied official attempts to intimidate them. Threatened in 1866 with official action if he did not curb his noisy Revival meetings, a Westmoreland leader responded that 'he would bring a thousand people from Hanover and he would see who could hinder him.' The official fumed: 'These people are under the impression that they can do what they like in their own place....' He was right. They did.[28]

The Myal tradition formed the core of a strong and self-confident counter-culture. It guaranteed that none of the evils of the post-slavery period would be accepted passively, but would be fought ritually and publicly. This would lead inevitably to periodic confrontations with island authorities or any group considered to be the perpetrators of misfortune, destroyers of harmony, the most dangerous sorcerers of a particular time.[29]

Notes

1. See, for example, George Eaton Simpson, 'Religions of the Caribbean', and Raymond T. Smith, 'Religion in the Formation of West Indian Society: Guyana and Jamaica', in Martin L. Kilson and Robert I. Rotberg *The African Diaspora: Interpretive Essays* (Cambridge, 1976), pp. 280-11, 312-41.
2. For a study of such movements see Willy de Craemer, Jan Vansina, and Renée C. Fox, 'Religious Movements in Central Africa: A Theoretical Study'. *Comparative Studies in Society and History*, No. 18, No. 4 (October 1976): 458-75; for the attributes of such movements and their goals see especially pp. 460-61, 467-68. I am grateful to Professor Jan Vansina for bringing this article to my attention.
3. Leonard E. Barrett, *The Rastafarians: A Study in Messianic Cultism in Jamaica*, Caribbean Monograph Series, No. 6 (Rio Pedras, 1968), pp. 193-94. Barrett cites Madeline Kerr, *Personality and Conflict in Jamaica* (Liverpool, 1963) on the subject of the religious nature of Jamaican political movements.
4. It is possible that the word *myal* is of Central African origin. Descendants of Central African immigrants in St. Thomas parish, members of the Kumina cult, describe powerful possession by ancestral spirits as 'catching myal'. Since from the start the Myal religion seems to have been associated with no one African group, it was probably a blend of West and Central African beliefs that arose out of the needs and traditions of plantation slaves of diverse ethnic origins. Although de Craemer *et al.* have limited their analysis to Central Africa, the area they know best, their findings may be at least partially applicable to West Africa. See de Craemer *et al.*, *op. cit.*, pp. 465-74.
5. A member of the Solanaceae family, called West Indian spinach, and apparently narcotic when soaked, uncooked, in cold water.
6. Edward Long, *The History of Jamaica*, 3 vols (London, 1970), 2:416-17; Orlando Patterson. *The Structure of Slavery: An Analysis of the Origins, Development, and Structure of Negro Slave Society in Jamaica* (London, 1967; Rutherford, N. J., 1969), pp. 186-87.
7. Many Myal doctors worked in plantation hospitals during slavery. Reverend Hope Masterson Waddell, *Twenty-Nine Years in the West Indies and Central Africa* (London, 1970), pp. 137-38; James M. Philippo, *Jamaica, Its Past and Present States* (London, 1969), pp. 248-49; T. W. Jackson to Robert Bruce, 4 November 1842, enclosed in No. 64, Earl of Elgin to Lord Stanley, 28 December 1842, CO 137/264.
8. In Jamaica, sorcery is known as *obeah*. All African societies have believed that sorcery is essentially anti-social, have tended to attribute most forms of misfortune to it and, consequently, fear sorcerers. See Mary Douglas, *Purity and Danger* (New York, 1966), pp. 107-08; John S. Mbiti, *African Religion and Philosophy* (New York, 1970), pp. 261-63.
9. Patterson, *op. cit.*, pp. 141-46, 153-54; Monica Schuler, 'Akan Slave Rebellions in the British Caribbean', *Savacou*, I, No. 1 (June, 1970): 8-31; Philip D. Curtin, *The Atlantic Slave Trade: A Census* (Madison, Wis., 1969), p. 160. There is now a growing realization that religions like Myalism constituted vital self-governing communities. See, for instance, Edward Kamau Brathwaite, 'Caliban, Ariel, and Unprospero in the Conflict of Creolization: A Study of the Slave Revolt in Jamaica in 1831-32', in Vera Rubin and Arthur Tuden (Eds), *Comparative Perspectives on Slavery in New World Plantation Societies* (New York, 1977), p. 57.
10. For 1798 rebellion see *Journals of the House of Assembly of Jamaica*, 1797-1802. pp. 106-14.
11. For the history of Black Baptists in Jamaica see W. J. Gardner, *A History of Jamaica* (London, 1971), pp. 343-53, 357-60; Waddell, *op. cit.*, pp. 25-27, 35-36; Philip D. Curtin, *Two Jamaicas: The Role of Ideas in a Tropical Colony, 1830-1865* (New York, 1970), pp. 32-33; Beverly Brown, 'George Liele: Black Baptist and Pan-Africanist, 1750-1826', *Savacou*, 11/12

(September 1975): 58–67. The practice of demanding visions as signs of conversion was still common among Jamaican Revivalists in the early twentieth century; see Martha Beckwith, *Black Roadways: A Study of Jamaican Folk Life* (Chapel Hill, 1929), pp. 163, 165, 166–67. This practice appears to be a feature of African diaspora religion; see, for instance, Melville J. Herskovits and Frances Herskovits, *Trinidad Village* (New York, 1964), pp. 199–202; George P. Rawick (Ed.), *God Struck Me Dead*, 19 vols, Vol. 19, *The American Slave: A Composite Biography* (Westport, 1972); Joseph G. Moore, 'Religion of Jamaican Negroes: A Study of Afro-Jamaican Acculturation', Ph.D. diss. (Evanston, Ill., 1953), p. 150. In the 1920s Beckwith noted the continued symbolism of water among Revivalists. See also her transscription of a Revivalist hymn dating back to the 1840s: 'River Jordan,' Beckwith, *op. cit.*, pp. 167–68, 175, 181.

12. Mary Reckord, 'The Slave Rebellion of 1831', *Jamaica Journal*,3 (June 1969): 25–31; Curtin, *Two Jamaicas*, pp. 85–88; Waddell, *Twenty-Nine Years*, pp. 50, 52, 55–56, 63, 74. Barry Higman has noted the essentially rural nature of the 1831–32 rebellion, stressing that it occurred in 'monocultural sugar areas where the system of colour and status was most highly developed, and where the heavy rate of natural decrease was placing stress on the system.' See Barry Higman, *Slave Population and Economy in Jamaica, 1807–1834* (Cambridge, 176), p. 230. For slave mortality between 1817 and 1832 see pp. 105–06. The context of the 1841–42 Myal movement was essentially the same. For a rebellion in Demerara see Shuler, 'Akan Slave Rebellions', pp. 24–27.
13. Douglas Hall, *Free Jamaica, 1838–1865: An Economic History* (London and Edinburgh, 1969), pp. 8, 10, 20–21, 117–18, 158, 168–69, 171, 172, 182–83, 193, 235. Sir Lionel Smith to Lord Glenelg, No. 8, 5 January 1839, and enclosed Stipendiary Magistrates' reports, CO 137/241; *idem*, No. 74, 6 April 1839, and enclosed Stipendiary Magistrates' reports, CO 137/242; *idem*, No. 53, 25 February 1839, and enclosed Stipendiary Magistrates' reports, CO 137/242. Hugh Paget, 'The Free Village System in Jamaica', in *Apprenticeship and Emancipation* (Mona, Jamaica), pp. 45–48. State of Agriculture, *Votes of the House of Assembly of Jamaica* (VHAJ), October–December 1845, Appendix No. 66, p. 713.
14. Monica Schuler, '"Yerri, Yerri, Koongo": A Social History of Liberated African Immigration into Jamaica, 1841–1867', Ph.D. diss. (University of Wisconsin, 1977). Lord Olivier, *Jamaica: The Blessed Isle* (London, 1936), pp. 135–37, 197.
15. The reference to deaths on Spring estates suggests that the high mortality noted by Higman in the last years of slavery was still a significant factor as the decade of the 1840s opened. Higman, *op. cit.*, pp. 105–16. Walter Finlayson Report, 31 December 1838, enclosed in No. 11, Sir Lionel Smith to Lord Glenelg, 5 January 1839, CO 137/241. *Jamaica Standard and Royal Gazette*, n.s., 64, 308, 30 September 1842, 1:2–4; 320, 14 October 1842, 1:2–3; 322, 17 October 1942, 1:4; 326, 21 October 1842, 2:3; 334, 31 October 1842, 2:3–4; 341, 8 November 1842, 3:1–2, 350, 18 November 1842, 2:2–3. Waddell, *op. cit.*, pp. 53, 137, 191–94; J. H. Buchner, *The Moravians in Jamaica, History of the Mission of the United Brethren's Church to the Negroes in the Island of Jamaica, From the Year 1754 to 1854* (London, 1854), p. 139.
16. The concept of a dual soul is central to Myal beliefs. See William Bascom, *The Yoruba of Southwestern Nigeria* (New York, 1969), p. 71; Moore, 'Religion of Jamaica', pp. 33–34, 152; George Eaton Simpson, 'The Shango Cult in Nigeria and Trinidad', *American Anthropologist* 64, No. 6 (December 1962): 1213; Geoffrey Parrinder, *West African Religion: A Study of Beliefs and Practices of the Akan, Ewe, Yoruba, Ibo, and Kindred People* (London, 1961), pp. 113–14; Karl Laman, *The Kongo*, 3 vols (Lund, 1962), 3:75, 95–98, for African beliefs in a dual soul. See also *Jamaica Standard*, n.s., 64, 320, 14 October 1842, 1:1; 308, 30 September 1842, 1:2; Buchner, *op. cit.*, 139; Waddell, *op. cit.*, quoting from *Cornwall Chronicle*, pp. 192–93.
17. Waddell, *op. cit.*, p. 188; *Jamaica Standard*, n.s., 64, 308, 30 September 1842, 1:3–4; 320, 14 October 1842, 1:1; 334, 31 October 1842, 2:3.
18. *Jamaica Standard*, n.s., 64, 320, 14 October 1842, 1:3, 18 November 1842, 2:2–3; Buchner, *op. cit.*, p. 139; Waddell, *op. cit.*, pp. 193–94. Drums and rattles were not mentioned in any of the eyewitness accounts of the 1841–42 Myal ceremonies, but Beckwith observed the use of both in the 1920s. Beckwith, *op. cit.*, pp. 148–49.
19. Sir Charles Metcalfe to Lord John Russell, No. 80, 18 May 1840, CO 137/249; Daniel Kelly to Robert Bruce, 14 June 1843, enclosed in No. 140; Earl of Elgin to Lord Stanley, 29 July 1843, CO 137/274; Waddell, *op. cit.*, pp. 188, 193–94; *Jamaica Standard*, n.s., 64, 308, 30 September, 1842, 1:3; 350, 18 November 1842, 2:2–3, Hall, *op. cit.*, pp. 208–09. Higman's analysis of the stress that resulted from increased competition for skilled plantation jobs after 1820 and that contributed to the 1831 rebellion is relevant here. See Higman, *op. cit.*, pp. 231–32. The Myal specialist who diagnosed the problem of the head stillerman in 1842 used a stone called an 'amber' in the divination process. This was still used by Myalists in the early twentieth century. See Beckwith, *op. cit.*, pp. 154, 159.
20. *Jamaica Standard*, n.s., 64, 308, 30 September 1842, 1:2–4; 326, 21 October 1842, 1:3–4.
21. Waddell, *op. cit.*, pp. 190–92; *Jamaica Standard*, n.s., 64, 308, 30 September 1842, 1:2; Buchner, *op. cit.*, pp. 140–41.
22. Curtin, *Two Jamaicas*, pp. 92–93, 159–60, 162–69; Inez Sibley, *The Baptists of Jamaica, 1793–1965* (Kingston, 1965), pp. 30–31.
23. Magistrate Lawson to Robert Bruce, 1 May 1843, enclosed in No. 140, Earl of Elgin to Lord Stanley, 29 July 1843, CO 137/274; *Falmouth Post*, Vol. 12, 34, 25 August 1846, 2:1; Bourke Grievance, December 1859, VHAJ, November–December 1859, Appendix No. 4, pp. 224–25; Alexander Fyfe to Hugh Austin, 24 January 1654, enclosed in No. 4, Sir Henry Barkly to Duke of Newcastle, 21 February 1854, Co 137/322; J. A. Dillon to W. G. Stewart, 14 August 1856, enclosed in No. 58, E. W. Bell to Henry Labouchere, 25 November 1856, CO 137/332. See also Curtin, *Two Jamaicas*, p. 170.
24. Hall, *Free Jamaica*, pp. 88–97; Curtin, *Two Jamaicas*, pp. 151–52. William Bell to Hugh Austin, 17 July 1854, enclosed in No. 101, Major Berkeley to Earl Grey, 18 September 1854, CO 137/324. For Toll Gate Riots see Charles Darling to Edward Bulwer-Lytton, No. 84, 25 March 1859, CO 137/344 and enclosures. For Trelawny disturbances see Darling to Duke of Newcastle, No. 103, 9 August 1859, and *idem*, No. 114, 5 September 1859, CO 137/346.
25. For the Great Revival see Curtin, *Two Jamaicas*, pp. 168–71. Martha Beckwith recognized the Myal ancestry of nineteenth-century Revivalism in Jamaica. See Beckwith, *Black Roadways*, p. 59, especially, but also pp. 142–82 for discussion of Myal and Revival sects and practices.

26. de Craemer *et al.*, *op. cit.*, p. 467.
27. 'Intelligence from Lucea,' in *Falmouth Post*, 31, No. 47 (16 June 1865): 2. The reference to a sword coming out of America may have been a result of the impact of the Civil War and rumors of the expansion of United States slavery into the Caribbean.
28. E. Alcock to H. A. Whitelocke, 17 December 1866, enclosed in No. 32, Sir John Grant to Earl of Carnarvon, 23 February 1867, CO 137/422. Reverend Anthony Davidson, Rector of Hanover, claimed that around April–May 1865 he had noticed a dramatic reduction in church attendance from about 2,000 to 1,400, and that at the time of the Morant Bay disturbance in October, attendance had dwindled to 'exceeding few' and had not increased since the end of the disturbances. He credited the decrease to the people's attending their own revival meetings. See Reverend Anthony Davidson evidence, Jamaican Royal Commission, 1866, Part II, P. P. 1866, XXX (3683–I), 638:1–2.
29. For two twentieth-century manifestations of this type of confrontation see the prophet Bedward's announcement in 1920 that he would ascend into heaven, the whites would be destroyed, and the reign of Bedwardism (the Jamaica Baptist Free Church was his creation) would commence on earth, Beckwith, *op. cit.*, pp. 168–71; and the various teachings and manifestations of Rastafarianism, Barrett, *The Rastafarians*. Rastafarian leaders are politically astute, and have a sophisticated understanding of the causes of contemporary Jamaican problems, as Barrett demonstrates. The time is now ripe for a reconsideration of such movements in the light of African religious tradition.

The Other Face of Slave Labor: Provision Grounds and Internal Marketing in Martinique

DALE W. TOMICH

The slaves' working activity was not confined to the production of export commodities. The planters of Martinique were under constant pressure to reduce the costs of their operations. The easiest and most readily available means to do this was simply to squeeze more out of the slaves. The latter were obliged to produce for their own subsistence in their 'free' time, that is outside the time devoted to producing the plantation's commercial crop. Instead of receiving the legally required amounts of food and clothing, the slaves were commonly given plots of marginal land and a free day on Saturday in order to provide for at least a portion of their own consumption needs on their own accounts. (Some planters gave only half a day on Saturday and continued to supply a part of the slaves' rations themselves.) By encouraging the slave to work for himself, the master could avoid the effort and expense of the large-scale cultivation of provisions. Instead, he had to furnish only some clothing, a fixed weekly ration of salt meat or fish and perhaps rum, and occasional medical care.[1]

This arrangement directly benefited the master, because the expense of maintaining the slave population placed a heavy economic burden on him. Goods imported for consumption were always expensive and their supply was often irregular, while both land and time for provision cultivation emerged almost naturally from the conditions of sugar production itself. The planters perceived it in their interest to spend as little money, time, or energy as possible on slave maintenance. This perception did not change appreciably, at least as long as the slave trade lasted, and for many it went beyond the end of the slave trade and even of slavery itself. Allowing the slaves to produce for their own subsistence from resources already at hand instead of purchasing the necessary items on the market represented a saving to the master and a reduction of the cash expenses of the estate. The burden of reproduction costs was shifted directly to the slaves themselves, and they were kept usefully employed even during periods when there was no work to be done on the sugar crop. Althouth it meant that after long hours of toil in the canefields the slaves had to work still more just to secure the basic necessities of life, many planters hoped that it would give them a stake in the plantation and instill regular habits and the virtues of work and property.[2]

The possibility of self-organized subsistence production emerged from the contradictory nature of the slave relation itself. The same social relation that shaped labor as a mass, disciplined, cooperative force also created the possibility for autonomous individual subsistence production and marketing by the slaves. The commodification of the person of the laborer compressed these two kinds of labor — commodity production and the reproduction of the labor force — into the same social space and defined the relation between them. Slavery thus made possible, and in some respects even required, the development of provision crop cultivation by the slaves as a means of reducing or avoiding market expenditures for their maintenance. But this labor of reproduction developed within the antagonistic relation between master and slave. For the master, the provision ground was the means of guaranteeing cheap labor. For slaves, it was the means of elaborating an autonomous style of life. From these conflicting perspectives evolved a struggle over the conditions of material and social reproduction in which the slaves were able to appropriate aspects of these activities and

Slavery in the Circuit of Sugar: Martinique and The World Economy, 1830–1848 (Baltimore, 1990), pp. 259–80.

develop them around their own interests and needs.

These simultaneously complementary and antagonistic processes crystallized in the practices and embryonic property relations that Sidney Mintz has described as the formation of a 'proto-peasantry'. He uses this term to characterize those activities that allowed the subsequent adaptation to a peasant way of life by people while they were still enslaved. As Mintz emphasizes, the formation of this proto-peasantry was both a mode of response and a mode of resistance by the enslaved to the conditions imposed upon them by the plantation system. Thus, it was not a traditional peasantry attacked from the outside by commodity production, the market economy, and the colonial state; rather, it was formed from within the processes of the historical development of slavery and the plantation system. The cultivation and marketing of provision crops and the acquisition of the necessary agricultural and craft skills emerged seemingly as a matter of course from the interstices of the slave plantation. They were interstitial, not just in the sense that final authority over the use of the land and the disposition of labor resided with the master, but also because the time and space for such activities arose out of the rhythm of plantation life and labor. These were not activities and relations separate from the plantation system but were intertwined with its logic; they developed within, and were dependent upon, its temporal and spatial constraints. Slave provision-ground cultivation was thus intimately linked to the organization of export commodity production and developed in close association with it.[3]

Mintz has been primarily concerned to demonstrate the originality of the proto-peasant and subsequent peasant adaptations that were precipitated out of Caribbean slavery. I would like to extend and qualify this concept by examining the historical interrelation between the various types of laboring activities performed by the slave population. Rather than looking toward the formation of an independent peasantry, as some readers of Mintz have done (though not Mintz himself), I would suggest that the focal point of the development of these autonomous cultivation and marketing activities was the struggle between master and slave over the conditions of labor and of social and material life within slavery. Beyond the formal juridical distinction between free and unfree labor, these activities indicate the substantive complexity of slave labor, which combined both 'proletarian' labor in the canefields, mill, and boiling house, and the 'peasant labor' of the provision ground. This 'peasant' dimension of slave labor emerged within its 'proletarian' dimension and formed a counterpoint to it. While provision-ground cultivation arose from the planter's attempts to reduce costs and create an interest for the slave in the well-being of the estate, its further elaboration depended upon the slaves' assertion of their own individual and collective needs within and against the predominant slave relation. The condition of the development of autonomous provision-ground cultivation and marketing was the slaves' appropriation of a portion of the estate's labor time. This struggle for 'free' time entailed, and was reinforced and conditioned by, struggles to appropriate physical space and to establish the right to property and disposition over their own activity. In turn, the consolidation of slave autonomy in provision-ground cultivation provided leverage for more struggles over the conditions of staple crop production. These interrelated practices transformed and subverted the organization of labor within slavery as they reinforced it.[4]

This process reveals both the contradictoriness and the historically developing character of the master-slave relation. As the assertion of slave autonomy had a continual tendency to push 'beyond' the limits of the slave relation, the master was compelled to try to recapture and rationalize labor under these changing conditions. Thus, for example, task work may be seen as an attempt to create a new, more effective form of labor discipline whose premise was autonomous slave self-interest. Industrial discipline depended on the existence of provision grounds and adequate material incentives recognized by both parties, though meaning something different to each. Slave struggles for autonomy and planter efforts to contain them within the bounds of the prevailing relations of production developed the slave relation to its fullest extent and created both the embryo of post-emancipation class structure within slavery and the conditions for the transition to 'free labor'. Seen from this perspective, the reconstruction of the post-emancipation plantation system was not simply a unilateral and functional shift to a more adequate and rational 'capitalist' form of organization. Rather, it was a process whose outcome was problematic, requiring violence and compulsion to recapture labor in the face of material and social resources acquired by the laboring population while still enslaved. The struggle over conditions of labor and of social and material life was continued in a new historical context.

Slavery and Subsistence

While the slaves had been given small gardens to supplement their rations since the beginning of slavery in the French colonies, the practice of giving the slaves gardens and a free day each week to grow their own food was brought by Dutch refugees from Pernambuco who introduced sugar cane into the French Antilles during the first half of the seventeenth century. The origins of this practice can be traced back to São Tomé in the sixteenth century. Thus, the diffusion of sugar cane entailed not merely the movement of a commodity but the spread of a whole way of life. With the appearance of sugar cultivation in the French Caribbean, subsistence crops for the slaves were neglected in favor of planting cane, and the 'Brazilian custom' was rapidly adapted by planters eager to reduce their expenses. Masters no longer distributed rations to their slaves. Instead, the latter were expected to provide their own food, shelter, clothing, and other material needs from the labor of their 'free' day.[5]

But this practice had negative consequences. Food production was chaotic, and the slaves were often poorly nourished. Indeed, frequent food shortages prevented the masters from dispensing altogether with the distribution of rations. Critics of the custom of free Saturdays claimed that it gave the slaves too much freedom and encouraged theft and disorder. The metropolitan authorities were in agreement with the critics and sought both to stop what they perceived to be the excesses resulting from the free Saturday and to ensure adequate treatment for the slave population. The proclamation of the Royal Edict of 1685 (the *Code noir*) by the metropolitan govenment was the first attempt to establish a uniform dietary standard for slaves in all the French colonies and to put an end to the prevailing disorder. It sought to make the master totally responsible for the maintenance of his slaves and to prescribe standards for food, shelter, and clothing to be provided to the slaves. The practice of individual slave gardens and free Saturdays in lieu of rations was to be suppressed, and regular weekly food allowances of determined composition and quanity (the *ordinaire*) were mandated.[6]

This edict remained the fundamental legislation governing slavery in the French colonies throughout the *ancien régime*. The distribution of slave rations seems to have been more widely practiced in Martinique than elsewhere in the French Antilles, and the slaves there had the reputation of being better fed than elsewhere in the French colonies during the *ancien régime*. Even so, the writings of administrators in Martinique throughout the course of the eighteenth century complain continuously that the slaveowners were concerned only with sugar, and if they provided a part of the slaves' nourishment, they obliged them to secure the rest on their own account. The persistent failure to regulate slave diet and treatment and especially to prohibit the practice of slave provision grounds is evidenced by the succession of declarations, edicts, ordinances, regulations, and decrees, too numerous to recount, promulgated on these matters by both metropolitan and colonial authorities during the seventeenth and eighteenth centuries. The colonial authorities lacked the means to enforce the regulations in a society dominated by slaveholders, who were usually hostile to any tinkering with their 'property rights', particularly if it cost them time or money. Planters expressed their preference for slave self-subsistence, and the reluctance to spend money on slave maintenance, especially food, persisted throughout the *ancien régime* and into the nineteenth century. Far from dying out, the practice of free Saturdays and private provision grounds expanded and increasingly became an established part of colonial life during those years.[7]

Ordinances enacted in 1784 and 1786 revised the *Code noir* and represent an important attempt to ameliorate the lot of slaves and reconcile the law with the growing importance of provision grounds in the colonies. The practice of the free Saturday was still forbidden, but, instead of prohibiting slave provision grounds, this legislation recognized their existence and attempted to regulate their use. It decreed that each adult slave was to receive a small plot of land to cultivate on his or her own account. However, the produce of these plots was to supplement the *ordinaire*, not to replace it. The distribution of rations was still required by the law. This prohibition against substituting the free Saturday for the legal ration was restated by the Royal Ordinance of October 29, 1828, which reformed the Colonial Penal Code. However, the custom was stronger than the law, and ministerial instructions advised colonial authorities to tolerate this arrangement when it was voluntary on the part of the slave.[8]

This legislation was a step toward recognizing the realities of colonial life, but provision-ground cultivation was still regarded as only a supplemental activity, and the slave codes continued to insist on the distribution of *ordinaire* as the primary means of providing for slave maintenance. However, postwar economic conditions made complete dependence on the ration impractical, and scarcities caused planters to increase their reliance on provision-ground cultivation. According to evidence presented before the commission of inquiry into the sugar industry, before 1823 the majority of plantations could only rarely provide their slaves with the *ordinaire* and had to abandon them to the necessity of providing for their own subsistence, thus depriving themselves of the labor of their slaves. In his testimony before the commission, Jabrun stated that the slaves were better fed, better dressed, and better housed than they had been some years previously. However, he added that the lack of affluence and shortage of credit — and, consequently, the difficulty in obtaining provisions opportunely — still caused some planters to substitute the free Saturday for the ration. De Lavigne testified that in general this practice had ceased in Martinique. Almost all the Negroes now received the quantity of codfish and other food prescribed by the regulations, and provision grounds supplemented the ration. While this claim seems exaggerated, De Lavigne also suggests a cyclical aspect of provision-ground cultivation. In contrast to periods of low sugar prices, when land and labor could be given over to provision grounds, with the high prices of the sugar boom of the 1820s many planters may have preferred to devote their attention entirely to sugar cultivation and purchase necessary provisions. Undoubtedly, a variety of individual strategies were possible, and while the historical continuity of provision-ground cultivation may be demonstrated for the colony as a whole, it may not necessarily have been the case for individual estates.[9]

Despite the shortcomings and abuses of the practice of free Saturdays and slave provision grounds and the repeated attempts to suppress or regulate them, the scale of these activities increased steadily, and by the nineteenth century they had become more and more central to the functioning of the colonial economy. By the 1830s, the masters, with few exceptions, were encouraging their slaves to grow their own foodstuffs, and the substitution of free Saturdays for rations had become widespread. The slaves were given as much land as they could cultivate. They not only produced but also marketed their crops without supervision, and the colony became dependent upon their produce for a substantial portion of its food. As one observer stated, 'The plantations which produce foodstuffs (*habitations vivrières*) and the slaves who cultivate gardens more than guarantee that the colony is supplied with local produce.' Measures prohibiting these activities were disregarded with the common consent of both masters and slaves. Enforcement not only would have inhibited the efforts of the independent slave cultivators but also would have reduced the island's food supply.[10]

By the 1840s, colonial authorities no longer regarded these practices as threats to order but, rather, felt that they contributed to social harmony. The reports of local officials particularly stressed the social benefits of independent cultivation by slaves. One of them expressed the opinion that the free Saturday was an 'effective means of giving [the slave] the taste for property and well-being, and consequently, to make them useful craftsmen and agriculturalists desirous of family ties.' For another, writing in 1842, it means nothing less than bringing the slaves up to the standards of the civilized world: 'But the slaves, for whom the custom of free Saturdays is established, prefer it to the ration because they work on their own account and find some profit from that state of affairs. It is clear evidence that man, even though a slave, has an interest in money and likes to enjoy the fruits of his labors while freely disposing of that which belongs to him. The black is forced to enter into types of social transaction that can only serve as a means of civilizing him.' This latter aspect was seen to be especially important because of the imminent prospect of emancipation. The report continued: 'In this regard, the custom of the free Saturday must be preferred to the legally sanctioned ration because, beyond everything else, it is a road toward free labor.'[11]

Thus, slavery, instead of separating the direct producers from the means of subsistence, provided them with the means of producing a livelihood. While the slaves acquired access to the use of property and the possibility of improving the material conditions of life, for them the price of subsistence was work beyond that required for sugar production. With these developments, the time devoted to the slaves' reproduction became separate from commodity production, and a de facto distinction between time belonging to the master and time belonging to the slave was created. However, instead of permitting the rationalization of the labor process, this distinction blocked it. The relation between time devoted to commodity production and time devoted to the reproduction of the labor force became fixed and rigid. The prevailing conditions of production were thereby reinforced. The economy of time and labor was dissolved into the maintenance and reproduction of a given body of laborers and the regular performance of a predetermined quantity of labor: it thus resolved itself into a social-political question as the master-slave relation was challenged from within.

The Self-Appropriation of the Appropriated

The successful development of autonomous provision-ground cultivation and marketing in Martinique depended upon the response of the enslaved. It was the result of the slaves' adapting to New World conditions and acquiring the skills and habits necessary to produce and market these crops. One contemporary document stresses the importance of cultural adaptation on the part of the slaves in developing subsistence agriculture and also suggests that slave provision grounds became more prevalent after the slave trade was abolished.

> Thus, previously, the progress of the population did not take place in accordance with the laws of nature. Each year, the irregular introduction of considerable numbers of blacks increased the possibility of a scarce food supply in the country. These new arrivals in the colonies, knowing neither the soil, the climate, nor the special agriculture of the Antilles, could not count on themselves for their support. It was necessary to provide sufficient and regular nourishment for them, but they had no skills to contribute. Thus, the proprietors were quite properly compelled to plant a certain amount of provisions since their slaves did not know how or were unable to plant enough. . . . . The slaves required more prompt and rigorous discipline (than today) because of the savage stage in which almost all of them had been taken, their ignorance of the work of a sugar plantation, the tiring labor to which they had perhaps not been accustomed, and their sorrow for their country which could lead some of them to commit crimes . . . . The slaves of today have less need of constant tutelage than previously. They are able to supply themselves without depending upon the generosity of their masters. The latter hardly plant provisions at all any more because the slaves plant well beyond the amount that is necessary for consumption.

Indeed, nineteenth-century accounts indicate that the slaves by and large preferred to have an extra day to themselves and to raise their own provisions rather than to receive an allowance of food from the master. 'This practice,' observed one government official, 'is completely to the advantage of the slave who wants to work. A day spent by him cultivating his garden or in some other manner, will bring him more than the value of the nourishment the law prescribes for him. I will add that there is no *atelier* which does not prefer this arrangement to the execution of the edict [*Code noir*]. Once it has been set, it would be dangerous for the master to renounce it.'[12]

The provision grounds and 'proto-peasant' activities were not merely functional for the reproduction of the social and material relations of the slave plantation. They also offered a space for slave initiative and self-assertion that cannot simply be deduced from their economic form. Through them the slaves themselves organized and controlled a secondary economic network that originated within the social and spatial boundaries of the plantation, but that allowed them to begin to construct an alternative way of life that went beyond it. In this process, the bonds of dependence of the slave upon the master slowly began to dissolve, and the activities of the slaves gradually transformed the foundations of slave society itself. The changing role and meaning of these activities was both cause and response to the increased pressure on the plantation system during the first half of the nineteenth century. While these practices had existed virtually since the beginning of slavery in the colony, they assumed new importance with the changing economic and political conditions of those decades and the imminent prospect of emancipation.

The reforms of the July Monarchy were a decisive step in the recognition of existing practices in the colonies and prepared the way for emancipation. The law of July 18 and 19, 1845, known as the Mackau Law, allowed the substitution of provision grounds for the *ordinaire*. While the land itself remained the property of the master, its produce belonged to the slave, and the law recognized the latter's legal personality and right to chattel property. The slaves could not represent themselves in civil action, but they had the right to administer their personal property and dispose of it as they saw fit in accordance with the civil code. This legislation confirmed and regularized what was already a customary practice and gave it the sanction of law. It thus extended the scope of previous legislation and further legitimized the existing custom. In the words of its authors, 'The law only recognizes a state that has long existed in practice and makes it a right to the great advantage of the black and without detriment to the master.' These legally enforceable rights were less precarious and dependent upon the proprietor's whim than was the previous custom. The slaves could now assert their purposes with the backing of the colonial state. The authorities saw in these practices not the source of disorder but the means to regulate slavery and provide a transition to free labor. The purpose of the legislation was to ease the transition to freedom by giving slaves skills, property, and therefore a stake in society. 'On the eve of complete emancipation, it is in the interest of the masters to see the taste for labor and the spirit of economy develop in the slaves. Now, without property there is no industrious activity. It is only for oneself that one has the heart to work. Without property there is no economy. One does not economize for another.'[13]

The Royal Ordinance of June 5, 1846, allowed the slaves to choose between the Saturday and the *ordinaire*. Upon request, each adult slave over 14 years of age could have the disposition of one free day per week to provide his or her own nourishment in place of the weekly ration. The minimum size of the plot to be allotted to each individual slave was set at six ares for slaves on a sugar estate, four ares for a coffee plantation, and three ares for other types of estates, and the master was not to make deductions for plots claimed by other members of the same family. The plot was to be located no more than one kilometer from the center of the plantation unless approved by the authorities. In addition, the master was also to supply the seeds and tools necessary to begin cultivation for the first year, but he was not obliged to renew the supply of these items. The extent of these plots could be reduced by half if the master could justify to colonial authorities that the total arable land at his disposal compared to the number of slaves made it necessary. The slave could be made to leave the assigned plot only when (1) it had been at his disposition for at least a full year; (2) his harvest was completed, and he had been advised not to plant again; and (3) a plot equivalent in size and as far as possible in quality was put at his disposal. Further, on the day reserved to him, the slave had the right to rent himself out, either to his master or to another proprietor in the commune on the condition that he demonstrate that his provision grounds were well maintained.[14]

The slave who claimed a free day had to provide only for his or her own personal nourishment from the provision ground. The husband, wife, children, or other family members to whom the disposition of a free day did not apply were to continue receiving the *ordinaire*, which this new legislation set at 6 liters of manioc flour, 6 kilograms of rice or 7 kilograms of corn, and $1\frac{1}{2}$ kilograms of cod or salt beef for an adult slave over 14 years. (Although there were some complaints about the lack of meat, all observers, including abolitionists like Schoelcher, reported that the diet of the slaves who received the *ordinaire* was adequate, if plain, and that planters supplemented the legal requirements with salt and rice.) However, an arrangement could be made between the master and the slave mother or father to replace the ration due to the children with additional free time. In this case, the size of the plot allotted was to be increased by one-sixth for each child over six years of age. But the right to this supplemental land ended when the child for whom it was claimed reached 14 years of age. Such arrangements also had to be submitted to the local authorities for approval.[15]

In order to prevent abuses of this system and to ensure adequate maintenance of the slaves, the request for the free day was to be made verbally in the presence of four adult slaves of the *atelier*, and each planter was to present a list of the slaves on his estate to the justice of the peace with an indication of those who requested the free day. The judge, on his own office or at the planter's request, could void the arrangement when the slave was recognized as incapable of providing his nourishment by his own labor, when he neglected the cultivation of his plot, or when he abused the time at his disposal. This arrangement could also be suspended or annulled at the slave's request, but in this case he could not claim the right to a provision ground again for at least six months without showing sufficient motive to the justice of the peace.[16]

Table 1 indicates the extent of provision-ground cultivation and the practice of free Saturdays in Martinique in the 1840s. However, it must be noted that these figures refer to the number of visits made by the inspecting magistrates, not to the number of plantations or slaves in the colony. Many estates were visited several times. Between May 1841 and May 1843, the colonial magistrates charged under the law with inspecting slave conditions made 968 visits

Table 1 Summary of Magistrates' Inspection Reports on Slave Conditions 1841–43

	Arrondissement		
	St. Piere	Fort Royal	Total
Number of plantations visited			
Sugar	205	309	514
Coffee	38	176	214
Provision & minor crops	112	100	212
Mixed crops	16	12	28
Total	371	597	968
Number of slaves			
Below 14 years old	6,556	9,670	16,226
14–60 years old	14,491	21,548	36,039
Over 60 years old	1,520	2,173	3,693
Total	22,567	33,391	55,958
Food distribution (by plantation)			
Legally prescribed ration	67	129	196
Free Saturday	252	400	652
Mixed regime	33	60	93
No information	19	8	27
Clothing distribution (by plantation)			
Legally prescribed ration	244	256	500
Partial ration	54	52	106
No distribution	60	287	347
No information	13	2	15
Gardens (by plantation)			
Well or adequately cultivated	304	384	688
Poorly cultivated	49	159	208[a]
No gardens	14	48	62
No information	12	6	18

Source: Ministère de la Marine et des Colonies, *Exposé générale des résultats de patronage*, pp. 89–90.
[a]Table gives figure as 200. Presumed addition error.

to plantations (of these, 514 were to sugar plantations, 214 to coffee plantations, and 240 to other types of plantation).[17]

With few exceptions, masters encouraged their slaves to grow their own foodstuffs wherever possible. Among the estates included in this sample, the practice of giving free Saturdays to the slaves appears to have been far more common than the distribution of the legally prescribed *ordinaire* as the means of providing for slave subsistence. The substitution of free Saturdays for the legal ration was almost general throughout the colony, while garden plots were almost universal and appear to have existed even where the *ordinaire* was distributed. For example, according to one report, in Lamentin, where free Saturdays were denied on almost all the plantations and the slaves received the legal allotments, the slaves nevertheless kept well-tended gardens and drew considerable revenues from selling to the local markets. Alternatively, many planters, especially if they were well-to-do, like the owners of the large plantations in Sainte Marie, preferrred to give rations to their slaves rather than to allow them to cultivate gardens independently. Not surprisingly, the distribution of clothing allowances was more widely practiced than food rations, although the plantation inspection reports reveal that many planters expected their slaves to provide their own clothing as well as their food from the income of their gardens. This practice was especially widespread among the less prosperous planters, particularly in the poorer southern *arrondissement* of Fort Royal. Only planters who were well-off could afford to buy clothing to give to their slaves. Others could do so only when the harvest was good, if at all. Several public prosecutors objected to making the slaves provide their own clothing and admonished the planters to stop the practice. Thus, while there were diverse combinations and possibilities of conditions of subsistence, the slaves appear to have provided a substantial amount of their maintenance through their independent labors beyond their toil in the canefields, and the gardens and free Saturdays were a widespread experience of the majority of the slaves.[18]

However, not all parts of the island nor all planters were amenable to the cultivation of provision grounds. The instances where there were no gardens or where they were reported as poorly cultivated appear to be overrepresented in the arid and poorer southern part of the island (the *arrondissement* of Fort Royal). In Vauclin, Marin, Sainte Anne, Diamant, Anses d'Arlets, Trois Ilets, and parts of Carbet, dry weather and poor soil prevented the slaves from producing enough to feed themselves and contributed to the malaise of the plantations as well. In 1843, a public prosecutor inspecting plantations in Vauclin wrote: 'In the *quartier*, the masters could not substitute the free Saturday for allowances of food without compromising the existence of their *ateliers*. The drought and the quality of the soil would prevent the slaves from satisfying their needs by their own labor. For several years, the products of some very important plantations have not covered their expenses.'[19]

For even the most industrious slave, the paternalism of the planter was inescapable. As Schoelcher remarked, 'The greater or lesser wealth of the slaves depends a great deal on the benevolence of the master.' Whichever mode of providing for the slaves was adopted, one inspection report noted, 'their nourishment is assured everywhere, and the master is always ready . . . to come to the aid of the slave when the latter has need of him.' Indeed, seasonal fluctuations could require the master to come to the assistance of his slaves. 'In years of great drought,' de Cassagnac writes, 'subsistence crops do not grow. Then planters who previously gave the free Saturday once again give the *ordinaire*. Those are disastrous years.'[20]

Although the actual cultivation of the crops was not subject to the direct discipline of the planter, this labor could be compulsory. According to the inspection report of one public prosecutor: 'the good or bad state of his provision is the doing of the slave. However, the master can be accused of negligence if he does not use all the means of encouragement or of correction in his power to compel the slave to work for himself and thus improve his lot. Also, I have given my approval to those planters who have told me that they are just as severe or even more so with the slave who will not cultivate his garden than with the one who will not work with them.' But compulsion was not usually necessary, and often individual planters went to great lengths to support the efforts of their slaves. Sieur Telliam-Maillet, who managed the Ceron plantation in Diamant, had the land that his slaves were going to use for their provision grounds plowed. Even though he supplied his slaves with the *ordinaire*, M. Delite-Loture, who owned nearly 300 slaves in the *quartier* of Sainte Anne, bought or rented land in the highlands of Rivière Pilote which he cleared so his slaves could work it for themselves. Each week, he had them taken nearly two leagues from the plantation to these gardens, and he paid for the transport of their produce as well. Schoelcher reports that in some *quartiers*, the masters provided the slaves who worked such gardens with tools, carts, mules, and a *corvée* of workers, and the masters and the slave cultivators divided the harvest in half. Other masters considered such an arrangement beneath their dignity and simply abandoned the land to the slaves.[21]

According to Schoelcher, the garden was the principal source of well-being available to the slaves in Martinique. Customarily, slaves who were given half a free day a week were given only half a ration, while those who received a full day were to provide their food by themselves. In addition, Sundays belonged to the slaves and could also be devoted to subsistence activities, as could rest periods and evenings during the week. Schoelcher records that on a great number of plantations in Martinique, this arrangement had become a sort of exchange between the master and his slaves. 'This transaction', he writes, 'is very favorable for the master who no longer has capital to lay out to ensure the supply of provisions. And it is accepted with good will by the black who in working Saturday and Sunday in his garden derives great benefits.'[22]

The slaves who wanted to plant gardens were given as much land as they could cultivate. The provision grounds were usually on the uncultivated lands on the margins of the estate, often scattered in the hills above the canefields. However, both de Cassagnac and Schoelcher write that some planters in the 1840s used the gardens to practice crop rotation. When the sugar cane had exhausted the soil in a field, the slaves were permitted to plant provisions there until the land was again fit for cane. The gardens were then shifted to other fields. (According to historian Gabriel Debien, larger gardens located away from the slave quarters appeared only after 1770, but these were still intended to supplement the rations provided by the master rather than to furnish the main items of the slave diet. The staples of the slave diet, manioc, potatoes, and yams, were grown by the master in the gardens belonging to the plantation.) The plots were frequently quite extensive, as much as one or two *arpents*, according to Schoelcher (1 *arpent* = 0.85 acre). All the available sources agree that the slave provision grounds were very well kept. The produce of the gardens was abundant, and the land was not allowed to stand idle. Manioc, the principal source of nourishment of the slave population, was harvested as often as four times a year. Besides manioc, the slaves raised bananas, potatoes, yams, and other vegetables on these provision grounds.[23]

In addition to the provision grounds, there were also small gardens in the yards surrounding the slave cabins. They were intended to supplement the weekly ration, not replace it, and all the slaves, including those who received the *ordinaire*, had them. There the slaves grew sorrel (*oiselle de Guinée*), a type of squash (*giraumon*), cucumbers from France and Guinea (*concombres de France et de Guinée*), green peppers (*poivrons*), hot peppers (*piment z'oiseau*), calabash vines (*liane à calebasse*), okra (*petites racines gombo*), and perhaps some tobacco. They also planted fruit trees and, if the master permitted, kept a few chickens there as well.[24]

The 'little Guineas', as the provision ground have been called, allowed collective self-expression by the slaves and form what Roger Bastide describes as a 'niche' within slavery where Afro-Caribbean culture could develop. The slaves had complete responsibility for the provision grounds and were able to organize their own activity there without supervision. The use of these parcels and their product was not simply a narrow economic activity but was integrated into broader cultural patterns. The work of preparing the soil, planting, cultivating, harvesting, and the disposition of the product were organized through ritual, kinship, and community and were important aspects of slave life as diverse as kinship, cuisine, and healing practices. These activities provided an avenue for the slaves to exercise decision making and to demonstrate self-worth otherwise closed off by slavery. But, except for Schoelcher's vague comment that the slaves cultivated them 'communally', there is little detailed information on how the slaves organized their activities. This lack of documentation is perhaps mute testimony to the genuine autonomy that the slaves enjoyed in the conduct of these activities.[25]

Even at best, the slaves who produced their own provisions were exposed to risk and uncertainty. They were generally given land of inferior quality that was incapable of supporting sugar or coffee. At times, the planters deprived them of their free day under various pretexts. If for some reason they fell ill and could not work, their food supply was jeopardized. Drought or bad weather might make cultivation impossible. The prospect of theft and disorder was then increased, and at the extreme the physical well-being of the labor force was threatened.[26]

Nevertheless, this arrangement could be advantageous for an industrious slave. Access to this property meant that the slaves' consumption was no longer entirely dependent on the economic condition of the master. Rather, they could use their free time and the produce of their gardens to improve their standard of living. They demonstrated exceptional initiative and skill and used the opportunities presented to them to secure at least relative control over their subsistence and a degree of independence from the master. According to one contemporary estimate, the incentive provided by the gardens doubled slave output, while Higman's data suggest an inverse relation between provision-ground cultivation and mortality on Jamaican sugar estates. With the free day and the other free time that could be husbanded during the week during rest periods and after tasks were finished, the slave could produce beyond his or her immediate subsistence needs. The slaves sold this produce in the towns and cities and developed a network of markets that was an important feature of the economic and social life of the colony. The sale of this surplus in the town market allowed the slaves to improve both the quantity and the quality of goods available to them and to satisfy tastes and desires that the master could not. Thus, improvement in the slaves' well-being was due to their own effort, not to any amelioration of the regime.[27]

Of course, not all slaves were willing or able to endure the burden of extra work which the provision grounds represented. Infants, the aged, the infirm, expectant mothers or those nursing children — all those who could not provide for themselves received a food allowance from the master, even on the plantations where the slaves grew their own foodstuffs. Also included among this number were those slaves who refused to raise a garden. In Fort Royal, a public prosecutor wrote, 'Only the lazy receive a ration and they are almost ashamed of it.' Of these 'lazy' slaves, Schoelcher commented. 'We do not want to deny, however, that there are many Negroes who show a great indifference to the benefit of free Saturdays. It is necessary to force them to work for themselves on that day. It does not surprise us that beings, saturated with disgust and struck by malediction, are litte concerned to improve their lot during the moments of respite that are given to them. Instead, they prefer to surrender to idleness or become intoxicated to the point of delirium from the melancholy agitation of their African dances.' The free Saturday, while generally received enthusiastically by the slaves, was not universally accepted. For many slaves, it simply meant more work, and they refused. They withdrew their voluntary cooperation and threw the burden of maintenance back on the master. De Cassagnac expressed surprise that on many plantations, if the slaves were given the free Saturday, they would not work. They had, in his view, to be treated like children and be forced to work for themselves. It was necessary to have a driver lead them to the gardens and watch them as carefully as when they were working for the estate.[28]

Long before the promulgation of the Mackau Law, the slaves established rights and prerogatives with regard not only to the produce of the land but to the provision grounds and gardens themselves that the masters were compelled to recognize. 'The masters no longer acknowledge any rights over the gardens of the *atelier*. The slave is the sovereign master over the terrain that is conceded to him,' admitted the Colonial Council of Martinique. 'This practice has become a custom for the slaves who regard it as a right which cannot be taken from them without the possibility of disrupting the discipline and good order of the *ateliers*,' reported one official. The slaves regarded the provision grounds as their own. When they died, the garden and its produce was passed on to their relatives. 'They pass them on from father to son, from mother to daughter, and, if they do not have any children, they bequeath them to their nearest kin or even their friends,' wrote Schoelcher. Often, if no relatives remained on the estate, it was reported that kinsmen came from other plantations to receive their inheritance with the consent of the master. Here as elsewhere the autonomous kinship organization of the slave community served as a counterpoint to the economic rationality of the plantation, and the master was obliged to respect its claims.[29]

The slaves defended their rights even at the expense of the master, and there was often a subtle game of give-and-take between the two parties. While traveling through the *quartier* of Robert, Schoelcher was surprised to find two small patches of manioc in the midst of a large, well-tended canefield. M. Tiberge, the proprietor, explained that the slaves had planted the manioc when the field had been abandoned. When he wanted to cultivate the field he offered to buy the crop, but they demanded an exorbitant price. The master then called upon the other slaves to set what they considered to be a fair price, but this too was rejected by the slaves who had planted the manioc. 'I'll have to wait six or seven months until that damned manioc is ripe,' Tiberge continued. Another planter, M. Latuillerie of Lamentin, upon returning from a long trip, found that his slaves had abandoned the plots allotted to them in favor of his canefields. He could not simply reclaim his land, but instead he first had to agree to give the occupants another field. Schoelcher also observed large mango trees in the middle of canefields which stunted the cane plants in their shadow. The masters would have cut them down, but they remained standing because they were bequeathed to some yet-unborn slave. He continued, 'There are some planters who do not have fruit trees on their plantations because tradition establishes that such and such a tree belongs to such and such a Negro, and they (the planters) have litte hope of ever enjoying them because the slave bequeaths his tree just like the rest of his property.'[30]

The Fruits of Their Labour

Beyond filling the personal consumption needs of the slaves, the provision grounds produced a marketable surplus of food that was sold to the plantations and in the towns and cities. The main source of revenue for the slaves was the sale of manioc flour and other agricultural products, and among the main customers were the plantations themselves. Almost all of the manioc consumed on the majority of medium and large estates was purchased from the slaves. The planters bought these provisions to replace or supplement provisions cultivated as an estate crop and to distribute as rations to those slaves who were unable to provide their own food. The abundance of slave produce, especially in the years when agricultural conditions were favorable, caused the price of provisions on the local markets to fall sharply. When this happened, the more prosperous planters bought manioc flour from their slaves at a constant price above that of the market and, according to De Moges, gave it right back to them as a ration. One official observed that 'every time that manioc flour is cheap, the master buys it from them, usually at a price above the market price. Sometimes he pays double the market price.' The report of a deputy public prosecutor in 1843 describes the difficulties caused by low provision prices:

> The worthless price to which provisions, especially manioc flour, . . . sometimes falls causes even the most industrious slave to become disgusted with labor. In these circumstances, many masters, I believe one could say the majority of them, come to the aid of their slaves, buying from them the quantity of flour which is necessary for the needs of their plantations at a price well above the market price. But sometimes the discouragement of men whose hopes for a better price for their labor have been betrayed is such that they do not plant at all in the following year. Thus dearth often follows abundance.

By subsidizing their slaves' production in hard times, the planters hoped to encourage them to continue growing provisions and thereby avoid a scarcity that would drive prices up, increase the colony's reliance on food imports, and disrupt general economic activity. Instead, they could keep prices low and guarantee a stable supply of essential provisions by supporting the market.[31]

The slaves also developed a network of markets beyond the plantation that was an important feature of the economic and social life of Martinique, and the colony came to rely on the produce of the slave gardens for a substantial portion of its food. Important market towns such as the ones at Lamentin, François, Trinité, and Robert attracted slaves from all parts of the island and brought them into contact with the world beyond the plantation. Soleau describes the Lamentin market: 'This town is one of the most frequently visited by the slaves of the colony. It has a fairly large market where they come to sell their produce on Sunday. I have been told that the number of slaves that gather there is often as high as five or six thousand. I passed through there that day while going to the *quartier* of Robert, and encountered many blacks on the road who were going to the town. All were carrying something that they were doubtlessly going to sell — manioc flour, potatoes, yams, poultry, etc.' Sunday was the major market day in the towns; however, smaller markets were held on other days. These markets allowed the masters to have their slaves acquire goods that were not available on the plantation and would otherwise have to be purchased. An astonishing variety of goods were exchanged at the town markets. These, of course, included manioc, fruits, vegetables, yams, fresh or salted fish, animals, and slave handicrafts, but also manufactured goods such as shoes, dry goods, porcelain, crystal, perfume, jewelry, and furniture. Undoubtedly, barter played a large part in these exchanges, especially in local markets, but the money economy was significant, and prices were set in major towns for the main articles of trade. The scale of exchanges at these town markets was so great that they caused the urban merchants to complain, but, in the words of Sainte Croix, they were nevertheless a great resource for the interior of the island.[32]

The Sunday market was as much a social event as an occasion for exchanging goods. Slaves went to town to attend mass, meet friends from other parts of the island, drink tafia, smoke, eat roast corn, exchange news and gossip, and perhaps dance, sing, or gamble. It was an opportunity for display, and the slaves wore their best. One observer paints a striking picture of the appearance made by the slaves at the Lamentin market: 'These slaves are almost always very well dressed and present the exterior signs of material well-being. The men have trousers, shirts, vests, and hats of oilskin or straw. The women have skirts of Indian cotton, white blouses, and scarves, some of which are luxurious, as well as earrings, pins and even some chains of gold.' According to Soleau, the signs of prosperity presented by the slaves of Martinique on market day were unusual in the Caribbean and even in rural France: 'One thing struck me that I have never seen in Cayenne, Surinam, or Demerara. It is the cleanliness and the luxury of the clothing of the slaves that I encountered. The lazy, having nothing to sell, remained on the plantations, but in France, generally, the peasants, except for their shoes, were not better dressed on Sunday and did not wear such fine material.'[33]

The colorful and bustling markets punctuated the drudgery and isolation of plantation life. Slaves from town and country, young and old, male and female, as well as freedmen, sailors, merchants, planters — anyone who wanted to buy or sell — mingled in the crowds. Such gatherings were potentially dangerous and posed a threat to order and security in a slave society, as Governor Mathieu recognized: 'I have posted thirty men and an officer at St. Esprit. This measure was welcomed by the entire commune. St. Esprit is a center of commerce. A great number of people, including many strangers, gather there for the markets that are held each week, especially on Sundays. Thus, police measures are necessary and are linked to those that have been established to prevent bad subjects from stirring up the *ateliers* and inciting unrest.'[34]

These markets offered incentives to the slaves and enabled them to improve the material conditions of life as well as to acquire skills, knowledge, and social contacts that increased their independence and allowed them to assert their individuality and vary the texture of their lives. Their initiative led to the development of new economic and social patterns and the mobilization of productive forces that otherwise would have remained dormant.

They were able to obtain money and to purchase a range of goods that would otherwise be unavailable to them. Particularly important were items of clothing, and the more industrious slaves were able to forgo the ration and provide for themselves. According to one inspection report: 'In general, the slaves are well-dressed. The most industrious of them renounce the distribution of clothing and are well enough off to consider it a disgrace to ask the master for a shirt or a pair of trousers. On the other hand, the laziest of them sometimes oblige the masters to give them more than the regulations prescribe.' With the ability to acquire their own clothing, dress became an important expression of independence and status during their free time. While they were working, the slaves dressed poorly. Schoelcher marveled at the tatters they wore. But on 'their' time the slaves' appearance could undergo a drastic transformation. On Sundays or special occasions, the slaves wore frock coats and well-made outfits with satin vests, ruffled shirts, boots, and the ever-present umbrella. A public prosecutor described the appearance of slaves at a New Year's celebration on one plantation: 'The costumes of some dancers were luxurious so to speak. For the women, there were skirts of fine material, cambric shirts, coral or jet necklaces, and gold earrings. For the men, costumes of linen or broadcloth. Shoes had been abandoned as unnecessary encumbrances.' Another attorney reported a runaway slave who wore a black frock coat, boots, and a new silk hat, and who passed for a freedman for several days. 'Meeting them like this,' wrote Schoelcher, 'one does not suspect that they are the same men that were seen the day before working in rags.' Boots or shoes were an especially important status symbol among the slaves. In the early days of the colony, they were forbidden to wear shoes. Although these ordinances were no longer enforced, most slaves went barefoot. Schoelcher wrote that it was not uncommon to meet a well-dressed slave on the road to town carrying his shoes and putting them on only after his arrival.[35]

Household goods also figured prominently among the items bought by the slaves. The more prosperous of them often furnished their cabins elaborately. Commentators on slave conditions, both official and unofficial, in favor of slavery and opposed to it, noted such articles as chairs, tables, chests of drawers, mirror wardrobes, and even four-poster beds with pillows, sheets, and mattresses. However, as Schoelcher emphasized, such relative luxury could be found only among a privileged few such as artisans and *commandeurs*. The less prosperous had only a broken-down bedstead, a chair or bench, some crockery, a cooking pot, a storage box or two, and an earthen floor, while the poorest possessed only a cooking pot, a board or mat to sleep on, a bamboo stalk to store water, and a few pieces of tattered clothing hanging from a string stretched across the room.[36]

The slaves often made great efforts to increase their property during their free time, and in the process they developed a variety of skills. Many slaves raised chickens, rabbits, pigs, sheep, cows, and even horses. Slave-owned herds could be surprisingly large. In addition to their provision grounds, the slaves on the Lacouet plantation had 25 hectares on which to graze their animals. The slaves on the Fabrique plantation in Rivière Salée owned 15 head of cattle. The head carpenter on the plantation of Peter Maillet in Saint Esprit personally owned seven cows in addition to pigs, chickens, and rabbits, while the *commandeur* on the same plantation had two horses. Schoelcher reports a herd of 100 sheep belonging to the slaves of M. Douville on the neighboring island of Guadeloupe. Slaves also found other means of augmenting their income or acquiring property if circumstances did not permit them to have provision grounds. Where the soil was poor and little garden produce could be grown, slaves cut wood and made charcoal for sale. Fishing was an important resource for slaves near the coast, although their activities were curtailed after 1837 by an ordinance, designed to prevent slaves from escaping to freedom in the neighboring British islands, which forbade slaves to use boats. Slaves on plantations near towns cut guinea grass during their midday break and carried bundles of it into the town to sell as fodder after work in the evening. A young lawyer from Martinique remarked to Schoelcher that the slaves sometimes walked as far as a league with bundles of fodder weighing up to 75 livres merely in order to earn 20 francs a month. Other slaves earned money by hiring themselves out during their free time, either on or off the plantation. In the context of such opportunities to earn money, any skills a slave could acquire were an extremely important resource. A notable example of this was a cook in Vauclin who acquired considerable wealth by preparing most of the banquets in the *quartier*. He was given his freedom when his master died, and he bought his wife's freedom for 1,500 francs.[37]

The provision grounds could be very profitable for industrious slaves. Lavollée estimated that the revenue from $1\frac{1}{2}$ hectares near the Pitons du Carbet, which was worked by three male and three female slaves, was no less than 10 francs per day. Schoelcher wrote that a slave could earn between 200 and 400 francs yearly with free Saturdays — men a little more and women a little less. An official source puts the figure at 700–800 francs per year. One public prosecutor reported that many slaves on one exemplary plantation had savings amounting to more than three times their purchase price but had not thought of buying their freedom. According to another public prosecutor, the slaves at the Grand-Ceron plantation had 18,000 francs in doubloons and quadruples, while a third attorney claimed that the slaves of another plantation had more than 5,000 doubloons worth 432,000 francs. Such estimates must be judged with caution, since we do not know the basis upon which they were made nor the number of slaves involved. Neither is it very likely that the slaves made a habit of showing their money to visiting public officials. Nevertheless, it is certain that slaves in Martinique were able to accumulate substantial sums of cash as well as other property.[38]

Perhaps the most surprising and extraordinary aspect of the independent economic life of the slaves in Martinique is that some slaves used their earnings to hire other slaves or freedmen to work in their gardens, and a few even owned slaves themselves. One public prosecutor commented on the practice of slaves hiring other slaves and on the source of their labor force: 'The Negroes have as much land as they can cultivate. It has reached the point that several of them hire Negroes from outside or belonging to the plantation to work in their gardens. This supposes that the latter do not cultivate the land on their own account. In fact, on almost all the plantations there are lazy slaves who do not have gardens. But these men, who cannot be motivated to work by the hope of a harvest for which one must wait several months, can be drawn by the lure of an immediate gain, at least to satisfy the needs of their moment.' Not only did slaves hire other laborers, including free men to work for them, but there are also recorded instances of slaves owning other slaves. On the Perpigna plantation in Vauclin, the *commandeur* owned a slave, but this *commandeur*, like so many other slaveowners, found that his slave was 'never as industrious as he could be'. There were several slaves on the plantation of Sieur Telliam-Maillet who owned slaves. 'It is a reward from a master who is very happy with his slave,' wrote a public prosecutor. 'He permits him to buy slaves to replace him when he does not want to work, even in the master's fields.' This is probably the ultimate expression of the slave's access to property in a slave society. With it the gap between slave and master, bondman and free man, was narrowed considerably. But, at the same time, such conditions cannot be exaggerated. The slave's access to property and the opportunity for independent activity are extremely important for understanding the contradictions of the slave system as well as the role of the slaves in shaping their New World environment. However, only a small minority ever acquired even moderate property, and independence was always limited and conditional upon the benevolence of the master. The social distance between the most prosperous and industrious slave and the most impoverished and recalcitrant slave was always much less than between the former and the most destitute master.[39]

This process of the slaves' appropriating the free Saturday and elaborating these 'proto-peasant' activities had far-reaching consequences for the development of slavery in the French West Indies and was itself an aspect of the crisis of the slave system. It was an initiative by a population that, over the course of its historical experience, had learned to adapt to the labor routine, discipline, and organization of time of the slave plantation and confronted slavery within its own relations and processes. The result was simultaneously to strengthen and to weaken the slave system. On the one hand, the slaves became more effectively integrated into slavery and responsive to its rewards and punishments. The operating expenses of the plantation were reduced, and a greater surplus was available to the planter. On the other hand, the slaves were able to appropriate aspects of these processes and to establish a degree of control over their own subsistence and reproduction. They claimed rights to property and disposition over time and labor that the masters were forced to recognize, and they were able to resist infringements upon them. While it meant more work for the slaves, they were able to improve their material well-being substantially and to increase their independence from the master. They restricted his capacity to exploit labor and presented a fixed obstacle to surplus production. The amount of labor time at the disposition of the planter was frozen, and the slaves acquired a means of resisting the intensification of work at the very moment that the transformation of the world sugar market demanded higher levels of productivity and greater exploitation of labor from French West Indian planters.

In this process, the character of the slave relation itself was altered. The assertion of these rights and the exercise of autonomy by the slaves reduced their dependence on the master and undermined his authority. Custom, consent, and accommodation assumed greater weight in the conduct of daily life where coercion had prevailed. The acquisition of skills and property and the establishment of economic and social networks enabled the enslaved to realize important material and psychological gains. The slaves thus began to fashion an alternative way of life that played an important role not only in eroding the slave regime but also in forming a transition to a new society. In it can be seen nuclei of the post-emancipation social structure. Significantly, after emancipation the system of petty production and marketing organized by the slaves was to play an important part in helping them to resist the new encroachments of plantation agriculture and shape a new relation between labor and capital.[40]

The ability to elaborate autunomous provision-ground cultivation and marketing within slavery provided the slaves with an alternative to plantation labor after emancipation and allowed them to resist its reimposition. The very activities that the planters had encouraged during slavery now incurred their wrath. Carlyle scorned Quashee and his pumpkin; but far from representing the 'lazy Negro', it is a testimony to the capacity of the Afro-Caribbean population to learn, adapt, create, and articulate an alternative conception of their needs despite the harshness of slavery. Probably few could escape the plantation entirely after emancipation, but for the great majority of the freed slaves the existence of provision-ground cultivation and marketing networks enabled them to struggle effectively over the conditions of their labor. Jamaican historian Douglas Hall suggests that upon emancipation the freed slaves sought to separate their place of residence from their place of work. Where planters tried to compel a resident labor force, the workers left to establish free villages on lands off the plantations. In either case, the skills, resources, and associations formed through 'proto-peasant' activities during slavery were of decisive importance in enabling the free population to secure control over their own conditions of reproduction and to establish an independent bargaining position vis-à-vis the planters.[41]

The immediate consequence of emancipation throughout the French and British Caribbean was the withdrawal of labor, particularly the labor of women and children, from the plantation sector, and struggles with the planters over time, wages, and conditions of work in which the laboring population was able to assert a great deal of independence and initiative. It represented, in Walter Rodney's expression, an attempt to impose the rhythm of the village on the plantation. The successful separation of work and residence forced a new relation of production and reproduction on the plantation system itself as the planters attempted to recapture the labor of the emancipated population or find a substitute for it under conditions that guaranteed profitability. This resulted in the formation of new coercive control over subsistence activities and petty commodity production to one degree or another. This transformation of the plantation system and the transition from one form of coerced labor to another was not the inevitable result of unfolding capitalist rationality but rather is best understood as the product of the contradictory relation between production and social reproduction within the relations of slavery and of the struggle between masters and slaves over alternative purposes, conceptions of needs, and modes of organization of social and material life.[42]

Notes

1. A. Soleau, *Notes sur les Guyanes francaise, hollandaise, anglaise, et sur les Antilles francaises*, (Cayenne, Surinam, Demerary, La Martinique, La Guadeloupe) (Paris, 1835), pp. 9-10; Ministère de la Marine et des Colonies, Commission, 26 (1840), p. 205.
2. Félix Sainte Croix, *Statistique de la Martinique*, Vol. 2 (Paris, 1822), p. 105.
3. Sidney W. Mintz, *Caribbean Transformations* (Baltimore, 1974), pp. 132-33; Ministère de la Marine et des Colonies, *Exposé général des résultats du patronage* (Paris, 1844), pp. 303-05.
4. Walter Rodney, 'Plantation Society in Guyana', *Review*, 4, No. 4 (1981), pp. 643-66; Sidney W. Mintz, 'Descrying the Peasantry', *Review*, 6, No. 2 (1982), pp. 209-25.
5. Gabriel Debien, *Les esclaves aux Antilles françaises, XVIIe-XVIIIe siècles*, (Basse-Terre: Société d'histoire de la Guadeloupe; Fort-de-France, 1974), pp. 178-86; Lucien Peytraud, *L'esclavage aux Antilles francaises avant 1789 d'après des documents inédits des Archives Coloniales*, (Guadeloupe, 1973), p. 217.
6. Debien, *op. cit.*, pp. 176-86; Peytraud, *op. cit.*, pp. 216-24.
7. Debien, *op. cit.*, pp. 176-77, 181, 183-86, 215; Antoine Gisler, *L'esclavage aux Antilles françaises, XVIIe-XIXe siècles: Contribution au problème de l'esclavage* (Fribourg, 1965), pp. 23-25, 35-38.
8. Victor Schoelcher, *Des colonies francaises: Abolition immédiate de l'esclavage* (Paris, 1842), pp. 8-9.
9. Ministère du Commerce et des Manufactures, *Enquête sur les sucres* (Paris, 1829), pp. 23, 52, 67, 156, 248.
10. Sainte Croix, *Statistique*, 2:p. 105. P. Lavollée, *Notes sur les cultures et la production de la Martinique et de la Guadeloupe* (Paris, 1841), p. 10.
11. Ministère de la Marine et des Colonies, *Exposé général des résultats du patronage* (Paris, 1844), pp. 183-84, 290.
12. *Ibid.*, pp. 104-05, 180-88, 290.
13. Ministère de la Marine et des Colonies, *Exposé général*, pp. 177-88, 288-91, 332-33.
14. Archives Nationales — Section Outre — Mer (A.N.S.O.M.), Généralités 167 (1350).
15. *Ibid.*
16. *Ibid.*
17. Ministère de la Marine et des Colonies, *Exposé général*, pp. 89-90.
18. *Ibid.*, pp. 89-90, 182-85, 177, 219-25, 288-91, 332-33.
19. Ministère de la Marine et des Colonies, *Exposé général*, pp. 183-85; Gisler, *op. cit.*, p. 48; Schoelcher, *op. cit.*, p. 7.
20. Ministère de la Marine et des Colonies, *op. cit.*, Schoelcher, *op. cit.*, pp. 12-13; A.N.S.O.M., Martinique 7 (83), Dupotêt à Ministre de la Marine et des colonies, Fort Royal, 5 April 1832.
21. *Ibid.*; Adolphe Granier de Cassagnac, *Voyage aux Antilles*, (Paris, 1842), pp.174-75.
22. Schoelcher, *op. cit.*, p. 11; Lavollée, *Notes sur les cultures*, p. 123.
23. Debien, *op. cit.*, pp. 178-91, 205-07; Sainte Croix, *Statistique*, 2, p. 105.
24. Ministère de la Marine et des Colonies, *Exposé général*, pp. 180-88; Schoelcher, *op. cit.*, pp. 9-13; A.N.S.O.M., Généralités 144 (1221); Debien, *op. cit.*, pp. 178-91; Mintz, *op. cit.*, pp. 225-50.
25. Melville Herskovits, *Life in a Haitian Valley* (New York, 1937), pp. 67-68, 76-81; M. G. Lewis, *Journal of a West India Proprietor, 1815-1817* (Boston, 1929), p. 88; Roger Bastide, *The African Religions of Brazil* (Baltmiore, 1978), p. 58.
26. Soleau, *op. cit.*, pp. 9-10; Lavollée, *Notes sur les culvures*, p. 123.
27. Ministère de la des Colonies, *Exposé général*, pp. 110-188, 305; Barry Higman, *Slave Population and Economy of Jamaica, 1807* (Cambridge, 1976), p. 129; A.N.S.O.M., Martinique, 7 (83).
28. De Cassagnac, *op. cit.*, p. 176; Schoelcher, *op. cit.*, p. 12.
29. Schoelcher, *op. cit.*, pp. 9-13; A.N.S.O.M., Généralités, 144 (1221), Ministère de la Marine et des Colonies, *Exposé général*, pp. 180-88, 290.
30. *Ibid.*
31. A.N.S.O.M., Martinique 9 (99); Schoelcher, *op. cit.*, p. 11; Ministère de la Marine et des colonies, Commission 26, May 1840, p. 206.
32. Soleau, *op. cit.*, p. 59; Herskovits, *op. cit.*, pp. 81-85; A.N.S.O.M., Généralités, 144 (1221); A.N.S.O.M., Martinique 7 (83); Sainte Croix, *Statistique*, Vol. 2, pp. 13-15; M. Le Comte E. De la Cornillère, *La Martinique en 1842: Intérêts coloniaux, souvenirs du voyage* (Paris, 1843), pp. 123-24.
33. Cornillère, *op. cit.*, pp.123-24; Soleau, *op. cit.*, p. 59; Ministère de la Marine et des Colonies, *Exposé général*, p. 102.
34. A.N.S.O.M., Martinique 7 (83), Mathieu à Ministre de la Marine et des Colonies, 10 March 1847, No. 1508.
35. *Ibid.*; Benoît Duschene-Devernay, *Mémoire sur la Martinique avec des notes explicatives* (Paris, 1832), p. 22-27; Schoelcher, *op. cit.*, pp. 4-7, 14-15.
36. Schoelcher, *op. cit.*, pp. 1-3; Ministère de la Marine et des Colonies, *Exposé général*, pp. 111, 268-77, 288-91, 332-33.
37. *Ibid.*; A.N.S.O.M., Martinique 7 (83), Duschene-Duvernay, *op. cit.*, pp. 17-19.
38. Ministère de la marine et des Colonies, *Exposé général*, p. 100, 111, 332-33; Schoelcher, *op. cit.*, p. 11; Lavollée, *Notes sur les cultures*, p. 10.
39. *Ibid.*; Sidney W. Mintz, 'Was the Plantation Slave a Proletarian?', *Review*, Vol. 2. No. 1 (1978), 81-98.
40. Mintz, *op. cit.*
41. *Ibid.*; Douglas Hall, 'The Flight from the Plantations Reconsidered: The British West Indies, 1838-1842', *Journal of Caribbean History*, Vol 10-11 (1978), pp. 7-23.
42. Rodney, 'Plantation Society in Guyana'.

The Origins of the Jamaican Internal Marketing System

SIDNEY MINTZ AND DOUGLAS HALL*

This paper deals with the origins and growth of the Jamaican internal market system and the local small-scale agriculture whose products are served by that system. The Jamaica Census of 1943 indicates that out of an agricultural labor force of 221,376, there were 49,200 peasants operating holdings of ten acres or less, while 16,972 operators had larger holdings. Moreover, a significant proportion of the agricultural labor force listed as wage earners was simultaneously engaged in cultivating owned land in plots of less than one acre, or in cultivating rented land (Cumper, n.d.).

The Jamaican peasantry of today originated within the physical boundaries of the slave-worked sugar estates and within the normal pattern of slave-estate administration of two centuries ago. Since the slave plantation elsewhere in much of the Caribbean region, as in Puerto Rico, served to destroy the peasantry rather than to create it (Mintz, 1951, 1959), the forces at work in the Jamaican case are of interest, and what is known of the history of Jamaican internal marketing is closely intermeshed with the rise of that country's peasant class (Mintz, 1955).

In the British Caribbean under slavery, the owners and managers of estates faced the problem of feeding their slaves. The alternative extremes were either to use the slaves to produce as much as possible of their own diet, by compulsion or by incentive, or else to import all of what they ate. Of these two courses the first, though not always practicable, was ideally the more desirable. If the slaves could feed themselves the estates would be saved expenditure of money on imported foods and avoid the risks contingent upon importation. When warfare disturbed merchant shipping, as occurred so often in the eighteenth century, and shortages of imported food resulted, food prices rose (Ragatz, 1927). Moreover, when shortages of imports prevailed, the slaves could not be adequately fed even if the planter could afford to purchase at high prices. Prolonged interference with the importation of food introduced a vicious circle of high prices, malnutrition, and reduced production and profits.

Yet there were often difficulties in the way of local food production, and it is no accident that today in the British Caribbean the peasantry and food production are found chiefly in mountain areas or in areas otherwise, by reason of location, or of soil or weather conditions, unsuitable for sugar production. Until the 1830s land and slave labor were the essential factors of sugar production. Capital equipment and technical know-how became important only after the emancipation and the opening of the British sugar market to foreign competition in the second half of the nineteenth century (Goveia, 1959).

On this emphasis on land and labor rested the expedient decisions of the sugar planter who wanted to plant sugar wherever it could profitably be planted, but at the same time had either to provide land for food growing for his labor force or risk the uncertainties of the food-import trade. Generally speaking, where land was flat and fertile the cane was planted; where it was not, food was grown for the slaves and the dependence on food imports was considerably reduced. Thus, throughout the archipelago as a whole, the flat or gently sloping islands (e.g.

The authors are grateful to Mr H. P. Jacobs of Kingston, Jamaica, and to Mr Peter Newman of the University College of the West Indies, Mona, Jamaica, for reading this paper and offering helpful criticism.

Papers in Caribbean Anthropology, No. 57 (New Haven, 1970), pp. 3–26.

Barbados, Antigua, St. Kitts) were almost entirely planted in sugar, whereas in the mountainous islands (e.g. Grenada, St. Vincent, Jamaica) planters, limited by topography in their sugar cultivation, had at their disposal relatively extensive areas which might be allotted to the growing of food crops.

Jamaica, largest of the British islands, contains distinctive coastal plains and interior valleys as well as mountain areas. In this island, therefore, both patterns developed (Beckford, 1790, 1: 154–70). On the few estates which lay quite apart from steep mountain slopes the food-import plan tended to prevail; but on those estates (the majority by far) which included rough hills or slopes or other poor-quality sugar land within their boundaries, the tendency was to food production. Clearly, whatever might be the individual planter's preference in the choice between food importing and food producing for his slaves, his actual practice was much influenced by sugar prices, the lay of his land, and the condition of the soil.

Where food production was undertaken the planter had to decide whether to include the work in the regular supervised agricultural program of the estate, or whether to offer inducements to the slaves to undertake the work voluntarily. It will be demonstrated that a thoroughgoing dependence on the regulated production of food was never achieved; in large measure, food production by the slaves grew in the absence of compulsion, and under conditions which implicitly acknowledged their responsiveness to the same incentives which operated for the free Jamaican.

In short, there was no generally accepted policy for supplying the slaves with food. Where an estate had land not wanted for cane, the slaves were usually allowed to cultivate provisions on it in their spare time. When war threatened or when for other reasons the importations of food were insufficient to meet the demand for them, laws were usually passed requiring estate owners to undertake the cultivation of a stipulated quantity of land in foodstuffs as an estate operation (Leslie, 1739: 233; Edwards, 1793, 2: 132). It is relevant that in years of warfare the prices offered for sugar tended to rise, thus encouraging the expansion of cane fields. In Jamaica the laws requiring local food production were customarily honored only in the breach. In all the islands, and especially in those in which the food-import system prevailed, the provident planter attempted to time his purchases of imported foods judiciously in order to keep his costs down and his stocks ready in case of shortage (Pares, 1950: 126–7, 136). At the same time, unsupervised cultivation of food stocks by the slaves themselves grew steadily more important, whenever the estate contained land to support their activity.

The slaves used such lands to produce a variety of foods, such as tree crops, vegetables, edible herbs and roots, as well as craft materials. This produce was primarily intended for their own domestic use. But eventually — and the details of the process are regrettably dim — surpluses came to be taken to local markets and exchanged for other commodities, or sold for cash. The proceeds of these transactions accrued entirely to the slaves, apparently from the very first. Market day, customarily held on Sunday so as not to interfere with estate cultivation, became an important social and economic institution.

Consideration of the system of agricultural production and marketing by slaves briefly noted above raises questions which are a prime concern of this paper. It is not at first apparent, for instance, why this food production should have been left to the slaves' initiative and not have been more commonly regulated as a part of the estate's program of cultivation. It is even less apparent why the slaves were permitted to go to market, sell or exchange surplus produce, and retain the goods or money received. Further, there is the question of the origins of the markets themselves. Also, we may ask precisely what crops the slaves chose to cultivate, why these were chosen, and with what skill and proficiency the enterprises of production and marketing were executed.

Exact and wholly satisfactory answers to these questions are not yet possible. For most of them we have been able to formulate reasonable explanations based on the available data, and it is convenient to begin with the subjects of crops and agricultural skills.

There had been a background for cultivation and for its associated processes before the English conquest of Jamaica and the rise of plantation agriculture, and even before the Spanish discovery and conquest of the island. To some extent at least, later patterns of subsistence were derivative from these older adjustments. Jamaica was occupied by Arawak Indian cultivators at the time of its discovery and early colonization by Spain.

Parry writes that the native Arawak cultivated cassava and perhaps a soft variety of maize, and gathered shellfish, roots, and berries (Parry, n.d.:30). Further information suggests that the Jamaican aboriginal crop repertory included 'tannier' (*Xanthosoma* sp.), arrowroot, sweet potatoes, coconuts, plantain, and a variety of uncultivated fruits. The diet was apparently sufficient and well-balanced (Sauer, 1950: 487–543; 1954: 20–1).

The Spanish settlement of Jamaica substantially eliminated the Arawak, but not their crops. Las Casas and others note the continued cultivation of the foods mentioned above, and the only important innovations mentioned are the raising of livestock and the curing of pork and bacon (Cundall and Pietersz, 1919: 15). Nonetheless, some of the earliest references to cultivated plants after the English occupation in 1655 make it clear that new crops had been added during the Spanish period, or introduced very early after the English landed. The Spaniards certainly were responsible for the introduction of the banana, nearly all the then known varieties of citrus, and the sugar cane. The English may, perhaps, be accredited with the introduction of the potato (Blome, 1672: 25; Hickeringill, 1661: 20; Parry, n.d.: 31).

The root crops which emerged as so important in later peasant agriculture and diet are of great interest, some of them spanning the three periods. Cassava and sweet potatoes, as we have noted, were cultivated aboriginally. Arrowroot and tannier were probably present, possibly cultivated. The 'yampee' or 'cushcush', a true New World cultivated yam (*Dioscorea trifida*), is popular to this day in Jamaica. Sloane did not mention it in his exhaustive botanical work (1707), and Parry thinks it fair to assume it was introduced from the American mainland after that time. Sloane does mention *Dioscorea cayenensis*, the 'yellow Guinea yam', which came to Jamaica from Oceania, probably via West Africa in the eighteenth century, Parry believes. By the start of the nineteenth century, there were at least six cultivated yam varieties in Jamaica, and there were the taros, the so-called 'eddoes, dasheens, and cocoes or cocoyams', which are of Oceanian origin and probably became established in Jamaican peasant cultivation and cuisine in the eighteenth century. Finally, there are several important plants whose dates of entry can be precisely fixed. Parry (1955) refers to the ackee (from West Africa, 1778), the mango (from Oceania, 1782), and the breadfruit (from Oceania, 1793, carried by Bligh on his second voyage).

From these enumerations, it will be seen that the crop possibilities open for Jamaican cultivators were considerable indeed. But very little, unfortunately, is ever afforded in the early reports concerning the agricultural methods themselves. Beckford, writing in 1790, probably provides the fullest description, and that all too sketchy and vague:

> When a tract of negro-provisions is regularly planted, is well cultivated, and kept clean, it makes a very husbandlike and a beautiful appearance; and it is astonishing of the common necessaries of life it will produce. A quarter of an acre of this description will be fully sufficient for the supply of a moderate family, and may enable the proprietor [read 'cultivator') to carry some to market besides; but then the land must be of a productive quality, be in a situation that cannot fail of seasons, be sheltered from the wind, and protected from the trespass of cattle, and the theft of negroes.
>
> If a small portion of land of this description will give such returns, a very considerable number of acres, if not attended to, will on the contrary, yield but little; and those negroes will hardly ever have good grounds, and of consequence plenty of provisions, who are not allowed to make for themselves a choice of situation, and who are not well assured that it will be well guarded and protected (Beckford, 1790, 1: 256–7).

At a later point, Beckford states:

> All kinds of ground provisions and corn are, as well as the plantain, successfully cultivated in the mountains; but as this is done by the negroes in their own grounds [i.e., provided individually by the owner or overseer] and on those days which are given to them for this particular purpose, it does not enter into the mass of plantation-labor. . . . (Beckford, 1790, 2: 129–30).

And further:

> The manner in which the negroes occupy themselves in their grounds is rather an employment than a toil, particularly if the wood be felled, and the land be cleared: but if they have heavy timber to cut down, the labour will be much, and the danger will be great; for they often get maimed or killed in this precarious operation, in which are required not only strength but likewise foresight.
>
> They generally make choice of such sorts of land for their grounds as are encompassed by lofty mountains; and I think that they commonly prefer the sides of hills, which are covered with loose stones, to the bottoms upon which they are not so abundant. Some will have a mixture of both, and will cultivate the plantain-tree upon the flat, and their provisions upon the rising ground; and some will pursue a contrary method; for in the choice as well as change of situation, they seem to be directed more by novelty and caprice, than by convenience or expediency.
>
> They prepare their land, and put in their crops on the Saturdays that are given to them, and they bring home their provisions at night; and if their grounds be

at a considerable distance from the plantation, as they often are to the amount of five or seven miles, or more, the journey backwards and forwards makes this rather a day of labour and fatigue, than of enjoyment and rest; but if, on the contrary, they be within any tolerable reach, it may be said to partake of both.

The negroes, when working in their grounds, exhibit a picture of which it will be difficult to give a minute description. They scatter themselves over the face, and form themselves into distinct parties at the bottom of the mountains; and being consequently much divided, their general exertions can only be observed from a distance.

If the land be hilly, it is generally broken by rocks, or encumbered by stones; the first they cannot displace, but the last they gently remove as they proceed in their work, and thus make a bed for the deposit of the plantain-sucker and the coco, or of the corn and yam.

Upon these occasions they move, with all their family, into the place of cultivation; the children of different ages are loaded with baskets, which are burdened in proportion to their strength and age; and it is pleasing to observe under what considerable weights they will bear themselves up, without either murmur or fatigue. The infants are flung at the backs of the mothers, and very little incommode them in their walks or labour.

The provision-grounds in the mountains, or polinks as they are called in the Island, admit of not much picturesque variety. Upon these are cultivated, and particularly upon those in Liguanea (a fertile tract of ground in the neighbourhood of Kingston), all kinds of fruit and garden stuff, or coffee, coco, ginger and other minor productions of the country (Beckford, 1790, 2: 151–87, *passim*).

It is known that the slave cultivators burned off the land they were preparing to plant. This technique, contemptuously referred to as 'fire-stick cultivation' in Jamaica, is of doubtful origin. It may have been continuous with aboriginal practice, but this cannot easily be proved.

The provision grounds, which normally lay at some distance from the huts of the slaves grouped near the center of the estate, were set apart agriculturally from the tiny house plots or 'yards'. On the patches of land around their huts, the slaves cultivated fruit trees, garden herbs, and crops which were very easily stolen, or very delicate. The distinction between house plot and provision ground persists to the present and is characteristic of Jamaican peasant agriculture. Stewart, writing in the first quarter of the nineteenth century, makes clear reference to the distinction between house plot and 'polink':[1]

Adjoining to the house is usually a small spot of ground, laid out into a sort of garden, and shaded by various fruit-trees. Here the family deposit their dead, to whose memory they invariably, if they can afford it, erect a rude tomb. Each slave has, besides this spot, a piece of ground (about half an acre) allotted to him as a provision ground. This is the principal means of his support; and so productive is the soil, where it is good and the seasons regular, that this spot will not only furnish him with sufficient food for his own consumption, but an overplus to carry to market. By means of this ground, and of the hogs and poultry which he may raise (most of which he sells), an industrious negro may not only support himself comfortably, but save something. If he has a family, an additional proportion of ground is allowed him, and all his children from five years upward assist him in his labours in some way or other (Stewart, 1823: 267).

The major local source of food appears to have been the provision grounds, or polinks. That these normally lay upon the slopes where cane was not grown suggests that the particular techniques of cultivation were adjusted to the terrain, a pattern which persisted long after emancipation and still largely characterizes peasant agriculture in Jamaica. This is of more than passing importance. Peasant agriculture in Jamaica has been repeatedly criticized for its erosive effects. It is true that failure to make long-range investment of labor and materials on such land is destructive. But it ought to be borne in mind that it is not necessarily the cultivation methods as such, or even the crops, which are destructive.

The 'choice' of hilly land for such cultivation followed from the monopolization of coastal plains and interior valleys by the plantations. It has never been conclusively proved, in fact, that the small-scale production of the Jamaican peasantry is in itself inherently less productive or more destructive than other systems of production *on the same land*. (This does not contradict the justifiable claim that productivity would be increased and erosion slowed by proper terracing, crop rotation, manuring, and the building of retainer structures, and so on.)

Sauer has written very explicitly of the *conuco*, or garden plot of the Antilles:

When Indians gave way to Negro slaves, the latter took over for themselves, rather than for their masters, the cultivation of the Indian crops, and added thereto such African things as the greater yam, the pigeon pea or *guandul* [*sic*], okra, and the keeping of fowls.

The food potential of the traditional *conuco* planting, or provision ground, is hardly appreciated by ourselves, be we agricultural scientists, economists, or planners, because its tradition as well as content are so different from what we know and practice. Yields are much higher than from grains, production is continuous the year round, storage is hardly needed, individual kinds are not grown separately in fields but are assembled together in one planted ground, to which our habits of order would apply neither the name of field or garden. And so we are likely to miss the merits of the system.

The proper *conuco* is, in fact an imitation by man of tropical nature, a many-storied cultural vegetation, producing at all levels, from tubers underground through the understory of pigeon peas and coffee, a second story of cacao and bananas, to a canopy of fruit trees and palms. Such an assemblage makes full use of light, moisture, and soil — its messy appearance to our eyes meaning really that all of the niches are filled. A proper planting of this sort is about as protective of the soil as is the wild vegetation. The *conuco* system can make intensive use of steep slopes and thereby may encounter erosion hazards that should not be blamed on the system itself, as commonly they have been (Sauer, 1954: 21–2).

Sauer's contentions, while unproved, certainly demand reflection. In fact, the whole nature of the adjustment of Caribbean peasantries to the aftermath of slavery, to the circumstances of a ruined economy, and to freedom, deserves more study than it has yet received. Such study can profitably examine the view that the patterns of human and horticultural occupance, the system of cultivation, the paths of distribution of products, and the economic relationships of the peasantry to other classes, form one interwoven system. We contend that this system had begun to evolve long before the emancipation.

Information on the agricultural implements used by the slaves is discouragingly scanty. The most important were the bush knife, or cutlass, and the short-handled hoe. We have been unable to ascribe an origin to these tools; a case might be made for either England or Africa. It is likely that at first they were provided by the plantation, and this might argue against an African origin (Public Record Office, 1836).

Both with regard to the crops generally preferred for cultivation and to cuisine, our information is again less than satisfactory. Several early authors suggest that the slaves preferred to cultivate plantains (and bananas?), corn, and vegetables rather than root crops, attributing this preference either to imprudence or to laziness. The planters themselves preferred to see root crops planted since these would better survive hurricanes (Edwards, 1793, 2: 132). Renny (1807: 87) believed it was the slaves' taste preference for plantains and corn that led them to neglect the root crops. And yet yams, sweet potatoes, dasheen, tanniers, cassava, etc, could hardly have become embedded in peasant taste choices only after the start of the nineteenth century. It seems fair to suppose, therefore, that any favoritism the slave cultivators may have shown for plantain, corn, and vegetables over root crops could have arisen as much from the market situation as from anything else, and it is possible that these items were supplied in significant quantities to naval and merchant vessels. That the planters never actively interfered with the slave cultivators' crop choices in any case is of great interest, and seems to underline the mutual respect of customary arrangements which held between the estate owners or managers and the slaves. It also explains the vagueness of the accounts given by Beckford and others of the cultivation of the provision grounds. The only points which these commentators make with clarity are the distinction between house plots and polinks, the 'high' productivity of the latter if conscientiously cultivated, and the fact that the slaves were allowed to take surpluses to market, dispose of them, and keep the proceeds.

The first of these points is of interest because it indicates that even where estates were limited in size and did not contain slave provision grounds, the slaves were not absolutely dependent on imports. Even in Barbados and St. Kitts, for example, there were house plots (Coleridge 1826: 132). But it is upon the polinks that the foundations of the free peasantry were established, and here we turn to the local trading of the slaves, and the origins and early growth of the market places.

Extracts from the writings of two West Indian proprietors of the late eighteenth century will serve to give the planter's view of the relative advantages of food production as against food importation and to suggest one very powerful motive for the reluctance of masters to supervise production on the polinks.

FRIDAY, FEB. 10TH, 1792. My voyage to Antigua has put me in full possession of the question concerning the best mode of feeding the negroes. I am speaking of the difference in this situation in regard to plenty and comfort, when fed by allowance from the master, as in Antigua; or when by provision grounds of their own, as in St. Vincent. In the first case, oppression may, and certainly in some instances, and in different degrees doth actually exist, either as to quantity or quality of food; besides the circumstances of food for himself, the negro too suffers in his poultry and little stock, which are his wealth. The maintenance of his pigs, turkeys, or chickens must often subtract from his own dinner, and that perhaps a scanty one, or he cannot keep stock at all; and a negro without stock, and means to purchase tobacco, and other little conveniences, and some finery too for his wife, is miserable.

In the second case, of the negro feeding himself with his own provisions, assisted only with salt provisions from his master (three pounds of salt-fish, or an adequate quantity of herrings, per week as in St. Vincent's) the situation of the negro is in proportion to his industry; but generally speaking, it affords him a plenty that amounts to comparative wealth, viewing any peasantry in Europe (Young, 1801: 287–8).

Bryan Edwards, a contemporary observer whose main experience was of Jamaica, wrote on the same subject:

The practice which prevails in Jamaica of giving the Negroes lands to cultivate, from the produce of which they are expected to maintain themselves (except in times of scarcity, arising from hurricanes and droughts, when assistance is never denied them) is universally allowed to be judicious and beneficial; producing a happy coalition of interests between the master and the slave. The negro who has acquired by his own labour a property in his master's land, has much to lose, and is therefore less inclined to desert his work. He earns a little money, by which he is enabled to indulge himself in fine clothes on holidays, and gratify his palate with salted meats and other provisions that otherwise he could not obtain; and the proprietor is eased, in a great measure, of the expense of feeding him (Edwards, 1793, 2: 131).

Both these observers mention the advantages of having the slaves produce their own food, but it is interesting that Edwards, the Jamaican planter, is more explicit about the consequent savings enjoyed by the master. In the small, relatively flat, arable islands such as Barbados or Antigua, the planter could allot land to food cultivation only by impinging on areas which, generally, could be more profitably planted in cane. He tended therefore to restrict the land at the disposal of the slaves to small house plots, to depend heavily on imports of food, and, when the food trade was disturbed, to include, however reluctantly, some food production in the general estate program.

In St. Vincent and the other mountainous islands of the Windwards, the planter's decision was affected by the relative unsuitability of his land for sugar production. The 'sacrifice' of allotting land to food cultivation was not so strong a deterrent, and the advantages of having a comparatively well-fed slave force and of reduced dependence on food imports were clear.

In Jamaica, the largest of the British islands, with the largest estates and the greatest variety of soil, topography, and climate, the planter usually had land on his estate which, except in periods of unusually high sugar prices, he would never consider using for cane. There is much evidence that in Jamaica the area in sugar cultivation expanded and contracted under the influence of rising and falling sugar prices (Hall, 1959: 13). As prices fell, marginal sugar areas became submarginal and were, at least temporarily, thrown out of cane cultivation. But even when the process worked the other way and cane fields were extended in response to the promise of higher prices, there was generally a significant area which, because of its high unsuitability, would remain beyond the sugar line.

It is worth noting that in Barbados and the Leewards (except Montserrat which is mountainous) there is still a heavy reliance on food imports; that in the Windward Islands and in Montserrat the sugar industry declined under the competitive conditions of nineteenth-century free trade in sugar, and these islands now export foodstuffs to Barbados and the Leewards; and that only in Jamaica have food production and sugar production managed to survive together.

But, from the two extracts quoted above, the decision whether or not to allow the slaves to cultivate foodstuffs was apparently affected by more than 'classical' considerations of diminishing returns to land. We have shown that even where polinks were not usually allowed house plots were, and in many of the contemporary explanations of the system there is a sort of medievalism modified by the realities of colonial slave-plantation life in the eighteenth-century. There is the implied concept of the estate community, of the advantages to be gained from 'a happy coalition of interests between the master and the slave'; and indeed, the eighteenth century sugar estate with its great house and surrounding fields, its 'village' of workshops and slave quarters, its unfree agricultural population, and its complement of skilled craftsmen, was, superficially, not unlike the medieval manor. Even further, although sugar cultivation was the basic occupation, the workers had access to estate 'waste' land (the polinks), where they labored on their own behalf, not only growing food but also grazing small livestock and collecting the raw materials for their handicraft products. But superficialities apart, there was a second very important reason why masters should be concerned with securing this happy coalition of interest. It was simply that, since there was neither ethical nor economic basis for any such coalition (and here we begin to diverge from the medieval pattern), they must try to introduce and stimulate it. At any rate, the wiser masters would because, as our two writers argued, the slave with a better diet, a small source of income, and a feeling of proprietorship in land was less discontented, less likely to run away, and less dangerous as a potential rebel.[2]

For this reason, too, the slave was not supervised in his food cultivation, and this activity was never included, except in brief periods of shortage or threatening shortage of food, in 'the mass of plantation-labor.' Supervised field labor was repugnant to the slaves, and in the social hierarchy of the slave population the field slaves sat on the lowest rung (Smith, 1953). Supervised cultivation of food would have necessitated either a reduction of the time spent in cane cultivation, which the masters would not have willingly conceded, or an increase of the daily hours of compulsory estate labor, which would have encouraged disaffection and rebellious sentiments among the slaves.

But the accounts quoted above were written more than a century after the practice of allowing slaves to cultivate estate backlands, or polinks, had been established. The writers, therefore, might simply have been trying to explain, in the light of their own experience, the reasons for a custom of which the beginning and original intention were unknown to them. They tell us not how the practice began but only why it was still favored in the late eighteenth century.

Blome, writing in 1672 from the notes of Governor Sir Thomas Lynch, in Jamaica, gives detailed instructions for the setting up of a 'Cocao [sic] Walk' or plantation, and his advice includes careful explanations of the need for provision grounds for servants and slaves (Blome, 1672: 15–21). Sloane's introductory notes to his great work on the flora of Jamaica, published 1707–25, say of the slaves:

> They have *Saturdays* in the Afternoon, and *Sundays*, with *Christmas* Holidays, *Easter* call'd little or *Piganinny*, Christmas, and some other great Feasts allow'd them for the Culture of their own Plantations to feed themselves from Potatoes, Yams and Plantains, etc., which they plant in Ground allow'd them by their Masters, beside a small Plantain-Walk they have by themselves (Sloane, 1707, 1: 52).

Leslie, writing in 1739, states:

> Their owners set aside for each a small Ground, and allow them the Sundays to manure it: In it they generally plant Maiz, Guiney Corn, Plantanes, Yams, Cocoes, Potatoes, Etc. This is the food which supports them . . . (Leslie, 1739: 322).

Though we have not been able to establish a precise date for the beginning of this practice, Blome's statements, coming but 17 years after the English occupation, make it clear that it was generally adopted even on the earliest estates.

We do not know if it became the practice to provide slaves with provision grounds immediately upon the establishment of a new plantation, however. Conceivably, the managers of a new estate might attempt to supervise food production as a matter of course at the time it was set up. But this would not be likely. Precisely at the time that a new estate was brought into being, when slaves were being bought, land cleared, buildings erected, and factory machinery installed, managerial attention would be almost exclusively directed toward the main objective of getting the first sugar away to market. Probably imported foods would bulk large in the first years. If food production by the estate slaves were undertaken, it would doubtless be in their free time. When such production became stabilized, the need for imports would presumably decline. Much of this is surmise, but we have so far found no contrary evidence. Estate-supervised production of provisions never seems to have been undertaken without pressure from the island legislature and, as we have stressed, unsupervised cultivation by the slaves goes back to the early years of the occupation and may have been conjoined with the start of the estates. By the late eighteenth century what might have begun as a conveniently casual system of industrial feeding had become a tradition with which it would have been profitless and dangerous to interfere.

In these circumstances the emergence of local marketing arrangements is not surprising. The unsupervised production of food crops by the slaves provided the very basis of an open market system. Each slave cultivated as, and what, he wanted to cultivate. His primary concern, originally, might well have been his own household needs. But because his neighbors also had free choice of whether to plant, what to plant, and how much of it, the range of small transactions which might take place even among the slaves of a single estate was considerable. For instance, the volume of exchange would have been increased by the fact that some slaves would prefer to produce minor handicrafts, some to raise small livestock, some to grow food, and some to find profit by acting as intermediaries among these diverse interests. The Jamaican higgler, or middleman, also finds his prototype in the slave society (Lewis, 1861: 41). Under a straight system of estate-organized food production this variety of interests could never have emerged. It would have been choked off by the routine and the compulsory conformity of estate agriculture.

Exactly how the first slave producers came to market their surplus stock is not known; nor can we pin down with assurance the date of founding of the first market in Jamaica. The first legally established market place, however, was created in Spanish Town (Santiago de la Vega) in the year 1662, seven years after the English occupation, at the request of English settlers.

> Whereas the settlement of our Island of Jamaica is much hindered or obstructed for want of a Faire or Markett for the sale and buying of Horses, Mares, Mules, Assinegoes, Cowes, Bulls and other Cattle and many other necessaries for the use of our subjects there and whereas our Towne of Snt. Jago de la Vega in our said Island is commodiously situated for the keeping of wuch a Faire or Markett therein . . . [we] by this our present Charter doe grant and confirm that . . . [the] inhabitants of our said Towne of Snt. Jago de la Vega for ever have a Faire or Markett in our said Towne . . . four times in every year . . . for the sale of horses, mares, mules, assinegoes, cows, bulls, and all or any other cattle and all or any other goods and commodities whatsoever of the groweth or produce of our said Island and all or any goods, wares and merchandizes whatsoever with all liberties . . . according to the usage and customs of our kingdome of England (Institute of Jamaica, 1895: 146).

The emphasis in this statement is upon the establishment of a market for livestock. Furthermore, this is a quarterly market only, and one may judge that its original intent was to serve the free population of Jamaica. Yet we learn that the need for a market place had been recognized and acted upon less than a decade after the occupation; it is also worth noting that the market here described was set up quite matter-of-factly according to English law. Though the slaves came to play a central role in Jamaican internal marketing, it is clear that this first legal market was English, not African, in conception and form.

Edward Long, describing events in the 1660s, tells of large numbers of small cultivators who produced food for the markets of Spanish Town (the capital) and of Port Royal, then a headquarters of the buccaneers where

> the great consumption of provisions of all sorts in that town, and for the outfit of so many privateers, created a very large demand for cattle, sheep, hogs, poultry, corn, and every other similar supply furnished by planters and settlers. . . . And it is owing to this cause that we find such a prodigious number of these little settlements grouped together in all the environs of St. Jago de la Vega [Spanish Town], and in the maritime parts not far from Port Royal harbour, which were then full of people, all subsisting well by their traffic with that town . . .

But, he continues, the suppression of the buccaneers and the founding of the sugar industry led to 'the declension of Port Royal, and the dissipation of the petty settlers, who from that period began to spread themselves more into the inland parts', while the establishment of large estates led to the buying out of many of these small settlers 'by the more opulent planters or merchants' (Long, 1774, 1: 282–3).

But as settlement and the sugar industry and trade increased, activity in the capital town and in the ports of the island would also have grown. New demands for food supplies would have arisen to be met, not by those early European small-scale farmers whom Long described, and mainly in whose interest this first market had been officially established, but by their successors in the business of food production. The great majority of these successors, we believe, were slaves working in their spare time on estate lands, and selling their produce in officially designated and other market places.

Since it was the individual slaves or slave households who produced provisions on the estate backlands, then clearly it would be they who would sell any surplus produce. Either individual slaves would go marketing, or else they would make voluntary agreements among themselves for marketing each other's produce. Certainly no sane estate manager would ever have conceived the idea of collecting and selling produce from separate slave provision grounds. The effort would have been pointless. If the estate kept all or even a share of the proceeds, voluntary food production by the slaves would be discouraged. In any case, the prevention of competitive transactions between slaves of the same estate, or even of adjacent estates would have been physically impossible for the limited and generally inefficient subordinate managerial staff.

Undoubtedly, the earliest transactions between slave producers were not conducted in markets. What seems probable is that the establishment of markets on the English model afforded a setting in which the slave producer could most readily buy and sell what he wished. The slave's part in market activity probably grew swiftly more important, but the details are nearly all obscure. Hickeringill (1661) and Blome (1672), two of the earliest observers, do not refer directly to markets, though Blome does state that '*provisions* are very dear' in Kingston at the time of his writing, and the reference seems to be to locally produced foodstuffs (Blome, 1672: 32). Cundall mentions a passing reference to a market for the year 1685, less than a quarter of a century after the first legally recognized market was established, in revealing terms: 'In May, the negroes at a usual Saturday market at Passage Fort having made some little disturbance, the market was suppressed by the Council' (Cundall, 1936: 99). That this market was 'usual', and that Negroes were in it, bears noting.

Leslie (1739) provides an abstract of laws in force, compiled mostly under the second government of Sir Thomas Lynch (1671–74), and these laws make plain that a number of markets were established, formalized, and maintained under government provision even in this early period. Laws regarding the weighing of meats, occasions of sale, market days, etc, were put into force in the seventeenth century (Leslie, 1739: 170–8).

Formal legal acknowledgment of the slaves' rights to market had been given, in negative form at least, as early as 1711: 'Hawking about and selling goods (except provisions, fruits, and other enumerated articles) to be punished, on conviction before a magistrate, by whipping, not exceeding *thirty-one lashes*' (Long, 1774, 2: 486–7). The exception is more important than the law, since it read: 'This restraint is construed to extend only to beef, veal, mutton and saltfish; and to manufactures, except baskets, ropes of bark, earthen pots and such like' (Long, 1774, 2: 486). In 1735, the law is stated in positive terms: 'Slaves may carry about, and sell, all manner of provisions, fruits, fresh fish, milk, poultry, and other small stock of all kinds, having a ticket from their owner or employer' (Long, 1774, 2: 492). It is interesting to compare the lists of goods which slaves were allowed to trade. The purpose of restriction was, of course, to prevent them from dealing in stolen goods. A slave with a carcass of beef was, prima facie, guilty of having slaughtered his owner's cattle. A slave offering metalware or saltfish, neither of which was produced in the island, was clearly suspect of having raided the estate stores. But clearly, between 1711 and 1735 there was some change. In the first year, slaves are forbidden to sell 'beef, veal, mutton and saltfish', in 1735 they are permitted to trade 'fresh fish, milk, poultry, and other small stock of all kinds'. This suggests either a belated legal acknowledgment of the range of slave production or, more likely because the laws were generally permissive and not restrictive in this matter, a fairly rapid extension of productive activities by the slaves in response to a growing market for their produce. Accounts of the later eighteenth century and after almost invariably list pigs, goats, fish, poultry, eggs, and milk,[3] as sold by the slaves. It will be a matter for further discussion that later laws restricting the free movement of slaves always excepted their marketing operations.

The importance, in the third quarter of the eighteenth century, of slaves to the Jamaican domestic economy is revealed at length in the intelligent and thorough discussions provided by Long, one of the most careful and thoughtful writers of the eighteenth century. In 1774, by Long's estimate, of the £50,000 in currency circulating in the island at least £10,000, or 20 per cent, was in the hands of the slaves, most of it in the form of small coins. Money was scarce, and this scarcity adversely affected daily commerce and interfered with transactions. The island had serious need of small silver to

> enable the housekeepers and Negroes to carry on their marketing for butchers meat, poultry, hogs, fish, corn, eggs, plantains and the like (Long, 1774, 2: 562).
>
> . . . a small copper coin might be found extremely convenient here, as enabling the lower class of inhabitants not only to exchange their silver without a drawback, but likewise to keep down the prices of the small necessaries of life: which is a matter that has been thought of great importance to every trading community; and is especially of moment to this island, where the Negroes, who supply the market with small stock, and other necessaries, as well as the white families supplied from those markets, must be very much distressed, if they should ever be wholly deprived of a minor currency accommodated to their dealings with each other (Long, 1774, 2: 570).

Long describes a number of markets, but his description of Kingston market is particularly revealing:

> At the bottom of the town, near the water side, is the market place, which is plentifully supplied with butchers meat, poultry, fish, fruits, and vegetables of all sorts. Here are found not only a great variety of American, but also of European, vegetables: such as pease, beans, cabbage, lettuce, cucumbers, French beans, artichokes, potatoes, carrots, turnips, radishes, celery, onions, etc. These are brought from

the Liguanea mountains, and are all excellent in their kind. Here are likewise strawberries, not inferior to the production of our English gardens; grapes and melons in the utmost perfection; mulberries, figs, and apples, exceedingly good, but in general gathered before they are thoroughly ripe. In short, the most luxurious epicure cannot fail of meeting here with sufficient in quantity, variety, and excellence, for the gratification of his appetite the whole year round. The prices are but little different from those of Spanish Town: but, where they disagree, they are more reasonable at Kingston, the supplies being more regular, and the market superintended by the magistracy. The beef is chiefly from the pastures of Pedro's, in St. Ann; the mutton, from the salt-pan lands, in St. Catherine's: what they draw from the penns in St. Andrew's parish being very indifferent meat (Long, 1774, 2: 105).

Long did not criticize the virtual monopoly which the slaves had come to exercise in internal marketing; rather, he repeatedly suggested means to broaden and extend it. He objected to the pay system in country barracks of the Army, where the officers disbursed the pay. It would have been better, he argued, had the common soldiers received their pay directly:

with the money in their hands, the men might purchase much better in quality, and more in quantity, of fresh meat and wholesome victuals... every country-barrack would attract a market for the sale of hogs, poultry, fresh fish, fruits, and roots, which are articles produced and vended by almost all the Negroes (Long, 1774, 2: 303–4).

Indeed, by the time Long was writing, the slaves were not only central to the economy as the producers of the cash export commodities, principally sugar, but had also become the most important suppliers of foodstuffs and utilitarian craft items to all Jamaicans.

The customs of slave-based subsistence farming and marketing clearly provided the slaves with their best opportunities to accumulate liquid capital, as Hall (1954: 161–3) and others have demonstrated. Long, too, writes:

even among these slaves, as they are called, the black grandfather, or father, directs in what manner his money, his hogs, poultry, furniture, cloaths, and other effects and acquisitions, shall descend, or be disposed of, after his decease. He nominates a sort of trustees, or executors, from the nearest of kin, who distribute them among the legatees, according to the will of the testator, without any molestation or interruption, most often without the enquiry, of their master; though some of these Negroes have been known to possess from £50 to £200 at their death; and few among them, that are at all industrious and frugal, lay up less than £20 or £30. For in this island they have the greatest part of the small silver circulating among them, which they gain by sale of their hogs, poultry, fish, corn, fruits, and other commodities, at the markets in town and country (Long, 1774, 2: 410–1).

Thus, one century after the first legal Jamaican market was created, the slaves had made a place for themselves in the free economic activity of the country which would never thereafter be challenged.

Our continuing emphasis upon the slaves' role in supplying and maintaining the internal markets, however, should not obscure another aspect of the economy as it was constituted under slavery. At the end of the eighteenth century, Jamaica's major exports, measured either in bulk or in value, were typical plantation products: cotton, coffee, ginger, and pimento to a lesser extent, and most important, sugar and rum. But other items also reached foreign markets, and quantities of these were derived from slave holdings; that is, they were produced on estate backlands by the slaves. Here may be mentioned gums, arrowroot, castor oil, turmeric, hides, supplejacks, oil nuts, cows' horns, goatskins, and wood products. These items were exported through a growing class of small merchants resident in towns and doing their business in conjunction with local markets. There is scarcely any descriptive information on these traders and their commercial relationships with slave producers; yet such relationships, well reported in the years after emancipation (Sewell, 1861: 219–20, 248–51), must have taken on their characteristic form under slavery. Large quantities of imported goods consumed by the slaves passed through the hands of local importers, the largest traffic being in clothes, household wares, and other items of comfort and convenience not provided by the estate owners.

By the start of the nineteenth century, reports by observers on slave production of provisions and acquisition of buying power had become quite matter of fact in character. Dallas, writing in 1803, reports:

Every proprietor is compelled by law, to cultivate in ground provisions (of course indestructible by hurricanes) one acre for every ten negroes; besides the allotment of negro territory. To cultivate this allotment, one day in every fortnight, belongs to the slaves, exclusive of Sundays and holidays. Thus they raise vegetables, poultry, pigs, or goats, which they consume, bestow, or sell. While some raise provisions, others fabricate coarse chairs, baskets, or common tables. These are bartered for salted meat, or pickled fish, utensils, or gaudy dresses; of which they are very fond. Their right of property in what they thus acquire, is never questioned; but seems completely established by custom (Dallas, 1803, 1: cviii).

It will be seen that certain customary arrangements had been secured, and these appear to have been observed by master and slave alike. The marketing arrangements, the increasing dependence of townsmen and free people on slave production, the customary system of slave inheritance, and the slave's attitudes concerning his property rights in the fruits of his labors, all must have grown up gradually and to some extent at least outside the law. They were maintained and accepted by the small group which wielded overwhelming power in the society because they were economically and socially convenient, even necessary, once they had taken shape.

By the time the nineteenth-century observers had begun to write of the markets and the slaves' role in them, the pattern had well over a century of traditional practice behind it. No really important new crops would be introduced after 1800, to enter into the slaves' cultivation, diet, or marketing; the slave code which guaranteed rights to market was long in force. After emancipation, many new markets would appear, and the scope of economic activity open to the freedmen would be much increased. But emancipation, insofar as marketing and cultivation practices were concerned, widened opportunities and increased alternatives; apparently it did not change their nature substantially.

Matthew Gregory ('Monk') Lewis, an estate owner, reported on his 1815–17 visit to his Jamaica estates:

In my evening's drive I met the negroes returning from the mountains, with baskets of provisions sufficient to last them for the week. By law they are only allowed every other Saturday for the purpose of cultivating their own grounds, which, indeed, is sufficient; but by giving them every alternate Saturday into the bargain, it enables them to perform their task with so much ease as almost converts it into an amusement; and the frequent visiting their grounds makes them grow habitually as much attached to them as they are to their houses and gardens. It is also advisable for them to bring home only a week's provisions at a time, rather than a fortnight's; for they are so thoughtless and improvident that, when they find themselves in possession of a larger supply than is requisite for their immediate occasions, they will sell half to the wandering higglers, or at Savannah la Mar, in exchange for spirits; and then, at the end of the week, they find themselves entirely unprovided with food, and come to beg a supply from the master's storehouse (Lewis, 1861: 41).

Lewis's comments indicate that the slaves were inclined to make much of their provision grounds. Certainly they must have found it a relief to escape from the regimen of labor in the cane fields and to work on 'their own' cultivations. His observations of their attachments to these far-off fields are even shrewder than he knew. The assumption some observers had made that the slave, once free, would be unable to give up his residence at the center of the estate, because of his emotional attachment to his house and garden there, turned out to be very mistaken. The slaves must also have responded well to the feeling of autonomy which work on their provision grounds afforded. As the day of emancipation approached, other observers, particularly missionaries intent on establishing the slaves' capacity for freedom, tried to confirm this:

If the vices of the slave belong then to his condition, that condition should be changed before the nature of the negro is deemed incapable of elevation, or susceptible of improvement. That his defects are redeemed by no good qualities would be a bold assertion; that they are mingled with so many good ones as they are, is to me a matter of the greatest wonder.

To say that he is not industrious without reference to the object for which his exertions are employed would be an absurd remark; to say he is indolent, where his labour is exacted without reward, is to prove nothing.

But where the negro labours on his own ground, for his own advantage, — where his wife and children have the price of his own commodities to fetch him from the market-town, no matter how many miles they have to trudge, or how heavy the load they have to bear, — where the wages he received for his services are at his own disposal, — where his own time is duly paid for, not in shads and herrings, but in money a little more than equivalent to the advantages he deprives his own ground of, by transferring his extra time to the estate he is employed on — the negro is not the indolent slothful being he is everywhere considered, both at home and in the colonies (Madden, 1835, 1: 136–7).

In fact, the marketing system in which the slave had been long involved not only prepared him for freedom but, in the way in which he rose to make the fullest use of it, established his capacity to live as a freedman.

At the same time that the missionaries used all their means to work courageously for emancipation, they deplored the Sunday markets. Their pronouncements provide some useful (though rather mournful) information on the markets themselves. Bickell describes a market in Kingston on the day of his arrival in August, 1819:

It was on a Sunday, and I had to pass by the Negro Market, where several thousands of human beings, of various nations and colours, but principally Negroes, instead of worshipping their Maker on His Holy Day, were busily employed in all kinds of traffick in the open streets. Here were Jews with shops and standings as at a fair, selling old and new clothes, trinkets and small wares at cent. per cent. to adorn the Negro person; there were some low Frenchmen and Spaniards, and people of colour, in petty shops and with stalls; some selling their bad rum, gin, tobacco, etc.; others, salt provisions, and small articles of dress; and many of them bartering with the Slave or purchasing his surplus provisions to retail again; poor free people and servants also, from all parts of the city to purchase vegetables, etc., for the following week (Bickell, 1835: 66).

Concern that the slave did his marketing on Sunday was not restricted to the missionaries, however. The shopkeepers who kept the Sabbath were effectively cut off from sharing in the consumer market the slave represented. Long, in 1774, had sought to demonstrate that there was more to the profaning of the Sabbath than met the eye. He noted the comment of a contemporary:

It is certain that the sabbath-day, as at present it is passed, is by no means a respite from labour: on the contrary, the Negroes, either employing it on their grounds, or in travelling a great distance to some market, fatigue themselves much more on that day, than on any other in the week. The forenoon of that day, at least, might be given to religious duties; but I think it rather desirable than otherwise, that the after-part of it should be spent on their grounds, instead of being uselessly dissipated in idleness and lounging, or (what is worse) in riot, drunkenness, and wickedness. If such an alteration should take place, Thursday might be assigned for the market day, instead of the sabbath, and prove of great advantage to all Christian shop-keepers and retailers; the Jews now grossing the whole business of trafficking with the Negroes every Sunday, at which time there is a prodigious resort of them to the towns, and a vast sum expended for drams, necessaries, and manufactures. This alteration would therefor place the Christian dealers upon an equal footing, which they do not at present enjoy (Long, 1774, 2: 492).

'No Sunday markets' was probably the only issue in Jamaican history on which missionaries and proslavery writers were able to agree, though their reasons were wholly different.

The significance of this concern is the proof it offers that the marketing activities of the slaves were in fact very important to the Jamaican economy. The economy itself rested on the plantation system and slave labor; but the circumstances were such that the slaves could make a second valuable capital-building contribution through their individual efforts. And the same observers who debated whether the slaves were capable of learning even the fundamentals of Christian teaching were surely aware of their very human capacity for creating and employing wealth by cultivation and commerce. Had it not been for the slaves' skills as producers and distributors and their needs as consumers, there could scarcely have appeared in the Jamaican economy a numerous class of middlemen, import and export dealers, retailers, etc. The importance of slave marketing was legally recognized in the laws which regulated the behavior of the slave population. Renny cites a law in 1807 which is revelatory of this:

And whereas it is absolutely necessary, that the slaves in this island should be kept in due obedience to their owners, and in due subordination to the white people in general, and, as much as in the power of the legislature, all means and opportunities of slaves committing rebellious conspiracies, and other crimes, to the ruin and destruction of the white people, and others in this island, prevented, and that proper punishments should be appointed for all crimes to be by them committed; be it further enacted by the authority aforesaid, that no slave, *such only excepted as are going with firewood, grass, fruit, provisions, or small stock and other goods, which they may lawfully sell, to market, and returning therefrom,* shall here after be suffered or permitted to go out of his or her master or owner's plantation or settlement, or to travel from one town or place to another, unless such slave shall have a ticket from his master, owner, employer, or overseer.... (Renny, 1807: 255 [italics ours])

For the marketing practices of the slaves, even the sharpest vigilance was relaxed, and the exceptions cry for explanation. It would be hard to explain this wholly and with certainty. But it may be fair to contend that the growth of town populations and the demand for the products of the slaves' spare time labor encouraged the participation of slaves as sellers and suppliers; that the growth of the market and the emergence of new demands enlarged the quantity and the variety of items which reached the markets; that the activity of the markets increased the slaves' buying power, and led in turn to increases in the numbers of local merchants, retailers, moneylenders, etc, who became dependent on the slaves' surpluses and buying needs for their share of profits from the economy; that the free people in the towns gradually grew reliant upon the slaves' marketing activities for their daily needs; and that long before emancipation came, the markets and all of the related institutions which maintained them had become core features of Jamaican society and economy. Such seems to have been the situation in Jamaica in 1834, when slavery ended and the 'apprenticeship system' began.

In most of the British West Indian colonies an attempt was made to bridge the gap between slavery and freedom by the intervention of a number of years of 'apprenticeship' during which masters and slaves were to condition themselves for the new order of a free society. But the 'apprenticeship system' asked too much of mere mortals. It allowed the masters the labor of their slaves for a stated number of hours per week. Beyond this limit the slaves (or 'apprentices') had the right either to refuse to work for their masters or to demand wages for what they did. The apprenticeship system failed to serve its purposes, however, and was curtailed. It was too much to ask that a man should be a slave on weekdays and a wage earner over the weekend. The Monday morning master found the Friday evening transition to wage-labor employer beyond his power. The apprenticeship system ended at midnight, July 31, 1838, exactly four years after it had begun, and the expected disagreements between ex-masters and ex-slaves set in.

The great variety of those disagreements need not detain us. They have been fully described elsewhere (Burn, 1937; Hall, 1953) and our present concern is with only one of the sources of discontent. Estate slaves had been housed in huts or tenements provided by their owners, and they had been allowed to cultivate estate backlands. Now, as free wage workers, they were asked to pay rents for huts and land, and ex-masters and ex-slaves faced each other as landlord employers and tenant employees.

This situation was full of potential misunderstanding and reprisal. Under slavery the Jamaican planters had made much of the freedom which they allowed the slaves in their cultivation of the backlands.

> I do not believe that an instance can be produced of a master's indifference with his Negroes in their *peculium* thus acquired. They are permitted also to dispose at their deaths of what little property they possess; and even to bequeath their grounds or gardens to such of their fellow-slaves as they think proper. These principles are so well established, that whenever it is found convenient for the owner to exchange the negro-grounds for other lands, the Negroes must be satisified, in money or otherwise, before the exchange takes place. It is universally the practice (Edwards, 1793, 2: 133).

There, precisely stated, are three points of immediate and important relevance to the post-emancipation squabbles over rents and wages. The first is that slaves were allowed to acquire and bequeath property of various kinds; the second, that they were even allowed to bequeath their provision grounds, or gardens; and the third, that planters so fully recognized the slaves' rights to these grounds that they offered compensation wherever it became necessary to convert an area of slave cultivation to estate purposes.

There is no need to discuss further the reasons why the slaves were allowed to keep the money and goods they received in their marketing transactions, and as they were allowed to keep them it was thus logical to allow bequests. The alternative would have been an unworkable estate tax system of 100 per cent death duties on the 'property' of deceased slaves. It would have been impossible without the full cooperation of the slaves themselves to assess the property of any individual slave in the crowded living conditions of the slave quarters and in the circumstances of a lifetime of unaccounted small purchases and transactions.

The fact that planters usually compensated slaves who were made to give up provision grounds to estate uses is reasonable enough. If the slaves were to provide most of their own food they would clearly have to have the necessary resources at their disposal. If they were to be deprived of certain plots of provision grounds they would have to be given other grounds with yielding crops, or a supply of food, or else money with which to fulfill their needs until other land was allowed them and they could collect their first harvest. From the planter's point of view this would be an obvious need unless he were disposed to see his slaves starve.

It is the fact that slaves were allowed to bequeath provision grounds which is least clearly explicable. At first glance this would seem to imply that for each estate a time would come when, all of the backlands having been appropriated, there would be no marginal areas left free for cultivation by newly arrived slaves. Yet this could never happen, in part because of the high rate of slave mortality, more so because of the way in which newly imported slaves were absorbed into the estate organization.

The practice is that of distributing the newly-imported Africans among the old Negroes, as pensioners (with some little assistance occasionally given), on their little *peculium*, and provision-grounds (Edwards, 1793, 2: 126).

Thus, new arrivals were simply taken into the existing pattern of provision ground production, and slave importation did not necessitate the setting aside of more land for spare-time cultivation.

The system appears to have been favored by all concerned. From our point of view, it is of interest because it was the course of action least likely to encourage continued introduction of West African methods into Jamaican slave estate agriculture. Admittedly, the newly arrived slaves would, by their language and behavior, revive memories of Africa among a few of the longer enslaved, but in their new households they were the newcomers, the trainees, and the minority voice. As Edwards points out, the new slaves were in fact pleased with the arrangement,

and afterwards considered themselves as the adopted children of those by whom they were thus protected, calling them parents, and venerating them as such; and I never knew an instance of the violation of a trust thus solicited and bestowed. In the course of eight or ten months, provided they are mildly used and kept free of disease, new people, under these circumstances, become reconciled to the country; begin to get well established in their families, their houses and provision-grounds; and prove in all respects as valuable as the native or Creole negroes (Edwards, 1793, 2: 127).

The new slaves thus became operators on the household's provision grounds, and later, perhaps, as heads of the households in a succeeding generation, inherited the right of use of the land. And this is where the emphasis must be placed, for as Edwards himself showed, no slaves held provision grounds by legal right of property in land (1793, 2: 147). The land belonged to the estate owner. The use of it was allowed to the slaves. What slaves were permitted to bequeath was certainly not a plot of land, but rather the right to continue to cultivate a certain piece of land for as long as the owner or estate manager permitted that land to be cultivated in provisions. The slaves, never disillusioned in the matter, may well have considered a certain piece of land as their 'property'; the master, under no illusions, recognized the arrangement for what it was, namely, a free letting of land in return for which he hoped to have a well-fed and contented slave labor force. After emancipation, of course, employers were no longer directly concerned with the condition of their workers' minds and stomachs, the *peculium* was quickly forgotten, and money rents were imposed.

The emancipation was the most important event in Jamaican history after the English conquest of the island. The Jamaican freedman of 1838 had to work out his style of life anew. The material needs of daily living would be met by personal effort and because of personal motivation; the hated compulsion of the planter was no longer a spur to effort and the freedman easily learned to live without it.

The freedman's most important means for establishing his independence was by repudiating his previous status as an estate laborer and becoming a peasant, that is, an agriculturist who produced the bulk of his own food needs and a surplus for sale, wholly or mainly on his own land. The inspiring transformation of the Jamaican people into a free and independent peasantry has been written about many times in the large; but the immediate concern is with the freedman's preparation for this transformation. Aside from the basic question of funds for the acquisition of land and housing, the freedman needed to have skills and knowledge which would enable him to live independently. In this he had been prepared for independence by certain conditions of slavery, notably the initial insistence or concession that he provide his own food (Mintz, 1955, 1958). At the same time it must be made clear that the newly enslaved Africans carried to Jamaica and absorbed into the estate system and the slave household did not have to learn everything anew. Some of native America's most important foods, such as maize and cassava, were carried to West Africa as early as the sixteenth century and were adopted there with incredible rapidity and success. Later, food-bearing plants had been brought from West Africa to the West Indies. In certain major crops, therefore, and perhaps in the technology and equipment of cultivation, there was much that was already familiar.

Nevertheless, we have largely avoided dealing with the important question of Africanisms, either in agriculture or in marketing. In the case of Jamaican agriculture, the available historical data have not yet been totally and thoroughly analyzed, while sufficient data simply are not available to assess the degree to which Jamaican marketing could have been derived directly from West African practices. Such common West African features as separate royal and commoner markets, royal monopolies in certain products, and price fixing by the court (Herskovits, 1938) were of course absent and could not have been expected to occur. The first formal Jamaican market was a wholly English innovation, and there is no need to look to Africa in this connection. It is true that women carry on most marketing activity in Jamaica today, as they do, and did, in large part in much of West Africa. But even this likeness may be a parallel rather than a historical derivation. Until specific historical documentation for such a derivation can be amassed, to claim this division of labor to be an Africanism is no more than an unproved assertion.

Slavery meant forced removal from familiar landscapes, institutions, and, often, kinsfolk. It meant sudden introduction into an estate system with a social order and an economic objective quite foreign to the newly arrived slave (Hall, 1954: 153–4). And because among each shipload of new arrivals the men usually far outnumbered the women, slavery demanded a total reconsideration of the place and functions of men and women in society, beginning with fundamental questions about new mating patterns.

In Jamaica, life was as the master ordered it; the master was European, or oriented toward Europe (Curtin, 1955: 42ff.), with his eyes on overseas markets, prices, laws, and fashions. What we have seen already of the rise of slave-based food production and activity in the markets should make it abundantly clear that what may have survived from Africa was what the master ignored, or permitted to survive. Yet admittedly, the African content of this aspect of slave culture remains unassessed. Its weighing will not depend on a search for likenesses, but on precise and detailed historical research.

We do not attempt here to carry the description of Jamaican markets and marketing further forward in time than those first years following the emancipation. Nor can our findings be claimed to do more than state some of the fundamental features of the market system in the early period of Jamaica's history as a British possession. We think it established that both the peasant economy and its marketing pattern originated within the slave population. We feel the role of European culture and culture history may have been slighted in the past tendency to attribute so many features of Jamaican peasant culture to the African culture stream. Adequate study, both historical and ethnographic, of the Jamaican peasantry, is only now beginning. As Ansell Hart has said:

> Plantation economy, absentee proprietorship and the overlordship of Britain combined to produce Jamaican traits of delegation, dependence, and 'tek a chance', above which however, tower the Jamaican's humor, sentiment, physique, capacity for hard work and generosity. There are of course many strands to the story of the undesirable traits which emerges from the plantation economy: neglect, economic insufficiency, malnutrition, disease, etc. Subsistence economy on the other hand developed into the main source of supply of staple food; and besides giving the slave a 'bellyful', produced directly by himself for himself, also gave him access to the Sunday market, a money economy, important social contacts in field and market and some degree of self-reliance and independence. The cultural and economic effect of what began as subsistence production was immense (Hart, 1955: 1).

Bibliography

Beckford, William, *A Descriptive Account of the ISLAND OF JAMAICA*, 2 vols. (London, 1790).

Bickell, Reverend R., *The West Indies as They Are* (London, 1835).

Blome, Richard, *Description of Jamaica* (London, 1672).

Burn, W. L., *Emancipation and Apprenticeship in the British West Indies* (London, 1937).

Coleridge, H. N., *Six Months in the West Indies in 1825* (London, 1826).

Cumper, George, *The Social Structure of Jamaica* (Mona, Jamaica, n.d.).

Cundall, Frank, *The Governors of Jamaica in the Seventeenth Century* (London, 1936).

Cundall, Frank, and Pietersz, J., *Jamaica under the Spaniards* (Kingston, Jamaica, 1919).

Curtin, Philip, *Two Jamaicas* (Cambridge, Mass., 1955).

Dallas, R. C., *The History of the Maroons*, 2 vols. (London, 1803).

Edwards, Bryan, *The History, Civil and Commercial, of the British Colonies in the West Indies*, 2 vols. (London, 1793).

Goveia, Elsa, 1959, *Comment* in 'Labour and Sugar in Puerto Rico and Jamaica', *Comparative Studies in Society and History*, Vol. 1, No. 3 (1959), pp. 281–83.

Hall, Douglas, The Apprenticeship Period in Jamaica, 1834–1838, *Caribbean Quarterly*, Vol. 3, No. 3 (1953), pp. 142–66.

Hall, Douglas, 'The Social and Economic Background to Sugar in Slave Days', *Caribbean Historical Review*, Nos. 3-4 (1954), pp. 149–69.

Hall, Douglas, *Free Jamaica* (New Haven, 1959).

Hart, Ansell, 'Causeries', *Monthly Comments*, Vol. 1, No. 15 (1955), p. 1.

Herskovits, M. J., *Dahomey*, 2 vols. (New York, 1938).

Hickeringill, Edmund, *Jamaica Viewed* (London, 1661).

Institute of Jamaica, 'Notes and Queries: Early Fairs in Jamaica', *Journal of the Institute of Jamaica*, Vol. 2, No. 2 (1895), p. 146.

Leslie, Charles, *A New and Exact Account of Jamaica* (Edinburgh, 1739).
Lewis, M. G., *Journal of a Residence Among the Negroes in the West Indies* (London, 1861).
Long, Edward, *The History of Jamaica*, 3 vols. (London, 1774).
Madden, R. R., *A Twelvemonth's Residence in the West Indies*, 2 vols. (London, 1835).
Mintz, Sidney W., 'The Role of Forced Labour in Nineteenth Century Puerto Rico', *Caribbean Historical Review*, No. 2 (1951), pp. 134–41.
Mintz, Sidney W., 'The Jamaican Internal Marketing Pattern', *Social and Economic Studies*, Vol. 4, No. 1 (1955), pp. 95–103.
Mintz, Sidney W., 'Historical Sociology of the Jamaican Church-Founded Free Village System', *De West-Indische Gids*, Vol. 38, Nos. 1–2 (1958), pp. 46–70.
Mintz, Sidney W., 'Labor and Sugar in Puerto Rico and Jamaica, 1800–1850', *Comparative Studies in Society and History*, Vol. 1, No. 3 (1959), pp. 273–83.
Pares, Richard, *A West India Fortune* (London, 1950).
Parry, John H., 'Salt Fish and Ackee', *Caribbean Quarterly*, Vol. 2, No. 4 (n.d.), pp. 29–35.
Parry, John H., 'Plantation and Provision Ground', *Revista de Historia*, No. 39 (1955), pp. 1–20.
Public Record Office, Letter from Magistrate Harris to the Governor, 27 July, 1856, *Colonial Office Documents*, No. 137/216, 'Jamaica Apprentices', Pt 3 (London, 1836).
Ragatz, L. J., *Statistics for the Study of British Caribbean Economic History, 1763–1833* (London, 1927).
Renny, Robert, *An History of Jamaica* (London, 1807).
Sauer, Carl O., Cultivated Plants of South and Central America, in *Handbook of South American Indians*, edited by Julian Steward, *Bulletin*, Bureau of American Ethnology, Vol. 6, No. 143 (1950), pp. 487–543.
Sauer, Carl O., 'Economic Prospects of the Caribbean', in *The Caribbean: Its Economy*, edited by A. C. Wilgus (Gainesville, Florida, 1954), pp. 15–27.
Sewell, William G., *The Ordeal of Free Labour in the British West Indies* (New York, 1861).
Sloane, Sir Hans, *A Description of a Voyage to the Islands of Madera, Barbados, Etc. . . .*, Vol. 1 (London, 1707).
Smith, M. G., 'Some Aspects of Social Structure in the British Caribbean About 1820', *Social and Economic Studies*, Vol. 1, No. 4 (1953), pp. 55–80.
Stewart, J., *A View of the Past and Present State of the Island of Jamaica* (Edinburgh, 1823).
Young, Sir William, *A Tour Through the Several Islands of Barbados, St. Vincent, Antigua, Tobago and Grenada, in the Years 1791 and 1792* (London, 1801).

Notes

1. Mr H. P. Jacobs has suggested a connection between the words 'polink' and 'palenque', the latter being a place where the Negro hunters of Spanish times lived and cultivated foodstuffs. In Cuba, the term 'palenque' was used to refer to a palisaded village established by runaway slaves.
2. It would be of interest to test this opinion by comparing data on slave desertions, riots, and other indices of disaffection in, for example, Antigua and St. Vincent. But such a comparison would have to take into account the disincentives to desertion, etc, in flat, fully occupied, and small islands, and the greater chances for success in the larger, mountainous, and less fully occupied islands.
3. It may have been goats' milk or perhaps cows' milk bought by the slaves from the estate owners for retail trading. Yet the cattle may have been owned by the slaves themselves. In his journal entry for March 2, 1816, Lewis (1861: 102–3) writes that he purchased from his slaves at 15 pounds per head, cattle which they owned and used to graze on the estate's pastures.

Slaves' Use of Their 'Free' Time in the Danish Virgin Islands in the Later Eighteenth and Early Nineteenth Century

N. A. T. HALL

Europe's expansion into the New World and the African diaspora that, by forced march, accompanied the former's progress had as one of their unforeseen consequences, a process of cultural change. That process has from time to time been described as 'acculturation', but the use of that conceals a value judgement, a presumption of a *terminus ad quem*, and the accommodation by the enslaved majority to the normative values of the white minority. Conceptualized in this way, the interaction of Europe and Africa in the New World locates the African exclusively as object, never as subject; and by a kind of hubristic Eurocentrism, ignores the double process of 'transculturation', in which each cultural legacy is stimulated by and responds to the other.

Bronislaw Malinowski observed in this regard that, 'the two races exist[ed] upon elements taken from Europe as well as from Africa... from both stores of culture. In so doing both races transform[ed] the borrowed elements and incorporate[d] them into a completely new and independent cultural reality.'[1] Recently, Edward Brathwaite, in examining this cultural process, which he describes as creolization, not only concurs implicitly with Malinowski's basic propositions, but also goes further to identify this process as 'the single most important factor in the development of Jamaica',[2] affecting whites no less than slaves. Further, in situations of cross-cultural contact, as Serghei Arutuniev has concluded, 'the dissimilarities, the morphological heterogeneities and the polymorphism existing even within the same population will... serve man as a means to cultural adaptation. The fact is that the plurality of cultures and of cultural variants... constitutes the adaptation mechanism which enables man to develop by selection of the best elements and renewal of his cultural heritage.'[3]

The cultural cross-currents of the Danish Virgin Islands in the period under review flowed from a variety of sources, and involved the intermingling of several cultural influences of the Danish official classes, Dutch and German missionaries, Jewish and French traders and craftsmen, English and Irish plantation owners and Scots-Irish overseers with an African cultural input that was itself by no means monolithic. Following Arutuniev's analysis, the foundations for the adaptation mechanism would have been well established by the middle of the eighteenth century, when the maximal exploitation of the Danish Virgin Islands began under Crown Rule.

What this paper sets out to do, as closely as the sources will permit, is to investigate one region of 'the world the slaves made', to shed some light on the process of cultural change, on the interplay of adaptation and adoption, or in Arutuniev's words, 'the independent creation of a new element (invention), and... the borrowing of an existing element from another culture... the first resembl[ing] mutation, the second, cross breeding'.[4] It would be idle to pretend that what is being attempted is in any way exhaustive. Nevertheless, it is the basic premise of this paper that the heterogeneous aggregate of Danish Virgin Islands slaves — more than 20,000 by the beginning of the nineteenth century — originating in an area that extended from Upper Guinea to Angola, came to comprise a community, achieve coherence, and evolve a discrete slave culture, involving, to precis Handler and Lange, behavioural patterns that were shared by the slaves as a group, and socially learned and transmitted.[5] The slaves' use of leisure, or if the phrase is not a contradiction in terms, 'free' time, will provide, it is hoped, important indicators of transculturation and a deeper understanding of this particular slave society.

Journal of Caribbean History, Vol. 13 (1980), pp. 21–43.

Despite the all-encompassing nature of slavery in these islands, as elsewhere in the Caribbean, it is nevertheless true to say that the slaves' occupational spread and the nature of the work routine allowed many slaves to have discretionary time. Those slaves, for example, who were involved in roles and specialities independent of plantation production and associated activities, viz. — urban jobbers and artisans, wharf and warehouse porters and seamen, were in no way bound by the sunrise to sunset regimen of the plantations. Even on the plantations themselves, custom not to mention self-interest had come to dictate that one day in the week, namely Sunday, was to be allowed to the slaves to rest from their labours. There were moreover individual planters who, in addition to Sunday, were in the habit of giving slaves an extra day for purposes of cultivating their provision grounds in lieu of plantation rations.[6] Long before 1843, therefore, when Saturday was legally created into a 'free' day and Sunday, the feast of the Lutheran Church and royal birthdays, likewise, there was ample opportunity for slaves in the towns and on the plantations to have discretionary leisure.

Both before and after 1843, a significant proportion of the work-free Sunday was spent in religious observance. The slaves of ten responded with fair enthusiasm to the stimulus of missionary proselytizing. Although the state Lutheran church was not itself a vigorous campaigner for slaves' souls, there were other denominations that entered the field with official concurrence and with varying degrees of success. The Moravians who were earliest in the field by 1732 had by far the largest number of slave adherents, followed by the Roman Catholics, the Anglicans, the Dutch Reformed Church and the Methodists in that order. Among slaves who became Moravians it was not uncommon to spend part of a week-day evening receiving instruction from a Moravian brother on the plantation, or walking to the nearest mission station.[7] Attendance at church on Sunday had also assumed significance before the end of the eighteenth century. One observer noted in 1788 as many as 200 slaves from a single estate on their way to church on Sunday. His description of the phenomenon, moreover, suggests strongly that those occasions had also been seized as opportunities for group activity and social interaction, for the display by some of 'chintz and other finery, such that a stranger would not think they were slaves'.[8]

At the beginning of the nineteenth century, church affiliation among slaves had achieved significant levels. The first complete figures indicate, as Table 1 illustrates, that in all three islands church affiliation exceeded 50 per cent of the total slave population. As the century grew older, despite the fact that the slave population was declining in all the islands except St. Thomas, as Table 2 shows, the numbers of church affiliated slaves had grown not only relatively but also absolutely. In the island of St. Croix, those numbers had reached an astonishing 99 per cent.

It is therefore surprising, given this significant response to the religion of the Europeans, that the slaves of the Danish Virgin islands showed no inclination whatever to graft their African religious beliefs and practices onto Christianity, to produce a syncretic religion of their own or to indigenize Christianity. There were no Moses Bakers or George Leisles, nor the emergence of any sect like the 'native' Baptists, as in Jamaica. The explanation probably inheres in the fact, firstly, that the missionary penetration was thorough, particularly on the part of the Moravians. Secondly, that penetration was a function of two variables: the islands' relatively small size, and their topography. None of these islands exceeded 85 sq. miles in area, and it was

Table 1 Christian Slaves in the Danish Virgin Islands, 1805

Island	Baptised slaves	Total slave population	Baptised slaves as % of total
St. John	1,294	2,417	53.5
St. Thomas	2,103	3,344	62.8
St. Croix	14,603	22,076	66.1
Total	18,000	27,837	64.6

Source: Dokumenter Vedkommende Kommissionen for Negerhandelens bedre Indrething og Ophaevelse, samt Efterrethinger om Negerhandelen og Slaveriet i Vestindien, 1783–1806, Rigsarkiv, Copenhagen.

Table 2 Christian Slaves in the Danish Virgin Islands, 1835

Island	Baptised slaves	Total slave population	Baptised slaves as % of total
St. John	1,636	1,943	84.1
St. Thomas	5,064	5,315	85.2
St. Croix	19,692	19,876	99.0
Total	26,392	27,134	87.2

Source: Originale Forestillinger fra Kommission Angaaende Negernes Stilling i Vestindien 1834–43, (5), Governor General von Scholten's Report, 2 January 1839, Bilag 16 B. Rigsarkiv, Copenhagen.

possible for a denomination as indefatigable as the Moravians, or as zealous as the Roman Catholics, to saturate an island like St. Croix, with its relatively easy topography, with Christian teaching. It is worthy of note that the missionaries' efforts were relatively less rewarding in St. John; not, one suspects, because the slaves on that island were any more resistant. Its breathtaking vistas notwithstanding — indeed precisely because of them — St. John is an island of notoriously difficult terrain. The lower percentages of converts from that island indicated in Tables 1 and 2 have a direct correlation with this geophysical fact.

Thirdly, there are grounds for believing that as the slave population became more and more creole or native-born after the slave trade's abolition in 1802, it was distanced with each passing year from aspects of its African roots. Missionary endeavour, it would seem, had pre-empted the population's leadership cadres, lessening the possibility thereby of cultural continuities, at least so far as religion went. Such a co-opted leadership could also help to explain why, between the aborted conspiracy of 1759 in St. Croix[9] and the uprising of 1848 which brought emancipation, there was neither conspiracy nor uprising. As the process of pre-emption and co-option took place, African magico-religious practices *pari-passu* fell into abeyance. Whereas in the eighteenth century, proscriptions against obeah figure very prominently in the slave codes and the proposed drafts for codes,[10] in the nineteenth century neither regulatory ordinances nor the accounts of contemporary travellers have anything to say on the subject of obeah.

It is not to be assumed, however, that the culture contact between European and African religions, was unidirectional. The flow in the other direction was equally noteworthy. The slaves' adoption of Christianity compelled the acquisition and more widespread use by the Europeans of the slaves' *lingua franca*, 'creolsk'. Dutch based, creole originated in St. Thomas from the need for a common medium of communication between the original Dutch colonizers and the multiple language slave community. Creole became a compound of African idiomatic expressions and sentence construction, with a vocabulary drawn from German and Dutch, Danish, French, Spanish and the Portuguese of the Sephardic Jewish community. It was a linguistic situation from which the English in the islands remained aloof, although their children, like other white children, learned creole from their slave nurses.[11] At a time when the 'art of writing a book was so seldom practised in Denmark',[12] two ABC creole books, a creole grammar, a hymnal and a catechism had been produced by 1770; a creole translation of the New Testament in 1779; a translation of the Old Testament, unpublished, in 1781; and in the remaining years before emancipation an impressive run of readers (1798, 1827); hymnals (1799, 1823); children's Bibles (1822); and catechisms (1827). By invention and cross-breeding a new element was created in creole and the *de facto* domination of Malinowski's 'new and independent cultural reality' remained basically unchanged, until the introduction by Governor General von Scholten of a Lancastrian school system for slaves in 1838, with English as the official medium of instruction.[13]

At its introduction von Scholten's school system catered for younger children aged four to eight on Monday to Friday mornings, and older children, up to age fourteen, on Saturday mornings and Sunday afternoons. When the school system was finally formalized in 1846, instruction to the older children was confined to three morning hours of the 'free' day, Saturday, established in 1843.[14] In St. Croix, where eight of the eleven schools were located, all the contemporary accounts bear witness to the children's enthusiasm. According to one account, they were attentive and responsive and showed a quicker grasp than white children in general. Their parents were no less enthusiastic about what they had missed, and obviously made special efforts to send their children to school clean and well dressed.[15]

I have argued elsewhere that this positive response on the part of the slaves to increased leisure and its opportunities, bears a direct causal relationship with the uprising of 1848. The availability of education at state expense, the adjustments to plantation routines which it necessitated, between them heightened the slaves' perception of their own worth. The Law of Free Birth of 28 July 1847 simply reinforced that perception and acted as a catalyst on the impatience which had slowly emerged in the previous decade with the introduction of education and the 'free' day associated with it.[16]

The declaration of that 'free' day in 1843 also introduced Saturday as market day, rescheduling it from Sunday on which it was traditionally held. By the middle of the eighteenth century the markets were well established in the islands' towns. They represent an important contribution on the slaves' part to the internal distribution system, no less important than what Hall and Mintz have identified for Jamaica in the eighteenth century.[17] The markets moreover provided an important opportunity for social interaction among the slaves from different plantations, an opportunity further to supplement their rations by barter or purchase, and to earn cash.

The market in Christianstead was usually open until 8 p.m., but as it got dark by 7 p.m., the slaves lit their stalls with candles. A variety of products was offered for sale: vegetables such as cabbages, green pulses and tomatoes; peas; poultry, pigeons, eggs; yams, potatoes, maize, guinea corn and cassava, known collectively as Indian provisions; pumpkins; melons, oranges, wild plums and berries from the hills on St. Croix's north side; rope tobacco; cassava bread, which many whites, particularly creoles, were especially fond of; fish, firewood and fodder.[18]

Market regulations were first codified as part of the Slave *Reglement* of 1775, and they called for two white market supervisors and the permission of slaves' owners, as a deterrent to the sale of stolen goods.[19] The convention was also established in the course of the eighteenth century that slaves could not offer for sale any of the export staples such as cotton and sugar or rum.[20] The *Reglement* was never enforced and in practice supervision appears to have been lax. Nevertheless there is little evidence to suggest that goods sold in the markets were stolen, or that the markets provided an outlet for illegal trafficking in the way that itinerant vending did. The available market produce was, overwhelmingly, the result of the slaves' creative initiative in the use of their 'free' time, particularly in the cultivation of their provision grounds. The literary evidence in the eighteenth century certainly identifies the same kind of goods for sale in the market as were grown on the provision grounds.[21] This creative initiative was particularly in evidence in identifying and satisfying the market demands for grass and firewood. Hans West who lived in St. Croix in the 1780s reckoned that the sale of these two items in Christianstead and Frederickstead amounted to the not inconsiderable sum of 61,488 *Rigsdaler* per annum,[22] and Thurlow Weed who wrote in the 1840s supplies evidence for the continuing vigour of this traffic.[23] What the evidence also helps to identify was that there was a rationalization of this activity, and a sex-specific distribution of the work involved at least by the 1840s. Like itinerant huckstering, market vending was largely a female monopoly; work on the provision grounds was largely the province of the males.[24] For West Indian purposes, the slaves had adopted the prevalent practice of the Gold Coast, from which many of them had originated.

The cultivation of provision grounds and the Sunday, subsequently Saturday, market apart, a major portion of slaves' discretionay time was spent in dancing. As early as the first codified slave laws of 1733, there were indications that 'fetes, balls, dances and divertissements with Negro instruments' were sufficiently established to warrant the imposition of conditions under which they could be held.[25] In the 1740s Governor Moth's *Articuler for Negerne* stipulated that such revelries should end at sundown or at 8 p.m. on moonlight nights.[26] In St. Thomas in the 1760s a proclamation of Governor de Gunthelberg extended the time limit to 10 p.m.; thereafter police permission was required but in no circumstances was the use of Goombay drums permitted.[27]

Understandably, dancing or the opportunity and energy to engage in it, was a greater likelihood for urban slaves. In St. Croix in the 1770s Governor General Clausen permitted dances in town but not beyond the 8 p.m. curfew. The same proclamation allowed free people of colour to hold dances until 10 p.m. but both slaves and whites were prohibited, on pain of severe punishment in the one case, and fines and imprisonment in the other, from either attending or participating.[28] The prohibition would suggest that in the towns at least the inflexible lines of slavery were being both bent and breached by the compelling attractions such as that contained in Lindemann's draft slave code for 1783.[29] There are, therefore, strong presumptive grounds for believing that some slaves and some whites by deliberate choice shared, in the eighteenth century at least, one common social activity, albeit illegally and under the cover of darkness.

Such violence to the society's implicit premises was not the only remarkable feature of the slaves' preoccupation with the dance. In 1791 Hans West reported that dances were held several times per week, with an entrance fee as much as three *Rigsdaler* per couple. It was this frequency he concluded, that was a prime consideration in the limitation of the activity.[30] Carl Holten, brother of Christian, the commandant of St. Thomas in 1815, was another contemporary observer who shed some light on the subject of slave dances. With a good eye for detail, Holten noted that formal styles of address were often in use at these occasions: Mister, Mrs., Councillor, Captain, etc. Holten put this down to mere mimicry. But that hardly exhausts the possibilities. It might just as probably have been ridicule, and there is the third alternative that the slaves could have been investing the occasion with special significance by the adaptation of European styles of address and the usages in contemporary 'society'. At any rate the adaptations were subject to the slaves' own sobering sense of the appropriate, an eye for the absurd, and a capacity to poke fun at each other. The point is well borne out by one of Holten's numerous anecdotes:

> Jeg mindes iblandt andet en Haarskjaerer, som anskaffede sig et Par Briller til at valse med, fordi han havde seet Waltersdorffs Secretair Captain Manthey at gjore dette, og at han, da de andre Couleurte dog fandte dette vel latterligt, svarede den ganske muggent: 'I ere nogle Tosser, some vide at dette er Mode ved Hoffet'.[31]

Non-dancing parties, at which tea and coffee were served, was another favourite diversion of slaves. The evidence, however, points to this being a particularly urban activity. They had become popular enough by the 1770s to attract the notice of officialdom, and the Burgher Council of St. Croix gave it their attention in 1778, declaring that those entertainments had got completely out of hand. Some slave owners not only turned a blind eye to these occurrences, but also used permission to attend them as a means of granting favours to some slaves. An entrance fee was charged, as with the dances on which West reported. The payments involved were more than likely one use to which the proceeds of marketeering or own-account jobbing were put. Like the dances too, these tea and coffee parties were opportunities for social intercourse among legally segregated strata of the society. The parties were attended by free people of colour, whose 'connections and too great familiarity' with slaves were, in the Burgher Council's opinion, a cause for concern. They thought these revelries should be either limited or forbidden altogether.[32]

Above all, the parties gave the slaves a chance to bring out their finery, finery of the sort that was the subject of a detailed sumptuary ordinance in 1786. The ordinance mentions accessories of gold and silver and precious stones, silk, lace and other expensive fabrics as items all prohibited to field and house slaves alike, although the latter were allowed a silver clasp of simple design.[33] The implication was that the silks and jewellery were, if not cast offs, stolen. The Danish West Indian, like the British West Indian, slave law tended to view the slave as above all a potential criminal. However, Governor General Schimmelmann, who drew up the ordinance, did not calculate for the slaves' insistence on carving out of the wilderness of servitude the oasis of his own humanity by individual idiosyncracies of dress or dressing up when he had unencumbered time. How effective the 1786 ordinance was is difficult to judge, but in 1814 the police chief of St. Croix, Gjellerup, issued a notice referring to 'wearing apparel, jewellery and beads too numerous to specify found at a slave ball', and inviting their 'owners' to claim them.[34] Despite Schimmelmann, the slaves had clearly not ceased to wear their best to balls, whether that best was the end product of their own sweat or borrowed surreptitiously from their masters' or mistresses' wardrobes, as the police chief broadly implied.

By convention and latterly by royal instructions of 1 May 1840, slaves were allowed all the recognized feast days and high holy days of the state Lutheran church, as well as the monarch's birthday. No special significance appears to have been attached to these by the slave population, although it can be assumed that where appropriate they would have gone to church. Of the public holidays, the two days of Christmas and the New Year stand in a category by themselves. According to Thurlow Weed who visited in 1844–45, in the week that intervened 'they contrive . . . to do very little work. . . . And on these occasions the slaves' cup of enjoyment fills to the brim.'[35] These days produced their own kinds of diversion and dynamics. The European practice of throwing firecrackers and letting off fireworks was a particularly pervasive practice among slaves in this holiday period; indeed, before — during the 'several weeks preceding' in which they were 'busied with preparations for their festivities' — and after.[36] Proclamations over several decades, particularly in St. Thomas, had failed to arrest the practice.[37]

A colonial law officer commenting in 1783 blamed it on the indolence of the police. But in part the explanation also lay in the fact that 'the throwing of fire-crackers was reckoned to be one of those innocent pleasures wherewith one distinguished special from ordinary days, and even whites themselves participated'.[38] Annual ordinances, issued by the police prefects just before Christmas, continued into the nineteenth century.[39] Their very issuance, however, are grounds for believing that this was one 'innocent pleasure' in which whites and slaves found common enjoyment.

Itinerant minstrelsy at Christmas and New

Year was well enough established by 1759 for Governor General von Prøck to issue a proclamation against it. It involved the use of violins, 'other instruments' which von Prøck did not specify, and begging for money as minstrels everywhere did and still do. It was also the practice among some slave owners to have these slaves playing for them, and it can also be reasonably inferred from the proclamation that they were sent to, or were hired by, other owners to perform.[40] Lindemann's draft slave laws of 1783 and van der Østen's of 1785 repeat the prohibitory paragraph of 1759, and indicate that the practice could not be legislated away.[41] It seems hardly likely that these slave musicians were performing African music on the violin for an audience of Europeans. It can safely be assumed therefore, that the music was, if not European, at the very least a creolized variant of it.

In connection with the New Year festivities, Johann Nissen who lived in St. Thomas for 46 years from 1792, noted in 1832:

> It is the custom here, especially among the coloured persons to celebrate old year's night with music, dancing, singing and in short, making a great noise. They commenced this uproar as early as 4 o'clock in the afternoon, passing in great crowds through all the streets, crying out in their creole tongue, 'Old Year's night'.[42]

These street processions to which Nissen calls attention were probably not new in 1832. Some 80 years before, von Prøck in condemning the minstrels with their violins, makes mention of '*de andre Negere som ombløber*': the other negroes who go around.[43] This is hardly conclusive, although tantalizingly suggestive.

Nissen further remarked:

> At 9 o'clock they pass through all the streets with music and continue to do so through the whole night. Some of them have a certain place, where they have put up a tent of coconut leaves, and dance there during the night. Many of them again dance in their own rooms, which are certainly very small, and are so full that the dancers have scarcely room to move.[44]

In St. Thomas then, the dance took over at the New Year's festivities, and the Goombay did duty here as with other dances. Nissen did not think a great deal of the slaves' dancing. Their free-form improvisatory style contrasted sharply in his mind with the then prescribed European measures of his day. Dancing was something which 'well-educated' people learnt and performed. On the other hand, 'the dances of the negroes are of one sort; turning and moving about — they have no regular dances'.[45]

In St. Croix, nominally more Christian by far, the situation described by Weed at the beginning of 1845 is not very different. Indeed, he describes dancing as the slaves' 'only festive resource' and notes that for the New Year frolic, there was 'turban, calico, ribbon, gewgaw and trinket' in abundance. Estate slaves elected Kings and Queens, Princes and Princesses, Maids of Honour and Pages; a somewhat more formalized structure than anything reported for St. Thomas. The dance was opened with 'much gravity' by the King and Queen, to the accompaniment of ballads led by a 'Prima Donna' supported by a chorus, and the ubiquitous Goombay 'discours[ing] most eloquent music'. As the dance progressed, the enthusiasm rose, as did the Prima Donna's voice, the chorus swelled, the drummer was carried away and the Queen eventually swooned, to be revived by her attendants sprinkling bay rum and plying their fans. But once recovered she joined the dance with renewed energy, having called upon the Princess to replace her as leader; she in her turn, and the King and Princess in theirs, calling on those of 'inferior rank' when exhausted. The chorus accompaniment did not actually join in the dance; indeed they constituted, according to Weed, the greater proportion of those present. 'Towards the close of the festivities, however, all join in the dance, all, at the same time, singing most vociferously.'[46]

Weed enables us to see not only the all-consuming nature of the event for the slave population. His information enables us equally to see the event's all-encompassing character for the entire population:

> The first privilege (or duty as they esteem it) of the slaves on Christmas day New Year's day, is to pay their respects, in a body, to their master, before whom they dance for an hour or more, paying tribute, in their songs to his liberality, generosity &c., after which they are regaled with cakes, cordial &c., and generally receive presents from their mistress.[47]

While plantation whites were touched in this way, the free coloureds confined to the towns residentially, were in their turn touched by the celebrations of the urban slave population. Both groups, we are told, 'form their parties, elect their Kings, Queens &c., and dance in like manner'.[48]

The renditions of the Prima Donna and chorus were not mere accompaniments to the dance. They were sometimes complimentary — to greet, impromptu, some passer-by; or congratulatory — to the King, Queen Victoria or the Americans. In this regard the slaves were displaying in song a good grasp of current events. But nowhere was this grasp put to better use than in the songs of incisive social comment, indeed of social protest;

All we girls must keep heads together; King Christian have sent to free us all; Governor SHOLTON had a vote for us; King Christian have sent to grant us all; we have signed for liberty; our Crown Prince had a vote in it; our Gracious Queen had the highest vote; King Christian have sent to say he will crown us all.
Oh yes! oh, yes! hurra! hurra!
All we girls must keep head together.[49]

Some 60 years before Schmidt had warned that slaves sang songs for the courage to rebel; that if Europeans paid more attention to them than they did the possibilities of uprising would be considerably lessened.[50] Weed, an outsider visiting from North America, may very well have recorded without realising it, the first audible rumble of the eruption which took place three years later.

There are no explicit references in the literature to end of year mummery of the John Canoe type, which Brathwaite has argued was an African retention in Jamaica.[51] However, the Jamaican procession of 'Set Girls' had an inexact equivalent in the organised processions from some estates that went into town on New Year's morning. The rivalries between the women of different estates was certainly as intense as that between the 'Set Girls'. They abused each other roundly for the poverty of parsimoniousness of their masters, cast slurs on the colour of mistresses, and did not cavil to use that most approbrious of epithets, 'Guinea Bird'.[52]

At least one slave diversion could be classified under the heading of the martial arts. Particularly among plantation or country slaves who had long distances to travel, it was not unusual for them to walk with a stick for support. Indeed, the surviving newspapers of the eighteenth century bear this out. On the longest journey the slave could contemplate, namely when he ran away, the advertisements almost invariably represented him with a stick. The sticks were obviously large enough to be considered cudgels, and could be gnarled, pointed, metal-tipped or banded with metal. The slave's staff had the potential for becoming a murderous weapon, and was so regarded by white authority, which proceeded to ban it.[53] But the ban of the Bangelar, as it was known, was never very successful. It was difficult to suppress like Goombay drumming, and perhaps for the same reason: probable ritual significance, definite entertainment value and a high degree of skill required, in the case of the Bangelar, for its effective use. At the same time, white encouragement is also to be accounted a causal factor in its survival. According to Clausen, whites not only found pleasure in the spectacle of these stick-fighting contests but attended to egg on the contestants.[54] Stick-fighting, like cock-fighting which survived into the nineteenth century and was favoured among whites no less than slaves,[55] was a blood sport; a brutal business for a brutal time. Whites and slaves could both find pleasure in the structured violence the contest involved, for co-existing in a society based upon an identical premise, neither could escape its logic.

One other pastime which served a second function as defence in situations of conflict, was the use of stones with and without slingshots. In 1873, a colonial law officer deemed stone-throwing a habit dangerous enough to merit 20 lashes. The habit, he said, was acquired in childhood: the slave child's first amusement as soon as it began to creep being stone throwing. It persisted into adult life, and stones were used not only for chasing dogs, pigs, goats and other animals but were also employed against each other in moments of irritation or during disputes:

Sielden seer man en Neger paa Gaden uden en Steen i Haanden. Det gaar endog saavidt, at man ei kan vaere sikker i huusene og paa Gallerierne for saadan letsindig Steenkasten hen i Veiret. Man hitter allerede paa at bruge Slynger. En saadan Øvelser, naar de blev almindelig, vist blive en farlig Tidsfordriv og Fornøielse.[56]

These remarks which apply to St. Croix, could equally have applied to St. Thomas. That island's commandant in the 1780s, de Maleville, reported with concern the growing proportions that stone-throwing had assumed. In the years 1774, 1775, 1776, for several nights at a particular time of the year which de Maleville did not specify, stones rained down upon the houses and galleries of Charlotte Amalie from the sea and from the hill above. Those stones were large enough to kill and made it unsafe to sit outside after dark.[57] If one rules out a poltergeist theory, the only likely explanations with which one is left, are gestures of defiance towards whites — a not uncommon phenomenon in the urban setting of Charlotte Amalie[58] — or a stone 'war' between individual slaves or groups of slaves under the cover of darkness.

If the facility with stones for diversion and

defence was African in origin, there is evidence of cultural cross-breeding in the West Indies. Lindemann suggested in his draft slave code that slaves should not be allowed to play 'Kag'.[59] But that game was almost certainly metropolitan Danish, for it is described in Verner Dahlerup's *Ordbog over det Danske Sprog* (Dictionary of the Danish Language) not as a game of African origin, but simply as: 'Name of a children's game, the object of which is to hit down with a stonethrow, the uppermost stone in a pyramid-formed stone-heap; or to knock over a ninepin or a forked stick'. Borrowing from a European children's game, the slaves had made it theirs, transformed it into an adult's game and used it as target practice to sharpen their stone-throwing skills.

Gaming was an important social activity among whites in Virgin Island slave society. Card games such as *L'Hombre*, whist and boston with 300 *piastre* stakes were an important part of official entertaining, at least under Governor General von Scholten; among the *haute monde* in the elegant public salons of Charlotte Amalie in the 1840s or among the less respectable and in secret in St. Croix.[60] Slaves no less than their masters were given to games of chance, especially to cards and dice. However, none of the official proclamations from Gardelin's time in the 1730s takes any notice of the practice before the 1770s. Since it is unlikely that slaves could have played without attracting attention to themselves, one possible conclusion is that gambling as 'leisure' time activity became popular after mid-century, and is probably one index of the creolization process. Calusen, in prohibiting all forms of gambling among slaves in 1774, claimed that 'daily experience had taught that slaves had an insatiable lust for gambling' which had gone completely out of control. It was taking place, it would appear, not only in houses and on galleries, but also on the streets.[61] This suggested a largely urban manifestation. Lindemann's draft code of 1783 on the other hand is not specific as to place in recommending prohibition of 'dice, cards . . . or any such games',[62] but Van der Østen's does speak of gambling in the towns.[63] However, the St. Croix Burgher Council did indicate in 1787 that there was gambling on the plantation as well; during the religious feast days and fast days, on Sundays and the two days of Christmas and the New Year.[64] De Maleville, writing in the same year from St. Thomas, also expressed concern about the extent of card playing and all forms of gambling among the slave population, and the participation of free coloureds in these games of chance.[65]

Gambling was associated in the minds of some whites with other 'vices' such as rum drinking, which officialdom did its best to discourage if it could not stop.[66] Some publicans apparently allowed slaves to sit in their rum shops when they were open on weekdays, Sundays and holidays. Some officials thought slaves should only be sold from the back yards of the shops and not permitted to loiter; others that such loitering and the gambling to which it gave rise was allowed and encouraged by the publicans for pecuniary advantage or for trafficking in stolen goods.[67] Rum, traditionally, was never sold on the plantations, so that a slave 'on his own time' wanting to acquire his own liquor without stealing or to buy himself a drink had to wait until there was an opportunity to be in town and have cash: an opportunity which the market provided. The market's attraction as an opportunity for release from the boredom and brutality of plantation life, was enormously enhanced, therefore, by the prospect of a few drams of 'kill-devil'.

A similar kind of release appears to have been found in horseback riding. The imperatives of the society, however, with its high premiums on discipline and deference, made such use of slaves' time in an essentially individualistic activity, problematic in the extreme — particularly if slaves were given to hard riding. For both whites and slaves, it was as if the physical act of mounting a horse had a corresponding metaphysical significance, lessening the status gap between both groups. Lindemann in drafting his slave code in 1783, emphasised white concern in this regard. Any mounted slave should either dismount or ride slowly out of the way for approaching whites, but in no circumstances was he to gallop past, nor ride side by side with, whites.[68] This was in the spirit of Gardelin's earlier code of 1733, which had insisted on similar shows of public submissiveness, even when the situations were reversed and the slave on foot.[69] In Van der Østen's draft code of 1785, we again meet with this continuing concern with the slaves on horseback. In his view, slaves' use of horses without permission was to be regarded as theft and punished accordingly.[70]

The abandon with which slaves apparently rode, as they savoured these brief moments of glory, was the occasion of adverse white comment from time to time, for as a group whites were as much concerned about 'public order' as they were about deference. Indeed, in their minds the two were closely related, if not synonymous. Governor General von Prøck noted in 1756 that hard riding in the streets of Christianstead had become a daily and dangerous practice on the part of slaves, and proceeded to prohibit it.[71] Lindemann too would have prohibited slaves riding in streets of towns or their immediate environs, unless there were evidence of some urgent errand. He remarked further that more often than not, the offenders were small boys,[72] who obviously rode with no less enthusiasm than their elders.

If there were constraints on this method of release in the towns and their vicinity, the country roads offered better opportunity. Estate slaves who were not professional jockeys like John Jones who ran away in 1815,[75] nevertheless continued to organize their own equestrian diversion. The following public notice in 1815 signed by the Chief of Police, Mouritzen, in St. Croix, suggests a well established practice, involving as dancing and stick-fighting did, whites no less than slaves, and conducted in such a way as to avoid official attention:

It has been reported to this office that it has been customary even among slaves to run Horse Races on the high-roads in the Country: This being contrary to the Laws and good order, each and every one is admonished to desist from such bad practice; and, it is requested, that any one who might know of such races give information to this office, where the offended will be treated as the Law directs.[74]

Horse racing as a sport did not have any currency before the first two decades of the nineteenth century. This was the period, at any rate, during which it was considered important enough to be advertised in the public prints.[75] The slaves had not only co-opted the sport among themselves for pleasure and, where possible, profit; they had also played a clear part in their role as jockeys in establishing the sport for whites.

In the last hundred years or so of slavery in the Danish Virgin Islands, the slaves by the use of the discretionary time, legally and illegally at their disposal, had created certain modes of being and behaviour that were distinctly theirs. The use of 'free' time was far more conducive to this purpose, having regard to the demanding nature of the routines and discipline associated with plantation production. By emancipation they had created a culture, neither wholly African nor yet European, retaining, adapting, borrowing and adopting. The transition from disaggregation to community was only possible by a process of cultural change. As Mintz and Price have observed, 'in order for slave communities to take shape, normative patterns of behaviour had to be established, and these patterns could be created only on the basis of particular forms of social interaction'.[76]

The creation was taking place not in a vacuum but in a dynamic context: of interaction among themselves and contact, sometimes intimate, with the other dominant cultural elements which were European. Masters as well as slaves were caught up in the process of cultural interchange. They enjoyed, or learnt to enjoy, foods like cassava bread, and some at any rate, slaves' sports like stick-fighting. Donors of their religions, they became recipients of the slaves' language, and in several respects provide empirical justification for the conclusion that 'the role of the powerless in affecting, and even controlling important parts of the lives of the masters was also typical of slave colonies'.[77]

Notes

1. B. Malinowski, 'Methods of Study of Culture Contract in Africa', *Institute of African Languages and Cultures*, Memorandum XV (1938), p. xvii.
2. Edward Brathwaite, *The Development of Creole Society in Jamaica 1770–1820* (Oxford, 1971), p. 296.
3. S. Arutuniev, 'Cultural Paradigms: The Process of Change Through Cultural Borrowings', *Cultures*, Vol. 5, No. 1 (1978):p. 95.
4. *Ibid.*, p. 95.
5. J. S. Handler and F. W. Lange, *Plantation Slavery in Barbados. An Archaeological and Historical Investigation*, (Cambridge, Mass, 1978), p. 289 n. 1.
6. Rigsarkiv, Copenhagen (cited hereafter as R/A), *Originale Forestillinger fra en Commission angaaende Negernes Stilling i Vestindien m.m. og dertil hørende Kongelige Resolutioner 1834–1843*, von Scholten to Christian VIII, 15 January 1841, Encl. 3, d/d 29 October 1840; Encl. 5, d/d 26 May 1840. For an earlier instance see I. Schmidt, 'Blandede Anmaearkninger', *Samleren*, Vol. 2, No. 42, (1788): p. 244.
7. Schmidt, *op. cit.*, p. 239. See also R/A, *Kommissions Forslag og Anmaerkning ang. negerhandelen med genparter af anordninger og publikationer* (1785), Bind 2. Commandant de Malevilles Bataenkninger, 19 October 1787, f. 92.
8. Schmidt, *op. cit.*, p. 245
9. R/A, *Udkast og Betaenkning ang, negerloven m. bilag*, No. 4, Philip Gardelin's Placat (cited hereafter as Gardelin), 5 September 1733, para. 13 Cf. *ibid.*, No. 24, Forslag til en Neger Lov for de Kongelife Danske Vestindicke Eylande, 1783 (cited hereafter as Lindemann), Pt 1, para. 10. Cf. also *Kommissions Forslag og Anmaerkning* .... Bind 1, Negerlov for de Danske Vestindiske Eylande (cited hereafter as *Van der østen*), Pt 3, para. 18.
10. Monica Schuler, 'Akan Slave Rebellions in the British Caribbean', *Savacou*, Vol. 1., No. 1 (June 1970): pp. 21–23.
11. Jens Larsen, *Virgin Islands Story* (Philadelphia, 1950), Chaps. 10 and 11 give an extremely useful survey of these developments.
12. H. B. Dahlerup, *Mit Livs Begivenheder* (Copenhagen, 1909), Vol. 2, p. 277.

13. This subject is dealt with by N. A. T. Hall, 'Establishing a Public Elementary School System for Slaves in the Danish Virgin Islands 1732–1846', *Caribbean Journal of Education* (January 1979).
14. *Ibid.*
15. Dahlerup, *Mit Livs*, Vol. 2, pp. 296–97. See also Dahlerup, 'Skizzer fra et kort Besog paa vore vestindiske Øer i Sommeren 1841', *Nyt Archiv for Søvaesnet, 1* (1842): p. 28.
16. N. A. T. Hall, 'Establishing a Public Elementary School System'.
17. Sidney Mintz and D. G. Hall, 'The origins of the Jamaican internal marketing system'. In Mintz S. (ed.), *Papers in Caribbean Anthropology*, (New Haven, 1960).
18. On the market see H. West, *Bidrag til Beskrivelse over Eylandet St. Croix i America in Vestindien* (Copenhagen, 1793), pp. 75–76; West, *Beretning om det dansk Eilande St. Croix i Vestindien* (Copenhagen, 1791), pp. 72–74; Schmidt, *op. cit.*, pp. 242–44; J. P. Nissen, *Reminiscences of a 46 years' residence in the Island of St. Thomas in the West Indies* (Nazareth, Pa, 1838), p. 34 and Thurlow Weed, *Letters from West Indies* (Albany, 1866), pp. 353–55.
19. R/A, *Udkast og Betaenkning*, No. 2, paras 14 and 15.
20. R/A, *Udkast og Betaenkning*, No. 27, Governor Clausen's Placat, 11 August 1767, paras 1–5.
21. West, *Beretning*, p. 72. Cf. Schmidt, *op. cit.*, pp. 241–43.
22. West, *Bidrag*, pp. 75–76.
23. Weed, *op. cit.*, p. 354.
24. Weeds, *op. cit.*, p. 353.
25. Gardelin, para. 16.
26. R/A, *Udkast og Betaenkning*, No. 1, 11 December 1941, para. 6. Cf. *ibid.*, No. 27, #18, Governor von Prøck's Placat, 17 May 1756, para. 7.
27. *Ibid.*, No. 27 #29, 9 February 1765, para. 9.
28. *Ibid.*, No. 27, #38, 5 October 1774, para. 6.
29. Lindemann, Pt 3, paras 33-36.
30. West, *Berentning*, p. 77. Although he does not specifically say so, it is likely that his remarks were based on his own observations of, or reports on, the situation in Christiansted, not on the plantations.
31. Carl Holtens Dagbog. In Clausen, J., & Rist, F. P. (Eds), *Memoirer og Breve*, ix (1909): 53. I recall among the other things a barber who got himself a pair of spectacles to waltz in, because he had seen Walterstoff's secretary Capt. Manthey doing so and when the other coloureds found this entirely ridiculous, replied surlily: 'You are a bunch of fools if you don't know that is the style at court.'
32. R/A, *Udkast og Betaenkning*, no. 27, #43, 2 December 1778, para. 5.
33. R/A, *Kommissions Forslag og Anmaerkning* .... Bind 1, Schimmelmann's Placat, 26 May 1786, paras 1 and 2.
34. *St. Croix Gazette*, 27 July 1814.
35. Weed, *op. cit.*, p. 346.
36. *Ibid.* See also R/A, *Udkast og Betaenkning*, No. 33, Clausen's Placat, 21 October 1770.
37. For representative samples of proclamations see R/A, *Udkast og Betaenkning*, No. 1, 30 December 1758, *ibid*, No. 27, 12 December 1761; *ibid*, No. 33, 21 October 1170; *ibid*, No. 41, 21 October 1777.
38. Lindemann, Pt. 1, para. 93. My emphasis.
39. See for example *St. Croix Gazette*, 25 December. 1813.
40. R/A, *Udkast og Betaenkning*, No. 27, #22, 23 December 1758, Para. 3.
41. Lindemann, Pt 1, para. 98, Van der Østen, Pt 3, para. 104.
42. Nissen, *Reminiscences*, p. 164.
43. R/A, *Udkast og Betaenkning*, No. 27, #22, 23 December 1759, para. 3.
44. Nissen, *Reminiscences*, p. 164.
45. *Ibid.*, pp. 164-65. My emphasis.
46. Weed, *op. cit.*, pp. 346–47.
47. *Ibid.*, p. 347.
48. *Ibid.*
49. *Ibid.*, p. 348.
50. Schmidt, *op. cit.*, pp. 232–33.
51. Brathwaite, *The Development of Creole Society*, p. 230.
52. Weed, *op. cit.*, pp. 349-350. On 'Set Girls', see Brathwaite, *The Development of Creole Society*, p. 231.
53. R/A, *Udkast og Betaenkning*, No. 27, #38, Governor General Clausen's Proclamation, 5 Oct. 1774, paras 1 and 5. Cf. *Lindemann*, Pt 1, para. 87; Van der Østen, Pt 3, para. 74.
54. R/A, *Udkast og Betaenkning*, No. 27, #38, 5 October 1774, para. 5.
55. Dahlerup, *Mit Livs*, p. 48. See also *Dansk Vestindisk Regerings Avis*, 25 August 1836.
56. Lindemann, Pt. 1, para. 94. One does not often see a Negro on the street without a stone in his hand. It has gone so far that one can no longer be secure in one's house or gallery from such careless stone-throwing Already they have hit upon using sling shots. If such a practice became common, it would be a dangerous pastime.
57. R/A, *Kommissions Forslag og Anmaerkning* ... Bind 2, Commandant de Maleville's Bataenkninger, 19 October 1787.
58. See for example R/A, *Udkast og Betaenkning*, No. 27, #29, Commandant de Gunthelberg's Proclamation, 9 February 1765.
59. Lindemann, Pt 1, para. 76.
60. Dahlerup, *Mit Livs*, pp. 47–48, 274.
61. R/A, *Udkast og Betaenkning*, No. 27, #38, 5 October 1774, para. 3.
62. Lindemann, Pt 1, para. 77.
63. Van der Østen, Pt 3, para. 73.
64. R/A, *Kommissions Forslag og Anmaerkning* .... Bind 2, 1 August 1787, f. 68.
65. *Ibid.*, de Maleville's Betaenkninger, 19 October 1787, f. 91.
66. Lindemann, Pt 1, para. 84.
67. Van der Østen, Pt 3, para. 98. Cf. R/A, *Kommissions Forslag og Anmaerkning*, Bind 2, 1 August 1787, f. 76, and *ibid.*, Etatz Raad Colbiornsens Anmaerkninger, 24 September 1788.
68. Lindemann, Pt 1, para. 2.
69. Gardelin, para. 11.
70. Van der Østen, Pt 3, para. 59.
71. R/A, *Udkast og Betaenkning*, No. 27, #18, 17 May 1756, paras, 8, 22. Cf. *ibid.*, #22, 23 December 1759, para. 12 and *St. Croix Gazette*, 7 July 1812, Police Chief Gjellerup's Ordinance.
72. Lindemann, Pt 1. para. 97.
73. *St. Croix Gazette*, 14 January 1815. Cf. *St. Croix Gazette*, 5 October 1814 wich announces the running away of 'mulatto Michael', another slave jockey.
74. *Dansk Vestindisk Regerings Avis*, 13 May 1815.
75. See for example *St. Croix Gazette*, 9 February 1807; 5 October 1814.
76. Mintz, S. W. and Price Richard, *An Anthropological Approach to the Afro-American Past: A Caribbean Perspective* (Philadelphia, 1976), p. 10.
77. *Ibid.*, p. 16.

SECTION NINE
Control, Resistance and Revolt

Caribbean slave societies were able to persist partly because of the complex and pervasive structures of control and regulation. Imperial control agencies were primarily concerned with the lowest social levels of colonial society, though they did not ignore the colonial elites. Spanish and French governments asserted greatest external control over their colonies, a factor which cannot be ignored and is a major argument in explaining the occurrence of the first successful slave revolt in a French colony, and why creole nationalism reached its most revolutionary potential in Spanish territories.

Goveia's essay suggests that differences in the stage of material and ideological development of imperial countries determined to a large extent the nature of control systems, though their effectiveness resulted significantly from the peculiarity of problems encountered in the region. Slaves, free coloureds, poor whites and Amerindians constantly opposed internal socio-political arrangements. Indeed, historians are now in agreement that in the Caribbean, anti-slavery revolt was endemic; and it has been suggested that the period of slavery was characterized primarily by one protracted war launched by slaves against slave owners. Detailed studies of the patterns and forms of resistance are now available. It is possible, therefore, to identify the major events and ideas that have shaped the development of Caribbean anti-slavery. Though highly structured revolts and long-term marronage have been considered the most advanced rebellious acts, the relations between such levels of political organizations and the more spontaneous day-to-day slavery responses have not been adequately assessed. This record of resistance illustrates, nonetheless, that there was hardly a generation of slaves in the Caribbean who did not take their anti-slavery actions to the level of violent armed encounters in the pursuit of freedom.

The West Indian Slave Laws of the Eighteenth Century

ELSA V. GOVEIA*

The West Indian slave laws of the eighteenth century mirror the society that created them. They reflect the political traditions of the European colonizers and the political necessities of a way of life based upon plantation slavery.

The foundation of these laws was laid in the earliest days of colonization; and the body of slave laws existing in the eighteenth century included a substantial proportion of laws made at an earlier time. The thirteenth-century code of laws, known as the *Siete Partidas*, was from the beginning incorporated in the common law of the Spanish colonies and provided a series of principles for the government of slaves.[1] The great slave code of the French West Indies, which came to be called the *Code Noir*, was promulgated during the seventeenth century. The early slave laws of the British colonies, though they were not codified in this way, were generally retained as part of the slave law of the islands during the eighteenth century; and even when these laws were repealed in detail, a continuity of principle can be traced. The early laws were elaborated. Their emphasis changed with changes in the life of the islands. But the structure of the eighteenth-century slave laws rested upon older laws and was moulded by forces, early at work in the islands, which had shaped not only the law but also the society of these slave colonies.

Both in the creation and in the maintenance of the slave laws, opinion was a factor of great significance. Law is not the original basis of slavery in the West India colonies, though slave laws were essential for the continued existence of slavery as an institution. Before the slave laws could be made, it was necessary for the opinion to be accepted that persons could be made slaves and held as slaves. To keep the slave laws in being, it was necessary for this opinion to persist. Without this, the legal structure would have been impossible. Spain's role in establishing slavery as part of the pattern of European colonization in the West Indies is thus of primary importance. Of equal importance, is the influence exerted by developments within the West Indies in sustaining the legal structure, first introduced by the Spaniards, and, to a greater or lesser extent, transforming its content.

Slavery was an accepted part of Spanish law at the time of the discovery. It was legal to hold slaves, and it was accepted in law that slavery was transmitted by birth, through the mother to her children. This was the core of the system of enslavement transferred from Spain to the West Indies.[2] But in Spain, at this time, slavery was a relatively insignificant and declining institution, and by no means the dominant force that it was to become in the West Indies. The early and vigorous growth of plantations and slavery in the Spanish West Indies, though it was sharply checked, revealed the dynamic, expansive force of slavery in the new environment. With the growth of the French and English plantation colonies, slavery came to provide the economic

---

*Elsa V. Goveia is Professor of West Indian History at the University of the West Indies, Jamaica. She is the author of *Slave Society in the British Leeward Islands at the End of the 18th Century* (1965) and a recognized authority on West Indian history.

Reprinted from Elsa V. Goveia, 'The West Indian Slave Laws of the Eighteenth Century,' *Revista de Ciencias Sociales*, IV, No. 1 (March, 1960), 75–105, by permission of the *Revista de Ciencias Sociales*.

Revista de Ciencias Sociales, IV, No. 1 (1960), pp. 75–105. Also in Laura Foner and Eugene Genovese (eds), Slavery in the New World: A Reader in Comparative History (New Jersey, 1969).

and social framework of a whole society. Both the institution and the society were radically transformed.

In the Spanish colonies, the decline of the plantation system, after its first phase of rapid growth, created a situation still different from that of Spain, but different also from the classic pattern of plantation slavery to be found elsewhere in the West Indies. The Spanish slave laws were less completely adapted to the will of the slave-owning 'planter' than was the case elsewhere, during the eighteenth century. In addition, the strong conservatism of the Spanish crown and government made possible the retention of some of the fundamental concepts borrowed originally from the slave laws of Spain.

These concepts are very clearly expressed in the *Siete Partidas*, in which may be found what is chronologically the earliest legal view of the slave and slavery in the history of the West Indian slave laws. In the *Siete Partidas*, the slave is considered as part of the 'familia', and the distinction between slaves and serfs is not clear-cut. The term 'servitude', which may cover the unfree condition of both, is defined, as is the concept of liberty, which is its opposite. According to the *Siete Partidas*: 'Servitude is an agreement and regulation which people established in ancient times, by means of which men who were originally free became slaves and were subjected to the authority of others contrary to natural reason.' (Partida IV, Tít. XXI, Ley i). Slavery is defined as 'something which men naturally abhor and . . . not only does a slave live in servitude, but also anyone who has not free power to leave the place where he resides.' (Partida VII, Tít. XXXIV, Reg. ii) Logically then, liberty is 'the power which every man has by nature to do what he wishes, except where the force of law or *fuero* (privilege) prevent him'. The preamble to the section on liberty states: 'All creatures in the world naturally love and desire liberty, and much more do men, who have intelligence superior to that of others.' (Part. IV, Tít. XXII).

Deriving from these premises, the principle of the Spanish slave law was, on the whole, a principle friendly to the protection of the slave and to his claims of freedom. For the *Partidas* envisaged the slave as a 'persona' and not as 'mere property'. The master was regarded as having duties toward his slaves, as well as rights over them: 'A master has complete authority over his slave to dispose of him as he pleases. Nevertheless, he should not kill or wound him, although he may give cause for it, except by order of the judge of the district, nor should he strike him in a way contrary to natural reason, or put him to death by starvation.' (Part. IV, Tit. XXI). In the *Partidas*, slavery is undoubtedly accepted as legal. It is not accepted as good. Liberty is the good which the law strives to serve: 'it is a rule of law that all judges should aid liberty, for the reason that it is a friend of nature, because not only men, but all animals love it.' (Partida IV, Tít. XXXIV, Reg. i).

The liberty of these principles relating to slaves cannot be denied, though it may be doubted whether they were ever fully enforced in Spain. In the *Partidas*, it is clear that slavery is looked upon as a misfortune, from the consequences of which slaves should be protected as far as possible, because they are men, and because man is a noble animal not meant for servitude. The growth of enslavement in the West Indies undermined and even reversed this view; and many later apologists of slavery attempted to prove that enslavement is not an evil but a good. The myth of 'inevitable progress' has prevented for long an appreciation of the fact that humaneness predates humanitarianism. The truth is that this 'medieval' slave code was probably the most humane in its principles ever to be introduced in the West Indies. It appears to have been the one section of the West India slave law in which was made the unequivocal assertion that liberty is the natural and proper condition of man.

The case of the *Siete Partidas* illustrates that, within the general agreement that slavery could legally exist, a considerable latitude of opinion about the institution itself was possible. The slave laws of the Spanish West Indies tended positively to favor the good treatment of slaves and their individual emancipation. From the beginning, under the provisons of the *Sieta Partidas*, the slave was legally protected in life and limb. As the celebrated jurist Solórzano pointed out, the slave was, in law, entitled to the protection and intervention of the law on his behalf, and the master could actually lose his property in the slave as a result of proved maltreatment of him.[3] Failure to subsist the slave adequately was, from the standpoint of the law, a serious abuse. So was the infliction upon the slave of inordinate work. In addition, slaves might be compulsorily manumitted for specific kinds of abuse — for example, in the case of women slaves, for violation or prostitution of the slave by her owner.[4] Under the Spanish slave laws codified in 1680, *audiencias* were instructed to hear cases of slaves who claimed to be free, and to see that justice was done to them.[5] When slaves of mixed blood were to be sold, it was provided that their Spanish fathers, if willing, should be allowed to buy them so that they might become free.[6] Orders were also given that peaceful settlements of free Negroes were not to be molested, and, throughout the eighteenth century, Puerto Rico followed the practice of giving asylum to fugitive slaves from non-Spanish islands, with very little variation from the principle that, once they had embraced the Roman Catholic religion, they were not to be returned.[7]

Custom, as well as law, appears to have favored the growth of the free colored group. By the custom of *coartación*, slaves by degrees bought themselves free from the ownership of their masters.[8] When the customary institution was incorporated in the slave laws, it had to be made clear that the master retained his property in the slave undiminished until the last payment was made. The law, which was more severe than custom had been, acknowledged a right in the master to claim all the *coartado*'s time if he wished.[9]

Customary *coartación* was widespread in the Spanish islands in the eighteenth century, and it was probably of great importance in increasing the numbers of freed men in these territories at the time. One estimate of Cuban population in 1774, which Friedlander apparently considers not too wide of the mark, gives a total of 171,620, of whom 96,440 were whites, 30,847 were free colored, and only 44,333 were slaves.[10] Figures for Puerto Rico, which was even slower than Cuba in turning to sugar and the great plantation, are equally interesting. As late as 1827, Puerto Rico was still a country with a predominantly free and even predominantly white population, though here the margin of difference between whites and non-whites was less than in Cuba of 1774.

The spirit of the Spanish slave laws, which was relatively liberal, undoubtedly influenced the form of these societies, in particular by aiding the growth of the free colored group. In turn, the less rigid and less slave-centered societies of these islands enabled the liberality of the Spanish law to survive and to exercise its influence upon them. When the changeover to sugar and the great plantation came in real earnest, the processes consequent on this changeover had to be worked out in a social environment different from that of other islands which had suffered transformation during the seventeenth and early eighteenth centuries. Despite the brutalities of the nineteenth century, slavery in the Spanish islands was, on the whole, milder than was the case elsewhere in the West Indies.

Nevertheless, this is a contrast which can be overemphasized. As Ortiz points out in his illuminating study *Los negros esclavos*, the attitude of the Cuban upper class throughout its history has not been so far different from that of the slave-owners of other islands as the difference in their slave laws might suggest. The relative despotism of the Spanish government acted as a check on the local oligarchies, which did not necessarily share the view of slavery expressed in the *Siete Partidas*. In fact Ortiz suggests that, if the task of making slave laws had been placed as firmly in the hands of these men as it was in the hands of a slave-owning ruling class in the British islands, there might not be so much to choose between Spanish and English slave laws.[11] Certainly, when this class became strong enough in Cuba to resist official policy successfully, one of its earliest successes was the defeat of the humane Slave Code of 1789, in which the Spanish government had attempted to provide for the amelioration of conditions among a growing slave population. Certainly also, it is generally agreed that the increase in the numbers of slaves in Cuba, which accompanied the expansion of the sugar industry there, brought a marked and general deterioration in their treatment. As Cuba became a sugar colony, its slave conditions more approximately resembled those of the other sugar colonies.[12]

What is more, even in the period of relatively mild treatment of slaves in the Spanish colonies, enacted law and practice were not one and the same thing.[13] The custom of *coartación*, which existed before it was recognized in law, serves to illustrate a case where custom was in advance of the law from the point of view of the slaves. In other cases, the law was decidedly more humane than was custom. The existence of the slave laws of the *Siete Partidas*, and of later enactments, did not prevent the existence of numbers of slaves who were underfed, overworked, and badly treated.

Lastly, though this is by no means of least importance, the humane regulations do not tell the whole story of the enacted slave law in the Spanish colonies. In addition to the structure of protective regulations already described, there existed other and different laws governing slaves and free colored, and these show the direct influence of the necessities of the slave system which depended in part upon force for its maintenance. In his discussion of the Cuban slave laws, Ortiz has pointed out how much the Spanish and local governments were concerned with the problem of slavery as a problem of public order. He shows that in the evolution of the slave laws, as in the restictions on the slave trade in the Spanish colonies, political considerations were often of great weight. The slave laws very clearly reflect this concern.[14]

In the Code of 1680,[15] for example, the police regulations governing slaves already outnumber all others, and there were also several restrictions on the free colored. (Vol. II, Lib. 7, Tít. 5). All of these were based upon the determination to preserve public order. It was provided, for instance, that Negroes were subject to a curfew in cities; and the magistrates were enjoined to try them for any disturbances which they might commit. (Leyes 12, 13.) No Negro, whether slave or free, and no person of Negro descent, except in special cases, was to be permitted to carry arms. (Leyes 14–18.) There were several regulations for the policing of runaway slaves. (Leyes 20–25.) One provided for their protection by forbidding that they should be mutilated in punishment. (Ley 24.) But it is fair to say that this was exceptional. Most of the provisions were made with an eye to the control and suppression of the runaways as a threat to public order. Finally, there were regulations for preventing, defeating, and punishing the risings of slaves, and for the summary arrest of any Negro found wandering or engaged in similar suspicious activities. (Ley 26.)

As for the free colored, they were supposed to live under the supervision of a patron, even though free; and, by a special law, they were forbidden to wear gold, silk, cloaks, or other kinds of clothing considered unsuitable to their station in society. (Leyes 3, 28). From the first too, the Spanish government tried to prevent race mixture in its colonies between Spaniards, Indians, and Negroes, whether slave or free. (Ley 5). In this, it was, of course, generally unsuccessful.

Among the provisions made to secure public order in Cuba during the seventeenth century, Ortiz lists laws prohibiting the sale of wine to slaves, regulations governing the work of hired slaves, the perennial restrictions against the bearing of arms by slaves, and provisions for the pursuit of runaways and their punishment. These, rather than purely protective measures, continued most to occupy the active attention of the authorities until the ameliorative codification of 1789.

This code included provisions regulating the work and recreation of slaves, their housing and medical care, their maintenance in old age, their marriages and similar subjects, their punishments, and their formal protection in law. Besides providing for the protection of slaves, the code of 1789 made provision for the detection and punishment of abuses by the colonists in the management of slaves. Unlike the police regulations, this code ran into strong opposition from the colonists, especially in Cuba, where the resistance was so determined that the government was forced virtually to withdraw the new code in 1791.[16]

There was in Puerto Rico a comparative neglect of those regulations which affected the activities of the master, while the laws penalizing the criminal actions of slaves were far more effectively enforced.[17] The intention behind protective regulations could thus be defeated, and the law was given an emphasis in practice which does not emerge to the same extent in its enactment. Even in these relatively liberal slave islands, therefore, it can be seen that slavery presented a minimum requirement of rigor, which pressed upon the slave because of his status, and because of the necessity to maintain it.

In the British islands, during the eighteenth century, the marks left by the slave system upon the law are less ambiguous. This is not only because the plantation system had here taken a very firm hold, but also because of the nature of the British political tradition. England, which was earlier freed of slavery and even of serfdom than was Spain, had no *Siete Partidas* to transfer to her West India colonies when they were acquired, even though these colonies quickly adopted the slave system brought to the West Indies by the Spaniards. The English government never, until the nineteenth century, showed so careful and sustained an interest in the subject of slave regulations as did the government of Spain from earliest times. Most important of all, perhaps, tradition of representative government determined that the slave laws of the British colonies were made directly by a slave-owning ruling class. These laws were, therefore, an immediate reflection of what the slave-owner conceived to be the necessities of the slave system.

It has often been said that the greater freedom incorporated in the British constitutional system helped to breed respect for the property of the subject, as well as for his liberty. This may be part of the explanation of the legal convention which, in the British slave colonies, left the power of the master over his property, the slave, virtually unlimited, even in some cases as to life and limb. For this convention to apply, however, it had to be made clear that the slave was property and subject to police regulations. In fact, the experience of the British colonies makes it particularly clear that police regulations lay at the very heart of the slave system and that, without them, the system became impossible to maintain.

This was the moral of Somersett's case decided by the Chief Justice, Lord Mansfield, in 1771–72, and also of the case of the slave Grace decided by Lord Stowell in 1827.[18] Given police regulations, the English law in the West Indies worked against the slave, because he was there mere property or something very near it. In the absence of such regulations, the slave had to be regarded as an ordinary man; and, in this context, the respect for liberty of the subject, which was also a part of the English legal tradition, worked in his favor. Somersett's case illustrates the operation of the principle of liberty of the subject. There was no law against slavery in England. But the absence of a law providing sanctions for slavery enabled Somersett to win his freedom by refusing any longer to be held as a slave. The case of the slave Grace shows the potency of police provisions in maintaining the slave system. For on returning voluntarily to Antigua, she lost the temporary freedom gained by a visit to England.

English respect for the liberty of the subject was thus restricted by the erection of a slave system, and had to be so restricted to keep the slave system in being. Under the English slave system in the West Indies, the slave was not regarded as a subject, but as a property; and when the English humanitarians attempted to take the view that he was a subject, they were advocating an innovation which only slowly gained acceptance in the controversies over amelioration and emancipation.

The basic conception of the English law in relation to the slave was not, as with the Spaniards, that he was an inferior kind of subject. It was rather that he was a special kind of property. First of all, he was merchandise when bought and sold in the course of the slave trade. Once acquired by a planter, the slave became private property — regarded in part as a chattel, in part as real property. As a chattel, for instance, he could be sold up for debts if other moveable assets were exhausted. But in other cases, he was subject to the laws of inheritance of real estate. He could be entailed, was subject to the widow's right of dower, and could be mortgaged.[19]

These aspects of the law appeared both in the law of the West Indies and in the law of England. Under both, trading in slaves was a recognized and legal activity. Under both, there were provisions for regulating the mortgage of slaves and obliging their sale as chattels in cases of debt.[20] This point is worth stressing. The idea of slaves as property was as firmly accepted in the law of England as it was in that of the colonies; and it was not for lack of this provision that Somersett had to be freed. It was the lack of the superstructure raised on this basis — in the form of police law governing slaves — which made it impossible for Somersett to be held in slavery by force in England. Before and after the Somersett case, slaves were taken to and from England, as the case of the slave Grace shows; and, so long as they did not refuse to serve, as Somersett did, it may be said that they remained property and did not become subjects in fact, though in theory this change was supposed to take place on their arrival in England.

In the West Indies, they were slaves because the superstructure, lacking in England, was there available. By the eighteenth century, it was elaborate and, generally speaking, comprehensive. On the basic idea of the slave as property, a whole system of laws was built up. Some concerned the disposal of the slaves as property, others governed the actions of slaves as an aspect of public order. Some gave slaves a species of legal protection. But, up to the time when organized humanitarian agitation began in the 1780s, the protective enactments were relatively few and sometimes rather ambiguous. Police regulations occupied the most ample proportion of the attention of the British West India legislators.

Some of the regulations made are clearly related to the conception that the slave was property, but even those border on the idea of police. Thus, owners whose slaves suffered the judicial penalty of death were usually compensated for the loss. Obviously, this was because their property in the slave was recognized. But the intention was also to reduce the temptation of owners to conceal criminal slaves from justice. Again, persons who employed or hired the slaves of others without proper consent were guilty of a form of trespass, which was subject to both civil and criminal proceedings. Taking the slaves of another by violence was robbery. To carry off a slave from the provisions safeguarded the slave as private property. They also penalized those aiding runaways, either by enabling them to support themselves away from the master or by aiding their flight directly. They are part of a whole series of laws which penalized all persons, whether slave or free, who sheltered or otherwise assisted the runaway slave.[21]

Every island passed laws for the pursuit, capture, suppression, and punishment of runaway slaves; and these laws were usually severe. Similar police regulations were made in islands other than those of the British. Slaves were not to wander abroad without written passes, they were not to have any firearms or to assemble together in numbers. Usually they were forbidden to beat drums and blow horns, since these were means of communication which might be used to help runaways.[22] All such activities were dangerous, too, as means of concerting uprisings — another reason for the existence of these laws. Not all of them were enforced at all times with equal rigor. Slave dances, feasts, and drumming were often allowed; and even the pass laws were not strictly observed. The laws remained in force, however, and they were used when necessary to prevent or to control emergencies.

The function served by the laws may be illustrated by a comparison. In Barbados, under an early law of the seventeenth century, it was provided that if a Negro slave died under punishment by his master and no malice was proved, the master killing his own slave was to pay a fine of £15. If the slave belonged to another master, the fine to be paid was £25, and an additional payment of double the slave's value was to be made to compensate his owner.[23] This law was made notorious by abolitionist criticism. It is one of the worst of its type, but its singularity lay rather in the lowness of its fines than in its principle. It was a brutal law, but its brutality flowed in well defined, socially accepted channels. This is why a struggle was necessary to achieve a change of principle. Few islands in the British West Indies, until the later eighteenth century, showed any willingness to recognize that the willful killing of a slave was an act of homicide or murder. It was usually regarded in theory, though not always in practice, as a criminal offence. But generally it was a criminal offence of a lesser order, to which it was not felt necessary to attach so heavy a penalty as that of death.

By contrast, heavy penalties were attached to the commission of a crime, the gravity of which depended entirely on its social context. For striking or insulting a white, slaves were subject to the penalties of whipping, mutilation, or death; and usually the law provided that if the white was in any way hurt or if the blow drew blood, then the more severe punishments should be inflicted.[24] Even free persons of color were often made liable to similar punishments for similar offences against whites — and this meant all whites, from the great planter to the poor white, and white indenture servant.[25] The contrast in treatment of the crime of striking or abusing a white is due in each case to the social significance attached to the crime.

Yet the slave was a special kind of property, as these laws attest. For to kill even one's own slave maliciously was penalized, though not usually as much as the killing either of the slave of another or of a free man. The law with regard to the striking or wounding of whites also had to envisage the slave as something more than a 'thing'. The dilemma was that he was not 'mere property', as the law wished to suppose him, but a creature possessing volition, and the capacity for resistance which must be checked, indeed crushed, if the society were to survive. Obviously, the slaves were also regarded as a special kind of property in the laws governing them as runaways, and punishing them as conspirators or rebels. If the slave had been truly a thing in fact, as well as in the fiction of the law, such legislation would not have been necessary. Because he was a person, he posed a problem of public order, which the police regulation tended to cover. The law was forced to allow the slave some kind of 'persona' for the purpose of dealing with him under this aspect of his activity as a special kind of property.

In the earlier British slave laws, and even up to the beginning of the humanitarian controversy, the dominant tendency was to recognize the slave as a 'persona' in a sphere far more limited than that allowed him in either Spanish or French slave law. Early English slave law almost totally neglects the slave as a subject for religious instruction, as a member of a family, or as a member of society possessing some rights, however inferior. Insofar as the slave is allowed personality before the law, he is regarded chiefly, almost solely, as a potential criminal.

This is true of the police regulations governing the movements of slaves. It is true of the regulations to restrain and punish thefts by slaves, which were numerous. It is true even of the regulations governing the economic activities of slaves, in which may be traced a constant preoccupation with the problems of running away and theft, as well as a desire to limit the economic competition of slaves with whites.

The humanitarians, in their criticism of the

West India slave laws, attacked this limited legal concept of the slave, and, in the course of their long struggle with the West Indians, substantial changes were made in the laws by the island legislatures. In particular, attempts were made, during the controversies over amelioration, to define the duties of masters towards their slaves, and the degree of protection to which slaves were entitled in law. During this phase, the status of the slave as a 'persona', in the eyes of the law, was significantly broadened. But this development came relatively late, and was, to a considerable extent, due to the pressure built up by the humanitarian critics of the West Indies.

Before the beginning of the humanitarian assault, the British West India slave laws included relatively few protective clauses, and even these often seem to rest on an ambiguous view of the slave. Indeed, it is misleading to regard many of these regulations as providing anything comparable to the 'positive protection' sought for in later laws. There was, for instance, a Montserrat regulation of 1693, which provided that one acre of provisions should be cultivated for every eight slaves belonging to a plantation. But this is only one clause of an extremely severe act intended to punish thefts by slaves, and especially thefts of provisions. The act was concerned with a problem of public order, rather than with any idea of the rights of slaves to sufficient food in return for their services.[26]

Provisions for holidays to be given to slaves at particular times reflect similar police problems. In these laws, fines were often imposed on those who gave more, as well as those who gave less, than the prescribed holidays, and this practice only gradually came to be modified later in the eighteenth century.[27]

Laws to prevent old and disabled slaves from being abandoned by their masters have a similar ambiguity. For wandering and destitute slaves always constituted a serious problem of public order; and local authorities usually refused to have them become a burden on poor relief. The most obvious expedient was, therefore, to insist upon the master's obligation to keep even useless slaves, rather than have this burden thrown on the public.[28] Here, for once, the idea that the slave was private property operated against, rather than in favor of, the master's will. The result of this insistence upon the private responsibility of the master was not always favorable to the slave, however. For it led to severe laws providing life sentences of hard labor for destitute slaves whose masters could not be found, and to an unwillingness on the part of the legislators to permit even the manumission of able-bodied slaves unless the public was indemnified beforehand against the possibility that the new freedman might become destitute. During the second half of the eighteenth century, in particular, several laws were passed, imposing a tax for this purpose upon manumissions.[29] Even where the object was not directly to check the growth in numbers of the free population, the effect was certainly to make the achievement of manumission more difficult, because more costly.

In the British West India slave laws in force during the eighteenth century, there were, of course, some unambiguous protective clauses. But some of these carry little weight in comparison with the other kinds of regulation. For example, Barbados in 1668 had provided that slaves should be given clothing once a year, specifying drawers and caps for men, and petticoats and caps for women. The penalty for failure to comply with this law was 5 shillings per slave.[30] In the newer colonies of the eighteenth century, for instance, St. Vincent and Dominica, heavier fines were imposed, but the amount of clothing provided as a compulsory allowance was still either small or inadequately defined in the law.[31] Even under the consolidated slave law passed at Jamaica in 1781, where the penalty of £50 was inflicted for neglect, the allowances to be made to slaves were stated without proper definition.[32] It can hardly be doubted that such weaknesses must have lessened the effectiveness of these protective laws.

Other more considerable regulations for the protection of slaves were also instituted. But their comparatively small number indicates that they were exceptional. It has already been noticed that the willful killing of slaves was not generally considered to be murder, but was nevertheless judged to be a criminal offense of some gravity. Jamaica, from relatively early days, went a step further than the other islands by providing under an act of 1696 that anyone found guilty of a second offense of willingly, wantonly, or 'bloodymindedly' killing a Negro or slave, should be convicted of murder. The first offence was declared a felony, and, as this was found to be an insufficient deterrent, an additional punishment of imprisonment was provided in 1751.[33]

There were also laws penalizing the dismemberment or mutilation of slaves, by fine or imprisonment or both. The range of fines ran from a minimum fine of £20, provided at Antigua in 1723, to the much heavier fine of

£500, provided by the St. Kitts legislature 60 years later.[34] But such provisions were by no means ubiquitous, and in many of the islands it remained true that, as one report of 1788 states: 'Very little Measure appears to have been assigned by any general laws, to the Authority of the Master in punishing Slaves.'[35] In particular, the regulation of lesser punishments by laws was very generally neglected, and the partial nature of such legislation is illustrated by the fact that a St. Vincent law which provided against mutilation of slaves also contained a clause inflicting a £10 fine on persons taking off iron collars and similar instruments of punishment from slaves, without the consent of the master.

When the controversy over abolition of the slave trade drew attention to the inadequacy of statutory protection offered slaves in the matter of punishment and maltreatment, defenders of the West India interest had recourse to the argument that common law protection was available, where statutory protection was lacking.[36] Insofar as this was clearly true, however, it affected the slave as a piece of property rather than as a person. The master had the right to bring suit for damages against anyone harming his slave, even where there was no statutory provision for this. Indeed, acts which added a criminal penalty for such offenses generally made specific reference to this civil right. The more dubious part of the case concerns not this right, but the right of slaves to personal protection, without the intervention of the owner, or against the owner or his representatives.[37] A thorough search of judicial records throughout the Britsh islands at this time would be necessary to determine whether, before the matter became a contentious one, cases against owners and their representatives were normally, or even occasionally, brought to the common law courts in any of the islands.

The evidence already available does not suggest that the personal protection of slaves under the common law was very effective. As late as 1823, when Fortunatus Dwarris, as a member of the legal commission of the West Indies, investigated this matter, he was forced to report a 'want of remedy' for slaves at common law in Barbados, and a conflict of opinion on the subject there and throughout the British islands.[38] Dwarris wished to have the situation clarified and recommended that

> it might be advantageous, that in the Windward as well as in the Leeward Islands, the common law of England should be declared to be the 'certain rule for all descriptions of persons being subjects of His Majesty, and to obviate all doubts real or pretended upon this head, it might be recited and set forth explicitly in such declaratory law, that all African, or Creole slaves admitted within the King's allegiance, are, and shall at all times be taken and held to be, entitled to the protection, and subject to the penalties, of the common law; and to this, the slave code carefully compiled would properly be supplemental.'[39]

Yet he doubted that even when this had been done, the common law would protect the slave from other than scandalous abuse.[40]

Dwarris' report, and his doubts, reflect an uncertainty as to the degree of protection offered under the common law. At St. Kitts, in 1786, a jury trying a case of maltreatment involving a slave also questioned whether 'immoderate correction of a slave by the Master be a Crime indictable'.[41] On this occasion, the judge decided that it was. But, what the attorney-general of Dominica said in 1823 of the whole question of common law protection is true here too: 'the rule upon this subject is so vague, and so little understood in the colonies, that decisions founded upon it will be often contradictory.'[42]

Even graver doubts about the application of the common law to slaves were current in the West Indies, and these may have sprung from an unwillingness to recognize the slave as having personal status in law. In 1823, Dwarris reported many assertions made by the judge and crown law officer of St. Kitts to the effect that 'the justices have no jurisdiction over slaves except what is expressly given them by Colonial Acts'. It was not their duty, or even their right, to hear and deal with the complaints of slaves.[43]

The existence of this belief in the West Indies underlines the contrast, already noted in the discussion of Somersett's case and of the case of the slave Grace, between the situation of the slave in England and in the West Indies. Somersett's freedom was due to the common law, the slavery of Grace was secured by enacted law. In the West Indies, the slave was a 'thing' rather than a person, a 'property' rather than a subject. The same conception, which led to inadequate protection of slaves under enacted law, explains the uncertainty regarding their protection under the common law. The legal nullity of the slave's personality, except when he was to be controlled or punished, was the greatest obstacle to his adequate personal protection.

The law of evidence with regard to slaves reveals both the nullity and the anomaly of the conception of the slave as property. Any free man could give evidence against or for a slave. But during the eighteenth century, the evidence of slaves was not admitted for or against free persons in the British islands. Nevertheless, at the discretion of the courts, the evidence of slaves was admitted for or against other slaves. Thus the legal disability of the slave reinforced his inferior position. Still exposed to detection for his own crimes, he was deprived of protection against the crimes of all but his fellow slaves. He had no real redress against those very abuses of power to which his inferior position already exposed him.

The existence of special forms of trial for slaves in the British islands, as well as the limited validity of their evidence, served to mark them off from the rest of the body politic. In many cases, they were placed under the summary jurisdiction of judges, acting without a jury, for the trial even of capital crimes.[44] When a solemn form of trial was provided, as for instance in Montserrat, where capital cases were tried by the Governor in Council, the form of trial still differed from that given to free men.[45] The Barbados legislature put the matter succinctly in 1688, when it provided a solemn court for capital cases but omitted the usual jury of twelve men, on the ground that the accused 'being British Slaves, deserve, not from the Baseness of their condition, to be tried by the legal trial of twelve men of their Peers, or Neighbourhood, which truly neither can be rightly done, as the Subjects of England are.'[46]

Every aspect of the slave law of the British islands reveals the fundamental political concern with the subordination and control of slaves. This emphasis was characteristic right up to the beginning of the abolitionist struggle and beyond. In 1784, when their first cautious ameliorated slave code, the Act of 1781, expired, the members of the Jamaican legislature were apparently too busy to bring in a new improved slave law. But this did not prevent them from passing an act providing for parties to hunt runaway slaves, nor from reviving the very severe laws under which thefts and destruction of horses and cattle by slaves were visited with the punishment of death.[47] It seems fair to conclude not only that these were less controversial than improvements in the slave laws, but also that they were regarded as being more urgently necessary than, for instance, the new provisions against mutilation and dismemberment of slaves which lapsed when the Act of 1781 did.

It was not that the West Indians were always disinclined to serve the cause of humanity, but simply that they considered the cause of self-preservation infinitely more important. The primary function of the British West India slave laws was either directly or indirectly repressive. For, as Bryan Edwards, who was himself a planter and a slave-owner, put it: 'In countries where slavery is established, the leading principle on which the government is supported is fear: or a sense of that absolute coercive necessity which, leaving no choice of action, supercedes all questions of right. It is vain to deny that such actually is, and necessarily must be, the case in all countries where slavery is allowed.'[48]

The French West Indies, unlike the British islands, had, after 1685, a slave code drawn up by the metropolitan government as the basis of their slave laws.[49] However, the contrast between these groups of islands, with regard to their slave laws, was not as great as that between the Spanish and British islands. The *Siete Partidas* was a code of Spanish laws, containing provisions relating to slaves. The *Partidas* came into existence long before the creation of a West Indian empire. They were not framed to deal with the circumstances of the West Indies, though they were incorporated into the law of the Spanish colonies there. But the *Code Noir*, though drawn up in France, was never intended to be a code of French laws. Like the laws of the British islands, the *Code Noir* of the French West Indies was made with West Indian conditions firmly in mind, and for the purpose of dealing with problems already posed by the existence and acceptance of slavery in the West Indian colonies. The *Code Noir* bears some resemblance to the *Siete Partidas* because both were influenced to some extent, by the concepts of Roman and canon law. Nevertheless, it more fundamentally resembles the slave laws of the British West Indies by reason of its intention and function.

The fact that the *Code Noir* was a metropolitan code is, nevertheless, important. Even in the early 1680s, the French monarchical government was less limited than that of England, a difference reflected in the government of the French and English colonies. In the English colonies, the crown's legislative power was incorporated in the structure of a representative legislature, including council and assembly. In the French colonies, the crown retained more autonomous powers of legislation. The laws of the French colonies were made by the royal government in France, by the royal officials in the West Indies, and by the local councils. The *Code Noir* is described as a metropolitan code, because it was made by the exercise of the legislative power of the royal government in France.

However, the *Code*, although made in France, was based upon earlier local laws and was prepared in consultation with the local authorities in the West Indies. Even after promulgation, it was revised to meet strong local criticisms on some points. Long before the *Code Noir* was prepared, local authorities had concerned themselves with the problems of religious conformity, with the regulation of the status and conduct of slaves, with the necessity for public security, and with the protection to be given to slaves as property and as persons. These were the matters which also occupied the framers of the *Code Noir*; and a few examples will show the similarities between the earlier laws and the later *Code*.

As early as 1638, it was provided that Protestants should not be allowed to own slaves in the islands; and, by later laws, made by representatives of the crown in the West Indies, provisions were added for the punishment of blasphemers, and the regulation of Jews and non-Catholics, and also to encourage the Christianization of slaves.[50] Undoubtedly, the crown may be regarded as having special interests in religious conformity; and it is hardly surprising that the *Code Noir*, which was promulgated in the same year that saw the Revocation of the Edict of Nantes, should have given great prominence and emphasis to the provisions enforcing religious conformity. But the regulations of the crown in this matter already had precedents in the accepted local law, and did not arouse much local opposition. On the one subject — the abolition of Negro markets on Sundays and holidays — where local opinion showed itself immediately hostile to the provisions of the crown for enforcing religious observance, the crown quickly gave way.[51] In the matter of religious conformity, the predilections of the crown enjoyed the general support of a large body of local opinion.

As for regulations concerned more directly with slaves, a good many may be cited which occur in the earlier laws and recur in some form in the *Code Noir*. They illustrate that, before the *Code Noir* was instituted, the French colonies already possessed a fairly comprehensive series of slave laws, and that the *Code Noir* really may be regarded as an extended codification of these laws.

Some of these laws were made by officials and some by the Council; and perhaps it is significant that the Council appears to have concerned itself mainly with police laws. It is notable, however, that the Council, as a court, heard cases arising from the cruelty of masters to their slaves, and already, before 1685, had made judgments punishing cruelty.[52] This point is probably significant of a contrast in attitudes in the British and French islands arising from a contrast in their political traditions.

In British law, the tendency was to limit the sphere of interference of the crown, and to foster, in particular, a respect for the rights of private property. In France and its colonies, because the power of the crown was less limited, its sphere of interference, even with private property, was commonly accepted to be much wider. The slave, by being private property, did not cease to be in his person a matter of public concern; and public interference in the management of slaves was more taken for granted at this stage of development in the French West Indies than it was in the British islands at the same time. With the continued growth of slavery in the French West Indies, and with the related development of a feeling of white solidarity in those colonies, two very important changes of sentiment with regard to slaves made themselves felt. Public concern for their welfare declined rapidly, and public acceptance of interference between the master and his property became less and less certain.

An analysis of the content of the *Code Noir* reveals the same concern for public order which marks the slave laws of the British West Indies. But the *Code Noir* was, nevertheless, based on a wider conception of the slave as a 'person' and on a different conception of the elements of public order. The contents of the code may be placed under a number of heads. Provisions regarding religious conformity are laid down in the earlier clauses; provisions governing the status of slaves and their political control follow. The protection of slaves is then provided for, after which their civil disabilities are carefully listed. These disabilities arose, of course, from the legal view that the slave was property, though as in the British law, he had to be admitted to be a peculiar kind of property. The element of political control over slaves, which was inseparable from their regulation as property, appears clearly in the section of the code which deals with the slave as property, as it does in the slave laws elsewhere. In this section however, the police regulations are accompanied by protective regulations; and, in fact, these two categories make up a large part of the code. Lastly, there are clauses providing for the manumission of slaves and for the regulation of the status of freedom. Underlying these provisions is the assumption that all groups in the community are subject to the will and direction of the state.

A short summary of the more important clauses of the code shows this assumption in operation. Under the provisions of the code, Jews were to be expelled from the colonies, and Protestants were subjected to religious and civil disabilities — such as incapacity for legal marriage by their own rites. The object was to secure public conformity of all, and not even the slaves were excluded. They were to be baptized and instructed as Catholics; and their overseers could be of no other religious persuasion. They were to observe Sundays, and the holidays of the church, to be married, and if baptized, buried on holy ground. The concubinage of free men with slaves was penalized, except in those cases where the irregular union was converted into marriage. (Cls. 1-11) Under this section, conformity to the state religion is the duty enforced on all.

The regulations concerning slavery provided that children should take the status of the mother in all cases. (Cls. 12, 13) The slave mother being property, the slave child was property. This property was to be kept in a state of subordination by the usual means. Slaves were forbidden to carry arms or other weapons, to assemble together, to engage in certain kinds of trade, to strike the master or mistress or to use violence against free persons. Penalties were provided for those slaves who were guilty of thefts, and for those slaves who were guilty of running away. Finally, it was expressly provided that slaves could be criminally prosecuted, without involving the master if he was not responsible for the crime. (Cls. 15-21, 33-38) As in the British law, therefore, the slave was subject to coercion; and was treated as being personally responsible to the state before the law.

He was also viewed as, to some extent, a person in a state of dependence. As such, the master who owned him was obliged to give him fixed allowances of food and clothing, to care for old and disabled slaves, to avoid concubinage with his slaves, and to leave them free to observe the rules of the church. His property in the slaves was regarded as conferring on him the right to punish them by whipping, or by putting them in irons. But he was expressly prohibited from torturing or mutilating them; and a master killing a slave was to be prosecuted as a criminal, and penalized 'according to the atrocity of the circumstances'. The clergy were enjoined not to marry slaves without the master's consent, but also not to constrain slaves to marry if they were unwilling to do so. Under the law, families were not to be broken up when slaves were sold; and those slaves between the ages of 14 and 60 who were employed in sugar — or indigo — works and plantations were attached to the soil and could not be sold except with the estate. Slaves not falling within these categories were, however, regarded as chattels. (Cls. 9-11, 22-25, 27, 42, 43, 47-54)

As a piece of property, rather than a person, the slave was incapable of legally possessing property or of legally making contracts, and he was, of course, incapable of holding any public office or acting legally as a responsible agent. The code declared that slaves could not legally be parties to a trial, though they themselves were subject to criminal prosecution. Masters received compensation for their loss when criminal slaves were executed. But they were also liable to make good losses caused by their slaves. (Cls. 28, 30-32, 37, 40)

All these clauses with regard to the protection and disabilities of the slave assumed that the master, in return for public recognition of the dependency of the slave, accepted certain conditions of obligation laid down by the state. His property in the slave was held subject to these obligations, and could be forfeited as a result of failure to observe the limitations on his authority, imposed by the state as a condition of its support. Under the British slave laws, where the disabilities arising from the slave's dependency were the same, the conditions of this dependency, as they affected the master, were less carefully defined. In both British and French slave law, the inferior position of the slave was accepted. But in the British slave law, the state showed far greater unwillingness to interpose in the relations between masters and slaves.

The inferior position of the slave, though it was recognized in the French slave laws, was not directly reflected in the forms of trial provided for slaves under the *Code Noir*. The slave was to be tried before the ordinary judges, and he had the right of appealing his case to the Council — 'the process to be carried on with the same formalities as in the case of free persons'. (Cl. 32) In 1711, however, the slave's right of appealing against his sentence was restricted to capital cases and sentences of hamstringing.[53] This was one of the symptoms of the change which gradually transformed the French West Indian slave code. But, at the time of the promulgation of the *Code Noir*, concern for the protection of the slave in law was still strong. Clause 30 of that code, which provided that slave evidence was inadmissible except against slaves, was immediately protested by the Martinique Council, on the grounds that this would result in an impunity for many crimes committed against slaves. As a result of this protest, the crown, in 1686, amended the code so as to allow the admission of evidence by slaves, in the absence of evidence by whites, in all cases except against their own masters.[65]

Even here, at one of the most touchy points in the whole slave system, the *Code Noir* provided for the protection of the slave in law, by enabling him, under clause 26, to make complaints to the crown's *procureur-général* against his master in cases where the master failed to give him subsistence, or treated him cruelly. The attorney-general was thus given a status as protector of slaves which compensated, to some extent, for the unwillingness to admit slave evidence against masters. In keeping with this relative liberality, manumissions were made easy for all masters who had attained their legal majority; and, once freed, the former slave was to be treated as a freeborn subject of the king, entitled to the same rights as other subjects, so long as he lived in obedience to the law and performed the duties of the subject — with this difference only that he was expected to give due respect to his former master, the source of his freedom. (Cls. 26, 55–59)

In one respect, the provisions of the *Code Noir* regarding manumissions were restrictive. Until the promulgation of the code, it was customary for children of mixed blood to be freed during their teens.[55] But the crown, in its desire to secure religious conformity, was most anxious to discourage concubinage; and therefore, it provided that the illegitimate offspring and their mothers could never be free, except by the marriage of the parents. (Cl. 9) But in this matter, the will of the crown was at variance with the will of the local society, and was defeated. Masters continued to engage in irregular sexual unions with their slaves and continued to free their offspring. In the end, the crown itself expressly withdrew from its former position, in the belief that the mulattoes, being sworn enemies of the Negroes, might safely be freed.[56]

While the special provisions against manumission of mulattoes fell into disuse, the general provisions for manumission became more difficult. Early in the eighteenth century, the royal representatives in the colonies made it a rule that their written permission was necessary to validate all manumissions of slaves.[57] In 1713, this rule was confirmed by the crown, and it continued to be enforced during the century.[58] Instead of encouraging manumissions, the crown and its officers in the colonies showed a constant determination to control the accession of slaves to freedom. Even in France, where it was an accepted axiom of law that slaves became free on entering the realm, the crown proved willing to protect West Indian property by altering the law so as to nullify this usage.[59] The crown and its officers also allowed the wide privileges, originally granted to freedmen under the *Code Noir*, to be gradually contracted, and joined with the councils in multiplying laws against them and in subjecting them to increasing disabilities.[60]

This series of changes in the laws reflects the process by which the law was adapted to fit in with the development of society in the French colonies. In framing the *Code Noir*, the metropolitan government had shown itself generally disposed to follow local practice and to respect local opinion, even though, as in the case of the mulattoes, it occasionally rejected local customs. Unlike the Spanish government which, for long, showed a tendency to limit the increase of slaves in its colonies, the government in France was early committed to a policy of increasing slave numbers and even, though somewhat more reluctantly, to encouraging the growth of large plantations. In line with mercantile thought, it regarded these as the means of acquiring wealth and power from its West India possessions. Slavery must be maintained if these benefits were to be secured and enjoyed.

In his monumental study of French West Indian slavery, Peytraud supports the view that Colbert, who was largely responsible for preparing the *Code Noir*, was moved to protect the slaves by commercial, rather than humane, considerations.[61] Material considerations, a concern for public security, and a strengthening of race prejudice later produced a much greater hardening in the attitude of the crown and its officials towards the Negroes. The crown's desire for order, which had led the regulation of masters as well as of slaves under the *Code Noir*, led on to a certain tolerance of the abuses committed by masters against their slaves.

In 1713, the crown expressed great indignation on learning that masters were torturing their slaves barbarously.[62] In 1742, disapproval was also expressed, this time concerning a case in which a slave had been killed.[63] But the crown was now rather more concerned with the need for maintaining subordination among the Negroes. In the following year, the crown declared that 'while the Slaves should be maintained and favorably treated by their Masters, the necessary precautions should also be taken to contain them within the bounds of their duty, and to prevent all that might be feared from them.'[64]

The humaneness of the *Code Noir* itself can be overstated. The allowances of food and clothing fixed in the code were small. In the matter of punishments, the code prohibited the private infliction of torture and mutilation, but did not prevent their use by judicial authorities. Slaves could still be tortured in official investigations, and judges were left free to sentence slaves to be burnt alive, to be broken on the wheel (a favorite punishment), to be dismembered, to be branded, or to be crippled by hamstringing — a penalty expressly provided for runaways under the code.[65] Masters maltreating or killing slaves were liable to prosecution, and there are records of cases having been brought against them, although no master appears to have suffered the death penalty for killing a slave. By contrast, atrocious sentences were usually passed on slaves guilty of killing whites; and even for the crime of raising a hand against one of the children of his mistress, a slave was sentenced to have his hand cut off and to be hanged.[66] The attorney-general, who was appointed as guardian of slaves under the *Code Noir*, was far oftener engaged in prosecuting slaves, or in complaining of abuses by them, than in presenting the abuses committed against them. Like his employer, the crown, he was preoccupied with the task of securing public order.

A glance through the very numerous police regulations, passed with the object of enforcing or of supplementing the police clauses in the *Code Noir*, shows that many of these were initiated by a complaint on the part of the *procureur-général*, citing incipient or actual disorders. Thus, at the beginning of the eighteenth century, the Council of Léogane passed laws forbidding slaves to carry arms, or to assemble together, and providing for a hunt of runaways. At Le Cap, a pass-system was enforced; and the attention of masters was again called to the prohibitions against slaves carrying arms. Later, the council at Port-au-Prince penalized those selling arms and ammunitions to slaves without the master's written authority.[67]

The attorney-general also occupied himself with the suppression of thefts by slaves and with the restrictions on their trading. In 1710, complaint was made that the clauses of the *Code Noir* regulating trade by slaves were not being properly enforced. In the same year, the council at Petit-Goâve, on advice from the crown attorney, forbade gold- and silver-smiths to buy anything from slaves without express permission. Neglect of the rules against trading with slaves in the staple crops at Guadeloupe was similarly brought to the attention of the council there during the eighteenth century.[68]

Even in performing those duties which might be regarded as protective, the *procureur-général* showed a tendency to consider the public interest rather than the slave. Thus, one source of unfailing annoyance was the practice adopted by masters in giving their slaves Saturday or some other day of the week to work for themselves, instead of giving an allowance. This was presented as an abuse, not only because it might lead to thefts of provisions by slaves, or to want among those who paid no attention to their cultivations, but also because the gain made by industrious slaves as a result of this practice 'has made them so proud that they can scarcely be recognized for what they are.'[69] The laws for the planting of provisions by estates, constantly reiterated and constantly neglected, were not motivated only by the desire to protect the slaves.[70] Similarly, though the attorney-general complained when colonists had their slaves beaten in the streets, the disorder caused in the towns by this practice was obviously important in calling forth an objection to it.[71]

The crown, the royal officials, and the councils did not need much urging to concern themselves with police regulations in any case. These made up the large majority of the laws passed after the *Code Noir* was instituted. The subjects of these laws are, generally speaking, those to which attention has already been drawn in discussing the complaints made by the crown's attorney — the control of runaways, the general subordination of slaves and the need to prevent them from concerting risings, the prevention and detection of thefts, and the limiting of their economic opportunities, as well as of their physical mobility. The laws emphasized their dependence, because it was an element of social stability, directly related to their subordination. The regulations occasionally made, enforcing the allowances fixed under the *Code Noir*, have to be seen in this context.

In 1712, the crown returned to its insistence that slaves should not be privately tortured, and the cases brought against masters from time to time for cruelty to slaves were a reminder that the principle of governmental supervision was not forgotten.[72] But the crown would have needed to maintain a much closer watch than it did, if it had meant to enforce those protective clauses which were included in the *Code Noir*. Religious instruction, at first so much insisted on, was neglected or prevented by the colonists, and their attitudes were in turn defeated by government officials like Fénelon, who had come to believe that: 'The safety of the Whites, less numerous than the slaves, surrounded by them on their estates, and almost completely at their mercy, demands that the slaves be kept in the most profound ignorance.'[73] Pierre Regis Desalles, himself a colonist, writing in the second half of the eighteenth century, admitted that regulations favoring the marriage of slaves, and providing fixed allowances of food and clothing for them, were generally neglected. The laws against concubinage were notoriously ineffective. Abuse against slaves went undetected because 'No one cares to inform on his neighbor; and it is so dangerous to let Negroes make complaints against their masters.'[74]

All evidence points to one conclusion. As they were actually administered during the eighteenth century, the French slave laws differed far less from their English counterparts than might be imagined. The enforcement of the *Code Noir* during this period, in fact, shows a well-defined emphasis markedly similar to that already noticed in the British slave laws before the period of amelioration. Thus the provisions safeguarding the slave as 'persona' were either laxly enforced or neglected. His religious instruction, his protection against ill-treatment, his right to food, clothing, and care, provided for in the law, depended in practice far more on the will of the master than on enacted regulations. The law tended to become more and more a dead letter in these matters. Changes in the law made his manumission less easy, and deprived him, when free, of equality with other free men. Thus, the benefits which the law had originally conferred upon the slave and the freedman were either lost or reduced in their value by practice or by legislative change. Meanwhile, the part of the law which was provided for his control and submission continued in vigor — as the activities of the crowns' attorney serve to make abundantly clear. As in the British islands, so in practice in the French, police laws were the heart of the slave code. They were not neglected because the continuance of slavery depended upon them, and was understood to depend upon them. The law actually and continuously enforced was here, as in the Spanish colonies, different from the law as enacted. As Peytraud says: 'Reality is sometimes far from corresponding to legal prescriptions.'[75]

The will to bring about a correspondence was also much weaker than it had been. In 1771, the crown issued official instructions which show this change at work:

> It is only by leaving to the masters a power that is nearly absolute, that it will be possible to keep so large a number of men in that state of submission which is made necessarry to their numerical superiority over the whites. If some masters abuse their power, they must be reproved in secret, so that the slaves may always be kept in the belief that the master can do no wrong in his dealing with them.[76]

That the feeling of white solidarity had grown even stronger in the colonies is indicated by the well-known case involving the coffee-planter, Le Jeune, who was alleged to have killed four slaves and to have severely burnt two others, in the course of torturing them. Heavy pressure was brought to bear upon the governor; and the judges, afraid to go against local opinion, dismissed the case. The Council also refused to see Le Jeune punished, and he suffered no legal penalty whatever for his crimes.[77]

The Le Jeune case occurred in 1788, about four years after the crown had made several new provisions for the protection of slaves in its act 'concerning Attorneys and Managers of Estates situated in the Leeward Islands'. This order which was intended to correct abuses at St. Domingue, where the Le Jeune case occurred, contained clauses limiting the working hours of slaves and fixing their holidays, and allowing them to cultivate small plots of land for their own profit, besides compelling proprietors to plant provisions and to make allowances of food and clothing to their slaves. Provision was also made for the care of pregnant women and the sick, and for encouraging child-bearing. The protection against physical maltreatment given the slaves under the *Code Noir* was renewed, and a limitation was placed on the number of lashes which a master might give his slave.[78] These last clauses did not prevent Le Jeune's escape, and it is difficult to believe that the rest of the code can have been much more effective. Peytraud appears to be justified in his conclusion that 'the material condition of the Negroes did not cease to be miserable. As for their legal condition, so for their moral education, the advances achieved were very small. The facts cry aloud the condemnation of slavery, which reduced so many human beings to being scarcely more than beasts of burden.'[79]

The rule of force inherent in slavery produced comparable results in the Spanish, British, and French colonies in the West Indies, though variations were introduced by the degree of their dependence on slavery and by differences in their political traditions. The experience of the Dutch and Danish colonies supports this conclusion. Westergaard, in his study of the Danish islands, has said that the slave laws, which were made by the local government, 'became more severe as the ratio of negro to white population increased.' He cites repressive measures against runaways, who were specially aided by the nearness of the islands to Puerto Rico, and against thefts and the trading carried on by slaves without the permission of their owners.[80] In particular, he refers to the very severe ordinance of 1733, which, in his opinion, precipitated the serious slave rebellion of that year at St. John's. This ordinance provided such punishments for the crimes of slaves as pinching and branding with hot irons, dismemberment, hanging, and flogging. It was a police law, entirely concerned with the prevention of revolts and conspiracies, the control of runaways, thefts, and slave assemblies. It forbade the carrying of weapons by slaves, and punished severely any Negro found guilty of raising his hand against a white. These were the elements which attracted most attention in the government of slaves. Other laws protected the master's property in the slaves, and masters were indemnified for their losses when their slaves were judicially punished.[81] There was also supposed to be official supervision of the punishment of slaves, but, generally speaking, their protection was left to custom rather than law. The Company, which governed the islands, was more interested in the slaves as objects of trade and sources of manual labor for the production of wealth, than as persons. Here as elsewhere, they were subject to public repression and private tyranny.

The Danish West Indies under Company rule were at once entrepôts and plantation colonies. The Dutch also held both plantation colonies and trading colonies in the region; but these were geographically separate. In the main trading centres, Curaçao and St. Eustatius, and in the other small islands held by the Dutch, planting was of almost negligible importance. They lived by trade. The Guiana colonies, by contrast, developed a planting economy.

Throughout these Dutch colonies, the slaves were considered in law as things rather than as persons.[82] But the difference in the economic functions of the two types of colonies was reflected in a difference of slave conditions within them, despite their common basic law. The slaves in the Guiana colonies were subject to very harsh conditions of enslavement. The resident slave populations of the trading colonies — as distinct from the slave cargoes merely brought to be sold through these ports — generally enjoyed more humane treatment. In the Guianas, also, the slave laws, especially those for the control of runaways, were extremely severe in comparison with the laws of the islands. The influence of the plantation economy on slavery is thus again demonstrated.

In many of its aspects, the Dutch slave law resembled the slave law of the French West Indies — a resemblance due no doubt to their common origins in Roman law. Under the Dutch law, slaves could be bought and sold as chattels, and slave status was transmitted by birth through the mother. Plantation slaves were attached to the soil, and could only be sold with the estate. The dependency of the slave on his master was held to imply an obligation on the master to feed, clothe, and otherwise care for his slave; and a degree of protection was, in principle, made available to the slave through the fiscal of each colony. For a time, also, the Dutch West India Company showed some interest in the religious instruction of slaves, and made provisions to prevent their masters from forcing them to work on Sundays.

But the divorce of law and practice was as characteristic of the Dutch as of other colonies in the West Indies. In general, the Dutch Company, like the Danish, regarded the slaves primarily as objects of profit; and the settlers in the Dutch colonies took a similar view. The police regulations, which were numerous and often severe, were constantly invoked. Extra-legal and illegal punishments were privately inflicted on slaves, especially in the Guiana colonies, where the existence of bands of runaway slaves in the hinterland encouraged a brutal stringency in estate discipline. Fear of the Bush Negro threat increased also the repressive tendencies of public policy. Inhuman punishments were inflicted on slaves, not merely by masters privately and illegally, but also by the judicial authorities acting under the law.

As in the French colonies, a conflict arose between the principle of repression and that of protection; and, on the whole, it was repression that triumphed.

Scandalous mistreatment of slaves by plantation-managers and others, acting on their own authority, was more than once punished by banishment or otherwise; but the persons responsible for the punishment were themselves slave-holders and this was reflected in the kind of punishment inflicted. The slave laws, which were revised from time to time, also failed to achieve the end in view. Those who administered them were all slave-holders. At the beginning of the nineteenth century, there was humane treatment of the slaves because of the abolition of the slave trade, but long after that time very crude punishments were apparently still in existence and the slaves were looked upon as a sort of cattle.[83]

Both in their content and in their enforcement, the West India slave laws follow a remarkably consistent pattern, imposed by the function of the law in maintaining the stability of those forms of social organization on which rested the whole of the West India colonies during the eighteenth century.

Notes

1. Samuel P. Scott, C. S. Lobingier, and John Vance (Eds), *Las Siete Partidas* (New York, 1931) is an English translation of the code, based upon the 1834–44 edition of the text of the original printed editions by Gregorio López (Salamanca: 1st edn, 1555; 2nd edn, 1565–98).
2. See C. Verlinden, *L'Esclavage dans l'Europe médievale* Vol. I, *Péninsule Ibérique-France*, (Bruges, 1955).
3. Juan de Solórzano, *Politica indiana*, 5 vols (Madrid and Buenos Aires, 1930), Vol. I, Lib. 2, c. 4, n. 34 and c. 7, n. 77.
4. *Ibid.*, Vol. I, Lib. 2, c. 7, n. 13 and Vol. II, Lib. 3, c. 17, n. 23.
5. *Recopilación de leyes de las Indias* 3 vols. (Madrid, 1943), Vol. II, Lib. 7, tít. 5, ley 8.
6. *Ibid.*, ley 6.
7. *Ibid.*, ley 19. See also Luis M. Díaz Soler, *Historia de la esclavitud negra en Puerto Rico* (Madrid, 1953), p. 235; Fernando Ortiz, *Los negros esclavos, estudio sociológico y de derecho público* (Havana, 1916), p. 351; Arturo Morales Carrión, *Puerto Rico and the Non-Hispanic Caribbean* (Río Piedras, 1952).
8. On *coartación* see H. H. S. Aimes, 'Coartación', *Yale Review* (February, 1909), 412–31; Díaz Soler, *op. cit.*, especially Chap. X; Ortiz, *op. cit.*, especially Chap. XVII.
9. Aimes, *op. cit.*, pp. 424–25.
10. H. E. Friedlaender, *Historia economica de Cuba* (Havana, 1944), p. 84.
11. Ortiz, *op. cit.*, pp. 335–44.
12. *Ibid.*, *passim*. See also H. H. S. Aimes, *A History in Cuba, 1511–1865* (New York, 1907).
13. For an illustration see Javier Malagón, *Un documento del siglo XVIII para la historia de la esclavitud en las Antillas* (Havana, 1956).
14. Ortiz, *op. cit.*, pp. 342 ff.
15. *Recopilación*.
16. Ortiz, *op. cit.*, Chap. XX.
17. Díaz Soler, *op. cit.*, pp. 192–93.
18. H. T. Catterall, *Judicial Cases Concerning American Slavery and the Negro*, 5 Vols. (Washington, 1926–36), vol. I, pp. 1–8, 14–18, 34–37.
19. A good summary of the basic provisions of the British West Indian slave law during the eighteenth century is given in Reeves' 'General View of the Principles on which this System of Laws Appears to have been Originally Founded' in House of Commons Accounts and Papers, Vol. XXVI (1789), No. 646a, Part III. See the section dealing with 'Slaves Considered as Property'.
20. Statute 5 Geo. II, c. 7, and Statute 13 Geo. III, c. 14. For a West Indian example see *Laws of Jamaica*, 2 vols. (St. Jago de la Vega, 1792), Vol. II, 23 Geo. III, c. 14.
21. See for example *Laws of the Island of Antigua*, 4 vols., London, 1805), Vol. I, No. 130 (1702), No. 176 (1723).
22. Reeves, 'General Views', *loc. cit.*
23. *Ibid.*, section on 'Punishment by Masters'. See Act No. 82 (1688) in *Acts Passed in the Island of Barbados (1643–1762)* (London, 1764); a ms. copy is in C. O. 30/5, P.R.O. London.
24. For examples, see the Virgin Islands slave act (1783) in C. O. 152/67, the St. Kitts Act No. 2 (1711) 'for the better government of Negroes and other slaves' in C. O. 240/4, and the St. Vincent Act (July 11, 1767) in C. O. 262/1, P.R.O. London.
25. See the Antigua Act No. 130 (1702) and the Virgin Islands Slave Act (1783).
26. Montserrat Act No. 36 (1693)
27. Compare Antigua Act No. 176 (1723) and Antigua Act No. 390 (1778) in *Laws... of Antigua, op. cit.*, Vol. I.
28. Virgin Islands Slave Act (1783).
29. See Reeves, 'General View', *loc. cit.*, section 'of Manumissions.'
30. Barbados Act No. 82 (1688).
31. St. Vincent Act (July 11, 1767), in C. O. 262/1, P.R.O. London
32. 22 Geo. III, in *Laws* (Spanish Town, Jamaica), Lib. 8, I. R. O.
33. Jamaica Acts 8 Wm. III, c. 2, and 24 Geo. II, c. 17, in *Laws* (Spanish Town, Jamaica), Lib. 4, R. O.
34. Antigua Act No. 176 (1723); St. Kitts Act (1783) in C. O. 152/66, P. R. O. London.
35. Reeves. 'General View', *loc. cit.*
36. For instance, evidence given by James Tobin before a Select Committee of the House of Commons (1790), printed in House of Commons Accounts and Papers, Vol. XXIX (1790), No. 695/5, esp. pp. 272–73.
37. This view of the case is put by Drewry Ottley, Chief Justice of St. Vincent, in his evidence, reported in House of Commons Accounts and Papers, Vol. XXIV (1790–91), No. 476, pp. 158 ff.
38. F. Dwarris, 'Substance of the Three Reports of the Commissioners of Enquiry into the Administration of Civil and Criminal Justice in the West Indies', extracted from the *Parliamentary Papers* (London, 1827), pp. 113ff., 431ff.
39. *Ibid.*, p. 433.
40. *Ibid.*, pp. 114–16.
41. House of Commons Accounts and Papers, Vol. XXVI (1789), No. 646a. Pt 3 (St. Kitts), Appendix A.
42. Dwarris, *op. cit.*, p. 543.
43. *Ibid.*, pp. 431ff., 113ff.
44. Antigua Act No. 130 (1702).
45. Reeves, 'General View', *loc. cit.*
46. Barbados Act No. 82 (1688).
47. 25 Geo. III, c. 23 and 22, in *Laws of Jamaica, op. cit.*, Vol. II.
48. Bryan Edwards, *History of the British Colonies in the West Indies*, 3 vols (London, 1801), Vol. III, p. 36.
49. See the definitive text of the *Code Noir* of 1685 in L. Peytraud, *L'Esclavage aux Antilles Françaises avant 1789* (Paris, 1897), pp. 158–66.
50. France, Archives Nationales. Colonies F3 247, p. 63

(Martinique), règlement of September 1, 1638; F3 221, pp. 477–80 (Guadeloupe), ordonnance of September 14, 1672. Louis Elie Moreau de St.-Méry, *Loix et constitutions des colonies français de l'Amérique sous le vent*, 6 vols (Paris, 1784–90), Vol. I, pp. 117–22 (règlement of June 19, 1664).

51. *Ibid.*, Vol. I, pp. 447–48 (arrêt of October. 13, 1686).
52. *Ibid.*, Vol. I, p. 203 (arrêt of October 20, 1670). Arch. Nat. Cols. F3 247, pp. 825–26 (Martinique), arrêt of May 10, 1671.
53. Moreau de St.-Méry, *op. cit.*, Vol. II, pp. 241, 242–43 (letter and ordonnance of April 20, 1711).
54. *Ibid.*, Vol. I, pp. 447–48 (arrêt of October 13, 1686).
55. See R. P. DuTertre, *Histoire général des Antilles habitées par les françois*, 3 vols (Paris, 1667–71), Vol. II, pp. 511–13; H. A. Wyndham, *The Atlantic and Slavery* (Oxford, 1935), pp. 256–57.
56. Moreau de St.-Méry, *op. cit.*, Vol. III, pp. 453–54 (letter of March 29, 1735).
57. *Ibid.*, Vol. II, pp. 272–73 (ordonnance of August 15, 1711). Arch. Nat. Cols. F^3 222, pp. 189–90.
58. Moreau de St.-Méry, *op. cit.*, Vol. II, pp. 398–99 (ordonnance of Oct. 24, 1713). Wyndham, *op. cit.*, pp. 256–57. An instance of a later law regulating manumissions is found in Arch. Nat. Cols. F^3 233 (Guadeloupe), ordonnance of March 3, 178.
59. Arch. Nat. Cols. F^3 249, p. 818 (Martinique). Moreau de St.-Méry, *op. cit.*, Vol. II, pp. 535–28.
60. Wyndham, *op. cit.*, pp. 367ff.
61. Peytraud, *op. cit.*, pp. 150–57.
62. *Ibid.*, p. 326.
63. Arch. Nat. Cols. F^3 225, p. 777 (Guadeloupe), letter of May 17, 1742.
64. Moreau de St.-Méry, *op. cit.*, Vol. III, pp. 727–29 (déclaration of February 1, 1743); pp. 500–502, (jugement of November 11, 1691); Vol. II, p. 103 (arrêt of August 1, 1707).
65. For examples see *ibid.*, Vol. I, p. 805 (arrêt of December II, 1777); Vol. I, Arch. Nat. Cols. F^3 221, pp. 925–28 (Guadeloupe), arrêt of March 4, 1698. Also, *Code Noir*, Cl. 38.
66. Moreau de St.-Méry, *op. cit.*, Vol. V, p. 744 (arrêt of November 20, 1776); Vol. IV, p. 136 (arrêt of November 5, 1753).
67. *Ibid.*, Vol. II, pp. 25–27 (arrêt of March 16, 1705), p. 117 (arrêt of May 9, 1708), pp. 568–69 (ordonnance of July 1, 1717); Vol. III, pp. 177–78 (arrêts of July 2 and 8, 1726); Vol. V, pp. 97–98 (arrêt of March 9, 1767).
68. *Ibid.*, Vol. II, pp. 208, 213 (arrêts of September 1 and October 6, 1710). Arch. Nat. Cols. F^3 223, pp. 717–23 (Guadeloupe), arrêt of September 6, 1725; F^3 225, pp. 139–45, arrêt of Nov. 8, 1735.
69. Arch. Nat. Cols. F^3 226, pp. 269–82 (Guadeloupe), arrêt of July 9, 1746.
70. Moreau de St.-Méry, *op. cit.*, Vol. IV, pp. 401–03 (ordonnance of August 19, 1761).
71. *Ibid.*, Vol. IV, p. 566 (ordonnance of March 24, 1763).
72. Arch. Nat. Cols. B.34, ordonnance of December 30, 1712.
73. Peytraud, *op. cit.*, pp. 193–94.
74. Adrien Desalles, *Histoire générale des Antilles* (Paris, 1847), III, pp. 21ff.
75. Peytraud, *op. cit.*, p. 150.
76. Pierre de Vaissière, *St. Domingue (1629–1789)* (Paris, 1909), p. 181.
77. *Ibid.*, pp. 186–89.
78. Arch. Nat. Cols. F^3 233, pp. 231–35 (Guadeloupe), ordonnance of December 17, 1784.
79. Peytraud, *op. cit.*, p. 241.
80. W. Westergaard, *The Danish West Indies under Company Rule (1671–1754)* (New York, 1917), pp. 158ff.
81. *Ibid.*, pp. 162ff.
82. The discussion of the Dutch West Indian slave law is based upon the article 'Slavernij' in *Encyclopaedie van Nederlandsch West Indie* (The Hague, 1914–17), pp. 637ff.
83. *Ibid.*, p. 640.

Caribbean Anti-Slavery: The Self-Liberation Ethos of Enslaved Blacks

HILARY McD. BECKLES

It is now commonly accepted by historians that in the British West Indies anti-slavery conflict was frequently of a revolutionary nature. In earlier articles, I have suggested that the many slave revolts and plots in these territories between 1638 and 1838 could be conceived of as the '200 Years' War' — one protracted struggle launched by Africans and their Afro-West Indian progeny against slave owners. Such endemic anti-slavery activity represented, furthermore, the most immediately striking characteristic of the West Indian world. Current anglophone historiography outlines in detail the empirical contours of this struggle — what amounts to an indigenous anti-slavery movement — though its philosophical and ideological aspects remain less researched.[1]

Anglophone literature on anti-slavery, however, has emphasised above other features, its trans-atlantic dimension. This perspective has enriched significantly our general understanding of the diverse forces that succeeded ultimately in toppling the region's heterogeneous slave regimes. To some extent, this panoramic vision of the anti-slavery movement results from a more theoretical reading of slave resistance which suggests the need for closer investigation of slaves' political culture. Such an examination is necessary not only for an empirical understanding of resistance, but also for a fuller evaluation of slaves' consciousness and depth of political awareness. Such insights would make it possible for the historian to illustrate more precisely those linkages, real or imaginary, that existed between plantation-based politics and the international anti-slavery ethos.[2]

Many historians have responded to this challenge, and the theme of slave resistance or, more appropriately, the blacks' anti-slavery movement, has now become a leading growth area in Caribbean historiography. From the works of leading scholars, particularly Orlando Patterson, Michael Craton, Edward Brathwaite, Barry Gaspar, Mary Turner, Barbara Kopytoff and Monica Schuler, it is possible to demarcate some structural features in the development of Caribbean anti-slavery. Three basic stages have so far been identified. The first stage relates to early plantation construction, and corresponds approximately with the period 1500–1750. The second basic stage is characterised by mature plantation society and declining dependency on slave importation — 1750–1800. The third stage relates to the 'general crisis' in plantation slavery; it is linked with the impact of Haitian politics and serious anti-slavery discussions in the metropole — 1804–1838.

Within these three general phases, three types/levels of anti-slavery struggle have been described — though no systematic effort has been made to articulate them within the historical continuum. Firstly, a proliferation of acts of 'day-to-day' resistance are identified; these were generally designed not to overthrow the slave system, but to undermine its efficiency in order to hasten its eventual abandonment. Secondly, evidence is adduced of the large number of unsuccessful plots and revolts which were characterised by collective organisation with reformist and revolutionary objectives. Thirdly, there is the incidence, 'successful' rebellion, from long-term marronage to the St. Domingue revolution.[3]

Highly structured revolts, considered generally as the most advanced rebellious acts, have been given more research attention within the wide range of anti-slavery politics. Unfortunately, no attempt has been made to

Journal of Caribbean History, Vol. 22, Nos. 1–2 1988, pp. 1–19.

illustrate how, and under what conditions, non-violent day-to-day anti-slavery protest evolved into violent revolutionary designs.[4] According to Robert Dirks there are references within the literature to some 70 slave uprisings between 1649 and 1833, including large-scale insurrections that engulfed entire colonies and small-scale violence limited to single estates. Of this total, Dirks states that some 32 revolts did not materialise due to discovery, and some were undoubtedly the invented product of planters' paranoia. Craton's chronology of resistance between 1638 and 1837, however, lists some 75 aborted revolts and actual rebellions; in this computation some of these actions have been grouped together and appear as one event.[5] This record of resistance illustrates that there was hardly a generation of slaves in the English West Indies that did not confront their masters collectively with arms in pursuit of freedom. In this sense, therefore, the relations between slaves and masters in the West Indies can be shown as characterised by ongoing psychological warfare and intermittent bloody battles.

It is now a major concern of scholars interpreting this extensive record of resistance to assess the extent to which slaves' rebellious actions were informed by ideological choices in the context of maturing political consciousness. It has taken scholars many years of revising interpretations to arrive at this position in regard to slave politics, though it remains an influential argument that slaves wanted much less than what some recent historians now suggest. This interpretive inertia reflects, in part, a compulsive assumption within western historical science that the working classes rarely perceived effectively their group interest, an argument supported by what some refer to as irrationality and inhibiting conservatism in their collective responses to oppression.

Not surprisingly, recent revisionist literature produced by most Caribbean, European and American scholars, has centred upon the need to distinguish as clearly as possible the Caribbean and metropolitan anti-slavery movements, and to assess their relative potency. Technically, this is an important development because slave resistance had long been conceived of as a lower species of political behaviour, lacking in ideological cohesion, intellectual qualities and a philosophical direction. Generally considered as marginally more advanced than basic primitive responses to a crude and oppressive material and social world, it was not seen to be possessing anything resembling theoretical significance. These perceptions have survived in spite of C. L. R. James' 1938 classic work, *The Black Jacobins*, which sought, perhaps with too much theoretical enthusiasm, to link rebel slaves in colonial St. Domingue with the philosophically progressive Jacobin equalitarianism of France that ultimately weakened the ideological hegemony of slave holders in that colony. The 'Black Jacobins' seized the colonial state and established an independent republic in 1804 — an achievement that cannot be divorced, according to James, from its European theoretical roots.[6]

At first glance the immediate goals of the Caribbean and European anti-slavery movements seem ideologically polarised and at variance. The metropolitan movement was essentially philosophical and respectably radical in character. It relied initially upon a strong moral perspective, though with an increasing reliance upon economic arguments in latter years. The Caribbean movement, on the other hand, spearheaded by enslaved blacks, with some Amerindian and free coloured support, was also generally non-violent, but occasionally erupted into revolutionary warfare. The metropolitan movement depended upon popular mobilisation and parliamentary lobbying in a legislative approach to emancipation. The slaves' approach, it may be implied, was more complex; they wanted freedom by all means necessary or possible, and engaged in activities which ranged from self-purchase to violent armed struggle for territory and political sovereignty.

There is some evidence, fragmented though it is, to suggest that more informed slaves saw their anti-slavery actions as articulated to those of metropolitan lobbyists, though they were not prepared to lose the initiative in terms of striking for freedom when circumstances, local or foreign, dictated autonomous actions. Some slaves, whether in revolutionary St. Domingue or rebellious Barbados and Jamaica in 1816 and 1831 respectively, had knowledge, considered crude and inaccurate by most historians, of developments in metropolitan anti-slavery ideas and strategies. This information base, it has been argued, assisted in shaping their costly movement for liberation (measured in human life) and thus illustrating, even if in a tamed manner, the internationalism of their political consciousness.[7]

Evaluating the relative potency of the two segments of the transatlantic anti-slavery movement cannot be an easy task for the historian. Contemporaneous writers on the English Caribbean did not attempt such analyses. Indeed, they generally saw the slaves' movement, most of the time, as having little more than nuisance value, and on those infrequent occasions when they recognised within it revolutionary proportions, their analyses degenerated into negrophobic descriptions and commentaries.[8] Such outpourings were based, in varying degrees, upon the racist notion of angry and savage blacks in a vengeful and mindless lust for blood and white women.[9]

The most sophisticated pro-slavery writer, Jamaica's Edward Long, does not best illustrate this particular point, but he does demonstrate in the clearest manner slave owners' reluctant recognition of slaves' maturing anti-slavery consciousness. Furthermore, he understood fully what it meant for the Caribbean world in particular and the politics of abolitionism in general.

Long was aware of the contradiction inherent in white colonists' claims for 'liberty' within the late eighteenth-century Whig ideological framework, while at the same time denying black colonists any legitimate right to their own liberty. He admitted, moreover, that the 'spirit of liberty' was also a deep-rooted feature of the slave community, though for him this consciousness had its origins in the white community — the blacks being ideological victims of its 'contagious fever'.[10] The resolution of this contradiction within Long's thought was found in a headlong plunge into racial arguments, the structure of which had long been a feature of colonial elite social consciousness. He argued, for example, that the condition of colonial slavery for blacks was in itself an advancement in their claim to liberty. That is, blacks in general enjoyed more social and material rights on the West Indian plantations than they did in West Africa where their lot was generally one of abject poverty and submission to monarchical tyranny. Gordon Lewis suggests that social relations within eighteenth-century planter ideology were based on the tenet that the slave required patronage in return for his labour. Long articulates this point by stating that the slave, once settled in his new home, enters into a limited freedom supervised by the master who is his 'friend and father'. This authority, Long adds,

> is like that of an ancient patriarch: conciliating affection by the mildness of its exertion, and claiming respect by the justice and propriety of its decisions and discipline, it attracts the love of the honest and good; while it awes the worthless into reformation.[11]

This unrealistic view of stability in master–slave relations fell apart precisely at the stage where slaves rejected those reforms which meant the abandonment of their claim to liberty. The extensive record of rebellion and protest provides the empirical and theoretical evidence to support their stance on this question. It points, furthermore, to a refusal within the slave community to accept as legitimate any kind of slave-relation whatsoever, and the search for avenues to freedom was persistent.

Ideally, it could be said that rebel slaves and metropolitan anti-slavery lobbyists shared the same goals, and hence their respective movements ought to be considered as different levels of a general process. The attractiveness of this position is partly betrayed by its simplicity, and is easily abandoned when tested under the weight of empirical evidence. It may very well be suggested that slaves wanted more than legal freedom on many occasions; that they also wanted political power and economic autonomy. These were certainly objectives that most 'humanitarians' preferred blacks not to have. The records of slave rebellion also show, it is true, that in some instances slaves might well have wanted only the right to reasonable wages and conditions of work under their old masters. The 1831 Sam Sharpe rebellion of Jamaica has recently been so interpreted.[12] But rebellions in St. Domingue, 1791–1804, and Barbados in 1816 also suggest that blacks understood that meaningful freedom could be guaranteed only by means of seizing the organs of law and government and by imposing a revolutionary constitutionalism thereafter in order to enforce the reality of freedom.

Wilberforce, for instance, had no time for slaves' revolutionary approach to emancipation in the English colonies, and considered such actions, in spite of his friendship with King Henry of Haiti, as detrimental to the survival of English authority in America — not only in terms of economic and political leverage, but also in terms of the hegemony of western civilisation. The scenario of black revolution and the formation of Afro-Caribbean republics or monarchies, in addition to the subsequent freezing of 'things European', did not excite English anti-slavery lobbyists.[13] From this point of view, then, it may be suggested that the two segments of the transatlantic anti-slavery movement were heading in different directions most of the time. It was not simply a matter of the divergence of strategies and radically different levels of procedure, but also a matter of the kind of worlds that were to be created in the aftermath.

A simple statistical analysis might show that given some 400,000 blacks who gained revolutionary freedom in St. Domingue, together with the large numbers who freed themselves by means of marronage and otherwise, no concrete basis exists for the claim that European legislative emancipation should be given an obvious right to first consideration. Though the numbers analysis is not necessarily the best way to proceed on this question, it would perhaps impose some demographic constraints upon the ideological charge involved in the argument that, by and large, freedom was brought to the blacks, and that self-attained freedom was of marginal significance. In addition, it would illustrate more clearly the impressive record of achievement of slave communities as sponsors of the libertarian ideology.

Such an analysis is particularly relevant at this stage partly because one of the most striking features of the recent historiography has been the establishment of a dichotomous core/periphery structure within the transatlantic anti-slavery movement. Eric Williams was perhaps first to pose this dichotomous paradigm when he argued that, while metropolitan anti-slavery lobbyists intensified their campaign, during the early nineteenth century, the slaves had done likewise. By 1833, he said, 'the alternatives were clear', 'emancipation from above or emancipation from below, but Emancipation'.[14] Not surprisingly, only radical scholars seem perturbed by the assignment of the peripheral status to the slaves' movement and the core status to the metropolitan lobbyists. This has been the case in spite of a revisionist attempt to give greater value within the emancipation process to the autonomous anti-slavery actions of blacks. That is, whereas the traditional interpretations crudely negated the slaves' role, the modernist view sought the subordination of slaves' struggle within international abolitionism. The hands-on political movement of slaves, then, is yet to free itself conceptually of the hegemonic constraints imposed by a revised anti-slavery interpretation. Symbolically, the images of Wilberforce, Schoelcher, *et al.* still stalk the literature, transcending those of slave leaders such as Bussa, Kofi and Sam Sharpe.

It is not clear, however, why the slaves' struggle for freedom should be considered secondary or peripheral to the activities of European emancipationists. No coherent arguments have been given for this outside of the general statement that ultimately it was imperial law rather than colonial war which terminated the 'not very peculiar' institution of slavery. Michael Craton, for example, after evaluating the record of slave resistance in the English colonies, though in a rather technical and 'eventist' manner, considered it necessary to add, by way of not distancing himself from what he perceived to be substantial empirical evidence, that white abolitionists won the day, though black abolitionists helped in no small way. He has also treated us to other variations on this theme. There is the view, for example, that slaves created in part the ideological context for parliamentary legislation by rendering their societies irretrievably unstable. In this way they assisted in forcing the imperial legislature into action in order to protect colonial life (white) and property (black and non-human). In addition, there is the argument that slave rebels had illustrated by 1832 that the colonial elite could rule in the long term only by means of extreme repression, and that Parliament was not prepared to pay the economic nor political cost implied, and acted to defuse an increasingly explosive situation.[15]

Whatever the perspectives, the perception that rebel slaves were featured in abolitionist debates by the imperial governments cannot be ignored. If these arguments have any weight, then it becomes less clear what precisely was the overwhelming and more critical role of the 'humanitarians'. Unfortunately, analyses of these and related matters are hampered by insufficient data on specific ways in which the imperial government perceived the political action of slaves in relation to that of its own anti-slavery members.

The assignment of a peripheral status within anti-slavery thought to slaves is also to be found in the 'intellectual' work of David Brion Davis and more so in Roger Anstey's several accounts of British abolitionism. Following Davis, it could be argued that while the conceptual separation of Caribbean and European processes are perhaps inevitable, owing to different historiographic and philosophical traditions, the projection of an hierarchical order in the emergence of democratic ideology, and in the partial and full attainment of freedom, constitutes a major problem of anti-slavery in western culture.[16]

Two recent works on anti-slavery, the first by

a long-standing anti-Marxist American scholar of British abolitionism, and the other by an English Marxist political historian, best illustrate this historiographical condition. First, in Seymour Drescher's 1986 work, *Capitalism and Anti-Slavery*, which represents a mild revision of Anstey's thesis, there are no references to Caribbean anti-slavery activities in the opening chapter entitled the 'Foundations of anti-slavery'. Drescher, however, offered what can be interpreted as a dismissive aside in his summary where it is stated that 'the expansion of freedom was the central problem of abolitionists (including the slaves)'.[17] Second, Robin Blackburn in his recent impressively comprehensive study, *The Overthrow of Colonial Slavery*, argues in the opening chapter on the 'origins of anti-slavery' that since the publication of Thomas Clarkson's seminal work on British slave trade abolition (1808), 'it has been common to identify the origins of anti-slavery within the works of the learned men who first published critiques of slavery or the slave trade.'[18]

Recognising the persistence of this perspective in the study of anti-slavery, Marxist historians such as C. L. R. James, Richard Hart and Gordon Lewis, among others, have been suggesting for some time that slave politics be conceived of as the 'on the ground' (core) dimension of a general struggle to remove slavery from Caribbean and European political culture. James has long been concerned with illustrating how revolutionary ideology transcended the political barriers implicit in colonial slavery and racism. He insists that there should be no surprise in the fact that Caribbean slaves hammered out a political reality of anti-slavery with the assistance of European thought.

The equally vintage work of Hart on Jamaican slave resistance and rebellion now represents an historiographic core that illustrates as well as any other source the evolution of a hardened anti-slavery consciousness among blacks in that country. For him, the core of the anti-slavery movement resided undoubtedly within the Caribbean, and his personal political feel for contemporary consciousness gives a strong sense of continuity in his analysis.[19] Lewis, in addition, in his well-known style, attempted to flesh out the theoretical and conceptual dimensions of international anti-slavery ideology, and gave full credit to the intellectual contribution of Caribbean slaves. He is not the kind of scholar who is limited by what has been said already. Furthermore, he had the courage to travel along uncharted areas in search of the 'hidden' ideological elements of the past world. What he found were the outer limits of a grand Caribbean anti-slavery tradition, whose actors were not only black and coloured, but also Amerindian and creole white. Conceptually, he does not detract from the achievements of Wilberforce, Clarkson, Buxton and Schoelcher, but he does suggest that the world created, even if temporarily, by the anti-slavery energies of Toussaint and Dessalines, Sam Sharpe, Tackey and other slave leaders, seemed comparatively more 'hell-bent' on destroying Caribbean slavery.[20]

English abolitionist leaders, of course, perceived themselves as constituting the vanguard of anti-slavery thought and practice, a vision which historians have continued to perpetuate. This perception, not surprisingly, has managed to survive long after the 1790s when blacks in St. Domingue overthrew the slave regime and established in 1804 the state of Haiti which boasted an aggressive anti-slavery constitution and foreign policy.[21] Haiti had emerged regionally and internationally as the real symbol and manifestation of anti-slavery, Toussaint having beforehand eclipsed Wilberforce in the watchful eyes of the western world as the prime anti-slavery leader. For the hard-working and determined English abolitionists, however, the presence of Haiti was, in general, more of a hindrance to their crusade than an asset, and they continued to see anti-slavery as being endangered by Caribbean slaves' impatient tendency to resort to arms. Eltis suggests that this is why abolitionists, in general, were in favour of the establishment of a strong police force, an independent magistracy, draconian vagrancy laws and increased missionary activity.[22]

Historians have had little difficulty in endorsing the humanitarians' claim to possession of the philosophic 'mind' — and hence the core — of anti-slavery, and by extension in suggesting that slaves lived out at best the cruder socio-material aspects of the movement. According to David Geggus, no major figure appears to have openly approved of violent self-liberation by blacks. Wilberforce thought them still unready for freedom, however obtained, and he deplored the 'cruel' and 'dreadful' revolt in St. Domingue. Even Charles James Fox, the well-known radical and abolitionist, uttered negrophobic statements which culminated in his call for an assurance by his government that the spirit of revolt would not find roots within English colonies. Thomas Clarkson, however, respected for his unemotional consistency on the question of anti-slavery, rejected the popular sentiments of abolitionists, and spoke of Haiti as representing, not the upsurge of brutish savagery, but the affirmation of the 'unalterable Rights of Men' to freedom. Clarkson had only few supporters within the abolitionists' camp, the most famous being the long-standing abolitionist, Percival Stockdale, who saw in the St. Domingue experience a movement against tyranny, led by Africans 'acting like men', fulfilling the most honourable destiny of mankind as directed by 'Nature and by God'.[23]

It was the treacherous removal of Toussaint from St. Domingue, the scene of the greatest single anti-slavery triumph, that allowed the best in England's journalism and the finest in its philosophic and artistic tradition to address the real meaning of Caribbean anti-slavery. In 1802, for example, the *Annual Register* voted him the man of the year, while Samuel Coleridge rated him in terms of 'true dignity of character' the better of Napoleon, his captor.[24] William Wordsworth, perhaps, more so than any other thinker, concretised in 1802 the value of Toussaint to mankind's search for liberty in general and the anti-slavery cause specifically with his sonnet, 'To Toussaint L'Ouverture':[25]

Though fallen thyself, never to rise again,
Live and take comfort. Thou has left behind
Powers that will work for thee; air, earth, and skies;
There's not a breathing of the common wind
That will forget thee; thou hast great allies;
Thy friends are exultations, agonies,
And love, and man's unconquerable mind.

But Wordsworth, like Toussaint, did not breathe 'the common wind', as Geggus assures us in his treatment of British opinion on black self-liberation in the Caribbean. On the St. Domingue question, Geggus asserts: 'Among the abolitionists, with the exception of a few fringe figures, the black rebels found apologists rather than supporters; most avoided the question of the legitimacy of the use of violence, and none seem to have spoken out against Britain's brief, but traumatic attempt to restore slavery in the colony'. Geggus is not surprised that 'the response of the British Romantics' to this struggle for personal freedom and national self-liberation was 'surprisingly slight', since the evidence suggests that although 'the blacks' resistance won them respect, prejudice persisted'.[26]

Persistent anti-black prejudice within western thought, Eric Williams affirmed, has influenced considerably the development of British and European colonial historiography, which forces us to examine the extent to which it remains a feature of the theoretical claims of anti-slavery literature.[27] It can be argued, within the limits of reasonable deductions from the data available, that English abolitionists' rejection of the slaves' revolutionary approach to freedom suggests that they had conceived liberation strictly in legal and sociological terms. That is, they did not support slave politics which sought to undermine the hegemony of the planter elite and the supportive Christian missions. They wished slaves legally free and to some extent recognised as social and biological equals to whites. But they did argue, however, that the economic dependency and political subordination of blacks to whites were necessary and desirable for their own advancement as well as for the continued growth of the Caribbean. Blacks, they generally believed, had nothing of superior merit to offer the new world in advancing its civilisation, and therefore they were to play a submissive role in the expansion of Eurocentric culture via the white-controlled plantation economic regime.[28]

The racism implied within this perception of black liberation was an entrenched feature of abolitionists' thought. Emancipation was not conceived in terms of liberation from Europeans' power, values and domination. From this point of view, then, it was only when Toussaint showed himself, like King Christophe did at a later date, to be receptive of the European educational and religious mission and its cultural-language baggage, that he received some measure of ideological acceptance by English statesmen and humanitarians. Furthermore, the abolitionists' tendency to conceive of slaves as unfortunate children to be liberated from tyrannical parents, with the moral outrage which that implied for the reasonable mind, served to deepen the racist perception of their audience and enhance a fear among them that blacks seeking independence, economic autonomy and political power, were irresponsible, rash, ungrateful, in addition to being naive.

With these ideological tenets so deeply embedded in abolitionist perceptions of blacks in struggle, it would have been a formidable, but necessary task for historians to transcend or penetrate them in order to observe as objectively as possible the intellectual features of the political culture of blacks. This remains a most necessary precondition for a proper evaluation of the Caribbean anti-slavery tradition as well as for an understanding of how it is related to the European movement.

Logically, then, a feature of anti-slavery that should have been addressed at the outset is the history of blacks' political consciousness in the general evolution of their conceptual understanding of their wants, needs and means. To do this, it would have been necessary to say something meaningful about the 'slave mind' — hence ideology. Gordon Lewis quite perceptively punctuated his fascinating treatment of Caribbean anti-slavery with this reference to the state of the 'slave mind' within the historiography:

> If, then, there was a planter mind, there was also a slave mind. This has not always been fully appreciated, even by authors sympathetic to the slave cause.[29]

Refusal to recognise black rebels at this level of consciousness, more than any other factor, has held back the advance of the kind of conceptual analysis which is necessary for an incisive understanding of slave resistance, and the subject remains today a soft spot within the modern anti-slavery literature.

To conceive rebel slaves as intelligent political activists (in spite of their material and socio-legal oppression), who were capable of evaluating pro-slavery strengths and weaknesses, has not been an easy task for most historians. Occasionally, references are made to this inhibition in terms of it being rooted within a racist perception of blacks which, in part, relates to the abolitionist view of slaves as primitive, anti-intellectual beings in need simply of paternalistic and moral care. Take Michael Craton's conceptual development, for example. For many years he worked diligently on slave resistance in the English Caribbean. In 1974 he presented what he described as a typology, morphology and etiology of resistance — neatly packaged in what he also termed 'a sequential model'. Since then he has published several works on slave resistance, illustrating a praiseworthy need to revise and fine-tune his analysis. Indeed, he is generally considered to be a leading authority within this aspect of Caribbean historiography. It is interesting to note, however, what happened when he encountered the need to comment on the 'slave mind' — an encounter which resulted from a general recognition that structuralist models based squarely on demographic, topographic and economic forces were insufficient in explaining why the slaves rebelled and what their motivating ideas were. He ran into the minefield of his own [unconscious] race attitude and attempted to deal with it as follows:

> Because of my seduction by the neat model and simple causes, I went so far as to dismiss the influence upon the British West Indies slaves of all the ideology of the Age of Revolution (1775–1815), even of the slave rebellion in Haiti between 1791 and 1804 . . . , finally, it seems to me now that to deprive the slaves of an ideology such as that normally ascribed to the rebellious Americans, the French Revolutionaries . . . is to be guilty once more of a racist denigration.[30]

Having cleared this hurdle, a major achievement within Euro-American historiography of black struggle, Craton goes on to assert what for him was the ideology of the rebel slaves throughout Caribbean history; it 'was that of all unfree men — that is the vast majority throughout history — freedom to make, or create, life of their own'.[31]

Craton's admission and subsequent assertion came some 30 years after C. L. R. James had illustrated quite remarkably in *The Black Jacobins* that a proliferation of conflicting ideas and socio-political visions existed within the Haitian revolutionary ranks on the issues of foreign policy, economic strategy, race relations, education and government. Indeed one could argue that, like Lenin, Stalin, and Trotsky, the Haitian leaders, Toussaint, Dessalines and Christophe, differed fundamentally from each other on ideology, and thus the revolution was characterised by deep-rooted conceptual heterogeneity.[32] The real tribute to slaves in Craton's point, then, is perhaps to be found more succinctly stated in Gordon Lewis' political theorem — 'without intelligence there can be no ideology'.[33]

Leading on from these conceptual developments, though not in a logical manner, is the belief, now generally associated with the work of Sidney Mintz and Douglas Hall, that rebel slaves wanted a limited measure of economic and social autonomy as represented by a peasant culture rather than formal political power.[34] It is not clearly stated whether this objective was that of rebel leaders or the generally non-violent majority of slaves. Neither is it clearly stated whether this 'peasanthood' was considered the end product of their politics — that is, after they had defeated their masters — or merely a base for a future revolutionary onslaught upon planter power. For Craton, 'the black majority' wanted to be 'free to work for planters or themselves as and when they wished', ambitions he considered to be 'comparatively moderate', but in 'consonance with what seems to have been the wishes of the mass following'.[35]

It is not difficult to recognise that these projections of rebel slaves' objectives represent the most conservative and restricted interpretation of their ascribed ideology — 'freedom to make a life of their own'. Is it not a little odd to state that rebel slaves would have used whatever means possible to win their freedom and then to suggest that this end could be realised by a 'moderate' peasanthood cocooned within a plantation/planter dominated world? Would slaves not have realised that this idea as an end itself was unattainable under plantation hegemony? If we look solely at the British West Indies where slaves failed, after 200 years, to wrest political power from masters by means of arms, we also see that, in the period 1838–1870, landownership was used as a political tool with far-reaching constitutional implications, especially for Jamaica where the peasantry was numerically most advanced.

Where slaves succeeded in freeing themselves, whether in Haiti, in long-lasting maroon communities, and in temporary slave regimes, the value of political power to their sense of freedom was considered critical. The labourers' and peasants' riots and voting practices in the mid-nineteenth-century British West Indies clearly illustrate that blacks were aware that without political power their 'reconstituted' peasant culture could not deliver the quality of freedom envisaged. Historians, then, seemed to have taken one step forward in the recognition of a slave ideology of struggle, but have taken two backwards in implying that it was a depoliticised peasant world, dialectically opposed to plantation hegemony, which rebel slaves pursued.

More recently, this regressive trend within the historiography has received a significant boost from Dirks in what he describes as an analysis of 'conflict and its ritual expression' on British West Indian slave plantations. Dirks' thesis is that slaves possessed a 'proclivity to turn the holidays [especially Christmas] into a bloodbath and to try to topple their masters' regime'.[36] He computes that of the 70 slave revolts reported, aborted, imagined and actual, some 37 occurred in the month of December, producing what he terms the 'darkside of Christmas'.[37] Dirks' analysis of this time-based phenomenon falls within the category identified by Craton as racist denigration — dark for whom! For him, the slaves were not driven by a political and military understanding, sophisticated or otherwise, of the impact of the Christmas festivities within the white community, but by forces of the belly rather than the brain. The month of December, he claims, without the presentation of adequate supportive data, was associated with a rather sudden increase in slave nutrition — preceding months being characterised by extensive hunger:

> The onset of dry weather in December brought immediate and dramatic relief. The energy-rich fields of cane started to ripen. At the same time yams, sweet potatoes, maize, plantains, and bananas, as well as a great number of other fruits and vegetables, began to mature. Field-work slackened off for a brief interlude before the cane harvest. And the end of the hurricane season brought hundreds of vessels laden with provisions, much of it for holiday distribution. Together these events broke the pattern of hunger and lethargy and disease of the previous months and gave way to vigor and better health all around.

'This upsurge in available food energy,' Dirks argues, 'is also related to tumultous celebrations' and aggressiveness among slaves in general. He asserts that 'the effect of this nutritional boost and the availability of other fresh sources of nourishment was nothing short of explosive'. Typically, some of this excessive energy went into 'jolly sport', but most went into 'extraordinary aggressiveness'.[38]

One of Dirks' achievements is that he has managed to turn upside down the traditional analysis without attempting to remove it from nutritional or biological levels of conception. In 1974, for example, Richard Sheridan had argued that slaves 'tended to revolt when they were underfed, overworked, and maltreated'.[39] We are now told by Dirks that, on the contrary, they tended to revolt when overfed, underworked and well-treated. The assumption underlying both arguments is that it was possible to produce in a general way an anti-rebellious consciousness by a sensitive, well-planned manipulation of labour and nutritional factors. This suggests an objection to the notion that slaves practised 'politics' on a sophisticated and intellectually conscious level. Yet, the evidence illustrates fully that slaves made definite political analyses of the power structures they encountered, and used almost every force — natural and human — in their struggle. They rebelled when they could, and accommodated when they had to. The ebb and flow of rebellion and accommodation suggest that they understood 'time', including Christmas time, as a political factor in struggle. As a result, some planters were forced to appreciate the political skills and conscious determination of rebel slaves, in spite of the negrophobic nature of their social commentaries.

It can no longer be generally accepted, then, that slaves existed in an atheoretical world which was devoid of ideas, political concepts and an alternative socio-political vision. Their tradition of anti-slavery activity impacted upon the social culture and polity of the Caribbean world in more fundamental ways than anti-slavery lobbyists ever did in metropolitan societies. Indeed, the entire Caribbean reality was shaped and informed by the persistent forces of slavery and anti-slavery as long as the slave regimes lasted. From a Caribbean perspective, slaves' struggle for freedom should not be diminished when placed alongside the legislative interventions of European parliaments. These metropolitan actions were part of the final episode in an epic struggle — initiated and propelled by its greatest sufferers — the slave population. Only in Haiti were blacks able to overthrow the slave regime and achieve their freedom. Yet, slaves throughout the region consistently rebelled in order to gain freedom, employing over time a wide range of political tools and methods in their struggle.

In terms of the Caribbean anti-slavery movement, no iron laws of slave resistance exist, and consequently most scholars have tended to emphasise the uniqueness of each colony's case. While recognising, at least philosophically, the temporal and spatial uniqueness of each historical moment, one can still illustrate that the fundamental ideological core of anti-slavery was almost identical: the slaves were saying to their masters, 'we want to be free, and we will pursue that freedom by all means necessary.' This was the essential stream of thought that ran through the region, from colony to colony, from plantation to plantation. Indeed, it was anti-slavery rather than sugar production which stamped the most prominent unifying marks upon the region. In this sense, then, black-led anti-slavery resided at the root of the Caribbean experience, and represented a critical element of the core of what was perhaps the first international political movement of the modern era — transatlantic abolitionism.

Notes

1. Hilary Beckles, 'The 200 Years War: Slave Resistance in the British West Indies: An Overview of the Historiography', *Jamaican Historical Review*, 13 (1982), 1-10; also 'Slave Ideology and Self-Emancipation in the British West Indies', *Bulletin of Eastern Caribbean Affairs*, 10:4 (1984), 1-8. See also Michael Craton, 'The Passion to Exist: Slave Rebellion in the British West Indies, 1650-1832', *Journal of Caribbean History*, 13, 1 (1980); Edward Long, *The History of Jamaica*, (London, 1774, rpt 1970), 348-55, 465-69; Bryan Edwards, *The History, Civil and Commercial of the British Colonies in the West Indies* (London, 1794), 1, 60-65.
2. See, for example, the following revisionist analyses of slave resistance: Barry Gaspar, *Bondsmen and Rebels: A Study of Master-Slave Relations in Antigua (with Implications for colonial British America)* (Baltimore, 1985), xiv-20. Michael Craton, *Testing the Chains: Resistance to Slavery in the British West Indies* (London, 1982), 19-51. Hilary Beckles, *Black Rebellion in Barbados: The Struggle Against Slavery, 1627-1838* (Bridgetown, 1984), 1-8.
3. See Orlando Patterson, 'Slavery and Slave Revolts: A Socio-historical Analysis of the First Maroon War, Jamaica 1655-1740', *Social and Economic Studies*, 19:3 (1970), 289-325. Michael Craton, *Sinews of Empire: A Short History of British Slavery* (New York, 1974), 225-40. Edward Braithwaite, *Wars of Respect: Nanny, Sam Sharpe and the Struggle* (Kingston, 1977); also 'Caliban, Ariel and Unprospero in the Conflict of Creolisation: A Study of the Slave Revolt of Jamaica, 1831-32', in V. Rubin and A. Tuden (eds), *Comparative Perspectives on Slavery in New World Plantation Societies* (New York, 1977), 41-62. Barbara Kopytoff, 'The Early Political Development of Jamaican Maroon Societies', *William and Mary Quarterly*, 35:2 (1978), 287-307; 'The Development of Jamaican Maroon Ethnicity', *Caribbean Quarterly*, 22 (1976), 35-50. Monica Schuler, 'Akan Slave Rebellion in the British Caribbean', *Savacou*, I:1 (1970); also 'Ethnic Slave Rebellions in the Caribbean and the Guianas', *Journal of Social History*, 3 (1970), 374-85. Barry Gaspar, 'The Antigua Slave Conspiracy of 1736: A Case Study of the Origins of Collective Resistance', *William and Mary Quarterly*, 35:2 (1978), 308-24. Mary Reckord-Turner, 'The Jamaican Slave Rebellion of 1831', *Past and Present*, No. 40 (July 1968), 108-25.
4. See Monica Schuler, 'Day-to-Day Resistance to Slavery in the Caribbean during the Eighteenth Century', *African Studies Association of the West Indies*, Bulletin 6 (December 1973), 57-77. Also, Richard Sheridan, 'The Jamaican Slave Insurrection Scare of 1776 and the American Revolution', *Journal of Negro History*, 61:3 (1976), 290-308.
5. Robert Dirks, *The Black Saturnalia: Conflict and its ritual expression on British West Indian Slave Plantations* (Gainesville, 1987). M. Craton, *Testing the Chains*, 335-39.
6. C. L. R. James, *The Black Jacobins: Toussaint L'Ouverture and the San Domingo Revolution* (rpt. 1963). See also Gordon K. Lewis, *Main Currents in Caribbean Thought: The Historical Evolution of Caribbean Society in its Ideological Aspects, 1492-1900* (Baltimore, 1983), 171-239.
7. For example, the Report of the House of Assembly's Select Committee which investigated the causes of the 1816 rebellion in Barbados concluded that the rebellion originated 'solely and entirely in consequence of the

intelligence imparted to the slaves, which intelligence was obtained from the English newspapers, that their freedom had been granted them in England'; and that their hopes for emancipation were 'kept alive' by the information that 'party in England and particularly in Wilberforce . . . were exerting themselves to ameliorate their condition, and ultimately effect their emancipation'. (*Report from a Select Committee Appointed to Inquire into the Origins, Causes, and Progress of the Late Insurrection — April 1816*, Barbados, 1818)

8. For example, J. Oldmixon (*The British Empire in America*, London, 1708) wrote of the rebels involved in the 1692 slave conspiracy in Barbados: 'Did they imagine that Christians would have suffered them to set up a Negro Monarchy, or Republick, in the midst of their Governments? . . . The English, Dutch and French . . . would rather have leagued than suffer this unnatural and dangerous independence. . . . They would have been looked upon as common enemies by all nations . . .' (p. 53). See Beckles, *Black Rebellion*, 48.
9. See Craton, *Testing the Chains*, 109; Beckles, *Black Rebellion*, 110.
10. Edward Long, *The History of Jamaica* (London, 1774); (rpt. 1970), 1, 25.
11. Lewis, *Main Currents*, 111; Long, 11, 270–271.
12. See Mary Turner, *Slaves and Missionaries: The Disintegration of Jamaican Slave Society, 1787–1834* (Chicago, 1982), 153–54, 158; Craton, *Testing the Chains*, 301.
13. See David Geggus, 'British Opinion and the Emergence of Haiti, 1791–1805', in James Walvin (ed.), *Slavery and British Society, 1776–1846* (London, 1982), 123–50; Michael Craton, 'Slave Culture, Resistance and the Achievement of Emancipation in the British West Indies, 1783-1838', in J. Walvin (ed.) *Slavery and British Society, 1776–1846* (Macmillan, 1982), 100–123. See also Hilary Beckles, 'Emancipation by War or Law? Wilberforce and the 1816 Barbados Slave Rebellion', in David Richardson (ed.), *Abolition and its Aftermath: The Historical Context, 1790–1916* (London, 1985), 80–105.
14. Eric Williams, *Capitalism and Slavery* (London, 1944), (rpt. 1964), 208.
15. Craton, 'Slave Culture', 122; also 'Proto-Peasant Revolts? The Late Slave Rebellions in the British West Indies, 1816–1832', *Past and Present*, No. 85 (1979), 99–126; 'What and Who to Whom and What: The Significance of Slave Resistance', in Barbara Solow and Stanley Engerman (eds), *British Capitalism and Caribbean Slavery: The Legacy of Eric Williams* (New York, 1987), 259–82.
16. Davis, in *The Problem of Slavery in the Age of Revolution, 1770–1823* (Ithaca, 1975), marginalised the philosophical impact which persistent slave rebellions in the Caribbean had upon English (European) anti-slavery thought, though conceptually this matter would have been critical to the thought of Locke and Hegel, both of whom he dealt with extensively. He attempted to address the matter in a rather peripheral manner by means of an epilogue entitled 'Toussaint L'Ouverture and the Phenomenology of Mind', which does no justice to the historical and philosophical vision of either Toussaint or Hegel. See Roger Anstey's two most impressive works: *The Atlantic Slave Trade and British Abolition, 1769–1810* (London, 1975); 'Parliamentary Reform, Methodism, and Anti-Slavery Politics, 1829–1833', *Slavery and Abolition*, 2:3 (1981), 209–26.
17. Seymour Drescher, *Capitalism and Anti-Slavery: British Mobilisation in Comparative Perspective* (London, 1986), 162.
18. Robin Blackburn, *The Overthrow of Colonial Slavery, 1776–1848* (London, 1988), 35.
19. Richard Hart, 'The Formation of a Caribbean Working Class', *The Black Liberator*, 2:2 (1973/74), 131–48; *Slaves who Abolished Slavery: Vol. 1 Blacks in Bondage* (Kingston, 1980); *Blacks in Rebellion* (Kingston, 1985); *Black Jamaicans' Struggle Against Slavery* (London, 1977); 'Cudjoe and the First Maroon War in Jamaica', *Caribbean Historical Review*, 1 (1950), 46–79.
20. See G. Lewis, *Main Currents*, Chap. 4, for an exciting analysis of Caribbean anti-slavery thought and actions.
21. For an interesting case of Haiti's anti-slavery foreign policy in action, see Richard Sheridan, 'From Jamaican Slavery to Haitian Freedom: The Case of the Black Crew of the Pilot Boat, Deep Nine', *Journal of Negro History*, 67:4 (1982), 328–39. See also David Geggus, 'The Enigma of Jamaica in the 1790s: New Light on the Causes of Slave Rebellions', *William and Mary Quarterly*, 44:2 (1987), 274–79.
22. D. Eltis, 'Abolitionist Perceptions of Society after Slavery', in James Walvin (ed.), *Slavery and British Society*, 202–03.
23. Geggus, 'British Opinion', 127.
24. *Annual Register*, 1802, 210–20.
25. Published in the *Morning Post*, 9 November 1802.
26. Geggus, 'British Opinion', 149.
27. Eric Williams, *British Historians and the West Indies* (Trinidad, 1964), 1–13.
28. For an excellent analysis of this theme, see David Eltis, 'Abolitionist Perceptions of Society after Slavery', 195–214. See also W. A. Green, 'Was British Emancipation a Success? The Abolitionist Perspective', in David Richardson (ed.) *Abolition*, 183–203.
29. Lewis, *Main Currents*, 182.
30. Craton, 'The Passion to Exist', 2.
31. *Ibid.*, p. 18.
32. See Beckles, *Black Rebellion*, 4.
33. Lewis, *Main Currents*, 180.
34. See Sidney Mintz and Douglas Hall, 'The Origins of the Jamaican Internal Marketing System', in this volume.
35. Craton, 'Slave Culture', 118. He further states: 'The chief of these aspirations was, naturally, to be free. Yet the form of that freedom seems to have become visualised as that of an independent peasantry, about which the slaves had quite clear notions and of which, in most cases, they already had considerable experience.'
36. Dirks, *Black Saturnalia*, xvi–xvii.
37. *Ibid.*, 167.
38. *Ibid.*, 171.
39. Richard Sheridan, *Sugar and Slavery: An Economic History of the British West Indies, 1625–1775* (Bridgetown, 1974), 254.

Akan Slave Rebellions in the British Caribbean

MONICA SCHULER

I

It is a well-established fact that African slaves in Western hemisphere societies did not accept their bondage with resignation. Rather, they resisted in a variety of ways. This resistance may be traced back to the very ships which transported Africans across the Atlantic. There, many Africans refused to eat, jumped overboard, refused to take medicine, and on occasion tried to seize control of their floating prisons.[1] In the New World one of the first acts of resistance was suicide.[2] Many undoubtedly managed to come to uneasy terms with their enslavement accommodating themselves as best they could to a regimen of daily toil interspersed with subsistence farming, Sunday market, and occasional holidays at Easter and Christmas. The records show, however, that even within this framework of adjustment most slaves could, and probably did, resist in innumerable and subtle ways. A whole range of misdemeanors was reported which could be considered as day-to-day resistance.[3] These included a display of insolence to overseers, managers and owners, malingering, various types of negligence or outright destruction of property such as ill-treatment of animals, and arson. Slaves sometimes staged work strikes, and frequently stole from their masters. Desertion was chronic. Murder was frequently resorted to, especially by poison.

A more spectacular type of resistance was large-scale armed revolt aimed at the seizure of part or all of a European colony. A major subdivision of this type of insurrection was national or ethnic revolt — an armed uprising dominated by a specific African ethnic group possessed of a clear sense of identity and a set of goals which excluded other groups of slaves. As long as the Atlantic slave trade continued to channel new shipments of black cargo into Western hemisphere ports the main thrust of these rebellions seems to have been toward enabling the slaves to seize territory and escape entirely from the 'system'[4] and to do so primarily along ethnic lines. Thus the slave rebellions discussed in this paper will be grouped into two sections. The first set occupy a rather large time-span, stretching from the seventeenth century until the end of the eighteenth century. The second group of rebellions covers a much shorter period, namely, the first third of the nineteenth century. The British abolition of the slave trade in 1807 is taken as the turning point, as being symbolic of other trends and changes, for the most part originating in Britain, which led slaves to de-emphasize ethnic differences, and to re-orient their resistance to slavery within the framework of the existing system. In this time-period the aim of rebellion seems to have been merely to force local assemblies to carry out changes and improvements in the system which the slaves thought the British monarch and Parliament had ordered. The goal of taking over territory seems to have disappeared for the most part.

Certain ethnic groups appear to have dominated revolts in various New World societies. The Fon and neighbouring groups from Dahomey were pre-eminent in the French colony of Saint Domingue, especially in the opening stages of the great slave rebellion of 1791.[5] In nineteenth-century Brazil a series of abortive revolts in Bahia and its environs were led by the Islamized Hausa people of Northern Nigeria.[6] Bantu-speaking people from the region of the Congo and Angola were often credited with being timid and 'faithful' slaves, but usually in areas where they were outnumbered by other ethnic groups.[7] Evidence from the little island of Montserrat contradicts this

Savacou, Vol. 1, no. 1(June 1970).

stereotype, however. 'You Congo Nigra' is reported to be a common epithet even in twentieth century Montserrat, being employed to describe a proud, pugnacious individual. This correlates with reports of the ethnic exclusiveness, hostility and involvement in rebellious conspiracies of what appears to have been a Bantu-speaking majority.[8] Ethnic exclusiveness might operate in relation in other African-born slaves of other ethnic groups, or it might pit itself against the Creole slaves. The latter, at least until the end of the eighteenth century, might almost be considered as a separate ethnic group for they were born in the New World and had to some extent imbibed the culture of their masters. There is evidence that Creoles considered themselves different from, and perhaps better than, the African-born, to whom they often applied the epithet 'salt-water Negroes.'[9]

The records of slave rebellions from the Virgin Islands to Suriname, from the seventeenth through the nineteenth century, show that the rebel slaves *par excellence* were the Akan and Ga/Adangme speaking peoples who originated in the area of modern Ghana. These are the 'Kormantine' or 'Caromantees,' 'Delminas' or 'Elminas' of the slave traders' and planters' descriptions. The terms Kormantine and Elmina were derived from the names of two trading posts on the Gold Coast of West Africa. There were also local coastal communities bearing these names. The people shipped from these ports were, however, from a number of political units which belonged to two major language groups (Akan and Ga/Adangme) and shared similar culture traits.[10] Once in the New World they were particularly distinguished, especially in the records of slave trials by their belief in obeah — a supernatural force given to man to protect and heal him (the term also refers to the charms which derive their power from this force), and by their Akan day-names.[11]

The question immediately arises: why were the Akan so prominent in the Caribbean and the Guianas? The answer provided by the case of Jamaica, where we find the highest frequency of Akan rebellions is particularly striking. That island saw a steadily increasing influx of Akan slaves from 1655 almost to the very eve of the abolition of the slave trade in 1807. This reflected both a preference of Jamaican planters for Akan slaves as well as the presence on the Gold Coast of British slave traders. But a third factor was even more important — the incidence of wars resulting from state building in that area of West Africa, particularly on the part of the Kingdom of Ashanti during the eighteenth century. This released a flood of war captives as slaves to the West Indies.[12] In his recent study, *The Atlantic Slave Trade: A Census*, Philip Curtin, after analyzing projected exports and imports, concluded that for the period 1751–1790 Jamaica purchased about one fourth of the total British slaves traded in the New World. Of the Gold Coast slaves included in the total British consignment, however, Jamaica purchased as much as eighty per cent.[13] It must be remembered, however, that some of these people may have been re-exported to other territories. A tabie [14] illustrating the Akan importations is most enlightening, for during every time-period for which import figures are given, Akan slaves could be found rebelling in Jamaica:

	1655–1701	1702–25	1726–50	1751–75	1776–91	1792–1807
Gold Coast	5,500	22,300	31,700	67,300	47,100	19,900
%	6.3	34.8	27.1	39.0	38.3	8.1

Only after 1776 were Gold Coast slaves outnumbered by another group, those coming from the Bight of Biafra. This might have contributed to a gradual decline in Akan exclusiveness, but there were other factors as well, which will be discussed in the context of nineteenth century rebellions.

Statistics for other territories are not as detailed; however it is known that the planters of Barbados, during the seventeenth century, tended to buy all their slaves from the Royal African Company, and most of these slaves would thus have come from the Gold Coast. However, the Barbados Assembly later passed a law banning the importation of Akan slaves.[15] Both the Dutch and the Danes held forts for a time on the Gold Coast, hence a portion of the Danish Virgin Island and Dutch Guianese slaves must have come from that area. Importation figures from around 1778 provide a picture of the Dutch and Danish trade that is suggestive for most of the eighteenth century. The Dutch in 1778 purchased 1,500 slaves on the Gold Coast and the same number in the area of Angola. The Danes purchased 1,000 on the Gold Coast and 200 in the Bight of Benin.[16]

What attracted a wide spectrum of planters to Akan slaves? Certainly their abilities as labourers made them most attractive but Governor Christopher Codrington of the Leeward Islands felt there was more to the Akan people than mere brawn. In 1701 he wrote:

> . . . they are not only the best and most faithful of our slaves, but are really all born Heroes. There is a difference between them and all other negroes beyond what 'tis possible for your Lordship to conceive. There

never was a raskal or coward of yt nation, intrepid to the last degree, not a man of them but will stand to be cut to pieces without a sigh or groan, grateful and obedient to a kind master, but implacably revengeful when ill-treated. My father, who had studied the genius and temper of all kinds of negroes 45 years with a very nice observation, would say, Noe man deserved a Coramantoe that would not treat him like a friend rather than a slave, and all my Coramantes preserve that love and veneration for him that they constantly visit his grave, make their libations upon it, hold up their hands to Heaven with violent lamentations and promise when they have done working for his son they will come to him and be his faithful slaves in the other world.[17]

The significance of this encomium is that it formed part of the Governor's report to the Council of Trade and Plantations concerning a minor uprising in 1701 of fifteen new Akan slaves on the property of a Major Martin of Antigua. The only casualty of this short-lived episode was Major Martin himself.[18] The Governor concluded in his report that the Major must have been guilty of 'some unusual act of severity, or rather some indignity' towards his slaves to stir them to such extreme action.[19]

After the occurrence of a number of Akan rebellions in Jamaica a committee of the Assembly of Jamaica recommended around 1760 a bill '... for laying an additional higher duty upon all Fantin, Akim and Ashantee Negroes, and all others commonly called Coromantins.' The planter-legislators, despite their concern over Akan rebelliousness and the subsequent destruction of property, opposed the bill, and it was dropped.[20] This ambivalence of Jamaican planters towards the Akan people is well illustrated by Bryan Edwards, the planter-historian of the West Indies, who gravitated between admiration and detestation of them:

The circumstances which distinguish the Koromantyn, or Gold Coast negroes, from all others, are firmness both of body and mind: a ferociousness of disposition; but withal, activity, courage, and a stubbornness, or what an ancient Roman would have deemed an elevation of soul, which prompts them to enterprizes of difficulty and danger; and enables them to meet death, in its most horrible shape, with fortitude or indifference. They sometimes take to labour with great promptitude and alacrity, and have constitutions well adapted for it; for many of them have undoubtedly been slaves in Africa ....

....

On the other hand ... there cannot be a doubt, that many of the captives taken in battle, and sold in the European settlements, were of free condition in their native country, and perhaps the owners of slaves themselves. It is not wonderful that such men should endeavour, even by means the most desperate, to regain the freedom of which they have been deprived; nor do I consider, that any further circumstances are necessary to prompt them to action, than that of being sold into captivity in a distant country.[21]

Yet Edwards, the planter and property owner whose very livelihood was based on slaveholding, and was threatened in a very tangible way by an Akan rebellion, could not help deploring in strong language the 'savage manner' of the 1760 Akan revolt. But a few pages later he is admiring again, describing the courage of Akan boys when faced with the branding iron, and concluding regretfully:

One cannot surely but lament, that a people thus naturaly amulous and intrepid, should be sunk into so deplorable a state of barbarity and superstition; and that their spirits should ever be broken down by the yoke of slavery! Whatever may be alleged concerning their ferociousness and implacability in their present notions of right and wrong, I am persuaded that they possess qualities, which are capable of, and well deserve cultivation and improvement.[22]

Edward's mixture of approbation and disapproval is probably far more representative of planter views of the Akan than is Christopher Codrington's paean of praise. Both Englishmen seem to have found in the Akan slave the 'noble savage' so dear to men of the eighteenth century. Where the Akan slaves themselves were concerned, this debate about their heroic qualities must surely have seemed rather irrelevant, for it did not alter their status as slaves. Further, most of the evidence suggests that the slaves possessed their own sub-culture, with customs and mores which they determined and controlled. J. Stewart, who lived in Jamaica from 1800 to 1821, described law courts conducted in secret by the slaves. The principals in these courts were the leading plantation slaves. They pronounced decisions on all disputes and complaints of the slaves. Steward, who was sometimes appealed to by the losing parties, found the sentences frequently severe, and sometimes partial and unjust. He tried on several occasions to abolish the courts, but found to his surprise that they were 'countenanced' and desired by the principal negroes and their adherents,' and so they persisted.[23] These peaceful pursuits, involving a recognized and fairly stable leadership, and involving considerable slave co-operation; demonstrate their independent attitude and their industry and initiative in conducting their own affairs in ways not always visible to their masters, and certainly *not* dependant on their approval. Accordingly, the nature of the Akan experience in the New World can best be judged, not by Europeans' opinions of them, but by their folk literature, religious beliefs and practices, economic achievements and skills, and finally by that activity of which historical records speak most frequently, loudly, and eloquently — their resistance to bondage.

II

Jamaica was the scene of the greatest number of Akan-led revolts. When a group of about 300 Akan slaves in the Parish of St. Ann rebelled in 1673 and took to the woods as fugitives,[24] they were certainly not the first to have done so in Jamaica. While the British were driving the Spaniards off the island in the 1650's many Spanish-owned slaves fled to the uninhabited areas. These constituted Jamaica's first Maroon (fugitive slave) communities. The slaves held by the Spaniard's were not likely to have been of Akan origin,[25] however, so the St. Ann rebels were the nucleus of the island's predominantly Akan Maroons.

In 1690 there occurred the next major Akan outburst, on the Sutton estate in the Parish of Clarendon in South Central Jamaica. About 400 slaves set fire to the plantation and escaped into the woods. They were at first content to live in small groups under various leaders, living off neighbouring plantation provision grounds. Their raids on English settlements prompted retaliation, however, and the fugitives decided that unity was necessary. An Akan named Kwadwo was chosen to command them, with his brothers Accompong and Johnny as his immediate subordinates, and with two other men, Kofi and Kwaw as sub-captains. Evantually the Maroons in the east (mainly St. George's Parish) and in Clarendon amalgamated. English attempts to establish new settlements in the northeast were foiled by their attacks. Slaves were in close contact with these Maroons, and the English colonists feared a general slave insurrection. Accordingly the campaign against the Maroons was accelerated. The English brought in Mosquito Indians from Honduras, recruited slave companies (commonly called 'blackshot') as well as free people of color. The Clarendon Maroons, following guerrilla tactics, retreated into the inaccessible Cockpit country of craggy mountains and caves, in Trelawny Parish. Accompong was placed in command of a group of Maroons on the northern boundary of St. Elizabeth Parish. From these superior locations they harassed the parishes of St. James, Hanover, Westmoreland and St. Elizabeth.[26] In time a third Maroon group was established in Hanover in the northwestern part of the island.[27]

Eventually, the island's authorities decided that pacification might be more successful than warfare, and in 1739 succeeded in arranging a treaty with Kwadwo in Trelawny. This Maroon group was granted in perpetuity 1,500 acres of land. The following year a similar treaty was signed wth the Maroons in St. George. They had thus secured official recognition of what was already a *fait accompli* — their freedom. They were forbidden, however, to admit any new runaway slaves into their communities, and agreed to 'take, kill, suppress or destroy' any rebel slaves in the island, either on their own initiative or by command of the Governor of Jamaica. The line of descent of Maroon chiefs or captains was specified, and two Europeans, appointed by the Governor, were to reside with the Maroons and their descendants in order to act as mediators between them and the English settlers.[28] The dominant Akan culture of the Maroons, as well as their promises to discourage runaways and prevent slave rebellions were to prove significant in relation to the Akan slave revolte which now followed.

In 1742, recently arrived Akan slaves on the Forster estate, situated in either St. James or Trelawny, formulated a plot to revolt. The plan, according to later testimony, hinged on the participation of Akan Maroons. Participants later revealed that they envisaged the Akan Maroons murdering all blacks born in the woods (Creoles), or who belonged to other ethnic groups. In turn, the plotters, together with African-born Akan of other plantations, would murder all the white people and join their Maroon compatriots in the wilds. The plans did not mature completely, however, and when the Forster slaves rose up, they were not joined by their Maroon countrymen. Instead, Colonel Kwadwo and Captain Accompong of the Trelawny Town Maroons armed some of their subjects and, in accordance with the terms of their recent treaty, attacked the rebels, killed some, captured others, and drove the rest back to their respective plantations. They also meted out similar treatment to a number of Maroons suspected of conspiring with the slaves.[29]

In 1745, according to information divulged by Deborah, a slave woman who feared for the life of the English child in her care, 900 slaves had been planning an uprising in St. David's Parish, during which they intended in murdering all the whites in the area. Conspiracies ought to be considered quite apart from actual insurrections, but on this occasion some slaves did rebel after the accusations of Deborah had been made. They killed an Englishman and four women in the vicinity of Bull Bay. They then retreated to Yallahs, further east, where they killed another English settler, stole arms and ammunition, and headed for the hills. More than a week elapsed before a search party could be equipped to pursue them. In a settlement above some falls on the Banana River they were finally trapped and defeated. Among those killed were two men described as 'negro captains'. Nine guns, ammunition and other stolen goods were seized.[30]

It was never an easy matter to single out the ringleaders in a slave rebellion, let alone one that did not get far past the conspiracy stage. The authorities made it easier for themselves by allowing the testimony of a single slave woman to condemn 11 slaves to transportation off the island (one of whom was a woman), and 3 to execution. In all 10 slave men were executed. Among these 10 there were 7 owners represented; among the 11 transported, 9 owners. Thus the conspiracy must have been fairly extensive. A number of the slaves listed as executed or banished had Akan day-names such as Kweku, Kofi, and Abena. Another was named Accra, showing, Gold Coast origin. There is no other evidence, however, that the rebellion was a specifically Akan one. Nevertheless, if as many as 900 slaves were originally involved in the plot, it is likely that the Akan were the most prominent.[31]

In 1760 the neighboring plantations of Trinity and Frontier in St. Mary's Parish, Jamaica, owned by Zachary Bayly and Ballard Beckford, respectively, acquired between them more than one hundred Gold Coast slaves. Bayly visited Trinity just before Easter to inspect his new Akan slaves and to distribute to them in person new clothing and knives. A rebellion broke out on Easter Sunday, beginning on Beckford's Frontier and Whitehall plantations, Bayly's Trinity, and a fourth estate, Heywood Hall.[32] But the rising was not limited to St. Mary's parish. Open rebellion or conspiracy was rife in Westmoreland, St. John, St. Thomas-in-the-East, St. James, Clarendon, St. Dorothy and in the city of Kingston. In all these places the finger of guilt pointed to the Akan slaves.

The various parish risings were apparently not intended to be simultaneous. St. Mary was to be the starting point, possibly because there were not many British people in the parish; it had extensive wooded areas, and a good supply of food. These factors might provide that initial success which could pursuade other parishes to join. The aim of the enterprise was supposed to be 'the entire extirpation of the white inhabitants; the enslaving of all such Negroes as might refuse to join them; and the partition of the island into small principalities in the African mode; to be distributed among their leaders and men.'[33] On May 25, 1760 Westmoreland became the second theatre of war in the Akan rebellion. A detachment of the 49th Regiment, the militia, and a group of Maroons, marched against the Westmoreland revels. The troops eventually routed them, killed many and took other prisoners. Many rebels committed suicide.[34]

While Westmoreland was in arms, risings occurred and conspiracies were discovered in other areas. An unusual aspect of the conspiracy in Kingston was the discovery of the 'Queen of Kingston.' She was Abena, an Akan slave belonging to a Kingston Jewess. Abena presided at secret meetings of the Akan conspirators in Kingston, sitting in state under a canopy, a robe around her shoulders, a crown on her head. Women are not often mentioned in the records of these revolts, but from those few whose names do enter history, we may infer that they played an active and important role. Was Abena cast in the role of a traditional Akan Queen-Mother? The only other information we possess about her is that she was ordered to be banished to Cuba, but managed to return and go into hiding. She was discovered, however, and this time her fate was execution. Also in Kingston a wooden sword was discovered 'of a peculiar structure, with a red feather stuck in the handle.' This was apparently to be used as a war signal.[35]

The process of quelling all the rebellious slaves was a long-drawn-out affair. In St. Mary it took the death of Tacky, the leader in that parish, to dishearten the rebels. Tacky was felled by the bullets of a Maroon who also killed Jamaica, another leader. The survivors of this encounter moved away a distance of about two miles to a cave, and there committed suicide — an end considered the only honourable one for Ashanti military commanders, and certainly preferable to capture. Later on, in the final stages of resistance in St. James and Westmoreland, the milita told of coming upon spots in the woods where seven or eight rebels could be found hanging from trees.[36] It is impossible to say whether these were the suicides of men who considered themselves primarily as slaves, or as Akan warriors. This rebellion is well-documented, and the details inadvertently recorded by Europeans certainly demonstrate many Akan, and perhaps even Ashanti, traits.

The role of the obeah man in the Akan slave rebellions, for instance, is very like the role of priests and magicians in Ashanti military campaigns. Before a military campaign the principal commanders of the Ashanti army met with the priests at night and participated in a ceremony designed to weaken the enemy each time it was repeated. Priests also recommended propitious days for advancing and attacking, usually after consulting oracles. Individual soldiers and companies also had recourse to magic. Each company had a shrine and a priest of its own. The priests (*esamankwafa*) also accompanied the soldiers on their campaigns and provided them with protective charms and amulets, some of which were believed to make their wearers invulnerable to bullets. Oaths were administered by these priets at the outset of war:

> Ashanti commanders in chief swore, as the original Osci Tutu had done, to pursue the war vigorously, not retreat, and to return the state sword encrusted with the blood of the enemy. The force of this oath was such that, rather than return to Kumasi a failure, defeated commanders might blow up themselves and their regalia with a barrel of powder.[37]

An obeah man was discovered among the rebels during the 1760 insurrection and Edward Long, the planter-historian of Jamaica, has left us a description of his appearance and his function:

> He was an old Coromantin, who, with others of his profession, had been a chief in counselling and instigating the credulous herd, to whom these priests administered a powder, which, being rubbed on their bodies was to make them invulnerable; they persuaded them into a belief that Tacky, their generalissimo in the woods, could not possibly be hurt by the white men, for that he caught all the bullets fired at him in his hand, and hurried them back with destruction to his foes. This old impostor was caught whilst he was tricked up with all his feathers, teeth, and other implements of magic, and in this attire suffered military execution by hanging . . .[38]

The solemn religious oath administered by the obeah man was administered in the following manner:

> Into a quantity of rum, with which some gunpowder and dirt taken from a grave had been mingled, blood was put, drawn in succession from the arm of each confederate. With certain . . . ceremonies this cup was drunk from by each person, and then came the council.[39]

So powerful was this oath that it was considered to be binding for life. When the 1760 rebellion was finally over, several of the oath takers managed to escape punishment and bided their time. Five years later another explosion rocked St. Mary's parish and many of the same plantations which had been involved in the 1760 affair. Many future Akan revolts were to exhibit, in differing degrees, the same cultural features as those just described.

III

At the beginning of 1763 the Dutch South American colony of Berbice was a small, relatively young settlement consisting of about 346 Europeans, 3,833 African and 244 Amerindian slaves. There were 84 privately-owned plantations, and a smaller number belonging to the Directors of the Berbice Company, proprietors of the colony. Most of the black slaves were employed by the privately-owned plantations. The colony was surrounded by communities of free Amerindians. Dutch policy dictated that the Indians were to be left alone and not to be ill-treated by the planters. The Indian slaves previously mentioned were an exception since they were war captives who originated in the far interior. Dutch Indian policy paid off handsomely in terms of trade and also in time of slave rebellion, for the Indians could generally be counted on to help subdue rebellious slaves.[40]

The situation of the Europeans along the Canje, Courentyne and Berbice rivers was much more precarious than even the slave-white ratio of 11:1 suggests. Wooden forts were rotting; arms and ammunition were in short supply; illness had sapped the strength of many. A mere handful of soldiers, mercenaries from many nations who had a history of mutinies, plus the sickly burgher militia, were the only defenders of the colony.[41] Berbice Company officials were poorly paid and undependable. The attitude of the whole lot — planters, soldiers and officials — can be summed up in the remark of the Governor's secretary shortly after the slaves revolted in February: 'I can't get enough for myself and wife, and don't feel bound to stand here and be shot at for twenty guilders a month.'[42] The situation in the neighboring colonies of Demerara and Essequibo was not much better. It is not surprising, then, that Berbice was wracked by a series of slave uprisings from 1733 through 1762. On February 23, 1763 there broke out a rebellion which seemed the culmination of all of these, and which came very close to success.

The rising began on Plantation Magdelenenburg on the Canje river. The slaves murdered the manager and the carpenter and then moved on to La Providence, a neighboring plantation. Ten slaves joined them and, after plundering the manager's house, the rebels crossed to the other side of the river. Apparently this group had planned to escape overland to the Courentyne river, and thence into the colony of Suriname. The contagion spread, however, and by early March the slaves had revolted on other estates on the Canje and Berbice rivers. Insurgents passed from one plantation to another, murdering some Europeans, imprisoning others, and driving even more as refugees in a painful retreat down river to the coast, or else overland to Demerara.[43] The rebellious slaves held the offensive from February to November of 1763. In November the tide turned with the arrival of European forces from abroad. Expeditions advanced up the rivers in November and December, scattering the rebels, engaging some in battle. Mopping-up operations, punishment, trials and executions occupied the months from January to June, 1764.

The roster of rebel leaders gives some clue to the ethnic rivalry and disunity which eventually undermined the initially superior position of the insurgents. At the top was Kofi or Cuffy, an Akan who, with his 'Captain' Accra, came from the Barkey estate, (Lillenburg) on the Berbice river. This plantation alone provided four rebel leaders. Kofi was elected headman or governor and in turn he appointed others as his officers. His background was typical of many other slave leaders. He had arrived in Berbice as a boy. He showed some talent and his owner first employed him as a domestic servant and then taught him the coopering trade. Kofi lived with a certain degree of style as Governor of the Berbice rebels. He lodged in the Council House at Fort Nassau, guarded by two cannon set in the doorway. He was waited upon by a mulatto captive. Amidst the posturing and parading of the newly victorious slaves, Kofi struck a practical and moderate note. He assigned some of the rebels to harvest the sugar cane and to make rum. This led to complaints that life under the new regime was no different from life under the old. Nevertheless, in the first flush of victory, the rebels managed to have a good time. According to one rather sour European report, they

> spent most of their time in revelry, debauchery and drink, dressing themselves up in the clothes which they found on plantations; over and above that, painting their faces as was their wont and imitating the planters for the rest. They had themselves rowed about in tentboats and called their wives 'madam', sleeping in cotton hammocks, fastidious in their eating and drinking . . .[44]

From Kofi's headquarters there issued a series of fascinating letters to Governor Hoogenheim. Kofi used white prisoners, the rebel slave, Prince, and Suriname mercenaries who had mutinied and been forced to join the rebels, as secretaries. The messengers who delivered the letters included Indians and freed captives. The first of these letters reached Governor Hoogenheim in March, 1768. The first letter warned the Governor to depart immediately for Holland, to leave all slaves behind, and also outlined the cause of the rebellion. The second letter was milder and more compromising, but still firm:

> Coffy, Governor of the Negroes of Berbice and Captain Akkara send their greetings to Your late Honourable. We don't want war: we see clearly that you do want war.
>
> Barkey and his servant de Graaf, Schook, Dell van Lentzing and Frederick Botgen, but more especially Mr. Barkey and his servant, and de Graaf, are the principal originators of the riot which occurred in Berbice. The Governor [Kofi] was present when it commenced, and was very angry at it. The Governor of Berbice asks Your Honour that Your Honour will come and speak with him; don't be afraid: but if you won't come, we will fight as long as one Christian remains in Berbice. The Governor will give your Honour half of Berbice and all the negroes will go high up the river, but don't think they will remain slaves. Those negroes that your honour has on the ships, they can remain slav.s. The Governor greets your Honour.[45]

The Indians brought other letters from Kofi. With the third letter he sent the Governor a present of a pair of gold shoe buckles, and a verbal message to the effect that he 'was sorry the Governor also had to suffer because of those whom the negroes had treated so badly, but that they were fond of him and wished him no harm.' In this letter also appeared the first indication that Kofi's power and his desire for restraint were being challenged. He had no evil aims, he reassured the Governor, but his followers were bitter and would not rest until the Europeans were destroyed.[46]

Kofi's sun was already sinking before the last of his letters, dated July 1763, reached Governor Hoogenheim. Back in May, the rebels, ignoring Kofi's wishes, began planning an attack on Daargradt, the last major planter outpost. Discord reached such a peak that Kofi's opponents set up another Governor, Atta, also an Akan. A struggle now broke out in May and June 1763 between Atta and Kofi, and many of the latter's supporters were killed. Kofi, in traditional Akan fashion, saw no way open for him but death. He had a small amount of gunpowder hidden, and rather than let things get into the hands of his rivals, he had it buried, and then himself killed the man who carried out the task. He then shot himself. Two Europeans were reportedly sacrificed on his grave. Accra, who had broken with him, was not allowed to share Atta's triumph, however, for he was reduced to the status of a slave for the ruling group. He was later to give himself up to the Dutch and offered to hunt down other rebels in return for his freedom.

A whole new power structure came into being with Atta's supremacy. It continued to be primarily Akan however. He appointed various subordinate officers — Kweku, Baube and Accabre, Kees, Goussari, Fortuin, Kwabena and others. There is no evidence that Atta ever tried to contact Governor Hoogenheim. He was a warlike leader, and succeeded in inspiring his followers with courage. When Captain von Oyen later led an attack against Atta's forces they returned his fire boldly, continuously shouting their war cry which was simply 'Atta! Atta!'[47]

Accabre was apparently an important leader too. He was described as 'a fine and well proportioned fellow with the bearing of a prince.' His ethnic origin is something of a puzzle. He was an obeah man, and after Kofi's death was chosen as chief of 600 Bantu-speaking rebels.[48] It is doubtful that an Akan obeah man would be accepted as leader of Bantu people, so he may have been Bantu-speaking. Baube, who was appointed a chief by Atta, was at the head of a group of Bantu-speaking rebels known as the 'Guango'. These people were often accused of cannibalism by Akan slaves in Guyana and Suriname.[49] They may well have been the Imbangala from what is now Angola. They had been moving into the area of the Kwanza and Kwango rivers over a period of years, and the Portuguese encountered them in the late sixteenth century. 'Guango' seems to be a rendering of 'Kwango.' The Imhangala were known as a fierce group of marauders. They seemed to operate as slave traders, but it is not unlikely that many may have been captured in war and sold as slaves. According to Birmingham,

> They lived entirely from plunder and raised neither cattle nor crops of their own. To make them more mobile in their campaigns the Imbangala did not rear their children but killed them at birth and adopted adolescents from among their defeated enemies. They appear to have been genuinely cannibal in their eating habits and did not, like some other peoples, eat human flesh primarily for the spiritual strength which it might give. Their chief luxury was palm wine and they travelled far and wide over Angola to obtain a plentiful supply. One Imbangala troop reached the coast south of the Kwanza river and sold twenty slaves to Andrew Buttell, an Englishman who spent twenty years in Angola as a captive of the Portuguese.[50]

Kofi's death seems to indicate the point at which disunity took over among the rebels. Certainly the reports of rivalry among Akan leaders suggest this. Also, the mention of two groups of Bantu-speaking slaves fighting as separate units suggests the extent to which ethnic groups maintained their separatism in this rebellion. Specific reports said that 'the Delmina slaves played the master, having either murdered most of the Angola slaves or hunted them into the bush and had forced the Creole into their service.' Creole slaves later accused the Africans of having tempted them to rebel, and they threatened to put both Kofi and Accra to death. The Africans kept an eye on the Creoles, and would not give them any positions of leadership. Most of the Creoles seem to have belonged to Berbice Company plantations as if the Company had deliberately chosen to stock its properties with the least rebellious type of slaves. Many of these Company slaves openly resisted the rebels, but were finally forced to submit to their superior strength. In addition, there is evidence that there was not much *rapport* between the Canje and the Berbice rebels. As the Dutch were regaining control of the colony, a number of Canje rebels crossed over to the Berbice area but found only hostility from their fellow rebels. A struggle ensued and many Canje people were killed.[51]

Some of this internal strife may be accounted for by the fact that as the pressure from Dutch troops mounted, the slaves were becoming desperate. Their flight ahead of Dutch troops was disorderly. Their weapons were depleted, and hunger was everywhere, making tempers short. Atta no longer commanded all the rebels and apparently held in subjugation a number of reluctant slaves from several plantations. Six rebels were found decapitated on Plantation Debora. Sometimes as many as 60 rebels at a time surrendered to a much smaller group of soldiers. Accra and Goussari, the turncoats, brought in 30 to 40 rebels at a time, including, finally, Atta himself.[52] By February 1764, an exact year after the rebellion started, the first Court of Criminal Justice sat in judgment of the rebels.

IV

Two noteworthy conspiracies to rebel were discovered on the islands of Antigua and S. Croix, Virgin Islands in the eighteenth century which merit attention for a number of reasons. First of all, they are rather well documented as conspiracies go; secondly, Akan slaves were involved; and thirdly, because two of the Antigua conspirators were banished to St. Croix and became involved in the St. Croix conspiracy, the two plots are linked, if only accidentally.

The Antiguan conspiracy, discovered in 1736,[53] involved two types of slaves — Akan and Creole — a combination that was most unpromising in the early eighteenth century. Both groups had leaders drawn from slaves who were skilled artisans, drivers and domestic servants. The two main leaders were Court, an Akan who had been brought to Antigua as a boy of ten, and who was though to be 'of a considerable family in this own country . . . and covertly assumed among his countrymen here the title of king,' and Tomboy, a Creole master-carpenter. Other Creoles involved in the plot were Hercules, Jack, Scipio, Ned, Fortune, Toney, and two French Creole slaves, Secundy and Jacko.

The plotting seems to have started around November 1735. It was carried out, as in so many other cases, under cover of dancing and feasting. On various such occasions numbers of slaves took the traditional Akan oath 'by drinking a health in liquor with grave-dirt and sometimes cock's blood infused, and sometimes the person swearing laid his hand on a live cock.' One man is supposed to have taken the oath at the house of John Obia, from his surname, an obeah man, although the oath was said to have been administered by Secundy. The general aim of the conspiracy was to murder the Europeans, seize control of the island, and set up a new government with Court, the Akan, as king. It is on this point that the customary rivalry between the Akan and the Creoles asserted itself. The suggestion was made during the investigation of the conspiracy that the Creoles planned to control the new regime themselves, and to make slaves of the Akan, an interesting reversal of the usual Creole-Akan roles. There is also evidence that the Akan themselves planned to retain control of the movement. A detailed report was given of a dance which was performed on October 3, 1736 as the organisation of the rebellion was being finalised. This was an *ikem* dance, purportedly a military ceremonial of the Akan. The English judges discovered from the slaves that

> It is the custom of Africa when a coromantee king has resolved on war to give public notice that the ikem-dance will be performed. The king appears at the place appointed under a canopy with his officers of state, guards and music, the people forming a semicircle about him. The king then begins the dance, carrying an ikem or shield of wicker and a lance: when fatigued, he delivers the ikem to the next dancer. When several have danced, the king dances again with his general and swears an oath to behave as a brave prince should or forfeit his life. If he is answered by three huzzas from these present it signifies a belief that the king will observe his oath and an engagement to join him in the war.

This, then, was the dance which Court performed on that October day. The Akan slaves cheered three times, knowing, as the Creoles apparently did not, the meaning of the ritual. Some other Akan slaves apparently tried to stop the performance, but their reason for doing so is not clear.

The action to which this ceremony committed Court and his followers was this: Tomboy, the Creole leader and master-carpenter, was to contract with the Europeans concerned to make the seats for a grand ball to be held on October 11, and to be attended by the island's best families. Gunpowder was to be placed in strategic places in the building and set off during the ball. Then three or four groups consisting of 300 to 400 slaves each were to enter the town and massacre the Europeans. Simultaneously the forts and all ships in the harbor were to be seized. Unfortunately for the conspirators, the ball was postponed until October 30. An agrument ensued in which some slaves insisted on going ahead with the rebellion as planned. Court, however, persuaded them to wait for the end of the month. By this time the activities of the conspirators began to attract attention, an inquiry was ordered, and the plot exposed.

Initially twelve slaves were executed, but this did not deter the other conspirators. It was reported that at least fifty more slaves took the oath to rebel after the execution of the twelve on October 26. Thereafter, thirty-five more slaves were executed and forty-two banished. Two slaves fled, and four free people of color were imprisoned, awaiting execution for their supposed part in the conspiracy. The prompt action of the courts in making an example of the plotters reflected the insecurity of the European residents. There were a total of 24,000 slaves in a colony of only 8,000 Europeans who had only a small force of regular soldiers and a poorly-armed militia to defend them.[54] The conspirators were their most trusted slaves.

Apparently at least two conspirators were banished to St. Croix, a small island purchased by the Danes from the French in 1734. One of these exiles was Sam Hector whose Akan day-name was Kwaw. He had been between eighteen and twenty years old when transported. His father had been accused of participating in the 1736 conspiracy, and Kwaw had turned King's evidence against him, helping to send him to his death by hanging. Kwaw could read and write, an unusual accomplishment for a slave in those days. The other exile was George Foot who had also testified against his father, Jupiter. He claimed that his father had tried to coerce him into joining the conspirators, and had punished him severely when he refused. Jupiter was burned at the stake as a rebel.[55] Precisely why these two took part in the conspiracy which occurred on St. Croix, in 1750 is not known. Perhaps they were bitter that they had not been better rewarded for turning King's evidence in Antigua, or perhaps they regretted having turned against their fathers.

The blacks on St. Croix outnumbered the Europeans 7:1. Most of them were slaves, and most of the slaves were African-born. In 1746 there had been a short-lived slave rebellion. The slaves showed considerable restlessness thereafter. St. Croix was in a poor state of defence. The forts were flimsy structures. Their cannon did not work. The soldiers were on starvation rations and were consequently apathetic.[56] It is not surprising, then, that some slaves should have decided to take advantage of the situation.

A free black, William Davis and three slaves, Kwaw (Sam Hector), Kewku, another Akan, and Michel, seem to have been the leaders. The rising was set for the Christmas holidays of 1759. The slaves were to kill their masters and overseers and seize what guns and ammunition they could find. They were to form into two groups. Near Christianstaed they were to assemble under Kewku's command. In the west they were to assemble at Fort Friderlchswaern and, under Kwaw's command, seize the fort and its ammunition. Christianstead and Christianswaern were then to be attacked in succession. After the island was taken William Davis was to become Governor General, Michel second-in-command, and Kwaw Captain of Christianstead. The conspirators were bound by the familiar oath. An unusual aspect of this one was the swearing 'By Jesus, I will,' after swallowing the grave dirt.[57]

The oath signified a vow of secrecy, but someone was indiscreet. The governor ordered an investigation. Kwame, an Akan voluntarily testified that Kwadwo, another Akan, had spoken of revolt in his presence. Kwadwo eventually conceded that William Davis had broached the subject of rebellion some days earlier. He also named a number of others who were involved in the conspiracy. Davis made a full confession, was imprisoned, and committed suicide in his cell. Ten slaves with Akan names were brought to trial. In all, thirteen men were executed and, following a familiar pattern, ten were transported.[58]

V

By the early nineteenth century, the pattern of revolts was changing. The slaves seemed more interested now in redefining their position within the system. Perhaps this was because the system seemed to promise changes for the better. Slave uprisings did not cease, but their causes, organization, goals and methods changed; and the ethnic exclusivism which had focused attention on the Akan people in previous centuries seemed to decline, although Akan participation in rebellions did not itself decline.

In British territories such as Barbados and Jamaica, and the recently acquired colonies of Demerara and Essequibo, the advent of Protestant sectarian missionaries to work among the slaves, the news of the British Abolitionist movement, and its influence on Parliament, introduced new and disturbing elements — disturbing, that is, from the viewpoint of the planters, but hopeful from the viewpoint of the slaves. The London Missionary Society was established in Demerara in 1808 at the invitation of a Dutch-born planter. Hermanus Post, who built Bethel Chapel on his plantation, Le Resouvenir.[59] After initial failures the Methodists succeeded in settling an English missionary in Demerara in 1814. Both denominations drew most of their converts from among free people of color and slaves. They made rapid progress, but not without considerable opposition from Governors as well as planters. Missionary activity developed in like manner in Jamaica, the Methodists and Baptists were predominating, and in Barbados and Trinidad . The British government protected these Protestant dissenters as best it could fom a distance, disallowing colonial laws which hindered their activities.[60] The missionaries, in turn, tried to do their Christian duty to the slaves without offending the planters. London Missionary Society instructions, for example, exhorted the preacher to 'inculcate religious doctrine on the minds of the slaves, without exhibiting to them views of referring to their lot in society''[61] — a difficult, if not impossible task. Colonial governors were openly sceptical that this mission could be performed without prejudice to the security of their slave colonies. Governor Woodford of Trinidad singled out a significant aspect of the missionaries' work when he complained that they allowed the slaves to preach.[62] The hallmark of the L.M.S. Baptists and Methodists was that they developed new forms of leadership among the slaves, based on their own Church government — the system of elders, deacons, class leaders (catechists), etc. was common to all these sects, and slaves who qualified were chosen for these responsible positions.[63] It often developed that slaves who were already distinguished on the plantations as skilled workers became Church leaders.

In 1807 the abolitionists won an important victory with the passage of a bill to abolish the British slave trade. Measures for the closer regulation of slavery and also for its amelioration followed. In 1815 a Bill was introduced in the House of Commons to establish a Registry of slaves in all slave colonies. William Wilberforce published his 'Appeal to the Religion, Justice and Humanity of the Inhabitants of the British Empire, in behalf of the Negro slaves in the West Indies' in March, 1823. The Anti-Slavery Society was also founded at this time, and Thomas F. Buxton's motion, introduced in Parliament on May 15, 1823, advocated the gradual abolition of slavery.[64] On May 28, 1823. Bathurst issued an Order in Council prescribing measures for the amelioration of the conditions of slavery in Crown Colonies. The despatch prohibited the flogging of slave women, the use of the whip by slave drivers, and limited the working day to nine hours.[65]

These events were widely discussed in the colonies — in the legislative assemblies, at the dinner table, sometimes in church, in the street, in slave huts. Precisely what the slaves made of it all is not too clear. They seemed to understand that ultimately it was their freedom which was being debated. Many do not seem to have distinguished between such concepts as registration, amelioration and emancipation. Thus, in July, 1812, Governor Carmichael reported to England that the slaves on several Demerara plantations 'Had shown a disposition of insubordination and in some cases had taken to the woods and formed camps of runaways . . . '. An anonymous white man was reported to have gone among the various estates announcing that 'the Prince Regent had sent out orders to give freedom to the slaves and arm them in their own defence.'[66] The report is vaguely written, but the premature expectation of emancipating, the feeling that the monarch was on their side — these are common elements of nineteenth century slave unrest in British colonies.

A similar event took place in Barbados on Easter Sunday, April 14, 1816, a few months after the debate on the Registry Bill. This was a short-lived but fierce armed rebellion.[67] Several free men of color were implicated, and accused of telling the slaves that 'a law was being passed in England to make them free, and that as the King was giving them their freedom the king's troops would not be employed against them.' The First West India Regiment captured a flag from the rebels, bearing the 'figure of a general officer (supposed to be intended for the King), placing a crown in the hands of a negro who had a white woman on his arm. Beneath these figures was the following motto: "Brittanic are happy to assist all such friends as endeavourance."' Lieutanent-Colonel Edward Codd, commander of the Barbadian militia wrote to the Lieutenant Governor of the island that he was convinced, after interrogating slaves, that the main cause of the rebellion was the slaves' misunderstanding of the intention of the Slave Registry Bill. There is no firm evidence that the slaves in Barbados intended to do more than force the planters to give them their freedom. The Barbados rebellion seems to have been part of a new pattern of rebellions which became less and less violent as time went by — rebellions characterized by public demonstration aimed at forcing local governing assemblies to implement reforms which were suspected by the slaves of having been ordered by Great Britain.

The rebellions in Demerara in 1829 and Jamaica in 1831 both began as versions of the modern work strike, coupled with other acts of defiance, but not with killing. Only when the local militia retaliated with force, assuming that this was another armed uprising, did such an occurrence actually take place.[68] In Demerara a number of Akan slaves were involved, chief among them being a father and son, Kwame and Jack, both of Success Plantation. Slaves mentioned their ethnic origin during the trials, but casually, as if it were not very important. Many of the Akan who were involved had been in the colony for some time. Others, like Jack, were second generation Akan, and hence really Creoles. Slaves of other ethnic groups were invited to join the movement. Kwame was the First Deacon of Bethel Chapel. Many of the participants were members of this Chapel. The records of the Jamaican rebellion do not speak of ethnic origins — for almost the first time in the history of Jamaican slave rebellions. This rising was known as the Baptist War,[69] and it is clear that both Demerara and Jamaica, the slave had detached the L.M.S. and Baptist church organizations from missionary control, and used them as organizations of social protest. If anything, a 'creolization' of slave protest had taken place, and slaves seemed anxious to find a better place for themselves *within* the traditional plantation society of their respective territories.

The aims of these two rebellions were somewhat confused, but suggestive, nevertheless, of the changed nature of slave rebellion. Governor Murray of Demerara went among the rebels at Plantation Le Resouvenir and tried to pacify them by explaining the contents of Bathurst's directive to the Court of Policy which had apparently touched off the rebellion. Murray promised them amelioration, 'But they declared they would be free.'[70] Lieutenant Colonel Leahy testified that at Plantation Bachelor's Adventure where he spoke to some of the rebels,

> The negroes spoke differently as to what they wanted; some wanted three days [to farm their provision grounds] and the Sunday to go to church; some wanted two days, and the Sunday to go to church; some said they wanted their freedom; and some wanted to tie me up... In half-an-hour afterwards... I wanted to know the reason why they did not lay down their arms, but the people who then came to me, said they wanted to be free...[71]

Militiaman John Croal spoke to Jack of Success Plantation, one fo the leaders:

> ... he said he thought it was very hard for the negroes to work all the week, and have not ime for themselves, and that he wished for Saturday; some other negroes called out they wanted three days... before I turned my horse to go away I said to Jack, then your demand is for Saturday; he said yes.[72]

In the case of the Baptist War in Jamaica, Samuel Sharp, one of the prime leaders, deliberately set the slaves to thinking about gaining freedom, although his most immediate aim seems to have been to organize a strike for wages.[73] It may well be, however, that he actually believed the rumours which he spread. The time of emancipation was, after all, very near. European planters in the West Indies and the Guianas had their own ideas as to what constituted a slave insurrection. They could not be counted on to see the difference between a full-blown insurrection of the Saint-Domingue type and a strike or non-violent demonstration. This was probably asking too much of them. After all, the strike was not as yet an accepted weapon of the English working class.

VI

The desire for freedom, then, inspired the majority of Akan slaves to rebel, but it also persuaded some of them that collaboration was a surer way to attain that freedom. The tensions in slave communities must have been, as a result, too sharp, perhaps, to allow for many successful armed revolts.

A number of factors were necessary for success. A prerequisite was European weakness, especially if aggravated by preoccupation with problems in the mother country; shrewd leaders; rugged terrain; superior tactics, in particular, gurerrilla warfare; and allies such as Maroons were necessary. Undoubtedly the most important factor was a large number of rebels united at least in their determination to fight a long war to the bitter end. In this respect the determination of the Akan to wage ethnic rebellions often militated against unity, for wherever there were non-Akan minorities there were spies in their midst. In addition, the dependence on religious factors such as charms, spells and so forth to guarantee invincibility meant that once a leader had been proved vulnerable through death, then the whole structure of rebellion might crumble.

There was also, as we have seen, discussion among the Akan themselves. Ethnic slave rebellion, therefore, although persistent, and in many cases spectacular, in terms of initial surprise and success, were not effective in the long run. They were, however, most representative of the manner in which men who were still African in culture and loyalties attempted to free themselves from bondage in the West Indies and the Guianas up to the end of the eighteenth century.

Perhaps however, only in the seventeenth and eighteenth centuries, when European colonies were weak, could the Akan have hoped to gain their freedom through armed revolt as the

Maroons had done. By the time they had dispensed with their ethnic pride and seen the value of inter-ethnic co-operation, in the first third of the nineteenth century, European strength had apparently increased to such a stage that rebellions could be coped with, if not easily, then adequately. Ultimately it was an Act of Parliament, and not an act of rebellion, which brought freedom. An act of Parliament in 1833 could do nothing of course, for all those thousands who had endured slavery in earlier centuries and who had died in desperate tries for freedom. It is not surprising, then, that the Akan over the years should have preferred to place their faith in self-help, and continued to do so even after the conscience of Europe, and its economic interests, worked to end the enslavement of Africans.

Notes

1. Melville J. Herskovits, The Myth of the Negro Past (Boston, 1964), pp. 87–89.
2. See J. Bennett, Bondsmen and Bishops: Slavery and Apprenticeship on the Codrington Plantations of Barbados, 1710–1836 (Berkeley, 1958), p. 49; also Richard Ligon, A True and Exact History of the Island of Barbados (London, 1873), p. 50; and Herskovits, *op. cit.*, pp. 36, 95.
3. For examples of day-to-day resistance see William Dickson, Letters on Slavery . . . to which are Added, Address to the Whites, and to the Free Negroes of Barbadoes and Accounts of Some Negroes Eminent for their Virtues and Abilities (London, 1789), pp. 10, 18–19, 20, 35, 41, 42, 56–57. For the slaves' knowledge and use of poisons see L. Peytraud, L'esclavage aux Antilles francaises avant 1789, d'après des documents inedits des archives colonies (Paris, 1897), pp. 315–22, 325, 334.
4. The 'system' may be defined as plantation colonies controlled by a European nation and by European planters employing forced labor.
5. See C. L. R. James, The Black Jacobins; Toussaint L'Overture and the San Domingo Revolution (2nd edn, revised; New York, 1963); also Herskovits, *op. cit.*, 34–53.
6. Raymond Kent, 'A Revolt in Bahia, January 24–25, 1835'. Unpublished paper, The University of Wisconsin, Madison, 1963.
7. Melville J. Herskovits, Life in a Haitian Valley (New York, 1937), p. 21.
8. John C. Messenger, 'The Influence of the Irish in Montserrat', Caribbean Quaterly, No. 2 (June, 1967), 16.
9. See Edward Long, The History of Jamaica 3 vols (London, 1 774), pp. 411; also Raymond T. Smith, British Guiana (London, 1964), p. 29.
10. See Madeline Manourian, Akan and Gu-Adangme Peoples, Daryll Forde (ed.) Ethnographic Survey of Africa, Western Africa, Part 1 (London, 1964), Hereafter the term 'Akan' will be used wherever 'Akan and Ga-Adangme' are intended.
11. The list of Akan day-names is taken from W. T. Balmer and F. C. F. Grant, A Grammar of the Fante-Akan Language (London, 1929), p. 64. The West Indian versions of these names are taken from Frank Wesley Pitman, 'Slavery on British West India Plantations in the Eighteenth Century', in Journal of Negro History, XI, No. 4 (October, 1916), 641. Pitman does not seem to have been completely accurate, however, and changes have been made where they seemed called for by other evidence.

Born on	Masculine	Common Form	Feminine	Common Form	W. Indian Version Masc.	Fem.
Sun: Kwesida	Kwies		Esi, Akwesiwa	Akosuwa	Quashy	Quashiba
Mon: Dwowda	Kwadwo	Kodwo	Adowa		Cudjo	Juba
Tue: Benada	Kwabana	Kubena	Abenaba, Abena	Araba	Cubena	Cuba, Bennio
Wed: Wukuda	Kweku		Ekuwa		Quaco	
Thu: Yawda	Kwaw, Kwaa		Aba		Quao, Quuw	Ahha
Fri: Fida	Kwefi	Kofi	Efiwa	Efua	Cuffy	Pheba
Sat: Memendo	Kwamena, Kwame		Amba, Amma		Quamino, Quamina	Bennaba, Amha

12. Philip D. Curtin, the Atlantic Slave Trade: A Census (Madison Press, 1969), p. 227; See also Ivor Wilkes, 'Ashanti Government', in D. Forde and P. M. Kaberry, West African Kingdoms in the Nineteenth Century (London, 1967). pp. 206–38; and Ivor Wilks, 'The Rise of the Akwamu Empire: 1650–1710', in Transactions of the Historical Society of Ghana, III (1957), 99–136.
13. Curtin, *op. cit.*, p. 161.
14. Taken from Curtin, *op. cit.*, p. 160.
15. Orlando Patterson, The Sociology of Slavery: An Analysis of the Origins, Developmental and Structure of Negro Slave Society in Jamaica (London, 1967), pp. 135, 139.
16. Curtin, *op. cit.*, p. 223.
17. 'Governor Codrington to the Council of Trade and Plantations, December 30, 1701', Calendar of State Papers, Colonial Series, America and the West Indies, Cecil Headlam (ed.) XIX (London. 1910), No. 1132, pp. 720–21.
18. 'Mr. Gamble to Governor Codrington, December 29, 1701', Calendar of State Papers, XIX, No. 1132, II, pp. 721–22.
19. 'Governor Codrington to the Council of Trade and Plantations, December 30, 1701,' Calendar of State Papers, XIX, No. 1132, pp. 720–21.
20. Long, *op. cit.*, II, 471.
21. Bryan Edwards, The History, Civil and Commercial of the British West Indies, vol. II 4 vols (Philadelphia, 1806), 267–68.
22. Edwards, *op. cit.*, II, 276.
23. J. Stewart, An Account of Jamaica and Its Inhabitants (London, 1808), pp.258–60.
24. Patterson, *op. cit.*, p. 267.
25. Various estimates for 1526–1640 show that Spanish slave imports came from the Senegambia, Guinea-Bissau, Sierra Leone, Cape Mount to Cameroons, and Angola areas, not from the Gold Coast. See Curtin, *op. cit.*, pp. 95–116.
26. R. C. Dallas, The History of the Maroons from their Origin to the Establishment of their Chief Tribe at Sierra Leone, 2 vols (London, 1803), I, 30–34.
27. Patterson, *op. cit.*, p. 270.
28. Dallas, *op. cit.*, I, 36, 45, 61, 64–65.
29. 'Report of Mr. Fuller, May 1, 1742', Journals of the Assembly of Jamaica, III, 594; hereafter referred to as JAJ.
30. William James Gardner, A History of Jamaica (London, 1873), pp. 126, 127; also 'Report by Arundale for the Committee, appointed to enquire into the

insurrection of the rebellious negroes, in and about Kingston and the Windward Parts, April 5, 1746,' JAJ IV, II, e, 2-12, e.1.
31. Gardner, *op. cit.*, p. 127; also 'Report of Mr. Palmer for Committee Appointed to enquire what Negroes were convicted in the late conspiracy, April 23, 1746', JAJ, IV: 26, c. 2-27, c.1.
32. Bryan Edwards, The History, Civil and Commercial of the British West Indies, 5th edn, 5 vols (London, 1819) II: 75, 76: also Long, *op. cit.*, II: 448.
33. Long, *op. cit.*, II, 447, 453.
34. Long, *op. cit.*, II, 452, 455.
35. Long, *op. cit.*, II, 455; also 'Report on the Clandestine return to Jamaica of a Woman transported for conspiring to rebel, December 5, 1760', JAJ, V: 233, c.2.
36. Long, *op. cit.*, II, 457-58, 460-62.
37. James Patrik Hubbard, Ashanti Military Affairs in the Nineteenth Century. Unpublished Master's Thesis, University of Wisconsin, Madiscon (1969), pp. 11-13.
38. Long, *op. cit.*, II, 451-52.
39. Quoted in J. J. Williams, Voodoos and obeah (New York, 1932), p. 165.
40. James Rodway, History of British Guiana from the Year 1488 to the Present Time, 3 vols (Georgetown, 1891), I: 159-60.
41. Rodway, *op. cit.*, 1: 175-76, 166-67, 195-98.
42. Rodway, *op. cit.*, 1: 182.
43. J. J. Harsainck, 'The Story of the Slave Rebellion in Berbice, 1762', Journal of the British Guiana Museum and Zoo and the Royal Agricultural and Commercial Society, 8 parts, Nos 20-27, (December 1958-September, 1960), I, 39-40.
44. Harsainck, *op. cit.*, I: 38, II: 39, III: 50, IV: 49, V: 49, 53.
45. Harsainck, *op. cit.*, I: 38, II: 47; also Rodway, *op. cit.*, I: 192-93.
46. Harsainck, *op. cit.*, III: 48
47. Harsainck, *op. cit.*, IV: 44, V: 53, VI: 58, VII: 64, 66.
48. Harsainck, *op. cit.*, VIII: 67.
49. Harsainck, *op. cit.*, VIII: 62; see also J. A. Stedman, Narrative of a five year expedition against the Revolted Negroes of Surinam, in Guinea on the Wild Coast of South America: from the year 1772 to 1777, 2 vols (London, 1796), II: 267-69.
50. David Birmingham, The Portuguese Conquest of Angola (London, 1965), pp. 18-19; see also Jan Vansina, Kingdoms of the Savana (Madison, 1968), pp. 65-69. Birmingham's assessment of the nature of Imbangala cannibalism has not been proved conclusively. It is notable that Vansina, a specialist on Central Africa, does not attempt to characterize Imgangala cannibalism at all, although he does ascribe cannibalism to them. Another name for the Imbangala was Jaga.
51. Harsainck, *op. cit.*, III: 53; IV, 23, 43, 48; V: 56, VI: 56-57.
52. Harsainck, *op. cit.*, VI: 62, 63; VII: 63, 65.
53. The account of the Antigua conspiracy of 1736 is taken from 'Report to Governor Mathew of an enquiry into the negro conspiracy. Antigua, 30 December 1736.' Calendar of State Papers, Colonial Series, America and West Indies, K. G. Davies, editor. XLIII (London, 1963), 20, iii, pp. 10-15.
54. 'Petition of John Yeomans, agent for Antigua, and of the planters and merchants whose names are subscribed to the King'. Calender of State Papers, XLIII; 99, p. 50.
55. W. C. Wesergaard, 'Account of the Negro Rebellion on St. Croix, Danish West Indies, 1759', in Journal of Negro History, XI (January, 1926), 55, 60. Hereafter the Journal is referred to a JNH.
56. Westergaard, *op. cit.*, JNH, XI: 51-52, 56.
57. Westergaard, *op. cit.*, JNH, XI: 55-57.
58. Westergaard, *op. cit.*, JNH, XI: 54-55, 58, 61.
59. Edwin, A. Wallbridge, The Demerara Martyr, Memoirs of the Rev. John Smith, Missionary to Demerara (London, 1848), pp. 16, 17.
60. Eric Williams, Documents on British West Indian History, 1607-1633 (Port-of-Spain, 1952), p. 224.
61. Speech of Wilmot Horoin, Hansard, Series 2, XI, 1000, e.2.
62. Governor Woodford to Bathurst, August 4, 1816, in Williams, Documents, pp. 241-242.
63. Philip D. Curtin, Two Jamaicas the Role of Ideas in a Tropical Colony, 1830-1848 (Cambridge, Mass., 1955), pp. 36-38.
64. Smith, British Guiana, p. 35.
65. 'British Guiana: Lord Bathurst to Governor John Murray and Lieut-Governor Henry Beard, 28 May, 1923', in Vincent Harlow and Frederick Madden, British Colonial Developments, 1774-1834; Select Documents (Oxford, 1955), pp. 560-61.
66. Acting Governor Carmichael to Bathurst, July 31, 1812, in Williams, Documents, pp. 240-241.
67. Account taken from A. B. Ellis, The History of the First West India Regiment (London, 1885), pp. 166-68.
68. See Murrary to Bathurst, August 26, 1823, Parliamentary Papers (hereafter referred to as P.P.), 1824, XXIII (333), p. 462; and Testimony of J. P. Slingards before Board of Evidence, P.P., 1824, XXIII (333), p. 498.
69. Curtin, Two Jamaicas, p. 86, and O. G. Findlay and W. W. Holdsworth, The History of the Wesleyan Methodist Missionary Society, 5 vols (London, 1921), II: 85-86.
70. Murray to Bathurst, August, 24, 1823, P.P., 1824, XXIII (333), p. 459.
71. The London Missionary Society, Report of the Proceedings against the Rev. John Smith of Demerara (London: 1824), p. 106.
72. Trial of Jack of Success, P.P. 1824, XXIII (333), p. 529.
73. See references in footnote 69.

Maritime Maroons: *Grand Marronage* from the Danish West Indies

N. A. T. HALL

The islands of St. Croix, St. Thomas, and St. Jan — now the Virgin Islands of the United States — were Denmark's outposts of empire in the Caribbean. Denmark was a late entrant in the seventeenth-century scramble for West Indian colonies. Its colonization of St. Thomas, beginning in 1671, and of St. Jan in 1718, occurred at a time when England, France, and Holland had long since broken, de facto and de jure, Spain's monopoly in the hemisphere and were consolidating their New World gains. Denmark's choice was limited in the extreme; its acquisition of St. Thomas and St. Jan was determined not by choice but by lack of feasible alternatives. St. Croix, bought from France in 1733, was the last of the Lesser Antilles to come under European rule, and the purchase has the dubious distinction of bringing to a close the first century of non-Hispanic colonization in the Caribbean. The acquisition completed Denmark's territorial empire in the New World. Apart from two British occupations during the Napoleonic Wars, in 1801 and again from 1807 to 1815, the islands remained in Denmark's possession until 1917, when they were sold to the United States.[1]

The geological origins of the Lesser Antilles fall between the Eocene and Pliocene intervals of the tertiary period, when tectonic activity produced the collision of the floors of the Atlantic Ocean and Caribbean Sea that created an inner arc of volcanic islands to which the Danish West Indies belonged. These islands, unlike those of the outer arc such as Antigua or Barbuda, are characterized by serrated ridges and rugged peaks. St. Thomas and St. Jan rise respectively to 517 meters (1,700 feet) and 396 meters (1,300 feet). St. Croix has a range of hills along its northern coast rising to 367 meters (1,200 feet) in its northwestern corner but contains in its center and south an area of flat and fairly well-watered land totaling about 100 square kilometers (39 square miles) that is particularly well adapted to agriculture. This fact, combined with its greater area of 217 square kilometers (84 square miles), determined that neither St. Thomas, with an area of 72 square kilometers (28 square miles), nor St. Jan, 52 square kilometers (20 square miles), ever rivaled St. Croix in sugar production.[2]

Sugar integrated these tropical islands into the economy of their metropolitan center, and it was notoriously labor-intensive. Although the use of white indentured workers was attempted,[3] African slave labor soon became the exclusive basis of the monocrop culture of each island. As Table 1 demonstrates, the eighteenth century was a period of almost unvaryingly upward growth in the number of slaves, which peaked at the turn of the nineteenth century, coincident with Denmark's decision in 1792 to abolish the transatlantic slave trade in 1802 and with consequent feverish importations during that ten-year grace period.[4] Relatively and absolutely, the increments of growth were largest for St. Croix. As the

A version of this article was presented at the XVIth annual conference of the Association of Caribbean Historians, Bridgetown, Barbados, April 1984. Acknowledgments: the author would like to thank Teresita Martínez Vergne and Richard Price for their helpful suggestions of additional material relating to Puerto Rico, Julius Scott and Lorna Simmonds for material relating respectively to St. Domingue and Jamaica, Poul Olsen for identifying the William Gilbert letter, Dahlia Riedel for translations from the German, and the Department of Geography, University of the West Indies, for assistance with the map. Their generosity in no way implicates them in any shortcomings the article may have.

William and Mary Quarterly, 3rd Sents, Vol. XLII, October 1985, pp. 476–97.

Table 1 Slave, White and Freedman Populations of the Danish West Indies, 1688–1846

	St. Croix			St. Thomas			St. Jan		
Year	Slaves	Whites	Freedmen	Slaves	Whites	Freedmen	Slaves	Whites	Freedmen
1688				422	317				
1691				547	389				
1715				3,042	555				
1733				**	**	**	1,087	208	**
1755	8,897	1,303*		3,949	325	138	2,031	213*	
1770	18,884	1,515	**	4,338	428	67	2,302	118	**
1789	22,488	1,952	953	4,614	492	160	2,200	167	16
1797	25,452	2,223	1,164	4,769	726	239	1,992	113	15
1815	24,330	1,840	2,840	4,393	2,122	2,284	2,306	157	271
1835	19,876	6,805*		5,315	8,707*		1,943	532*	
1846	16,706	7,359*		3,494	9,579*		1,790	660*	

*These figures include freedmen as well as whites.
**No data.
Note: Between 1688 and 1715, neither St. Jan nor St. Croix had been acquired by the Danes. St. Jan was acquired in 1718 and was Danish at the time of the slave uprising there in 1733.
Sources: *Forskellige Oplysninger*, VI, General Toldkammer, Rigsarkiv, Copenhagen; Oxholm's 'Statistik Tabelle over de danske Amerikanske Eilande St. Croix, St. Thomas og St. Jan, 1797', *Dokumenter vedkommende Kommissionen for Negerhandelen, ibid.*; 'Viisdomsbog', *Diverse Dokumenter, Vestindiske Sager, ibid.*; *Originale Forestillinger fra Kommissionen angaaende Negernes Stilling, ibid.*; Westergaard, *op. cit.*; J. O. Bro-Jørgensen, *Vore Gamle Tropekolonier* (Copenhagen, 1966); Hans West, *Beretning om det dansk eilande St. Croix i Vestindien* (Copenhagen, 1791).

nineteenth century progressed, however, all the Danish islands experienced a gradual decline of slave populations as rates of mortality exceeded those of birth.[5]

But even as their numbers dwindled, slaves remained in the majority, a position held almost from the outset of each island's exploitation. Even after 1835, when freedmen, having obtained their civil liberties, were enumerated with whites in the category 'free', slaves never lost numerical superiority vis-à-vis non-slaves. St. Thomas, however, had become an exception in this regard by 1835, and the explanation inheres in that island's large number of freedmen, who then composed well above 70 per cent of the entire population.[6]

The increase of freedmen was closely related to the expansion of mercantile activity in St. Croix's port towns of Christiansted and Frederiksted and, most dramatically, in St. Thomas's port of Charlotte Amalie. That growth also greatly enlarged the number of slaves in those towns. By 1838, slaves composed some 26 per cent of Charlotte Amalie's population. Many were women, engaged mostly as domestics and constituting, in St. Croix, some 62 per cent of the urban slave population in 1839.[7] The data for male slaves do not permit quantification of their employment, although it is a fair assumption that most were occupied in maritime work — loading and unloading vessels, driving the wains that delivered or removed cargo, and laboring in warehouses or as crew in inter-island or other seagoing traffic. As market centers the towns drew slaves from the countryside to sell fruit, vegetables, poultry, grass, and firewood.[8] At least in St. Thomas and St. Croix, almost the entire slave population was thus in constant contact with the port towns.

The sex distribution of slaves reflected, for the eighteenth century, a general preference for males in plantation America, since planters assumed that females were less able to withstand the rigors of labor. Indeed, the Danish Slave Trade Abolition Commission, in order to redress the imbalance and promote self-sustaining growth, exempted female slaves imported after 1792 from the usual taxes.[9] For St. Croix, for example, the bias against females and its reversal over time is indicated by a comparison of the sex composition of that island's slave population of 1792 (when abolition was announced), 1804 (when the trade had just ended), 1815, 1835, and 1840, eight years before emancipation. Table 2 shows a dramatic half-century shift from a ratio of 85.8 female slaves to 100 males in 1792 to a ratio of 109 to 100 in 1840.

This change does not appear to have resulted in larger numbers of females than males among the slaves who escaped from the islands. Maroons from the Danish West Indies, as from Jamaica, Surinam, and Brazil, were preponderantly male.[10] The reason was not that women were physically less resilient or robust than men, but, more probably, that men were

Table 2 Sex Distribution of the Slave Population of St. Croix, 1792–1840.

Year	Female	Male	Total	Ratio of females per 100 males
1792*	7,364	8,579	15,943	85.8
1804	10,475	11,601	22,076	90.2
1815	12,250	12,080	24,330	101
1835	10,423	9,453	19,876	110
1840	9,714	8,891	18,605	109

*Figures do not include disabled and runaway slaves, numbering 96 and 2,082 respectively.
Sources: Oxholm's 'General Tabelle for St. Croix, 1792', *Dokumenter vedkommende Kommissionen for Negerhandelen*, General Toldkammer, Rigsarkiv; *Forskellige Oplysninger*, VI, *ibid.*; 'Extract af General Tabellerne over Folkmængden paa de danske vestindiske Øer, den 1ste Oktober 1835', *Originale Forestillinger fra Kommissionen angaaende Negernes Stilling*, *ibid.*; G. W. Alexander, *Om den moralske Forpligtelse til og den hensigtsmæssige af strax og fuldstændigt at ophæve Slaveriet i de dansk-vestindiske Kolonier* (Copenhagen, 1843).

more likely to have acquired skills needed to survive in forests, swamps, or at sea, while, in addition, women were rendered less mobile by pregnancy or the responsibilities of maternity. In the Danish West Indies, moreover, women began to predominate in the slave population at a time when the creolization of that population was well advanced. (See Table 3.) By the nineteenth century, creole slave women were arguably further deterred from deserting by attachments of family, sentiment, or a sense of place.

Table 3 Creoles and Africans in the Slave Population of the Danish West Indies, 1804–05.

	Creoles	Africans	Total	% Creoles
St. Croix	11,530	10,546	22,076	52.2
St. Thomas	2,096	1,248	3,344	62.7
St. Jan	1,521	896	2,417	62.9
Total	15,147	12,690	27,837	54.4

Source: Raw data from *Forskellige Oplysninger*, V, General Toldkammer, Rigsarkiv.

The three islands lie within sight of each other just east of Puerto Rico and at the northern end of the eastern Antillean chain as it curves gently westward in the vicinity of 18 degrees north latitude. Under Danish administration, they constituted a wedge, as it were, between Spanish Puerto Rico with its dependencies to the west and Britain's Virgin Islands to the east. This factor of insular proximity in a patchwork of national properties had an important bearing on how *grand marronage* from the Danish West Indies developed. There were significant differences from the pattern in the rest of the hemisphere, where aggregates of single fugitives created discrete communities that threatened the plantation system militarily and economically. Irrespective of their location, the viability of such communities, as Richard Price has noted, was a function of topography.[11] Natural barriers such as jungle, swamp, and hardly penetrable mountain fastnesses enabled maroon communities to develop in isolation and successfully defend themselves against attack. Slaves on the Danish islands enjoyed none of these advantages. The extensive cutting of forests to make way for sugar plantations removed nature's only benefaction from which maroons could profit. The experience of the Danish West Indies therefore provides empirical foundation for a theorem: that in small islands where geographical factors were hostile to the formation of permanent maroon communities, *grand marronage* tended to mean maritime *marronage*.

Grand marronage was the most viable of alternatives to servitude short of the supreme act of rebellion. From the beginning of Danish colonization to the time of emancipation in 1848, this form of resistance was continuous, indicating that its incidence was not significantly affected by the degree of acculturation or creolization of the slave population or by the changing proportions of male and female slaves. The numbers involved, however, were never very great. Hans West, a Danish pedagogue in St. Croix, reported 1,340 slaves at large in 1789, when the slave population stood at 22,448 — a mere 5.9 per cent.[12] P. L. Oxholm, a military engineer who later became governor-general, identified 96 deserters in 1792, only 0.5 per cent[13] of Croix's 18,121 slaves. In St. Thomas the 86 known deserters in 1802 constituted 2.7 per cent of the slave population of 3,150.[14]

The evidence indicates that *grand marronage* commenced shortly after the settlement of St.

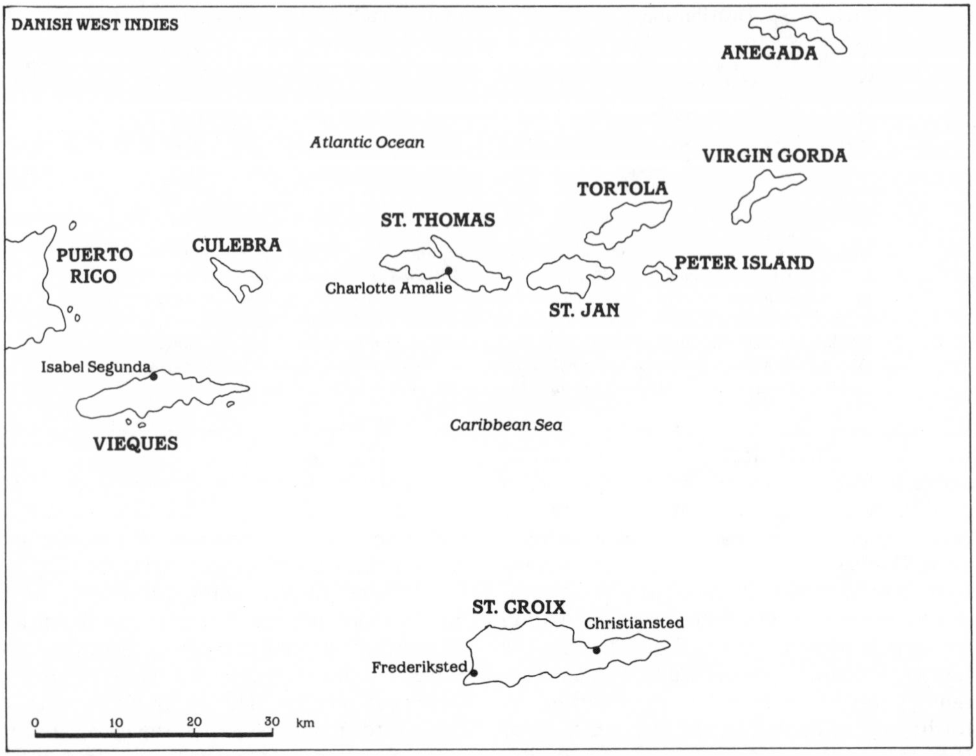

Thomas and the beginnings of that island's development as a plantation colony, which Waldemar Westergaard dates at 1688.[15] During the governorship of Johan Lorentz in the 1690s, proclamations were issued on the subject of runaways,[16] and the Privy Council of St. Thomas resolved early in 1706 to take action against *grand marronage*. Accordingly, it was ordered on October 2 that all trees on the island from which slaves could make canoes were to be cut down; a proclamation of December 30 offered a reward of fifty Rigsdaler for the return of any slave dead or alive who had escaped to Puerto Rico.[17]

The proclamations of 1706 demonstrate two factors that had an important bearing on the phenomenon of *marronage* immediately and over time: environment and geography. In the early years of settlement, before the apotheosis of sugar, the primeval forest provided superb cover and supplied wood for canoes in which slaves could seek freedom in nearby islands. The 'marine underground' to Puerto Rico and Vieques (Crab Island), and farther afield to islands in the northern Leewards and elsewhere, ultimately became a major route of escape.

When the expansion of the plantations removed the forest cover, in St. Thomas and St. Jan by the 1730s and a generation or so later in St. Croix,[18] the best chances for permanent escape lay overseas, although, as we shall see, the islands' towns, as their populations grew, also provided havens. J. L. Carstens, who was born in St. Thomas in 1705 and died there in 1747, noted in his memoirs that in those early years runaways occupied the island's coastal cliffs, where they sheltered in almost inaccessible caves. Those first maroons chose well, with a keen strategic eye, for the cliffs could not be scaled from the seaward side and vegetation obstructed the landward approaches. Such refugees went naked and subsisted on fish, fruit, small game such as land turtles, or stolen provender. Slave hunts, organized three times a year, could neither loosen their grip on freedom nor dislodge them from the cliffs.[19]

Regrettably, Carstens recorded nothing of the size and social organization of this early community or its relationship with plantation slaves. It was the only such community that St. Thomas ever had, and it did not last long. The Danish authorities could ill afford to stand idly by, especially when St. Thomas was not yet self-sustaining.[20] During the War of the Spanish Succession they began to organize the *klappe jagt* or slave hunt more effectively, using planters, soldiers, and trusty slaves.[21] The forests then became less safe, while at the same time the agricultural exploitation of St. Thomas, peaking in the 1720,[22] reduced the vegetational cover. As a result, slaves turned to the sea. Their line of escape led west, with favorable northeast trade winds and currents, toward Puerto Rico and other islands, none of which lay more than 60 kilometers from St. Thomas. Slaves had opportunities to become familiar with the surrounding waters on fishing expeditions for sea turtles around Vieques, and the same boats they manned on their masters' behalf could be used to make a break for Puerto Rico.[23] In 1747, 19 slaves deserted from St. Croix, and the following year 42 seized a sloop there and sailed to comparative freedom among the Spaniards.[24]

Puerto Rico, which became their preferred destination, was sparsely populated before the *Cédula de Gracias* of 1815, and its authorities, perhaps for this very reason, looked leniently if not encouragingly on runaways from the Danish islands. As early as 1714, Gov. Don Juan de Rivera organized 80 deserters from Danish and other islands into a community at San Mateo de Cangrejos east of San Juan, gave them public land, and required them to function as an auxiliary militia.[25] The Spanish government ratified these arrangements in *cédulas* of 1738 and 1750, and in the latter decreed freedom for runaways who embraced Catholicism.[26] Eugenio Fernández Méndez has argued that the Spanish acted largely from religious motives.[27] But there was also an element of calculating realpolitik: in addition to providing manpower, maroons were potential sources of useful intelligence in the event of hostilities. It is instructive to note that slaves from South Carolina found an equally agreeable haven in Spanish Florida in the early eighteenth century and were used by the Spaniards in border incursions that kept the British colony in a state of apprehension.[28]

Early legislative prescriptions against *grand marronage* authorized such physical deterrents as leg amputations, hamstring attenuation, and leg irons or neck collars.[29] Such measures hampered but did not prevent escape by water. Later laws elaborated rules for access to and use of boats. Even before 1750, legislation limited the size of canoes and barges that whites could keep and specified conditions of ownership.[30] Although mutilations and hardware such as neck irons fell out of use pari passu with the disappearance of the forests,[31] regulation of boats persisted until the very end of the era of slavery. The ordinance of October 2, 1706, was the forerunner of many, the necessity for which was proof of the problem they sought to eradicate. But despite a flurry of laws in the 1740s and 1750s, probably inspired by the beginning of the agricultural exploitation of St. Croix, *grand marronage* could not be suppressed.

Reimert Haagensen, who lived in St. Croix in the 1750s, noted in an account of that island that planter families were being ruined by the running away of slaves in groups of as many as 20–25 in a single night. He instanced occasions when slaves seized boats by surprise attack and forced their crews to sail to Puerto Rico. Many plantation owners, Haagensen complained, had '*capital staaende iblandt de Spanske, hvoraf dog ingen Interesse svares*.'[32] It was commonly supposed in the Danish islands that a year in the service of the Spanish crown brought freedom. This Haagensen said he could neither confirm nor deny; but he had personal knowledge of slaves who had escaped to Spanish territory, lived well and in freedom, and sent back messages of greeting to their former masters and slave companions.[33] Similarly, C. G. A. Oldendorp, a Moravian missionary inspector, writing in the 1760s, noted that Maronbjerg — Maroon Mountain, in the northwestern corner of St. Croix — was no longer a secure retreat, and that as a result the proximity of Puerto Rico and the promise of freedom there acted as powerful stimulants. The still largely African-born slave population demonstrated the same levels of inventiveness and daring that Haagensen observed in the previous decade. Slaves secretly built canoes large enough to accommodate whole families, commandeered when they could not build, forced sailors to take them to Puerto Rico, and, when all else failed, bravely swam out to sea in hope of accomplishing the same objective.[34]

Legislation dealing with *marronage* at the end of the eighteenth century and in the early years of the nineteenth shows a continuing preoccupation with the problem. Gov.-Gen. Ernst von Walterstorff attempted to introduce a boat registry in St. Croix in 1791 and insisted that all canoes must have bungs that were to be put away, along with oars and sails, when the canoes were not in use. All craft were to be stamped with the royal arms and bear a registration number as well as the owner's name; none was to be sold or rented outside the towns' harbors.[35] In 1811 the police chief of Christiansted announced a fine of ten *pistoles* for employing slaves on the wharves or on boats in the harbor without a police permit.[36] The Danish West Indian government in 1816 expressed concern at the persistence of escapes by boat and contemplated introducing regulatory measures such as prohibition of boat ownership except in towns.[37] Finally, as late as 1845, three years before emancipation, Adam Søbøtker, the acting governor-general, promulgated a decree permitting plantations to keep only flat-bottomed boats, as slaves were unlikely to try to escape in such craft.[38] By then, however, the marine underground had other destinations than Puerto Rico, as will be shown below.

Over time, legislation to cauterize the hemorrhage proved only minimally effective. The failure of preventative measures prompted a search for other solutions. The absence of a formal extradition convention had enabled runaways to Puerto Rico to cock their snooks at former owners, a form of salutation that Haagensen for one found less than amusing.[39] The establishment of such a convention, it was thought, would resolve the difficulty. Accordingly, a series of cartels between Spain and Denmark in 1742, 1765, 1767, and 1776 established that deserters would have to be claimed within one year by their owners; that the latter would pay the expenses of their slaves' maintenance for that period; that reclaimed fugitives would not be punished; that those who embraced Catholicism would be allowed to remain in Puerto Rico; and, finally, that a Catholic church and residence for its priest would be built in St. Thomas at Denmark's expense.[40]

These diplomatic initiatives, however, proved disappointing. The cartels applied to future deserters but not to slaves already in Puerto Rico. The Spanish authorities, moreover, were less than expeditious in dealing with claims. The Danish West India Company filed a claim in 1745 for the return of some 300 deserters known to be in San Mateo de Cangrejos, but 21 years passed before it was adjusted.[41] Less than a decade after the 1767 convention, Gov.-Gen Clausen was engaged in a brisk correspondence with Don Miguel de Muesos, captain general of Puerto Rico. Several slaves had decamped from St. Thomas early in 1775, but the envoy sent to claim them was met by Spanish professions of ignorance of their whereabouts.[42] *Grosso modo*, the Spaniards showed little inclination to cooperate in the matter of runaways. Occupation of the Danish West Indies in the early years of the nineteenth century by Spain's wartime ally England appears to have made little difference. The British lieutenant governor of St. Croix in 1811, Brig. G.W. Harcourt, issued a proclamation asserting that slaves had been carried off in Puerto Rican boats and declared that such boats found illegally four weeks thereafter in any harbor except Christiansted and Frederiksted would be seized and confiscated.[43] Two months later, the British authorities invited persons who had recently lost slaves and believed them to be in Puerto Rico to submit information on the slaves' age, sex, appearance, and time of desertion.[44]

As late as 1841, the 'long-standing difficulties' with Puerto Rico were the subject of exchanges between the Danish West Indian governor-general and King Christian VIII, each hoping that the new Puerto Rican captain general, Mendez Vigo, would be more disposed to 'friendly conclusions' than some of his predecessors had been.[45] An incident reported by Van Dockum in the early 1840s reveals the nature of the difficulties. Acting on information that two slaves had been spirited away to Vieques in boats from that island, the authorities in St. Croix sent the frigate on patrol duty in the West Indies to reclaim them. When the frigate arrived at Isabel Segunda, the main town of Vieques, that island's governor, though full of conviviality and consideration, would admit only that a boat had in fact taken slaves from St. Croix to Vieques.[46] It appears that the shortage of labor in the Spanish islands after the legal suspension of the slave trade in the 1820s bred illegal trafficking, often with the collusion of Spanish authorities.[47] The episode to which Van Dockum referred seems to have been an instance of labor piracy willingly embraced by the slaves of St. Croix as an avenue of *grand marronage*.

Taking refuge in forested hills and fleeing to Puerto Rico or Vieques were the most dramatic early acts of *grand marronage*. While slaves continued to escape by water, the disappearance of primeval vegetation prompted others to find ways of deserting without leaving the islands. Sugar served their needs and turn. Harvesting began in late December or early January when the canes approached maturity and had grown high enough to conceal even the tallest person. Until the end of the 'crop' or reaping season in July, therefore, each unreaped field provided an artificial forest in which slaves could continue to conceal themselves over a six-month period. The work of these months of harvest made the most strenuous and exacting demands on slaves' endurance. This was also the dry season, before high summer brought the heavy showers associated with the movement of the intertropical convergence zone. A slave thus had multiple inducements: he could find cover, escape the period of hardest labor, and keep dry. A Danish official in the late eighteenth century noted that the expansion of plantations on St. Croix made it difficult for runaway slaves to find shelter in forests that were disappearing or in fields that no longer contained scrub. The alternative, he observed, rendered them secure but posed a constant fire hazard: 'Fleeing to the cane fields in which the cane and leaves can exceed a man's height, they put down poles of about a meter and a half and make a bower over these with the leaves of the nearest canes plaited together. In this way they form a little hut about four and a half feet by six to seven feet around. Having cleared the ground in the hut of dry leaves and left an opening, they then use the place to lie up, to store whatever ground provisions they can, and as a fireplace.'[48] The existence of maroon hideouts in the cane fields was authenticated by discoveries of corner posts, ashes, and coal. A causal link between such hideouts and cane fires was also established by remnants of pork and other meat abandoned to and partially consumed by fires out of control.[49]

Another variant of *grand marronage* was desertion to the coastal towns. Christiansted and Frederiksted in St. Croix, and Charlotte Amalie in St. Thomas, grew in population and commercial importance in the prosperous years of the late eighteenth century: plantations flourished, trade expanded, and Charlotte Amalie was established as a free port.[50] For slaves on islands as small as the Danish West Indies, towns offered advantages of comparative anonymity; a prospect of work on the wharves, in warehouses, and aboard coastal or other vessels; the likelihood of finding a sympathetic reception and succor in the areas of these towns designated by law for free persons of color; concealment, incongruously enough, by whites; and the chance of using the town as a staging post in what might become a step-migration to freedom.

Anonymity was enormously enhanced when a slave on the run shipped from one Danish island to another. One cannot quantify this type of *marronage*, but it was known to have taken place, and as the bustle of free-port commerce in Charlotte Amalie arguably rendered that town a more impersonal place than either Christiansted or Frederiksted, it must be presumed that the tendency would have been toward St. Thomas. Newspaper advertisements appear to support such a hypothesis, although there is also evidence of *marronage* from Charlotte Amalie to St. Jan and St. Croix. Most notorious was the case of Jane George, who in an advanced state of pregnancy escaped from St. Thomas in a canoe with a white man early in September 1815 paddling for St. Jan or St. Croix.[51] Another runaway, James Dougharty, an artisan apprentice, headed for St. Jan in 1822. A reward of $20 was offered for information, 'as it [was] not likely [he] had walked all the way.'[52] By and large, however, advertisements for maroons in St. Thomas over the first 15 years of the publication of the *Sankt Thomæ Tidende* (1815–30) show approximately twice as many desertions to St. Thomas as to St. Croix or St. Jan from St. Thomas.

The variety of employment in the growing towns facilitated *grand marronage* into them, and the anonymity they offered was compounded by the notorious laxity of the Danish West Indian police,[53] so that it was possible for runaways to sustain a livelihood in wharf-related work or itinerant vending without too great a risk of discovery.[54] Fugitives enjoyed the normally supportive presence of freedmen in their legally prescribed areas of residence, the Free Guts. With freedmen, urban slaves, and poor whites, deserters composed a demi-monde of the marginalized. Governor-General Clausen in St. Croix in the 1770s and Lt. Gov. Thomas de Maleville in St. Thomas in the 1780s expressed only more explicitly than most the sense of community that prevailed among runaways and freedmen in the Guts.[55] Poor whites involved in petty retail trading or artisan trades were known to consort with and provide shelter for runaways. The latter were potential sources of stolen goods and, if they had an artisanal skill, could be hired out to earn an income for their protectors. Throughout the late eighteenth and early nineteenth centuries, therefore, one finds legislation aimed at curtailing the mutually reinforcing liaison of fugitives and their patrons, especially in the towns. The preamble to an ordinance issued by Gov.-Gen. Adrian Bentzon in 1817 spoke of the long history of this liaison; the ordinance prescribed severe penalties for whites and free persons of color who either hired or hid slaves on the run.[56] As late as 1831, Adam Søbøtker, acting as governor-general, was still vainly attempting to curb that sort of collusion.[57]

For runaways, the coastal towns were above all a porthole of opportunity to a wider world. *Marronage* overseas to foreign destinations, before the significant growth of the towns, had been limited to Vieques and Puerto Rico. However, as towns grew, they attracted an increasing number of vessels from distant ports, widening the escape hatch for slaves. The schooners, brigs, sloops, yawls, and snows that called at these towns, especially Charlotte Amalie as it became a Caribbean entrepôt, brought St. Domingue/Haiti and Jamaica in the Greater Antilles, the islands of the Leewards and Windwards, the North American continent, and even Europe within reach, though after 1802 Denmark ruled itself out as a haven for escapees. A Supreme Court decision that year in the case of the slave Hans Jonathan decreed that the free soil of the mother country did not confer freedom on the enslaved.[58]

Access to avenues of flight depended in some measure on the collusion of masters of vessels. Service at sea in the eighteenth and early nineteenth centuries was such as to suggest a parallel between masters of vessels and slave masters, between ships and regimented slave plantations, between crews and enslaved estate labor. Ship masters, not surprisingly, had their own problems of *marronage* in the form of desertion. It was not unusual for crewmen, singly or in numbers, to jump ship in West Indian waters. One Swedish sloop, the *William*, Capt. Joseph Almeida, lost five hands in St. Thomas harbor on February 5, 1827.[59] Such incidents meant that additional or substitute crews were often needed, and since the white population of Caribbean coastal towns was too small to meet the need, it was unlikely that runaway slaves who offered themselves would be interrogated closely, if at all, about their status. Black crewmen were therefore commonplace. Many of Almeida's men were Africans of unspecified status, and slave shiphands were by no means extraordinary. One such, Jan Maloney, deserted from a vessel of British registry in St. Thomas in 1819.[60]

In 1778 regulations were adopted to obstruct this avenue of *grand marronage* by forbidding shipboard employment of any slave without a sailor's pass and written permission from his owner. Significantly, it was considered necessary to reissue these regulations in 1806.[61] The 1833 royal proclamation of Frederik VII, by offering the extravagant reward of 1,500 *pistoles* for information on masters of vessels secretly exporting slaves, suggests that the problem still persisted even at that late date.[62] The size of the reward indicated the seriousness with which the problem was viewed, particularly at a time when the slave population of the Danish islands was steadily declining.[63]

Some ship captains, even before the end of the eighteenth century, were free persons of color. One such was Nicholas Manuel, whose ship, the *Trimmer*, plied between St. Thomas and Jeremie, St. Domingue, in 1796.[64] In such a vessel, arguably, a slave could find the maritime equivalent of a house of safety in a Free Gut. The legislation directed at captains thus took into account a potential collaborator, the colored shipmaster, while it also expressed the paranoia prevailing after the revolution in St. Domingue and accompanying disturbances in the French West Indies. Vulnerability to revolutionary contamination from these trouble spots was a recurring concern of Danish West Indian authorities, who lived in constant fear that their slaves would emulate the St. Domingue example. The years from 1791 to about 1807 were therefore punctuated by measures to establish a *cordon sanitaire* against St. Domingue. These involved, *inter alia*, the confiscation of any boats arriving from St. Domingue/Haiti and the imposition of a fine of 1,000 Rigsdaler. Yet there is evidence to suggest that such prophylaxis achieved only indifferent results. The traffic to St. Domingue/Haiti, especially from St. Thomas, continued, and in the early 1840s Governor-General von Scholten felt moved to remark on the 'significant' number of 'unavoidable' desertions to that island.[66]

Legislation could not prevent desertions, for the movement of inter-island maritime traffic depended to a degree on slave crews, and the law permitted slaves with seamen's passes to be so engaged, making a pragmatic virtue out of necessity, considering the shallowness of the white labor pool.[67] Engaged as crews in their island of origin, slaves embraced the opportunity to escape on reaching a foreign port. Jamaica was one such destination in the western Caribbean at which goods from the emporium that was St. Thomas were arriving well before the end of the eighteenth century. Both the *Royal Gazette* and the *Jamaica Courant* carried information that confirms that slaves considered any port a station in the maritime underground. The St. Thomas sloop *Martha*, Capt. John Simmons Blyden, arrived in Kingston in August 1788 and promptly lost Jack, a sailor aged 25, and Tony, 23, described as a 'waiting man and occasional fiddler'. Another St. Thomas sloop, the *Hope*, Capt. John Winfield, lost George, aged 19, at about the same time.[68] Joe, 25, jumped ship in Kingston from the schooner *Eagle*, registered in St. Croix, in May 1806.[69] Not all the deserting slave seamen from the Danish West Indies appear to have made it to freedom. Some like

Sam, a St. Thomas creole who arrived in Kingston on a sloop commanded by Captain Capp in 1797, were apprehended.[70] No doubt a reasonable competence in an English creole tongue must have helped a slave negotiate the narrows of early freedom in a strange English-speaking island, and in this regard slaves from St. Croix may have enjoyed an advantage. In that island, step by step with the creolization of the slave population, there developed an English-based creole lingua franca, whereas in St. Thomas it was Dutch-based.[71] Having an employable skill in addition to seafaring would also have helped. Another Sam, for example, who deserted from a Danish island schooner in Kingston late in 1793, was a hairdresser by trade. Since he was American-born and spoke good English,[72] he stood a doubly good chance of gettng past the exit turnstiles of this station in the maritime underground.

In the Caribbean, the same flows of trade that took vessels to St. Domingue/Haiti or farther away to Jamaica also took Danish West Indian vessels to the Lesser Antilles in the opposite direction. These flows presented like opportunities to slave for employment as crew, and such employment, legitimate or illegitimate, created chances for desertion to the Leewards, Windwards, and elsewhere. That traffic, moreover, complemented the trade originating to leeward of St. Thomas and St. Croix, thereby widening the possibilities for maritime *marronage*. This branch of eastern Carribean intercourse in the early nineteenth century was part of the expanding seaborne commerce into St. Thomas[73] and opened a major escape route for runaways to St. Thomas from islands in the northern Leewards and from as far away as Curaçao and Barbados.[74] Danish slaves were not slow to exploit the situation. One reported example from St. Thomas in 1819 indicates that eight slaves — seven men and one woman — probably crew on the 17-ton inter-island schooner *Waterloo*, stole the ship when it arrived in St. Vincent in the British Windwards.[75]

This episode is remarkable for its daring and also for the fact that it is the only incident of running away to the non-Danish islands of the eastern Caribbean, excluding Tortola, that the newspapers report. Though one of the best sources for the study of all forms of *marronage*, the Danish West Indian newspapers are in fact less helpful than one would like on maritime *marronage* to the foreign islands of the eastern Caribbean — perhaps understandably so, for the logical place in which to advertise for deserters was the *terminus a quo* or point of escape. The Danish West Indian papers therefore report desertions from other islands more fully than desertions from the Danish islands. The local advertisement placed in the *Sankt Thomœ Tidende* by James Hazel, owner of the above-mentioned *Waterloo*, was thus unusual. Recovery of this lost schooner and slaves would have been better served by insertions in the foreign press. But perhaps the size of his loss — schooner, cargo, and eight slaves — obliged him to issue, in modern police parlance, an all points bulletin.[76]

From the inception of Danish colonization, slaves showed their capacity for creating possibilities for *grand marronage* overseas from each new set of circumstances. They responded ingeniously to the openings presented by the islands' ecology, the proximity of the Spanish islands, and the growing volume of traffic to and from the Danish ports. But of all the circumstances affecting *grand marronage*, none appears to have had a more quickening effect than emancipation in the neighboring British Leeward Islands, particularly Tortola. Desertions to Tortola began to increase from 1839, the year after the post-emancipation period of apprenticeship ended in the British West Indies.[77] Especially in St. Jan, no more than a cannon shot's distance from Tortola, the urge to run away then appears to have become irresistible.

Slaves were well aware that once they set foot on Tortola their freedom was secure, for the effect of the British Emancipation Act of 1833 was to confer on them on arrival the free status that the West Indian slave James Somerset had acquired in England in 1772 only after litigation at the highest level. For example, in reporting the incident of the early 1840s involving the two slaves from St. Croix, Van Dockum noted that before proceeding to Vieques they had requested to be taken to Tortola, where they went ashore. The authorities in Vieques used this fact to explain why they could not return persons who were in law free men.[78] The difficulties that British West Indian emancipation posed for the Danish authorities were practically insurmountable. Louis Rothe, an observant judge of probate who came to St. Croix in the 1840s, noted that desertions from St. Jan were almost impossible to control — and not only because of the proximity of Tortola. Overlooked by precipitous cliffs, St. Jan's innumerable bays made coastal patrols for the most part ineffective. Moreover, the patrols were too few to police bays that, even when contiguous, did not permit observation of one from another. Deserters crossed the straits by boats and improvised rafts from St. Jan. Boats also originated from Tortola; some even came by appointment to fetch a slave or group of slaves. In Tortola, Rothe observed, 'all classes receive them with open arms and emissaries await with tempting offers of money and free transportation to larger islands, and promises of high wages and little work.' For the years 1840–46, he reported desertion by 70 slaves.[79] Though the total seems insignificant, it was more than double the number of runaways from St. Thomas over the same period.[80] If Rothe was correct — and he admitted that no official records were kept — an important fact emerges. St. Jan's slave population declined from 1,970 in 1840 to 1,790 in 1846.[81] The 70 slaves therefore represented nearly 40 per cent of the decline over that period.[82]

As the 1840s began, the Danish West Indian government sought to close this route to freedom by using frigates on the naval station. Governor-General von Scholten's orders were apparently to shoot to kill, although his long-term objective, as expressed in a letter to Christian VIII, was to reduce the attractions of desertion by progressive amelioration of conditions for slaves.[83] In 1840, a slave woman attempting to reach Tortola by canoe was killed by naval fire. Two others in the party, a mother and child, were apprehended, but two escaped by swimming.[84] In Denmark, the newspaper *Fædrelandet* observed in righteous indignation that 'blood ought not to be shed to compensate for an inability to reconcile the slaves to their existence' and found a sinister significance in the recent erection of 'an enormous prison' in St. Croix.[85] Von Scholten and the authorities were for the moment impervious to such voices of humanitarian protest, but it was another matter when pursuit of slaves involved firing upon them in ill-defined territorial waters claimed by the British. An ensuing British protest led to an investigation in 1841 by a senior Danish naval officer, Hans Birch Dahlerup. Formal charges were brought against a Lieutenant Hedemann for the killing of the woman and violation of British waters. The investigation ended in a court martial in Copenhagen and two months' imprisonment for Hedemann — 'more to satisfy England and its then powerful abolitionist lobby,' Dahlerup concluded, 'than for the offence with which he was charged.'[86]

The year 1845 was a particularly successful one for slaves bidding for freedom in Tortola. The administration's preoccupation, if not panic, was by then plain. Acting Governor-General Søbøtker, reported to the crown in tones of anguish a sequence of escapes. On October 26, six slaves — five men and a woman[87] — from plantations on St. Croix's north side, got hold of a fishing canoe and made it to Tortola, although police and fire corps went in immediate pursuit. The Tortolan authorities returned the boat but not the people. Of particular interest is the fact that the leadership of this escape was attributed to a seasoned maritime maroon who some years previously had deserted from Dutch Saba and had been recaptured and resold in St. Croix.[88]

Less than a month after this incident the most spectacular episode of *grand marronage* from St. Jan to Tortola occurred. On the night of November 15, 37 slaves, including six from one plantation, deserted from southside St. Jan in two English boats sent from Tortola for that purpose. The maroon patrol, such as it was, was based on the island's north side, closest to Tortola, leaving the south side unguarded. For some time planters in St. Jan had been allowed to get their supplies of salt from Tortola in boats from that island, but they were less than vigilant in this instance. No satisfaction was to be expected, Søbøtker felt, as the government of the British Leeward Islands was unlikely to make reparations and would take no action against the two Tortolan boatmen who were accessories. 'The established principle since emancipation,' he pointed out, 'was that no one who had helped an unfree person to gain freedom could be punished for it.' The best the frustrated Søbøtker could do was to issue stern warnings to plantation owners, increase night patrols by his inadequate militia, and make new regulations respecting planters' ownership of boats.[89]

Grand marronage by David West Indian slaves lasted from the beginning of colonization, when the slave population was exclusively African-born, until slavery's end in 1848, when it was largely creole. In the decade or so before that date, emancipation in the British West Indies, particularly in neighboring Tortola, stimulated desertions on a scale that, especially in St. Jan, threatened to destabilize the slave system. In the 1840s such desertions, though they may have robbed the slave population of its potentially most revolutionary leadership, nevertheless prefigured and arguably acted as a catalyst for the successful rebellion of 1848.

Later commentators, like earlier observers, rationalized *grand marronage* in a variety of ways, some self-serving, others perceptive. These included depravity, overwork, fear of punishment or impending trial, arbitrary owners, the attractions of a work-free Sunday on other islands, and scarcity of food.[90] Whenever the occasion arose, officals were given to asserting, in an access of obtuseness or arrogant self-satisfaction, that fugitives would willingly return if only they could enjoy more discretionary time.[91] One of the 37 who fled to Tortola in 1845 seized a boat and did indeed return to St. Jan early in 1846. The records do not disclose his reasons but do report him as having said that others were equally ready to return, 'which was not improbable,' the authorities smugly concluded, 'having regard to the prevailing destitution in Tortola.'[92] But there is no evidence that these escapees came back to St. Jan, nor did this one swallow make a summer. On the occasion of the 1759 slave conspiracy in St. Croix, the examining magistrate, Engebret Hesselberg, made the surprisingly enlightened observation that 'the desire for freedom is an inseparable part of the human condition'.[93] Oldendorp, no libertarian himself, concurred, although with less generosity of spirit. 'It is extraordinarily difficult,' he noted, 'to convince the . . . Negroes that the rights their masters exercise over them are their due rights. They follow their uncontrollable nature and consider every means of gaining their freedom justified. . . . [T]hey run away from their masters . . . and seek violent means of escaping from their service.'[94]

By running away as they had always done, and in the numbers they did to Tortola, slaves reinforced the truth of Hesselberg's observation. In the 1840s they began to press the issue of their freedom by bringing the metropolitan authorities urgently to consider concrete measures for emancipation. Their initiatives helped embolden liberal opinion in Denmark, already critical of absolute monarchy and colonial policy and favorably disposed to emancipation on economic as well as humanitarian grounds.[95] The newspaper *Fœdrelandet*, organ of the opposition, declared it 'impossible for all practical purposes to place limits on the longing for freedom'.[96]

Indeed, when a deserted slave spoke into the record, he gave poignant endorsement to *Fœdrelandet's* sentiments. Such a man was William F.A. Gilbert, the only escaped slave from the Danish West Indies from whom we have a personal written testament. We do not know when or how he reached Boston, Massachusetts, but it was from that city on August 12, 1847, a year before emancipation, that he addressed to Christian VIII an impassioned plea not only on his own behalf but for every member of his race who had ever been or was still oppressed by slavery:

To His Supreme Magistrate, King Christian VIII, Copenhagen, Denmark. Sir: I taken my pen in hand a runaway slave, to inform your excelcy of the evil of slavery. Sir Slavery is a bad thing and if any man will make a slave of a man after he is born free, i, should think it anoutrage becose i was born free of my Mother wom and after i was born the Monster, in the shape of a man, made a slave of me in your dominion now Sir i ask your excelcy in the name of God & his kingdom is it wright for God created man Kind equal and free so i have a writ to my freedom I have my freedom now but that is not all Sir. i want to see my Sisters & my Brothers and i now ask your excelcy if your excelcy will grant me a free pass to go and come when ever i fail dispose to go and come to Ile of St. Croix or Santacruce the west indies Sir i ask in arnist for that pass for the tears is now gushing from mine eyes as if someone had poar water on my head and it running down my Cheak. Sir i ask becose i have some hopes of geting it for i see there your Nation has a stablished Chirches and Schools for inlightning the Slave. that something the American has not done all though she is a republican my nam is Frederick Augustus Gilbert now i has another name thus

Wm F. A. Gilbert

Sir, when i see such good sines i cannot but ask for such a thing as liberty and freedom for it is Glorius. Sir i make very bold to write to a King but i cannot helpit for i have been a runaway slave i hope your excelcy will for give me if i is out in order Please to sind you answer to the Deinish Council in Boston

His withered hands he hold to view
With nerves once firmly strung,
And scarcely can believe it true
That ever he was yong,
And as he thinks o'er all his ills,
Disease, neglect, and scorn,
Strange pity of himself he feels
That slave is forlane

William F. A. Gilbert.[97]

Notes

1. Useful introductory material on the Danish West Indies published in English can be found in Isaac Dookhan, *A History of the Virgin Islands of the United States* (Epping, 1974); Jens Larsen, *Virgin Islands Story* (Philadelphia, 1950); and Waldemar Westergaard, *The Danish West Indies under Company Rule (1671–1754)* . . . (New York, 1917).
2. See John Macpherson, *Caribbean Lands: A Geography of the West Indies, (Kingston, Jamaica, 3rd edn, 1973), 123, and P. P. Sveistrup, 'Bidrag til de Tldligere Dansk-Vestindiske* øers Økonomiske Historie, med ærligt

Henblik paa Sukker-production og Sukkerhandel', *National Økonomiske Tidsskrift for Samfindsspørgsmaal Økonomi og Handel*, LXXX (1942), 65, 87.
3. J. L. Carstens, 'En almindelig Beskrivelse om Alle de danske Amerikanske eller West-Indiske Eylande', H. Nielsen (ed.), *Danske Magazin*, III, No. 8, Pts. 3 and 4 (1960–70), 260–61.
4. Svend E. Green-Pedersen, 'The Economic Considerations behind the Danish Abolition of the Negro Slave Trade', in Henry A. Gemery and Jan S. Hogendorn (eds), *The Uncommon Market: Essays in the Economic History of the Atlantic Slave Trade* (New York, 1979), 407–08, and 'Slave Demography in the Danish West Indies and the Abolition of the Danish Slave Trade', in David Eltis and James Walvin (eds), *The Abolition of the Atlantic Slave Trade: Origins and Effects in Europe, Africa, and the Americas* (Madison, Wis., 1981), 234; also in this volume.
5. Green-Pedersen, 'Slave Demography,' *loc. cit.*, 245.
6. N.A.T. Hall, 'The 1816 Freedman Petition in the Danish West Indies: Its Background and Consequences', *Boletín de Estudios Latinoamericanos y del Caribe*, 29 (1980), 56.
7. N.A.T. Hall, 'Slavery in Three West Indian Towns: Christiansted, Fredericksted and Charlotte Amalie in the Late Eighteenth and Early Nineteenth Century', in B. W. Higman (ed.), *Trade, Government and Society in Caribbean History, 1700–1920: Essays Presented to Douglas Hall* (Kingston, Jamaica, 1983), 18.
8. *Ibid.*, 23.
9. Green-Pedersen, 'Economic Considerations,' *loc. cit.*, 408.
10. Richard Price (ed.), *Maroon Societies: Rebel Slave Communities in the Americas* (New York, 1973), 9.
11. *Ibid.*, 3.
12. That number is not to be taken at face value since West made no distinction between *petit* and *grand marronage*. West, *Beretning*, 'Mandtal Optaget for 1789'.
13. Oxholm's General Tabell, St. Croix, 1792, *Dokumenter vedkommende Kommissionen for Negerhandelens bedre Indretning og Ophæ*velse, samt Efterretninger om Negerhandelen og Slaveriet i Vestindien, 1783–1806, General Toldkammer, Rigsarkiv.
14. *Recapitulation of the State of the Different Quarters of the Island of St. Thomas, May 13, 1802*, Den Engelske Okkupation 1801, 1807, General Toldkammer, Rigsarkiv.
15. Westergaard, *op. cit.*, 121.
16. *Copies of Orders Issued during Governorships, 1672–1727*, Bancroft Papers, Z–A 1, 3, University of California, Berkeley.
17. *Kongelig Secretaire Schwartkopp's Report*, October 13, 1786, *ibid.*, Z–A 1, 48.
18. In the case of St. Croix, contemplated legislation in 1783 against illegal felling of trees was justified on the basis that 'since almost all the forests have been cut down, illegal felling of trees is of greater importance than previously' (*Udkast og Betæ*nkning angaaende Neger Loven med bilag 1783–1789, No. 24, Pt. i, Article 48, General Toldkammer, Rigsarkiv.
19. Carstens, 'En almindelig Beskrivelse', *op. cit.*, 225, 259.
20. N. A. T. Hall, 'Empire without Dominion: Denmark and Her West Indian Colonies, 1671–1848', seminar paper (University of the West Indies, Mona, 1983), 3–10.
21. Bro-Jørgensen, *Vore Gamle Tropekolonier*, 225.
22. Westergaard, *op. cit.*, 160.
23. *Ibid.*, 161.
24. Arturo Morales Carrión, *Albores Históricos del Capitalismo en Puerto Rico* (Barcelona, 1972), 83.
25. Luis M. Diaz Soler, *Historia de la Esclavitud Negra en Puerto Rico* (Rio Piedras, 1974), 233, 236.
26. Cayetano Coll y Toste (ed.), *Boletín Histórico de Puerto Rico* (San Juan, 1914), I, 16, 20.
27. Fernández Méndez, *Historia Cultural de Puerto Rico, 1493–1968* (San Juan, 1971), 165.
28. Peter H. Wood, *Black Majority: Negroes in Colonial South Carolina from 1670 through the Stono Rebellion* (New York, 1974), 305–07.
29. Westergaard, *op. cit.*, 162. See also C.G.A. Oldendorp, *Geschichte der Mission der evangelischen Brüder* (Barby, 1777), I, 496, and N. A. T. Hall, 'Slave Laws of the Danish Virgin Islands in the Later Eighteenth Century', New York Academy of Sciences, *Annals*, CCXCII (1977), 174–86.
30 Gov.-Gen. Walterstorff's Placat of November 21, 1791, quoting earlier proclamations of 1742, 1744, 1750, and 1756, Bancroft Papers, Z–A 1, 52.
31. Oldendorp mentions amputations for which the definitive slave code of 1733 made provision (*Geschichte*, I, 396). But by the 1780s there were already voices critical of the code's provisions as barbaric. See, for example, Judge Colbiørnsen's Opinion, September 3, 1785, Miscellaneous Papers, *Udkast og Betænkning*, General Toldkammer, Rigsarkiv, and General Toldkammer Skrivelse to Danish West Indian Government, Dec. 23, 1782, *Kommissions Forslag og Anmærkning angaaende Negerloven*, Bind 1, 1785, *ibid.*
32. 'Capital invested among the Spaniards that yeilds no interest' (Haagensen, *Beskrivelse over Eylandet St. Croix i America i Vestindien* [Copenhagen, 1758], 42).
33. *Ibid.*, 43.
34. Oldendorp, *Geschichte*, I, 396–97. Oldendorp did not say whether he knew of any slaves who managed to reach Puerto Rico or adjacent islands by swimming.
35. Gov.-Gen. Walterstorff's Placat, November 21, 1791, Bancroft Papers, Z–A 1, 52.
36. *St. Croix Gazette*, March 12, 1811.
37. *Akter Vedkommende Slaveemancipation*, Frikulørte 1826, 1834, Dansk Vestindisk Regerings Deliberations Protocoller, April 30, 1816, General Toldkammer, Rigsarkiv.
38. Søbøtker to Christian VIII, December 13, 1845, Record Group 55, Box 9, National Archives, Washington, D.C.
39. Haagensen, *Beskrivelse*, 43.
40. Oldendorp, *Geschichte*, I, 396–97; E. V. Lose, *Kort Udsigt over den danskelutherske Missions Historie paa St. Croix, St. Thomas og St. Jan* (Copenhagen, 1890), 22–23; Diaz Soler, *Historia de la Esclavitud*, 234–236; Morales Carrión, *Albores Históricos*, 67; *Kommissions Forslag*, Bind 2, fols. 74, 89, General Toldkammer, Rigsarkiv.
41. Westergaard, *op. cit.*, 161. Diaz Soler is of the view that the settlement of the claim under the 1767 convention was facilitated by the demise of the Danish West India Company, whose illicit trading withPuerto Rico had always been an obstacle to negotiations (*op. cit.*, 234).
42. Clausen to de Muesos, July 4, 1775, Bancroft Papers, Z–A 1, 43.
43. *St. Croix Gazette*, February 8, 1811.
44. *Ibid.*, April 9, 1811.
45. Von Scholten to Christian VIII, Jan. 13, 1841, in which reference is also made to an unfiled letter of Nov. 18, 1840, *Originale Forestillinger fra Kommissionen angaaende Negernes Stilling i Vestindien med Resolutioner*, General Toldkammer, Rigsarkiv. See also Christian VII to von Scholten, October 7, December 4,

1840, August I, 1841, Privatarkiv 6795, Rigsarkiv.

46. C. Van Dockum, *Livserindringer* (Copenhagen, 1893), 74–77.
47. Andrés Ramos Mattei, *La Hacienda Azucarera: Su Crecimiento y Crisis en Puerto Rico (Siglo XIX)* (San Juan, 1981), 23–24. Demand for labor inspired the decree of 1849 establishing an obligatory work regimen for free labor in Puerto Rico. See *ibid.*, 24, and Labor Gomez Acevedo, *Organización y Reglamentación del Trabajo en el Puerto Rico del Siglo* XIX (San Juan, 1970), 449–53.
48. Etats Raad Laurbergs Erinderinger, Jan. 12, 1784, *Kommissions Forslag*, Bind 2, fols. 10–11, General Toldkammer, Rigsarkiv, cf. *ibid.*, Bind 1, fol. 326.
49. It is possible that cane-field deserters were simply engaging in short-term absenteeism. The length of absence and the construction of shelter that made absence of that duration possible would suggest, more plausibly, an intention to remain at large and ultimately leave the island.
50. Hall, 'Slavery in Three West Indian Towns', in Higman (ed.), *Trade, Government and Society*, 19–20.
51. *Sankt Thomœ* Tidende, September 16, 1815.
52. *Ibid.*, March 5, 1822.
53. Hall, 'Slave Laws', *op. cit.*, 184.
54. Hall, 'Slavery in Three West Indian Towns', in Higman (ed.), *loc. cit.*, 27, 29, 30.
55. Clausen's Placat, 39, July 29, 1775, *Udkast og Betænkning* ... No. 27, General Toldkammer, Rigsarkiv; de Maleville's *Anmærkning*, April 7, 1784, and de Maleville's *Betænkning*, October 19, 1787, *Kommissions Forslag*, Bind 2, fols. 33, 84, *ibid.*
56. Bentzon's Ordinance of September 11, 1817, *Forskellige Oplysninger*, V, fol. 315, General Toldkammer, Rigsarkiv.
57. Søbøtker's Proclamation of July 22, 1831, *ibid.*, VI, fol. 216.
58. A.S. Ørsted, 'Beholdes Herredømmet over en vestindisk Slave, naar han betræder dansk-europæisk Grund', *Arkiv for Retsvidenskaben og dens Anvendelse*, I (1824), 459–85.
59. *Sankt Thomœ Tidende*, Feb. 9, 1827.
60. *Ibid.*, March 9, 1819.
61. *Dansk Vestindisk Regerings Avis*, May 15, 1806.
62. *Sankt ThomœTidende*, March 9, 1833.
63. Green-Pedersen, 'Slave Demography', *loc. cit.*, 245. See also Alexander, *Om den moralske Forpligtelse*, 5–7.
64. Calendar of Records, High Court of Vice Admiralty, Jamaica, 1796, fol. 17. Jamaica Government Archives, Spanish Town. Freedmen sometimes also owned their own vessels. The brothers Jacob and August Dennerey jointly owned a boat in St. Thomas in 1820. See Hall, '1816 Petition', *Boletín de Estudios Lationoamericanos*, No. 29 (1980), 70.
65. General Toldkammer Skrivelse to Dansk Vestindisk Regering, November 23, 1793, and Dansk Cancelli to General Toldkammer, August 8, 1807, enclosure 4, October 29, 1805, *Akter Vedkommende Slaveemancipation*, Frikulørte 1826, 1834, General Toldkammer, Rigsarkiv. For further examples of boat legislation directed at St. Domingue/Haiti see N.A.T. Hall, 'Forslag til Ordning af Vestindisk Forfatningsforhold Angaaende Negerne med Mere', Bureau of Libraries, Museums and Archaeological Services–Department of Conservation and Cultural Affairs, Occasional Paper No. 5 (1979), 3, 7, n. 16.
66. Von Scholten's comments on G. W. Alexander's 'Anmærkninger til Kongen af Danmark m.h.t. de danske Øer' [n.d.], *Akter Vedkommende Slaveemancipation* 1834–47, II, General Toldkammer, Rigsarkiv.
67. The scarcity of white labor was a continuous problem, especially for plantations, forcing von Scholten to pass deficiency legislation in the 1830s. See Hall, 'Empire without Dominion', 26.
68. *Royal Gazette*, Supplement, August 8–15, 1788.
69. *Jamaica Courant*, May 17, 1806.
70. *Royal Gazette.*, December 2–9, 1797.
71. Hall, 'Empire without Dominion', 18.
72. *Royal Gazette.*, November 7, 1792.
73. The total tonnage of shipping into St. Thomas, 1821–30, doubled that of the previous decade. There was an annual average of 2,890 vessels with a total tonnage of 177,441. See Westergaard, *op. cit.*, 252.
74. Hall, 'Slavery in Three West Indian Towns', *loc. cit.*, 30.
75. *Sankt Thomœ* Tidende, April 10, 1819.
76. The newspapers of the Leewards, Windwards, Barbados, and elsewhere in the eastern and southern Caribbean can be expected to be good sources for *marronage* from the Danish West Indies. It has not been possible at this writing to consult such sources.
77. Louis Rothe, 'Om Populations Forhold i de danske vestindiske Colonier og fornemlig paa St. Croix' [n.p.], *Neger Emancipation Efter Reskript af 1847*, General Toldkammer, Rigsarkiv.
78. Van Dockum, *Livserindringer*, 74–77.
79. Rothe, 'Om Populations Forhold' [n.p.], *Neger Emancipation Efter Reskript*, General Toldkammer, Rigsarkiv.
80. *Ibid.*
81. The figures for 1840 are derived from Alexander, *Om den moralske Forpligtelse*, 7. Those for 1846 are from Sveistrup, 'Bidrag', *National Økonomiske Tidsskrift*, LXXX (1942), 78–79.
82. Rothe did not make any attempt to quantify the effect of *grand marronage* from St. Jan, but he did state that *marronage* to Tortola would have a 'conclusive influence upon the structure of [St. Jan's] slave population' ('Om Populations Forhold' [n.p.], *Neger Emancipation Efter Reskript*, General Toldkammer, Rigsarkiv).
83. Von Scholten to Christian VIII, January 15, 1841, *Originale Forestillinger fra Kommissionen angaaende Negernes Stilling*, General Toldkammer, Rigsarkiv.
84. Alexander, *Om den moralske Forpligtelse*, 15.
85. *Fædrelandet*, December 15, 22, 1840.
86. Dahlerup, *Mit Livs Beginvenheder* (Copenhagen, 1909), II, 270, 289, and 'Skizzer fra et kort Besøg paa vore vestindiske Øer i Sommeren 1841', *Nyt Archiv for Sovæsnet*, I (1842), I.
87. Statistics on the sex distribution of deserters or groups of deserters are not abundant, but the available data do point to a heavy preponderance of males. For example, of the 86 deserters in St. Thomas in 1802 (see above, n. 14), 73 were male and 13 female. The 7 men and 1 woman in the incident in 1819 (see above, n. 75) represent a not dissimilar proportion. The party of 5 in 1840 (see above, n. 84), assuming the two escapees were men, appears to be almost evenly balanced. But that distribution, on the basis of other evidence, can be considered unusual.
88. Søbøtker to Christian VIII, November 11, 1845, No. 3, Copies of Letters Sent to the King, Record Group 55, Box 9, fols. 2–3, Natl. Archs.
89. For letters reporting the incident see November 28, December 13, 1845, January 27, 28, 1846, Nos. 4–7, *ibid.*
90. For examples see Gardelin's Placat, Sept. 5, 1733,

Udkast og Betænkning . . . No. 4, General Toldkammer, Rigsarkiv; Walterstorff to General Toldkammer, July 20, 1802, *Akter Vedkommende Slaveemancipation*, Frikulørte, 1826, 1824, *ibid*.; and von Scholten to Christian VIII, May 14, 1842, *Originale Forestillinger fra Kommissionen*, *ibid*.; Søbøter to Christian VIII, January 28, June 12, 1846, Nos. 7, 19, Record Group 55, Box 9, Natl. Archs.; and Haagensen, *Beskrivelse*, 35.

91. Von Scholten to Christian VIII, May 14, 1842, *Originale Forestillinger fra Kommissionen*, General Toldkammer, Rigsarkiv.
92. Søbøtker to Christian VIII, January 28, 1846, No. 7, Record Group 55, Box 9, Natl. Archs.
93. 'Species Facti over den paa Eilandet St. Croix Intenderede Neger Rebellion Forfattet efter Ordre af Byfoged Engebret Hesselberg' [n.p.], *Udkast og Betænkning* . . . No. 3, General Toldkammer, Rigsarkiv.
94. Oldendorp, *Geschichte*, I, 394.
95. For a detailed discussion of opposition liberal and other positions on the emancipation debate in Denmark see Grethe Bentzen, 'Debatten om det Dansk Vestindisk Negerslaveri 1833–1848 med sæligt Henslik paa de igennem Tidsskrieft pessem og Stænderdebatterne udtrykt Holdninger' (M.A. thesis, Aarhus University, 1976).
96. *Fædrelandet*, Jan. 5, 1941.
97. *Henlagte Sager*, Vestindisk Journal, No. 141, 1848, General Toldkammer, Rigsarkiv.

SECTION TEN
Revolution, Reform and Emancipation

Though slaves launched a complex and relentless assault on the system of slavery over a period of 300 years, slave-owners were able to assert their power so as to contain such actions. The Haitian revolution stands out as the grand exception to the generalization. In French San Domingue slaves were able to defeat the masterclass, and their imperial allies, declare the abolition of slavery, and establish the republic of Haiti. The slaves of Danish St. Croix revolted on July 2, 1848, and by so doing created the context in which Danish officials proclaimed emancipation. Such cases represent acts of self-liberation by revolutionary opposition to slave-owners, and illustrates that slaves were first to implement emancipation schemes within the Caribbean.

As slave societies matured and became more creolised, their internal contradictions, and difficulties in their external ideological and economic relations, became increasingly problematic. Anti-slavery forces were not only internal, but by the end of the eighteenth century were supplemented by metropolitan individuals and organizations determined to remove slavery from the culture of western civilization. In addition, the rise of the industrial complex in the world economy posed certain difficulties for the decaying mercantile structures that had supported the slave systems of the region. Between 1794 and the last quarter of the nineteenth century, the region's slave systems collapsed in a drawn-out programme of legislation emancipation. Explanations for this progress are varied and this section provides a sample of the arguments used by historians to account for the diverse nature and specific timing of imperial-sponsored emancipations.

The Haitian Revolution

DAVID GEGGUS

Racial equality, the abolition of slavery, decolonization, and nationhood first came to the Caribbean with the Haitian Revolution. Between 1791 and 1803 the opulent French colony of Saint Domingue was transformed by the largest and most successful of all slave revolts. After twelve years of desolating warfare, Haiti emerged in 1804 as the first modern independent state in the Americas after the United States. For slaves and slave owners throughout the New World, the Haitian Revolution was an inspiration and a warning. The most productive colony of the day had been destroyed, its economy ruined, its ruling class eliminated. Few revolutions in world history have had such profound consequences.

Saint Domingue in the 1780s

In the period between the American and French revolutions, Saint Domingue produced close to one half of all the sugar and coffee consumed in Europe and the Americas, as well as substantial amounts of cotton, indigo, and ground provisions. Though scarcely larger than Maryland, and little more than twice the size of Jamaica, it had long been the wealthiest colony in the Caribbean and was hailed by publicists as the 'Pearl of the Antilles' or the 'Eden of the Western World'. Moreover, it was still expanding. In the long-settled coastal plains, the number of sugar plantations grew only slowly but the mountainous interior was the scene of bustling pioneer activity, where new coffee estates were being cut out of the mountain forests to meet rising demand in Europe and North America.

By 1789 Saint Domingue had about 8,000 plantations producing crops for export. They generated some two-fifths of France's foreign trade, a proportion rarely equalled in any colonial empire. Saint Domingue's importance to France was not just economic, but fiscal (in customs revenue) and strategic, too, since the colonial trade provided both seamen for the national navy in wartime and foreign exchange to purchase vital naval stores from northern Europe (hemp, mast trees, saltpeter). In the Môle Saint Nicolas, the colony also contained the most secure naval base in the West Indies.

Although colonial statistics are not very reliable, Saint Domingue's population on the eve of the French Revolution consisted of approximately 500,000 slaves, 40,000 whites (including transient seamen), and over 30,000 free coloreds, who constituted a sort of middle class. In broad outline, Saint Domingue society thus conformed to the three-tier structure common to all sugar colonies. However, there were some significant differences.

The tiny white community was united by racial solidarity but also divided to an unusual degree along class lines. The resulting tensions pitted sugar and coffee planters against each other as well as against merchants and lawyers, and separated all of these from the turbulent *petits blancs*, or poor whites, an amorphous group that included plantation managers, artisans, clerks, shopkeepers, seamen, and peddlers. Such tensions reflected the wealth and diversity of Saint Domingue's economy. Also, because France was a much more populous country than Great Britain or Spain, and possessed fewer colonies, Saint Domingue inevitably attracted uncommonly large numbers of indigent young men seeking employment. The richest planters, on the other hand, were able to reside in Europe living off their revenues. This was typical of West Indian sugar colonies.

The Modern Caribbean (University of North Carolina Press), 1989,pp. 21–50.

At the same time, however, the extent of less profitable secondary economic enterprises such as coffee, indigo, and cotton meant that Saint Domingue also possessed a sizable resident planter class, like the southern United States or Cuba. Residence in the colony, its competitive position in the world market, and its ability to produce much of its own food were factors that encouraged some planters to envisage its eventual independence.

Saint Domingue's free colored sector was exceptional both for its size and its wealth. Elsewhere in the Caribbean free coloreds were generally a very small minority and they rarely rose above the position of prosperous artisan. In Saint Domingue, however, the *gens de couleur* outnumbered the whites in two of the colony's three provinces, and they included in their number rich and cultivated planters who had been educated in France. In Saint Domingue anyone with a black ancestor, no matter how remote, was subject to the humiliating restrictions of the legal system of separation typical of all slave colonies in the eighteenth century. Free coloreds were banned from public office and the professions, and forbidden to wear fine clothing, ride in carriages, or sit with whites in church or when eating. They were not only unequal before the law but also suffered extra-legal harassment, especially from poor whites with whom they competed for jobs.

The gens de couleur thus covered an extremely broad social range, from recently freed black slaves to rich landowners and tradesmen who were almost indistinguishable in appearance or culture from their white counterparts. They constituted merely a legal category (those neither slave nor white) rather than a class. Probably a majority of the men were artisans or smallholders. The women were usually petty traders or white men's mistresses. As most were of mixed racial descent, the term 'mulatto' was often applied to the entire free colored community. Many had both whites and slaves for relatives. Their position within Saint Domingue society was therefore highly ambiguous. Though held in subjection by the whites, they were often slave owners themselves or acted as slave catchers in the rural police force.

Despite the spread of liberal ideas in Europe, the laws governing the free coloreds in France, as well as Saint Domingue, grew increasingly severe in the late eighteenth century — a paradox of the French Enlightenment. At the same time, the free coloreds grew rapidly in number, and in wealth as they profited from the coffee boom. By the 1780s they not only dominated the rural police force but in addition formed the backbone of the colonial militia.

Saint Domingue's slave population was easily the largest in the Caribbean. It was nearly twice the size of Jamaica's, its closest rival. The imbalance between slave and free, black and white, was not unusually extreme, but for most of the 1780s the number of slaves grew at a faster rate than probably anywhere else. During the period 1785–90 over 30,000 manacled Africans were imported each year. Despite the influx of white immigrants and the growing community of free coloreds, Saint Domingue was actually becoming increasingly African. Young men around twenty years old comprised a significant proportion of the black population.

The slave community was not at all homogeneous, being even more segmented than the white and free colored groups. Split up into small units, tied six days a week to plantation labor, the slaves constituted a random agglomeration of individuals from diverse cultures, speaking different languages and at different stages of assimilation into colonial society. On a typical sugar estate of two hundred slaves there would be Africans from twenty or more different linguistic groups. Mountain plantations were much smaller and even more isolated. Everywhere in Saint Domingue, however, Bantu slaves known as 'Congoes' constituted the largest of the African groups, and formed a third of the population in the plains and well over half in the mountains.

On the lowland sugar plantations about half the adults were Creoles — that is, individuals born locally and raised in slavery; they made up perhaps one-third of the total slave population. Accustomed to producing their own food and marketing the surplus, they tended to be better off than the Africans. Fluent in the local Creole tongue, superficially Christianized, and united by at least limited family ties, they constituted the slave upper class. From their ranks were chosen the domestics, artisans, and slave drivers who formed the slave elite. Elite slaves would have some familiarity with French, the language of the master class, and a few could read and write.

Little is known about how these groups interrelated. Plantation labor, social interaction, and the common experience of slavery inevitably imposed some sort of solidarity, which was symbolized in songs of call and response, networks of fictive kin, and a strong sense of locality. Moreover, slaves from different estates could meet at weekly markets, at Saturday night dances, and in more secret assemblies associated with the Voodoo cult. Voodoo apparently served to integrate different religious traditions — West African, Bantu, and Christian — and doubtless helped release anomic tensions. Nevertheless, the diversity of the slave community must be accounted one reason why, in a comparative context, Saint Domingue's slaves seem to have been remarkably unrebellious. It is true that in the twenty years before the American Revolution poisoning scares swept the colony, but these had as much to do with white paranoia as with real resistance; in the 1780s little was said about poison. Compared to the British or Dutch colonies, organized, violent resistance in Saint Domingue was relatively slight.

This paradox underlying the greatest of all slave revolts has received little scholarly attention. The planters themselves tended to attribute the absence of slave revolts to Saint Domingue's military-style government, which precluded the democratic dissensions of the self-governing British colonies, and which placed far more stress on militia training. Certainly the slaves seem to have been no better treated than in any other sugar colony. Perhaps most importantly, the colony's size and low population density meant that slave discontent was most easily channelled into running away to the mountains and forests. Other slaves fled over the frontier into the even more sparsely populated Spanish colony of Santo Domingo, as well as to towns such as Port-au-Prince and Cap Français. While some runaways formed armed bands which attacked travelers or isolated plantations, they were never very numerous and the 1780s saw a definite downturn in such activities. Although this is a controversial area, it seems clear that desertions were usually short-term and offered little threat to the system. Moreover, in 1777 an extradition treaty was signed with Santo Domingo. As new settlements spread into the remaining frontier regions, and as the colony's forests were felled, it was becoming increasingly hard to be a successful maroon. it may be, therefore, that by the 1780s slave dissidents were coming to see revolt as a more viable alternative.

The Influence of the American Revolution

Vulnerability to slave rebellion and foreign invasion made all West Indian colonies especially dependent on their mother countries for military and naval protection. Nevertheless, the desire for self-government had a long history in Saint Domingue, and among a minority of radical planters it was notably strengthened after the North American colonists won their independence from England. Apart from its ideological impact, the American Revolution gave Saint Domingue a tempting taste of free trade. When France intervened in the conflict, it opened the colony's ports to Yankee traders, who supplied its needs more cheaply than could French merchants. These commercial contacts were sustained after the war through a new sytem of free ports, but the trade was heavily taxed and subject to frustrating prohibitions. Moreover, smuggling was severely curtailed by new measures reminiscent of British action in North America twenty years before. Such conflicts of interest encouraged planters to think of themselves as 'Americans' rather than Frenchmen.

The War of Independence, perhaps, had its greatest impact on the free colored community. A special regiment of free coloreds was raised and sent to Georgia to fight alongside the rebel colonists. It included André Rigaud, Jean-Baptiste Chavannes, J. B. Villatte, Henry Christophe, Jean-Pierre Lambert, and Louis-Jacques Beauvais; its muster roll reads like a roll call of future revolutionaries. These men returned to Saint Domingue with military experience and a new sense of their own importance. Leading mulattoes secretly drew up a report attacking the caste system and in 1784 sent a representative to France. The government, however, for fear of offending the whites or exciting the slaves, dared not yield an inch.

The abolition of slavery in Massachusetts and other northern states had been much discussed in Saint Domingue by American seamen and local whites, but it is not known how this affected the slaves. By the end of the 1780s news was anyway arriving from France itself of a French anti-slavery society, the Amis des Noirs. At the same time, government reforms aimed at limiting abuses on the plantations outraged the planter class. Hitherto, whites had presented a solid front on the question of slavery. Now cracks were starting to appear in what had been a monolithic white power structure.

The Impact of the French Revolution, 1789–92

Historians do not agree on just how close Saint Domingue came to having a revolution in the

1780s. Whether the whites' desires for autonomy, the free coloreds' for equality, or the slaves' for liberty would of themselves have led to violent conflict must remain a matter for speculation. No one doubts, however, that the French Revolution of 1789 precipitated the colony's destruction. If Saint Domingue was a dormant volcano, as contemporaries liked to say, it needed only the shock waves of the political earthquake in Paris to provoke its eruption.

The ideological impact of the French Revolution is not easy to distinguish from its political impact. The ideals of liberty, equality, and fraternity proclaimed by the revolutionaries in Paris were peculiarly dangerous for Caribbean societies, which represented their complete negation. But at the same time, the overthrow of the Old Regime in France also directly undermined the traditional sources of authority in the French West Indies — governor, intendant, law courts, garrison, militia, police. The French Revolution thus inflamed social and political aspirations, while weakening the institutions that held them in check.

The influence of the French Revolution was felt first at the peak of the social pyramid and thereafter worked its way inexorably downward. Although colonists were not invited when the States-General was summoned in 1788 to recommend sweeping changes in French government, wealthy planters in both Paris and Saint Domingue met in secret committees to elect deputies and ensure their representation. Their activities in fact merged with movements already under way to protest against recent government reforms in the colonies. It was the fall of the Bastille, however, and the creation of a National Assembly in the summer of 1789 that overturned the Old Regime in Saint Domingue as well as France. While mobs of poor whites adopted the tricolor cockade and celebrated riotously the news from Paris, planters, merchants, and lawyers became politicians and elected assemblies in each of the colony's three provinces. In many parishes and towns, elected committees and municipalities emerged alongside or replaced local military commanders. The militia was converted into a National Guard dominated by the plantocracy. The intendant, former strongman of the administration, was driven out of the colony, and the governor, uncertain of support from France, was forced to accept what he could not prevent.

From April to August 1790, a Colonial Assembly met in the town of Saint Marc. Though illegal, it declared itself sovereign and boldly drew up a constitution severely restricting French control even over matters of trade. Its most radical deputies openly discussed the idea of independence. The extremism of these *Patriotes* brought about a backlash, which temporarily united the Assembly of the North with the governor and military. In 1789 the elegant northern capital of Cap Français had been in the forefront of the revolution. Thereafter its big merchants and establishment lawyers became a moderating influence, and sprawling and shabby Port-au-Prince took over as the center of colonial radicalism. Lower-class whites came to exercise increasing control over its politics, notably after its garrison mutinied in March 1791 and caused the governor to flee to Le Cap.

Colonial politics was an affair of factions and demagogues. Without previous political experience. Saint Domingue's whites threw up local leaders of ephemeral fame who maintained the Creole's reputation for turbulence and impulsive egotism. Divided by regional, class, and political loyalties, colonists disagreed as to what degree of autonomy Saint Domingue should seek, how much militancy they should employ, what classes of whites should vote and serve together in the militia, and whether the colony should be represented in the National Assembly or cooperate directly with the king's ministers. The great majority agreed, nonetheless, on two things — that no one should tamper with the institution of slavery, and that the system of white supremacy should be rigorously maintained. Increasingly, however, the revolution in France came to be seen as a threat to both these pillars of colonial society.

In 1789 the society of the Amis des Noirs gained new prominence as the revolution provided a platform for its leading members (Mirabeau, Brissot, Condorcet). It campaigned only for the abolition of the slave trade and for equal rights for free coloreds, and disclaimed any desire to interfere with slavery. However, to the colonial mind which saw racial discrimination as an essential bulwark of slavery, such action endangered white lives in the West Indies. Encouraged by the Amis des Noirs, free coloreds in Paris demanded that the National Assembly live up to its Declaration of the Rights of Man. Were they not men, too? At the same time, the autumn of 1789, free colored property owners in Saint Domingue also gathered to demand equal rights with whites. Some also seem to have called for the freeing of mixed-race slaves, and those in Paris spoke of an eventual, though distant, abolition of slavery. In general, however, the free coloreds acted like the slave owners they were and were careful not to have their cause confused with that of the black masses.

In a few parts of the colony, the early days of the French Revolution saw free coloreds and whites attending meetings together and sitting on the same committees, but this was rare. The mulattoes' request to adopt the tricolor cockade created great unease among whites. Before long they and their few whites allies became the victims of intimidatory acts of violence, including murder. Fears for the stability of the slave regime reinforced deep-seated prejudice, so that by 1790 it was clear that the colonists were determined to maintain the status quo and keep the free coloreds out of politics. The Assembly of the West even demanded from them a humiliating oath of obedience. Faced by mounting persecution, some now fortified their plantations, but a small armed gathering in the spring in the Artibonite plain was easily dispersed. The free colored militia joined the governor's forces which suppressed the Colonial Assembly, but the administration proved no more willing than the colonists to grant concessions.

Meanwhile, however, the mulattoes were acquiring leaders from among wealthy non-whites now returning from France, men who had been accustomed to equal treatment. These included Villatte, J.B. Lapointe, and Pierre Pinchinat, but it was the light-skinned Vincent Ogé (an unsuccessful small merchant) who decided to force the whites' hand. He had been a prominent spokesman of the free colored activists in Paris, where he had tried and failed to gain the cooperation of the absentee colonists. On of his brothers apparently was killed in the skirmish in the Artibonite. In October, Ogé secretly returned to his home in the mountains of the North Province. With Jean-Baptiste Chavannes he rapidly raised an army of over three hundred free coloreds and demanded that the governor put an end to racial discrimination. Despite the urging of Chavannes, Ogé refused to recruit any slaves. Free coloreds were not numerous in the North; and though they initially created great panic among the whites, Ogé's men were soon routed. Mass arrests and a lengthy trial followed. Twenty rebels were executed, Ogé and Chavannes suffering the excruciating punishment of being broken on the wheel. In the West and South, free coloreds had also taken up arms but there they were peaceably persuaded to disperse by royalist officers. Military men were often more sympathetic to the mulattoes' cause, if only because they saw them as a counterweight to the colonial radicals. In the North, all free coloreds were disarmed except a few fugitives from Ogé's band who remained in hiding in the forests.

Up until now the National Assembly in Paris had maintained an ambiguous silence on the color question. France's revolutionary politicians were extremely embarrassed by events in the Caribbean and the issues that they raised. Colonial self-government, racial equality, and freedom for the slaves all posed serious threats to France's prosperity. The news of the barbarous execution of Ogé and Chavannes, however, shocked the National Assembly into making a compromise gesture. On May 15, 1791, free coloreds born legitimately of free parents were declared equal in rights to whites. Although the measure concerned a very small proportion of free coloreds, news of the Assembly's vote created a violent backlash in Saint Domingue. Whites, now meeting to elect a second colonial assembly, seemed determined to resist the decree with force. A few talked of secession. When the governor announced he would not promulgate the decree, the patience of the free coloreds was exhausted. In August, those of the West and South began to gather in armed bands in the parishes where they were strongest. At the same time, news arrived from France that King Louis XVI had revealed his hostility to the revolution by attempting to flee from Paris.

It was in this rather complicated political situation, with civil war brewing between whites and free coloreds, with tensions rising between conservatives and radicals, with rumors circulating of secession and counter-revolution and a new assembly gathering in Cap Français, that the slaves took everyone by surprise. At the end of August 1791, an enormous revolt erupted in the plain around Le Cap. Beating drums, chanting, and yelling, slaves armed with machetes marched from plantation to plantation, killing, looting, and burning the cane fields. From the night it began, the uprising was the largest and bloodiest yet seen in an American slave society. Spreading swiftly across the plain and into the surrounding mountains, the revolt snowballed to overwhelming proportions. Whites fled pell-mell from the plain, and military sorties from Cap Français proved ineffective against the rebels' guerrilla tactics. By the end of September, over a thousand plantations had been burned and hundreds of whites killed. The number of slaves slaughtered in indiscriminate reprisals was apparently much greater, but this merely served to swell the ranks of the insurgents. Nevertheless, a cordon of military camps managed to confine the revolt to the central section of the North Province.

Most slave conspiracies in the Americas were betrayed before reaching fruition, and most rebellions were quashed within a few days. The circumstances surrounding the August uprising are therefore of great interest. The divided and distracted state of the whites and the alienation of the free coloreds probably explain much of the rebels' success, both in gathering support and in overcoming opposition. Their aims, however, are less clear. Many slaves appear to have believed they were fighting to gain a freedom already granted them by the king of France but which the colonists were withholding. They in fact rebelled, not in the name of the Rights of Man, but as defenders of church and king. How far this was a deliberate ploy (perhaps designed to win aid from their conservative Spanish neighbors), is hard to say, but the influence of French revolutionary ideology on the revolt would seem slight. Since 1789 slaves had called the tricolor cockade the symbol of the whites' emancipation, but in revolt they adopted the white cockade of the royalists. Rumors of a royal emancipation decree had circulated in Saint Domingue in the autumn of 1789, along with news of an insurrection in Martinique, which was itself prompted by similar rumors that may have had their roots in late ancien régime reforms. The Saint Domingue uprising was one of the first of a new type of slave revolt, soon to become typical, in which the insurgents claimed to be already officially emancipated. Apparently beginning with the Martinique rebellion of August 1789, this development probably owed more to the anti-slavery movement than to French revolutionary ideals.

Contemporary interrogations of captives revealed that the slave revolt was organized by elite slaves from some two hundred sugar estates. Later sources connect their meetings with the voodoo cult. The colonists, however, refused to believe that the slaves acted alone. Royalists counter-revolutionaries, the Amis des Noirs, secessionist planters, the remnants of Ogé's band, and the free coloreds in general were all accused by one group or another in the devastating aftermath of the rebellion. However, if any outside elements were involved, they soon found that the slaves were determined to decide their own fate. Their early leaders, Jean-François and Biassou, imposed an iron discipline on the disparate bands that they formed into armies. Yet, when they attempted, fearing famine and defeat, to negotiate in December a sell-out peace with the planters, their followers forced them back onto the offensive.

Free coloreds from the parishes of Ogé and Chavannes certainly did join the slave rebels when the northern mountains were overrun, but in this they had little option. Elsewhere in the North, free coloreds fought against the slaves until they learned that the May 15 decree had been withdrawn. This was a fatal move by the wavering National Assembly. Although civil war between whites and free coloreds had broken out in the western and southern provinces, the whites had been swiftly compelled to accept the mulattoes' demands in these regions where the free coloreds predominated and showed exceptional military skill. Now, however, fighting began all over again. The towns of Port-au-Prince and Jacmel were burned and, as in the North, fearful atrocities were committed by all sides, making future reconciliation the more difficult. In parts of the West, white and colored planters combined to fight urban white radicals. In the South, they divided along color rather than class lines, while in the North free coloreds joined the slave rebels. All sides began to arm slaves to fight for them, and plantation discipline slackened. Slave revolts broke out intermittently in the West and South, but the rebels were usually bought off with limited concessions, so that in general the slave regime remained intact though shaken.

Beginning in December 1791, troop reinforcements started to arrive in small numbers from strife-torn France. The soldiers died rapidly, however, from tropical diseases, and, needed everywhere in the colony, they had little impact on an enemy that avoided pitched battles. Not until France finally granted full citizenship to all free persons in April 1792 did the situation begin to stabilize. Prejudice and resentment remained strong; but in most areas outside the main towns, white and mulatto property owners now grudgingly came to terms and turned their attention to the slaves. However, the civil commissioners who arrived in September to enforce the decree rapidly alienated most sections of the white population. Léger-Félicité Sonthonax and Etienne Polverel were dynamic and zealous radicals who scorned colonial opinion and who immediately adopted the cause of the Republic on learning that the French monarchy had been overthrown. After deporting the governor, they dissolved the Colonial Assembly, all municipalities, and political clubs. Royalist officers, autonomist planters, and racist small whites were imprisoned and deported in large numbers, and free coloreds were promoted to public office in their stead.

Separated from the race war, the slave rebellion assumed more manageable proportions. The 6,000 troops and National Guards who came out with the civil commissioners were left inactive for months, but the northern plain was nonetheless easily retaken in November 1792. When a full offensive was eventually mounted in January 1793, Jean-François and Biassou were driven from one after another of their mountain camps, and thousands of slaves surrendered. By this time, however, the new French Republic was being propelled by its leaders into a world war that would leave Europe and Saint Domingue irrevocably changed.

War and the Rise of Toussaint Louverture, 1793–98

By refuting the ideology of white supremacy and destroying the governmental structure that imposed it, the French Revolution thus brought the free coloreds to power in most parts of Saint Domingue in alliance with the Republican officials from France. This transfer of power to the free coloreds also gained impetus from the outbreak of war with England and Spain in the spring of 1793. The colonists looked to foreign invasion to free them from the civil commissioners, who in turn grew intolerant of any white in a position of power. Port-au-Prince was bombarded into submission by Sonthonax and its jails were filled with recalcitrant colonists. The southern coast was already a free colored stronghold, but, following a massacre of whites in Les Cayes in July, it became effectively autonomous under the mulatto goldsmith André Rigaud. In the plain of Arcahaye the ruthless J. B. Lapointe established himself as a local dictator, while in the plain of Cul-de-Sac behind Port-au-Prince, Pinchinat, Lambert, and Beauvais became the dominant influences. At Cap Français, Villatte would achieve a similar local dominance after the burning of the town in June and the flight of some 10,000 whites to North America.

With the white colonists eclipsed and the slave revolt close to suppression, the spring of 1793 represents the high point of mulatto control in Saint Domingue. The rest of the colony's history, indeed that of independence Haiti, may be viewed as a struggle between the emergent power of the black masses and the predominantly brown-skinned middle class. Whether the slave revolt in the North could actually have been suppressed, and whether slavery on the plantations of the South and West would have continued as before, of course no one can say. However, the onset of war quite clearly transformed the situation not only of the veteran fighters in the northern mountains but also of all the blacks in Saint Domingue.

As soon as war was declared, both the Republican French and the Spaniards, preparing to invade from Santo Domingo, began competing to win over the black rebels. They offered them employment as mercenaries and personal freedom for themselves. Both in Europe and Saint Domingue, the fortunes of the new Republic were at their lowest ebb. Half of the soldiers sent to the colony in 1792 were already dead, and no more could be expected from a France racked by civil war and itself facing invasion. The civil commissioners' rhetoric about Republican virtues therefore had little impact on Jean-François, Biassou, and the other black chiefs. They preferred to take guns, uniforms, and bribes from the Spaniards and continued to attack Frenchmen and free coloreds in the name of the king. Increasingly, Sonthonax and Polverel were compelled to turn to the masses in general to shore up Republican rule. First they liberalized the plantation regime, then freed and formed into legions slaves who had fought in the civil wars. To forestall a counter-revolution by the new governor, they offered rebel bands the sack of Cap Français; and when an English invasion was imminent, they abolished slavery completely on August 29, 1793.

The decree of General Emancipation was felt in the colony like an electric shock. It was greeted with hostility by mulatto and white planters and with some skepticism by the blacks; Sonthonax had acted unilaterally and might yet be overruled by the French government. Sonthonax's intention was to convert the slaves into profit-sharing serfs, who were to be tied to their estates and subject to compulsory but remunerated labor. Almost nothing is known about how this system of forced labor functioned, either in 1793 or later years, but among the decree's initial effects were a disruption of plantation discipline and an increasing assertiveness on the part of the blacks. The hitherto powerless began to fully appreciate their latent power.

British and Spanish troops, sent from the surrounding colonies and welcomed by the planters, were to preserve slavery in most of the West and part of the South, but in some of the districts they occupied their arrival itself provoked uprisings and the burning of the plantations. Even without such militant action a social revolution was quietly proceeding, for where planters abandoned the countryside, work in the fields ceased and the blacks adopted a peasant life-style centered on their provision grounds. Moreover, to supplement their scanty forces the British, like the Spanish, were to recruit thousands of blacks as soldiers, further weakening the plantation regime. Above all, to repel the invaders, the Republican forces were also, during five years of warfare, to arm thousands of former slaves who until then had not left their plantations. As to the psychological effects of participating in a war of liberation, one can only guess, but in military terms the results were obvious. The civil commissioners in the North and West, André Rigaud in the South, the Spanish, and eventually the British all came to rely on armies predominantly made up of blacks.

One may argue, therefore, that though the Spanish and British occupations were intended to save the slave regime and the plantation economy, they had precisely the opposite effect. The outbreak of the European war greatly extended the effects of the slave revolt, breaking down the mental and physical shackles of slavery and plantation habit, and enabling the ex-slaves to develop the military skills with which to defend their freedom. At the same time, it made the former free coloreds increasingly dependent on the martial ability of the blacks. More than this, foreign intervention completely divided the *anciens libres* (as the free coloreds were now called) and isolated the large communities of the West from their cousins in the North and South. Slave emancipation was a fatal dilemma for the members of this classically unstable class. The Republic had guaranteed their civil rights but then took away their property and offended their prejudices. Many, therefore, opted to support the Spanish and British, though of these a large number soon changed their minds. Rigaud and Villatte remained committed to the Republic, but friction between them and Sonthonax and the French general Laveaux mounted as the latter looked more and more to the blacks for support.

While this gradual shift in the internal balance of power lay in the logic of the political situation, it also came to acquire enormous impetus from the meteoric career of a single black general, Toussaint Bréda, who in August 1793 adopted the name Louverture. A few months before, he had joined the Spaniards independently of Jean-François and Biassou, under whose command he had served. During the next ten years, he was to emerge as a military commander, diplomat, and political leader of consummate ability. He would achieve international renown and be acknowledged in some quarters as one of the great men of his day. Of the previous fifty years of his life little can be said with certainty.

Like the majority of slave leaders who achieved prominence, Toussaint was a Creole who had belonged to the slave elite. He had been a coachman and in charge of the livestock on the Bréda estate just outside of Cap Français, whose manager appears to have favored him. At some point he had become a devout Christian. Though his command of French would always remain fairly basic, he had learned to read, and late in life (between 1779 and 1791) to write his name. Despite his degree of acculturation, Toussaint did not lose touch with his African roots. He is said to have spoken fluently the language of his 'Arada' father — apparently the son of a chief — and to have enjoyed speaking it with other slaves of his father's ethnic group. He seems also to have become skilled in the medicinal use of plants and herbs. Such slaves who lived at the interface between white and black society needed to know the ways of both worlds. To maintain their standing in both communities, they had to be shrewd observers of human nature and skilled performers of a number of roles. It is not so surprising, then, if among Toussaint's dominant characteristics in later life were his ability to manipulate and his virtuoso use of deception. The plantation house was in this respect a good school.

This is perhaps one reason why it has only recently been discovered that Toussaint was no longer a slave at the time of the French Revolution. He had actually been freed around the age of thirty. While he appears to have maintained a close connection with the Bréda estate and its manager, he also owned and rented at different times both slaves and small properties. He thus belonged to the class of free colored slaveholders, into whose lower ranks he and his children married. One gets a picture, then, of a man of diverse experience, who was at home in various social milieus: among the white colonists, who thought well of him; among creole slaves and free blacks; and among *bossales* newly arrived from Africa.

Two versions exist of Toussaint's behavior during the August 1791 insurrection, both shakily supported by contemporary documentation. Most historians suppose that Toussaint had nothing to do with the uprising and at first protected the Bréda plantation, until after a few months he threw in his lot with the rebels. Others suggest that Toussaint himself secretly organized the rebellion. They claim he acted as an intermediary for counter-revolutionary whites, using his contacts among leaders of the slave community but remaining shrewdly in the background. Similar puzzles exist with regard to many other events in his life. It is certain, however, that within three months of the August uprising he had achieved prominence among the rebel blacks and was apparently one of Biassou's advisers. He interceded successfully for the lives of white prisoners, and, as one of the free colored negotiators used by the slave leaders, he transmitted their offer to the whites to help suppress the rebellion in return for the freedom of a few score leaders. Despite the amnesty France offered to free coloreds in rebellion, Toussaint stayed with the slave rebels through the dark days of 1792. His relations with Jean-François, who called himself the 'Grand Admiral', and with Biassou, self-styled 'Generalissimo', seem to have been stormy, but he remained one of their leading subordinates commanding a small force of his own with the rank of field marshal.

After he joined the Spaniards around June 1793, Toussaint's star rose rapidly. In the great jumble of mountains of the North Province, he immediately won a series of startling military victories against the French and free coloreds. These early campaigns reveal at once a leader of acute intelligence, who was adept at ambush and at totally confusing his opponents. They also reveal a man both ruthless and humane, capable of making barbarous threats but of sparing even those who had double-crossed him. This policy reaped rewards. White and mulatto property owners surrendered to him, knowing his reputation for mercy. As arms and ammunition fell into his hands, so his tiny army grew. Lances and machetes were exchanged for muskets. Free colored and even French soldiers joined its ranks and helped train its levies. If the essence of things creole is creative adaptation, this was a truly creole army. In nine months, it grew from a few hundred to several thousand men.

Meanwhile, the Spanish troops stayed cautiously on the Santo Domingo frontier, paralyzed by a series of epidemics. The forces of Jean-François and Biassou, for their part, gave up campaigning for quarreling among themselves and for living it up outrageously at the expense of the king of Spain. The Spaniards soon realized that they had bitten off far more than they could chew. Such successes as they had, they owed almost entirely to Toussaint. The handsome Jean-François they found vain and fickle, and the impetuous Biassou, gross and overbearing. But in Toussaint, Spanish officers recognized a military commander of ability and a man of honor and personal dignity. They were also much impressed by his piety and the hours he spent in church. Nonetheless, however much the Spanish might respect piety, honor, and military ability, they found themselves stuck with Jean-François and Biassou and compelled to recognize them as principal commanders.

This raises the difficult question of Toussaint's volte-face, his sudden desertion of the Spaniards in the spring of 1794 and his rallying to the French Republic. According to one interpretation, it was frustrated ambition and increasing friction with Biassou that led Toussaint to leave the Spanish and seek promotion under the French. Others attribute the changeover to a desire to win freedom for all the blacks in Saint Domingue. Specifically, they link his change of direction to the decree of February 4, 1794, by which the French government ratified Sonthonax's actions and abolished slavery in all France's colonies. However, though it would seem logical that these two great events were connected, the decree was not in fact known in the colony until long after Toussaint began negotiating with the French general Laveaux, and not for at least a month after he had turned on his Spanish allies.

Even so, Toussaint's volte-face was not a simply self-interested affair. His concern for the liberty of the blacks was genuine. Although in 1791–92 he was prominent among the chiefs who offered to force their followers back into slavery on the plantations, this was at moments when defeat seemed certain. Unlike Jean-François and Biassou, Toussaint never rounded up plantation blacks for sale to the Spaniards, and at least by mid-1793 he had become associated with the idea of General Emancipation. There is some evidence that his delay in joining the Spaniards was specifically due to his attempts to get the French to declare slavery abolished. His refusal to join the French thereafter was probably attributable to the Republic's precarious position. Anyway, having joined the Spanish, Toussaint played a double game, fighting to preserve the plantation regime but at the same time speaking to the blacks of liberty and equality. This doubtless helps explain why his army grew so rapidly. It was also at this time that he adopted the name Louverture ('the opening') with its cryptic connotation of a new beginning.

Matters came to a head early in 1794. After Spanish troops had arrived from Cuba and Venezuela, hundreds of French refugees began returning to the occupied districts. Only now, after almost a year of inaction, could the Spanish seriously contemplate restoring slavery on the plantations and launching an attack on Cap Français. Resistance came from various quarters — from plantation blacks who had not taken up arms but who refused to be coerced back into the fields, from free coloreds disenchanted with their treatment by the Spanish, and from some of the black mercenary troops as well. It was behind this movement that Toussaint decided to fling his weight as of the beginning of May 1794. For several months, nevertheless, he kept up his astonishing double game while he assessed the political situation. Though he told the French general Laveaux he was fighting hard for the Republic, he remained largely on the defensive, assuring the Spaniards that such hostilities as occurred should be blamed on his disobedient subordinates. At the same time, he tried to allay the suspicions of Jean-François and he also promised his allegiance to the British forces who were threatening him from the south. In the meantime, news trickled through from Europe of Republican victories and of the abolition of slavery, while in Saint Domingue the spring rains brought fevers that decimated the Spanish and British troops. Cunningly choosing his moment, Toussaint then fell on each of his opponents in turn with devastating effect.

Whether motivated by idealism or ambition, Toussaint's volte-face was therefore tortuous, cautious, and protracted, and it was not a single-handed initiative. It was nonetheless the turning point of the Haitian Revolution. Now associated with the ideology of the French Revolution, black militancy became unequivocally directed toward the complete overthrow of slavery for perhaps the first time in the Americas. The balance of power tipped against the alliance of slave owners and foreign invaders, and French rule in Saint Domingue would be saved for another decade; but having gained a leader of genius, the movement for black self-liberation henceforth held center stage.

The next four years were a period of almost constant warfare. For much of this time, Toussaint's ragged soldiers, 'as naked as earthworms' as he graphically described them, were perpetually short of food, clothing, and ammunition. They died by the hundred in their attacks on the well-entrenched positions of the British and Spanish, but in the process was forged a formidable army. The development should not be taken for granted. Unlike the free coloreds, who had a reputation as horsemen and sharpshooters, few slaves can have had much experience of firearms or artillery, even if they had been warriors in Africa. Since 1791 they had shown themselves skillful in their use of surprise and in exploiting terrain, capable of great endurance, and difficult to pin down. To these qualities Toussaint added the ability to maneuver in large numbers, heightened esprit de corps, and a tactical brilliance few could equal. He gathered around him an experienced officer corps, which was mainly black and ex-slave but included many mulattoes and a few whites as well. Already prominent by the end of 1794 were the youthful Moise, whom Toussaint called his nephew, and the vigorous and stern Jean-Jacques Dessalines.

By then, the Spaniards and their black auxiliaries were almost a spent force in Saint Domingue. They had lost half of their conquests and even their own frontier towns of San Raphael and San Michel on the grassy central savanna, stormed by Toussaint in October. They held the strategic northeastern seaport of Fort Dauphin, but the massacre there of 800 French colonists by Jean-François's soldiers, smarting from defeat, had ended all hopes of reviving the plantation regime. Instead, Spanish and black officers cooperated in stripping the sugar estates and sending their slaves and equipment to Cuba. Defeated in Europe and the Caribbean, Spain withdrew from the war in July 1795 and became an ally of the French Republic the following year. Santo Domingo, Spain's oldest colony, had become untenable and was surrendered to France, which for the time was too weak to occupy it. Jean-François and Biassou with 800 of their followers went into pensioned exile in different parts of the Spanish Empire. In the mountains of the northeast, however, many of their soldiers fought on in the name of the king until 1797.

Toussaint's forces occupied a cordon of some thirty camps stretching from the central mountains of the North Province along the fringe of the Artibonite plain to the port of Gonaives. He thus controlled access from the North to the West. Most of the northern littoral, however, was in the hands of Villatte and other semi-independent mulatto leaders. Laveaux, now governor, was confined with his few surviving white troops to the northwestern port of Port-de-Paix. The broad flood plain of the Artibonite became something of a no-man's-land, but the whole of the West Province to the south of it eventually fell to the British and their planter allies, although independent bands of blacks continued to harry them from various mountain strongholds. The British also held the naval base of the Môle Saint Nicolas and, at the tip of the southern peninsula, the prosperous coffee-growing region of the Grand Anse. The rest of the southern peninsula was a mulatto fief ruled from Les Cayes by André Rigaud. Launching successive attacks against the Grand Anse and Port-au-Prince, Rigaud, like Toussaint, built up an army mainly consisting of ex-slaves. By 1798 he commanded some 10,000 soldiers and Toussaint around 20,000.

Up to 1796, the British government had hoped to conquer Saint Domingue and add it to its tropical empire. Thereafter, it became resigned to failure but dared not withdraw for fear the black revolution would be exported to its own colonies. During their first two years in Saint Domingue (the only time they had any prospect of success), the British forces averaged barely 2,000 men. Though they were massively reinforced in 1796, British commanders continued with a mainly defensive strategy that condemned most of their troops to die in the seaports of epidemic diseases. Throughout these years of war, yellow fever flourished in the Caribbean, fueled by the huge influx of non-immune European troops and their concentration in the region's ports. During the five-year occupation of Saint Domingue, the British lost 15,000 of the 25,000 soldiers they sent there. The British also gravely blundered early on by alienating the free coloreds, many of whom deserted them. Even so, the most valuable part of the occupied zone was the plain of Arcahaye, where the local commander, the ancien libre Lapointe, kept the plantations in full production. By 1798 the costs of occupation were found to be prohibitive; and under mounting pressure from Toussaint and Rigaud, the British staged a gradual evacuation. Only then for some 60,000–70,000 blacks did slavery come to an end.

During these years Toussaint's position within the Republican zone grew steadily more dominant. Early in 1796, Villatte and the anciens libres of the North Province attempted to overthrow Governor Laveaux in an apparent bid for independence, which seems to have been secretly supported by André Rigaud in the South. According to some sources, Toussaint knew of the planned coup and with supreme cunning actually encouraged its instigators. But once it had broken out, he intervened in force and crushed it. The French government was left in no doubt on whom it depended for keeping Saint Domingue in French hands. Toussaint, the ex-slave, was proclaimed deputy-governor.

For the time being, however, the Republican position remained precarious. Not only were the British now pouring troops into the colony, but also dissension was rife in the Republican zone. Having fled to France in 1794, Sonthonax returned to Saint Domingue in May 1796 with four other civil commissioners and 900 white soldiers. Their attempts to centralize control of both the war effort and the economy of the Republican parishes quickly made enemies. As Laveaux had found, mulatto leaders who had become accustomed to complete local autonomy resented attempts to take over abandoned property they themselves were exploiting. Efforts to raise the productivity of the surviving plantations also spread fears among the ex-slaves (now called 'cultivators') of a restoration of slavery. This was especially true of the northwestern peninsula, where the plantations had suffered relatively little, and whose coffee was sold to American traders for food and munitions, as in the mulatto South. From the failure of Villatte's coup to the end of 1796, the Northwest witnessed a succession of uprisings by black cultivators, in which were killed the few remaining white colonists in the region. Local mulattoes were probably behind at least some of these revolts. They show, nevertheless, that even in these districts least affected by the slave revolution a complete break with the past had by now occurred in the minds of the rural blacks. This did not mean, however, that such blacks were willing to defend their freedom by leaving their homes and becoming soldiers in Toussaint's army. Sonthonax had distributed guns to plantation workers; but when in a moment of crisis he tried to conscript all young males for military service, the extent of rebellion increased. At the same time, the mulatto South broke away from French rule, when the tactless commissioners sent to Les Cayes were expelled by André Rigaud and more whites were massacred.

The Republic was to weather these crises but only at the cost of seeing more and more power pass into the hands of Toussaint Louverture. It was his homespun diplomacy that finally pacified the blacks of the Northwest. The African General Pierre Michel, hero of the northeastern campaigns and a favorite of Sonthonax, was then arrested. Earlier rivals of Toussaint had already disappeared. With the aristocratic Governor Laveaux, Toussaint had formed a remarkably close friendship, referring to him in his correspondence as 'Papa', though the two men were about the same age. Even so, by the autumn of 1796 Toussaint was intimating that Laveaux could best serve Saint Domingue if he were in Paris, where angry planters were demanding the restoration of West Indian slavery; Laveaux was promptly elected a deputy for Saint Domingue and returned home to France. Next it was the turn of Commissioner Sonthonax. In the summer of 1797, Toussaint suddenly accused him of plotting to make Saint Domingue independent. Though still popular with the blacks, he also was forced to depart.

Smitten with life in the West Indies and threatened by political reaction in Paris, Sonthonax may indeed have wished to see Saint Domingue sever ties with France. Nevertheless, Toussaint's accusation suggests a neat sense of irony. While continuing to play the role of a loyal servant of the French Republic, he eliminated one by one all his rivals within the colony. The French government was becoming alarmed and in 1798 dispatched a new representative, General Hédouville. In six months, he, too, was deftly outmaneuvered, though with all due courtesty, and driven out of Saint Domingue by a supposedly spontaneous uprising. Whether or not Toussaint was aiming for independence, or even supreme power, at this time, historians will probably never agree. However, the growth of Toussaint's power was inexorable.

The Ascendancy of Toussaint Louverture, 1798–1802

Toussaint's expulsion of Sonthonax facilitated a rapprochement with Rigaud, which enabled the two men to cooperate in driving out the British. Thereafter, only Rigaud himself stood between Toussaint and complete domination of Saint Domingue. Rigaud now controlled all the southern peninsula; Toussaint, all the North and West. Once their common enemy had been eliminated, relations between them rapidly deteriorated. Even today, the conflict between Toussaint and Rigaud is regarded by Haitians as one of the most sensitive topics in their history. It has become known as the War of Knives. Although it was in essence a regional power struggle, it tended to divide the light-skinned anciens libres from the new class of black military officers, though most of the troops on both sides were black ex-slaves. Many of Toussaint's light-skinned officers, though they had been with him for years, sided with Rigaud; and when Toussant invaded the South, they staged rebellions against him. The fighting was desperate, and Toussaint's reprisals were brutal, although prudently delegated to subordinates. The details are disputed, but the black general Dessalines has been accused of waging something like a war of genocide against the southern mulattoes. Toussaint later reproved him: 'I ordered you to prune the tree not to uproot it.' Rigaud and most of the leaders fled to France.

By the middle of 1800, Toussaint ruled supreme in Saint Domingue and of necessity was recognized as its governor. A small, wiry man, very black, with mobile, penetrating eyes, he greatly impressed most who met him, even those who thought him ugly. He had lost in battle his upper set of front teeth and his ears were deformed by wearing heavy gold earrings, but his presence was commanding and suggested enormous self-control. Whether socializing with white planters or pacifying angry plantation workers, his manner was reserved but dignified. In private, the whites might mock his rusticity (his headscarf, his limited French) or his 'pretensions' (his huge watch chains, his moralizing piety), but in his presence no one laughed. Though Toussaint maintained the external pomp of previous colonial governors and he acquired much landed property, his private life was frugal. Wary of being poisoned, he ate little, and he slept only a few hours each night, invariably working late with his secretaries. His prodigious activity astonished people, as did the air of mystery he deliberately cultivated. Still an excellent horseman, he often rode over one hundred miles a day, making frequent changes of direction so that no one could be sure where he would appear next.

With the war ended in the south, Toussaint could now set about rebuilding the colony and restoring its shattered economy. Although fiercely committed to the liberty of the blacks, he believed it essential that the plantation regime be revived in order to restore Saint Domingue's prosperity. With no export economy, there would be no revenue to maintain his army of 20,000–40,000 men. And without the army, the gains of the revolution would be at the mercy of France's unstable politics. Toussaint therefore continued with the schemes of Commissioner Sonthonax, whereby the ex-slaves were compelled to work on the plantations in return for a share of the produce. It was a difficult policy to implement, for increasingly the blacks preferred to establish smallholdings of their own and had little desire to work for wages. This was especially true of the sugar estates, which depended on regimented gang labor and where the working day was long and arduous. Already accustomed to marketing their own food crops, most blacks preferred to concentrate on extending their family provision grounds, cheerfully letting the fields of cane and coffee choke with weeds. Toussaint, however, refused to break up the great estates. He used the army to impose the regime of forced labor and sanctioned the use of corporal punishment; he even supported the reintroduction of the slave trade to make up the loss of manpower. As most estates had been abandoned by their owners, they were leased out usually to army officers and other privileged figures in the new regime. In addition, Toussaint also encouraged the return from exile of the white planters to take charge of their properties and to work toward the creation of a new Saint Domingue.

The return of the planters, of course, raised grave suspicions among the plantation blacks and also among some of Toussaint's officers. They also resented the white advisers he appointed, and the pleasure he evidently took in inviting planters and merchants to his social gatherings. A naturally taciturn man, he seemed to be becoming increasingly remote. These tensions were given violent expression when the very popular General Moise staged a revolt in the northern plain, which caused the deaths of several of the returned planters. When Toussaint had him executed, many thought his policies where going awry. It is usually argued that Toussaint thought the technical expertise of the whites and their social polish were necessary to the rebuilding of the colony, and that he therefore was committed to a multiracial Saint Domingue. Recent work, however, has stressed that, although Toussaint encouraged the whites to return, he rarely gave them back their estates. These tended to remain in the hands of his army officers who constituted a new, black, landholding class. The return of the planters served to camouflage this development, and also to provide hostages.

It is by no means clear how successful Toussaint was in reviving the plantation economy. Export figures for the twelve months following the war against Rigaud (1800–01) show coffee production at two-thirds the 1789 level, raw sugar down by four-fifths, and semi-refined sugar, the most valuable item, almost non-existent. On the other hand, it is likely that trade figures were deliberately understated to allow the amassing of secret funds and the stockpiling of munitions. The administrative confusion and the autonomy of local army commanders, of which white officials complained, probably fulfilled the same function. According to his critics, Toussaint kept his generals' loyalty by allowing them to amass personal fortunes. Their troops went unpaid but the soldiers in turn were allowed to exercise a petty tyranny over the cultivators, whose provision grounds were subject to army requisitions. Only on the generals' plantations, however, were the labor laws effectively applied. Other commentators painted a more enthusiastic picture of the regime, insisting that a new spirit was abroad in the colony. Race prejudice was diminishing fast. Towns were being rebuilt. Justice was administered impartially. Even some schools were established (though this was a French initiative). All one can say with certainty is that the new regime was given very little time to prove itself.

Late in 1799, France, like Saint Domingue, also acquired a military strongman for a ruler. Napoleon Bonaparte and Toussaint Louverture had much in common. Both were seen as defenders of basic revolutionary gains of the previous decade, particularly of new land settlements. Both were autocrats who extinguished all political liberty in their respective countries. Both were destroyed by their own ambition. In July 1801, shortly before Napoleon proclaimed himself consul for life, Toussaint promulgated a constitution for Saint Domingue which flagrantly concentrated all power in his hands and which made him governor for life with the right to choose his successor. Drawn up by planters with a secessionist background, the document came within a hairbreadth of a declaration of independence. Toussaint had anticipated by 160 years the concept of associated statehood. Napoleon was infuriated. However, the first consul had already determined that French rule should be restored in what had been France's most valuable possession.

There was, nevertheless, nothing inevitable about the epic clash between Toussaint and Napoleon. Although he was constantly under pressure from vengeful planters, merchants, and colonial officials, bonaparte had resisted for well over a year their clamor for a military expedition. His original policy was to leave Toussaint in control of Saint Domingue and to use the colony as a springboard for expanding French power in the Americas. Black troops would be sent to conquer the slave colonies of France's rivals. As part of the plan, Louisiana was purchased from Spain. However, by the spring of 1801 it was apparent that, under its black governor, Saint Domingue would be of little use to France; it was de facto already an independent state. Though France was at war with Great Britain, and unofficially with the United States, too (the Quasi-War of 1798–1800), Toussaint had made a secret commercial treaty and non-aggression pact with both these powers. This involved expelling French privateers from the colony. His purpose was to preserve the trade on which Saint Domingue, and his army, depended. The United States supplied vital foodstuffs, livestock, and munitions; the British navy controlled the sea-lanes and would otherwise have blockaded Saint Domingue. This is why, when the French and mulattoes tried to foment a slave rebellion in Jamaica, and sent agents there from Saint Domingue, Toussaint betrayed the plot to the Jamaican administration. Whatever his interest in black liberation, he needed to keep on good terms with his neighbors so as to preserve his autonomy.

In spite of Toussaint's independent foreign policy and his ambiguous behavior toward the planters, Napoleon's intention remained down to March 1801 to work with the black leader, not against him. However, the last straw for Napoleon came when Toussaint suddenly annexed without reference to France the adjoining colony of Santo Domingo, which was then French territory. The ex-slave thereby became master of the entire island of Hispaniola. It was the high point of his career. Suspicious of French intentions, Toussaint aimed to deny a potential invasion force use of Santo Domingo's harbors. But it was precisely this event that persuaded Napoleon that an invasion was necessary. Toussaint's new constitution merely enraged him further. Nevertheless, the fatal decision to attempt to restore slavery in Saint Domingue was not taken for another year, long after the invasion force had landed. Although usually presented as an act of vicious megalomania, the Napoleonic invasion of Saint Domingue was more like a last-ditch attempt to keep the plantation regime in French hands.

Toussaint had grossly miscalculated. If he was willing to antagonize Napoleon to this degree, some say, he should have gone all out and declared complete independence, rallying the black masses behind him. Instead, he kept up the fiction of loyalty to France, sending envoys to Napoleon to explain each act of defiance. He continued to assure local whites of his goodwill and to admonish the blacks on the necessity of hard work. The ambivalence of his double game was to critically weaken black resistance to the coming invasion. Toussaint's failure to declare independence was doubtless due to a number of factors. Caution, the need for white administrative personnel, and the fear of alienating the slaveholding Americans and British were probably the most important. By stopping short of de jure independence, Toussaint evidently thought that Napoleon would negotiate rather than fight. Perhaps he overrated the military lession he had taught the Spanish and British. Or perhaps he believed that the British navy would prevent a French fleet from crossing the Atlantic.

The British, however, would support the black governor's rule only so long as it weakened France's war effort, and the Anglo-French war was now drawing to a temporary close. The British government feared both Toussaint and Napoleon, but regarded the latter as the lesser of two evils. To see the two embroiled in internecine conflict would be a perfect compromise solution to a threatening situation. In October 1801, as soon as peace preliminaries were signed, the British gave their assent to an invasion of Saint Domingue.

The War of Independence, 1802–03

Napoleon's brother-in-law, General Leclerc, landed in Saint Domingue at the beginning of February 1802 with some 10,000 soldiers. By sending out a large force in the healthy winter months and deploying it rapidly, Napoleon avoided the worst mistakes of the British and Spanish. His troops were also far superior to those previously sent there, and their numbers were doubled within two months. Leclerc's orders were nevertheless to seize the colony by ruse, winning over where possible the black generals. Only later, once he had allayed their suspicions, was he to disarm their soliders and then deport all the black officers. The plantations would be returned to their owners. Slavery would be restored in Santo Domingo, where it had never been officially abolished, but in Saint Domingue the forced labor regime would be retained. Leclerc both said and thought he was re-establishing French rule but not slavery.

Uncertain of French intentions, the blacks failed to offer any concerted resistance and Leclerc quickly occupied all the colony's ports. Cap Français, under the eye of Toussaint, was burned by its commander, Henry Christophe, as was Saint Marc by Dessalines, but several of the generals surrendered without a fight. They were now planters themselves and had property to protect. Toussaint, Christophe, and Dessalines, however, took to the mountains, fighting heroic rearguard actions and destroying all that they left behind. Battle casualties were heavy and from the beginning the war was marked by frightful atrocities on both sides. Fearing the return of slavery, the rural population rallied to the black army and produced guerrilla leaders of their own. However, as successive generals surrendered, their troops were turned against those who still held out. Through the month of April Toussaint kept up a vigorous guerrilla campaign with great persistence but dwindling resources. He surrendered early in May and retired to private life on one of his plantations. Christophe, Dessalines, and the other generals were maintained in their posts and used by the French to mop up remaining guerrilla resistance.

It may be that all three leaders were biding their time. Leclerc's army was already severely weakened and the blacks well knew that during the summer it would be decimated by disease. Nevertheless, when within a month Toussaint was accused of plotting rebellion, it was Dessalines and Christophe who helped denounce him. The old leader was kidnapped, hastily deported, and died in a French dungeon in April 1803. Despite this devious maneuvering by the military chiefs, small bands of insurgents fought on in the mountains in the tradition of the maroons. As Toussaint declared on leaving the colony: the French had felled only the trunk of the tree of liberty; it had strong roots and would grow again.

The situation changed dramatically in July 1802, when it was learned (by the blacks and Leclerc almost simultaneously) that the French government had decided to restore slavery in all France's colonies. Attempts to disarm the rural population now met with massive resistance, just when hundreds of French soldiers each week were dying of yellow fever. The campaign of terror launched by Leclerc proved counterproductive. As thousands of black prisoners, men and women, went stoically to their deaths, a new sense of unity was forged based on racial solidarity. By the autumn, the French were fighting the entire non-white population of Saint Domingue. Even the free coloreds who had fled the South in 1800 and returned in Leclerc's army now combined with their former opponents. Led by Rigaud's protégé, Alexandre Pétion, they accepted the overall leadership of Jean-Jacques Dessalines, who finally deserted the French in late September. As Toussaint's inspector of agriculture, the conqueror of the mulatto South, and then Leclerc's chief collaborator, Dessalines had been responsible for the deaths of very many blacks and anciens libres. However, he was the ideal person to lead the struggle to expel the French, and not only because he was the senior general. A menial slave under the old regime, he had none of the liking for white society which Toussaint, and the former domestic Christophe, shared with the mulattoes. He spoke only Créole, the language of the cultivators. And he was possessed of demonic energy, his battle cry being, 'Burn houses, cut off heads!'

After Leclerc himself died of yellow fever, the repugnant General Rochambeau openly waged a war of genocide against the black population, but to no avail. No one can say how far Napoleon would have gone in this hopeless venture, but once war was resumed with Great Britain in May 1803 he had to admit defeat. Until then he had sent 44,000 troops to Saint Domingue. Thereafter the British navy prevented any reinforcements from crossing the Atlantic. Napoleon's western design was at an end. Louisiana was sold to the United States. With British ships blockading the coast of Saint Domingue, and Dessalines's forces besieging the coastal towns, the remains of the French army evacuated the colony in November. Since 1791, some 70,000 European soldiers and seamen had died in the attempt to maintain slavery. Of the few thousand whites who optimistically stayed behind, most died in a series of massacres in the following months.

International Repercussions

On January 1, 1804, Dessalines declared Saint Domingue independent and gave it the aboriginal Amerindian name of 'Haiti'. 'I have given the French cannibals blood for blood,' he proclaimed. 'I have avenged America.'[1] During the war of independence some of the blacks referred to themselves as 'Incas' (perhaps an echo of the Peruvian uprising of 1780), and some European writers also fancifully depicted the ex-slaves as avenging the Arawaks exterminated in the sixteenth century. Archaeological finds probably made for a general awareness among the blacks of these fellow victims of colonialism, whose patrimony they were now inheriting. While anchoring the new state to the American past, the country's new name meant above all a symbolic break with Europe. All whites were henceforth forbidden to own land in Haiti.

Having destroyed the wealthiest planter class in the New World and defeated the armies of France, Spain, and England, the former slaves and free coloreds now went about making laws for themselves and erecting a state apparatus. In a world dominated by Europeans and where slavery and the slave trade were expanding, the new state was a symbol of black freedom and a demonstration of black accomplishments. For both abolitionists and the pro-slavery lobby, Haiti was a great experiment, a crucial test case for ideas about race, slavery, and the future of the Caribbean. In Haiti itself, publicists and statesmen spoke out against racism, colonialism, and enslavement. Nevertheless, all the early Haitian statesmen took pains to disclaim any intention of intervening in neighboring colonies. Like Toussaint, they wished to do nothing that might provoke a maritime blockade or an invasion by the slave-holding powers. The exception to this policy was the annexation of Santo Domingo, which Dessalines attempted in 1805 and was finally accomplished in 1822. As in the 1790s, rumors about the activity of Haitian 'agents' continued to circulate, and these are given credence by some historians, but official involvement in any of the slave conspiracies or rebellions of the post-1804 period has yet to be proven. The only clear case we have of subversive proselytizing is by agents of the French Republic during the 1790s, most particularly by Victor Hugues, who from Guadeloupe helped foment rebellions among the French-speaking free coloreds of Grenada and Saint Vincent. Haiti nonetheless did make a major contribution to the abolition of slavery (and to decolonization) in the New World. This was in 1815, when Alexandre Pétion gave vital assistance to Simon Bolívar that enabled him to relaunch his campaign for South American independence. Pétion demanded as payment that the planter aristocrat declare slavery in his homeland abolished, which he did on his return to South America.

From 1792 onward laws were passed all around the Caribbean and in North America restricting immigration from strife-torn Saint Domingue. Even when the likelihood of direct interference was not considered strong, slave owners feared the revolution's inflammatory example. Within a month of the August 1791 revolt, slaves in Jamaica were singing songs about the uprising, and before long whites in the West Indies and North America were complaining uneasily of a new 'insolence' on the part of their slaves. Several plots and insurrections were partly inspired by events in Saint Domingue and the Emancipation Decree of 1794. Most notable of these were the conspiracies organized by free coloreds in Bahia (1798), Havana (1812), and Charleston (1822). However, many factors were at work in the slave rebellions of the period, and to suppose that mere inspiration from abroad was critical in provoking resistance would be to underestimate the difficulties confronting dissidents in this age of strong colonial garrisons.

France did not abandon its claims to its former colony until 1825, when the Haitian government agreed to pay a large indemnity to the expelled colonists. The debt the country thereby incurred was among the factors retarding its growth in the nineteenth century, and the concessions then given to French merchants further shifted the export economy into foreign hands. Britain and the United States had early established trade relations with the new state (later interrupted by Jefferson as a favor to Napoleon), but full diplomatic recognition was withheld by these countries until they had abolished slavery and no longer deemed Haiti a threat.

The Legacy of Revolution

Created from a unique experience of slavery, war and revolution, Haiti was to be like no other state. The fledgling black republic began life with its towns and plantations in ruins and under constant threat of another French invasion. Its population had been decimated; it was severely lacking in technical skills and almost totally without experience in administration or government.

Despite the attempts to maintain production on the plantations, the ex-slaves had for a decade been building new lives for themselves as either soldiers or peasant cultivators. Fear of invasion and institutional self-interest were to burden Haiti with an exceptionally large army for the rest of the century. The earliest governments, particularly that of Henry Christophe (1806–20), continued the struggle to revive the sugar plantations with forced labor. However, the masses' desire for land and hatred of estate work, and the falling world price of sugar, forced the attempt to be finally abandoned by 1830. Haiti became essentially a country of peasant smallholders who grew food crops and a little coffee, either on land distributed by the government or on which they squatted. The postwar population was presumably young and mainly female, and therefore grew rapidly. The relative abundance of land meant that the peasants probably lived reasonably well in the nineteenth century. The Voodoo religion, though persecuted by all the early leaders as subversive to authority, became entrenched in the countryside.

Government revenues came primarily from taxing coffee exports. As in colonial times and during the revolution, the government remained military and authoritarian in character, though constitutional forms were to vary widely and regimes change rapidly. After declaring himself emperor, Dessalines was assassinated in 1806 and for the next fourteen years Haiti was divided between a mulatto republic in the South and West and a northern state, ruled by Henry Christophe, which became a monarchy in 1811. Dessalines had made great efforts to preserve the fragile wartime alliance between blacks and anciens libres but tensions continued to run deep, even after the reunification of the country in 1820. Haitian politics developed as a struggle between the uneducated black officer corps which controlled the army, and the brown-skinned professional and business class which made up most of the country's elite.

This conflict was mirrored more broadly in the elaboration of two competing ideologies, one 'black', the other 'mulatto'. In Haitian society the color line was not at all absolute, but these two opposing camps, fronted by the Liberal and National parties, tended to be divided by phenotype as well as by culture, religion, and attitudes toward national development and toward the country's revolutionary past.

Note

1. Archives Nationales Paris, Cols.,CC9B/23, proclamation of 28 April 1804.

The Victor Vanquished: Emancipation in St. Croix; Its Antecedents and Immediate Aftermath[1]

N. A. T. HALL

Introduction

The slave uprising of 2–3 July 1848 in St. Croix, Danish West Indies, belongs to that splendidly isolated category of Caribbean slave revolts which succeeded if, that is, one defines success in the narrow sense of the legal termination of servitude. The sequence of events can be briefly rehearsed. On the night of Sunday 2 July, signal fires were lit on the estates of western St. Croix, estate bells began to ring and conch shells blown, and by Monday morning, 3 July, some 8,000 slaves had converged in front of Frederiksted fort demanding their freedom. In the early hours of Monday morning, the governor general Peter von Scholten, who had only hours before returned from a visit to neighbouring St. Thomas, summoned a meeting of his senior advisers in Christiansted (Bass End), the island's capital. Among them was Lt. Capt. Irminger, commander of the Danish West Indian naval station, who urged the use of force, including bombardment from the sea to disperse the insurgents, and the deployment of a detachment of soldiers and marines from his frigate *Ørnen*. Von Scholten kept his own counsels. No troops were despatched along the arterial Centreline road and, although he gave Irminger permission to sail around the coast to beleaguered Frederiksted (West End), he went overland himself and arrived in town sometime around 4 p.m. before Irminger did. No sooner had he alighted from his coach than he addressed the swarming multitude of slaves insisting on their freedom: 'Now you are free, you are hereby emancipated.' (Von Petersen 1855: 94–142; Larsen 1928: 252–67; Lawaetz 1940: 174–91; Vibæk 1966: 286–96; Hansen 1970: 355–96).

Emancipation by gubernatorial fiat abruptly terminated 16 hours of riotous but surprisingly bloodless activity. The absence of bloodshed and the *dénouement* of freedom distinguishes this uprising from other 'late' slave rebellions in the Caribbean. Bussa's 1816 rebellion in Barbados, the Demerara uprising in 1823 and the Jamaica Christmas rebellion of 1831 were all characterised by spectacular blood-letting and no immediate consequential change in the slaves' legal status (Craton 1982: 254–321). None of those uprisings in the British West Indies had been predicated on the declared, as distinct from the rumoured, intent of the metropolitan government to emancipate the slave population. The slaves in the Danish West Indies, on the other hand, had had the Crown's assurance in the previous year that general emancipation would take place in 1859, with an interim dispensation of Free Birth to take effect from 28 July 1847 (R/A, GTk, NEER 1847). Nevertheless, the St. Croix rebellion shares common ground with those above-mentioned in the British West Indies, in that it derived as much from aroused expectations as it did from a perception of oppression.

The uprising followed more than a decade and a half of ameliorative changes introduced under the liberalising stewardship of Von Scholten, governor general since 1828. During the 1830s, the work day's length was strictly regulated; slave owners' discretionary powers of punishment drastically reduced; public auctions banned and the keeping of plantation journals for regular inspection made mandatory (R/A, GTk, CANS 1834–43: passim). In the 1840s, Saturday was conceded as a free day, to facilitate its use as a market day in place of Sunday, which was now consecrated to religious observance and secular instruction, Wage payments at the rate of 4 Reales per day were

Nieuwe West-Indische Gids, Vol. 58, Nos. 1–2, (1984)m pp. 3–36.

introduced for plantation work undertaken on the prescribed free day (Ørsted 1844: 259–61). Significant improvements were also registered in the quality of slave housing which was approvingly viewed by an eye as critical as Victor Schoelcher's (Schoelcher 1843: 20–21). The first publicly supported elementary schools for slave children were opened with appropriate ceremony in 1841, and by 1846 their existence had been formalised by an ordinance authorising 17 schools distributed between St. Croix, St. Thomas and St. Jan, the establishment of a board, a curriculum, examination procedures, etc. (Hall 1979: 1–45). Von Scholten's strategy was based on a calculation of the inevitability of emancipation in the Danish, once emancipation had taken place in the British, West Indies. Since he deemed it no longer a question of whether but when, he sought by this reforming dispensation to smooth the transition to full freedom when it should arrive (R/A, GTk, CANS 1834–43: 1834a; 1834b). His metropolitan principals and the increasingly vocal Liberal politicians in Denmark's provincial assemblies gradually came to share the governor general's emancipationist perspective (Jensen 1931–34: 608–11) and by 1847 the issue had been sealed by royal proclamation.

For all the world therefore, the Danish West Indies appeared set on a course for an untraumatic termination of chattel slavery. Amelioration and the royal proclamation apart, there were other favourable auguries which suggested a smooth passage. There was no well-developed tradition of slave revolts. The Danish West Indies, unlike Jamaica, had passed but once through the fiery crucible of actual revolt, and that 1733 uprising in St. Jan (Westergaard 1917) had been conclusively put down with assistance from the French. Ethnic rebellions of the sort which frequently plagued Jamaica, Barbados, the Leeward and Windward islands while their slave populations were predominantly African, were never a feature of the Danish West Indian experience. As for conspiracies, only that in St. Croix in 1759 (R/A, GTk 1760; Westergaard 1926) created a briefly sustained ripple of anxiety. Nor were there to be further conspiracies, actual or attempted revolts, as the slave populations of the Danish West Indies became increasingly creolised after the late eighteenth century. In St. Croix itself, a useful index of the creolisation process was the astonishingly high incidence of church affiliation, which by 1835 was 99 per cent of the island's total slave population (Hall 1980a: 25). Yet those confessional affinities appear, if anything, to have reinforced the quest for 'respectability' at the expense of 'reputation' (Wilson 1973). That emphasis, and its concomitant, an accommodating rather than an adversary mind-set, is perhaps best explained not so much by religion's opiate effect, as by the structures within those denominations permitted to practise in the Danish West Indies: the state Lutheran Church, the Roman Catholics, the Moravians, and to a lesser extent the Dutch Reformed Church. None of these offered the same possibilities as the non-conformist Baptists and Methodists for slave leadership within the congregation; nor, by the same token, the possibilities for the emergence of movements such as the 'native Baptists' with their potential for political radicalisation (Turner 1982).

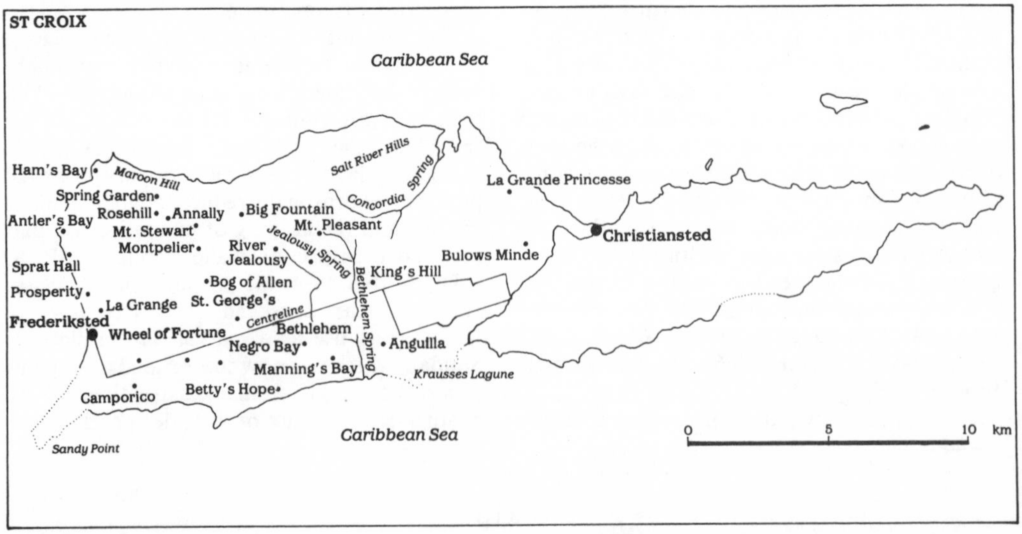

Notwithstanding the apparent order and calm of mature creolised slave society in the Danish West Indies, there were persons, as late as 1847, who recognized that the will to resist was as constant as servitude itself; that the grace period — virtually apprenticeship before emancipation — could conceivably be interrupted by what was euphemistically called 'unforeseen circumstances' (Hall 1983b: 52). The slaves for their part had responded to the Law of Free Birth not with unalloyed enthusiasm as might have been anticipated, but rather with impatience born of dissatisfaction that their children were beneficiaries of an imperial largesse which they would have to wait more than a decade to enjoy (Hall 1979: 33). Free Birth as policy had a respectable international pedigree: the Venezuelans had implemented it in 1821 (Lombardi 1971: 48–53); Buxton had canvassed it in the British Parliament in 1823 (Klingberg 1968: 182). But in the Danish West Indies, the asymmetry which it established was productive of the very tensions the metropolitan government sought to avoid.

There is evidence, moreover, which indicates that since at least 1800, the slaves particularly in St. Croix, were less and less in thrall to whiteness as a megalithic instrument of social control. Its erosion as a formidable deterrent had been promoted by intimate contact with a growing cadre of Anglo-Irish plantation supervisory personnel which did not exactly command respect. Nor were there grounds to be in awe of a colonial polity whose power traditionally had been less than hegemonic. Most particularly, its exiguous resources of force, which had virtually invited the 1733 uprising, encouraged the conspiracy of 1759 and had proved visibly inadequate to respond to the British invasions of 1801 and 1807, were no more prepossessing in 1848 than they had ever been (Hall 1983b). Whatever other calculations the slaves might have made in 1848, there is very little doubt that they considered the odds favourable because of the feebleness of the colonial military posture.

Emancipation by gubernatorial fiat foreclosed the possibility of the Akan-style alternative polity envisaged by some earlier Caribbean slave rebellions, and of which the regime of Dessalines, as Michael Craton has perceptively noted, was the ultimate expression (Craton 1982: 251). The St. Croix insurgents had no such political order in contemplation. Their aspirations, like those of their Jamaican counterparts in 1831 or Barbadian equivalents in 1816 (Craton 1982: 252, 257, 294, 332) did not transcend the regularisation of a proto-peasant status well established by 1848 (Hall 1980a; 1983a). Victory achieved through the mediation of state approval also left intact, with the exception of legal slavery, the institutional structures of the colonial polity, including the mechanisms for the administration of law and order. Many of the predominantly non-Danish planter class and some sectors of officialdom, moreover, shared little of Von Scholten's reforming enthusiasm or racial optimism, however guarded (Hall 1979: 15–22). Soured by an emancipation which they thought premature, angered by a rebellion which they deemed impertinent, they sought an early opportunity to restore the social order which had prevailed up to Monday 3 July 1848.

The court martial: provenance, significance and purpose

In the early hours of Tuesday morning, a group of the recently emancipated was shot down just outside Christiansted. There was retaliatory looting and destruction for the next three days on estates in the centre, south, west and north of the island. On Thursday, Von Scholten suffered what would now be diagnosed as a nervous collapse, and the lieutenant governor of St. Thomas, Frederik Oxholm, was invited to assume command of the civil government (Von Petersen 1855: 94–142; Larsen 1928: 252–67; Lawaetz 1940: 174–91; Vibæk 1966: 286–96; Hansen 1970: 355–96). Oxholm arrived on Saturday and the 530 troops which he requested of the governor of Puerto Rico arrived on Friday (N/A, RG 55 Box 9, 1848a, 1848b). But long before then, Irminger had moved decisively to assert the power of constituted authority, to demonstrate to the newly emancipated that freedom was not licence. On Tuesday, Frederiksted was put under a state of emergency by a commission consisting of Irminger, Capt. Frederik von Scholten, the governor general's brother, Capt. Castonier, the fort commandant, and Chief of Police Øgaard: if the freedmen came back to town and assembled in groups of more than ten, they would be fired on by the fort cannon and the frigate, still at anchor in the harbour (Von Petersen 1855: 126–27).

Irminger's role as *primus inter pares* in this commission can be assumed from the superiority of his rank and the fact that he commanded resources far superior to anything Castonier had at his disposal. By Wednesday he had manifestly taken charge, relieving

Castonier, albeit temporarily, of the command of the fort, and using his marines to demolish a block of buildings obscuring the fort's line of fire towards the landward approaches from the north and east. By Thursday 6 July, the commission had been enlarged to include the commanding officer of Frederiksted's Fire Corps, Major Gyllich, and Crown Prosecutor Sarauw (Von Petersen 1855: 126–27). This enlarged commission issued a second proclamation on Thursday which had the effect of extending the emergency beyond Frederiksted: 'any person or persons opposing the authorities or in any other manner combining for illegal or violent purposes will be dealt with as rioters and instantly shot' (Von Petersen 1855: 129).[2] The mass arrests began the same day and the court martial proceedings in Frederiksted on Friday 7 July.

The court sat uninterruptedly for the next five weeks. It examined more than 100 prisoners, heard evidence from other recently emancipated slaves, from freedmen before emancipation, from estate owners, agents, overseers, book-keepers and from government officials. Those apprehended were far more than could be accommodated in the very fort to which most of the terrified whites of western St. Croix had fled only a few days before. The overflow were confined on the *Ørnen* and on cargo boats in harbour (Hansen 1970:394). The court consisted essentially of the members of the commission mentioned above, with High Court Assessor Louis Rothe as chairman. Irminger did not participate, but the draconian spirit of the trials breathed his love of discipline and strong measures as the only effective method to deal with the perpetrators of the uprising and participants in its destructive aftermath. Within a week, eight persons had been executed on charges ranging from felonious wounding and arson to riotous assembly.

In resorting to the court martial, Irminger and the commission drew upon an instrument with the best antecedents. In the previous century a parallel had been drawn with frequency and facility between the slave society of the Danish West Indies and one in which martial law or the articles of war were in force. The population disparity between slaves and whites fostered a desire for absolute obedience and a state-of-siege mentality which manifested themselves in actual or proposed provisions of the slave codes and the manner of their administration (Hall 1977). Summary justice of the drumhead variety followed in the wake of the 1759 conspiracy (R/A, GTk 1760) and there were resonances of approval from eighteenth-century commentators such as Hans West (West 1793: 134) and a governor general in the 1780s, Major General Schimmelmann (R/A, GTk 1785a).

Above all, however, the elaboration and justification of the military parallel was the work of State Counsellor Lindemann, who produced in 1783 one of the better known draft slave codes. More than a quarter of those 43 articles dealing with 'Slaves and Punishment for Misdeeds' had their inclusion justified on the basis of similar provisions in the military code (R/A, GTk 1783a). Proposed punishments for theft and perjury were similarly based, as were proposals for the maintenance of law and order (R/A, GTk 1783b). In those paragraphs dealing with unlawful and riotous assembly aimed at rebellion, Lindemann provided the most explicit bases for the court martial of 1848. With Danish war articles 600 and 601 to guide him, Lindemann proposed that punishment should be terrifying and as summarily swift as a military court. Experience had shown, he said, that slave cases were not only costly but time consuming, and as a result the significance of the punishment was lost by the time it came to be administered. To obviate protracted hearings, Lindemann called for the use of military process, specifically the 'Stand Ret' or court martial (R/A, GTk 1783c).

Riotous assembly on the part of slaves aimed at rebellion had thus been deemed mutiny as far back as 1783. Little did Lindemann realise that his prescriptions would come to apply where the 'mutiny' had 'succeeded'. Those who were the paradoxical foundations on which free society was established in St. Croix. The victors were made to suffer the fate of the vanquished. But this was the heavy price required of those who dared to turn the wheel but not full circle. That price was inherent in a strategy of revolution which eschewed violence and had objectives of too limited a character to disturb the balance of power relations. Free society's parturition in such inauspicious circumstances boded ill for its healthy growth. The cataclysmic eruption of the 'Great Fire Burn' in St. Croix 30 years later can only be fully understood in the light of the unresolved tensions of 1848 (Skrubbeltrang 1967: 189–218; Marsh 1981: 78–91).

At another level of significance, the court martial through its depositions[3] provides the only source from which the revolted slaves of 1848 speak. For comparable trials conducted during the slave period the reliability of the evidence, invariably given under duress, must always be treated with a certain caution. In the instant case, however, the fact that those on trial were freedmen, of however recent vintage, is an important distinction lending weight to a presumption of greater reliability. Moreover, in its totality, the evidence, from ex-slave as well as other deponents, has a degree of internal consistency which puts its plausibility beyond reasonable doubt. The trial transcript is thus an important source of information. *Inter alia*, it sheds light on the modalities of planning and mobilisation; the leadership role of individuals; the objectives of the planned revolt; collective expectations and attitudes; the particular role of women, now, no less than before, somewhat more than silent bystanders in Afro-Caribbean resistance to oppression.[4] It demonstrates the rage and passion with which the freedmen settled old scores, and provides from the inventory of destruction brief glimpses of the life-style of plantation whites and the internal appointments of their houses.

The officers of the court, for their part, were motivated by a range of concerns somewhat narrower than those which might preoccupy subsequent historians. Apart from the dispensation of exemplary punishments, the purpose of the court martial from their perspective was twofold: to enquire into the origins of the emancipation movement and to determine the extent of, participation in, and culpability for the disturbances between Tuesday and Thursday. Naturally, they led evidence to establish foreknowledge, preparation, motive, timing and leadership; and, attempting to anticipate the thrust of the eventual metropolitan enquiry (Lawaetz 1940: 192–216) to probe the connection, if any, between the governor general and those who planned it.[5] Reading through the transcript, the distinct impression prevails that the members of the court merely went through the motions in the interrogations relating to the post-emancipation disorders. One senses them springing to life, alert and more attentive in the heat and tedium of those long tropical summer days, when there was evidence bearing on the emancipation movement, even though involvement in it could not be deemed an offence after 3 July.

The trial evidence: Prologomenon to revolt

As was the case with so many previous slave uprisings in the Caribbean, that in St. Croix derived some of its inspiration from rumour, garbled intelligence and misplaced belief in the imminence of emancipation. A great many of the freedmen examined confessed to having heard months before that emancipation was impending. Such talk of emancipation, it appears, gathered momentum after the provisional government of the Second Republic had decreed general emancipation in the French islands in April 1848. This was the tenor of the depositions respectively of Cuby from Envy and Jack from Prosperity (R/A, VLA 1848: 132, 167–68). Johannes from Bog of Allen said that at least since June he had heard slaves out in the country say:

> it was their understanding that the King had already for some time past granted freedom to people here, but that this emancipation had not been publicised because the planters opposed it (R/A, VLA 1848: 140).[6]

This view, that emancipation had already been granted, reoccurs in the examination of Frederik from Mt. Pleasant. Chamberlain Ferral's recollection was that when the emancipation proclamation was read on that estate on Tuesday 4 July, Frederik had remarked that if the proclamation had not been printed that day, 'it had stuck in the throats for a very long time'. Frederik denied the remark, but conceded having said that the proclamation was printed neither on Monday nor on Tuesday. This was a view shared by many slaves in Frederiksted on Monday. According to Frederik they claimed that they had been free for a long time but that the proclamation had been withheld (R/A, VLA 1848: 176, 178–79). If Moses from Butler's Bay is to be believed, at least one white person felt similarly, namely a Mrs. Beech whom he alleged to have heard berating her husband on Tuesday for being a party to withholding the promulgation (R/A, VLA 1848: 158). None of these deponents, however, admitted to knowing anything about the planned march on Frederiksted before Sunday night.

There were others who had heard from a week before that Monday was the target day on which they would withdraw their labour and demand their freedom (R/A, VLA 1848: 177). A slave, George Francis, was alleged to have told the Rosehill workforce on Saturday to turn out with sugar bills and sticks on Monday, but nothing was said about going to Frederiksted. Similar advice had also been given at Rosehill by Richard from neighbouring Mt. Stewart, and Patrick from Punch, another northside estate. Adam from Rosehill admitted, before being sentenced for setting fire to a canefield, that a week in advance Gotleib Bordeaux, also known as General Buddoe, an artisan from La Grange, had told him they should all 'look to their time' and to inform others (R/A, VLA 1848: 39). But Buddoe himself denied knowing anything about the planned events of Monday before Sunday afternoon. Indeed, Buddoe claimed that his source of information was Charles of Butler's Bay. But the latter denied that allegation, insisting he knew nothing prior to Sunday evening (R/A, VLA 1848: 32, 204–05). Martin King, whom the court said was commonly believed to be a leader of the emancipation movement, also denied any foreknowledge of a plan before Sunday evening. If he is to be believed, he did not fancy its chances of success even as late as Monday morning (R/A, VLA 1848: 111).

As it transpired, none of the persons examined admitted knowledge of a plan earlier than the preceding Friday. On that day, Moses of Butler's Bay said he heard slaves on the way to and from the West End saying there would be no work on Monday. Even so, he knew nothing of a concrete development before he heard the conch shells, known in local creole as *tuttue* (Schmidt 1788: 204), being blown on Sunday night (R/A, VLA 1848: 140). There was even one witness who claimed to have heard nothing before Monday at lunch time (R/A, VLA 1848: 171). It is also interesting to notice that not even those freedmen from Martin King's Bog of Allen or Buddoe's La Grange seemed to have, or admitted to having, any previous information as to what was to transpire. One witness from Bog of Allen told the court that when the bells started to ring and the shells were being blown on Sunday evening, neither he nor anyone else on the estate, so far as he knew, had any idea of what was afoot. Joseph from Prosperity, who lived on neighbouring La Grange, said he knew nothing before Sunday evening (R/A, VLA 1848: 122, 132).

Counsels of discretion aside, this suggests that the plan had been conceived and passed on to a few chosen persons whose task was to organise their individual estates, and to sound the signals on Sunday night. Limiting knowledge of the plot to a few trusted lieutenants explains the success with which disciplined secrecy was maintained to such a remarkable degree in the planning of the uprising. Further, it enabled its implementation to enjoy all of the optimal advantages of surprise. There were no betrayers in a total slave population of nearly 20,000. The compact size, favourable terrain and intense development of St. Croix, where no estate was ever much more than a kilometre from its neighbour, facilitated ease of communication between the leadership without the need to rely on intermediaries of questionable trustworthiness.

Leadership

Whilst the evidence led at the trial is not especially forthcoming with details of prior planning, it positively identifies leadership roles and suggests the identity of ultimate leadership. Specific individuals either unilaterally assumed, or, more plausibly, were delegated specific tasks for the occupation of Frederiksted. On Monday morning when the crowd there was in front of the office of the Chief of Police, a building which was subsequently destroyed, Augustus from Concordia was self-confessedly 'in command to get the crowd in line'. His leadership role was emphasised by the sword he had in hand, and by way of further emphasis, the blood of a duck, killed by the same sword, smeared on the front of his shirt (R/A, VLA 1848: 21–22). On Monday evening, still in his bloodstained shirt, he was at Hogensborg estate shouting that he had orders 'to decapitate anyone who didn't declare himself free since all were now free'. One man for whom the notion of general emancipation was too much to accept, told Augustus he was not free since he had not been manumitted by his master. Augustus promised to decapitate him too. His role as leader is also confirmed by his participation on Monday in a symbolic act of climactic catharsis: the rooting up of the beating post, the *Justits Støt*, in Frederiksted's market square and its dumping into the sea (R/A, VLA 1848: 22, 24).

The first shred of evidence relating to ultimate leadership came from Will of Annally estate. Questioned about his activities in Frederiksted on Monday, he admitted being there and having in his possession a demi-john of rum stolen from the premises of the grocer Moore. But the demi-john was 'taken from him or rather smashed'. He did not say by whom (R/A, VLA 1848: 110). However, Frederik von Scholten in his eye-witness account published subsequently, pointed out that the crowd in front of the fort and adjacent to Moore's grocery was being commanded by Buddoe. He forcibly prevented the looting of goods and spirits and 'smashed the containers with his sword' (Von Petersen 1855: 110). Will either suffered a genuine bout of amnesia, or like so many other witnesses, would give nothing away regarding preparation or leadership. One other shred of evidence on leadership came from Edward of Rosehill estate. He told the Court that when George Francis enjoined the workforce on Saturday to turn out on Monday, he made it sound as though Moses of Butler's Bay was the 'chief organiser' (R/A, VLA 1848: 178).

Despite intensive interrogation, neither Buddoe nor Martin King admitted to organising the uprising. Such an admission in any case, with emancipation accomplished, would have been a work of supererogation. However, there was a direct attribution of leadership to Buddoe and Martin King from the four men condemned to death on 11 July: Decatur from Bethlehem for rioting and theft; Friday from Castle for a similar offence; Augustus from Concordia for felonious wounding and Adam from Rosehill for arson. In his original examination on 9 July, Friday deposed that Martin King was to be blamed for everything. On the day he was sentenced, Friday first admitted to using the general's name, i.e. Buddoe, not the governor general, to stir up the crowd, but later came back at his own request to inform the court that 'Bordeaux was at the head of everything' (R/A, VLA 1848: 20, 28, 35, 41).

Decatur, who admitted breaking open Moore's iron safe from which a lot of money had been removed, also asked to make a statement to the court after his death sentence had been pronounced. As far as the court could make out, he explained that it was Buddoe who made the slaves on northside estates rise for freedom and come into town (R/A, VLA 1848: 38, 39). Adam too, asking the court to make a statement after his condemnation, reaffirmed his earlier testimony that Buddoe had instructed slaves that they should take their freedom by fair means or foul. Augustus for his part reinforced these statements by adding that on Sunday Buddoe had told slaves that come Monday, they should 'tell the white man they would no longer be slaves' (R/A, VLA 1848: 41, 42).

What is of further interest about this group of testimonies, is that with the exception of Friday, they all stated in the most emphatic terms that Buddoe gave no orders for looting or destruction. Friday claimed that Buddoe gave him instructions on Tuesday to destroy Carlton estate (R/A, VLA 1848: 41). But there was an abundance of countervailing evidence from other ex-slaves, from white plantation help and government officials that Buddoe strove to maintain order on Monday and on the days following (R/A, VLA 1848: 61, 62, 89, 120).[7] Friday's statement about Tuesday, even if true, does not alter the weight of the evidence from the other three in relation to Monday. One would have good grounds to believe that Decatur, Augustus and Adam, their minds wonderfully clarified by the prospect of impending execution, were unlikely to have given collectively misleading testimony. There was nothing to be gained by exonerating Buddoe from instigating violence on Monday. If that part of their testimony stands the test of reliability, so should the other portion relating to Buddoe's ultimate leadership.

Strategy and Objectives

If the proceedings help to clarify the locus of leadership, they also shed some light on organisational strategies. None of the testimony is explicit on this point, but there were enough statements at the trial to indicate that the slaves intended to use the strike weapon as a lever to force the issue of their freedom. Industrial action as a form of ultimate protest was no novelty among Caribbean slave populations. It had been advocated, though unsuccessfully, by Nanny Grigg in Barbados in 1816, Deacon Quamina in Demerara in 1823 and more recently by Sam Sharpe in the Jamaica Christmas uprising of 1831 (Craton 1982: 261, 281, 300). The predetermined signal for Monday's strike was the blowing of *tuttues* and the ringing of plantation bells. Both signalled emergencies such as fire, or work start and stoppage. But when the signals were given, Frederik von Scholten, whose house lay high enough for a good view of the countryside, could see no fire (Von Petersen 1855: 94, 96). At that time of night, work could not, obviously, be beginning. This was indeed an emergency signal, but for a final work stoppage.

The most concrete testimony of the connection between withdrawal of labour and its use as a bargaining counter for freedom, came from the condemned Augustus. Buddoe, according to him, had told slaves on Sunday that they were not to go to work on Monday *and* to tell the whites they would no longer be slaves. The connection was also made explicit by Edward of Rosehill. Where the connection was not explicit, others nevertheless showed awareness of an impending strike. Moses from Butler's Bay, as mentioned earlier, had heard about this on Friday, and Robert Lucas, the carpenter at Betty's Hope, said that when he went to town on Saturday to buy turpentine, 'several persons' had informed him that there was to be no work on Monday (R/A, VLA 1848: 42, 177–78, 140, 157, 94).

The seriousness with which the work stoppage was enforced is well illustrated by Martin King's experience on Monday. By his own account, the workforce at Bog of Allen had gone to work on Monday, a circumstance which raises questions about his leadership influence up to this point. On instructions from the overseer, Williams Naest, King took the plantation wain to drive to the West End. Having descended the escarpment to the Centreline as far as St. George's, where his wife Severine lived (R/A, VLA 1848: 123), Martin King stopped to get a cart whip. He was met by an angry crowd, led by Decatur among others, who unhitched the mule and drove the cart into the cane piece, telling Martin he was not to drive to the West End. It may well be that Martin wanted to use the opportunity of his instructions to be present in Frederiksted for reasons connected with the events of later that day. But so far as Decatur and the others were concerned, the mere appearance of collaboration on Monday morning, which driving the cart symbolised, was a betrayal. Phillipus of Mt. Pleasant was sufficiently enraged to hit Martin over the arm with a cutlass and force him to join in the march to the West End (R/A, VLA 1848: 112).

The difficulty of implementing a work stoppage aimed at emancipation is illustrated not only by what Martin King reported as happening at Bog of Allen on Monday morning. Habits of a lifetime were not easily dispelled. Even at Mt. Pleasant to which the enraged Phillipus was attached, some work had begun on Monday morning. The driver there, Jorgen, told the court, however, that he was threatened with decapitation for this lapse by John Simmons, one of the men eventually condemned, and two others (R/A, VLA 1848: 71). Whatever the difficulty of its implementation, the strategy obviously struck a responsive chord. Forced labour was the essential badge of a servitude they were being asked to endure patiently for another eleven years until general emancipation in 1859. But in the meantime freedom had already come since 1847 for their newborn children; since 1838 for the British West Indies, including Tortola scarcely a cannon shot from St. Jan; and more recently since April for the French West Indies.

The deeply felt resentment is expressed in the language and behaviour of Decatur, Phillipus and John Simmons. Comparable freedom, to work not at all, or on their own terms, was the substance of that independence they hoped to achieve that Monday and to maintain thereafter. This was the spirit which informed the behaviour of Edward of Rosehill on the morrow of emancipation. In an encounter with his erstwhile owner Van Brackle from neighbouring Spring Garden on the northside, Edward announced: 'Mr. van Brackle here is your hoe and your cutlass. I will no longer work for you and if I work I will buy them for myself.' Whereupon, he threw the tools at Van Brackle's feet (R/A, VLA 1848: 175–76). The principle of voluntary work on freely negotiated terms was, before Monday and after, the only acceptable and dignified basis on which to establish the status of a free peasantry to which they aspired. It would take another generation to achieve. But for the present the objective was a powerful motivating force, and the strategy had a certain attractiveness, particularly when it promised the circumscription at worst and the avoidance at best of bloodshed.

Violence Manquée: 2–3 July 1848

St. Croix's birthday of freedom was not, however, entirely bloodless nor characterised by an absolute absence of violence. Only incredible levels of discipline, universally applied, could have restrained physical assault on persons and property on that day. Yet the evidence indicates that those levels of discipline were in large measure realised. Two incidents involving attacks on white persons were proof of the rule by the proverbial exception. The first is not contained in the trial transcript but in Frederik von Scholten's account. It involved Major Gyllich, commander of the Fire Corps. Riding into town on Monday, he was chopped at by someone as he passed through a crowd, managed to parry the blow and after shouting, 'I am a friend not an enemy', and throwing his sword on the ground, was allowed to pass (Von Petersen 1855: 102). Gyllich subsequently proved his *bona fides* by riding around on Tuesday, accompanied by Buddoe, and attempting to restore calm without force on several mid-island estates (R/A, VLA 1848: 121–22). The conviction that he was sympathetic may have saved Gyllich when discipline briefly disintegrated on Monday morning.

The second incident involved Augustus from Concordia and John Lang, owner of Paradise, on the road between that estate and Good Hope on Monday afternoon. Each gave a slightly different version of how the incident began, but they concurred on how it developed, namely, that Lang who was unarmed took a stick from an old man and fetched Augustus two smart blows. In retaliation Augustus slashed with his sword at Lang inflicting a serious wound to the arm and a less serious wound to the hand (R/A, VLA 1848: 22, 33–34). By Augustus' own admission, and that of William McFarlane who saw him shortly after the event, he was pretty far gone in drink (R/A, VLA 1848: 29). There were thus important extenuating circumstances attending Augustus' loss of self-control.

The other exceptional incidents of violence immediately preceding emancipation involved the destruction and plunder of three houses in Frederiksted in the course of Monday: the Police Station and residence of Frederiksted's Chief of Police Andresen; Police Adjutant Didrichsen's house and Moore the grocer's shop cum house. The evidence led at the trial is not especially helpful as to motive in the case of the first two. It is possible to infer, however, that Peter von Scholten's absence in St. Thomas was widely known among the slave community and that in his absence the revolting slaves directed their protest at those whom they perceived as representing authority. This would help in accounting for the assault on Major Gyllich. Such an interpretation also lessens, if not discredits, the conspiratorial theory which suggests links between the governor general and the plot to revolt (Von Petersen 1855: 132; Prosch 1848: 416–17). Frederik von Scholten records it as his understanding that the slaves had come into town on Monday morning to 'negotiate' with Frederiksted's Chief of Police for their freedom (Von Petersen 1855: 101). The destruction of the Police Station and the Police Adjutant's house must therefore be construed as a consequence of the slaves' frustration at not being able to extract freedom from this quarter (Hansen 1970: 373–75), as an expression of the seriousness of their intent and a symbolic gesture of defiant uncompromising militancy. No examinee confessed to being in either police building and the trial record thus contains nothing to convey the electric atmosphere of that highly charged morning. The closest it comes is in the deposition of Malvina of Big Fountain who, standing outside Didrichsen's house, was unable to get in 'as it was filled with people' (R/A, VLA 1848: 87).

A similar crushing throng was present at grocer Moore's. The sack of his building on Strandgade (Waterfront Street), in close proximity to and in full view of the fort, was inspired by the slaves' belief that Moore had advised the Fort Commander to 'shoot them down like dogs'. Moore's cook, Edward, who was present, heard the crowd shouting the accusation. There was such an enormous crowd that he was unable to identify anyone as particularly responsible or who led the charge. They burst through the street door which gave access via a staircase to the rooms above, which were locked. The doors to them were broken down by crow bars and axes obtained from the cellar (R/A, VLA 1848: 169–70).

It was impossible for the court to apportion individual responsibility for the destruction and sack of any of the three houses, although Decatur's condemnation was specifically related to the rifling of Moore's iron safe (R/A, VLA 1848: 36). But on the day in question, the destruction of Moore's house gave the slaves an important psychological boost by emphasising their considerable advantage in tactical and strategic terms. It would have been easy to follow Moore's alleged advice, strafe Strandgade and mow down the insurgents either from the water battery or the gun emplacements at the fort's entrance. But this was not an option the whites could exercise. The slaves, in effective control of the town, had accomplished this without bloodshed in it. A burst of grape shot would have indiscriminately killed those in the streets while the looters in Moore's shop needed only to go through the back entrance into the street behind. This was the reason that Irminger demolished all the buildings obstructing the cannons' line of sight towards the north and east on Wednesday. Had the Fort Commander opened fire on Monday, the likelihood was that the slaves would not only have killed whites in retaliation but also put fire to Frederiksted (Von Petersen 1855: 104).

The vulnerability of the towns to fire was notorious. The slaves knew this and it led them to deploy a strategy in which the threat of Frederiksted's total destruction was their ultimate bargaining counter. When Frederik von Scholten ventured out of the fort with the Roman Catholic priest and some of the more courageous whites to calm the slaves in the streets, one of the leaders told him: 'We can't fight the soldiers since we have no weapons, but we can burn and destroy if we don't get our freedom — and we will do it.' This was no idle boast; it was clearly part of a well laid plan:

> close to the fort, behind a corner house and out of the cannons' reach was a large group of slave women with trash and dry cane leaves which, at the first volley from the fort, they would have lit and thrown through windows and doors. Since most householders had by

then left their houses there would thus have been nothing to prevent such a fire spreading rapidly through the town (Von Petersen 1855: 103).

Attitudes to the Future: Race and Class

The proceedings of the court martial also help to answer the question whether the slaves had developed ideas relating to a future less immediate than the acquisition of freedom. Accompanying the desire for freedom was an aspiration to property in land. There even seemed to be a sense in which that aspiration was aborn of a conception of land as *patria* to which they and not the whites had an exclusive claim. A similar view prevailed among the equally creolised slave population of Barbados in 1816 (Craton 1982: 258). Nelson, interestingly enough a *bosal*, who had worked at Mt. Pleasant, declared on Tuesday that if anyone attempted to arrest him he would cut them down 'since the land belonged to them'. A virtually identical expression came from Andreas of Envy, who told John Randall Findlay, a freedman before emancipation, that 'the land would now belong to them, namely the blacks' (R/A, VLA 1848: 51, 74). Land as property was the indispensable basis of their independence as peasants. Beyond that, however, there were visions that transcended mere peasant subsistence and looked to the continuance of the mono-crop export economy run by freedmen. John Simmons told Richard Doute the book-keeper at Big Fountain that there was enough land to plant cane and that they could build their own ships to bring provisions in (R/A, VLA 1848: 46). James Heyliger, one of those executed, made an important distinction between the destruction of plantation buildings and the destruction of cane in the field, since the latter 'would be the country's loss' (R/A, VLA 1848: 4). This desire to own land and to maintain on it the production of cane as an export staple, probably explains why Adam's arson attempt at Rosehill was the only one such.

The corollary of those ambitions was that the whites would have to leave the estates or remain on them on a footing of equality at best or subordination at worst. The collective attitude of the slaves, where it did not celebrate their own race, condemned whites *qua* whites, denigrated them as figures of authority and judged them unflatteringly in terms of class. By the 1840s a great many of the overseers and book-keepers on estates in the Danish West Indies were Irish or Anglo-Irish, usually humble crofters in search of their fortune. More often than not, they were less familiar with plantation routine and management techniques than the slaves they were supposed to supervise. Their penchant for liaisons with slave women had a long history and this, with a predilection for drink and general hell-raising, made them a disruptive force on most plantations (R/A, GTk 1785b; *Fædrelandet* 1841a, 1841b). Such white estate help did not invite the respect of the slave gangs. Karen Fog Olwig has graphically illustrated this in the case of St. Jan, instancing an 1847 case in which a slave Johannes abused the overseer Glasco in the most derogatory and scatological terms: 'You are a come-and-go, my master is head-judge. You pskaw! You a shitting ass (sic) Blanco' (Olwig 1977: 405 n. 19). The heat and excitement of the emancipation uprising and its aftermath was an opportunity for the expression of race consciousness; for the vilification of whites generally and plantation help in particular; for expressions of challenge to and rejection of their authority.

Racial consciousness inspired the threat on Tuesday by Martin William of Hamsbay to Emilia of the same estate that 'he would take off her head if she was on the white people's side' (R/A, VLA 1848: 78). Charles of Butler's Bay on the previous Sunday evening had threatened anyone taking the whites' side with similar punishment. John Simmons, for his part, had a utilitarian concept of racial solidarity: he told the book-keeper at Montpelier that it was a good thing to proceed against whites as they had, or it would be the worse for blacks (R/A, VLA 1848: 32, 46). From racial consciousness and solidarity it was an easy transition to racial animosity. According to Eveline, a domestic in Frederiksted, Christian, a former house servant to the regimental surgeon, took very unkindly to a remark from a white school teacher to behave himself on Tuesday. Christian's reply was that he would not permit any white man to speak to him like that, and he would consider it a small matter to sever his head from his body. Christian denied the remark, but conceded that he was unable to recall everything he had done, drunk as he was at the time (R/A, VLA 1848: 57, 58). Indeed, even before the disturbances began on Sunday evening, racial animosity was in evidence. At Montpelier, Henry, incensed at the overseer's rebuke for impertinence on Sunday afternoon, declared that 'his spirit was such that white people should be very careful with him' (R/A, VLA 1848: 80).

The decision to revolt was an effect of the renting of that veil of respect which clothed whites in slave society. But it was also cause. Several incidents involving manhandling, attempted manhandling and abusive remarks on and after Monday 3 July, demonstrate the extent to which the blacks of St. Croix were no longer contained by the established devices of social control. At Envy on Tuesday, several blacks from Negro Bay armed with machetes charged the book-keeper, who was only rescued by the timely intervention of some of Envy's workforce. Charles Conally, overseer at Hope, had a similar experience on Tuesday when he lost a silver watch and a watch chain (R/A, VLA 1848: 10, 162–63). Comparable examples can be cited from Camporico, Carlton, Sprathall, Mt. Pleasant and Spring Garden estates in the period beween Monday and Tuesday (R/A, VLA 1848: 48, 54, 62, 71, 90).

What this as product suggests, is a process of 'demystification' of whites, and it was exemplified pre-eminently in the behaviour of Isaac of Prosperity, from Tuesday a close associate of Buddoe. On Thursday at Hamsbay, Buddoe arrived with Isaac and others to remind the owner, John Elliot, that slavery was abolished and along with it, the whip from the field. Elliot was told that if he did not agree to working conditions which the freedmen found acceptable, the plantation would be taken from him and any other like-minded white. To emphasise the point, Isaac struck the floor with his sword, declaring, 'No nonsense Elliot.' On Wednesday at Prosperity, again accompanying Buddoe, Isaac let his old book-keeper know that he had 'an account to settle with him' and that it was a good thing he had not met him. The rapid evaporation of deference which this signifies is well illustrated by the third incident involving Isaac. With Buddoe at the estate The William on Tuesday, they both wanted to know who had given orders for work to resume there. Thomas Murphy, the overseer, assured them that he had given the orders and that the workforce would be paid. Whereupon, Isaac grabbed Murphy by the scruff of the neck, told him to behave himself and be quiet or he would rough him up (R/A, VLA 1848: 32, 38, 108, 133, 134).

Hated and disrespected, overseers and book-keepers were also objects of distrust. An important aspect of the immediate management of freedom, therefore, appears to have been to get white plantation help to leave the estates and to disarm them. The first objective was consonant with an aspairation to property; the second with a desire to minimise their vulnerability and to protect themselves, if the need arose, with weapons other than sugar-bills and cudgels. The depositions at the trial do not suggest by their number that the desire to drive the whites from the estates was a widespread phenomenon. But its existence on widely separated estates points not so much to spontaneous indignation on the part of individuals, as to a pre-arranged plan. At Adventure on Wednesday, Peter from Kingshill, a central estate along the Centreline, exclaimed: 'Why is this white man still on the plantation?' (R/A, VLA 1848: 91). At Sprathall on the northside, 'a large part of the workforce' demanded on Tuesday that the overseer, book-keeper and owner should never set foot on the property again (R/A, VLA 1848: 29). At Montpelier, another northside estate on Wednesday, Henry, cutlass in hand, told Hewson the overseer in threatening tones that he wanted whites 'cleared away from the estates' and that it was best if they hid themselves (R/A, VLA 1848: 79–81). Moorehead, the lessee of Camporico in the south, was similarly threatened on Wednesday (R/A, VLA 1848: 16). The geographical spread of these estates — Kingshill from which Peter derived, in the island's centre; Sprathall in the northwest; Montpelier in the north; Adventure in the south and Camporiso in the southwest — is sufficiently wide to discount pure spontaneity as an explanation.

The plan to disarm whites on Tuesday and subsequently was said to have originated with Buddoe. Samuel and John from Camporico, both of whom engaged in a spectacular if unsuccessful horseback chase to seize the book-keeper's gun, claimed to have received such orders (R/A, VLA 1848: 15). Buddoe disclaimed responsibility, although he admitted to riding around to several estates on the northside on Tuesday, requiring the usual distribution of food allowances and enjoining the workforce to look after animals (R/A, VLA 1848: 32, 105). There is no doubt, however, that he used the occasion to get overseers and others to hand over their firearms. Such was the case, for example, at The William on Tuesday, when in the company of Isaac from Prosperity, he demanded and got overseer Murphy's gun (R/A, VLA 1848: 133).

Buddoe's denial has the ring of veracity. If he intended to collect the guns himself, he might well have given no order. The fact is that the discipline which had prevailed up to Monday, had begun to wear thin by Tuesday and individuals like Samuel and John simply took matters into their own hands. The breakdown was facilitated, in the absence of regular rations in those confused days, by hunger and by drink. The continuance of the allowance arose as a specific issue on Tuesday at several estates (R/A, VLA 1848: 61, 101, 133, 152). A cow was slaughtered at Montpelier; sheep there and at Concordia; pigs at Sprathall and at Mt. Stewart where ducks were also slaughtered (R/A, VLA 1848: 79, 80, 100, 115, 134). Numerous witnesses confessed to being heavily under the influence of drink after emancipation was declared (R/A, VLA 1848: 24–26, 29, 38, 67, 81, 97, 103, 112, 126). There is some evidence too that some of the rum consumed so extensively might have been ritually drunk to symbolise binding engagement. Cuby testified that on Wednesday morning he was offered a mixture of rum and gunpowder by some of the workforce from Negro Bay (R/A, VLA 1848: 179–80).[8] In such circumstances the revolting freedmen were less susceptible to the restraints of leadership. It is interesting to observe that after Buddoe had collected arms at The William, the workforce from Sprathall arrived some hours later to make the same demand on overseer Murphy (R/A, VLA 1848: 83, 84). At Carlton on the southside on the same day, there was also an attempt to seize the book-keeper's gun (R/A, VLA 1848: 59, 82). At Montpelier on Tuesday a freedman, Frederik, had already come into possession of a firearm. Asked to give it up by the Roman Catholic priest accompanying the party to read the emancipation proclamation, Frederik is alleged to have claimed that they had taken all the overseers' guns in the country. Making allowances for hyperbole, the remark if true, reinforces the view that the disarming of white plantation help by Buddoe alone, or by increasingly indisciplined subordinates, was a cardinal feature of the planning post-Monday. More importantly, Frederik is again alleged to have said that the guns would only be returned when they could have greater trust in overseers, or when they behaved better (R/A, VLA 1848: 176, 179).[9]

Here, distilled, was the very essence of the matter. Oversers and book-keepers, standard bearers of the *mission civilisatrice*, had been weighed in the scales and found severely wanting. They generated hatred, animosity, contempt, distrust and bitterness. Augustus at Concordia smashed up the sick house precisely 'because he had been locked up in it many times'. Others too like Catherine from Carlton or Isaac from Prosperity, mentioned earlier, equally victims of arbitrary detention and the whip, had searing recollections as the basis for settling old scores (R/A, VLA 1848: 22, 82). Persistent bitterness inspired Joseph from Anguilla to shout threateningly at Envy estate: 'Where is that fellow Lorentz? It's him I want' (R/A, VLA 1848: 83, 85). It would equally explain the insistence independently by Neddy from Grove Place and Present from Jealousy that Lucas' house at Mt. Pleasant should be destroyed, as it was a prison (R/A, VLA 1848: 51, 172). The fact that Thomas Clarke was overseer at both Jealousy and Mt. Pleasant which was contiguous (R/A, VLA 1848: 71) was, in all probability, not an unrelated circumstance.

Property Destruction: 4–5 July 1848

Against this background, it is no matter for surprise that the extensive looting and destruction which characterised Tuesday and Wednesday, 4–5 July, were directed almost exclusively at the houses and personal effects of white plantation personnel.[10] The trial transcript is replete with instances, not of mere destruction of such property on several estates, but symbolic acts of violation and humiliation fuelled by extremities of rage. The many occasions (R/A, VLA 1848: 6, 43, 47, 48, 51, 58, 59, 69, 76, 160) on which ex-slaves bedecked themselves with three-cornered hats, swords, military jackets and belts of whites who had fled in terror, were not so much gasconade as calculated demonstrations of the fact that the mighty had fallen. The looting of food supplies — salted fish and beef, flour, cornmeal, sugar, rum, beer and wine from the provision cellars of several estates (R/A, VLA 1848: 10, 18, 24) — answered similarly not merely to the needs of hunger. Such looting represented as well the symbolic rejection of that authority in which control of plantation rations was vested. Chopping off the locks of provision cellars or breaking down the doors to them was arguably a form of cathartic release no less satisfying than the uprooting of the *Justits Støt* on Monday.

The almost endless catalogue of destroyed houses and personal property belonging to overseers and book-keepers invites a similar interpretation. Mannings Bay, Envy, Lower Love, Castle, Concordia, Adventure, Golden Grove, Jealousy, Sprathall, Hamsbay, Diamond, Ruby, St. George, Wheel of Fortune, Mt. Pleasant, Mt. Stewart, Good Hope among others, suffered in varying degrees. Apart from houses partially or wholly destroyed, the inventory of items most frequently mentioned as destroyed or stolen included clothing, bed linen, beds, bedsteads, wardrobes, cupboards, washstands, dining tables, porcelain, glassware, silverware, gold plate, objets d'art (R/A VLA 1848: 8, 18, 23, 29, 72, 83, 86, 112, 115–17).

Another common *leitmotiv*, which informs all the accounts of destruction, is the extraordinary violence. The explanation inheres only in part in the freedom with which rum was available from plantation stores. It inheres even less in Adam's religious assignment of cause to 'the devil in his head' for setting fire to the fields at Rosehill. One has to look elsewhere for the springs of that volcanic passion which led individuals systematically to demolish a dining room at Concordia; reduce a divan, clock and clock-stand there to splinters; or impale Lucas' globe at Mt. Pleasant on an improvised bayonet (R/A, VLA 1848: 51, 115–17). The effects in question could simply have been taken away as booty. Rum and 'the devil' merely quickened an impulse to destroy whose roots lay deep in the long suffered indignities and abuses of servitude.

Women

One interesting aspect of the rampage between Tuesday and Thursday was the important contribution of women. It was pointed out earlier that they had assembled the trash with which to set fire to Frederiksted, should that prove necessary. At Negro Bay on Wednesday they again comprised another trash detail when Big Robert threatened to burn the owner's house down (R/A, VLA 1848: 8). Frederik von Scholten in this connection made the very interesting observation that:

> Among the black population, women play a role of great importance. They do the same work that the men do and their physical build and size render them formidable adversaries in the rough and tumble of a fight. Throughout the disturbances they were more aggressive, vengeful and altogether more violent in their passion than the men (Von Petersen 1855: 117).

The trial transcript bears this out substantially. Rosaline, described by her former owner Jane Jackson as giddy-headed and childish, underwent no instant metamorphosis when she made the soberingly pointed remark: 'Is there a war on? That can't be for in that case they would have burnt the town just as in St. Domingue' (R/A, VLA 1848: 135).

Women displayed a rage no less primordial than the men's. Slavery had after all made no distinction as to gender, and their sex had laid them open to the additional disadvantage of harassment, not to mention the perversion of normal maternal relations. It is no wonder therefore that Mathilda from Frederiksted was an active instigator outside Moore's grocery; that a woman was co-leader with Big Robert in the sack of Negro Bay; that Sey, a woman from neighbouring Manning's Bay, was also identified as a moving spirit at Negro Bay (R/A, VLA 1848: 54, 55). Another Manning's Bay woman, Sara, chopped off the legs of Knight's piano at Negro Bay, and was only prevented from chopping up the rest when Martha, who belonged to the estate workforce, lay on top of it to protect it (R/A, VLA 1848: 143). At Lucas' Mt. Pleasant, Penny from adjoining River took the first blow at the door with a cudgel, and when it did not give, proceeded to attack another door. The overseer Thomas Clarke commented that Penny distinguished herself with 'threats of murder and cutting people's heads off'. At the same estate, Present from Jealousy who had described Lucas' house as a prison to be destroyed, chopped up a cupboard (R/A, VLA 1848: 71, 172–73). It was Rachel wielding an axe who reduced the divan at Concordia to splinters (R/A, VLA 1848: 115). Violent in destruction, the women were remarkably resourceful in plunder. Unable to remove a whole mattress at Sprathall, Else removed the ticking and took the cover (R/A, VLA 1848: 135). Women were the main removers of plunder at Concordia and a large number of other estates (R/A, VLA 1848: 87, 116, 142–43, 174).

Differential Responses

It should be emphasised that not all the freedmen succumbed to such transports of fury. Notwithstanding the fact that Buddoe's writ had ceased to run island-wide since the morning of Tuesday 4 July, and such influence as Martin King possessed had begun to wane, their stand against destruction and plunder, of which the court took note (R/A, VLA 1848: 32, 41–42, 120), apparently had some effect. For some freedmen, the psychological bond with familiar things and places, masters' as well as their own, or a *Weltanschauung* defined by the plantation as world, was not readily rupturable by the transition to freedom. Many drivers were as resistant to plundering as others were active in instigating it. Some like Jacob Washington, former crookgang driver at Spring Garden and son of the book-keeper Jasper Washington, perhaps had special reason to resist the rioters (R/A, VLA 1848: 90). The same would be true of William Borch, former driver of the same estate, who had a reputation for excessive use of the whip in the field, and from whom a number of freedmen sought 'satisfaction' (R/A, VLA 1848: 80, 96). But there are no special circumstances to explain why John Peru, former driver at Upper Love, or Isaac at Paradise, both attempted to prevent destruction and pillaging on Wednesday (R/A, VLA 1848: 27, 152). Drivers apart, there were many former slaves, male as well as female, who protected property on many estates in the immediate aftermath of emancipation. They hid household effects in the quarters, in canefields and in trash, or bravely barred entrance to provision cellars at Enfield Green, Camporico, Bog of Allen, Rosehill, Carlton, Mt. Pleasant, Negro Bay, Adventure, Envy and elsewhere (R/A, VLA 1848: 5, 15, 30, 38, 53, 60, 69, 89, 179).

Among those free before emancipation, the events on and immediately after Monday 3 July also produced no unilinear response. In Frederiksted there was a strong suspicion of this group as originators of the plot and potential allies of the insurgents. Nevertheless, it was their restraining influence, Frederik von Scholten reports, which accounted for the destruction in town being limited to three houses (Von Petersen 1855: 98–99, 101, 105). That restraining influence was also in evidence in the rural milieu, where by a growing convention in violation of a 1747 law, some freedmen before emancipation were allowed to live. Thus Edward Hein who lived on Negro Bay did his best to prevent destruction at neighbouring Golden Grove; Richard Gumbs disarmed the leader of the invading band at Hamsbay, and Samuel William openly deplored the use of violence at Bog of Allen (R/A, VLA 1848: 30, 54, 85). The latter's wife and five children were slaves up to emancipation. But his response is in radical contrast with that of Mathaeus, another freedman before emancipation, whose wife Sally had also been a slave. Mathaeus was the driver of one of the carts in which effects were removed from Negro Bay. At Negro Bay too, it was another *ancien libre*, Christopher from Manning's Bay, who allegedly helped in the removal of a hogshead of rum (R/A, VLA 1848: 44, 55). No common pattern of behaviour thus emerges. But this is hardly a matter for surprise in view of the disparities of economic achievement, aspirations and status among pre-emancipation freedmen (Hall 1980b: 69–72).

Epilogue

The evidence from the trial establishes that the slaves of St. Croix pursued their purpose of achieving emancipation with unwavering single-mindedness. However, on the very morrow of emancipation there were signs of atomisation. In the trial itself freedmen freely accused other freedmen for their part in the events after Monday. Those who had achieved freedom earlier were themselves no more united programmatically. Such internal divisions weighted the scales in favour of constituted authority which remained intact despite the upheavals. The executions, and Buddoe's deportation at his own request (R/A, VLA 1848: 105), robbed the freedmen of their best potential leadership. Vanquished victors, the freedmen of St. Croix were poorly placed to confront the challenges of the first generation of freedom.

Notes

1. An earlier version of this paper was presented at the XIIIth Annual Conference of the Association of Caribbean Historians, Guadeloupe, April 1981. I would like to thank Arnold Sio and Richard Price, both of whom made constructive comments and offered some useful suggestions.
2. All translations from the Danish are by the author who accepts sole responsibility for their accuracy.
3. The transcript records are in Danish although the depositions themselves were most probably rendered in English creole, the *lingua franca* of St. Croix slaves long before the end of the eighteenth century (West 1793: 325).
4. The Danish Slave Trade Abolition Ordinance of 1792 abolished import duties on female slaves until the trade's final cessation in 1802, and exempted such slaves from poll tax if used for field work, while doubling that tax on male slaves (Green-Pedersen 1979: 408). This policy reversed a well-established bias towards males in St. Croix's slave population. By 1840 of a total of 18,605, female slaves comprised some 52.2 per cent (Alexander 1843: 6). The preponderance was even more marked in the towns of St. Croix where in 1839 they accounted for some 62.6 per cent of the slave population (Hall 1983a: 19–20; Tables 2.4 and 2.5).
5. The popular literature holds that Gotlieb Bordeaux (General Buddoe) who played a leadership role of some significance during and just after the revolt, was an intimate of the governor general's (Ramløv 1967).
6. It certainly would not have been the first demonstration of obstructionist behaviour by the plantocracy to official policy. Frederik V's *Reglement for Slaverne* was withheld for this reason (Vibæk 1966: 146–47), and they were not exactly models of cooperation with the governor general's reforms in the 1840s (Hall 1979).
7. These are the testimonies respectively of an ex-slave from Sprathall estate, a book-keeper from the same estate, an overseer from Adventure and Major Gyllich, Commander of Frederiksted Fire Corps.

8. The absence of grave dirt was significant. Its use for ritually binding engagements in the 'African' period of slavery has been noted for example by Handler and Lange in the case of Barbados (Handler and Lange 1978: 202, 207–08), and it figured prominently in the preparations for the 1759 St. Croix conspiracy (Schuler 1970: 23). It may well be that the absence of grave dirt in 1848 constitutes a usable index of creolisation at that point.
9. Frederik denied the remark although Chamberlain Ferral, Van Brackle and Edward from Rosehill each independently corroborated the others' testimony.
10. Only two houses belonging to owners appear to have been destroyed: the notorious Lucas' at Mt. Pleasant and Richard Knight's at Negro Bay (R/A, VLA 1848: 47, 121). Remarkably high levels of absenteeism seem to have prevailed in St. Croix in the 1840s, thereby reinforcing the position of overseers, etc, as the predominant point of contact with white authority on the estates. Of a sample of 83 estates in St. Croix in 1840, 41 or 49.3 per cent belonged to owners who were absentee. Richard Knight also appears to have been a recent purchaser of Negro Bay as in 1840 it was owned by the heirs of John Cooper and managed by Hugh Kerr, attorney for several other estates (R/A, GTk, CANS 1834–43: 1840).

References

The following abbreviations have been used in the reference citations: CANS (Originale Forestillinger fra en Commission angaaende Negrenes Stilling i Vestindien m.m. og dertil hørende Kongelige Resolutioner. Copenhagen: Rigsarkiv), manuscript material; GTk (General Toldkammer papers, Copenhagen: Rigsarkiv), manuscript material; N/A (National Archives, Washington, D.C.); NEER (Neger Emancipation efter Reskript af 1847, Copenhagen: Rigsarkiv), manuscript material; R/A (Rigsarkiv, Copenhagen); RG (Record Group, National Archives, Washington, D.C.); VLA (Vestindiske Lokale Arkiver, Copenhagen: Rigsarkiv), manuscript material.

Alexander, G. W., *Om den moralske Forpligtelser til og hensigtmassige af strax of fulstændigt at ophave Slaveriet i de danske Vestindiske Kolonier* (Copenhagen, 1843).

Craton, Michael, *Testing the Chains. Resistance to Slavery in the British West Indies*, (Ithaca, 1982).

Fædrelandet, Newspaper (a) 2 April 1841, (b) 17 October 1841.

Green-Pedersen, Svend E., 'The Economic Considerations behind the Danish Abolition of the Negro Slave Trade', in Gemery, Henry and Hogendorn, Jan (eds.), *The Uncommon Market. Essays in the Economic History of the Atlantic Slave Trade* (New York, San Francisco, London, 1979), pp. 399–418.

Hall, N. A. T., 'Slave Laws of the Danish Virgin Islands in the Later Eighteenth Century', in Rubin, Vera and Tudin, Arthur (eds.) *Comparative Perspectives on Slavery in New World Plantation Societies* (New York, 1977, 292), pp. 174–86.

Hall, N. A. T., 'Establishing a Public Elementary School System for Slaves in the Danish Virgin Islands 1732–1846', *Caribbean Journal of Education*, 9 (1979): 1–45.

Hall, N. A. T., 'Slaves' Use of their "Free" Time in the Danish Virgin Islands in the later Eighteenth and early Nineteenth Century', *Journal of Caribbean History*, 13 (1980a): 21–43; and this volume.

Hall, N. A. T., 'The 1816 Freedman Petition in the Danish West Indies. Its Background and Consequences', *Boletin de Estudios Latinoamericanos y del Caribe*, 29 (1980b): 55–73.

Hall, N. A. T., 'Slavery in Three West Indian Towns: Christiansted, Frederiksted and Charlotte Amalie in the late Eighteenth and early Nineteenth Century', in Higman, Barry (ed.), *Trade, Government and Society in Caribbean History 1700–1920. Essays presented to Douglas Hall* (Kingston, 1983a), pp. 17–38.

Hall, N. A. T., 1983b, 'Empire Without Dominion. Denmark and her West Indian Colonies 1671–1848', University of the West Indies, Mona, Seminar Paper: 1–53.

Handler, Jerome and Lange, Frederick, *Plantation Slavery in Barbados. An Archaeological and Historical Investigation* (Cambridge, Mass. and London, 1978).

Hansen, Thorkild, *Slavernes Øer* (Copenhagen, 1970).

Jensen, Hans, *De Danske Stænderforsamlingers Historie 1830–1848*, Vol. 2 (Copenhagen, 1931–34).

Klingenberg, Frank, *The Anti-Slavery Movement in England. A study in English Humanitarianism* (Hampden, Conn., 1968).

Larsen, Kay, *Dansk Vestindien 1666–1917* (Copenhagen, 1928).

Lawaetz, Herman, *Peter von Scholten. Vestindiske Tidsbilleder fra den sidste Generalguvern65rs Dage* (Copenhagen, 1940).

Lombardi, John V., *The Decline and Abolition of Negro Slavery in Venezuela 1820–1834* (Westport, Conn., 1971).

Marsh, Clifton, *A Socio-Historical Analysis of the Emancipation of 1848 and the Labor Revolts of 1878 in the Danish West Indies* (St. Thomas, 1981).

N/A, RG 55, Box 9, 1848. 1848a: Frederik Oxholm to Frederik VII, 13 July 1848. 1848b: Frederik Oxholm to Frederik VII, 27 July 1848.

Olwig, Karen Fog, *Households, Exchange and Social Reproduction. The Development of Caribbean Society*, University of Minnesota, Ph.D. dissertation, 1977.

Ørsted, A. S. (ed.), *Collegial-Tidende for Danmark* (Copenhagen, 1840).

Prosch, Victor, 'Om Slave Emancipation paa de dansk-vestindiske Øer', *Dansk Tidsskrift* 2 (1848): 385–431.

R/A, GTk, Species Facti over den paa Eilandet Sainte Croix Aaret 1760 Intenderede Neger Rebellion forfattet efter Ordre af Byfoged' (Hesselberg, 1760).

R/A, GTk, Udkast og Betænkning angaaende Negerloven med bilag, No. 24 Pt 1: Articles 1–4, 6, 8, 18–21, 32, 36 (1783a).

R/A, GTk, Udkast og Betænkning angaaende Negerloven med bilag, No. 24 Pt 1: Articles 45, 49, 51–58, 60, 69, 74, 75, 79, 80 (1783b).

R/A, GTk, Udkast og Betænkning angaaende Negerloven med bilag, No. 24. Pt 1: Articles 18, 19, 84; Pt 4: Articles 2, 3 (1783c).

R/A, GTk, Kommissions Forslag og Anmærkning angaaende Negerloven med genparter af anordninger og publikationer, Bind 2: Hr. Gen. Maj. Schimmelmanns Anmærkninger, 20 April 1784, f. 38 (1785a).

R/A, GTk, Kommissions Forslag og Anmærkning angaaende Negerloven med genparter af anordninger og publikationer, Bind 2: de Malevilles Betænkninger, 29 October 1787, f. 93 (1785b).

R/A, GTk, CANS, 1834–43, Afskrift af det af Generalgouverneuren forfattede Udkast til en Emancipations Plan for Slaverne paa de danske vestindiske Øer, 13 October 1834 (1834a). Commissions Betænkning, 13 November 1834 (1834b). von Scholten to Christian VIII, 15 January 1841, enclosing Proprietors and Administrators of Estates to von Scholten, 29 October 1840 (1840).

R/A, GTk, NEER, Neger Emancipation Efter Reskript af 1847 (1847).
R/A, VLA, Frederiksfort Stand Ret 7 July–12 August 1848 (1848).
Ramløv, Preben, *Massa Peter* (Copenhagen, 1967).
Schmidt, I., 'Blandede Anmærkninger samlede paa og over Eylandet St. Croix i Amerika', *Samleren* 2, Nos. 39–43 (1788): 199–260.
Schoelcher, Victor, *Colonies Etrangères et Haiti. Resultats de l'Emancipation Anglaise*, Vol. 2 (Paris, 1843).
Schuler, Monica, 'Akan Slave Rebellions in the British Caribbean', *Savacou*, 1 (1970): 8–31.
Skubbeltrang, Fridlev, *Vore Gamle Tropekolonier*, Vol. 3 (Copenhagen, 1967).
Turner, Mary, *Slaves and Missionaries. The Disintegration of Jamaican Slave Society 1787–1834* (Urbana, Chicago and London, 1982).
Vibæk, Jens, *Vore Gamle Tropekolonier*, Vol. 2 (Copenhagen, 1966).
Von Petersen, *En Historisk Beretning om de danske vestindiske øer St. Croix, St. Thomas og St. Jan* (Copenhagen, 1855).
West, Hans, *Bidrag til Beskrivelse over St. Croix* (Copenhagen, 1793).
Wilson, Peter, *Crab Antics. The Social Anthropology of English Speaking Negro Societies of the Caribbean* (New Haven, 1973).
Westergaard, Waldemar, *The Danish West Indies under Company Rule* (New York, 1917).
Westergaard, Waldemar, 'Account of the Negro Rebellion on St. Croix, Danish West Indies, 1759', *Journal of Negro History*, XI (1926): 50–61.

The State of the Debate on the Role of Capitalism in the Ending of the Slave System

SELWYN CARRINGTON

The callousness of the trading interest beyond the sea to the distresses of the kidnapped servitors and the miseries of the slave trade, gradually roused a philanthropic sentiment, which was eventually to exercise a powerful influence on the condition of labour at home.

...Comparative little progress was made till the philanthropic agitation was reinforced by political and economic reasons for abandoning the trade as detrimental.

W. Cunningham, *The Growth of English Industry and Commerce in Modern Times* (Cambridge, 1907), p. 607.

No historical work in the twentieth century has elicited more controversy about the abolition of the slave trade and the final emancipation of slaves than Eric Williams' *Capitalism and Slavery*, 1944. Although almost 50 years have elapsed since the book first appeared, it has continued to send ripples throughout academic circles. Probably, this is because the themes of the work are as topical today as they were 150 years ago; it is certainly not because the academic world has reached a consensus on the scholarly and other achievements of the study. In fact, one historian, commenting on *Capitalism and Slavery*, points out that 'no history is timeless' and that, although the work has enjoyed 'enduring acclaim', it has also been severely criticised. Its methodological framework as well as its theoretical basis has 'begun to exhibit advancing age' in a world where modern technology has been applied to historical research. Yet he has warned historians, economists and other commentators to desist from writing the book's 'obituary' because 'Whenever in the past Williams' work has appeared irreparably discredited some new academic physician has breathed fresh life into the old pages.'[1]

The attainment of freedom by the former slaves in 1834–38, like the abolition of the slave trade in 1807, must certainly be viewed as one of the truly momentous events in the annals of British history. Britain was the first industrial country to abolish the slave trade and then pass legislation in 1833 to emancipate the slaves in her colonies. The reasons for these decisions are less clear, and have led to a continuing lively debate among historians. As early as 1907, Cunningham had noted that three factors played important roles. In the first place, there was a 'philanthropic sentiment', but this had more impact on the condition of labour in Britain than on the slave trade or slavery in the colonies. While philanthropy played its part, however, it had to be reinforced by 'political and economic reasons' in order to achieve any success. This paper is an attempt to assess the economic reasons for abolition, and to investigate the state of the 'decline thesis'.

The Decline Thesis

Lowell J. Ragatz (1928) was the first modern historian to argue that the British West Indies were in decline after the 1750s because successive events conjoined to place great stress on the sugar plantation system at the end of the eighteenth century. Ragatz's *The Fall of the Planter Class in the British West Indies, 1763–1833* examines a series of events which occurred within the chronological period of his study and which in the long run led to the demise of the planter class. The decline of the British West Indies coincided with the rise of the movement for the abolition of the slave trade,

Journal of Caribbean History, 22, 1–2 (1988), pp. 20–41.

and Ragatz further observes that 'with the estate owners at the height of prosperity, the undermining of the old plantation system in the British West Indies was begun'.[2]

At first glance, one would immediately place Ragatz and Drescher in the same camp. On closer examination, however, it becomes clear that the time periods are different. While Ragatz sees West Indian prosperity, at least that of the old plantation system, as ending in the 1760s, Drescher has elected the post-1783 period as representing the height of West Indian economic prosperity.

While Ragatz had conceived of but had not developed the economic interpretation of abolition, he had intimated this position; but it was left to *Capitalism and Slavery* to establish the link between a declining British West Indian economy and the success of the movement in Britain to abolish the slave trade and to emancipate the slaves. It is clear that Williams had realised that, while the humanitarian movement was central to the process of abolition, it was in the words of William Cunningham, a 'philanthropic sentiment' until it 'was reinforced by political and economic reasons'. Williams had for the first time placed the British abolition 'in English works in economic history'.[3] He had challenged the traditional view of the role of the humanitarians and had subordinated it to the economic forces which had been largely overlooked by British scholars.

Pre-Williams Advocates

William Darity, Jr has recently examined the question of capitalism and slavery before the Williams thesis. He writes: 'Some British economic historians writing before Williams were struck equally by the ironies of British abolition. Williams could have turned to some British scholars themselves to make his case.'[4] However, Darity is worried by the absence of any mention of the works of William Cunningham, William E. H. Lecky and Samuel T. Coleridge. After offering several reasons for the omission of their work from Williams' study, Darity shows that the decline thesis, as it correlated to the abolition of the slave trade, was available in scholarship on English economic history during the Victorian period. However, he argues that it was Williams who brought a complexity and subtleness to an understanding of how the economic motives and patterns at work in British society conjoined to bring about the abolition movement. *Capitalism and Slavery* successfully linked the rise of capitalism to the changes in the structure of the British imperial economic system which affected fundamentally the economic relationship between Britain and her colonies. This enabled Parliament to pass legislation affecting the economy of the colonies.

Cunningham's work established that there were several problems in the West Indian slave plantation economy in the late eighteenth century. It shows that the islands were no longer the props to British commerce, and it contends that the older colonies were finding it difficult to cope with the successful rivalry of St. Domingue, especially since British policy had created an invaluable trade between the United States and the French islands. It had restricted a free flow of goods and ships between the United States and British sugar colonies, and thus it triggered the existing latent problems which sent the sugar economy into a downward spiral.

Between 1775 and 1783, in addition to the decline of West Indian production, the trade between the local merchants and those in Spanish and Portuguese America fell off. By the end of the war, British merchants had established direct trade with the region, especially Brazil, and the new trade diverted a stream of commerce which had hitherto been very profitable to the West Indian merchants. Cunningham viewed this occurrence as 'a serious matter'. Furthermore, by the end of the eighteenth century, the decline in West Indian production and trade clearly indicated that 'there had always been something a little artificial in their... [British West Indian] prosperity'. Hence, it is clear to Cunningham that abolition resulted because there was 'the existence of deeper roots than the evangelical fervour for the movement to overturn the slave trade'.[5]

Darity supports Coleridge's assessment of Pitt's role in the humanitarian movement. He agrees that Pitt made no sincere effort to prohibit the slave trade to the newly conquered colonies and allowed the planters to accumulate slaves as a precautionary measure against the abolition of the trade. The advance of the sugar industry in the new colonies speeded up the decline of the old plantations and reduced the value of West Indian products as prices fell. The sugar dealers thus joined in support of the movement for the abolition of the slave trade. This action was certainly not based on humanitarian grounds or even evangelical fervour: it was intended to protect the interests of an important element of the British economy.

In addition, many abolitionists favoured the continuation of slavery. They believed that the existing slave population in the British West Indies could be sustained, even allowing growth, by improving the conditions and diet of the slaves. There also emerged during this period a commerce with Africa in order to secure raw material. This in Darity's opinion led to a new policy of exploiting Africans at home rather than in the West Indies. The Coleridge/Lecky assessment stresses the point that the abolition of the slave trade was not the consequence of humanitarianism. When it occurred, it did not result in any significant loss to the old plantation system. This view has been developed by Barbara Solow. Coleridge and Lecky were certain, in the view of Darity, that abolition did 'not evolve as an exclusive or necessary consequence of humanitarianism'.

William Darity therefore makes it evident that the main tenets of the Williams thesis are to be found in the writings of British economic historians in the late nineteenth and early twentieth century. Even Reginald Coupland had found little disagreement with the economic argument since it was under his supervision that the thesis was prepared, and he did acknowledge that he had neglected this aspect of the investigation. But, if Williams had neglected the works of British scholars, he certainly owed much to three other scholars — Lowell J. Ragatz, to C. L. R. James, (*The Black Jacobins*), and to German historian, Franz Hockstetter (*Die wirtschaftslichen und politischen Motu für der Abochuffung des brifischen Sklavenhandels*).[7]

Williams and His Support

Williams' provocative study, which examined the relationship between British economic growth and the West Indian plantation system, addressed the question of western capitalism and its dependence on the exploitation of labour through the slave trade and slavery. Williams argued that the British West Indies were pivotal to significant capital formation in Britain, which laid the foundation for the industrial revolution. It was not only the trade and the plantation system which maintained the West Indian hegemony. The West India interest, which attained its greatest success in 1763 when it forced Britain to retain Canada in preference to Guadeloupe, a major threat to the British sugar planters, had been severely weakened by the American War of Independence. Compounding this was the creation of the United States, which led to an irreversible economic decline from which there was only periodic recovery to the status quo ante-bellum; but there was certainly no growth.[8] Compounding the secular decline in the West Indian economy which gave rise to abolition, Williams argued that the short-run features of 'overproduction in 1833 demanded abolition'; and that 'overproduction in 1807 demanded emancipation'.[9] In his claim that overproduction gave rise to the abolition of the slave trade in 1807, Williams is again guilty of not citing his authorities effectively. He could have called upon further British support. Likewise, there is no indication that he was aware of the evidence which has been cited by Sheridan:

> No less an authority than Lord Castlereagh can be cited to challenge Drescher's argument that the concept of overproduction did not enter into the decision for abolition. Writing to the governor of Jamaica on January 19, 1808, Castlereagh said that at a time when the world market was overstocked by the 'too great increase of colonial produce', an experiment for putting an end to the slave traffic had been undertaken . . . [10]

The American Revolution and Adam Smith

The beginning of the American War of Independence coincided with the publication of Adam Smith's *Wealth of Nations*. This work initiated a protracted debate over the issue of free trade, and postulated claims that Great Britain derived nothing but loss from the colonies. Hence the view of the West Indies changed from islands of great economic value to colonies that drained the British Treasury.[11] This negative view led to an atmosphere in which the very industries which depended on the West Indian trade found the sugar planters' monopoly of the home market irksome and influenced many in Britain to support the adoption of the principles of free trade while at the same time imposing mercantilist doctrines against the colonial trade with the United States.[12]

Compounding the problems of shortages and high costs of plantation supplies, the loss of credit from continental merchants, the drainage of cash from the islands, and the loss of a major consumer market for East Indian rum and other minor products, several internal factors making for decline were highlighted. For example, by the end of the eighteenth century, the islands suffered from outdated agricultural techniques, inability to maximise production, indebtedness, exhausted soii, and an inefficient labour force which made sugar production unprofitable. In his examination of the issue of the profitability of slavery at the end of the eighteenth and the beginning of the nineteenth century, William Dickson wrote:

> it is a historical fact that Slaves could not be bought at the full value, without ultimate loss . . . excepting always, those few cases where the returns of their labour were uncommonly great, or where none of them died in seasoning, and they afterwards kept up or increased their numbers by births.[13]

By the time the official debate over the abolition of the slave trade began at the end of the 1780s, the downward spiral in the economy in the British West Indies had been established for over a decade.[14] The artificial nature of the plantation system of the British West Indian colonies was glaringly clear to financiers who saw better possibilities for investment in new areas more suited to sugar production.

The publication of *Capitalism and Slavery* was certainly overshadowed by war. Scholars were both cautious and muted in their appraisal, and there was also no unanimity among the critics. Many pointed to several economic factors which had plagued the sugar planters at the end of the eighteenth century, and they agreed that the economic decline of the West Indies had made it possible for the abolitionists to gain support for the termination of the slave trade. Yet these very scholars were not prepared to hand Williams all the kudos. They opposed his 'single mindedness' and his 'economic determinism' which had led him to establish the pre-eminence and the primacy of the economic forces at the expense of the humanitarians in the abolition movement.[15]

The next two decades of the history of the decline thesis could be accurately termed 'the calm before the storm'. The international scene changed dramatically. The Second World War ended; the United Nations Organization was created; black countries were emerging; racial segregation was being attacked; and television was highlighting the plight of blacks, the sons and daughters of slavery. Williams became the prime minister of a former sugar colony. The 'third world' had been created in the minds of people in the developed world; and historians and other scholars pondered over the theses, set in a compelling literary style of *Capitalism and Slavery*, which had become the guidebook for many scholars from developing societies which were struggling against capitalist exploitation by imperialist powers, and against the persisting plantation system.

Opponents to Williams — Pre-Drescherian

The reprint of *Capitalism and Slavery* in 1964 began the reassessment of the decline thesis. In conference papers, Roger Anstey and C. Duncan Rice concentrated on the claim by Williams that 'Britain's changing attitude to slavery and the slave trade was essentially a function of her changing economic situation and interest', and that this in part explains the abolition of the slave trade. Anstey also set out to reinterpret the claims against Pitt's conduct of the abolition movement and Lord Palmerston's policy on the suppression of the slave trade. It was his intention to resurrect the view that the movement for the abolition of slavery sprang from a new doctrine of Christianity associated with evangelical philosophy and the philanthropy of the Enlightenment which placed emphasis on the human soul and hence the individual.[16]

But Anstey, like his predecessors, was inconclusive on the Williams thesis. In the 1965 unpublished version of the conference paper, he wrote that 'much of Williams' general evidence is persuasive'. Yet in the published version he modified his initial statement: 'Williams' argument is to an extent persuasive'. Despite this minor alteration, Anstey willingly conceded:

> It is difficult not to think that the radical change in the position of the British West Indies in the later eighteenth century did not affect English attitudes to the slave trade and slavery, whilst some of the figures Williams quotes are significant. For example, he shows that . . . the West Indies became relatively less important as a mart for British exports and that British sugar imports from Brazil, Cuba and Mauritius increased considerably whilst British Caribbean production remained stationary. Again . . . by 1807 the slave trade had become much less important to Liverpool, the British port most engaged in it.[17]

Having agreed with the principle of decline, Anstey was reluctant to follow Williams' lead and link it to the abolition of the slave trade. However, in the case of the passage of the Emancipation Act of 1833, Anstey contended that the Williams argument 'seems, *prima facie*, more convincing', and he concluded that by this time the British taxpayers were subsidising West Indian sugar on the European market in order to enable it to compete with foreign sugar. A decade later, Anstey, still conscious of the issue of decline, and turning to the relative economic importance of the slave trade, wrote: 'The Slave

Trade of the European nations with Western Africa was a commerce which reached its peak in the half century before British abolition.'[18] While, like David Richardson, Anstey undoubtedly favoured a link between abolition and evangelical Christianity in an effort to suppress the decline thesis, he had not lost sight of the fact that, in Parliament at the end of the eighteenth century, the humanitarians' cause was best served by James Stephen, who linked the West Indian condition to the question of abolition:

> A more generalised but deep-rooted sense of the importance of the West Indies for British prosperity amongst the political nation, especially as represented in Parliament, was the critically important obstacle and it was this which made Stephen's discernment of how the cause of abolition would be linked to the chariot of national interest so important . . . [19]

Although only peripherally connected to the decline thesis, three articles published between 1973 and 1978 support the overall view of the profitability of the West Indian economy right down to the time of emancipation. J. R. Ward, whom Drescher has co-opted as an ally, employing as limited a methodology as W. A. Green and R. K. Aufhauser, contends however that West Indian profitability had fallen below the 40–55 per cent of the early years. According to Ward, profits declined throughout the eighteenth century to modest levels of approximately 10 per cent in the period 1744–55, 14 per cent in 1756–62, 9.3 per cent in 1763–75, 3.4 per cent in the war years, 1776–82, and 8.5 per cent in the decade 1783–93.[20] Other statistical information analysed by Carrington corroborates this trend. Profits fell from 12 per cent in the 1790s to 6 per cent in 1801–04 and to only 3 per cent for well-run estates by 1805–06.[21] All profits virtually disappeared by 1807 when the act abolishing the slave trade was passed.[22] A good example of this seemingly irreversible trend is the Worthy Park plantation during the 1780s, clearly identified by Michael Craton and James Walvin.[23]

On the question of declining profits and the negative image of the West Indian islands, no one makes the point more succinctly than David Brion Davis. He is very conscious, and rightly so, that 'opposition to slavery cannot be divorced from the vast economic changes that were intensifying social conflicts and heightening class consciousness', and that in Britain these changes contributed to a 'larger ideology' that ensured stability while initiating social change. By the end of the eighteenth century, and even before the American Revolution, the West Indian sugar colonies were overvalued but only because 'sugar was a crucial symbol of national power'.[24] Davis writes:

> The West Indies decline thus appeared all the more dramatic. Sugar and slaves were not a source of opulence, one discovered, but of debt, wasted soil, decayed properties and social depravity. . . . In the popular view there was thus a total dissociation between the old empire of plantation slavery and the new imperial search for raw materials and world markets. The emergence of the second empire involved a repudiation of the first. The second might depend on millions of involuntary labourers, but it was, by definition, a 'free world'.[25]

Not only was there 'decline and stagnation' of the British West Indian economy but, at the end of the eighteenth century, this reinforced and confirmed the contention 'that slave labour itself was inefficient, unprofitable and an impediment to economic growth'.[26] These were indeed the negative perceptions of the sugar economy which prevailed among capitalists at a time when the abolitionists were initiating their campaign against the slave trade.

Econocide and the Decline Thesis: Acclaim and Opposition

The most serious attack on the decline/abolition thesis of Eric Williams has been launched by Seymour Drescher in his *Econocide: British Slavery in the Era of Abolition* (1977). Countering the Ragatz/Williams position, Drescher challenged the claim that the West Indies had lost its relative position in British trade and in importance to the imperial power. He adopted the view that the economies of the sugar colonies were growing both in absolute and relative value which, after 1783, reached levels above those of any putative 'golden age' before the American Revolution. Unlike Anstey, Drescher argued that the slave trade was expanding at the turn of the nineteenth century and that Britain was altruistic in her economic policy because she abolished the trade when she stood to make significant profits. This interpretation has now been endorsed by David Brion Davis, and is repeatedly used, although not convincingly, by David Eltis in his recent monograph.[27] Because the American Revolution is considered a watershed period in the history of the West Indies, Drescher and his allies inadvisedly dismiss this event as having little or no negative impact on the economy of the sugar islands.[28]

Econocide, like *Capitalism and Slavery*, has had mixed reviews. Many hailed the work as having discredited the thesis of Eric Williams, and they concluded that Drescher's findings illustrate that decline followed abolition. Most of the reviewers who support the claims of Seymour Drescher are not themselves specialists in the area, and they are therefore emotionally following *Econocide's* assumptions. A few, like James Walvin and Philip D. Curtin, have had to overturn the positions they had adopted in highly acclaimed works. For example, Walvin had written of decline on a West Indian plantation in the 1780s as irreversible and symptomatic of a broader/general problem.[29] Curtin, who defended charges of biased research made by Joseph Inikori,[30] has succumbed to the Drescher mystique and admitted that his figures were wrong.[31]

Caribbeanists were less confused by Drescher's argument. Craton, while supporting many of his statistical offerings, concluded that the book was weakened by 'omissions and obscurities' and that 'his overall dynamics of abolition verges on the simplistic'. Craton disagrees that the slave trade was profitable and concludes that *Econocide* succeeded only in obscuring the debate.[32] Elsa Goveia pointed to several contradictions in Drescher's interpretation of the statistical evidence. Mary Turner and Richard Sheridan argue that the West Indian interest was concerned about over-production and the declining share of the British re-export trade.[33] Sheridan quoted Lord Castlereagh in contradicting Drescher's claim that there is no evidence that over-production gave rise to abolition in 1807. Walter Minchinton cited Lord Grenville's use of the over-production theme when moving for abolition in 1807.[34]

It was Minchinton who established that many of the claims of an advancing/increasing West Indian economy at the end of the eighteenth century made by Drescher have fallen short of their mark, and that the arguments are less compelling than were heralded by his supporters. Examining the same table which Drescher used to oppose the decline thesis, Minchinton observed:

> Drescher has chosen his dates with care to support his argument but the full table enables a different interpretation to be presented. In his statement, Drescher made no reference to the period 1773–87 yet the peak quinquennium for the whole period 1713–1832 is 1778–82 (21.0 per cent) — a figure distorted by the American Revolution — and the position in 1803–12 is no more than a recovery to that level (20.8, 20.9).

Minchinton uses the table comprehensively to show that overall the British West Indies were in decline. Furthermore, he shows that the figures do not support the claim that the West Indies were more valuable to Britain in the period 1813–22 than the years 1773–87. On the basis of those figures, he concludes that 'Drescher has not done "brilliant demolition job".... If Drescher's case rests in the British West Indian share of total British trade... then the case is not proven. If these figures do not support the Ragatz-Williams doctrine of West Indian decline neither do they support the Drescher thesis of growth.'[35] Another interesting observation is that the upswings in British trade with the West Indies occurred during the years of war, and it is surprising that the trade figures for 1778–82 were better than those for 1803–07 or 1808–12, especially in light of the fact that during the former period the West Indian sugar economy was in shambles;[36] trade to the United States was prohibited; and the sugar economy depended totally on the British market.

Barbara Solow, in her assessment of the debate, stressed that the declining state of the West Indian economy had become an issue which had political consequences for abolition. Thus, she notes that by 1807 the act abolishing the slave trade had no negative impact on the British economy as would have been the case half a century earlier. Hence, 'abolition came when the economic development made it unimportant, not when it would have mattered a lot'.[37]

In the last five years, the debate over the Williams/decline thesis and the Drescher/non-decline interpretation has been intensified. Selwyn H. H. Carrington (the present author) produced one of the first full critiques of Drescher's arguments in his article, ' "Econocide" — Myth or Reality — The Question of West Indian Decline, 1783–1806' (1984). Carrington set out to show that Drescher's work only confused the issue. Decline was evident during the American War of Independence, unlike the case during other eighteenth-century wars. What appeared to Drescher to be growth of the British West Indian economy during the French Revolutionary and Napoleonic Wars was a return to pre-1776 wartime conditions in the West Indies.[38] During the latter wars, increased prices resulting from the social and economic disruptions in the

French islands caused the value of West Indian goods to appreciate.[39] But even when prices rose, costs increased faster and led to diminished profits, as shown by J. R. Ward. Carrington utilised a staple analysis approach to arrive at a better understanding of the decline question. A crop by crop performance examination shows that, as with sugar, there was no overall increase in production in the older islands except in the case of cotton which expanded until about 1790 when United States production quickly overshadowed that of the islands. Evaluating Drescher's view of growing slave profits as a feature of British West Indian economy which was indicative of the viability of the slave system, Carrington denies that these profits reflect a healthy British West Indian economy. He shows that the number of slaves retained on the islands declined in the period after 1783.[40] More recently, Carrington has reassessed Drescher's claims and his use of the slave trade as an indicator of the continued value of the sugar colonies to Britain.[41]

New information provided by David Richardson shows that the total number of slaves imported into the sugar colonies declined as the profits of the planters dwindled. Richardson found a direct but lagged relationship between changes in Jamaican planters' gross receipts from sugar shipments to England between 1748 and 1775 and the number of slaves retained on the island. Richardson further argues that the peaks in slave imports into the British West Indies occurred in the 1720s–30s and in the years shortly before the American Revolution, and certainly not in the years cited by Drescher, although imports in some years were excessively high. During the years 1763–75, 'British vessels carried more slaves from Africa than in any previous or subsequent period of thirteen consecutive years.'[42]

William Darity has also turned his scholarship to an assessment of the Drescher hypothesis, and he 'takes a different line of defence of the Williams position', according to Walter Minchinton.[43] Darity argues that it is the interpreters of Williams' thesis who 'assume that his position hinges on the belief that the plantation system was in decline'. Darity's research establishes that the plantation system could have emerged as a 'millstone' around the neck of Britain, even though the islands were profitable in themselves. Hence, Darity shows that at the foundation of the thesis is indeed the belief that not only did the plantation system emerge as not valuable to furthering the interest of industrial capitalism, but also that there was a transition of 'the thinking elements of Britain's governing elite away from principles of the mercantile system towards the *laissez-faire* principles of Adam Smith'.[44]

A most interesting observation is offered by David Brion Davis in his earlier interpretation of the state of the West Indian economy. Here, he agreed that American independence marked the end of one British empire with slavery as the major labour system, and the rise of the second British empire with an emphasis on capitalist exploitation which called for free or involuntary labour, and opposed to slavery. His vision was a declining West Indian economy lumbered by absenteeism, continued white depopulation, depleted soil, indebtedness, declining crop production levels and limited markets for slaves which established the illusion of slave labour as inefficient, wasteful, unprofitable and a retardation of economic growth.[45] This position seems very much in keeping with Darity's view that the West Indies could have still been profitable and have their supply of slaves removed by the British Parliament.

This was the view articulated by Adam Smith in his *The Wealth of Nations* where he sought to establish the groundwork for a free trade economy. Although Smith was technically incorrect, he identified two factors which countered the long-standing positions of the planter-historians. First, he credited the prosperity of the sugar colonies 'to the great riches of England, of which a part has overflowed' upon them. But, probably the more damaging claim was that 'Great Britain derived nothing but loss from the dominion which she assumes over her colonies'.[46] This latter claim, and certainly the loss of the American colonies, must have convinced the embattled conservative upper class that the future of Britain lay in a policy which favoured Englishmen at home. This was therefore not incongruent with the adoption of mercantilist restrictions on colonial trade with the United States on the one hand, and the movement to free trade on the other with the abolition of the slave trade in 1807.

Smith's polemical work has found support in the studies of modern economists who have attempted to discredit the Williams thesis. One of the best known works which adopts wholesale the Smithsonian concept of the colonies as a 'net loss' to Britain and as retarding the growth of the national economy is Robert Paul Thomas' article, 'The Sugar Colonies of the Old Empire: Profit or Loss for Great Britain'. Thomas employed a cost/benefit analysis to show that the British consumers paid more for colonial sugar under the mercantile system which gave preferential duties to the planters. Thomas' contention certainly enhances the idea that the West Indies were burdensome to British capitalists.[47] But Darity argues that this line of thinking does not detract from the Williams conclusion that British policy-makers became concerned about the colonial/mercantile system, but only after it had served its purpose in spurring British industrial growth and expansion in the eighteenth century.[48] Thomas' methodology has been criticised for being biased and too focused on 'consumer welfare'. It can also be argued that the successes of West Indian planters in securing protectionism made them appear in the end as burdensome to the metropole in their effort to maintain their self-interest.

Following the lead of Thomas, other writers have concentrated on the theme of the sugar colonies as a 'drain' on the British Treasury because of the monopolistic structures and the costs of administering and defending these colonies. Looking at the period 1768–72, Coelho concludes that the West Indian islands cost the British government an estimated £1.1 million annually. This work is basically a naive restatement of Adam Smith's criticism of the colonial-mercantile system.[49] One of its more serious flaws is the claim that the eighteenth century led to substantial net capital transfers to the colonies from Britain. Although these transfers did not occur, it was definitely good propaganda on the part of the free traders. It is a historical fact that the financial relationship between the planters and their merchant houses/factors in Britain, as it was emerging in the American colonies in the post-Seven Years War period, functioned on a credit/debit system.

A recent paper, highly critical of 'Drescherian history', was written by Cecil Gutzmore for the Hull Sesquicentennial in 1983. Drescher ignores this work in his 'The Decline Thesis of British Slavery since Econocide', which is his attempt to answer his critics. But the Gutzmore paper received a better fate at the hands of Minchinton, who notes that Gutzmore raises fundamental issues 'without dealing in detail with any of Drescher's arguments', and condemns Drescher as a 'bourgeois historian who . . . has misunderstood and misrepresented Williams'. According to Minchinton, Gutzmore accuses Drescher of 'empirical falsifications' which neither interrogate nor demolish the Williams-Ragatz decline thesis, and he 'dissents from the view that the "lengthy procession of British and other bourgeois scholars" have effectively "restored the claims of the British historical tradition in the matter of the humanitarian explanation of abolition and emancipation"'.[50]

Support for the overall concept of decline as a feature of abolition in slave economies can be found in an interesting article on comparative history. In this work, Gavin Wright draws attention to similarities between the British West Indies and the American South. For example, slavery contributed to industrialisation but showed a reluctance to expand. In the West Indies there was also evidence of stagnation and retardation; most sugar planters had little West Indian identity, and wealthy members of the West India interest did not reinvest in the colonies. As signs of a faltering economy, Wright suggests white depopulation as illustrated by ineffective deficiency laws; discouraged white immigration; increased reinvestments in other locations; and slave owners' interest in restricting imports as a way of raising prices and safeguarding their own investments. This was especially so in the older islands and was 'a factor in the success of the abolition movement'. Agreeing with Davis's earlier position, Wright contends that the birth of the movement for the abolition of the slave trade coincided with the destruction of the first British empire and the publication of *The Wealth of Nations*.

> The 'Age of Adam Smith' in which growth was dominated by expansion of trade and commerce and by exploitation of the gains from trade and the market, gave way to the 'Age of Schumpeter' as entrepreneurship moved into search for innovation in technology and improvements in the process of production. The resemblance to Williams' conception is not hard to see. Slavery encouraged commerce by accelerating the production of exotic commodities in far-off places. As entrepreneurial energies moved into home-based production of manufactured goods, the sugar islands came to seem more remote and irrelevant to the important things in economic life, as indeed they were.[51]

Reborn Humanitarianism

Although it is certainly correct to link the decline thesis to the economic argument for abolition and emancipation, Williams also argued that mature capitalism had destroyed the very links which had fostered its growth. Wright compares this feature in the West Indies and the southern United States and reaches very much the same conclusion when he contends that, as the industrial revolution with its emphasis on domestic manufacturing took hold in Britain, the sugar islands and their slave economies seemed remote and irrelevant to economic growth in the metropole. David Eltis and Seymour Drescher remain opposed, preferring to base their interpretation of the period on speculative/'if' history.

Recent studies by Eltis and Drescher, although not primarily concerned with the decline thesis, uses the hypothesis formulated in *Econocide* to reaffirm the contention that the British had sacrificed a quicker rate of economic growth for 'the humanitarian cause' of abolition. Eltis accepts and expands Drescher's argument against the putative decline of slavery in his study which traces the relationship between slavery and industrial growth in Europe. Thus, he reconstructs the costs, profits and methods of the nineteenth-century Atlantic slave trade. The first part of the work which concerns us here is the section in which he restates many of Drescher's assumptions without himself, analysing and testing claims such as 'The Caribbean islands certainly experienced lower returns. But the long-run economic data testify to continuing vitality of the British West Indies well into the nineteenth century.' His evidence for this is Seymour Drescher's argument that the value and prospects of the slave trade and slavery to Britain were brighter 'when the British Parliament severed the umbilical link with Africa in 1807'. Reminiscent of Drescher, he therefore argues that it was British anti-slave policy that had destroyed the relative world position of the British plantations and resulted in the absolute decline of the sugar colonies. Eltis ignores the evidence that clearly indicates that the British West Indies were in decline at the end of the eighteenth century. This section conveys to the reader a morbid feeling as he examines the contention that had Britain not outlawed the slave trade and emancipated the slaves, her economic advance/growth would have been sustained at a much faster rate. This neoclassical analytic approach depends to a large extent on speculative analysis of an historical topic and on a *bourgeois* conceptualisation of the relationship between human labour and the market-place.[52] More importantly, however, this interpretation shows a limited knowledge of eighteenth-century West Indian history. It also illustrates a misreading of the British West Indian economic conditions by metropolitan historians in their effort to discredit Williams' *Capitalism and Slavery*.

Seymour Drescher's *Capitalism and Anti-Slavery* seems to be the brain-child of a reborn humanitarian who has moved away from the moral vision to the emergence and expression of a political culture which conjoined with other forces to sweep the Augean stables clean of slaves but to leave the stench. The work is very little concerned with denying the role of capitalism in the abolition of slavery. Instead, it seeks to show how Englishmen 'for the only time in their lives' could cut across class lines to abolish slavery because of political consciousness and activism. Then, they went to sleep because, as in the words of Lord Nelson at Trafalgar, 'Thank God [We] have done my [our] duty'. In some miraculous way, Drescher has been able to find the emergence of the British tradition of liberty in the anti-slavery movement one which was born of widespread literacy and political consciousness within the popular movement which witnessed mass petition campaigns against slavery between 1806 and 1838, never to reappear as far as blacks are concerned. Drescher's Britain differed significantly from Eltis'. The latter has shown in his work that throughout the early decades of the nineteenth century the British share in the slave trade increased despite the government's efforts at its suppression. Hence, in dissimilar ways, Drescher and Eltis trace/highlight, without acknowledging it as such, the development of British hypocrisy, which is nowhere more clearly expressed than in its attitude to race.

Capitalism and Anti-Slavery ignores many of the most serious criticisms levied against *Econocide*. However, Drescher acknowledges the economic decline of the British West Indies when he writes:

> For more than three decades after 1807, the British planters were faced with a diminishing, mobile and more expensive work force. The British colonial system, which accounted for more than half of North Atlantic sugar in 1808, languished helplessly as its share of world production dropped throughout the first half of the nineteenth century.[53]

It is not clear whether Drescher's decline began in 1800, as the first half of 'the nineteenth century' would imply, or in the post-1807 period, as his thesis in *Econocide* indicates. But it was this diminishing importance of the islands and not his opposition to abolition, as claimed by Drescher, that led John Pinney of Nevis to write to his uncle:

Our situation is truly alarming. What with the shortness of our present crop and the low ebb of West Indian credit, united with our present unhappy contest.... Provisions and all plantations necessaries are so excessively dear, that the expense of supporting our slaves and keeping up our Estates in a proper condition, swallows up the greatest part of the produce. For these reasons, I want to contract my concerns here and fix a fund in England — not solely to depend upon estates subject to every calamity.[54]

Conclusion

This article has attempted an analysis of the major themes, issues and works on the question of decline. It has shown that the recent article by William Darity, Jr has undoubtedly established precedents for Williams' linking of the decline thesis with the increased movement for abolition and emancipation in the British West Indies. Caribbeanists who have supported the decline argument have analysed critically the performance of the islands' economies, demonstrating that these were in decline. Even anti-decline theorists, such as J. R. Ward, whose main research interest is profitability, demonstrate conclusively that profits had declined after the outbreak of the American Revolutionary War. The fact that profits recovered in the French Revolutionary War, representing a return to trends in these economies during wartime in the eighteenth century, has been neglected. These trends have been evaluated as growth. This is particularly the case in the approach of Seymour Drescher who has, however, joined forces with the decline theorists in the period after 1807. There is undoubtedly something amiss with the Drescherian perception of the abolition of the slave trade and its 'impact' on the economy of Britain. One cannot help but feel that Drescher's return to a school of historical thought which neither squares with history nor reflects British attitudes to race in the post-slavery period is an attempt to *whitewash* the issue, especially when at times the material used as evidence is misquoted.

The question of the role of 'mature capitalism' and its impact on the slave trade and slavery has basically been ignored by most critics of Eric Williams. Yet, it is one salient area which would undoubtedly shed light on the question of the relationship between advancing capitalism and slavery, and is clearly demonstrated by Gavin Wright. Cuban writers, in assessing the growth of capitalism in the Spanish sugar economy, have established that the adoption of capitalist principles was a factor in the final abolition of slavery. Advancing industrialisation in Britain was certainly incompatible with a slave labour system in the productive areas because the raw material could be more advantageously and cheaply procured from satellite economies. The retention of mercantilist principles in some areas of the economy was also not incompatible with free trade in others. Self-interest was the hallmark of British policy makers, and since it became increasingly more common for Britain to legislate for the colonies after the American Revolution, the decision to abolish the slave system was initiated without the existence of a liberal political tradition towards blacks. It was simply the case of the mother country embarking on an economic policy initiated by political action to protect British self-interest. After 150 years, British economic interest continues to dictate its policy towards the question of freedom for blacks. Would British humanitarians lay claim to their 'traditional' place in the history of the struggle for freedom in South Africa?

Notes

1. William A. Green, 'Race and Slavery: Considerations on the Williams Thesis' in Barbara Solow and S. L. Engerman (eds), *British Capitalism and Caribbean Slavery. The Legacy of Eric Williams* (Cambridge, 1987), 25.
2. L. J. Ragatz, *The Fall of the Planter Class in the British Caribbean, 1763–1833* (New York, 1928), 240.
3. William Darity, Jr, 'The Williams Abolition Thesis Before Williams', *Slavery and Abolition*, Vol. 9: 1 (May 1988), 32–33.
4. *Ibid.*, 31. See D. Eltis, *Economic Growth and the Ending of the Atlantic Slave Trade* (New York, 1987).
5. Darity, *op. cit.*, 33–34. See S. H. Carrington, *The British West Indies during the American Revolution* (Holland, 1988), especially Chap. 7.
6. Darity, *op. cit.*, 37.
7. See Walter Minchinton, 'Abolition and Emancipation: British West Indies since 1975', unpublished Paper. I wish to thank Professor Minchinton for sending me a copy of this paper.
8. For a full examination, see Carrington, The British West Indies; 'The American Revolution and the British West Indies', *Journal of Interdisciplinary History*, 17:5 (1987), 823–50; 'Econocide — Myth or Reality; The Question of West Indian Decline, 1783–1806'. *Boletin de Estudios Latinamericanos y del Caribe* (1984), 36.
9. Eric Williams, *Capitalism and Slavery* (Chapel Hill, N.C, 1944), 152: Minchinton, *op. cit.*, 2.
10. Richard B. Sheridan, Review of *Econocide: British Slavery in the Era of Abolition* in *Journal of Economic History* 38:3 (1978), 765.
11. Barbara L. Solow, 'Caribbean Slavery and British Growth: The Eric Williams Hypothesis'. Unpublished Paper. See also Barbara Solow, 'Capitalism and Slavery in the Exceedingly Long Run', *Journal of Interdisciplinary History*, 17:4, 711–37, for a lengthy

discussion of the Williams hypothesis on the profitability of slavery and the slave trade to Britain.
12. Carrington, *The British West Indies*, Chap. XI.
13. William Dickson, *Mitigation of Slavery* (London, 1814), 198.
14. Carrington, 'Econocide — Myth or Reality?'; Carrington, *The British West Indies*, 164–81.
15. *Times Literary Supplement*, 26 May 1945, 250.
16. Richard Anstey, 'Capitalism and Slavery: A Critique'; C. Duncan Rice, 'Critique of the Eric Williams Thesis: The Anti-Slavery Interest and the Sugar Duties, 1841–1853' in *The Atlantic Slave Trade from West Africa* (University of Edinburgh, 1965).
17. Roger Anstey, *The Atlantic Slave Trade and British Abolition, 1760–1810* (London, 1975), 403.
18. *Ibid.*
19. *Ibid.*, 407. By this time Anstey had found an ally in Seymour Drescher, and he cited Drescher's work in support of his contention that the islands were still highly valuable to the imperial economy.
20. J. R. Ward, 'The Profitability of Sugar Planting in the British West Indies, 1650–1834', *Economic History Review*, 31:2 (1978), 197–213; See also W. A. Green, 'The Planter Class and British West Indian Sugar Production Before and After Emancipation'. *Economic History Review*, 26 (1973); R. K. Aufhauser, 'Profitability of Slavery in the British Caribbean', *Journal of Interdisciplinary History*, 5:1 (1974); S. Drescher, 'The Decline Thesis of British Slavery Since Econocide', *Slavery and Abolition*, 7:1 (1986).
21. Carrington, 'British West Indian Economic Decline and Abolition, 1775–1807; Revisiting *Econocide*', unpublished paper (September, 1987), 20; J. R. Ward, *British West Indian Slavery, 1750–1834: The Process of Amelioration* (Oxford, 1988), 49.
22. S. Drescher, '*Econocide: British Slavery in the Era of Abolition* (Pittsburg, 1977), 53.
23. Michael Craton and James Walvin, *A Jamaican Plantation: The History of Worthy Park, 1670–1970* (London, 1970), 118.
24. David Brion Davis, 'Reflections on Abolitionism and Ideological Hegemony', *The American Historical Review*, 92:4 (1987), 797–812.
25. David Brion Davis, *The Problem of Slavery in the Age of Revolution 1770–1823* (Ithaca, 1975), 62.
26. *Ibid.*, 61.
27. See Eltis, *Economic Growth*.
28. For an opposing view of the impact of the American Revolution on the British West Indian economy, see Carrington, *The British West Indies*.
29. Craton and Walvin, *op. cit.*, 118.
30. Joseph E. Inikori, 'Measuring the Atlantic Slave Trade: An Assessment of Curtin and Anstey'. *Journal of African History*, 17 (1976).
31. See Curtin's review of *Econocide in Journal of Interdisciplinary History*, 9:3 (1979), 539–41.
32. See Craton's review of *Econocide* in the *Canadian Journal of History*, 13:2 (1978).
33. For the viewpoint of the Caribbeanists, see *William and Mary Quarterly*, 3rd series, 35:4 (1978), *Peasant Studies*, 8:4 (1978); *Journal of Economic History*, 38:3 (1978).
34. Walter Minchinton, 'Williams and Drescher: Abolition and Emancipation', *Slavery and Abolition*, 4:2 (1983), 91.
35. *Ibid.*, 86.
36. Carrington, *The British West Indies.*
37. See Barbara Solow's review of *Econocide* in the *Journal of Economic Literature*, 17 (1979).
38. One of the most significant studies which would have enabled Drescher to understand the fluctuations in the West Indian sugar economy in times of peace and war is Richard Pares' *War and Trade in the West Indies 1739–1763* (London, 1963).
39. Isaac Dookhan, 'War and Trade in the West Indies, 1763–1815. Preliminary Survey', *Journal of the College of the Virgin Islands*, 1 (1975).
40. Carrington, 'Econocide — Myth or Reality?', 36–45.
41. Carrington, 'British West India Economic Decline and Abolition, 1775–1807: Revisiting *Econocide*, unpublished paper (1987).
42. David Richardson, 'The Slave Trade, Sugar and British Economic Growth 1748 to 1776', *Journal of Interdisciplinary History*, 17:4 (1987), 742.
43. Minchinton, 'Abolition and Emancipation', 14.
44. William Darity, Jr, 'A General Equilibrium Model of the Eighteenth Century Atlantic Slave Trade: A Least-Likely Test for the Caribbean School'. *Research in Economic History*, 7, 289.
45. Davis Brion Davis, *Slavery and Human Progress* (New York, 1984), 335, n. 121, 178–79. In this work, Davis veers towards the position of Drescher without good reason or evidence.
46. Adam Smith (ed. E. Cannan), *An Inquiry into the Nature and Causes of the Wealth of Nations* (London, 1961), 362. See Abbé Raynal, *A Philosophical and Political History of the Settlement and Trade of the European Countries in the East and West Indies* (London, 1798), Vol. V, 106–07; E. Long, *History of Jamaica*, 3 vols (London, 1774); Bryan Edwards, *The History, Civil and Commercial of the British Colonies in the West Indies* (London, 1805), Vol. 1.
47. Robert Paul Thomas, 'The Sugar of the Old Empire: Profit or Loss for Great Britain', *Economic History Review*, 2nd ser. 21 (1968), 30–45.
48. Darity, 'A General Equilibrium Model', 292.
49. P. R. Coelho, 'The Profitability of Imperialism: The British Experience in the West Indies, 1768–1771', *Explorations in Economic History*, 10 (1973).
50. Minchinton, 'Abolition and Emancipation', 11.
51. Gavin Wright, 'Capitalism and Slavery on the Islands: A Lesson from the Mainland', *Journal of Interdisciplinary History*, 17:4 (1987), 867–69.
52. Eltis, *Economic Growth*, Section I.
53. Seymour Drescher, *Capitalism and Anti-Slavery. British Mobilization in Comparative Perspective* (Oxford, 1986).
54. John Pinney to Simon Pretor, 12 June, 1977. Pinney Papers: Letter Book 2, p. 114. See Richard Pares. *A West India Fortune* (London, 1950), 93–94; Drescher, *Capitalism and Anti-Slavery*, 83.

Victor Schoelcher and Emancipation in the French West Indies

ANDRE MIDAS

(*Translated from the French by Mrs V. O. Aicalá*)

The recent celebration of the centenary of the Revolution of 1848 in France, and of one of its most immediate and important consequences — the abolition of slavery — has revived interest in the action of the French abolitionists. Speeches were made, articles published and new editions of old texts appeared, on this occasion. Victor Schoelcher, the greatest of these gallant men who were called, not without a certain amount of irony, 'the philanthropists', received special mention, and his memory was revived throughout the nation by the transfer of his ashes to the Panthéon where illustrious Frenchmen are interred. Thus, a humanitarian enterprise of the highest order, involving men from various walks of life who differed fundamentally in their intellectual development, ideas and character, was commemorated. As was natural, this crusade aroused bitter controversies and unrelenting opposition in its time.

There is no doubt that Victor Schoelcher and the part that he played at a crucial turning point in colonial history are little known today in France, outside a small circle of scholars, and still less known in foreign lands. It is fair to add, however, that his name never ceased to be loaded with significance and fame in the minds of those whom he liberated and of later generations of their descendants. It is indeed difficult, outside of the French West Indies, to assess the importance of the position he held in those islands, almost the entire populations of which suddenly recovered their liberty. There are Schoelcher Streets, Schoelcher libraries and a Schoelcher High School in Martinique. A symbolic figure, a beacon for his fellowmen, an architect of justice, Schoelcher was all this in the eyes of sensitive and grateful human beings who worshipped him with mystic devotion and resigned themselves to his spiritual guidance with absolute confidence. They called him their father and, in his honour, they composed a very popular song, 'The Mountain is Green', a verse of which reads: 'Schoelcher must shine like a star in the East'. For many a year after his death, West Indian homes were decorated on the anniversary of his birth, with an improvised altar richly ornamented or more modest according to the financial resources available, where his portrait was displayed.[1] All the burning love of the West Indian soul and the shrewdness of a people who knew instinctively where homage was due were expressed in this pious gesture.

The outstanding part played by Schoelcher in the abolition of slavery cannot be exaggerated. Schoelcher was a man with a single idea, continually reiterated, sifted and strengthened, and fighting a single cause brought to a successful conclusion with implacable severity. Victor Schoelcher's history provides this point of interest, *viz.*, that he did not achieve that fierce strictness which he made his guiding principle, at the very start. At a certain stage of his evolution he said: 'It is no more possible to regulate slavery humanely than it is to regulate murder.' From then onwards that was his golden rule, and his goal — the immediate liberation of the slaves without compromise or equivocation.

Victor Schoelcher was a middle-class citizen in easy circumstances. His father, a porcelain

Caribbean Historical Review Vol. 1 (1950), pp. 110–30.

merchant of the Rue Grange-Batelière in Paris, wished Victor to follow in his footsteps, the normal wish of a good father of a family, who is anxious to assure his child's future. The idea did not appeal to Victor Schoelcher who threw himself into a worldly life on leaving the Lycée Louis le Grand and frequented the literary circles. He engaged in politics, was active in the ranks of the liberals, and belonged to the Freemasonry. His father then sent him on a business trip to the United States and Mexico for the purpose of selling some merchandise. On his return, Victor Schoelcher published a series of articles entitled 'Letters about Mexico', in the *Revue de Paris*, from May to November, 1830. In these articles he recounted his first experience of slavery. In Cuba he saw the system functioning at close quarters, and his contact with 'ebony wood' (the name given to the slaves) certainly brought him a certain amount of disillusionment. He stressed the responsibilities of the masters who, under the slave system, possessed all rights. He was equally plain spoken, however, in dealing with the Negroes. 'I admit,' he said, 'that the Negroes, as they exist at present in slavery, constitute the most wretched, abject and immoral class that can be imagined.' Such were the conclusions of this young man of 26 years who treated the problem of slavery, with interest certainly, but without deep conviction and, above all, without passion. In his opinion, consideration must be given 'to the great task of emancipating the slaves'. It was necessary, however, to proceed with calm and caution and without undue haste: 'Leave it to the great healer, Time, to effect the cure,' were the words he used then.[2] The only measure on which he suggested immediate action was a rigorous suppression of the slave trade in order to dry up the very source of slavery.

When Victor Schoelcher's interest in the question of slavery, faint though it might be, first became apparent, it was clear that he shared generally the views of those who considered the problem before him. Prudent and moderate action was the course advocated by the Duc de Broglie who, for several years, had been working within the 'Society of Christian Morals' for the abolition of slavery. He, too, felt that the first step should be complete suppression of the slave trade and he discussed these views at great length, in a magnificent discourse delivered in the Chamber of Peers on March 28, 1822. Without any difficulty, he established the fact that traffic in slaves continued after the official abolition of the slave trade by France (Napoleon's Decree of March 29, 1815, confirmed by Louis XVIII on July 30 of the same year). His efforts in this direction were moderately successful. To the very end he gave no thought to immediate liberation and when, after three years, the Commission over which he presided published its report on the measures for effecting the emancipation of the slaves, the conclusions were very vague. De Broglie, who was responsible for them, offered two solutions: general emancipation at the end of ten years or partial and progressive emancipation. On July 7, 1845, de Broglie made another speech in the Chamber of Peers recommending the passage of certain draft bills providing for the re-purchase, education and welfare of the slaves, but not for their liberation. All the other contemporary defenders of the slaves showed a similar prudence and moderation in their views. Hypolite Passy, who presented a draft bill in connection with emancipation to the Chamber of Deputies on February 10, 1838, provided only for the freedom of children born to slave parents. Neither Lamartine, who made noble and moving speeches on the question of slavery, nor yet Montalembert, Remusat, Tocqueville and Wallon, who devoted their efforts and talents to the cause of the slaves, thought of immediate emancipation. The various petitions presented to the Chamber of Deputies on behalf of the slaves, the petition of the workers of Paris and Lyons in 1844, and the more representative one made by the whole nation in 1847, did not request any radical and immediate action. Ledru-Rollin, inspired and briefed by Schoelcher, was the first to demand the immediate abolition of slavery, from the gallery of the Chamber of Deputies in April, 1847.

After his first stand in 'Letters about Mexico', Victor Schoelcher, unlike his companions in the struggle, experienced a profound evolution in his way of thinking. In 1833 he published his first work entitled *De l'Esclavage des Noirs et de la Legislation Coloniale*. It is a violent, impassioned book, inspired by a great generosity, in which we find the origin of Victor Schoelcher's dedication of his life to the abolition of slavery. Why did he devote himself with such ardour to the cause of the slaves? He gave the reason in the very first lines of his foreword: it was idealism and natural generosity.[3]

Meanwhile he continued to display great clearsightedness and assessed the slaves without illusion.[4] Nevertheless, this man who, in 1842, became the uncompromising champion of immediate liberation of the Negroes,[5] was resolutely opposed to the idea nine years earlier.[6] About that time he published draft legislation couched in very general terms, in which the following statement occurs: 'It should be understood that slaves are men and, therefore, their masters should treat them as such.' This draft, comprising thirty articles altogether, springs undoubtedly from a generous inspiration, but seems hardly applicable at that period. Briefly, Schoelcher was in precisely the same position as the Duc de Broglie, with one voyage more (certainly a matter of importance), and several works, studies, conferences and political speeches less, to his credit.

What changed Schoelcher's outlook was the voyage which he made to the French West Indies in 1840.

Mr Périnelle, one of the most important proprietors in Martinique, was aboard the sailing ship that took Schoelcher to the West Indies. Quite willingly, this planter, who was well aware of Victor Schoelcher's convictions, secured him access to the different plantations on the island, thereby permitting him to gain direct experience of the functioning of the slave system. Victor Schoelcher revised his values in the light of facts. He irrevocably condemned the institution itself, being by then firmly convinced that it should be unconditionally abolished, and, at the same time, his opinion of both planters and slaves underwent a change. He did not think that all planters were fundamentally corrupt and, when he met slave owners who were humane and temperate (according to their own code of ethics), he said so loyally. Indeed, he emphasised that: 'They (the planters) fear one another and tremble before the tyranny of their own public opinion which drowns the voice of the good and the wise.' He saw instances where slaves did not seem unhappy, and cases where they enjoyed the rights of property, acquired by means of some form of regulation, and scrupulously respected by their masters. On the question of colour prejudice, he admitted that 'a great deal might be said in defence of the planters'. However, he also cited definite instances of extraordinary cruelty on the part of colonials who were acquitted of guilt by the colonial judiciary. The case of Brafin, estate owner at Rivière Salée in Martinique,[7] and that of Douillard-Mahaudière, a planter in Guadeloupe, men who tortured slaves and were acquitted by the courts, were eloquent examples of the complicated circumstances in which the slaves were caught.

Schoelcher's book, moving in its sincerity and its constant attention to facts in recounting events and allotting responsibility, drew the amply justified conclusion that slavery must be abolished without delay. Henceforward this was Schoelcher's opinion, which was strengthened still more by his voyages to Haiti, Egypt and Senegal.

Therein lies one of the dominant characteristics of Victor Schoelcher. He was not merely an abstract and 'ivory tower' idealist. When he cited the wretched condition of existence of the Negro slaves in support of his opinions, he was speaking of things he had seen in various countries and at different periods. In Cuba, he witnessed the sale of a slave in the public market and he described 'this unfortunate woman . . . dirtily clad, cold and indifferent to her fate, surrounded by passers-by and purchasers . . .' In his book on *Les Colonies Françaises*, he again described a sale of slaves by auction, which he witnessed in 1841, and he revived this scene in his *Histoire de l'Esclavage au cours des Deux Dernières Années*, published in 1847. He saw slaves whipped[8] and visited their prisons. He knew the 'commander's' power and all the degrading circumstances linked with slavery. He derived the force of his convictions and the ardour of his opinions, which he expressed both by spoken word and in writing, from a store of experience which he could bring to bear vigorously, against those metropolitan advocates of slavery who, like Granier de Cassagnac,[10] visited the West Indies in search of fresh arguments in support of their thesis. This direct contact, for which there is no substitute, was lamentably lacking in the other abolitionists of his time.

This argument did not escape the metropolitan advocates of slavery, the planters' friends and defenders. Seizing on an idea rashly expressed by Lamartine, the Parisian newspaper *La Globe* emphasised one of the weaknesses of the abolitionists' position. 'It is indeed true,' this paper said, 'that the philanthropists do not know, have never seen and probably will never see the men whose regeneration they seek. That is why their doctrines are misleading.' On the eve of emancipation in 1848, Schoelcher had already gained the friendship of the Negroes. He was in Africa at the outbreak of the Revolution of 1848. What was he doing there? He was continuing his research indefatigably, studying the African way of life and adding yet more documents to his file.

In the first half of the nineteenth century, Victor Schoelcher was, with the exception of

Thomas Clarkson in England, to whom he bears a marked resemblance, unquestionably the greatest European specialist on the question of slavery. This fact was appreciated in France where his republican friends made him a member of the government after his headlong return from Africa. He was entrusted with the task of solving the multiple problems which slavery posed. In a despatch to colonial territories, the new Minister of the Navy and the Colonies, François Arago, reminded all citizens that their first duty was 'to submit to the existing laws and authorities'. Would the republican régime continue the excuses and delaying policy of Louis Philippe's government, in so far as slavery was concerned? It is clear that Arago was uncertain. Moreover, the defenders of the planters in Paris, the Chambers of Commerce of the great seaports, who fully appreciated the gravity of the situation, devoted themselves with feverish activity to the task of lessening the significance of an eventual emancipation. Perrinon, a native of the West Indies, who was in Paris, was of the opinion that the interim government had not the right to abolish slavery, and concluded a letter addressed to the West Indians with these words: 'Patience, hope, unity, order and work, these are the things I recommend to all.'[12] The position was, therefore, unchanged and the liberation of the slaves seemed doubtful.

Schoelcher arrived in Paris on March 3, 1848, and conferred immediately with Arago. One of his first victories, according to Arago, in his *Memoirs*, was to persuade the new minister to end slavery and to present his colleagues with 'a decree of immediate emancipation'. Victor Schoelcher was appointed Under Secretary of State for the Navy and the Colonies. On March 4, the provisional government of the Republic, 'taking into consideration the fact that no French territory may countenance slavery', appointed a Commission responsible for preparing 'the order for immediate emancipation in all the colonies of the Republic, at its earliest convenience'. Victor Schoelcher, who, in the eyes of the government, personified the struggle against slavery which was nearing the end, was appointed President of this Commission. The Commission, composed of five members, one of whom was Perrinon, then a Major of the 'Marines', began its work immediately.

The planters and their representatives did not accept the event that was forecast, and took more and more steps to ward it off. The Council of Delegates from the Colonies (that is, from the planters) sent a letter to the Commission over which Schoelcher presided, on March 7, 1848, stating clearly that only the National Assembly was competent 'to pass two inseparable measures, Emancipation and Indemnity'. This letter went on to describe, in the blackest terms possible, the conditions that would result from a hasty liberation of the slaves: ruin of industries, decline of agriculture, impoverishment of society, ruin of trade with the colonies. The Chambers of Commerce of Marseilles, Nantes and Le Havre sent delegates to Paris to intercede with the Ministers.

Opinion was not unanimous even within the Commission. Certain members, like Mestro, Director of the Colonies, and Gatine, a lawyer, were concerned about the judicial aspect of the problem and the effects of abolition on the planters' right of ownership. Schoelcher maintained and won his point in the matter of immediate abolition. He used another argument very successfully, *viz.*, that any government that had the right of expropriation for public purposes might well exercise this right where moral issues were involved. Schoelcher also maintained forcefully that the newly liberated slaves should thenceforward be *citizens*. In opposition to Perrinon, who claimed that French slaves were inferior politically to English slaves, in opposition to Mestro and the delegates from Guadeloupe (Jabrun, Reizet), Réunion and Martinique, Schoelcher insisted that the liberated slaves enjoy the full rights of citizenship. Froidefont-Desfarges, the planters' delegate from Martinique, stated that 'the Negroes are big children equally incapable of recognising either their rights or their duties'. Schoelcher refused to believe this. He expressed his faith in the Negro race, and his decisions were adopted.

On April 27, 1848, the provisional government, acting on the Commission's proposals, abolished slavery in all the French colonies, and in the following year the National Assembly fixed the indemnity due to the planters at 126 million francs.[14]

Thus, within a few years, France repeated the action taken by England in 1833, when she decreed the abolition of slavery in her overseas possessions. The action of the English philanthropists was strongly supported by British commercial and industrial circles — cotton producers, shipowners, sugar refiners — and by the most important business centres, London, Manchester, Liverpool, etc. The monopoly of the British West Indies, and slavery on which this monopoly rested, offered no further interest from the economic standpoint, though both had contributed largely to the prosperity of the metropolitan country, particularly in the eighteenth century. In exchange for its exports, Great Britain received raw materials. The monopoly guaranteed to the British West Indies excluded foreign sugar from this trading arrangement and constituted an obstacle to British industry.[15] Great Britain, the workshop of the world, technologically ahead of its competitors in the world market, found the West Indian colonies doubly irksome in the early nineteenth century: they purchased insignificant quantities of British manufactures, whilst their monopoly of the British sugar market hampered the potentialities of British trade with such rival sugar producers as Cuba and Brazil.

The emancipation of the slaves in the French West Indies had its economic aspect also. Beet sugar production, first stimulated by Bonaparte and the Prussians as the answer to Britain's continental blockade, had, by 1848, become an established commercial fact. The French beet producers stressed the large white population involved in the cultivation and manufacture of beet sugar, their superior standard of living, and their greater importance to French capitalists.[16] They took the lead, therefore, in pressing for emancipation of the slaves in the French colonies — on humanitarian grounds, ostensibly, but in reality, for their own economic advantage.

There is some evidence that certain British abolitionists were closely identified with those economic vested interests which opposed the West Indian planters. As regards Schoelcher, however, there is no evidence to suggest that his conduct was even partially inspired by the defence of economic interests. Gaston Martin, whose *Histoire de l'Esclavage dans les Colonies Françaises*, published in 1948, is one of the most recent works on the question, makes no such inference. Augustin Cochin, in his *Abolition de l'Esclavage*, which appeared in 1861, makes no mention of such a possibility. However, Schoelcher's whole life, the struggle he kept up indefatigably, the nobility of feeling which appears in his writings, all these bear high testimony of his sincerity and disinterestedness.

His work accomplished, Schoelcher who had no further political ambitions, resigned his post as Under Secretary of State. His struggle for emancipation, however, had won him very great popularity among the newly liberated Negroes. In August, 1848, he was elected the people's representative both in Martinique and Guadeloupe, by 19,117 votes and 16,038 votes, respectively. He elected to be deputy for Guadeloupe.[17]

On December 2, 1851, Victor Schoelcher, a fervent republican, refused to accept Louis Napoleon Bonaparte's *coup d'état*. He joined the resistance group which was immediately formed and in which Victor Hugo was a notable figure. He flung himself into the defence of the barricades of Paris, where the deputy, Baudin, who became famous by his resistance to Bonaparte and sacrificed his life to his political convictions, was killed at his side. Then he went into voluntary exile to England where he spent eighteen years.

Schoelcher returned to France only in August, 1870, after the military disaster sustained by France at Sedan, and was appointed Colonel of the National Guard. At the elections, a few months later, he was appointed to the National Assembly by the Department of the Seine, French Guiana and Martinique. He chose to represent Martinique. He was next elected Senator for life.

The abolition of slavery in 1848 constituted an economic and social experiment of the greatest significance in the French West Indies. We have seen that the planters had predicted the worst disasters. Naturally, a period of transition and reorganisation of the system of labour was necessary. The government had recourse to immigration and two decrees, February 13, and March 27, 1852, provided for the introduction of European, African or Asiatic labour into the French colonies. Further, on July 1, 1861, the British and French Governments concluded an agreement providing for the recruitment of Indian labourers for the French West Indies. In the course of debates which took place in the Conseil Général of Martinique in December, 1884, as a result of which authorised immigration was suppressed, it was revealed that 25,509 Indian immigrants had been brought into Martinique by 55 convoys from 1853 to 1884, and that 13,271 of them still existed there.[18]

Schoelcher examined the problem in his work, *Polémique Coloniale*,[19] but gave somewhat different figures. 'From the commencement of immigration in 1854 to June 30, 1876,' he wrote, '31,640 Indians have been brought in (to Martinique). Of this number only 3,307 were repatriated when their contract expired; 17,890 are still living in the island; 10,443 are dead.' He drew the following conclusion: 'In 22 years, therefore, a third of these men have died more or less in their prime in a civilised country.' Did Indian immigration assist in the economic development of Martinique? Was it worth the cost? Schoelcher did not think so. He emphasised the fact that the Indians 'are of weak constitution', 'only fit for light work' and 'certainly figure in the debts on which interest at the rate of 10 and 12 per cent devours the best part of the revenue of the inhabitants'. Referring again to the figure in *The Yearbook of Martinique*, which fixes the number of workers 'employed in the different cultivations and sugar factories' at 57,000 in 1876, he estimated, further, that there were about 10,000 immigrants supplying regular agricultural labour. It was, therefore, on the 47,000 local workers that 'the largest part of the Colony's production depended'. Schoelcher concluded therefrom that the immigrants were far from being indispensable: 'We should do much better without them,' he added, 'for as fast as they disappeared we should see a certain number of native workers returning to the plantations, since the latter dislike being brought into contact with Indians whose introduction has been responsible for lowering wages'.

On his return to France, following the defeat of Sedan, Schoelcher renewed his close relations with the Caribbean islands. He was then able to determine the tangible results of his action in 1848. Towards the end of his life, he saw the birth and rise of the coloured generation, the descendants of the liberated slaves.

In 1880, Schoelcher reviewed the work accomplished, in the presence of men of colour from Martinique, Guadeloupe and Cochin China, who presented him with a work of art purchased with their subscriptions, as a mark of gratitude: 'What gigantic strides the emancipated class has made in such a short space of time!' he says, 'what immense moral and material progress it has made!' Then he stressed the fact that the population of African origin 'furnished this consoling testimony that, given equal education, all human races are equal'.

Indeed, he continued the bitter attack, which he had led against the planters who were bent on claiming their privileges as slave owners, on behalf of the coloured men who had so recently gained access to the social life of their territories. With an enthusiasm and ardour altogether youthful, Schoelcher rushed to the assistance of the young coloured class of Saint Pierre (Martinique) in the face of the fierce and bitter hostility of the old privileged class. It was inevitable that Schoelcher, in taking up this position again, should draw down on his head the fury of the planters of that period. By his very nature he must displease them. He did not believe in God, whom he confessed that he had sought unsuccessfully, and on March 23, 1882, before the French Senate, he had made a public declaration of atheism which caused scandal. Schoelcher was a republican. Further, the planters declared in their paper, *Les Antilles*: 'We do not like the Republic because in 1848 and 1870 it handed us over as a prey to Mr Schoelcher.'[20] The paper of Saint Pierre, *La Défense Coloniale*, in April, 1882, reprinted an article entitled 'The Atheist of Luxembourg' from the *Figaro* of Paris, in which Schoelcher was ridiculed. He was described as 'a tall, thin man, with pointed features, pointed and jutting ears'. Souquet-Basiège, who published a biased and controversial work on *Le Préjugé de Race aux Antilles Françaises*, denounced Victor Schoelcher as 'this embodiment of hatred, coldly proud, a sophist masquerading in the guise of a stickler for humanitarian doctrines.' The newspapers of Saint Pierre, in their opposition to Schoelcher, multiplied their attacks against him, accusing him of seeking the 'substitution' of one race for another, of having sworn 'Hannibal's oath against Martinique', and exciting rebellion and violation of property. 'Hatred of white people, their annihilation and disappearance, that is the programme, and Schoelcher has dictated it,' they said.[21]

When we read the two volumes of *Polémique Coloniale*,[22] a collection of attacks against Victor Schoelcher, and public refutations published by him and the newspapers published at Saint Pierre during this period, we cannot fail to be struck by the extreme violence of the controversy. The young generation, represented by brave and brilliant lawyers and journalists — Marius-Hurard, president of the local General Council and Martinique's deputy, Clavius-Marius, Césaire Lainé, Deproge, who also became one of Martinique's deputies — vigorously defended their newly won position in Martinique society. From Paris, Schoelcher watched events closely. In the eyes of young West Indians he was a wise Nestor, full of experience and aggressive courage. Nothing escaped him. He read the various colonial papers carefully and knew the strength of the forces mustered. Clearsighted, with abundant references always at his disposal, he answered untiringly the exasperated and often unjust criticisms which his adversaries levelled at him.

He contributed in Paris to *L'Homme Libre*, *L'Opinion Nationale*, *Le Rappel*, *XIXe Siècle*. These were so many forums from which he kept metropolitan public opinion informed of the position in the Colonies. He followed with interest the progress of the paper, *Les Colonies*, which Marius-Hurard founded in 1878 at Saint Pierre. On that occasion he wrote the following to him: 'I have received the first two numbers of your paper. I find it very good. . . . Fight colour prejudice whenever it appears. It is the greatest scourge of the French West Indies. Point out calmly, without irritation but firmly, all the evil that it causes in the present and all the dangers with which it is fraught for the future; as long as it survives there will be no peace or well-being for colonial society.'[23] Wherever he saw an instance of iniquity in the new social conditions of the French West Indies, he denounced it vigorously. He revolted against colour prejudice in all its many and frequent manifestations, quoted definite facts, dates and names.[24] He desired equality in education,[25] equality in justice.[26] To Mr Champvallier, who opposed representation for the colonies in a speech to the Chamber, because of the 'small number of voters at all colonial elections', Schoelcher replied that the colonies had always felt the urgent need in the past of defending their particular interests in the metropolitan assemblies. In support of his contention, he drew attention to the fact that, under Louis Philippe, the colonies 'hired the services of Mr Charles Dupin and Mr Jollivet at a cost of 20,000 francs per year, each, to plead their cause in the Chamber of Peers and in the Chamber of Deputies, respectively.'[27]

When Paul Leroy-Beaulieu, the distinguished French economist, expressed some doubt concerning the civic sense of the coloured population of Martinique and Guadeloupe in the re-issue of his work, *De la Colonisation chez les Peuples Modernes*, Schoelcher protested indignantly against his views.[28]

Schoelcher received letters from all quarters, informing him of the situation in the West Indies or asking his opinion, advice or intervention.[29] He never rested, and always went to the assistance of those whom he considered his *protégés*. The planters in the French West Indies, at least those among them whom Schoelcher called the 'Incorrigibles', knew the influence that he had acquired in France, and they wrote, not without bitterness: 'Mr Schoelcher is the perpetual minister of the colonies. He elaborates the programme everyone must follow, he it is who distributes blame or praise, punishment or reward.'[30]

According to them, he exercised 'unlimited influence' on the Department of the Navy (which was also responsible for the Colonies). They charged that the Ministers were placed there for the sole purpose of initiating his *protégés*.

Commenting ironically on these accusations, Schoelcher stressed the point that, if any credence must be given to the palnters of Saint Pierre, they, Admiral Pothuau, Admiral de Dompierre d'Hornoy, Admiral Montaignac, Admiral Fourichon, Admiral Jaureguiberry, Admiral Cloué, general officers 'holding political opinions that are opposed and different in character', have 'resigned the power into his hands'.

There was an obvious exaggeration in this charge which Schoelcher vigorously attacked. 'Behold!' he wrote, 'the ridiculous ideas spread by certain agitators shut up in St. Pierre, in their narrow circle, who neither see nor look at anything happening in the world, apart from their old prejudices and who detest anyone that does not share these.'

Schoelcher owed the enormous prestige which he enjoyed at the time to his unalterable fidelity to his ideal and to the uprightness of his life. His good faith was unassailable. This austere old man, robed in a long frock-coat, had voluntarily assumed certain responsibilities with regard to the slaves, and he intended to fulfil them to the end. At least he was not mistaken in the hopes that had constantly inspired his action. Events at the end of the century amply justified the daring risks he had taken.

Looking over the road traversed and the promise the future held, he jubilantly exclaimed: 'Bravo, "African savages", continue your self-enlightenment . . . and preserve your scorn for those who insult you. Your astounding progress speaks for itself.' This irony *à la* Montesquieu and this affection are both striking and moving.

His death, on December 26, 1893, brought dismay to the West Indies.

Notes

1. Robert Caddy, *Le Roman de Mayotte* (Fort de France, 1922).
2. *La Revue de Paris*, Vol. 20, No. 2, 1830.
3. *De l'Esclavage des Noirs et de la Législation Coloniale* (Paris, 1853).
4. *Ibid.*, p. 34.
5. *Des Colonies Françaises: Abolition Immédiate de l'Esclavage* (Paris, 1842).

6. *De l'Esclavage des Noirs*, p. 41.
7. *Des Colonies Françaises*, p. 34.
8. *Ibid.*, p. 84.
9. *Ibid.*, p. 84.
10. Granier de Cassagnac, *Voyage aux Antilles* (Paris, 1842).
11. Victor Schoelcher, *L'Immigration aux Colonies* (Paris, 1883), p. 67.
12. *Courrier de la Martinique*, 27 March 1848.
13. Gaston-Martin, *Histoire de l'Esclavage dans les Colonies Françaises* (Paris, 1948), p. 293.
14. *Ibid.*, p. 295.
15. Eric Williams, *Capitalism and Slavery* (Chapel Hill, N.C., 1944), p. 154.
16. See, for example, T. Lestiboudois, *Des Colonies Sucrières et des Sucreries Indigènes* (Lille, 1839), p. 11, 12, 17, 52–53; T. Dehay, *Les Colonies et la Métropole, le Sucre Exotique et le Sucre Indigène*, (Paris, 1839), pp. 29, 54, 183, 285.
17. *Biographie Impartiale des Représentants du Peuple à l'Assemblée Nationale* (Paris, 1848).
18. Eugène Revert, *La Martinique* (Paris, 1949), p. 241.
19. Victor Schoelcher, *Polémique Coloniale* (Paris, 1882), Vol. I, p. 241.
20. Victor Schoelcher, *Evènements des 18 et 19 Juillet* (Paris, 1882), p. 15.
21. *Ibid.*, p. 15.
22. *Polémique Coloniale*, Vol. I; Vol. II (Paris, 1886).
23. *Ibid.*, I, p. 281.
24. *Ibid.*, I, p. 281.
25. *Ibid.*, I, p. 66.
26. *Ibid.*
27. *Ibid.*, I, p. 13.
28. *Ibid.*, II, p. 119.
29. Victor Schoelcher, *Lettres Martiniquaises* (Paris, 1935).
30. *Evènements des 18 et 19 Juillet*, 9.

Explaining Abolition: Contradiction, Adaptation, and Challenge in Cuban Slave Society, 1860–86

REBECCA J. SCOTT

In the middle decades of the nineteenth century, as slavery was disappearing elsewhere in the New World, slave-based plantation production of sugar in Cuba reached remarkable heights of technological sophistication and output. In 1868 Cuba produced 720,250 metric tons of sugar, more than 40 per cent of the cane sugar reaching the world market in that year.[1] Yet just as production reached these levels, the abolition of slavery in Cuba was initiated, beginning a process of slave emancipation that was to last nearly 20 years. This concurrence of events raises the questions: What was the relationship between slavery and the development of sugar production? Why did emancipation in Cuba take place when and as it did?

My analysis of these questions takes a comparative perspective in two respects. First, it is partly in implicit comparison to other New World slave societies that the very late abolition of slavery in Cuba — 1886 — poses a problem of explanation. Second, and more important, an explicitly comparative analysis of the course of emancipation in distinct regions *within* Cuba can help to identify the forces that advanced, and those that retarded, emancipation, and thus can contribute to a fuller interpretation of the causes and nature of abolition.

The predominant explanations generally put forward for Cuban abolition invoke large-scale forces and internal contradictions. One argument, enunciated most fully by Cuban historian Manuel Moreno Fraginals, goes roughly as follows. There was a contradiction between slave-based production and necessary technological innovation. For the sugar industry to advance, it had to break free of this outmoded organization of production. Indeed, as the industry advanced, slavery itself decayed. Formal abolition was thus merely the de jure recognition of a de facto disintegration of slavery.[2] A complementary argument has been made about the attitudes of Cuban slave holders. Eugene Genovese compares planters in the United States with those in Cuba and concludes that major Cuban planters had only an economic attachment to the institution of slavery and were quite prepared to abandon it in order to advance and modernize.[3]

An alternative hypothesis, advanced by Arthur Corwin in his study of Spain and Cuba, sees abolition as part of a worldwide political and diplomatic campaign resulting from a basic ideological shift away from bound labor. Cuban abolition, in this view, results from Spanish colonial policies designed to end the institution of slavery, thus protecting the colonies from outside interference while bringing Spain in line with what were seen as more advanced and civilized modes of labor organization.[4]

The underlying explanatory problem posed is a challenging one, not so much because it has

This essay is part of a larger project that was funded by the Social Science Research Council, the Fulbright-Hays Program, and the Latin American Program of Princeton University. The author would like to thank David Davis, Seymour Drescher, Stanley Engerman, Albert Hirschman, Thoms Holt, Franklin Knight, Sidney Mintz, Magnus Mörner, David Murray, Stuart Schwartz, and Gavin Wright for their comments, and Manuel Moreno Fraginals for numerous discussions of the issue of slavery and abolition. This essay first appeared in *Comparative Studies in Society and History*, 26 (January 1984): 83–111. Parts in Rebecca Scott, *Slave Emancipation in Cuba: The Transition to Free Labor, 1860–1899*, to be published in 1985 by the Princeton University Press.

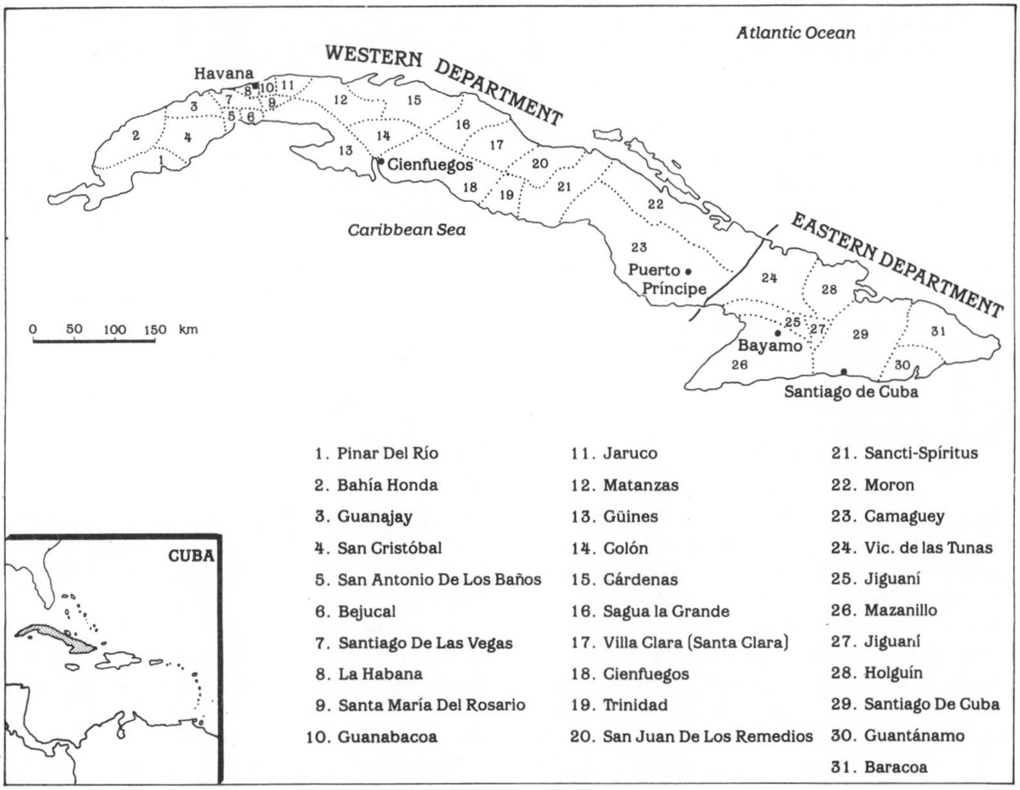

historiographical implications but because it obliges one to look at large-scale explanations and then at small-scale patterns of events and ask how well the explanations actually account for the patterns observed. The point is not simply to juxtapose the particularities or uniqueness of a given case against the large-scale explanation and conclude that one must reject simplifying generalities. Rather, it is to hypothesize appropriate links between the different levels at which the historical explanation might operate and then to determine whether the observed patterns of historical reality generally match the patterns anticipated from the explanation. For example, if it is the case that 'mechanization, the conversion of manufacture into large industry, unquestionably brings about the abolition of slavery'[5] then technologically advanced areas might be expected to shift toward free labor first, with the most advanced estates giving up the use of slave labor. If, on the other hand, abolition were the result of colonial policy, then emancipation might be expected to occur more or less evenly across provinces, closely tied chronologically to key legal changes.

The Chronology and Geography of Abolition

Let us begin with the background to abolition and the key events that marked the ending of slavery. In 1860 the island of Cuba was the world's largest producer of cane sugar and contained some 1,400 sugar mills. The majority of Cuban mills operated by steam power, and a minority (located primarily in the central province of Matanzas) also used advanced processing equipment.[6] The slave population was approximately 370,000, and by far the largest single occupation of slaves was that of sugar worker.[7] Production increased rapidly in the decade of the sixties, growing from 428,800 metric tons in 1860 to 720,250 tons in 1868.[8]

Despite the apparent prosperity and productivity of the sugar industry, problems were rising to the surface. The slave trade, illegal since 1817 according to a treaty between Spain and England, had nonetheless flourished as a vigorous contraband. But after a large upswing in slave imports in the latter part of the 1850s, the 1860s saw a rapid and permanent decline as British pressure and changing United States policy finally blocked off the trade.[9] Since the Cuban slave population did not fully reproduce itself, the work force would necessarily decline in size unless other steps were taken. One response to the labor supply problem was to import indentured Chinese workers, but this practice was halted by a treaty between Spain and China in the 1870s. Another was to institute a policy of what was referred to as 'good treatment', intended to encourage slave reproduction. This was to some extent successful, though not enough so as to maintain the size of the slave labor force.

The impact of these problems over the short term should not be exaggerated, however. Profits continued to be made in Cuban sugar production, and world prices for sugar remained relatively steady in the 1860s and early 1870s. Though planters had difficulties with agricultural credit, and resorted to extensive mortgaging, output continued to climb. Despite competition from beet sugar, Cuba's share of the world market in sugar remained about 25 per cent.[10] In the minds of larger planters, moreover, there were strong forces supporting both slavery and colonialism. Slavery was a form of labour organization that permitted the exaction of an extraordinary amount of labor from the men, women, and children who toiled under it. Planters were unsure whether free persons would willingly labor under the grueling regime prevalent in the cane fields and sugar-boiling houses of Cuba. At the same time, to most planters in the sugar areas Spanish colonialism was a known quantity, an extractive presence but a protective one, a bulwark against social disruption, and the ultimate guarantor of peace on the plantations.

It was in this environment that the rebellion of 1868, later to be called the Ten Years' War, broke out. Small-scale planters in the eastern end of the island, provoked by heavy new taxes and by a financial crisis in 1867, rose in rebellion against Spanish domination. The insurrection, begun by relatively conservative men, some sympathetic to the possibility of annexation to the United States, rapidly became more radical as its social base expanded. Though the rebellion was not successful, three results significant for the future of slavery emerged from the conflict.[11]

First, in order to gain the support of slaves and free blacks, the insurgents declared the qualified freedom of slaves under their control, a measure that quickly went beyond the limited aims of its initiators and undermined the social relations of slavery throughout the war zone. Second, because the Spanish hoped to capture the apparent moral high ground and avoid appearing as retrograde defenders of slavery in the eyes of potential black recruits to the insurrection, as well as to potential international allies of the insurgents, Spain in 1870 adopted the Moret Law. This measure declared free all children born after 1868 and all slaves over the age of 60 and also promised some form of emancipation of the rest when Cuban deputies were seated in the Spanish parliament once the war was over. This was an extremely cautious form of gradual abolition and did not generally affect those of working age, but it did signal Spain's intention eventually to abolish the institution. Third, the 1878 peace treaty ending the Ten Years' War freed those slaves who had fought on either side. The Spanish government saw this policy as a necessary precondition for pacification — there would be little reason otherwise for slaves among the insurgents to lay down arms — but it was both controversial and disruptive.[12]

The following year, in 1879, the remaining slaves in the eastern provinces unexpectedly challenged their masters, refusing to work unless they were granted freedom *como los convenidos* — like those freed by the peace treaty. Eastern planters backed down, promising freedom in four years and wages during the interim. The Spanish government, already under pressure from abolitionists in Spain, backed down as well and declared both the end of slavery and the immediate transformation of slaves into 'apprentices' called *patrocinados*.[13] This intermediate status, under which former slaves were obliged to work for their former masters, was intended to last until 1888. Attacked by Spanish abolitionists and by the handful of Cuban abolitionists, and undermined by the behavior of masters and apprentices themselves, the interim arrangement was instead ended prematurely in 1886, finishing the legal process of abolition.

This, in effect, is the political sequence of events that comprised the abolition of slavery in Cuba. If we turn the search for underlying causes and mechanisms to examining the phenomenon regionally and demographically, however, it becomes clear that the process of emancipation, the actual achievement of legal freedom by slaves, followed a pattern quite different from abolition.

The rate of decay of slavery varied widely from province to province (Tables 1 and 2). Matanzas and Santa Clara, the major sugar provinces and the ones with most of the

Table 1 Slave and *Patrocinado* Population by Province, 1862–86

Province	1862	1867	1871	1877	1883	1885	1886
Pinar del Río	46,027	44,879	36,031	29,129	13,885	8,110	3,937
Havana	86,241	84,769	63,312	41,716	18,427	10,419	5,693
Matanzas	98,496	102,661	87,858	70,849	38,620	19,997	9,264
Santa Clara	72,116	68,680	56,535	42,049	23,260	12,987	5,648
Puerto Príncipe	14,807	14,889	7,167	2,290	246	153	101
Santiago de Cuba	50,863	47,410	36,717	13,061	5,128	1,715	738
Total	368,550	363,288	287,620	199,094	99,566	53,381	25,381

Source: See Appendix.

Table 2 Slave and *Patrocinado* Population Retained, Percentage by Province, 1862–86 (1862 = 100)

Province	1862	1867	1871	1877	1883	1885	1886
Pinar del Río	100	98	78	63	30	18	9
Havana	100	98	73	48	21	12	7
Matanzas	100	104	89	72	39	20	9
Santa Clara	100	95	78	58	32	18	8
Puerto Príncipe	100	101	48	15	2	1	1
Santiago de Cuba	100	93	72	26	10	3	1
Total	100	99	78	54	27	14	7

Source: See Appendix.

technically advanced mills, showed the greatest persistence of slavery into the early 1880s. Pinar del Río, in the west, where about one-third of the slaves in 1862 were living on tobacco farms and slightly over one-third on sugar plantations, showed a similar pattern. Havana, a province that contained the island's major urban area (about 25,000 slaves lived in the city of Havana in 1862) showed a substantially more rapid decline. By 1877 it held less than half of its 1862 slave population; by 1883, about one-fifth. The eastern provinces of Puerto Príncipe, a cattle area, and Santiago de Cuba, an area of some backward sugar mills and much small-scale farming and coffee growing, lost slave population very rapidly after 1867. These were the two provinces most involved in the Ten Years' War, which led to the destruction, both direct and indirect, of many plantations. Some had to cease operation for want of labor when their slaves fled; others were burned, which often resulted in de facto freedom for the slaves.

This pattern reveals that the course of emancipation was by no means uniform across the island, suggesting that the pace of achievement of freedom was determined by factors other than Spanish colonial policy. Moreover, the result of the unequal rates of emancipation was to concentrate slavery increasingly in the more technologically advanced sugar zones. In 1862 Matanzas and Santa Clara had 46 per cent of Cuba's slave population; by 1883 they had 62 per cent of the *patrocinados*. The freeing of slaves thus cannot be attributed solely to the requirements of the advanced sugar plantations, either, for as emancipation proceeded these plantations held proportionately more, not fewer, of Cuba's slaves.[14]

The chronology of the process is also significant. During the 1860s and 1870s, whatever the 'contradictions' facing the sugar industry, the major sugar areas were holding on to their slaves. In Matanzas in 1862 the slave population was around 98,500. About 20 per cent of those slaves would have been under the age of ten or over the age of 60, leaving approximately 78,800 between those ages.[15] In 1877 all slaves were by definition between the ages of nine and 59, as a result of the Moret Law, but about 70,850 slaves remained in Matanzas. The slave population of working age had indeed fallen in the intervening 15 years but only about 10 per cent, an amount plausibly attributable to deaths and a shift in the age structure, partially counteracted by some in-migration. There is no support in these figures for the idea of large-scale abandonment of slaves or of slavery by the owners of plantations in Matanzas.

There was significant decline, however, in the areas of backward technology and political unrest — Puerto Príncipe and Santiago de Cuba — where slaves and insurgents fought directly for an end to slavery. Decline was also marked in the province containing a large city, Havana, where lawsuits and self-purchase by slaves were facilitated by access to courts and by money earned through hiring out. Official tabulations of appeals by slaves for *coartación* (partial self-purchase) and freedom show disproportionate representation for the city of Havana.[16]

The strong persistence of slavery through the 1870s in major sugar areas suggests that the notion of an irreconcilable conflict between the existence of slavery and the technological advancement of plantations needs revision. Sugar production expanded in the 1860s and 1870s as planters with capital bought vacuum pans and other modern processing apparatus, increasing the output of sugar per unit of land planted. Additional workers appeared on estates. (The Chinese population of Cuba increased 35 per cent between 1862 and 1877, while the island's total population grew only slightly.) Some discharged Spanish soldiers and other Spanish immigrants also worked on the plantations. But the slave population, though diminishing, remained crucial. In enumerating the *dotaciones* (labor forces) of sugar estates, the 1877 agricultural census found 90,516 slaves working on the estates of their owners, 20,726 *alquilados y libres* (hired and free), and 14,597 Chinese. Slaves thus comprised at least 72 per cent of the *dotaciones*, and quite probably more, since the category *alquilados y libres* included not only hired laborers but rented slaves and some young and elderly former slaves who had been freed by the Moret Law and were not full-time workers.[17]

The regional and chronological pattern of persistence of the slave population suggests that the strategy of large planters was to maintain continued control over their slaves, even while expanding their labor force in other ways — to adapt, rather than repudiate, slavery. Thus the contradictions of Cuban slavery (of which the failure of the slave population to maintain its numbers was the most urgent) did not have to impel abolition as such. An observer sympathetic to Cuban planters noted dryly in 1873: 'The slave-owners in Cuba are convinced of the necessity of manumitting their slaves; but readily as they acknowledge the evils of the slave system, they are not persuaded of the wisdom of any measure by which it may be brought to an end.' He described planters' advocacy of a gradual substitution of free labor for the declining slave population, rather than support for actual suppression of the institution of slavery.[18]

The Plantation Work Force

The most distinctive characteristic of the plantation work force in the mid-1870s, then, was its diversity. Plantation slaves, rented slaves, indentured Asians, and black, white, and mulatto wage workers all labored on the estates. Plantation employers did not face a homogeneous supply of labor but rather a segmented labor force, with different forms and quantities of payment due different types of worker. Wages were paid by the day, the task, the month, the trimester, or the year; the amount paid varied widely; workers sometimes did and sometimes did not receive maintenance; compensation occurred in coin, bills, credit, goods, or shares.[19]

This is the situation that has been interpreted as chaotic, symptomatic of the internal collapse of slavery.[20] But one must examine carefully the argument that the diversity of forms of labor in the 1870s was indicative of a disintegration of Cuban slavery in the face of unavoidable contradictions.

The argument has several parts. One claim is, in a sense, definitional: that the slave who received a bonus, cultivated a provision ground, or was rewarded for learning a skill was in some sense no longer a true slave and that these developments were symptomatic of the disintegration of slavery. Although such concessions certainly affected slaves' lives, and in some cases hastened self-purchase, they had appeared in many slave systems long before abolition and do not, by definition or ortherwise, necessarily constitute disintegration. They were attempts to resolve a variety of problems within slavery, but they certainly did not need to lead to its demise.[21]

A second claim deals with the response of planters to the reduction in the slave trade. Aware that their supply of labor was being cut off, some Cuban planters had resolved to take better care of their existing slaves and to encourage reproduction. But, it has been argued, the policy of 'good treatment' inevitably led to a decline in the productivity of the slave work force because the proportion of the very young and the very old increased, eventually making the enterprise unprofitable. Moreno Fraginals's study of plantation records shows convincingly that the proportion of slaves of working age did decline on some Cuban estates through the first half of the nineteenth century.[22] But even if one accepts the argument that maintaining a self-reproducing slave labor force would eventually have undermined profitability for Cuban planters (in a way that it apparently did not, for example, in the American south), the question remains: Given the very late cessation of the contraband slave trade to Cuba, how far had this process actually proceeded on Cuban plantations by the time of abolition?

Though plantation lists for an adequately

representative range of estates in the 1870s have not survived, there is an extremely comprehensive source for one district: the manuscript returns of an 1875 slave count from Santa Isabel de las Lajas in the province of Santa Clara. Lajas was a prosperous area in the jurisdiction of Cienfuegos and contained both old and new plantations. In 1861 the district had a slave population of 1,930 and contained 17 *ingenios* (plantations, including fields and mill). In 1875, when the manuscript listing was drawn up, there were 15 *ingenios* and a slave population of 1,852.[23] The exceptional persistence of slavery in the region was no doubt due in part to the presence of estate owners, such as Tomás Terry and Agustín Goytisolo, who were both prosperous and tied to the slave trade. The district is thus not typical of the island as a whole, but analysis of its population reflects the labor situation facing large and small planters in an important sugar area in the mid-1870s.

Of the slaves on *ingenios* in Lajas in 1875, 58 per cent had been born in Cuba and 42 per cent in Africa; 61 per cent were male and 39 per cent female. It was a population that plainly had relied recently and heavily on imported slaves, probably during the boom in the contraband trade in the 1850s. The age structure of the plantation population is also quite striking, considering the date — just five years before the legal abolition of slavery and the establishment of apprenticeship. It was not an aged population: while 28 per cent were between the ages of 31 and 40, only 6 per cent were between the ages of 51 and 60, even though one might have expected this latter group to include some slaves over age 60 whose ages had been falsified by their masters to evade the Moret Law. Nor was there a high proportion of young slave children. Those born since September 1868 were technically free, and those between the ages of six and ten constituted only 7.5 per cent of the population. Even though those born since 1868 were still the responsibility of the plantation, the total burden was probably relatively small, for in some instances slave parents maintained their *liberto* children directly or later reimbursed the master for their maintenance. What is most significant is that the 16–40 age group, of prime working age, constituted fully 63 per cent of the plantation slave population and 66 per cent of the males (see Table 3 and Figure 1). One can contrast this with the situation in the coffee-producing municipality of Vassouras in Brazil, where the age 15–40 sector of the plantation population fell from a high of 62 per cent of the total labor force during 1830–49 to a low of 35

Figure 1 Age Pyramid for Slaves on *Ingenios* in Santa Isabel de las Lajas, 1875

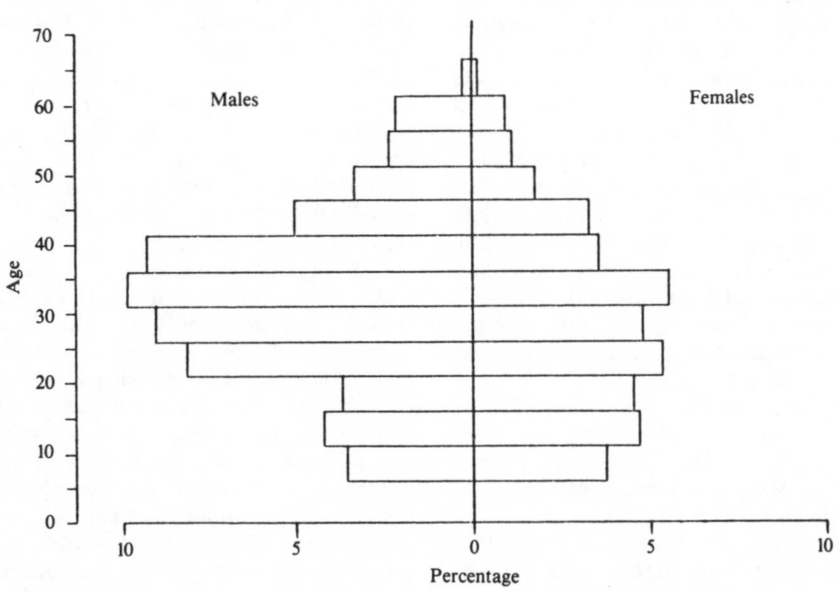

Source: See Table 3.

Table 3 Ages of Slaves in *Ingenios* in Santa Isabel de las Lajas, 1875

Ages	Males	Females	All slaves	Percentage of total
6–10[a]	49	51	100	7.5
11–15	56	61	117	8.8
16–20	51	58	109	8.2
21–25	108	69	177	13.3
26–30	120	64	184	13.8
31–35	132	72	204	15.3
36–40	124	46	170	12.8
41–45	69	44	113	8.5
46–50	45	24	69	5.2
51–55	31	15	46	3.5
56–60	29	10	39	2.9
61–65[a]	2	1	3	0.2
Total	816	515	1,331	100.0

Source: Archivo Nacional de Cuba, Misc. de Expedientes, leg. 3748, exp. B, Capitanía Pedánea de Santa Isabel de las Lajas, núm. 3, Padrón general de esclavos, 1875.

[a] All of those under age 6 or over age 60 should legally have been free under the Moret Law. Some of those age 6 were free.

per cent in the last eight years of slavery, thus bringing about a true age-related crisis of labor supply.[24]

The plantation population of Lajas was, at least potentially, a quite productive one. The Moret Law had so streamlined it that 100 per cent of the legally enslaved population was between the ages of 6 and 60, and between those limits the population was further weighted toward those of working age. The largest single groups consisted of males aged 31 through 40 and 21 through 30. Lajas plantations were not carrying a terrible burden of young and old slaves. Masters were not sustaining the full cost of reproduction of their work force. They were still operating with a carefully selected labor force built up primarily through purchase. The difficult future of slavery now that the trade had ended was apparent in the small number coming up through the ranks — there were less than half as many males aged 11 through 20 as aged 21 through 30 (see Table 3). But this problem would not be expected to make itself fully felt until some years later.

Though they were also using some Chinese laborers, free workers, and rented slaves, sugar plantations in Lajas remained heavily committed to slavery. Indeed, if one can trust the ambiguous figures from the 1877 agricultural census, the large Lajas plantations relied even more heavily on slave labor than the small. The Santa Catalina, Caracas, San Agustín, Amalia, and San Isidro estates, each with a work force of over 100, had a total of 701 slaves, 161 *alquilados y libres* (which could include *libertos* and rented slaves as well as free workers), and 89 Chinese. The smaller plantations of Sacramento, Dos Hermanas, Adelaida, Santa Elena, Maguaraya, and Destino together had 235 slaves and 105 *alquilados y libres*.[25]

Large planters in Lajas were not yet facing an internal collapse of slavery. Though the demographic structure of their slave populations indicated trouble in the long run, suggesting that free laborers would have to be attracted sooner or later, this fact motivated only a theoretical acceptance of an eventual transition, not a willingness to give up control over the existing work force. It is therefore not surprising that the *hacendados* of Cienfuegos, like those elsewhere in the western part of the island, held meetings during the 1870s to oppose immediate abolition.[26]

Slavery and Technology

A further element in the argument for the internal dissolution of slavery is the positing of an incompatability between slave labor and the needs of technology. This is often stated as a contradiction between slave labor, which is seen as brute labor, and advanced machinery, which is thought to require the motivations characteristic of free labor.[27] This argument also fits the image of a labor force whose quality was steadily deteriorating, based on the concept of slaves as instruments of production whose productivity depended simply on physical strength and whose value therefore dropped sharply once they were past their prime. The argument is coherent but not necessarily empirically correct. One needs to ask how slaves actually behaved and how they were viewed by planters.

It is suggestive that an owner of 300 slaves in Cuba, in a pamphlet addressed to the Spanish colonial minister in 1868, estimated the average value of male slaves aged 31–50 as *higher* than that of slaves aged 16–30, remarking that in the older group were those with skills, such as machinists, carpenters, masons, blacksmiths, and *paileros* (those who worked with boiling pans), among others.[28] Corroboration of this portrait would require an analysis of actual sale prices to determine the effect of various factors on the market value of slaves. But the statement does suggest that a slave work force with an age structure similar to that in Lajas was not necessarily experiencing sharply declining productivity and that planters did not invariably regard slaves as mere brute labor.

A more important challenge to the incompatability thesis is the direct evidence that slaves were used extensively in the large advanced mills. The *ingenio* España, for example, was one of the most advanced plantations in Cuba in the 1870s. Its work force in 1873 was composed of 530 slaves, 86 Asians, and just 19 whites. That is, the work force was more than 80 per cent slave, and 97 per cent unfree labor, if the Chinese were indentured, as is likely. The *ingenio* Álava, whose technological apparatus Moreno Fraginals has used to illustrate the industrial revolution on Cuban plantations, was operating in 1877 with 550 slaves and 71 Asians. It listed no free wage workers or rented slaves.[29] The Las Cañas plantation has been described as 'Cuba's most modern mill in 1850', in which, up to 1880, new machinery was being added 'in a continuous system of renovation'. Its work force in 1873 numbered 450 slaves, 230 Asians, and 27 whites. Again, the number of free white workers was very small, and they held the same jobs that they had always held on Cuban plantations: administrator, *mayordomo*, machinist, and so forth. On Las Cañas, the Asians do seem to have been treated differently from slaves and were concentrated in the processing sector.[30]

These examples do not really test the claim that technological advancement encouraged a shift to free labor — for that, one would need reliable statistics on the work forces of a large sample of Cuban plantations and detailed data on the internal division of labor. But these cases do suggest that major technological advances did not require the extensive use of fully free labor. In fact, the only substantial concession to the supposed necessity of a shift to free labor made on some major Cuban plantations in the 1870s involved the employment of Chinese. This was a limited step, for although the structure of incentives and motivations for the indentured Chinese, working on eight-year contracts bought and sold by planters, was somewhat different from that of slaves, it was not that of free wage workers.[31]

One could go further and argue that technological innovation is, under certain circumstances, quite compatible with a labor force that for one reason or another lacks motivation or elements of internalized industrial labor discipline. One economist has suggested that 'process-centered' industrial activities — of which sugar manufacture is a good example — which are often capital intensive, can be appropriate to a less socialized labor force because to some extent the machinery itself provides a pace and discipline to the work.[32] Although this hypothesis is not immediately adaptable to the circumstances of slavery, it does imply that the introduction of technology may cut both ways: advanced machinery can facilitate the labor and the pacing of labor of less experienced or less willing workers, even if at the same time it requires higher levels of skill and motivation for the performance of certain associated tasks.

Both slavery and indentured Asian labor did make labor costs in part a form of fixed capital, reducing the amount of capital immediately available from internal sources for investment in machinery. But the total available for further capital investment would depend on profitability and access to credit, which might in fact be facilitated by the purchase of slaves. Furthermore, individual planters often used rented slaves in order to mitigate the problem of fixed labor costs within the system of slavery. Rental permitted the shifting of the existing slave labor supply to areas of greatest profitability; it did not necessarily weaken slavery as an institution or loosen the bonds on slaves.[33]

Plantation records reveal the range of adaptations utilized on Cuban *ingenios* in the 1870s and convey a sense of the nature and tempo of change. The *ingenio* Angelita, for example, owned by J. A. Argudín and located in the jurisdiction of Cienfuegos, enumerated its work force several times between 1868 and 1877. On June 10, 1868, the plantation had 414 slaves; 20 'employees and workers of the estate', most of them white; and 35 *colonos*, in this case indentured Chinese laborers. By September 1868 the work force had increased with the addition of more Chinese workers, bringing their total to 74. In 1870 an epidemic of cholera hit, resulting in many deaths, and by September of that year the *dotación* consisted of 397 slaves and 58 Asians (see Table 4).

Another document lists the Angelita work force in January 1877, and an accompanying inventory confirms the impression that it was a mechanized plantation, complete with steam-powered grinding apparatus and vacuum pans, centrifuges, and the older Jamaica trains for processing. By this date the number of slaves had fallen to 247, although there were also 37 *libertos* over the age 60 and 29 children under age 8, clearly still part of the plantation population, who were not counted because of the Moret Law. The total comparable to the

Table 4 Work Force on the *Ingenios* Angelita, June 1868 and January 1877

1868		1877	
	Employees		
Administrator	1	Administrator	1
Doctor	1	*Mayordomo*	1
Overseer	1	Accountant	1
Mayordomos	2	Overseer	1
Machinest	1	Nurse (male)	1
Cattle handlers	2	Machinist	1
Carpenters	3	Carpenter	1
Distiller	1	Sugarmaster	1
[Illegible]	2	*Maestro de tacho*	1
Tachero		Plowmen	2
(works the *tacho*, or boiling pan)	1	Cattle handler	1
Sugarmasters	2	Overseer of the *batey* (mill area)	1
Mason	1	Supervisor of *colonos*	1
Montero	1	Mason	1
Asian, job unspecified	1	Barrel makers	2
		Overseer of the *potrero*	1
		Montero	1
		Messenger	1
		Head of the volunteers	1
		Movilizados (soldiers)	23
Total employees	20	Total employees	44
	Slaves		
Males	212	Males	126
Females	202	Females	121
Total slaves (all ages)	414	Total slaves; (excludes 29 children and 37 elderly)	247
	Chinese Laborers		
Total Chinese	35	Total Chinese	45
	Others		
		Free blacks (jobs unspecified)	8
		Rented slaves (owned by administrator)	6
		Sharecroppers (93 family members)	11
Total	469	Total (454 including families)	361

Source: Archivo Nacional de Cuba, Misc. de Libros, núm. 11536, Libro Diario del Ingenio 'Angelita' de la propiedad de Sr. J. A. Argunín, 1868–71, pp. 1–13; Archivo Nacional de Cuba, Misc. de Libros, núm. 10789, Libro Diario del Ingenio Angelita Argudín, 1877, pp. 2, 3, 17, 18.

1870 figure of 397 slaves would thus be 313, a drop of 84 in six years. The work force also now included 8 free blacks, all apparently former slaves of Argudín, and 6 rented slaves. There were the usual 20 or so white employees, but also about 20 *movilizados*, soldiers presumably stationed on the plantation or released for employment there. A new category, *partidario* (sharecropper), had appeared by 1877 and included 11 heads of family and numerous family members. Forty-five *colonos asiáticos* were employed at the time of the count, and at harvest time additional gangs of Asians were hired to cut cane (see Table 4).

Despite the increase in the complexity and variety of the work force on Angelita by 1877, the importance of the nucleus of 247 slaves between the ages of 9 and 59 remains apparent. The sharecroppers, though included in the plantation population, seem primarily to have been engaged in supplying food to the plantation rather than working in cane, though the evidence is not unequivocal. The increase in the number of free workers suggests that they were making inroads into some areas previously dominated by slaves, but it seems unlikely that either the temporary *movilizados* or the sharecroppers were performing any of the more technical tasks. Nor does it seem likely that all of the Asians worked in the more mechanized sectors, since this too was a fluctuating population, often rented out from the *depósito de cimarrones*, and prone to flight. In short, it seems that at Angelita it was not the introduction of technology but the death of slaves — and the necessity of replacing them — that initially brought the increased use of free labor.

After 1877 the decline in forced labor at Angelita accelerated. Asians persisted in fleeing, and replacements were not always available. Slaves became more likely to purchase their freedom. Although in the late 1860s such purchases were infrequent (just one man and his daughter obtained their freedom between June 1868 and September 1870), by the late 1870s they had become more common. In Feburary 1878 four women and two children freed themselves, apparently after having visited the *síndico* (protector of slaves) to have their prices set. In April, Secundina, a 30-year-old Creole, paid 750 pesos for herself and another 187 pesos to free her *liberto* children. That same month the slave Gervasia went to Cienfuegos to have her price set at 700 pesos, and in August her mother, Jacoba Lucumí, age 50, made a down payment of 500 pesos on that amount. As this was going on, the plantation began to increase the rewards given to slaves. At the beginning of the 1878 grinding season, tobacco, money, and bread were distributed.[34]

Reading through the daybook, one gets the sense that relations within the plantation were shifting as slaves, particularly women, found ways to buy their freedom and as the plantation increased the use of monetary incentives. Most of the money that slaves used for self-purchase probably came from their sales of pork and crops to the plantation, and such sales are frequently recorded. When the plantation accepted 700 pesos from a slave as payment for freedom, it was thus recouping some of what had been paid to that slave for goods produced, as well as recovering part of the investment in the slave. The master, unsurprisingly, might well come out ahead. But a circuit of money exchanges had been introduced — and not necessarily at the planter's initiative.

The records of other plantations in the 1870s show many of these same characteristics. Multiple forms of labor gathered around a slowly diminishing core of slave workers; 'gratuities' were paid to slaves more frequently; rent of slaves and the contracting of Asians provided considerable flexibility. None of these adaptations, however, suggests a repudiation of slavery, only a search for supplementary forms of labor and some modifications of the slave regime. Nor do the moves toward wages and compensation appear to be correlated closely with work on machinery — they are as likely to be payment simply for Sunday work or as a general incentive at the beginning of the harvest. Indeed, the repudiation of forced labor in the 1870s comes largely not from planters but from the slaves and Chinese indentured laborers themselves, through self-purchase and through flight.[35]

As late as 1879 most sugar planters appear to have remained strongly attached to the control that slavery gave them over their work force, though they were increasingly obliged by political circumstances to contemplate some shifts in its form. The Spanish government, however, had by 1879 come under pressure from domestic abolitionists, from rebels in Cuba, and from slaves in the east who refused to work. An apparent solution was to abolish the name of slavery, while keeping much of its substance.[36]

The *Patronato*

In February 1880 the Spanish parliament decreed the end of slavery and the beginning of apprenticeship, or *patronato*. All slaves were henceforth to be called *patrocinados* and remained obliged to work for their former masters until freed. Masters owed a stipend of 1–3 pesos monthly to their former slaves, and *patrocinados* could purchase their freedom for a specified and gradually diminishing amount. Limited rights were granted to *patrocinados*, such as the right to charge one's master with a violation of the regulations, with full freedom the reward if he were convicted. But masters also retained substantial prerogatives, including control over physical mobility, the setting of hours and conditions of labor, and, until 1883, the right to use corporal punishment. Beginning in 1885, one-quarter of the remaining *patrocinados* were to be freed each year, in descending order of age, under a complex system that was to conclude in 1888.

The previous discussion of the evolution of the nature and organization of labor in the 1870s suggests why planters might grudgingly accede to, though they did not initiate, such a gradualist solution. They wished to find substitutes for the diminishing slave work force, and nominal abolition might help attract new laborers, since European emigrants were believed to prefer non-slave societies. Both landowners and the government also wished if possible to defuse the emotional issue of abolition. At the same time, many planters sought to maintain the essentials of slavery and to keep their slaves on the plantation, which the *patronato*, in theory, would allow them to do.

The conservative nature of the law establishing the *patronato* meant that May 8, 1880, the date it went into effect, could come and go without an immediate impact on the plantations. Administrators shifted from paying irregular bonuses to paying stipends, increasing their need for cash but not severely disrupting the routine. Indeed, it appeared initially that a considerable degree of continuity was possible. For instance, while in the British West Indies masters had often withdrawn traditional indulgences from slaves when apprenticeship was established, on some Cuban plantations the old rhythm of holidays and rewards was maintained. On the *ingenio* Nueva Teresa, the New Year arrived just as the 1881–82 harvest was about to begin. On December 30 an ox was slaughtered, and the *dotación*, which included approximately 175 *patrocinados*, was given the day off. The following day, fresh meat, bread (a luxury), and salt were distributed, and *criollitos* were baptized in the *casa de vivienda* (plantation house). The first two days of January were also given as holidays; on the fourth and fifth the workers began to cut and haul cane; and at six o'clock on the morning of the sixth day the grinding began.[37]

Patronos may have felt it appropriate to observe these customs in order to maintain their own sense of legitimacy or to encourage productivity among the *patrocinados*. Since the government regulations were not being strictly enforced, masters may also have been less seized by a spirit of vengeance than their British West Indian counterparts. The usual rewards of the harvest could be maintained because the usual level of exploitation was being maintained. During the harvest of 1880–81 on Nueva Teresa, Sunday rest was ignored, and *patrocinados* received only one day of respite between March 17 and April 15. At the end of May, the harvest ended, and a cow was killed for the *dotación*, a calf for additional hired hands. Stipends for the *patrocinados*, due weeks earlier, were finally paid. The withholding of stipends seems clearly to have been a means for maintaining work discipline, not a problem of cash flow; the man who regularly brought the money for stipends from Havana had arrived at the estate three weeks before.[38]

The law of 1880 nonetheless changed the rules of the game, and after a certain lag the impact began to be felt on plantations. By the 1882–83 harvest the administration on Nueva Teresa was becoming scrupulous about paying stipends on time. At the same time, *patrocinados* were beginning to obtain full freedom on their own by self-purchase. This was to have a complicated effect on the economics of running a plantation. On the one hand, working *patrocinados* who obtained their freedom would have to be paid wages or replaced by hired hands. On the other, the purchase of freedom of children, the aged, or the infirm could be a net financial gain to the estate. In any event, such purchases subsidized the wage bill: on the *ingenio* Nueva Teresa, deposits made for purchases of freedom covered almost 70 per cent of the amount paid in stipends during 1883–84, and between 1882 and 1886 approximately 80 *patrocinados* and *libertos* on the estate obtained full legal freedom through payment.[39]

On the *ingenio* Mapos in Sancti Spíritus, the number of working *patrocinados* initially fell only slightly. Early in 1882, however, a group of 35 *patrocinados* fled the estate to present their grievances to the local Junta de Patronato, the board established to oversee the enforcement of the 1880 law. They returned to the plantation, but a year later the effect of the challenge appeared when the estate's *patrocinado* population fell abruptly by almost one-quarter, as more than 60 *patrocinados* were freed by order of the junta, some on the grounds of age, others through self-purchase. The success of these initiatives, combined with the ever-lengthening period during which *patrocinados* could be accumulating funds, led to a steady stream of self-purchases after the harvest of 1883. By August 1884, Mapos retained only 135 of its original 277 *patrocinados*.[40]

The acceleration of emancipation throughout the island in the 1880s, well before the gradual freeings by age began, is evident in the figures gathered by the Juntas de Patronato. In the first year 6,000 *patrocinados* obtained full freedom; in the second 10,000; in the third 17,000; in the fourth 27,000 (see Table 5). Evidently many *patrocinados* learned to use the new situation to hasten their own emancipation. Some

Table 5 *Patrocinados* Legally Achieving Full Freedom, May 1881–May 1886, by Category and Year

Year May to May)	Mutual accord	Renunciation by master	Indemnification by *Patrocinado*	Master's failure to Fulfill Article 4[a]	Other causes	By Article 8[b] (1885 and 1886 only)	Total[c]
1881–82	3,476	3,229	2,001	406	1,137	—	10,249
	(34)	(43)	(20)	(4)	(11)	—	(100)
1882–83	6,954	3,714	3,341	1,596	1,813	—	17,418
	(40)	(21)	(19)	(9)	(10)	—	(100)
1883–84	9,453	3,925	3,452	1,764	7,923	—	26,517
	(36)	(15)	(13)	(7)	(30)	—	(100)
1884–85	7,360	4,405	2,459	2,431	2,514	15,119	34,288
	(21)	(13)	(7)	(7)	(7)	(44)	(100)
1885–86	7,859	3,553	1,750	1,226	837	10,190	25,415
	(31)	(14)	(7)	(5)	(3)	(40)	(100)
Total	35,102	18,826	13,003	7,423	14,224	25,309	113,887
	(31)	(17)	(11)	(7)	(12)	(22)	(100)

Source: Archivo Histórico Nacional, Ultramar, leg. 4814, exp. 273 and exp. 289; *ibid.*, leg. 4926, exp. 144; Manuel Villanova, *Estadística de la abolición de la esclavitud* (Havana, 1885).

[a] Article 4 of the 1880 law listed the obligations of the *patrono*: to maintain his *patrocinados*, clothe them, assist them when ill, pay the specified monthly stipend, educate minors, and feed, clothe, and assist in illness the children of his *patrocinados*.

[b] Article 8 called for one in four of the *patrocinados* of each master to be freed in 1885, and one in three in 1886, in descending order of age. In the event that several *patrocinados* were of the same age, a lottery was to be held.

[c] Some rows do not add to 100 per cent because of rounding.

purchased their freedom; some brought charges against their masters; some found that they were unregistered and sued for freedom on those grounds. Even in rural Matanzas province more than 2,000 *patrocinados* successfully charged their masters with failure to fulfill the obligations of the 1880 law, and more than 3,000 others obtained their freedom through self-purchase between May 1881 and May 1886.[41]

Many masters tried to block such initiatives, through isolation, threats, or legal measures. The institution of the plantation store, for example, though a harbinger of controls that would be imposed on wage labor, helped for the moment to sustain the *patronato* system. In the 1880s local shopkeepers initiated a debate on the tax status of such stores, an occurrence interesting primarily for the attitudes it reveals among planters. Freely acknowledging that the main purpose of the stores was control, planters from several sugar areas made it clear that they wished to prevent their workers and particularly their *patrocinados* from setting foot off the plantation. They were not prepared to accept the physical mobility associated with fully free labor.[42]

Other masters, however, tried to come to some kind of agreement with *patrocinados* on the terms of freedom, which could include informal payment by the *patrocinado*, or an arrangement concerning future wages, resulting in emancipation by 'mutual accord'. Some masters actually renounced their rights over individual *patrocinados*, and a few of these were acclaimed in the liberal press for their benevolence. Such manumissions, however, declined in relative importance after 1881–82, and renunciation was generally most frequent not in the sugar areas of Matanzas or Santa Clara but in the province of Havana. Freedom in Santa Clara or Matanzas was more likely to come through 'mutual accord', as masters exacted concessions in return (see Tables 5 and 6).[43]

By 1883 the total number of *patrocinados* on the island had fallen to about 99,600 (half of the number of slaves six years earlier) even though the gradual freeings by age had yet to begin. In an 1884 debate within the Consejo de Administración in Havana, two councillors argued that the *patronato* had led to the worst of both worlds, providing neither the stimulus of corporal punishment nor the fear of dismissal. They urged that the system be ended, claiming that there was a labor surplus and that, if freed, *patrocinados* would work for their former masters for low wages. The majority of the councillors rejected the argument for abolition of the *patronato*, however, and clung to the compulsion that it provided.[44]

A look at the municipality of Lajas may suggest why. Lajas recorded 1,852 slaves in 1875 and 1,137 *patrocinados* in 1883.[45] Approximately 100 slaves would probably have obtained their freedom in the interval on reaching age 60; thus other losses through

Table 6 *Patrocinados* Legally Achieving Full Freedom, May 1881–May 1886, Percentage by Province and Category

Terms of freedom	Number freed	Pinar del Río	Havana	Matanzas	Santa Clara	Puerto Príncipe	Santiago de Cuba
Mutual accord	35,102	9	10	43	32	0	6
Renunciation	18,826	15	36	19	19	1	10
Indemnification of service	13,003	16	16	27	24	0	17
Master's failure to fulfill Article 4	7,423	14	46	28	6	1	5
Other causes	14,224	13	21	31	23	1	11
Article 8 (1885 and 1886 only)	25,309	17	14	41	25	0	3
Total freed	113,887	13	20	34	25	1	8

Source: Same as Table 5.
Notes: Some rows do not add to 100 per cent because of rounding.

emancipation and death had been kept to only about one-third. For those in areas like Lajas, where the line had been held, extra-economic control over this nucleus of the labor force was still worth defending.

Simply retaining legal control over *patrocinados* was not enough, however. On the *ingenio* Nueva Teresa, for example, which in 1884 still held 150 *patrocinados*, it was necessary to use new incentives tied to productivity. In February 1884, apparently for the first time, the *patrocinado* Evaristo was paid 6 pesos as first prize for the quantity of cane hauled, and others received amounts in decreasing size for second through fifth prize. In March prizes were given to the first ten *patrocinados*, and again in April prizes appeared.[46] By the 1884–85 harvest, the picture at Nueva Teresa had changed still further, and the mobilization of labor began strongly to foreshadow post-abolition arrangements. About a dozen tenants brought cane and wood to the mill, drew supplies on credit, and in some cases hired laborers from the estate. Gangs of Chinese workers contracted to perform specific tasks, particularly in the *casa de calderas* (boiling house). Many *patrocinados* purchased their freedom, and some hired on as free workers at 18 pesos monthly for women and 20 pesos for men, plus rations. The work force was increasingly seasonal, with Chinese contract laborers providing much of the flexibility, whether they wanted to or not. The harvest of 1885 ended on August 16, and on September 4 the *cuadrilla* (gang) of Chinese found themselves 'expelled' by order of the administrator. Maintenance off season was no longer the planter's responsibility.[47]

By 1885, the year the gradual freeings by age were to begin, the *patronato* was already in a state of decay. Only 53,381 *patrocinados* remained in the island, about half of the number two years before, and many fewer than had been anticipated in the original plan. In 1883–84, 26,517 *patrocinados* had obtained their freedom, 36 per cent through mutual accord, 15 percent through renunciation by the *patronato*, 13 per cent through formal self-purchase, 7 per cent through successfully charging their masters with violation of the laws, and 30 per cent through other means, probably including proof of non-registration. The process of emancipation had gained sufficient momentum that the interim institution could not possibly last. The financial crisis of 1884, brought on in part by a drop in sugar prices, may have further encouraged the abandonment of slavery, though renunciation still accounted for fewer than 15 per cent of the freeings in the island between 1884 and 1886 (see Table 5).

By the time of the harvest of 1885–86, the number of *patrocinados* on Nueva Teresa, for example had fallen to 50 or 60. The estate contracted out an increasing proportion of the cutting and hauling of cane, and paid by the cartload, while similarly contracting for wood. The contractors, generally white, took their pay in money and in sugar. Some of the estate's former slaves continued to be directly employed there at a monthly wage of 17–20 pesos, but not as many as had received their freedom. A Chinese contractor provided workers to serve in the field and at the centrifuges, and they were paid both by weight of sugar processed and by the month (at 40 pesos). Individual Chinese workers hired on at about 35 pesos and rations, as did gangs of wage workers of unspecified origin.[48]

On October 7, 1886, a royal decree, following a parliamentary resolution, abolished the *patronato*. When definitive abolition finally arrived, it merely confirmed an existing state of affairs. The number of *patrocinados* had fallen to about 25,000, and almost everyone, including the Planters' Association, was willing to see the *patronato* go.[49] The reality that the law ratified, however, had to a considerable extent been brought about in the immediately preceding years by the slaves and *patrocinados* themselves, both directly — through self-purchase, flight, and suits before the juntas — and indirectly — through the negotiation of agreements of mutual accord. Sheer abandonment of slavery by masters was not the main source of freedom for slaves and *patrocinados*.

Conclusions

At the beginning of this chapter it was suggested that a careful regional and chronological examination of the pattern of transition could help one to evaluate alternative explanations of the process of slave emancipation in Cuba. The evidence and arguments presented show that what is needed is a blending of elements from several hypotheses. The challenge is to make this blending coherent rather than eclectic and ad hoc.

It is true that Cuban slaveholders by the late 1870s had relatively little emotional attachment to the formal institution of slavery. Though some of their representatives continued to defend the institution as a benevolent one, the possibility of a controlled, gradual abolition did not put them up in arms.[50] The Moret Law had already in 1870 guaranteed the eventual demise of slavery by freeing the children of slaves, and demographic patterns were pushing in the same direction. There would not be enough slave workers to replenish the system; new sources and forms of labor had to be found.

This decay of the slave system during the 1870s must, however be interpreted with great care. Young and elderly slaves achieved formal freedom by decree; assertive slaves, particularly in cities and in the east, sometimes obtained their freedom through litigation or self-purchase; many slaves died or became free as a result of war. The gaps thereby created were often filled with free workers. Mixed work forces were indeed common, but it does not appear, as has sometimes been argued, that the plantations invariably were driven to free labor either by the needs of the new technology or by a decline in the quality of the slave labor force caused by an excess of the young and the aged. Large plantations with available capital had often purchased Africans in the last years of the slave trade and still had substantial *dotaciones* of African and Creole slaves. An essential core of slaves of working age continued to be held in bondage in the major sugar areas, helping to maintain high levels of production during the 1870s despite the sharp drop in the total number of slaves.

If Cuba's planters by the end of the 1870s were no longer fully committed to the indefinite maintenance of an institution called slavery, they remained committed to many of the realities of slavery: its work rhythms, social relations, and power relations. They still extracted labor from substantial numbers of workers through extra-economic compulsion. This is why they wanted the control afforded by the *patronato* and why they generally did not engage in mass manumissions.

The *patronato*, however, contained contradictions of its own, particularly in the granting of limited rights and partial access to redress. The social relations of slavery are by their nature difficult to maintain. Alterations in the relative bargaining power and legal rights of masters and slaves may weaken those relations irreparably. In this sense, the passage of the 1880 law was not merely a reflection in law of an existing state of affairs. Mechanisms provided by the law, however inadvertently, emerged as significant for the actual process of emancipation. But it was the shifting interests and resources of apprentices and their masters, not the legislature's intentions, that determined the uses to which they were put.

What, then, remains of the internal contradiction argument? It does contain a key insight concerning the difficulty of achieving capital-intensive development with forced labor, the maintenance expense of which must be borne year-round. But even this contradiction, though perceived by some planters, did not push them to the abandonment of slavery. They sought instead to segment the labor force: to add flexibility through slave rentals, to add workers through immigration, and to maintain as much control as possible over their existing slaves. Their use of Chinese laborers, contract workers, convicts, and rented slaves is sometimes cited as proof that the slave system was dissolving in the 1870s. But one could just as easily see this as evidence of its resilience. That such mixtures of forms of labor were brought together *without* the abandonment of slavery is striking. And that the men who ran these mixed plantations continued to oppose abolition is further evidence of the gap between the seeming contradictions within slavery and the forces actually driving abolition forward.

It may have come as something of a surprise to planters that their strategy could not work indefinitely. But there is a sense in which these continued improvizations and innovations did undermine slavery. It is a social one, a kind of second-order contradiction. Free labor and indentured labor were *economically* complementary to slavery: indentured Chinese workers often dealt with the centrifuges while slaves handled other tasks; white woodcutters on contract relieved the plantation of direct responsibility for providing fuel; the employment of free workers during the harvest diminished the problem of year-round maintenance of all workers. But the use of these complementary forms of labor had indirect effects on the social structure necessary to sustain slavery. Plantation slavery as a social system depended to a large degree on isolation. The incorporation of free workers, beyond those supervisors and artisans rigidly and traditionally separated from the slave work force, broke some of that isolation. It made obvious to slaves the existence of alternatives, created new sources of information, and made possible new alliances — both of individuals and of groups. Such alliances could be a matter of a union between a slave woman and a Chinese man, both interested in freedom for their children; of communication between free black workers and those who remained enslaved; of assistance from a newly freed slave to other members of the family. These alliances and examples aided slaves in their efforts at challenge and self-purchase and, in extreme cases (as in the east during the Ten Years' War), encouraged flight and rebellion.

This should not imply that slavery in Cuba inherently was always socially brittle. But in this specific political context, when abolition was already on the agenda, when insurgency was a reality, and when there was division within the white population, innovations and adaptations carried serious risks.

The abolition of slavery in Cuba, then, should not be seen simply as an imposition from the metropolitan power nor as the result of an inevitable collapse of the system of bondage in the face of internal economic contradictions. The planters' desire to maintain a high degree of control over their work force meant that as a practical matter most of them inhibited, rather than facilitated, emancipation, up to the very last years of the 18-year process. Slaves and *patrocinados*, on the other hand, took advantage of the legal openings provided in the 1870 and 1880 legislation and in other ways resisted submitting to their masters' control. Their initiatives served in part as a countervailing force and tended to accelerate emancipation. Thus the actual course of emancipation can be fully perceived only through an understanding of the interaction of the groups involved. Emancipation was, throughout, a social process in which the struggle between master and slave, *patrono* and *patrocinado*, employer and worker, shaped the character, the timing, and the terms of the transition from slavery to free labor.

Although these internal dynamics may be the most interesting part of the story of Cuban abolition, one ought to return, at least momentarily, to the search for large-scale explanations and ask how one would begin to reconstruct an explanation from what remains of the original hypotheses about causation. This chapter therefore concludes with a few observations about three aspects of such a large-scale explanation: the importance of political pressures, the nature of slaveholder attitudes, and the relationship between slavery and technology. For each of these three aspects, what was initially proposed as a primary cause has emerged as a complicated kind of contributing factor, not in the simple sense of yet another in a great list of factors mechanically bringing about abolition but rather as a conditioning circumstance that determined the constraints under which the process of emancipation would operate.

First, there is no question but that international diplomacy and domestic political unrest narrowed the options of Cuban slaveholders. The ending of the transatlantic slave trade — an event explicable almost entirely in terms of forces external to Cuba, crucial among them British diplomacy and the outcome of the Civil War in the United States — set in motion a long-term problem of labor supply. As long as Cuba's slave population was not fully self-reproducing, then new labor forms would have to be found. And to the extent that the existence of slavery inhibited the free immigration that might provide such laborers, a powerful argument against slavery would continue to build, even before the actual demographic crisis of labor supply had made itself felt. At the same time, domestically, the existence of an anticolonial rebellion that took on abolition as a rallying cry, however opportunistically, changed the climate in which slavery existed. The insurrection opened new options, while creating new stresses.

What has become clear through an examination of the process of abolition is that both kinds of political forces — international and domestic — could to some extent be contained and that for most of the 18 years of gradual emancipation neither planters nor policy makers were prepared to deal with them by making substantial concessions. But these forces nonetheless conditioned the environment in which both slaves and slaveholders adopted strategies and sought to maintain or further their interests.

This brings us to a second general question involved in the search for large-scale explanations: the issue of slaveholder attitudes. It would be wrong to see modernizing Cuban planters as the prime movers behind abolition itself. The initiative simply did not come from them. Though most Cuban planters were not willing to give up slavery in pursuit of economic modernization, however, they were prepared to add free workers to their plantation work forces and to acquiesce in schemes of gradual emancipation, if these seemed to guarantee continuity of authority. Because they thought that they could control the inevitable through very gradual emancipation, they did not mount a last-ditch stand against it. They were to an extent wrong in the expectation that they could control the transition to free labor, and they were certainly wrong in thinking that they could fully control emancipation itself. But the fact that they were not utterly intransigent was a crucial circumstance as partial concessions grew beyond their intended dimensions.

Finally, on the issue of slavery and technology, there is a kind of irony in the post-emancipation history of the Cuban sugar industry. I have rejected the assumption that abolition was, or was even seen as, inherently necessary in order to adopt new technologies. Yet soon after abolition there was a rapid adoption of new modes of organization of production, including the extensive use of advanced processing equipment. The early 1890s saw a dramatic increase in capital investment in machinery, extensive consolidation of estates, and a great boom in sugar production. Several external factors having little to do with abolition stimulated this boom — including the fall in the prices of steel rails that made cane transport cheaper over long distances and shifts in the United States tariff policy that favored Cuban sugar. So the rapid development of central mills with very modern equipment, processing cane from several sources, cannot be fully attributed to the elimination of slavery. Even more important, the boom was by no means uniformly advantageous for former slaveholders. Many found their estates swallowed up in the new central mills and either lost their land entirely or became growers of cane rather than producers of sugar. It is not surprising that those who foresaw that abolition might be followed by such a change in their status would have opposed emancipation. But even those who stood to benefit from the development of central mills saw no reason for relinquishing any control over their workers along the way.[51]

The unfolding of emancipation and the development of post-emancipation society were processes so complex that one cannot infer from the post-emancipation experience of technological innovation and growth that a perceived need for such innovation actually motivated abolition. Moreover, as one moves away from the invocation of internal contradictions or diplomatic pressures as explanations for abolition, and shifts the focus to the dialectic of, on the one hand, stalling and improvization by slaveowners and, on the other, pressure and initiatives from slaves, gradual emancipation emerges as a form of social change largely controlled by planters and the state, but which nonetheless drew much of its character and timing from slaves and insurgents. Large-scale explanations and small-scale historical events can thus be linked in the case of Cuban abolition, but only by multiple threads of interaction and adaptation, woven together over time.

Appendix: Notes on Census Data Used in Tables 1 and 2

The figures cited in Tables 1 and 2 are based on several official tabulations. Those for 1862 are from Cuba, Centro de Estadística, *Noticias estadísticas de la isla de Cuba en 1862* (Havana, 1864). I have derived provincial totals by aggregating the population figures for the 1862 *jurisdicciones* to match the provincial boundaries established in 1878. (For details on redistricting and the method of compilation, see Rebecca J. Scott, 'Slave Emancipation and the Transition to Free Labor in Cuba, 1868–1895' [Ph.D. dissertation, Princeton University, 1982], Chap. 4, note 2.) Returns from the 1867 slave count are neither reliable nor consistent and are included here only for the purpose of comparison. They can be found, divided by jurisdiction, in the 'Resumen general de los esclavos que segun el censo de 1867 . . . existían a la terminación de ese censo en las jurisdicciones que componían el territorio de la Isla', in the Archivo Histórico Nacional, Madrid, Sección de Ultramar (hereinafter AHN, Ultramar), legajo 4884, tomo 8, expediente 160. The 1871 figures are from the 'Resumen de los esclavos comprendidos en el padrón de 1871 . . . ', in AHN, Ultramar, leg. 4882, tomo 4. The 1877 census has often been considered unreliable, but the article by Fe Iglesias García, 'El censo cubano de 1877 y sus diferentes versiones', *Santiago*, 34 (June 1979): 167–211, presents new evidence that in its final version the census was more accurate than previously imagined. I have used her totals for 1877. The figures for the 1880s are from AHN, Ultramar, leg. 4926, exp. 144, and leg. 4814, exp. 289, and are based on records of the provincial Juntas de Patronato.

Notes

1. Manuel Moreno Fraginals, *El ingenio: complejo económico social cubano del azúcar*, 3 vols (Havana, 1978), 3:37.
2. The thesis of the incompatability of slave labor and technology is argued by Moreno Fraginals in *El ingenio*, and he expresses it succinctly in several articles, including 'El esclavo y la mecanización de los ingenios,' *Bohemia* (June 13, 1969): 98–99, and 'Desgarramiento azucarero e integración nacional,' *Casa de las Américas* ,11 (September-October 1970): 6–22.
3. Eugene D. Genovese, *The World the Slaveholders Made: Two Essays in Interpretation* (New York, 1971). pp. 69–70.
4. Arthur F. Corwin, *Spain and the Abolition of Slavery in Cuba, 1817–1886* (Austin, 1967).
5. Moreno Fraginals, 'El esclavo y la mecanización de los ingenios', pp. 98–99.
6. Carlos Rebello, *Estados relativos a la producción azucarera de la isla de Cuba* (Havana, 1860).
7. Cuba, Centro de Estadística, *Noticias estadísticas de la isla de Cuba, en 1862* (Havana, 1864).
8. Moreno Fraginals, *El ingenio*, 3: 36–37.
9. David R. Murray, *Odious Commerce: Britain, Spain and the Abolition of the Cuban Slave Trade* (Cambridge, 1980).
10. Moreno Fraginals, *El ingenio*, 3: 36–37.
11. The best analyses of the Ten Years' War are to be found in Raúl Cepero Bonilla, *Azúcar y abolición* (Havana, 1948); Ramiro Guerra y Sánchez, *Guerra de los Diez Años* (Havana, 1950–52); and Franklin Knight, *Slave Society in Cuba during the Nineteenth Century* (Madison, 1970).
12. For a fuller analysis of the effects of the war on slavery, see Rebecca J. Scott, *Slave Emancipation in Cuba: The Transition to Free Labor, 1860–1899* (Princeton, 1985), Chap. 2.
13. For evidence on the events of 1879, see the opinion of José Bueno y Blanco in Archivo Histórico Nacional, Madrid, Sección de Ultramar (hereafter AHN, Ultramar) leg. 4882, tomo 5, 'Documentos de la Comisión . . . 1879', and AHN, Ultramar, leg. 4882, tomo 3, exp. 76, telegram from the Governor General to the Minister of Ultramar, September 11, 1879. José Martí vividly described the pressure on Spain from rebellious slaves in the east of Cuba and the double-edged response of abolition and increased military presence. See José Martí's speech given in Steck Hall, New York, January 24, 1880, printed in Hortensia Pichardo (ed.), *Documentos para la historia de Cuba*, 2 vols (Havana, 1976, 1977) 1: 424–49.
14. For these and other provincial totals, see Appendix.
15. The figure of 20 per cent was derived by using the age distribution of slaves in Cuba in the 1862 census. Of those listed, around 22 per cent were over age 60 or under age 10 (Cuba, *Noticias*). I have assumed that the proportion would be somewhat smaller in a plantation area, which would have a higher concentration of imported Africans. This estimate also coincides with the age pyramids derived by Moreno Fraginals from plantation accounts. Moreno Fraginals, *El ingenio*, 2: 90.
16. See Archivo Nacional de Cuba (hereafter ANC), Misc. de Expendientes, leg. 3814, exp. A. Expediente promovido pot este Gob° Gral para conocer las operaciones paracticadas en todas las Sindicaturas de la Isla durante el quinquenio de 1873 a 1877. Of the 3,359 *coartaciones* in the island, 1,413 were in the city of Havana.
17. For area planted in cane, see Rebello, *Estados*, and the *Revista de Agricultura* (Havana), 3 (March 31, 1879), 75. Population figures are from the 1862 census and from Fe Iglesias García, 'El censo cubano de 1877 y sus diferentes versiones', *Santiago* 34 (June 1979): 167–211. On the categories of workers in sugar, see the *Revista de Agricultura* cited above.
18. A. Gallenga, *The Pearl of the Antilles* (London, 1873), pp. 96, 105.
19. This picture emerges from censuses, account books, and observers' reports. See the 1877 agricultural census, the plantation records cited in notes 33–35 and F. de Zayas, 'Estudios de agricultura: II. El trabajador, el jornal', *Revista de Agricultura*, 1 (April 30, 1879): 83.
20. Moreno Fraginals puts foward this argument in 'Abolición o desintegración? Algunas preguntas en torno a un centenario', *Granma* (January 23, 1980), and in 'Plantations in the Caribbean: Cuba, Puerto Rico, and the Dominican Republic in the Late Nineteenth Century', in M. Fraginals, F. Moya Pons, S. Engerman (eds), *Between Slavery and Free Labor: The Spanish-speaking Caribbean in the Nineteenth Century* (Baltimore, 1985).
21. For an examination of the ways in which 'contradictions' within slavery are resolved, and in some cases give rise to new contradictions, see Sidney Mintz, 'Slavery and the Rise of Peasantries', in Michael Craton (ed.), *Roots and Branches: Current Directions*

in Slave Studies (Toronto, 1979), pp. 213–42. The point is that such things as bonuses and provision grounds may or may not signal disintegration, depending on the surrounding circumstances. In some cases, they may even strengthen slavery.

22. Moreno Fraginals, *El ingenio*, 2: 83–90. He states that the conscious policy of 'good treatment', aimed at creating a self-reproducing slave work force, was 'the most visible symptom of the dissolution of slavery' (p. 90).
23. See the 1862 census and Enrique Edo y Llop. *Memoria histórica de Cienfuegos y su jurisdicción* (Cienfuegos, 1888), appendix, pp. 5–6. The manuscript slave list is in ANC, Misc. de Expendientes, leg. 3748, exp. B, Capitanía Pedánea de Santa Isabel de las Lajas, núm, 3, Padrón general de esclavos, 1875.
24. Stanley J. Stein, *Vassouras: A Brazilian Coffee County, 1850–1900* (New York, 1974), p. 78.
25. See *Revista Económica*, 2 (June 7, 1878): 13. The Armantina and Manaca estates, excluded from the comparisons because their 1875 slave data are incomplete, had 122 slaves and 17 *alquilados y libres*.
26. Edo y Llop, *op. cit.*, p. 629. For evidence of planter hostility to abolition in the 1870s, see Corwin, *op. cit.*, Chap. 14.
27. In Cuba, this argument dates at least to Ramón de la Sagra in the mid-nineteenth century and is repeated by Moreno Fraginals. See *El ingenio*, 2: 30.
28. AHN, Ultramar, leg. 4759, exp. 85, 'Exposición del Excmo. Señor Cordede Vega Mar' (Madrid, 1868).
29. Fermín Rosillo y Alquier, *Noticias de dos ingenios y datos sobre la producción azucarera de la isla de Cuba* (Havana, 1873), describes the work force on España. For Álava, see the 1877 agricultural census in *Revista Económica*, 2 (June 7, 1878): 11.
30. The description of Las Cañas as 'Cuba's most modern mill' is from *El ingenio*, 1: 250. The figures on the work force are from Rosillo, *Noticias*. Observations on the treatment of the Chinese are from Juan Pérez de la Riva, 'Duvergier de Hauranne: un joven francés visita el ingenio Las Cañas en 1865', *Revista de la Biblioteca Nacional José Martí*, 56 (October–December 1965): 85–114.
31. On the Chinese in Cuba see Juan Pérez de la Riva, 'Demografía de los culíes chinos en Cuba (1853–1877)' and 'La situación legal del culí en Cuba', in his *El barracón y otros ensayos* (Havana, 1975), pp. 469–507, 209–45. See also Denise Helly, *Idéologie et ethnicité: les chinois Macao à Cuba, 1847–1886* (Montreal, 1979). The question of whether the Chinese should, for the purposes of analysis, be considered wage workers is a difficult one. The extra-economic coercion to which they were subjected was so great, and so similar to that inflicted on slaves, that I am inclined to doubt the substance of their 'freeness'. If in Cuba they were seen as particularly suited for work with machinery, this may in part have reflected employers' high expectations of the Chinese relative to their low expectations of slaves. It may also have reflected actual differences in performance, but these differences could have had as much to do with the cultural background of the Chinese and their anticipation of a future freedom as they did with any alleged juridicial freedom while under contract, a freedom often violated.
32. See Albert O. Hirschman. *The Strategy of Economic Development* (New Haven, 1958), ch. 8.
33. See, for example, the records of slave rentals on the Ingenio Delicias in ANC, Misc. de Libros, núm. 10802, Libro Diario del Ingenio Delicias, 1872–82.
34. Data on the work force at Angelita are from ANC, Misc. de Libros, núm. 11536, Libro Diario del Ingenio 'Angelita' de la propiedad de St. J. A. Argudín, 1868–71, and ANC, Misc. de Libros, núm. 10789, Libro Diario del Ingenio Angelita Argudín, 1877.
35. Other daybooks and slave lists for the 1870s include Archivo Provincial de Sancti Spíritus, Fondo Valle-Iznaga (hereafter APSS, Valle-Iznaga), leg. 27, Libro con la dotación de esclavos del ingenio La Crisis; ANC, Misc. de Libros, núm. 10806, Libro Diario al parecer de un ingenio, 1879–81; and ANC, Misc. de Libros, núm, 11245, Libro Mayor del Ingenio Nueva Teresa, 1872–85.
36. Fur a further discussion of the politics of abolition, see Corwin, *op. cit.*, and Knight, *op. cit.*
37. ANC, Misc. de Libros, núm. 10831, Libro Diario del Ingenio Nueva Teresa, 1880–86.
38. *Ibid.*
39. ANC, Misc. de Libros, núm. 11245, Libro Mayor del Ingenio Nueva Teresa, 1872–85.
40. APSS, Valle-Iznaga, leg. 24, Libro que contiene documentos del estado general de la finca Mapos.
41. For provincial figures on emancipation, see AHN, Ultramar, leg. 4814, exp. 273 and exp. 289; leg. 4926, exp. 144; and Manuel Villanova, *Estadística de la abolición de la esclavitud* (Havana, 1885).
42. For the debate, see AHN, Ultramar, leg. 4818, exp. 84, Sobre pago de contribuciones de las tiendas de los Ingenios.
43. For a more detailed discussion of the operation of the *patronato*, see Rebecca J. Scott, 'Gradual Abolition and the Dynamics of Slave Emancipation in Cuba, 1868–86', *Hispanic American Historical Review*, 63 (August 1983): 449–77.
44. AHN, Ultramar, leg. 4926, exp. 144, núm. 300, Informe del Consejo de Administración, August 8, 1884.
45. Edo y Llop, *op. cit.*, pp. 988–89.
46. ANC. Misc. de Libros, núm. 11245, Libro Mayor del Ingenio Nueva Teresa, 1872–85.
47. ANC, Misc. de Libros, núm. 10831, Libro Diario del Ingenio Nueva Teresa, 1880–86.
48. *Ibid.*
49. See AHN, Ultramar, leg. 4926, exp. 144, núm. 323, telegram from the Governor General of Cuba to the Minister of Ultramar, Havana, August 12, 1886.
50. For the debates in the Spanish parliament, see Spain, Cortes, 1879–80, *Discursos de la ley de abolición de la esclavitud en Cuba* (Madrid, 1879–80).
51. A good example of the later would be Francisco Feliciano Ibáñez, *Observaciones sobre la utilidad y conveniencia del establecimiento en esta isla de grandes ingenios centrales* (Havana, 1880).

Select Bibliography

The following lists contain a limited selection of published and some unpublished works, bibliographies and guides to sources which are intended to provide supplementary reading for the Reader.

Bibliographies and Guides to Sources

Brathwaite, Kamau. *Our Ancestral Heritage: A Bibliography of the Roots of Culture in the English-Speaking Caribbean* (Kingston, 1977).

Goveia, Elsa. *A Study of the Historiography of the British West Indies to the End of the Nineteenth Century* (Washington, DC, 1980).

Green, William A. 'Caribbean Historiography 1600–1800', *Journal of Interdisciplinary History*, 7, 3 (1977), 509–530.

Handler, Jerome S. *A Guide to Source Materials for the Study of Barbados History, 1627–1834* (Carbondale & Edwardville, Illinois, 1971).

Higman, Barry W. 'Theory, Method and Technique in Caribbean Social History', *Journal of Caribbean History*, 20, 1 (1985).

Ingram, K. E. N. (ed.), *Sources for West Indian Studies* (Switzerland, 1983).

Marshall, Woodville K. 'A Review of Historical Writing on the Commonwealth Caribbean since *ca* 1940', *Social and Economic Studies*, 24, 3 (1975).

Miller, Joseph C. and Borus, D. H. 'Slavery: A Supplementary Teaching Bibliography', *Slavery and Abolition*, 1, 1 (1980).

Miller, Joseph C. 'Slavery: Annual Bibliographical Supplement (1981)', *Slavery and Abolition*, 2, 2 (1981).

Miller, Joseph C. 'Slavery: Annual Bibliographical Supplement Part I', *Slavery and Abolition* 3, 2 (1982).

Miller, Joseph C. and Brown, L. V. 'Slavery: Annual Bibliographical Supplement (1982)', Part II, *Slavery and Abolition*, 3, 3 (1982).

Miller, Joseph C. 'Slavery: Annual Bibliographical Supplement (1983)', Part I, *Slavery and Abolition*, 4, 2 (1983).

Miller, Joseph C. 'Slavery: Annual Bibliographical Supplement, (1983)', Part II, *Slavery and Abolition*, 4, 3 (1983).

Miller, Joseph C. and Skalnik, J. V. 'Slavery: Annual Bibliographical Supplement (1984)', *Slavery and Abolition*, 6, 1 (1985).

Miller, Joseph C. 'Slavery: Annual Bibliographical Supplement', *Slavery and Abolition*, 7, 3 (1986).

Miller, Joseph C. and Appleby, D. 'Slavery: Annual Bibliographical Supplement', *Slavery and Abolition*, 8, 3 (1987).

Miller, Joseph C. 'Slavery: Annual Bibliographical Supplement (1987)', *Slavery and Abolition*, 9, 2 (1988).

Oostindie, Gert J. 'Historiography on the Dutch Caribbean (1985): Catching Up?', *Journal of Caribbean History*, 21, 1 (1985).

Williams, Eric. *British Historians and the West Indies* (Port-of-Spain, 1964).

General

Bisnauth, D. *A History of Religions in the Caribbean* (Kingston, 1989).

Blackburn, R. *The Overthrow of Colonial Slavery, 1776–1848* (Verso Press, 1988).

Bolland, Nigel O. 'Slavery in Belize', *Journal of Belizean Affairs*, 6 (1978).

Brathwaite, Kamau. *The Development of Creole Society in Jamaica 1770–1820* (Clarendon Press, Oxford, 1971).

Cohen, D. and Greene, J. *Neither Slave Nor Free: The Freedom of African Descent in the Slave Societies of the New World* (Johns Hopkins Univ. Press, 1972).

Craton, M. *Testing the Chains: Resistance to Slavery in the British West Indies* (Cornell Univ. Press, 1982).

Curtin, P. D. *The Atlantic Slave Trade: A Census* (Univ. of Wisconsin Press, 1969).

Diaz Soler, L. J. *Historia de la Esclavitud Negra en Puerto Rico* (Rio Piedras, 1965).

Dookhan, I. *A History of the Virgin Islands 1652–1970* (Caribbean Univ. Press, 1975).

Dunn, R. *Sugar and Slaves: The Rise of the Planter Class in The English West Indies 1624–1713* (Univ. of North Carolina Press, 1972).

Fraginals, M., Pons F. M. and Engerman, S. L. *Between Slavery and Freedom: The Spanish-Speaking Caribbean in the Nineteenth Century* (Johns Hopkins Univ. Press, 1985).

Goveia, E. 'The West Indian Slave Laws of the 18th Century', in L. Foner, *Slavery in the New World* (Prentice-Hall, 1969).

Higman, B. W. *Slave Population and Economy in Jamaica 1807-1834* (Cambridge Univ. Press, 1976).
Higman, B. W. *Slave Populations of the British Caribbean 1807-1834* (John Hopkins Univ. Press, 1984).
Klein, H. S. *African Slavery in Latin America and the Caribbean* (Oxford Univ. Press. 1982).
Knight, F. W. *Slave Society in Cuba During the Nineteenth Century* (Univ. of Wisconsin Press, 1970).
Lewis, G. K. *Main Currents in Caribbean Thought: The Historical Evolution of Caribbean Society in its Ideological Aspects 1492-1900* (Heinemann, 1983).
Leyburn, J. G. *The Haitian People* (Yale Univ. Press, 1966).
Midlo Hall, G. *Social Control in Plantation Societies: A Comparison of St. Domingue and Cuba* (Baltimore, 197 1).
Mintz, S. *Caribbean Transformations* (Johns Hopkins Univ. Press, 1984).
Munford, C. J. 'Slavery in the French Caribbean 1625–1715: A Marxist Analysis', *Journal of Black Studies*, 17, 1 (1986).
Packwood, C. O. *Chained to the Rock: Slavery In Bermuda* (New York, 1975).
Proesmans, Father R. 'Notes on the Slaves of the French', in *Aspects of Dominican History* (Rosseau, 1972).
Saunders, G. *Slavery in the Bahamas 1648–1838* (Nassau Guardian, 1985).
Sheridan, R. *Doctors and Slaves: A Medical and Demographic History of Slavery in the B.W.I. 1680–1834* (Cambridge Univ. Press, 1985).
Smith, J. E. *Slavery in Bermuda* (Vantage Press, 1976).
Spingham, L. P. 'Slavery in the Danish West Indies', *American Scandinavian Review*, 45, 1 (1957).
Stein, R. *The French Sugar Business in the Eighteenth Century* (Louisiana State Univ. Press, 1988).
Van Lier, R. 'Negro Slavery in Suriname', *Caribbean Historical Review*, 3-4 (1954).
Williams, E. *Capitalism and Slavery* (Chapel Hill, 1944).

Section 1: Amerindians and Slavery

Beckles, H. McD, 'Origins of a Slave Society', in H. McD. Beckles, *Black Rebellion in Barbados: The Struggle Against Slavery 1627-1838* (Antilles Publications, Barbados, 1984).
Beckles, H. McD, 'The First Barbadians, c. 1650–1540: Amerindian Civilization', in H. McD. Beckles, *A History of Barbados: From Amerindian Settlement to Nation-State* (Cambridge Univ. Press, 1990).
Beckles, H. McD, 'English Colonization 1625–1644', in H. McD. Beckles, *A History of Barbados, op. cit.*, above.
Broomert, Arie. 'The Arawaks of Trinidad and Coastal Guiana, ca. 1500-1650', *Journal of Caribbean History*, 19, 2 (1984).
Borome, Joseph A. 'Spain and Dominica, 1493–1647', in *Aspects of Dominican History* (Government Printing Office, Dominica, 1972).
Borome, Joseph A. 'The French and Dominica, 1699–1763', in *Aspects of Dominican History, op. cit.*, above.
Cook, S. F. and Borah, W. *Essays in Population History: Mexico and the Caribbean*, 2 vols. (Berkeley and Los Angeles, 1971 and 1974).
Davis, Nicholas D. 'The Caribs of Guiana: As Enemies of the Spaniards and as Allies of the Dutch 1733–1789' (Pamphlet, U.W.I., Mona, W.I.C.).
Denevan, William M. (ed.), *The Native Population of the Americas in 1492* (Madison, 1976).
Dieve, Carlos E. *El Indio, el Negro y la Vida Tradicional Dominicana* (Santo Domingo: Museo del Hombre Dominicano, 1970).
Fernandez Mendez, Eugenio. *Las Encomiendas y Esclavitud de los Indios de Puerto Rico 1508–1550* (Univ. of Puerto Rico, 1976).
Hulme, Peter. *Colonial Encounters: Europe and the Native Caribbean 1492–1797* (Methuen, London, 1976).
Newson, Linda. *Aboriginal and Spanish Colonial Trinidad: A Study in Culture Contact* (London/New York, 1976).
Sauer, Carl O. *The Early Spanish Main* (Berkeley, 1966).
Shepherd, Charles. *An Historical Account of the Island of St. Vincent* (London, 1831).
Williamson, J. A. *English Colonies in Guiana and the Amazon* (Clarendon Press, Oxford, 1923).

Section 2: Origins of Large-scale Slavery

Beckford, George. *Persistent Poverty* (Oxford Univ. Press, 1972).
Beckles, H. McD. 'The Economic Origins of Black Slavery in the B.W.I.: A Tentative Analysis of the Barbados Model, 1643-1680', *Journal of Caribbean History*, 16 (1982).
Beckles, H. McD. and Downes, Andrew. 'An Economic Formalization of the Origins of Black Slavery in the B.W.I., 1624–1645', *Social and Economic Studies*, 34 (1985).
Beckles, H. McD. 'The Economics of Transition to the Black Labour System in Barbados, 1630–1680', *Journal of Interdisciplinary History*, 18, 2 (1987).
Beckles, H. McD. 'Sugar and Slavery, 1644–1692', in H. McD. Beckles, *A History of Barbados from Amerindian Settlement to Nation State* (Cambridge, 1990).
Bryan, Patrick. 'The Transition to Plantation Agriculture in The Dominican Republic, 1770–1844', *Journal of Caribbean History*, 10 and 11 (1970).
Chandler, A. D. 'The Expansion of Barbados', *Journal of the Barbados Museum and Historical Society*, 13 (1946).
Chardon, Roland, E. 'Sugar Plantations in the Dominican Republic', *Geographical Review*, 74, 4 (1984).
Curet, Jose, 'About Slavery and the Order of Things: Puerto Rico, 1845-1873', in Fraginals, Pons and Engerman (eds.), *Between Slavery and Freedom, op. cit.*, see General section above.
Curtin, P. D. *The Atlantic Slave Trade, op. cit.*, see General Section above.
Curtin, P. D. 'A Planting Economy', in Curtin, P. D. *Two Jamaicas: The Role of Ideas in a Tropical Colony 1830–1865* (Atheneum Press New York, 1970).

Curtin, P. D. 'The Sugar Revolution and the Settlement of the Caribbean', in P. D. Curtin, *The Rise and Fall of the Plantation Complex: Essays in Atlantic History* (Cambridge Univ. Press, 1990).
Debien, G. *Une Plantation de Saint-Domingue: La Sucretie Galbad du Fort 1690–1802* (Cairo, 1941).
Dunn, R. *Sugar and Slaves op. cit.*, see General Section.
Fraginals, M. *The Sugarmill: The Socio-Economic Complex of Sugar in Cuba 1760–1860* (New York, 1976).
Galenson, D. W. 'The Atlantic Slave Trade and the Early Development of the English West Indies', in D. W. Galenson, *Traders, Planters and Slaves: Market Behaviour in Early English America* (Cambridge Univ. Press, 1986).
Galloway, J. H. 'The Atlantic Sugar Industry *c*. 1450–1680', in J. H. Galloway, *The Sugar Cane Industry: A Historical Geography From Its Origins to 1914* (Cambridge Univ. Press, 1989).
Galloway, J. H. 'The American Sugar Industry in the 18th century', in Galloway, *The Sugar Industry, op. cit.*, above.
Greenfield, S. 'Plantations, Sugarcane and Slavery', in M. Craton (ed.), *Roots and Branches: Current Directions in Slave Studies* (Toronto, 1979).
Klein, H. S. 'Sugar and Slavery in the Caribbean in the 17th and 18th Centuries' in H. S. Klein, *African Slavery in Latin America and the Caribbean* (Oxford Univ. Press, 1982).
Pitman, F. W. 'The Settlement and Financing of the B.W.I. Plantations in the 18th Century', in *Essays Presented to C. Andrews* (New Haven, 1971).
Ratekin, Mervyn. 'The Early Sugar Industry in Espaniola', *Hispanic American Historical Review*, 34 (1954).
Scarano, Fransicso A. 'Ponce: The Making of a Sugar Economy', in Francisco A. Scarano, *Sugar and Slavery in Puerto Rico: The Plantation Economy of Ponce* (Univ. of Wisconsin Press, 1984).
Sheridan, Richard. 'The Plantation Revolution and the Industrial Revolution, 1625–1775', *Caribbean Studies*, 9, 3 (1969).
Sheridan, Richard. *The Development of the Plantations to 1750* (Caribbean Univ. Press, 1970).
Sheridan, Richard. *Sugar and Slavery: An Economic History of the B.W.I., 1624–1775* (Barbados, 1974).
Watts, D. 'The Extension of the West Indian Sugar Estate Economy 1665–1833', in D. Watts, *The West Indies: Patterns of Development, Culture and Environmental Change Since 1492* (Cambridge Univ. Press, 1987).

Section 3: Production, Profitability and Markets

Aufhauser, R. K. 'Profitability of Slavery in the British Caribbean', *Journal of Interdisciplinary History*, 5, 1 (1974).
Aufhauser, R. K. 'Slavery and Technological Change', *Journal of Economic History*, 34 (1974).
Barrett, W. 'Caribbean Sugar Production Standards in the 17th Century and 18th Century', in J. Parker (ed.), *Merchants and Scholars: Essays in the History of Exploration and Trade* (Minneaplis, 1965).
Claypole, W. A. and Buisserett, D. 'Trade Patterns in Early English Jamaica', *Journal of Caribbean History*, 5 (1972).
Coelho, P. 'The Profitability of Imperialsim: The British Experience in the W.I., 1768–1772', *Explorations in Economic History*, 10, 3 (1972–73).
Craton, M. and Walvin, J. *A Jamaican Plantation: The History of Worthy Park* (London, 1970).
Craton, M. *Searching for the Invisible Man: Slaves and Plantation Life in Jamaica* (Harvard Univ. Press, 1978).
Dookhan, 'Era of Prosperity and Decline', in I Dookhan, *A History of the Virgin Islands 1672–1970* (Caribbean Univ. Press, 1975).
Dunn, Richard. 'The Barbados Census of 1680: Profile of the Richest Colony in English America', *William and Mary Quarterly*, 26 (1969).
Fraginals, Manuel M. 'Plantations in the Caribbean: Cuba, Puerto Rico and the Dominican Republic in the late 19th Century', in Fraginals, Pons and Engerman *Between Slavery and Freedom op. cit.*, see General Section above.
Garcia, Fe Iglesias, 'The Development of Capitalism in Cuban Sugar Production, 1860–1900', in Fraginals, Pons and Engerman, *op. cit.*, above.
Green, W. 'The Planter Class and B.W.I. Sugar Production Before and After Emancipation', *Economic History Review*, 26 (1973).
Hall, D. G. 'Incalculability as a Feature of Sugar Production During the 18th Century', *Social and Economic Studies*, 10 (1961).
Hall, D. G. *In Miserable Slavery: Thomas Thistlewood in Jamaica, 1750–1786* (Mcmillan, London, 1989).
Lamur, H. 'Profitability of Vossenburg and Wayampibo Plantations in Dutch Suriname', in Lamur, The Production of Sugar and the Reproduction of Slaves at Vossenburg, Suriname, 1705–1863 (Amsterdam, 1987).
Monteith, K. 'The Coffee Industry in Jamaica 1790–1850', Staff/Postgraduate Seminar Paper, U.W.I. Mona 1988.
Nelson, George H. 'Contraband Trade Under the Asiento, 1730–1739', *American Historical Review*, 1 (1945).
Nettles, Curtis P. 'England and the Spanish American Trade, 1680–1715', *Journal of Modern History*, 111, 1 (1931).
Pares, Richard. *War and Trade in the West Indies* (Frank Cass, 1963).
Pares, Richard. *Yankees and Creoles: The Trade Between North America and the West Indies Before the American Revolution* (Hampden, Conn., 1968).
Pares, Richard. 'The London Sugar Market, 1740–1769', *Economic History Review*, 9 (1956/57).
Ramos Mattei, Andres. 'Technical Innovations and Social Change in the Sugar Industry of Puerto Rico, 1870–1880', in Fraginals, Pons and Engerman, *op. cit.*, see General Section above.
Sheridan, R. B. 'The Wealth of Jamaica in the 18th Century', *Economic History Review*, 18, 2 (1965).
Sheridan, R. B. *An Era of West Indian Prosperity, 1750–1775*. Chapters in Caribbean History, I (Caribbean Univ. Press, 1970).
Ward, J. R. *British West Indian Slavery, 1750–1834: The Process of Amelioration* (Clarendon Press, Oxford, 1988).
Zahadieh, Nuala. 'The Merchants of Port Royal, Jamaica and the Spanish Contraband Trade, 1655–1696', *William and Mary Quarterly*, 3rd Ser., 43 (1986).
Zahadieh, Nuala. 'Trade, Plunder and Economic Development in Early English Jamaica, 1655–1689', *Economic History Review*, 39 (1988).

Section 4: Caribbean Slavery and the Capitalist World Economy

Carrington, S. H. H. *The West Indies During the American Revolution* (London, 1987).
Carrington, S. H. H. 'The American Revolution and the British West Indies Economy', *Journal of Interdisciplinary History*, 17, 4 (1987).
Carrington, S. H. 'Econocide: Myth or Reality?: Question of West Indian Decline, 1738–1806', *Boletin de Estudios Latino-americanos y del Caribe*, 36 (1986).
Carrington, S. H. 'The State of the Debate on the Role of Capitalism in the Ending of the Slave System', *Journal of Caribbean History* 22, 1 and 2 (1988).
Drescher, S. 'Capitalism and the Decline of Slavery', in V. Rubin and A. Tuden (eds), *Comparative Perspectives in New World Plantation Societies* (New York, 1977).
Drescher, S. *Econocide: British Slavery in the Era of Abolition* (Univ. of Pittsburgh Press, 1977).
Dupuy, Alex. 'French Merchant Capital and Slavery in St. Dominique', *Latin American Perspectives*, 12, 3 (1985).
Nettles, Curtis P. 'England and the Spanish American Trade, 1680–1715', *Journal of Modern History*, III, 1 (1945).
Pares, Richard. 'The London Sugar Market, 1740–1769', *Economic History Review*, 9 (1956/57).
Pares, Richard. *Yankees and Creoles: The Trade Between North America and the West Indies Before the American Revolution* (Hampden, Conn., 1968).
Sheridan, R. B. 'The West India Sugar Crisis and British Slave Emancipation 1830–1833', *Journal of Economic History*, 21, 4 (1961).
Thomas, Robert. 'The Sugar Colonies of the Old Empire: Profit and Loss for Great Britian?', *Economic History Review*, 21 (1968).
Tomich, Dale W. *Slavery in the Circuit of Sugar: Martinique and the World Economy, 1830–1948* (Johns Hopkins Univ. Press, 1990).
Ward, J. R. *British West Indian Slavery 1750–1834: The Process of Amelioration* (Clarendon Press, Oxford, 1988).
Williams, Eric. 'The Exclusive', in E. Williams, *From Columbus to Castro: The History of the Caribbean 1492–1969* (André Deutsch, 1970).

Section 5: Race, Colour and Ideology

Beckles, H. McD. 'On the Backs of Blacks: The Barbados Free Coloureds' Pursuit of Civil Rights and the 1816 Rebellion', *Immigrants and Minorities*, 3, 2 (1984).
Beckles, H.McD. ' "Black Men in White Skins": The Formation of a White Proletariat in West Indian Slave Society', *The Journal of Imperial and Commonwealth History*, 15, 1 (1986).
Beckles, H. McD. 'Black Over White: The "Poor White" Problem in Barbados Slave Society', in *Immigrants and Minorities*, 7, 1 (1988).
Boa, S. 'Free Black and Coloured Women in a White Man's Slave Society: Jamaica 1760–1843', M. Phil U.W.I. Mona 1985.
Brathwaite, Kamau. *The Development of Creole Society in Jamaica 1770–1820* (Clarendon Press, Oxford, 1970).
Campbell, Elaine, 'Oroonoko's Heir: The West Indies in late 18th Century Novels by Women', *Caribbean Quarterly*, 25, 1, 2 (1979).
Campbell, M. *The Dynamics of Change in a Slave Society: A Socio-Political History of the Free Coloureds in Jamaica 1800–1865* (Associated Presses, 1976).
Cox, Edward. *Free Coloureds in the Slave Societies of St. Kitts and Grenada, 1763–1833* (Univ. of Tennessee Press, 1984).
Cox, Edward. 'The Free Coloureds and Slave Emancipation', *Journal of Caribbean History*, 22, 1 and 2 (1989).
Curtin, P.D. 'European Jamaica: The White and Coloured Castes', in P. D. Curtin, *Two Jamaicas: The Role of Ideas in a Tropical Colony 1830–1865* (Atheneum Press, New York, 1970).
Edmondson, Locksley. 'Trans-Atlantic Slavery and the Institutionalization of Race', *Caribbean Quarterly*, 22, 2 and 3 (1976).
Hall, D. G. 'Jamaica', in D. Cohen and J. P. Greene (eds), *Neither Slave Nor Free, op. cit.*, see General Section.
Hall, N. A. T. 'Anna Heegaard — Enigma', *Caribbean Quarterly*, 22, 2 and 3 (1976).
Handler, Jerome, *The Unappropriated People: Freedmen in the Slave Society of Barbados* (Johns Hopkins Univ. Press, 1974).
Heuman, G. 'White Over Brown Over Black: The Free Coloureds In Jamaican Society During Slavery and After Emancipation' *Journal of Caribbean History*, 14 (1981).
Heuman, G. *Between Black and White: Race, Politics and the Free Coloureds in Jamaica, 1792–1865* (Greenwood, Conn., 1981).
Heuman, G. 'Free Coloureds in Jamaican Slave Society', in G. Heuman, *Between Black and White, op. cit.*, above.
Hoetink, H. 'Surinam and Curacao', in D. Cohen and J. P. Greene (eds), *Neither Slave Nor Free, op. cit.*, above.
Leo, Elizabeth, 'The French Antilles', in Cohen and Greene (eds), *Neither Slave Nor Free, op. cit.*, above.
Lewis, G. K. 'The Eighteenth and Nineteenth Centuries: Pro-slavery Ideology', in G. K. Lewis, *op. cit.*, see General Section.
Lewis, G. K. 'The Eighteenth and Nineteenth Centuries: The Antislavery Ideology', in G. K. Lewis, *op. cit.*, see General Section.
Lokke, C. C. 'Malouet and the St. Domingue Mullatto Question in 1793', *Journal of Negro History*, 24, 4 (1939).
Nicholls, D. 'Race, Couler et Independance en Haiti 1804–1825', *Revue d'Histoire Moderne et Contemporaine*, 25, 2 (1978).
Puckrein, Gary A. 'Race, Racism and the Imperial System', in G. A Puckrein, *Little England: Plantation Society and Anglo-Barbadian Politics, 1607–1700* (New York Univ. Press, 1984).
Shepherd, V. A. 'Livestock Farmers and Marginality in Jamaica's Sugar Plantation Society: A Tentative Analysis', Association of Caribbean Historians Conference, Trinidad 1990.
Sio, Arnold. 'Race, Colour and Miscegenation; The Free Coloureds of Jamaica and Barbados', *Caribbean Studies*, 16, 1 (1976).

Smith, M. G. 'Some Aspects of Social Structure in the British Caribbean about 1820', *Social and Economic Studies*, 1 (1953).
Stein, R. 'The Free Men of Colour and the Revolution of St. Domingue', *Histoire Sociale*, 14, 27 (1981).
Trouillot, M. R. 'Motion in the System: Coffee, Colour and Slavery in 18th-Century St. Domingue', *Review* 5, 3, (1982).
Watson, Karl. *The Civilized Island: Barbados, A Social History* (Bridgetown, 1979).

Section 7: Slave Women, Family and Households

Brathwaite, Kamau, 'Caribbean Women During the Period of Slavery', *Caribbean Contact*, May 1984 (Pt 1), and June 1984 (Pt 2).
Bush, B. '"White Ladies", Coloured "Favourites" and Black "Wenches": Some Considerations on Sex, Race and Class Factors in Social Relations in White Creole Society in the British Caribbean', *Slavery and Abolition*, 2 (1981).
Bush, B. *Slave Women in Caribbean Society 1650–1838* (Indiana Press/Heinemann Caribbean 1990).
Cousins, W. 'Slave Family Life in the British Colonies 1800–1834', *Sociological Review*, 27 (1935).
Higman, B. W. 'The Slave Family and Households in the British West Indies, 1800–1834', *Journal of Interdisciplinary History*, 7 (1975).
Higman, B. W. 'Methodological Problems in the Study of Slave Family', in V. Rubin and A. Tuden (eds), *Comparative Perspectives on Slavery in New World Plantation Societies* (New York, 1977).
Higman, B.W. 'African and Creole Slave Families in Trinidad', in Margaret E. Graham and Franklin W. Knight (eds), *Africa and the Caribbean: Legacies of a Link* (Johns Hopkins Univ. Press, 1979).
Higman, B. W. 'Domestic Service in Jamaica Since 1750', in B. W. Higman (ed.) *Trade, Government and Society in Caribbean History 1700–1920* Kingston (1983).
Higman, B. W. 'Terms for Kin in the B.W.I. Slave Community: Differing Perceptions of Masters and Slaves', in R. T. Smith (ed.), *Kinship, Ideology and Practice in Latin America* (Univ. of North Carolina Press, 1984).
Mair, L. Mathurin. 'A Historical Study of Women in Jamaica 1655–1844', Ph.D. diss., U.W.I., Mona (1974).
Mair, L. Mathurin. *Women Field Workers in Jamaica During Slavery* (Elsa Goveia Memorial Lecture, 1986).
Morrissey, M. *Slave Women in the New World: Gender Stratification in the Caribbean* (University Press of Kansas, 1989).
Reddock, Rhoda. 'Women and Slavery in the Caribbean: A Feminist Perspective', *Latin American Perspectives*, Issue 44, 12:1 (1985).

Section 6: Health, Nutrition and The Crisis of Social Reproduction

Butler, Mary, 'Mortality and Labour on the Codrington Estates, Barbados', *Journal of Caribbean History*, 19, 1 (1984).
Craton, M. 'Jamaican Slave Mortality: Fresh Light from Worthy Park, Longville and the Tharp Estates', *Journal of Caribbean History*, 3 (1971).
Craton, M. *Searching for the Invisible Man, op. cit.*, see Section 3.
Craton, M. 'Hobbesian or Panglossian?: The Two Extremes of Slave Conditions in the British Caribbean, 1739–1834', *William and Mary Quarterly*, 2nd Ser., 35, (1978).
Dunn, R. 'A Tale of Two Plantations: Slave Life at Mesopotamia in Jamaica and Mt. Airy in Virginia 1799–1828', *William and Mary Quarterly*, 34 (1977).
Dunn, R. 'Dreadful Idlers in the Cane Fields: The Slave Labour Pattern on a Jamaican Sugar Estate 1767–1831', *Journal of Interdisciplinary History*, 17 (1987).
Eblen, Jack. 'On the Natural Increase of Slave Populations: The Example of the Cuban Black Population, 1775–1900', in S. L. Engerman and E. Genovese (eds), *Race and Slavery in the Western Hemisphere: Quantitative Studies* (Princeton, 1974).
Engerman, S. L. 'Some Economic and Demographic Comparisons of Slavery in the United States and the B.W.I.', *Economic History Review*, 2nd Ser., 29 (1976).
Galenson, D. 'Population Turnover in the English West Indies in the late 17th Century: A Comparative Perspective', *Journal of Economic History*, 42 (1982).
Green-Pedersen, S. E. 'Slave Demography in the Danish West Indies and the Abolition of the Danish Slave Trade', in D. Eltis and J. Watuin (eds) The Abolition of the Atlantic Slave Trade, (Madison, 1981).
Higman, B. W. *Slave Population and Economy, op. cit.*, see General Section.
Higman, B.W. *Slave Population and Economy, op. cit.*, see General Section.
Higman, B. W. 'Growth in Afro-Caribbean Slave Populations', *American Journal of Physical Anthropology*, 1 (1979).
Johansen, Hans C. 'Slave Demography of the Danish West Indian Islands', *Scandinavian Economic History Review*, 29, 1 (1981).
Kiple, K. *The Caribbean Slave: A Biological History* (Cambridge University Press, 1984).
Koplan, J. P. 'Slave Mortality in 19th Century Grenada', *Social Science History*, 7, 3 (1983).
Lamur, Humphrey. 'The Impact of Maroon Wars on Population Policy During Slavery in Suriname', *Journal of Caribbean History*, 23 (1990).
Lamur, Humphrey. 'Demography of Surinam Plantation Slaves in the Last Decade Before Emancipation: The Case of Catharina Sophia' in V. Rubin and A. Tuden (eds), *Comparative Perspectives, op. cit.*
Lowenthal, D. and Clarke, C. 'Slave Breeding in Barbuda: The Past of a Negro Myth', in V. Rubin and A. Tuden (eds), *Comparative Perspectives, op. cit.*
Meredith, John A. 'Plantation Slave Mortality in Trinidad', *Population*, 42, 2 (1988).
Meredith, John A. *The Plantation Slaves of Trinidad 1783–1816: A Mathematical and Demographic Enquiry* (Cambridge Univ. Press, 1988).
Molen, P. 'Population and Social Patterns in Barbados in the early 18th Century', *William and Mary Quarterly*, 28 (1971).
Sheridan, Richard B. 'Sweet Malefactor: The Social Cost of Slavery and Sugar in Jamaica and Cuba, 1807–1854', *Economic History Review*, 29 (1976).

Sheridan, Richard B. 'Slave Demography in the B.W.I. and the Abolition of the Slave Trade', in D. Ellis and J. Walvin (eds.), *The Abolition of the Atlantic Slave Trade* (Wisconsin, 1981).
Sheridan, R. B. 'The Crisis of Slave Subsistence in the British West Indies During and After the American Revolution', *William and Mary Quarterly*, 33 (1976).
Sheridan, R. B. *Doctors and Slaves, op. cit.*, see General Section.
Ward, J. R. *British West Indian Slavery 1750–1834: The Process of Amelioration* (Clarendon Press, Oxford, 1988).
Wessman, James. 'The Demographic Structure of Slavery in Puerto Rico: Some Aspects of Agrarian Capitalism in the late 19th Century', *Journal of Latin American Studies*, 12, 2 (1980).
Wood, B. C. and Clayton, T. R. 'Slave Birth, Death and Diseases on Golden Grove Estate, Jamaica, 1765–1810', *Slavery and Abolition*, 6 (1985).

Section 8: Social Culture and Autonomy

Abrahams, R. and Szwed, J. *After Africa* (Yale Univ. Press, 1983).
Bisnauth, D. 'Africans and Africanism in the Caribbean', in D. Bisnauth, *A History of Religions in the Caribbean, op. cit.*, see General Section.
Brathwaite, Kamau. *Folk Culture of the Slaves in Jamaica* (New Beacon Books, London, 1970).
Brathwaite, Kamau. *The Development of Creole Society in Jamaica, op. cit.*, see General Section.
Cave, Roderick. 'Four Slave Songs from St. Bartholomew', *Caribbean Quarterly*, 25, 1 and 2 (1979).
Courlander, H. 'Vodoun: Its Origins and Meanings', in H. Courlander and Remy Bastien, *Religion and Politics in Haiti* (Institute of Cross-Cultural Research, Washington, 1966).
Curtin, P. D. 'African Jamaica', in P. D. Curtin (ed.), *Two Jamaicas: The Role of Ideas in a Tropical Colony 1830–1865* (Atheneum Press, New York, 1970).
Dirks, R. 'Slaves Holidays', *Natural History*, 84, 10 (1972).
Gaspar, B. 'Slavery, Amelioration and Sunday Markets in Antigua, 1823–1831', *Slavery and Abolition*, 9, 1 (1988).
Hall, D. *In Miserable Slavery: Thomas Thistlewood in Jamaica*, 1750–1786 (Mamillan, London, 1989).
Hall, Neville. 'Slavery in Three West Indian Towns', in B. W. Higman (ed.), *Trade, Government and Society in Caribbean Society 1700–1920: Essays Presented to Douglas Hall* (Kingston, 1983).
Handler, Jerome. 'An Archaeological Investigation of the Domestic Life of Plantation Slaves in Barbados', *Journal of the Barbados Museum and Historical Society*, 34, 2 (1972).
Jesse, C. 'Religion Among the Early Slaves in the French Antilles', *Journal of the Barbados Museum and Historical Society*, 28, 1 (1960).
Lange, F. W. 'Slave Mortuary Practices, Barbados W.I', in *Actas del XLI Congreso Internacional de Americanistas* (Mexico, 1974; Mexico, 1976), Vol. 2, pp. 477–83.
Leyburn, J. G. *The Haitian People, op. cit.*, see General Section.
Mintz, Sydney and Hall, Douglas. 'Economic Roles and Cultural Traditions' in Filomena Steady (ed.), *The Black Woman Cross-Culturally* (Schenkmann Publishing Co., Cambridge, Mass., 1981).
Patterson, O. *The Sociology of Slavery* (MacGibbon and Kee, London, 1967; see also under Section II).
Paute, Jean-Pierre. 'Musica y Sociedad Esclavista en Cuba', *Anuario de Estudios Americanos*, 43 (1986).
Schuler, M. 'Afro-American Slave Culture', in M. Craton (ed.), *Roots and Branches: Current Directions in Slave Studies* (Toronto, 1979).
Shepherd, V. A. 'Alternative Husbandry: Slaves on Livestock Farms in Jamaica', paper presented at the ILAS/ICS confernece 'Farm Chattel to Wage Slavery', May 1991 London.
Turner, M. 'Chattel Slaves into Wage Slaves: A Jamaican Case Study', in G. Heuman and M. Gross (eds), Labour in the Caribbean: From Emancipation to Independence (Macmillan 1988).

Section 9: Control, Resistance and Revolt

Bailey, Wilma. 'Social Control in the Pre-Emancipation Society of Kingston, Jamaica', *Boletin de Estudios Latinoamericanos del Caribe*, 24 (1978).
Beckles, H. McD. 'Masters and Servants', in H. McD. Beckles, *White Servitude and Black Slavery in Barbados 1627–1715* (Univ. of Tennessee Press, 1989).
Beckles, H. McD. 'The 200 Years War: Slave Resistance in the B.W.I.: An Overview of the Historiography', *Jamaican Historical Review*, 12 (1982).
Beckles, H. McD. 'Rebels Without Heroes: Slave Politics in Seventeenth Century Barbados', *Journal of Caribbean History*, 18, 2 (1984).
Beckles, H. McD. *Black Rebellion in Barbados: The Struggle Against Slavery, 1627–1838* (Antilles Publications, 1984).
Beckles, H. McD. 'The Slave Drivers' War: Bussa and the 1816 Barbados Slave Uprising', *Boletin de Estudios Latinoamericanos y del Caribe*, 39 (1985).
Beckles, H. McD. 'From Land to Sea: Runaway Barbados Slaves and Servants 1630–1700', in G. Heuman (ed.), *Out of the House of Bondage: Runaways, Resistance and Marronage in Africa and the New World* (Frank Cass, 1986).
Beckels, H. McD. and Watson, Karl. 'Social Protest and Labour Bargaining: The Changing Nature of Slaves' Responses to Plantation Life in Eighteenth Century Barbados', *Slavery and Abolition*, 8, 3 (1987).
Beckles, H. McD. *Afro-Caribbean Women and Resistance to Slavery in Barbados* (Karnak House, 1988).
Blair, B. L. 'Wolfert Simon van Hoogenheim in the Berbice Slave Revolt of 1763–64', *Bijdragen tot de taal — Landen Volkenkunde*, 140, 1 (1984).

Blouet, O. M. 'To Make Society Safe for Freedom: Slave Education in Barbados 1823–1833', *Journal of Negro History*, 65, 2 (1980).
Brace, J. 'From Chattel to Person: Martinique 1635–1848', *Plantation Society in the Americas*, 2, 1 (1983).
Brace, J. 'The Evolution of the Laws of Slavery 1635–1848', *Plantation Society in the Americas*, 1, 2 (1979).
Brace, R. and Brace, J. 'Code Noir: Intention and Practice, 1685–1794', in *Proceedings of the Second Meeting of the Western Society for French History*, November 1974, Austin, Texas (San Francisco, 1975).
Brathwaite, Kamau. *The Development of Creole Society in Jamaica, op. cit.*, see General Section above.
Brathwaite, Kamau. 'Attitudes of Whites to Non-Whites', in Kamau Brathwaite, *The Development of Creole Society in Jamaica 1770–1820, op. cit.*
Brathwaite, Kamau. *White Power in Jamaica: The Inter-Dynamics of Slave Control*, ISER, Mona (forthcoming).
Brathwaite, Kamau. *Nanny, Sam Sharpe and the Struggle for People's Liberation* (Agency for Public Information, Kingston, 1976).
Brathwaite, Kamau. 'The Slave Rebellion in the Great River Valley of St. James, 1831/32', *Jamaican Historical Review*, 13 (1982).
Breathett, G. 'Catholic Missionary Activity and the Negro Slave in Haiti', *Phylon*, 23, 3 (1962).
Bush, B. 'Defiance or Submission? The Role of the Slave Woman in Slave Resistance in the British Caribbean', *Immigrants and Minorities*, 1 (1982).
Bush, B., 'Towards Emancipation: Slave Women and Resistance to Coercive Labour Regime in the British West Indian Colonies 1770–1838', in D. Richardson (ed.), *Abolition and its Aftermath: The Historical Context 1790–1916* (Frank Cass, 1985).
Bush, B., '"The Family Tree is Not Cut": Women and Cultural Resistance in Slave Family Life in the British Caribbean', in G. Okihiro (ed.), *In Resistance: Studies in African, Caribbean and Afro-American History* (Univ. of Massachusetts Press, 1986).
Caldecott, A. 'The Church in the Slavery Period', in A. Caldecott, *The Church in the West Indies* (Frank Cass, 1970).
Campbell, M. *The Maroons of Jamaica 1655–1796: A History of Resistance, Collaboration and Betrayal* (Granby, Mass., 1988).
Carrington, S. H. H. 'West Indian Opposition to British Policy: Barbadian Politics 1774–82', *Journal of Caribbean History*, 17, (1982).
Carrington, S. H. H. 'Eighteenth Century Political Change in the British Empire: A Case Study of St Vincent, 1775–1779', *Journal of Caribbean History*, 20, 2 (1985).
Corwin, Charles D. 'Efforts of the Dutch Colonial Pastors for the Conversion of the Negroes', *Journal of the Presbyterian Historical Society*, 12, 7 (1927).
Craton, 'Proto-Peasant Revolts? The Late Slave Rebellions in the B.W.I. 1816–1832', *Past and Present*, 85 (1979).
Craton, 'The Passion to Exist: Slave Rebellions in the B.W.I. 1650–1832', *Journal of Caribbean History*, 13 (1980).
Craton, *Testing the Chains, op. cit.*, see General Section.
Craton, 'We Shall Not Be Moved: Pompey's Slave Revolt in Exuma Island, Bahamas, 1830', *Nieuwe West Indische Gids*, 57, 1–2 (1983).
Cripps, L. L. *The Spanish Caribbean From Columbus to Castro* (G. K. Hall, Boston, 1979).
Curtin, P. D. 'European Jamaica: The White and Coloured Castes', P. D Curtin *Two Jamaicas, op. cit.*
Curtin, P. D. 'Defenses Against Revolution', in P. D. Curtin, *Two Jamaicas, op. cit.*
Curtin, P. D. 'The Jamaican Revolution', in P. D. Curtin, *Two Jamaicas, op. cit.*
Curtin, P. D. 'Revolution in the French Antilles', in P. D. Curtin, *The Rise and Fall of the Plantation Complex: Essays in Atlantic History* (Cambridge Univ. Press, 1990).
Debein, G. 'Le Marronage Aux Antilles Francaises au xvii siècle', *Caribbean Studies*, 6, 3 (1966).
Degroot, S. 'Les Marrons de Saint Domingue en 1764', *Jamaican Historical Review*, 6 (1960).
Dirks, R. *The Black Saturnalia: Conflict and its Ritual Expression on British West Indian Slave Plantations* (Gainesville, 1987).
Duran, V. A. 'Ordenanzas para el Gobierno de los Negros de la Isla Espaniola', *Anales de la Universidad de Santo Domingo*, 16, 57–60 (1951).
Fergus, H. 'The Early Slave Laws of Montserrat 1688–1780: The Legal Schema of a Slave Society', *Caribbean Quarterly*, 24, 1, 2 (1978).
Furley, O. 'Moravian Missionaries and Slaves in the West Indies', *Caribbean Studies*, (1965).
Gaspar, Barry. *Bondsmen and Rebels: A Study of Master-Slave Relations in Antigua: With Implications for Colonial British America* (Johns Hopkins Univ. Press, 1984).
Gaspar, B. 'The Antigua Slave Conspiracy of 1736: A Case Study of the Origins of Collective Resistance', *William and Mary Quarterly*, 3rd Ser., 33 (1978).
Gaspar, B. '"To Bring the Offending Slaves to Justice": Compensation and Slave Resistance in Antigua 1669–1763', *Caribbean Quarterly*, 30, 3–4 (1984).
Geggus, D. 'Jamaica and the St. Domingue Slave Revolt 1791–1793', *Americas*, 38, (1981).
Geggus, D. 'The Enigma of Jamaica: New Light on the Causes of Slave Rebellions', *William and Mary Quarterly*, 44 (1987).
Goveia, Elsa. *Slave Society in the British Leeward Islands at the End of the 18th Century* (Greenwood Press, 1965).
Hall, G. Mildo. *Social Control in Plantation Societies: A Comparison of St. Domingue and Cuba* (Baltimore, 1971).
Hall, Richard. *Acts Passed in the Islands of Barbados from 1643–1762 Inclusive* (London, 1764).
Hall, N. A. T. 'Establishing a Public Elementary School for Slaves in the Danish Virgin Islands 1732–1846', *Caribbean Journal of Education*, 6, 1 (1979).
Hall, N. A. T. 'The Judicial System of a Plantation Society: Barbados on the Eve of Emancipation', *Colloque d'Histoire Antillaise*, 1.
Hart, Richard. 'Church, State and Status' in Richard Hart, *Slaves Who Abolished Slavery*, Vol. I, Blacks in Bondage (ISER, UWI, Mona, 1980).

Hartsinck, J. J. 'The Story of the Slave Rebellion in Berbice' (translated by W. E. Ruth), *Journal of the British Guiana Museum and Zoo*, 20-27 (1958).
Heuman, G. 'Runaway Slaves in 19th Century Barbados', in G. Heuman, *Out of the House of Bondage, op. cit.*
Lane, C. A. 'Concerning Jamaica's 1760 Slave Rebellions', *Jamaica Journal*, 7, 4 (1973).
Marshall, Bernard. 'Religion as an Agent of Social Control and Social Instability in the Slave Plantations of the British Windward Islands', *Journal of Ethnic Studies*, 10, 1, (1982).
Marshall, B. 'Marronage in Slave Plantation Societies: A Case Study of Dominica', *Caribbean Quarterly*, 22 (1976).
Marshall, B. 'Slave Resistance and White Reaction in the Britsh Windward Islands, 1763–1833', *Caribbean Quarterly*, 28, 3 (1982).
Mathurin, Lucille. *The Rebel Woman in the B. W.I. During Slavery* (African Caribbean Publications, Institute of Jamaica, 1975).
Mecham, J. *Church and State in Latin America* (Univ. of South Carolina Press, 1966).
Morales-Carron, A. *Puerto Rico and the Non-Hispanic Caribbean* (Univ. of Puerto Rico Press, 1952).
Moore,Samuel. *The Public Acts in Force: Passed by the Legislature of Barbados from May 11, 1762 to April 8, 1800* (London, 1801).
Patterson, O. *The Sociology of Slavery* (Sangster's Bookstores Ltd and Granada Pub., 1973 rpt).
Patterson, O. 'Slavery and Slave Revolts: A Sociohistorical Analysis of the First Maroon War', *Social and Economic Studies*, 19, 3 (1970).
Patterson, O. 'The General Causes of Slave Revolts' in L. Foner and E. Genovese (eds), *Slavery in the New World* (Prentice-Hall, 1969).
Paula, A. F. '1795: The Slave Insurrection on the Island of Curaçao: Possible Connections Between the Curaçao and Venezuela Revolts in 1795', *Cimarrons*, 2.
Price, R. *Maroon Societies: Rebel Slave Communities in the Americas* (Johns Hopkins Univ. Press, 1973).
Reynolds, C. Roy, 'Tacky and the Great Slave Rebellions of 1760', *Jamaica Journal*, 6, 2 (1972).
Rooke, Patricia. 'The "New Mechanic" in Slave Society: Socio-Psychological Motivations and Evangelical Missionaries in the B.W.I.', *Journal of Religious History*, 11, 1 (1980).
Schuler, M. 'Ethnic Slave Rebellions in the Caribbean and the Guianas', *Journal of Social History*, 3 (1970).
Schuler, M 'Day to Day Resistance to Slavery in the Caribbean in the 18th Century', *ASAWI Bulletin*, 1, iv (1973).
Scott, Rebecca. 'Insurrection and Slavery', in Rebecca Scott, *Slave Emancipation in Cuba: The Transition to Free Labour 1860–1899* (Princeton Univ. Press, 1985).
Sheridan, R. 'The Jamaican Slave Insurrection Scare of 1776 and the American Revolution', *Journal of Negro History*, 61, 3 (1976).
Smith, M. G. 'Some Aspects of Social Structure in the British Caribbean About 1870', in M. G. Smith, *The Plural Society of the B. W.I.* (Sangster's Bookstores Ltd and Univ. of California Press, 1965).
Smith, R. W. 'The Legal Status of Jamaican Slaves Before the Anti-Slavery Movement', *Journal of Negro History*, 30, 3 (1945).
Taylor, C. 'Planter Comment on Slave Revolts in Jamaica', *Slavery and Abolition*, 3, 3 (1982).
Thompson, Alvin, 'Dutch Colonial Society', in Alvin Thompson, *Colonialism and Underdevelopment in Guyana 1580–1803* (Caribbean Research and Publication Inc., Barbados, 1987).
Thompson, Vincent B. 'Divide and Rule', in V. B. Thompson, *The Making of the African Diaspora in the Americas 1441–1900* (Longman Group, 1987).
Thompson, Vincent B. 'The Treatment of Slaves', in V. B. Thompson, *The Making of the African Diaspora, op. cit.*
Thompson, V. B. 'African Resistance to Slavery in the Americas', in V. B. Thompson, *The Making of the African Diaspora in the Ameircas 1441–1900* (Longman, 1987).
Thompson, V. B. 'The Haitian Revolution', in V. B. Thompson, *op. cit.*
Thompson, A. *Brethren of the Bush: A Study of the Runaways and Bush Negroes in Guyana* (Cave Hill, ISER, 1976).
Turner, Mary. 'The Bishop of Jamaica and Slave Insurrection in Jamaica', *Journal of Ecclesiastical History*, 26, 4 (1975).
Turner, Mary. 'Chattel Slaves into Wage Slaves: A Jamaican Case Study', in G. Heuman and M. Gross (eds), *Labour in the Caribbean: From Emancipation to Independence* (Mcmillan, 1988).
Turner, Mary. 'The Missionaries and the Slaves', in Mary Turner, *Slaves and Missionaries: The Disintegration of Jamaican Slave Society 1787–1834* (Univ. of Illinois Press, 1982).
Wrong, H. 'The Old Representative System Before the Abolition of Slavery', in H. Wrong, *Government of the West Indies* (Negro Univ. Press, 1969).

Section 10: Revolution and Emancipation

Anstey, R. *The Atlantic Slave Trade and Abolition* (London, 1975).
Anstey, R. 'Parliamentary Reform Methodism and Anti-Slavery Politics, 1829–1833', *Slavery and Abolition*, 2 (1981).
Bartlett, Christopher. 'Britain and the Abolition of Slavery in Puerto Rico and Cuba', *Journal of Caribbean History*, 23, 1 (1990).
Blackburn, Robin. *The Overthrow, op. cit.*, see General Section.
Brace, J. 'From Chattel to Person. Martinique 1635–1848', *Plantation Society in the Americas*, 2, 1 (1988).
Butler, M. 'Fair and Equitable Consideration: The Distribution of Slave Compensation in Jamaica and Barbados', Journal of Caribbean History 22:1 and 2.
Campbell, M. 'The Price of Freedom: On Forms of Manumission. A Note on the Comparative Study of Slavery', *Revista/Review Interamericana*, 6, 2 (1976).

Cesaire, Aimé. *Toussaint L'Overture: la Révolution Française et la Problème Coloniale* (Paris, 1960).
Corwin, A. F. *Spain and the Abolition of Slavery in Cuba 1817–1866* (Univ. of Texas Press, 1967).
Cox, Edward. 'The Free Coloureds and Slave Emancipation', *Journal of Caribbean History*, 22, 1 and 2 (1990).
Craton, M. 'Emancipation from Below?: The Role of the British West Indian Slaves in the Emancipation Movement', in J. Hayward (ed.), *Out of Slavery: Abolition and After* (London, 1985).
Craton, M. 'Slave Culture, Resistance and the Achievement of Emancipation in the B.W.I., 1738–1828', in J. Walvin (ed.), *Slavery and British Abolition, 1776–1848* (London, MacMillan, 1982).
Curtin, P. D. 'The End of Slavery in the Americas', in Curtin P. D. *The Rise and Fall of the Sugar Plantation Complex* (Cambridge Univ. Press, 1990).
Dauvergne, R. 'La Guadeloupe à l'epoque de l'abolition de l'esclavage', *Bulletin de la Société d'Histoire Moderne*, Ser. 1, 53, nos. 11–12, (1954).
De Groot, S. W. 'The Maroons of Suriname: Agents of their own Emancipation', David Richardson, (ed) Abolition and its Aftermath: The Historical Content (Frank Cass, 1985).
Diaz Soler, L. M. 'The Abolition of Slavery in Puerto Rico 1868–1878', *Caribbean Historical Review*, 2 (1951).
Drescher, S. 'Capitalism and the Decline of Slavery', in V. Rubin and A. Tuden (eds), *Comparative Perspectives on Slavery in New World Plantation Societies* (New York, 1977).
Drescher, S. 'The Decline Thesis of British Slavery Since Econocide', *Slavery and Abolition*, 7, 1 (1980).
Drescher, S. *Econocide: British Slavery in the Era of Abolition* (Univ. of Pittsburgh Press, 1977).
Eltis, D. The Economic Impact of the Ending of the African Slave Trade to the Americas', *Social and Economic Studies* 37, 1 and 2 (1988).
Eltis, D. and Walvin, J. *The Abolition of the Atlantic Slave Trade: Origins and Effects in Europe, Africa and the Americas* (Univ. of Wisconsin Press, 1981).
Emmer, P. 'The Abolitionist Movement Abroad in the Ending of Caribbean Slavery: The Case of Surinam', *Caribbean Societies* (ICS), 11: Collected Seminar Papers, No. 34 (1985).
Engerman, S. L. 'Slavery and Emancipation in Comparative Perspectives: A Look at Some Recent Debates', *Journal of Economic History* 46 (1986).
Frucht, R. 'Emancipation and Revolt in the West Indies, St. Kitts, 1834', *Science and Society*, 39, 2 (1975).
Green, W. *British Emancipation: The Sugar Colonies and the Great Experiment 1830–1865* (Oxford, 1976).
Hart, Richard. *Slaves Who Abolished Slavery* II (Institute of Social and Economic Research, Mona, 1985).
Hiss, D. *Netherlands America: The Dutch Territories in the West* (Sloane and Pearce, New York, 1943).
Hoetink, H. 'La Abolicion de la Esclavitud en las Antillas Hollandesas', *La Torre*, 21, 81–82 (1973).
James, C. L. R. *The Black Jacobins* (London, 1938).
Jenkins, H. J. K. 'Guadeloupe, Savagery and Emancipation: British Comment of 1794–96', *Revue Française d'Histoire d'Outre-Mer*, 65, 2 no. 240, (1978).
Knight, F. W. 'The Ten Year War and the Abolition of Slavery', in F. W. Knight *Slave Society*, *op. cit.*, see General Section.
Levy, C. 'Barbados: The Last Years of Slavery 1823-33', *Journal of Negro History*, 44, 4 (1959).
Leyburn, J. *The Haitian People*, *op. cit.*, see General Section.
Milsome, John R. *Olaudah Equiano: The Slave Who Helped to End the Slave Trade* (Longman, 1969).
Nistal-Moret, Benjamin. 'Problems in the Social Structure of Slavery in Puerto Rico During the Process of Abolition, 1872', in Fraginals, Pons and Engerman, *op. cit.*, see General Section.
Otto, T. O. *The Haitian Revolution 1789–1804* (Univ. of Tennessee Press, 1973).
Ragatz, L. J. *The Fall of the Planter Class in the B.W.I. 1763–1833* (New York, 1928).
Richardson, R. K. *Moral Imperium(?): Afro-Caribbeans and the Transformation of British Rule* (Connecticut, 1987).
Schuler, M. 'Plantation Labourers, The London Missionary Society and Emancipation in West Demerara, Guyana', *Journal of Caribbean History*, 22, 1 and 2 (1990).
Scott, Rebecca. 'Gradual Abolition and the Dynamics of Slave Emancipation in Cuba 1868–1886', *Hispanic American Historical Review* (1983).
Segrera, F. L. 'Cuba: Dependence, Plantation Economy and Social Classes, 1762–1902', in Fraginals, Pons and Engerman, *Between Slavery and Freedom*, *op. cit.*, under General section above.
Sheridan, R. B. 'From Jamaican Slavery to Haitian Freedom: The Case of the Black Crew of the Pilot Boat, Deep Nine', *Journal of Negro History*, 67 (1982).
Siwpersad, J. P. 'Emancipation in British Guiana and its Influence on Dutch Policy Regarding Surinam', in D. Richardson (ed.), *Abolition and Its Aftermath: The Historical Content, 1790–1916* (Frank Cass, 1985).
Stein, R. 'The Abolition of Slavery in the North, West and South of St. Domingue', *Americas*, 41, 3 (1985).
Stein, R. 'The Revolution of 1789 and the Abolition of Slavery', *Canadian Journal of History*, 17, 3 (1982).
Thompson, V. B. 'Antislavery', in V. B. Thompson, *The Making of the African Diaspora*, *op. cit.*
Thompson, V. B. 'The Haitian Revolution', in V. B. Thompson, *The Making of the African Diaspora*, *op. cit.*
Tocqueville, Alexis de. *Report on the Abolition of Slavery in the French Colonies* (Negro Universities Press, 1970 rpt).
Turner, Mary. 'The Baptist War in Abolition', *Jamaican Historical Review*, 23 (1982).
Turner, Mary. *Slaves and Missionaries: The Disintegration of Jamaican Slave Society 1787–1834* (Illinois, 1982).
Tyson, George F. Jr. (ed.). *Toussaint L'Ouverture* (Prentice-Hall, 1973).
Ward, J. R., 'Emancipation and Planters', *Journal of Caribbean History*, 22, 1 and 2 (1990).
Williams, E. *Capitalism and Slavery*, *op. cit.*, see General Section.